씨뮬이 제안하는 가장 효율적인 학습법!

온·오프 블렌디드 러닝 (on/off Blended Learning)

1 STEP ONE OFF-LINE

기출은 수능 대비의 기본! 기본에 가장 충실한 씨뮬로 실전연습하자

- 다양한 구성의 기출문제집으로 목표에 맞는 학습 가능
- 씨뮬 교재를 풀면 온라인에서 자동채점 & 성적분석 가능

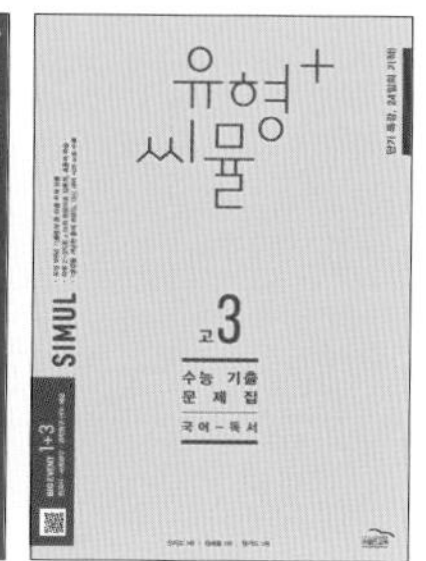

2 STEP TWO ON-LINE

스터디센스 STUDY SENSE

QR 찍고 회원가입 → 씨뮬 문제 풀기→ 자동채점 → 성적분석

- 내 등급컷과 취약 유형까지 완벽 분석
- AI 문제 추천으로 취약 유형을 한 번 더 학습
- 오답노트로 복습 또 복습해서 틀린 문제 정복하기

3 STEP THREE OFF-LINE

모의고사 맞춤제작 OneUP

'원하는 문제만 골라서 맞춤 교재'를 만들고 싶다면? OneUP

- 원하는 제본 형태로 제작 가능
- 학평, 모평, 수능, 종로 사설 모의고사 맞춤 제작

CONTENTS

고 3 ▸ 영어 — 독해

목표	단원		페이지	학습 체크
DAY 01	01 글의 목적		001	
	문법 플러스 1. 주어 • 동사	숙어플러스 1. 수능 필수 숙어 1회	005 / 006	
DAY 02	02 심경 • 분위기		007	
	문법 플러스 2. 목적어, 보어	숙어플러스 2. 수능 필수 숙어 2회	011 / 012	
DAY 03	03 필자의 주장		013	
	문법 플러스 3. 동사의 종류	숙어플러스 3. 수능 필수 숙어 3회	017 / 018	
DAY 04	04 함축 · 지칭 추론		019	
	문법 플러스 4. 동사의 시제	숙어플러스 4. 수능 필수 숙어 4회	023 / 024	
DAY 05	05 글의 요지		025	
	문법 플러스 5. 동명사	숙어플러스 5. 수능 필수 숙어 5회	029 / 030	
DAY 06	06 글의 주제		031	
	문법 플러스 6. 부정사	숙어플러스 6. 수능 필수 숙어 6회	035 / 036	
DAY 07	07 글의 제목		037	
	문법 플러스 7. 분사, 분사구문	숙어플러스 7. 수능 필수 숙어 7회	041 / 042	
DAY 08	08 도표 정보 파악		043	
	문법 플러스 8. 준동사	숙어플러스 8. 수능 필수 숙어 8회	047 / 048	
DAY 09	09 내용 일치 · 불일치		049	
	문법 플러스 9. 조동사	숙어플러스 9. 수능 필수 숙어 9회	053 / 054	
DAY 10	10 안내문		055	
	문법 플러스 10. 수동태	숙어플러스 10. 수능 필수 숙어 10회	059 / 060	
DAY 11	11 어법 정확성 파악		061	
	문법 플러스 11. 가정법	숙어플러스 11. 수능 필수 숙어 11회	065 / 066	
DAY 12	12 어휘 적절성 파악		067	
	문법 플러스 12. 대명사	숙어플러스 12. 수능 필수 숙어 12회	071 / 072	

유형+ 씨뮬

목표	단원		페이지	학습 체크
DAY 13	13 빈칸 추론 (1) 어휘, 짧은 어구		073	
	문법 플러스 13. 관계대명사	숙어플러스 13. 수능 필수 숙어 13회	077 / 078	
DAY 14	14 빈칸 추론 (2) 긴 어구, 문장		079	
	문법 플러스 14. 형용사, 부사	숙어플러스 14. 수능 필수 숙어 14회	083 / 084	
DAY 15	15 흐름에 무관한 문장 찾기		085	
	문법 플러스 15. 비교 구문	숙어플러스 15. 수능 필수 숙어 15회	089 / 090	
DAY 16	16 문단 내 글의 순서 파악		091	
	문법 플러스 16. 관계부사	숙어플러스 16. 수능 필수 숙어 16회	095 / 096	
DAY 17	17 주어진 문장의 위치 파악		097	
	문법 플러스 17. 병렬 구조	숙어플러스 17. 수능 필수 숙어 17회	101 / 102	
DAY 18	18 문단 요약		103	
	문법 플러스 18. 수의 일치	숙어플러스 18. 수능 필수 숙어 18회	107 / 108	
DAY 19	19 장문의 이해 (1)		109	
	문법 플러스 19. 접속사, 전치사	숙어플러스 19. 수능 필수 숙어 19회	113 / 114	
DAY 20	20 장문의 이해 (2)		115	
	문법 플러스 20. 특수 구문	숙어플러스 20. 수능 필수 숙어 20회	119 / 120	
DAY 21	미니 고난도 Test 1회		121	
DAY 22	미니 고난도 Test 2회		123	
DAY 23	미니 고난도 Test 3회		125	
DAY 24	미니 고난도 Test 4회		127	

구성 + 특징

01

내신 대비 서브 노트

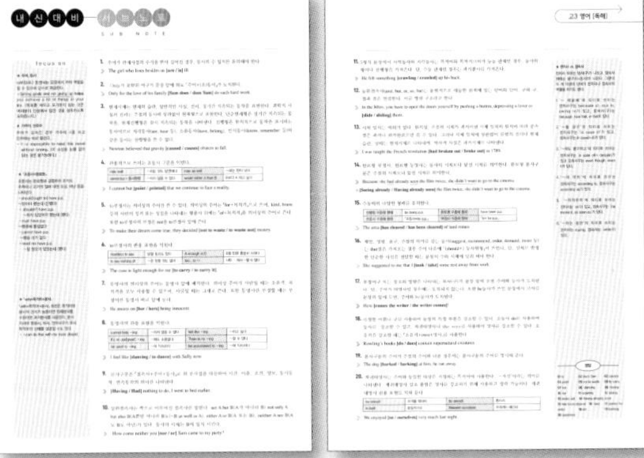

고3 영어 독해 시험에 자주 나오는 문법 내신 요약입니다.

내신 영어 독해 시험에 자주 나오는 문법 사항을 정리한 학습 자료입니다. 서브 노트를 활용하여 중간 · 기말고사 직전에 빠르게 영어 문법을 익혀 봅시다.

02

가장 효율적인 24일의 학습 체계

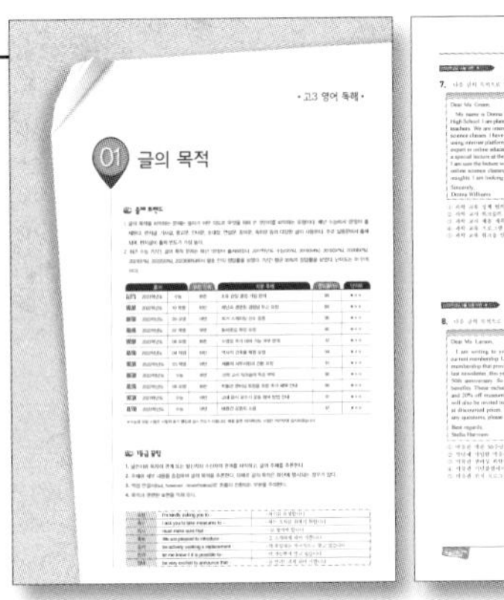

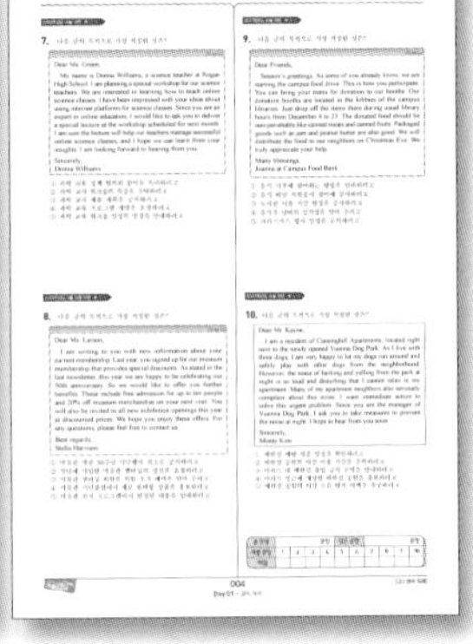

유형 학습이 처음이라 불안하다면? 수능 체계를 잘 모른다면?
더욱더 학습 효과가 큰 교재입니다.

❶ 최신 기출 순서로 엄선된 학평, 모평, 수능 기출 문제를 24일 동안 학습합니다.

❷ 매일매일 10개 내외의 지문으로 압축적, 효율적 학습이 가능하며 채점을 간단히 매일 할 수 있게 체크 박스를 붙였습니다.

❸ 각 지문마다 난이도, 소요 시간, 출처를 안내하였습니다. 난이도는 정답률 85% 이상이면 별 1개(★), 정답률 60~84%이면 별 2개(★★), 정답률 59% 이하는 별 3개(★★★)를 주었습니다.

❹ 참고로, 출처 중에 수능과 모평 시험은 시험지 표기 명칭을 따랐습니다. 예를 들면, 2023학년도 6월 모평 시험은 실제로는 2022년 6월에 실시된 시험입니다.

03

출제 트렌드와 대표 기출

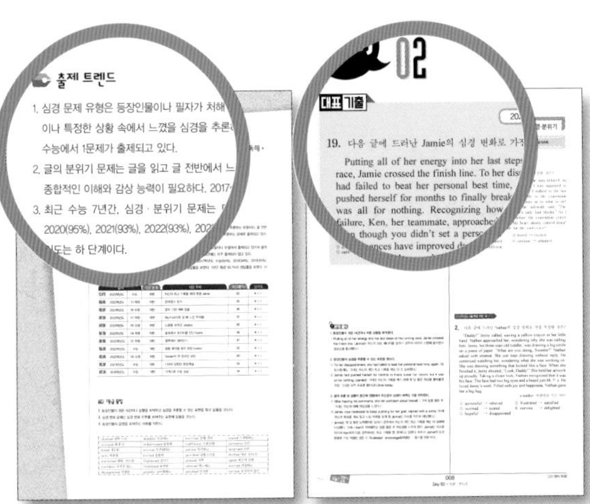

기출 문제 분석을 통해 공부의 올바른 '방향'을 설정합니다.

❶ 최신 출제 트렌드와 1등급 꿀팁을 제공합니다. 수능 영어를 대비해 무엇이 중요한지, 어떻게 공부해야 할지 7년간의 수능 출제 경향과 꿀팁을 정리했습니다.

❷ 각 유형의 대표 기출 문제를 통해 출제 핵심을 파악할 수 있습니다.

STRUCTURE & FEATURES

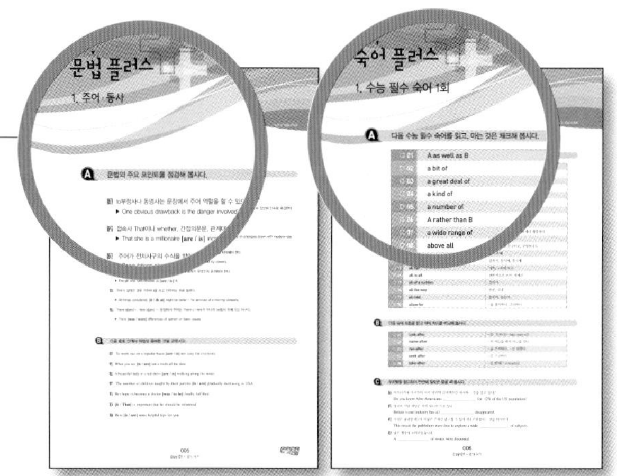

04

문법 플러스 / 숙어 플러스

문법과 어휘를 알면 영어 독해에 자신감이 생깁니다.

❶ 독해의 기본 재료는 언어형식(문법)과 어휘입니다. 수능 어법 문제로 잘 출제되거나, 문장의 뼈대를 이루는 기본 문법 20개를 정리했습니다. 최근 4년간의 어법 문제를 활용해 문법의 주요 포인트를 점검했습니다.

❷ 독해 실력을 높이기 방법 중 하나는 어휘력 증가입니다. 20회 동안 매일 25개씩 수능 필수 숙어 500개를 학습합니다. 독해 학습의 기본 중의 기본이니 부지런히 마스터하기를 권합니다.

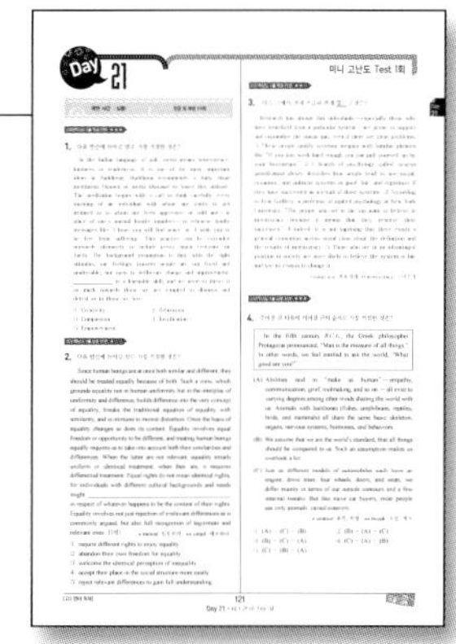
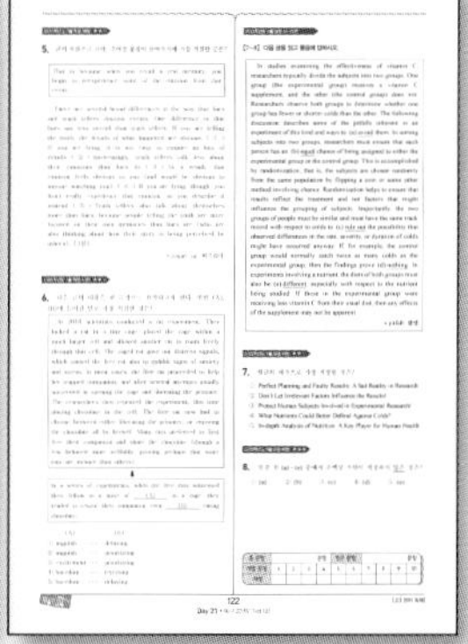

05

미니 고난도 Test

21~24일은 간단하게 미니 테스트를 할 수 있습니다.

❶ 영어 절대 평가의 변별력을 좌우할 수 있는 고난도 문제로 자신의 실력을 점검할 수 있도록 하였습니다.

❷ 빈칸 문제, 전체 흐름, 글의 순서, 주어진 문장의 위치 파악, 문단 요약, 장문의 이해(1), 장문의 이해(2) 위주로 문제를 수록하였습니다.

06

체계적이고 효율적인 해설

어려운 문항은 상세하게, 쉬운 문항은 명료하게~ 효율적인 똑똑한 해설입니다.

❶ 각 지문의 어려운 내용을 이해하기 쉽게 풀이하며 많이 틀린 문항에 대해서는 상세하게 풀이를 제시합니다.

❷ 직독직해를 통해 영문의 기본 구조를 마스터하도록 하였습니다.

❸ 골드교육 홈피 학습 지원 자료 코너에서 지문에 나온 어휘를 한글 파일 형태로 다운받을 수 있습니다.

내신대비 서브노트

SUB NOTE

focus on

★ 주어, 동사

to부정사나 동명사는 문장에서 주어 역할을 할 수 있으며 단수로 취급한다.

• Setting goals and not giving up helps you achieve a lot of things in your life. (목표를 세우고 포기하지 않는 것은 여러분이 인생에서 많은 것을 성취하도록 도와줍니다.)

★ 가주어, 진주어

주어가 길어진 경우 가주어 it을 쓰고 진주어는 뒤로 돌린다.

• It is impossible to read this novel without crying. (이 소설을 눈물 없이 읽는 것은 불가능하다.)

★ 「조동사+완료형」

조동사는 완료형과 결합하여 과거의 추측이나 과거의 일에 대한 유감, 비난 등을 나타낸다.

• should[ought to] have p.p. ~했어야 했는데 (안했다)
• shouldn't have p.p. ~하지 않았어야 했는데 (했다)
• must have p.p. ~했음에 틀림없다
• cannot have p.p. ~했을 리가 없다
• need not have p.p. ~할 필요가 없었는데 (했다)

★ 「with+목적어+분사」

「with+목적어+분사」 표현은 목적어와 분사의 관계가 능동이면 현재분사를, 수동이면 과거분사를 사용한다. 분사 자리에 형용사, 부사, 전치사구가 와서 목적어의 상태를 설명할 수도 있다.

• I can do that with my eyes closed.

1. 주어가 관계사절의 수식을 받아 길어진 경우, 동사의 수 일치를 유의해야 한다.

≫ The girl who lives besides us **[are / is]** ill.

2. Only가 포함된 어구가 문장 앞에 와도 「주어+(조)동사」가 도치된다.

≫ Only for the love of his family **[Sam does / does Sam]** do such hard work.

3. 현재시제는 현재의 습관, 일반적인 사실, 진리, 장기간 지속되는 동작을 표현한다. 과학적 사실과 진리는 주절의 동사에 상관없이 현재형으로 표현한다. 단순현재형은 장기간 지속되는 동작을, 현재진행형은 잠시 지속되는 동작을 나타낸다. 진행형은 원칙적으로 동작을 표시하는 동사이므로 지각동사(see, hear 등), 소유동사(have, belong), 인식동사(know, remember 등)와 같은 동사는 진행형을 쓸 수 없다.

≫ Newton believed that gravity **[caused / causes]** objects to fall.

4. 관용적으로 쓰이는 조동사 구문을 익힌다.

may well	~하는 것도 당연하다	may as well	~하는 편이 낫다
cannot but + 동사원형	~하지 않을 수 없다	would rather A than B	B보다 A 하고 싶다

≫ I cannot but **[point / pointed]** that we continue to face a reality.

5. to부정사는 의미상의 주어를 쓸 수 있다. 의미상의 주어는 「for+목적격」으로 쓰며, kind, brave 등의 사람의 성격 또는 성질을 나타내는 형용사 뒤에는 「of+목적격」을 의미상의 주어로 쓴다. 또한 to부정사의 부정은 not을 to부정사 앞에 쓴다.

≫ To make their dream come true, they decided **[not to waste / to waste not]** money.

6. to부정사의 관용 표현을 익힌다.

needless to say	말할 필요도 없이	A enough to B	B할 만큼 충분히 A하다
to say nothing of	~은 말할 것도 없이	too... to ~	너무 … 해서 ~할 수 없다

≫ The case is light enough for me **[to carry / to carry it]**.

7. 동명사의 의미상의 주어는 동명사 앞에 배치한다. 의미상 주어가 사람일 때는 소유격, 목적격을 모두 사용할 수 있으며, 사물일 때는 그대로 쓴다. 또한 동명사를 부정할 때는 부정어를 동명사 바로 앞에 둔다.

≫ He insists on **[her / hers]** being innocent.

8. 동명사의 관용 표현을 익힌다.

cannot help -ing	~하지 않을 수 없다	feel like -ing	~하고 싶다
It's no use[good] -ing	~해도 소용없다	There is no -ing	~할 수 없다
be used to -ing	~에 익숙하다	be accustomed to -ing	~에 익숙하다

≫ I feel like **[dancing / to dance]** with Sally now.

9. 분사구문은 「접속사+주어+동사」로 된 부사절을 대신하며 시간, 이유, 조건, 양보, 동시동작, 연속동작의 의미를 나타낸다.

≫ **[Having / Had]** nothing to do, I went to bed earlier.

10. 상관접속사는 짝으로 이루어진 접속사를 말한다. not A but B(A가 아니라 B) not only A but also B(A뿐만 아니라 B도(=B as well as A), either A or B(A 또는 B), neither A nor B(A도 B도 아닌)가 있다. 동사의 시제는 B에 일치 시킨다.

≫ How come neither you **[nor / or]** Sam came to my party?

11. 5형식 문장에서 사역동사와 지각동사는 목적어와 목적격보어가 능동 관계인 경우, 동사원형이나 진행형을 가져온다. 단, 수동 관계인 경우는 과거분사를 가져온다.

≫ He felt something **[crawling / crawled]** up his back.

12. 등위접속사(and, but, or, so, for)는 문법적으로 대등한 관계에 있는 단어와 단어, 구와 구, 절과 절을 연결한다. 이를 병렬 구조라고 한다

≫ In the Mtro, you have to open the doors yourself by pushing a button, depressing a lever or **[slide / sliding]** them.

13. 시제 일치는 예외가 있다. 원칙상, 주절의 시제가 과거이면 시제 일치의 원칙에 따라 종속절은 과거나 과거완료로만 쓸 수 있다. 그러나 시제 일치에 상관없이 불변의 진리나 현재 습관, 상태는 현재시제로 나타내며, 역사적 사실은 과거시제로 나타낸다.

≫ I was taught the French revolution **[had broken out / broke out]** in 1789.

14. 완료형 부정사, 완료형 동명사는 동사의 시제보다 앞선 시제를 의미한다. 완료형 분사구문은 주절의 시제보다 앞선 시제를 의미한다.

≫ Because she had already seen the film twice, she didn't want to go to the cinema.
= **[Seeing already / Having already seen]** the film twice, she didn't want to go to the cinema.

15. 수동태의 다양한 형태를 유의한다.

진행형 수동태 형태	be being p.p.	완료형 수동태 형태	have been p.p.
조동사 수동태 형태	「조동사+be p.p.」	부정사 수동태 형태	「to+ be p.p.」

≫ The area **[has cleared / has been cleared]** of land mines.

16. 제안, 명령, 요구, 주장의 의미를 갖는 동사(suggest, recommend, order, demand, insist 등)는 that절을 가져오는 경우 주어 다음에 「(should+) 동사원형」이 쓰인다. 단, 실제로 발생한 단순한 사실을 전달할 때는 문장의 수와 시제에 맞춰 써야 한다.

≫ She suggested to me that I **[took / take]** some rest away from work.

17. 부정어구 또는 장소와 방향을 나타내는 부사(구)가 문장 앞에 오면 주어와 동사가 도치된다. 단, 주어가 대명사인 경우에는 도치되지 않는다. 또한 be동사가 쓰인 문장에서 보어를 문장의 앞에 두면, 주어와 be동사가 도치된다.

≫ Here **[comes the writer / the writer comes]**!

18. 특정한 어휘나 구를 사용하여 문장의 특정 부분을 강조할 수 있다. 조동사 do를 사용하여 동사를 강조할 수 있고, 재귀대명사나 the very를 사용하여 명사를 강조할 수 있다. 소유격을 강조할 때는「소유격+own+명사」를 사용한다.

≫ Rowling's books **[do / does]** contain supernatural creatures.

19. 분사구문의 주어가 주절의 주어와 다른 경우에는 분사구문의 주어를 명시해 준다.

≫ The dog **[barked / barking]** at him, he ran away.

20. 재귀대명사는 주어와 동일한 대상을 지칭하는 목적어에 사용한다. '~자신'이라는 의미를 나타낸다. 재귀대명사 강조 용법은 명사를 강조하기 위해 사용하고 생략 가능하다. 재귀대명사 관용 표현도 익혀 둔다.

for oneself	자기를 위하여	by oneself	혼자서
in itself	본질적으로	Between ourselves	우리끼리 얘긴데

≫ We enjoyed **[us / ourselves]** very much last night.

★ 전치사 vs. 접속사

전치사 뒤에는 명사(구)가 나오고, 접속사 뒤에는 절(주어+동사)이 나온다. 그런데 두 개 이상의 단어가 전치사나 접속사의 역할을 하기도 한다.

1. '~ 때문에'의 의미로 쓰이는 전치사구는 because of, due to, owing to가 있고, 접속사(구)는 because, now that, in that이 있다.
2. '~할 경우'의 의미로 쓰이는 전치사구는 in case of가 있고, 접속사구는 in case(= if)가 있다.
3. '~에도 불구하고'의 의미로 쓰이는 전치사구는 in spite of(= despite)가 있고 접속사구는 even though, even if가 있다.
4. '~에 따라'의 의미로 쓰이는 전치사구는 according to, 접속사구는 according as가 있다.
5. '~하자마자'의 의미로 쓰이는 전치사는 on이 있고, 접속사구는 the moment, as soon as가 있다.
6. '~하는 동안'의 의미로 쓰이는 전치사는 during, 접속사는 while이 있다.

정답

01 is 02 does Sam 03 causes
04 point 05 not to waste 06 to carry
07 her 08 ancing 09 Having
10 nor 11 crawling 12 sliding
13 broke out 14 Having already seen
15 has been cleared 16 take
17 comes the writer 18 do 19 barking
20 ourselves

고3 영어 [독해]

※문법 / 숙어 플러스는 정답 및 해설 참조

DAY 01 글의 목적

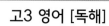

1 ⑤　2 ③　3 ④　4 ④　5 ③
6 ①　7 ②　8 ③　9 ①　10 ⑤

DAY 02 심경·분위기

1 ①　2 ④　3 ④　4 ①　5 ⑤
6 ③　7 ⑤　8 ①　9 ①　10 ①

DAY 03 필자의 주장

1 ①　2 ①　3 ①　4 ②　5 ①
6 ⑤　7 ③　8 ①　9 ①　10 ①

DAY 04 함축·지칭 추론

1 ①　2 ⑤　3 ①　4 ④　5 ⑤
6 ②　7 ④　8 ②　9 ②　10 ④

DAY 05 글의 요지

1 ①　2 ⑤　3 ⑤　4 ①　5 ②
6 ②　7 ①　8 ①　9 ①　10 ①

DAY 06 글의 주제

1 ③　2 ①　3 ⑤　4 ②　5 ①
6 ②　7 ⑤　8 ④　9 ③　10 ⑤

DAY 07 글의 제목

1 ⑤　2 ②　3 ①　4 ①　5 ①
6 ①　7 ①　8 ②　9 ②　10 ②

DAY 08 도표 정보 파악

1 ⑤　2 ⑤　3 ④　4 ③　5 ⑤
6 ⑤　7 ④　8 ②　9 ⑤　10 ④

DAY 09 내용 일치·불일치

1 ⑤　2 ③　3 ③　4 ③　5 ③
6 ⑤　7 ③　8 ③　9 ⑤　10 ⑤

DAY 10 안내문

1 ④　2 ④　3 ③　4 ⑤　5 ③
6 ④　7 ④　8 ④　9 ④　10 ③

DAY 11 어법 정확성 파악

1 ④　2 ②　3 ③　4 ③　5 ②
6 ②　7 ④　8 ⑤　9 ⑤　10 ④

DAY 12 어휘 적절성 파악

1 ⑤　2 ④　3 ⑤　4 ②　5 ④
6 ③　7 ④　8 ③　9 ⑤　10 ④

DAY 13 빈칸 추론 (1) 어휘, 짧은 어구

1 ②　2 ②　3 ⑤　4 ④　5 ⑤
6 ④　7 ①　8 ⑤　9 ②　10 ③

DAY 14 빈칸 추론 (2) 긴 어구, 문장

1 ⑤　2 ④　3 ①　4 ④　5 ②
6 ②　7 ①　8 ②　9 ①　10 ②

DAY 15 흐름에 무관한 문장 찾기

1 ③　2 ④　3 ④　4 ③　5 ③
6 ④　7 ④　8 ③　9 ③　10 ③

DAY 16 문단 내 글의 순서 파악

1 ②　2 ④　3 ②　4 ⑤　5 ④
6 ②　7 ②　8 ⑤　9 ②　10 ⑤

DAY 17 주어진 문장의 위치 파악

1 ④　2 ④　3 ②　4 ⑤　5 ⑤
6 ③　7 ⑤　8 ④　9 ④　10 ④

DAY 18 문단 요약

1 ①　2 ①　3 ②　4 ①　5 ③
6 ⑤　7 ①

DAY 19 장문의 이해 (1)

1 ①　2 ④　3 ②　4 ③　5 ③
6 ④　7 ⑤　8 ④

DAY 20 장문의 이해 (2)

1 ⑤　2 ②　3 ③　4 ③　5 ③
6 ②　7 ③　8 ⑤　9 ④　10 ③
11 ②　12 ③

DAY 21 미니 고난도 Test 1회

1 ③　2 ①　3 ④　4 ②　5 ③
6 ①　7 ②　8 ⑤

DAY 22 미니 고난도 Test 2회

1 ②　2 ④　3 ④　4 ③　5 ②
6 ④　7 ⑤

DAY 23 미니 고난도 Test 3회

1 ②　2 ⑤　3 ④　4 ⑤　5 ③
6 ①　7 ②　8 ③

DAY 24 미니 고난도 Test 4회

1 ①　2 ⑤　3 ③　4 ②　5 ④
6 ③　7 ②　8 ⑤

01 글의 목적

출제 트렌드

1. 글의 목적을 파악하는 문제는 필자가 어떤 의도로 무엇을 위해 쓴 것인지를 파악하는 유형이다. 매년 수능에서 1문항이 출제된다. 편지글, 기사글, 광고문, 안내문, 초대장, 연설문, 항의문, 축하문 등의 다양한 글이 사용된다. 주로 실용문에서 출제되며, 편지글이 출제 빈도가 가장 높다.
2. 최근 수능 7년간, 글의 목적 문제는 매년 1문항이 출제되었다. 2017학년도 수능(95%), 2018(94%), 2019(97%), 2020(97%), 2021(91%), 2022(93%), 2023(98%)에서 괄호 안의 정답률을 보였다. 7년간 평균 95%의 정답률을 보였다. 난이도는 하 단계이다.

출처			문항 번호	지문 주제	정답률(%)	난이도
대표	2023학년도	수능	18번	조류 관찰 클럽 가입 문의	98	★☆☆
1	2022학년도	10 학평	18번	재난과 관련된 경험담 투고 요청	88	★☆☆
2	2023학년도	09 모평	18번	피겨 스케이팅 선수 응원	96	★☆☆
3	2022학년도	07 학평	18번	등하굣길 확장 요청	96	★☆☆
4	2023학년도	06 모평	18번	수영장 추가 대여 가능 여부 문의	97	★☆☆
5	2022학년도	04 학평	18번	역사적 건축물 복원 요청	94	★☆☆
6	2022학년도	03 학평	18번	제품의 세부사항과 견본 요청	91	★☆☆
7	2022학년도	수능	18번	과학 교사 워크숍의 특강 부탁	96	★☆☆
8	2022학년도	06 모평	18번	박물관 멤버십 회원을 위한 추가 혜택 안내	96	★☆☆
9	2021학년도	수능	18번	교내 음식 모으기 운동 참여 방법 안내	91	★☆☆
10	2020학년도	수능	18번	애완견 공원의 소음	97	★☆☆

※수능과 모평 시험은 시험지 표기 명칭과 실시 연도가 다릅니다. 예를 들면 2023학년도 시험은 2022년에 실시되었습니다.

1등급 꿀팁

1. 글쓴이와 독자의 관계 또는 발신자와 수신자의 관계를 파악하고, 글의 주제를 추론한다.
2. 주제와 세부 내용을 종합하여 글의 목적을 추론한다. 대체로 글의 목적은 하단에 명시되는 경우가 많다.
3. 역접 연결사(but, however, nevertheless)로 흐름이 전환되는 부분을 주의한다.
4. 목적과 관련된 표현을 익혀 둔다.

요청	I'm kindly asking you to ~	~하기를 요청합니다
촉구	I ask you to take measures to ~	~하는 조치를 취하기 원합니다
지시	must make sure that ~	~를 챙겨야 합니다
홍보	We are pleased to introduce ~	~을 소개하게 되어 기쁩니다
공지	be actively seeking a replacement ~	~의 후임자를 적극적으로 찾고 있습니다
문의	let me know if it is possible to~	~이 가능한지 알고 싶습니다
안내	be very excited to announce that ~	~를 알려드리게 되어 기쁩니다

제한 시간 : 15분 | 정답 및 해설 002쪽

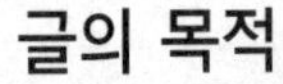

대표 기출

2023학년도 수능 18번

18. 다음 글의 목적으로 가장 적절한 것은?

To whom it may concern,

My name is Michael Brown. I have been a bird-watcher since childhood. I have always enjoyed watching birds in my yard and identifying them by sight and sound. Yesterday, I happened to read an article about your club. I was surprised and excited to find out about a community of passionate bird-watchers who travel annually to go birding. I would love to join your club, but your website appears to be under construction. I could not find any information except for this contact email address. I would like to know how to sign up for the club. I look forward to your reply.

Sincerely,
Michael Brown

① 조류 관찰 클럽에 가입하는 방법을 문의하려고
② 조류 관찰 시 주의해야 할 사항을 전달하려고
③ 조류 관찰 협회의 새로운 규정을 확인하려고
④ 조류 관찰과 관련된 웹 사이트를 소개하려고
⑤ 조류 관찰 시 필요한 장비를 알아보려고

문제 풀이

1. 수신자와 발신자 간의 관계를 파악하고 글의 주제를 추론해 본다.

수신자	관계자 분께
발신자	Michael Brown
글의 주제	조류 관찰 클럽에 가입하는 방법을 문의하려고

2. 글의 세부 내용을 파악한다.

① Yesterday, I happened to read an article about your club. (어제 저는 우연히 귀하의 클럽에 대한 기사를 읽었습니다.)

② I was surprised and excited to find out about a community of passionate bird-watchers who travel annually to go birding. (저는 조류 관찰을 하러 매년 여행하는 열정적인 조류 관찰자들의 공동체에 대해 알게 되어 놀랐고 신이 났습니다.)

③ I would love to join your club, but your website appears to be under construction. (저는 귀하의 클럽에 가입하기를 몹시 원하지만, 귀하의 웹 사이트가 공사 중인 것 같습니다.)

④ I could not find any information except for this contact email address. I would like to know how to sign up for the club. (이 이메일 주소 외에 다른 정보를 찾을 수가 없었습니다. 클럽에 가입하는 방법을 알고 싶습니다.)

3. 글의 주제와 세부 내용을 종합하여 글의 목적을 파악한다.

• 조류 관찰 클럽에 대한 기사를 읽은 후 클럽에 가입하는 방법을 알고 싶어서 쓴 글이므로, 글의 목적으로 가장 적절한 것은 ① '조류 관찰 클럽에 가입하는 방법을 문의하려고'이다.

2022학년도 10월 학평 18번 ★☆☆

1. 다음 글의 목적으로 가장 적절한 것은?

Dear Readers,

As you've seen throughout my books, I've learned a great deal from people who have sent me their stories and advice. Let's keep it going. If you would like to send me an email about your experiences with disasters and what you've learned about escaping them, please send it to nodisaster@smail.com. I want you to note that, by sending me your story, you are giving me permission to use it in the books that I write. But I promise not to use your name unless you give me explicit permission. Thank you.

Very truly yours,
Robert Brown

① 신간 도서 출판 기념회에 초대하려고
② 저작물 사용에 대한 허락을 구하려고
③ 개인 정보의 무단 사용에 대해 항의하려고
④ 재난에 적절히 대처하는 요령을 안내하려고
⑤ 재난과 관련한 경험담을 보내 줄 것을 요청하려고

2023학년도 9월 모평 18번 ★☆☆

2. 다음 글의 목적으로 가장 적절한 것은?

Dear Natalie Talley,

My name is Olivia Spikes, the mayor of Millstown. Before you attend the world championships next month, on behalf of everyone in Millstown, I wish to let you know that we are supporting you all the way. As you are the first famous figure skater from Millstown, we are all big fans of yours. Our community was so proud of you for winning the national championships last year. Your amazing performance really moved us all. We all believe that you are going to impress the entire nation again. Your hometown supporters will cheer for you whenever you perform on the ice. Good luck!

Best wishes,
Olivia Spikes

① 지역 사회 홍보 대사로 활동해 줄 것을 제안하려고
② 이웃 도시와 예정된 친선 경기 취소를 통보하려고
③ 지역 사회 출신 피겨 스케이팅 선수를 응원하려고
④ 시청에서 주관하는 연례 자선 행사를 홍보하려고
⑤ 피겨 스케이팅 경기장 건립을 위한 기부를 요청하려고

2022학년도 7월 학평 18번 ★☆☆

3. 다음 글의 목적으로 가장 적절한 것은?

To whom it may concern,

Thank you very much for faithfully responding to our request six months ago and taking corresponding measures. Even after the installation of road traffic safety facilities, we still need more for the safety of our students. It is a problem with the school road, which students use on their way to and from school. The width of the current school road is barely wide enough for two people to walk side by side. So, there are risks of collision with vehicles on the road where students walk and accidents if many students flock to the narrow school road. Therefore, we ask you to expand the school road for students' safety. I would appreciate it if you could respond as soon as possible.

Sincerely,
Alisha Lee

① 교통 신호등 추가 설치를 제안하려고
② 도로 교통 안전 법규 개정을 촉구하려고
③ 학교 앞 교통 지도 인원의 증원을 건의하려고
④ 학생 안전을 위해 등하굣길 폭의 확장을 요청하려고
⑤ 학교 주변 불법 주정차 차량 단속 강화를 요구하려고

2023학년도 6월 모평 18번 ★☆☆

4. 다음 글의 목적으로 가장 적절한 것은?

Dear Hylean Miller,

Hello, I'm Nelson Perkins, a teacher and swimming coach at Broomstone High School. Last week, I made a reservation for one of your company's swimming pools for our summer swim camp. However, due to its popularity, thirty more students are coming to the camp than we expected, so we need one more swimming pool for them. The rental section on your website says that there are two other swimming pools during the summer season: the Splash Pool and the Rainbow Pool. Please let me know if an additional rental would be possible. Thank you in advance.

Best Wishes,
Nelson Perkins

① 수영 캠프 참가 날짜를 변경하려고
② 수영장 수용 가능 인원을 확인하려고
③ 수영 캠프 등록 방법에 대해 알아보려고
④ 수영장 추가 대여 가능 여부를 문의하려고
⑤ 수영장 대여 취소에 따른 환불을 요청하려고

2022학년도 4월 학평 18번 ★☆☆

5. 다음 글의 목적으로 가장 적절한 것은?

To whom it may concern,

I sometimes travel to Summerland to visit friends. One of the first landmarks to captivate me there years ago was the Mackenzie-Brown House. Last week, I visited again after a long time away, and I was shocked at the state of the house — yard overgrown and stains on the beautiful walls. I am particularly sensitive to historic sites falling into disrepair. I certainly can't understand why you have neglected such a landmark, and I ask that you please restore the Mackenzie-Brown House. I cannot imagine how heartbreaking it must be for the residents of Summerland to witness the decline of this historic building.

With kind regards,
Holly Bebernitz

① 역사적 건축물 견학 프로그램을 홍보하려고
② 관광객 유치를 위한 아이디어를 제안하려고
③ 지역의 역사적 건축물 복원을 요청하려고
④ 박물관 보수 공사 일정 조정을 부탁하려고
⑤ 유적지 관리 실태 조사 결과를 공유하려고

2022학년도 3월 학평 18번 ★☆☆

6. 다음 글의 목적으로 가장 적절한 것은?

Dear Lorenzo Romano,

I heard from Antonio Ricci of Rome that you are producing handmade gloves for export in a variety of natural leathers. I read about your business on your website. There is a steady demand in my country for high quality leather gloves, and I am able to charge good prices. Please let me know full details of the gloves you would recommend. It would also help if you could provide me with some samples of the gloves you produce. I hope to hear from you soon.

Sincerely yours,
Jonathan Turner

① 제품의 모든 세부 사항과 견본을 요청하려고
② 신제품의 가격 인상 요인에 대해 설명하려고
③ 수출할 제품에 대한 전수 검사를 의뢰하려고
④ 웹 사이트에 게시한 정보의 수정을 촉구하려고
⑤ 제조업체에 품질 개선을 위한 회의를 제안하려고

2022학년도 수능 18번 ★☆☆

7. 다음 글의 목적으로 가장 적절한 것은?

Dear Ms. Green,

My name is Donna Williams, a science teacher at Rogan High School. I am planning a special workshop for our science teachers. We are interested in learning how to teach online science classes. I have been impressed with your ideas about using internet platforms for science classes. Since you are an expert in online education, I would like to ask you to deliver a special lecture at the workshop scheduled for next month. I am sure the lecture will help our teachers manage successful online science classes, and I hope we can learn from your insights. I am looking forward to hearing from you.

Sincerely,
Donna Williams

① 과학 교육 정책 협의회 참여를 독려하려고
② 과학 교사 워크숍의 특강을 부탁하려고
③ 과학 교사 채용 계획을 공지하려고
④ 과학 교육 프로그램 개발을 요청하려고
⑤ 과학 교육 워크숍 일정의 변경을 안내하려고

2022학년도 6월 모평 18번 ★☆☆

8. 다음 글의 목적으로 가장 적절한 것은?

Dear Ms. Larson,

I am writing to you with new information about your current membership. Last year, you signed up for our museum membership that provides special discounts. As stated in the last newsletter, this year we are happy to be celebrating our 50th anniversary. So we would like to offer you further benefits. These include free admission for up to ten people and 20% off museum merchandise on your next visit. You will also be invited to all new exhibition openings this year at discounted prices. We hope you enjoy these offers. For any questions, please feel free to contact us.

Best regards,
Stella Harrison

① 박물관 개관 50주년 기념행사 취소를 공지하려고
② 작년에 가입한 박물관 멤버십의 갱신을 요청하려고
③ 박물관 멤버십 회원을 위한 추가 혜택을 알려 주려고
④ 박물관 기념품점에서 새로 판매할 상품을 홍보하려고
⑤ 박물관 전시 프로그램에서 변경된 내용을 안내하려고

2021학년도 수능 18번 ★☆☆

9. 다음 글의 목적으로 가장 적절한 것은?

Dear Friends,

Season's greetings. As some of you already know, we are starting the campus food drive. This is how you participate. You can bring your items for donation to our booths. Our donation booths are located in the lobbies of the campus libraries. Just drop off the items there during usual library hours from December 4 to 23. The donated food should be non-perishable like canned meats and canned fruits. Packaged goods such as jam and peanut butter are also good. We will distribute the food to our neighbors on Christmas Eve. We truly appreciate your help.

Many blessings,
Joanna at Campus Food Bank

① 음식 기부에 참여하는 방법을 안내하려고
② 음식 배달 자원봉사 참여에 감사하려고
③ 도서관 이용 시간 변경을 공지하려고
④ 음식물 낭비의 심각성을 알려 주려고
⑤ 크리스마스 행사 일정을 문의하려고

2020학년도 수능 18번 ★☆☆

10. 다음 글의 목적으로 가장 적절한 것은?

Dear Mr. Kayne,

I am a resident of Cansinghill Apartments, located right next to the newly opened Vuenna Dog Park. As I live with three dogs, I am very happy to let my dogs run around and safely play with other dogs from the neighborhood. However, the noise of barking and yelling from the park at night is so loud and disturbing that I cannot relax in my apartment. Many of my apartment neighbors also seriously complain about this noise. I want immediate action to solve this urgent problem. Since you are the manager of Vuenna Dog Park, I ask you to take measures to prevent the noise at night. I hope to hear from you soon.

Sincerely,
Monty Kim

① 애완견 예방 접종 일정을 확인하려고
② 애완견 공원의 야간 이용 시간을 문의하려고
③ 아파트 내 애완견 출입 금지 구역을 안내하려고
④ 아파트 인근에 개장한 애완견 공원을 홍보하려고
⑤ 애완견 공원의 야간 소음 방지 대책을 촉구하려고

총 문항				문항	맞은 문항					문항
개별 문항	1	2	3	4	5	6	7	8	9	10
채점										

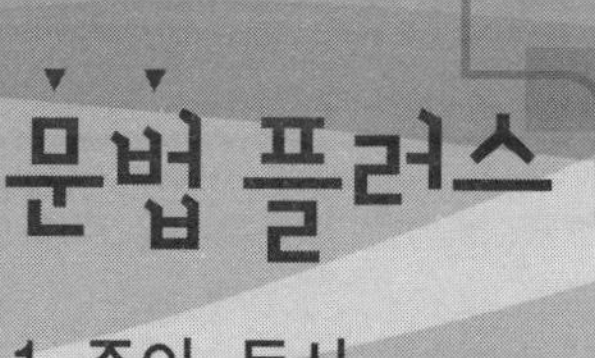

문법 플러스

1. 주어·동사

정답 및 해설 005쪽

A 문법의 주요 포인트를 점검해 봅시다.

1 to부정사나 동명사는 문장에서 주어 역할을 할 수 있으며 단수로 취급한다.
▶ One obvious drawback is the danger involved; knowing that it exists **[does / do]** nothing to reduce it.

2 접속사 That이나 whether, 간접의문문, 관계대명사 what, 복합관계대명사가 이끄는 절은 주어 역할을 할 수 있으며 단수로 취급한다.
▶ That she is a millionaire **[are / is]** incredible.

3 주어가 전치사구의 수식을 받아 길어진 경우, 주어, 동사를 잘 파악해야 한다.
▶ Speculations about the meaning and purpose of prehistoric art **[relies / rely]** heavily on analogies drawn with modern-day hunter-gatherer societies.

4 주어가 분사구, to부정사구의 수식을 받아 길어진 경우, 문장의 주어, 동사를 잘 파악해야 한다.
▶ A weekly program dealing with social issues **[was / were]** loved by viewers.

5 주어가 관계사절의 수식을 받아 길어진 경우, 문장의 동사가 무엇인지 유의해야 한다.
▶ The girl who lives besides us **[are / is]** ill.

6 주어가 길어진 경우 가주어 it을 쓰고 진주어는 뒤로 돌린다.
▶ All things considered, **[it / that]** might be better to ask for the services of a moving company.

7 There is[are]~, Here is[are] ~ 문장에서 주어는 There나 Here가 아니라 be동사 뒤에 오는 어구다.
▶ There **[was / were]** differences of opinion on basic issues.

B 다음 괄호 안에서 어법상 올바른 것을 고르시오.

1 To work out on a regular basis **[are / is]** not easy for everyone.

2 What you see **[is / are]** not a truth all the time.

3 A beautiful lady in a red dress **[are / is]** walking along the street.

4 The number of children taught by their parents **[is / are]** gradually increasing in USA.

5 Her hope to become a doctor **[was / to be]** finally fulfilled.

6 **[It / That]** is important that he should be informed.

7 Here **[is / are]** some helpful tips for you.

숙어 플러스

1. 수능 필수 숙어 1회

정답 및 해설 006쪽

A 다음 수능 필수 숙어를 읽고, 아는 것은 체크해 봅시다.

□ 01	A as well as B	B뿐만 아니라 A도(= not only A but also B)
□ 02	a bit of	조금의, 한 조각의
□ 03	a great deal of	다량의, 많은(= a large amount of)
□ 04	a kind of	일종의, 유사한
□ 05	a number of	많은
□ 06	A rather than B	B라기 보다는 A
□ 07	a wide range of	광범위한, 다양한
□ 08	above all	무엇보다
□ 09	account for	설명하다, (비율을) 차지하다
□ 10	act on	~에 영향을 미치다, ~에 따라 행동하다
□ 11	adjust A to B	A를 B에 맞추다
□ 12	after all	결국, ~에도 불구하고, 무엇보다도
□ 13	after a while	잠시 후에
□ 14	all at once	갑자기, 불시에, 동시에
□ 15	all but	거의, ~외에 모두
□ 16	all in all	전반적으로 보아, 대체로
□ 17	all of a sudden	갑자기
□ 18	all the way	줄곧, 내내
□ 19	all told	합쳐서, 통틀어
□ 20	allow for	~을 참작하다, 고려하다

B 다음 숙어 표현을 읽고 의미 차이를 비교해 봅시다.

□ 21	look after	~를 돌보다(= take care of)
□ 22	name after	~의 이름을 따서 이름을 짓다
□ 23	run after	~을 추적하다, ~를 뒤쫓다
□ 24	seek after	~를 추구하다
□ 25	take after	~를 닮다(= resemble)

C 우리말을 참고하여 빈칸에 알맞은 말을 써 봅시다.

1 아프리카계 미국인이 미국 국민의 12퍼센트를 차지하는 것을 알고 있니?
Do you know Afro-Americans ________________ for 12% of the US population?

2 영국의 석탄 산업은 거의 사라져 가고 있다.
Britain's coal industry has all ________________ disappeared.

3 이것은 출판업자들이 폭넓은 주제를 탐구할 수 있게 자유로워졌다는 것을 의미한다.
This meant the publishers were free to explore a wide ______________ of subjects.

4 많은 쟁점이 논의되었습니다.
A ______________ of issues were discussed.

02 심경·분위기

출제 트렌드

1. 심경 문제 유형은 등장인물이나 필자가 처해 있는 상황이나 사건을 통해 그들을 느꼈을 심경을 추론하는 유형이다. 글 전반이나 특정한 상황 속에서 느꼈을 심경을 추론하는 문제와 앞부분과 뒷부분의 심경 변화를 추론하는 문제로 출제되고 있다. 수능에서 1문제가 출제되고 있다.
2. 글의 분위기 문제는 글을 읽고 글 전반에서 느끼는 분위기를 추론하는 유형이다. 소설이나 수필에서 출제되고 있으며 글의 종합적인 이해와 감상 능력이 필요하다. 2017~2018년도에는 출제되었지만, 최근에는 자주 출제되지 않고 있다.
3. 최근 수능 7년간, 심경 · 분위기 문제는 매년 1문항이 출제되었다. 2017학년도 수능(94%), 2018(94%), 2019(95%), 2020(95%), 2021(93%), 2022(93%), 2023(92%)에서 괄호 안의 정답률을 보였다. 7년간 평균 93.7%의 정답률을 보였다. 난이도는 하 단계이다.

	출처		문항 번호	지문 주제	정답률(%)	난이도
대표	2023학년도	수능	19번	자신의 최고 기록을 깨지 못한 Jamie	92	★☆☆
1	2022학년도	10 학평	19번	콘퍼런스 참석	95	★☆☆
2	2023학년도	09 모평	19번	딸이 그린 아빠 얼굴	96	★☆☆
3	2022학년도	07 학평	19번	Big Foot으로 갈 때 느낀 두려움	91	★☆☆
4	2023학년도	06 모평	19번	노을을 보러간 Jessica	96	★☆☆
5	2022학년도	04 학평	19번	숲속에서 코끼리를 만난 Karim	95	★☆☆
6	2022학년도	03 학평	19번	절벽에서 내려오기	87	★☆☆
7	2022학년도	수능	19번	공룡 화석을 찾지 못한 Evelyn	93	★☆☆
8	2022학년도	06 모평	19번	Natalie의 첫 온라인 상담	90	★☆☆
9	2021학년도	수능	19번	기대와 달랐던 현장학습	95	★☆☆
10	2019학년도	수능	19번	가까스로 서핑 성공	95	★☆☆

1등급 꿀팁

1. 등장인물이 겪은 사건이나 상황을 파악하고 심경을 추론할 수 있는 표현을 찾고 밑줄을 긋는다.
2. 심경 변화 문제는 심경 변화 전후를 보여주는 표현에 밑줄을 긋는다.
3. 등장인물의 감정을 보여주는 어휘를 익힌다.

alarmed 깜짝 놀란	doubtful 의심하는	horrified 겁에 질린	scared 두려워하는
annoyed 화가 난	embarrassed 당황한	indifferent 무관심한	sorrowful 슬픈
bored 지루한	envious 부러워하는	jealous 시기하는	surprised 놀란
calm 차분한	excited 흥분한	panicked 당황스러운	thrilled 아주 신이 난
comforted 편한, 안도한	frightened 겁먹은	pleased 기쁜	upset 마음이 상한
confident 자신감 있는	frustrated 좌절한	relieved 안도하는	worried 걱정하는
disappointed 실망한	grateful 고마워하는	satisfied 만족한	curious 호기심이 많은

Day 02

제한 시간 : 15분 | 정답 및 해설 006쪽

대표 기출

2023학년도 수능 19번

19. 다음 글에 드러난 Jamie의 심경 변화로 가장 적절한 것은?

Putting all of her energy into her last steps of the running race, Jamie crossed the finish line. To her disappointment, she had failed to beat her personal best time, again. Jamie had pushed herself for months to finally break her record, but it was all for nothing. Recognizing how she felt about her failure, Ken, her teammate, approached her and said, "Jamie, even though you didn't set a personal best time today, your performances have improved dramatically. Your running skills have progressed so much! You'll definitely break your personal best time in the next race!" After hearing his comments, she felt confident about herself. Jamie, now motivated to keep pushing for her goal, replied with a smile. "You're right! Next race, I'll beat my best time for sure!"

① indifferent → regretful　② pleased → bored
③ frustrated → encouraged　④ nervous → fearful
⑤ calm → excited

문제 풀이

1. 등장인물이 겪은 사건이나 처한 상황을 파악한다.

- Putting all of her energy into her last steps of the running race, Jamie crossed the finish line. (Jamie는 자신의 모든 에너지를 달리기 경주의 마지막 스텝에 쏟으면서 결승선을 통과했다.)

2. 등장인물의 심경을 추론할 수 있는 표현을 찾는다.

① To her disappointment, she had failed to beat her personal best time, again. (실망스럽게도, 그녀는 자신의 개인 최고 기록을 깨는 데 또 실패했다.)

② Jamie had pushed herself for months to finally break her record, but it was all for nothing. (Jamie는 기어코 자신의 기록을 깨기 위해 몇 달 동안 자신을 몰아붙였지만, 그것은 모두 수포로 돌아갔다.)

3. 글의 흐름 및 상황이 중간에 전환되어 주인공의 심경이 바뀌는 것을 파악한다.

① After hearing his comments, she felt confident about herself. (그의 말을 들은 후, 그녀는 자신에 대해 자신감을 느꼈다.)

② Jamie, now motivated to keep pushing for her goal, replied with a smile. (이제 자신의 목표를 계속 밀고 나갈 의욕을 갖게 된 Jamie는 미소를 지으며 대답했다.)

- Jamie는 몇 달 동안 노력했지만 달리기 경주에서 자신의 개인 최고 기록을 깨는 데 실패해 낙심했다. 그러나 Ken이 격려해주는 말을 들은 후 자신감을 느끼게 된다. Jamie는 미소를 지으며 Ken에게 다음 경주에서는 최고 기록을 깰 것이라고 답한다. 따라서 Jamie의 심경 변화로 가장 적절한 것은 ③ 'frustrated→encouraged (좌절한 → 용기를 얻은)'이다.

2022학년도 10월 학평 19번 ★☆☆

1. 다음 글에 나타난 'I'의 심경 변화로 가장 적절한 것은?

I was going to a conference and my plane was delayed, so by the time I got to my hotel everyone I was supposed to meet had already left for the conference. I walked to the bus stop, but to my dismay the last shuttle to the convention center had already gone. I was at a loss as to what to do! Then a young man standing on the sidewalk said, "The convention center isn't very far. It's only four blocks." So I started walking. It wasn't long before the convention center appeared in front of my eyes. My heart slowly calmed down! Fortunately, I was just in time for the conference!

① frustrated → relieved　② bored → excited
③ angry → embarrassed　④ envious → ashamed
⑤ doubtful → indifferent

2023학년도 9월 모평 19번 ★☆☆

2. 다음 글에 드러난 Nathan의 심경 변화로 가장 적절한 것은?

"Daddy!" Jenny called, waving a yellow crayon in her little hand. Nathan approached her, wondering why she was calling him. Jenny, his three-year-old toddler, was drawing a big circle on a piece of paper. "What are you doing, Sweetie?" Nathan asked with interest. She just kept drawing without reply. He continued watching her, wondering what she was working on. She was drawing something that looked like a face. When she finished it, Jenny shouted, "Look, Daddy!" She held her artwork up proudly. Taking a closer look, Nathan recognized that it was his face. The face had two big eyes and a beard just like his. He loved Jenny's work. Filled with joy and happiness, Nathan gave her a big hug.

* toddler: 아장아장 걷는 아이

① sorrowful → relieved　② frustrated → satisfied
③ worried → scared　④ curious → delighted
⑤ hopeful → disappointed

2022학년도 7월 학평 19번 ★☆☆

3. 다음 글에 나타난 'I'의 심경으로 가장 적절한 것은?

One night a buddy and I decided we were going to go find that Big Foot. We were in my old truck and we set off across the fields heading toward the tallest hill. The fields were rough, with only the slightest trail to follow. Along the way there were small trenches dug in the fields. I never figured out why. As we got closer and closer to the top of the hill, I was actually becoming scared, which was kind of rare, because at that age I was pretty fearless. As we got to the top of the hill, there was a loud thump! My truck sunk down like something heavy had just jumped in the bed. We were too terrified to look in the back. I panicked and decided to throw the truck into reverse and back down the hill. As I did so, there was another thump and a loud roar now came out like I'd never, ever heard before.

① relieved and relaxed
② pleased and delighted
③ bored and indifferent
④ alarmed and frightened
⑤ dissatisfied and angry

2023학년도 6월 모평 19번 ★☆☆

4. 다음 글에 나타난 Jessica의 심경 변화로 가장 적절한 것은?

The island tour bus Jessica was riding on was moving slowly toward the ocean cliffs. Outside, the sky was getting dark. Jessica sighed with concern, "I'm going to miss the sunset because of the traffic." The bus arrived at the cliffs' parking lot. While the other passengers were gathering their bags, Jessica quickly got off the bus and she ran up the cliff that was famous for its ocean views. She was about to give up when she got to the top. Just then she saw the setting sun and it still shone brightly in the sky. Jessica said to herself, "The glow of the sun is so beautiful. It's even better than I expected."

① worried → delighted
② bored → confident
③ relieved → annoyed
④ joyful → indifferent
⑤ regretful → depressed

2022학년도 4월 학평 19번 ★☆☆

5. 다음 글에 드러난 Karim의 심경 변화로 가장 적절한 것은?

Karim was deep within the dense forest alone. He began to notice the strangeness of his surroundings. Scared, he hid under a tree, and he heard the "thump−thump" sound. Moments later, he saw a large elephant running toward him! He trembled uncontrollably and could hardly move. Suddenly, he remembered what he had read about elephants: Elephants are scared of loud noises. He also thought of the firecrackers in his pack. Quick as a flash, he lit them. The firecrackers burst with a loud noise, scaring away the elephant. Then, Karim ran away as fast as he could. By the time he reached his campsite, he was sure there was nothing dangerous around him. He could finally breathe easily. He put his hand on his chest, feeling his heartbeat slow back to its normal pace.

① hopeful → nervous
② fulfilled → regretful
③ jealous → satisfied
④ ashamed → grateful
⑤ terrified → relieved

2022학년도 3월 학평 19번 ★☆☆

6. 다음 글에 드러난 'I'의 심경 변화로 가장 적절한 것은?

Finally, it came to my turn. I was supposed to walk backward off the cliff. Just looking down the cliff made my legs begin to shake. I knew there was a safety rope around me in case I should black out. I had an intellectual understanding of the whole situation and an intellectual sense of security. Nevertheless, my hair stood on end and I shivered all over. That first step off the cliff was the most difficult moment, but I made it — as did others. I arrived safely at the bottom, overjoyed by the success of meeting the challenge. I felt as though I was walking on air.

① relaxed → nervous
② angry → ashamed
③ terrified → delighted
④ envious → sympathetic
⑤ disappointed → hopeful

2022년도 수능 19번 ★☆☆

7. 다음 글에 나타난 Evelyn의 심경 변화로 가장 적절한 것은?

It was Evelyn's first time to explore the Badlands of Alberta, famous across Canada for its numerous dinosaur fossils. As a young amateur bone-hunter, she was overflowing with anticipation. She had not travelled this far for the bones of common dinosaur species. Her life-long dream to find rare fossils of dinosaurs was about to come true. She began eagerly searching for them. After many hours of wandering throughout the deserted lands, however, she was unsuccessful. Now, the sun was beginning to set, and her goal was still far beyond her reach. Looking at the slowly darkening ground before her, she sighed to herself, "I can't believe I came all this way for nothing. What a waste of time!"

① confused → scared
② discouraged → confident
③ relaxed → annoyed
④ indifferent → depressed
⑤ hopeful → disappointed

2022학년도 6월 모평 19번 ★☆☆

8. 다음 글에 드러난 Natalie의 심경 변화로 가장 적절한 것은?

As Natalie was logging in to her first online counseling session, she wondered, "How can I open my heart to the counselor through a computer screen?" Since the counseling center was a long drive away, she knew that this would save her a lot of time. Natalie just wasn't sure if it would be as helpful as meeting her counselor in person. Once the session began, however, her concerns went away. She actually started thinking that it was much more convenient than expected. She felt as if the counselor were in the room with her. As the session closed, she told him with a smile, "I'll definitely see you online again!"

① doubtful → satisfied
② regretful → confused
③ confident → ashamed
④ bored → excited
⑤ thrilled → disappointed

2021학년도 수능 19번 ★☆☆

9. 다음 글에 드러난 Jonas의 심경 변화로 가장 적절한 것은?

Looking out the bus window, Jonas could not stay calm. He had been looking forward to this field trip. It was the first field trip for his history course. His history professor had recommended it to the class, and Jonas had signed up enthusiastically. He was the first to board the bus in the morning. The landscape looked fascinating as the bus headed to Alsace. Finally arriving in Alsace after three hours on the road, however, Jonas saw nothing but endless agricultural fields. The fields were vast, but hardly appealed to him. He had expected to see some old castles and historical monuments, but now he saw nothing like that awaiting him. "What can I learn from these boring fields?" Jonas said to himself with a sigh.

① excited → disappointed
② indifferent → thrilled
③ amazed → horrified
④ surprised → relieved
⑤ worried → confident

2019학년도 수능 19번 ★☆☆

10. 다음 글에 드러난 Dave의 심경 변화로 가장 적절한 것은?

The waves were perfect for surfing. Dave, however, just could not stay on his board. He had tried more than ten times to stand up but never managed it. He felt that he would never succeed. He was about to give up when he looked at the sea one last time. The swelling waves seemed to say, "Come on, Dave. One more try!" Taking a deep breath, he picked up his board and ran into the water. He waited for the right wave. Finally, it came. He jumped up onto the board just like he had practiced. And this time, standing upright, he battled the wave all the way back to shore. Walking out of the water joyfully, he cheered, "Wow, I did it!"

① frustrated → delighted
② bored → comforted
③ calm → annoyed
④ relieved → frightened
⑤ pleased → upset

총 문항				문항	맞은 문항					문항
개별 문항	1	2	3	4	5	6	7	8	9	10
채점										

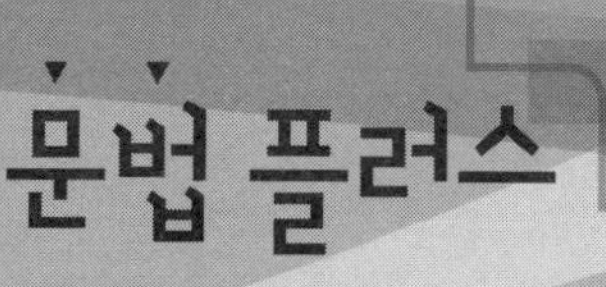

문법 플러스

2. 목적어, 보어

정답 및 해설 010쪽

A 문법의 주요 포인트를 점검해 봅시다.

1 주격보어는 주어를 설명해 주는 말로, 명사(구), 형용사(구)뿐만 아니라, to부정사(구), 동명사(구), 현재분사, 과거분사, 명사절이 주격보어가 될 수 있다.
▶ The liliacs on the table smell **[sweet / sweetly]**.

2 to부정사와 동명사는 문장에서 목적어의 역할을 할 수 있다.

to부정사만을 목적어로 취하는 동사	동명사를 목적어로 취하는 동사
want, wish, plan, agree, decide, refuse	finish, mind, enjoy, avoid, deny, escape

▶ Sam refused **[letting / to let]** anyone come into the room.

3 직접의문문이 다른 문장의 주어, 목적어, 보어 자리에 들어간 간접의문문은 문장구조가 [의문사 또는 if/whether]+ 주어+동사의 어순을 갖는다.
▶ She didn't know how old **[was he / he was]**.

4 문장에서 목적어가 길어지면, 가목적어 it을 쓰고, (진)목적어를 문장 뒤로 보낸다.
▶ Jack made **[it is / it]** clear that he disagreed.

5 목적보어는 목적어의 상태나 성질을 설명해 주는 말로, 명사(구), 형용사, to부정사, 원형부정사, 현재분사, 과거분사가 목적격보어가 될 수 있다.
▶ We did our part by keeping our rooms **[neatly / neat]**.

6 지각[사역]동사의 목적보어는 동사원형이 나온다. 지각동사는 진행형이 나올 수도 있다. 단, 지각[사역]동사의 목적어와 목적보어가 수동관계인 경우는 과거분사가 나온다.
▶ I watched a beautiful smile **[flashed / flashing]** across her face.

7 allow, cause, enable, encourage, tell, urge, want 동사는 목적격보어로 to부정사가 나온다.
▶ Today many countries do not allow foreigners **[stay / to stay]** without visa.

B 다음 괄호 안에서 어법상 올바른 것을 고르시오.

1 This milk smells **[badly / bad]**.

2 This Sally narrowly escaped **[to be / being]** run over.

3 I don't know where **[they are / are they]** hiding.

4 I find **[myself / it]** difficult to talk to her about anything serious.

5 Three hours will be enough for us to make your home **[freely / free]** of any dirt.

6 Sally had her purse **[steal / stolen]** on the bus.

7 The latest technology allowed us **[get / to get]** access to the Internet all the time.

숙어 플러스

2. 수능 필수 숙어 2회

정답 및 해설 010쪽

A 다음 수능 필수 숙어를 읽고, 아는 것은 체크해 봅시다.

□ 01	amount to	~이 되다, ~와 같다
□ 02	and so forth[on]	~등등
□ 03	and the like	기타 등등
□ 04	anything but	~이 결코 아닌
□ 05	apart from	~을 제외하고, ~뿐만 아니라
□ 06	apologize to A for B	B에 대해 A에게 사과하다
□ 07	appeal to	~에 호소하다, ~의 마음을 끌다
□ 08	approve of	~을 승인하다, ~을 찬성하다
□ 09	as a matter of fact	사실은(= in fact)
□ 10	as a (general) rule	대체로
□ 11	as a result of	~의 결과로서, ~때문에
□ 12	as far as	~까지, ~하는 한
□ 13	as for	~에 대해서 말하자면
□ 14	as it is	현재로서는
□ 15	as to	~에 관해서는
□ 16	ascribe A to B	A를 B의 탓으로 돌리다
□ 17	aside from	~을 제외하고, ~외에
□ 18	assent to	~에 동의하다, 찬성하다
□ 19	at (the) best	기껏해야
□ 20	at a time	한 번에

B 다음 숙어 표현을 읽고 의미 차이를 비교해 봅시다.

□ 21	break down	고장나다
□ 22	hand down	(후세에) 전하다
□ 23	look down on	경멸하다 (↔ look up to 존경하다)
□ 24	turn down	(볼륨, 가스불 등을) 줄이다 (↔ turn up)
□ 25	upside down	거꾸러, 뒤집어서, 뒤죽박죽, 엉망으로

C 우리말을 참고하여 빈칸에 알맞은 말을 써 봅시다.

1 당면한 위험이 없을 때는 간섭하지 말고 아이의 놀이를 인정해 주는 것이 대개 제일 좋다.
When there is no immediate danger, it is usually best to ________________ of the child's play without interfering.

2 제조업에 종사하는 근로자들은 소음의 결과로 오는 심각한 건강 문제 때문에 고통 받기 쉽다.
Workers in manufacturing jobs are likely to suffer serious health problems as a ________________ of the noise.

3 이러한 기본적인 두 관계는 제쳐두고라도, 그것은 주위에 있는 다른 동·식물에 직·간접적으로 무수한 영향을 받을 수 있다.
________________ from these two basic relationships, it may be affected directly or indirectly in countless different ways by other plants and animals around it.

4 당신은 반드시 그 상처에 대해 그녀에게 사과해야 할 것이다.
You must ________________ to her for that hurt.

필자의 주장

출제 트렌드

1. 글에서 제시된 근거를 바탕으로 필자의 주장을 찾는 유형이다. 수능에서 매년 거의 1문제가 출제되고 있다.
2. 논설문, 연설문, 독자 투고, 수필 등 필자의 주관이나 의도가 강하게 개입되어 있는 글을 대상으로 출제된다.
3. 필자의 주장을 고르는 문제는 요지 추론의 일종으로 볼 수 있지만, 요지가 객관적인 진술인 반면 주장은 주관적인 진술이다.
4. 최근 수능 5년간, 필자의 주장 문제는 2017학년도 수능을 제외하고 2018학년도부터 매년 1문항이 출제되었다. 2018학년도 수능(91%), 2019(88%), 2020(89%), 2021(83%), 2022(83%), 2023(80%)에서 괄호 안의 정답률을 보였다. 6년간 평균 85.6%의 정답률을 보였다. 난이도는 하 단계이다.

	출처		문항 번호	지문 주제	정답률(%)	난이도
대표	2023학년도	수능	20번	더 나은 선택을 하는 방법	80	★★☆
1	2022학년도	10 학평	20번	창의성을 유지하는 방법	75	★★☆
2	2023학년도	09 모평	20번	타 문화 사람들과 교류를 잘하는 방법	94	★☆☆
3	2022학년도	07 학평	20번	경험의 가치	92	★☆☆
4	2023학년도	06 모평	20번	성과를 얻기 위해 선수들이 활용해야 할 정신적 추진력	71	★★☆
5	2022학년도	04 학평	20번	불확실성 해결 방안	78	★★☆
6	2022학년도	03 학평	20번	임상 연구 윤리	89	★☆☆
7	2022학년도	수능	20번	기업이 소셜 미디어를 활용할 때 주의해야 할 점	83	★★☆
8	2022학년도	06 모평	20번	과학의 대중화를 위한 방법	89	★☆☆
9	2020학년도	수능	20번	어른의 놀이에 장애가 되는 규범	89	★☆☆
10	2019학년도	수능	20번	전쟁과 적을 추상적이고 획일적으로 개념화하는 것을 경계해야 한다	88	★☆☆

1등급 꿀팁

1. 우리말 선택지를 먼저 읽고 난 후, 글을 읽고 특정 개념과 관련된 어구 또는 반복되는 어구를 통해 필자의 주장을 파악한다.
2. 필자가 말하고자 하는 바를 확인하면서 필자의 주장을 추론한다.
3. 글의 중간이나 결론에서 강조되고 있는 내용에 유의해야 한다.
4. 필자의 주장을 찾는 문제는 주장(must, have to)이나 당위(should, natural), 필요(need, necessary), 권유(had better)의 표현에 유의한다. I think[believe] ~, In my opinion 표현 뒤에 필자의 주장이 나타나기도 한다.
5. 필자의 주장을 보여주는 기본 표현을 익힌다.

▪ 주장	It's clear we should ~	우리가 ~해야 하는 것은 명백하다
	The thing is: You have to ~	중요한 것은 이것이다. 당신이 ~해야 한다는 것이다
	We need to ~	우리는 ~해야 할 필요가 있다
	must be seen ~	~에 비추어 살펴보아야 한다
	be clear about ~	~에 관해 명확하게 밝혀야 한다
	but you have to let A B	하지만 당신은 A가 B하도록 해야 한다

필자의 주장

제한 시간 : 15분 | 정답 및 해설 011쪽

대표 기출

2023학년도 수능 20번

20. 다음 글에서 필자가 주장하는 바로 가장 적절한 것은?

At every step in our journey through life we encounter junctions with many different pathways leading into the distance. Each choice involves uncertainty about which path will get you to your destination. Trusting our intuition to make the choice often ends up with us making a suboptimal choice. Turning the uncertainty into numbers has proved a potent way of analyzing the paths and finding the shortcut to your destination. The mathematical theory of probability hasn't eliminated risk, but it allows us to manage that risk more effectively. The strategy is to analyze all the possible scenarios that the future holds and then to see what proportion of them lead to success or failure. This gives you a much better map of the future on which to base your decisions about which path to choose.

* junction: 분기점 ** suboptimal: 차선의

① 성공적인 삶을 위해 미래에 대한 구체적인 계획을 세워야 한다.
② 중요한 결정을 내릴 때에는 자신의 직관에 따라 판단해야 한다.
③ 더 나은 선택을 위해 성공 가능성을 확률적으로 분석해야 한다.
④ 빠른 목표 달성을 위해 지름길로 가고자 할 때 신중해야 한다.
⑤ 인생의 여정에서 선택에 따른 결과를 스스로 책임져야 한다.

문제 풀이

1. 먼저, 글에 전반적으로 언급된 소재나 논제를 이해한다.

• Turning the uncertainty into numbers (불확실성을 숫자로 바꾸는 것)

2. 필자가 말하고자 하는 바를 확인하면서 필자의 주장을 추론한다.

① Turning the uncertainty into numbers has proved a potent way of analyzing the paths and finding the shortcut to your destination. (불확실성을 숫자로 바꾸는 것은 여러분의 목적지로 가는 길을 분석하고 지름길을 찾는 강력한 방법으로 입증되었다)

② The mathematical theory of probability hasn't eliminated risk, but it allows us to manage that risk more effectively. (확률에 대한 수학적 이론은 위험을 제거하지는 않았지만, 우리가 그 위험을 더 효과적으로 관리할 수 있게 해준다.)

③ The strategy is to analyze all the possible scenarios that the future holds and then to see what proportion of them lead to success or failure. (그 전략은 미래가 안고 있는 모든 가능한 시나리오를 분석한 다음, 그것들이 성공이나 실패로 이어질 비율이 얼마나 되는지를 살펴보는 것이다.)

④ This gives you a much better map of the future on which to base your decisions about which path to choose. (이것은 여러분이 어떤 길을 선택할 것인지에 관한 결정을 내릴 때 그 근거로 삼을 수 있는 미래에 대한 훨씬 더 좋은 지도를 여러분에게 제공한다.)

• 이 글은 인생의 여정에서 우리가 하는 모든 선택은 불확실성을 포함하게 되는데 불확실성을 확률적으로 분석하는 것은 목적지로 가는 지름길을 찾는 강력한 방법으로 위험을 더 효과적으로 관리할 수 있게 해준다는 내용이다. 그러므로 필자가 주장하는 바로 가장 적절한 것은 ③이다.

2022학년도 10월 학평 20번 ★★☆

1. 다음 글에서 필자가 주장하는 바로 가장 적절한 것은?

Bringing incredible creative projects to life demands much hard work down in the trenches of day-to-day idea execution. Genius truly is "1 percent inspiration and 99 percent perspiration." But we cannot forget the flip side of that 99 percent — it's impossible to solve every problem by sheer force of will. We must also make time for play, relaxation, and exploration, the essential ingredients of the creative insights that help us evolve existing ideas and set new projects in motion. Often this means creating a routine for breaking from your routine, working on exploratory side projects just for the hell of it, or finding new ways to hotwire your brain's perspective on a problem. To stay creatively fit, we must keep our minds engaged and on the move — because the greatest enemy of creativity is nothing more than standing still.

① 창의성을 유지할 다양한 경험과 활동을 지속해야 한다.
② 내적 비판과 성찰을 통해 숨은 잠재력을 일깨워야 한다.
③ 일상에서의 관찰을 통해 새로운 아이디어를 얻어야 한다.
④ 혁신적 아이디어를 내려면 기존 사고의 틀을 버려야 한다.
⑤ 추상적인 생각을 뛰어넘어 구체적인 적용을 모색해야 한다.

2023학년도 9월 모평 20번 ★☆☆

2. 다음 글에서 필자가 주장하는 바로 가장 적절한 것은?

Becoming competent in another culture means looking beyond behavior to see if we can understand the attitudes, beliefs, and values that motivate what we observe. By looking only at the visible aspects of culture — customs, clothing, food, and language — we develop a short-sighted view of intercultural understanding — just the tip of the iceberg, really. If we are to be successful in our business interactions with people who have different values and beliefs about how the world is ordered, then we must go below the surface of what it means to understand culture and attempt to see what Edward Hall calls the "hidden dimensions." Those hidden aspects are the very foundation of culture and are the reason why culture is actually more than meets the eye. We tend not to notice those cultural norms until they violate what we consider to be common sense, good judgment, or the nature of things.

① 타 문화 사람들과 교류를 잘하려면 그 문화의 이면을 알아야 한다.
② 문화 배경이 다른 직원과 협업할 때 공정하게 업무를 나눠야 한다.
③ 여러 문화에 대한 이해를 통해 공동체 의식을 길러야 한다.
④ 원만한 대인 관계를 위해서는 서로의 공통점을 우선 파악해야 한다.
⑤ 문화적 갈등을 줄이려면 구성원 간의 소통을 활성화해야 한다.

2022학년도 7월 학평 20번 ★☆☆

3. 다음 글에서 필자가 주장하는 바로 가장 적절한 것은?

Placing value on and investing in experiences provides us with a greater sense of vitality. Our experiences make us feel alive and give us greater opportunities to grow. Any time you consider purchasing a new possession, stop yourself and think about what kind of experience it will give you. Ask yourself: How much joy will this bring me? Will the joy be temporary or long-lasting? Will the purchase be something I can share with others? If it becomes clear the purchase will provide only short-term benefit to you, think about an experience you could purchase instead that would provide you with longer-term benefits. For instance, if you have your eye on a new pair of shoes for $150, ask yourself what kind of experience you could enjoy for that same amount. Maybe you'd enjoy a concert with friends or a dinner cruise during the summer. Once you think of an experience you'd enjoy, seriously consider diverting the money for the purchase from possession to experience.

① 소유보다 경험에 가치를 두고 소비해야 한다.
② 물품 구매 시 품질을 우선으로 고려해야 한다.
③ 경제 흐름을 분석한 후 투자 대상을 선정해야 한다.
④ 단기 목표를 설정하여 잦은 성취 경험을 가져야 한다.
⑤ 경험하지 않은 것에 대해 선불리 옳고 그름을 판단해서는 안 된다.

2023학년도 6월 모평 20번 ★★☆

4. 다음 글에서 필자가 주장하는 바로 가장 적절한 것은?

Consider two athletes who both want to play in college. One says she has to work very hard and the other uses goal setting to create a plan to stay on track and work on specific skills where she is lacking. Both are working hard but only the latter is working smart. It can be frustrating for athletes to work extremely hard but not make the progress they wanted. What can make the difference is drive — utilizing the mental gear to maximize gains made in the technical and physical areas. Drive provides direction (goals), sustains effort (motivation), and creates a training mindset that goes beyond simply working hard. Drive applies direct force on your physical and technical gears, strengthening and polishing them so they can spin with vigor and purpose. While desire might make you spin those gears faster and harder as you work out or practice, drive is what built them in the first place.

* vigor: 활력, 활기

① 선수들의 훈련 방식은 장점을 극대화하는 방향으로 이루어져야 한다.
② 선수들은 최고의 성과를 얻기 위해 정신적 추진력을 잘 활용해야 한다.
③ 선수들은 단기적 훈련 성과보다 장기적 목표 달성에 힘써야 한다.
④ 선수들은 육체적 훈련과 정신적 훈련을 균형 있게 병행해야 한다.
⑤ 선수들은 수립한 계획을 실행하면서 꾸준히 수정하여야 한다.

2022학년도 4월 학평 20번 ★★☆

5. 다음 글에서 필자가 주장하는 바로 가장 적절한 것은?

We try to avoid uncertainty by overanalyzing. But we don't have complete control over how the future will play out. You may feel that if you can just answer your "worry question" once and for all, you will be satisfied and you can finally drop your rumination, but has this ever actually happened to you? Has there ever been an answer that allowed you to stop worrying? There is only one way out of this spiral, and that is not to try to gain control, but to give it up. Instead of pushing back against uncertainty, embrace it. Instead of trying to answer your worry question, deliberately practice leaving it unanswered. Don't ask others and don't think about it. Tell yourself that analysis is *not* the solution, but really just more of the same problem.

* rumination: 반추(反芻) ** spiral: 소용돌이

① 분석을 통해 미래의 불확실성을 통제하기보다 수용해야 한다.
② 타인에게 의존하기보다는 스스로 문제 해결력을 길러야 한다.
③ 걱정을 유발하는 문제 상황을 객관적으로 판단해야 한다.
④ 문제의 해결책을 찾기 전에 원인을 먼저 분석해야 한다.
⑤ 만일의 상황에 대비하여 꼼꼼하게 계획을 세워야 한다.

2022학년도 3월 학평 20번 ★☆☆

6. 다음 글에서 필자가 주장하는 바로 가장 적절한 것은?

Conflicts between the goals of science and the need to protect the rights and welfare of human research participants result in the central ethical tension of clinical research. The statement "Bad science is bad ethics" is true. Putting humans at risk if the study design does not permit a reasonable expectation of valid findings is never ethical. Even a study that presents no risk presents at least an inconvenience to participants and is in that sense disrespectful. The statement "Good science is good ethics," however, is false. Study design may be scientifically valid, yet the risk of harming human participants is too great to accept. Although achieving the appropriate scientific ends is always the necessary goal of a study, protection of the rights and welfare of human participants must override scientific efficiency.

① 참가자에게 임상 연구 결과를 투명하게 공개해야 한다.
② 임상 연구 과정에서 진행자의 편견이 배제되어야 한다.
③ 인간을 대상으로 하는 다양한 임상 연구를 시도해야 한다.
④ 임상 연구 설계 시 연구 목적을 구체적으로 설정해야 한다.
⑤ 임상 연구에서 참가자의 권리와 복지 보호가 우선되어야 한다.

2022학년도 수능 20번 ★★☆

7. 다음 글에서 필자가 주장하는 바로 가장 적절한 것은?

One of the most common mistakes made by organizations when they first consider experimenting with social media is that they focus too much on social media tools and platforms and not enough on their business objectives. The reality of success in the social web for businesses is that creating a social media program begins not with insight into the latest social media tools and channels but with a thorough understanding of the organization's own goals and objectives. A social media program is not merely the fulfillment of a vague need to manage a "presence" on popular social networks because "everyone else is doing it." "Being in social media" serves no purpose in and of itself. In order to serve any purpose at all, a social media presence must either solve a problem for the organization and its customers or result in an improvement of some sort (preferably a measurable one). In all things, purpose drives success. The world of social media is no different.

① 기업 이미지에 부합하는 소셜 미디어를 직접 개발하여 운영해야 한다.
② 기업은 사회적 가치와 요구를 반영하여 사업 목표를 수립해야 한다.
③ 기업은 소셜 미디어를 활용할 때 사업 목표를 토대로 해야 한다.
④ 소셜 미디어로 제품을 홍보할 때는 구체적인 정보를 제공해야 한다.
⑤ 소비자의 의견을 수렴하기 위해 소셜 미디어를 적극 활용해야 한다.

2022학년도 6월 모평 20번 ★☆☆

8. 다음 글에서 필자가 주장하는 바로 가장 적절한 것은?

New ideas, such as those inspired by scientific developments, are often aired and critiqued in our popular culture as part of a healthy process of public debate, and scientists sometimes deserve the criticism they get. But the popularization of science would be greatly enhanced by improving the widespread images of the scientist. Part of the problem may be that the majority of the people who are most likely to write novels, plays, and film scripts were educated in the humanities, not in the sciences. Furthermore, the few scientists-turned-writers have used their scientific training as the source material for thrillers that further damage the image of science and scientists. We need more screenplays and novels that present scientists in a positive light. In our contemporary world, television and film are particularly influential media, and it is likely that the introduction of more scientist-heroes would help to make science more attractive.

① 과학의 대중화를 위해 여러 매체에서 과학자를 긍정적으로 묘사해야 한다.
② 작가로 전업한 과학자는 전공 지식을 작품에 사실적으로 반영해야 한다.
③ 공상 과학 작가로 성공하려면 과학과 인문학을 깊이 이해해야 한다.
④ 과학의 저변 확대를 위해 영화 주인공으로 과학자가 등장해야 한다.
⑤ 과학 정책 논의에 과학자뿐만 아니라 인문학자도 참여해야 한다.

2020학년도 수능 20번 ★☆☆

9. 다음 글에서 필자가 주장하는 바로 가장 적절한 것은?

Probably the biggest roadblock to play for adults is the worry that they will look silly, improper, or dumb if they allow themselves to truly play. Or they think that it is irresponsible, immature, and childish to give themselves regularly over to play. Nonsense and silliness come naturally to kids, but they get pounded out by norms that look down on "frivolity." This is particularly true for people who have been valued for performance standards set by parents or the educational system, or measured by other cultural norms that are internalized and no longer questioned. If someone has spent his adult life worried about always appearing respectable, competent, and knowledgeable, it can be hard to let go sometimes and become physically and emotionally free. The thing is this: You have to give yourself permission to improvise, to mimic, to take on a long-hidden identity.

* frivolity: 경박함 ** improvise: 즉흥적으로 하다

① 어른도 규범에 얽매이지 말고 자유롭게 놀이를 즐겨야 한다.
② 아동에게 사회 규범을 내면화할 수 있는 놀이를 제공해야 한다.
③ 개인의 창의성을 극대화할 수 있는 놀이 문화를 조성해야 한다.
④ 타인의 시선을 의식하지 않고 자신의 목표 달성에 매진해야 한다.
⑤ 어른을 위한 잠재력 계발 프로그램에서 놀이의 비중을 늘려야 한다.

2019학년도 수능 20번 ★☆☆

10. 다음 글에서 필자가 주장하는 바로 가장 적절한 것은?

War is inconceivable without *some* image, or concept, of the enemy. It is the presence of the enemy that gives meaning and justification to war. 'War follows from feelings of hatred', wrote Carl Schmitt. 'War has its own strategic, tactical, and other rules and points of view, but they all presuppose that the political decision has already been made as to who the enemy is'. The concept of the enemy is fundamental to the moral assessment of war: 'The basic aim of a nation at war in establishing an image of the enemy is to distinguish as sharply as possible the act of killing from the act of murder'. However, we need to be cautious about thinking of war and the image of the enemy that informs it in an abstract and uniform way. Rather, both must be seen for the cultural and contingent phenomena that they are.

* contingent: 불확정적인

① 전쟁과 적을 추상적이고 획일적으로 개념화하는 것을 경계해야 한다.
② 적에 따라 다양한 전략과 전술을 수립하고 적용해야 한다.
③ 보편적 윤리관에 기초하여 적의 개념을 정의해야 한다.
④ 전쟁 예방에 도움이 되는 정치적 결정을 해야 한다.
⑤ 어떠한 경우에도 전쟁을 정당화하지 말아야 한다.

총 문항			문항	맞은 문항					문항
개별 문항	1	2	3	4	5	6	7	8	9	10
채점										

문법 플러스

3. 동사의 종류

정답 및 해설 015쪽

A 문법의 주요 포인트를 점검해 봅시다.

1 동사는 목적어와 보어의 유무에 따라 몇 가지로 분류할 수 있다.

종류	목적어	보어
완전자동사	X	X
불완전자동사	X	O
타동사	O	X
수여동사	O	X
불완전타동사	O	O

▶ Contrary to what he thought, she looked very **[calmly / calm]**.

2 타동사로 착각하기 쉬운 자동사가 있는데 주의해야 한다. 목적어를 취하려면 자동사 뒤에 전치사를 가져와야 한다.

apologize to ~에 사과하다	complain about ~을 불평하다	consist of ~으로 구성되다
deal with ~을 처리하다	object to ~에 반대하다	interfere with ~을 방해하다

▶ Water **[consists / consists of]** hydrogen and oxygen.

3 자동사로 착각하기 쉬운 타동사가 있는데 주의해야 한다. 타동사이기 때문에 전치사 없이 목적어를 취한다.

approach ~에 접근하다	contact ~에 연락하다	discuss ~와 토론하다
enter ~에 들어가다	marry ~와 결혼하다	mention ~을 언급하다

▶ Peter is going to **[marry / marry with]** Sally.

4 4형식 동사는 간접목적어(~에게)와 직접목적어(~을)을 둘 다 취하는 동사이다. 4형식 문장은 3형식 문장으로 전환할 수 있다.

▶ He gave the athlete a gold medal. = He gave a gold medal **[to / for]** the athlete.

5 지각동사(see, hear, listen to 등)는 목적어와 목적보어가 능동 관계인 경우 동사원형, 현재분사를 목적보어로 쓰고, 수동 관계인 경우 과거분사를 쓴다.

▶ I could see a small group of cattle **[to graze / grazing]** in the field.

6 사역동사(have, make, let 등)는 목적어와 목적보어가 능동 관계인 경우 동사원형을 쓰고, 수동 관계인 경우 과거분사를 쓴다.

▶ They said that they would never let their children **[play / played]** with toy guns.

7 타동사+부사의 구동사는 목적어가 대명사인 경우 타동사와 부사 사이에 나온다.

▶ Could you **[put me up / put up me]** a few nights?

B 다음 괄호 안에서 어법상 올바른 것을 고르시오.

1 After Sally heard the news, she got **[angry / angrily]**.

2 He must **[apologize / apologize to]** his teacher for being late to class.

3 Our heads do not **[resemble with / resemble]** steam kettles in which negative feelings builds up pressure.

4 Sarah made a doll **[for / to]** me.

5 She saw a lot of books and notes **[piling / piled]** up on the desk.

6 Where do you normally have your hair **[doing / done]**?

7 The most effective way to focus on your goal is to **[write them down / write down them]**.

숙어 플러스

3. 수능 필수 숙어 3회

정답 및 해설 015쪽

A 다음 수능 필수 숙어를 읽고, 아는 것은 체크해 봅시다.

□ 01	at ease	마음 편히
□ 02	at hand	(거리가) 가까운, 가까운 미래에
□ 03	at issue	논쟁 중인, 고려 중인
□ 04	at last	마침내
□ 05	at odds with	~와 의견이 일치하지 않는
□ 06	at length	상세히, 한참 후에
□ 07	at one time	예전에, 동시에
□ 08	at other times	다른 때에는, 평소에는
□ 09	at present	현재는, 지금은
□ 10	at the cost of	~을 희생하고, ~의 비용을 지불하고
□ 11	at the earliest	(아무리) 빨라도
□ 12	at the moment	바로 지금
□ 13	attach A to B	A를 B에 붙이다(첨부하다)
□ 14	attribute A to B	A를 B의 탓으로 돌리다
□ 15	avail oneself of	~을 이용하다
□ 16	back and forth	앞뒤로
□ 17	be all ears	주의 깊게 듣다
□ 18	be apt to	~하는 경향이 있다, ~하기 쉽다
□ 19	be bound to	반드시 ~하다, ~할 의무가 있다
□ 20	be engaged in	~에 종사하다

B 다음 숙어 표현을 읽고 의미 차이를 비교해 봅시다.

□ 21	give away	거저 주다, 넘겨 주다
□ 22	keep away from	피하다, ~을 멀리하다
□ 23	pass away	죽다(= die)
□ 24	run away	도망치다(= flee)
□ 25	throw away	버리다

C 우리말을 참고하여 빈칸에 알맞은 말을 써 봅시다.

1 남바위는 한국의 가장 오래된 전통 겨울용 모자 중 하나이다. 비단띠가 귀마개에 부착되어 있다.
The Nambawi is one of the oldest traditional winter hats in Korea. Silk sashes are ______________ to the ear flaps.

2 동물은 식량 공급을 위해, 다른 살아 있는 동물, 궁극적으로는 식물에 의존해야만 한다.
An animal is ________________ to depend on other living creatures, ultimately plants, for its food supply.

3 종종 어린아이들은 자신들의 예술을 버리거나 나누어 준다.
Often young children throw their art away or give it ________________.

4 그럼에도 불구하고, 그들은 대개 과일에서 영양분이 매우 풍부한 부분인 껍질을 버린다.
Nonetheless, they usually ________________ away a very nutritious part of the fruit — the peel.

04 함축·지칭 추론

출제 트렌드

1. 함축적 추론 문제 유형은 '밑줄 친 ~가 다음 글에서 의미하는 바로 가장 적절한 것'을 고르는 문제이다. 글의 흐름상 중요한 개념을 담고 있는 어구를 밑줄로 제시한 후 내포된 의미를 찾도록 출제된다.
2. 함축적 추론 문제는 변별력을 가릴 수 있는 고난이도 독해 문제이다. 2019학년도 수능은 역대급 불수능이었는데, 특히 23번 함축 의미 추론이 난이도가 높게 출제되었다.
3. 지칭 추론 문제 유형은 글에서 대명사가 가리키는 대상이 나머지와 다른 하나를 찾는 유형이다. 최근 수능과 학력 평가에서는 단일 문항으로는 출제되지 않고, 세트 문제인 1지문 3문항 문제에서 1문제가 출제되고 있다.
4. 최근 수능 7년간, 함축 · 지칭 추론 문제는 2017–2018학년까지 지칭 문제가 매년 1문제씩 출제되다가, 2019학년도 이후 함축 문제가 매년 1문제씩 출제되고 있다. 2017학년도 수능(86%), 2018(86%), 2019(54%), 2020(72%), 2021(63%), 2022(35%), 2023(68%)에서 괄호 안의 정답률을 보였다. 평균적으로 2년 동안 지칭 문제는 86%, 5년 동안 함축 문제는 58.4%의 정답률을 보였다. 난이도는 각각 하, 상 단계에 해당한다.

출처			문항 번호	지문 주제	정답률(%)	난이도
대표	2022학년도	06 모평	21번	창조적인 작업을 위해 차단의 필요성	56	★★☆
1	2023학년도	수능	21번	일기의 기능	68	★★☆
2	2022학년도	10 학평	21번	소비주의의 문제점	44	★★★
3	2023학년도	09 모평	21번	알고리즘의 특징	55	★★★
4	2022학년도	07 학평	21번	인간을 노예로 만든 기술이 부여한 여가	72	★★☆
5	2023학년도	06 모평	21번	세계에 대한 우리의 관점	59	★★☆
6	2022학년도	04 학평	21번	뉴스의 특성	61	★★☆
7	2022학년도	03 학평	21번	전깃불과 전기 시스템의 기술적, 경제적 중요성	65	★★☆
8	2022학년도	수능	21번	전문가에 대한 신뢰	35	★★★
9	2021학년도	수능	21번	환경 기자의 역할	63	★★☆
10	2018학년도	10 학평	30번	디저트를 먹는 Chloe와 할머니	82	★★☆

1등급 꿀팁

1. 함축적 의미 추론은 먼저 밑줄 친 부분의 글자 그대로의 의미를 파악한다.
2. 밑줄 친 부분이 글의 전반부에 있는 경우 거기까지 의미를 파악하고 선택지에서 답을 추측해 본다.
3. 끝까지 지문을 읽고 답을 고른 후 문맥 속에 선택지의 의역된 의미를 대입하여 흐름이 자연스러운지를 확인한다.
4. 지칭 추론 문제에서 대명사는 앞에서 언급한 명사를 가리키므로, 밑줄 친 부분 바로 앞 문장을 주의 깊게 읽는다.

Day 04

제한 시간 : 15분 | 정답 및 해설 016쪽

대표 기출

2022학년도 6월 모평 21번

21. 밑줄 친 an empty inbox가 다음 글에서 의미하는 바로 가장 적절한 것은? [3점]

The single most important change you can make in your working habits is to switch to creative work first, reactive work second. This means blocking off a large chunk of time every day for creative work on your own priorities, with the phone and e-mail off. I used to be a frustrated writer. Making this switch turned me into a productive writer. Yet there wasn't a single day when I sat down to write an article, blog post, or book chapter without a string of people waiting for me to get back to them. It wasn't easy, and it still isn't, particularly when I get phone messages beginning "I sent you an e-mail *two hours ago*...!" By definition, this approach goes against the grain of others' expectations and the pressures they put on you. It takes willpower to switch off the world, even for an hour. It feels uncomfortable, and sometimes people get upset. But it's better to disappoint a few people over small things, than to abandon your dreams for an empty inbox. Otherwise, you're sacrificing your potential for the illusion of professionalism.

① following an innovative course of action
② attempting to satisfy other people's demands
③ completing challenging work without mistakes
④ removing social ties to maintain a mental balance
⑤ securing enough opportunities for social networking

문제 풀이

1. 주제문을 통해 글의 주제를 파악한다.

• 주제문: The single most important change you can make in your working habits is to switch to creative work first, reactive work second. (일하는 습관에서 이뤄낼 수 있는 가장 중요한 단 한 가지 변화는 창조적인 일을 먼저 하고 대응적인 일을 그 다음에 하는 쪽으로 전환하는 것이다.)

2. 글의 흐름을 따라가며 글의 주제를 뒷받침하는 세부 사항을 파악한다.

① This means blocking off a large chunk of time every day for creative work on your own priorities, with the phone and e-mail off. (이것은 전화기와 이메일을 끈 채, 자신의 우선순위에 따라 창조적인 작업을 위해 매일 많은 시간을 차단하는 것을 의미한다.)
② Making this switch turned me into a productive writer. (이렇게 전환하자 나는 생산적인 작가가 되었다.)
③ But it's better to disappoint a few people over small things, than to abandon your dreams for an empty inbox. (하지만 빈 수신함을 위해 자신의 꿈을 포기하는 것보다 사소한 것에 대해 몇 사람을 실망케 하는 것이 낫다.)

3. 글의 주제와 관련해서 밑줄 친 부분의 함축적 의미를 추론한다.

• 밑줄 친 부분 바로 뒤에 보면 자신의 전문가다움을 고객에게 보여줄 수 있을지는 모르지만, 작가로서의 가능성(창작 활동)을 희생하게 된다고 했다. 그러므로 밑줄 친 부분 'an empty inbox(빈 수신함)'은 자신의 창조적인 일을 중지하고 고객이나 의뢰인이 전화나 이메일로 요청하는 내용을 바로바로 답변해서 수신함을 비워 주는 것을 의미한다. 정답은 ② 'attempting to satisfy other people's demands(다른 사람의 요구를 만족시켜 주려고 시도하는 것)'이다.

2023학년도 수능 21번 ★★☆

1. 밑줄 친 make oneself public to oneself가 다음 글에서 의미하는 바로 가장 적절한 것은? [3점]

Coming of age in the 18th and 19th centuries, the personal diary became a centerpiece in the construction of a modern subjectivity, at the heart of which is the application of reason and critique to the understanding of world and self, which allowed the creation of a new kind of knowledge. Diaries were central media through which enlightened and free subjects could be constructed. They provided a space where one could write daily about her whereabouts, feelings, and thoughts. Over time and with rereading, disparate entries, events, and happenstances could be rendered into insights and narratives about the self, and allowed for the formation of subjectivity. It is in that context that the idea of "the self [as] both made and explored with words" emerges. Diaries were personal and private; one would write for oneself, or, in Habermas's formulation, one would make oneself public to oneself. By making the self public in a private sphere, the self also became an object for self-inspection and self-critique.

* disparate: 이질적인 ** render: 만들다

① use writing as a means of reflecting on oneself
② build one's identity by reading others' diaries
③ exchange feedback in the process of writing
④ create an alternate ego to present to others
⑤ develop topics for writing about selfhood

2022학년도 10월 학평 21번 ★★★

2. 밑줄 친 do not have the ears to hear it이 다음 글에서 의미하는 바로 가장 적절한 것은? [3점]

Far from a synonym for capitalism, consumerism makes capitalism impossible over the long term, since it makes capital formation all but impossible. A consumer culture isn't a saving culture, isn't a thrift culture. It's too fixated on buying the next toy to ever delay gratification, to ever save and invest for the future. The point is elementary: you can't have sustainable capitalism without capital; you can't have capital without savings; and you can't save if you're running around spending everything you've just earned. But the confusion has grown so deep that many people today do not have the ears to hear it. Indeed, the policies of our nation's central bank seem to reinforce this habit by driving down interest rates to near zero and thereby denying people a material reward — in the form of interest on their banked savings — for foregoing consumption.

* fixated: 집착하는 ** gratification: 욕구 충족 *** forego: 단념하다

① disagree with the national policy of lowering interest rates
② ignore the fact that consumerism is a synonym for capitalism
③ believe that consumerism doesn't really do much for well-being
④ form a false assumption that savings can make nations prosper
⑤ fail to understand that consumption alone can't sustain capitalism

2023학년도 9월 모평 21번 ★★★

3. 밑줄 친 <u>send us off into different far corners of the library</u>가 다음 글에서 의미하는 바로 가장 적절한 것은? [3점]

You may feel there is something scary about an algorithm deciding what you might like. Could it mean that, if computers conclude you won't like something, you will never get the chance to see it? Personally, I really enjoy being directed toward new music that I might not have found by myself. I can quickly get stuck in a rut where I put on the same songs over and over. That's why I've always enjoyed the radio. But the algorithms that are now pushing and pulling me through the music library are perfectly suited to finding gems that I'll like. My worry originally about such algorithms was that they might drive everyone into certain parts of the library, leaving others lacking listeners. Would they cause a convergence of tastes? But thanks to the nonlinear and chaotic mathematics usually behind them, this doesn't happen. A small divergence in my likes compared to yours can <u>send us off into different far corners of the library</u>.

* rut: 관습, 틀 ** gem: 보석 *** divergence: 갈라짐

① lead us to music selected to suit our respective tastes
② enable us to build connections with other listeners
③ encourage us to request frequent updates for algorithms
④ motivate us to search for talented but unknown musicians
⑤ make us ignore our preferences for particular music genres

2022학년도 7월 학평 21번 ★★☆

4. 밑줄 친 <u>this civilization of leisure was, in reality, a Trojan horse</u>가 다음 글에서 의미하는 바로 가장 적절한 것은? [3점]

It seemed like a fair deal: we would accept new technologies, which would modify our habits and oblige us to adjust to certain changes, but in exchange we would be granted relief from the burden of work, more security, and above all, the freedom to pursue our desires. The sacrifice was worth the gain; there would be no regrets. Yet it has become apparent that <u>this civilization of leisure was, in reality, a Trojan horse</u>. Its swelling flanks hid the impositions of a new type of enslavement. The automatons are not as autonomous as advertised. They need us. Those computers that were supposed to do our calculations for us instead demand our attention: for ten hours a day, we are glued to their screens. Our communications monopolize our time. Time itself is accelerating. The complexity of the system overwhelms us. And leisure is often a costly distraction.

* flank: 측면, 옆구리 ** automaton: 자동 장치

① Doing leisure activities increased communication between colleagues.
② Labor was easily incorporated with leisure by the media.
③ People's privacy was attacked because of low security.
④ Technology's promise for leisure actually made people less free.
⑤ Technological innovations did not improve hierarchical working culture.

2023학년도 6월 모평 21번 ★★★

5. 밑줄 친 <u>"view from nowhere"</u>가 다음 글에서 의미하는 바로 가장 적절한 것은? [3점]

Our view of the world is not given to us from the outside in a pure, objective form; it is shaped by our mental abilities, our shared cultural perspectives and our unique values and beliefs. This is not to say that there is no reality outside our minds or that the world is just an illusion. It is to say that our version of reality is precisely that: *our* version, not *the* version. There is no single, universal or authoritative version that makes sense, other than as a theoretical construct. We can see the world only as it appears to us, not "as it truly is," because there is no "as it truly is" without a perspective to give it form. Philosopher Thomas Nagel argued that there is no <u>"view from nowhere,"</u> since we cannot see the world except from a particular perspective, and that perspective influences what we see. We can experience the world only through the human lenses that make it intelligible to us.

* illusion: 환영

① perception of reality affected by subjective views
② valuable perspective most people have in mind
③ particular view adopted by very few people
④ critical insight that defeats our prejudices
⑤ unbiased and objective view of the world

2022학년도 4월 학평 21번 ★★☆

6. 밑줄 친 <u>news 'happens'</u>가 다음 글에서 의미하는 바로 가장 적절한 것은? [3점]

Journalists love to report studies that are at the "initial findings" stages — research that claims to be the first time anyone has discovered a thing — because there is newsworthiness in their novelty. But "first ever" discoveries are extremely vulnerable to becoming undermined by subsequent research. When that happens, the news media often don't go back and inform their audiences about the change — assuming they even hear about it. Kelly Crowe, a CBC News reporter writes, quoting one epidemiologist, "There is increasing concern that in modern research, false findings may be the majority or even the vast majority of published research claims." She goes on to suggest that journalists, though blameworthy for this tendency, are aided and abetted by the scientists whose studies they cite. She writes that the "conclusions" sections in scientific abstracts can sometimes be overstated in an attempt to draw attention from prestigious academic journals and media who uncritically take their bait. Even so, Crowe ends her piece by stressing that there is still an incompatibility between the purposes and processes of news and science: Science 'evolves,' but <u>news 'happens.'</u>

* epidemiologist: 전염병학자 ** aid and abet: 방조하다

① News follows the process of research more than the outcome.
② News focuses not on how research changes but on the novelty of it.
③ News attracts attention by criticizing false scientific discoveries.
④ Reporters give instant feedback to their viewers, unlike scientists.
⑤ Reporters create and strengthen trust in the importance of science.

2022학년도 3월 학평 21번 ★★☆

7. 밑줄 친 carries the stamp of this age가 다음 글에서 의미하는 바로 가장 적절한 것은? [3점]

Thomas Edison's name is synonymous with invention, and his most famous invention, the electric light bulb, is a familiar symbol for that flash of inspired genius traditionally associated with the inventive act. Besides being the exemplar of the "bright idea," however, Edison's electric light is worthy of study for other reasons. The technical and economic importance of the light and of the electrical system that surrounded it matches that of any other invention we could name, at least from the last two hundred years. The introduction and spread of electric light and power was one of the key steps in the transformation of the world from an industrial age, characterized by iron and coal and steam, to a post-industrial one, in which electricity was joined by petroleum, light metals and alloys, and internal combustion engines to give the twentieth century its distinctive form and character. Our own time still largely carries the stamp of this age, however dazzled we may be by the electronic, computerized, and media wonders of the twenty-first century.

* alloy: 합금

① combines creative ideas from various disciplines
② strives to overcome limitations of the industrial age
③ is a theoretical background for academic exploration
④ is under the influence of earlier electrical innovations
⑤ is dependent on resources reserved for future generations

2022학년도 수능 21번 ★★★

8. 밑줄 친 whether to make ready for the morning commute or not이 다음 글에서 의미하는 바로 가장 적절한 것은? [3점]

Scientists have no special purchase on moral or ethical decisions; a climate scientist is no more qualified to comment on health care reform than a physicist is to judge the causes of bee colony collapse. The very features that create expertise in a specialized domain lead to ignorance in many others. In some cases lay people — farmers, fishermen, patients, native peoples — may have relevant experiences that scientists can learn from. Indeed, in recent years, scientists have begun to recognize this: the Arctic Climate Impact Assessment includes observations gathered from local native groups. So our trust needs to be limited, and focused. It needs to be very *particular*. Blind trust will get us into at least as much trouble as no trust at all. But without some degree of trust in our designated experts — the men and women who have devoted their lives to sorting out tough questions about the natural world we live in — we are paralyzed, in effect not knowing whether to make ready for the morning commute or not.

* lay: 전문가가 아닌 ** paralyze: 마비시키다 *** commute: 통근

① questionable facts that have been popularized by non-experts
② readily applicable information offered by specialized experts
③ common knowledge that hardly influences crucial decisions
④ practical information produced by both specialists and lay people
⑤ biased knowledge that is widespread in the local community

2021학년도 수능 21번 ★★☆

9. 밑줄 친 the role of the 'lion's historians'가 다음 글에서 의미하는 바로 가장 적절한 것은?

There is an African proverb that says, 'Till the lions have their historians, tales of hunting will always glorify the hunter'. The proverb is about power, control and law making. Environmental journalists have to play the role of the 'lion's historians'. They have to put across the point of view of the environment to people who make the laws. They have to be the voice of wild India. The present rate of human consumption is completely unsustainable. Forest, wetlands, wastelands, coastal zones, eco-sensitive zones, they are all seen as disposable for the accelerating demands of human population. But to ask for any change in human behaviour — whether it be to cut down on consumption, alter lifestyles or decrease population growth — is seen as a violation of human rights. But at some point human rights become 'wrongs'. It's time we changed our thinking so that there is no difference between the rights of humans and the rights of the rest of the environment.

① uncovering the history of a species' biological evolution
② urging a shift to sustainable human behaviour for nature
③ fighting against widespread violations of human rights
④ rewriting history for more underrepresented people
⑤ restricting the power of environmental lawmakers

2018학년도 10월 학평 30번 ★★☆

10. 밑줄 친 부분이 가리키는 대상이 나머지 넷과 다른 것은?

When the tea tray was being carried across the room to their table, Chloe's eyes rounded and she almost gasped out loud. There were lots of tiny desserts and mini sandwiches and small biscuit-looking things. Where to start? Where to start? Her grandmother smiled and winked at ① her from across the table. Chloe winked back. ② She took a sip of the sweet tea and waited for her grandmother to make the first move. ③ She carefully mirrored her grandmother's actions and started with a small, delicate sandwich. It was good. She ate it up and selected another. After a time, all the sandwiches were eaten up and Chloe boldly chose the biscuit-looking thing before her grandmother. "Aren't the scones lovely, dear?" asked her grandmother, as ④ she spread cream and jam on hers. Scones, was that what they were called? Chloe had already started to eat hers without the cream and jam; in fact, it was mostly all in ⑤ her mouth already.

총 문항				문항	맞은 문항					문항
개별 문항	1	2	3	4	5	6	7	8	9	10
채점										

문법 플러스

4. 동사의 시제

정답 및 해설 022쪽

A 문법의 주요 포인트를 점검해 봅시다.

1 현재시제는 현재의 습관, 일반적인 사실, 진리, 장기간 지속되는 동작을 표현한다. 과학적 사실과 진리는 주절의 동사에 상관없이 현재형으로 표현한다. 단순현재형은 장기간 지속되는 동작을, 현재진행형은 잠시 지속되는 동작을 나타낸다. 진행형은 원칙적으로 동작을 표시하는 동사이므로 지각동사(see, hear 등), 소유동사(have, belong), 인식동사(know, remember 등)와 같은 동사에는 진행형을 쓸 수 없다.

▶ Newton believed that gravity **[caused / causes]** objects to fall.

2 시간과 조건을 나타내는 부사절은 미래 의미를 현재시제로 나타낸다. 명사절은 미래 의미를 나타내는 경우, 미래시제로 표현한다.

▶ Sam will be happy when Sally **[shows / will show]** up to the party.

3 과거시제는 과거의 동작, 상태, 습관을 표현하며, 과거를 뚜렷하게 나타내는 부사(구)(ago, yesterday, last week ~)가 있는 문장은 현재완료가 아닌, 과거시제로 나타내야 한다.

▶ He **[have met / met]** her last week and they fell in love at first sight.

4 현재완료형은 과거의 행위나 상태가 현재에 미치는 경우 사용한다.

▶ Sally has **[gone / been]** to London. She is not here now.

5 과거완료형은 과거 이전에 일어난 일(대과거)에 대해서 말하거나, 대과거에 일어난 일이 과거의 어느 한 시점에 영향을 미칠 때 사용된다.

▶ When she returned home, Sally discovered that she **[had lost / lost]** her door key.

6 미래를 표현하는 구문에는 단순미래형, 미래진행형, 미래완료형 등이 있다. 특히 미래의 특정 시점까지 계속을 나타내고 싶을 때는 미래완료형이 사용된다. 또한 일정상 확실한 미래는 현재형이나 현재진행형으로 미래를 나타낼 수 있다.

▶ By this Sunday Becky and I **[will have been / will be]** together for 100 days.

7 시제 일치는 예외가 있다. 원칙상, 주절의 시제가 과거이면 시제일치의 원칙에 따라 종속절은 과거나 과거완료로만 쓸 수 있다. 그러나 시제일치에 상관없이 불변의 진리나 현재 습관, 상태는 현재시제로 나타내며, 역사적 사실은 과거시제로 나타낸다. 또한 주절에 주장(insist), 제안(suggest), 요구(demand), 명령(order) 등의 동사가 나오면 that이 이끄는 종속절은 「(should+)동사원형」으로 표현한다. 단, 실제로 발생한 단순한 사실을 전달할 때는 문장의 수와 시제에 맞춰 써야 한다.

▶ I was taught French Revolution **[had broken out / broke out]** in 1789.

B 다음 괄호 안에서 어법상 올바른 것을 고르시오.

1 Water boils at 100°C and **[froze / freezes]** at 0°C.

2 By the time Sally **[will get / gets]** home, her father will have left for Paris.

3 The movie **[have started / started]** about 5 minutes ago.

4 He was supposed to be here half an hour ago, but he **[hadn't shown / hasn't shown]** up yet.

5 They **[hadn't / haven't]** made a reservation, so they didn't get a table.

6 The plane **[leaves / left]** for Paris at 9 0'clock tonight.

7 Galileo believed that the earth **[moves / moved]** around the sun.

숙어 플러스

4. 수능 필수 숙어 4회

정답 및 해설 022쪽

A 다음 수능 필수 숙어를 읽고, 아는 것은 체크해 봅시다.

□ 01	be fed up with	~에 진저리가 나다
□ 02	be free of	~에서 자유롭다, ~이 없다
□ 03	be in charge of	~을 떠맡다, 담당하다, 책임지다
□ 04	be in control of	~을 관리하다
□ 05	be in fashion	유행하고 있다
□ 06	be known for	~으로 유명하다
□ 07	be on board	승선하다
□ 08	be likely to	~할 것 같다
□ 09	be said that	~라고 말해지다
□ 10	be short of	~이 부족하다
□ 11	be through	끝내다, ~와 관계를 끊다
□ 12	be to blame for	~에 대해 책임이 있다
□ 13	be tired of	~에 싫증이 나다
□ 14	be used to	~에 익숙하다(= get used to)
□ 15	be worth -ing	~할 가치가 있다
□ 16	bear fruit	열매를 맺다
□ 17	before long	곧
□ 18	beware of	주의하다, 조심하다
□ 19	beyond one's power	능력밖인
□ 20	beyond description	말로 표현할 수 없을 정도인

B 다음 숙어 표현을 읽고 의미 차이를 비교해 봅시다.

□ 21	account for	~을 설명하다(= explain)
□ 22	apply for	~을 신청하다 cf. apply to ~에 지원하다
□ 23	call for	~을 강력히 요구하다
□ 24	care for	~을 돌보다(= look after)
□ 25	long for	~을 갈망하다(= be anxious for)

C 우리말을 참고하여 빈칸에 알맞은 말을 써 봅시다.

1 저는 Jane Wilson이고 Terra 벼룩시장을 조직하는 일을 맡고 있습니다.
I'm Jane Wilson, and I'm in ____________ of organizing the Terra Flea Market.

2 사람들은 친구의 시간과 관심에 대해 거의 모든 권리를 주장하는 것 같다.
One is ____________ to claim an almost total right to his friend's time and attention.

3 아빠, 위층에서 나는 소음에 질렸어요.
Dad, I'm ____________ of the noise from upstairs.

4 식물이 어떻게 열매를 맺는가를 설명하신 그 방법이 전 좋아요.
I liked the way you explained how plants ____________ fruit.

05 글의 요지

출제 트렌드

1. 글의 요지란 글을 통해 말하고자 하는 중심 내용(main idea)이라고 할 수 있다. 주장이 필자의 주관적인 진술이라고 한다면, 요지는 필자의 객관적인 진술이이라고 말할 수 있다. 주로 논설문이나 설명문을 대상으로 출제되지만 시사적인 글에서 출제되기도 한다.
2. 글을 읽고 중심 내용을 찾는 유형으로 선택지는 주로 우리말로 제시하고 있다.
3. 최근 수능 7년간, 글의 요지 문제는 매년 1문제가 출제되었다. 2017학년도 수능(92%), 2018(87%), 2019(82%), 2020(78%), 2021(89%), 2022(89%), 2023(78%)에서 괄호 안의 정답률을 보였다. 7년간 평균 85% 정도 정답률이 나왔으며 난이도는 하 단계이다.

출처			문항 번호	지문 주제	정답률(%)	난이도
대표	2023학년도	수능	22번	도시에서 효율적인 운송 수단	78	★★☆
1	2022학년도	10 학평	22번	정보의 양보다는 유용한 사용이 중요함	90	★☆☆
2	2023학년도	09 모평	22번	조세 입법에 있어 중요한 것	92	★☆☆
3	2022학년도	07 학평	22번	리더가 진실을 말해야 하는 이유	91	★☆☆
4	2023학년도	06 모평	22번	주체적인 소비자가 되는 방법	61	★★☆
5	2022학년도	04 학평	22번	인간의 지능 발달의 원인	90	★☆☆
6	2022학년도	03 학평	22번	인간이 지각하지 못하는 화학 신호로 가득 찬 세상	86	★☆☆
7	2022학년도	수능	22번	개인이 피하기 어려운 유해 환경 요인에 대한 대처	89	★☆☆
8	2022학년도	09 모평	22번	전문직과 사회의 관계	55	★★★
9	2021학년도	수능	22번	음악 비평의 변화	89	★☆☆
10	2020학년도	수능	22번	문자 기록을 이끈 고대 사회의 경제 활동	78	★★☆

1등급 꿀팁

1. 특정 개념과 관련된 어구 또는 반복되는 어구를 통해 글의 요지를 파악한다.
2. 요지는 필자가 궁극적으로 전달하려고 하는 중심 내용이므로 주제문을 찾는 것이 중요하다. 주제문은 글의 맨 앞부분이나 마지막 부분에 주어지는 경우가 많다.
3. 글에서 예시를 보여주는 경우, 바로 앞 문장이 주제문으로 나올 수 있다. 문단 마지막 부분의 경우, 결론, 요약을 이끄는 표현 뒤에 주제문이 나올 수 있다. 글의 흐름이 반전되거나 필자의 태도가 바뀌는 부분 뒤에 주제문이 나올 수 있다.
4. 주제문과 관련된 단서가 되는 표현에 유의한다.

주제문 위치	단서	주제문 위치
[주제문] +	[예시] for example, for instance	
	[결론] therefore, consequently, as a result, in conclusion	+[주제문]
	[요약] in short, in brief	+[주제문]
	[반전] however, yet, but, nevertheless	+[주제문]

제한 시간 : 15분 | 정답 및 해설 022쪽

대표 기출

2023학년도 수능 22번

22. 다음 글의 요지로 가장 적절한 것은?

Urban delivery vehicles can be adapted to better suit the density of urban distribution, which often involves smaller vehicles such as vans, including bicycles. The latter have the potential to become a preferred 'last-mile' vehicle, particularly in high-density and congested areas. In locations where bicycle use is high, such as the Netherlands, delivery bicycles are also used to carry personal cargo (e.g. groceries). Due to their low acquisition and maintenance costs, cargo bicycles convey much potential in developed and developing countries alike, such as the *becak* (a three-wheeled bicycle) in Indonesia. Services using electrically assisted delivery tricycles have been successfully implemented in France and are gradually being adopted across Europe for services as varied as parcel and catering deliveries. Using bicycles as cargo vehicles is particularly encouraged when combined with policies that restrict motor vehicle access to specific areas of a city, such as downtown or commercial districts, or with the extension of dedicated bike lanes.

① 도시에서 자전거는 효율적인 배송 수단으로 사용될 수 있다.
② 자전거는 출퇴근 시간을 줄이기 위한 대안으로 선호되고 있다.
③ 자전거는 배송 수단으로의 경제적 장단점을 모두 가질 수 있다.
④ 수요자의 요구에 부합하는 다양한 용도의 자전거가 개발되고 있다.
⑤ 세계 각국에서는 전기 자전거 사용을 장려하는 정책을 추진하고 있다.

문제 풀이

1. 글의 핵심, 주요 어구 또는 반복적인 어구를 찾는다.

• 글의 주요 어구: urban delivery vehicles(도시의 배송 수단), bicycles(자전거)

2. 주제에 대한 필자의 생각을 확인하면서, 글의 요지를 추론한다.

① The latter have the potential to become a preferred 'last-mile' vehicle, particularly in high-density and congested areas. (후자(자전거)는 특히 밀도가 높고 혼잡한 지역에서 선호되는 '최종 단계' 운송 수단이 될 잠재력이 있다.)
② In locations where bicycle use is high, such as the Netherlands, delivery bicycles are also used to carry personal cargo (e.g. groceries). (네덜란드와 같이 자전거 사용이 많은 지역에서 배달 자전거가 또한 개인 짐(예를 들어 식료품)을 운반하기 위해 사용된다.)
③ Due to their low acquisition and maintenance costs, cargo bicycles convey much potential in developed and developing countries alike, such as the becak (a three-wheeled bicycle) in Indonesia. (매입과 유지 비용이 낮아서 짐 자전거는 선진국에서 그리고 인도네시아의 becak(바퀴가 세 개 달린 자전거)와 같이 개발도상국에서 똑같이 많은 잠재력을 전달한다.)
④ Using bicycles as cargo vehicles is particularly encouraged when combined with policies that restrict motor vehicle access to specific areas of a city, such as downtown or commercial districts, or with the extension of dedicated bike lanes. (자전거를 화물 운송 수단으로 사용하는 것은 도심이나 상업 지구처럼 도시의 특정 지역에 자동차 접근을 제한하는 정책이나 자전거 전용 도로의 확장과 결합될 때 특히 장려된다.)

3. 주제문을 통해 글의 요지를 확인하고 요지를 드러내는 선택지를 고른다.

• 이 글은 혼잡하고 밀도가 높은 도심에서 자전거가 배달 운송 수단으로 많은 잠재력을 갖고 있으며, 실제 많은 나라에서 자전거를 운송 수단으로 사용하는 서비스가 점차 늘고 있다는 내용의 글이다. 따라서 글의 요지로 가장 적절한 것은 ①이다.

2022학년도 10월 학평 22번 ★☆☆

1. 다음 글의 요지로 가장 적절한 것은?

Many people say that we should take full advantage of the privileges of the Internet by forever learning more and more. They see no limit to how much information a person ought to consume and never acknowledge the emotional and psychological cost of cramming facts into our brains. If we aren't using the wealth of available data to make ourselves more productive and useful to society, what's the point of having it? While access to information is a privilege, it's also a burden. This is especially true when we treat being well-read as an obligation that can't be escaped. Constant exposure to upsetting news can be traumatic. An unending flood of information makes it hard to pause and reflect on anything you've learned. At some point, even the most voracious of readers needs to pull the plug and stop the constant drip of facts, figures, and meaningless Internet fights. We're living in an era of information overload — and the solution is not to learn more but to step back and consume a smaller amount of data in a more meaningful way.

* voracious: 매우 열심인, 만족을 모르는

① 정보 습득의 양보다 정보의 유의미한 사용이 더 중요하다.
② 인터넷상의 정보를 비판적으로 바라보는 태도가 필요하다.
③ 인터넷 기술의 발전으로 인해 평생 학습이 실현되고 있다.
④ 인터넷을 통한 의사소통은 사회적 갈등을 유발할 수 있다.
⑤ 정보는 받아들이는 사람의 관점에 따라 달리 해석될 수 있다.

2023학년도 9월 모평 22번 ★☆☆

2. 다음 글의 요지로 가장 적절한 것은?

Historically, drafters of tax legislation are attentive to questions of economics and history, and less attentive to moral questions. Questions of morality are often pushed to the side in legislative debate, labeled too controversial, too difficult to answer, or, worst of all, irrelevant to the project. But, in fact, the moral questions of taxation are at the very heart of the creation of tax laws. Rather than irrelevant, moral questions are fundamental to the imposition of tax. Tax is the application of a society's theories of distributive justice. Economics can go a long way towards helping a legislature determine whether or not a particular tax law will help achieve a particular goal, but economics cannot, in a vacuum, identify the goal. Creating tax policy requires identifying a moral goal, which is a task that must involve ethics and moral analysis.

* legislation: 입법 ** imposition: 부과

① 분배 정의를 실현하려면 시민 단체의 역할이 필요하다.
② 사회적 합의는 민주적인 정책 수립의 선행 조건이다.
③ 성실한 납세는 안정적인 정부 예산 확보의 기반이 된다.
④ 경제학은 세법을 개정할 때 이론적 근거를 제공한다.
⑤ 세법을 만들 때 도덕적 목표를 설정하는 것이 중요하다.

2022학년도 7월 학평 22번 ★☆☆

3. 다음 글의 요지로 가장 적절한 것은?

Giving honest information may be particularly relevant to integrity because honesty is so fundamental in discussions of trustworthiness. Unfortunately, leaders are often reluctant to tell the truth. During times of crisis and change, business leaders are often faced with the challenge of either telling an uncomfortable truth, remaining silent, or downplaying the severity of the situation. There are plenty of other situations in which, in the short term, it may be more comfortable not to tell the truth to followers. Ultimately, however, even dishonesty that was meant to protect employee morale will eventually be exposed, undermining trustworthiness at a time when commitment to the organization is most vital. Even concerted efforts at secrecy can backfire, as employees may simply "fill in the gaps" in their understanding with their own theories about the leader's behavior. Therefore, leaders need to take steps to explain the true reasons for their decisions to those individuals affected by it, leaving less room for negative interpretations of leader behavior.

① 조직이 처할 위기를 예측하여 사전 대책 수립이 필요하다.
② 리더는 업무 효율 향상을 위해 구성원의 사기를 높여야 한다.
③ 조직에 대한 과도한 헌신을 강조하는 것은 역효과를 초래한다.
④ 리더는 구성원의 비판적 의견을 수용하는 자세를 가져야 한다.
⑤ 리더는 조직 내 신뢰 유지를 위해 구성원에게 진실을 알려야 한다.

2023학년도 6월 모평 22번 ★★☆

4. 다음 글의 요지로 가장 적절한 것은?

Often overlooked, but just as important a stakeholder, is the consumer who plays a large role in the notion of the privacy paradox. Consumer engagement levels in all manner of digital experiences and communities have simply exploded — and they show little or no signs of slowing. There is an awareness among consumers, not only that their personal data helps to drive the rich experiences that these companies provide, but also that sharing this data is the price you pay for these experiences, in whole or in part. Without a better understanding of the what, when, and why of data collection and use, the consumer is often left feeling vulnerable and conflicted. "I love this restaurant-finder app on my phone, but what happens to my data if I press 'ok' when asked if that app can use my current location?" Armed with tools that can provide them options, the consumer moves from passive bystander to active participant.

* stakeholder: 이해관계자 ** vulnerable: 상처를 입기 쉬운

① 개인정보 제공의 속성을 심층적으로 이해하면 주체적 소비자가 된다.
② 소비자는 디지털 시대에 유용한 앱을 적극 활용하는 자세가 필요하다.
③ 현명한 소비자가 되려면 다양한 디지털 데이터를 활용해야 한다.
④ 기업의 디지털 서비스를 이용하면 상응하는 대가가 뒤따른다.
⑤ 타인과의 정보 공유로 인해 개인정보가 유출되기도 한다.

2022학년도 4월 학평 22번 ★☆☆

5. 다음 글의 요지로 가장 적절한 것은?

To overcome death as the obstacle that was hindering the evolution of human intelligence, our ancestors developed the killer app that propelled our species forward, ahead of all others: namely, spoken and written language in words and maths. I believe communication was, and still is, our most valuable invention. It has helped us preserve the knowledge, learning, discoveries and intelligence we have gained and pass them on from person to person and from generation to generation. Imagine if Einstein had had no way of telling the rest of us about his remarkable understanding of the theory of relativity. In the absence of our incredible abilities to communicate, each and every one of us would need to discover relativity on his or her own. Leaps of human intelligence have happened, then, as a response to the way human society and culture developed. A lot of our intelligence resulted from our interaction with each other, and not just in response to our environments.

① 인간의 언어는 환경과의 상호 작용을 통해 발달한다.
② 인간의 지능 발달은 상호 간 의사소통의 결과물이다.
③ 과학의 발전은 인간 사회의 문화 보존에 필수적이다.
④ 언어의 변화가 세대 간 의사소통의 단절을 초래한다.
⑤ 기술에 대한 의존이 인간의 학습 능력 발달을 저해한다.

2022학년도 3월 학평 22번 ★☆☆

6. 다음 글의 요지로 가장 적절한 것은?

Just imagine that we have invented special glasses that give us the power to see the odorous world the way that other organisms perceive it. Put your pair on and walk outside for just a moment. As the bright sunlight hits our eyes, we would encounter a world far different from what we would normally expect. The air is full of molecules carried by breezes. Chemical signals would flood our eyes just as surely as sounds overwhelm our ears at a cocktail party. Stare at any plant and you would see compounds being released into the air from leaves, bark, and roots. A squirrel in a tree exudes carbon dioxide and other compounds with each breath. Glance along its brown body and notice that specific points (scent glands) appear to be slowly releasing chemical signals. If we could translate these signals into language, we would see phrases, sentences, statements, songs, and other messages waiting to be intercepted and interpreted.

* exude: 발산하다 ** gland: (분비)샘

① 인간이 보지 못하는 것을 볼 수 있는 유기체가 매우 많다.
② 세상은 인간이 지각하지 못하는 화학 신호로 가득 차 있다.
③ 동물과 식물의 감각 기관은 외부 자극에 일정하게 반응한다.
④ 동물과 식물은 화학 물질의 발산을 통해 스스로를 보호한다.
⑤ 시각적 인식이 다른 모든 감각에 의한 인식보다 더 우선한다.

2022학년도 수능 22번 ★☆☆

7. 다음 글의 요지로 가장 적절한 것은?

Environmental hazards include biological, physical, and chemical ones, along with the human behaviors that promote or allow exposure. Some environmental contaminants are difficult to avoid (the breathing of polluted air, the drinking of chemically contaminated public drinking water, noise in open public spaces); in these circumstances, exposure is largely involuntary. Reduction or elimination of these factors may require societal action, such as public awareness and public health measures. In many countries, the fact that some environmental hazards are difficult to avoid at the individual level is felt to be more morally egregious than those hazards that can be avoided. Having no choice but to drink water contaminated with very high levels of arsenic, or being forced to passively breathe in tobacco smoke in restaurants, outrages people more than the personal choice of whether an individual smokes tobacco. These factors are important when one considers how change (risk reduction) happens.

* contaminate: 오염시키다 ** egregious: 매우 나쁜

① 개인이 피하기 어려운 유해 환경 요인에 대해서는 사회적 대응이 필요하다.
② 환경오염으로 인한 피해자들에게 적절한 보상을 하는 것이 바람직하다.
③ 다수의 건강을 해치는 행위에 대해 도덕적 비난 이상의 조치가 요구된다.
④ 환경오염 문제를 해결하기 위해서는 사후 대응보다 예방이 중요하다.
⑤ 대기오염 문제는 인접 국가들과의 긴밀한 협력을 통해 해결할 수 있다.

2022학년도 9월 모평 22번 ★★★

8. 다음 글의 요지로 가장 적절한 것은?

Historically, the professions and society have engaged in a negotiating process intended to define the terms of their relationship. At the heart of this process is the tension between the professions' pursuit of autonomy and the public's demand for accountability. Society's granting of power and privilege to the professions is premised on their willingness and ability to contribute to social well-being and to conduct their affairs in a manner consistent with broader social values. It has long been recognized that the expertise and privileged position of professionals confer authority and power that could readily be used to advance their own interests at the expense of those they serve. As Edmund Burke observed two centuries ago, "Men are qualified for civil liberty in exact proportion to their disposition to put moral chains upon their own appetites." Autonomy has never been a one-way street and is never granted absolutely and irreversibly.

* autonomy: 자율성 ** privilege: 특권 *** premise: 전제로 말하다

① 전문직에 부여되는 자율성은 그에 상응하는 사회적 책임을 수반한다.
② 전문직의 권위는 해당 집단의 이익을 추구하는 데 이용되어 왔다.
③ 전문직의 사회적 책임을 규정할 수 있는 제도 정비가 필요하다.
④ 전문직이 되기 위한 자격 요건은 사회 경제적 요구에 따라 변화해 왔다.
⑤ 전문직의 업무 성과는 일정 수준의 자율성과 특권이 부여될 때 높아진다.

2021학년도 수능 22번 ★☆☆

9. 다음 글의 요지로 가장 적절한 것은?

Prior to file-sharing services, music albums landed exclusively in the hands of music critics before their release. These critics would listen to them well before the general public could and preview them for the rest of the world in their reviews. Once the internet made music easily accessible and allowed even advanced releases to spread through online social networks, availability of new music became democratized, which meant critics no longer had unique access. That is, critics and laypeople alike could obtain new music simultaneously. Social media services also enabled people to publicize their views on new songs, list their new favorite bands in their social media bios, and argue over new music endlessly on message boards. The result was that critics now could access the opinions of the masses on a particular album before writing their reviews. Thus, instead of music reviews guiding popular opinion toward art (as they did in preinternet times), music reviews began to reflect — consciously or subconsciously — public opinion.

* laypeople: 비전문가

① 미디어 환경의 변화로 음악 비평이 대중의 영향을 받게 되었다.
② 인터넷의 발달로 다양한 장르의 음악을 접하는 것이 가능해졌다.
③ 비평가의 음악 비평은 자신의 주관적인 경험을 기반으로 한다.
④ 오늘날 새로운 음악은 대중의 기호를 확인한 후에 공개된다.
⑤ 온라인 환경의 대두로 음악 비평의 질이 전반적으로 상승하였다.

2020학년도 수능 22번 ★★☆

10. 다음 글의 요지로 가장 적절한 것은?

In retrospect, it might seem surprising that something as mundane as the desire to count sheep was the driving force for an advance as fundamental as written language. But the desire for written records has always accompanied economic activity, since transactions are meaningless unless you can clearly keep track of who owns what. As such, early human writing is dominated by wheeling and dealing: a collection of bets, bills, and contracts. Long before we had the writings of the prophets, we had the writings of the profits. In fact, many civilizations never got to the stage of recording and leaving behind the kinds of great literary works that we often associate with the history of culture. What survives these ancient societies is, for the most part, a pile of receipts. If it weren't for the commercial enterprises that produced those records, we would know far, far less about the cultures that they came from.

* mundane: 세속의 ** prophet: 예언자

① 고대 사회에서 경제 활동은 문자 기록의 원동력이었다.
② 고전 문학을 통해 당대의 경제 활동을 파악할 수 있다.
③ 경제 발전의 정도가 문명의 발달 수준을 결정한다.
④ 종교의 역사는 상업의 역사보다 먼저 시작되었다.
⑤ 모든 문명이 위대한 작가를 배출한 것은 아니다.

총 문항			문항	맞은 문항					문항
개별 문항	1	2	3	4	5	6	7	8	9	10
채점										

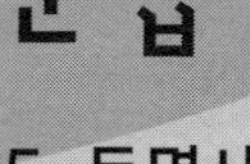

문법 플러스

5. 동명사

정답 및 해설 027쪽

A 문법의 주요 포인트를 점검해 봅시다.

1 동명사는 문장 속에서 명사 역할을 한다. 즉 주어, (동사나 전치사의) 목적어, 보어로 사용될 수 있다.
한편, 동명사가 주어일 경우, 동사는 단수동사를 사용한다.

▶ **[Set / Setting]** goals and not giving up helps you achieve a lot of things in your life.

2 finish, enjoy, mind, give up 등의 동사(구)는 동명사를 목적어로 취한다. 일부 동사는 to부정사와 동명사를 목적어로 가져올 수 있지만 의미 차이가 있다.

「regret+동명사」	~한 것을 후회하다	「regret+to부정사」	~해야 해서 유감이다
「try+동명사」	시험 삼아 ~해보다	「try+to부정사」	~하려고 노력하다

▶ Sam regrets **[having done / have done]** such a silly thing.

3 전치사의 목적어는 동명사를 사용한다. 특히 전치사 to 뒤에 to부정사를 쓰지 않도록 유의한다.

look forward to -ing	~을 기대하다	object to -ing	~에 반대하다
contribute to -ing	~에 헌신하다	devote oneself to -ing	~에 헌신하다

▶ This summer, my son is really looking forward to **[learn / learning]** how to scuba-dive.

4 동명사는 –ing형(단순형)과 「having+p.p형」(완료형)으로 시제를 나타낸다. 단순형은 술어 동사와 시제가 같다.

▶ Sam is sure that she was a singer. = Sam is sure of her **[being / having been]** a singer.

5 동명사의 의미상의 주어는 동명사 앞에 배치한다. 의미상 주어가 사람일 때는 소유격, 목적격을 모두 사용할 수 있으며, 사물일 때는 그대로 쓴다. 또한 동명사를 부정할 때는 부정어를 동명사 바로 앞에 둔다.

▶ He insists on **[her / hers]** being innocent.

6 수동형동명사 「being+p.p.」와 「having been+p.p.」는 의미상의 주어와 수동의 의미 관계를 갖는다.

▶ The boy doesn't like **[being / having been]** treated like a child.
= The boy doesn't like that he is treated like a child.

7 동명사의 관용 표현을 익힌다.

cannot help –ing	~하지 않을 수 없다	feel like –ing	~하고 싶다
It's no use[good] –ing	~해도 소용없다	There is no –ing	~할 수 없다 (~하는 것이 불가능하다)
be used to –ing	~에 익숙하다	be accustomed to –ing	~에 익숙하다

▶ I feel like **[dancing / to dance]** with Sally now.

B 다음 괄호 안에서 어법상 올바른 것을 고르시오.

1 **[Understand / Understanding]** why historic events took place is important.

2 My boss enjoyed **[to fish / fishing]** in the river during the weekend.

3 One of the keys to **[succeed / succeeding]** in life is to live it with some sense of balance.

4 She is sorry for **[being / having been]** late. = She is sorry that she is late.

5 The man objected to **[cars / cars']** being parked here.

6 Sally can't stand **[treating / being treated]** unequally.

7 It's no use **[to cry / crying]** over spilt milk.

숙어 플러스

5. 수능 필수 숙어 5회

정답 및 해설 027쪽

A 다음 수능 필수 숙어를 읽고, 아는 것은 체크해 봅시다.

□ 01	boast of	~을 자랑하다, 뽐내다
□ 02	break down	부수다, 고장나다
□ 03	break into	침입하다, (대화) 방해하다
□ 04	break off	갑자기 그만두다
□ 05	break out	발생하다, 발발하다
□ 06	break up	부수다, (관계를) 끝내다, 해산시키다
□ 07	break (up) with	관계를 끊다, 절교하다
□ 08	breathe in	숨을 들이마시다
□ 09	bring about	초래하다, 야기하다
□ 10	bring back	돌려주다, 기억나게 하다
□ 11	bring down	(짐을) 내리다, 낮추다, 줄이다
□ 12	bring out	발휘되게 하다, 눈에 띄게 만들다
□ 13	bring ~ to light	밝히다, 폭로하다
□ 14	bring to an end	끝내다, 끝나다
□ 15	bring up	~을 기리다, (의견, 문제 등을) 꺼내다
□ 16	burst into	갑자기 ~하기 시작하다
□ 17	but for	~을 제외하고, ~이 없다면(없었더라면)
□ 18	by and large	전반적으로, 대체로
□ 19	by degrees	서서히, 조금씩, 점차로
□ 20	by far	단연코

B 다음 숙어 표현을 읽고 의미 차이를 비교해 봅시다.

□ 21	apart from	~을 제쳐 놓고(= aside from)
□ 22	far from	~에서 멀리, 전혀(결코) ~이 아닌
□ 23	free from	~이 없는, ~의 염려가 없는
□ 24	hear from	~로부터 (직접) 소식을 듣다
□ 25	result from	~로부터 생기다(↔ result in 결과를 낳다)

C 우리말을 참고하여 빈칸에 알맞은 말을 써 봅시다.

1 불행하게도 내 차가 방금 고장 났어.
Unfortunately, my car has just ________________ down.

2 대화를 깨고 그녀가 물었다. "얼마나 체중을 줄였는지 물어봐도 되니?"
Breaking ________________ the conversation, she asked, "May I ask how much you lost?"

3 이번 사건이 심각한 문제를 야기할지도 모른다.
This event may bring ________________ serious trouble.

4 그러나 심리학에 대한 이런 모든 어려움들에 비하여, 과학적인 방법의 이점은 연구 결과가 반복 가능하다는 것이다.
But ________________ all of these difficulties for psychology, the payoff of the scientific method is that the findings are replicable.

06 글의 주제

출제 트렌드

1. 글의 주제란 글의 중심이 되는 사상이나 제재를 말한다. 따라서 주제 찾기는 글이 중점적으로 다루고 있는 대상이 무엇인지를 파악하는 문제라고 할 수 있다.
2. 글의 중심 내용을 파악할 수 있는지 글에 대한 종합적 이해 능력을 측정하는 문제로서 수능에서 매년 1문항이 출제되고 있다.
3. 글의 주제 문제는 글의 핵심 내용과 방향이 뚜렷하고 문장 간의 연결이 긴밀한 지문이 제시된다. 주로 주제문은 지문의 처음이나 끝부분에 명시적으로 제시되지만, 글 전체에 대한 추론적 이해 여부를 묻기 위해 명시적으로 드러나지 않을 수도 있다. 주제가 글 속에 숨어 있는 경우에는 글에 대한 종합적인 이해가 필요하다.
4. 최근 수능 7년간, 글의 주제 문제는 매년 1문제가 출제되었다. 2017학년도 수능(73%), 2018(84%), 2019(51%), 2020(65%), 2021(62%), 2022(77%), 2023(68%)에서 괄호의 정답률을 보였다. 난이도는 중 단계이다. 2019, 2021학년도 수능에서 3점 문제로 출제되었고, 7년간 평균 68.6% 정도 정답률을 보이고 있다.

	출처		문항 번호	지문 주제	정답률(%)	난이도
대표	2023학년도	수능	23번	정보 공개의 이점	68	★★☆
1	2022학년도	10 학평	23번	조기 직업 선택의 문제점	82	★★☆
2	2023학년도	09 모평	23번	농업에서 경험적인 관찰 사용의 한계	73	★★☆
3	2022학년도	07 학평	23번	신체 감각에 대한 뇌의 해석	84	★★☆
4	2023학년도	06 모평	23번	문화에 따라 달라지는 감정 표현	63	★★☆
5	2022학년도	04 학평	23번	바로크 시대 회화의 특징	67	★★☆
6	2022학년도	03 학평	23번	사고 기술 교육의 한계	66	★★☆
7	2022학년도	수능	23번	과학자들의 연구에서 패러다임의 역할	77	★★☆
8	2022학년도	06 모평	23번	아동기와 청소년기의 놀이	66	★★☆
9	2021학년도	수능	23번	자동화된 시스템에서의 문제	62	★★☆
10	2020학년도	수능	23번	도덕성에 미치는 유전자와 환경의 작용	65	★★☆

1등급 꿀팁

1. 글의 주제 및 제목을 찾는 데 있어서 가장 중요한 것은 주제문을 찾는 것이다. 주제문은 보통 글의 앞이나 뒤에 주어지지만 생략된 경우도 있다. 이런 경우 반복 어구나 핵심 어구를 통해 주제를 파악한다. 선택지는 핵심 어구를 포함하는 경우가 많으므로 글을 읽으면서 핵심 어구에 표시를 한다.
2. 선택지를 고를 때는 하위 개념들을 포괄하는 상위 개념을 생각하고 글의 일부에만 해당하거나 지나치게 광범위한 주제는 피하도록 한다.
3. 역접 연결어가 나오는 문장에 중심 내용이 담겨 있는 경우가 많다.
4. 지문을 읽을 때 글쓴이가 전달하고자 하는 내용을 영어로 한 마디를 써 보는 습관을 갖는다.

제한 시간 : 15분 | 정답 및 해설 028쪽

대표 기출

2023학년도 수능 23번

23. 다음 글의 주제로 가장 적절한 것은? [3점]

An important advantage of disclosure, as opposed to more aggressive forms of regulation, is its flexibility and respect for the operation of free markets. Regulatory mandates are blunt swords; they tend to neglect diversity and may have serious unintended adverse effects. For example, energy efficiency requirements for appliances may produce goods that work less well or that have characteristics that consumers do not want. Information provision, by contrast, respects freedom of choice. If automobile manufacturers are required to measure and publicize the safety characteristics of cars, potential car purchasers can trade safety concerns against other attributes, such as price and styling. If restaurant customers are informed of the calories in their meals, those who want to lose weight can make use of the information, leaving those who are unconcerned about calories unaffected. Disclosure does not interfere with, and should even promote, the autonomy (and quality) of individual decision-making.

* mandate: 명령 ** adverse: 거스르는 *** autonomy: 자율성

① steps to make public information accessible to customers
② benefits of publicizing information to ensure free choices
③ strategies for companies to increase profits in a free market
④ necessities of identifying and analyzing current industry trends
⑤ effects of diversified markets on reasonable customer choices

문제 풀이

1. 글에서 반복적으로 제시된 핵심 개념을 파악한다.
- an important advantage of disclosure(정보 공개의 이점)

2. 핵심 개념에 대해 필자가 제시하는 견해를 찾는다.

① An important advantage of disclosure, as opposed to more aggressive forms of regulation, is its flexibility and respect for the operation of free markets. (공개의 중요한 이점은 더 공세적인 형태의 규제와는 반대로 자유 시장의 작용에 대한 유연성과 존중이다.)

② Information provision, by contrast, respects freedom of choice. If automobile manufacturers are required to measure and publicize the safety characteristics of cars, potential car purchasers can trade safety concerns against other attributes, such as price and styling. (반대로 정보 제공은 선택의 자유를 존중한다. 자동차 제조업체가 자동차의 안전 특성을 측정하고 공개해야 한다면, 잠재적인 자동차 구매자는 가격과 스타일 같은 다른 속성과 안전에 대한 우려를 맞바꿀 수 있다.)

③ If restaurant customers are informed of the calories in their meals, those who want to lose weight can make use of the information, leaving those who are unconcerned about calories unaffected. Disclosure does not interfere with, and should even promote, the autonomy (and quality) of individual decision-making. (식당 손님들에게 식사에 들어 있는 칼로리를 알려주면, 살을 빼고 싶은 사람들은 그 정보를 이용할 수 있고, 칼로리에 신경 쓰지 않는 사람들은 영향을 받지 않은 채로 있게 된다. 공개는 개인 의사 결정의 자율성(과 품질)을 방해하지 않으며 심지어 촉진할 것이다.)

3. 핵심 개념과 필자의 견해를 고려하여 글의 주제를 추론한다.
- 규제는 다양성을 무시하는 경향이 있으며 심각한 역효과를 낳지만, 정보 공개는 자유 시장에서 소비자가 스스로 자유롭게 의사 결정을 내릴 수 있는 자율성을 촉진한다는 내용의 글이다. 따라서 글의 주제로 가장 적절한 것은 ② '자유로운 선택을 보장하기 위해 정보를 공개하는 것의 이점'이다.

2022학년도 10월 학평 23번 ★★☆

1. 다음 글의 주제로 가장 적절한 것은?

Most of us make our career choices when we are about eighteen. At eighteen, you have limited experience, very limited skills and most of what you know comes from your parents, your environment and the structured school system you have gone through. You are usually slightly better at some skills because you have spent a bit more time on them. Maybe someone in your environment was good at something and passionate enough to get you interested in spending more time in that area. It is also possible that you might have a specific physical feature — such as being tall — that might make you better at certain activities, such as playing basketball. In any case, most people make a decision regarding their career and direction in life based on their limited experiences and biases in their childhood and teenage years. This decision will come to dominate their life for many years to come. No wonder so many get it wrong! It is easier to get it wrong than to get it right, because statistically, there are more wrong ways than right ways.

① social factors that make employment unstable
② useful statistics for making a right career choice
③ reasons that an early career choice can go wrong
④ necessity to find one's aptitude as early as possible
⑤ how to overcome biases in making one's career choices

2023학년도 9월 모평 23번 ★★☆

2. 다음 글의 주제로 가장 적절한 것은? [3점]

Environmental learning occurs when farmers base decisions on observations of "payoff" information. They may observe their own or neighbors' farms, but it is the empirical results they are using as a guide, not the neighbors themselves. They are looking at farming activities as experiments and assessing such factors as relative advantage, compatibility with existing resources, difficulty of use, and "trialability" — how well can it be experimented with. But that criterion of "trialability" turns out to be a real problem; it's true that farmers are always experimenting, but working farms are very flawed laboratories. Farmers cannot set up the controlled conditions of professional test plots in research facilities. Farmers also often confront complex and difficult-to-observe phenomena that would be hard to manage even if they could run controlled experiments. Moreover farmers can rarely acquire payoff information on more than a few of the production methods they might use, which makes the criterion of "relative advantage" hard to measure.

* empirical: 경험적인 ** compatibility: 양립성 *** criterion: 기준

① limitations of using empirical observations in farming
② challenges in modernizing traditional farming equipment
③ necessity of prioritizing trialability in agricultural innovation
④ importance of making instinctive decisions in agriculture
⑤ ways to control unpredictable agricultural phenomena

2022학년도 7월 학평 23번 ★★☆

3. 다음 글의 주제로 가장 적절한 것은?

From your brain's perspective, your body is just another source of sensory input. Sensations from your heart and lungs, your metabolism, your changing temperature, and so on, are like ambiguous blobs. These purely physical sensations inside your body have no objective psychological meaning. Once your concepts enter the picture, however, those sensations may take on additional meaning. If you feel an ache in your stomach while sitting at the dinner table, you might experience it as hunger. If flu season is just around the corner, you might experience that same ache as nausea. If you are a judge in a courtroom, you might experience the ache as a gut feeling that the defendant cannot be trusted. In a given moment, in a given context, your brain uses concepts to give meaning to internal sensations as well as to external sensations from the world, all simultaneously. From an aching stomach, your brain constructs an instance of hunger, nausea, or mistrust.

* blob: 형태가 뚜렷하지 않은 것

① influence of mental health on physical performance
② physiological responses to extreme emotional stimuli
③ role of negative emotions in dealing with difficult situations
④ necessity of staying objective in various professional contexts
⑤ brain's interpretation of bodily sensations using concepts in context

2023학년도 6월 모평 23번 ★★☆

4. 다음 글의 주제로 가장 적절한 것은? [3점]

Considerable work by cultural psychologists and anthropologists has shown that there are indeed large and sometimes surprising differences in the words and concepts that different cultures have for describing emotions, as well as in the social circumstances that draw out the expression of particular emotions. However, those data do not actually show that different cultures have different emotions, if we think of emotions as central, neurally implemented states. As for, say, color vision, they just say that, despite the same internal processing architecture, how we interpret, categorize, and name emotions varies according to culture and that we learn in a particular culture the social context in which it is appropriate to express emotions. However, the emotional states themselves are likely to be quite invariant across cultures. In a sense, we can think of a basic, culturally universal emotion set that is shaped by evolution and implemented in the brain, but the links between such emotional states and stimuli, behavior, and other cognitive states are plastic and can be modified by learning in a specific cultural context.

* anthropologist: 인류학자 ** stimuli: 자극 *** cognitive: 인지적인

① essential links between emotions and behaviors
② culturally constructed representation of emotions
③ falsely described emotions through global languages
④ universally defined emotions across academic disciplines
⑤ wider influence of cognition on learning cultural contexts

2022학년도 4월 학평 23번 ★★☆

5. 다음 글의 주제로 가장 적절한 것은?

By the start of the 16th century, the Renaissance movement had given birth to the Protestant Reformation and an era of profound religious change. The art of this period reflected the disruption caused by this shift. Appropriately named the Baroque, meaning irregular or distorted, European painting in the 16th century largely focused on capturing motion, drama, action, and powerful emotion. Painters employed the strong visual tools of dramatic composition, intense contrast of light and dark, and emotionally provocative subject matter to stir up feelings of disruption. Religious subjects were often portrayed in this era through new dramatic visual language, a contrast to the reverential portrayal of religious figures in earlier traditions. In order to capture the social disruption surrounding Christianity and the Roman Catholic Church, many artists abandoned old standards of visual perfection from the Classical and Renaissance periods in their portrayal of religious figures.

* Protestant Reformation: 종교 개혁 ** reverential: 경건한

① characteristics of Baroque paintings caused by religious disruption
② impacts of the Baroque on the development of visual perfectionism
③ efforts of Baroque painters to imitate the Renaissance style
④ roles of Baroque artists in stabilizing the disrupted society
⑤ reasons of idealizing religious figures in Baroque paintings

2022학년도 3월 학평 23번 ★★☆

6. 다음 글의 주제로 가장 적절한 것은?

Skills-based approaches to teaching critical thinking now have a long history and literature, but what has become clear through more than 25 years of work on critical thinking theory and pedagogy is that teaching students a set of thinking skills does not seem to be enough. Students may learn to write an adequate article critique in one class, but fail to use those skills in another. They may learn how to evaluate research methodology in other students' research designs, but completely miss the flaws in their own. They may learn to recognize thinking biases in the classroom, but still use badly flawed reasoning in their own decision making. Too often students think our courses are either about memorizing a great deal of material, or about learning the rules for and playing one more idiosyncratic academic game. Students regularly fail to understand what we are trying to teach them or they fail to transfer and generalize thinking skills across contexts and classes.

* pedagogy: 교수법 ** idiosyncratic: 특유한

① importance of critical thinking in school learning
② limitations of teaching thinking skills to students
③ impacts of thinking biases on academic performance
④ application of various teaching methods in classrooms
⑤ necessity of evaluating students' critical thinking skills

2022학년도 수능 23번 ★★☆

7. 다음 글의 주제로 가장 적절한 것은? [3점]

Scientists *use* paradigms rather than believing them. The use of a paradigm in research typically addresses related problems by employing shared concepts, symbolic expressions, experimental and mathematical tools and procedures, and even some of the same theoretical statements. Scientists need only understand *how* to use these various elements in ways that others would accept. These elements of shared practice thus need not presuppose any comparable unity in scientists' beliefs about what they are doing when they use them. Indeed, one role of a paradigm is to enable scientists to work successfully without having to provide a detailed account of what they are doing or what they believe about it. Thomas Kuhn noted that scientists "can agree in their *identification* of a paradigm without agreeing on, or even attempting to produce, a full *interpretation* or *rationalization* of it. Lack of a standard interpretation or of an agreed reduction to rules will not prevent a paradigm from guiding research."

① difficulty in drawing novel theories from existing paradigms
② significant influence of personal beliefs in scientific fields
③ key factors that promote the rise of innovative paradigms
④ roles of a paradigm in grouping like-minded researchers
⑤ functional aspects of a paradigm in scientific research

2022학년도 6월 모평 23번 ★★☆

8. 다음 글의 주제로 가장 적절한 것은? [3점]

Children can move effortlessly between play and absorption in a story, as if both are forms of the same activity. The taking of roles in a narratively structured game of pirates is not very different than the taking of roles in identifying with characters as one watches a movie. It might be thought that, as they grow towards adolescence, people give up childhood play, but this is not so. Instead, the bases and interests of this activity change and develop to playing and watching sports, to the fiction of plays, novels, and movies, and nowadays to video games. In fiction, one can enter possible worlds. When we experience emotions in such worlds, this is not a sign that we are being incoherent or regressed. It derives from trying out metaphorical transformations of our selves in new ways, in new worlds, in ways that can be moving and important to us.

* pirate: 해적 ** incoherent: 일관되지 않은

① relationship between play types and emotional stability
② reasons for identifying with imaginary characters in childhood
③ ways of helping adolescents develop good reading habits
④ continued engagement in altered forms of play after childhood
⑤ effects of narrative structures on readers' imaginations

2021학년도 수능 23번 ★★☆

9. 다음 글의 주제로 가장 적절한 것은? [3점]

Difficulties arise when we do not think of people and machines as collaborative systems, but assign whatever tasks can be automated to the machines and leave the rest to people. This ends up requiring people to behave in machine-like fashion, in ways that differ from human capabilities. We expect people to monitor machines, which means keeping alert for long periods, something we are bad at. We require people to do repeated operations with the extreme precision and accuracy required by machines, again something we are not good at. When we divide up the machine and human components of a task in this way, we fail to take advantage of human strengths and capabilities but instead rely upon areas where we are genetically, biologically unsuited. Yet, when people fail, they are blamed.

① difficulties of overcoming human weaknesses to avoid failure
② benefits of allowing machines and humans to work together
③ issues of allocating unfit tasks to humans in automated systems
④ reasons why humans continue to pursue machine automation
⑤ influences of human actions on a machine's performance

2020학년도 수능 23번 ★★☆

10. 다음 글의 주제로 가장 적절한 것은?

Human beings do not enter the world as competent moral agents. Nor does everyone leave the world in that state. But somewhere in between, most people acquire a bit of decency that qualifies them for membership in the community of moral agents. Genes, development, and learning all contribute to the process of becoming a decent human being. The interaction between nature and nurture is, however, highly complex, and developmental biologists are only just beginning to grasp just how complex it is. Without the context provided by cells, organisms, social groups, and culture, DNA is inert. Anyone who says that people are "genetically programmed" to be moral has an oversimplified view of how genes work. Genes and environment interact in ways that make it nonsensical to think that the process of moral development in children, or any other developmental process, can be discussed in terms of nature *versus* nurture. Developmental biologists now know that it is really both, or nature *through* nurture. A complete scientific explanation of moral evolution and development in the human species is a very long way off.

* decency: 예의 ** inert: 비활성의

① evolution of human morality from a cultural perspective
② difficulties in studying the evolutionary process of genes
③ increasing necessity of educating children as moral agents
④ nature versus nurture controversies in developmental biology
⑤ complicated gene-environment interplay in moral development

총 문항				문항	맞은 문항				문항
개별 문항	1	2	3	4	5	6	7	8	9	10
채점										

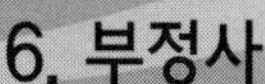

문법 플러스

6. 부정사

정답 및 해설 033쪽

A 문법의 주요 포인트를 점검해 봅시다.

1 to부정사는 문장 속에서 명사 역할을 한다. 즉 주어, 목적어, 보어로 사용될 수 있다.
▶ His great ambition is **[emigrated / to emigrate]** to USA.

2 plan, agree, refuse, decide 등의 동사는 to부정사를 목적어로 취한다.
▶ People will refuse **[paying / to pay]** the new tax.

3 start, begin, continue, like, hate 동사는 to부정사와 동명사를 모두 목적어로 취한다. 의미 차이가 없다. 일부 동사는 to부정사와 동명사를 목적어로 가져올 수 있지만 의미 차이가 있다. stop은 뒤에 동명사를 목적어로 가져오면 '~하는 것을 멈추다'의 의미이며, stop 뒤에 to부정사가 오는 경우, 부사적 용법으로서 '~하기 위해 멈추다'의 의미를 가지고 있다.

「remember+동명사」	(과거) ~했던 것을 기억하다	「remember+to부정사」	(미래) ~할 것을 기억하다
「forget+동명사」	(과거) ~했던 것을 잊다	「forget+to부정사」	(미래) ~할 것을 잊다

. ▶ Don't forget **[to get / getting]** your own food to the party this Saturday.

4 to부정사는 형용사처럼 문장 속에서 명사를 수식하거나 「be동사+to부정사」 구문의 형태로 사용될 수 있다.
▶ Her refusal **[to cooperate / cooperate]** was embarrassing.

5 to부정사는 부사 역할을 할 수 있으며 목적, 원인, 결과, 조건 등을 나타낸다.
▶ Peter came home **[finding / to find]** his house on fire.

6 to부정사의 관용 표현을 익힌다.

needless to say	말할 필요도 없이	A enough to B	B할 만큼 충분히 A하다
to say nothing of	~은 말할 것도 없이	too... to ~	너무 … 해서 ~할 수 없다

▶ The case is light enough for me **[to carry / to carry it]**.

7 to부정사는 의미상의 주어를 쓸 수 있다. 의미상의 주어는 「for+목적격」으로 쓰며, kind, brave 등의 형용사 뒤에는 「of+목적격」을 의미상의 주어로 쓴다. 또한 to부정사의 부정은 not을 to부정사 앞에 쓴다.
▶ To make their dream come true, they decided **[not to waste / to waste not]** money.

B 다음 괄호 안에서 어법상 올바른 것을 고르시오.

1 My Job is **[to report / reported]**, not comment or judge.

2 They decided **[to take / taking]** a 15 minutes' break after CEO's speech.

3 I remember **[to swim / swimming]** in the river when I was a kid.

4 The company's failure **[to modernize / modernize]** caused its decline.

5 **[See / To see]** her walk, you'd never know she is blind.

6 The tiger is **[fat too / too fat]** to climb up the tree.

7 It was very kind **[of / for]** you to help such poor children.

숙어 플러스

6. 수능 필수 숙어 6회

정답 및 해설 034쪽

A 다음 수능 필수 숙어를 읽고, 아는 것은 체크해 봅시다.

□ 01	by itself	저절로, 혼자
□ 02	by nature	본래, 선천적으로
□ 03	by no means	결코 ~이 아닌
□ 04	call for	~을 요구하다, ~을 큰 소리로 부르다
□ 05	call on	요청하다, 방문하다
□ 06	call out	큰 소리로 외치다, (사람 등을) 부르다
□ 07	can afford	~할 여유가 있다
□ 08	cannot help but + 동사원형	~하지 않을 수 없다 (=cannot help -ing)
□ 09	cannot wait to ~	~하기를 몹시 바라다
□ 10	care about	~에 마음 쓰다 ~에 관심을 가지다
□ 11	carry off	잘 해내다
□ 12	carry out	이행하다, 완수하다
□ 13	catch a cold	감기에 걸리다
□ 14	catch one's yes	~의 눈길을 끌다
□ 15	catch up with	따라가다, 따라잡다
□ 16	clear A of B	A에게서 B를 제거하다
□ 17	check in	투숙[탑승] 절차를 밟다
□ 18	come about	(일, 사건 등이) 발생하다, 일어나다
□ 19	come across	이해되다, 인상을 주다, ~을 우연히 만나다
□ 20	come along	나타나다, 동행하다, 나아지다

B 다음 숙어 표현을 읽고 의미 차이를 비교해 봅시다.

□ 21	come down with	병에 걸리다
□ 22	go wrong with	일이 잘못되다
□ 23	hang out with	어울려 다니다
□ 24	in connection with	~과 관련하여
□ 25	keep company with	~와 사귀다

C 우리말을 참고하여 빈칸에 알맞은 말을 써 봅시다.

1 나는 그녀를 좋아하지 않을 수 없었다.
I cannot ______________ but like her.

2 나는 다른 소녀들을 따라 가려고 연습하고 또 연습했다.
I practiced and practiced, trying to ______________ up with the other girls.

3 적어도 출발 한 시간 전에 탑승 수속을 밟으세요.
Please ______________ in at least an hour before departure.

4 Sally는 오랫동안 말을 했지만 그녀가 의미하는 바는 제대로 전달이 되지 않았다.
Sally spoke for a long time but her meaning didn't really come ______________.

07 글의 제목

출제 트렌드

1. 글의 제목이란 글의 내용을 명시하거나 암시하는 간략한 표현을 말한다. 제목은 글의 주제와 내용을 간결하고 압축적으로 표현한 것을 선택한다.
2. 제목 찾기는 글을 읽고 필자가 전달하고자 하는 중심 내용을 파악할 수 있는지 글에 대한 종합적 이해 능력을 측정하는 문제로서 수능에서 매년 1문항이 출제된다. 다양한 글감에서 출제되며, 선택지가 영어로 제시된다.
3. 최근 수능 7년간, 글의 제목 문제는 2017학년도 2문제, 2018학년도 이후 매년 1문제가 출제되었다. 2017학년도 수능 22번(80%), 23번(75%), 2018(71%), 2019(68%), 2020(69%), 2021(54%), 2022(52%), 2023(78%)에서 괄호의 정답률을 보였다. 7년간 평균 68.3% 정도 정답률을 보였다. 난이도는 중 단계이다. 이 문제 유형은 2021, 2022학년도 수능이 다른 해에 비해 상대적으로 어렵게 출제되었다. 제목 문제가 어렵게 출제될 수 있어, 주의가 필요하다.
4. 글의 중심 내용을 물어보는 글의 요지, 주제, 제목 문제 유형의 5년간 평균 정답률을 비교하면 요지(85%) 〉 주제(68.6%) 〉 제목(68.3%) 순서였다. 제목 문제가 약간 더 어려운 것을 알 수 있다.

	출처		문항 번호	지문 주제	정답률(%)	난이도
대표	2023학년도	수능	24번	뇌세포의 시각적 인식 방식	78	★★☆
1	2022학년도	10 학평	24번	동물 모방 의식을 보여주는 동굴 예술	79	★★☆
2	2023학년도	09 모평	24번	음악 연주에서 변주의 가치	86	★☆☆
3	2022학년도	07 학평	24번	영양의 눈이 두개골의 측면에 위치하는 이유	77	★★☆
4	2023학년도	06 모평	24번	인간과 로봇의 혼합팀	76	★★☆
5	2022학년도	04 학평	24번	챔팬지의 사냥 방식	75	★★☆
6	2022학년도	03 학평	24번	생물 다양성 보존의 중요성	87	★☆☆
7	2022학년도	수능	24번	기계가 대신할 수 없는 수리	52	★★★
8	2021학년도	03 학평	24번	F. Yates의 대학 시절 일화	59	★★★
9	2021학년도	수능	24번	촉각의 본질	54	★★★
10	2020학년도	수능	24번	생물다양성과 생태계 보존	69	★★☆

1등급 꿀팁

1. 글의 제목은 주제 추론 유형보다 내용을 좀 더 종합적으로 파악해야 한다. 보통 제목은 주제를 압축해 표현하거나 비유적, 상징적인 어구로 나타낸다.
2. 반복적으로 나오는 어구 또는 특정 개념과 관련된 어구를 통해 글의 내용을 추측하고, 특정 개념에 대해 필자가 어떤 견해를 제시하고 있는지 유의한다.
3. 역접이나 결과, 요약 연결어 다음에 나오는 내용에 유의한다.
4. 선택지로 제시된 제목이 너무 지엽적이거나 너무 포괄적인 경우 답안에서 배제한다.

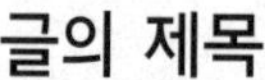

글의 제목

제한 시간 : 15분 | 정답 및 해설 034쪽

대표 기출

2023학년도 수능 24번

24. 다음 글의 제목으로 가장 적절한 것은?

Different parts of the brain's visual system get information on a need-to-know basis. Cells that help your hand muscles reach out to an object need to know the size and location of the object, but they don't need to know about color. They need to know a little about shape, but not in great detail. Cells that help you recognize people's faces need to be extremely sensitive to details of shape, but they can pay less attention to location. It is natural to assume that anyone who sees an object sees everything about it — the shape, color, location, and movement. However, one part of your brain sees its shape, another sees color, another detects location, and another perceives movement. Consequently, after localized brain damage, it is possible to see certain aspects of an object and not others. Centuries ago, people found it difficult to imagine how someone could see an object without seeing what color it is. Even today, you might find it surprising to learn about people who see an object without seeing where it is, or see it without seeing whether it is moving.

① Visual Systems Never Betray Our Trust!
② Secret Missions of Color-Sensitive Brain Cells
③ Blind Spots: What Is Still Unknown About the Brain
④ Why Brain Cells Exemplify Nature's Recovery Process
⑤ Separate and Independent: Brain Cells' Visual Perceptions

문제 풀이

1. 글에서 반복적으로 나오는 어구 또는 특정 개념과 관련된 어구를 통해 글의 내용을 추측한다.

반복적인 어구: the brain's visual system(뇌 시각 시스템)

2. 특정 개념에 대해 필자가 제시하는 견해를 찾는다.

① Different parts of the brain's visual system get information on a need-to-know basis. (뇌 시각 시스템의 다양한 부분들은 꼭 필요한 때 꼭 필요한 것만 알려주는 방식으로 정보를 얻는다.)

② Cells that help your hand muscles reach out to an object need to know the size and location of the object, but they don't need to know about color. (여러분의 손 근육이 어떤 물체에 닿을 수 있도록 돕는 세포들은 그 물체의 크기와 위치를 알아야 하지만 색깔에 대해 알 필요는 없다.)

③ However, one part of your brain sees its shape, another sees color, another detects location, and another perceives movement. (하지만, 여러분 뇌의 한 부분은 그것의 모양을 보고, 다른 한 부분은 색깔을 보며, 또 다른 부분은 위치를 감지하고, 또 다른 한 부분은 움직임을 인식한다.)

④ Consequently, after localized brain damage, it is possible to see certain aspects of an object and not others. (따라서 국부적 뇌 손상 후 물체의 특정한 측면은 볼 수 있으면서 다른 측면은 볼 수 없는 것이 가능하다.)

3. 선택지를 살펴보고 글의 요지를 정확하게 담고 있는 제목을 선택한다.

• 이 글은 뇌의 시각 시스템은 꼭 필요한 때 꼭 필요한 것만 알려 주는 방식으로 정보를 얻기 때문에, 국부적 뇌 손상을 받으면, 특정 뇌세포가 인지하는 물체의 측면을 다른 뇌세포는 인지하지 못하는 경우가 생길 수 있다는 내용이다. 따라서 글의 제목으로 가장 적절한 것은 ⑤ '분리되고 독립적인: 뇌세포의 시각적 인식'이다.

2022학년도 10월 학평 24번 ★★☆

1. 다음 글의 제목으로 가장 적절한 것은?

In making sense of cave art, anthropologists have turned to surviving hunter-gatherer societies that continue to paint inside caves, particularly the San peoples, who live in communities across a wide region of southern Africa. What began to fascinate anthropologists who studied the San was their detailed imitations of the animals they hunt. The hunters, in some sense, become animals in order to make inferences about how their prey might behave. This spills over into ritual. The San use hyperventilation and rhythmic movement to create states of altered consciousness as part of a shamanistic culture. In the final stage of a trance, Lewis-Williams writes, 'people sometimes feel themselves to be turning into animals and undergoing other frightening or exalting transformations'. For anthropologist Kim Hill, identifying and observing animals to eat and those to escape might merge into 'a single process' that sees animals as having humanlike intentions that 'can influence and be influenced'.

* hyperventilation: 과호흡 ** trance: 무아지경
*** exalt: 의기양양하게 하다

① Cave Paintings: The Dawn of Human Creativity
② Early Humans' Communication Through Cave Art
③ Hardships of Early Humans Depicted in Cave Art
④ Shamanistic Culture for Paying Honor to Ancestors
⑤ Animal Imitation Rituals and Understanding Cave Art

2023학년도 9월 모평 24번 ★★☆

2. 다음 글의 제목으로 가장 적절한 것은?

Not only musicians and psychologists, but also committed music enthusiasts and experts often voice the opinion that the beauty of music lies in an expressive deviation from the exactly defined score. Concert performances become interesting and gain in attraction from the fact that they go far beyond the information printed in the score. In his early studies on musical performance, Carl Seashore discovered that musicians only rarely play two equal notes in exactly the same way. Within the same metric structure, there is a wide potential of variations in tempo, volume, tonal quality and intonation. Such variation is based on the composition but diverges from it individually. We generally call this 'expressivity'. This explains why we do not lose interest when we hear different artists perform the same piece of music. It also explains why it is worthwhile for following generations to repeat the same repertoire. New, inspiring interpretations help us to expand our understanding, which serves to enrich and animate the music scene.

* deviation: 벗어남

① How to Build a Successful Career in Music Criticism
② Never the Same: The Value of Variation in Music Performance
③ The Importance of Personal Expression in Music Therapy
④ Keep Your Cool: Overcoming Stage Fright When Playing Music
⑤ What's New in the Classical Music Industry?

2022학년도 7월 학평 24번 ★★☆

3. 다음 글의 제목으로 가장 적절한 것은?

On an antelope's skull, the eye sockets are situated on the side of the head. This is because this animal spends a lot of its time with its head bent down to eat a low-nutrient food: grass. While the animal is busy grazing, there will be predators out stalking for their food, so the antelope needs the greatest possible range of vision so that it has the maximum chance of seeing its predator and making an escape. With the eye sockets at the back of the head and on the side, it can see nearly 360° around itself. The eye of the antelope is also at the back of its head, giving it a long nose. If the eyes were at the front of the skull, vision would be obscured by long grass, so its long nose also gives an evolutionary advantage.

① Better Predator Detection: Eyes' Location Matters!
② Escaping as a Primary Defense Tactic in a Field
③ Closer Eyes, Less Accurate Distance Perception
④ A Win-Win Survival Strategy for Prey and Predator
⑤ Why Do Animals Have Longer Noses than Humans?

2023학년도 6월 모평 24번 ★★☆

4. 다음 글의 제목으로 가장 적절한 것은?

The approach, *joint cognitive systems*, treats a robot as part of a human-machine team where the intelligence is synergistic, arising from the contributions of each agent. The team consists of at least one robot and one human and is often called a *mixed team* because it is a mixture of human and robot agents. Self-driving cars, where a person turns on and off the driving, is an example of a joint cognitive system. Entertainment robots are examples of mixed teams as are robots for telecommuting. The design process concentrates on how the agents will cooperate and coordinate with each other to accomplish the team goals. Rather than treating robots as peer agents with their own completely independent agenda, joint cognitive systems approaches treat robots as helpers such as service animals or sheep dogs. In joint cognitive system designs, artificial intelligence is used along with human-robot interaction principles to create robots that can be intelligent enough to be good team members.

① Better Together: Human and Machine Collaboration
② Can Robots Join Forces to Outperform Human Teams?
③ Loss of Humanity in the Human and Machine Conflict
④ Power Off: When and How to Say No to Robot Partners
⑤ Shifting from Service Animals to Robot Assistants of Humans

2022학년도 4월 학평 24번 ★★☆

5. 다음 글의 제목으로 가장 적절한 것은?

Chimpanzees are known to hunt and eat red colobus monkeys. Although a solo male typically initiates a hunt, others often join in, and hunting success is much higher when chimps hunt as a group rather than individually. During the hunt, chimpanzees adopt different roles: one male might flush the monkeys from their refuge, while another blocks the escape route. Somewhere else, an ambusher hides, ready to make his deadly move. Although this sounds a lot like teamwork, recent work offers a simpler interpretation. Chimps are more likely to join others for hunts because larger hunting groups increase each *individual's* chance of catching a monkey — they aren't interested in collective goals. The appearance of specialised roles in the hunt may also be an illusion: a simpler explanation is that each chimp places himself where his own chance of catching a monkey is highest, relative to the positions the others have already taken. Collaboration in chimps seems to emerge from an 'every chimp for himself' mentality.

* refuge: 은신처 ** ambusher: 복병

① Chimps' Group Hunt: It's All about Myself, Not Ourselves
② Obstacles to Chimps in Assigning Roles for Group Hunting
③ How One Selfish Chimp Can Ruin a Cooperative Group Hunt
④ Hunting in Concert with Other Chimps Determines Social Status!
⑤ Which Are Better Hunters, Cooperative or Competitive Chimps?

2022학년도 3월 학평 24번 ★☆☆

6. 다음 글의 제목으로 가장 적절한 것은?

As much as we like to think of ourselves as being different and special, humans are a part of Earth's biosphere, created within and by it. Ultimately, it is the living, breathing elements of this world that we need more than inanimate supplies, such as coal, gas, or bauxite ore. We can live without cars or beer cans, but we cannot without food and oxygen. As nations around the globe try to band together to attack the problems of greenhouse gas emissions and the shrinking availability of fresh drinking water, in all corners of the world thousands of species quietly go extinct. E. O. Wilson, the renowned Harvard biologist, recently presented the problem our species faces in a succinct law: "If you save the living environment, the biodiversity that we have left, you will also automatically save the physical environment, too. But if you only save the physical environment, you will ultimately lose both."

* biosphere: 생물권 ** ore: 광석 *** succinct: 간결한

① Save Biodiversity to Save the Earth
② Invasive Alien Species Threaten Biodiversity
③ Potentiality and Utilization of Renewable Energy
④ Tackling Climate Change Has a Long Way to Go
⑤ Worldwide Efforts to Protect Endangered Species

2022학년도 수능 24번 ★★★

7. 다음 글의 제목으로 가장 적절한 것은?

Mending and restoring objects often require even more creativity than original production. The preindustrial blacksmith made things to order for people in his immediate community; customizing the product, modifying or transforming it according to the user, was routine. Customers would bring things back if something went wrong; repair was thus an extension of fabrication. With industrialization and eventually with mass production, making things became the province of machine tenders with limited knowledge. But repair continued to require a larger grasp of design and materials, an understanding of the whole and a comprehension of the designer's intentions. "Manufacturers all work by machinery or by vast subdivision of labour and not, so to speak, by hand," an 1896 *Manual of Mending and Repairing* explained. "But all repairing *must* be done by hand. We can make every detail of a watch or of a gun by machinery, but the machine cannot mend it when broken, much less a clock or a pistol!"

① Still Left to the Modern Blacksmith: The Art of Repair
② A Historical Survey of How Repairing Skills Evolved
③ How to Be a Creative Repairperson: Tips and Ideas
④ A Process of Repair: Create, Modify, Transform!
⑤ Can Industrialization Mend Our Broken Past?

2021학년도 3월 학평 24번 ★★★

8. 다음 글의 제목으로 가장 적절한 것은?

There is a story about F. Yates, a prominent UK statistician. During his student years at St. John's College, Cambridge, Yates had been keen on a form of sport. It consisted of climbing about the roofs and towers of the college buildings at night. In particular, the chapel of St. John's College has a massive neo-Gothic tower adorned with statues of saints, and to Yates it appeared obvious that it would be more decorous if these saints were properly attired in surplices. One night he climbed up and did the job; next morning the result was generally much admired. But the College authorities were unappreciative and began to consider means of divesting the saints of their newly acquired garments. This was not easy, since they were well out of reach of any ordinary ladder. An attempt to lift the surplices off from above, using ropes with hooks attached, was unsuccessful. No progress was being made and eventually Yates came forward and volunteered to climb up in the daylight and bring them down. This he did to the admiration of the crowd that assembled.

* decorous: 품위 있는 ** surplice: 흰 가운 *** divest: 벗기다

① A Scary Legend About the Statues at St. John's College
② A Student Who Solved a Problem of His Own Making
③ Standards of Beauty Varying from Person to Person
④ A Smart Professor Who Identified a Criminal
⑤ A Success Story of a Mysterious Architect

2021학년도 수능 24번 ★★☆

9. 다음 글의 제목으로 가장 적절한 것은?

People don't usually think of touch as a temporal phenomenon, but it is every bit as time-based as it is spatial. You can carry out an experiment to see for yourself. Ask a friend to cup his hand, palm face up, and close his eyes. Place a small ordinary object in his palm — a ring, an eraser, anything will do — and ask him to identify it without moving any part of his hand. He won't have a clue other than weight and maybe overall size. Then tell him to keep his eyes closed and move his fingers over the object. He'll most likely identify it at once. By allowing the fingers to move, you've added time to the sensory perception of touch. There's a direct analogy between the fovea at the center of your retina and your fingertips, both of which have high acuity. Your ability to make complex use of touch, such as buttoning your shirt or unlocking your front door in the dark, depends on continuous time-varying patterns of touch sensation.

* analogy: 유사 ** fovea: (망막의) 중심와(窩) *** retina: 망막

① Touch and Movement: Two Major Elements of Humanity
② Time Does Matter: A Hidden Essence of Touch
③ How to Use the Five Senses in a Timely Manner
④ The Role of Touch in Forming the Concept of Time
⑤ The Surprising Function of Touch as a Booster of Knowledge

2020학년도 수능 24번 ★★☆

10. 다음 글의 제목으로 가장 적절한 것은?

Invasions of natural communities by non-indigenous species are currently rated as one of the most important global-scale environmental problems. The loss of biodiversity has generated concern over the consequences for ecosystem functioning and thus understanding the relationship between both has become a major focus in ecological research during the last two decades. The "biodiversity-invasibility hypothesis" by Elton suggests that high diversity increases the competitive environment of communities and makes them more difficult to invade. Numerous biodiversity experiments have been conducted since Elton's time and several mechanisms have been proposed to explain the often observed negative relationship between diversity and invasibility. Beside the decreased chance of empty ecological niches but the increased probability of competitors that prevent invasion success, diverse communities are assumed to use resources more completely and, therefore, limit the ability of invaders to establish. Further, more diverse communities are believed to be more stable because they use a broader range of niches than species-poor communities.

* indigenous: 토착의 ** niche: 생태적 지위

① Carve Out More Empty Ecological Spaces!
② Guardian of Ecology: Diversity Resists Invasion
③ Grasp All, Lose All: Necessity of Species-poor Ecology
④ Challenges in Testing Biodiversity-Invasibility Hypothesis
⑤ Diversity Dilemma: The More Competitive, the Less Secure

총 문항			문항	맞은 문항					문항
개별 문항	1	2	3	4	5	6	7	8	9	10
채점										

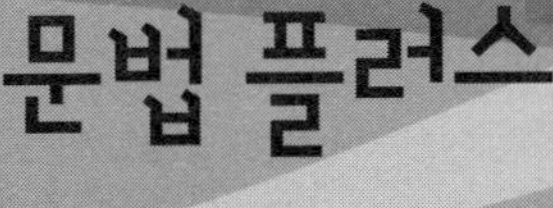

7. 분사, 분사구문

정답 및 해설 039쪽

A 문법의 주요 포인트를 점검해 봅시다.

1 분사는 형용사처럼 명사를 수식하거나 주격보어나 목적격보어 역할을 할 수 있다. 현재분사는 능동, 진행의 의미를 나타내고, 과거분사는 수동, 완료의 의미를 나타낸다.

▶ When considered in this light, the visual preoccupation of early humans with the nonhuman creatures **[inhabiting / inhabited]** their world becomes profoundly meaningful.

2 주어와 주격보어의 관계가 능동 관계이면 현재분사를, 수동 관계이면 과거분사를 사용한다.

▶ He is a interesting writer, and I'm very **[interesting / interested]** in the subjects that he writes about.

3 목적어와 목적격보어의 관계가 능동 관계이면 현재분사를, 수동 관계이면 과거분사를 사용한다.

▶ Sam felt something **[clawing / clawed]** up his back.

4 분사구문은 「접속사+주어+동사」로 된 부사절을 대신하며, 시간, 이유, 조건, 양보, 동시동작, 연속동작의 의미를 나타낸다.

▶ A cell is "born" as a twin when its mother cell divides, **[produced / producing]** two daughter cells.

5 완료분사구문은 주절의 시제보다 앞선 시제를 나타낸다. 또한 수동형 분사구문에서 being이나 having been은 생략 가능하다.

▶ **[Having found / Finding]** a hotel(= After they had found), they looked for somewhere to have dinner.

6 「with+목적어+분사」 표현은 목적어와 분사의 관계가 능동이면 현재분사를, 수동이면 과거분사를 사용한다.
분사 자리에 형용사, 부사, 전치사구가 와서 목적어의 상태를 설명할 수도 있다.

▶ I can do that with my eyes **[closing / closed]**.

7 분사구문의 주어가 주절의 주어와 다른 경우 분사구문의 주어를 분사 앞에 명시해 주어야 한다. 부정어는 분사 바로 앞에 배치한다.

▶ Even the most complex cell has only a small number of parts, each **[being / is]** responsible for a distinct, well-defined aspect of cell life.

B 다음 괄호 안에서 어법상 올바른 것을 고르시오.

1 Scientists who experiment on themselves can, functionally if not legally, avoid the restrictions **[associating / associated]** with experimenting on other people.

2 Sam's job is boring, so he is **[boring / bored].**

3 I'm sorry to have kept you **[waited / waiting]**.

4 **[Situated / Situating]** at an elevation of 1,300 meters, the city enjoys a warm climate year-round.

5 **[Having seen / Seen]** an accident, she stopped her car.

6 He jogs everyday with his dog **[following / followed]** him.

7 **[Not knowing / Knowing not]** the way, they soon got lost.

숙어 플러스

7. 수능 필수 숙어 7회

정답 및 해설 040쪽

A 다음 수능 필수 숙어를 읽고, 아는 것은 체크해 봅시다.

□ 01	come around	~에 들르다, 다시 의식을 차리다
□ 02	come by	얻다, 구하다, 잠깐 들르다
□ 03	come down with	병에 걸리다
□ 04	come of	~의 결과로 일어나다
□ 05	come over	우연히 들르다
□ 06	come through	통과하다, 견뎌내다, 해내다
□ 07	come true	실현되다
□ 08	come up to	~까지 오다, 미치다, 이르다
□ 09	confess A to B	A를 B에게 자백하다
□ 10	confine A to B	A를 B로 제한하다
□ 11	contribute A to B	A를 B에 기부하다
□ 12	convince A of B	A에게 B를 확신시키다
□ 13	cool off	시원해지다, 진정하다
□ 14	cope with	대처하다
□ 15	count on	~에 의지하다
□ 16	cover up	감추다, 은폐하다
□ 17	cure A of B	A에게서 B를 낫게 하다
□ 18	cut off	잘라내다, 중단하다
□ 19	cut out	제거(삭제)하다, 그만두다
□ 20	dare to + 동사원형	감히 ~하다

B 다음 숙어 표현을 읽고 의미 차이를 비교해 봅시다.

□ 21	be amused at	~에 즐거워하다
□ 22	be delighted at	~에 기뻐하다
□ 23	be shocked at	~에 충격을 받다
□ 24	be amazed at	~에 놀라다
□ 25	be surprised at	~에 놀라다

C 우리말을 참고하여 빈칸에 알맞은 말을 써 봅시다.

1 그들은 자신들의 꿈을 실현시키기 위해서 돈을 낭비하지 않기로 결정했다.
In order to make their dream ______________ true, they decided not to waste money.

2 음악회는 내가 기대한 정도는 아니었다.
The concert did not come ______________ to my expectations.

3 그는 점진적인 과정을 통해 그것들에 대처할 수 있게 될지도 모른다.
He may become able to __________with them in a step-by-step process.

4 그는 내가 믿을 수 있는 유일한 사람이야.
He is the only one I can _________________ on.

도표 정보 파악

출제 트렌드

1. 세부 내용 파악하기 읽기 유형에는 도표 정보 파악, 내용 일치 · 불일치, 안내문 파악하기 문제가 있다.
2. 도표 정보 파악 문제 유형은 '다음 도표[표]의 내용과 일치하지 않는 것'을 고르는 문제이다.
3. 통계 자료나 정보를 한 눈에 볼 수 있도록 도식화한 것을 도표라고 한다. 도표 정보 파악 문제는 제시된 정보와 선택지의 내용이 일치하는지 판단하는 능력을 측정한다. 언어 학습의 실용성 측면에서 이 문제 유형은 의미가 크다. 수능에서 최근 매년 1문항이 출제되고 있다. 최근에는 도표가 복잡해지고 도표를 서술하는 정보도 어려워지고 있다. 도표 외에도 표가 나오기도 한다.
4. 최근 수능 7년간, 도표 정보 파악 문제는 2017학년도 이후 매년 1문제가 출제되고 있다. 2017학년도 수능(94%), 2018(94%), 2019(91%), 2020(95%), 2021(93%), 2022(93%), 2023(94%)에서 괄호 안의 정답률을 보였다. 7년간 평균 93.4% 정도 정답률을 보였다. 난이도는 하 단계이다.

	출처		문항 번호	지문 주제	정답률(%)	난이도
대표	2023학년도	수능	25번	미국인이 선호하는 거주지 유형	94	★☆☆
1	2022학년도	10 학평	25번	미국 디지털 비디오 소비자 점유율	95	★☆☆
2	2023학년도	09 모평	25번	가장 많은 재생에너지 발전 용량을 가진 유럽 상위 4개국	96	★☆☆
3	2022학년도	07 학평	25번	2016년 EU 국가들의 플라스틱 포장 쓰레기 처리법	91	★☆☆
4	2023학년도	06 모평	25번	거주자 특허 출원	93	★☆☆
5	2022학년도	04 학평	25번	연료 종류별 유럽 연합에서의 신차 점유율	92	★☆☆
6	2022학년도	03 학평	25번	차량 대 선박의 이산화 탄소 배출량	86	★☆☆
7	2022학년도	수능	25번	세계 중산층의 점유율 비교	93	★☆☆
8	2022학년도	06 모평	25번	미국 성인의 나이 연령대별 책 소비	86	★☆☆
9	2021학년도	수능	25번	소매 판매의 온라인 점유율	93	★☆☆
10	2020학년도	수능	25번	세계 인구의 전기 이용	95	★☆☆

1등급 꿀팁

1. 도표 상단의 제목과 가로축과 세로축의 정보를 보고 무엇에 관한 도표인지 파악한다.
2. 도표나 표를 보면서 특이하거나 중요한 정보를 찾아본다. 선택지 순서대로, 도표나 표를 보면서 기술한 내용이 맞는지 체크한다.
3. 다양한 도표(막대 그래프, 꺾은선 그래프, 파이 그래프)를 접해 보고 그 내용을 분석하는 연습을 해본다.
4. 도표(표)와 관련된 표현을 익혀 둔다.

증가	rise, increase, go up, grow, soar
감소	fall, decrease, go down, drop, decline
증감	drastically/rapidly (급격하게), gradually(점차로), slowly (천천히)
배수	a half (1/2배), double (2배), twice (2배), three times (3배)
	be more than three times (3배 이상이다), 배수사+as 원급 as (~배 만큼 …한)
비교	be larger than (~보다 더 크다), be less than (~보다 적다), be fewer than (~보다 적다)
	compared with (~과 비교하여), the most (가장 ~한), the second most (두 번째로 ~한)
비율	a rate of A to B (A와 B의 비율), more than A out of B (B중에서 A 이상)
기타	the gap of ~ (~의 차이), rank lower (보다 낮은 순위를 차지하다), likewise(마찬가지로)

제한 시간 : 15분 | 정답 및 해설 040쪽

대표 기출

2023학년도 수능 25번

25. 다음 도표의 내용과 일치하지 않는 것은?

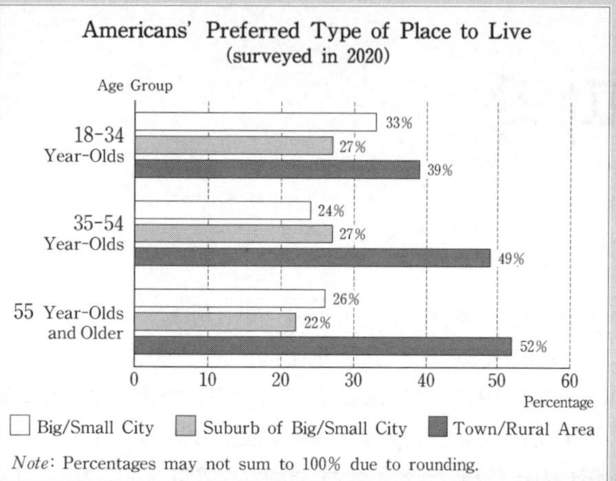

The above graph shows the percentages of Americans' preferred type of place to live by age group, based on a 2020 survey. ① In each of the three age groups, Town/Rural Area was the most preferred type of place to live. ② In the 18-34 year-olds group, the percentage of those who preferred Big/Small City was higher than that of those who preferred Suburb of Big/Small City. ③ In the 35-54 year-olds group, the percentage of those who preferred Suburb of Big/Small City exceeded that of those who preferred Big/Small City. ④ In the 55 year-olds and older group, the percentage of those who chose Big/Small City among the three preferred types of place to live was the lowest. ⑤ Each percentage of the three preferred types of place to live was higher than 20% across the three age groups.

문제 풀이

1. 도표 제목 및 가로축과 세로축 정보를 파악한다.

① 제목: Americans' preferred type of place to live(미국인이 선호하는 거주지 유형)
② 가로축: 퍼센트(%) 세로축: age group(나이 그룹)

2. 글의 도입부를 통해 표 이해를 위한 개요를 파악한다.

① The above graph shows the percentages of Americans' preferred type of place to live by age group, based on a 2020 survey. (위의 그래프는 2020년 조사를 기반으로 연령대별로 미국인이 선호하는 거주지 유형의 비율을 보여준다.)

3. 도표와 선택지의 내용이 서로 일치하는지 확인한다.

① 각기 세 연령대에서 읍내/시골 지역이 가장 선호되는 거주지 유형이었다.
② 18~34세 그룹에서는 대도시/소도시를 선호하는 비율이 대도시/소도시 근교를 선호하는 비율보다 더 높았다.
③ 35~54세 연령층에서는 대도시/소도시 근교를 선호하는 비율이 대도시/소도시를 선호하는 비율을 앞질렀다.
⑤ 세 가지 선호하는 거주지 유형의 각각의 비율은 세 연령대에 걸쳐 20%보다 더 높았다.

• ④ In the 55 year-olds and older group, the percentage of those who chose Big/Small City among the three preferred types of place to live was the lowest. (55세 이상 연령층에서는 세 가지 선호하는 거주지 유형 중에서 대도시/소도시를 선택한 비율이 가장 낮았다.) 55세 이상 연령층에서 대도시/소도시 근교를 선택한 사람들의 비율이 22%로 가장 낮았으므로, 도표의 내용과 일치하지 않는 것은 ④이다.

2022학년도 10월 학평 25번 ★☆☆

1. 다음 도표의 내용과 일치하지 않는 것은?

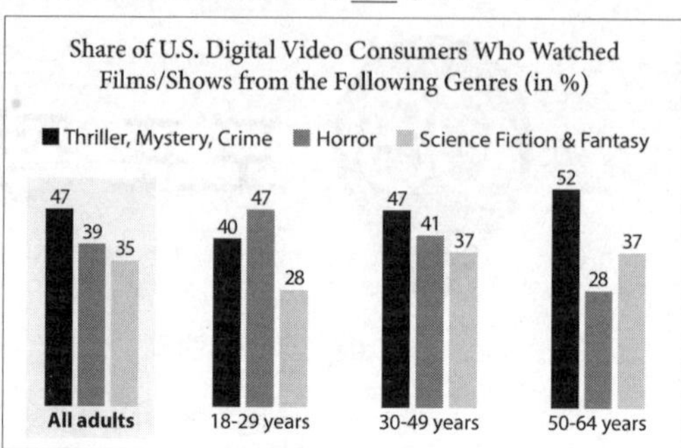

The graph above shows the share of U.S. digital video consumers who watched films/shows from three genres between April 2021 and March 2022. ① "Thriller, Mystery, Crime" was the most watched genre by American adults with the percentage of 47, followed by "Horror" and "Science Fiction & Fantasy," which accounted for 39% and 35% respectively. ② In the 18−29 age group, "Horror" was the most watched genre, while "Science Fiction & Fantasy" was the least watched genre. ③ Each of the three genres was watched by more than 35 percent of the consumers in the 30−49 age group. ④ The percentage of people who watched "Science Fiction & Fantasy" in the 30−49 age group was the same as that in the 50−64 age group. ⑤ In the 50−64 age group, the percentage of those who watched "Thriller, Mystery, Crime" was twice as large as the percentage of those who watched "Horror."

2023학년도 9월 모평 25번 ★☆☆

2. 다음 도표의 내용과 일치하지 않는 것은?

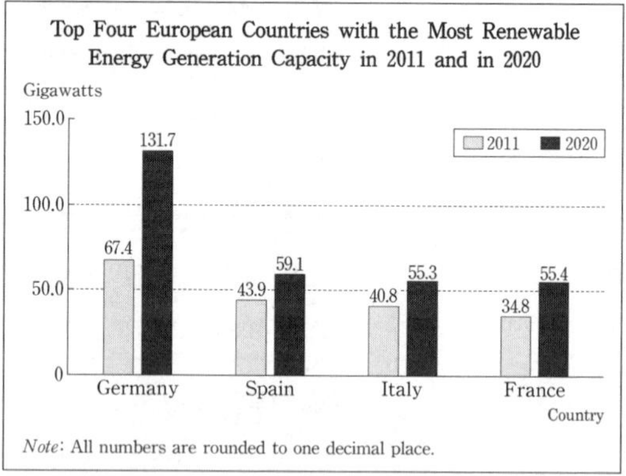

The graph above shows the top four European countries with the most renewable energy generation capacity in 2011 and in 2020. ① Each of the four countries in the graph had a higher capacity to generate renewable energy in 2020 than its respective capacity in 2011. ② Germany's capacity to generate renewable energy in 2011 reached more than 50.0 gigawatts, which was also the case in 2020. ③ Among the countries above, Spain ranked in second place in terms of renewable energy generation capacity in 2011 and remained in second place in 2020. ④ The renewable energy generation capacity of Italy in 2020 was lower than that of Spain in the same year. ⑤ The renewable energy generation capacity of France was higher than that of Italy in both 2011 and 2020.

* decimal: 소수의

2022학년도 7월 학평 25번 ★☆☆

3. 다음 도표의 내용과 일치하지 않는 것은?

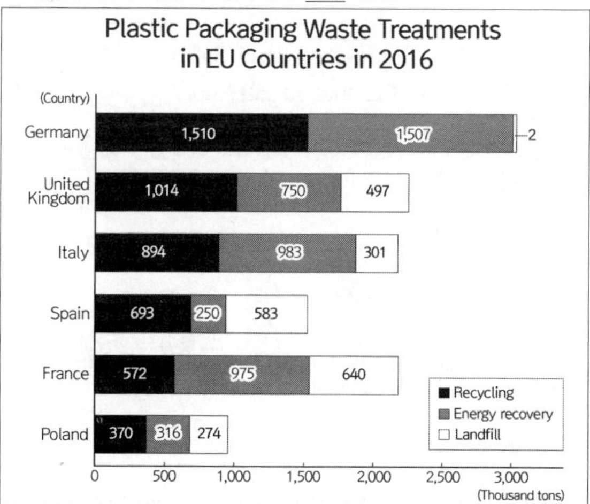

The graph above shows the plastic packaging waste treatments in EU countries in 2016. ① Among the six countries represented in the graph, Germany had the highest amount of both recycling and energy recovery while France had the highest amount of landfill. ② In the United Kingdom, the combined amount of energy recovery and landfill was more than half the total amount of plastic packaging waste treated. ③ In Italy, plastic packaging waste recycled and plastic packaging waste recovered for energy each amounted to more than 800 thousand tons. ④ The amount of plastic packaging waste used for energy recovery in France was more than four times that of Spain. ⑤ The total amount of plastic packaging waste treated in Poland was less than the amount of plastic packaging waste recycled in the United Kingdom.

2023학년도 6월 모평 25번 ★☆☆

4. 다음 표의 내용과 일치하지 않는 것은?

Resident Patent Applications per Million Population for the Top 6 Origins, in 2009 and in 2019

2009			2019		
Rank	Origin	Resident patent applications per million population	Rank	Origin	Resident patent applications per million population
1	Republic of Korea	2,582	1	Republic of Korea	3,319
2	Japan	2,306	2	Japan	1,943
3	Switzerland	975	3	Switzerland	1,122
4	Germany	891	4	China	890
5	U.S.	733	5	Germany	884
6	Finland	609	6	U.S.	869

Note: The top 6 origins were included if they had a population greater than 5 million and if they had more than 100 resident patent applications.

The above tables show the resident patent applications per million population for the top 6 origins in 2009 and in 2019. ① The Republic of Korea, Japan, and Switzerland, the top three origins in 2009, maintained their rankings in 2019. ② Germany, which sat fourth on the 2009 list with 891 resident patent applications per million population, fell to fifth place on the 2019 list with 884 resident patent applications per million population. ③ The U.S. fell from fifth place on the 2009 list to sixth place on the 2019 list, showing a decrease in the number of resident patent applications per million population. ④ Among the top 6 origins which made the list in 2009, Finland was the only origin which did not make it again in 2019. ⑤ On the other hand, China, which did not make the list of the top 6 origins in 2009, sat fourth on the 2019 list with 890 resident patent applications per million population.

2022학년도 4월 학평 25번 ★☆☆

5. 다음 표의 내용과 일치하지 않는 것은?

New Cars in the EU by Fuel Type in 2018 and in 2020

Type	Share of New Cars (%) 2018 (A)	Share of New Cars (%) 2020 (B)	Gap (B−A)
Gasoline	55.6	47.5	−8.1
Diesel	36.7	28	−8.7
Hybrid Electric	4	11.9	7.9
Alternative Fuels	1.8	2.1	0.3
Battery Electric	1	5.4	4.4
Plug−in Hybrid	0.9	5.1	4.2

The table above shows the share of new cars in the EU by fuel type in 2018 and in 2020. ① Compared to 2018, the share of both gasoline and diesel cars decreased in 2020. ② However, gasoline cars still held the largest share of new cars in 2020, followed by diesel vehicles, which made up more than a quarter of new cars in the same year. ③ Hybrid electric cars increased by 7.9 percentage points in the share of new cars from 2018 to 2020. ④ In 2018, the share of new cars powered by alternative fuels was larger than that of battery electric cars, but in 2020, the share of battery electric cars was more than twice that of cars using alternative fuels. ⑤ Plug−in hybrid vehicles were the only type of vehicle which accounted for less than 1% of new cars in 2018, and their share remained the smallest among all types of vehicle in 2020.

2022학년도 3월 학평 25번 ★☆☆

6. 다음 도표의 내용과 일치하지 않는 것은?

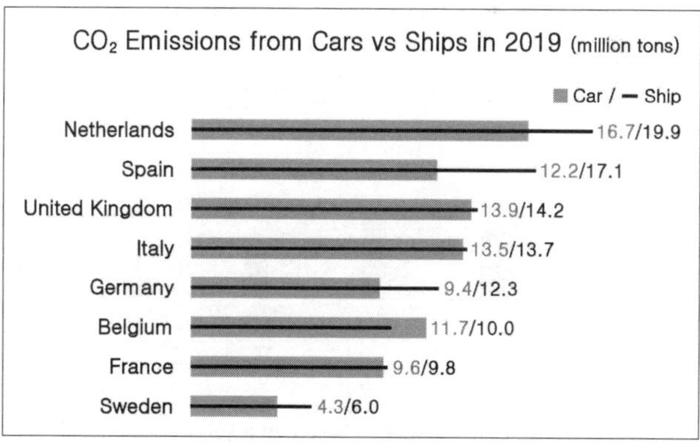

The graph above shows the CO_2 emissions from cars versus ships in Europe in 2019. ① Among the eight countries, the CO_2 emissions from ships were larger than those from cars except for Belgium. ② The Netherlands had the largest CO_2 emissions from both cars and ships, whereas Sweden had the smallest CO_2 emissions from both. ③ The CO_2 emissions from ships were larger in Spain than in the United Kingdom, but the CO_2 emissions from cars were larger in the United Kingdom than in Spain. ④ Germany's CO_2 emissions from ships were more than twice those of Sweden. ⑤ The gap between the CO_2 emissions from cars and ships was the largest in the Netherlands and the smallest in Italy and France.

2022학년도 수능 25번 ★☆☆

7. 다음 도표의 내용과 일치하지 않는 것은?

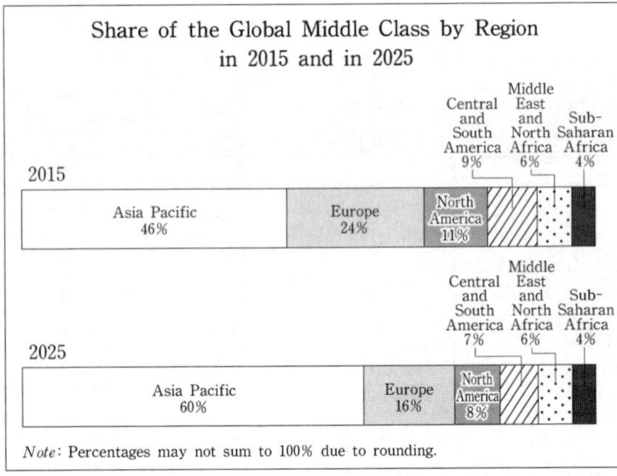

The above graphs show the percentage share of the global middle class by region in 2015 and its projected share in 2025. ① It is projected that the share of the global middle class in Asia Pacific will increase from 46 percent in 2015 to 60 percent in 2025. ② The projected share of Asia Pacific in 2025, the largest among the six regions, is more than three times that of Europe in the same year. ③ The shares of Europe and North America are both projected to decrease, from 24 percent in 2015 to 16 percent in 2025 for Europe, and from 11 percent in 2015 to 8 percent in 2025 for North America. ④ Central and South America is not expected to change from 2015 to 2025 in its share of the global middle class. ⑤ In 2025, the share of the Middle East and North Africa will be larger than that of sub-Saharan Africa, as it was in 2015.

2022학년도 6월 모평 25번 ★☆☆

8. 다음 도표의 내용과 일치하지 않는 것은?

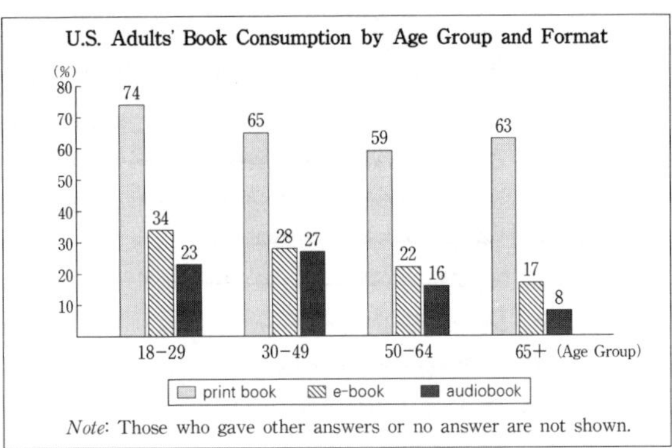

The above graph, which was based on a survey conducted in 2019, shows the percentages of U.S. adults by age group who said they had read (or listened to) a book in one or more of the formats — print books, e-books, and audiobooks — in the previous 12 months. ① The percentage of people in the 18-29 group who said they had read a print book was 74%, which was the highest among the four groups. ② The percentage of people who said they had read a print book in the 50-64 group was higher than that in the 65 and up group. ③ While 34% of people in the 18-29 group said they had read an e-book, the percentage of people who said so was below 20% in the 65 and up group. ④ In all age groups, the percentage of people who said they had read an e-book was higher than that of people who said they had listened to an audiobook. ⑤ Among the four age groups, the 30-49 group had the highest percentage of people who said they had listened to an audiobook.

2021학년도 수능 25번 ★☆☆

9. 다음 도표의 내용과 일치하지 않는 것은?

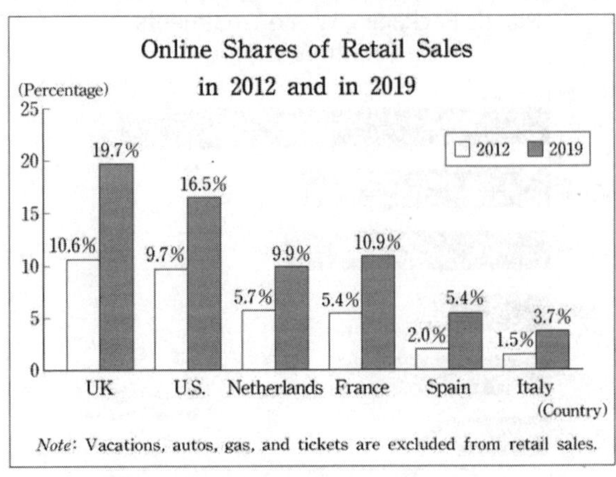

The graph above shows the online shares of retail sales for each of six countries in 2012 and in 2019. The online share of retail sales refers to the percentage of retail sales conducted online in a given country. ① For each country, its online share of retail sales in 2019 was larger than that in 2012. ② Among the six countries, the UK owned the largest online share of retail sales with 19.7% in 2019. ③ In 2019, the U.S. had the second largest online share of retail sales with 16.5%. ④ In 2012, the online share of retail sales in the Netherlands was larger than that in France, whereas the reverse was true in 2019. ⑤ In the case of Spain and Italy, the online share of retail sales in each country was less than 5.0% both in 2012 and in 2019.

2020학년도 수능 25번 ★☆☆

10. 다음 도표의 내용과 일치하지 않는 것은?

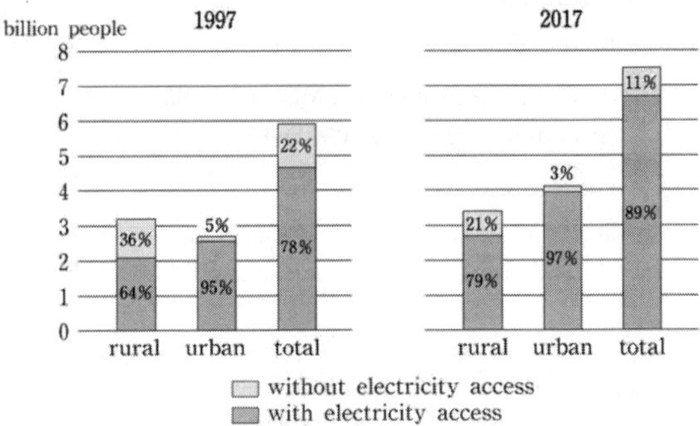

The above graph shows the world population access to electricity in 1997 and in 2017. ① The percentage of the total world population with electricity access in 2017 was 11 percentage points higher than that in 1997. ② Both in 1997 and in 2017, less than 80% of the rural population had access to electricity while over 90% of the urban population had access to electricity. ③ In 1997, 36% of the rural population did not have electricity access while 5% of the urban population did not have access to electricity. ④ The percentage of the rural population without electricity access in 2017 was 20 percentage points lower than that in 1997. ⑤ The percentage of the urban population without electricity access decreased from 5% in 1997 to 3% in 2017.

총 문항				문항	맞은 문항					문항
개별 문항	1	2	3	4	5	6	7	8	9	10
채점										

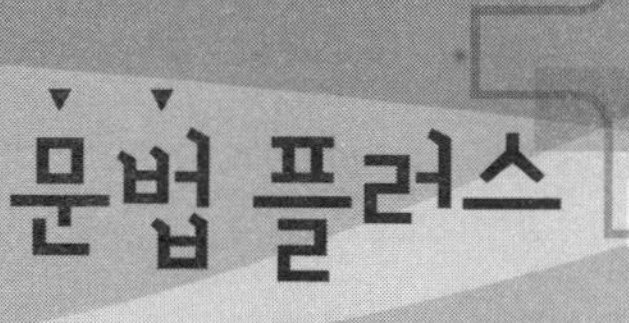

8. 준동사

정답 및 해설 043쪽

A 문법의 주요 포인트를 점검해 봅시다.

1 완료형 부정사, 완료형 동명사는 동사의 시제보다 앞선 시제를 의미한다.

부정사 단순형 : to+동사원형	부정사 완료형 : to have p.p.
동명사 단순형 : 동사원형 -ing	동명사 완료형 : having p.p.

▶ He is believed **[to leave / to have left]** the country. = It is believed that he left the country.

2 완료 분사구문은 주절의 시제보다 앞선 시제를 의미한다.

분사 단순형 : 동사원형 -ing	분사 완료형 : having p.p.

▶ Because she had seen the film twice, she didn't want to go to the cinema.
= **[Seeing already / Having already seen]** the film twice, she didn't want to go to the cinema.

3 준동사도 수동태를 나타낼 수 있다. 주어와 준동사의 관계가 수동이면 to부정사는 「to be+p.p.」로 표현하고, 동명사와 분사는 「being+p.p.」로 표현한다.

수동형	부정사 : to be p.p.	동명사 : being p.p.	분사 : (being) p.p.

▶ Sally disconnected the phone so as not to **[be / being]** disturbed.

4 명사와 분사의 관계가 능동이면 현재분사를 쓰고 수동이면 과거분사로 쓴다.
▶ As a form of expression, fashion contains a host of ambiguities, enabling individuals to recreate the meanings **[associating / associated]** with specific pieces of clothing.

5 분사구문이 주절의 주어와 능동 관계이면 현재분사로, 수동 관계이면 과거분사로 쓴다.
▶ Fashion can also strengthen agency in various ways, **[opened / opening]** up space for action.

6 준동사는 의미상의 주어를 나타낼 수 있다.

의미상 주어	동명사 : 소유격 / 목적격	동명사가 문장의 주어로 문두에 나오는 경우 소유격을 쓴다.
	부정사 : 「for+목적격」	성품 형용사(kind, nice 등)는 「of+목적격」을 쓴다.
	분사 : 분사구문의 주어가 주절의 주어와 다른 경우에는 분사구문의 주어를 명시해 준다.	

▶ **[His / Him]** knowing I returned home unexpectedly is strange.

7 준동사 부정은 바로 앞에 not을 둔다.
▶ I'm surprised at **[not his / his not]** having noticed.

B 다음 괄호 안에서 어법상 올바른 것을 고르시오.

1 I'm sorry for **[wasting / having wasted]** your time. (= I'm sorry that I wasted your time.)

2 After she had completed the work, she took a vacation.
= **[Completing / Having completed]** the work, she took a vacation.

3 Sam says nothing without **[being spoken to / speaking to]**.

4 I saw Mark **[taking / taken]** away by the police.

5 His drama director, **[frustrating / frustrated]** with his acting, shouted at him.

6 It was careless **[for / of]** him to leave his smart phone in the bus.

7 **[Not wanting / Wanting not]** to interrupt the conversation, he stood quietly.

숙어 플러스

8. 수능 필수 숙어 8회

정답 및 해설 044쪽

A 다음 수능 필수 숙어를 읽고, 아는 것은 체크해 봅시다.

□ 01	dawn on(upon)	생각나다
□ 02	day and night	밤낮으로
□ 03	deal in	취급하다, 거래하다
□ 04	decide on	~으로 결정되다
□ 05	depart from	~에서 출발하다, ~에서 벗어나다
□ 06	deprive A of B	A에게서 B를 빼앗다
□ 07	devote oneself to + -ing	~에 전념하다, 헌신하다
□ 08	die from	~으로 죽다
□ 09	die of	~으로 죽다
□ 10	dig up	땅을 파내다, (비밀 등을) 알아내다
□ 11	do a favor	부탁을 들어주다
□ 12	do away with	~을 그만두다, ~을 제거하다
□ 13	do harm	해를 입히다
□ 14	dress up	잘 차려입다
□ 15	drop by	잠깐 들르다
□ 16	drop off	잠깐 졸다, 줄어들다, (차로) 내려주다
□ 17	drop out	빠지다, 중퇴하다
□ 18	due to	~ 때문에(= because of)
□ 19	engage in	~에 종사하다
□ 20	ever since	~이후로 줄곧

B 다음 숙어 표현을 읽고 의미 차이를 비교해 봅시다.

□ 21	clear A of B	A에게서 B를 제거하다
□ 22	convince A of B	A에게서 B를 확신시키다
□ 23	cure A of B	A에게서 B를 낫게 하다, 치유하다
□ 24	inform A of B	A에게서 B를 알리다
□ 25	remind A of B	A에게서 B를 생각나게 하다

C 우리말을 참고하여 빈칸에 알맞은 말을 써 봅시다.

1. 그들은 가난하고 희망이 없는 사람들을 위해 몇 시간의 무보수 일을 하는 데 헌신했다.
   They devoted themselves ___________ hours of unpaid work for the poor and helpless.
2. 그녀는 애벌레가 양배추에게 해를 끼친다는 것을 알았다.
   She knew caterpillars did _____________ to cabbages.
3. 대부분의 자전거 사고는 부품 고장, 날씨 조건 그리고 운전자의 부주의에 기인한다.
   Most bike accidents are ____________ to equipment failure, weather conditions and biker carelessness.
4. 제 부탁 좀 들어주실 수 있나요?
   Can you do me a ___________?

09 내용 일치·불일치

출제 트렌드

1. 내용 일치 · 불일치 문제 유형은 '~에 관한 다음 글의 내용과 일치하지 않는 것/일치한 것'을 고르는 문제이다.
2. 글의 내용을 토대로 선택지가 글의 내용과 일치하는지 여부를 판단하는 능력을 측정하는 문제로 수능에서는 두 문항씩 출제되다가 2014년 이후에는 매년 1문항이 출제되고 있다.
3. 동 · 식물, 사물에 대한 설명문, 개인의 전기나 일화를 소재로 문제가 나온다.
4. 최근 수능 7년간, 내용 일치 · 불일치 문제는 2017학년도 이후 매년 1문제가 출제되고 있다. 2017학년도 수능(93%), 2018(95%), 2019(96%), 2020(94%), 2021(96%) 2022(97%) 2023(96%)에서 괄호 안의 정답률을 보였다. 7년간 평균 95.2% 정도 정답률을 보였다. 난이도는 하 단계이다.

출처			문항 번호	지문 주제	정답률(%)	난이도
대표	2023학년도	수능	26번	Niklas Luhmann	96	★☆☆
1	2022학년도	10 학평	26번	미국 초상화의 아버지 Gilbert Stuart	97	★☆☆
2	2023학년도	09 모평	26번	Leon Festinger	98	★☆☆
3	2022학년도	07 학평	26번	Eric Carle의 삶	96	★☆☆
4	2023학년도	06 모평	26번	William Buckland	92	★☆☆
5	2022학년도	04 학평	26번	Antonia Brico	96	★☆☆
6	2022학년도	03 학평	26번	사진작가 Josef Sudek	92	★☆☆
7	2022학년도	수능	26번	Donato Bramante	97	★☆☆
8	2022학년도	06 모평	26번	육상 선수, Emil Zátopek	97	★☆☆
9	2021학년도	수능	26번	Frank Hyneman Knight	96	★☆☆
10	2020학년도	수능	26번	나일강의 누에르족	94	★☆☆

1등급 꿀팁

1. 글의 전반부에서 소재를 파악하고 무엇에 관한 정보인지 파악한다.
2. 선택지를 미리 읽어 보면 지문의 내용을 빨리 이해하는데 도움이 된다.
3. 선택지 순서대로 지문에서 관련된 내용을 찾아 일치 여부를 판단한다.
4. 일반적인 상식이 아니라 글에서 언급된 정보를 토대로 일치 여부를 판단해야 한다.
5. 일치, 불일치 문제는 부정 관련 표현을 정확하게 알아야 한다.

hardly[scarcely/barely]	거의 ~하지 않는	no better than	~할 정도로 어리석지 않은
fewer than ~	~ 보다 더 적은	no more A than B	B가 아닌 것과 마찬가지로 A가 아니다
not necessarily	(부분 부정) 반드시 ~한 것은 아닌	no ~ more	더 이상 ~않는 (= not ~ any more)
not completely	(부분 부정) 완전히 ~한 것은 아닌	despite	~임에도 불구하고

제한 시간 : 15분 | 정답 및 해설 045쪽

대표 기출

2023학년도 수능 26번

26. Niklas Luhmann에 관한 다음 글의 내용과 일치하지 <u>않는</u> 것은?

Niklas Luhmann, a renowned sociologist of the twentieth century, was born in Lüneburg, Germany in 1927. After World War II, he studied law at the University of Freiburg until 1949. Early in his career, he worked for the State of Lower Saxony, where he was in charge of educational reform. In 1960–1961, Luhmann had the chance to study sociology at Harvard University, where he was influenced by Talcott Parsons, one of the most famous social system theorists. Later, Luhmann developed his own social system theory. In 1968, he became a professor of sociology at the University of Bielefeld. He researched a variety of subjects, including mass media and law. Although his books are known to be difficult to translate, they have in fact been widely translated into other languages.

① 제2차 세계 대전 이후에 법을 공부했다.
② State of Lower Saxony에서 교육 개혁을 담당했다.
③ Harvard University에 있을 때 Talcott Parsons의 영향을 받았다.
④ 다양한 주제에 관해 연구했다.
⑤ 그의 책은 번역하기가 쉽다고 알려져 있다.

문제 풀이

1. 글의 전반부에서 소재를 파악하고 무엇에 관한 정보인지 파악한다.
- Niklas Luhmann, a renowned sociologist of the twentieth century, was born in Lüneburg, Germany in 1927. (20세기의 유명한 사회학자 Niklas Luhmann은 1927년 독일 Lüneburg에서 태어났다.)

2. 보통, 글이 전개되는 순서로 선택지 내용이 나온다. 선택지를 읽고 난 후, 글을 읽으며 빠르게 일치 여부를 확인한다.

① 제2차 세계 대전 이후에 법을 공부했다.
→ After World War II, he studied law at the University of Freiburg until 1949.
② State of Lower Saxony에서 교육 개혁을 담당했다.
→ Early in his career, he worked for the State of Lower Saxony, where he was in charge of educational reform.
③ Harvard University에 있을 때 Talcott Parsons의 영향을 받았다.
→ Luhmann had the chance to study sociology at Harvard University, where he was influenced by Talcott Parsons, one of the most famous social system theorists.
④ 다양한 주제에 관해 연구했다.
→ He researched a variety of subjects, including mass media and law.

3. 지문과 일치하지 않는 선택지를 찾는다.
- 글의 마지막 부분에서 Luhmann의 책들이 번역하기 어렵다(Although his books are known to be difficult to translate,~)고 알려져 있다고 했으므로, 글의 내용과 일치하지 않는 것은 ⑤이다.

2022학년도 10월 학평 26번 ★☆☆

1. Gilbert Stuart에 관한 다음 글의 내용과 일치하지 <u>않는</u> 것은?

Gilbert Stuart grew up in the American colony of Rhode Island before the United States was an independent nation. He traveled to Scotland, England, and Ireland to study art. He then returned to America about the time the war for independence broke out, but he returned to Europe once again because the war made his career as an artist difficult. Even so, he didn't find much success until he came back to the United States in 1795, when he painted a portrait of George Washington. Stuart is called the "father of American portraiture" because he painted pictures of all the famous people of early America. One of his paintings of George Washington was hung in the White House. The image of Washington on the U.S. one-dollar bill came from one of Stuart's most famous paintings of Washington. In 1824, Stuart suffered a stroke which left him partially paralyzed, but he still continued to paint for two years until his death on July 9, 1828.

① 미술 공부를 위해 스코틀랜드, 잉글랜드, 아일랜드로 갔다.
② 독립 전쟁으로 인해 화가로서 일하는 것이 어려워졌다.
③ 초기 미국의 모든 유명인의 초상화를 그렸다.
④ 그가 그린 초상화가 미국 1달러 지폐에 사용되었다.
⑤ 뇌졸중을 겪은 후 더 이상 그림을 그리지 않았다.

2023학년도 9월 모평 26번 ★☆☆

2. Leon Festinger에 관한 다음 글의 내용과 일치하지 <u>않는</u> 것은?

Leon Festinger was an American social psychologist. He was born in New York City in 1919 to a Russian immigrant family. As a graduate student at the University of Iowa, Festinger was influenced by Kurt Lewin, a leading social psychologist. After graduating from there, he became a professor at the Massachusetts Institute of Technology in 1945. He later moved to Stanford University, where he continued his work in social psychology. His theory of social comparison earned him a good reputation. Festinger actively participated in international scholarly cooperation. In the late 1970s, he turned his interest to the field of history. He was one of the most cited psychologists of the twentieth century. Festinger's theories still play an important role in psychology today.

① 러시아인 이민자 가정에서 태어났다.
② 사회 심리학자 Kurt Lewin에게 영향을 받았다.
③ Stanford University에서 사회 심리학 연구를 중단했다.
④ 국제 학술 협력에 활발하게 참여했다.
⑤ 1970년대 후반에 역사 분야로 관심을 돌렸다.

2022학년도 7월 학평 26번 ★☆☆

3. Eric Carle에 관한 다음 글의 내용과 일치하지 <u>않는</u> 것은?

Eric Carle was an American writer and illustrator of children's literature. Born in Syracuse, New York, in 1929, he moved with his parents to Germany when he was six years old. He was educated there, and graduated from an art school in Stuttgart, Germany. He moved back to the United States and worked as a graphic designer at *The New York Times*. In the mid-1960s, children's author Bill Martin Jr. asked Carle to illustrate a book he was writing. In 1967, they published their first collaboration: *Brown Bear, Brown Bear, What Do You See?* His best-known work, *The Very Hungry Caterpillar*, has been translated into more than 66 languages and sold over 50 million copies. In 2002, Carle and his wife opened the Eric Carle Museum of Picture Book Art, which collects and features the work of children's book illustrators from around the world.

① 독일에서 예술 학교를 졸업했다.
② *The New York Times*에서 그래픽 디자이너로 일했다.
③ 1960년대 초반에 Bill Martin Jr.와의 첫 합작품을 출판했다.
④ *The Very Hungry Caterpillar*는 66개가 넘는 언어로 번역되었다.
⑤ 아내와 Eric Carle Museum of Picture Book Art를 개관했다.

2023학년도 6월 모평 26번 ★☆☆

4. William Buckland에 관한 다음 글의 내용과 일치하지 <u>않는</u> 것은?

William Buckland (1784−1856) was well known as one of the greatest geologists in his time. His birthplace, Axminster in Britain, was rich with fossils, and as a child, he naturally became interested in fossils while collecting them. In 1801, Buckland won a scholarship and was admitted to Corpus Christi College, Oxford. He developed his scientific knowledge there while attending John Kidd's lectures on mineralogy and chemistry. After Kidd resigned his position, Buckland was appointed his successor at the college. Buckland used representative samples and large-scale geological maps in his lectures, which made his lectures more lively. In 1824, he announced the discovery of the bones of a giant creature, and he named it *Megalosaurus*, or 'great lizard'. He won the prize from the Geological Society due to his achievements in geology.

① 태어난 곳은 화석이 풍부하였다.
② John Kidd의 강의를 들으며 자신의 과학 지식을 발전시켰다.
③ John Kidd의 사임 전에 그의 후임자로 임명되었다.
④ 자신의 강의에서 대축척 지질학 지도를 사용하였다.
⑤ 1824년에 거대 생물 뼈의 발견을 발표하였다.

2022학년도 4월 학평 26번 ★☆☆

5. Antonia Brico에 관한 다음 글의 내용과 일치하지 <u>않는</u> 것은?

Antonia Brico was born in the Netherlands in 1902 and immigrated to the United States at the age of six. After attending a park concert when she was young, she was so inspired that she made up her mind to study music and become a conductor. In 1927, she entered the Berlin State Academy of Music and became the first American to graduate from its master class in conducting. In 1930, Brico made her debut as a professional conductor, for which she received positive reviews. She made an extensive European tour, and during the tour she was invited by Jean Sibelius to conduct the Helsinki Symphony Orchestra. Brico settled in Denver, where she continued to work as a conductor of the Denver Businessmen's Orchestra, later renamed the Brico Symphony Orchestra. In 1974, her most famous student, folk singer Judy Collins, made a documentary film about her, which was nominated for an Academy Award.

① 네덜란드에서 태어나 6살에 미국으로 이주했다.
② 공원 콘서트에 참석한 후 지휘자가 되기로 결심했다.
③ 전문 지휘자로서의 데뷔에서 부정적인 평가를 받았다.
④ Denver에 정착해서 지휘자로 계속 일했다.
⑤ 그녀에 관한 영화가 아카데미상 후보에 올랐다.

2022학년도 3월 학평 26번 ★☆☆

6. Josef Sudek에 관한 다음 글의 내용과 일치하지 <u>않는</u> 것은?

Josef Sudek was born in the Czech Republic. Originally a bookbinder, Sudek was badly injured during World War I, resulting in the loss of his right arm. After the injury, he spent three years in various hospitals, and began to take photographs out of boredom. In 1922, he enrolled at the State School of Graphic Arts in Prague, where he studied photography for two years. His army disability pension allowed him to make art without worrying about an income. He photographed many night-scapes of Prague and the wooded landscapes of Bohemia. Sudek didn't let his disability get in the way and, despite having only one arm, he used very heavy and bulky equipment. Often known as the 'Poet of Prague,' Sudek never married, and was a shy and retiring person. He never appeared at his exhibition openings. He died on 15 September 1976, when he was 80 years old.

① 제1차 세계 대전 중 심한 부상으로 오른팔을 잃었다.
② Prague에 있는 학교에서 2년 동안 사진술을 공부했다.
③ 연금을 받아서 수입 걱정 없이 예술 창작을 할 수 있었다.
④ 매우 무겁고 부피가 큰 장비를 사용했다.
⑤ 자신의 전시회 개막식에 항상 참석했다.

2021학년도 9월 모평 26번 ★☆☆

7. Donato Bramante에 관한 다음 글의 내용과 일치하지 <u>않는</u> 것은?

Donato Bramante, born in Fermignano, Italy, began to paint early in his life. His father encouraged him to study painting. Later, he worked as an assistant of Piero della Francesca in Urbino. Around 1480, he built several churches in a new style in Milan. He had a close relationship with Leonardo da Vinci, and they worked together in that city. Architecture became his main interest, but he did not give up painting. Bramante moved to Rome in 1499 and participated in Pope Julius II's plan for the renewal of Rome. He planned the new Basilica of St. Peter in Rome — one of the most ambitious building projects in the history of humankind. Bramante died on April 11, 1514 and was buried in Rome. His buildings influenced other architects for centuries.

① Piero della Francesca의 조수로 일했다.
② Milan에서 새로운 양식의 교회들을 건축했다.
③ 건축에 주된 관심을 갖게 되면서 그림 그리기를 포기했다.
④ Pope Julius II의 Rome 재개발 계획에 참여했다.
⑤ 그의 건축물들은 다른 건축가들에게 영향을 끼쳤다.

2022학년도 6월 모평 26번 ★☆☆

8. Emil Zátopek에 관한 다음 글의 내용과 일치하지 <u>않는</u> 것은?

Emil Zátopek, a former Czech athlete, is considered one of the greatest long-distance runners ever. He was also famous for his distinctive running style. While working in a shoe factory, he participated in a 1,500-meter race and won second place. After that event, he took a more serious interest in running and devoted himself to it. At the 1952 Olympic Games in Helsinki, he won three gold medals in the 5,000-meter and 10,000-meter races and in the marathon, breaking Olympic records in each. He was married to Dana Zátopková, who was an Olympic gold medalist, too. Zátopek was also noted for his friendly personality. In 1966, Zátopek invited Ron Clarke, a great Australian runner who had never won an Olympic gold medal, to an athletic meeting in Prague. After the meeting, he gave Clarke one of his gold medals as a gift.

① 독특한 달리기 스타일로 유명했다.
② 신발 공장에서 일한 적이 있다.
③ 1952년 Helsinki 올림픽에서 올림픽 기록을 깨지 못했다.
④ 올림픽 금메달리스트인 Dana Zátopková와 결혼했다.
⑤ 자신의 금메달 중 하나를 Ron Clarke에게 주었다.

2021학년도 수능 26번 ★☆☆

9. Frank Hyneman Knight에 관한 다음 글의 내용과 일치하지 <u>않는</u> 것은?

Frank Hyneman Knight was one of the most influential economists of the twentieth century. After obtaining his Ph.D. in 1916 at Cornell University, Knight taught at Cornell, the University of Iowa, and the University of Chicago. Knight spent most of his career at the University of Chicago. Some of his students at Chicago later received the Nobel Prize. Knight is known as the author of the book *Risk, Uncertainty and Profit*, a study of the role of the entrepreneur in economic life. He also wrote a brief introduction to economics entitled *The Economic Organization*, which became a classic of microeconomic theory. But Knight was much more than an economist; he was also a social philosopher. Later in his career, Knight developed his theories of freedom, democracy, and ethics. After retiring in 1952, Knight remained active in teaching and writing.

* entrepreneur: 기업가

① 20세기의 가장 영향력 있는 경제학자들 중 한 명이었다.
② 경력의 대부분을 University of Chicago에서 보냈다.
③ 그의 학생들 중 몇 명은 나중에 노벨상을 받았다.
④ *Risk, Uncertainty and Profit*의 저자로 알려져 있다.
⑤ 은퇴 후에는 가르치는 일은 하지 않고 글 쓰는 일에 전념했다.

2020학년도 수능 26번 ★☆☆

10. The Nuer에 관한 다음 글의 내용과 일치하지 <u>않는</u> 것은?

The Nuer are one of the largest ethnic groups in South Sudan, primarily residing in the Nile River Valley. The Nuer are a cattle-raising people, whose everyday lives revolve around their cattle. They have various terms related to cattle, so they can distinguish between hundreds of types of cows, based on color, markings, and shape of horns. They prefer to be called by the names of the cattle they raise. The commonest daily foods for the Nuer are dairy products, especially milk for the young and soured milk, like yogurt, for adults. And wild fruits and nuts are favorite snacks for the Nuer. The Nuer also have a culture of counting only older members of the family. They believe that counting the number of children one has could result in misfortune and prefer to report fewer children than they have.

① 주로 Nile River Valley에 거주한다.
② 소와 관련된 다양한 용어를 가지고 있다.
③ 자신들이 기르는 소의 이름으로 불리는 것을 선호한다.
④ 가장 일반적인 일상 음식은 유제품이다.
⑤ 어린 자녀의 수를 세는 것이 행운을 가져온다고 믿는다.

총 문항			문항	맞은 문항					문항
개별 문항	1	2	3	4	5	6	7	8	9	10
채점										

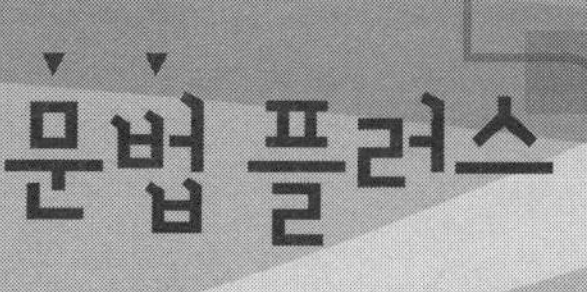

문법 플러스

정답 및 해설 049쪽

9. 조동사

A 문법의 주요 포인트를 점검해 봅시다.

1 조동사는 몇 가지 특성과 의미 차이가 있다. 조동사 뒤에는 동사원형을 써야 하며, 조동사는 두 개를 나란히 쓸 수 없다. must not은 '~해서는 안 된다'는 의미이며 'don't have to'는 '~할 필요가 없다'는 의미이다.

▶ You **[will can / will be able to]** do your homework.

2 준동사와 같은 표현이 있다. 이것들은 조동사처럼 뒤에 동사원형을 쓰며 동사의 의미를 보충해 준다.

ought to	~해야 한다	used to	하곤 했다, 이전에는 ~했었다
had better	~하는 편이 낫다	be supposed to	~하기로 되어 있다
cf. be used+ to 부정사 : ~하기 위해 사용되다 cf. be used to + 동명사 : ~하는 데 익숙하다			

▶ You had better **[to tell / tell]** him that you won't be able to come to his party.

3 조동사는 완료형과 결합하여 과거의 일에 대한 유감, 비난이나 과거의 추측 등을 나타낸다.

should[ought to] have p.p.	~했어야 했는데	shouldn't have p.p.	~하지 않았어야 했는데
must have p.p.	~했음에 틀림없다	cannot have p.p.	~했을 리가 없다
may have p.p.	~했을지도 모른다	need not have p.p.	~할 필요가 없었는데

▶ I regret having paid little attention to him. In other words, I **[should be paid / should have paid]** more attention to him.

4 제안, 명령, 요구, 주장의 의미를 갖는 동사(suggest, order, demand, insist 등) 다음의 that절에서 주어 다음에 「(should+) 동사원형」이 쓰인다. 단, 실제로 발생한 단순한 사실을 전달할 때는 문장의 수와 시제에 맞춰 써야 한다.

▶ She suggested to me that I **[took / take]** some rest away from work.

5 관용적으로 쓰이는 조동사 구문을 익힌다.

may well	~하는 것도 당연하다	may as well	~하는 것이 낫다
cannot but	~하지 않을 수 없다	would rather A than B	B보다 A 하고 싶다

▶ I cannot but **[point / pointed]** that we continue to face a reality.

6 had better를 부정할 때는 바로 뒤에 not을 쓴다.

▶ You'd better **[wake not / not wake]** Billy up when you come in.

7 조동사 may와 can의 과거형 might와 could는 과거의 의미를 나타내기보다는 좀 더 불확실한 추측을 나타낸다. 하지만 주절이 과거인 경우, 시제 일치의 규칙에 따라 종속절에는 might와 could를 사용한다.

▶ He asked me if he **[may / might]** come to see me that evening.

B 다음 괄호 안에서 어법상 올바른 것을 고르시오.

1 That will **[do / did]** beautifully.

2 He used to **[smoke / smoking]** a pipe; now he smokes e-cigarettes.

3 She **[needn't have cooked / don't need to cook]** so much food, but she cooked so much food.

4 He suggested that the conference **[should be / is]** put off.

5 I would rather walk the 5 miles to school than **[to ride / ride]** the bus again.

6 You don't look very well. You'd better **[not go / go not]** to work today.

7 Tom said that she **[may / might]** be twenty nine the following year.

숙어 플러스

9. 수능 필수 숙어 9회

정답 및 해설 049쪽

A 다음 수능 필수 숙어를 읽고, 아는 것은 체크해 봅시다.

□ 01	face to face	마주보고
□ 02	fade away	(소리, 기억이) 서서히 사라지다
□ 03	fall asleep	잠들다
□ 04	fall in love	사랑에 빠지다
□ 05	fall off	(아래로) 떨어지다, (수량 등이) 줄어들다
□ 06	fall on	~에 덤며 들다, ~의 책임이다
□ 07	fall over	~에 걸려 넘어지다
□ 08	fill out	(서류, 빈칸) 채우다, 작성하다
□ 09	fit in	시간을 내다, 잘 어울리다
□ 10	for nothing	무료로, 헛되이
□ 11	for one thing	우선, 첫째로
□ 12	for sure	확실히, 틀림없이
□ 13	for the most part	대개, 보통
□ 14	free of charge	무료로
□ 15	from time to time	가끔, 이따금
□ 16	get along	~와 잘 지내다
□ 17	get lost	길을 잃다
□ 18	get off	손을 떼라, (버스, 지하철) 내리다 (↔ get on)
□ 19	get on with	(중단된 일을) 계속하다
□ 20	get over	극복하다, (병) 회복되다, (슬픔) 잊다

B 다음 숙어 표현을 읽고 의미 차이를 비교해 봅시다.

□ 21	be covered with	~로 덮여 있다
□ 22	be filled with	~로 가득 채워져 있다
□ 23	be satisfied with	~에 만족하다
□ 24	be interested in	~에 관심이(흥미가) 있다
□ 25	be disappointed in	~에 실망하다

C 우리말을 참고하여 빈칸에 알맞은 말을 써 봅시다.

1 음악계에 종사하면서, 나는 스피커 위의 유리컵이 떨어져 깨지는 것을 본 적이 있다.
Working in the music business, I have seen glasses ____________ off speakers and break.

2 오셔서 서류를 작성하고 인터뷰 약속을 해야 합니다.
You would have to come in, ____________ out a form, and make an appointment for an interview.

3 만일 이 지역에 거주한다면, 도서 카드를 무료로 얻을 수 있다.
If you reside in this area, you may get a library card free of ____________.

4 나는 이 문제를 어떻게 극복해야 할지 모르겠어.
I don't know how to get ____________ this problem.

10 안내문

출제 트렌드

1. 안내문 문제 유형은 안내문을 제시하고 '~에 관한 안내문의 내용과 일치하지 않는 것'을 고르는 문제이다.
2. 실생활에서 접할 수 있는 안내문이나 포스터를 보고 제시된 정보와 선택지의 내용이 서로 일치하는지 판단하는 능력을 측정한다. 수능에서 매년 2문항이 출제되고 있다.
3. 관광, 공연, 행사, 전시회, 강좌, 관람 등과 관련된 실용문이 제시된다.
4. 최근 수능 7년간, 안내문(실용 자료 내용) 문제는 2017학년도 이후 매년 2문제가 출제되고 있다. 2017학년도 수능(96%/94%), 2018년도 수능(95%/93%), 2019학년도 수능(97%/95%), 2020학년도 수능(97%/95%), 2021학년도 수능(96%/95%), 2022학년도 수능 (97%/96%), 2023학년도 수능 (97%/96%)에서 괄호 안의 정답률을 보였다. 7년간 평균 95.6%의 정답률을 보였다. 난이도는 하 단계이다.

	출처		문항 번호	지문 주제	정답률(%)	난이도
대표	2023학년도	수능	27번	보수 공사 공지	97	★☆☆
1	2023학년도	수능	28번	2022 Valestown 재활용 포스터 대회	96	★☆☆
2	2023학년도	10 학평	27번	Glass Bottom Boat Adventure 안내문	97	★☆☆
3	2022학년도	10 학평	28번	Annual Car Wash Fundraiser 안내문	94	★☆☆
4	2023학년도	09 모평	27번	2022 K-차 문화 프로그램	97	★☆☆
5	2022학년도	09 모평	28번	빅 데이터 전문가와 함께하는 직업의 날	97	★☆☆
6	2022학년도	07 학평	27번	Black Box Short Play Festival 안내문	96	★☆☆
7	2022학년도	07 학평	28번	Newport Hackathon 2022에 관한 안내문	91	★☆☆
8	2023학년도	06 모평	28번	별똥별 보기 행사	96	★☆☆
9	2021학년도	수능	27번	Sittka 시 공영자전거 공유 서비스	96	★☆☆
10	2020학년도	수능	27번	디자인 대회	97	★☆☆

1등급 꿀팁

1. 글의 전반부에서 소재를 파악하고 무엇에 관한 정보를 파악한다.
2. 선택지의 핵심 정보를 확인하고 글의 내용을 예측한다.
3. 주로 본문에 언급된 순서대로 선택지가 나열된다. 선택지 순서대로 관련 내용을 찾아 일치 여부를 빨리 판단한다.
4. 안내문과 관련된 표현을 익힌다.

advanced 상급의	details 세부 사항	register 등록하다
age requirement 나이 제한	entries 출품작	registration 등록
award 상	evaluation criteria 평가 기준	safety instruction 안전 교육
be submitted 제출하다	participants 참가자	snacks and water 간식과 물
competition theme 대회 주제	price 가격	snacks provided 간식 제공됨
deadline 마감 일시	prize 상	visit 방문하다

제한 시간 : 15분 | 정답 및 해설 050쪽

대표 기출

2023학년도 수능 27번

27. 다음 Renovation Notice의 내용과 일치하지 않는 것은?

Renovation Notice

At the Natural Jade Resort, we are continually improving our facilities to better serve our guests. Therefore, we will be renovating some areas of the resort, according to the schedule below.

Renovation Period: November 21 to December 18, 2022
- Renovations will take place every day from 9:00 a.m. to 5:00 p.m.

Areas to be Closed: Gym and indoor swimming pool

Further Information
- All outdoor leisure activities will be available as usual.
- Guests will receive a 15% discount for all meals in the restaurant.
- Guests may use the tennis courts for free.

We will take all possible measures to minimize noise and any other inconvenience. We sincerely appreciate your understanding.

① 보수 공사는 2022년 11월 21일에 시작된다.
② 보수 공사는 주말에만 진행될 것이다.
③ 체육관과 실내 수영장은 폐쇄될 것이다.
④ 모든 야외 레저 활동은 평소와 같이 가능할 것이다.
⑤ 손님은 무료로 테니스장을 이용할 수 있다.

문제 풀이

1. 글의 전반부에서 소재를 파악하고 무엇에 관한 정보인지 파악한다.
- 소재: Renovation Notice(보수 공사 공지)
- 전반부: At the Natural Jade Resort, we are continually improving our facilities to better serve our guests. Therefore, we will be renovating some areas of the resort, according to the schedule below. (Natural Jade 리조트는 투숙객들에게 더 나은 서비스를 제공하기 위해 지속적으로 시설을 개선하고 있습니다. 그래서 우리는 아래 일정에 따라 리조트의 몇몇 구역을 보수 공사하려고 합니다.)

2. 선택지의 핵심 정보를 확인하고 글의 내용을 예측한다.

① 보수 공사는 2022년 11월 21일에 시작된다.
→ Renovation Period: November 21 to December 18, 2022
② 보수 공사는 주말에만 진행될 것이다.
→ Renovations will take place every day from 9:00 a.m. to 5:00 p.m.
③ 체육관과 실내 수영장은 폐쇄될 것이다.
→ Areas to be Closed: Gym and indoor swimming pool
④ 모든 야외 레저 활동은 평소와 같이 가능할 것이다.
→ All outdoor leisure activities will be available as usual.
⑤ 손님은 무료로 테니스장을 이용할 수 있다.
→ Guests may use the tennis courts for free.

3. 선택지를 읽고 난 후, 글을 읽으며 빠르게 일치 여부를 확인한다.
- 보수 공사는 해당 기간 중 매일 진행된다(Renovations will take place every day from 9:00 a.m. to 5:00 p.m.)고 했으므로, ②번이 안내문의 내용과 일치하지 않는다.

2023학년도 수능 28번 ★☆☆

1. 2022 Valestown Recycles Poster Contest에 관한 다음 안내문의 내용과 일치하는 것은?

2022 Valestown Recycles Poster Contest

Join this year's Valestown Recycles Poster Contest and show off your artistic talent!

Guidelines
- Participation is only for high school students in Valestown.
- Participants should use the theme of "Recycling for the Future."

Submission Format
- File type: PDF only
- Maximum file size: 40MB

Judging Criteria
- Use of theme - Creativity - Artistic skill

Details
- Submissions are limited to one poster per person.
- Submissions should be uploaded to the website by 6 p.m., December 19.
- Winners will be announced on the website on December 28.

For more information, please visit www.vtco.org.

① Valestown의 모든 학생들이 참여할 수 있다.
② 참가자는 포스터의 주제 선정에 제약을 받지 않는다.
③ 출품할 파일 양식은 자유롭게 선택 가능하다.
④ 심사 기준에 창의성이 포함된다.
⑤ 1인당 출품할 수 있는 포스터의 수에는 제한이 없다.

2022학년도 10월 학평 27번 ★☆☆

2. Glass Bottom Boat Adventure에 관한 다음 안내문의 내용과 일치하지 않는 것은?

Glass Bottom Boat Adventure

Enjoy all day aquarium admission plus an exclusive glass bottom boat ride across our oceanarium. You'll see how our team care for our marine species and see our animals from a different point of view.

Cost:
- Adult (16+): $80 / Child (4–15): $65
- Activity Pack: $8
  - Includes Activity Trail Map, Magnifying Glass, Picture Puzzle and more!

Please note:
- Children ages 0–3 cannot participate in the boat tour.
- Boat departs every hour from 10:00 a.m. – 4:00 p.m.
- Please arrive AT LEAST 20 minutes prior to your boat departure.

① 바닥이 유리로 된 보트를 탄다.
② 활동 꾸러미에는 돋보기가 포함된다.
③ 3세 이하 아이는 보트 투어에 참가할 수 없다.
④ 보트는 오전 10시부터 30분마다 출발한다.
⑤ 적어도 보트 출발 20분 전에 도착해야 한다.

2022학년도 10월 학평 28번 ★☆☆

3. Annual Car Wash Fundraiser에 관한 다음 안내문의 내용과 일치하는 것은?

Annual Car Wash Fundraiser

Join us for our Annual Car Wash Fundraiser! Have your car washed and do your part to help homeless pets!

- When: 8:30 a.m. – 10:30 a.m., Saturday, 5th November
- Where: Cranberry College — Eastern Street Carpark
- Cost: $10 per vehicle
  (A free beverage is offered in the waiting area.)
- Car Wash Time Slots — 10 car wash bookings available per half-hour time slot:
  - 8:30 a.m. – 9:00 a.m.
  - 9:00 a.m. – 9:30 a.m.
  - 9:30 a.m. – 10:00 a.m.
  - 10:00 a.m. – 10:30 a.m.

Please select the most convenient time to have your car washed. You should collect your car in person 20 minutes after your selected time slot.

① 불우 이웃을 돕기 위한 행사이다.
② 토요일 오전에 3시간 동안 진행된다.
③ 대기 장소에서 음료가 무료로 제공된다.
④ 30분 시간대마다 20대의 세차 예약이 가능하다.
⑤ 세차가 끝나면 차주에게 차를 가져다 준다.

2023학년도 9월 모평 27번 ★☆☆

4. 2022 K-Tea Culture Program에 관한 다음 안내문의 내용과 일치하지 <u>않는</u> 것은?

2022 K-Tea Culture Program

Evergreen Tea Society invites you to the second annual K-Tea Culture Program! Come and enjoy a refreshing cup of tea and learn about traditional Korean tea culture.

Program Includes:
1) Watching a short video about the history of Korean tea culture
2) Observing a demonstration of a traditional Korean tea-ceremony (*dado*)
3) Participating in the ceremony yourself
4) Tasting a selection of teas along with cookies

When: Saturday, September 24, 3:00 p.m. – 5:00 p.m.

Where: Evergreen Culture Center

Participation Fee: $20 per person (traditional teacup included)

Reservations should be made online (www.egtsociety.or.kr) at least one day before your visit.

① 한국의 차 문화 역사에 관한 영상을 시청한다.
② 한국 전통 다도 시연을 본다.
③ 쿠키와 함께 차를 맛본다.
④ 참가비에는 전통 찻잔이 포함되어 있다.
⑤ 예약은 방문 일주일 전까지 해야 한다.

2023학년도 9월 모평 28번 ★☆☆

5. Career Day with a Big Data Expert에 관한 다음 안내문의 내용과 일치하는 것은?

Career Day with a Big Data Expert

Meet a Big Data expert from a leading IT company! Jill Johnson, famous data analyst and bestselling author, will be visiting Sovenhill High School to give a lecture on careers related to Big Data.

Participation:
- Sovenhill High School students only
- Limited to 50 students

When & Where:
- October 15, 10:00 a.m. to 11:30 a.m.
- Library

Registration: Scan the QR code to fill in the application form.

Note:
- Drinking beverages is not permitted during the lecture.
- The lecture will be followed by a Q&A session.
- All participants will receive a free copy of the lecturer's book.

① 학부모도 참여할 수 있다.
② 참석 인원에 제한이 없다.
③ QR 코드를 스캔하여 신청서를 작성한다.
④ 강연 중에 음료수를 마실 수 있다.
⑤ 참석자 중 일부만 강연자의 책을 무료로 받는다.

2022학년도 7월 학평 27번 ★☆☆

6. Black Box Short Play Festival에 관한 다음 안내문의 내용과 일치하지 <u>않는</u> 것은?

Black Box Short Play Festival

The annual Black Box Short Play Festival is waiting for you. This festival aims to showcase new playwrights by allowing their works to be performed onstage. Come and enjoy!

Date and Place
- August 12 – 14, 2022
- The Black Box Theater, 530 Fifth Avenue, New York

Performance Schedule

	Friday, August 12	Saturday, August 13	Sunday, August 14
The Midnight Salesmen	8 p.m.	2 p.m.	
Shrink to Fit		8 p.m.	2 p.m.
Casting the Villain Aside	2 p.m.		8 p.m.

Tickets
- Early Bird: $10 per play (reserve before July 31, 2022)
- Regular Price: $15 per play
- Reserve tickets online at www.theblackboxtheater.com.

Notes
- No late entries will be permitted.
- Children under 10 are not allowed.

① 3일간 진행된다.
② The Black Box Theater에서 열린다.
③ *Shrink to Fit*은 8월 13일과 14일에 상연된다.
④ 조기 예매 시 관람료는 연극당 15달러이다.
⑤ 10세 미만의 어린이는 입장할 수 없다.

2022학년도 7월 학평 28번 ★☆☆

7. Newport Hackathon 2022에 관한 다음 안내문의 내용과 일치하는 것은?

Newport Hackathon 2022

Newport Hackathon 2022 is a website-coding marathon to promote creativity, collaboration, and innovative thinking.

Event Information
- Who: Newport University students
- When: Friday, September 23, 1 p.m. – Saturday, September 24, 9 a.m.
- Where: Newport University Student Center

How to Participate
- You can participate individually or as a team of up to 4.
- You must register between August 23 and August 31.

Requirements and Rules
- Participants will have 20 hours to code a website according to the theme announced on the day of the event.
- Submissions must include a video explaining the website. (Less than 5 minutes in length)
- Participants may use open source code while developing their websites.

① 금요일 하루 동안 진행된다.
② 개인으로는 참가할 수 없다.
③ 8월 31일부터 참가 등록이 시작된다.
④ 주제는 행사 당일에 공지된다.
⑤ 제출하는 영상의 길이는 5분 이상이어야 한다.

2023학년도 6월 모평 27번 ★☆☆

8. Shooting Star Viewing Event에 관한 다음 안내문의 내용과 일치하는 것은?

Shooting Star Viewing Event

Would you like to watch the rare shooting star, coming on Sunday, July 24? The Downtown Central Science Museum is the perfect spot to catch the vivid view!

Registration
- Online only — www.dcsm.org
- From July 1 to July 14
- The number of participants will be limited to 50.

Schedule on July 24
- 8:00 p.m.: Participants will gather at the hall and then move to the rooftop.
- 8:30 p.m.: Guides will explain how to observe the shooting star.
- 9:00 p.m. – 11:00 p.m.: We will share the experience of the shooting star.

Notes
- If the event is cancelled due to the weather conditions, notice will be given via text message.
- Outside food and drinks are not allowed.

① 현장 등록이 가능하다.
② 참가 인원에 제한이 없다.
③ 참가자들은 오후 9시에 홀에서 모여 옥상으로 이동할 것이다.
④ 기상 상황으로 인한 행사 취소 시 문자 메시지로 공지될 것이다.
⑤ 외부 음식과 음료는 허용된다.

2021학년도 수능 27번 ★☆☆

9. City of Sittka Public Bike Sharing Service에 관한 다음 안내문의 내용과 일치하지 않는 것은?

City of Sittka Public Bike Sharing Service

Are you planning to explore the city?
This is the eco-friendly way to do it!

Rent
- Register anywhere via our easy app.
- Payment can be made only by credit card.

Fee
- Free for the first 30 minutes
- One dollar per additional 30 minutes

Use
- Choose a bike and scan the QR code on the bike.
- Helmets are not provided.

Return
- Return the bike to the Green Zone shown on the app.
- Complete the return by pressing the OK button on the bike.

① 신용 카드 결제만 가능하다.
② 처음 30분은 무료이다.
③ 자전거의 QR 코드를 스캔해서 이용한다.
④ 헬멧이 제공된다.
⑤ 자전거의 OK 버튼을 눌러서 반납을 완료한다.

2020학년도 수능 27번 ★☆☆

10. Green Tea Packaging Design Competition에 관한 다음 안내문의 내용과 일치하지 않는 것은?

Green Tea Packaging Design Competition

Take the opportunity to design the packaging box for brand-new green tea products of TIIS Tea in the competition!

Deadline: December 2, 2019, 6:00 p.m.
Participants: Lokota County residents only
Details
- Our company name "TIIS Tea" should appear on the design.
- The competition theme is "Go Green with Green Tea."
- Entries (JPG format only) should be submitted by email to designmanager@tiistea.com.

Evaluation Criteria
- Functionality
- Creativity
- Eco-friendliness

Awards
- 1st place: $1,000
- 2nd place: $500
- 3rd place: $250

(The first-place winner's signature will be printed on the packaging box.)

Please visit www.tiistea.com to learn more about the competition.

① 신제품 녹차를 위한 포장 상자 디자인 대회이다.
② Lokota County 주민들만 참가할 수 있다.
③ 출품작은 직접 방문하여 제출해야 한다.
④ 평가 기준에 창의성이 포함된다.
⑤ 1등 수상자의 서명이 포장 상자에 인쇄될 것이다.

총 문항				문항	맞은 문항					문항
개별 문항	1	2	3	4	5	6	7	8	9	10
채점										

10. 수동태

정답 및 해설 052쪽

A 문법의 주요 포인트를 점검해 봅시다.

1 진행형, 완료형의 수동태 형태와 조동사와 함께 쓰일 경우 수동태 형태를 유의한다.

진행형 수동태 형태	be **being** p.p.	완료형 수동태 형태	
조동사 수동태 형태	「조동사+be p.p.」		

▶ The area **[has cleared / has been cleared]** of land mines.

2 동사구는 하나의 동사로 취급해 수동태를 만든다.

▶ The pain **[was put up with / was put up]** by her.

3 4형식 문장은 수동태를 만들 때 유의해야 한다. 동사에 따라서는 간접목적어만 또는 직접목적어만 수동태가 가능한 경우가 있다.

▶ He **[is given / was given]** a chance to speak yesterday.

4 to부정사, 동명사, 현재분사의 수동태 형태를 유의한다.

to부정사 수동태 형태	(단순형) to be p.p	동명사 수동태 형태	(단순형) being p.p.
	(완료형) to have been p.p		(완료형) having been p.p
* Would you help me if you saw me **being mugged** in the street? (현재분사 수동태)			

▶ The girl was afraid **[to be left / being left]** alone at night.

5 지각, 사역동사가 들어 있는 문장을 수동태로 바꿀 경우, 목적격보어인 원형부정사는 to부정사로 바뀌진다.

▶ My son was heard **[sing / to sing]** by himself at midnight.

6 「It+be+p.p.+that절」은 사람들의 말과 생각과 같은 일반적인 정보를 전달한다. say, think, believe 등의 동사가 that절을 목적어로 가지는 경우 (1) 「It+be+p.p.+that절」 형태의 수동태와 (2) that절 속의 주어를 문장 전체의 주어로 한 수동태가 가능하다.

▶ People say that she is a trustworthy person. → (1) It **[says / is said]** that she is a trustworthy person.
(2) She is said to be a trustworthy person.

7 자동사(appear, disappear)와 상태 동사(have, resemble, lack, fit 등)는 수동태로 쓸 수 없다. 태에 유의해야 할 동사구가 있다. consist of(~로 구성되다)는 능동태로 쓴다. 수동태로 나타내려면 be composed of, be made up of로 표현한다.

▶ Sally **[was suddenly disappeared / suddenly disappeared]** into the darkness.

B 다음 괄호 안에서 어법상 올바른 것을 고르시오.

1 Data can be useful only after it **[has collected / has been collected]** and processed.

2 The baseball game **[called off / was called off]** because of heavy rain.

3 The baseball bat was bought **[to / for]** me by my dad.

4 Sam doesn't know how to get over **[being dumped / to be dumped]**.

5 Unlike a stream, a glacer cannot be seen **[to move / move]**.

6 It **[thinks / is thought]** that the launch of the euro brought about an increase in the cost of living.

7 You **[are resembled / resemble]** your mom very much.

숙어 플러스

10. 수능 필수 숙어 10회

정답 및 해설 052쪽

A 다음 수능 필수 숙어를 읽고, 아는 것은 체크해 봅시다.

□ 01	get rid of	~을 제거하다
□ 02	get through	통과하다, 견뎌내다
□ 03	give away	기부하다, 수여하다
□ 04	give it a try	시도하다
□ 05	give off	(빛, 가스, 냄새 등을) 발산하다
□ 06	give out	나눠주다, 발산하다
□ 07	give rise to	~이 생기게 하다
□ 08	go ahead	앞서가다, (일 등이) 진행되다
□ 09	go along	계속하다, 진행되다
□ 10	go by	(시간) 흐르다, (장소) 지나가다
□ 11	go off	떠나다, 발사되다, (경보기 등이) 울리다
□ 12	go through	~을 살펴보다, (절차) 거치다, (어려움) 겪다
□ 13	hand in hand	손에 손을 맞잡고
□ 14	hand in	제출하다
□ 15	hand out	나눠주다
□ 16	hang up	(옷, 그림 등을) 걸다, 전화를 끊다
□ 17	have a look at	~을 한 번 보다
□ 18	have an influence on	~에 영향을 미치다
□ 19	have difficulty (in) -ing	~하는 데 어려움을 겪다
□ 20	have in common	공통점을 지니다

B 다음 숙어 표현을 읽고 의미 차이를 비교해 봅시다.

□ 21	call off	취소하다
□ 22	keep off	막다, 못 들어오게 하다
□ 23	put off	미루다, 연기하다(= postpone)
□ 24	see off	배웅하다, 전송하다
□ 25	take off	(비행기가) 이륙하다, (옷)을 벗다

C 우리말을 참고하여 빈칸에 알맞은 말을 써 봅시다.

1 예약을 진행하시겠어요?
Would you like to go ____________ with the reservation?

2 들판이 숲으로 변하려면 여러 단계를 거쳐야만 한다.
An open field must go ____________ several stages to turn into a forest.

3 여러분은 다음 주말까지 모두 과제물을 제출해야 해요.
You must all ____________in your projects by the end of next week.

4 새로운 연구에 의하면, 구름은 지구 온난화에 영향이 미친다.
According to a new study, clouds have an ____________ on global warming.

11 어법 정확성 파악

출제 트렌드

1. 어법 정확성 문제는 지문의 문장 구조를 이해하는지 유무를 판단하는 유형이다. 지문 속에 밑줄을 그어놓고 '밑줄 친 부분 중, 어법상 틀린 것을 고르는' 문제와 '각 네모 안에서 어법에 맞는 유형'을 고르는 문제가 출제되었다.
2. 2014년 이후에는 두 문항 중 한 문항이 출제되고, 최근 2019학년도 이후 수능에서는 '밑줄 친 부분 중, 어법상 틀린 것을 고르는' 문제 유형이 출제되고 있다. 고난이도 문제로 출제되고 있다. 선택지 중 1~2개가 어려워 오답률이 높은 유형이다.
3. 최근 수능 7년간, 어법 정확성 파악 문제는 2020학년도를 제외하고, 3점 문항으로 출제되었다. 2017학년도 수능(48%), 2018(51%), 2019(35%), 2020(54%), 2021(61%), 2022(54%), 2023(40%)에서 괄호 안의 정답률을 보였다. 7년간 평균 49%의 정답률을 보였다. 난이도는 상 단계이다. 수능에서 가장 어려운 문제 유형 중 하나라고 할 수 있다.

	출처		문항 번호	지문 주제	정답률(%)	난이도
대표	2023학년도	수능	29번	패션의 역할	40	★★★
1	2022학년도	10 학평	29번	지도자가 될 수 있게 해 주는 특성	54	★★★
2	2023학년도	09 모평	29번	기업 윤리의 이해	57	★★★
3	2022학년도	07 학평	29번	스파이더 차트	73	★☆☆
4	2023학년도	06 모평	29번	생태계들의 구성과 범위	54	★★★
5	2022학년도	04 학평	29번	국가 통제주의와 자본주의에서의 독점 문제	52	★★★
6	2022학년도	03 학평	29번	고대 그리스 음악의 소리	22	★★★
7	2022학년도	수능	29번	세포 주기	54	★★★
8	2022학년도	06 모평	29번	규칙성과 예측 가능성을 위한 도구	59	★★★
9	2021학년도	수능	29번	자기를 실험하는 것의 장점과 단점	61	★★☆
10	2020학년도	수능	29번	초기 인류의 자연 세계와 인간 사회의 관계	54	★★★

1등급 꿀팁

1. 평소 글을 읽으면서 주어와 동사가 무엇인지 살펴보는 습관이 필요하다.

2. 기출 문제를 철저히 분석하고, 기출 문제에 나오는 문법 사항들을 좀더 심도있게 공부하는 것이 좋다.

■ 주어와 동사의 수 일치	Speculations about the meaning and purpose of prehistoric art **rely** heavily on analogies hunter-gatherer society
■ 병렬 구조	But now the tools of the digital age give us a way to easily get, share, and **act** on the information in new ways.
■ 분사	Scientists who experiment on themselves can, functionally if not legally, avoid the restrictions **associated** with experimenting on other people.
■ 동명사	Finally, Simb stopped **breathing**.
■ to부정사	We've done everything we can **to contain** costs without compromising quality.
■ 관계사	The dual expressions of this tendency are anthropomorphism and totemism both of **which** spread through the visual art and the mythology of primitive cultures.
■ 접속사	Experimental results derived from a single subject are, therefore, of limited value; there is no way to know **whether** the subject's responses are typical or atypical of the response of humans as a group.

대표 기출

2023학년도 수능 29번

29. 다음 글의 밑줄 친 부분 중, 어법상 틀린 것은?

Trends constantly suggest new opportunities for individuals to restage themselves, representing occasions for change. To understand how trends can ultimately give individuals power and freedom, one must first discuss fashion's importance as a basis for change. The most common explanation offered by my informants as to why fashion is so appealing is ① that it constitutes a kind of theatrical costumery. Clothes are part of how people present ② them to the world, and fashion locates them in the present, relative to what is happening in society and to fashion's own history. As a form of expression, fashion contains a host of ambiguities, enabling individuals to recreate the meanings ③ associated with specific pieces of clothing. Fashion is among the simplest and cheapest methods of self-expression: clothes can be ④ inexpensively purchased while making it easy to convey notions of wealth, intellectual stature, relaxation or environmental consciousness, even if none of these is true. Fashion can also strengthen agency in various ways, ⑤ opening up space for action.

문제 풀이

1. 전반부를 읽고 글의 전개 방향을 염두한다.

- Trends constantly suggest new opportunities for individuals to restage themselves, representing occasions for change. (유행은 사람들이 자신을 재조정할 새로운 기회를 계속해서 제시하고, 변화의 경우를 나타낸다.)

2. 문맥과 어법을 고려하여 밑줄 친 부분의 어법성을 판단한다.

① [접속사 that] 뒤에 문장 성분을 모두 갖춘 완전한 문장이 왔으므로, 문장의 보어 역할을 하는 명사절을 이끄는 접속사 that이 온 것은 적절하다.
③ [과거분사] '연관된'이라는 의미로 앞의 명사 the meanings를 수식하는 과거분사가 되어야 하므로, associated가 온 것은 적절하다.
④ [부사] 과거분사 purchased를 수식하므로 부사로 inexpensively가 온 것은 적절하다.
⑤ [분사구문] 분사구문이 와야 하는데, '행동을 위한 공간을 열어주면서'라는 능동의 의미이므로, 현재분사 opening이 온 것은 적절하다.

3. 어법상 틀린 것으로 생각되는 선택지를 숙고해 분석하고 답을 확정한다.

- ② [재귀대명사] '사람들이 자신들을 세상에 제시하는'이라는 의미가 되어야 하는데 주어 people과 목적어가 가리키는 대상이 같으므로, them을 재귀대명사 themselves로 바꿔 써야 한다.

제한 시간 : 15분 | 정답 및 해설 052쪽

2022학년도 10월 학평 29번 ★★★

1. 다음 글의 밑줄 친 부분 중, 어법상 틀린 것은? [3점]

The idea that leaders *inherently* possess certain physical, intellectual, or personality traits that distinguish them from nonleaders ① was the foundational belief of the trait-based approach to leadership. This approach dominated leadership research from the late 1800s until the mid-1940s and has experienced a resurgence of interest in the last couple of decades. Early trait theorists believed that some individuals are born with the traits that allow ② them to become great leaders. Thus, early research in this area often presented the widely stated argument ③ that "leaders are born, not made." Also, some of the earliest leadership studies were grounded in what ④ referred to as the "great man" theory because researchers at the time focused on identifying traits of highly visible leaders in history who were typically male and associated with the aristocracy or political or military leadership. In more recent history, numerous authors have acknowledged that there are many enduring qualities, ⑤ whether innate or learned, that contribute to leadership potential. These traits include such things as *drive, self-confidence, cognitive ability, conscientiousness, determination, intelligence,* and *integrity.*

* resurgence: 되살아남 ** aristocracy: 귀족

2023학년도 9월 모평 29번 ★★★

2. 다음 글의 밑줄 친 부분 중, 어법상 틀린 것은?

Recognizing ethical issues is the most important step in understanding business ethics. An ethical issue is an identifiable problem, situation, or opportunity that requires a person to choose from among several actions that may ① be evaluated as right or wrong, ethical or unethical. ② Learn how to choose from alternatives and make a decision requires not only good personal values, but also knowledge competence in the business area of concern. Employees also need to know when to rely on their organizations' policies and codes of ethics or ③ have discussions with co-workers or managers on appropriate conduct. Ethical decision making is not always easy because there are always gray areas ④ that create dilemmas, no matter how decisions are made. For instance, should an employee report on a co-worker engaging in time theft? Should a salesperson leave out facts about a product's poor safety record in his presentation to a customer? Such questions require the decision maker to evaluate the ethics of his or her choice and decide ⑤ whether to ask for guidance.

2022학년도 7월 학평 29번 ★★★

3. 다음 글의 밑줄 친 부분 중, 어법상 <u>틀린</u> 것은? [3점]

The spider chart, also called a radar chart, is a form of line graph. It helps the researcher to represent their data in a chart ① <u>that</u> shows the relative size of a response on one scale for interrelated variables. Like the bar chart, the data needs to have one scale which is common to all variables. The spider chart is drawn with the variables spanning the chart, ② <u>creating</u> a spider web. An example of this is seen in a research study looking at self-reported confidence in year 7 students across a range of subjects ③ <u>have taught</u> in their first term in secondary school. The researcher takes the responses from a sample group and ④ <u>calculates</u> the mean to plot on the spider chart. The spider chart allows the researcher to easily compare and contrast the confidence level in different subjects for the sample group. The chart, like the pie chart, can then be broken down for different groups of students within the study ⑤ <u>to elicit</u> further analysis of findings.

2023학년도 6월 모평 29번 ★★☆

4. 다음 글의 밑줄 친 부분 중, 어법상 <u>틀린</u> 것은? [3점]

Ecosystems differ in composition and extent. They can be defined as ranging from the communities and interactions of organisms in your mouth or ① <u>those</u> in the canopy of a rain forest to all those in Earth's oceans. The processes ② <u>governing</u> them differ in complexity and speed. There are systems that turn over in minutes, and there are others ③ <u>which</u> rhythmic time extends to hundreds of years. Some ecosystems are extensive ('biomes', such as the African savanna); some cover regions (river basins); many involve clusters of villages (micro-watersheds); others are confined to the level of a single village (the village pond). In each example there is an element of indivisibility. Divide an ecosystem into parts by creating barriers, and the sum of the productivity of the parts will typically be found to be lower than the productivity of the whole, other things ④ <u>being</u> equal. The mobility of biological populations is a reason. Safe passages, for example, enable migratory species ⑤ <u>to survive</u>.

* canopy: 덮개 ** basin: 유역

2022학년도 4월 학평 29번 ★★★

5. 다음 글의 밑줄 친 부분 중, 어법상 <u>틀린</u> 것은?

The actual problems with monopolies are caused by statism, not capitalism. Under a statist social system, taxes, subsidies, tariffs, and regulations often serve to protect existing large players in the marketplace. Those players often use crony tactics to retain or expand the protections: a new tariff preventing foreign competition, a subsidy making it harder for new players ① <u>to compete</u> with them, or a regulatory measure that a large company has the resources to comply with. Under a capitalist social system, on the other hand, the government has no say in how ② <u>dominantly</u> a company may become in its industry or how companies take over and merge with one another. Furthermore, a capitalist society doesn't have rights-violating taxes, tariffs, subsidies, or regulations ③ <u>favoring</u> anybody nor does it have antitrust laws. Under capitalism, dominance can only be achieved by becoming really good at ④ <u>what</u> you're doing. And to maintain dominance, you have to continue to stay ahead of the competition, which sees your dominance and profits as a sign ⑤ <u>that</u> there is money to be made by others as well.

* statism: 국가 통제주의 ** crony: 정실(사사로운 정에 이끌리는 일)
*** antitrust law: 독점 금지법

2022학년도 3월 학평 29번 ★★★

6. 다음 글의 밑줄 친 부분 중, 어법상 <u>틀린</u> 것은? [3점]

We don't know what ancient Greek music sounded like, because there are no examples of it in written or notated form, nor ① <u>has it</u> survived in oral tradition. Much of it was probably improvised anyway, within certain rules and conventions. So we are forced largely to guess at its basis from the accounts of writers such as Plato and Aristotle, who were generally more concerned with writing about music as a philosophical and ethical exercise ② <u>as</u> with providing a technical primer on its practice. It seems Greek music was predominantly a vocal form, ③ <u>consisting</u> of sung verse accompanied by instruments such as the lyre or the plucked kithara (the root of 'guitar'). In fact, Plato considered music in which the lyre and flute played alone and not as the accompaniment of dance or song ④ <u>to be</u> 'exceedingly coarse and tasteless'. The melodies seem to have had a very limited pitch range, since the instruments ⑤ <u>generally</u> span only an octave, from one E (as we'd now define it) to the next.

* primer: 입문서 ** lyre: 수금(竪琴) *** coarse: 조잡한

2022학년도 수능 29번 ★★★

7. 다음 글의 밑줄 친 부분 중, 어법상 틀린 것은? [3점]

Like whole individuals, cells have a life span. During their life cycle (cell cycle), cell size, shape, and metabolic activities can change dramatically. A cell is "born" as a twin when its mother cell divides, ① producing two daughter cells. Each daughter cell is smaller than the mother cell, and except for unusual cases, each grows until it becomes as large as the mother cell ② was. During this time, the cell absorbs water, sugars, amino acids, and other nutrients and assembles them into new, living protoplasm. After the cell has grown to the proper size, its metabolism shifts as it either prepares to divide or matures and ③ differentiates into a specialized cell. Both growth and development require a complex and dynamic set of interactions involving all cell parts. ④ What cell metabolism and structure should be complex would not be surprising, but actually, they are rather simple and logical. Even the most complex cell has only a small number of parts, each ⑤ responsible for a distinct, well-defined aspect of cell life.

* metabolic: 물질대사의 ** protoplasm: 원형질

2022학년도 6월 모평 29번 ★★★

8. 다음 글의 밑줄 친 부분 중, 어법상 틀린 것은?

Most historians of science point to the need for a reliable calendar to regulate agricultural activity as the motivation for learning about what we now call astronomy, the study of stars and planets. Early astronomy provided information about when to plant crops and gave humans ① their first formal method of recording the passage of time. Stonehenge, the 4,000-year-old ring of stones in southern Britain, ② is perhaps the best-known monument to the discovery of regularity and predictability in the world we inhabit. The great markers of Stonehenge point to the spots on the horizon ③ where the sun rises at the solstices and equinoxes — the dates we still use to mark the beginnings of the seasons. The stones may even have ④ been used to predict eclipses. The existence of Stonehenge, built by people without writing, bears silent testimony both to the regularity of nature and to the ability of the human mind to see behind immediate appearances and ⑤ discovers deeper meanings in events.

* monument: 기념비 ** eclipse: (해·달의) 식(蝕)
*** testimony: 증언

2021학년도 수능 29번 ★★☆

9. 다음 글의 밑줄 친 부분 중, 어법상 틀린 것은? [3점]

Regulations covering scientific experiments on human subjects are strict. Subjects must give their informed, written consent, and experimenters must submit their proposed experiments to thorough examination by overseeing bodies. Scientists who experiment on themselves can, functionally if not legally, avoid the restrictions ① associated with experimenting on other people. They can also sidestep most of the ethical issues involved: nobody, presumably, is more aware of an experiment's potential hazards than the scientist who devised ② it. Nonetheless, experimenting on oneself remains ③ deeply problematic. One obvious drawback is the danger involved; knowing that it exists ④ does nothing to reduce it. A less obvious drawback is the limited range of data that the experiment can generate. Human anatomy and physiology vary, in small but significant ways, according to gender, age, lifestyle, and other factors. Experimental results derived from a single subject are, therefore, of limited value; there is no way to know ⑤ what the subject's responses are typical or atypical of the response of humans as a group.

* consent: 동의 ** anatomy: (해부학적) 구조
*** physiology: 생리적 현상

2020학년도 수능 29번 ★★★

10. 다음 글의 밑줄 친 부분 중, 어법상 틀린 것은?

Speculations about the meaning and purpose of prehistoric art ① rely heavily on analogies drawn with modern-day hunter-gatherer societies. Such primitive societies, ② as Steven Mithen emphasizes in *The Prehistory of the Modern Mind*, tend to view man and beast, animal and plant, organic and inorganic spheres, as participants in an integrated, animated totality. The dual expressions of this tendency are *anthropomorphism* (the practice of regarding animals as humans) and *totemism* (the practice of regarding humans as animals), both of ③ which spread through the visual art and the mythology of primitive cultures. Thus the natural world is conceptualized in terms of human social relations. When considered in this light, the visual preoccupation of early humans with the nonhuman creatures ④ inhabited their world becomes profoundly meaningful. Among hunter-gatherers, animals are not only good to eat, they are also *good to think about*, as Claude Lévi-Strauss has observed. In the practice of totemism, he has suggested, an unlettered humanity "broods upon ⑤ itself and its place in nature."

* speculation: 고찰 ** analogy: 유사점
*** brood: 곰곰이 생각하다

총 문항				문항	맞은 문항					문항
개별 문항	1	2	3	4	5	6	7	8	9	10
채점										

11. 가정법

정답 및 해설 059쪽

A 문법의 주요 포인트를 점검해 봅시다.

1 가정법 과거는 현재 사실과 반대되는 것을 가정한다.

「If+주어+과거동사 ~, 주어+조동사 과거형+동사원형~」	만일 ~하면 ~할 것이다

▶ If it were not for you, I would be lonely. (네가 아니었다면, 나는 외로웠을 거야.)

▶ If I **[have / had]** some money, I would lend it to him.

2 가정법 과거완료는 과거의 사실과 반대되는 것을 가정한다.

「If+주어+had+과거분사 ~, 주어+조동사 과거형+have+과거분사~」	만일 ~했다면 ~했을 것이다

▶ Without (= But for) your advice, I would have failed. (너의 충고가 없었다면 나는 실패했을 텐데.)

▶ If he **[had / had had]** a basketball, he could have started a game.

3 가정법 미래는 미래에 일어날 가능성이 거의 없는 상황에 쓰인다. 혼합가정법은 과거의 일이 현재에 영향을 미칠 때 사용한다.

가정법 미래: 「If+주어+should[were to]+동사원형~, 주어+조동사 과거형+동사원형~」	혹시라도 ~한다면 ~할 텐데
혼합가정법: 「If+주어+had+과거분사 ~, 주어+조동사 과거형+동사원형~」	(과거에) 만일 ~했다면, (지금) ~할 것이다

▶ If she **[took / had taken]** my advice then, she might still be alive.

4 「I wish+가정법 과거[과거완료]」는 이루기 어려운 소망을 나타내며, 「I wish+가정법 과거」는 주절과 종속절이 나타내는 시제가 동일할 때 쓰인다. 「I wish+가정법 과거완료」는 주절보다 종속절의 시제가 앞선 경우에 사용한다.

▶ I wish he **[weren't / hadn't been]** here now.

5 「as if+가정법과거[과거완료]」는 '마치 ~인(이었던)것처럼'이라는 의미이다. 「as if+가정법 과거」는 주절과 종속절이 나타내는 시제가 동일할 때 쓰인다. 「as if+가정법 과거완료」는 주절보다 종속절의 시제가 앞선 경우에 사용한다. 「as if+직설법」은 as if 다음의 내용이 사실인지 아닌지 모르는 상태에서 사용한다.

▶ He looked as if **[had had / have]** some bad news.

6 가정법 「If+주어+동사~」에서 If가 생략되면, 「동사+주어」로 문장이 도치된다.

▶ **[Had she known / She had known]** it was dangerous, she wouldn't have gone climbing the mountain.

7 It's time that 뒤에는 가정법 과거 표현이 사용된다. '~할 때이다'는 의미이다. 또한 주장(insist), 제안(suggest), 요구(demand), 명령(order)을 나타내는 동사에 이어지는 that절에서는 「주어+(should)+동사원형」을 쓴다. 하지만 실제로 발생한 단순한 사실을 전달할 때는 문장의 수와 시제에 맞추어 써야 한다.

▶ He demanded that she **[returns / return]** the books she had borrowed from him.

B 다음 괄호 안에서 어법상 올바른 것을 고르시오.

1 What would you do if it **[snowed / snows]** on your wedding day?

2 If I had known you were coming, I would **[prepare / have prepared]** dinner.

3 If you had followed my advice then, you would **[have had / be]** happier now.

4 I really wish I **[hadn't quit / quit]** school last year.

5 Sally behaves as if she **[were / is]** queen. In fact, she is not queen.

6 **[Had / Did]** Sam not told her to wear a seatbelt, she might have been more seriously injured.

7 It's time you **[settled / had settled]** your differences with your wife.

숙어 플러스

11. 수능 필수 숙어 11회

정답 및 해설 059쪽

A 다음 수능 필수 숙어를 읽고, 아는 것은 체크해 봅시다.

□ 01	have in mind	~을 염두하다
□ 02	have no choice but to	~할 수밖에 없다
□ 03	have nothing to do with	~와 관련이 없다
□ 04	head for	~로 향하다
□ 05	hear from	~에게서 연락을 받다
□ 06	hear out	~의 말을 끝까지 듣다
□ 07	help oneself	자기 스스로 하다
□ 08	hold down	억제하다
□ 09	hold on to	~을 붙잡다, 고수하다, ~을 맡아주다
□ 10	hold out	내밀다, 지속하다
□ 11	hold to	고수하다, (약속) 지키게 하다
□ 12	hold up	손들다, 견디다
□ 13	in a minute	곧, 즉시
□ 14	in a sense	어떤 의미에서는
□ 15	in a way	어느 정도는, 어느 면에서는
□ 16	in brief	간략히 하면, 요약하면
□ 17	in charge of	~을 담당하고 있는
□ 18	in conclusion	결론적으로
□ 19	in danger	위험에 처해 있는
□ 20	in detail	상세하게

B 다음 숙어 표현을 읽고 의미 차이를 비교해 봅시다.

□ 21	be into	~에 관심이 많다, ~을 좋아하다
□ 22	burst into	…에 난입하다, 갑자기 …하다
□ 23	look into	조사하다, 주의 깊게 살피다
□ 24	put effort [work / labor] into	힘을 들이다
□ 25	run into	~와 충돌하다, 우연히 만나다

C 우리말을 참고하여 빈칸에 알맞은 말을 써 봅시다.

1 당신 사무실을 방문하는 수밖에 없다.
I have no ____________ but to visit your office.

2 나는 그 문제와 아무 관련이 없다.
I have _______________ to do with the matter.

3 이것은 연구자들이 향유고래의 사회 집단에 대해 자세하게 설명할 수 있도록 해 주었다.
This has allowed researchers to describe sperm whale social groups in _____________.

4 결론적으로, 당신은 운전 시 타 운전사를 고려해야 한다.
In _______________, you should think of others when driving.

12 어휘 적절성 파악

출제 트렌드

1. 어휘 적절성 문제는 구체적으로 살펴보면, '밑줄 친 부분 중 문맥상 낱말의 쓰임이 적절하지 않는' 것을 고르는 문제와 '(A), (B), (C)의 각 네모 안에서 문맥에 맞는 낱말로 적절한' 것을 고르는 문제로 출제되고 있다.
2. 수능에서는 2문항이 출제되다가, 2014학년도부터 전자의 문항만 1문항이 출제되고 있다. 3점 고난이도 문제로 출제될 때가 많다. 주제가 분명하고 글의 흐름이 뚜렷한 글을 사용해 문제가 출제되고 있다.
3. 최근 수능 7년간, 어휘 적절성 파악 문제는 2017학년도 수능(57%), 2018(49%), 2019(57%), 2020(55%), 2021(73%), 2022(55%), 2023(58%)에서 괄호 안의 정답률을 보였다. 7년간 평균 57.7%의 정답률을 보였다. 난이도는 상 단계이다.

	출처		문항 번호	지문 주제	정답률(%)	난이도
대표	2022학년도	06 모평	30번	스포츠의 정서적 격렬함	64	★★☆
1	2023학년도	수능	30번	새로운 기술의 적응	58	★★★
2	2022학년도	10 학평	30번	음반에 대한 음악 공연자와 방송사들의 인식	65	★★★
3	2023학년도	09 모평	30번	인터넷의 부정적인 면	61	★★☆
4	2022학년도	07 학평	30번	전통적 양적 성장 개념의 변경 필요성	40	★★★
5	2023학년도	06 모평	30번	자동차 수요 관리	54	★★★
6	2022학년도	04 학평	30번	고객 점유율을 높이기	42	★★★
7	2022학년도	03 학평	30번	기술의 발달과 그 결과 예측	54	★★★
8	2022학년도	수능	30번	유기농법의 단점	55	★★★
9	2021학년도	수능	30번	빛의 속도 측정에서 편승 효과의 발생	73	★★☆
10	2020학년도	수능	30번	잘못된 선택의 오류	55	★★★

1등급 꿀팁

1. '밑줄 친 부분 중 문맥상 낱말의 쓰임이 적절하지 않는' 문제는 적절하지 않는 어휘 대신에 어떤 단어를 써야 할지 숙고해 본다.

2. '(A), (B), (C)의 각 네모 안에서 문맥에 맞는 낱말로 적절한' 것을 고르는 문제는 네모 안에 반의어, 유의어가 쌍으로 제시되는 경우가 많으므로 단어 공부를 할 때, 반의어, 유의어 학습을 부지런히 하도록 한다.

3. 반의어, 유의어, 헷갈리는 어휘를 익힌다.

easily 쉽게	laboriously 힘들게	promote 촉진하다	disrupt 중단시키다
concede 인정하다	deny 부정하다	evade 피하다	undertake 맡다
follow 따르다, 순응하다	resist 저항하다	inadequate 불충분한	adequate 충분한
satisfactory 만족스러운	unsatisfactory 불만족스러운	eliminate 없애다	preserve 지키다
compatible 양립하는	competitive 경쟁하는	allow ~할 수 있게 하다	forbid 금지하다
enhance 향상시키다	neglect 무시하다	hinder 방해하다	cooperate 협력하다
mostly 주로, 대체로	never 전혀 ~이 아닌	fuse 융합하다	replace 대체하다

어휘 적절성 파악

제한 시간 : 15분 | 정답 및 해설 059쪽

대표 기출

2022학년도 6월 모평 30번

30. 다음 글의 밑줄 친 부분 중, 문맥상 낱말의 쓰임이 적절하지 않은 것은?

Sport can trigger an emotional response in its consumers of the kind rarely brought forth by other products. Imagine bank customers buying memorabilia to show loyalty to their bank, or consumers ① identifying so strongly with their car insurance company that they get a tattoo with its logo. We know that some sport followers are so ② passionate about players, teams and the sport itself that their interest borders on obsession. This addiction provides the emotional glue that binds fans to teams, and maintains loyalty even in the face of on-field ③ failure. While most managers can only dream of having customers that are as passionate about their products as sport fans, the emotion triggered by sport can also have a negative impact. Sport's emotional intensity can mean that organisations have strong attachments to the past through nostalgia and club tradition. As a result, they may ④ increase efficiency, productivity and the need to respond quickly to changing market conditions. For example, a proposal to change club colours in order to project a more attractive image may be ⑤ defeated because it breaks a link with tradition.

* memorabilia: 기념품 ** obsession: 집착

문제 풀이

1. 글의 앞부분을 읽으며 글의 중심 소재를 파악하고 글 전체를 빠르게 읽으며 요지를 파악한다.

① 중심 소재: Sports can trigger an emotional response in its consumers of the kind rarely brought forth by other products. (스포츠는 그것의 소비자에게 다른 제품이 좀처럼 일으키지 못하는 종류의 정서적 반응을 촉발시킬 수 있다.)

② 글의 요지: While most managers can only dream of having customers that are as passionate about their products as sport fans, the emotion triggered by sport can also have a negative impact. (대부분의 관리자는 스포츠팬만큼 그들 제품에 열정적인 고객을 가지기를 오직 꿈꾸지만, 스포츠로 인해 촉발되는 감정은 또한 부정적인 영향을 미칠 수 있다.)

2. 글의 문맥을 바탕으로 문장 간 또는 문장 내 논리적인 흐름을 통해 밑줄 친 낱말의 적절성을 파악한다.

선지 ④ increase: 그 결과, 그것[조직]은 효율성, 생산성 및 변화하는 시장 상황에 신속하게 대응해야 할 필요성을 늘릴(→ 무시할) 수도 있다.

3. 문맥상 적절해 보이지 않는 ④ increase의 대안을 생각해 보고 문맥을 점검하여 답을 정한다.

- 대부분의 관리자는 스포츠팬만큼 그들 제품에 열정적인 고객을 가지기를 꿈꾸지만, 스포츠로 인해 촉발되는 감정은 또한 부정적인 영향을 미칠 수 있다. 예를 들면, 조직이 향수와 클럽 전통을 통해 과거에 대한 강한 애착을 가질 수 있는데, 이로 말미암아 조직이 효율성, 생산성과 변화하는 시장 상황에 신속하게 대응해야 할 필요성을 무시할 수도 있다. 정답은 ④번이며 increase를 ignore로 바꿔야 한다.

2023학년도 수능 30번 ★★★

1. 다음 글의 밑줄 친 부분 중, 문맥상 낱말의 쓰임이 적절하지 않은 것은? [3점]

Everywhere we turn we hear about almighty "cyberspace"! The hype promises that we will leave our boring lives, put on goggles and body suits, and enter some metallic, three-dimensional, multimedia otherworld. When the Industrial Revolution arrived with its great innovation, the motor, we didn't leave our world to go to some ① remote motorspace! On the contrary, we brought the motors into our lives, as automobiles, refrigerators, drill presses, and pencil sharpeners. This ② absorption has been so complete that we refer to all these tools with names that declare their usage, not their "motorness." These innovations led to a major socioeconomic movement precisely because they entered and ③ affected profoundly our everyday lives. People have not changed fundamentally in thousands of years. Technology changes constantly. It's the one that must ④ adapt to us. That's exactly what will happen with information technology and its devices under human-centric computing. The longer we continue to believe that computers will take us to a magical new world, the longer we will ⑤ maintain their natural fusion with our lives, the hallmark of every major movement that aspires to be called a socioeconomic revolution.

* hype: 과대광고 ** hallmark: 특징

2022학년도 10월 학평 30번 ★★☆

2. 다음 글의 밑줄 친 부분 중, 문맥상 낱말의 쓰임이 적절하지 않은 것은?

Musical performers and their labor union did not perceive early recordings as a threat to their livelihoods because the recordings were mostly of poor quality. It was not long before musicians began to wonder whether recordings of popular artists or songs would ① undermine the demand for live music. For a time, however, recorded music was too scratchy to pose a serious threat, even though it played in commercial places and offered a few performers a way to ② supplement their income. Additionally, during the early days of recording, radio stations ③ preferred using live musicians on their programs. Sound from live performances was better quality, and stations at this time rarely used recordings. Broadcasters ④ rejected union demands for employment and decent wages, because the alterative use of recordings was even less attractive. They made efforts to employ orchestras, bands, and vocalists to perform on radio programs. There was relative balance between live music and technology in the early innovation stages. With increased ⑤ improvements in electrical recording, however, this balance soon changed.

* alterative: 대체하는

2023학년도 9월 모평 30번 ★★☆

3. 다음 글의 밑줄 친 부분 중, 문맥상 낱말의 쓰임이 적절하지 않은 것은?

Although the wonders of modern technology have provided people with opportunities beyond the wildest dreams of our ancestors, the good, as usual, is weakened by a downside. One of those downsides is that anyone who so chooses can pick up the virtual megaphone that is the Internet and put in their two cents on any of an infinite number of topics, regardless of their ① qualifications. After all, on the Internet, there are no regulations ② preventing a kindergarten teacher from offering medical advice or a physician from suggesting ways to safely make structural changes to your home. As a result, misinformation gets disseminated as information, and it is not always easy to ③ differentiate the two. This can be particularly frustrating for scientists, who spend their lives learning how to understand the intricacies of the world around them, only to have their work summarily ④ challenged by people whose experience with the topic can be measured in minutes. This frustration is then ⑤ diminished by the fact that, to the general public, both the scientist and the challenger are awarded equal credibility.

* put in one's two cents: 의견을 말하다 ** disseminate: 퍼뜨리다 *** intricacy: 복잡성

2022학년도 7월 학평 30번 ★★★

4. 다음 글의 밑줄 친 부분 중, 문맥상 낱말의 쓰임이 적절하지 않은 것은? [3점]

In poorer countries many years of fast growth may be necessary to bring living standards up to acceptable levels. But growth is the means to achieve desired goals, not the ① end in itself. In the richer world the whole idea of growth — at least as conventionally measured — may need to be ② maintained. In economies where services dominate, goods and services tailored to our ③ individual needs will be what determine the advance of our societies. These could be anything from genome-specific medicines to personalized care or tailored suits. That is different from more and more stuff, an arms race of growth. Instead, it means improvements in ④ quality, something that GDP is ill equipped to measure. Some fifty years ago one US economist contrasted what he called the "cowboy" economy, bent on production, exploitation of resources, and pollution, with the "spaceman" economy, in which quality and complexity replaced "throughput" as the measure of success. The ⑤ move from manufacturing to services and from analog to digital is the shift from cowboy to spaceman. But we are still measuring the size of the lasso.

* throughput: (일정 시간 내에 해야 할) 처리량
** lasso: (카우보이가 야생마를 잡는 데 사용하는) 올가미 밧줄

2023학년도 6월 모평 30번 ★★★

5. 다음 글의 밑줄 친 부분 중, 문맥상 낱말의 쓰임이 적절하지 않은 것은?

In recent years urban transport professionals globally have largely acquiesced to the view that automobile demand in cities needs to be managed rather than accommodated. Rising incomes inevitably lead to increases in motorization. Even without the imperative of climate change, the physical constraints of densely inhabited cities and the corresponding demands of accessibility, mobility, safety, air pollution, and urban livability all ① limit the option of expanding road networks purely to accommodate this rising demand. As a result, as cities develop and their residents become more prosperous, ② persuading people to choose *not* to use cars becomes an increasingly key focus of city managers and planners. Improving the quality of ③ alternative options, such as walking, cycling, and public transport, is a central element of this strategy. However, the most direct approach to ④ accommodating automobile demand is making motorized travel more expensive or restricting it with administrative rules. The contribution of motorized travel to climate change ⑤ reinforces this imperative.

* acquiesce: 따르다 ** imperative: 불가피한 것 *** constraint: 압박

2022학년도 4월 학평 30번 ★★★

6. 다음 글의 밑줄 친 부분 중, 문맥상 낱말의 쓰임이 적절하지 않은 것은?

One of the most productive strategies to build customer relationships is to increase the firm's share of customer rather than its market share. This strategy involves abandoning the old notions of ① acquiring new customers and increasing transactions to focus instead on more fully serving the needs of existing customers. Financial services are a great example of this. Most consumers purchase financial services from ② different firms. They bank at one institution, purchase insurance from another, and handle their investments elsewhere. To ③ solidify this purchasing pattern, many companies now offer all of these services under one roof. For example, Regions Financial Corporation offers retail and commercial banking, trust, mortgage, and insurance products to customers in a network of more than 1,500 offices. The company tries to more fully serve the financial needs of its ④ current customers, thereby acquiring a larger share of each customer's financial business. By creating these types of relationships, customers have ⑤ little incentive to seek out competitive firms to fulfill their financial services needs.

2022학년도 3월 학평 30번 ★★★

7. 다음 글의 밑줄 친 부분 중, 문맥상 낱말의 쓰임이 적절하지 않은 것은?

Just as there's a tendency to glorify technological progress, there's a countertendency to expect the worst of every new tool or machine. In Plato's *Phaedrus*, Socrates bemoaned the ① development of writing. He feared that, as people came to rely on the written word as a ② substitute for the knowledge they used to carry inside their heads, they would, in the words of one of the dialogue's characters, "cease to exercise their memory and become forgetful." And because they would be able to "③ receive a quantity of information without proper instruction," they would "be thought very knowledgeable when they are for the most part quite ignorant." They would be "filled with the conceit of wisdom instead of real wisdom." Socrates wasn't ④ right — the new technology did often have the effects he feared — but he was shortsighted. He couldn't ⑤ foresee the many ways that writing and reading would serve to spread information, spark fresh ideas, and expand human knowledge (if not wisdom).

* bemoan: 한탄하다 ** conceit: 자만심

2022학년도 수능 30번 ★★★

8. 다음 글의 밑줄 친 부분 중, 문맥상 낱말의 쓰임이 적절하지 않은 것은?

It has been suggested that "organic" methods, defined as those in which only natural products can be used as inputs, would be less damaging to the biosphere. Large-scale adoption of "organic" farming methods, however, would ① reduce yields and increase production costs for many major crops. Inorganic nitrogen supplies are ② essential for maintaining moderate to high levels of productivity for many of the non-leguminous crop species, because organic supplies of nitrogenous materials often are either limited or more expensive than inorganic nitrogen fertilizers. In addition, there are ③ benefits to the extensive use of either manure or legumes as "green manure" crops. In many cases, weed control can be very difficult or require much hand labor if chemicals cannot be used, and ④ fewer people are willing to do this work as societies become wealthier. Some methods used in "organic" farming, however, such as the sensible use of crop rotations and specific combinations of cropping and livestock enterprises, can make important ⑤ contributions to the sustainability of rural ecosystems.

* nitrogen fertilizer: 질소 비료 ** manure: 거름
*** legume: 콩과(科) 식물

2021학년도 수능 30번 ★★☆

9. 다음 글의 밑줄 친 부분 중, 문맥상 낱말의 쓰임이 적절하지 않은 것은?

How the bandwagon effect occurs is demonstrated by the history of measurements of the speed of light. Because this speed is the basis of the theory of relativity, it's one of the most frequently and carefully measured ① quantities in science. As far as we know, the speed hasn't changed over time. However, from 1870 to 1900, all the experiments found speeds that were too high. Then, from 1900 to 1950, the ② opposite happened — all the experiments found speeds that were too low! This kind of error, where results are always on one side of the real value, is called "bias." It probably happened because over time, experimenters subconsciously adjusted their results to ③ match what they expected to find. If a result fit what they expected, they kept it. If a result didn't fit, they threw it out. They weren't being intentionally dishonest, just ④ influenced by the conventional wisdom. The pattern only changed when someone ⑤ lacked the courage to report what was actually measured instead of what was expected.

* bandwagon effect: 편승 효과

2020학년도 수능 30번 ★★★

10. 다음 글의 밑줄 친 부분 중, 문맥상 낱말의 쓰임이 적절하지 않은 것은? [3점]

Suppose we know that Paula suffers from a severe phobia. If we reason that Paula is afraid either of snakes or spiders, and then ① establish that she is not afraid of snakes, we will conclude that Paula is afraid of spiders. However, our conclusion is reasonable only if Paula's fear really does concern either snakes or spiders. If we know only that Paula has a phobia, then the fact that she's not afraid of snakes is entirely ② consistent with her being afraid of heights, water, dogs or the number thirteen. More generally, when we are presented with a list of alternative explanations for some phenomenon, and are then persuaded that all but one of those explanations are ③ unsatisfactory, we should pause to reflect. Before ④ denying that the remaining explanation is the correct one, consider whether other plausible options are being ignored or overlooked. The fallacy of false choice misleads when we're insufficiently attentive to an important hidden assumption, that the choices which have been made explicit exhaust the ⑤ sensible alternatives.

* plausible: 그럴듯한 ** fallacy: 오류

총 문항			문항	맞은 문항					문항
개별 문항	1	2	3	4	5	6	7	8	9	10
채점										

문법 플러스

12. 대명사

정답 및 해설 065쪽

A 문법의 주요 포인트를 점검해 봅시다.

1 인칭대명사는 주격, 소유격, 목적격과 단수형, 복수형이 있다. 대명사가 목적어일 때, 「타동사+대명사+부사」의 어순으로 써야 한다.

▶ They can also sidestep most of the ethical issues involved: nobody, presumably, is more aware of an experiment's potential hazards than the scientist who devised **[them / it]**.

2 재귀대명사는 주어와 동일한 대상을 지칭하는 목적어에 사용한다. '~자신'이라는 의미를 나타낸다. 재귀대명사 강조 용법은 명사를 강조하기 위해 사용하고 생략 가능하다. 재귀대명사 관용 표현도 익혀 둔다.

for oneself	자기를 위하여	by oneself	혼자서	in itself	본질적으로	between ourselves	우리끼리 얘긴데

▶ In the practice of totemism, he has suggested, an unlettered humanity "broods upon **[it / itself]** and its place in nature."

3 소유대명사는 「소유격+명사」를 대신하는 말이고 '~의 것'이라는 의미를 나타낸다.

▶ Are those his books? - No, they are **[her / hers]**.

4 지시대명사 this/that은 앞에 언급된 어구나 내용을 받는다. this[these]는 가까운 것, that[those]은 먼 것을 가리킨다. 명사의 반복을 피하기 위해 that이나 those를 쓸 수 있다.

▶ It is said that China's economy could be 2.5 times **[those / that]** of US by 2030.

5 부정대명사 either, neither, someone, anyone, no one, everyone 등은 단수로 취급한다. both는 복수로 취급한다. 막연한 것을 지칭할 때는 부정대명사 one[some], 구체적인 것을 지칭할 때는 it을 쓴다.

one..., the other ~	(둘 중에서) 하나는 …, 다른 하나는 ~
one..., another ~, the other~	(셋 중에서) 하나는 …, 다른 하나는 ~, 또 다른 하나는 ~
some... others~	(막연한 다수 중) 일부는 …, 다른 일부는 ~
some... the others~	(한정된 다수 중) 일부는 …, 나머지 일부는 ~

▶ We have two puppies; one is white and **[the other / another]** is black.

6 의문대명사는 who, whose, whom, which, what이 있다. 직접의문문이 다른 문장의 일부로 들어가는 경우, 의문사가 있는 경우, 「의문사+주어+동사」의 간접의문문 형식을 갖는다. 의문사가 없는 경우에는 「whether[if]+주어+동사」의 형태를 취한다.

▶ Can you tell me **[what you like / what do you like]** most about your job?

7 구체적인 지칭은 it/ they를 사용하고, 막연한 지칭은 one / some을 사용한다.

▶ In a sense, the fine art object is valued because **[it / one]** can be reproduced for popular consumption.

B 다음 괄호 안에서 어법상 올바른 것을 고르시오.

1 Possibly the most effect way to focus on your goals is to **[write them down / write down them]**.

2 Clothes are part of how people present **[themselves / them]** to the world, and fashion locates them in the present, relative to what is happening in society and to fashion's own history.

3 I have my pencil; have you got **[you / yours]**?

4 The picture I am referring to is **[this / these]** here.

5 Some tourists went to the beach; **[the others / others]** explored the town.

6 There are six books. One is mine, and **[others / the others]** are my brother's.

7 Did any letters come for me? Yes, **[they / some]** came.

숙어 플러스

12. 수능 필수 숙어 12회

정답 및 해설 065쪽

A 다음 수능 필수 숙어를 읽고, 아는 것은 체크해 봅시다.

□ 01	in effect	사실상, (법, 규정 등이) 시행 중인
□ 02	in favor of	~에 찬성하여, ~을 위하여
□ 03	in full	전부, 빠짐없이
□ 04	in itself	그 자체로, 본질적으로
□ 05	in need of	~이 필요한
□ 06	in need	어려움에 처한
□ 07	in no time	즉시, 당장
□ 08	in order	순서대로, 알맞은, 적절한
□ 09	in person	몸소, 직접
□ 10	in place	제자리에 있는, 가동 중인
□ 11	in place of	~대신에
□ 12	in shape	건강 상태가 좋은
□ 13	in terms of	~에 관하여, ~면에서
□ 14	in that	~라는 점에서
□ 15	in the distance	먼 곳에
□ 16	in the end	마침내, 결국 (= after all)
□ 17	in the first place	우선, 먼저, 첫째로
□ 18	in the long run	결국에는, 긴 안목으로 보면
□ 19	in the meantime	그 사이에
□ 20	keep ~ in mind	~을 명심하다(= bear ~ in mind)

B 다음 숙어 표현을 읽고 의미 차이를 비교해 봅시다.

□ 21	consist in	~에 있다 cf. consist of ~로 구성되다
□ 22	drop in	(잠깐) 방문하다
□ 23	get in(to)	(택시 등을) 타다(↔ get off)
□ 24	hand in	~을 제출하다(= submit)
□ 25	move in	이사 오다(↔ move out 이사 가다)

C 우리말을 참고하여 빈칸에 알맞은 말을 써 봅시다.

1 사실상, 흡혈박쥐들은 일종의 상호 보험 체계를 만들어 낸다.
In __________, the vampire bats have created a kind of mutual insurance system.

2 가격 면에 있어서는 비교가 안 된다.
In _________ of price, there's no comparison.

3 걱정 마. 곧 나아서 돌아다니게 될 거야.
Don't worry. I'll be up and running in no ___________.

4 외부와의 경험과 균형을 맞추어 독서를 하는 것이 중요하다는 것을 명심하라.
Keep in _________ the importance of balancing reading with outside experiences.

13 빈칸 추론 (1) 어휘, 짧은 어구

출제 트렌드

1. 빈칸 추론 유형은 '빈칸에 들어갈 말로 가장 적절한 것'을 고르는 문제이다.
2. 빈칸 추론은 총 4문항이 출제된다. 그 중에서 빈칸에 들어갈 어휘나 짧은 어구를 추론하는 유형은 수능에서 거의 2문항이 출제된다. 논리적이고 종합적 사고력을 요구하는 문제로 난이도와 변별력이 높게 출제된다.
3. 최근 수능 7년간, 빈칸 추론(1) 단어, 짧은 어구 문제는 주로 31번, 32번 문항으로 출제되었다. 2017학년도 수능에서 (45/43%), 2018(64/60%), 2019(57/63%), 2020(43/65%), 2021(54/57%), 2022(67/47%), 2023(47/68%)에서 괄호 안의 정답률을 보였다. 평균 55.7%의 정답률을 보였으며, 난이도는 상 단계이다.

출처			문항 번호	지문 주제	정답률(%)	난이도
대표	2023학년도	수능	31번	스포츠 저널리스트 지위의 역설적인 측면	47	★★☆
1	2023학년도	수능	32번	언어 혁신이 일어나는 장소	68	★★☆
2	2022학년도	10 학평	31번	정치적 리스크의 불확실성	60	★★☆
3	2022학년도	10 학평	32번	생태 건강을 파괴하는 광물 또는 화합물의 채굴	32	★★★
4	2023학년도	09 모평	32번	팬덤의 즐거움의 원천	65	★★☆
5	2023학년도	06 모평	31번	컴퓨터 미술가의 소멸	37	★★★
6	2023학년도	06 모평	32번	형식주의의 관점에서의 문학	47	★★★
7	2022학년도	수능	31번	유머의 특징	67	★★☆
8	2022학년도	수능	32번	뉴스의 구성	47	★★★
9	2021학년도	수능	31번	수메르 사회에서 사원의 역할과 문자의 발달	54	★★★
10	2021학년도	수능	32번	환경의 영향을 받아 달라지는 생존 전략	57	★★★

1등급 꿀팁

1. 글의 주제나 요지가 빈칸으로 제시되는 경우가 많으므로 지문의 주제나 요지를 확인하다.
2. 글의 소재 및 중심 요지를 파악하고 핵심 어구에 줄을 그으며 읽어 간다.
3. 글을 읽을 때 특히 빈칸 전후 부분을 살펴보면서 빈칸에 들어갈 단서를 찾아본다.
4. 글의 앞부분에 빈칸이 있는 경우, 주로 주제문에 해당하며 이어지는 내용은 부연 설명이나 예시가 일반적이다.
5. 빈칸 추론의 핵심 단서가 될 수 있는 연결어에 유의한다.

that is	즉	similarly	마찬가지로
in sum	요약해 보면	in short	간단히 말해서
while	반면에	however	그러나(= but)
in other words	다시 말해서	besides	게다가
as a result	결국	moreover	더욱이, 게다가

빈칸 추론 (1) 어휘, 짧은 어구

제한 시간 : 15분 | 정답 및 해설 066쪽

대표 기출

2023학년도 수능 31번

다음 빈칸에 들어갈 말로 가장 적절한 것은?

31. There is something deeply paradoxical about the professional status of sports journalism, especially in the medium of print. In discharging their usual responsibilities of description and commentary, reporters' accounts of sports events are eagerly consulted by sports fans, while in their broader journalistic role of covering sport in its many forms, sports journalists are among the most visible of all contemporary writers. The ruminations of the elite class of 'celebrity' sports journalists are much sought after by the major newspapers, their lucrative contracts being the envy of colleagues in other 'disciplines' of journalism. Yet sports journalists do not have a standing in their profession that corresponds to the size of their readerships or of their pay packets, with the old saying (now reaching the status of cliché) that sport is the 'toy department of the news media' still readily to hand as a dismissal of the worth of what sports journalists do. This reluctance to take sports journalism seriously produces the paradoxical outcome that sports newspaper writers are much read but little ________.

* discharge: 이행하다 ** rumination: 생각
*** lucrative: 돈을 많이 버는

① paid ② admired
③ censored ④ challenged
⑤ discussed

문제 풀이

1. 글의 도입부에 제시된 글의 소재를 파악하고 글의 내용을 예측한다.

• 글의 소재: the professional status of sports journalism(스포츠 저널리즘의 전문적 지위)

2. 전개 부분을 읽고 글의 주제를 추론해 본다.

① The ruminations of the elite class of 'celebrity' sports journalists are much sought after by the major newspapers, their lucrative contracts being the envy of colleagues in other 'disciplines' of journalism. ('유명인급' 스포츠 저널리스트 중 엘리트 계층의 숙고의 결과는 주요 신문사들이 많이 원하고, 그들의 수익성이 좋은 계약은 저널리즘의 다른 '부문'에 있는 동료들의 부러움의 대상이 된다.)

② Yet sports journalists do not have a standing in their profession that corresponds to the size of their readerships or of their pay packets, with ~. (하지만 스포츠 저널리스트는 ~과 더불어 그들의 독자 수나 급여 액수의 크기에 상응하는 그들 전문성에서의 지위를 갖지 못한다.)

③ This reluctance to take sports journalism seriously produces the paradoxical outcome that sports newspaper writers are much read but little ~. (이렇게 스포츠 저널리즘을 진지하게 여기기를 꺼리는 것은 스포츠 신문 작가들이 많이 읽히지만 거의 ~ 받지 못하는 역설적인 결과를 얻는다.)

3. 도입과 전개 부분을 통해 파악한 글의 주제를 염두하고 빈칸 내용을 추론한다. 특히 빈칸과 인접한 문장에서 단서를 찾는다.

• 스포츠 저널리즘의 전문적 지위에 대해서는 역설적이라고 하면서, 스포츠 저널리스트들은 독자들이 그들의 글을 많이 찾아 읽고 신문사들도 많이 원하고 돈도 많이 벌지만, 뉴스 매체에서는 그들의 독자 수나 급여 규모의 액수에 상응하는 전문적인 지위를 갖지 못한다고 했다. 따라서 빈칸에는 ②'admired'가 들어가서 빈칸을 포함한 문장이 '이렇게 스포츠 저널리즘을 진지하게 여기기를 꺼리는 것은 스포츠 신문 작가들이 많이 읽히지만 거의 존경받지 못하는 역설적인 결과를 얻는다.'가 되는 것이 적절하다.

2023학년도 수능 32번 ★★☆

1. 다음 빈칸에 들어갈 말로 가장 적절한 것은?

People have always wanted to be around other people and to learn from them. Cities have long been dynamos of social possibility, foundries of art, music, and fashion. Slang, or, if you prefer, "lexical innovation," has always started in cities — an outgrowth of all those different people so frequently exposed to one another. It spreads outward, in a manner not unlike transmissible disease, which itself typically "takes off" in cities. If, as the noted linguist Leonard Bloomfield argued, the way a person talks is a "composite result of what he has heard before," then language innovation would happen where the most people heard and talked to the most other people. Cities drive taste change because they ________________________________, who not surprisingly are often the creative people cities seem to attract. Media, ever more global, ever more far-reaching, spread language faster to more people.

* foundry: 주물 공장 ** lexical: 어휘의

① provide rich source materials for artists
② offer the greatest exposure to other people
③ cause cultural conflicts among users of slang
④ present ideal research environments to linguists
⑤ reduce the social mobility of ambitious outsiders

2022학년도 10월 학평 31번 ★★☆

2. 다음 빈칸에 들어갈 말로 가장 적절한 것은?

Much of what we call political risk is in fact ___________. This applies to all types of political risks, from civil strife to expropriations to regulatory changes. Political risk, unlike credit or market or operational risk, can be unsystematic and therefore more difficult to address in classic statistical terms. What is the probability that terrorists will attack the United States again? Unlike earthquakes or hurricanes, political actors constantly adapt to overcome the barriers created by risk managers. When corporations structure foreign investments to mitigate risks of expropriations, through international guarantees or legal contracts, host governments seek out new forms of obstruction, such as creeping expropriation or regulatory discrimination, that are very hard and legally costly to prove. Observation of a risk changes the risk itself. There are ways to mitigate high-impact, low-probability events. But analysis of these risks can be as much art as science. [3점]

* expropriation: 몰수 ** mitigate: 줄이다

① injustice ② uncertainty
③ circularity ④ contradiction
⑤ miscommunication

2022학년도 10월 학평 32번 ★★★

3. 다음 빈칸에 들어갈 말로 가장 적절한 것은?

Ecological health depends on keeping the surface of the earth rich in humus and minerals so that it can provide a foundation for healthy plant and animal life. The situation is disrupted if the soil loses these raw materials or if ____________________. When man goes beneath the surface of the earth and drags out minerals or other compounds that did not evolve as part of this system, then problems follow. The mining of lead and cadmium are examples of this. Petroleum is also a substance that has been dug out of the bowels of the earth and introduced into the surface ecology by man. Though it is formed from plant matter, the highly reduced carbon compounds that result are often toxic to living protoplasm. In some cases this is true of even very tiny amounts, as in the case of "polychlorinated biphenyls," a petroleum product which can cause cancer.

* humus: 부식토, 부엽토 ** protoplasm: 원형질

① the number of plants on it increases too rapidly
② it stops providing enough nourishment for humans
③ climate change transforms its chemical components
④ alien species prevail and deplete resources around it
⑤ great quantities of contaminants are introduced into it

2023학년도 9월 모평 32번 ★★☆

4. 다음 빈칸에 들어갈 말로 가장 적절한 것은?

Fans feel for feeling's own sake. They make meanings beyond what seems to be on offer. They build identities and experiences, and make artistic creations of their own to share with others. A person can be an individual fan, feeling an "idealized connection with a star, strong feelings of memory and nostalgia," and engaging in activities like "collecting to develop a sense of self." But, more often, individual experiences are embedded in social contexts where other people with shared attachments socialize around the object of their affections. Much of the pleasure of fandom ____________________. In their diaries, Bostonians of the 1800s described being part of the crowds at concerts as part of the pleasure of attendance. A compelling argument can be made that what fans love is less the object of their fandom than the attachments to (and differentiations from) one another that those affections afford.

* embed: 끼워 넣다 ** compelling: 강력한

① is enhanced by collaborations between global stars
② results from frequent personal contact with a star
③ deepens as fans age together with their idols
④ comes from being connected to other fans
⑤ is heightened by stars' media appearances

2023학년도 6월 모평 31번 ★★★

5. 다음 빈칸에 들어갈 말로 가장 적절한 것은?

Young contemporary artists who employ digital technologies in their practice rarely make reference to computers. For example, Wade Guyton, an abstractionist who uses a word processing program and inkjet printers, does not call himself a computer artist. Moreover, some critics, who admire his work, are little concerned about his extensive use of computers in the art-making process. This is a marked contrast from three decades ago when artists who utilized computers were labeled by critics — often disapprovingly — as computer artists. For the present generation of artists, the computer, or more appropriately, the laptop, is one in a collection of integrated, portable digital technologies that link their social and working life. With tablets and cell phones surpassing personal computers in Internet usage, and as slim digital devices resemble nothing like the room-sized mainframes and bulky desktop computers of previous decades, it now appears that the computer artist is finally __________.

① awake
② influential
③ distinct
④ troublesome
⑤ extinct

2023학년도 6월 모평 32번 ★★★

6. 다음 빈칸에 들어갈 말로 가장 적절한 것은?

The critic who wants to write about literature from a formalist perspective must first be a close and careful reader who examines all the elements of a text individually and questions how they come together to create a work of art. Such a reader, who respects the autonomy of a work, achieves an understanding of it by ____________________. Instead of examining historical periods, author biographies, or literary styles, for example, he or she will approach a text with the assumption that it is a self-contained entity and that he or she is looking for the governing principles that allow the text to reveal itself. For example, the correspondences between the characters in James Joyce's short story "Araby" and the people he knew personally may be interesting, but for the formalist they are less relevant to understanding how the story creates meaning than are other kinds of information that the story contains within itself.

* entity: 실체

① putting himself or herself both inside and outside it
② finding a middle ground between it and the world
③ searching for historical realities revealed within it
④ looking inside it, not outside it or beyond it
⑤ exploring its characters' cultural relevance

2022학년도 수능 31번 ★★☆

7. 다음 빈칸에 들어갈 말로 가장 적절한 것은?

Humour involves not just practical disengagement but cognitive disengagement. As long as something is funny, we are for the moment not concerned with whether it is real or fictional, true or false. This is why we give considerable leeway to people telling funny stories. If they are getting extra laughs by exaggerating the silliness of a situation or even by making up a few details, we are happy to grant them comic licence, a kind of poetic licence. Indeed, someone listening to a funny story who tries to correct the teller — 'No, he didn't spill the spaghetti on the keyboard and the monitor, just on the keyboard' — will probably be told by the other listeners to stop interrupting. The creator of humour is putting ideas into people's heads for the pleasure those ideas will bring, not to provide __________ information.

* cognitive: 인식의 ** leeway: 여지

① accurate ② detailed
③ useful ④ additional
⑤ alternative

2022학년도 수능 32번 ★★★

8. 다음 빈칸에 들어갈 말로 가장 적절한 것은?

News, especially in its televised form, is constituted not only by its choice of topics and stories but by its ____________________________. Presentational styles have been subject to a tension between an informational-educational purpose and the need to engage us entertainingly. While current affairs programmes are often 'serious' in tone sticking to the 'rules' of balance, more popular programmes adopt a friendly, lighter, idiom in which we are invited to consider the impact of particular news items from the perspective of the 'average person in the street'. Indeed, contemporary news construction has come to rely on an increased use of faster editing tempos and 'flashier' presentational styles including the use of logos, sound-bites, rapid visual cuts and the 'star quality' of news readers. Popular formats can be said to enhance understanding by engaging an audience unwilling to endure the longer verbal orientation of older news formats. However, they arguably work to reduce understanding by failing to provide the structural contexts for news events.

① coordination with traditional display techniques
② prompt and full coverage of the latest issues
③ educational media contents favoured by producers
④ commitment to long-lasting news standards
⑤ verbal and visual idioms or modes of address

2021학년도 수능 31번 ★★★

9. 다음 빈칸에 들어갈 말로 가장 적절한 것은?

In the classic model of the Sumerian economy, the temple functioned as an administrative authority governing commodity production, collection, and redistribution. The discovery of administrative tablets from the temple complexes at Uruk suggests that token use and consequently writing evolved as a tool of centralized economic governance. Given the lack of archaeological evidence from Uruk-period domestic sites, it is not clear whether individuals also used the system for __________________. For that matter, it is not clear how widespread literacy was at its beginnings. The use of identifiable symbols and pictograms on the early tablets is consistent with administrators needing a lexicon that was mutually intelligible by literate and nonliterate parties. As cuneiform script became more abstract, literacy must have become increasingly important to ensure one understood what he or she had agreed to.

* archaeological: 고고학적인 ** lexicon: 어휘 목록
*** cuneiform script: 쐐기 문자

① religious events
② personal agreements
③ communal responsibilities
④ historical records
⑤ power shifts

2021학년도 수능 32번 ★★★

10. 다음 빈칸에 들어갈 말로 가장 적절한 것은?

Choosing similar friends can have a rationale. Assessing the survivability of an environment can be risky (if an environment turns out to be deadly, for instance, it might be too late by the time you found out), so humans have evolved the desire to associate with similar individuals as a way to perform this function efficiently. This is especially useful to a species that lives in so many different sorts of environments. However, the carrying capacity of a given environment ____________________________. If resources are very limited, the individuals who live in a particular place cannot all do the exact same thing (for example, if there are few trees, people cannot all live in tree houses, or if mangoes are in short supply, people cannot all live solely on a diet of mangoes). A rational strategy would therefore sometimes be to *avoid* similar members of one's species.

① exceeds the expected demands of a community
② is decreased by diverse means of survival
③ places a limit on this strategy
④ makes the world suitable for individuals
⑤ prevents social ties to dissimilar members

총 문항				문항	맞은 문항					문항
개별 문항	1	2	3	4	5	6	7	8	9	10
채점										

13. 관계대명사

정답 및 해설 071쪽

A 문법의 주요 포인트를 점검해 봅시다.

1 관계대명사는 문장 내에서 「접속사+대명사」의 역할을 하며, 주격, 소유격, 목적격이 있다. 선행사 앞에 최상급, all, every, 서수, the only 등이 오면 that을 쓴다. 관계대명사는 관계사절 안에서 대명사 역할을 하기 때문에 뒤에 불완전 문장이 온다.

선행사	주격	목적격	소유격
사람	who	who(m)	whose
사물/동물	which	which	of which 또는 whose
사람/사물/동물	that	that	–

▶ The dual expressions of this tendency are anthropomorphism (the practice of regarding animals as humans) and totemism (the practice of regarding humans as animals), both of **[whom /which]** spread through the visual art and the mythology of primitive cultures.

2 관계대명사 what(= the thing(s) which[that])은 선행사를 포함하고 있으므로, 따로 선행사가 앞에 나와 있지 않는다.

▶ **[What / Which]** is most important in life is love.

3 관계대명사 계속적 용법은 관계대명사 앞에 콤마(,)를 쓴다. that은 계속적 용법으로 쓰지 않는다. 또한 which의 계속적 용법은 앞의 구나 절 등을 받을 수 있다.

▶ She discussed it with her friend, **[that / who]** is a lawyer.

4 관계대명사가 타동사나 전치사의 목적어로 쓰인 경우에는 생략할 수 있다. 단, 관계대명사가 전치사의 목적어일 때는 전치사를 문장 가장 뒤로 보낸 후, 관계대명사를 생략할 수 있다. 전치사가 앞에 있을 때는 생략할 수 없다. 또한 「주격관계대명사+be동사」도 생략할 수 있다.

▶ The lady **[that / which]** I talked with is my aunt.

5 접속사인 as, but than이 관계대명사처럼 쓰이는 경우 '유사관계대명사'라고 한다. 선행사 앞에 as, such, the same 등이 올 때 as를 쓴다. 부정어가 있을 때 유사관계대명사 but을 쓴다.

▶ This is the same watch **[but / as]** the one I lost.

6 선행사 앞에 비교급이 올 때 유사관계대명사 than을 쓴다.

▶ He has more money **[as / than]** is needed.

7 관계대명사에 −ever를 붙이면 복합관계대명사가 된다. 복합관계대명사는 명사절이나 양보의 부사절로 사용할 수 있다.

▶ **[Whoever / Whatever]** breaks this law will be punished.

B 다음 괄호 안에서 어법상 올바른 것을 고르시오.

1 **[What / That]** cell metabolism and structure should be complex would not be surprising, but actually, they are rather simple and logical.

2 Do you believe in **[that / what]** you cannot see?

3 Sally slid on the ice, **[who / which]** made everyone laugh.

4 The man who **[was / were]** working as an usher was looking for a new job.

5 Choose such friends **[but / as]** will help you.

6 She has **[more / but]** books than I have.

7 You can take **[which / whichever]** you like.

숙어 플러스

13. 수능 필수 숙어 13회

정답 및 해설 072쪽

A 다음 수능 필수 숙어를 읽고, 아는 것은 체크해 봅시다.

□ 01	keep away from	멀리하다, 가까이 하지 않다
□ 02	keep in touch	연락하며 지내다
□ 03	keep on	계속 ~하다
□ 04	keep one's word	약속을 지키다
□ 05	keep track of	~을 기록하다, ~에 대해 계속 파악하다
□ 06	keep up with	~와 연락하고 지내다, 뒤떨어지지 않다
□ 07	kind of	약간, 어느 정도
□ 08	lay out	~을 펼치다, ~을 배치하다
□ 09	leave ~ behind	~을 훨씬 앞서다, ~을 두고 가다
□ 10	leave alone	그대로 두다, 내버려 두다
□ 11	leave for	~을 향해 떠나다
□ 12	leave out	생략하다
□ 13	let alone	~은 말할 것도 없이
□ 14	line up	줄을 서다
□ 15	live up to	(기대, 요구 등에) 부응하다
□ 16	long for	~을 간절히 바라다
□ 17	look after	돌보다, 보살피다
□ 18	look back	회상하다, 되돌아보다
□ 19	look in	잠깐 들르다
□ 20	look into	들여다보다, 조사하다

B 다음 숙어 표현을 읽고 의미 차이를 비교해 봅시다.

□ 21	in advance	우선
□ 22	in case of	~의 경우에, 만약 ~하면
□ 23	in place of	~대신에(= instead of)
□ 24	in short	요약하면(= in brief)
□ 25	in fact	사실은

C 우리말을 참고하여 빈칸에 알맞은 말을 써 봅시다.

1 너 Sally와 계속 연락하고 지내니?
Do you keep in ______ with Sally?

2 고래들은 다시 잠수할 때, 바다 표면에 피부 조각들을 남겨둔다.
The whales leave ______ the bits of skins on the surface when they re-submerge.

3 개미들은 개미 풀 안에서 사는 애벌레를 돌보기도 한다.
The ants also look ______ a caterpillar which lives inside the ant plant.

4 우리는 늦어도 4시까지는 공항으로 출발해야 한다.
We need to leave ______ the airport no later than four o'clock.

14 빈칸 추론 (2) 긴 어구, 문장

출제 트렌드

1. 빈칸 추론 유형은 '빈칸에 들어갈 말로 가장 적절한 것'을 고르는 문제이다.
2. 빈칸 추론은 총 4문항이 출제된다. 그 중에서 빈칸에 들어갈 긴 어구나 절을 추론하는 유형은 종합적 사고력을 요구하는 문제로 난이도와 변별력이 매우 높게 출제된다. 빈칸 앞뒤에 제시되는 내용을 논리적으로 이해하고 있는지 글의 흐름을 종합적으로 파악할 수 있는지를 측정하는 문제로 수능에서 2문제가 출제된다. 3점 배점이 집중되는 유형이다.
3. 설명문이나 논설문 등 논리성이 있는 글을 중심으로 출제된다. 후반부의 결론 부분에 빈칸이 있는 경우가 가장 많다.
4. 2018학년도 수능은 최초로 영어 과목이 절대 평가로 시행되었다. 2018학년도부터 최근까지 수능 영어의 킬러 문항은 비연계 지문으로 출제한 34번 빈칸 추론이었다. 등급의 당락을 결정짓는 어려운 문제였다.
5. 최근 수능 7년간, 빈칸 추론(2) 긴 어구, 문장 문제는 33, 34번 문항으로 고정되어 출제되었다. 2017학년도 수능(33/52%), 2018(52/53%), 2019(32/32%), 2020(48/45%), 2021(55/43%), 2022(50/31%), 2023(47/21%)에서 괄호 안의 정답률을 보였다. 평균 42.6%의 정답률을 보였으며, 난이도는 상 단계에 속한다. 수능에서 가장 어려운 고난이도 문제 그룹에 속한다.

	출처		문항 번호	지문 주제	정답률(%)	난이도
대표	2023학년도	수능	33번	벌들의 댄스 플로어에서 정보 교환의 결과	47	★★★
1	2023학년도	수능	34번	시간에 대한 의식	21	★★★
2	2022학년도	10 학평	33번	과학적 발견의 장벽을 무너뜨리는 방법	28	★★★
3	2023학년도	10 학평	34번	우리의 믿음이 사실을 해석하는 방식에 영향을 미침	44	★★★
4	2023학년도	09 모평	33번	의상 디자이너에 대한 인식 변화	48	★★★
5	2023학년도	06 모평	33번	제조업자들의 혁신 과정 설계 방식	35	★★★
6	2023학년도	06 모평	34번	음악 작품에서 전개부	36	★★★
7	2022학년도	수능	33번	공유지 문제 해결책	50	★★★
8	2022학년도	수능	34번	역사적 통찰의 특징	31	★★★
9	2021학년도	수능	33번	뇌 발달 과정	55	★★★
10	2021학년도	수능	34번	교육 기술의 성공적인 통합	43	★★★

1등급 꿀팁

1. 빈칸이 첫 문장이나 마지막 문장에 있는 경우, 글의 주제나 요지가 될 가능성이 높다.
2. 빈칸은 주로 중요 문장이 들어가므로 중심 내용을 먼저 찾는다.
3. 전체적인 내용을 종합하여 빈칸에 들어갈 말을 논리적으로 추론한다.
4. 선택지를 선택한 후에는 빈칸에 넣고 문맥상 적절한지 확인해 본다.
5. 글을 요약하거나 완성하는 연습을 꾸준히 한다.

빈칸 추론 (2) 긴 어구, 문장

제한 시간 : 15분 | 정답 및 해설 072쪽

대표 기출

2023학년도 수능 33번

다음 빈칸에 들어갈 말로 가장 적절한 것은?

33. The entrance to a honeybee colony, often referred to as the dancefloor, is a market place for information about the state of the colony and the environment outside the hive. Studying interactions on the dancefloor provides us with a number of illustrative examples of how individuals changing their own behavior in response to local information ______________________. For example, upon returning to their hive honeybees that have collected water search out a receiver bee to unload their water to within the hive. If this search time is short then the returning bee is more likely to perform a waggle dance to recruit others to the water source. Conversely, if this search time is long then the bee is more likely to give up collecting water. Since receiver bees will only accept water if they require it, either for themselves or to pass on to other bees and brood, this unloading time is correlated with the colony's overall need of water. Thus the individual water forager's response to unloading time (up or down) regulates water collection in response to the colony's need. [3점]

* brood: 애벌레 ** forager: 조달자

① allow the colony to regulate its workforce
② search for water sources by measuring distance
③ decrease the colony's workload when necessary
④ divide tasks according to their respective talents
⑤ train workers to acquire basic communication patterns

문제 풀이

1. 글의 도입부에 제시된 글의 소재를 파악하고 글의 내용을 예측한다.

• 글의 소재: interactions on the dancefloor(댄스 플로어에서의 상호 작용)

2. 전개 부분을 읽고 글의 주제를 추론해 본다.

① Studying interactions on the dancefloor provides us with a number of illustrative examples of how individuals changing their own behavior in response to local information ~. (댄스 플로어에서의 상호 작용을 연구하는 것은 우리에게 지역의 정보에 반응하여 어떻게 그들 자신의 행동을 바꾸는 개체들이 ~에 대한 많은 예증이 되는 예시들을 제공한다.)

② For example, upon returning to their hive honeybees that have collected water search out a receiver bee to unload their water to within the hive. (예를 들면, 물을 모아온 꿀벌들은 자신들의 벌집으로 돌아오자마자 자신들의 물을 벌집 안으로 넘겨주기 위해 물을 받아줄 벌을 찾는다.)

③ If this search time is short then the returning bee is more likely to perform a waggle dance to recruit others to the water source. (만약 이 (물을 받을 벌을) 찾는 시간이 짧으면, 그 돌아오는 벌은 물이 있는 곳으로 데려갈 다른 벌들을 모집하기 위해 8자 춤을 출 가능성이 더 높다.)

④ Thus the individual water forager's response to unloading time (up or down) regulates water collection in response to the colony's need. (그러므로 (시간이 늘어나든 혹은 줄어들든 간에) 물을 넘겨주는 시간에 대한 개별적인 물 조달자의 반응은 군집의 수요에 맞춰서 물 수집을 조절한다.)

3. 도입과 전개 부분을 통해 파악한 글의 주제를 염두하고 빈칸 내용을 추론한다.

• 빈칸 뒤에서 댄스 플로어에서 물을 넘겨주는 데 걸리는 시간에 따라 물을 조달하는 벌들의 행동이 달라지는 예에 대해 설명하고 있다. 이것은 개별적인 벌들이 댄스 플로어(무도장)에서 정보를 교환하여 그것에 맞게 행동을 바꿈으로써 결국 군집 전체의 노동력을 조절하게 되는 예에 해당하므로, 빈칸에 들어갈 말로 가장 적절한 것은 ① 'allow the colony to regulate its workforce(군집이 군집의 노동력을 조절할 수 있게 하는지)'이다.

2023학년도 수능 34번 ★★★

1. 다음 빈칸에 들어갈 말로 가장 적절한 것은?

We understand that the segregation of our consciousness into present, past, and future is both a fiction and an oddly self-referential framework; your present was part of your mother's future, and your children's past will be in part your present. Nothing is generally wrong with structuring our consciousness of time in this conventional manner, and it often works well enough. In the case of climate change, however, the sharp division of time into past, present, and future has been desperately misleading and has, most importantly, hidden from view the extent of the responsibility of those of us alive now. The narrowing of our consciousness of time smooths the way to divorcing ourselves from responsibility for developments in the past and the future with which our lives are in fact deeply intertwined. In the climate case, it is not that ______________________. It is that the realities are obscured from view by the partitioning of time, and so questions of responsibility toward the past and future do not arise naturally. [3점]

* segregation: 분리 ** intertwine: 뒤얽히게 하다
*** obscure: 흐릿하게 하다

① all our efforts prove to be effective and are thus encouraged
② sufficient scientific evidence has been provided to us
③ future concerns are more urgent than present needs
④ our ancestors maintained a different frame of time
⑤ we face the facts but then deny our responsibility

2022학년도 10월 학평 33번 ★★★

2. 다음 빈칸에 들어갈 말로 가장 적절한 것은?

Magical thinking, intellectual insecurity, and confirmation bias are all powerful barriers to scientific discovery; they blocked the eyes of generations of astronomers before Copernicus. But as twenty-first-century researchers have discovered, these three barriers can all be destroyed with a simple teaching trick: transporting our brain to an environment outside our own. That environment can be a nature preserve many miles from our home, or a computer-simulated Mars, or any other space that our ego doesn't associate directly with our health, social status, and material success. In that environment, our ego will be less inclined to take the failure of its predictions personally. Certainly, our ego may feel a little upset that its guesses about the nature preserve or Mars were wrong, but it was never really that invested in the guesses to begin with. Why should it care too much about things that have no bearing on its own fame or well-being? So, in that happy state of apathy, our ego is less likely to get data manipulative, mentally threatened, or magically minded, leaving the rest of our brain free to ______________________. [3점]

* apathy: 무관심

① do away with irregularity and seek harmony
② justify errors by reorganizing remaining data
③ build barriers to avoid intellectual insecurity
④ abandon failed hypotheses and venture new ones
⑤ manipulate the surroundings and support existing ideas

2022학년도 10월 학평 34번 ★★★

3. 다음 빈칸에 들어갈 말로 가장 적절한 것은?

If you are unconvinced that ____________________, consider the example of the "flying horse." Depictions of galloping horses from prehistoric times up until the mid-1800s typically showed horses' legs splayed while galloping, that is, the front legs reaching far ahead as the hind legs stretched far behind. People just "knew" that's how horses galloped, and that is how they "saw" them galloping. Cavemen *saw* them this way, Aristotle *saw* them this way, and so did Victorian gentry. But all of that ended when, in 1878, Eadweard Muybridge published a set of twelve pictures he had taken of a galloping horse in the space of less than half a second using twelve cameras hooked to wire triggers. Muybridge's photos showed clearly that a horse goes completely airborne in the third step of the gallop with its legs *collected* beneath it, not splayed. It is called the moment of suspension. Now even kids draw horses galloping this way. [3점]

* gallop: 질주(하다) ** splay: 벌리다 *** gentry: 상류층

① our beliefs influence how we interpret facts
② what we see is an illusion of our past memories
③ even photographs can lead to a wrong visual perception
④ there is no standard by which we can judge good or bad
⑤ we adhere to our intuition in spite of irresistible evidence

2023학년도 9월 모평 33번 ★★★

4. 다음 빈칸에 들어갈 말로 가장 적절한 것은?

There was nothing modern about the idea of men making women's clothes — we saw them doing it for centuries in the past. In the old days, however, the client was always primary and her tailor was an obscure craftsman, perhaps talented but perhaps not. She had her own ideas like any patron, there were no fashion plates, and the tailor was simply at her service, perhaps with helpful suggestions about what others were wearing. Beginning in the late nineteenth century, with the hugely successful rise of the artistic male couturier, it was the designer who became celebrated, and the client elevated by his inspired attention. In a climate of admiration for male artists and their female creations, the dress-designer first flourished as the same sort of creator. Instead of the old rule that dressmaking is a craft, ____________________ was invented that had not been there before. [3점]

* obscure: 무명의 ** patron: 후원자
*** couturier: 고급 여성복 디자이너

① a profitable industry driving fast fashion
② a widespread respect for marketing skills
③ a public institution preserving traditional designs
④ a modern connection between dress-design and art
⑤ an efficient system for producing affordable clothing

2023학년도 6월 모평 33번 ★★★

5. 다음 빈칸에 들어갈 말로 가장 적절한 것은?

Manufacturers design their innovation processes around the way they think the process works. The vast majority of manufacturers still think that product development and service development are always done by manufacturers, and that their job is always to find a need and fill it rather than to sometimes find and commercialize an innovation that ____________________. Accordingly, manufacturers have set up market-research departments to explore the needs of users in the target market, product-development groups to think up suitable products to address those needs, and so forth. The needs and prototype solutions of lead users — if encountered at all — are typically rejected as outliers of no interest. Indeed, when lead users' innovations do enter a firm's product line — and they have been shown to be the actual source of many major innovations for many firms — they typically arrive with a lag and by an unusual and unsystematic route. [3점]

* lag: 지연

① lead users tended to overlook
② lead users have already developed
③ lead users encountered in the market
④ other firms frequently put into use
⑤ both users and firms have valued

Day 14

2023학년도 6월 모평 34번 ★★★

6. 다음 빈칸에 들어갈 말로 가장 적절한 것은?

Development can get very complicated and fanciful. A fugue by Johann Sebastian Bach illustrates how far this process could go, when a single melodic line, sometimes just a handful of notes, was all that the composer needed to create a brilliant work containing lots of intricate development within a coherent structure. Ludwig van Beethoven's famous Fifth Symphony provides an exceptional example of how much mileage a classical composer can get out of a few notes and a simple rhythmic tapping. The opening da-da-da-DUM that everyone has heard somewhere or another ____________________ throughout not only the opening movement, but the remaining three movements, like a kind of motto or a connective thread. Just as we don't always see the intricate brushwork that goes into the creation of a painting, we may not always notice how Beethoven keeps finding fresh uses for his motto or how he develops his material into a large, cohesive statement. But a lot of the enjoyment we get from that mighty symphony stems from the inventiveness behind it, the impressive development of musical ideas. [3점]

* intricate: 복잡한 ** coherent: 통일성 있는

① makes the composer's musical ideas contradictory
② appears in an incredible variety of ways
③ provides extensive musical knowledge creatively
④ remains fairly calm within the structure
⑤ becomes deeply associated with one's own enjoyment

2022학년도 수능 33번 ★★★

7. 다음 빈칸에 들어갈 말로 가장 적절한 것은?

Elinor Ostrom found that there are several factors critical to bringing about stable institutional solutions to the problem of the commons. She pointed out, for instance, that the actors affected by the rules for the use and care of resources must have the right to ______________________________. For that reason, the people who monitor and control the behavior of users should also be users and/or have been given a mandate by all users. This is a significant insight, as it shows that prospects are poor for a centrally directed solution to the problem of the commons coming from a state power in comparison with a local solution for which users assume personal responsibility. Ostrom also emphasizes the importance of democratic decision processes and that all users must be given access to local forums for solving problems and conflicts among themselves. Political institutions at central, regional, and local levels must allow users to devise their own regulations and independently ensure observance. [3점]

* commons: 공유지 ** mandate: 위임

① participate in decisions to change the rules
② claim individual ownership of the resources
③ use those resources to maximize their profits
④ demand free access to the communal resources
⑤ request proper distribution based on their merits

2022학년도 수능 34번 ★★★

8. 다음 빈칸에 들어갈 말로 가장 적절한 것은?

Precision and determinacy are a necessary requirement for all meaningful scientific debate, and progress in the sciences is, to a large extent, the ongoing process of achieving ever greater precision. But historical representation puts a premium on a proliferation of representations, hence not on the refinement of one representation but on the production of an ever more varied set of representations. Historical insight is not a matter of a continuous "narrowing down" of previous options, not of an approximation of the truth, but, on the contrary, is an "explosion" of possible points of view. It therefore aims at the unmasking of previous illusions of determinacy and precision by the production of new and alternative representations, rather than at achieving truth by a careful analysis of what was right and wrong in those previous representations. And from this perspective, the development of historical insight may indeed be regarded by the outsider as a process of creating ever more confusion, a continuous questioning of ______________________________, rather than, as in the sciences, an ever greater approximation to the truth. [3점]

* proliferation: 증식

① criteria for evaluating historical representations
② certainty and precision seemingly achieved already
③ possibilities of alternative interpretations of an event
④ coexistence of multiple viewpoints in historical writing
⑤ correctness and reliability of historical evidence collected

2021학년도 수능 33번 ★★★

9. 다음 빈칸에 들어갈 말로 가장 적절한 것은?

Thanks to newly developed neuroimaging technology, we now have access to the specific brain changes that occur during learning. Even though all of our brains contain the same basic structures, our neural networks are as unique as our fingerprints. The latest developmental neuroscience research has shown that the brain is much more malleable throughout life than previously assumed; it develops in response to its own processes, to its immediate and distant "environments," and to its past and current situations. The brain seeks to create meaning through establishing or refining existing neural networks. When we learn a new fact or skill, our neurons communicate to form networks of connected information. Using this knowledge or skill results in structural changes to allow similar future impulses to travel more quickly and efficiently than others. High-activity synaptic connections are stabilized and strengthened, while connections with relatively low use are weakened and eventually pruned. In this way, our brains are ______________________________. [3점]

* malleable: 순응성이 있는 ** prune: 잘라 내다

① sculpted by our own history of experiences
② designed to maintain their initial structures
③ geared toward strengthening recent memories
④ twinned with the development of other organs
⑤ portrayed as the seat of logical and creative thinking

2021학년도 수능 34번 ★★★

10. 다음 빈칸에 들어갈 말로 가장 적절한 것은?

Successful integration of an educational technology is marked by that technology being regarded by users as an unobtrusive facilitator of learning, instruction, or performance. When the focus shifts from the technology being used to the educational purpose that technology serves, then that technology is becoming a comfortable and trusted element, and can be regarded as being successfully integrated. Few people give a second thought to the use of a ball-point pen although the mechanisms involved vary — some use a twist mechanism and some use a push button on top, and there are other variations as well. Personal computers have reached a similar level of familiarity for a great many users, but certainly not for all. New and emerging technologies often introduce both fascination and frustration with users. As long as ______________________________ in promoting learning, instruction, or performance, then one ought not to conclude that the technology has been successfully integrated — at least for that user. [3점]

* unobtrusive: 눈에 띄지 않는

① the user successfully achieves familiarity with the technology
② the user's focus is on the technology itself rather than its use
③ the user continues to employ outdated educational techniques
④ the user involuntarily gets used to the misuse of the technology
⑤ the user's preference for interaction with other users persists

총 문항			문항	맞은 문항					문항
개별 문항	1	2	3	4	5	6	7	8	9	10
채점										

문법 플러스

14. 형용사, 부사

정답 및 해설 078쪽

A 문법의 주요 포인트를 점검해 봅시다.

1 정관사 the가 형용사 앞에 붙으면 형용사가 명사처럼 사용되기도 한다. 「the+형용사」는 일반적으로 복수 보통명사의 의미를 나타내고, 단수 보통명사, 추상명사의 의미를 나타내기도 한다.

▶ Why **[do / does]** the elderly live alone?

2 형용사는 명사를 수식하거나 주어나 목적어의 보어로서 서술적 용법으로 사용된다. 형용사 alike, alive, awake, asleep, ashamed, afraid 등은 서술적 용법으로 사용된다. 형용사 drunken, main, live, mere 등은 한정적 용법으로 사용된다.

▶ They are not family, but they look **[like, alike]**.

3 부사는 형용사, 동사, 다른 부사를 수식한다. 빈도부사는 대개 일반동사 앞에, 조동사와 be동사 사이에 위치한다.

▶ Nonetheless, experimenting on oneself remains **[deep / deeply]** problematic.

4 ① 형용사와 형태가 같은 부사와 ② -ly가 붙은 부사의 의미 차이에 유의한다.

deep(깊게)	deeply(매우)	high(높이)	highly(매우)
dear(비싸게)	dearly(마음으로부터)	late(늦게)	lately(최근에)
free (공짜로)	freely(자유롭게)	near(가까이)	nearly(거의)
hard(열심히)	hardly(좀처럼 ~하지 않는)	pretty(대단히)	prettily(예쁘게)

▶ I was **[high / highly]** pleased and full of expectations about being in a new place.

5 most(대부분의)가 형용사일 때는 '대부분의' 의미이다. most가 대명사로 쓰일 때는 「most of+한정어(the, these, those, 소유격)+복수명사」의 형태로 쓴다. '~의 대부분'의 의미이다. almost(거의)는 부사로 쓰인다. almost 뒤에는 종종 all, every, any 등이 온다.

▶ **[Most / Almost]** people like apples.

6 동사와 부사가 결합된 동사구에서 목적어가 대명사일 경우에는 「동사+대명사+부사」의 어순이 되어야 한다.

▶ I told her to turn down the volume, not to **[turn it up / tun up it]**.

7 「enough+to부정사」 구문에서 enough가 형용사[부사]를 수식하는 경우, 「형용사[부사]+enough+to부정사」 순서로 나온다.

▶ He is not **[old enough / enough old]** to watch that program.

B 다음 괄호 안에서 어법상 올바른 것을 고르시오.

1 The English **[talks / talk]** about the weather a lot.

2 My uncle enjoys eating **[live / alive]** octopus.

3 Fashion is among the simplest and cheapest methods of self-expression: clothes can be **[inexpensively / inexpensive]** purchased while making it easy to convey notions of wealth, intellectual stature, relaxation or environmental consciousness, even if none of these is true.

4 The brother's kite rose **[high / highly]** in the sky.

5 She's **[most / almost]** always punctual for appointments.

6 Do your science homework now. Don't **[put off it / put it off]** until tomorrow.

7 Those tomatoes aren't **[ripe enough / enough ripe]** to eat.

숙어 플러스

14. 수능 필수 숙어 14회

정답 및 해설 079쪽

A 다음 수능 필수 숙어를 읽고, 아는 것은 체크해 봅시다.

□ 01	look over	~을 살펴보다
□ 02	look through	~을 빠르게 훑어보다
□ 03	look up	(정보를) 찾다
□ 04	lose weight	살이 빠지다
□ 05	make a difference	차이를 가져오다, 차별을 두다
□ 06	make friends	~와 친구가 되다
□ 07	make it	해내다, 성공하다, 늦지 않게 도착하다
□ 08	make out	(문서를) 작성하다, ~을 이해하다, 지내다
□ 09	make sure	확실하게 하다
□ 10	make up	(이야기를) 꾸며 내다, ~을 형성하다
□ 11	make up for	(손해 등을) 보상하다, 만회하다
□ 12	make use of	~을 이용하다
□ 13	may well	~하는 것도 당연하다
□ 14	mean to do	~할 작정이다
□ 15	might as well	~하는 편이 낫다
□ 16	more or less	거의, 대략
□ 17	move on	(다음 주제로) 넘어가다
□ 18	much less	더구나 ~은 아니다
□ 19	name after	~의 이름을 따서 이름 짓다
□ 20	needless to say	말할 필요도 없이

B 다음 숙어 표현을 읽고 의미 차이를 비교해 봅시다.

□ 21	carry on	~을 계속하다
□ 22	depend on	~을 의지하다
□ 23	hold on	전화를 끊지 않고 기다리다
□ 24	take on	~을 떠맡다
□ 25	try on	(시험 삼아) 입어보다, 신어보다

C 우리말을 참고하여 빈칸에 알맞은 말을 써 봅시다.

1 저는 서둘러 사전에서 'flattering'이라는 단어를 찾았다.
I rushed to look __________ the word 'flattering' in the dictionary.

2 비행기는 15분 있으면 떠나. 절대 그들은 시간 내에 못 갈 거야.
The flight leaves in fifteen minutes—they'll never __________ it.

3 허비된 시간을 메우기 위해 우리는 서둘렀다.
She hurried on to make up __________ lost time.

4 말할 필요도 없이, 더 싼 것이 난 더 좋아요. 어떻게 생각하세요?
________________ to say, I prefer the cheaper one. How about you?

15 흐름에 무관한 문장 찾기

출제 트렌드

1. 간접 쓰기를 위해서는 글의 전체적인 맥락과 문장 간의 흐름을 파악하여 가상의 글쓰기에 적용할 수 있는 능력이 필요하다. 간접 쓰기 문항 유형에는 흐름에 무관한 문장 찾기, 글의 순서 파악하기, 주어진 문장의 적합한 위치, 문단 요약하기 문제가 있다.
2. 흐름에 무관한 문장 찾기 문제 유형은 '다음 글에서 전체 흐름과 관계 없는 문장'을 고르는 문제이다.
3. 흐름에 무관한 문장을 찾는 문제는 글의 주제와 무관하거나 글의 논지를 흐리는 문장을 찾아 이를 제거함으로써 응집성을 가진 글을 만들어낼 수 있는지 유무를 평가하는 문제이다. 수능에서 매년 1문제가 출제된다.
4. 앞부분에 주제가 드러나는 두괄식의 글이 주로 출제되며, 일관된 글의 흐름이 뚜렷하게 나타난 지문을 사용한다.
5. 최근 수능 7년간, 흐름에 무관한 문장 찾기 문제는 매년 1문항이 출제되었다, 2017학년도 수능(69%), 2018(86%), 2019(72%), 2020(68%), 2021(81%), 2022(74%), 2023(82%)에서 괄호 안의 정답률을 보였다. 7년간 평균 76%의 정답률을 보였다. 난이도는 중 단계이다.

출처			문항 번호	지문 주제	정답률(%)	난이도
대표	2022학년도	06 모평	35번	'수정 확대 가족'의 개념과 성격	83	★★☆
1	2023학년도	수능	35번	의사소통의 수단으로서의 목소리	82	★★☆
2	2022학년도	10 학평	35번	식품 보존 방식	83	★★☆
3	2023학년도	09 모평	35번	재해로부터 빨리 회복하는 식물의 능력	80	★★☆
4	2022학년도	07 학평	35번	서로 다른 가치를 지닌 다양한 형태의 에너지	67	★★☆
5	2023학년도	06 모평	35번	정보 수집과 동물의 의사 결정	82	★★☆
6	2022학년도	04 학평	35번	초기 근대 유럽에서 철학과 과학의 특징	62	★★☆
7	2022학년도	수능	35번	회사 간의 협력 형태의 변화	74	★★☆
8	2021학년도	10 학평	35번	실효성이 없는 국제 인권 조약	56	★★☆
9	2021학년도	수능	35번	조직 내에서 유머의 기능	81	★★☆
10	2020학년도	수능	35번	상반된 격언들의 모순	68	★★☆

1등급 꿀팁

1. 동일한 소재를 다루고 있으나 관점이 다른 문장을 무관한 문장으로 출제하는 경우가 많다.
2. 글의 흐름과 무관한 문장 찾기는 글의 초반부에 주목해야 한다. 첫 문장을 통해 글의 기본 흐름을 파악하고 뒤에 나오는 문장들이 같은 흐름으로 이어지고 있는지 확인한다.
3. 비교하는 표현이나, 연결어, 지시어 등의 흐름이 자연스러운지 확인한다.
4. 다양한 지문에서 글의 흐름, 요지, 주제 등을 파악하는 연습을 한다.

흐름에 무관한 문장 찾기

제한 시간 : 20분 | 정답 및 해설 079쪽

대표 기출

2022학년도 6월 모평 35번

35. 다음 글에서 전체 흐름과 관계 없는 문장은?

Kinship ties continue to be important today. In modern societies such as the United States people frequently have family get-togethers, they telephone their relatives regularly, and they provide their kin with a wide variety of services. ① Eugene Litwak has referred to this pattern of behaviour as the 'modified extended family'. ② It is an extended family structure because multigenerational ties are maintained, but it is modified because it does not usually rest on co-residence between the generations and most extended families do not act as corporate groups. ③ Although modified extended family members often live close by, the modified extended family does not require geographical proximity and ties are maintained even when kin are separated by considerable distances. ④ The oldest member of the family makes the decisions on important issues, no matter how far away family members live from each other. ⑤ In contrast to the traditional extended family where kin always live in close proximity, the members of modified extended families may freely move away from kin to seek opportunities for occupational advancement.

* kin: 친족 ** proximity: 근접

문제 풀이

1. 반복적인 어구 또는 특정 개념과 관련된 어구를 통해 글의 요지를 추측한다.

① 특정 개념 : modified extended families(수정 확대 가족)

② 글의 요지: In contrast to the traditional extended family where kin always live in close proximity, the members of modified extended families may freely move away from kin to seek opportunities for occupational advancement. (친족이 언제나 아주 가까이 사는 전통적인 확대 가족과는 대조적으로, 수정 확대 가족의 구성원들은 친족에게서 자유로이 멀리 이주해가서 직업상의 발전을 위한 기회를 추구할 수도 있다.)

2. 글의 요지를 고려하면서 흐름에서 벗어난 문장을 찾는다.

선지 ④ The oldest member of the family makes the decisions on important issues, no matter how far away family members live from each other. (가족 구성원들이 서로 아무리 멀리 떨어져 살지라도, 중요한 문제에 관해서는 그 가족의 최고 연장자가 결정을 내린다.)가 흐름에서 벗어나 보인다.

3. 글의 전개 방식을 확인하면서 ④가 부적절함을 확인한다.

- 이 글은 수정 확대 가족의 개념(다세대의 유대 관계가 유지되지만 세대 간 공동 거주에 기초를 두지 않음)과 성격(구성원이 상당히 멀리 떨어져 있어도 유지되므로, 구성원이 직업상의 발전 기회를 추구할 수 있음)을 설명하고 있는데, ④번에서는 가족의 의사결정 구조를 기술하고 있으므로, 본문의 흐름에서 벗어난다.

2023학년도 수능 35번 ★★☆

1. 다음 글에서 전체 흐름과 관계 없는 문장은?

Actors, singers, politicians and countless others recognise the power of the human voice as a means of communication beyond the simple decoding of the words that are used. Learning to control your voice and use it for different purposes is, therefore, one of the most important skills to develop as an early career teacher. ① The more confidently you give instructions, the higher the chance of a positive class response. ② There are times when being able to project your voice loudly will be very useful when working in school, and knowing that you can cut through a noisy classroom, dinner hall or playground is a great skill to have. ③ In order to address serious noise issues in school, students, parents and teachers should search for a solution together. ④ However, I would always advise that you use your loudest voice incredibly sparingly and avoid shouting as much as possible. ⑤ A quiet, authoritative and measured tone has so much more impact than slightly panicked shouting.

2022학년도 10월 학평 35번 ★★☆

2. 다음 글에서 전체 흐름과 관계 없는 문장은?

Except for grains and sugars, most foods humans eat are perishable. They deteriorate in palatability, spoil, or become unhealthy when stored for long periods. ① Surplus animal and crop harvests, however, can be saved for future use if appropriate methods of preservation are used. ② The major ways of preserving foods are canning, freezing, drying, salting, and smoking. ③ With all methods the aim is to kill or restrict the growth of harmful microbes or their toxins and to slow or inactivate enzymes that cause undesirable changes in food palatability. ④ Palatability is not static: it is always changing, based on the state of the individual, especially in regard to the time of food consumption. ⑤ For further protection during long periods of storage, preserved food is placed either in sterile metal cans or glass jars or frozen in airtight paper or plastic containers.

* palatability: (좋은) 맛 ** enzyme: 효소 *** sterile: 멸균한

2023년도 9월 모평 35번 ★★☆

3. 다음 글에서 전체 흐름과 관계 없는 문장은?

Because plants tend to recover from disasters more quickly than animals, they are essential to the revitalization of damaged environments. Why do plants have this preferential ability to recover from disaster? It is largely because, unlike animals, they can generate new organs and tissues throughout their life cycle. ① This ability is due to the activity of plant meristems — regions of undifferentiated tissue in roots and shoots that can, in response to specific cues, differentiate into new tissues and organs. ② If meristems are not damaged during disasters, plants can recover and ultimately transform the destroyed or barren environment. ③ You can see this phenomenon on a smaller scale when a tree struck by lightning forms new branches that grow from the old scar. ④ In the form of forests and grasslands, plants regulate the cycling of water and adjust the chemical composition of the atmosphere. ⑤ In addition to regeneration or resprouting of plants, disturbed areas can also recover through reseeding.

* revitalization: 소생

2022학년도 7월 학평 35번 ★★☆

4. 다음 글에서 전체 흐름과 관계 없는 문장은?

Some forms of energy are more versatile in their usefulness than others. For example, we can use electricity for a myriad of applications, whereas the heat from burning coal is currently used mostly for stationary applications like generating power. ① When we turn the heat from burning coal into electricity, a substantial amount of energy is lost due to the inefficiency of the process. ② But we are willing to accept that loss because coal is relatively cheap, and it would be difficult and inconvenient to use burning coal *directly* to power lights, computers, and refrigerators. ③ Finding an economical way to use coal to produce carbon fibers will help revitalize rural communities suffering from the decline in coal production. ④ In effect, we put a differing value on different forms of energy, with electricity at the top of the value ladder, liquid and gaseous fuels in the middle, and coal or firewood at the bottom. ⑤ Solar and wind technologies have an advantage in that they produce high-value electricity directly.

* versatile: 다용도의

2023학년도 6월 모평 35번 ★★☆

5. 다음 글에서 전체 흐름과 관계 없는 문장은?

The animal in a conflict between attacking a rival and fleeing may initially not have sufficient information to enable it to make a decision straight away. ① If the rival is likely to win the fight, then the optimal decision would be to give up immediately and not risk getting injured. ② But if the rival is weak and easily defeatable, then there could be considerable benefit in going ahead and obtaining the territory, females, food or whatever is at stake. ③ Animals under normal circumstances maintain a very constant body weight and they eat and drink enough for their needs at regular intervals. ④ By taking a little extra time to collect information about the opponent, the animal is more likely to reach a decision that maximizes its chances of winning than if it takes a decision without such information. ⑤ Many signals are now seen as having this information gathering or 'assessment' function, directly contributing to the mechanism of the decision-making process by supplying vital information about the likely outcomes of the various options.

2022학년도 4월 학평 35번 ★★☆

6. 다음 글에서 전체 흐름과 관계 없는 문장은?

What characterizes philosophy and science in early modern Europe and marks a break from earlier traditions is the concern to tailor theories to evidence rather than authority or tradition. ① Galileo Galilei, Francis Bacon, René Descartes, and others formulated explanations of the heavens, of the natural world around them, and of human nature and society not by appealing to the proclamations of earlier thinkers. ② Nor were religious principles and ecclesiastic dogma their guiding lights. ③ Rather, they took their lead from reason — what some thinkers called "the light of nature" — and experience. ④ The fierce debates on the superiority of reason or experience continued, but all serious thinkers ultimately abandoned experience in the development of modern science and philosophy. ⑤ Whether they proceeded according to the logic of deduction or through the analysis of empirical data, the modern scientific method they developed consists in testing theories according to reason and in light of the available evidence.

* ecclesiastic dogma: 교회의 교리 ** deduction: 연역

Day 15

2022학년도 수능 35번 ★★☆

7. 다음 글에서 전체 흐름과 관계 없는 문장은?

Since their introduction, information systems have substantially changed the way business is conducted. ① This is particularly true for business in the shape and form of cooperation between firms that involves an integration of value chains across multiple units. ② The resulting networks do not only cover the business units of a single firm but typically also include multiple units from different firms. ③ As a consequence, firms do not only need to consider their internal organization in order to ensure sustainable business performance; they also need to take into account the entire ecosystem of units surrounding them. ④ Many major companies are fundamentally changing their business models by focusing on profitable units and cutting off less profitable ones. ⑤ In order to allow these different units to cooperate successfully, the existence of a common platform is crucial.

2021학년도 10월 학평 35번 ★★☆

8. 다음 글에서 전체 흐름과 관계 없는 문장은?

A group of academics, mainly political scientists, assumed that human rights treaties did *not* have any effect on the behavior of countries. ① Indeed, these academics, who typically called themselves "realists," assumed that international law generally did not affect the behavior of states. ② They saw the international arena as a security competition among different states, a zero-sum game in which one state's gain was another state's loss. ③ International lawyers and human rights advocates assumed that human rights treaties caused countries to improve their treatment of their citizens. ④ In such conditions, states could gain little by cooperating with each other — except in temporary military alliances or security agreements that could fall apart at a moment's notice. ⑤ International law could play a minimal role or none at all, and was perhaps just an illusion, a sophisticated kind of propaganda — a set of rules that would be swept away whenever the balance of power changed.

2021학년도 수능 35번 ★★☆

9. 다음 글에서 전체 흐름과 관계 없는 문장은?

Workers are united by laughing at shared events, even ones that may initially spark anger or conflict. Humor reframes potentially divisive events into merely "laughable" ones which are put in perspective as subservient to unifying values held by organization members. Repeatedly recounting humorous incidents reinforces unity based on key organizational values. ① One team told repeated stories about a dumpster fire, something that does not seem funny on its face, but the reactions of workers motivated to preserve safety sparked laughter as the stories were shared multiple times by multiple parties in the workplace. ② Shared events that cause laughter can indicate a sense of belonging since "you had to be there" to see the humor in them, and non-members were not and do not. ③ Since humor can easily capture people's attention, commercials tend to contain humorous elements, such as funny faces and gestures. ④ Instances of humor serve to enact bonds among organization members. ⑤ Understanding the humor may even be required as an informal badge of membership in the organization.

* subservient: 도움이 되는

2020학년도 수능 35번 ★★☆

10. 다음 글에서 전체 흐름과 관계 없는 문장은?

Although commonsense knowledge may have merit, it also has weaknesses, not the least of which is that it often contradicts itself. For example, we hear that people who are similar will like one another ("Birds of a feather flock together") but also that persons who are dissimilar will like each other ("Opposites attract"). ① We are told that groups are wiser and smarter than individuals ("Two heads are better than one") but also that group work inevitably produces poor results ("Too many cooks spoil the broth"). ② Each of these contradictory statements may hold true under particular conditions, but without a clear statement of when they apply and when they do not, aphorisms provide little insight into relations among people. ③ That is why we heavily depend on aphorisms whenever we face difficulties and challenges in the long journey of our lives. ④ They provide even less guidance in situations where we must make decisions. ⑤ For example, when facing a choice that entails risk, which guideline should we use — "Nothing ventured, nothing gained" or "Better safe than sorry"?

* aphorism: 격언, 경구(警句) ** entail: 수반하다

총 문항				문항	맞은 문항				문항
개별 문항	1	2	3	4	5	6	7	8	9	10
채점										

문법 플러스

15. 비교 구문

정답 및 해설 084쪽

A 문법의 주요 포인트를 점검해 봅시다.

1 원급 비교는 「as+형용사/부사+as」의 형태로, 둘 사이에 비교의 정도가 같음을 나타낸다. 부정은 not as ~as로 표현하고 몇 가지 관용 표현을 익히는 것이 좋다.

not so much A as B	A라기 보다는 B다	as ~ as possible	가능한 한 ~하게

▶ Sam is as **[diligent / diligently]** as his brother.

2 비교급 비교는 「비교급+than」의 형태로, 비교되는 대상의 우열을 나타낸다. 비교급을 강조하는 경우 비교급 앞에 much, even, still, far, a lot 등을 쓴다. 몇 가지 관용 표현을 익혀야 한다.

비교급 and 비교급	점점 더 ~한	the 비교급... the 비교급 ~	…하면 할수록 더 ~하다

▶ Sally is **[very / much]** wiser than her friends.

3 비교급은 정관사 the를 붙이지 않지만, of the two가 나오면 비교급에 정관사 the를 붙인다.

▶ Peter is **[taller / the taller]** of the two.

4 최상급은 「the+최상급」 형태로 셋 이상 중에서 하나가 최고인 것을 나타낸다. 몇 가지 주의할 표현이 있다.

「one of the 최상급+ 복수명사」	가장 ~중의 하나
「the+서수+최상급」	…번째로 ~한
비교급 than any other 단수명사	다른 어떤 ~보다도 더 …하게
비교급 than all the other 복수명사	다른 모든 ~보다도 더 …하게
「the 최상급+주어+have[has] ever p.p.」	지금껏 ~한 것들 중 가장 ~하게
「as ~ as any+단수명사」	다른 어떤 …못지 않게 ~한

▶ He is one of the best **[novelist / novelists]** in Korea.

5 최상급은 정관사 the를 붙이지만, 동일 대상 내에서나 부사의 최상급은 정관사 the를 붙이지 않는다.

▶ Since you know her **[the best / best]**, you should ask her.

6 「부정주어+원급 / 비교급」으로 최상급의 의미를 나타낼 수 있다.

부정주어 ~ as 원급 as	어떤 ~도 …만큼 ~하지 않다
부정주어 ~ 비교급 than	어떤 ~도 …보다 ~하지 않다

▶ Nothing is more precious **[as / than]** health.

7 기타 주의해야 할 비교 구문 관용 표현이 있다.

no more than	단지(= only)	not more than	기껏해야(= at most)
no less than	~만큼(= as much as)	not less than	적어도(= at least)
▶ A is no more than B C is D A가 B가 아닌 것은 C가 D가 아닌 것과 같다			

▶ A child must sleep not **[more / less]** than eight hours.

B 다음 괄호 안에서 어법상 올바른 것을 고르시오.

1 Sally is not **[more / as]** beautiful as her sister.

2 Sarah is **[prettier / pretty]** than Jane.

3 Of the two pens this one is **[longer / the longer]**.

4 Jack is as brave as any **[boy / boys]** in his class.

5 This lake is **[the deepest / deepest]** here.

6 To me, nothing in the world is funnier **[than / as]** fishing.

7 Tom is not **[more / less]** than(= at most) an average salesman.

숙어 플러스

15. 수능 필수 숙어 15회

정답 및 해설 084쪽

A 다음 수능 필수 숙어를 읽고, 아는 것은 체크해 봅시다.

□ 01	no more than	단지 ~에 지나지 않는
□ 02	not entirely	전적으로 ~인 것은 아닌
□ 03	not to mention	~은 말할 것도 없고
□ 04	now and then	때때로, 가끔
□ 05	of all ages	모든 연령의, 모든 시대의
□ 06	of itself	저절로
□ 07	of use	유용한
□ 08	on (the) air	방송 중인
□ 09	on behalf of	~을 대표하여
□ 10	on earth	도대체
□ 11	on foot	도보로
□ 12	on leave	휴가로, 휴가를 얻어
□ 13	on one's own	혼자 힘으로, 혼자서
□ 14	on the contrary	~와는 반대로
□ 15	on the other hand	한편으로는, 반면에
□ 16	on the way	~가는 중인, ~하는 도중에
□ 17	once upon a time	옛날에
□ 18	one another	서로
□ 19	one by one	하나씩
□ 20	only a few	소수의

B 다음 숙어 표현을 읽고 의미 차이를 비교해 봅시다.

□ 21	get over	극복하다
□ 22	hand over	양도하다
□ 23	look over	~너머로 보다, 자세히 살피다
□ 24	run over	(차가) 치다
□ 25	take over	(책임 등을) 떠맡다, 인계받다

C 우리말을 참고하여 빈칸에 알맞은 말을 써 봅시다.

1 면접은 단지 당신 자신을 표현하는 것에 불과합니다.
Interviewing is ____________________ more than expressing yourself.

2 물질적 부유함이 본질적으로 그리고 그 자체로서 반드시 의미를 만들어 내는 것은 아니다.
Material wealth in and ____________ itself does not necessarily generate meaning.

3 반대로, 몇몇의 스타급 선수들은 그들의 의견에 동의하지 않는다.
On the ________________, some star players disagree with them.

4 반면에, 참된 감상자는 견문이 넓고 감상할 줄 안다.
True observers, on the other ______________, are informed and appreciative.

16 문단 내 글의 순서 파악

출제 트렌드

1. 글의 순서 파악 문제 유형은 '주어진 글 다음에 이어질 글의 순서로 가장 적절한 것'을 고르는 문제이다.
2. 주어진 글을 포함한 네 부분의 글을 논리적 흐름 또는 시간적 흐름에 맞게 바른 순서로 배열할 수 있는지 측정한다.
3. 최근 수능에서 2문항이 출제되고 있으며 난이도가 높은 편이다. 출제되는 2문항 중에서 1문항은 연결어로 힌트를 제시하는 평이한 문항이 출제되고, 다른 1문항은 3점 문항으로 지문도 길고 고난이도 문항이다.
4. 글의 응집성과 논리적인 흐름을 파악하는 능력을 평가한다.
5. 최근 수능 7년간, 문단 내 글의 순서 파악 문제는 매년 2문항이 출제되었다. 36, 37번 문항으로 출제되었는데, 37번 문항이 난이도가 더 높다. 2017학년도 수능(72/54%), 2018(75/41%), 2019(59/36%), 2020(62/52%), 2021(76/49%), 2022(71/67%), 2023(60/33%)에서 괄호 안의 정답률을 보였다. 7년간 평균 57.6%의 정답률을 보였다. 난이도는 상 단계이다. 36번과 37번 문항 비교 시 36번이 5년간 평균 67.9%, 37번이 47.4% 정답률을 보였다.

	출처		문항 번호	지문 주제	정답률(%)	난이도
대표	2022학년도	06 모평	36번	공간 기준의 상대적 크기	30	★★★
1	2023학년도	수능	36번	적응적 가소성	60	★★☆
2	2023학년도	수능	37번	승소 시 보수 약정	33	★★★
3	2022학년도	10 학평	37번	진화적 조정을 촉발한 직립 보행	43	★★★
4	2023학년도	09 모평	36번	운하 건설에서 자연 수역의 수위 차이 보완 방법	69	★★☆
5	2022학년도	07 학평	37번	디지털 세계의 잘못된 지시 전략	47	★★★
6	2023학년도	06 모평	37번	매몰 비용 오류의 장단점	47	★★★
7	2022학년도	수능	36번	가격 인상의 결과	71	★★☆
8	2022학년도	수능	37번	허구의 세계 vs. 현실의 세계	67	★★☆
9	2021학년도	수능	36번	정치적 의도가 있는 전쟁의 속성	76	★★☆
10	2021학년도	수능	37번	에너지 효율 투자에서 비용 효율	49	★★★

1등급 꿀팁

1. 주어진 글 바로 다음에 이어질 첫 문장을 찾는 것이 매우 중요하다.
2. 연결사는 문장 간의 논리적 관계를 나타내므로 연결사를 단서로 문장의 순서를 정한다.
3. 대명사와 지시어는 앞에서 언급된 대상을 지칭하므로, 대명사와 지시어가 가리키는 말을 찾는다.
4. 정관사 the는 글의 순서를 정하는 중요한 단서가 된다.
5. 문장과 문장 간의 연결고리 역할을 하는 표현을 익힌다.

인칭대명사	성과 수가 일치하는 명사 뒤에 위치한다.
this [these], that[those], it, such	명사가 언급된 명사 뒤에 위치한다.
others, the others	some과 상관적으로 쓰인 경우 some 뒤에 나온다.
for the reason	앞에 나온 원인들 뒤에 결론을 이끌 때 쓴다.

Day 16

문단 내 글의 순서 파악

제한 시간 : 15분 | 정답 및 해설 085쪽

대표 기출

2022학년도 6월 모평 36번

주어진 글 다음에 이어질 글의 순서로 가장 적절한 것은?

36.

> Spatial reference points are larger than themselves. This isn't really a paradox: landmarks are themselves, but they also define neighborhoods around themselves.

(A) In a paradigm that has been repeated on many campuses, researchers first collect a list of campus landmarks from students. Then they ask another group of students to estimate the distances between pairs of locations, some to landmarks, some to ordinary buildings on campus.

(B) This asymmetry of distance estimates violates the most elementary principles of Euclidean distance, that the distance from A to B must be the same as the distance from B to A. Judgments of distance, then, are not necessarily coherent.

(C) The remarkable finding is that distances from an ordinary location to a landmark are judged shorter than distances from a landmark to an ordinary location. So, people would judge the distance from Pierre's house to the Eiffel Tower to be shorter than the distance from the Eiffel Tower to Pierre's house. Like black holes, landmarks seem to pull ordinary locations toward themselves, but ordinary places do not.

* asymmetry: 비대칭

① (A) − (C) − (B)　② (B) − (A) − (C)
③ (B) − (C) − (A)　④ (C) − (A) − (B)
⑤ (C) − (B) − (A)

문제 풀이

1. 주어진 문장을 통해 글의 소재 및 핵심 어구와 전개 방향을 파악한다.

① 주어진 문장: Spatial reference points are larger than themselves. This isn't really a paradox: landmarks are themselves, but they also define neighborhoods around themselves. (공간 기준점(공간적으로 기준이 되는 장소)은 자기 자신보다 더 크다. 이것은 그다지 역설적이지 않은데, 랜드마크(주요 지형지물)는 그 자체이기도 하지만, 또한 자기 자신 주변 지역을 (자신의 범위로) 규정하기도 한다.)

② 핵심 어구: spatial reference points(공간 기준점), landmark(랜드마크), distance(거리)

2. 주어진 문장으로부터 논리적 전개를 파악한다. 파악할 때 연결어구와 지시어를 활용한다.

주어진 문장이 공간 기준점(랜드마크)의 상대적 크기에 대해 설명하고 있다.

(A) 캠퍼스에서 공간 기준점 실험을 하게 되었다. 연구원들이 학생들로부터 캠퍼스 랜드마크 목록을 수집한 후, 연구원들이 다른 학생 집단에게 쌍으로 이루어진 두 장소 사이의 거리가 얼마인지 추정하라고 요청한다.

(C) 실험 결과 평범한 장소에서 랜드마크까지의 거리가 랜드마크에서 평범한 장소까지의 거리보다 더 짧다고 추정되었다.

(B) 이 실험적 의미는 거리에 관한 추정은 반드시 일관성이 있는 것은 아니라는 것이다.

• 그러므로 이 글의 문단 순서는 ① '(A) - (C) - (B)'이다.

2023학년도 수능 36번 ★★☆

1. 주어진 글 다음에 이어질 글의 순서로 가장 적절한 것은?

> A fascinating species of water flea exhibits a kind of flexibility that evolutionary biologists call *adaptive plasticity*.

(A) That's a clever trick, because producing spines and a helmet is costly, in terms of energy, and conserving energy is essential for an organism's ability to survive and reproduce. The water flea only expends the energy needed to produce spines and a helmet when it needs to.

(B) If the baby water flea is developing into an adult in water that includes the chemical signatures of creatures that prey on water fleas, it develops a helmet and spines to defend itself against predators. If the water around it doesn't include the chemical signatures of predators, the water flea doesn't develop these protective devices.

(C) So it may well be that this plasticity is an adaptation: a trait that came to exist in a species because it contributed to reproductive fitness. There are many cases, across many species, of adaptive plasticity. Plasticity is conducive to fitness if there is sufficient variation in the environment.

* spine: 가시 ** conducive: 도움되는

① (A) − (C) − (B)　② (B) − (A) − (C)
③ (B) − (C) − (A)　④ (C) − (A) − (B)
⑤ (C) − (B) − (A)

2023학년도 수능 37번 ★★★

2. 주어진 글 다음에 이어질 글의 순서로 가장 적절한 것은?

> The most commonly known form of results-based pricing is a practice called *contingency pricing*, used by lawyers.

(A) Therefore, only an outcome in the client's favor is compensated. From the client's point of view, the pricing makes sense in part because most clients in these cases are unfamiliar with and possibly intimidated by law firms. Their biggest fears are high fees for a case that may take years to settle.

(B) By using contingency pricing, clients are ensured that they pay no fees until they receive a settlement. In these and other instances of contingency pricing, the economic value of the service is hard to determine before the service, and providers develop a price that allows them to share the risks and rewards of delivering value to the buyer.

(C) Contingency pricing is the major way that personal injury and certain consumer cases are billed. In this approach, lawyers do not receive fees or payment until the case is settled, when they are paid a percentage of the money that the client receives. [3점]

* intimidate: 위협하다

① (A) − (C) − (B)　② (B) − (A) − (C)
③ (B) − (C) − (A)　④ (C) − (A) − (B)
⑤ (C) − (B) − (A)

2022학년도 10월 학평 37번 ★★★

3. 주어진 글 다음에 이어질 글의 순서로 가장 적절한 것은?

> Bipedalism, upright walking, started a chain of enormous evolutionary adjustments. It liberated hominin arms for carrying weapons and for taking food to group sites instead of consuming it on the spot. But bipedalism was necessary to trigger hand dexterity and tool use.

(A) This creates the ability to use each digit independently in the complex manipulations required for tool use. But without bipedalism it would be impossible to use the trunk for leverage in accelerating the hand during toolmaking and tool use.

(B) Hashimoto and co-workers concluded that adaptations underlying tool use evolved independently of those required for human bipedalism because in both humans and monkeys, each finger is represented separately in the primary sensorimotor cortex, just as the fingers are physically separated in the hand.

(C) Bipedalism also freed the mouth and teeth to develop a more complex call system as the prerequisite of language. These developments required larger brains whose energy cost eventually reached three times the level for chimpanzees, accounting for up to one-sixth of the total basal metabolic rate. [3점]

* hominin: 호미닌(인간의 조상으로 분류되는 종족)
** dexterity: (손)재주 *** sensorimotor cortex: 감각 운동 피질

① (A) – (C) – (B) ② (B) – (A) – (C)
③ (B) – (C) – (A) ④ (C) – (A) – (B)
⑤ (C) – (B) – (A)

2023학년도 9월 모평 36번 ★★☆

4. 주어진 글 다음에 이어질 글의 순서로 가장 적절한 것은?

> When two natural bodies of water stand at different levels, building a canal between them presents a complicated engineering problem.

(A) Then the upper gates open and the ship passes through. For downstream passage, the process works the opposite way. The ship enters the lock from the upper level, and water is pumped from the lock until the ship is in line with the lower level.

(B) When a vessel is going upstream, the upper gates stay closed as the ship enters the lock at the lower water level. The downstream gates are then closed and more water is pumped into the basin. The rising water lifts the vessel to the level of the upper body of water.

(C) To make up for the difference in level, engineers build one or more water "steps," called locks, that carry ships or boats up or down between the two levels. A lock is an artificial water basin. It has a long rectangular shape with concrete walls and a pair of gates at each end.

* rectangular: 직사각형의

① (A) – (C) – (B) ② (B) – (A) – (C)
③ (B) – (C) – (A) ④ (C) – (A) – (B)
⑤ (C) – (B) – (A)

2022학년도 7월 학평 37번 ★★★

5. 주어진 글 다음에 이어질 글의 순서로 가장 적절한 것은?

> One common strategy and use of passive misdirection in the digital world comes through the use of repetition.

(A) This action is repeated over and over to navigate their web browsers to the desired web page or action until it becomes an almost immediate, reflexive action. Malicious online actors take advantage of this behavior to distract the user from carefully examining the details of the web page that might tip off the user that there is something amiss about the website.

(B) The website is designed to focus the user's attention on the action the malicious actor wants them to take (e.g., click a link) and to draw their attention away from any details that might suggest to the user that the website is not what it appears to be on the surface.

(C) This digital misdirection strategy relies on the fact that online users utilizing web browsers to visit websites have quickly learned that the most basic ubiquitous navigational action is to click on a link or button presented to them on a website.

① (A) – (C) – (B) ② (B) – (A) – (C)
③ (B) – (C) – (A) ④ (C) – (A) – (B)
⑤ (C) – (B) – (A)

2023학년도 6월 모평 37번 ★★☆

6. 주어진 글 다음에 이어질 글의 순서로 가장 적절한 것은?

> In economics, there is a principle known as the *sunk cost fallacy*. The idea is that when you are invested and have ownership in something, you overvalue that thing.

(A) Sometimes, the smartest thing a person can do is quit. Although this is true, it has also become a tired and played-out argument. Sunk cost doesn't always have to be a bad thing.

(B) This leads people to continue on paths or pursuits that should clearly be abandoned. For example, people often remain in terrible relationships simply because they've invested a great deal of themselves into them. Or someone may continue pouring money into a business that is clearly a bad idea in the market.

(C) Actually, you can leverage this human tendency to your benefit. Like someone invests a great deal of money in a personal trainer to ensure they follow through on their commitment, you, too, can invest a great deal up front to ensure you stay on the path you want to be on. [3점]

* leverage: 이용하다

① (A) – (C) – (B) ② (B) – (A) – (C)
③ (B) – (C) – (A) ④ (C) – (A) – (B)
⑤ (C) – (B) – (A)

Day 16

2022학년도 수능 36번 ★★☆

7. 주어진 글 다음에 이어질 글의 순서로 가장 적절한 것은?

According to the market response model, it is increasing prices that drive providers to search for new sources, innovators to substitute, consumers to conserve, and alternatives to emerge.

(A) Many examples of such "green taxes" exist. Facing landfill costs, labor expenses, and related costs in the provision of garbage disposal, for example, some cities have required households to dispose of all waste in special trash bags, purchased by consumers themselves, and often costing a dollar or more each.

(B) Taxing certain goods or services, and so increasing prices, should result in either decreased use of these resources or creative innovation of new sources or options. The money raised through the tax can be used directly by the government either to supply services or to search for alternatives.

(C) The results have been greatly increased recycling and more careful attention by consumers to packaging and waste. By internalizing the costs of trash to consumers, there has been an observed decrease in the flow of garbage from households.

① (A) − (C) − (B)
② (B) − (A) − (C)
③ (B) − (C) − (A)
④ (C) − (A) − (B)
⑤ (C) − (B) − (A)

2022학년도 수능 37번 ★★☆

8. 주어진 글 다음에 이어질 글의 순서로 가장 적절한 것은?

In spite of the likeness between the fictional and real world, the fictional world deviates from the real one in one important respect.

(A) The author has selected the content according to his own worldview and his own conception of relevance, in an attempt to be neutral and objective or convey a subjective view on the world. Whatever the motives, the author's subjective conception of the world stands between the reader and the original, untouched world on which the story is based.

(B) Because of the inner qualities with which the individual is endowed through heritage and environment, the mind functions as a filter; every outside impression that passes through it is filtered and interpreted. However, the world the reader encounters in literature is already processed and filtered by another consciousness.

(C) The existing world faced by the individual is in principle an infinite chaos of events and details before it is organized by a human mind. This chaos only gets processed and modified when perceived by a human mind. [3점]

* deviate: 벗어나다 ** endow: 부여하다 *** heritage: 유산

① (A) − (C) − (B)
② (B) − (A) − (C)
③ (B) − (C) − (A)
④ (C) − (A) − (B)
⑤ (C) − (B) − (A)

2021학년도 수능 36번 ★★☆

9. 주어진 글 다음에 이어질 글의 순서로 가장 적절한 것은?

The objective of battle, to "throw" the enemy and to make him defenseless, may temporarily blind commanders and even strategists to the larger purpose of war. War is never an isolated act, nor is it ever only one decision.

(A) To be political, a political entity or a representative of a political entity, whatever its constitutional form, has to have an intention, a will. That intention has to be clearly expressed.

(B) In the real world, war's larger purpose is always a political purpose. It transcends the use of force. This insight was famously captured by Clausewitz's most famous phrase, "War is a mere continuation of politics by other means."

(C) And one side's will has to be transmitted to the enemy at some point during the confrontation (it does not have to be publicly communicated). A violent act and its larger political intention must also be attributed to one side at some point during the confrontation. History does not know of acts of war without eventual attribution.

* entity: 실체 ** transcend: 초월하다

① (A) − (C) − (B)
② (B) − (A) − (C)
③ (B) − (C) − (A)
④ (C) − (A) − (B)
⑤ (C) − (B) − (A)

2021학년도 수능 37번 ★★★

10. 주어진 글 다음에 이어질 글의 순서로 가장 적절한 것은?

Experts have identified a large number of measures that promote energy efficiency. Unfortunately many of them are not cost effective. This is a fundamental requirement for energy efficiency investment from an economic perspective.

(A) And this has direct repercussions at the individual level: households can reduce the cost of electricity and gas bills, and improve their health and comfort, while companies can increase their competitiveness and their productivity. Finally, the market for energy efficiency could contribute to the economy through job and firms creation.

(B) There are significant externalities to take into account and there are also macroeconomic effects. For instance, at the aggregate level, improving the level of national energy efficiency has positive effects on macroeconomic issues such as energy dependence, climate change, health, national competitiveness and reducing fuel poverty.

(C) However, the calculation of such cost effectiveness is not easy: it is not simply a case of looking at private costs and comparing them to the reductions achieved. [3점]

* repercussion: 반향, 영향 ** aggregate: 집합의

① (A) − (C) − (B)
② (B) − (A) − (C)
③ (B) − (C) − (A)
④ (C) − (A) − (B)
⑤ (C) − (B) − (A)

총 문항	문항				맞은 문항					문항
개별 문항	1	2	3	4	5	6	7	8	9	10
채점										

문법 플러스

16. 관계부사

정답 및 해설 090쪽

A 문법의 주요 포인트를 점검해 봅시다.

1 관계부사는 문장 내에서 「접속사+부사」의 역할을 한다.

▶ After getting married we bought a flat, where we lived for the next 10 years.

= After getting married we bought a flat, and we lived for the next 10 years **[there / then]**.

2 관계부사는 선행사가 시간이면 when, 장소이면 where, 이유이면 why, 방법이면 how를 사용한다. 관계부사 이하는 완전한 문장이 나온다.

때	장소	이유, 원인	방법
when / that	where / that	why / that	how / that
= in[at/on] which	= in[at/on] which	= for which	= in which

▶ There will be a time **[when / where]** you'll find true love.

3 관계부사 how는 선행사(the way)를 쓰든지, 관계부사를 쓰든지 하나만 써야 한다. 단, how를 in which로 바꾼 경우 the way in which처럼 써도 된다.

▶ I don't like **[the way / the way how]** he looks at me.

4 관계부사 when과 where는 계속적 용법으로 사용될 수 있으며, 이 경우 생략할 수 없다.

▶ They finally reached the mountaintop, **[when / where]** they could see nothing but clouds all around.

5 관계부사는 「전치사+관계대명사」로 바꾸어 쓸 수 있다.

▶ That's a vending machine **[from / for]** which you can get prescription drugs.

6 관계부사 when, where, why, how 대신 관계부사 that을 사용할 수 있으며, 생략할 수도 있다.

▶ They've come to the time **[that / where]** they have to make a decision.

7 관계부사 -ever를 붙이면 복합관계부사가 된다. 복합관계부사절은 주로 양보의 부사절로 사용될 수 있다.

복합관계부사	시간, 장소의 부사절	양보의 부사절
whenever	at any time when(~할 때는 언제나)	no matter when(언제 ~할지라도)
wherever	at any place where(~하는 곳은 어디나)	no matter where(어디에서 ~할지라도)
however	–	no matter how(아무리 ~할지라도)

▶ **[However / Whenever]** you need me, just call me. I can contact you at any time if you require my assistance.

B 다음 괄호 안에서 어법상 올바른 것을 고르시오.

1 We finally reached the top of Mt. Jiri, but **[then / there]** we could see nothing but clouds.

2 I don't know the reason **[when / why]** Sally refused my invitation.

3 I like **[the way / the place]** in which she looks at me.

4 My favorite month is February, **[where / when]** we celebrate Valentine's Day.

5 This is the place **[at / for]** which she lost her smartphone.

6 This is the way **[when / that]** migratory birds find their way.

7 **[Whenever / Wherever]** you are, I'll be there with you.

숙어 플러스

16. 수능 필수 숙어 16회

정답 및 해설 091쪽

A 다음 수능 필수 숙어를 읽고, 아는 것은 체크해 봅시다.

□ 01	on a diet	다이어트 중인
□ 02	on end	(어떤 기간 동안) 계속
□ 03	out of order	고장 난, 정리가 안 된, ~에 어긋나는
□ 04	out of place	제자리에 있지 않은, 부적절한
□ 05	over and over	반복해서
□ 06	pass away	사망하다
□ 07	pass by	(장소를) 지나가다, (시간이) 흘러가다
□ 08	pass down	(후대에) ~을 물려주다
□ 09	pass through	~을 통과하다
□ 10	pay back	(돈을) 갚다, 복수하다
□ 11	pay off	(빚을) 갚다, 성과를 올리다
□ 12	place an order	~을 주문하다
□ 13	play a role	역할을 맡다
□ 14	prevent A from B	A가 B하는 것을 막다
□ 15	provide A with B	A에게 B를 제공하다(= supply A with B)
□ 16	pull over	(차를) 길가에 대다
□ 17	put aside	따로 떼어 놓다, 무시하다
□ 18	put away	(물건을 제자리로) 치우다
□ 19	put off	~을 연기하다(= postpone), 미루다
□ 20	put together	조립하다

B 다음 숙어 표현을 읽고 의미 차이를 비교해 봅시다.

□ 21	break out	(전쟁, 질병) 갑자기 발생하다
□ 22	make out	서류를 작성하다, ~을 알아보다
□ 23	stand out	눈에 뜨다, 두드러지다
□ 24	put out	불을 끄다
□ 25	leave out	생략하다(= omit)

C 우리말을 참고하여 빈칸에 알맞은 말을 써 봅시다.

1 저 승강기는 지금 고장나있다.
That elevator is out of ______________ right now.

2 제가 2주 전에 한 주문을 확인하려고 전화를 했어요.
I'm calling to check on the order that I ______________ two weeks ago.

3 우리의 마음은 병과 치료에 중요한 역할을 할 수 있다.
Our mind could ____________ an important role in illness and healing.

4 여기에 당신이 할 수 있는 감기를 예방하기 위한 몇 가지 방법이 있습니다.
Here are something you can do to ______________ yourself from catching the flu.

17 주어진 문장의 위치 파악

출제 트렌드

1. 주어진 문장의 알맞은 위치를 찾아 하나의 완결한 글로 완성하는 유형이다. 지문에서 분리한 문장이 본래 위치했던 곳을 찾아내는 능력이 있는지 유무를 평가한다. 글의 흐름이 명확하거나 사건의 순서가 분명히 드러나는 글이 주로 출제된다.
2. 이 유형은 수능에서 난이도가 높게 2문항이 출제되고 있다. 2문항 중 1문항은 비연계 고난도 문항으로 출제되며 높은 수준의 논리적 판단 능력을 요구하고 있다.
3. 최근 수능 7년간, 주어진 문장의 적합한 위치 파악 문제는 매년 2문항이 출제되었다. 38, 39번 문항으로 출제되었는데, 39번 문항이 난이도 더 높다. 38번과 39번 문항 비교 시 5년간 평균 38번이 55.9%, 39번이 53% 정답률을 보였다. 2017학년도 수능(57/68%), 2018(66/55%), 2019(65/37%), 2020(69/40%), 2021(54/69%), 2022(31/47%), 2023(54/56%)에서 괄호 안의 정답률을 보였다. 7년간 평균 54.9%의 정답률을 보였다. 난이도는 상 단계에 속한다.

	출처		문항 번호	지문 주제	정답률(%)	난이도
대표	2023학년도	수능	38번	공원의 형태	54	★★★
1	2023학년도	수능	39번	협상가들의 문제 해결 전략	56	★★★
2	2022학년도	10 학평	38번	물 분자의 대기 순환 과정	64	★★★
3	2023학년도	09 모평	38번	집단의 정의	39	★★★
4	2023학년도	09 모평	39번	편리성과 보안의 관계	40	★★★
5	2022학년도	07 학평	38번	영국에서의 패션 디자인의 맞춤복에서 기성복으로 전환	44	★★★
6	2023학년도	06 모평	39번	집단 탐지의 역학	40	★★★
7	2022학년도	수능	38번	공장에 로봇 도입을 두려워하는 직원을 위해 할 일	31	★★★
8	2022학년도	수능	39번	영화의 가치	47	★★★
9	2021학년도	수능	38번	나쁜(bad)과 사악한(wicked)의 차이	54	★★★
10	2021학년도	수능	39번	저작권의 특징	69	★★☆

1등급 꿀팁

1. 주어진 문장은 대체로 큰 단락이 시작되거나 논리가 전환되는 부분의 첫 문장일 가능성이 높다.
2. 주어진 문장을 먼저 읽고 전후에 올 수 있는 내용을 추정해 보는 연습을 한다. 글을 읽다가 흐름이 끊기거나 논리적으로 자연스럽지 못한 부분을 찾아낸다. 대명사의 지칭 대상이 있는지, 연결사의 전후 내용이 논리적인지 확인한다.
3. 주어진 문장을 선택한 위치에 넣은 후 글의 연결성이 자연스러운지 재검토한다.
4. 문장의 위치 파악과 관련된 표현을 익힌다.

however 그러나	though 비록 ~일지라도	nonetheless 그렇더라도	nevertheless 그럼에도 불구하고
on the contrary 반대로	for example 예를 들어	besides ~외에도	in addition 게다가
moreover 더욱이	in addition 게다가,	likewise 비슷하게	therefore 그래서
as a result 결과적으로	consequently 그 결과	hence 따라서	thus 따라서
at first 처음에는	finally 끝으로	last 끝으로	in the end 결국

주어진 문장의 위치 파악

제한 시간 : 15분 | 정답 및 해설 091쪽

대표 기출

2023학년도 수능 38번

글의 흐름으로 보아, 주어진 문장이 들어가기에 가장 적절한 곳은?

38.

> There's a reason for that: traditionally, park designers attempted to create such a feeling by planting tall trees at park boundaries, building stone walls, and constructing other means of partition.

Parks take the shape demanded by the cultural concerns of their time. Once parks are in place, they are no inert stage — their purposes and meanings are made and remade by planners and by park users. Moments of park creation are particularly telling, however, for they reveal and actualize ideas about nature and its relationship to urban society. (①) Indeed, what distinguishes a park from the broader category of public space is the representation of nature that parks are meant to embody. (②) Public spaces include parks, concrete plazas, sidewalks, even indoor atriums. (③) Parks typically have trees, grass, and other plants as their central features. (④) When entering a city park, people often imagine a sharp separation from streets, cars, and buildings. (⑤) What's behind this idea is not only landscape architects' desire to design aesthetically suggestive park spaces, but a much longer history of Western thought that envisions cities and nature as antithetical spaces and oppositional forces.

* aesthetically: 미적으로 ** antithetical: 대조적인

문제 풀이

1. 도입부를 읽고 글의 전반적은 내용을 개략적으로 파악한다.

- Parks take the shape demanded by the cultural concerns of their time. (공원은 그것이 속한 시대의 문화적 관심사가 요구하는 형태를 취한다.)

2. 글의 주제와 요지를 염두에 두고 읽으면서 문장과 문장 사이의 흐름이 부자연스럽거나 단절된 곳을 파악한다.

(①) Indeed, what distinguishes a park from the broader category of public space is the representation of nature that parks are meant to embody. (실제로 공원을 더 넓은 범주의 공공 공간과 구별하는 것은 공원이 구현하려는 자연의 표현이다.)

(②) Public spaces include parks, concrete plazas, sidewalks, even indoor atriums. (공공 공간에는 공원, 콘크리트 광장, 보도, 심지어 실내 아트리움도 포함된다.)

(③) Parks typically have trees, grass, and other plants as their central features. (일반적으로 공원에는 그들의 중심적인 특색으로 나무, 풀, 그리고 다른 식물들이 있다.)

(④) When entering a city park, people often imagine a sharp separation from streets, cars, and buildings. (도시 공원에 들어갈 때, 사람들은 흔히 거리, 자동차, 그리고 건물과의 뚜렷한 분리를 상상한다.)

3. 주어진 문장의 내용을 숙지하고 글이 전개되는 흐름을 파악하여 주어진 문장이 들어가기에 가장 적절한 곳을 고른다.

- 주어진 문장의 such a feeling은 ⑤ 앞 문장에서 언급된 공원과 도시의 사물이 분리되는 느낌을 의미한다. 또한 주어진 문장의 '공원 설계자들이 전통적으로 공원 경계에 나무를 심고 돌담 및 다른 칸막이 수단을 세웠다'는 내용은 ⑤ 앞 문장에서 사람들이 도시 공원에서 갖게 되는 느낌의 이유에 해당된다. 따라서 주어진 문장이 들어가기에 가장 적절한 곳은 ⑤이다.

2023학년도 수능 39번 ★★★

1. 글의 흐름으로 보아, 주어진 문장이 들어가기에 가장 적절한 곳은?

> It may be easier to reach an agreement when settlement terms don't have to be implemented until months in the future.

Negotiators should try to find ways to slice a large issue into smaller pieces, known as using *salami tactics*. (①) Issues that can be expressed in quantitative, measurable units are easy to slice. (②) For example, compensation demands can be divided into cents-per-hour increments or lease rates can be quoted as dollars per square foot. (③) When working to fractionate issues of principle or precedent, parties may use the time horizon (when the principle goes into effect or how long it will last) as a way to fractionate the issue. (④) Another approach is to vary the number of ways that the principle may be applied. (⑤) For example, a company may devise a family emergency leave plan that allows employees the opportunity to be away from the company for a period of no longer than three hours, and no more than once a month, for illness in the employee's immediate family. [3점]

* increment: 증가 ** fractionate: 세분하다

2022학년도 10월 학평 38번 ★★★

2. 글의 흐름으로 보아, 주어진 문장이 들어가기에 가장 적절한 곳은?

> However, after all the available materials on the Earth's surface, mostly iron, had combined with the free oxygen, it began to appear in the atmosphere in sizable quantities.

Water molecules circulate through the atmosphere as a result of evaporation. (①) As water molecules rise high up in the atmosphere, they may split up into their constituent chemical elements, hydrogen and oxygen, under the influence of sunlight. (②) Whereas the much heavier oxygen either remains in the atmosphere or is captured on the Earth's surface, the hydrogen tends to escape into space, because it is so light that Earth's gravity cannot retain it. (③) As long as there was little or no free oxygen in the atmosphere that could capture hydrogen before it escaped into the cosmos, this process would have continued unhindered. (④) As soon as this happened, the free oxygen would have captured most of the free hydrogen by forming water molecules again, thus slowing down the loss of hydrogen. (⑤) Over the course of time, this process would have helped to retain water on Earth, while it also contributed to the emergence of oxygen in the atmosphere.

2023학년도 9월 모평 38번 ★★★

3. 글의 흐름으로 보아, 주어진 문장이 들어가기에 가장 적절한 곳은?

> In particular, they define a group as two or more people who interact with, and exert mutual influences on, each other.

In everyday life, we tend to see any collection of people as a group. (①) However, social psychologists use this term more precisely. (②) It is this sense of mutual interaction or inter-dependence for a common purpose which distinguishes the members of a group from a mere aggregation of individuals. (③) For example, as Kenneth Hodge observed, a collection of people who happen to go for a swim after work on the same day each week does not, strictly speaking, constitute a group because these swimmers do not interact with each other in a structured manner. (④) By contrast, a squad of young competitive swimmers who train every morning before going to school *is* a group because they not only share a common objective (training for competition) but also interact with each other in formal ways (e.g., by warming up together beforehand). (⑤) It is this sense of people coming together to achieve a common objective that defines a "team".

* exert: 발휘하다 ** aggregation: 집합

2023학년도 9월 모평 39번 ★★★

4. 글의 흐름으로 보아, 주어진 문장이 들어가기에 가장 적절한 곳은?

> On top of the hurdles introduced in accessing his or her money, if a suspected fraud is detected, the account holder has to deal with the phone call asking if he or she made the suspicious transactions.

Each new wave of technology is intended to enhance user convenience, as well as improve security, but sometimes these do not necessarily go hand-in-hand. For example, the transition from magnetic stripe to embedded chip slightly slowed down transactions, sometimes frustrating customers in a hurry. (①) Make a service too burdensome, and the potential customer will go elsewhere. (②) This obstacle applies at several levels. (③) Passwords, double-key identification, and biometrics such as fingerprint-, iris-, and voice recognition are all ways of keeping the account details hidden from potential fraudsters, of keeping your data dark. (④) But they all inevitably add a burden to the use of the account. (⑤) This is all useful at some level — indeed, it can be reassuring knowing that your bank is keeping alert to protect you — but it becomes tiresome if too many such calls are received. [3점]

* fraud: 사기

2022학년도 7월 학평 38번 ★★★

5. 글의 흐름으로 보아, 주어진 문장이 들어가기에 가장 적절한 곳은?

> By now designers worked predominately within factories and no longer designed for individuals but for mass markets.

Earliest indications of the need for inspiration for fashion direction are possibly evidenced by a number of British manufacturers visiting the United States in around 1825 where they were much inspired by lightweight wool blend fabrics produced for outerwear. The ready-to-wear sector was established much earlier in America than in Britain and with it came new challenges. (①) Previously garments were custom-made by skilled individuals who later became known as or recognized as being fashion designers. (②) These handmade garments that are now accepted as being the fashion garments of that time were only made for those with the means to pay for them. (③) The lesser-privileged mass market wore homemade and handed down garments. (④) Later, by the end of the industrial revolution, fashion was more readily available and affordable to all classes. (⑤) Thus the direct communication link between the designer and client no longer existed and designers had to rely on anticipating the needs and desires of the new fashion consumer.

2023학년도 6월 모평 39번 ★★★

6. 글의 흐름으로 보아, 주어진 문장이 들어가기에 가장 적절한 곳은?

> This makes sense from the perspective of information reliability.

The dynamics of collective detection have an interesting feature. Which cue(s) do individuals use as evidence of predator attack? In some cases, when an individual detects a predator, its best response is to seek shelter. (①) Departure from the group may signal danger to nonvigilant animals and cause what appears to be a coordinated flushing of prey from the area. (②) Studies on dark-eyed juncos (a type of bird) support the view that nonvigilant animals attend to departures of individual group mates but that the departure of multiple individuals causes a greater escape response in the nonvigilant individuals. (③) If one group member departs, it might have done so for a number of reasons that have little to do with predation threat. (④) If nonvigilant animals escaped each time a single member left the group, they would frequently respond when there was no predator (a false alarm). (⑤) On the other hand, when several individuals depart the group at the same time, a true threat is much more likely to be present. [3점]

* predator: 포식자 ** vigilant: 경계하는 *** flushing: 날아오름

2022학년도 수능 38번 ★★★

7. 글의 흐름으로 보아, 주어진 문장이 들어가기에 가장 적절한 곳은?

> Retraining current employees for new positions within the company will also greatly reduce their fear of being laid off.

Introduction of robots into factories, while employment of human workers is being reduced, creates worry and fear. (①) It is the responsibility of management to prevent or, at least, to ease these fears. (②) For example, robots could be introduced only in new plants rather than replacing humans in existing assembly lines. (③) Workers should be included in the planning for new factories or the introduction of robots into existing plants, so they can participate in the process. (④) It may be that robots are needed to reduce manufacturing costs so that the company remains competitive, but planning for such cost reductions should be done jointly by labor and management. (⑤) Since robots are particularly good at highly repetitive simple motions, the replaced human workers should be moved to positions where judgment and decisions beyond the abilities of robots are required.

2022학년도 수능 39번 ★★★

8. 글의 흐름으로 보아, 주어진 문장이 들어가기에 가장 적절한 곳은?

> As long as the irrealism of the silent black and white film predominated, one could not take filmic fantasies for representations of reality.

Cinema is valuable not for its ability to make visible the hidden outlines of our reality, but for its ability to reveal what reality itself veils — the dimension of fantasy. (①) This is why, to a person, the first great theorists of film decried the introduction of sound and other technical innovations (such as color) that pushed film in the direction of realism. (②) Since cinema was an entirely fantasmatic art, these innovations were completely unnecessary. (③) And what's worse, they could do nothing but turn filmmakers and audiences away from the fantasmatic dimension of cinema, potentially transforming film into a mere delivery device for representations of reality. (④) But sound and color threatened to create just such an illusion, thereby destroying the very essence of film art. (⑤) As Rudolf Arnheim puts it, "The creative power of the artist can only come into play where reality and the medium of representation do not coincide." [3점]

* decry: 공공연히 비난하다 ** fantasmatic: 환상의

2021학년도 수능 38번 ★★★

9. 글의 흐름으로 보아, 주어진 문장이 들어가기에 가장 적절한 곳은?

> I have still not exactly pinpointed Maddy's character since wickedness takes many forms.

Imagine I tell you that Maddy is bad. Perhaps you infer from my intonation, or the context in which we are talking, that I mean morally bad. Additionally, you will probably infer that I am disapproving of Maddy, or saying that I think you should disapprove of her, or similar, given typical linguistic conventions and assuming I am sincere. (①) However, you might not get a more detailed sense of the particular sorts of way in which Maddy is bad, her typical character traits, and the like, since people can be bad in many ways. (②) In contrast, if I say that Maddy is wicked, then you get more of a sense of her typical actions and attitudes to others. (③) The word 'wicked' is more specific than 'bad'. (④) But there is more detail nevertheless, perhaps a stronger connotation of the sort of person Maddy is. (⑤) In addition, and again assuming typical linguistic conventions, you should also get a sense that I am disapproving of Maddy, or saying that you should disapprove of her, or similar, assuming that we are still discussing her moral character.

* connotation: 함축

2021학년도 수능 39번 ★★☆

10. 글의 흐름으로 보아, 주어진 문장이 들어가기에 가장 적절한 곳은?

> Note that copyright covers the expression of an idea and not the idea itself.

Designers draw on their experience of design when approaching a new project. This includes the use of previous designs that they know work — both designs that they have created themselves and those that others have created. (①) Others' creations often spark inspiration that also leads to new ideas and innovation. (②) This is well known and understood. (③) However, the expression of an idea is protected by copyright, and people who infringe on that copyright can be taken to court and prosecuted. (④) This means, for example, that while there are numerous smartphones all with similar functionality, this does not represent an infringement of copyright as the idea has been expressed in different ways and it is the expression that has been copyrighted. (⑤) Copyright is free and is automatically invested in the author, for instance, the writer of a book or a programmer who develops a program, unless they sign the copyright over to someone else. [3점]

* infringe: 침해하다 ** prosecute: 기소하다

총 문항				문항	맞은 문항					문항
개별 문항	1	2	3	4	5	6	7	8	9	10
채점										

문법 플러스

17. 병렬 구조

정답 및 해설 096쪽

A 문법의 주요 포인트를 점검해 봅시다.

1 등위접속사(and, or, but 등)에 의해 연결되는 내용은 비슷한 구조로 병렬되어야 한다.

▶ It seizes the unsuspecting prey with a lightning-fast snap of the jaws, and **[swallows / to swallow]** the prey down head first.

2 등위접속사에 의해 연결되는 구조는 A가 동명사이면 B도 동명사로 해야 한다.

▶ She is looking forward to going to Italy and **[eat / eating]** wonderful pasta every day.

3 등위접속사에 의해 연결되는 구조는 A가 부정사이면 B도 부정사로로 해야 한다.

▶ But now the tools of the digital age give us a way to easily get, share, and **[acting / act]** on information in new ways.

4 상관접속사에 의해 연결되는 내용도 비슷한 구조로 병렬되어야 한다.

not A but B	A가 아니라 B	either A or B	A 또는 B
not only A but also B	A뿐만 아니라 B도	neither A nor B	A도 B도 아닌
B as well as A	A뿐만 아니라 B도	both A and B	A, B 둘 다

▶ The Mongol Empire was not a unified state **[but / nor]** a vast collection of territories held together by military force.

5 상관접속사 not A but B, not only A but also B, B as well as A, either A or B, neither A nor B에서 동사의 시제 일치는 B에 일치시킨다. 단, both A and B는 복수 취급한다.

▶ After the cell has grown to the proper size, its metabolism shifts as it either prepares to divide or matures and **[to differentiate / differentiates]** into a specialized cell.

6 비교 구문에서도 병렬 구조를 지켜야 한다.

▶ His idea is better than **[me / mine]**.

7 비교 구문이 병렬 구조를 이루는 경우, 명사의 반복을 피하기 위해 「the+명사」 대신에 that을 쓴다. 명사가 복수일 때는 those를 써야 한다.

▶ The population of Tokyo is larger than **[that / those]** of Seoul.

B 다음 괄호 안에서 어법상 올바른 것을 고르시오.

1 Sally is smart, beautiful and **[humorously / humorous]**.

2 The adults busied themselves preparing the food, supervising the children, and **[playing / played]** volleyball.

3 He hopes to go to London university and **[studying / study]** under Dr. Lee.

4 Neither Peter **[nor / or]** his wife mentions anything about moving house.

5 Either you or your sister **[have / has]** to stay here.

6 My Smartphone is similar to **[her / hers]** in color and shape.

7 Japan made an increase in electronic products, but the increase of Japan was smaller than **[that / those]** of South Korea.

숙어 플러스

17. 수능 필수 숙어 17회

정답 및 해설 097쪽

A 다음 수능 필수 숙어를 읽고, 아는 것은 체크해 봅시다.

□ 01	regardless of	~에 상관없이
□ 02	rich in	~이 풍부한
□ 03	rule out	~을 배제하다
□ 04	run away	달아나다, 도망가다
□ 05	run down	(자동차 등이) ~을 치다
□ 06	run for	~을 출마하다
□ 07	run into	~에 충돌하다, 우연히 만나다
□ 08	run out	다 써버리다
□ 09	run the risk	위험을 무릅쓰다
□ 10	see off	배웅하다
□ 11	send out	발송하다
□ 12	set aside	따로 떼어두다, ~을 한 쪽으로 치워놓다
□ 13	set off	(경보 등을) 울리다, 폭발시키다
□ 14	settle down	진정되다, 정착하다
□ 15	shake hands with	~와 악수하다
□ 16	show off	과시하다
□ 17	shut down	문을 닫다, (기계가) 멈추다
□ 18	side by side	나란히
□ 19	slip out	(비밀이 입에서) 무심코 튀어 나오다
□ 20	sort out	정리하다, 선별하다

B 다음 숙어 표현을 읽고 의미 차이를 비교해 봅시다.

□ 21	add to	~를 증가시키다(= increase)
□ 22	agree to	~에 동의하다
□ 23	lead to	~에 이르다, ~를 초래하다
□ 24	contribute to	~에 공헌하다, 기부하다
□ 25	due to	~ 때문에

C 우리말을 참고하여 빈칸에 알맞은 말을 써 봅시다.

1 개간된 토양은 미네랄과 영양분이 풍부하였고 상당한 양의 농작물을 산출하였다.
The cleared soil was ______________ in minerals and nutrients and provided substantial production yields.

2 빨간불인데도 달린다면, 당신은 다른 사람들을 죽일 수 있는 위험을 무릅쓰는 것이다.
If you run a red light, you are running the _________of killing others.

3 절 배웅하러 와주셔서 고마워요.
Thanks for coming to ______________ me off.

4 그 남자 모델들은 그들의 근육을 자랑한다.
The male models __________________ off their muscles.

18 문단 요약

출제 트렌드

1. 문단 요약 문제 유형은 '다음 글의 내용을 한 문장으로 요약하고자 한다. 빈칸 (A), (B)에 들어갈 말로 가장 적절한 것'을 고르도록 출제된다.
2. 글을 읽고 글 전체의 내용을 이해한 후 이것을 하나의 문장으로 완성하도록 요구하는 유형으로서 쓰기 능력을 간접적으로 평가하는 유형이다. 수능에서 매년 1문항이 출제되고 있다.
3. 글의 내용을 요약하는 문장에서 빈칸 두 개를 제시한다. 요약문의 빈칸에는 본문에 나오는 핵심어를 그대로 사용하거나, 핵심어의 동의어가 정답이 되기도 한다.
4. 최근 수능 7년간, 문단 요약하기 문제는 2017학년도 이후 매년 1문제가 출제되고 있다. 2017학년도 수능(64%), 2018(67%), 2019(74%), 2020(69%), 2021(57%), 2022(69%), 2023(75%)에서 괄호 안의 정답률을 보였다. 7년간 평균 67.9% 정도 정답률을 보였다. 난이도는 중 단계이다.
5. 간접 쓰기 유형 35-40번 문제 중 가장 어려운 문제는 문단 내 글의 순서 파악 37번 문항이다. 문제를 풀 때 시간이 부족한 경우, 빈칸 33, 34번과 37번 문항은 전략적으로 나중에 푸는 것이 좋다.

출처			문항 번호	지문 주제	정답률(%)	난이도
대표	2022학년도	06 모평	40번	영국 귀족에게 나무 심기의 의의	58	★★★
1	2023학년도	수능	40번	장인 정신	75	★★☆
2	2022학년도	수능	40번	두 가지 설명에 대한 철학적 이론	69	★★☆
3	2021학년도	10 학평	40번	마술 기법의 모방과 비밀 누설	79	★★☆
4	2022학년도	09 모평	40번	컴퓨터 정보 처리의 장단점	51	★★★
5	2021학년도	수능	40번	다른 문화의 정치 권력 이해	57	★★★
6	2020학년도	수능	40번	코끼리의 인사 행동	69	★★☆
7	2019학년도	수능	40번	즉각적인 생산물을 선호하는 경향	74	★★☆

1등급 꿀팁

1. 요약문은 글의 주제와 밀접한 관련이 있으므로 먼저 주제를 파악하는 것이 문제 해결의 핵심이다.
2. 요약문은 글에 나타난 두 핵심 개념의 관계를 주로 표현한다.
3. 제시된 요약문을 먼저 읽은 후에 본문의 내용을 읽고 판단한다. 글을 읽어 가면서 주제와 관련된 표현 및 핵심 어구에 표시를 한다.
4. 요약문을 완성한 후 다시 읽어 보면서 요지와 일치하는지 판단한다.
5. 원인과 결과 관계를 나타내는 서술 구조를 익힌다.

(문제의) 원인	cause, affect, bring about, result in, have influence on, lead to	(문제의) 결과
(문제의) 결과	depend on, attribute to, result from because of, thanks to, owing to, due to	(문제의) 원인

제한 시간 : 12분 | 정답 및 해설 097쪽

대표 기출

2022학년도 6월 모평 40번

40. 다음 글의 내용을 한 문장으로 요약하고자 한다. 빈칸 (A), (B)에 들어갈 말로 가장 적절한 것은?

The idea that *planting* trees could have a social or political significance appears to have been invented by the English, though it has since spread widely. According to Keith Thomas's history *Man and the Natural World*, seventeenth- and eighteenth-century aristocrats began planting hardwood trees, usually in lines, to declare the extent of their property and the permanence of their claim to it. "What can be more pleasant," the editor of a magazine for gentlemen asked his readers, "than to have the bounds and limits of your own property preserved and continued from age to age by the testimony of such living and growing witnesses?" Planting trees had the additional advantage of being regarded as a patriotic act, for the Crown had declared a severe shortage of the hardwood on which the Royal Navy depended.

* aristocrat: 귀족 ** patriotic: 애국적인

⬇

For English aristocrats, planting trees served as statements to mark the ___(A)___ ownership of their land, and it was also considered to be a(n) ___(B)___ of their loyalty to the nation.

	(A)		(B)
①	unstable	……	confirmation
②	unstable	……	exaggeration
③	lasting	……	exhibition
④	lasting	……	manipulation
⑤	official	……	justification

문제 풀이

1. 요약문과 선택지를 먼저 훑어봄으로써 글의 주제를 추론해 보고 빈칸에 들어갈 내용에 대한 단서를 확보한다.

- 17세기 18세기 영국 귀족들은 자신의 재산 정도를 표시하고 그 재산적 권리에 대한 영속성을 보여주기 위해 활엽수를 심기 시작했다. 또한 귀족들이 나무를 심는 것은 영국 해군이 의존하는 경재(단단한 나무)가 부족하다는 영국 군주의 요청에 대해 애국심을 보여 주는 반응이기도 했다.

2. 요약문을 통해 얻은 단서를 바탕으로 글을 읽는다.

(1) 글의 요지: 영국 귀족의 나무 심기는 자신의 재산 정도와 권리의 영속성을 보여주기 위함이며, 군주에 대한 충성심의 표현이기도 하다.

(2) 요지를 뒷받침하는 예

① ~aristocrats began planting hardwood trees, usually in lines, to declare the extent of their property and the permanence of their claim to it.

② Planting trees had the additional advantage of being regarded as a patriotic act, ~.

3. 글을 읽으면서 파악한 요지를 바탕으로 요약문의 빈칸에 들어갈 말로 가장 적절한 단어를 선택지에서 고른다.

- 영국의 귀족들에게, 나무를 심는 것은 자신의 땅에 대한 (A) 지속적인 소유권을 표시 하는 표현의 역할을 했고, 그것은 또한 국가에 대한 그들의 충성심을 (B) 표현하는 것으로 여겨졌다. 가장 적절한 답은 ③번이다.

2023학년도 수능 40번 ★★★

1. 다음 글의 내용을 한 문장으로 요약하고자 한다. 빈칸 (A), (B)에 들어갈 말로 가장 적절한 것은?

"Craftsmanship" may suggest a way of life that declined with the arrival of industrial society — but this is misleading. Craftsmanship names an enduring, basic human impulse, the desire to do a job well for its own sake. Craftsmanship cuts a far wider swath than skilled manual labor; it serves the computer programmer, the doctor, and the artist; parenting improves when it is practiced as a skilled craft, as does citizenship. In all these domains, craftsmanship focuses on objective standards, on the thing in itself. Social and economic conditions, however, often stand in the way of the craftsman's discipline and commitment: schools may fail to provide the tools to do good work, and workplaces may not truly value the aspiration for quality. And though craftsmanship can reward an individual with a sense of pride in work, this reward is not simple. The craftsman often faces conflicting objective standards of excellence; the desire to do something well for its own sake can be weakened by competitive pressure, by frustration, or by obsession.

* swath: 구획

⬇

Craftsmanship, a human desire that has ___(A)___ over time in diverse contexts, often encounters factors that ___(B)___ its full development.

	(A)		(B)
①	persisted	…	limit
②	persisted	…	cultivate
③	evolved	…	accelerate
④	diminished	…	shape
⑤	diminished	…	restrict

2022학년도 수능 40번 ★★☆

2. 다음 글의 내용을 한 문장으로 요약하고자 한다. 빈칸 (A), (B)에 들어갈 말로 가장 적절한 것은?

Philip Kitcher and Wesley Salmon have suggested that there are two possible alternatives among philosophical theories of explanation. One is the view that scientific explanation consists in the *unification* of broad bodies of phenomena under a minimal number of generalizations. According to this view, the (or perhaps, a) goal of science is to construct an economical framework of laws or generalizations that are capable of subsuming all observable phenomena. Scientific explanations organize and systematize our knowledge of the empirical world; the more economical the systematization, the deeper our understanding of what is explained. The other view is the *causal/mechanical* approach. According to it, a scientific explanation of a phenomenon consists of uncovering the mechanisms that produced the phenomenon of interest. This view sees the explanation of individual events as primary, with the explanation of generalizations flowing from them. That is, the explanation of scientific generalizations comes from the causal mechanisms that produce the regularities.

* subsume: 포섭(포함)하다 ** empirical: 경험적인

⬇

Scientific explanations can be made either by seeking the ____(A)____ number of principles covering all observations or by finding general ____(B)____ drawn from individual phenomena.

	(A)	(B)		(A)	(B)
①	least	··· patterns	②	fixed	··· features
③	limited	··· functions	④	fixed	··· rules
⑤	least	··· assumptions			

2021학년도 10월 학평 40번 ★★☆

3. 다음 글의 내용을 한 문장으로 요약하고자 한다. 빈칸 (A), (B)에 들어갈 말로 가장 적절한 것은?

Perhaps not surprisingly, given how long magicians have been developing their craft, a lot of creativity in magic is of the tweaking variety—some of the most skilled and inventive magicians gained fame by refining the execution of tricks that have been known for decades, or sometimes centuries. Nevil Maskelyne, one of magic's old masters, claimed that "the difficulty of producing a new magical effect is about equivalent to that of inventing a new proposition in Euclid." Whether it's because there's little that's completely new, or for some other reason, magicians seem to worry less about imitation. They do, however, worry a lot about *traitors*—those magicians who expose the secrets behind a trick to the public. Once a trick is exposed in this way, its value as "magic" is destroyed, and this harms everyone in the industry. For this reason, magicians' norms are focused mostly on punishing magicians who expose tricks to the public—even if the trick is the exposer's own invention.

* tweak: 살짝 변화를 주다 ** traitor: 배신자

⬇

Magicians, having long refined existing tricks, are not much worried about ____(A)____ tricks, but they are very strict about ____(B)____ the methods of tricks as it damages their industry.

	(A)		(B)
①	copying	········	blending
②	copying	········	disclosing
③	criticizing	········	distorting
④	modifying	········	evaluating
⑤	modifying	········	underestimating

2022학년도 9월 모평 40번 ★★★

4. 다음 글의 내용을 한 문장으로 요약하고자 한다. 빈칸 (A), (B)에 들어갈 말로 가장 적절한 것은?

The computer has, to a considerable extent, solved the problem of acquiring, preserving, and retrieving information. Data can be stored in effectively unlimited quantities and in manageable form. The computer makes available a range of data unattainable in the age of books. It packages it effectively; style is no longer needed to make it accessible, nor is memorization. In dealing with a single decision separated from its context, the computer supplies tools unimaginable even a decade ago. But it also diminishes perspective. Because information is so accessible and communication instantaneous, there is a diminution of focus on its significance, or even on the definition of what is significant. This dynamic may encourage policymakers to wait for an issue to arise rather than anticipate it, and to regard moments of decision as a series of isolated events rather than part of a historical continuum. When this happens, manipulation of information replaces reflection as the principal policy tool.

* retrieve: (정보를) 추출하다 ** diminution: 감소

⬇

Although the computer is clearly ____(A)____ at handling information in a decontextualized way, it interferes with our making ____(B)____ judgments related to the broader context, as can be seen in policymaking processes.

	(A)	(B)		(A)	(B)
①	competent	······ comprehensive	②	dominant	······ biased
③	imperfect	······ informed	④	impressive	······ legal
⑤	inefficient	······ timely			

Day 18

2021학년도 수능 40번 ★★★

5. 다음 글의 내용을 한 문장으로 요약하고자 한다. 빈칸 (A), (B)에 들어갈 말로 가장 적절한 것은?

From a cross-cultural perspective the equation between public leadership and dominance is questionable. What does one mean by 'dominance'? Does it indicate coercion? Or control over 'the most valued'? 'Political' systems may be about both, either, or conceivably neither. The idea of 'control' would be a bothersome one for many peoples, as for instance among many native peoples of Amazonia where all members of a community are fond of their personal autonomy and notably allergic to any obvious expression of control or coercion. The conception of political power as a *coercive* force, while it may be a Western fixation, is not a universal. It is very unusual for an Amazonian leader to give an order. If many peoples do not view political power as a coercive force, *nor as the most valued domain*, then the leap from 'the political' to 'domination' (as coercion), *and from there* to 'domination of women', is a shaky one. As Marilyn Strathern has remarked, the notions of 'the political' and 'political personhood' are cultural obsessions of our own, a bias long reflected in anthropological constructs.

* coercion: 강제 ** autonomy: 자율
*** anthropological: 인류학의

⬇

It is ___(A)___ to understand political power in other cultures through our own notion of it because ideas of political power are not ___(B)___ across cultures.

	(A)		(B)
①	rational	⋯	flexible
②	appropriate	⋯	commonplace
③	misguided	⋯	uniform
④	unreasonable	⋯	varied
⑤	effective	⋯	objective

2020학년도 수능 40번 ★★☆

6. 다음 글의 내용을 한 문장으로 요약하고자 한다. 빈칸 (A), (B)에 들어갈 말로 가장 적절한 것은?

Because elephant groups break up and reunite very frequently — for instance, in response to variation in food availability — reunions are more important in elephant society than among primates. And the species has evolved elaborate greeting behaviors, the form of which reflects the strength of the social bond between the individuals (much like how you might merely shake hands with a long-standing acquaintance but hug a close friend you have not seen in a while, and maybe even tear up). Elephants may greet each other simply by reaching their trunks into each other's mouths, possibly equivalent to a human peck on the cheek. However, after long absences, members of family and bond groups greet one another with incredibly theatrical displays. The fact that the intensity reflects the duration of the separation as well as the level of intimacy suggests that elephants have a sense of time as well. To human eyes, these greetings strike a familiar chord. I'm reminded of the joyous reunions so visible in the arrivals area of an international airport terminal.

* acquaintance: 지인 ** peck: 가벼운 입맞춤

⬇

The evolved greeting behaviors of elephants can serve as an indicator of how much they are socially ___(A)___ and how long they have been ___(B)___.

	(A)		(B)
①	competitive	⋯⋯	disconnected
②	tied	⋯⋯	endangered
③	responsible	⋯⋯	isolated
④	competitive	⋯⋯	united
⑤	tied	⋯⋯	parted

2019학년도 수능 40번 ★★☆

7. 다음 글의 내용을 한 문장으로 요약하고자 한다. 빈칸 (A), (B)에 들어갈 말로 가장 적절한 것은?

Biological organisms, including human societies both with and without market systems, discount distant outputs over those available at the present time based on risks associated with an uncertain future. As the timing of inputs and outputs varies greatly depending on the type of energy, there is a strong case to incorporate time when assessing energy alternatives. For example, the energy output from solar panels or wind power engines, where most investment happens before they begin producing, may need to be assessed differently when compared to most fossil fuel extraction technologies, where a large proportion of the energy output comes much sooner, and a larger (relative) proportion of inputs is applied during the extraction process, and not upfront. Thus fossil fuels, particularly oil and natural gas, in addition to having energy quality advantages (cost, storability, transportability, etc.) over many renewable technologies, also have a "temporal advantage" after accounting for human behavioral preference for current consumption/return.

* upfront: 선행 투자의

⬇

Due to the fact that people tend to favor more ___(A)___ outputs, fossil fuels are more ___(B)___ than renewable energy alternatives in regards to the distance between inputs and outputs.

	(A)		(B)
①	immediate	⋯⋯	competitive
②	available	⋯⋯	expensive
③	delayed	⋯⋯	competitive
④	convenient	⋯⋯	expensive
⑤	abundant	⋯⋯	competitive

총 문항			문항	맞은 문항					문항
개별 문항	1	2	3	4	5	6	7	8	9	10
채점										

문법 플러스

18. 수의 일치

정답 및 해설 101쪽

A 문법의 주요 포인트를 점검해 봅시다.

1 수 일치의 기본 원칙은 단수주어는 단수동사를, 복수주어는 복수동사를 사용한다.
▶ A famous professor and a musician **[is / are]** discussing the problem.

2 주어, 동사 사이에 수식어구나 관계사절이 있는 경우, 주어를 잘 찾은 후, 주어의 수에 맞게 동사를 일치시켜야 한다.
▶ Families that avoid conflict by ignoring unpleasant subjects or situations **[is / are]** weaker, not stronger for it.

3 관계대명사절 안의 동사는 선행사의 수에 일치시킨다. 선행사가 단수주어면 동사는 단수동사, 선행사가 복수주어이면 복수동사를 사용한다.
▶ Kids shouldn't watch TV programs which **[contains / contain]** violence.

4 It ... that ~ 강조 구문에서 주어가 강조되면, that 바로 뒤의 동사는 강조된 주어에 맞게 수를 일치시킨다. There is[are] 구문에서 be동사는 바로 뒤에 나오는 주어에 맞게 수를 일치시킨다.
▶ It is golf courses that **[has / have]** beautiful grass, plants and pretty ponds.

5 도치 구문은 뒤에 나오는 주어에 맞게 수를 일치시킨다.
▶ Only after her death **[were / was]** I able to appreciate her.

6 most of ~, some of ~, all of ~, a lot of ~, 「분수+of ~」 등이 주어로 쓰인 경우, 동사는 of 뒤에 나오는 명사(구)의 수에 일치시킨다. 「the number of+복수명사」는 뒤에 단수동사를 쓰고, 「A number of+복수명사」는 뒤에 복수동사를 쓴다.
▶ Some of her friends **[thinks / think]** she is silly to work and save for a smartwatch, but I don't agree with them.

7 명사를 대신하는 대명사는 그 명사의 수와 일치해야 한다.
▶ The tail of a rabbit is shorter than **[that / those]** of a cat.

B 다음 괄호 안에서 어법상 올바른 것을 고르시오.

1 A famous professor and musician **[are / is]** talking on the phone.

2 The custom decorating the body with jewels **[is / are]** ancient.

3 Doctors are contacting patients with cancer, who **[has / have]** taken the drugs in the last three months.

4 There **[is / are]** no subway station near my house.

5 Seldom **[do / does]** Sam say anything bad about people.

6 Most of the shelves **[is / are]** empty.

7 An opening airing of disagreements is an excellent way to manage family conflict and keep **[them / it]** within acceptable bounds.

숙어 플러스

18. 수능 필수 숙어 18회

정답 및 해설 102쪽

A 다음 수능 필수 숙어를 읽고, 아는 것은 체크해 봅시다.

□ 01	specialize in	~을 전공하다, ~을 전문으로 하다
□ 02	spend (money) on ~	~에 돈을 쓰다
□ 03	spread out	퍼지다, (접힌 것을) 펴다
□ 04	stand for	나타내다, 의미하다, 지지하다
□ 05	stand out	두드러지다
□ 06	stand up for	지지하다, 옹호하다, 지키다
□ 07	stay up	(늦게까지) 깨어 있다
□ 08	step in	(문제, 사건 등에) 개입하다
□ 09	step up	앞으로 나가다, ~을 증가시키다
□ 10	stick out	튀어나오다, 눈에 띄다
□ 11	stop by	잠깐 들르다
□ 12	subject to	~을 조건으로 하여
□ 13	succeed in	~에 성공하다
□ 14	take ~ into account	~을 고려하다
□ 15	take a break	휴식을 취하다
□ 16	take action	조치를 취하다
□ 17	take away	제거하다
□ 18	take in	이해하다, 섭취하다, 받아들이다
□ 19	take off	~을 벗다, (비행기가) 이륙하다
□ 20	take out	~을 꺼내다, ~을 데리고 나가다

B 다음 숙어 표현을 읽고 의미 차이를 비교해 봅시다.

□ 21	bring up	양육하다
□ 22	give up	포기하다
□ 23	make up	(이야기 등)을 꾸미다, 화장하다
□ 24	pick up	집어올리다, 마중나가다
□ 25	show up	나타나다(= turn up)

C 우리말을 참고하여 빈칸에 알맞은 말을 써 봅시다.

1 그래서 정확하게 그것은 무엇을 의미하는가?
So, what exactly does it _________________ for?

2 어젯밤을 꼬박 새웠는데 여전히 끝내지 못했어. 스트레스를 많이 받아!
I _________________ up all night but I still haven't finished it. I'm so stressed out!

3 그는 매우 수줍어 눈에 띄는 걸 별로 좋아하지 않았어요
He is very shy and does not wish to stick _________________ from the others

4 저는 매일 비행기가 하늘로 이륙하는 것을 보았죠.
Every day I watched the planes taking _________________ into the sky.

장문의 이해 (1)

출제 트렌드

1. 장문 1지문 2문항 문제 유형은 제1문항은 '윗글의 제목으로 가장 적절한 것'을 묻는 문제가 출세되고, 제2문항은 '밑줄 친 (a) ~ (e) 중에서 문맥상 밑줄 친 낱말의 쓰임이 적절하지 않은 것'을 묻는 문제가 출제된다.
2. 수능에서 매년 1세트씩 출제되었다. 한 문항은 제목을 묻는 문항으로, 다른 한 문항은 어휘 추론 3점 문제로 출제되고 있다. 2019학년도 수능은 역대급 불수능이었는데, 23번 함축 의미 추론과 42번 단일 장문의 어휘 추론이 새로운 유형으로 난이도가 높게 출제되었다.
3. 수필, 문학 작품과 같은 평이한 글이 제시될 수도 있고 철학, 사회 현상, 인간관계와 같은 추상적인 글이 제시되기도 한다. 비교적 난이도가 높은 유형이다.
4. 최근 수능 7년간, 장문의 이해 (1) 41–42번 문항은 매년 2문제가 출제되고 있다. 41번 문항은 고정적으로 제목 문제가 출제되었는데, 42번 문항은 2017–2018학년도 수능은 빈칸 문제로, 2019년 이후 수능은 문맥상 낱말의 쓰임이 적절하지 않는 문제로 출제되고 있다. 2017학년도 수능(71/51%), 2018(67/76%), 2019(72/54%), 2020(52/53%), 2021(66/73%), 2022(64/61%), 2023(57/62%)에서 괄호 안의 정답률을 보였다. 7년간 평균 62.8% 정도 정답률을 보였다. 난이도는 중 단계이다. 7년간 평균 41번 문항은 64.1%, 42번 문항은 61.4%의 정답률을 보였다.

출처			문항 번호	지문 주제	정답률(%)	난이도
대표	2022학년도	06 모평	41–42번	사생활에 대한 권리의 개념 변화	71 / 50	★★★
1~2	2023학년도	수능	41–42번	판단할 때, 단순한 공식의 중요성	57 / 62	★★★
3~4	2022학년도	수능	41–42번	언어의 분류적 특성	64 / 61	★★☆
5~6	2021학년도	수능	41–42번	동물 행동의 복잡성	66 / 73	★★☆
7~8	2020학년도	수능	41–42번	과학 학습에서 체험보다 중요한 사고	52 / 53	★★★

1등급 꿀팁

1. 문제를 먼저 살펴본 후 지문을 읽는 것이 효율적이다.
2. 글의 제목 문제는 글의 주제를 파악하고 주제를 담고 있는 제목을 선택한다.
3. 어휘 추론 문제는 그의 요지나 흐름에 적절하지 않는 어휘를 찾아낸다.

장문의 이해 (1)

제한 시간 : 12분 | 정답 및 해설 102쪽

대표 기출

2022학년도 6월 모평 41~42번

[41~42] 다음 글을 읽고, 물음에 답하시오.

The right to privacy may extend only to the point where it does not restrict someone else's right to freedom of expression or right to information. The scope of the right to privacy is (a) similarly restricted by the general interest in preventing crime or in promoting public health. However, when we move away from the property-based notion of a right (where the right to privacy would protect, for example, images and personality), to modern notions of private and family life, we find it (b) easier to establish the limits of the right. This is, of course, the strength of the notion of privacy, in that it can adapt to meet changing expectations and technological advances.

In sum, *what* is privacy today? The concept includes a claim that we should be unobserved, and that certain information and images about us should not be (c) circulated without our permission. *Why* did these privacy claims arise? They arose because powerful people took offence at such observation. Furthermore, privacy incorporated the need to protect the family, home, and correspondence from arbitrary (d) interference and, in addition, there has been a determination to protect honour and reputation. *How* is privacy protected? Historically, privacy was protected by restricting circulation of the damaging material. But if the concept of privacy first became interesting legally as a response to reproductions of images through photography and newspapers, more recent technological advances, such as data storage, digital images, and the Internet, (e) pose new threats to privacy. The right to privacy is now being reinterpreted to meet those challenges.

* arbitrary: 임의의

41. 윗글의 제목으로 가장 적절한 것은?

① Side Effects of Privacy Protection Technologies
② The Legal Domain of Privacy Claims and Conflicts
③ The Right to Privacy: Evolving Concepts and Practices
④ Who Really Benefits from Looser Privacy Regulations?
⑤ Less Is More: Reduce State Intervention in Privacy!

42. 밑줄 친 (a)~(e) 중에서 문맥상 낱말의 쓰임이 적절하지 않은 것은? [3점]

① (a) ② (b) ③ (c) ④ (d) ⑤ (e)

문제 풀이

1. 제목 문제를 풀 때는 글의 전반적인 흐름을 파악한다.

① 도입: The right to privacy may extend only to the point where it does not restrict someone else's right to freedom of expression or right to information. (사생활에 대한 권리는 다른 사람의 표현의 자유에 대한 권리나 정보에 대한 권리를 제한하지 않는 정도까지만 확대될 수 있다.)

② 요지: However, when we move away from the property-based notion of a right (where the right to privacy would protect, for example, images and personality), to modern notions of private and family life, we find it harder to establish the limits of the right. This is, of course, the strength of the notion of privacy, in that it can adapt to meet changing expectations and technological advances. (사생활에 대한 권리의 개념이 이미지와 인격 보호와 같은 속성에 기반을 둔 개념에서 사생활과 가족의 생활이라는 현대적 개념으로 바뀜에 따라 그 권리의 한계를 설정하기가 더 어려워졌고, 그것이 변화된 상황에 대처하기 위해 적응할 수 있다는 점에서 강점이기도 하다.)

③ 부연: 필자는 사생활의 개념, 발생 이유, 보호 방법에 대해 기술하고 있다.
-In sum, *what* is privacy today?
(사생활 개념의 정의: 오늘날 사생활이란 무엇인가?)
-*Why* did these privacy claims arise?
(발생 이유: '왜' 이러한 사생활 주장들이 생겼는가?)
-*How* is privacy protected?
(사생활 보호 방법: 사생활은 '어떻게' 보호되었는가?)

④ 결론: 사생활에 대한 권리는 개념과 실제가 변화하는 기대와 기술적 진보에 대처해 적응하고 있다.

• 41. 글의 내용을 종합적으로 파악하여 제목으로 적절한 선택지를 고른다. 오늘날 사생활에 대한 권리는 개념과 관행이 발전하고 있다고 했으므로 글의 제목으로 적절한 것은 ③ 'The Right to Privacy: Evolving Concepts and Practices (사생활에 대한 권리: 발전하는 개념과 관행)'가 가장 적절하다.

2. 글의 맥락에 맞게 어휘의 적절성을 파악하여 문맥에 맞지 않는 말을 고른다.

• 42. 사생활에 대한 개념이 이미지와 인격 보호와 같은 속성에 기반을 둔 개념에서 사생활과 가족의 생활이라는 현대적 개념으로 바뀜에 따라 그 권리의 한계를 설정하기가 어려워졌다고 해야 할 것이다. 그러므로 ② (b) easier가 어색하다. easier를 harder로 고치는 것이 적절하다.

2022학년도 6월 모평 41~42번

【1~2】 다음 글을 읽고 물음에 답하시오.

There is evidence that even very simple algorithms can outperform expert judgement on simple prediction problems. For example, algorithms have proved more (a) accurate than humans in predicting whether a prisoner released on parole will go on to commit another crime, or in predicting whether a potential candidate will perform well in a job in future. In over 100 studies across many different domains, half of all cases show simple formulas make (b) better significant predictions than human experts, and the remainder (except a very small handful), show a tie between the two. When there are a lot of different factors involved and a situation is very uncertain, simple formulas can win out by focusing on the most important factors and being consistent, while human judgement is too easily influenced by particularly salient and perhaps (c) irrelevant considerations. A similar idea is supported by further evidence that 'checklists' can improve the quality of expert decisions in a range of domains by ensuring that important steps or considerations aren't missed when people are feeling (d) relaxed. For example, treating patients in intensive care can require hundreds of small actions per day, and one small error could cost a life. Using checklists to ensure that no crucial steps are missed has proved to be remarkably (e) effective in a range of medical contexts, from preventing live infections to reducing pneumonia.

* parole: 가석방 ** salient: 두드러진 *** pneumonia: 폐렴

2023학년도 수능 41번 ★★★

1. 윗글의 제목으로 가장 적절한 것은?

① The Power of Simple Formulas in Decision Making
② Always Prioritise: Tips for Managing Big Data
③ Algorithms' Mistakes: The Myth of Simplicity
④ Be Prepared! Make a Checklist Just in Case
⑤ How Human Judgement Beats Algorithms

2023학년도 수능 42번 ★★★

2. 밑줄 친 (a)~(e) 중에서 문맥상 낱말의 쓰임이 적절하지 않은 것은?

① (a) ② (b) ③ (c) ④ (d) ⑤ (e)

2022학년도 수능 41~42번

【3~4】 다음 글을 읽고 물음에 답하시오.

Classifying things together into groups is something we do all the time, and it isn't hard to see why. Imagine trying to shop in a supermarket where the food was arranged in random order on the shelves: tomato soup next to the white bread in one aisle, chicken soup in the back next to the 60-watt light bulbs, one brand of cream cheese in front and another in aisle 8 near the cookies. The task of finding what you want would be (a) time-consuming and extremely difficult, if not impossible.

In the case of a supermarket, someone had to (b) design the system of classification. But there is also a ready-made system of classification embodied in our language. The word "dog," for example, groups together a certain class of animals and distinguishes them from other animals. Such a grouping may seem too (c) abstract to be called a classification, but this is only because you have already mastered the word. As a child learning to speak, you had to work hard to (d) learn the system of classification your parents were trying to teach you. Before you got the hang of it, you probably made mistakes, like calling the cat a dog. If you hadn't learned to speak, the whole world would seem like the (e) unorganized supermarket; you would be in the position of an infant, for whom every object is new and unfamiliar. In learning the principles of classification, therefore, we'll be learning about the structure that lies at the core of our language.

2022학년도 수능 41번 ★★☆

3. 윗글의 제목으로 가장 적절한 것은?

① Similarities of Strategies in Sales and Language Learning
② Classification: An Inherent Characteristic of Language
③ Exploring Linguistic Issues Through Categorization
④ Is a Ready-Made Classification System Truly Better?
⑤ Dilemmas of Using Classification in Language Education

2022학년도 수능 42번 ★★☆

4. 밑줄 친 (a)~(e) 중에서 문맥상 낱말의 쓰임이 적절하지 않은 것은?

① (a) ② (b) ③ (c) ④ (d) ⑤ (e)

Day 19

2021학년도 수능 41~42번

【5~6】 다음 글을 읽고 물음에 답하시오.

Our irresistible tendency to see things in human terms — that we are often mistaken in attributing complex human motives and processing abilities to other species — does not mean that an animal's behavior is not, in fact, complex. Rather, it means that the complexity of the animal's behavior is not purely a (a) product of its internal complexity. Herbert Simon's "parable of the ant" makes this point very clearly. Imagine an ant walking along a beach, and (b) visualize tracking the trajectory of the ant as it moves. The trajectory would show a lot of twists and turns, and would be very irregular and complicated. One could then suppose that the ant had equally complicated (c) internal navigational abilities, and work out what these were likely to be by analyzing the trajectory to infer the rules and mechanisms that could produce such a complex navigational path. The complexity of the trajectory, however, "is really a complexity in the surface of the beach, not a complexity in the ant." In reality, the ant may be using a set of very (d) complex rules: it is the interaction of these rules with the environment that actually produces the complex trajectory, not the ant alone. Put more generally, the parable of the ant illustrates that there is no necessary correlation between the complexity of an (e) observed behavior and the complexity of the mechanism that produces it.

* parable: 우화 ** trajectory: 이동 경로

2021학년도 수능 41번 ★★☆

5. 윗글의 제목으로 가장 적절한 것은?

① Open the Mysterious Door to Environmental Complexity!
② Peaceful Coexistence of Human Beings and Animals
③ What Makes the Complexity of Animal Behavior?
④ Animals' Dilemma: Finding Their Way in a Human World
⑤ Environmental Influences on Human Behavior Complexity

2021학년도 수능 42번 ★★☆

6. 밑줄 친 (a)~(e) 중에서 문맥상 낱말의 쓰임이 적절하지 않은 것은? [3점]

① (a) ② (b) ③ (c) ④ (d) ⑤ (e)

2020학년도 수능 41~42번

【7~8】 다음 글을 읽고 물음에 답하시오.

For quite some time, science educators believed that "hands-on" activities were the answer to children's understanding through their participation in science-related activities. Many teachers believed that students merely engaging in activities and (a) manipulating objects would organize the information to be gained and the knowledge to be understood into concept comprehension. Educators began to notice that the pendulum had swung too far to the "hands-on" component of inquiry as they realized that the knowledge was not (b) inherent in the materials themselves, but in the thought and metacognition about what students had done in the activity. We now know that "hands-on" is a dangerous phrase when speaking about learning science. The (c) missing ingredient is the "minds-on" part of the instructional experience. (d) Uncertainty about the knowledge intended in any activity comes from each student's re-creation of concepts — and discussing, thinking, arguing, listening, and evaluating one's own preconceptions after the activities, under the leadership of a thoughtful teacher, can bring this about. After all, a food fight is a hands-on activity, but about all you would learn was something about the aerodynamics of flying mashed potatoes! Our view of what students need to build their knowledge and theories about the natural world (e) extends far beyond a "hands-on activity." While it is important for students to use and interact with materials in science class, the learning comes from the sense-making of students' "hands-on" experiences.

* pendulum: 추(錘) ** metacognition: 초(超)인지
*** aerodynamics: 공기 역학

2020학년도 수능 41번 ★★★

7. 윗글의 제목으로 가장 적절한 것은?

① "Hands-on" Activities as a Source of Creativity
② Activity-oriented Learning Enters Science Education!
③ Figure Out What Students Like Most in Science Class
④ Joy and Learning: More Effective When Separated
⑤ Turn "Minds-on" Learning On in Science Class

2020학년도 수능 42번 ★★★

8. 밑줄 친 (a)~(e) 중에서 문맥상 낱말의 쓰임이 적절하지 않은 것은? [3점]

① (a) ② (b) ③ (c) ④ (d) ⑤ (e)

총 문항				문항	맞은 문항					문항
개별 문항	1	2	3	4	5	6	7	8	9	10
채점										

문법 플러스

19. 접속사, 전치사

정답 및 해설 106쪽

A 문법의 주요 포인트를 점검해 봅시다.

1 전치사 뒤에는 명사(구)가 나오고, 접속사 뒤에는 절(「주어+동사」)이 나온다. 그런데 두 개 이상의 단어가 하나의 전치사나 접속사의 역할을 하기도 한다.

의미	접속사	전치사
~때문에	because, now that, in that	because of, due to, owing to
~할 경우	in case(= if)	in case of
~에도 불구하고	even though, even if	in spite of(= despite)
~에 따라(기준)	according as	according to
~하자마자	the moment, as soon as	on
~에 관해	–	with regard to, as to
~하는 동안	while	during

▶ According **[as / to]** the demand increases, the price goes up.

2 등위접속사(and, but, or, so, for)는 문법적으로 대등한 관계에 있는 단어와 단어, 구와 구, 절과 절을 연결한다. 이를 병렬 구조라고 한다.

▶ I hope to go to that university and **[study / studying]** under Dr. Kim.

3 상관접속사는 짝으로 이루어진 접속사를 말한다. not A but B(A가 아니라 B), not only A but also B(A뿐만 아니라 B도(= B as well as A), either A or B(A 또는 B), neither A nor B(A도 B도 아닌), both A and B(A, B 둘 다) 등이 있다.

▶ How come neither you **[nor / or]** Sam came to my party?

4 명사절을 이끄는 접속사는 that, if, whether 등이 있고, 의문사가 명사절을 이끌기도 한다.

▶The most common explanation offered by my informants as to why fashion is so appealing is **[what / that]** it constitutes a kind of theatrical costumery.

5 종속접속사는 시간, 조건, 이유, 양보 등의 의미를 나타내는 부사절을 이끌 수 있다.

▶ Such primitive societies, **[than / as]** Steven Mithen emphasizes in *The Prehistory of the Modern Mind*, tend to view man and beast, animal and plant, organic and inorganic spheres, as participants in an integrated, animated totality.

6 「no sooner A than B」는 'A하자마자 B하다(= Hardly(Scarcely) A when(before) B)'의 의미이다. 이 경우, A에는 과거완료형이 나오고, B에는 과거시제가 나온다.

▶ Hardly had he come home **[when / than]** he started complaining.

7 「의문사+ever」는 양보의 부사절을 이끌 수 있다(= 「no matter+의문사」).

▶ I will stand by you **[whatever / whoever]** happens.

B 다음 괄호 안에서 어법상 올바른 것을 고르시오.

1 All the outdoor activities were canceled **[due to / because]** heavy snow.

2 He concentrated on improving his language ability and **[make / making]** friends in his school.

3 Their glory lies not in their achievements **[nor / but]** in their sacrifices.

4 Experimental results derived from a single subject are, therefore, of limited value; there is no way to know **[whether / what]** the subject's responses are typical or atypical of the response of humans as a group.

5 **[Because / Because of]** everything is interconnected, a change in one area may affect the other area.

6 No sooner had he finished a car washing **[when / than]** the rain began to fall.

7 **[Wherever, Whatever]** she goes, I will be right here waiting for her.

숙어 플러스

19. 수능 필수 숙어 19회

정답 및 해설 106쪽

A 다음 수능 필수 숙어를 읽고, 아는 것은 체크해 봅시다.

□ 01	take part in	~에 참여하다
□ 02	take place	개최되다, 일어나다
□ 03	take turns	번갈아 하다, ~을 교대로 하다
□ 04	tear down	파괴하다, 해체하다
□ 05	tell from	~과 구별되다
□ 06	that is	즉
□ 07	the former..., while the latter	~ 전자는 …인 반면, 후자는 ~
□ 08	the number of + 복수명사 + 단수동사	~의 수 cf. a number of + 복수명사(다수의)+ 복수동사
□ 09	the other day	일전에
□ 10	the ratio of 5 to 3	5대 3의 비율로
□ 11	think over	~을 숙고하다
□ 12	to be sure	틀림없이
□ 13	to one's surprise	놀랍게도
□ 14	to some extent	어느 정도까지
□ 15	to the point	간단명료한, 핵심적인
□ 16	try on	(옷을) 입어보다, (신을) 신어보다
□ 17	try one's best	최선을 다하다(=do one's best)
□ 18	turn around	방향을 바꾸다, 뒤돌아보다, (상황이) 호전되다
□ 19	turn down	(제안, 요구 등을) 거절하다(= reject)
□ 20	turn in	~을 반납하다, ~을 제출하다(= hand in)

B 다음 숙어 표현을 읽고 의미 차이를 비교해 봅시다.

□ 21	break with	~와 관계를 끊다
□ 22	deal with	~을 다루다, 처리하다
□ 23	dispense with	생략하다, 없애다, 제거하다(= get rid of)
□ 24	put up with	참다, 견디다
□ 25	correspond with	서신 왕래를 하다, 통신하다

C 우리말을 참고하여 빈칸에 알맞은 말을 써 봅시다.

1 전통적인 학교에서는, 학생들이 단체 운동과 동아리 활동에 참여할 수 있다.
In traditional schools, students may also _________ part in team sports and club activities.

2 각각의 학생들은 둥글게 둘러앉아, 돌아가며 다른 사람들에게 자신의 이름을 말했다.
Sitting in a circle, they took _____________ telling the others his or her name.

3 우리 대부분은 어느 정도까지는 속이는 방법을 알고 있는 것처럼 보인다.
It seems that most of us know how to fake it to some ___________.

4 Steve는 그 승진을 거절했다.
Steve turned ________________the promotion.

20 장문의 이해 (2)

출제 트렌드

1. 장문 1지문 3문항 문제 유형은 제1문항은 '주어진 글 (A)에 이어질 내용을 순서에 맞게 배열한 것으로 가장 적절한 것'을 묻는 문제가 출제되고, 제2문항은 '밑줄 친 (a) ~ (e) 중에서 가리키는 대상이 나머지 넷과 다른 것'을 묻는 문제가 출제된다. 제3문항은 '윗글의 ~에 관한 내용으로 가장 적절한 것을 묻는 문제가 출제된다.
2. 문단의 순서, 지칭 추론, 내용 일치 · 불일치 파악 등 다양한 문제로 출제되고 있다. 네 개의 문단으로 이루어진 글을 읽고 이에 따른 질문을 푸는 유형으로, 매년 수능에서 3문항이 출제되고 있다.
3. 빠른 독해력과 종합적인 사고력이 요구된다. 소설이나 수필에서 발췌한 글감을 토대로 비교적 쉬운 글이 제시되며 감동적이고 교훈적인 글이 출제된다.
4. 최근 수능 7년간, 장문의 이해 (2) 43–45번 문항은 매년 3문제가 출제되고 있다. 43번은 문단의 순서, 44번은 지칭 추론, 45번은 내용 일치 파악 문제로 출제되었다. 2017학년도 수능(71/79/86%), 2018(91/86/90%), 2019(91/90/88%), 2020(93/93/92%), 2021(91/87/92%), 2022(95/93/94%), 2023(91/85/86%)에서 괄호 안의 정답률을 보였다. 7년간 평균 88.8% 정도 정답률을 보였다. 난이도는 하 단계이다. 7년간 평균 43번 문항은 89%, 44번 문항은 87.6%, 45번 문항은 89.7%의 정답률을 보였다.
5. 난이도가 높지 않으므로, 난이도가 높은 빈칸 4문제를 먼저 풀지 말고 전략적으로 장문의 이해 (1), (2) 문제를 먼저 푸는 것이 유리하다.

출처			문항 번호	지문 주제	정답률(%)	난이도
대표	2023학년도	수능	43–45번	아빠에게 준 생일 선물	91 / 85 / 86	★☆☆
1~3	2023학년도	09 모평	43–45번	Van Gogh의 '해바라기'를 보기 위한 여정	89 / 92 / 93	★☆☆
4~6	2022학년도	수능	43–45번	태권도 연습에 나오지 못한 Cora	95 / 93 /94	★☆☆
7~9	2021학년도	수능	43–45번	동물 행동의 복잡성	91 / 87 /92	★☆☆
10~12	2020학년도	수능	43~45번	연어를 보고 용기를 낸 전 챔피언	93 /93 /92	★☆☆

1등급 꿀팁

1. 글을 읽기 전에 제시된 문제가 무엇인지 먼저 파악한다.
2. 제시된 사건의 순서를 파악한 후 글의 순서를 정해야 한다.
3. 등장인물들의 말과 행동을 이해한 후, 지칭 대상이 다른 것을 파악한다.
4. 사건의 세부 사항을 파악한 후 내용 일치 문제를 해결한다.

대표 기출

2023학년도 수능 43~45번

[43~45] 다음 글을 읽고, 물음에 답하시오.

(A)

"Hailey, be careful!" Camila yelled uneasily, watching her sister carrying a huge cake to the table. "Don't worry, Camila," Hailey responded, smiling. Camila relaxed only when Hailey had safely placed the cake on the party table. "Dad will be here shortly. What gift did (a) you buy for his birthday?" Camila asked out of interest. "Dad will be surprised to find out what it is!" Hailey answered with a wink.

(B)

"Dad, these glasses can help correct your red-green color blindness," said Hailey. He slowly put them on, and stared at the birthday presents on the table. Seeing vivid red and green colors for the first time ever, he started to cry. "Incredible! Look at those wonderful colors!" He shouted in amazement. Hailey told him in tears, "Dad, I'm glad you can now finally enjoy the true beauty of rainbows and roses. Red represents love and green represents health. You deserve both." Camila nodded, seeing how happy (b) her gift of the glasses had made their dad.

(C)

"Happy birthday! You're fifty today, Dad. We love you!" Camila said before (c) her sister handed him a small parcel. When he opened it, he discovered a pair of glasses inside. "Hailey, Dad doesn't have eyesight problems," Camila said, puzzled. "Actually Camila, I recently found out he has long been suffering from color blindness. He's kept it a secret so as not to worry us," Hailey explained.

(D)

"I bet (d) you bought a wallet or a watch for him," Camila said. In reply, Hailey answered, "No. I bought something much more personal. By the way, there's something (e) you should know about Dad..." They were suddenly interrupted by the doorbell ringing. It was their dad and they were overjoyed to see him. "My lovely ladies, thank you for inviting me to your place for my birthday." He walked in joyfully, hugging his daughters. They all walked into the dining room, where he was greeted with a rainbow-colored birthday cake and fifty red roses.

2023학년도 수능 43번 ★☆☆

43. 주어진 글 (A)에 이어질 내용을 순서에 맞게 배열한 것으로 가장 적절한 것은?

① (B) – (D) – (C) ② (C) – (B) – (D)
③ (C) – (D) – (B) ④ (D) – (B) – (C)
⑤ (D) – (C) – (B)

제한 시간 : 20분 | 정답 및 해설 107쪽

총 문항				문항	맞은 문항							문항
개별 문항	1	2	3	4	5	6	7	8	9	10	11	12
채점												

2023학년도 수능 44번 ★☆☆

44. 밑줄 친 (a)~(e) 중에서 가리키는 대상이 나머지 넷과 다른 것은?

① (a) ② (b) ③ (c) ④ (d) ⑤ (e)

2023학년도 수능 45번 ★★☆

45. 윗글에 관한 내용으로 적절하지 않은 것은?

① Hailey는 생일 케이크를 테이블로 무사히 옮겨 놓았다.
② 아버지는 생일 선물로 받은 안경을 직접 써 보았다.
③ Hailey는 아버지가 색맹이라는 사실을 최근에 알게 되었다.
④ Hailey와 Camila는 아버지의 집을 방문하였다.
⑤ 아버지는 자신의 나이와 똑같은 수의 장미를 받았다.

문제 풀이

1. 주어진 글 (A)를 읽고, 글 (B), (C), (D)의 첫 문장이나 마지막 문장을 통해 글의 순서를 추측해 본다.

글 (A): Camila와 Hailey가 아빠의 생일을 위해 케이크를 테이블에 올려놓고 생일 선물에 관해 이야기한다.

글 (D): 그들의 아버지가 그들의 집에 와서 무지개색 생일 케이크와 50송이의 빨간 장미를 받았다.

글 (C): 아빠가 오랫동안 색맹을 앓고 있다는 것을 비밀로 해온 것을 Hailey가 최근에 알게 되어 아빠를 위해 색맹 교정 안경을 생일 선물로 준비했다.

글 (B): 안경을 쓴 아빠가 경이롭게 선명한 색들을 보고 매우 행복해했다.

- 43. (A) 단락 끝부분에서 언니 Camila가 동생 Haeiley에게 아빠 선물로 무엇을 샀냐고 묻자, 동생은 답을 하지 않고 윙크를 했으므로 (D)와 같이 언니가 동생이 산 선물에 대해 추측하는 내용이 나올 수 있다. 동생은 아빠를 위해 더 개인적인 것을 샀다고 답한다. (C)에서는 동생이 아빠를 위해 준비한 개인적인 선물이 밝혀진다. 그것은 아빠를 위한 색맹 안경이었다. (B)에서는 선물로 받은 적록색명 안경을 쓰고 느끼는 아빠의 감정이 드러나 있으므로 글의 순서는 (A) 다음에 (D)-(C)-(B) 순서로 진행하는 것이 흐름상 자연스럽다. 그러므로 정답은 ⑤번이다.

2. 글의 흐름에 맞추어 글의 내용을 이해하고 글의 세부 사항을 확인한다.

- 44. (a), (b), (c), (d)는 모두 Hailey를 가리키지만, (e)는 Camila를 가리킨다. 그러므로 정답은 ⑤번이다.

3. 글의 세부 사항은 본문과 선택지 순서가 일치하게 전개된다.

① Hailey는 생일 케이크를 테이블로 무사히 옮겨 놓았다.
→ "Hailey, be careful!" Camila yelled uneasily, watching her sister carrying a huge cake to the table.

② 아버지는 생일 선물로 받은 안경을 직접 써 보았다.
→ He slowly put them on, and stared at the birthday presents on the table.

③ Hailey는 아버지가 색맹이라는 사실을 최근에 알게 되었다.
→ "Actually Camila, I recently found out he has long been suffering from color blindness.

⑤ 아버지는 자신의 나이와 똑같은 수의 장미를 받았다.
→ They all walked into the dining room, where he was greeted with a rainbow-colored birthday cake and fifty red roses.

- 45. (D)에서 아버지가 자기 생일에 그녀들의 집에 자신을 초대해줘서 고맙다("My lovely ladies, thank you for inviting me to your place for my birthday.")고 했으므로, 글의 내용으로 적절하지 않다. 그러므로 정답은 ④번이다.

2023학년도 9월 모평 43~45번 ★☆☆

[1~3] 다음 글을 읽고 물음에 답하시오.

(A)

Walking out of Charing Cross Station in London, Emilia and her traveling companion, Layla, already felt their hearts pounding. It was the second day of their European summer trip. They were about to visit one of the world's most famous art galleries. The two of them started hurrying with excitement. Suddenly, Emilia shouted, "Look! There it is! We're finally at the National Gallery!" Layla laughed and responded, "(a) Your dream's finally come true!"

(B)

"Don't lose hope yet! Which gallery is the special exhibition at?" Layla asked. Emilia responded, "Well, his *Sunflowers* is still in England, but it's at a gallery in Liverpool. That's a long way, isn't it?" After a quick search on her phone, Layla stated, "No! It's only two hours to Liverpool by train. The next train leaves in an hour. Why don't we take it?" After considering the idea, Emilia, now relieved, responded, "Yeah, but (b) you always wanted to see Rembrandt's paintings. Let's do that first, Layla! Then, after lunch, we can catch the next train." Layla smiled brightly.

(C)

However, after searching all the exhibition rooms, Emilia and Layla couldn't find van Gogh's masterpiece anywhere. "That's weird. Van Gogh's *Sunflowers* should be here. Where is it?" Emilia looked upset, but Layla kept calm and said, "Maybe (c) you've missed a notice about it. Check the National Gallery app." Emilia checked it quickly. Then, she sighed, "*Sunflowers* isn't here! It's been lent to a different gallery for a special exhibition. (d) I can't believe I didn't check!"

(D)

Upon entering the National Gallery, Emilia knew exactly where to go first. (e) She grabbed Layla's hand and dragged her hurriedly to find van Gogh's *Sunflowers*. It was Emilia's favorite painting and had inspired her to become a painter. Emilia loved his use of bright colors and light. She couldn't wait to finally see his masterpiece in person. "It'll be amazing to see how he communicated the feelings of isolation and loneliness in his work," she said eagerly.

1. 주어진 글 (A)에 이어질 내용을 순서에 맞게 배열한 것으로 가장 적절한 것은?

① (B) − (D) − (C)　② (C) − (B) − (D)
③ (C) − (D) − (B)　④ (D) − (B) − (C)
⑤ (D) − (C) − (B)

2. 밑줄 친 (a)~(e) 중에서 가리키는 대상이 나머지 넷과 다른 것은?

① (a)　② (b)　③ (c)　④ (d)　⑤ (e)

3. 윗글에 관한 내용으로 적절하지 않은 것은?

① Emilia와 Layla는 유럽 여행 중이었다.
② Layla는 Emilia에게 Liverpool로 가자고 제안했다.
③ Emilia는 기차를 점심 식사 전에 타자고 말했다.
④ National Gallery에는 van Gogh의 *Sunflowers*가 없었다.
⑤ Emilia는 van Gogh의 *Sunflowers*를 좋아했다.

2022학년도 수능 43~45번 ★☆☆

[4~6] 다음 글을 읽고 물음에 답하시오.

(A)

In the gym, members of the taekwondo club were busy practicing. Some were trying to kick as high as they could, and some were striking the sparring pad. Anna, the head of the club, was teaching the new members basic moves. Close by, her friend Jane was assisting Anna. Jane noticed that Anna was glancing at the entrance door of the gym. She seemed to be expecting someone. At last, when Anna took a break, Jane came over to (a) her and asked, "Hey, are you waiting for Cora?"

(B)

Cora walked in like a wounded soldier with bandages on her face and arms. Surprised, Anna and Jane simply looked at her with their eyes wide open. Cora explained, "I'm sorry I've been absent. I got into a bicycle accident, and I was in the hospital for two days. Finally, the doctor gave me the okay to practice." Anna said excitedly, "No problem! We're thrilled to have you back!" Then, Jane gave Anna an apologetic look, and (b) she responded with a friendly pat on Jane's shoulder.

(C)

Anna answered the question by nodding uneasily. In fact, Jane knew what her friend was thinking. Cora was a new member, whom Anna had personally invited to join the club. Anna really liked (c) her. Although her budget was tight, Anna bought Cora a taekwondo uniform. When she received it, Cora thanked her and promised, "I'll come to practice and work hard every day." However, unexpectedly, she came to practice only once and then never showed up again.

(D)

Since Cora had missed several practices, Anna wondered what could have happened. Jane, on the other hand, was disappointed and said judgingly, "Still waiting for her, huh? I can't believe (d) you don't feel disappointed or angry. Why don't you forget about her?" Anna replied, "Well, I know most newcomers don't keep their commitment to the club, but I thought that Cora would be different. She said she would come every day and practice." Just as Jane was about to respond to (e) her, the door swung open. There she was!

4. 주어진 글 (A)에 이어질 내용을 순서에 맞게 배열한 것으로 가장 적절한 것은?

① (B) − (D) − (C)　② (C) − (B) − (D)
③ (C) − (D) − (B)　④ (D) − (B) − (C)
⑤ (D) − (C) − (B)

5. 밑줄 친 (a)~(e) 중에서 가리키는 대상이 나머지 넷과 다른 것은?

① (a)　② (b)　③ (c)　④ (d)　⑤ (e)

6. 윗글에 관한 내용으로 적절하지 않은 것은?

① Anna는 신입 회원에게 태권도를 가르쳤다.
② Anna와 Jane은 Cora를 보고 놀라지 않았다.
③ Anna는 Cora에게 태권도 도복을 사 주었다.
④ Cora는 여러 차례 연습에 참여하지 않았다.
⑤ Anna는 Cora를 대다수의 신입 회원과 다를 것이라 생각했다.

2021학년도 수능 43~45번 ★☆☆

【7~9】 다음 글을 읽고 물음에 답하시오.

(A)

In this area, heavy snow in winter was not uncommon. Sometimes it poured down for hours and hours and piled up very high. Then, no one could go out. Today too, because of the heavy snow, Mom was doing her office work at the kitchen table. Felix, the high schooler, had to take online classes in his room. Five-year-old Sean, who normally went to kindergarten, was sneaking around in the house playing home policeman. (a) The kindergartener wanted to know what his family members were up to, and was checking up on everyone.

* sneak: 몰래 움직이다

(B)

"All right. I'm sure you're doing your work." Mom replied, and then sharply added a question. "Sean, what are *you* doing?" Sean's face immediately became blank, and he said, "Nothing." "Come here, Honey, and you can help me." Sean ran to the kitchen right away. "What can I do for you, Mom?" His voice was high, and Felix could sense that his brother was excited. Felix was pleased to get rid of (b) the policeman, and now he could concentrate on the lesson, at least till Sean came back.

(C)

While checking on his family, Sean interfered in their business as if it was his own. This time, (c) the playful and curious boy was interested in his brother Felix, who committed himself to studying no matter where he was. Sean secretly looked inside his brother's room from the door, and shouted toward the kitchen where Mom was working, "Mom, Felix isn't studying. He's just watching a funny video." Sean was naughtily smiling at his brother.

* naughtily: 짓궂게

(D)

Felix was mad because (d) his little brother was bothering him. Felix was studying science using a video posted on the school web site. He made an angry face at the naughty boy. Right then, Mom asked loudly from the kitchen, "What are you doing, Felix?" Felix's room was located next to the kitchen, and he could hear Mom clearly. "I'm watching a lecture video for my science class." Felix argued against Sean's accusation and mischievously stuck (e) his tongue out at his little brother.

* mischievously: 장난기 있게

7. 주어진 글 (A)에 이어질 내용을 순서에 맞게 배열한 것으로 가장 적절한 것은?

① (B) – (D) – (C)　② (C) – (B) – (D)
③ (C) – (D) – (B)　④ (D) – (B) – (C)
⑤ (D) – (C) – (B)

8. 밑줄 친 (a)~(e) 중에서 가리키는 대상이 나머지 넷과 다른 것은?

① (a)　② (b)　③ (c)　④ (d)　⑤ (e)

9. 윗글에 관한 내용으로 적절하지 않은 것은?

① 엄마는 폭설로 인해 집에서 업무를 보고 있었다.
② Sean은 엄마가 불러서 주방으로 달려갔다.
③ Sean은 몰래 형의 방을 들여다보았다.
④ Felix는 자신의 방에서 게임을 하고 있었다.
⑤ Felix의 방은 주방 옆에 있었다.

2020학년도 수능 43~45번 ★☆☆

【10~12】 다음 글을 읽고 물음에 답하시오.

(A)

The colors of the trees looked like they were on fire, the reds and oranges competing with the yellows and golds. This was Nina's favorite season, but she remained silent for hours while Marie was driving. Nina had been heartbroken after losing her championship belt. Now a former champion, she was thinking of retiring from boxing. Marie, her long-time friend and trainer, shared her pain. After another silent hour, Marie and Nina saw a sign: Sauble Falls. Marie thought this would be a good place for (a) them to stop.

(B)

Then, with a great push, a small one turned a complete circle and made it over the falls. "He made it!" Nina shouted at the success with admiration. More salmon then followed and succeeded. She felt ashamed to be looking at (b) them. After a moment, she turned to Marie and said, "Giving up is not in my vocabulary. Marie, I'll get my championship belt back." Marie nodded with a bright smile. "Our training begins tomorrow. It's going to be tough. Are you ready?" Walking up the path and back to the car, (c) they could still hear the fish splashing in the water.

* splash: 물을 튀기다

(C)

Marie pulled over into the parking lot. Marie and Nina went down a path to watch the falls. Another sign: Watch Your Step. Rocks Are Slippery. (d) They found the falls spilling out in various layers of rock. No one was there except them. "Look at them!" Marie pointed to movement in the water moving toward the falls. Hundreds of fish tails were flashing and catching light from the sun, moving upstream. Beneath them in the water, they saw salmon slowly moving their bodies.

(D)

While Marie and Nina kept watching the salmon, a big one suddenly leapt. It threw itself up and over the rushing water above, but in vain. (e) They were standing without a word and watching the fish struggling. Another jumped, its body spinning until it made it over the falls. Another one leapt and was washed back by the power of the water. Watching the salmon, Marie noticed Nina fixing her eyes on their continuing challenge. Nina's heart was beating fast at each leap and twist.

10. 주어진 글 (A)에 이어질 내용을 순서에 맞게 배열한 것으로 가장 적절한 것은?

① (B) – (D) – (C)　② (C) – (B) – (D)
③ (C) – (D) – (B)　④ (D) – (B) – (C)
⑤ (D) – (C) – (B)

11. 밑줄 친 (a)~(e) 중에서 가리키는 대상이 나머지 넷과 다른 것은?

① (a)　② (b)　③ (c)　④ (d)　⑤ (e)

12. 윗글에 관한 내용으로 적절하지 않은 것은?

① Marie가 운전하는 동안 Nina는 말이 없었다.
② Marie는 Nina의 오랜 친구이자 트레이너였다.
③ 폭포에서 Nina는 Marie에게 권투를 그만두겠다고 말했다.
④ 폭포에 있는 사람은 Marie와 Nina뿐이었다.
⑤ Nina는 폭포 위로 뛰어오르는 연어를 유심히 바라보았다.

문법 플러스

20. 특수 구문

정답 및 해설 111쪽

A 문법의 주요 포인트를 점검해 봅시다.

1 부정어(구)가 문장 앞에 오면 「주어+(조)동사」가 도치된다.

▶ Not only **[could they / they could]** see nothing in front of them, but they were tired and ill and could not walk any more.

2 Only가 포함된 어구가 문장 앞에 와도 「주어+(조)동사」가 도치된다.

▶ Only for the love of his family **[Sam does / does Sam]** do such hard work.

3 장소와 방향을 나타내는 부사(구)가 문장 앞에 오면 주어와 동사가 도치된다. 단, 주어가 대명사인 경우에는 도치되지 않는다. 또한 be동사가 쓰인 문장에서 보어를 문장의 앞에 두면, 주어와 be동사가 도치된다.

▶ Here **[comes the writer / the writer comes]**!

4 It is[was] ~ that 강조 구문은 주어, 목적어, 보어, 부사구를 It is[was] ~ that 사이에 넣어 강조한다. 강조되는 어구가 사람이면 who를, 사물이면 which를 that 대신에 쓸 수 있다.

▶ It is those explorers, through their unceasing trial and error, **[which / who]** have paved the way for us to follow.

5 특정한 어휘나 구를 사용하여 문장의 특정 부분을 강조할 수 있다. 조동사 do를 사용하여 동사를 강조할 수 있고, 재귀대명사나 the very를 사용하여 명사를 강조할 수 있다. 소유격을 강조할 때는 「소유격+own+명사」를 사용한다.

▶ Rowling's books **[do / does]** contain supernatural creatures.

6 전체를 나타내는 어구가 not과 함께 쓰이면 부분 부정의 의미를 나타낸다.

▶ **[Not every / Every not]** news on the Internet is true.

7 동격 관계를 나타내는 어구는 앞의 표현을 부가적으로 설명하는 기능을 한다. 문장에서 일정어구가 반복되거나 의미적으로 추론이 가능할 때 생략한다. 특히, 일반동사로 시작하는 어구가 반복되면 대동사 do를 사용하여 생략한다. 앞에 나온 동사가 be동사이며 반복을 피하기 위해 be동사를 대동사로 쓸 수 있다.

▶ Sally, my best friend, plays the piano better than I **[do / does]**.

cf. These experts **are** still with us, as a result so **is** the phrase.

(이 전문가들은 여전히 우리와 함께 하고 있으며, 결과적으로 이 문구도 그렇다.)

B 다음 괄호 안에서 어법상 올바른 것을 고르시오.

1 Hardly **[had she / she had]** gone when he began to speak ill of her.

2 Only after hard work **[can rest / rest can]** be truly enjoyed.

3 Blessed **[are the poor / the poor are]** in spirit.

4 It was not her remarks **[which / who]** we found very unpleasant.

5 She is **[does / the very]** woman who helped me the other day.

6 It's okay if you don't like me. **[Everyone not / Not everyone]** has a good taste.

7 Each daughter cell is smaller than the mother cell, and except for unusual cases, each grows until it becomes as large as the mother cell **[was / did]**.

숙어 플러스

20. 수능 필수 숙어 20회

정답 및 해설 111쪽

A 다음 수능 필수 숙어를 읽고, 아는 것은 체크해 봅시다.

□ 01	turn into	~으로 변하다
□ 02	turn off	(전기, 가스, 수도 등을) 끄다, 잠그다
□ 03	turn on	(전기, 가스, 수도 등을) 켜다
□ 04	turn to	의지하다, (성질이 ~로) 변하다
□ 05	turn up	(사람이) 도착하다, (기회가) 생기다
□ 06	under pressure	압박을 받는, 강요당하는
□ 07	up and down	위아래로, 왔다 갔다
□ 08	up to date	최신의
□ 09	upside down	거꾸로
□ 10	use up	다 써버리다
□ 11	used to + 동사원형	~하곤 했다, (과거에) ~이었다
□ 12	vote for	~에 찬성투표하다
□ 13	warm up	준비 운동을 하다
□ 14	warn ~ about	~에게 (위험 등)을 경고하다
□ 15	what is called	소위, 이른바
□ 16	wipe out	~을 완전히 파괴하다
□ 17	with respect to	~에 관하여
□ 18	work out	운동하다, 일이 잘 풀리다
□ 19	would rather + 동사원형	차라리 ~하고 싶다
□ 20	wrap up	(회의 등을) 마무리 짓다, 포장하다

B 다음 숙어 표현을 읽고 의미 차이를 비교해 봅시다.

□ 21	be about to do	막 ~ 하려고 하다
□ 22	be apt to do	~하기 쉽다, ~하는 경향이 있다
□ 23	be inclined to do	~하는 경향이 있다
□ 24	be anxious to do	~하기를 갈망하다
□ 25	be supposed to do	~하기로 되어 있다, ~해야 한다

C 우리말을 참고하여 빈칸에 알맞은 말을 써 봅시다.

1 부엌 전등은 껐니?
Did you ___________ off my kitchen light?

2 압박감을 받을 때 휴식에 좀 더 주의를 기울임으로써 이러한 방식에서 벗어나도록 하라.
Break out of this pattern by paying more attention to relaxation when you are under ________________.

3 인생은 롤러코스터를 타는 것과 같을 수 있다. 오르고 내리거나 심지어 거꾸로 뒤집힐 때가 존재한다.
Life can be like riding a roller coaster. There are ups and downs and even times when you're upside ________.

4 부산 국제 영화제가 흥분된 10일 간을 성공적으로 마쳤다.
The Busan International Film Festival wrapped ___________ ten days of excitement.

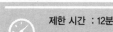

제한 시간 : 12분 | 정답 및 해설 112쪽

2022학년도 3월 학평 31번 ★★★

1. 다음 빈칸에 들어갈 말로 가장 적절한 것은?

In the Indian language of pali, *mettā* means benevolence, kindness or tenderness. It is one of the most important ideas in Buddhism. Buddhism recommends a daily ritual meditation (known as *mettā bhāvanā*) to foster this attitude. The meditation begins with a call to think carefully every morning of an individual with whom one tends to get irritated or to whom one feels aggressive or cold and — in place of one's normal hostile impulses — to rehearse kindly messages like 'I hope you will find peace' or 'I wish you to be free from suffering'. This practice can be extended outwards ultimately to include pretty much everyone on Earth. The background assumption is that, with the right stimulus, our feelings towards people are not fixed and unalterable, but open to deliberate change and improvement. ____________ is a learnable skill, and we need to direct it as much towards those we are tempted to dismiss and detest as to those we love.

① Creativity ② Relaxation
③ Compassion ④ Justification
⑤ Empowerment

2021학년도 9월 모평 33번 ★☆☆

2. 다음 빈칸에 들어갈 말로 가장 적절한 것은?

Since human beings are at once both similar and different, they should be treated equally because of both. Such a view, which grounds equality not in human uniformity but in the interplay of uniformity and difference, builds difference into the very concept of equality, breaks the traditional equation of equality with similarity, and is immune to monist distortion. Once the basis of equality changes so does its content. Equality involves equal freedom or opportunity to be different, and treating human beings equally requires us to take into account both their similarities and differences. When the latter are not relevant, equality entails uniform or identical treatment; when they are, it requires differential treatment. Equal rights do not mean identical rights, for individuals with different cultural backgrounds and needs might ____________________ in respect of whatever happens to be the content of their rights. Equality involves not just rejection of irrelevant differences as is commonly argued, but also full recognition of legitimate and relevant ones. [3점]

* monist: 일원론의 ** entail: 내포하다

① require different rights to enjoy equality
② abandon their own freedom for equality
③ welcome the identical perception of inequality
④ accept their place in the social structure more easily
⑤ reject relevant differences to gain full understanding

2021학년도 4월 학평 35번 ★★☆

3. 다음 글에서 전체 흐름과 관계 없는 문장은?

Research has shown that individuals — especially those who have benefited from a particular system — are prone to support and rationalize the status quo, even if there are clear problems. ① These people justify systemic inequity with familiar phrases like "If you just work hard enough you can pull yourself up by your bootstraps." ② A branch of psychology called *system justification theory* describes how people tend to see social, economic, and political systems as good, fair, and legitimate if they have succeeded as a result of those systems. ③ According to Erin Godfrey, a professor of applied psychology at New York University, "The people who are at the top want to believe in meritocracy because it means that they deserve their successes." ④ Indeed, it is not suprising that there exists a general consensus across social class about the definition and the results of meritocracy. ⑤ Those who are in an advantaged position in society are more likely to believe the system is fair and see no reason to change it.

* status quo: 현재 상태 ** meritocracy: 능력주의

2021학년도 9월 모평 36번 ★★★

4. 주어진 글 다음에 이어질 글의 순서로 가장 적절한 것은?

In the fifth century *B.C.E.*, the Greek philosopher Protagoras pronounced, "Man is the measure of all things." In other words, we feel entitled to ask the world, "What good are you?"

(A) Abilities said to "make us human" — empathy, communication, grief, toolmaking, and so on — all exist to varying degrees among other minds sharing the world with us. Animals with backbones (fishes, amphibians, reptiles, birds, and mammals) all share the same basic skeleton, organs, nervous systems, hormones, and behaviors.

(B) We assume that we are the world's standard, that all things should be compared to us. Such an assumption makes us overlook a lot.

(C) Just as different models of automobiles each have an engine, drive train, four wheels, doors, and seats, we differ mainly in terms of our outside contours and a few internal tweaks. But like naive car buyers, most people see only animals' varied exteriors.

* contour: 윤곽, 외형 ** tweak: 조정, 개조

① (A) – (C) – (B) ② (B) – (A) – (C)
③ (B) – (C) – (A) ④ (C) – (A) – (B)
⑤ (C) – (B) – (A)

2020학년도 7월 학평 38번 ★★☆

5. 글의 흐름으로 보아, 주어진 문장이 들어가기에 가장 적절한 곳은?

> That is because when you recall a real memory, you begin to reexperience some of the emotion from that event.

There are several broad differences in the way that liars and truth tellers discuss events. One difference is that liars say less overall than truth tellers. If you are telling the truth, the details of what happened are obvious. (①) If you are lying, it is not easy to conjure up lots of details. (②) Interestingly, truth tellers talk *less* about their emotions than liars do. (③) As a result, that emotion feels obvious to you (and would be obvious to anyone watching you). (④) If you are lying, though, you don't really experience that emotion, so you describe it instead. (⑤) Truth tellers also talk about themselves more than liars, because people telling the truth are more focused on their own memories than liars are (who are also thinking about how their story is being perceived by others). [3점]

* conjure up: 떠올리다

2020학년도 7월 학평 40번 ★★☆

6. 다음 글의 내용을 한 문장으로 요약하고자 한다. 빈칸 (A), (B)에 들어갈 말로 가장 적절한 것은?

> In 2010 scientists conducted a rat experiment. They locked a rat in a tiny cage, placed the cage within a much larger cell and allowed another rat to roam freely through that cell. The caged rat gave out distress signals, which caused the free rat also to exhibit signs of anxiety and stress. In most cases, the free rat proceeded to help her trapped companion, and after several attempts usually succeeded in opening the cage and liberating the prisoner. The researchers then repeated the experiment, this time placing chocolate in the cell. The free rat now had to choose between either liberating the prisoner, or enjoying the chocolate all by herself. Many rats preferred to first free their companion and share the chocolate (though a few behaved more selfishly, proving perhaps that some rats are meaner than others).

⬇

> In a series of experiments, when the free rats witnessed their fellow in a state of ___(A)___ in a cage, they tended to rescue their companion, even ___(B)___ eating chocolate.

	(A)		(B)
①	anguish	······	delaying
②	anguish	······	prioritizing
③	excitement	······	prioritizing
④	boredom	······	rejecting
⑤	boredom	······	delaying

2022학년도 9월 모평 41~42번

【7~8】 다음 글을 읽고 물음에 답하시오.

> In studies examining the effectiveness of vitamin C, researchers typically divide the subjects into two groups. One group (the experimental group) receives a vitamin C supplement, and the other (the control group) does not. Researchers observe both groups to determine whether one group has fewer or shorter colds than the other. The following discussion describes some of the pitfalls inherent in an experiment of this kind and ways to (a) <u>avoid</u> them. In sorting subjects into two groups, researchers must ensure that each person has an (b) <u>equal</u> chance of being assigned to either the experimental group or the control group. This is accomplished by randomization; that is, the subjects are chosen randomly from the same population by flipping a coin or some other method involving chance. Randomization helps to ensure that results reflect the treatment and not factors that might influence the grouping of subjects. Importantly, the two groups of people must be similar and must have the same track record with respect to colds to (c) <u>rule out</u> the possibility that observed differences in the rate, severity, or duration of colds might have occurred anyway. If, for example, the control group would normally catch twice as many colds as the experimental group, then the findings prove (d) <u>nothing</u>. In experiments involving a nutrient, the diets of both groups must also be (e) <u>different</u>, especially with respect to the nutrient being studied. If those in the experimental group were receiving less vitamin C from their usual diet, then any effects of the supplement may not be apparent.
>
> * pitfall: 함정

2022학년도 9월 모평 41번 ★★☆

7. 윗글의 제목으로 가장 적절한 것은?

① Perfect Planning and Faulty Results: A Sad Reality in Research
② Don't Let Irrelevant Factors Influence the Results!
③ Protect Human Subjects Involved in Experimental Research!
④ What Nutrients Could Better Defend Against Colds?
⑤ In-depth Analysis of Nutrition: A Key Player for Human Health

2022학년도 9월 모평 42번 ★★★

8. 밑줄 친 (a)~(e) 중에서 문맥상 쓰임이 적절하지 <u>않은</u> 것은?

① (a) ② (b) ③ (c) ④ (d) ⑤ (e)

총 문항				문항	맞은 문항					문항
개별 문항	1	2	3	4	5	6	7	8	9	10
채점										

Day 22

제한 시간 : 12분 | 정답 및 해설 116쪽

2021학년도 9월 모평 32번 ★★★

1. 다음 빈칸에 들어갈 말로 가장 적절한 것은?

Genetic engineering followed by cloning to distribute many identical animals or plants is sometimes seen as a threat to the diversity of nature. However, humans have been replacing diverse natural habitats with artificial monoculture for millennia. Most natural habitats in the advanced nations have already been replaced with some form of artificial environment based on mass production or repetition. The real threat to biodiversity is surely the need to convert ever more of our planet into production zones to feed the ever-increasing human population. The cloning and transgenic alteration of domestic animals makes little difference to the overall situation. Conversely, the renewed interest in genetics has led to a growing awareness that there are many wild plants and animals with interesting or useful genetic properties that could be used for a variety of as-yet-unknown purposes. This has led in turn to a realization that ______________________ because they may harbor tomorrow's drugs against cancer, malaria, or obesity.

* monoculture: 단일 경작

① ecological systems are genetically programmed
② we should avoid destroying natural ecosystems
③ we need to stop creating genetically modified organisms
④ artificial organisms can survive in natural environments
⑤ living things adapt themselves to their physical environments

2021학년도 9월 모평 34번 ★★★

2. 다음 빈칸에 들어갈 말로 가장 적절한 것은?

Protopia is a state of becoming, rather than a destination. It is a process. In the protopian mode, things are better today than they were yesterday, although only a little better. It is incremental improvement or mild progress. The "pro" in protopian stems from the notions of process and progress. This subtle progress is not dramatic, not exciting. It is easy to miss because a protopia generates almost as many new problems as new benefits. The problems of today were caused by yesterday's technological successes, and the technological solutions to today's problems will cause the problems of tomorrow. This circular expansion of both problems and solutions ______________________. Ever since the Enlightenment and the invention of science, we've managed to create a tiny bit more than we've destroyed each year. But that few percent positive difference is compounded over decades into what we might call civilization. Its benefits never star in movies. [3점]

* incremental: 증가의
** compound: 조합하다

① conceals the limits of innovations at the present time
② makes it difficult to predict the future with confidence
③ motivates us to quickly achieve a protopian civilization
④ hides a steady accumulation of small net benefits over time
⑤ produces a considerable change in technological successes

2021학년도 7월 학평 35번 ★★☆

3. 다음 글에서 전체 흐름과 관계 없는 문장은?

Cyber attacks on air traffic control systems have become a leading security concern. ① The federal government released a report in 2009 stating that the nation's air traffic control system is vulnerable to a cyber attack that could interrupt communication with pilots and alter the flight information used to separate aircraft as they approach an airport. ② The report found numerous security problems in airline computer systems, including easy-to-crack passwords and unencrypted file folders, issues that could give invaders easy access. ③ A cyber attack on air traffic has the potential to kill many people and could cripple the country's entire airline industry. ④ Unprecedented declines in consumer demand impacted the profitability of the airline industry, changing the face of aircraft travel for the foreseeable future. ⑤ Tightening airline computer security could be even more important than conducting security screenings of passengers, because in an increasingly cyber-oriented world, plane hijackers of the future may not even be on board.

* unencrypted: 암호화되지 않은 ** cripple: 무력하게 만들다

2020학년도 10월 학평 39번 ★★★

4. 글의 흐름으로 보아, 주어진 문장이 들어가기에 가장 적절한 곳은?

> These constraints may be helpful to facilitate agreement, as they put pressure on parties to come to agreement.

Any negotiation is bounded in terms of time allocated to it, and time constraints are especially important when it comes to constitutional negotiations. (①) Constitutions are typically, though not always, adopted in moments of high political drama, perhaps even violent crisis. (②) Often there are upstream constraints that limit the amount of time available to drafters—deadlines that are exogenously fixed and cannot be evaded. (③) But they also bound the negotiation and prevent the parties from spelling out a complete set of arrangements, and so the constitutional bargain will of necessity be incomplete. (④) Negotiators may focus only on the largest, most salient issues, leaving more minor ones unresolved. (⑤) Time pressures contribute to the introduction of structural mistakes in the constitutional text, seeding pitfalls for the immediate post-constitution-making period. [3점]

* exogenously: 외적인 요인으로 ** salient: 두드러진

2021학년도 9월 모평 43~45번

【5~7】 다음 글을 읽고 물음에 답하시오.

(A)

The children arrived at sunrise at their grandmother's house. They always gathered at this time of year to assist with her corn harvest. In return, their grandmother would reward them with a present and by cooking a delicious feast. The children were all in great spirits. But not Sally. She disliked working in the corn field as she hated the heat and the dust. (a) She sat silently as the others took a sack each and then sang their way to the field.

(B)

Sally just wanted to get her present and leave the field because she was starting to get hot and feel irritated. (b) She had only filled her sack twice, but the others were now taking their third sacks to the granary. Sally sighed heavily. Then an idea struck her. To make the sack lighter and speed things up, she quickly filled her last sack with corn stalks. Sally reached the granary first, and her grandmother asked (c) her to put aside the final load and write her name on it.

* granary: 곡물창고 ** stalk: 줄기

(C)

They reached the field and started to work happily. Soon after, Sally joined them with her sack. Around mid-morning, their grandmother came with ice-cold lemonade and peach pie. After finishing, the children continued working until the sun was high and their sacks were bursting. Each child had to make three trips to the granary. Grandmother was impressed by their efforts and (d) she wanted to give them presents accordingly.

(D)

Grandmother asked the other children to do the same thing. Then, all of the children enjoyed their grandmother's delicious lunch. "I am so pleased with your work," she told them after lunch. "This year, you can all take home your final load as a present!" The children cheered for joy, gladly thanked her, and lifted their sacks to take home. Sally was terribly disappointed. There was nothing but useless corn stalks in (e) her sack. She then made the long walk home, pretending that she was carrying a heavy load.

2021학년도 9월 모평 43번 ★★☆

5. 주어진 글 (A)에 이어질 내용을 순서에 맞게 배열한 것으로 가장 적절한 것은?

① (B) – (D) – (C)
② (C) – (B) – (D)
③ (C) – (D) – (B)
④ (D) – (B) – (C)
⑤ (D) – (C) – (B)

2021학년도 9월 모평 44번 ★☆☆

6. 밑줄 친 (a)~(e) 중에서 가리키는 대상이 나머지 넷과 다른 것은?

① (a) ② (b) ③ (c) ④ (d) ⑤ (e)

2021학년도 9월 모평 45번 ★★☆

7. 윗글에 관한 내용으로 적절하지 않은 것은?

① 아이들은 할머니의 옥수수 수확을 돕기 위해 모였다.
② Sally는 덥고 짜증나서 옥수수 밭을 떠나고 싶었다.
③ 아이들은 각자 세 번씩 옥수수가 담긴 자루를 곡물창고로 날라야 했다.
④ 할머니는 아이들에게 맛있는 점심을 제공했다.
⑤ Sally는 옥수수가 담긴 무거운 자루를 가지고 집으로 갔다.

총 문항				문항	맞은 문항					문항
개별 문항	1	2	3	4	5	6	7	8	9	10
채점										

제한 시간 : 12분 | 정답 및 해설 119쪽

2022학년도 4월 학평 31번 ★★★

1. 다음 빈칸에 들어갈 말로 가장 적절한 것은?

Not only was Eurasia by chance blessed with biological abundance, but the very ____________ of the continent greatly promoted the spread of crops between distant regions. When the supercontinent Pangea fragmented, it was torn apart along rifts that just so happened to leave Eurasia as a broad landmass running in an east–west direction — the entire continent stretches more than a third of the way around the world, but mostly within a relatively narrow range of latitudes. As it is the latitude on the Earth that largely determines the climate and length of the growing season, crops domesticated in one part of Eurasia can be transplanted across the continent with only minimal need for adaptation to the new locale. Thus wheat cultivation spread readily from the uplands of Turkey throughout Mesopotamia, to Europe, and all the way round to India, for example. The twin continents of the Americas, by contrast, lie in a north–south direction. Here, the spreading of crops originally domesticated in one region to another led to a much harder process of re–adapting the plant species to different growing conditions. [3점]

* fragment: 조각나다 ** rift: 갈라진 틈

① isolation
② orientation
③ diversity
④ conservation
⑤ instability

2022학년도 4월 학평 34번 ★★★

2. 다음 빈칸에 들어갈 말로 가장 적절한 것을 고르시오.

Imagine some mutation appears which makes animals spontaneously die at the age of 50. This is unambiguously disadvantageous — but only very slightly so. More than 99 per cent of animals carrying this mutation will never experience its ill effects because they will die before it has a chance to act. This means that it's pretty likely to remain in the population — not because it's good, but because the 'force of natural selection' at such advanced ages is not strong enough to get rid of it. Conversely, if a mutation killed the animals at two years, striking them down when many could reasonably expect to still be alive and producing children, evolution would get rid of it very promptly: animals with the mutation would soon be outcompeted by those fortunate enough not to have it, because the force of natural selection is powerful in the years up to and including reproductive age. Thus, problematic mutations can accumulate, just so long as ______________________. [3점]

* mutation: 돌연변이

① the force of natural selection increases as animals get older
② their accumulation is largely due to their evolutionary benefits
③ evolution operates by suppressing reproductive success of animals
④ animals can promptly compensate for the decline in their abilities
⑤ they only affect animals after they're old enough to have reproduced

2020학년도 6월 모평 35번 ★★☆

3. 다음 글에서 전체 흐름과 관계 없는 문장은?

When a dog is trained to detect drugs, explosives, contraband, or other items, the trainer doesn't actually teach the dog how to smell; the dog already knows how to discriminate one scent from another. Rather, the dog is trained to become emotionally aroused by one smell versus another. ① In the step-by-step training process, the trainer attaches an "emotional charge" to a particular scent so that the dog is drawn to it above all others. ② And then the dog is trained to search out the desired item on cue, so that the trainer can control or release the behavior. ③ This emotional arousal is also why playing tug with a dog is a more powerful emotional reward in a training regime than just giving a dog a food treat, since the trainer invests more emotion into a game of tug. ④ As long as the trainer gives the dog a food reward regularly, the dog can understand its "good" behavior results in rewards. ⑤ From a dog's point of view, the tug toy is compelling because the trainer is "upset" by the toy.

* contraband: 밀수품 ** tug: 잡아당김

2020학년도 7월 학평 36번 ★★★

4. 주어진 글 다음에 이어질 글의 순서로 가장 적절한 것은?

The reason why any sugar molecule — whether in cocoa bean or pan or anywhere else — turns brown when heated is to do with the presence of carbon.

(A) Further roasting will turn some of the sugar into pure carbon (double bonds all round), which creates a burnt flavor and a dark-brown color. Complete roasting results in charcoal: all of the sugar has become carbon, which is black.

(B) On the whole, it is the carbon-rich molecules that are larger, so these get left behind, and within these there is a structure called a carbon-carbon double bond. This chemical structure absorbs light. In small amounts it gives the caramelizing sugar a yellow-brown color.

(C) Sugars are carbohydrates, which is to say that they are made of carbon ("carbo-"), hydrogen ("hydr-"), and oxygen ("-ate") atoms. When heated, these long molecules disintegrate into smaller units, some of which are so small that they evaporate (which accounts for the lovely smell). [3점]

① (A) – (C) – (B)
② (B) – (A) – (C)
③ (B) – (C) – (A)
④ (C) – (A) – (B)
⑤ (C) – (B) – (A)

2021학년도 9월 모평 38번 ★★★

5. 글의 흐름으로 보아 주어진 문장이 들어가기에 가장 적절한 곳은?

> As long as you do not run out of copies before completing this process, you will know that you have a sufficient number to go around.

We sometimes solve number problems almost without realizing it. (①) For example, suppose you are conducting a meeting and you want to ensure that everyone there has a copy of the agenda. (②) You can deal with this by labelling each copy of the handout in turn with the initials of each of those present. (③) You have then solved this problem without resorting to arithmetic and without explicit counting. (④) There are numbers at work for us here all the same and they allow precise comparison of one collection with another, even though the members that make up the collections could have entirely different characters, as is the case here, where one set is a collection of people, while the other consists of pieces of paper. (⑤) What numbers allow us to do is to compare the relative size of one set with another.

* arithmetic: 산수

2020학년도 4월 학평 40번 ★★☆

6. 다음 글의 내용을 한 문장으로 요약하고자 한다. 빈칸 (A), (B)에 들어갈 말로 가장 적절한 것은?

A few scientists from Duke University and University College London decided to find out what happens inside our brains when we lie. They put people into an fMRI machine and had them play a game where they lied to their partner. The first time people told a lie, the amygdala weighed in. It released chemicals that give us that familiar fear, that sinking sense of guilt we get when we lie. But then the researchers went one step further. They rewarded people for lying. They gave them a small monetary reward for deceiving their partner without them knowing they'd been lied to. Once people started getting rewarded for lying and not getting caught, that amygdala-driven sense of guilt started to fade. Interestingly, it faded most markedly when the lie would hurt someone else but help the person telling it. So people started telling bigger and bigger lies. Despite being small at the beginning, engagement in dishonest acts may trigger a process that leads to larger acts of dishonesty later on.

* fMRI: 기능적 자기 공명 영상 ** amygdala: 편도체

⬇

> The experiment above suggests that when people receive a ___(A)___ for lying, their brain chemistry changes, affecting their sense of guilt and ___(B)___ engagement in bigger lies.

	(A)		(B)
①	prize	......	facilitating
②	prize	......	preventing
③	benefit	......	hindering
④	penalty	......	encouraging
⑤	penalty	......	inhibiting

2022학년도 4월 학평 41~42번

[7~8] 다음 글을 읽고 물음에 답하시오.

Evolutionary biologist Richard Dawkins and zoologist John Krebs, in a now classic 1978 paper, point out that deceptive signaling is, itself, an evolutionary adaptation, a trait that developed in our earliest animal ancestors, to gain survival and reproductive benefits. (Think about how hostile mammalian and avian vocalizations are built upon size bluffing through lowered pitch and noisy growling—a "dishonest signal.") According to Dawkins and Krebs, such false signaling is (a) <u>found</u> in *all* animal communication: the colors flashed by butterflies, the calls of crickets, the pheromones released by moths and ants, the body postures of lizards, and our acoustic signals. Nature is deceitful. Creatures will do what they can to *not die*—at least until they've (b) <u>succeeded</u> in winning a mate and passing along their genes.

But at the same time, Dawkins and Krebs tell us, the *receivers* of deceptive signals undergo their own coevolutionary "selection pressure" for *detecting* false communications. The coevolution of voice and ear initiated a biological "arms race." The "manipulating" vocalizer evolves, over vast spans of evolutionary time, finer and finer means for faking, by (c) <u>abandoning</u> greater neurological control over the vocal apparatus. Meanwhile, the listener, who has his own survival concerns, gets (d) <u>better</u> at picking out the particular blend of pitch, rhythm, timbre and volume that marks the vocalizer as a deceiver. This (e) <u>compels</u> the sender to further refine his "manipulations," which creates further pressure on the receiver to improve his acoustic "mindreading."

* bluff: 허세 부리다 ** vocal apparatus: 발성 기관

2022학년도 4월 학평 41번 ★★☆

7. 윗글의 제목으로 가장 적절한 것은?

① Decreased Trustworthiness of Warning Signals: A Cost of Deception
② Evolutionary Competition Between Deceiving Vocalizers and Detectors
③ Vocalizers Are Always the Winner in the Jungle of Deception!
④ Only the Strongest Send False Signals in the Animal World
⑤ On-going Arms Race in Nature: Major Cause of Migration

2022학년도 4월 학평 42번 ★★☆

8. 밑줄 친 (a)~(e) 중에서 문맥상 낱말의 쓰임이 적절하지 <u>않은</u> 것은?

① (a) ② (b) ③ (c) ④ (d) ⑤ (e)

총 문항				문항	맞은 문항					문항
개별 문항	1	2	3	4	5	6	7	8	9	10
채점										

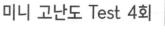

제한 시간 : 12분 | 정답 및 해설 123쪽

2022학년도 4월 학평 32번 ★★★

1. 다음 빈칸에 들어갈 말로 가장 적절한 것은?

When you are born, your neocortex knows almost nothing. It doesn't know any words, what buildings are like, how to use a computer, or what a door is and how it moves on hinges. It has to learn countless things. The overall structure of the neocortex is not random. Its size, the number of regions it has, and how they are connected together is largely determined by our genes. For example, genes determine what parts of the neocortex are connected to the eyes, what other parts are connected to the ears, and how those parts connect to each other. Therefore, we can say that the neocortex is structured at birth to see, hear, and even learn language. But it is also true that the neocortex doesn't know what it will see, what it will hear, and what specific languages it might learn. We can think of the neocortex as starting life ____________________ but knowing nothing in particular. Through experience, it learns a rich and complicated model of the world.

* neocortex: (대뇌의) 신피질

① having some built-in assumptions about the world
② causing conflicts between genes and environments
③ being able to efficiently reprocess prior knowledge
④ controlling the structure and processing power of the brain
⑤ fighting persistently against the determined world of genes

2020학년도 7월 학평 34번 ★★★

2. 다음 빈칸에 들어갈 말로 가장 적절한 것은?

In the longer term, by bringing together enough data and enough computing power, the data-giants could hack the deepest secrets of life, and then use this knowledge not just to make choices for us or manipulate us, but also to re-engineer organic life and to create inorganic life forms. Selling advertisements may be necessary to sustain the giants in the short term, but they often evaluate apps, products and companies according to the data they harvest rather than according to the money they generate. A popular app may lack a business model and may even lose money in the short term, but as long as it sucks data, it could be worth billions. Even if you don't know how to cash in on the data today, it is worth having it because it might hold the key to controlling and shaping life in the future. I don't know for certain that the data-giants explicitly think about it in such terms, but their actions indicate that they ____________________. [3점]

① acknowledge the need for the democratization of data
② underestimate the long-term effects of short-term losses
③ treat data as a by-product of operations, not a valuable asset
④ focus only on the return they can make on selling advertisements
⑤ value the accumulation of data more than mere dollars and cents

2019학년도 4월 학평 35번 ★★★

3. 다음 글에서 전체 흐름과 관계없는 문장은?

In the case of classical music performance, notwithstanding the perhaps increased psychological pressure to achieve "perfection," to a large extent it is the participation in a physical pursuit of excellence that links art to sports. ① Musicians and athletes both must attempt to create mistake-free performances that require finely tuned neural and muscle control enabled by countless hours of practice. ② For both activities, disciplining the body and mind is central to achieving what is typically considered a successful performance. ③ Standard descriptions of the actions of the muscles controlling the hand can give a misleading impression of the degree to which the fingers can be controlled independently. ④ Indeed one might assume that one of the prime objectives of art, as in sports, is to win recognition for the artist/performer's technical physical ability. ⑤ Thus, in essence, even music becomes a competition for performers, who compete against their own bodies, if not those of others, in attaining recognition for their performances.

2020학년도 7월 학평 37번 ★★☆

4. 주어진 글 다음에 이어질 글의 순서로 가장 적절한 것은?

In the 1980s and '90s, some conservationists predicted that orangutans would go extinct in the wild within 20 or 30 years. Fortunately that didn't happen. Many thousands more orangutans are now known to exist than were recognized at the turn of the millennium.

(A) In fact, the overall population of orangutans has fallen by at least 80 percent in the past 75 years. It's indicative of the difficulty of orangutan research that scientist Erik Meijaard is willing to say only that between 40,000 and 100,000 live on Borneo. Conservationists on Sumatra estimate that only 14,000 survive there.

(B) This doesn't mean that all is well in the orangutans' world. The higher figures come thanks to improved survey methods and the discovery of previously unknown populations, not because the actual numbers have increased.

(C) Much of this loss has been driven by habitat destruction from logging and the rapid spread of vast plantations of oil palm, the fruit of which is sold to make oil used in cooking and in many food products.

① (A) - (C) - (B)
② (B) - (A) - (C)
③ (B) - (C) - (A)
④ (C) - (A) - (B)
⑤ (C) - (B) - (A)

2021학년도 9월 모평 39번 ★★☆

5. 글의 흐름으로 보아, 주어진 문장이 들어가기에 가장 적절한 곳은?

> Rather, it evolved naturally as certain devices were found in practice to be both workable and useful.

Film has no grammar. (①) There are, however, some vaguely defined rules of usage in cinematic language, and the syntax of film — its systematic arrangement — orders these rules and indicates relationships among them. (②) As with written and spoken languages, it is important to remember that the syntax of film is a result of its usage, not a determinant of it. (③) There is nothing preordained about film syntax. (④) Like the syntax of written and spoken language, the syntax of film is an organic development, descriptive rather than prescriptive, and it has changed considerably over the years. (⑤) "Hollywood Grammar" may sound laughable now, but during the thirties, forties, and early fifties it was an accurate model of the way Hollywood films were constructed. [3점]

* preordained: 미리 정해진

2022학년도 6월 모평 43~45번

[6~8] 다음 글을 읽고 물음에 답하시오.

(A)

> Fighting against the force of the water was a thrilling challenge. Sophia tried to keep herself planted firmly in the boat, paying attention to the waves crashing against the rocks. As the water got rougher, she was forced to paddle harder to keep the waves from tossing her into the water. Her friends Mia and Rebecca were paddling eagerly behind her to balance the boat. They were soaked from all of the spray. Mia shouted to Sophia, "Are you OK? Aren't (a) you scared?"
>
> * paddle: 노를 젓다

(B)

> "You've got a good point. It's a real advantage to graduate from college with the mindset of a daring adventurer," Mia said. Rebecca quickly added, "That's why I went to Mongolia before I started my first job out of college. Teaching English there for two months was a big challenge for me. But (b) I learned a lot from the experience. It really gave me the courage to try anything in life." Listening to her friends, Sophia looked at (c) her own reflection in the water and saw a confident young woman smiling back at her.

(C)

> "I'm great!" Sophia shouted back excitedly. Even though the boat was getting thrown around, the girls managed to avoid hitting any rocks. Suddenly, almost as quickly as the water had got rougher, the river seemed to calm down, and they all felt relaxed. With a sigh of relief, Sophia looked around. "Wow! What a wonderful view!" (d) she shouted. The scenery around them was breathtaking. Everyone was speechless. As they enjoyed the emerald green Rocky Mountains, Mia said, "No wonder rafting is the best thing to do in Colorado!"

(D)

> Agreeing with her friend, Rebecca gave a thumbs-up. "Sophia, your choice was excellent!" she said with a delighted smile. "I thought you were afraid of water, though, Sophia," Mia said. Sophia explained, "Well, I was before I started rafting. But I graduate from college in a few months. And, before I do, I wanted to do something really adventurous to test my bravery. I thought that if I did something completely crazy, it might give (e) me more confidence when I'm interviewing for jobs." Now they could see why she had suggested going rafting.

2022학년도 6월 모평 43번 ★☆☆

6. 주어진 글 (A)에 이어질 내용을 순서에 맞게 배열한 것으로 가장 적절한 것은?

① (B) − (D) − (C) ② (C) − (B) − (D)
③ (C) − (D) − (B) ④ (D) − (B) − (C)
⑤ (D) − (C) − (B)

2022학년도 6월 모평 44번 ★☆☆

7. 밑줄 친 (a)~(e) 중에서 가리키는 대상이 나머지 넷과 다른 것은?

① (a) ② (b) ③ (c) ④ (d) ⑤ (e)

2022학년도 6월 모평 45번 ★★☆

8. 윗글에 관한 내용으로 적절하지 않은 것은?

① Mia와 Rebecca는 보트의 균형을 유지하려고 애썼다.
② Rebecca는 몽골에서 영어를 가르친 경험이 있다.
③ Sophia와 친구들이 함께 탄 보트는 바위에 부딪치지 않았다.
④ Sophia는 래프팅을 하기 전에는 물을 두려워했다.
⑤ Sophia는 용기를 시험할 모험을 대학 졸업 후에 하길 원했다.

총 문항				문항	맞은 문항					문항
개별 문항	1	2	3	4	5	6	7	8	9	10
채점										

BIG EVENT 1+3

씨뮬 교재를 구매하신 모든 분들께
고1, 2, 3 한국사 · 사회탐구 · 과학탐구 과목
중에서 학년에 상관없이 원하는 3과목의
최신 모의고사(과목별 4~12회 구성)
PDF 파일을 메일로 보내 드립니다.

❶ 설문지를 작성하고, "Big Event 1+3" 한국사 · 사회탐구 · 과학탐구 교재 목록에서 교재번호와 과목명을 확인한 후 'Big Event 1+3 교재 신청란'에 정확히 기입합니다.

❷ 설문지 부분을 핸드폰(또는 디지털 카메라)으로 찍어서 골드교육 홈페이지(www.goldedu.co.kr) 커뮤니티 → "1+3 이벤트" 게시판에 올리시면 됩니다.

❸ "Big Event 1+3"은 3과목까지 신청할 수 있으며, 여러 과목을 신청하면 임의대로 3과목을 선정하여 보내 드립니다.

★ 2023년 시행 모의고사를 신청하면 출간 일정상 2024년 2월부터 보내 드리오니 이용에 착오 없으시기 바랍니다. 그리고 이 책의 1+3 이벤트 유효 기간은 발행일로부터 3년입니다.

★ 개인 정보는 이벤트 목적 외에는 사용하지 않으며 이벤트 마감 이후 폐기함을 알려드립니다.

"Big Event 1+3" 한국사 · 사회탐구 · 과학탐구 교재 목록

1. 2022년 시행 모의고사 : 신청하시면 확인 후 바로 보내드리고 있습니다.

학년	과목(영역)	횟수	PDF 제공 교재
고1	한국사	4회	11-1 한국사
고2	한국사	4회	11-2 한국사
	사회탐구	4회	11-3 생활과 윤리, 11-4 윤리와 사상, 11-5 한국지리, 11-6 세계지리, 11-7 동아시아사, 11-8 세계사, 11-9 정치와 법, 11-10 경제, 11-11 사회 · 문화
	과학탐구	4회	11-12 물리학 Ⅰ, 11-13 화학 Ⅰ, 11-14 생명과학 Ⅰ, 11-15 지구과학 Ⅰ
고3	한국사	12회	11-16 한국사
	사회탐구	12회	11-17 생활과 윤리, 11-18 윤리와 사상, 11-19 한국지리, 11-20 세계지리, 11-21 동아시아사, 11-22 세계사, 11-23 법과 정치, 11-24 경제, 11-25 사회 · 문화
	과학탐구	12회	11-26 물리학 Ⅰ, 11-27 화학 Ⅰ, 11-28 생명과학 Ⅰ, 11-29 지구과학 Ⅰ
		11회	11-30 물리학 Ⅱ, 11-31 화학 Ⅱ, 11-32 생명과학 Ⅱ, 11-33 지구과학 Ⅱ

2. 2023년 시행 모의고사 : 2024년 2월부터 보내드릴 예정입니다.

학년	과목(영역)	횟수	PDF 제공 교재
고1	한국사	4회	12-1 한국사
고2	한국사	4회	12-2 한국사
	사회탐구	4회	12-3 생활과 윤리, 12-4 윤리와 사상, 12-5 한국지리, 12-6 세계지리, 12-7 동아시아사, 12-8 세계사, 12-9 정치와 법, 12-10 경제, 12-11 사회 · 문화
	과학탐구	4회	12-12 물리학 Ⅰ, 12-13 화학 Ⅰ, 12-14 생명과학 Ⅰ, 12-15 지구과학 Ⅰ
고3	한국사	11회	12-16 한국사
	사회탐구	11회	12-17 생활과윤리, 12-18 윤리와 사상, 12-19 한국지리, 12-20 세계지리, 12-21 동아시아사, 12-22 세계사, 12-23 법과 정치, 12-24 경제, 12-25 사회 · 문화
	과학탐구	11회	12-26 물리학 Ⅰ, 12-27 화학 Ⅰ, 12-28 생명과학 Ⅰ, 12-29 지구과학 Ⅰ
		10회	12-30 물리학 Ⅱ, 12-31 화학 Ⅱ, 12-32 생명과학 Ⅱ, 12-33 지구과학 Ⅱ

※ 과목별 수록 회차는 사정상 변경될 수 있습니다.

(주)골드교육 씨뮬 교재를 이용해 주셔서 감사합니다.
더 좋은 교재를 만들기 위해 독자 여러분의 의견을 귀담아 듣고자 합니다.

1. 이 책을 구입하게 된 동기는 무엇입니까?

① 학교/학원 교재 ② 선생님이 추천해 주셔서 ③ 선배나 친구들이 추천해서
④ 직접 서점에서 보고 ⑤ 광고나 입소문을 들어서 ⑥ 기타( )

2. 이 책의 전반적인 부분에 대한 질문입니다.

• 문제의 분량 : 많다□ 알맞다□ 적다□
• 책의 크기 : 크다□ 적당하다□ 작다□
• 책의 가격 : 비싸다□ 적당하다□ 싸다□
• 해설의 분량 : 많다□ 적당하다□ 부족하다□
• 이용 편의성 : 편하다□ 보통이다□ 불편하다□
• 책의 만족도 : 만족□ 보통□ 불만족□

3. 이 책에서 좋았던 점은 무엇입니까? (복수 응답 가능)

① 24일 학습 체계 ② 출제 트렌드 & 1등급 꿀팁 ③ 대표 기출 문제 풀이
④ 지문의 난이도 ⑤ 정답 및 해설 ⑥ 내신 대비 서브노트
⑦ 문법 플러스 ⑧ 숙어 플러스 ⑨ 기타( )

4. 내가 구매한 씨뮬 교재에 대한 독자서평을 작성해 주세요.
베스트 독자서평으로 채택되면 다음 씨뮬 교재에 수록해 드립니다.

Big Event 1+3 교재 신청란 〈유형+ 씨뮬 고3 영어 독해〉

이름

이벤트 신청은 위의 표를 보고 교재번호와 과목명을 빈칸에 정확히 적어 주시기 바랍니다. (교재번호 11-5, 과목명 한국지리)

	교재번호	과목명
신청 과목 1		
신청 과목 2		
신청 과목 3		

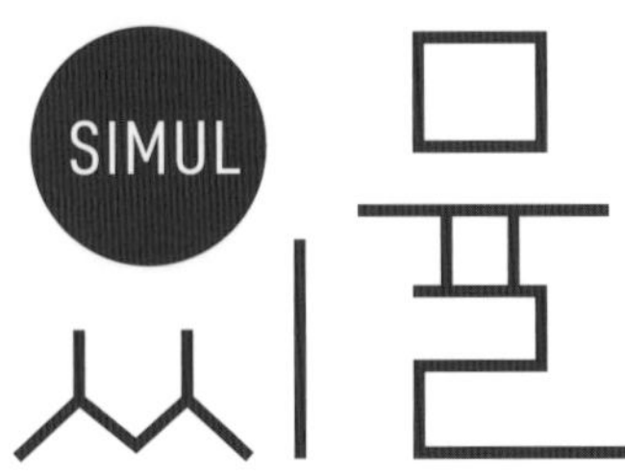
SIMUL
씨뮬

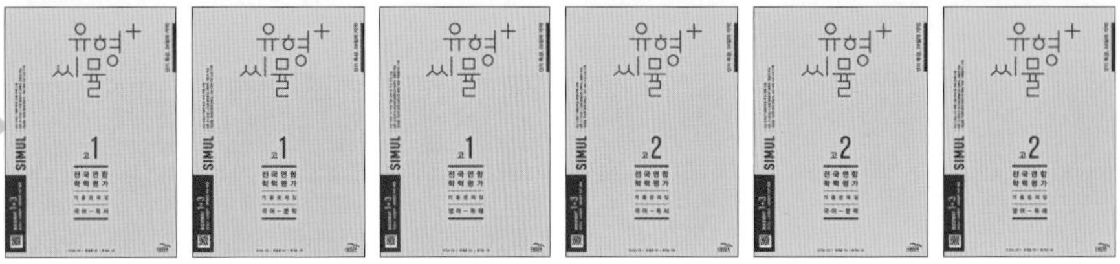

단기 특강, 24일의 기적!

유형+씨물

고3

수능기출 문제집

영어 – 독해

정답및해설

씨뮬과 함께하는 기출 완전정복 커리큘럼

씨뮬 = 실전 연습

내신, 학평, 수능까지 실전 대비 최고의 연습, 씨뮬

씨뮬과 함께 1등급, SKY, 의치한까지

01
예비 고1
예비 고1 3월 전국연합
3년간 모의고사
고등학교 첫 시험을 발 빠르게 준비하여
단 한 권으로 학습 주도권을 잡는 교재
※ 국어, 수학, 영어, 한국사, 사회, 과학 수록
02
고1~3
유형+ 씨뮬
학평, 수능의 문제 유형을 연습하고
출제 경향을 파악할 수 있는 교재
※ 고1~3 국어 독서/문학
※ 고1~3 영어 독해, 고3 영어 어법 · 어휘
03
고1~3
전국연합 3년간
최근 3년간 시행된 학평, 모평, 수능 문제들로
완벽한 수능 대비를 할 수 있는 기본 중의 기본서
※ 고1 통합사회, 통합과학
※ 고1~3 국어, 수학, 영어
04
고1~3
사설 3년간
종로, 이투스에서 출제된 고난도 모의고사
문제들을 연습할 수 있는 교재
※ 고1~3 국어, 영어
05
고3
6 · 9 · 수능 평가원 3/4년간
평가원에서 최근 3/4년간 출제한 6월,
9월 모평 및 수능 문제들이 수록된
수능 출제 경향 파악에 가장 적합한 교재
※ 고3 국어, 수학, 영어
06
고3
최신 1년간
최근 1년간 시행된 학평, 모평, 수능 문제 뿐
아니라 종로 모의고사까지 수록되어 최신 출제
경향을 한 권으로 파악할 수 있는 교재
※ 고3 국어, 수학, 영어

독자 여러분의 애정 어린 충고로

씨뮬은 해마다 새롭게 완성되어 갑니다!

실제 크기의 시험지와 OMR 카드를 제공해 주어서 실제 시험을 보는 것 같아 실제 시험에서 떨리지 않았고 문제에 대한 해설이 친절히 서술되어 있어 어려운 문제도 혼자만의 노력으로 이해할 수 있었어요. 역시 씨뮬!

—》 **황*현**

모의고사가 모아져 있는 책 중 씨뮬이 정말 최고예요. 특히 영어는 듣기 연습용 받아쓰기도 있어서 많은 도움이 되었습니다. 감사합니다.

—》 **조*빈**

회차별 영단어 핸드북뿐 아니라 책 마지막 부분에 있는 수능 필수 영숙어 파트가 도움이 많이 되었다. 수능에서뿐만 아니라 내신 시험에도 나오는 표현들이 많아 유용했다.

—》 **김*희**

모의고사를 대비하기 위해 구매하였습니다. 다른 문제집들은 실제 모의고사 시험지처럼 되어 있지 않아서 긴장감이 많이 떨어지는데, 씨뮬은 실제 시험지처럼 되어 있고 OMR 카드도 있어서 모의고사 대비하기 아주 좋아요!

—》 **김*연**

씨뮬 교재가 실제 모의고사 종이 크기이다 보니 실제 시험을 치는 듯한 느낌이 들어 더 집중이 잘 되는 것 같다. 해설도 꼼꼼하게 되어 있어 내가 어디서 해석이 안 되는지 바로 찾을 수 있어서 좋았다.

—》 **김*진**

국어에 자신감이 없어서 시작했는데 해설이 꼼꼼하고 추가적인 작품이나 문법이 수록돼 있어서 더 깊이 있게 공부할 수 있었어요.

—》 **배*진**

이 책을 구매했던 이유들 중 하나인, 실전과 비슷한 종이 재질 덕분에 더욱 실감나게 학습할 수 있었습니다. 그리고 맨 뒤에 부착되어 있는 OMR 카드로 체킹 실수를 줄이는 연습도 되었습니다. 꼼꼼한 해설지와 문제 풀이로 공부하면서 그 외에 실전 감각 또한 함양할 수 있는 씨뮬 모의고사입니다!

—》 **권*희**

백분위 95~96을 왔다갔다했어요. 수학 실력을 늘리기 위해 책을 구매해 풀어 본 후 높은 점수를 받게 되었습니다.

—》 **정*헌**

모의고사 볼 때처럼 큰 종이로 되어 있어 더 몰입감 있게 집중할 수 있었던 것 같습니다. 또 해설도 자세하고 고난도 문제와 등급컷도 알려 주어 좋았습니다!

—》 **서*준**

어느 정도 실력이 쌓이고 나면 모의고사로 실전 대비 훈련을 하며 실력을 굳혀 나가야 되죠. 그리고 그 연습 방법으로는 '씨뮬'이라는 교재가 정말 완벽한 것 같아요. 여러분들에게 '씨뮬' 적극 추천합니다.

—》 **백*민**

내신에서 학평까지 실전 연습은 씨뮬 기출 하나로 충분하다

전국연합학력평가 3년간 모의고사 | **11th 국영수 고1~3**

01 실제 시험 그대로 실전 감각 익히기

02 핵심을 짚어주는 명쾌한 해설

03 오답 노트 & OMR 카드

04 같은 작가 다른 작품(국어), 기출문법[구문] 모아보기(영어), 준 킬러 문항 연습(수학)

05 [12th] 전국연합 3년간 수학 교재의 중요 문항에 동영상 강의 제공 예정

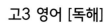

고3 영어 [독해]

※문법 / 숙어 플러스는 정답 및 해설 참조

DAY 01 글의 목적

1 ⑤ 2 ③ 3 ④ 4 ④ 5 ③
6 ① 7 ② 8 ③ 9 ① 10 ⑤

DAY 02 심경 • 분위기

1 ① 2 ④ 3 ④ 4 ① 5 ⑤
6 ③ 7 ⑤ 8 ① 9 ① 10 ①

DAY 03 필자의 주장

1 ① 2 ① 3 ① 4 ② 5 ①
6 ⑤ 7 ③ 8 ① 9 ① 10 ①

DAY 04 함축 • 지칭 추론

1 ① 2 ⑤ 3 ① 4 ④ 5 ⑤
6 ② 7 ④ 8 ② 9 ② 10 ④

DAY 05 글의 요지

1 ① 2 ⑤ 3 ⑤ 4 ① 5 ②
6 ② 7 ① 8 ① 9 ① 10 ①

DAY 06 글의 주제

1 ③ 2 ① 3 ⑤ 4 ② 5 ①
6 ② 7 ⑤ 8 ④ 9 ③ 10 ⑤

DAY 07 글의 제목

1 ⑤ 2 ② 3 ① 4 ① 5 ①
6 ① 7 ① 8 ② 9 ② 10 ②

DAY 08 도표 정보 파악

1 ⑤ 2 ⑤ 3 ④ 4 ③ 5 ⑤
6 ⑤ 7 ④ 8 ② 9 ⑤ 10 ④

DAY 09 내용 일치 • 불일치

1 ⑤ 2 ③ 3 ③ 4 ③ 5 ③
6 ⑤ 7 ③ 8 ③ 9 ⑤ 10 ⑤

DAY 10 안내문

1 ④ 2 ④ 3 ③ 4 ⑤ 5 ③
6 ④ 7 ④ 8 ④ 9 ④ 10 ③

DAY 11 어법 정확성 파악

1 ④ 2 ② 3 ③ 4 ③ 5 ②
6 ② 7 ④ 8 ⑤ 9 ⑤ 10 ④

DAY 12 어휘 적절성 파악

1 ⑤ 2 ④ 3 ⑤ 4 ② 5 ④
6 ③ 7 ④ 8 ③ 9 ⑤ 10 ④

DAY 13 빈칸 추론 (1) 어휘, 짧은 어구

1 ② 2 ② 3 ⑤ 4 ④ 5 ⑤
6 ④ 7 ① 8 ⑤ 9 ② 10 ③

DAY 14 빈칸 추론 (2) 긴 어구, 문장

1 ⑤ 2 ④ 3 ① 4 ④ 5 ②
6 ② 7 ① 8 ② 9 ① 10 ②

DAY 15 흐름에 무관한 문장 찾기

1 ③ 2 ④ 3 ④ 4 ③ 5 ③
6 ④ 7 ④ 8 ③ 9 ③ 10 ③

DAY 16 문단 내 글의 순서 파악

1 ② 2 ④ 3 ② 4 ⑤ 5 ④
6 ② 7 ② 8 ⑤ 9 ② 10 ⑤

DAY 17 주어진 문장의 위치 파악

1 ④ 2 ④ 3 ② 4 ⑤ 5 ⑤
6 ③ 7 ⑤ 8 ④ 9 ④ 10 ④

DAY 18 문단 요약

1 ① 2 ① 3 ② 4 ① 5 ③
6 ⑤ 7 ①

DAY 19 장문의 이해 (1)

1 ① 2 ④ 3 ② 4 ③ 5 ③
6 ④ 7 ⑤ 8 ④

DAY 20 장문의 이해 (2)

1 ⑤ 2 ② 3 ③ 4 ③ 5 ③
6 ② 7 ③ 8 ⑤ 9 ④ 10 ③
11 ② 12 ③

DAY 21 미니 고난도 Test 1회

1 ③ 2 ① 3 ④ 4 ② 5 ③
6 ① 7 ② 8 ⑤

DAY 22 미니 고난도 Test 2회

1 ② 2 ④ 3 ④ 4 ③ 5 ②
6 ④ 7 ⑤

DAY 23 미니 고난도 Test 3회

1 ② 2 ⑤ 3 ④ 4 ⑤ 5 ③
6 ① 7 ② 8 ③

DAY 24 미니 고난도 Test 4회

1 ① 2 ⑤ 3 ③ 4 ② 5 ④
6 ③ 7 ② 8 ⑤

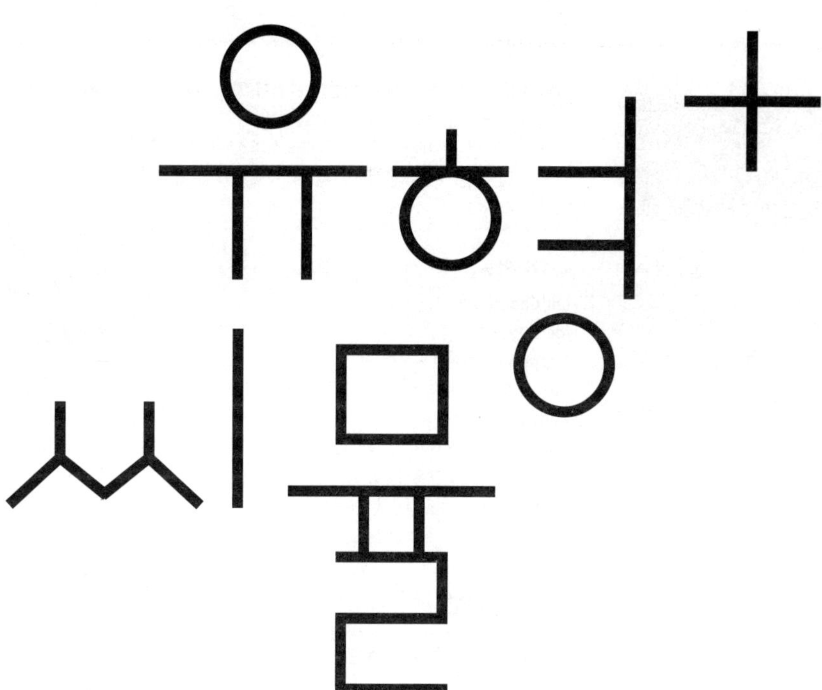

단기 특강, 24일의 기적!

정답 및 해설

고3 영어 독해

CONTENTS

Day 01	002	Day 13	066
Day 02	006	Day 14	072
Day 03	011	Day 15	079
Day 04	016	Day 16	085
Day 05	022	Day 17	091
Day 06	028	Day 18	097
Day 07	034	Day 19	102
Day 08	040	Day 20	107
Day 09	045	Day 21	112
Day 10	050	Day 22	116
Day 11	052	Day 23	119
Day 12	059	Day 24	123

01. 글의 목적

본문 002쪽

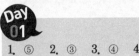

1. ⑤	2. ③	3. ④	4. ④	5. ③
6. ①	7. ②	8. ③	9. ①	10. ⑤

정답률 98%

대표 기출 ① 조류 관찰 클럽 가입 문의

직독/직해

To whom it may concern, 관계자분께
My name is Michael Brown.
제 이름은 Michael Brown입니다
I have been a bird-watcher / since childhood.
저는 조류 관찰자였습니다 / 어릴 때부터
I have always enjoyed watching birds in my yard /
저는 마당에서 항상 새들을 관찰하는 것을 즐겨 왔습니다 /
and identifying them / by sight and sound.
그리고 그것들을 식별하는 (것을 즐겨왔습니다) / 외모와 소리로
Yesterday, I happened to read an article about your club.
어제 저는 우연히 귀하의 클럽에 관한 기사를 읽었습니다
I was surprised and excited /
저는 놀랐고 신이 났습니다 /
to find out about a community of passionate bird-watchers /
열정적인 조류 관찰자들의 커뮤니티에 대해 알게 되어서 /
who travel annually to go birding.
조류를 관찰하러 매년 여행하는
I would love to join your club, /
저는 귀하의 클럽에 가입하고 싶습니다 /
but your website appears to be under construction.
하지만 귀하의 웹 사이트가 공사 중인 것 같습니다
I could not find any information / except for this contact email address.
다른 정보를 찾을 수가 없었습니다 / 이 이메일 주소를 제외한
I would like to know how to sign up for the club.
나는 클럽에 가입하는 방법을 알고 싶습니다
I look forward to your reply.
귀하의 회신을 기다리겠습니다
Sincerely, 진심으로
Michael Brown Michael Brown 드림

관계자분께
제 이름은 Michael Brown입니다. 저는 어릴 때부터 조류 관찰자였습니다. 저는 항상 마당에서 새들을 관찰하여 외모와 소리로 그것들을 식별하는 것을 즐겨왔습니다. 어제 저는 우연히 귀하의 클럽에 관한 기사를 읽었습니다. 저는 조류를 관찰하러 매년 여행하는 열정적인 조류 관찰자들의 커뮤니티에 대해 알게 되어서 놀랐고 신이 났습니다. 저는 귀하의 클럽에 가입하고 싶지만, 귀하의 웹 사이트가 공사 중인 것 같습니다. 이 이메일 주소를 제외한 다른 정보를 찾을 수가 없었습니다. 클럽에 가입하는 방법을 알고 싶습니다. 귀하의 회신을 기다리겠습니다.
진심으로,
Michael Brown 드림

문제풀이

'I was surprised and excited to find out about a community of passionate bird-watchers who travel annually to go birding.(저는 조류를 관찰하러 매년 여행하는 열정적인 조류 관찰자들의 커뮤니티에 대해 알게 되어서 놀랐고 신이 났습니다.)'과 'I would like to know how to sign up for the club.(클럽에 가입하는 방법을 알고 싶습니다.)'을 통해 조류 관찰 클럽에 관심이 있는 필자가 클럽에 가입하는 방법을 문의하기 위해 쓴 글임을 알 수 있다. 따라서 글의 목적으로 가장 적절한 것은 ① '조류 관찰 클럽에 가입하는 방법을 문의하려고'이다.

어휘·어구

childhood 어린 시절
identify 식별하다
happen to 우연히 ~하다
passionate 열정적인
annually 매년
under construction 공사 중인
except for ~을 제외하고는
sign up for ~에 가입하다

정답률 88%

1. ⑤ 재난과 관련된 경험담 투고 요청

직독/직해

Dear Readers,
독자 여러분께
As you've seen throughout my books, / I've learned a great deal from people /
저의 여러 책에서 보셨듯이 / 저는 사람들로부터 많은 것을 배웠습니다 /
who have sent me their stories and advice.
저에게 자신의 이야기와 조언을 보내 주신
Let's keep it going.
그 작업을 계속 이어 나갑시다
If you would like to send me an email / about your experiences with disasters /
저에게 이메일로 보내고 싶으시면 / 재난에 대한 여러분의 경험에 대해서 /
and what you've learned about escaping them, /
그리고 재난을 피한 경험을 통해 배운 것을 /
please send it to nodisaster@smail.com.
nodisaster@smail.com으로 보내 주십시오
I want you to note that, / by sending me your story, /
저는 여러분이 주의하기 바랍니다 / 이야기를 제게 보내 줌으로써 /
you are giving me permission to use it in the books that I write.
제가 쓰는 책에 그것을 사용할 수 있도록 허용하신다는 것을
But I promise not to use your name /
하지만 여러분의 이름을 사용하지 않겠다고 약속드립니다 /
unless you give me explicit permission.
여러분이 제게 허락을 명시하지 않는 한
Thank you. 감사합니다
Very truly yours, 진심을 담아서
Robert Brown Robert Brown 올림

독자 여러분께,
저의 여러 책에서 보셨듯이, 저는 저에게 자신의 이야기와 조언을 보내 주신 분들로부터 많은 것을 배웠습니다. 그 작업을 계속 이어 나갑시다. 재난에 대한 여러분의 경험, 그리고 재난을 피한 경험을 통해 배운 것을 저에게 이메일로 보내고 싶으시면, nodisaster@smail.com으로 보내 주십시오. 여러분이 이야기를 제게 보내 줌으로써 제가 쓰는 책에 그것을 사용할 수 있도록 허용하신다는 것을 알아두시기 바랍니다. 하지만 여러분이 제게 허락을 명시하지 않는 한, 여러분의 이름을 사용하지 않겠다고 약속드립니다. 감사합니다.
진심을 담아서,
Robert Brown 올림

문제풀이

작가가 자신의 책에 사용할 수 있도록 독자들에게 재난에 대한 경험과 재난을 피한 경험을 통해 배운 것을 이메일로 보내달라는 내용의 글이므로 글의 목적으로 가장 적절한 것은 '⑤ 재난과 관련한 경험담을 보내 줄 것을 요청하려고'이다.

어휘·어구

throughout ~을 통하여
permission 허락
explicit 명시적인

정답률 96%

2. ③ 피겨 스케이팅 선수 응원

직독/직해

Dear Natalie Talley, Natalie Talley 씨께
My name is Olivia Spikes, / the mayor of Millstown.
제 이름은 Olivia Spikes입니다 / Millstown의 시장
Before you attend the world championships / next month, /
세계 선수권 대회에 출전하기 전에 / 다음 달 /
on behalf of everyone in Millstown, /
Millstown의 모든 사람을 대신하여 /
I wish to let you know / that we are supporting you / all the way.
우리가 당신에게 알려드리고 싶습니다 / 우리가 당신을 응원하고 있음을 / 항상
As you are the first famous figure skater / from Millstown, /
당신이 최초의 유명한 피겨 스케이팅 선수이기 때문에 / Millstown 출신의 /
we are all big fans of yours.
우리는 모두 당신의 열렬한 팬입니다
Our community was so proud of you /
우리 지역 사회는 당신을 매우 자랑스럽게 생각했습니다 /
for winning the national championships last year.
당신이 작년에 전국 선수권 대회에서 우승한 것을
Your amazing performance / really moved us all.
당신의 놀라운 연기는 / 우리 모두를 감동하게 했습니다
We all believe / that you are going to impress the entire nation again.
우리는 모두 믿습니다 / 당신이 다시 온 나라를 감동하게 할 것이라고
Your hometown supporters will cheer for you / whenever you perform / on the ice.
당신의 고향의 서포터들이 응원할 것입니다 / 당신이 연기할 때마다 / 빙판 위에서
Good luck!
행운을 빕니다!
Best wishes,
Olivia Spikes Olivia Spikes 드림

Natalie Talley 씨께
제 이름은 Olivia Spikes이고, Millstown의 시장입니다. 다음 달 세계 선수권 대회에 출전하기 전에, Millstown의 모든 사람을 대신하여 우리가 당신을 항상 응원하고 있음을 알려드리고 싶습니다. 당신이 Millstown 출신의 최초의 유명한 피겨 스케이팅 선수이기 때문에 우리는 모두 당신의 열렬한 팬입니다. 우리 지역 사회는 당신이 작년에 전국 선수권 대회에서 우승한 것을 매우 자랑스럽게 생각했습니다. 당신의 놀라운 연기는 우리 모두를 감동하게 했습니다. 우리는 모두 당신이 다시 온 나라를 감동하게 할 것이라고 믿습니다. 빙판 위에서 연기할 때마다 고향의 서포터들이 응원할 것입니다. 행운을 빕니다!
Olivia Spikes 드림

문제풀이

'Before you attend the world championships next month, on behalf of everyone in Millstown, I wish to let you know that we are supporting you all the way.(다음 달 세계 선수권 대회에 출전하기 전에, Millstown의 모든 사람을 대신하여 우리가 당신을 항상 응원하고 있음을 알려드리고 싶습니다.)'를 통해 세계 피겨 스케이팅 선수권 대회에 출전하는 지역 사회 출신 선수에게 그 지역 시장이 응원의 메시지를 전하고 있다는 것을 알 수 있다. 따라서 글의 목적으로 가장 적절한 것은 ③ '지역 사회 출신 피겨 스케이팅 선수를 응원하려고'이다.

어휘·어구

mayor 시장
championship 선수권 대회

어휘·어구

mayor 시장
championship 선수권 대회
on behalf of ~을 대신하여
support 응원하다, 지지하다
all the way 내내
community 지역 사회, 공동체
performance 연기
impress 깊은 인상을 주다, 감동을 주다

정답률 96%

3. ④ 등하굣길 확장 요청

직독/직해

To whom it may concern,
관계자분께

Thank you very much / for faithfully responding to our request /
매우 감사합니다 / 우리의 요청에 충실하게 답변해 주신 것에 /

six months ago / and taking corresponding measures.
6개월 전 / 그리고 상응하는 조처를 해 주신 것에

Even after the installation of road traffic safety facilities, /
도로 교통안전 시설 설치 후에도 /

we still need more / for the safety of our students.
우리는 여전히 더 많은 것을 필요로 합니다 / 학생의 안전을 위해

It is a problem with the school road, / which students use /
그것은 등하굣길과 관련된 문제입니다 / 그것을 학생들이 사용합니다 /

on their way to and from school.
학교에 오가는 길에

The width of the current school road is barely wide /
현재 등하굣길의 폭은 겨우 너비가 됩니다 /

enough for two people to walk side by side.
나란히 두 사람이 걸을 정도의

So, there are risks of collision with vehicles / on the road where students walk /
그래서 차량과 충돌할 위험성이 있습니다 / 학생이 걷는 길에서 /

and accidents / if many students flock to the narrow school road.
그리고 사고의 (위험성) / 많은 학생이 좁은 등하굣길에 몰린다면

Therefore, / we ask you to expand the school road / for students' safety.
따라서 / 우리는 귀하에게 등하굣길을 확장해 줄 것을 요청합니다 / 학생의 안전을 위해

I would appreciate it / if you could respond as soon as possible.
감사하겠습니다 / 가능한 한 빨리 답변해 주시면

Sincerely, 진심을 담아서
Alisha Lee Alisha Lee 드림

관계자분께,
6개월 전 우리의 요청에 충실하게 답변해 주시고 상응하는 조처를 해 주신 것에 매우 감사합니다. 도로 교통안전 시설 설치 후에도 우리는 여전히 학생의 안전을 위해 더 많은 것을 필요로 합니다. 그것은 등하굣길과 관련된 문제이고, 그 등하굣길은 학생이 학교에 오가는 길에 이용하는 것입니다. 현재 등하굣길의 폭은 나란히 두 사람이 간신히 걸을 정도의 너비입니다. 그래서 학생이 걷는 길에서 차량과 충돌할 위험성과 많은 학생이 좁은 등하굣길에 몰린다면 사고가 날 위험성이 있습니다. 따라서 우리는 귀하에게 학생의 안전을 위해 등하굣길을 확장해 줄 것을 요청합니다. 가능한 한 빨리 답변해 주시면 감사하겠습니다.
진심을 담아서
Alisha Lee 드림

문제풀이

학생들의 등하굣길이 너무 좁아 차량과 충돌하거나, 학생들이 함께 몰리면 사고의 위험성이 있으므로 등하굣길을 확장해 달라고 요청하는 내용의 글이므로, 글의 목적으로 가장 적절한 것은 ④ '학생 안전을 위해 등하굣길 폭의 확장을 요청하려고'이다.

어휘·어구

faithfully 충실하게
correspond 상응
measure 조치
installation 설치
facility 시설
barely 간신히, 가까스로
collision 충돌
flock 모이다
expand 확장하다
appreciate 감사하다

정답률 97%

4. ④ 수영장 추가 대여 가능 여부 문의

직독/직해

Dear Hylean Miller, Hylean Miller 씨께

Hello, / I'm Nelson Perkins, /
안녕하세요 / 저는 Nelson Perkins입니다 /

a teacher and swimming coach / at Broomstone High School.
교사이자 수영 코치인 / Broomstone 고등학교

Last week, / I made a reservation / for one of your company's swimming pools /
지난주에 / 저는 예약했습니다 / 귀사의 수영장 중 한 곳을 /

for our summer swim camp.
저희 여름 수영 캠프를 위해서

However, due to its popularity, /
그런데 그것의 인기 때문에 /

thirty more students are coming to the camp than we expected, /
저희가 예상했던 것보다 학생들이 30명 더 캠프에 오게 되었습니다 /

so we need one more swimming pool for them.
그래서 저희는 그들을 위한 수영장 한 곳이 더 필요합니다

The rental section on your website says /
귀사 웹사이트의 대여란에 나와 있는데 /

that there are two other swimming pools / during the summer season: /
두 곳의 다른 수영장이 있다고 / 여름철 동안 /

the Splash Pool and the Rainbow Pool.
Splash Pool과 Rainbow Pool입니다

Please let me know / if an additional rental would be possible.
저에게 알려주시길 바랍니다 / 추가 대여가 가능할지를

Thank you in advance.
미리 감사드립니다

Best Wishes, 행복을 빕니다
Nelson Perkins Nelson Perkins 드림

Hylean Miller 씨께
안녕하세요, 저는 Broomstone 고등학교 교사이자 수영 코치인 Nelson Perkins입니다. 지난주에 저는 저희 여름 수영 캠프를 위해서 귀사의 수영장 중 한 곳을 예약했습니다. 그런데 그것의 인기 때문에, 저희가 예상했던 것보다 학생들이 30명 더 캠프에 오게 되어서 저희는 그들을 위한 수영장 한 곳이 더 필요합니다. 귀사 웹사이트의 대여란에 여름철 동안 두 곳의 다른 수영장이 있다고 나와 있는데, Splash Pool과 Rainbow Pool입니다. 추가 대여가 가능할지를 저에게 알려주시길 바랍니다. 미리 감사드립니다.
행복을 빕니다
Nelson Perkins 드림

문제풀이

'thirty more students are coming to the camp than we expected, so we need one more swimming pool for them(저희가 예상했던 것보다 학생들이 30명 더 캠프에 오게 되어서 저희는 그들을 위한 수영장 한 곳이 더 필요합니다)'와 'Please let me know if an additional rental would be possible.(추가 대여가 가능할지를 저에게 알려주시길 바랍니다.)'를 통해 필자가 여름 수영 캠프를 위해 수영장 한 곳을 예약했으나 예상보다 많은 학생이 참가하게 되어 다른 수영장을 추가로 대여할 수 있는지 알려줄 것을 요청하고 있다는 것을 알 수 있다. 따라서 글의 목적으로 가장 적절한 것은 ④ '수영장 추가 대여 가능 여부를 문의하려고'이다.

어휘·어구

make a reservation 예약하다
due to ~ 때문에
popularity 인기
rental 대여(의)
additional 추가의
in advance 미리, 사전에

정답률 94%

5. ③ 역사적 건축물 복원 요청

직독/직해

To whom it may concern,
관계자분께

I sometimes travel to Summerland / to visit friends.
저는 가끔 Summerland로 여행을 갑니다 / 친구들을 방문하기 위해 /

One of the first landmarks to captivate me there years ago /
몇 년 전 그곳에서 저를 사로잡았던 첫 번째 랜드마크 중 하나는 /

was the Mackenzie-Brown House.
Mackenzie-Brown House였습니다

Last week, / I visited again after a long time away, /
지난주 / 저는 오랜 시간이 지난 후에 다시 방문했습니다 /

and I was shocked at the state of the house — /
저는 그 집의 상태에 충격을 받았는데 /

yard overgrown and stains on the beautiful walls.
마당은 풀이 무성했고 아름다운 벽에는 얼룩이 있었습니다

I am particularly sensitive to historic sites / falling into disrepair.
저는 유적지들이 특히 민감합니다 / 황폐해지는 것에

I certainly can't understand /
저는 확실히 이해할 수 없습니다 /

why you have neglected such a landmark, /
귀하가 왜 그러한 랜드마크를 방치해 왔는지 /

and I ask / that you please restore the Mackenzie-Brown House.
그리고 저는 요청합니다 / 귀하가 Mackenzie-Brown House를 복원해 줄 것을

I cannot imagine / how heartbreaking it must be /
저는 상상할 수가 없습니다 / 틀림없이 얼마나 가슴 아픈 일인지 /

for the residents of Summerland / to witness the decline of this historic building.
Summerland 주민들이 / 이런 역사적 건축물의 쇠퇴를 목격하는 것이

With kind regards, / 친절한 안부를 담아
Holly Bebernitz / Holly Bebernitz 드림

관계자분께,
저는 가끔 친구들을 방문하기 위해 Summerland로 여행을 갑니다. 몇 년 전 그곳에서 저를 사로잡았던 첫 번째 랜드마크(주요 지형지물) 중 하나는 Mackenzie-Brown House였습니다. 지난주 저는 오랜 시간이 지난 후에 다시 방문했고 저는 그 집의 상태에 충격을 받았는데, 마당은 풀이 무성했고 아름다운 벽에는 얼룩이 있었습니다. 저는 유적지들이 황폐해지는 것에 특히 민감합니다. 저는 귀하가 왜 그러한 랜드마크를 방치해 왔는지 확실히 이해할 수가 없으며, 귀하가 Mackenzie-Brown House를 복원해 줄 것을 요청합니다. 저는 Summerland 주민들이 이런 역사적 건축물의 쇠퇴를 목격하는 것이 틀림없이 얼마나 가슴 아픈 일인지 상상할 수가 없습니다.
친절한 안부를 담아
Holly Bebernitz 드림

문제풀이

'I certainly can't understand why you have

neglected such a landmark, and I ask that you please restore the Mackenzie-Brown House.(저는 귀하가 왜 그런 랜드마크를 방치해 왔는지 확실히 이해할 수 없으며, 귀하에게 Mackenzie-Brown House를 복원해 줄 것을 요청합니다.)'를 통해 필자가 역사적 건축물이 방치되어 황폐해진 것을 보고 복원을 요청하고 있다는 것을 알 수 있다. 따라서 글의 목적으로 가장 적절한 것은 ③ '지역의 역사적 건축물 복원을 요청하려고'이다.

《 어휘·어구 》

landmark (주요 지형지물) 랜드마크
captivate ~의 마음을 사로잡다
state 상태
stain 얼룩
sensitive 예민한
historic 역사적인
fall into disrepair 황폐해지다
neglect 방치하다
restore 복원하다
heartbreaking 가슴이 미어지는 듯한
resident 주민
decline 쇠퇴하다

정답률 91%

6. ① 제품의 세부사항과 견본 요청

직독/직해

Dear Lorenzo Romano,
Lorenzo Romano 씨께
I heard from Antonio Ricci of Rome /
로마의 Antonio Ricci 씨로부터 들었습니다 /
that you are producing handmade gloves / for export /
귀하께서 수제 장갑을 생산하고 있다고 / 수출용의 /
in a variety of natural leathers.
다양한 천연 가죽으로
I read about your business on your website.
귀하의 웹 사이트에서 귀하의 사업에 대해 읽어 보았습니다
There is a steady demand in my country / for high quality leather gloves, /
우리나라에는 꾸준한 수요가 있습니다 / 고품질의 가죽 장갑에 대한 /
and I am able to charge good prices.
그리고 제가 좋은 가격을 매길 수 있습니다
Please let me know full details of the gloves /
장갑에 대한 모든 세부 사항을 알려 주시기 바랍니다 /
you would recommend.
귀하께서 추천하고 싶은
It would also help /
또한 도움이 될 것 같습니다 /
if you could provide me with some samples of the gloves you produce. /
귀하께서 생산하는 장갑의 견본을 몇 개 보내 주실 수 있으면
I hope to hear from you soon.
곧 답변을 들을 수 있기를 바랍니다.
Sincerely yours, Jonathan Turner
Jonathan Turner 드림

Lorenzo Romano 씨께
로마의 Antonio Ricci 씨로부터 귀하께서 다양한 천연 가죽으로 수출용 수제 장갑을 생산하고 있다고 들었습니다. 귀하의 웹 사이트에서 귀하의 사업에 대해 읽어 보았습니다. 우리나라에는 고품질의 가죽 장갑에 대한 수요가 꾸준하며, 제가 좋은 가격을 매길 수 있습니다. 귀하께서 추천하고 싶은 장갑에 대한 모든 세부 사항을 알려 주시기 바랍니다. 또한 귀하께서 생산하는 장갑의 견본을 몇 개 보내 주실 수 있으면 도움이 될 것 같습니다. 곧 답변을 들을 수 있기를 바랍니다.
Jonathan Turner 드림

문제풀이

'Please let me know full details of the gloves you would recommend. It would also help if you could provide me with some samples of the gloves you produce.(귀하께서 추천하고 싶은 장갑에 대한 모든 세부 사항을 알려 주시기 바랍니다. 또한 귀하께서 생산하는 장갑의 견본을 몇 개 보내 주실 수 있으면 도움이 될 것 같습니다.)'로 보아, 글의 목적으로 가장 적절한 것은 ① '제품의 모든 세부 사항과 견본을 요청하려고'이다.

《 어휘·어구 》

handmade 수제의
export 수출
a variety of 다양한
steady 꾸준한
demand 수요
quality 품질
charge (가격을) 매기다
price 가격
detail 세부 사항
recommend 추천하다

정답률 96%

7. ② 과학 교사 워크숍의 특강 부탁

직독/직해

Dear Ms. Green, Green 씨께
My name is Donna Williams, /
제 이름은 Donna Williams이고 /
a science teacher at Rogan High School.
Rogan 고등학교 과학 교사입니다
I am planning a special workshop /
저는 특별 워크숍을 계획하고 있습니다 /
for our science teachers.
우리 학교의 과학 교사들을 위해
We are interested in learning /
저희는 배우는 것에 관심이 있습니다 /
how to teach online science classes.
온라인 과학 수업을 가르치는 방법을
I have been impressed with your ideas /
저는 귀하의 아이디어에 감명받았습니다 /
about using internet platforms for science classes.
과학 수업에 인터넷 플랫폼을 사용하는 것에 관한
Since you are an expert in online education, /
귀하가 온라인 교육의 전문가이기 때문에 /
I would like to ask you / to deliver a special lecture /
저는 귀하에게 부탁드리고 싶습니다 / 특별 강연을 해 주시기를 /
at the workshop / scheduled for next month.
워크숍에서 / 다음 달에 계획된
I am sure / the lecture will help our teachers /
저는 확신합니다 / 강의가 저희 교사들에게 도움이 될 것이라고 /
manage successful online science classes, /
성공적인 온라인 과학 수업을 해내는 데 /
and I hope / we can learn / from your insights.
그리고 저는 바랍니다 / 저희가 배울 수 있기를 / 귀하의 통찰력으로부터
I am looking forward to hearing from you.
귀하의 답변을 기대하고 있겠습니다.
Sincerely, Donna Williams
Donna Williams 드림

Green 씨께
제 이름은 Donna Williams이고, Rogan 고등학교 과학 교사입니다. 저는 우리 학교의 과학 교사들을 위해 특별 워크숍을 계획하고 있습니다. 저희는 온라인 과학 수업을 가르치는 방법을 배우는 것에 관심이 있습니다. 저는 과학 수업에 인터넷 플랫폼을 사용하는 것에 관한 귀하의 아이디어에 감명받았습니다. 귀하가 온라인 교육의 전문가이기 때문에, 저는 다음 달에 계획된 워크숍에서 귀하가 특별 강연을 해 주시기를 부탁드리고 싶습니다. 저희 교사들이 성공적인 온라인 과학 수업을 해내는 데 강의가 도움이 될 것이라고 확신하며 귀하의 통찰력으로부터 저희가 배울 수 있기를 바랍니다. 귀하의 답변을 기대하고 있겠습니다.
Donna Williams 드림

문제풀이

'I am planning a special workshop for our science teachers.(저는 우리 학교의 과학 교사들을 위해 특별 워크숍을 계획하고 있습니다.)'와 'Since you are an expert in online education, I would like to ask you to deliver a special lecture at the workshop scheduled for next month.(귀하가 온라인 교육의 전문가이기 때문에, 저는 다음 달에 계획된 워크숍에서 귀하가 특별 강연을 해 주시기를 부탁드리고 싶습니다.)'를 통해 필자가 온라인 교육 전문가에게 자신의 학교 과학 교사들을 위한 워크숍에서 특별 강연을 해 달라고 부탁하고 있다는 것을 알 수 있다. 따라서 정답은 ② '과학 교사 워크숍의 특강을 부탁하려고'이다.

《 어휘·어구 》

impressed 감명[감동]을 받은
platform 플랫폼(사용 기반이 되는 컴퓨터 시스템·소프트웨어)
expert 전문가
education 교육
deliver (연설·강연 등을) 하다
lecture 강연, 강의
scheduled 예정된
manage (어떻게든) ~하다[해내다]
insight 통찰력
look forward to ~하기를 기대하다

정답률 96%

8. ③ 박물관 멤버십 회원을 위한 추가 혜택 안내

직독/직해

Dear Ms. Larson, Larson 씨에게
I am writing to you / with new information /
저는 귀하에게 편지를 씁니다 / 새로운 정보를 알려드리려고 /
about your current membership.
귀하의 현재 멤버십에 대한
Last year, / 작년에 /
you signed up for our museum membership /
귀하는 우리 박물관 멤버십을 신청하셨습니다 /
that provides special discounts.
특별 할인을 제공하는
As stated in the last newsletter, /
지난번 소식지에서 언급한 바와 같이 /
this year we are happy /
올해 저희는 행복합니다 /
to be celebrating our 50th anniversary.
저희의 50주년을 기념하게 되어
So we would like to offer you further benefits.
그래서 저희는 귀하에게 더 많은 혜택을 제공해 드리고 싶습니다
These include free admission for up to ten people /
이것에는 10명까지의 무료입장이 포함됩니다 /
and 20% off museum merchandise /
그리고 박물관 상품 20% 할인 혜택이 (포함됩니다) /
on your next visit.
귀하의 다음 방문 시
You will also be invited /
귀하는 또한 초대 될 것입니다. /
to all new exhibition openings this year /
올해 모든 새로운 전시회 개막식에 /
at discounted prices.
할인된 가격으로

We hope / you enjoy these offers.
저희는 바랍니다 / 귀하께서 이러한 제안을 즐기시길
For any questions, / please feel free to contact us.
질문이 있으시면 / 언제든지 저희에게 연락해 주세요
Best regards,
Stella Harrison Stella Harrison 드림

Larson 씨에게
귀하의 현재 멤버십에 대한 새로운 정보를 알려드리려고 편지를 씁니다. 작년에 귀하는 특별 할인을 제공하는 우리 박물관 멤버십을 신청하셨습니다. 지난번 소식지에서 언급한 바와 같이, 올해 저희는 저희의 50주년을 기념하게 되어 행복합니다. 그래서 저희는 귀하에게 더 많은 혜택을 제공해 드리고 싶습니다. 이것에는 귀하의 다음 방문 시 10명까지의 무료입장과 박물관 상품 20% 할인 혜택이 포함됩니다. 귀하는 또한 할인된 가격으로 올해 모든 새로운 전시회 개막식에 초대될 것입니다. 저희는 귀하께서 이러한 제안을 즐기시길 바랍니다. 질문이 있으시면 언제든지 저희에게 연락해 주세요.
Stella Harrison 드림

문제풀이

올해 50주년을 기념하여 박물관에서 박물관 멤버십 회원에게 추가적으로 제공하는 혜택 두 가지에 대해 알려 주고 있는 글이다. 따라서 글의 목적으로 가장 적절한 것은 ③ '박물관 멤버십 회원을 위한 추가 혜택을 알려 주려고'이다.

어휘·어구

current 현재의
sign up for ~을 신청하다
state (정식으로) 말하다, 쓰다
newsletter 소식지, 뉴스레터
celebrate 기념하다
anniversary 기념일
benefit 혜택
admission 입장료
merchandise 상품
exhibition 전시회

정답률 91%

9. ① 교내 음식 모으기 운동 참여 방법 안내

직독/직해

Dear Friends, 친구 여러분에게,
Season's greetings.
즐거운 크리스마스와 연말되세요
As some of you already know, /
여러분 중 일부가 이미 알고 있듯이 /
we are starting the campus food drive.
교내 음식 모으기 운동을 시작하고 있습니다
This is / how you participate.
다음은 ~입니다 / 여러분이 참여하는 방법
You can bring your items for donation /
기부할 음식을 가져오면 됩니다 /
to our booths. 저희 부스로
Our donation booths are located /
저희 기부 부스는 있습니다 /
in the lobbies of the campus libraries.
교내 도서관 로비에
Just drop off the items there /
그곳에 음식을 가져다 놓기만 하면 됩니다 /
during usual library hours /
정규 도서관 운영 시간 동안 /
from December 4 to 23.
12월 4일부터 23일까지
The donated food should be non-perishable /
기부된 음식은 상하지 않는 음식이어야 합니다 /
like canned meats and canned fruits.
통조림 고기와 통조림 과일 같은
Packaged goods such as jam and peanut butter /
잼이나 땅콩버터와 같은 포장된 제품도 /
are also good. 괜찮습니다
We will distribute the food to our neighbors /
저희는 그 음식을 이웃들에게 나누어줄 겁니다 /
on Christmas Eve. 크리스마스이브에
We truly appreciate your help.
여러분의 도움에 진심으로 감사드립니다
Many blessings, 많은 축복을 받기를.
Joanna at Campus Food Bank
Campus Food Bank의 Joanna 올림

친구 여러분에게,
즐거운 크리스마스와 연말되세요. 여러분 중 일부가 이미 알고 있듯이, 교내 음식 모으기 운동을 시작하고 있습니다. 다음은 여러분이 참여하는 방법입니다. 기부할 음식을 저희 부스로 가져오면 됩니다. 저희 기부 부스는 교내 도서관 로비에 있습니다. 12월 4일부터 23일까지 정규 도서관 운영 시간 동안 그곳에 음식을 가져다 놓기만 하면 됩니다. 기부된 음식은 통조림 고기와 통조림 과일 같은 상하지 않는 음식이어야 합니다. 잼이나 땅콩버터와 같은 포장된 제품도 괜찮습니다. 저희는 크리스마스이브에 그 음식을 이웃들에게 나누어줄 겁니다. 여러분의 도움에 진심으로 감사드립니다.
많은 축복이 있기를,
Campus Food Bank의 Joanna 올림

문제풀이

'As some of you already know, we are starting the campus food drive.(여러분 중 일부가 이미 알고 있듯이, 교내 음식 모으기 운동을 시작하고 있습니다.)'와 'This is how you participate.(다음은 여러분이 참여하는 방법입니다.)'를 통해 이 글이 교내 음식 모으기 운동이 시작되었다는 것을 알려주면서 그 운동에 참여하는 방법을 안내하고 있다는 것을 알 수 있다. 따라서 글의 목적으로 가장 적절한 것은 ① '음식 기부에 참여하는 방법을 안내하려고'이다.

어휘·어구

drive 운동
participate 참가하다, 참여하다
donation 기부
drop off ~을 가져다주다
non-perishable 쉽게 부패하지 않는
packaged 포장된
goods 제품
distribute 나누어 주다

정답률 97%

10. ⑤ 애완견 공원의 소음

직독/직해

Dear Mr. Kayne, / Kayne 씨에게 /
I am a resident of Cansinghill Apartments, /
저는 Cansinghill 아파트의 주민입니다 /
located right next to the newly opened Vuenna Dog Park. 새롭게 문을 연 Vuenna 애완견 공원 바로 옆에 위치한
As I live with three dogs, / 세 마리의 개와 함께 살고 있기에 /
I am very happy to let my dogs run around /
저는 제 개들이 뛰어다니게 해서 기쁩니다 /
and safely play with other dogs from the neighborhood.
그리고 이웃의 다른 개들과 안전하게 놀 수 있게 해서
However, the noise of barking and yelling from the
하지만 밤에 공원에서 들려오는 개가 짖고 소리를 지르는 소음은 /
park at night /
is so loud and disturbing that I cannot relax in my
너무 시끄럽고 방해가 되어 저는 아파트에서 쉴 수가 없습니다
apartment.
Many of my apartment neighbors also seriously
제 아파트의 많은 이웃 역시 이 소음에 대해 심하게 불평하고 있습니다
complain about this noise.
I want immediate action to solve this urgent problem.
저는 이 긴급한 문제를 해결할 즉각적인 조치를 원합니다
Since you are the manager of Vuenna Dog Park, /
귀하께서 Vuenna 애완견 공원의 관리자이기에 /
I ask you to take measures to prevent the noise at night. 저는 귀하가 밤의 소음을 막을 조치를 해 줄 것을 요청합니다
I hope to hear from you soon.
귀하로부터 곧 소식을 기대합니다
Sincerely, Monty Kim Monty Kim 드림

Mr. Kayne,
저는 최근 문을 연 Vuenna 애완견 공원 바로 옆에 Cansinghill 아파트의 주민입니다. 저는 세 마리의 애완견과 함께 살고 있기에, 제 애완견들이 뛰어다니고 이웃의 다른 애완견들과 함께 안전하게 놀 수 있게 해줄 수 있어 매우 기쁩니다. 하지만 밤에 그 공원에서 들려오는, 애완견이 짖고 소리를 지르는 소음이 너무 시끄럽고 방해가 되어 저는 아파트에서 쉴 수가 없습니다. 제 아파트의 많은 이웃 역시 이 소음에 대해 심하게 불평하고 있습니다. 저는 이 긴급한 문제를 해결할 수 있는 즉각적인 조치를 원합니다. 귀하께서 Vuenna 애완견 공원의 관리자이기에 저는 귀하께서 밤에 나는 그 소음을 막을 조치를 취해 줄 것을 요청합니다. 귀하로부터 곧 소식을 듣기를 기대합니다.
Monty Kim 드림

문제풀이

새로 개장한 Vuenna 애완견 공원에 접해 있는 아파트 주민이라고 자신을 소개한 필자는 'However, the noise of barking and yelling from the park at night is so loud and disturbing that I cannot relax in my apartment.(하지만 밤에 그 공원에서 들려오는, 개가 짖고 소리를 지르는 소음이 너무 시끄럽고 방해가 되어 저는 아파트에서 쉴 수가 없습니다.)' 그리고 'I want immediate action to solve this urgent problem.(저는 이 긴급한 문제를 해결할 수 있는 즉각적인 조치를 원합니다.)'라며 애완견 공원의 소음에 대한 조치를 촉구하고 있다. 따라서 글의 목적으로 가장 적절한 것은 ⑤임을 알 수 있다.

어휘·어구

resident 거주자
yell 소리 지르다
disturbing 방해가 되는
take measures 조치를 취하다
prevent 막다

본문 005쪽

문법 플러스 1. 주어·동사

A. 1. does 2. is 3. rely
4. was 5. is 6. it
7. were

1 [해석]▶ 한 가지 명백한 문제점은 (실험에) 수반되는 위험인데, 위험이 존재한다는 것을 안다고 해서 위험을 줄이기 위해 어떤 일을 하게 되는 것은 결코 아니다.
[해설]▶ 동명사구인 knowing that it exists가 문장의 주어이므로 술어 동사를 단수로 수 일치시킨 does가 어법상 적절하다.

2 [해석]▶ 그녀가 백만장자라는 것이 믿어지지 않는다.
[해설]▶ 접속사 That이 이끄는 절은 주어 역할을 할 수 있으며 단수로 취급한다.

3 [해석]▶ 선사 시대 예술의 의미와 목적에 대한 고찰은 현대의 수렵 채집 사회와의 사이에서 끌어낸 유사점에 많은 것을 의존한다.
[해설]▶ 복수 명사인 Speculations가 주어이므로 rely가 어법에 맞다.

4 [해석]▶ 시사적 문제를 다루는 주간 프로그램이 시청자들에 의해 사랑을 받았다.
[해설]▶ 주어가 분사구(현재분사)의 수식을 받아 길어진 경

우로 주어는 단수주어 A weekly program이므로 단수동사가 와야 한다.

5 [해석]▶ 우리 옆집에 사는 그 소녀는 아프다.
[해설]▶ 주어가 관계사절의 수식을 받아 길어진 경우로, 주어는 The girl이므로 동사는 단수동사 is를 써야 한다.

6 [해석]▶ 모든 것을 고려했을 때, 이사짐 회사의 서비스를 받는 것이 더 좋을 것 같다.
[해설]▶ 주어가 길어진 경우 가주어 it을 쓰고 진주어(to ask for the services of a moving company)는 뒤로 돌린다.

7 [해석]▶ 기본 쟁점에 대한 의견 차이가 있었다.
[해설]▶ There was/were ~ 문장에서 주어는 be동사 다음에 나온 어구(differences)가 복수이면 복수동사를 쓰고, 단수주어이면 단수동사를 쓰므로 복수동사가 맞다. .

본문 005쪽

B. 1. is　2. is　3. is
4. is　5. was　6. It
7. are

1 [해석]▶ 정기적으로 운동하는 것은 누구에게나 쉽지 않다.
[해설]▶ to부정사는 문장에서 주어 역할을 할 수 있으며 단수로 취급한다.

2 [해석]▶ 당신이 보는 것이 항상 진실인 것은 아닙니다.
[해설]▶ 관계사가 이끄는 절은 주어 역할을 할 수 있으며 단수로 취급한다.

3 [해석]▶ 빨간색 드레스를 입은 아름다운 여인이 거리를 걷고 있다.
[해설]▶ 주어가 전치사구의 수식을 받아 길어진 경우 주어, 동사를 잘 구분해야 한다. 주어는 단수주어 A beautiful lady이므로 단수동사가 나와야 한다.

4 [해석]▶ 미국에서 자기 부모에 의해서 교육을 받는 아이들의 수가 점진적으로 늘어나고 있다.
[해설]▶ 주어가 분사구(과거분사)의 수식을 받아 길어진 경우로 「The number of +복수명사」는 단수동사를 사용한다.

5 [해석]▶ 의사가 되고자 하는 그녀의 꿈이 마침내 이루어졌다.
[해설]▶ 주어가 to부정사구의 수식을 받아 길어진 경우로 하나의 문장에는 주어와 동사가 필요하므로 단수주어 Her hope에 해당하는 단수동사가 나와야 한다.

6 [해석]▶ 그에게 알리는 것이 중요하다.
[해설]▶ 문두에 주어가 길어진 경우 가주어 it을 쓰고 진주어(that he should be informed)는 뒤로 돌린다.

7 [해석]▶ 당신을 위해 유용한 조언이 몇 개 있다.
[해설]▶ Here is / are ~ 문장에서 주어는 be동사 다음에 나온 어구(some useful tips)이다. 어구가 복수이면 복수동사를 쓴다.

본문 006쪽

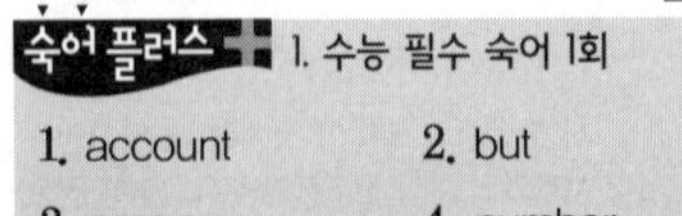

1. 수능 필수 숙어 1회

1. account　2. but
3. range　4. number

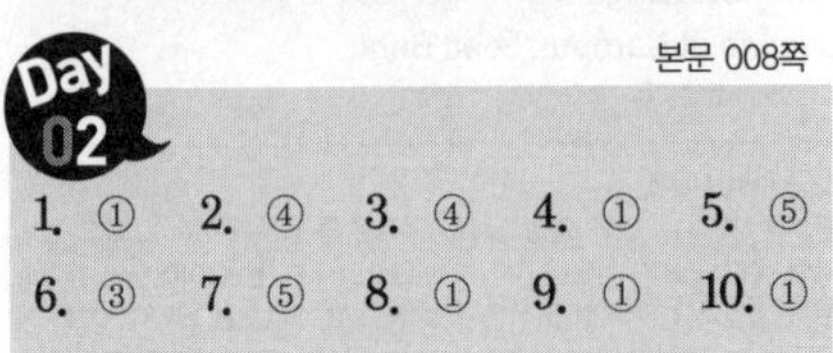

본문 008쪽

Day 02

1. ①　2. ④　3. ④　4. ①　5. ⑤
6. ③　7. ⑤　8. ①　9. ①　10. ①

정답률 92%

대표 기출 ③　자신의 최고 기록을 깨지 못한 Jamie

직독/직해

Putting all of her energy / into her last steps of the running race, /
자신의 모든 에너지를 쏟으면서 / 경주의 마지막 스텝에 /
Jamie crossed the finish line.
Jamie는 결승선을 통과했다
To her disappointment, / she had failed to beat her personal best time, again.
실망스럽게도 / 그녀는 자신의 개인 최고 기록을 깨는 것에 다시 실패했다
Jamie had pushed herself for months / to finally break her record, /
Jamie는 몇 달 동안 스스로 채찍질해왔다 / 기어코 자신의 최고 기록을 깨기 위해 /
but it was all for nothing.
하지만 그것은 모두 헛수고였다
Recognizing how she felt about her failure, /
그녀가 자신의 실패에 대해 어떻게 느끼는지 알아차린 /
Ken, her teammate, approached her and said, /
그녀의 팀 동료 Ken은 그녀에게 다가와 말했다 /
"Jamie, / even though you didn't set a personal best time today, /
Jamie / 비록 오늘 네가 개인 최고 기록을 세우지는 못했지만 /
your performances have improved dramatically.
너의 경기력은 극적으로 향상되었어
Your running skills have progressed so much!
너의 달리기 실력이 아주 많이 발전했어!
You'll definitely break your personal best time / in the next race!"
넌 분명 너의 개인 최고 기록을 깰 거야! / 다음 경주에서
After hearing his comments, / she felt confident about herself.
그의 말을 들은 후 / 그녀는 자신에 대해 자신감을 느꼈다
Jamie, / now motivated to keep pushing for her goal, / replied with a smile.
Jamie가 / 이제 자신의 목표를 계속 밀고 나갈 의욕이 생긴 / 미소를 지으며 대답했다
"You're right! 네 말이 맞아!
Next race, / I'll beat my best time for sure!"
다음 경주에서 / 나는 확실히 최고 기록을 깰 거야!

자신의 모든 에너지를 경주의 마지막 스텝에 쏟으면서 Jamie는 결승선을 통과했다. 실망스럽게도, 그녀는 자신의 개인 최고 기록을 깨는 것에 다시 실패했다. Jamie는 기어코 자신의 최고 기록을 깨기 위해 몇 달 동안 스스로 채찍질해왔지만, 그것은 모두 헛수고였다. 그녀가 자신의 실패에 대해 어떻게 느끼는지 알아차린 그녀의 팀 동료 Ken은 그녀에게 다가와 말했다. "Jamie, 비록 오늘 네가 개인 최고 기록을 세우지는 못했지만 너의 경기력은 극적으로 향상되었어. 너의 달리기 실력이 아주 많이 발전했어! 다음 경주에서 넌 분명 너의 개인 최고 기록을 깰 거야!" 그의 말을 들은 후, 그녀는 자신에 대해 자신감을 느꼈다. 이제 자신의 목표를 계속 밀고 나갈 의욕이 생긴 Jamie가 미소를 지으며 대답했다. "네 말이 맞아! 다음 경주에서 나는 확실히 최고 기록을 깰 거야!"

① 무관심한 → 후회하는　② 기쁜 → 지루해 하는
③ 좌절한 → 용기를 얻은　④ 초조한 → 무서워하는
⑤ 차분한 → 신이 난

문제풀이

달리기 경주에서 자신의 개인 최고 기록을 깨는 데 실패한 Jamie가 Ken이 격려해 주는 말을 들은 상황이다. 'Jamie had pushed herself for months to finally break her record, but it was all for nothing.(Jamie는 기어코 자신의 최고 기록을 깨기 위해 몇 달 동안 자신을 몰아붙였지만, 그것은 모두 헛수고였다.)'을 통해 처음에 Jamie가 좌절했다는 것을 알 수 있고, 'After hearing his comments, she felt confident about herself.(그의 말을 들은 후, 그녀는 자신에 대해 자신감을 느꼈다.)'를 통해 나중에 Jamie가 용기를 얻은 상태로 변했음을 알 수 있다. 따라서 정답은 ③ 'frustrated → encouraged(좌절한 → 용기를 얻은)'이다.

《 어휘·어구 》

push oneself 스스로 채찍질하다, 분투하다
break one's record ~의 기록을 깨다
for nothing 헛되이
recognize 알아차리다
approach 다가오다
dramatically 극적으로
definitely 분명히
comment 언급, 논평
motivate 의욕을 갖게 하다
for sure 확실히

정답률 95%

1. ①　콘퍼런스 참석

직독/직해

I was going to a conference / and my plane was delayed, /
나는 콘퍼런스에 가는 중이었다 / 그런데 비행기가 연착되었다 /
so by the time I got to my hotel / everyone I was supposed to meet /
그래서 내가 호텔에 도착했을 때에는 / 만나기로 한 모든 사람들이 /
had already left for the conference.
이미 콘퍼런스에 참석하기 위해 떠나버렸다
I walked to the bus stop, / but to my dismay /
나는 버스 정류장까지 걸어갔다 / 그러나 당황스럽게도 /
the last shuttle to the convention center had already gone.
컨벤션 센터로 가는 마지막 셔틀버스는 이미 가고 없었다
I was at a loss as to what to do!
나는 어떻게 해야 할지 막막했다
Then a young man standing on the sidewalk said, /
그때, 보도에 서 있던 한 청년이 말했다 /
"The convention center isn't very far. / It's only four blocks."
컨벤션 센터는 그리 멀지 않습니다 / 네 블록만 가면 됩니다
So I started walking.
그래서 나는 걸어가기 시작했다
It wasn't long before the convention center appeared / in front of my eyes.
얼마 지나지 않아 컨벤션 센터가 나타났다 / 눈앞에
My heart slowly calmed down!
내 마음은 천천히 차분해졌다
Fortunately, / I was just in time for the conference!
다행스럽게도 / 나는 콘퍼런스 시간에 딱 맞출 수 있었다

콘퍼런스에 가는 중인데 비행기가 연착되어, 내가 호텔에 도착했을 때에는 만나기로 한 모든 사람들이 이미 콘퍼런스에 참석하기 위해 떠나버렸다. 나는 버스 정류장까지 걸어갔지만, 당황스럽게도 컨벤션 센터로 가는 마지막 셔틀버스는 이미 가고 없었다. 나는 어떻게 해야 할지 막막했다! 그때, 보도에 서 있던 한 청년이 "컨벤션 센터는 그리 멀지 않습니다. 네 블록만 가면 됩니다."라고 말했다. 그래서 나는 걸어가기 시작했다. 얼마 지나지 않아 컨벤션 센터가 눈앞에 나타났다. 내 마음은 천천히 차분해졌다! 다행스럽게도 나는 콘퍼런스 시간에 딱 맞출 수 있었다!

① 좌절한 → 안도한
② 지루한 → 흥분한
③ 화난 → 당황한
④ 부러운 → 부끄러운
⑤ 의심이 많은 → 무관심한

문제풀이

비행기가 연착하는 바람에 만나기로 한 사람들이 콘퍼런스에 참여하기 위해 이미 모두 떠나 버렸고, 컨벤션 센터로 가는 마지막 셔틀버스도 이미 떠나 버려 매우 당황한 처지에 놓이게 되었는데, 한 청년이 컨벤션 센터가 그리 멀지 않다고 하여 걸어서 컨벤션 센터로 가서 다행스럽게 콘퍼런스에 늦지 않게 도착했다는 내용의 글이므로 'I'의 심경변화로 가장 적절한 것은 ① 'frustrated(좌절한) → relieved(안도한)'이다.

《 어휘·어구 》

delay 지연, 지체
by the time ~할 때까지
to one's dismay 당황스럽게도
convention 회의
be at a loss 당혹스러워하다
sidewalk 보도
in time 늦지 않게

정답률 96%

2. ④ 딸이 그린 아빠 얼굴

직독/직해

"Daddy!" / Jenny called, / waving a yellow crayon / in her little hand.
"아빠!" Jenny는 불렀다 / 노란색 크레용을 흔들면서 / 작은 손에 쥔

Nathan approached her, / wondering why she was calling him.
Nathan은 아이에게 다가갔다 / 아이가 왜 자신을 부르는지 궁금해하면서

Jenny, his three-year-old toddler, / was drawing a big circle on a piece of paper.
그의 걸음마를 하는 세 살배기 Jenny는 / 종이에 큰 원을 그리고 있었다

"What are you doing, Sweetie?" / Nathan asked with interest.
"무엇을 하고 있니, 얘야?" / Nathan은 관심을 가지고 물었다

She just kept drawing / without reply.
아이는 계속 그림을 그리고 있었다 / 대답하지 않고

He continued watching her, / wondering what she was working on.
그는 계속해서 아이를 보고 있었다 / 아이가 무엇을 하고 있는지 궁금해하며

She was drawing something / that looked like a face.
아이는 무언가를 그리고 있었다 / 얼굴처럼 보이는

When she finished it, / Jenny shouted, / "Look, Daddy!"
그것을 다했을 때 / Jenny는 소리쳤다 / "보세요, 아빠!"

She held her artwork up / proudly.
아이는 자기 작품을 들어 올렸다 / 자랑스럽게

Taking a closer look, / Nathan recognized / that it was his face.
더 자세히 보자 / Nathan은 알아챘다 / 그것이 자기 얼굴이라는 것을

The face had two big eyes and a beard / just like his.
그 얼굴에는 두 개의 큰 눈과 수염이 있었다 / 그의 것과 똑같은

He loved Jenny's work.
그는 Jenny의 작품이 마음에 들었다

Filled with joy and happiness, / Nathan gave her a big hug.
기쁨과 행복으로 가득 찬 / Nathan은 아이를 꼭 껴안아 주었다

"아빠!" Jenny는 작은 손에 쥔 노란색 크레용을 흔들면서 불렀다. Nathan은 아이가 왜 자신을 부르는지 궁금해하면서 아이에게 다가갔다. 그의 걸음마를 하는 세 살배기 Jenny는 종이에 큰 원을 그리고 있었다. "무엇을 하고 있니, 얘야?"라고 Nathan은 관심을 가지고 물었다. 아이는 대답하지 않고 계속 그림을 그리고 있었다. 그는 아이가 무엇을 하고 있는지 궁금해하며 계속해서 아이를 보고 있었다. 아이는 얼굴처럼 보이는 것을 그리고 있었다. 그것을 다했을 때, Jenny는 "보세요, 아빠!"라고 소리쳤다. 아이는 자기 작품을 자랑스럽게 들어 올렸다. 더 자세히 보자 Nathan은 그것이 자기 얼굴이라는 것을 알아챘다. 그 얼굴에는 그의 것과 똑같은 두 개의 큰 눈과 수염이 있었다. 그는 Jenny의 작품이 마음에 들었다. 기쁨과 행복으로 가득 찬 Nathan은 아이를 꼭 껴안아 주었다.

① 슬픈 → 안도하는
② 좌절된 → 만족한
③ 걱정하는 → 무서워하는
④ 궁금해하는 → 기쁜
⑤ 기대하는 → 실망한

문제풀이

Nathan은 딸 Jenny가 자신을 불러놓고 뭔가를 그리는 것을 곁에서 지켜만 보고 있다가, 완성된 딸의 그림이 자신의 얼굴이라는 것을 안 상황이다. 'Nathan approached her, wondering why she was calling him.(Nathan은 아이가 왜 자신을 부르는지 궁금해하면서 아이에게 다가갔다.)'과 'He continued watching her, wondering what she was working on.(아이가 무엇을 하고 있는지 궁금해하며 그는 계속해서 아이를 보고 있었다.)'을 통해 처음에 Nathan이 궁금해하고 있다는 것을 알 수 있고, 'Filled with joy and happiness, Nathan gave her a big hug.(기쁨과 행복으로 가득 찬 Nathan은 아이를 꼭 껴안아 주었다.)'를 통해 나중에 Nathan이 기쁜 상태로 변했음을 알 수 있다. 따라서 정답은 ④ 'curious → delighted(궁금해하는 → 기쁜)'이다.

《 어휘·어구 》

approach 다가가다
artwork 작품
recognize 알아보다
beard (턱)수염

정답률 91%

3. ④ Big Foot으로 갈 때 느낀 두려움

직독/직해

One night / a buddy and I decided / we were going to go find that Big Foot.
어느 날 밤 / 한 친구와 나는 결심했다 / 나는 그 Big Foot을 찾으러 가기로

We were in my old truck / and we set off across the fields /
우리는 내 오래된 트럭을 탔다 / 그리고 들판을 가로질러 출발했다 /

heading toward the tallest hill.
가장 높은 언덕을 향해

The fields were rough, / with only the slightest trail to follow.
들판은 거칠었다 / 따라갈 가장 좁은 길만이 있었고

Along the way / there were small trenches dug in the fields.
길을 따라 / 들판에 파인 작은 구덩이들이 있었다

I never figured out why.
나는 왜 그런지 전혀 알 수가 없었다

As we got closer and closer / to the top of the hill, /
우리가 점점 가까워질수록 / 언덕 꼭대기에

I was actually becoming scared, / which was kind of rare, /
나는 실제로 겁이 나기 시작했다 / 그것은 좀 드문 일이었다 /

because at that age I was pretty fearless.
왜냐하면 그 나이 때 나는 상당히 겁이 없었기 때문이었다

As we got to the top of the hill, / there was a loud thump!
우리가 언덕 꼭대기에 도착했을 바로 그때 / 크게 쿵 하는 소리가 났다

My truck sunk down / like something heavy had just jumped in the bed.
내 트럭이 내려앉았다 / 어떤 무거운 것이 (트럭 뒤편) 적재함에 뛰어든 것처럼

We were too terrified to look in the back.
우리는 너무 무서워서 뒤를 볼 수가 없었다

I panicked / and decided to throw the truck into reverse /
나는 공포에 사로잡혔다 / 그리고 트럭을 후진시키기로 결심했다 /

and back down the hill.
그리고 언덕 아래로 몰고 가기로

As I did so, / there was another thump / and a loud roar now came out /
내가 그렇게 했을 때 / 또 다른 쿵 하는 소리가 났다 / 그리고 엄청난 포효 소리가 났다 /

like I'd never, ever heard before.
전에 전혀 들어본 적이 없는 것 같은

어느 날 밤 한 친구와 나는 그 Big Foot을 찾으러 가기로 결심했다. 우리는 내 오래된 트럭을 타고 가장 높은 언덕을 향해 들판을 가로질러 출발했다. 들판은 거칠었고, 따라갈 가장 좁은 길만이 있었다. 길을 따라 들판에 파인 작은 구덩이들이 있었다. 나는 왜 그런지 전혀 알 수가 없었다. 우리가 언덕 꼭대기에 점점 가까워질수록, 나는 실제로 겁이 나기 시작했고, 그것은 좀 드문 일이었는데, 왜냐하면 그 나이 때 나는 상당히 겁이 없었기 때문이었다. 우리가 언덕 꼭대기에 도착했을 바로 그때, 크게 쿵 하는 소리가 났다! 어떤 무거운 것이 (트럭 뒤편) 적재함에 뛰어든 것처럼 내 트럭이 내려앉았다. 우리는 너무 무서워서 뒤를 볼 수가 없었다. 나는 공포에 사로잡혔고 트럭을 후진시켜 언덕 아래로 몰고 가기로 결심했다. 내가 그렇게 했을 때, 또 다른 쿵 하는 소리가 났고 그때 전에 전혀 들어본 적이 없는 엄청난 포효 소리가 났다.

① 안도하고 편안한
② 만족하고 기뻐하는
③ 지루하고 무관심한
④ 불안하고 두려운
⑤ 불만족스럽고 화가 난

문제풀이

트럭을 타고 Big Foot으로 가던 도중 알 수 없는 불안감을 느끼고 있을 때 트럭 뒤에서 들리는 쿵하는 소리와, 엄청난 포효소리를 듣고 무서워 뒤를 쳐다보지도 못하는 상황이므로 'I'의 심정으로 가장 적절한 것은 ④ 'alarmed and frightened(불안하고 두려운)'이다.

《 어휘·어구 》

set off 출발하다
head toward ~으로 향하다
trail 오솔길
trenches dug 구덩이
figure out 알아내다
rare 드문
fearless 두려움을 모르는
thump 쾅 치다
terrify 겁나게 하다
reverse 후진시키다
roar 포효, 고함

4. ① 노을을 보러간 Jessica

직독/직해

The island tour bus Jessica was riding on /
Jessica가 타고 있는 섬 관광버스는 /

was moving slowly toward the ocean cliffs.
바다를 면한 절벽 쪽으로 천천히 움직이고 있었다

Outside, / the sky was getting dark.
밖은 / 하늘이 점점 어두워지고 있었다

Jessica sighed with concern, /
Jessica는 걱정스럽게 한숨지었다 /

"I'm going to miss the sunset / because of the traffic."
나는 일몰을 놓치게 될 거야 / 교통체증 때문에

The bus arrived / at the cliffs' parking lot.
버스가 도착했다 / 절벽의 주차장에

While the other passengers were gathering their bags, /
다른 승객들이 자신들의 가방을 챙기는 동안 /

Jessica quickly got off the bus /
Jessica는 재빨리 버스에서 내렸다 /

and she ran up the cliff / that was famous for its ocean views.
그리고 절벽으로 뛰어 올라갔다 / 바다 전망으로 유명한

She was about to give up / when she got to the top.
그녀는 막 포기하려 했다 / 그녀는 정상에 도달했을 때

Just then she saw the setting sun / and it still shone brightly in the sky.
바로 그때 그녀는 지는 해를 보았다 / 그리고 그것은 여전히 하늘에서 밝게 빛나고 있었다

Jessica said to herself, / "The glow of the sun is so beautiful.
Jessica는 혼잣말을 했다 / 노을이 너무 아름답네

It's even better than I expected."
내가 기대했던 것보다 훨씬 더 좋아.

Jessica가 타고 있는 섬 관광버스는 바다를 면한 절벽 쪽으로 천천히 움직이고 있었다. 밖은 하늘이 점점 어두워지고 있었다. Jessica는 "나는 교통체증 때문에 일몰을 놓치게 될 거야."라고 말하며 걱정스럽게 한숨지었다. 버스가 절벽의 주차장에 도착했다. 다른 승객들이 자신들의 가방을 챙기는 동안, Jessica는 재빨리 버스에서 내려서 바다 전망으로 유명한 절벽으로 뛰어 올라갔다. 정상에 도달했을 때 그녀는 막 포기하려 했다. 바로 그때 그녀는 지는 해를 보았는데 그것은 여전히 하늘에서 밝게 빛나고 있었다. Jessica는 "노을이 너무 아름답네. 내가 기대했던 것보다 훨씬 더 좋아."라고 혼잣말을 했다.

① 걱정하는 → 기쁜 ② 지루한 → 자신감 있는
③ 안도한 → 짜증 난 ④ 즐거운 → 무관심한
⑤ 후회하는 → 우울한

문제풀이

Jessica는 일몰을 구경할 장소로 가고 있는 버스가 교통체증에 갇혀 있어 일몰을 놓칠 거라 생각했지만, 결국 도착하여 아름다운 일몰을 본 상황이다. 'Jessica sighed with concern, "I'm going to miss the sunset because of the traffic."(Jessica는 "나는 교통체증 때문에 일몰을 놓치게 될 거야."라고 말하며 걱정스럽게 한숨을 쉬었다.)'을 통해 처음에 Jessica가 걱정하고 있다는 것을 알 수 있고, 'It's even better than I expected.(내가 기대했던 것보다 훨씬 더 좋아.)'를 통해 나중에 Jessica가 기쁜 상태로 변했음을 알 수 있다. 따라서 정답은 ① 'worried → delighted(걱정하는 → 기쁜)'이다.

어휘·어구

cliff 절벽
sigh 한숨을 쉬다
concern 걱정, 우려
parking lot 주차장
passenger 승객
be about to do 막 ~하려 하다
give up 포기하다
glow 붉은 빛

정답률 95%

5. ⑤ 숲속에서 코끼리를 만난 Karim

직독/직해

Karim was deep within the dense forest / alone.
Karim은 울창한 숲속 깊은 곳에 있었다 / 혼자

He began / to notice the strangeness of his surroundings.
그는 시작했다 / 자신의 주변의 이상함을 알아차리기

Scared, / he hid under a tree, / and he heard the "thump-thump" sound.
겁에 질려 / 그는 나무 아래에 숨었다 / 그리고 그는 '쿵쿵' 소리를 들었다

Moments later, / he saw a large elephant running toward him!
잠시 후 / 그는 큰 코끼리 한 마리가 자신을 향해 달려오고 있는 것을 보았다

He trembled uncontrollably / and could hardly move.
그는 걷잡을 수 없이 떨었다 / 그리고 거의 움직일 수가 없었다

Suddenly, / he remembered / what he had read about elephants: /
갑자기 / 그는 기억했다 / 자신이 코끼리에 관해 읽었었던 것 /

Elephants are scared of loud noises.
즉, 코끼리가 큰 소음을 무서워한다는 것을

He also thought of the firecrackers / in his pack.
그는 또한 자신의 폭죽을 생각해 냈다 / 배낭 안에 있는

Quick as a flash, / he lit them.
순식간에 / 그는 그것들에 불을 붙였다

The firecrackers burst / with a loud noise, / scaring away the elephant.
그 폭죽이 터져 / 큰 소음을 내며 / 그 코끼리를 겁주어 쫓아 버렸다

Then, / Karim ran away / as fast as he could.
그러고 나서 Karim은 도망쳤다 / 자신이 할 수 있는 한 빨리

By the time he reached his campsite, /
그가 자신의 캠프장에 도착했을 때쯤에 /

he was sure / there was nothing dangerous around him.
그는 확신했다 / 자신의 주변에 위험한 것이 아무것도 없다고

He could finally breathe easily.
마침내 그는 안도의 한숨을 내쉴 수 있었다

He put his hand on his chest, /
그는 가슴에 자신의 손을 얹었고 /

feeling his heartbeat slow back to its normal pace.
자신의 심장 박동이 다시 정상 속도로 느려지는 것을 느꼈다

Karim은 혼자 울창한 숲속 깊은 곳에 있었다. 그는 자신의 주변의 이상함을 알아차리기 시작했다. 겁에 질려, 그는 나무 아래에 숨었고, 그는 '쿵쿵' 소리를 들었다. 잠시 후, 그는 큰 코끼리 한 마리가 자신을 향해 달려오고 있는 것을 보았다! 그는 걷잡을 수 없이 떨었고 거의 움직일 수가 없었다. 갑자기 그는 자신이 코끼리에 관해 읽었었던 것, 즉 코끼리가 큰 소음을 무서워한다는 것을 기억했다. 그는 또한 자신의 배낭 안에 있는 폭죽을 생각해 냈다. 그는 순식간에 그것들에 불을 붙였다. 그 폭죽이 큰 소음을 내며 터져 그 코끼리를 겁주어 쫓아 버렸다. 그러고 나서 Karim은 자신이 할 수 있는 한 빨리 도망쳤다. 그가 자신의 캠프장에 도착했을 때쯤에 그는 자신의 주변에 위험한 것이 아무것도 없다고 확신했다. 마침내 그는 안도의 한숨을 내쉴 수 있었다. 그는 가슴에 자신의 손을 얹었고 자신의 심장 박동이 다시 정상 속도로 느려지는 것을 느꼈다.

① 기대하는 → 긴장한 ② 만족한 → 후회하는
③ 질투하는 → 만족한 ④ 부끄러운 → 고마워하는
⑤ 겁에 질린 → 안도한

문제풀이

Karim이 혼자 숲속에 있을 때 코끼리를 만나 큰 소리가 나는 폭죽을 터뜨려 코끼리를 쫓아 버린 상황이다. 'He trembled uncontrollably and could hardly move.(그는 걷잡을 수 없이 떨었고 거의 움직일 수가 없었다.)'를 통해 처음에 Karim이 겁에 질렸다는 것을 알 수 있고, 'He could finally breathe easily.(마침내 그는 안도의 한숨을 내쉴 수 있었다.)'를 통해 나중에 Karim이 안도한 상태로 바뀌었다는 것을 알 수 있다. 따라서 정답은 ⑤ 'terrified → relieved(겁에 질린 → 안도한)'이다.

어휘·어구

dense 빽빽한
thump 쿵 하는 소리
tremble 떨다, 떨리다
uncontrollably 제어하기 힘들게, 통제할 수 없게
firecracker 폭죽
burst 터지다
breathe 숨을 쉬다, 호흡하다
heartbeat 심장 박동

정답률 87%

6. ③ 절벽에서 내려오기

직독/직해

Finally, / it came to my turn.
마침내 / 내 차례가 되었다

I was supposed to walk backward off the cliff.
난 절벽에서 뒤로 걸어가기로 되어 있었다

Just looking down the cliff / made my legs begin to shake.
절벽 아래를 내려다보기만 했는데도 / 다리가 후들거리기 시작했다

I knew there was a safety rope around me / in case I should black out.
몸에 안전 밧줄이 둘려 있다는 것은 알고 있었다 / 의식을 잃을 때에 대비해

I had an intellectual understanding of the whole situation /
머리로는 모든 상황을 이해했다 /

and an intellectual sense of security.
그리고 머리로는 안전하다고 느꼈다

Nevertheless, / my hair stood on end / and I shivered all over.
그럼에도 불구하고 / 내 머리카락은 곤두섰다 / 그리고 온몸이 떨렸다

That first step off the cliff was the most difficult moment, /
절벽에서 첫발을 내딛는 것이 가장 힘든 순간이었다 /

but I made it — / as did others.
그러나 나는 해냈다 / 다른 사람들이 해낸 것처럼

I arrived safely at the bottom, /
나는 무사히 바닥에 도착했다 /

overjoyed by the success of meeting the challenge.
도전에 성공한 것을 매우 기뻐하며

I felt / as though I was walking on air.
나는 느꼈다 / 마치 내가 하늘 위를 걷는 것처럼

마침내 내 차례가 되었다. 난 절벽에서 뒤로 걸어가기로 되어 있었다. 절벽 아래를 내려다보기만 했는데도 다리가 후들거리기 시작했다. 의식을 잃을 때에 대비해 몸에 안전 밧줄이 둘려 있다는 것은 알고 있었다. 머리로는 모든 상황을 이해했고, 머리로는 안전하다고 느꼈다. 그런데도 내 머리카락은 곤두섰고 온몸이 떨렸다. 절벽에서 첫발을 내딛는 것이 가장 힘든 순간이었지만, 다른 사람들이 해낸 것처럼, 나도 해냈다. 나는 도전에 성공한 것을 매우 기뻐하며 무사히 바닥에 도착했다. 나는 마치 하늘 위를 걷는 것 같은 기분이었다.

① 여유있는 → 긴장한
② 화가난 → 부끄러운
③ 두려운 → 기쁜
④ 시기하는 → 동정하는
⑤ 실망한 → 희망찬

문제풀이

처음에 절벽에서 내려가는 것에 대해 머리로는 안전하다는 것을 느꼈지만, 머리카락이 곤두서고, 온몸이 떨리는 것을 느꼈던 'I'가 무사히 다른 사람과 똑같이 무사히 바닥에 도착해서 매우 기뻐하고 있는 상황이므로 'I'의 심경 변화로 가장 적절한 것은 ③ 'terrified(무서운) → delighted(기쁜)'이다.

어휘·어구

turn 차례
backward 뒤로
cliff 절벽
shake 후들거리다, 떨리다
black out 의식을 잃다
security 안전, 보안
stand on end 곤두서다
shiver 떨다
overjoyed 매우 기쁜

정답률 93%

7. ⑤ 공룡 화석을 찾지 못한 Evelyn

직독/직해

It was Evelyn's first time /
Evelyn에게는 처음이었다 /

to explore the Badlands of Alberta, /
Alberta 주의 Badlands를 탐험하는 것이 /

famous across Canada /
캐나다 전역에서 유명한 /

for its numerous dinosaur fossils.
그곳의 많은 공룡 화석으로

As a young amateur bone-hunter, /
젊은 아마추어 뼈 발굴자로서 /

she was overflowing with anticipation.
그녀는 기대감에 가득 차 있었다
She had not travelled this far /
그녀는 이렇게 멀리 이동하지는 않았다 /
for the bones of common dinosaur species.
흔한 공룡 종의 뼈를 위해
Her life-long dream / to find rare fossils of dinosaurs /
그녀의 평생에 걸친 꿈이 / 희귀한 공룡 화석을 발견하고자 하는 /
was about to come true.
막 실현되려던 참이었다
She began eagerly searching for them.
그녀는 열심히 그것들을 찾기 시작했다
After many hours of wandering throughout the deserted lands, /
황량한 땅을 여러 시간 헤매고 다닌 후에도 /
however, / she was unsuccessful.
그러나 / 그녀는 성공적이지 않았다
Now, the sun was beginning to set, /
이제 해가 지기 시작하고 있었다 /
and her goal was still far / beyond her reach.
그리고 그녀의 목표는 여전히 먼 곳에 있었다 / 그녀의 손이 닿지 않는
Looking at the slowly darkening ground / before her, /
천천히 어두워지는 지면을 바라보면서 / 자신 앞의 /
she sighed to herself, /
그녀는 혼자 한숨을 쉬며 말했다 /
"I can't believe / I came all this way for nothing.
나는 믿을 수가 없어 / 내가 이렇게 먼 길을 와서 아무것도 못 얻었다니
What a waste of time!"
정말 시간 낭비야

캐나다 전역에서 그곳의 많은 공룡 화석으로 유명한 Alberta 주의 Badlands를 탐험하는 것이 Evelyn에게는 처음이었다. 젊은 아마추어 뼈 발굴자로서, 그녀는 기대감에 가득 차 있었다. 그녀는 흔한 공룡 종의 뼈를 위해 이렇게 멀리 이동하지는 않았다. 희귀한 공룡 화석을 발견하고자 하는 그녀의 평생에 걸친 꿈이 막 실현되려던 참이었다. 그녀는 열심히 그것들을 찾기 시작했다. 그러나 황량한 땅을 여러 시간 헤매고 다닌 후에도 그녀는 성공적이지 않았다. 이제 해가 지기 시작하고 있었고, 그녀의 목표는 여전히 그녀의 손이 닿지 않는 먼 곳에 있었다. 천천히 어두워지는 자신 앞의 지면을 바라보면서 그녀는 혼자 한숨을 쉬며 말했다. "이렇게 먼 길을 와서 아무것도 못 얻었다니 믿을 수가 없어. 정말 시간 낭비야!"

① 혼란스러운 → 무서워하는
② 낙담하는 → 자신감 있는
③ 여유 있는 → 짜증이 난
④ 무관심한 → 우울한
⑤ 기대하는 → 실망한

문제풀이

아마추어 공룡 뼈 발굴자인 Evelyn이 처음으로 공룡 화석으로 유명한 지역을 방문해서 공룡 화석을 발견하려고 했지만 아무것도 찾지 못한 상황이다. 'she was overflowing with anticipation(그녀는 기대감에 가득 차 있었다)'을 통해 처음에 Evelyn이 기대하고 있었다는 것을 알 수 있고, 'her goal was still far beyond her reach(그녀의 목표는 여전히 그녀의 손이 닿지 않는 먼 곳에 있었다)'와 'What a waste of time!(정말 시간 낭비야!)'을 통해 나중에 Evelyn이 실망한 상태로 변했음을 알 수 있다. 따라서 정답은 ⑤ 'hopeful(기대하는)' → 'disappointed(실망한)'이다.

어휘·어구

explore 탐험하다
numerous 많은
dinosaur 공룡
fossil 화석
amateur 아마추어, 비전문가
bone-hunter 뼈 발굴자
overflow 넘치다
anticipation 기대, 고대
species (생물의) 종
rare 희귀한
be about to do 막 ~을 하려고 하다
eagerly 열심히
wander 헤매다
deserted 황량한, 버려진
beyond ~ 너머
sigh 한숨을 쉬다

8. ① Natalie의 첫 온라인 상담

직독/직해

As Natalie was logging in /
Natalie는 로그인하면서 /
to her first online counseling session, /
자신의 첫 온라인 상담 시간에 /
she wondered, / 그녀는 궁금해했다 /
"How can I open my heart to the counselor /
내가 어떻게 상담사에게 나의 마음을 열 수 있을까 /
through a computer screen?"
컴퓨터 화면을 통해
Since the counseling center was a long drive away, /
상담 센터가 차로 오래 가야 하는 곳에 있어서 /
she knew / that this would save her a lot of time.
그녀는 알았다 / 이것이 자신에게 많은 시간을 절약해 줄 거라는 걸
Natalie just wasn't sure / if it would be as helpful /
단지 Natalie는 확신할 수 없었다 / 그것이 도움이 될지는 /
as meeting her counselor / in person.
상담사를 만나는 것만큼 / 직접
Once the session began, / however, /
일단 상담 시간이 시작되자 / 그러나 /
her concerns went away.
그녀의 걱정은 없어졌다
She actually started thinking /
사실 그녀는 생각하기 시작했다 /
that it was much more convenient than expected.
그것이 예상했던 것보다 훨씬 더 편리하다고
She felt / as if the counselor were in the room /
그녀는 느꼈다 / 마치 상담사가 방 안에 있는 것처럼 /
with her. 자신과 함께
As the session closed, / she told him with a smile, /
상담 시간이 끝났을 때 / 그녀는 미소를 지으며 그에게 말했다 /
"I'll definitely see you online / again!"
온라인에서 꼭 만날 거예요 / 다시

Natalie는 자신의 첫 온라인 상담 시간에 로그인하면서, "내가 컴퓨터 화면을 통해 상담사에게 어떻게 나의 마음을 열 수 있을까?"라며 궁금해했다. 상담 센터가 차로 오래 가야 하는 곳에 있어서, 그녀는 이것이 자신에게 많은 시간을 절약해 줄 거라는 걸 알았다. 단지 Natalie는 그것이 상담사를 직접 만나는 것만큼 도움이 될지는 확신할 수 없었다. 그러나 일단 상담 시간이 시작되자, 그녀의 걱정은 없어졌다. 사실 그녀는 그것이 예상했던 것보다 훨씬 더 편리하다고 생각하기 시작했다. 그녀는 마치 상담사가 자신과 함께 방 안에 있는 것처럼 느꼈다. 상담 시간이 끝났을 때, 그녀는 미소를 지으며 그에게 말했다. "온라인에서 꼭 다시 만날 거예요!"

① 의심하는 → 만족한
② 후회하는 → 혼란스러운
③ 자신만만한 → 부끄러운
④ 따분한 → 신이 난
⑤ 아주 흥분한 → 실망한

문제풀이

Natalie는 자신의 첫 온라인 상담 시간에 로그인하여 상담을 받은 상황이다. 'Natalie just wasn't sure if it would be as helpful as meeting her counselor in person.(단지 Natalie는 그것이 상담사를 직접 만나는 것만큼 도움이 될지는 확신할 수 없었다.)'를 통해 처음에 Natalie가 온라인 상담의 효과에 대해 의심하고 있다는 것을 알 수 있고, 'her concerns went away(그녀의 걱정은 없어졌다)'와 'She actually started thinking that it was much more convenient than expected.(사실 그녀는 그것이 예상했던 것보다 훨씬 더 편리하다고 생각하기 시작했다.)'를 통해 나중에 Natalie가 만족했다는 것을 알 수 있다. 따라서 정답은 ① 'doubtful(의심하는) → satisfied(만족한)'이다.

어휘·어구

counseling 상담
counselor 상담사
session 시간, 기간
in person 직접
concern 걱정, 우려
definitely 꼭, 분명히

정답률 95%

9. ① 기대와 달랐던 현장학습

직독/직해

Looking out the bus window, Jonas could not stay calm. 버스 창밖을 내다보면서 Jonas는 차분히 있을 수가 없었다
He had been looking forward to this field trip.
그는 이번 현장학습을 학수고대하고 있었다
It was the first field trip for his history course.
그것은 그의 역사 과목을 위한 첫 번째 현장 학습이었다
His history professor had recommended it to the class, /
그의 역사 교수님은 학생들에 그것을 추천했다 /
and Jonas had signed up enthusiastically.
그리고 Jonas는 열정적으로 신청했다
He was the first to board the bus in the morning.
그는 아침에 버스를 가장 먼저 탄 사람이었다
The landscape looked fascinating / as the bus headed to Alsace.
경치는 굉장히 아름다워 보였다 / 버스가 Alsace로 향하는 동안
Finally arriving in Alsace after three hours on the road, however, /
하지만 길을 세 시간 달려 마침내 Alsace에 도착했을 때 /
Jonas saw nothing but endless agricultural fields.
Jonas는 끝없이 농지 외에는 아무것도 볼 수 없었다
The fields were vast, but hardly appealed to him.
들판은 광대했지만 그에게는 전혀 매력적이지 않았다
He had expected to see some old castles and historical monuments, /
그는 몇몇 오래된 성들과 역사적인 기념물들을 보기를 기대 했었다 /
but now he saw nothing like that awaiting him.
하지만 지금 그를 기다리는 그러한 것은 전혀 못 봤다
"What can I learn from these boring fields?" /
이 지루한 들판에서 뭘 배울 수 있지? /
Jonas said to himself with a sigh.
Jonas는 한숨을 쉬며 혼잣말을 했다

버스 창밖을 내다보면서 Jonas는 차분히 있을 수가 없었다. 그는 이번 현장 학습을 학수고대하고 있었다. 그것은 그의 역사 과목을 위한 첫 번째 현장 학습이었다. 그의 역사 교수님은 학생들에 그것을 추천했고, Jonas는 열정적으로 신청했었다. 그는 아침에 버스를 가장 먼저 탄 사람이었다. 버스가 Alsace로 향하는 동안 경치는 굉장히 아름다워 보였다. 하지만 길을 세 시간 달려 마침내 Alsace에 도착했을 때 Jonas는 끝없이 펼쳐진 농지 외에는 아무것도 보지 못했다. 들판은 광대했지만 그에게는 전혀 매력적이지 않았다. 그는 몇몇 오래된 성들과 역사적인 기념물들을 보기를 기대했었지만, 이제 그를 기다리고 있는 그러한 것은 어떤 것도 보이지 않았다. "난 이 지루한 들판에서 무엇을 배울 수 있단 말인가?" Jonas는 한숨을 쉬며 혼잣말을 했다.

① 흥분한 → 실망한
② 무관심한 → 아주 신이 난
③ 매우 놀란 → 겁에 질린
④ 놀란 → 안심한
⑤ 걱정스러운 → 자신감 있는

문제풀이

Jonas가 큰 기대를 안고 현장 학습을 갔는데 기대와는 다른 풍경에 실망한 상황이다. 'He had been looking forward to this field trip.(그는 이번 현장학습을 학수고대하고 있었다.)' 그리고 'He was the first to board the bus in the morning.(그는 아침에 버스를 가장 먼저 탄 사람이었다.)' 등에서 현장 학습에 매우 흥분해 있는 상

태를 알 수 있고, "'What can I learn from these boring fields?" Jonas said to himself with a sigh.("난 이 지루한 들판에서 무엇을 배울 수 있단 말인가?" Jonas는 한숨을 쉬며 혼잣말을 했다.)'에서 몹시 실망했음을 알 수 있다. 따라서 글에 드러난 Jonas의 심경 변화로 가장 적절한 것은 ① '흥분한 → 실망한'이다.

어휘·어구

field trip 현장 학습
enthusiastically 열성적으로
board 올라타다
fascinating 굉장히 아름다운, 매력적인
monument (역사적) 기념물
await 기다리고 있다

정답률 

10. ① 가까스로 서핑 성공

직독/직해

The waves were perfect for surfing.
파도는 서핑하기에 완벽했다

Dave, however, / just could not stay on his board.
하지만 Dave는 / 그저 자신의 보드에 있을 수가 없었다

He had tried more than ten times / to stand up /
그는 열 차례 이상 시도했지만 / 일어서기 위해 /

but never managed it. 결코 그것을 해내지 못했다

He felt / that he would never succeed.
그는 느꼈다 / 그가 절대 성공하지 못할 것이라고

He was about to give up / when he looked at the sea one last time.
그는 포기하려던 참나였다 / 마지막으로 바다를 보았을 때

The swelling waves seemed to say, / "Come on, Dave. / One more try!"
넘실거리는 파도가 말하는 것 같았다 / 이봐, Dave. / 한 번 더 해 봐!

Taking a deep breath, / he picked up his board /
심호흡하고 나서 / 그는 자기 보드를 들고 /

and ran into the water. 바다로 뛰어들었다

He waited for the right wave. 그는 적당한 파도를 기다렸다

Finally, it came. 드디어, 그것이 왔다

He jumped up onto the board / just like he had practiced.
그는 보드 위로 점프해서 올라탔다 / 바로 자신이 연습했던 것처럼

And this time, / standing upright, /
그리고 이번에는 / 똑바로 서서 /

he battled the wave all the way back to shore.
그는 해변으로 돌아오는 내내 파도와 싸움을 벌였다

Walking out of the water joyfully, /
즐겁게 물 밖으로 걸어 나오면서 /

he cheered, / "Wow, I did it!"
그는 환호성을 질렀다 / 우와, 내가 해냈어!

파도는 서핑하기에 완벽했다. 하지만 Dave는 그저 자신의 보드에 있을 수가 없었다. 그는 일어서기 위해 열 차례 이상 시도했지만, 결코 그것을 해내지 못했다. 그는 절대 성공하지 못할 것이라고 느꼈다. 그는 포기하려던 찰나에 마지막으로 바다를 보았다. 넘실거리는 파도가 "이봐, Dave. 한 번 더 해 봐!"라고 말하는 것 같았다. 심호흡하고 나서, 그는 자기 보드를 들고 바다로 뛰어들었다. 그는 적당한 파도를 기다렸다. 드디어, 그것이 왔다. 그는 자신이 바로 연습했던 것처럼 보드 위로 점프해서 올라탔다. 그리고 이번에는 똑바로 서서 그는 해변으로 돌아오는 내내 파도와 싸움을 벌였다. 즐겁게 물 밖으로 걸어 나오면서, 그는 "우와, 내가 해냈어!"라고 환호성을 질렀다.

① **좌절한 → 기쁜** ② 지루한 → 편한
③ 차분한 → 짜증이 난 ④ 안도하는 → 겁먹은
⑤ 기쁜 → 화가 난

문제풀이

계속된 실패로 보드 타는 걸 포기하려는 찰나, 마지막 시도에서 보드 타기에 성공해서 환호성을 질렀다고 했으므로, 필자의 심경 변화로 ① frustrated(좌절한) → delighted(기쁜)'가 적절하다.

이렇게 풀자_ 'never managed it(결코 그것을 해내지 못했다)', 'he would never succeed(그는 결코 성공하지 못할 것이다)', 'was about to give up(포기하려는 찰나였다)', 'joyfully(즐겁게)', 'he cheered, "Wow, I did it!"('와, 내가 해냈어!'라고 그가 환호성을 질렀다)'에서 Dave의 심경 변화를 알 수 있다.

어휘·어구

swelling 넘실거리는
stand upright 똑바로 서다
battle 싸우다
cheer 환호성을 지르다

본문 011쪽

문법 플러스 2. 목적어, 보어

A. 1. sweet 2. to let 3. he was 4. it
5. neat 6. flashing 7. to stay

1 [해석]▶ 책상 위에 있는 라일락은 향기가 좋았다.
[해설]▶ 2형식 동사(smell)의 주격보어 자리에는 부사를 쓰지 않고 형용사를 사용한다.

2 [해석]▶ 샘은 아무도 방안으로 들어오지 못하게 했다.
[해설]▶ 동사 refuse는 뒤에 to부정사를 목적어로 가져온다.

3 [해석]▶ 그녀는 그가 몇 살인지 알지 못했다.
[해설]▶ 직접의문문 How old was he?가 타동사 목적어 자리에 들어가 있으므로, 간접의문문의 어순으로 전환해야 한다. 즉 how old he was로 고쳐야 한다.

4 [해석]▶ Jack은 동의하지 않는다는 점을 분명히 했다.
[해설]▶ 「make+가목적어+목적격보어+that」 구문이다.

5 [해석]▶ 우리는 방을 청결하게 유지함으로써 우리의 역할을 하였다.
[해설]▶「keep+목적어+형용사」는 '~을 …한 상태로 유지하다'라는 의미로서 목적격보어에 형용사가 나와야 한다.

6 [해석]▶ 나는 아름다운 미소가 그녀의 얼굴에 스치는 것을 보았다.
[해설]▶지각동사(watch) 다음에 목적어와 목적보어가 능동관계인 경우 목적보어는 동사원형 또는 진행형을 사용한다.

7 [해석]▶ 오늘날 많은 국가들은 비자 없이 외국인이 머무르는 것을 허락하지 않는다.
[해설]▶ 「allow+목적어+목적보어」의 구조로서 동사 allow는 목적격보어를 가져오는 경우, to부정사 형태를 취한다.

본문 011쪽

B. 1. bad 2. being 3. they are
4. it 5. free 6. stolen
7. to get

1 [해석]▶ 이 우유는 상한 냄새가 난다.
[해설]▶ 2형식 동사(smell)의 주격보어 자리에는 부사를 쓰지 않고 형용사를 사용한다.

2 [해석]▶ Sally는 가까스로 차에 치이는 것을 피했다.
[해설]▶ 동사 escape는 뒤에 동명사를 목적어로 가져온다.

3 [해석]▶ 나는 그들이 어디에 숨어 있는지 모른다.
[해설]▶ 직접의문문이 다른 문장의 일부로 들어간 경우, 간접의문문(의문사+주어+동사)의 형태를 취한다.

4 [해석]▶ 나는 그녀와 심각한 문제에 대하여 이야기하는 것이 어렵다.
[해설]▶ 「find+가목적어+목적격보어+that」 구문이다.

5 [해석]▶ 당신의 집을 먼지 하나 없이 깨끗하게 만드는 데는 3시간이면 충분합니다.
[해설]▶ 먼지 하나 없는 집을 만들어 준다'는 의미로서 동사 make의 목적격보어에 해당하는 free of가 와야 한다.

6 [해석]▶ 샐리는 버스에서 지갑을 도난당했다.
[해설]▶사역동사 had 뒤에 목적어 her purse와 목적격보어 stolen이 수동 관계이므로 과거분사가 나와야 한다.

7 [해석]▶ 최신 기술은 언제든지 우리가 인터넷에 접근하는 것을 가능하게 했다.
[해설]▶ allow 동사는 목적보어로 to부정사가 나온다.

본문 012쪽

숙어 플러스 2. 수능 필수 숙어 2회

1. approve 2. result
3. Apart 4. apologize

03. 필자의 주장

Day 03

본문 014쪽

1. ①	2. ①	3. ①	4. ②	5. ①
6. ⑤	7. ③	8. ①	9. ①	10. ①

정답률 80%

대표 기출 ③ 더 나은 선택을 하는 방법

직독/직해

At every step in our journey through life /
인생을 통해 우리 여정의 모든 단계에서 /

we encounter junctions with many different pathways / leading into the distance.
우리는 많은 다른 길이 있는 분기점을 만난다 / 먼 곳으로 이어지는

Each choice involves uncertainty /
각각의 선택은 불확실성을 수반한다 /

about which path will get you to your destination.
어떤 길이 여러분의 목적지로 데려다줄지에 대한

Trusting our intuition / to make the choice /
우리의 직관을 믿는 것은 / 선택하기 위해서 /

often ends up with us making a suboptimal choice.
종종 결국 우리가 차선의 선택을 하는 것으로 끝난다

Turning the uncertainty into numbers / has proved a potent way /
불확실성을 숫자로 바꾸는 것은 / 강력한 방법으로 증명되었다 /

of analyzing the paths and finding the shortcut to your destination.
여러분의 목적지로 가는 길을 분석하고 지름길을 찾는

The mathematical theory of probability / hasn't eliminated risk, /
확률에 대한 수학적 이론은 / 위험을 없애지는 않았다 /

but it allows us to manage that risk more effectively.
하지만 우리가 그 위험을 더 효과적으로 관리할 수 있도록 해 준다

The strategy is to analyze all the possible scenarios /
전략은 모든 가능한 시나리오를 분석하는 것이다 /

that the future holds / and then to see /
미래가 안고 있는 / 그러고 나서 살펴보는 것이다 /

what proportion of them lead to success or failure.
그것들이 성공이나 실패로 이어질 비율이 얼마나 되는지를

This gives you a much better map of the future /
이것은 미래에 대한 훨씬 더 좋은 지도를 여러분에게 제공해 준다 /

on which to base your decisions /
여러분이 결정을 내릴 때 그 근거로 삼을 수 있는 /

about which path to choose.
어떤 길을 선택할 것인지에 관한

인생을 통해 우리 여정의 모든 단계에서 우리는 먼 곳으로 이어지는 많은 다른 길이 있는 분기점을 만난다. 각각의 선택은 어떤 길이 여러분의 목적지로 데려다줄지에 대한 불확실성을 수반한다. 선택하기 위해서 우리의 직관을 믿는 것은 종종 결국 우리가 차선의 선택을 하는 것으로 끝난다. 불확실성을 숫자로 바꾸는 것은 여러분의 목적지로 가는 길을 분석하고 지름길을 찾는 강력한 방법으로 증명되었다. 확률에 대한 수학적 이론은 위험을 없애지는 않았지만, 우리가 그 위험을 더 효과적으로 관리할 수 있도록 해 준다. 전략은 미래가 안고 있는 모든 가능한 시나리오를 분석하고 나서, 그것들이 성공이나 실패로 이어질 비율이 얼마나 되는지를 살펴보는 것이다. 이것은 여러분이 어떤 길을 선택할 것인지에 관한 결정을 내릴 때 그 근거로 삼을 수 있는 미래에 대한 훨씬 더 좋은 지도를 여러분에게 제공해 준다.

문제풀이

인생의 여정에서 내리는 각각의 선택은 불확실성을 수반하게 되는데, 불확실성을 확률적으로 분석하는 것은 위험을 더 효과적으로 관리할 수 있게 해 준다고 했다. 따라서 필자가 주장하는 바로 가장 적절한 것은 ③ '더 나은 선택을 위해 성공 가능성을 확률적으로 분석해야 한다.'이다.

어휘·어구

encounter 만나다, 마주치다
uncertainty 불확실성
destination 목적지
intuition 직관
end up with 결국 ~하게 되다
potent 강한
probability 확률
eliminate 없애다, 제거하다
effectively 효과적으로
strategy 전략
analyze 분석하다
proportion 비율

정답률 75%

1. ① 창의성을 유지하는 방법

직독/직해

Bringing incredible creative projects to life demands much hard work /
삶에서 놀랍고도 창의적인 프로젝트를 실현하는 것은 많은 노력이 필요하다 /

down in the trenches of day-to-day idea execution.
매일 매일 아이디어를 실행하는 어려운 상황에서도

Genius truly is "1 percent inspiration and 99 percent perspiration."
천재는 정말로 '1퍼센트의 영감과 99퍼센트의 노력'이다

But we cannot forget the flip side of that 99 percent /
하지만 우리는 99%의 이면을 잊어서는 안 된다

— it's impossible to solve every problem / by sheer force of will.
모든 문제를 해결하는 것은 불가능하다 / 오로지 의지의 힘만으로

We must also make time for play, relaxation, and exploration, /
우리는 또한 놀이, 휴식, 탐구의 시간을 마련해야 한다 /

the essential ingredients of the creative insights /
창의적 통찰의 필수 요소인 /

that help us evolve existing ideas and set new projects in motion.
우리가 기존의 아이디어를 발전시키고 새로운 프로젝트를 진행하도록 돕는

Often this means creating a routine for breaking from your routine, /
자주, 이것은 여러분의 일상에서 벗어나기 위한 일상을 만드는 것을 의미한다 /

working on exploratory side projects just for the hell of it, /
단지 재미 삼아 부차적인 탐구 프로젝트를 하는 것을 /

or finding new ways to hotwire your brain's perspective on a problem.
또는 여러분의 뇌로 문제를 바라보는 관점을 발동할 새로운 방법을 찾는 것을

To stay creatively fit, / we must keep our minds engaged and on the move /
창의적이기 위한 최적의 상태를 유지하려면 / 정신을 바쁘게 하고 움직이게 해야 한다 /

— because the greatest enemy of creativity is nothing more than standing still.
왜냐하면 창의력의 가장 큰 적은 다름 아닌 정체해 있는 것이기 때문이다

놀랍고도 창의적인 프로젝트를 실현하려면 매일 매일 아이디어를 실행하는 어려운 상황에서도 많은 노력이 필요하다. 천재는 정말로 '1퍼센트의 영감과 99퍼센트의 노력'이다. 하지만 우리는 99%의 이면을 잊어서는 안 된다. 모든 문제를 오로지 의지의 힘만으로 해결하는 것은 불가능하다. 우리는 또한 우리가 기존의 아이디어를 발전시키고 새로운 프로젝트를 진행하도록 돕는 창의적 통찰의 필수 요소인 놀이, 휴식, 탐구의 시간을 마련해야 한다. 자주, 이것은 여러분의 일상에서 벗어나기 위한 일상을 만들거나, 단지 재미 삼아 부차적인 탐구 프로젝트를 하거나, 여러분의 뇌로 문제를 바라보는 관점을 발동할 새로운 방법을 찾는 것을 의미한다. 창의적이기 위한 최적의 상태를 유지하려면, 정신을 바쁘게 하고 움직이게 해야 한다. 왜냐하면 창의력의 가장 큰 적은 다름 아닌 정체해 있는 것이기 때문이다.

문제풀이

창의성을 유지하기 위해서는 기존의 아이디어를 발전시키고, 새로운 프로젝트를 진행하도록 돕는 놀이, 휴식, 탐구의 시간을 가져야 하고, 특히 창의력의 가장 큰 적은 정체에 있으므로 정신을 바쁘게 하고 움직이게 해야 한다는 내용의 글이므로 필자의 주장으로 가장 적절한 것은 ① '창의성을 유지할 다양한 경험과 활동을 지속해야 한다.'이다.

○ 이렇게 풀자 필자의 주장을 묻는 글에서 당위성을 나타내는 'must, should, have to, ought to, had better' 등이 포함된 문장이 주제문인 경우가 많다. 'We must also make time for play, relaxation, and exploration, the essential ingredients of the creative insights that help us evolve existing ideas and set new projects in motion.(우리는 또한 우리가 기존의 아이디어를 발전시키고 새로운 프로젝트를 진행하도록 돕는 창의적 통찰의 필수 요소인 놀이, 휴식, 탐구의 시간을 마련해야 한다.)'와 'To stay creatively fit, we must keep our minds engaged and on the move — because the greatest enemy of creativity is nothing more than standing still.(창의적이기 위한 최적의 상태를 유지하려면, 정신을 바쁘게 하고 움직이게 해야 한다. 왜냐하면 창의력의 가장 큰 적은 다름 아닌 정체해 있는 것이기 때문이다.)'에서 글의 주제가 잘 드러나 있다.

어휘·어구

down in the trenches 어려운 상황에서
day to day 매일매일
execution 실행
inspiration 영감
perspiration 노력
flip side 다른 면
sheer 오로지, 순전한
relaxation 휴식
exploration 탐구
ingredient 구성 요소
evolve 발전하다
routine 일상
just for the hell of it 단지 재미 삼아, 별다른 이유 없이
hotwire (열쇠 대신에) 철사를 이용하여 차에 시동을 걸다
perspective 관점
nothing more than ~에 불과한

2. ① 타 문화 사람들과 교류를 잘하는 방법

직독/직해

Becoming competent in another culture / means / looking beyond behavior /
다른 문화에서 유능해진다는 것은 / 의미한다 / 행동 너머를 살펴보는 것을 /

to see if we can understand the attitudes, beliefs, and values /
태도, 신념, 가치를 이해할 수 있는지 알아보기 위해 /

that motivate what we observe.
우리가 관찰하는 것의 이유가 되는

By looking only at the visible aspects of culture /
문화의 눈에 보이는 측면만을 봄으로써 /

— customs, clothing, food, and language — /
즉 관습, 의복, 음식, 언어 /

we develop a short-sighted view of intercultural understanding /
우리는 다른 문화 이해에 있어 근시안적 시각을 발달시킨다 /

— just the tip of the iceberg, really.
정말로 빙산의 일각에 불과한

If we are to be successful / in our business interactions /
우리가 성공하려고 한다면 / 사업상의 교류에서 /

with people / who have different values and beliefs /
사람들과의 / 다른 가치와 신념을 가진 /

about how the world is ordered, /
세상이 어떻게 질서를 세우는지에 대한 /

then we must go below the surface /
그렇다면 그 이면을 들여다볼 수 있어야 한다 /

of what it means to understand culture /
문화를 이해한다는 것이 의미하는 것의 /

and attempt to see / what Edward Hall calls the "hidden dimensions."
그리고 보려고 시도해야 한다 / Edward Hall이 '숨겨진 차원'이라고 부른 것을

Those hidden aspects / are the very foundation of culture /
그러한 숨겨진 측면이 / 바로 문화의 근간이다 /

and are the reason / why culture is actually more than meets the eye.
그리고 이유이다 / 왜 문화가 실제로는 눈에 보이는 것 이상인

We tend not to notice those cultural norms / until they violate /
우리는 그러한 문화적 규범들에 주목하지 않는 경향이 있다 / 규범들이 위반할 때까지 /

what we consider / to be common sense, good judgment, or the nature of things.
우리가 여기는 것을 / 상식, 올바른 판단 또는 사물의 본질이라고

다른 문화에서 유능해진다는 것은 우리가 관찰하는 것의 이유가 되는 태도, 신념, 가치를 이해할 수 있는지 알아보기 위해 행동 너머를 살펴보는 것을 의미한다. 문화의 눈에 보이는 측면, 즉 관습, 의복, 음식, 언어만을 봄으로써, 우리는 다른 문화 이해에 있어 정말로 빙산의 일각에 불과한 근시안적 시각을 발달시킨다. 세상이 어떻게 질서를 세우는지에 대한 다른 가치와 신념을 가진 사람들과의 사업상의 교류에서 성공하려고 한다면, 문화를 이해한다는 것이 의미하는 것의 그 이면을 들여다볼 수 있어야 하며 Edward Hall이 '숨겨진 차원'이라고 부른 것을 보려고 시도해야 한다. 그러한 숨겨진 측면이 바로 문화의 근간이며 왜 문화가 실제로는 눈에 보이는 것 이상인 이유이다. 우리는 그러한 문화적 규범들이 우리가 상식, 올바른 판단 또는 사물의 본질이라고 여기는 것을 어기고 나서야 비로소 그것들을 알아보는 경향이 있다.

문제풀이

다른 문화의 사람들과의 사업상의 교류에서 성공하려면, 문화의 눈에 보이는 측면만이 아니라 그 이면의 문화의 근간인 숨겨진 측면들을 들여다보아야 한다고 했다. 따라서 필자가 주장하는 바로 가장 적절한 것은 ① '타 문화 사람들과 교류를 잘 하려면 그 문화의 이면을 알아야 한다.'이다.

어휘·어구

competent 유능한
beyond ~ 너머
attitude 태도
motivate 동기를 부여하다
observe 관찰하다
visible 보이는, 가시적인
aspect 측면
short-sighted 근시안의
interaction 상호 작용
dimension 차원
foundation 토대, 기초
norm 규범
violate 어기다, 위반하다

3. ① 경험의 가치

Placing value on and investing in experiences /
경험에 가치를 두고 투자하는 것은 /

provides us with a greater sense of vitality.
우리에게 더 큰 생동감을 준다

Our experiences make us feel alive /
우리의 경험은 우리가 살아있음을 느끼게 해 준다 /

and give us greater opportunities to grow.
그리고 우리에게 성장할 더 큰 기회를 준다

Any time you consider purchasing a new possession, / stop yourself and think /
당신이 새로운 소유물 구입을 고려할 때마다 / 스스로를 멈추고 생각해 보아라 /

about what kind of experience it will give you.
그것이 당신에게 어떤 종류의 경험을 가져다줄지에 대해

Ask yourself: / How much joy will this bring me?
스스로에게 물어라 / 이것이 나에게 얼마나 큰 기쁨을 가져다줄 것인가

Will the joy be temporary or long-lasting?
그 기쁨은 일시적일 것인가 혹은 오래 지속될 것인가

Will the purchase be something I can share with others?
그 구매는 내가 다른 사람들과 공유할 수 있는 것인가

If it becomes clear / the purchase will provide only short-term benefit to you, /
명확해진다면 / 그 구매가 당신에게 단기적 혜택만을 줄 것임이 /

think about an experience / you could purchase instead /
경험에 대해 생각해 보아라 / 대신에 당신이 구매할 수 있는 /

that would provide you with longer-term benefits.
(그 구매는) 당신에게 장기적 혜택을 제공해 줄 것이다

For instance, / if you have your eye on a new pair of shoes for $150, /
예를 들어 / 만약 당신이 150달러에 새 신발 한 켤레를 눈여겨본다면 /

ask yourself / what kind of experience you could enjoy / for that same amount.
스스로에게 물어 보아라 / 어떤 종류의 경험을 누릴 수 있는지를 / 같은 액수로

Maybe you'd enjoy a concert with friends / or a dinner cruise during the summer.
어쩌면 당신은 친구들과의 콘서트를 즐길 수 있을 것이다 / 혹은 여름 동안의 디너 크루즈를 (즐길 수 있을 것이다)

Once you think of an experience you'd enjoy, /
일단 당신이 누리고 싶은 경험을 생각하고 나면 /

seriously consider diverting the money for the purchase /
그 구매 비용을 전환하는 것을 진지하게 고려해라 /

from possession to experience.
소유에서 경험으로

경험에 가치를 두고 투자하는 것은 우리에게 더 큰 생동감을 준다. 우리의 경험은 우리가 살아있음을 느끼게 해 주고 우리에게 성장할 더 큰 기회를 준다. 당신이 새로운 소유물 구입을 고려할 때마다 스스로를 멈추고 그것이 당신에게 어떤 종류의 경험을 가져다줄지에 대해 생각해 보아라. 스스로에게 물어라. 이것이 나에게 얼마나 큰 기쁨을 가져다줄 것인가? 그 기쁨은 일시적일 것인가 혹은 오래 지속될 것인가? 그 구매는 내가 다른 사람들과 공유할 수 있는 것인가? 그 구매가 당신에게 단기적 혜택만을 줄 것임이 명확해진다면, 대신에 당신이 구매할 수 있는, 당신에게 장기적 혜택을 제공해 줄 경험에 대해 생각해 보아라. 예를 들어, 만약 당신이 150달러에 새 신발 한 켤레를 눈여겨본다면, 같은 액수로 어떤 종류의 경험을 누릴 수 있는지를 스스로에게 물어 보아라. 어쩌면 당신은 친구들과의 콘서트 혹은 여름 동안의 디너 크루즈를 즐길 수 있을 것이다. 일단 당신이 누리고 싶은 경험을 생각하고 나면, 그 구매 비용을 소유에서 경험으로 전환하는 것을 진지하게 고려해라.

문제풀이

경험은 우리가 살아있음을 느끼게 해 주고 우리에게 성장할 더 큰 기회를 부여하므로, 소비할 때 단기적 혜택보다는 장기적 혜택을 줄 경험에 가치를 두고 소비해야 한다는 내용의 글이다. 따라서 필자의 주장으로 가장 적절한 것은 ① '소유보다 경험에 가치를 두고 소비해야 한다.'가 가장 적절하다.

어휘·어구

invest 투자하다
vitality 생동감
possession 소유물
temporary 일시적인
long-lasting 오래 지속되는
short-term 단기적인
benefit 혜택
cruise 유람선 여행
divert 전환시키다
possession 소유

4. ② 성과를 얻기 위해 선수들이 활용해야 할 정신적 추진력

직독/직해

Consider two athletes / who both want to play in college.
두 명의 운동선수를 생각해 보라 / 둘 다 대학에서 뛰고 싶어 하는

One says / she has to work very hard /
한 명은 말한다 / 매우 열심히 해야 한다고 /

and the other uses goal setting / to create a plan /
그리고 다른 한 명은 목표 설정을 이용한다 / 계획을 세우기 위해 /

to stay on track and work on specific skills / where she is lacking.
계속 진보하고 특정한 기술을 연마할 / 자신이 부족한

Both are working hard / but only the latter is working smart.
둘 다 열심히 하고 있다 / 하지만 오직 후자만이 영리하게 하고 있다

It can be frustrating / for athletes / to work extremely hard /
좌절감을 줄 수 있다 / 운동선수가 / 극도로 열심히 하는 것은 /

but not make the progress / they wanted.
하지만 진전을 이루지 못하는 것은 / 자신이 원하는

What can make the difference / is drive /
차이를 만들어낼 수 있는 것은 / 추진력이다 /

— utilizing the mental gear / to maximize gains /
정신적 장치를 활용하는 것이다 / 이점을 극대화하기 위해 /

made in the technical and physical areas.
기술과 신체 영역에서 이루어진

Drive provides direction (goals), / sustains effort (motivation), /
추진력은 방향(목표)을 제공하고 / 노력(동기부여)을 유지하며 /

and creates a training mindset / that goes beyond simply working hard.
그리고 훈련의 마음가짐을 만들어낸다 / 그냥 열심히 하는 것을 넘어선

Drive applies direct force / on your physical and technical gears, /
추진력은 직접적인 힘을 가하여 / 신체와 기술 장치에 /

strengthening and polishing them / so they can spin with vigor and purpose.
그것들을 강화하고 연마한다 / 그것들이 활력과 목적에 맞게 회전할 수 있도록

While desire might make you spin those gears faster and harder /
욕망은 그러한 장치가 더 빨리, 그리고 더 열심히 회전하게 만들지도 모르지만 /

as you work out or practice, /
여러분이 운동하거나 연습할 때 /

drive is what built them in the first place.
추진력은 애초에 그것들을 만드는 것이다.

대학에서 뛰고 싶어 하는 두 명의 운동선수를 생각해 보라. 한 명은 매우 열심히 해야 한다고 말하고, 다른 한 명은 계속 진보하고 자신이 부족한 특정한 기술을 연마할 계획을 세우기 위해 목표 설정을 이용한다. 둘 다 열심히 하고 있지만 오직 후자만이 영리하게 하고 있다. 운동선수가 극도로 열심히 하지만 자신이 원하는 진전을 이루지 못하는 것은 좌절감을 줄 수 있다. 차이를 만들어낼 수 있는 것은 추진력, 즉 기술과 신체 영역에서 이루어진 이점을 극대화하기 위해 정신적 장치를 활용하는 것이다. 추진력은 방향(목표)을 제공하고, 노력(동기부여)을 유지하며, 그냥 열심히 하는 것을 넘어선 훈련의 마음가짐을 만들어낸다. 추진력은 신체와 기술 장치에 직접적인 힘을 가하여, 그것들이 활력과 목적에 맞게 회전할 수 있도록 그것들을 강화하고 연마한다. 욕망은 여러분이 운동하거나 연습할 때 그러한 장치가 더 빨리, 그리고 더 열심히 회전하게 만들지도 모르지만, 추진력은 애초에 그것들을 만드는 것이다.

문제풀이

필자는 운동선수가 그냥 열심히 하는 것보다는 기술과 신체 영역에서 이루어진 이점을 극대화할 수 있도록, 방향을 제공하고, 노력을 유지하며, 훈련의 마음가짐을 만들어내는 추진력을 활용해야 한다고 했다. 따라서 필자가 주장하는 바로 가장 적

절한 것은 ② '선수들은 최고의 성과를 얻기 위해 정신적 추진력을 잘 활용해야 한다.'이다.

《 어휘·어구 》

athlete 운동선수
stay on track (계획대로) 계속 나아가다
specific 특정한
frustrating 좌절감을 주는
extremely 극도로
progress 진전, 진보
drive 추진력
utilize 활용하다
mental 정신적인, 정신의
gear 장치, 장비
maximize 극대화하다
sustain 유지시키다
motivation 동기 부여
mindset 마음가짐, 사고방식
strengthen 강화하다
polish 다듬다, 연마하다
in the first place 애초에

5. ① 불확실성 해결 방안

직독/직해

We try to avoid uncertainty / by overanalyzing.
우리는 불확실성을 피하려고 애쓴다 / 과도하게 분석함으로써

But we don't have complete control / over how the future will play out.
하지만 우리는 완전한 통제권을 갖고 있지 않다 / 미래가 어떻게 전개될지에 대해

You may feel / 여러분은 느낄 수도 있다 /

that if you can just answer your "worry question" once and for all, /
만약 여러분이 단지 여러분의 '걱정(되는) 문제'에 완전히 답할 수만 있다면 /

you will be satisfied / and you can finally drop your rumination, /
여러분은 만족할 것이다 / 그리고 마침내 반추(反芻)를 중단할 수 있다 /

but has this ever actually happened to you?
하지만 이런 일이 실제로 여러분에게 일어난 적이 있는가

Has there ever been an answer / that allowed you to stop worrying?
정답이 있었던 적이 있는가 / 여러분이 걱정을 그만하도록 허용해 주었던

There is only one way out of this spiral, /
이 소용돌이에서 벗어날 수 있는 유일한 한 가지 방법이 있다 /

and that is not to try to gain control, / but to give it up.
그리고 그것은 통제권을 쥐기 위해 노력하는 것이 아니라 / 그것을 포기하는 것이다

Instead of pushing back against uncertainty, / embrace it.
불확실성에 맞서 막으려 하는 대신 / 그것을 수용해라

Instead of trying to answer your worry question, /
여러분의 걱정 문제에 답하기 위해 노력하는 대신 /

deliberately practice / leaving it unanswered.
의도적으로 연습해라 / 그것을 해결이 되지 않은 채로 두는 것을

Don't ask others / and don't think about it.
타인에게 물어보지 말아라 / 그리고 그것에 대해 생각하지 말아라

Tell yourself / that analysis is *not* the solution, /
여러분 스스로에게 말하라 / 분석이 해결책이 '아니라' /

but really just more of the same problem.
실제로는 단지 오히려 동일한 문제라고

우리는 과도하게 분석함으로써 불확실성을 피하려고 애쓴다. 하지만 우리는 미래가 어떻게 전개될지에 대해 완전한 통제권을 갖고 있지 않다. 만약 여러분이 단지 여러분의 '걱정(되는) 문제'에 완전히 답할 수만 있다면, 여러분은 만족할 것이고 여러분은 마침내 반추(反芻)를 중단할 수 있다고 느낄 수도 있지만, 이런 일이 실제로 여러분에게 일어난 적이 있는가? 여러분이 걱정을 그만하도록 허용해 주었던 정답이 있었던 적이 있는가? 이 소용돌이에서 벗어날 수 있는 유일한 한 가지 방법이 있으며, 그것은 통제권을 쥐기 위해 노력하는 것이 아니라 그것을 포기하는 것이다. 불확실성에 맞서 막으려 하는 대신, 그것을 수용해라. 여러분의 걱정(되는) 문제에 답하기 위해 노력하는 대신, 그것을 해결이 되지 않은 채로 두는 것을 의도적으로 연습해라. 타인에게 물어보지 말고, 그것에 대해 생각하지 말아라. 분석이 해결책이 '아니라' 실제로는 단지 오히려 동일한 문제라고 여러분 스스로에게 말하라.

문제풀이

필자는 불확실성을 피하기 위해 분석을 하여 통제하는 것은 해결책이 아니라고 하면서 걱정이 되는 문제를 해결하는 유일한 방법은 불확실성을 받아들이는 것이라고 했다. 따라서 필자의 주장으로 가장 적절한 것은 ① '분석을 통해 미래의 불확실성을 통제하기보다 수용해야 한다.'이다.

《 어휘·어구 》

overanalyze 너무 자세히 분석하다
once and for all 최종적으로, 완전히
give up 포기하다
push back against ~에 대해 반박하다
uncertainty 불확실성
embrace 받아들이다, 수용하다
deliberately 고의로, 의도적으로
analysis 분석
solution 해결책

6. ⑤ 임상 연구 윤리

직독/직해

Conflicts between the goals of science and the need /
과학의 목표와 필요성 사이의 충돌은 /

to protect the rights and welfare of human research participants /
인간 연구 참가자의 권리와 복지를 보호할 /

result in the central ethical tension of clinical research.
임상 연구에서의 주요한 윤리적 긴장을 초래한다

The statement "Bad science is bad ethics" is true.
'나쁜 과학은 나쁜 윤리이다.'라는 말은 사실이다

Putting humans at risk /
인간을 위험에 빠뜨리는 것은 /

if the study design does not permit a reasonable expectation of valid findings /
연구 설계가 타당한 연구 결과에 대한 합리적 기대를 허용하지 않는다면 /

is never ethical.
결코 윤리적이지 않다

Even a study that presents no risk /
아무런 위험을 주지 않는 연구조차도 /

presents at least an inconvenience to participants /
적어도 참가자들에게 불편함을 준다 /

and is in that sense disrespectful.
그리고 그런 면에서 (참가자를) 존중하지 않는 것이다

The statement "Good science is good ethics," however, is false.
그러나 '좋은 과학은 좋은 윤리이다.'라는 말은 거짓이다

Study design may be scientifically valid, /
연구 설계가 과학적으로 타당할 수도 있다 /

yet the risk of harming human participants is too great to accept.
그러나 인간 참가자에게 해를 끼칠 위험성은 받아들이기에는 너무 큰 것이다

Although achieving the appropriate scientific ends is always the necessary goal of a study, /
비록 적절한 과학적 목적을 달성하는 것이 항상 연구의 필수 목표일지라도 /

protection of the rights and welfare of human participants / must override scientific efficiency.
인간 참가자의 권리와 복지 보호가 / 과학적 효율성보다 더 우선되어야만 한다

과학의 목표와 인간 연구 참가자의 권리와 복지를 보호할 필요성 사이의 충돌은 임상 연구에서의 주요한 윤리적 긴장을 초래한다. '나쁜 과학은 나쁜 윤리이다.'라는 말은 사실이다. 연구 설계가 타당한 연구 결과에 대한 합리적 기대를 허용하지 않는다면, 인간을 위험에 빠뜨리는 것은 결코 윤리적이지 않다. 아무런 위험을 주지 않는 연구조차도 적어도 참가자들에게 불편함을 주고 그런 면에서 (참가자를) 존중하지 않는 것이다. 그러나 '좋은 과학은 좋은 윤리이다.'라는 말은 거짓이다. 연구 설계가 과학적으로 타당할 수도 있지만, 인간 참가자에게 해를 끼칠 위험성은 받아들이기에는 너무 큰 것이다. 비록 적절한 과학적 목적을 달성하는 것이 항상 연구의 필수 목표일지라도, 인간 참가자의 권리와 복지 보호가 과학적 효율성보다 더 우선되어야만 한다.

문제풀이

필자는 인간을 위험에 빠뜨리거나 인간 참가자에게 불편함을 주는 임상 연구는 윤리적이지 못하므로 적절한 과학적 목적을 달성하는 것이 연구의 목표일지라도, 과학적 효율성보다 인간 참가자의 권리와 복지 보호가 더 우선 되어야 한다고 주장하고 있다. 따라서 필자의 주장으로 가장 적절한 것은 ⑤ '임상 연구에서 참가자의 권리와 복지 보호가 우선되어야 한다.'이다.

이렇게 풀자 필자의 주장을 묻는 문제는 특히 글의 마지막 부분을 주의 깊게 읽어야 한다. 또한 필자의 주장을 묻는 문제는 조동사 must나 should가 포함된 부분을 유의해야 한다. 특히 이 글의 마지막 문장은 양보의 부사절을 사용하여, 양보절의 주절이 주제문이라는 것을 명백히 보여주고 있다. 'Although achieving the appropriate scientific ends is always the necessary goal of a study, protection of the rights and welfare of human participants must override scientific efficiency.(비록 적절한 과학적 목적을 달성하는 것이 항상 연구의 필수 목표일지라도, 인간 참가자의 권리와 복지 보호가 과학적 효율성보다 더 우선되어야만 한다.)'에서 글의 주장을 파악할 수 있다.

《 어휘·어구 》

conflict 충돌, 상충, 갈등
result in ~을 초래하다
ethical 윤리적인
tension 긴장
clinical research 임상 연구
statement 말, 진술
reasonable 합리적인, 적당한
valid 타당한, 유효한
finding (연구) 결과
present 주다, 발표하다
disrespectful 존중하지 않는, 무례한
achieve 달성하다
override ~보다 더 우선하다[중요하다]

7. ③ 기업이 소셜 미디어를 활용할 때 주의해야 할 점

직독/직해

One of the most common mistakes /
가장 일반적인 실수 중 하나는 /

made by organizations /
조직이 저지르는 /

when they first consider experimenting with social media /
그들이 소셜 미디어로 실험하는 것을 처음으로 고려할 때 /

is / ~이다 /

that they focus too much on social media tools and platforms /
너무 지나치게 소셜 미디어 도구와 플랫폼에 집중한다는 것/

and not enough on their business objectives.
그리고 조직 자체의 사업 목표에는 충분히 집중하지 않는 것

The reality of success in the social web for businesses /
기업을 위한 소셜 웹에서의 성공의 실제는 /

is / ~이다 /

that creating a social media program / begins /

소셜 미디어 프로그램을 만드는 것이 / 시작된다는 것이다 /
not with insight / 통찰력이 아니라 /
into the latest social media tools and channels /
최신 소셜 미디어 도구와 채널에 대한 /
but with a thorough understanding of the organization's own goals and objectives.
조직 자체의 목적과 목표에 대한 철저한 이해와 함께
A social media program /
소셜 미디어 프로그램은 /
is not merely the fulfillment of a vague need /
그저 막연한 필요를 이행하는 것이 아니다 /
to manage a "presence" on popular social networks /
인기 소셜 네트워크상에서 '존재'를 관리해야 할 /
because "everyone else is doing it."
'다른 모든 이가 하고 있어서'
"Being in social media" /
'소셜 미디어에 있다는 것'은 /
serves no purpose in and of itself.
그 자체로는 아무런 이득이 없다
In order to serve any purpose at all, /
조금이라도 어떤 이득을 얻기 위해서는 /
a social media presence must either solve a problem /
소셜 미디어상의 존재는 문제를 해결해야 한다 /
for the organization and its customers /
조직과 조직의 고객을 위해 /
or result in an improvement of some sort /
또는 어떤 종류의 개선이라는 결과를 가져와야 한다 /
(preferably a measurable one).
되도록이면 측정 가능한 결과
In all things, / purpose drives success.
모든 일에서 / 목적이 성공을 끌어낸다
The world of social media is no different.
소셜 미디어의 세계도 전혀 다르지 않다

조직이 소셜 미디어로 실험하는 것을 처음으로 고려할 때 저지르는 가장 일반적인 실수 중 하나는 너무 지나치게 소셜 미디어 도구와 플랫폼에 집중하고 조직 자체의 사업 목표에는 충분히 집중하지 않는 것이다. 기업을 위한 소셜 웹에서의 성공의 실제는 소셜 미디어 프로그램을 만드는 것이 최신 소셜 미디어 도구와 채널에 대한 통찰력이 아니라 조직 자체의 목적과 목표에 대한 철저한 이해와 함께 시작된다는 것이다. 소셜 미디어 프로그램은 그저 '다른 모든 이가 하고 있어서' 인기 소셜 네트워크상에서 '존재'를 관리해야 할 막연한 필요를 이행하는 것이 아니다. '소셜 미디어에 있다는 것'은 그 자체로는 아무런 이득이 없다. 조금이라도 어떤 이득을 얻기 위해서는, 소셜 미디어상의 존재는 조직과 조직의 고객을 위해 문제를 해결하거나 어떤 종류의 개선이라는 결과(되도록이면 측정 가능한 결과)를 가져와야 한다. 모든 일에서, 목적이 성공을 끌어낸다. 소셜 미디어의 세계도 전혀 다르지 않다.

문제풀이

소셜 미디어 세계에서도 목적이 성공을 끌어낸다고 하면서, 조직이 소셜 미디어 프로그램을 활용할 때는 소셜 미디어 도구와 플랫폼에 중점을 두는 것이 아닌 조직 자체의 목적과 목표에 대한 철저한 이해를 바탕으로 시작해야 조금이라도 이득을 얻을 수 있다고 했다. 따라서 필자가 주장하는 바로 가장 적절한 것은 ③ '기업은 소셜 미디어를 활용할 때 사업 목표를 토대로 해야 한다.'이다.

어휘·어구

organization 조직, 단체
focus on ~에 집중하다, ~에 중점을 두다
objective 목표
thorough 철저한
merely 단지, 그저
fulfillment 이행, 수행
vague 막연한
in and of itself 그것 자체로는
improvement 개선
preferably 되도록이면
measurable 측정 가능한

8. ① 과학의 대중화를 위한 방법

직독/직해

New ideas, such as those inspired by scientific developments, /
과학 발전에 의해 영감을 받은 것과 같은 새로운 아이디어는 /
are often aired and critiqued / in our popular culture /
우리의 대중문화에서 종종 방송되고 비판되는데 /
as part of a healthy process of public debate, /
건전한 공개 토론 과정의 일부로 /
and scientists sometimes deserve the criticism /
과학자들은 때때로 비판을 받을 만하다 /
they get. 자신들이 받는
But the popularization of science /
하지만 과학의 대중화는 /
would be greatly enhanced /
크게 높아질 것이다
by improving the widespread images of the scientist.
널리 퍼진 과학자의 이미지를 개선함으로써
Part of the problem may be /
그 문제의 일부는 ~일지도 모른다 /
that the majority of the people /
대다수의 사람이 /
who are most likely to write novels, plays, and film scripts /
아마도 소설, 희곡, 그리고 영화 대본을 쓸 가능성이 높은 /
were educated in the humanities, /
인문학 분야에서 교육받았다는 것 /
not in the sciences. 과학이 아니라
Furthermore, / 게다가 /
the few scientists-turned-writers /
작가로 전업한 소수의 과학자가 /
have used their scientific training /
자신들이 받은 과학 교육을 사용해왔다 /
as the source material for thrillers /
스릴러물의 원자료로 /
that further damage the image of science and scientists.
과학과 과학자의 이미지를 더욱 해치는
We need more screenplays and novels /
우리는 더 많은 영화 대본과 소설이 필요하다 /
that present scientists in a positive light.
긍정적인 시각으로 과학자를 보여주는
In our contemporary world, /
우리의 현재의 세계에서 /
television and film are particularly influential media, /
텔레비전과 영화는 특히 영향력 있는 매체이다 /
and it is likely / 그리고 ~일 것이다 /
that the introduction of more scientist-heroes /
더 많은 과학자 영웅들을 주인공으로 도입한다면 /
would help to make science more attractive.
과학을 더 매력적이게 하는 데 도움이 될 것이다

과학 발전에 의해 영감을 받은 것과 같은 새로운 아이디어는 건전한 공개 토론 과정의 일부로 우리의 대중문화에서 종종 방송되고 비판되는데, 과학자들은 때때로 자신들이 받는 비판을 받을 만하다. 하지만 널리 퍼진 과학자의 이미지를 개선함으로써 과학의 대중화는 크게 높아질 것이다. 그 문제의 일부는 아마도 소설, 희곡, 그리고 영화 대본을 쓸 가능성이 높은 대다수의 사람이 과학이 아니라 인문학 분야에서 교육받았다는 것일지도 모른다. 게다가 작가로 전업한 소수의 과학자가 자신들이 받은 과학 교육을 과학과 과학자의 이미지를 더욱 해치는 스릴러물의 원자료로 사용해왔다. 우리는 긍정적인 시각으로 과학자를 보여주는 더 많은 영화 대본과 소설이 필요하다. 우리의 현재의 세계에서 텔레비전과 영화는 특히 영향력 있는 매체여서, 더 많은 과학자 영웅들을 주인공으로 도입한다면 과학을 더 매력적이게 하는 데 도움이 될 것이다.

문제풀이

필자는 과학자를 긍정적인 시각으로 보여주는 더 많은 영화 대본과 소설이 필요하다고 하면서, 여러 매체에서 과학자의 모습을 긍정적으로 묘사한다면 과학의 대중화가 크게 증진될 것이라고 했다. 따라서 필자가 주장하는 바로 가장 적절한 것은 ① '과학의 대중화를 위해 여러 매체에서 과학자를 긍정적으로 묘사해야 한다.'이다.

어휘·어구

inspire 영감을 주다
critique 비판하다, 비평하다
debate 토론
deserve 받을 만하다
popularization 대중화
enhance 높이다
widespread 널리 퍼진
majority 다수
educate 교육하다
humanities 인문학, 고전 문학
screenplay 영화 대본
contemporary 동시대의, 현대의
influential 영향력 있는
introduction 도입, 소개
attractive 매력적인

9. ① 어른의 놀이에 장애가 되는 규범

직독/직해

Probably the biggest roadblock to play for adults /
아마도 어른에게 있어서 노는 것에 가장 큰 장애물은 /
is the worry that they will look silly, improper, or
그들이 어리석거나, 부적절하거나, 혹은 바보같이 보일 것이라는 걱정이다
dumb / if they allow themselves to truly play.
/ 그들이 진정으로 놀 수 있도록 하면
Or they think that it is irresponsible, immature,
아니면 무책임하고, 미숙하며, 유치하다고 그들은 생각한다 /
and childish /
to give themselves regularly over to play.
노는 것에 자신을 정기적으로 맡기는 것은
Nonsense and silliness come naturally to kids, /
당찮음과 어리석음이 아이들에게는 자연스럽게 다가온다 /
but they get pounded out by norms that look down
하지만 '경박함'을 경시하는 규범이 그들을 계속 두들겨 댄다
on "frivolity."
This is particularly true for people who have been
이것은 성과 기준으로 평가되어 온 사람들에게 있어 특히 그러하다 /
valued for performance standards /
set by parents or the educational system, /
부모나 교육제도에 의해 정해진 /
or measured by other cultural norms /
또는 다른 문화 규범에 의해 측정되어 온 /
that are internalized and no longer questioned.
내면화되어 더 이상 의문시 되지 않는
If someone has spent his adult life /
만약 누군가가 성년기를 보냈다면 /
worried about always appearing respectable, competent, and knowledgeable, /
항상 존경할 만하고, 유능하며, 박식해 보이는 것에 대해 걱정하며 /
it can be hard to let go sometimes and become
때때로 내려놓고 육체적이고 감정적으로 자유로워지는 것은 어려울 수 있다
physically and emotionally free.
The thing is this: / 중요한 것은 이것이다 /
You have to give yourself permission /
스스로에게 허락해야 한다 /
to improvise, to mimic, to take on a long-hidden
즉흥적으로 하고, 흉내 내고, 오랫동안 숨겨둔 정체성을 나타내는 것을
identity.

아마도 어른에게 있어 노는 것에 대한 가장 큰 장애물은 그들이 정말로 놀기로 작정할 경우에 우스꽝스럽고, 부적절하고, 멍청해 보일 것이라는 걱정일 것이다. 또는 그들이 자기 자신을 정기적으로 놀이에 넘기는 것이 무책임하고, 미숙하며, 유치하다고 생각한다. 허튼 소리나 바보짓은 아이들에게 자연스럽게 일어나는데, 그들은 '경박함'을 얕보는 규범에 의해 공격을 당한다. 이것은 특히 부모나 교육제도에 의해 정해진 성과 기준 때문에 가치가 있다고 평가되었거나, 내면화되어 더 이상 의문을 받지 않는 다른 문화규범에 의해 측정된 사람들에게 해당된다. 만약 누군가가 항상 존경스럽고 유능하고 박식해 보이는 것에 대해 걱정하는 성년기를 보냈다면, 때때로 자제심을 잃고 육체적이고 감정적으로 자유로워지는 것은 어려울 수 있다. 중요한 것은 다음과 같은데, 즉 여러분은 여러분 자신에게 즉흥적으로 행동하고, 흉내를 내고, 오랫동안 숨겨져 있던 정체성을 나타내라는 허락을 해야 한다.

문제풀이

어른들은 부모, 교육제도, 문화규범 등에 의해 경박하다는 공격을 받을 것에 대한 걱정 때문에 아이들처럼 노는 것에 장애가 된다고 하면서 어른들도 스스로에게 즉흥적으로 행동하고, 흉내를 내고, 오랫동안 숨겨져 있던 정체성을 드러내도록 허락을 해야 한다고 했다. 따라서 필자의 주장으로 가장 적절한 것은 ① '어른도 규범에 얽매이지 말고 자유롭게 놀이를 즐겨야 한다.'이다.

이렇게 풀자_ 주장 찾기 유형에서는 명령문 또는 '~해야 한다'라는 의미의 표현인 must, have to, should 등이 포함된 문장에 필자의 주장이 직접적으로 드러난다. 여기서는 'You have to give yourself permission to improvise, to mimic, to take on a long-hidden identity.(즉흥적으로 하고, 흉내 내고, 오랫동안 숨겨져 있던 정체성을 나타낼 수 있도록 스스로에게 허락해야 한다는 것이다.)'에 주장이 잘 드러나 있다.

어휘·어구

- **roadblock** 장애물
- **immature** 미성숙한
- **pound** 맹공격하다
- **norm** 규범
- **look down on** ~을 얕보다
- **performance standard** 성과 기준
- **competent** 유능한
- **knowledgeable** 박식한
- **mimic** 흉내를 내다
- **take on** ~을 나타내다

10. ① 전쟁과 적을 추상적이고 획일적으로 개념화하는 것을 경계해야 한다

직독/직해

War is inconceivable / without *some* image, or concept, of the enemy.
전쟁은 상상할 수 없다 / 적에 관한 '어떤' 이미지나 개념 없이는

It is the presence of the enemy / that gives meaning and justification to war.
적의 존재이다 / 전쟁에 의미와 정당화를 부여하는 것은

'War follows from feelings of hatred', / wrote Carl Schmitt.
전쟁은 증오의 감정으로부터 나온다 / Carl Schmitt는 적었다

'War has its own strategic, tactical, and other rules and points of view, / but they all presuppose / that the political decision has already been made / as to who the enemy is'.
전쟁은 그것의 전략적, 전술적 그리고 다른 규칙들과 관점들을 가지고 있지만 / 그것들은 모두 전제로 한다 / 정치적 결정이 이미 정해졌다는 것을 / 적이 누군지에 관한

The concept of the enemy is fundamental / to the moral assessment of war: / 'The basic aim of a nation at war / in establishing an image of the enemy / is to distinguish as sharply as possible / the act of killing / from the act of murder'.
적의 개념은 중요하다 / 전쟁의 도덕적 결정에 있어 / 전쟁 중인 국가의 기본 목표는 / 적의 이미지를 만들어내는 데 있어 / 가능한 한 명확하게 구분하는 것이다 / 살인 행위를 / 죽이는 행위와

However, / we need to be cautious / about thinking of war and the image of the enemy / that informs it in an abstract and uniform way.
하지만 / 우리는 신중을 기해야 한다 / 전쟁과 적의 이미지에 관해 생각하는 것에 대해 / 추상적이고 획일적인 방식으로 전쟁에 생기를 불어넣는

Rather, / both must be seen for the cultural and contingent phenomena / that they are.
오히려 / 둘을 문화적이고 불확정적인 현상에 비추어 살펴보아야 한다 / 그들 본연의

전쟁은 적에 관한 '어떤' 이미지나 개념 없이는 상상할 수 없다. 전쟁에 의미와 정당화를 부여하는 것은 적의 존재이다. "전쟁은 증오의 감정으로부터 나온다. 전쟁은 그것의 전략적, 전술적 그리고 다른 규칙들과 관점들을 가지고 있지만, 그것들은 모두 적이 누군지에 관한 정치적 결정이 이미 정해졌다는 것을 전제로 한다."라고 Carl Schmitt는 적었다. 적의 개념은 전쟁의 도덕적 결정에 있어 중요하다. 적의 이미지를 만들어내는 데 있어 전쟁 중인 국가의 기본 목표는 살인 행위를 죽이는 행위와 가능한 한 명확하게 구분하는 것이다. 하지만 전쟁과 추상적이고 획일적인 방식으로 전쟁에 생기를 불어넣는 적의 이미지에 관해 생각하는 것에 대해 우리는 신중을 기해야 한다. 오히려, 둘을(전쟁과 적의 이미지) 그들 본연의 문화적이고 불확정적인 현상에 비추어 살펴보아야 한다.

문제풀이

전쟁과 적의 이미지를 추상적이고 획일적으로 생각하는 것에 신중을 기해야 하고, 오히려 전쟁과 적의 이미지를 그들 본연의 문화적이고 불확정적인 현상에 비추어서 살펴보아야 한다고 했으므로, 필자의 주장으로 ① '전쟁과 적을 추상적이고 획일적으로 개념화하는 것을 경계해야 한다.'가 가장 적절하다.

이렇게 풀자_ 글의 후반부에 제시된 'However, we need to be cautious ~ that informs it in an abstract and uniform way.'와 'Rather, both must be seen for the cultural and contingent phenomena that they are.'에 필자의 주장이 드러나 있다.

어휘·어구

- **inconceivable** 상상할 수 없는
- **presence** 존재
- **justification** 정당화
- **hatred** 증오, 혐오
- **strategic** 전략적인
- **tactical** 전술적인
- **presuppose** 전제하다
- **fundamental** 근간이 되는, 중요한
- **assessment** 평가
- **distinguish** 구별하다
- **cautious** 조심스러운, 신중한
- **inform** 생기를 불어넣다
- **abstract** 추상적인
- **uniform** 획일적인

본문 017쪽

문법 플러스 3. 동사의 종류

A. 1. calm 2. consists of 3. marry 4. to 5. grazing 6. play 7. put me up

1 [해석]▶ 그가 생각했던 것과 달리 그녀는 매우 차분해 보였다.
[해설]▶ look은 주격보어로 형용사를 취하여 '~하게 보이다'의 뜻으로 쓰인다.

2 [해석]▶ 물은 산소와 수소로 구성되어 있다.
[해설]▶ consist of(= be composed of / be made up of)는 '~으로 구성되다'는 의미로 consist는 자동사이기 때문에 전치사(of)와 함께 쓸 때만 목적어를 가져올 수 있다.

3 [해석]▶ 피터는 샐리와 결혼하고자 한다.
[해설]▶ marry는 '~와 결혼하다'의 의미로 타동사이므로 전치사 없이 목적어를 취한다.

4 [해석]▶ 그는 그 선수에게 금메달을 수여했다.
[해설]▶ 4형식의 「give+간접목적어+직접목적어」 문장은 3형식의 「give+직접목적어+전치사(to)+간접목적어」 문장으로 전환할 수 있다.

5 [해석]▶ 나는 작은 무리의 소들이 들녘에서 풀을 뜯어 먹고 있는 것을 볼 수 있었다.
[해설]▶ 지각동사(see)의 목적어와 목적보어가 능동 관계이므로 동사원형이나 현재분사를 사용해야 한다

6 [해석]▶ 그들은 결코 그들의 아이들이 장난감 총을 가지고 노는 것을 허락하지 않겠다고 말했다.
[해설]▶ 사역동사(let)는 목적어와 목적보어가 능동 관계인 경우 동사원형을 쓴다.

7 [해석]▶ 며칠간만 좀 묵어도 되겠습니까?
[해설]▶ 「타동사+부사」로 이루어진 구동사는 목적어가 대명사인 경우, 목적어를 타동사와 부사 사이에 취한다.

본문 017쪽

B. 1. angry 2. apologize to 3. resemble 4. for 5. piled 6. done 7. write them down

1 [해석]▶ Sally는 그 소식을 듣고, 화가 났다.
[해설]▶ 「get[grow/go/become]+형용사」는 '~하게 되다'는 의미이다.

2 [해석]▶ 그는 수업 시간에 늦게 온 것에 대해 선생님께 사과드려야 한다.
[해설]▶ apologize는 '~에게 사과하다'는 의미의 자동사로 뒤에 목적어를 가져오려면 자동사 바로 뒤에 전치사 to를 가져와야 한다.

3 [해석]▶ 우리의 머리는 부정적인 감정이 압력을 키우는 증기 주전자와는 닮지 않았다.
[해설]▶ resemble은 '~을 닮았다'는 의미의 타동사로서 뒤에 전치사 없이 목적어를 취한다.

4 [해석]▶ Sarah는 내게 인형을 만들어 주었다.
[해설]▶ 4형식의 「make+간접목적어+직접목적어」 문장은 3형식의 「make+직접목적어+전치사(for)+간접목적어」 문장으로 전환할 수 있다.

5 [해석]▶ 그녀는 책상 위에 많은 책과 노트가 쌓여 있는 것을 보았다.
[해설]▶ 지각동사(saw)의 목적어와 목적보어가 수동 관계이므로 과거분사를 사용해야 한다.

6 [해석]▶ 당신은 보통 어디서 머리를 하나요?
[해설]▶ 사역동사(have)는 목적어와 목적보어가 수동 관계인 경우 과거분사를 쓴다.

7 [해석]▶ 목표에 집중하는 가장 효과적인 방법은 그것들을 적는 것이다.
[해설]▶ 「타동사+부사」로 이루어진 구동사는 목적어가 대명사인 경우, 목적어를 타동사와 부사 사이에 취한다.

본문 018쪽

숙어 플러스 3. 수능 필수 숙어 3회

1. attached 2. bound 3. away 4. throw

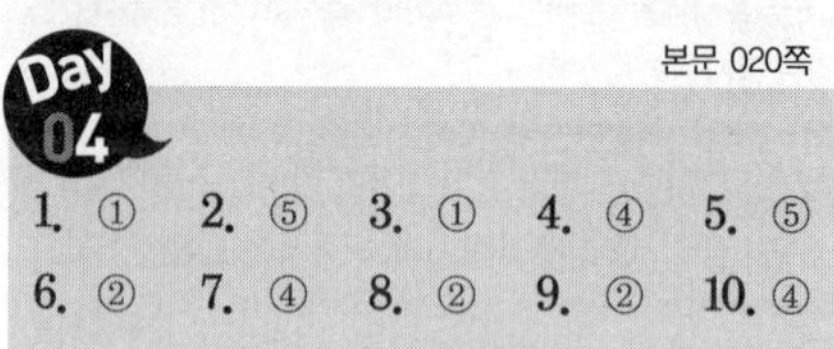

04. 함축 · 지칭 추론

본문 020쪽

1. ①	2. ⑤	3. ①	4. ④	5. ⑤
6. ②	7. ④	8. ②	9. ②	10. ④

정답률 56%

대표 기출 ② 창조적인 작업을 위해 차단의 필요성

직독/직해

The single most important change /
가장 중요한 단 하나의 변화는 /
you can make in your working habits /
여러분이 일하는 습관에서 할 수 있는 /
is to switch to creative work first, /
창조적인 일을 먼저 하는 쪽으로 전환하는 것이다 /
reactive work second.
대응적인 일은 다음으로 하는 것이다
This means / 이것은 의미한다 /
blocking off a large chunk of time every day /
매일 많은 시간을 떼어 두는 것을
for creative work / on your own priorities, /
창조적인 작업을 위해 / 여러분 자신의 우선순위에 따라 /
with the phone and e-mail off.
전화기와 이메일을 끈 채
I used to be a frustrated writer.
나는 좌절감을 느끼곤 하던 작가였다
Making this switch / turned me into a productive writer.
이렇게 전환하는 것이 / 나를 생산적인 작가로 변하게 했다
Yet there wasn't a single day / when I sat down /
그러나 단 하루도 없었다 / 내가 앉을 때마다 /
to write an article, blog post, or book chapter /
기사나 블로그 게시글 또는 책의 한 챕터를 쓰려고 /
without a string of people waiting /
여러 사람들이 기다리지 않은 /
for me to get back to them.
내가 그들에게 답장을 주기를
It wasn't easy, / and it still isn't, /
그것은 쉽지 않았다 / 아직도 쉽지 않다 /
particularly when I get phone messages /
특히 시작하는 전화 메시지를 받을 때는 /
beginning "I sent you an e-mail two hours ago...!"
"2시간 전에 이메일을 보냈어요..."라고 시작하는
By definition, / this approach goes against /
당연히 / 이런 접근 방식은 충돌하는 것이다 /
the grain of others' expectations /
다른 사람들의 기대와 /
and the pressures they put on you.
그리고 그들이 여러분에게 가하는 압박과
It takes willpower / to switch off the world, /
의지가 필요하다 / 세상에 대한 스위치를 끄는 데는 /
even for an hour. 단 한 시간 동안이라도
It feels uncomfortable, /
그것은 불편한 느낌이 든다 /
and sometimes people get upset.
그리고 때때로 사람들이 기분 상하기도 한다
But it's better / 하지만 더 낫다 /
to disappoint a few people over small things, /
사소한 일에 대해 몇 사람을 실망시키는 것이 /
than to abandon your dreams / for an empty inbox.
자신의 꿈을 버리는 것보다 / 빈 수신함을 위해
Otherwise, / you're sacrificing your potential /
그렇지 않으면 / 자신의 잠재력을 희생하고 있다 /
for the illusion of professionalism.
여러분은 전문가답다는 환상을 위해

여러분이 일하는 습관에서 할 수 있는 가장 중요한 단 하나의 변화는 창조적인 일을 먼저 하고 대응적인 일은 다음으로 하는 쪽으로 전환하는 것이다. 이것은 전화기와 이메일을 끈 채, 여러분 자신의 우선순위에 따라 창조적인 작업을 위해 매일 많은 시간을 떼어 두는 것을 의미한다. 나는 좌절감을 느끼곤 하던 작가였다. 이렇게 전환하는 것이 나를 생산적인 작가로 변하게 했다. 그러나 내가 기사나 블로그 게시글 또는 책의 한 챕터를 쓰려고 앉을 때마다 여러 사람들이 내가 그들에게 답장을 주기를 기다리지 않은 날이 단 하루도 없었다. 그것은 쉽지 않았고, 특히 "2시간 전에 이메일을 보냈어요...!"라고 시작하는 전화 메시지를 받을 때는 아직도 쉽지 않다. 당연히, 이런 접근 방식은 다른 사람들의 기대와 그들이 여러분에게 가하는 압박과 충돌하는 것이다. 단 한 시간 동안이라도 세상에 대한 스위치를 끄는 데는 의지가 필요하다. 그것은 불편한 느낌이 들고, 때때로 사람들이 기분 상하기도 한다. 하지만 빈 수신함을 위해 자신의 꿈을 버리는 것보다, 사소한 일에 대해 몇 사람을 실망시키는 것이 더 낫다. 그렇지 않으면, 여러분은 전문가답다는 환상을 위해 자신의 잠재력을 희생하고 있다.

① 혁신적인 행동 방침을 따르는 것
② 다른 사람들의 요구를 충족하려고 하는 것
③ 도전적인 일을 실수 없이 완수하는 것
④ 정신적 균형을 유지하기 위해 사회적 유대를 없애는 것
⑤ 소셜 네트워킹을 위해서 충분한 기회를 확보하는 것

문제풀이

창조적인 작업을 하기 위해 매일 많은 시간 동안 전화기나 이메일을 꺼 놓아 자신이 하는 일에 방해를 받지 않도록 차단하라고 하면서 빈 수신함을 위해 자신의 꿈을 포기하는 것보다 그냥 몇 사람을 실망하게 하는 것이 낫다고 했다. 따라서 밑줄 친 an empty inbox가 의미하는 바는 답장을 기다리는 사람에게 답장하는 것을 의미하므로, 밑줄 친 부분이 의미하는 바로 가장 적절한 것은 ② 'attempting to satisfy other people's demands(다른 사람들의 요구를 충족하려고 하는 것)'이다.

이렇게 풀자 밑줄 친 부분이 의미하는 바를 찾는 문제에서 밑줄 친 부분은 글의 중심 내용과 관계있는 경우가 많다. 'The single most important change you can make in your working habits is to switch to creative work first, reactive work second.(여러분이 일하는 습관에서 할 수 있는 가장 중요한 단 하나의 변화는 창조적인 일을 먼저 하고 대응적인 일은 그다음에 하는 쪽으로 전환하는 것이다.)'와 'This means blocking off a large chunk of time every day for creative work on your own priorities, with the phone and e-mail off.(이것은 전화기와 이메일을 끈 채, 여러분 자신의 우선순위에 따라 창조적인 작업을 위해 매일 많은 시간을 떼어 두는 것을 의미한다.)'를 통해 이 글의 주제를 알 수 있으며, 밑줄 친 '빈 수신함'이 답장을 기다리는 사람들에게 답장하는 것을 의미한다는 것을 알면 an empty inbox가 의미하는 바를 쉽게 유추해낼 수 있다.

어휘·어구

switch to ~로 전환하다
creative 창의적인
reactive 대응적인
block off ~을 막다
chunk 많은 양, 덩어리
priority 우선순위
frustrated 좌절감을 느끼는
a string of 여러 개의
by definition 당연히
willpower 의지력
go against ~에 위배되다
grain (나무의) 결, 기질
abandon 버리다
sacrifice 희생하다
potential 잠재력, 가능성
illusion 환상
professionalism 전문성
innovative 혁신적인
attempt to do ~하려고 시도하다
demand 요구
challenging 도전적인

정답률 68%

1. ① 일기의 기능

직독/직해

Coming of age in the 18th and 19th centuries, /
18세기와 19세기에 발달된 /
the personal diary became a centerpiece /
개인 일기는 핵심이 되었는데 /
in the construction of a modern subjectivity, /
현대적 주체성을 구축하는 데 /
at the heart of which is the application of reason and critique /
그것의 중심에는 이성과 비판의 적용이 있었고 /
to the understanding of world and self, /
세계와 자아에 대한 이해에 /
which allowed the creation of a new kind of knowledge.
이는 새로운 종류의 지식을 만들어질 수 있게 해 주었다
Diaries were central media /
일기는 중심 매체였다 /
through which enlightened and free subjects could be constructed.
그것을 통해 계몽되고 자유로운 주체가 구축될 수 있는
They provided a space / where one could write daily /
그것은 공간을 제공했다 / 개인이 매일 쓸 수 있는 /
about her whereabouts, feelings, and thoughts.
자신의 소재, 감정, 생각에 대해
Over time and with rereading, /
시간이 흐름에 따라 그리고 다시 읽음으로써 /
disparate entries, events, and happenstances could be rendered /
이질적인 항목, 사건 및 우연이 만들어질 수 있었다 /
into insights and narratives about the self, /
자신에 관한 통찰력과 이야기로 /
and allowed for the formation of subjectivity.
그리고 주체성의 형성을 가능하게 만들었다
It is in that context / that the idea of "the self /
바로 그런 맥락에서다 / 자아'라는 개념이 /
[as] both made and explored with words" emerges.
말로 만들어지고 혹은 탐구되는 (것으로의) 생겨나는 것은
Diaries were personal and private; /
일기는 개인적이고 사적인 것이었다 /
one would write for oneself, / or, in Habermas's formulation, /
사람들은 자신을 위해 쓰곤 했는데 / Habermas의 명확한 말을 빌리면 /
one would make oneself public to oneself.
자신을 자신에게 공개적으로 만들곤 했다
By making the self public in a private sphere, /
자아를 개인적인 영역에서 공적으로 만들면서 /
the self also became an object / for self-inspection and self-critique.
자아는 대상이 되었다 / 또한 자기 점검과 자기비판의

18세기와 19세기에 발달된 개인 일기는 현대적 주체성을 구축하는 데 핵심이 되었는데, 그것의 중심에는 세계와 자아에 대한 이해에 이성과 비판의 적용이 있었고, 이는 새로운 종류의 지식을 만들어질 수 있게 해 주었다. 일기는 그것을 통해 계몽되고 자유로운 주체가 구축될 수 있는 중심 매체였다. 그것은 개인이 자신의 소재, 감정, 생각에 대해 매일 쓸 수 있는 공간을 제공했다. 시간이 흐름에 따라 그리고 다시 읽음으로써, 이질적인 항목, 사건 및 우연이 자신에 관한 통찰력과 이야기로 만들어질 수 있었으며, 주체성의 형성을 가능하게 만들었다. '말로 만들어지고 혹은 탐구되는 (것으로의) 자아'라는 개념이 생겨나는 것은 바로 그런 맥락에서다. 일기는 개인적이고 사적인 것이었다. 사람들은 자신을 위해 쓰곤 했는데, Habermas의 명확한 말을 빌리면, 자신을 자신에게 공개적으로 만들곤 했다. 자아를 개인적인 영역에서 공적으로 만들면서, 자아는 또한 자기 점검과 자기비판의 대상이 되었다.

① 글을 자신을 반성하는 수단으로 사용하곤
② 다른 사람의 일기를 읽음으로써 자신의 정체성을 확립하곤

③ 글 쓰는 과정에서 피드백을 교환하곤
④ 다른 사람에게 제시하기 위한 대체 자아를 창조하곤
⑤ 자아에 관한 글을 쓰기 위한 주제를 발전시키곤

문제풀이

일기는 계몽되고 자유로운 주체를 구성할 수 있는 중심 매체로서 자신의 소재, 감정, 생각에 관해 쓸 수 있는 공간을 제공했고, 일기를 씀으로써 자아를 개인적인 영역에서 공적으로 만들게 되어 자아는 자기 점검과 자기비판의 대상이 되었다고 했다. 따라서 밑줄 친 make oneself public to oneself가 의미하는 바로 가장 적절한 것은 ① 'use writing as a means of reflecting on oneself(글을 자신을 반성하는 수단으로 사용하곤)'이다.

이렇게 풀자 밑줄 친 부분이 의미하는 바를 찾는 문제에서 밑줄 친 부분은 글의 중심 내용과 관계있는 경우가 많다. 이 글은 일기의 기능에 대해 이야기하고 있는데 'By making the self public in a private sphere, the self also became an object for self-inspection and self-critique.(자아를 개인적인 영역에서 공적으로 만들면서, 자아는 또한 자기 점검과 자기비판의 대상이 되었다.)'를 통해 일기를 쓰는 것이 자신을 개인을 어떻게 변화시켰고 그것이 자아에 어떤 영향을 미쳤는지를 이해하면 밑줄 친 부분의 의미를 쉽게 추론해 낼 수 있다.

어휘·어구

come of age (무엇이) 발달한 상태가 되다
centerpiece 중심물
subjectivity 주체성, 주관성
application 적용
critique 비판
self 자아
enlightened 계몽된
whereabouts 소재, 행방
entry 항목
happenstance (특히 좋은 결과로 이어지는) 우연
render 만들다
narrative 이야기
emerge 생겨나다
formulation 명확한 표현, 간명하게 말함
sphere 영역
as a means of ~의 수단으로서
reflect on ~을 반성하다
identity 정체성
alternate 대신인, 교대의
selfhood 자아

정답률 44%

2. ⑤ 소비주의의 문제점

직독/직해

Far from a synonym for capitalism, / consumerism makes capitalism impossible /
자본주의의 동의어이기는커녕 / 소비주의는 자본주의를 불가능하게 한다 /

over the long term, / since it makes capital formation all but impossible.
오랜 기간에 걸쳐 / 이는 그것이 자본 형성을 거의 불가능하게 하기 때문이다

A consumer culture isn't a saving culture, / isn't a thrift culture.
소비 문화는 저축 문화가 아니다 / 그리고 절약 문화도 아니다

It's too fixated on buying the next toy / to ever delay gratification, /
그것은 다음 장난감을 사는 데 너무 집착해서 / 결코 욕구 충족을 미루지 않는다 /

to ever save and invest for the future.
그리고 미래를 위해 결코 저축하고 투자하지도 않는다

The point is elementary: / you can't have sustainable capitalism without capital; /
요점은 기본적이다 / 자본이 없이는 지속 가능한 자본주의가 있을 수 없다 /

you can't have capital without savings; /
저축이 없이는 자본이 생길 수 없다 /

and you can't save / if you're running around spending everything /
그리고 저축할 수 없다 / 만일 모든 것을 쓰면서 돌아다닌다면 /

you've just earned.
방금 벌어들인

But the confusion has grown so deep /
하지만 혼동은 너무 깊어져서 /

that many people today do not have the ears to hear it.
많은 이들이 오늘날 그것을 들을 귀를 갖고 있지 않다

Indeed, / the policies of our nation's central bank seem to reinforce this habit /
실제로 / 우리 나라의 중앙은행 정책은 이런 습관을 강화하는 것 같다 /

by driving down interest rates to near zero /
이자율을 영에 가깝게 끌어내림으로써 /

and thereby denying people a material reward /
그리고 그로 인해 물질적 보상을 주기를 거부함으로써 /

— in the form of interest on their banked savings — /
사람들에게 은행 예금의 이자 형태로 /

for foregoing consumption.
소비를 단념하는 것에 대한

소비주의는 자본주의의 동의어이기는커녕 자본주의를 오랜 기간에 걸쳐 불가능하게 하는데, 이는 그것이 자본 형성을 거의 불가능하게 하기 때문이다. 소비 문화는 저축 문화도 아니고 절약 문화도 아니다. 그것은 다음 장난감을 사는 데 너무 집착한 나머지 결코 욕구 충족을 미루지도 않고, 미래를 위해 결코 저축하고 투자하지도 않는다. 요점은 기본적인데, 자본이 없이는 지속 가능한 자본주의가 있을 수 없고, 저축이 없이는 자본이 생길 수 없으며, 방금 벌어들인 모든 것을 쓰면서 돌아다닌다면 저축할 수 없다는 것이다. 하지만 혼동은 너무 깊어져서 많은 이들이 오늘날 그것을 들을 귀를 갖고 있지 않다. 실제로 우리 나라의 중앙은행 정책은 이자율을 영에 가깝게 끌어내려, 그로 인해 사람들에게 은행 예금의 이자 형태로, 소비를 단념하는 것에 대한 물질적 보상을 주기를 거부함으로써 이런 습관을 강화하는 것 같다.

① 금리 인하라는 국가 정책에 반대하다
② 소비주의가 자본주의의 동의어라는 사실을 무시하다
③ 소비주의는 실제로 행복에 별로 도움이 되지 않다고 믿는다
④ 저축이 나라를 번영시킬 수 있다는 그릇된 가정을 형성한다
⑤ 소비만으로는 자본주의를 유지할 수 없다는 것을 이해하지 못한다

문제풀이

소비주의는 자본 형성을 불가능하게 하고, 소비가 만연하면 저축과 투자가 없고, 저축이 없으면 자본이 축적되지 않아 지속 가능한 자본주의가 생길 수 없는데 오늘날 많은 사람들이 이런 사실을 이해하지 못하고 있다는 내용의 글이다. 따라서 밑줄 친 부분이 의미하는 바로 가장 적절한 것은 ⑤ 'fail to understand that consumption alone can't sustain capitalism(소비만으로는 자본주의를 유지할 수 없다는 것을 이해하지 못한다.)'이다.

구조 다시보기

주제	소비주의와 자본주의는 서로 다른 것임
상술	자본주의는 근검절약을 통해 자본을 축적함으로써 유지되는데 소비주의는 저축하지 않음
부연	국가가 소비를 촉진하는 정책을 시행함으로써 사람들에게 자본주의는 소비를 통해 유지되는 것으로 혼동하게 함

어휘·어구

synonym 동의어
term 기간
capitalism 자본주의
consumerism 소비주의
formation 형성
all but 거의
consumer 소비자
invest 투자하다
sustainable 지속[유지]할 수 있는
confusion 혼란
indeed 실제로
policy 정책
reinforce 강화하다
thereby 그렇게 함으로써
deny 거부하다
material 물질적
consumption 소비

정답률 55%

3. ① 알고리즘의 특징

직독/직해

You may feel / there is something scary /
당신은 느끼지도 모른다 / 무엇인가 무서운 것이 있다고 /

about an algorithm deciding what you might like.
당신이 좋아할 수도 있는 것을 결정하는 알고리즘에 대해

Could it mean / that, if computers conclude /
그것은 의미일 수 있는가 / 컴퓨터가 결론을 내린다면 /

you won't like something, /
당신이 무엇인가를 좋아하지 않을 것이라고 /

you will never get the chance / to see it?
당신은 기회조차 절대 얻지 못할 수도 있다는 / 그것을 볼

Personally, / I really enjoy being directed toward new music /
개인적으로 / 나는 새로운 음악 쪽으로 안내받는 것을 정말 좋아한다 /

that I might not have found by myself.
스스로는 발견할 수 없었을

I can quickly get stuck in a rut / where I put on the same songs over and over.
나는 틀에 빨리 갇힐 수도 있다 / 같은 노래를 반복해서 넣는

That's / why I've always enjoyed the radio.
그것이 ~이다 / 내가 항상 라디오를 즐겨 듣는 이유

But / the algorithms /
하지만 / 알고리즘은 /

that are now pushing and pulling me through the music library /
현재 뮤직 라이브러리를 통해 나를 밀고 당기는 /

are perfectly suited to finding gems / that I'll like.
보석을 찾는 데 완벽히 적합하다 / 내가 좋아할

My worry originally about such algorithms /
원래 그러한 알고리즘에 대한 나의 걱정은 /

was that they might drive everyone into certain parts of the library, /
모든 사람을 라이브러리의 특정 부분으로 몰고 갈 수도 있다는 것이었다 /

leaving others lacking listeners.
나머지 부분은 듣는 사람들이 적은 상태가 되게 만들 수 있다

Would they cause / a convergence of tastes?
그것은 초래할 것인가 / 취향의 수렴을

But / thanks to the nonlinear and chaotic mathematics usually behind them, /
하지만 / 일반적으로 그 배후에 있는 비선형적이고 혼란스러운 방식의 수학 덕분에 /

this doesn't happen.
이런 일은 일어나지는 않는다

A small divergence in my likes / compared to yours /
내가 좋아하는 것의 작은 갈라짐이 / 당신이 좋아하는 것과 비교하여 /

can send us off / into different far corners of the library.
우리를 보낼 수 있다 / 라이브러리의 다른 저 멀리 떨어진 구석들로

당신은 당신이 좋아할 수도 있는 것을 결정하는 알고리즘에 대해 무엇인가 무서운 것이 있다고 느낄지도 모른다. 그것은 당신이 무엇인가를 좋아하지 않을 것이라고 컴퓨터가 결론을 내린다면 당신은 그것을 볼 기회조차 절대 얻지 못할 수도 있다는 의미일 수 있는가? 개인적으로, 나는 스스로는 발견할 수 없었을 새로운 음악 쪽으로 안내받는 것을 정말 좋아한다. 나는 같은 노래를 반복해서 넣는 틀에 빨리 갇힐 수도 있다. 그것이 내가 항상 라디오를 즐겨 듣는 이유이다. 하지만 현재 뮤직 라이브러리를 통해 나를 밀고 당기는 알고리즘은 내가 좋아할 보석을 찾는 데 완벽히 적합하다. 원래 그러한 알고리즘에 대한 나의 걱정은 모든 사람을 라이브

러리의 특정 부분으로 몰고 가서 나머지 부분은 듣는 사람들이 적은 상태가 되게 만들 수 있다는 것이었다. 그것은 취향의 수렴을 초래할 것인가? 하지만 일반적으로 그 배후에 있는 비선형적이고 혼란스러운 방식의 수학 덕분에 이런 일은 일어나지는 않는다. 당신이 좋아하는 것과 비교하여 내가 좋아하는 것의 작은 갈라짐이 우리를 라이브러리의 다른 저 멀리 떨어진 구석들로 보낼 수 있다.

① 우리 각자의 취향에 맞도록 선택된 음악으로 우리를 이끌다
② 우리가 다른 청취자들과 관계를 맺을 수 있게 해 준다
③ 우리가 알고리즘을 위한 업데이트를 자주 요청하라고 권하다
④ 재능이 있지만 알려지지 않은 음악가들을 찾도록 우리에게 동기를 부여하다
⑤ 특별한 음악 장르에 대해서 우리의 선호를 무시하도록 만들다

문제풀이

알고리즘은 배후에 있는 비선형적이고 혼란스러운 방식의 수학 덕분에 모든 사람이 뮤직 라이브러리의 특정 부분으로 몰리지 않게 한다고 했으므로, 각자의 작은 선호의 차이 때문에 우리 취향이 다양성을 유지할 수 있다고 해야 한다. 따라서 밑줄 친 send us off into different far corners of the library가 의미하는 바로 가장 적절한 것은 ① 'lead us to music selected to suit our respective tastes(우리 각자의 취향에 맞도록 선택된 음악으로 우리를 이끌다)'이다.

이렇게 풀자 밑줄 친 부분이 의미하는 바를 찾는 문제에서 밑줄 친 부분은 글의 중심 내용과 관계있는 경우가 많다. 글의 중심 내용은 'But thanks to the nonlinear and chaotic mathematics usually behind them, this doesn't happen.(하지만 일반적으로 그 배후에 있는 비선형적이고 혼란스러운 방식의 수학 덕분에 이런 일은 일어나지는 않는다.)'에 잘 드러나 있는데, 이 문장에서 this가 가리키는 것이 'My worry originally about such algorithms was that they might drive everyone into certain parts of the library, leaving others lacking listeners.(원래 그러한 알고리즘에 대한 나의 걱정은 모든 사람을 라이브러리의 특정 부분으로 몰고 가서 나머지 부분은 듣는 사람들이 적은 상태가 되게 만들 수 있다는 것이었다.)'라는 것을 알면 밑줄 친 부분이 의미하는 바를 쉽게 유추해 낼 수 있다.

어휘·어구

algorithm 알고리즘
direct 안내하다, 알려 주다
get stuck in ~에 갇히다
over and over 반복해서
be suited to ~에 적합하다
lacking 부족한, ~이 모자라는
convergence 수렴, 한 점으로 집합함
nonlinear 비선형적인
chaotic 혼돈 상태인
respective 각자의, 각각의
ignore 무시하다
preference 선호

정답률 72%

4. ④ 인간을 노예로 만든 기술이 부여한 여가

직독/직해

It seemed like a fair deal: / we would accept new technologies, /
그것은 공정한 거래처럼 보였다 / 우리는 새로운 기술을 받아들일 것이었고 /
which would modify our habits /
그것은 우리의 습관을 바꾸고 /
and oblige us to adjust to certain changes, /
그리고 어쩔 수 없이 우리가 특정한 변화에 적응하게 할 것이었다 /
but in exchange / we would be granted relief from the burden of work, /
그러나 그 대가로 / 우리는 일의 부담의 경감을 얻을 것이었다 /
more security, / and above all, / the freedom to pursue our desires.
더 많은 보안 / 그리고 무엇보다도 / 우리의 욕망을 추구할 자유를
The sacrifice was worth the gain; / there would be no regrets.
그 희생에는 그 이득의 가치가 있었다 / 후회는 없을 것이었다
Yet it has become apparent / that this civilization of leisure was, / in reality, /
그러나 명백해졌다 / 여가로 인한 이러한 생활의 개선은 / 실제로 /
a Trojan horse.
트로이 목마였다는 것이
Its swelling flanks hid the impositions / of a new type of enslavement.
그것의 불룩한 옆구리는 부담을 숨겼다 / 새로운 형태의 노예화라는
The automatons are not as autonomous as advertised.
그 자동 장치는 광고되는 것처럼 자율적이지 않다
They need us. 그것들은 우리를 필요로 한다
Those computers / that were supposed to do our calculations for us /
그 컴퓨터들은 / 우리를 위해 계산을 해 주기로 되어 있던 /
instead demand our attention: / for ten hours a day, /
대신 우리의 주의를 요구한다 / 하루에 10시간 동안 /
we are glued to their screens.
우리는 그것들의 화면에 붙어 있다
Our communications monopolize our time.
우리의 통신은 우리의 시간을 독점한다
Time itself is accelerating.
시간 자체가 빨라지고 있다
The complexity of the system overwhelms us.
그 시스템의 복잡성은 우리를 어쩔 줄 모르게 만든다
And leisure is often a costly distraction.
그리고 여가는 종종 비용이 많이 드는 오락이다

그것은 공정한 거래처럼 보였다. 우리는 새로운 기술을 받아들일 것이었고, 그것은 우리의 습관을 바꾸고 어쩔 수 없이 우리가 특정한 변화에 적응하게 할 것이었지만, 그 대가로 우리는 일의 부담의 경감, 더 많은 보안, 그리고 무엇보다도 우리의 욕망을 추구할 자유를 얻을 것이었다. 그 희생에는 그 이득의 가치가 있었다. 후회는 없을 것이었다. 그러나 여가로 인한 이러한 생활의 개선은 실제로는 트로이 목마였다는 것이 명백해졌다. 그것의 불룩한 옆구리는 새로운 형태의 노예화라는 부담을 숨겼다. 그 자동 장치는 광고되는 것처럼 자율적이지 않다. 그것들은 우리를 필요로 한다. 우리를 위해 계산을 해 주기로 되어 있던 그 컴퓨터들은 대신 우리의 주의를 요구한다. 하루에 10시간 동안 우리는 그것들의 화면에 붙어 있다. 우리의 통신은 우리의 시간을 독점한다. 시간 자체가 빨라지고 있다. 그 시스템의 복잡성은 우리를 어쩔 줄 모르게 만든다. 그리고 여가는 종종 비용이 많이 드는 오락이다.

① 여가 활동을 하는 것은 동료들 간의 소통을 증가시켰다.
② 노동은 언론에 의해 여가와 쉽게 결합되었다.
③ 낮은 보안 때문에 사람들의 사생활이 공격당했다.
④ 레저에 대한 기술의 약속은 실제로 사람들을 덜 자유롭게 만들었다.
⑤ 기술 혁신은 계층적 작업 문화를 개선하지 못했다.

문제풀이

기술 발달을 수용함으로 우리는 일의 부담이 줄어들고, 우리의 욕망을 추구할 자유를 얻을 수 있을 것이라고 여겼지만, 실제로는 이러한 기술이 부여하는 여가가 오히려 우리를 더욱 노예화한다는 내용의 글이다. 따라서 밑줄 친 'this civilization of leisure was, in reality, a Trojan horse'가 의미하는 바로 가장 적절한 것은 ④ 'Technology's promise for leisure actually made people less free.(레저에 대한 기술의 약속은 실제로 사람들을 덜 자유롭게 만들었다.)'이다.

이렇게 풀자 밑줄 친 부분이 의미하는 바를 찾는 문제에서는 밑줄 친 부분을 포함한 문장 앞뒤에서 그 단서를 찾을 수 있다. 밑줄 친 부분을 포함한 문장의 'Yet'으로 보아 바로 앞 문장 'The sacrifice was worth the gain; there would be not regrets.(그 희생에는 그 이득의 가치가 있었다. 후회는 없을 것이었다.)'와는 상반되는 내용이 이어진다는 것을 알 수 있고, 밑줄 친 부분 다음의 자동화, 컴퓨터, 통신 등이 사실은 우리의 시간을 절약하는 것이 아니라 우리의 시간을 더 많이 요구한다는 내용에서 밑줄 친 부분의 의미를 유추할 수 있다.

어휘·어구

modify 바꾸다
oblige 강요하다
adjust to ~에 적응하다
exchange 교환하다
relief 경감
burden 부담
security 보안
apparent 명백한
swell 부풀다
imposition 부담
enslavement 노예화
calculation 계산
attention 주의
monopolize 독점하다
accelerate 가속하다, 촉진하다
complexity 복잡성, 복잡함
overwhelm 당황하게 하다
costly 많은 비용이 드는
distraction 오락

정답률 59%

5. ⑤ 세계에 대한 우리의 관점

직독/직해

Our view of the world is not given to us /
세계에 대한 우리의 관점은 우리에게 주어지는 것이 아니다 /
from the outside / in a pure, objective form; /
외부에서 / 순수하고 객관적인 형태로 /
it is shaped / by our mental abilities, /
그것은 형성된다 / 우리의 정신 능력에 의해 /
our shared cultural perspectives / and our unique values and beliefs.
우리의 공유된 문화적 관점(에 의해) / 그리고 우리의 독특한 가치관과 신념(에 의해)
This is not to say /
이것은 말하는 것이 아니다 /
that there is no reality outside our minds /
우리의 마음 바깥에 현실이 없다고 /
or that the world is just an illusion.
또는 세계는 환영일 뿐이라고
It is to say / that our version of reality is precisely that: /
그것은 말하는 것이다 / 우리가 가진 현실 버전은 바로 그것이다 /
our version, not *the* version.
'우리의' 버전이지 (유일한) '그' 버전은 아니라고
There is no single, universal or authoritative version /
단일하거나, 보편적이거나 권위 있는 버전은 없다 /
that makes sense, / other than as a theoretical construct.
이치에 맞는 / 이론적 구성물 외에
We can see the world / only as it appears to us, / not "as it truly is," /
우리는 세계를 볼 수 있는데 / 그것이 우리에게 보이는 대로만 / '진정한 그대로'가 아니라 /
because there is no "as it truly is" / without a perspective to give it form.
왜냐하면 '진정한 그대로'란 없기 때문이다 / 세계에 형태를 부여하는 관점 없이
Philosopher Thomas Nagel argued / that there is no "view from nowhere," /
철학자 Thomas Nagel은 주장했는데 / '입장이 없는 관점'은 없다고 /
since we cannot see the world /
왜냐하면 우리는 세계를 볼 수 없고 /
except from a particular perspective, /
특정한 관점에서 보는 경우를 제외하고는 /
and that perspective influences what we see.
그리고 그 관점이 우리가 보는 것에 영향을 주기 때문이다

We can experience the world /
우리는 세계를 세계를 경험할 수 있다 /

only through the human lenses / that make it intelligible to us.
인간의 렌즈를 통해서만 / 우리가 이해할 수 있게 해 주는

세계에 대한 우리의 관점은 순수하고 객관적인 형태로 외부에서 우리에게 주어지는 것이 아니라, 그것은 우리의 정신 능력, 우리의 공유된 문화적 관점, 그리고 우리의 독특한 가치관과 신념에 의해 형성된다. 이것은 우리의 마음 바깥에 현실이 없다거나 세계는 환영일 뿐이라고 말하는 것이 아니다. 그것은 우리가 가진 현실 버전은 바로 그것, 즉 '우리의' 버전이지 (유일한) '그' 버전은 아니라고 말하는 것이다. 이론적 구성물 외에 이치에 맞는 단일하거나, 보편적이거나 권위 있는 버전은 없다. 우리는 세계를 '진정한 그대로'가 아니라, 그것이 우리에게 보이는 대로만 볼 수 있는데, 왜냐하면 세계에 형태를 부여하는 관점 없이 '진정한 그대로'란 없기 때문이다. 철학자 Thomas Nagel은 '입장이 없는 관점'은 없다고 주장했는데, 왜냐하면 우리는 특정한 관점에서 보는 경우를 제외하고는 세계를 볼 수 없고, 그 관점이 우리가 보는 것에 영향을 주기 때문이다. 우리는 세계를 우리가 이해할 수 있게 해 주는 인간의 렌즈를 통해서만 세계를 경험할 수 있다.

① 주관적인 관점에 영향을 받는 현실 인식
② 대부분의 사람이 마음에 두고 있는 가치 있는 관점
③ 아주 소수의 사람이 채택하는 특정한 관점
④ 우리의 편견을 물리치는 비판적인 통찰
⑤ 편견 없는 객관적인 세계에 관한 관점

문제풀이

우리의 세계관은 순수하고 객관적인 형태로 외부로부터 우리에게 주어진 것이 아니며, 결국은 공유된 문화적 관심, 우리 자신의 가치관이나 신념을 통해 세상을 바라본다는 내용의 글이다. 밑줄 친 'view from nowhere'는 '입장이 없는 관점'을 뜻하는 데, 이는 '진정한 그대로' 우리에게 주어지는 객관적인 세계에 대한 관점을 의미하므로, 정답은 ⑤ 'unbiased and objective view of the world(편견 없는 객관적인 세계에 관한 관점)'이다.

이렇게 풀자 밑줄 친 부분이 의미하는 바를 찾는 문제에서 밑줄 친 부분은 글의 중심 내용과 관계있는 경우가 많다. 'Our view of the world is not given to us from the outside in a pure, objective form; it is shaped by our mental abilities, our shared cultural perspectives and our unique values and beliefs.(세계에 대한 우리의 관점은 순수하고 객관적인 형태로 외부에서 우리에게 주어지는 것이 아니라, 그것은 우리의 정신 능력, 우리의 공유된 문화적 관점, 그리고 우리의 독특한 가치관과 신념에 의해 형성된다.)'를 통해 세계에 대한 관점이 개인의 주관적인 가치관과 신념에 의해 형성된다는 것을 알면 답을 쉽게 찾을 수 있다. 단, 밑줄 친 부분 앞에 no가 왔으므로, 밑줄 친 부분이 이 글의 중심 내용과 반대되는 내용이 와야 한다는 점에 유의한다.

어휘·어구

pure 순수한
objective 객관적인
perspective 관점
version 버전, 견해, 설명
precisely 바로, 정확하게
universal 보편적인
authoritative 권위 있는, 권위적인
theoretical construct 이론적 구성물
other than ~외에
philosopher 철학자
intelligible 이해할 수 있는
perception 인식
subjective 주관적인
valuable 가치 있는
adopt 채택하다
critical 비판적인
insight 통찰력
prejudice 편견
unbiased 편견 없는

정답률 61%

6. ② 뉴스의 특성

직독/직해

Journalists love to report studies / that are at the "initial findings" stages —/
기자들은 연구들을 보도하기를 매우 좋아하는데 / '초기 결과' 단계에 있는 /

research that claims / to be the first time / anyone has discovered a thing —/
주장하는 연구를 / 최초로 / 누군가가 어떤 것을 발견했다고 /

because there is newsworthiness in their novelty.
왜냐하면 그것들의 새로움에 뉴스 가치가 있기 때문이다

But / "first ever" discoveries are extremely vulnerable to / becoming undermined /
하지만 / '사상 최초의' 발견들은 아주 쉽다(취약하다) / 약화되기가 /

by subsequent research.
후속 연구에 의해

When that happens, /
그것이 일어날 때 /

the news media often don't go back and inform /
뉴스 매체는 종종 돌아가서 알리지 않는다

their audiences about the change —/
그들에게 그것에 관해 /

assuming they even hear about it.
그들의 독자들이 그 변화에 관해 심지어 들을 것이라고 가정한 채

Kelly Crowe, a CBC News reporter writes, /
CBC News 기자인 Kelly Crowe는 쓴 적이 있다 /

quoting one epidemiologist, / "There is increasing concern /
한 전염병 학자의 말을 인용해서 / 증가하는 우려가 있다 /

that in modern research, / false findings may be the majority /
현대 연구에서 / 잘못된 결과가 다수일 수도 있다 /

or even the vast majority / of published research claims."
혹은 심지어 대다수(일 수도 있다) / 게재된 연구 주장의

She goes on to suggest / that journalists, / though blameworthy for this tendency, /
그녀는 이어서 시사한다 / 기자들이 / 이러한 경향에 있어 비난받을 만하지만 /

are aided and abetted by the scientists / whose studies they cite.
과학자들에 의해 방조되고 있음을 / 자신들이 인용하는 연구들의

She writes / that the "conclusions" sections in scientific abstracts /
그녀는 쓰고 있다 / 과학 초록의 '결론' 부분들이 /

can sometimes be overstated /
때때로 과장될 수 있다고 /

in an attempt to draw attention / from prestigious academic journals and media /
관심을 끌기 위한 시도에서 / 명성 있는 학술지와 매체로부터 /

who uncritically take their bait.
무비판적으로 그것들의 미끼를 무는

Even so, / Crowe ends her piece /
그럼에도 불구하고 / Crowe는 자신의 글을 끝마친다 /

by stressing / that there is still an incompatibility /
강조함으로써 / 여전히 상반된 점이 있다는 것 /

between the purposes and processes of news and science: /
뉴스와 과학의 목적과 과정 사이에는 /

Science 'evolves,' but news 'happens.'
과학은 '진화'하지만 뉴스는 '발생한다'는 것을

기자들은 '초기 결과' 단계에 있는 연구들, 즉 누군가가 최초로 어떤 것을 발견했다고 주장하는 연구를 보도하기를 매우 좋아하는데, 왜냐하면 그것들의 새로움에 뉴스 가치가 있기 때문이다. 하지만 '사상 최초의' 발견들은 후속 연구에 의해 약화되기가 아주 쉽다. 그것이 일어날 때 뉴스 매체는 그들의 독자들이 그 변화에 관해 심지어 들을 것이라고 가정한 채, 종종 돌아가서 그들에게 그것(그 변화)에 관해 알리지 않는다. CBC News 기자인 Kelly Crowe는 한 전염병 학자의 말을 인용해서 "현대 연구에서 잘못된 결과가 게재된 연구 주장의 다수 혹은 심지어 대다수일 수도 있다는 증가하는 우려가 있다."라고 쓰고 있다. 그녀는 기자들이 이러한 경향에 있어 비난받을 만하지만, 자신들이 인용하는 연구들의 과학자들에 의해 방조되고 있음을 이어서 시사한다. 그녀는 무비판적으로 그것들의 미끼를 무는 명성 있는 학술지와 매체로부터 관심을 끌기 위한 시도에서 과학 초록의 '결론' 부분들이 때때로 과장될 수 있다고 쓰고 있다. 그럼에도 불구하고, Crowe는 뉴스와 과학의 목적과 과정 사이에는 여전히 상반된 점이 있다는 것, 즉 과학은 '진화'하지만 뉴스는 '발생한다'는 것을 강조함으로써 자신의 글을 끝마친다.

① 뉴스는 결과보다 연구 과정을 더 따른다.
② 뉴스는 연구가 어떻게 변화하느냐가 아니라 그것의 새로움에 초점을 맞춘다.
③ 뉴스는 잘못된 과학적 발견을 비판함으로써 주목을 끈다.
④ 기자들은 과학자들과 달리 독자들에게 즉각적인 피드백을 준다.
⑤ 기자들은 과학의 중요성에 대한 신뢰를 만들고 강화한다.

문제풀이

필자는 기자들이 초기 결과 단계의 새 연구는 뉴스 가치가 있기 때문에 보도하기 좋아하지만, 후속 단계에 의해 약화된 연구는 잘 보도하지 않는다고 언급했다. 따라서 밑줄 친 news 'happens'는 뉴스는 변화보다 발생한 일만 강조한다는 것을 의미하므로 정답은 ② 'News focuses not on how research changes but on the novelty of it.(뉴스는 연구가 어떻게 변화하느냐가 아니라 그것의 새로움에 초점을 맞춘다.)'이다.

이렇게 풀자 밑줄 친 부분이 의미하는 바를 찾는 문제에서 밑줄 친 부분은 글의 중심 내용과 관계있는 경우가 많다. 'Journalists love to report studies that are at the "initial findings" stages — research that claims to be the first time anyone has discovered a thing — because there is newsworthiness in their novelty.(기자들은 '초기 결과' 단계에 있는 연구들, 즉 누군가가 최초로 어떤 것을 발견했다고 주장하는 연구를 보도하기를 매우 좋아하는데, 왜냐하면 그것들의 새로움에 뉴스 가치가 있기 때문이다.)'와 'When that happens, the news media often don't go back and inform their audiences about the change — assuming they even hear about it.(그것이 생겼을 때 뉴스 매체는 그들의 독자들이 그 변화에 관해 심지어 들을 것이라고 가정한 채, 종종 돌아가서 그들에게 그것에 관해 알리지 않는다.)'을 통해 뉴스가 어떻게 변화하는지보다 새롭게 일어난 일에만 초점을 맞춘다는 사실을 알면 답을 쉽게 찾을 수 있다.

어휘·어구

journalist 저널리스트, 기자
initial 최초의
claim 주장하다
novelty 새로움, 참신함
vulnerable 취약한, 연약한
undermine 약화시키다
subsequent 그 다음의, 차후의
assume 추정하다
quote 인용하다
concern 우려, 걱정
false 잘못된
majority 다수
vast 방대한, 엄청난
publish 출판하다
blameworthy 탓할 만한, 책임이 있는
tendency 경향
cite 인용하다
abstract (논문의) 초록
overstate 과장하다
prestigious 명망 있는, 일류의
uncritically 무비판적으로
bait 미끼
incompatibility 상반, 양립할 수 없음
evolve 진화하다
outcome 결과
criticize 비판하다
instant 즉각적인

7. ④ 전깃불과 전기 시스템의 기술적, 경제적 중요성

직독/직해

Thomas Edison's name is synonymous with invention, /
Thomas Edison의 이름은 발명과 동의어이다 /

and his most famous invention, the electric light bulb, /
그리고 그의 가장 유명한 발명품인 전구는 /

is a familiar symbol / for that flash of inspired genius /
친숙한 상징이다 / 영감을 받은 번득이는 그러한 천재성을 나타내는 /

traditionally associated with the inventive act.
전통적으로 창의적 행위와 연관되는

Besides being the exemplar of the "bright idea," / however, /
'총명한 아이디어'의 표본이라는 것 외에도 / 그러나 /

Edison's electric light is worthy of study for other reasons.
Edison의 전깃불은 다른 이유로 연구할 가치가 있다

The technical and economic importance of the light and of the electrical system /
전깃불과 전기 시스템의 기술적, 경제적 중요성은 /

that surrounded it / matches that of any other invention / we could name, /
그 주변을 둘러싸고 있는 / 다른 어떤 발명품의 그것에 필적한다 / 우리가 열거할 수 있는 /

at least from the last two hundred years.
적어도 지난 200년 이래

The introduction and spread of electric light and power /
전깃불과 전력의 도입과 확산은 /

was one of the key steps / in the transformation of the world /
핵심 단계 중 하나였다 / 세상의 전환에 있어서 /

from an industrial age, / characterized by iron and coal and steam, /
산업 시대에서 / 철, 석탄, 증기를 특징으로 하는 /

to a post-industrial one, / in which electricity was joined /
후기 산업 시대로의 / 전기가 결합된 /

by petroleum, light metals and alloys, and internal combustion engines /
석유, 경금속과 합금 그리고 내연 기관에 의해 /

to give the twentieth century its distinctive form and character.
20세기에 특유한 형태와 특성을 부여한

Our own time still largely carries the stamp of this age, /
우리 자신의 시대는 여전히 대체로 이 시대의 흔적을 지니고 있다 /

however dazzled we may be /
우리가 아무리 감탄할지라도 /

by the electronic, computerized, and media wonders of the twenty-first century.
21세기의 전자, 전산화 그리고 미디어의 경이에

Thomas Edison의 이름은 발명과 동의어이고, 그의 가장 유명한 발명품인 전구는 전통적으로 창의적 행위와 연관되는, 영감을 받은 번득이는 그러한 천재성을 나타내는 친숙한 상징이다. 그러나 Edison의 전깃불은 '총명한 아이디어'의 표본이라는 것 외에도 다른 이유로 연구할 가치가 있다. 전깃불과 그 주변을 둘러싸고 있는 전기 시스템의 기술적, 경제적 중요성은 적어도 지난 200년 이래 우리가 열거할 수 있는 다른 어떤 발명품의 기술적, 경제적 중요성에 필적한다. 전깃불과 전력의 도입과 확산은 세상이 철, 석탄, 증기를 특징으로 하는 산업 시대에서, 전기가 석유, 경금속과 합금 그리고 내연 기관과 결합해 20세기에 특유한 형태와 특성을 부여한, 후기 산업 시대로의 전환에 핵심 단계 중 하나였다. 우리가 21세기의 전자, 전산화 그리고 미디어의 경이에 아무리 감탄할지라도, 우리 자신의 시대는 여전히 대체로 이 시대의 흔적을 지니고 있다.

① 다양한 분야의 창의적 아이디어를 결합한다
② 산업 시대의 한계를 극복하기 위해 노력한다
③ 학문적 탐구의 이론적 배경이다
④ 이전의 전기 혁명의 영향력 하에 있다
⑤ 미래 세대를 위해 비축된 자원에 의존한다

문제풀이

이 글은 에디슨이 발명한 전깃불과 전기 시스템의 기술적, 경제적 중요성이 지난 200년 이래 어떤 다른 발명품의 중요성에 필적하고 전깃불과 전력의 도입과 확산이 산업 시대에서 20세기의 후기 산업 시대로의 전환에 핵심 단계 중 하나였다는 내용의 글이다. 따라서 밑줄 친 부분 'carries the stamp of this age(이 시대의 흔적을 지니고 있다)'가 의미하는 것으로 가장 적절한 것은 ④ 'is under the influence of earlier electrical innovations(이전의 전기 혁명의 영향력 하에 있다)'이다.

어휘·어구

synonymous 동의어의
invention 발명(품)
light bulb 전구
flash 번득임, 섬광
inspire 영감을 주다
genius 천재성, 천재
associated 연관된
inventive 창의적인
besides ~외에도
exemplar 표본
be worthy of ~의 가치가 있다
technical 기술적인
surround 둘러싸다
match 필적하다, 맞먹다
introduction 도입
spread 확산
transformation 전환, 변화, 탈바꿈
characterize 특징을 이루다, 특징짓다
post-industrial 후기 산업의
petroleum 석유
light metal 경금속
internal combustion engine 내연 기관
distinctive 특유한, 뚜렷이 구별되는
stamp 흔적, 발자취
dazzle 감탄하게 하다, 눈이 부시게 하다
wonder 경이, 기적; 궁금해하다

8. ② 전문가에 대한 신뢰

직독/직해

Scientists have no special purchase /
과학자들은 특별한 강점이 없으며 /

on moral or ethical decisions; /
도덕적 또는 윤리적 결정에 있어서 /

a climate scientist is no more qualified /
기후 과학자가 자격이 없는 것은 /

to comment on health care reform /
건강 의료 개혁에 대해 견해를 밝힐 /

than a physicist is to judge /
물리학자가 판단할 자격이 없는 것과 같다 /

the causes of bee colony collapse.
꿀벌 집단의 붕괴 원인을

The very features that create expertise in a specialized domain /
전문화된 영역에서의 전문 지식을 만들어 내는 바로 그 특성이 /

lead to ignorance / in many others.
무지로 이어진다 / 많은 다른 영역에서의

In some cases lay people /
일부의 상황에서 전문가가 아닌 사람들 /

— farmers, fishermen, patients, native peoples — /
농부, 어부, 환자, 토착민이, /

may have relevant experiences /
관련 경험을 가지고 있을 수 있다 /

that scientists can learn from.
과학자들이 그것으로부터 배울 수 있는

Indeed, in recent years, /
실제로, 최근 들어 /

scientists have begun to recognize this: /
과학자들은 이 점을 인식하기 시작했는데 /

the Arctic Climate Impact Assessment includes observations /
북극 기후 영향 평가는 관찰을 포함하고 있다 /

gathered from local native groups.
지역 토착 집단에게서 수집된

So our trust needs to be limited, and focused.
따라서 우리의 신뢰는 제한되고 초점이 맞춰져야 한다

It needs to be very *particular*.
그것은 매우 '특정할' 필요가 있다

Blind trust will get us /
맹목적 신뢰는 우리를 봉착하게 할 것이다 /

into at least as much trouble as no trust at all.
최소한 신뢰가 전혀 없는 것만큼이나 문제에

But / without some degree of trust /
그러나 / 어느 정도의 신뢰가 없다면 /

in our designated experts /
우리의 지정된 전문가들에 대한 /

— the men and women who have devoted their lives /
생애를 바친 남녀들 /

to sorting out tough questions /
어려운 질문들을 처리하는 데 /

about the natural world / we live in — /
자연 세계에 관한 / 우리가 사는 /

we are paralyzed, / in effect not knowing /
우리는 마비되고 / 사실상 알지 못할 것이다 /

whether to make ready for the morning commute or not.
아침 통근을 위해 준비해야 할지 말아야 할지를

과학자들은 도덕적 또는 윤리적 결정에 있어서 특별한 강점이 없으며, 기후 과학자가 건강 의료 개혁에 대해 견해를 밝힐 자격이 없는 것은 물리학자가 꿀벌 집단의 붕괴 원인을 판단할 자격이 없는 것과 같다. 전문화된 영역에서의 전문 지식을 만들어 내는 바로 그 특성이 많은 다른 영역에서의 무지로 이어진다. 일부의 상황에서, 전문가가 아닌 사람들, 즉 농부, 어부, 환자, 토착민이, 과학자들이 그것으로부터 배울 수 있는 관련 경험을 가지고 있을 수 있다. 실제로, 최근 들어 과학자들은 이 점을 인식하기 시작했는데, 북극 기후 영향 평가는 지역 토착 집단에게서 수집된 관찰을 포함하고 있다. 따라서 우리의 신뢰는 제한되고 초점이 맞춰져야 한다. 그것은 매우 '특정할' 필요가 있다. 맹목적 신뢰는 최소한 신뢰가 전혀 없는 것만큼이나 우리를 문제에 봉착하게 할 것이다. 그러나 우리의 지정된 전문가들, 즉 우리가 사는 자연 세계에 관한 어려운 질문들을 처리하는 데 생애를 바친 남녀들에 대한 어느 정도의 신뢰가 없다면, 우리는 마비되고, 사실상 아침 통근을 위해 준비해야 할지 말아야 할지를 알지 못할 것이다.

① 비전문가에 의해서 대중화된 의심스러운 사실
② 전문화된 전문가에 의해 제공되는 손쉽게 적용할 수 있는 정보
③ 중대한 결정에 거의 영향을 주지 못하는 흔한 지식
④ 전문가와 전문가가 아닌 사람들 모두에 의해 생산되는 실용적인 정보
⑤ 지역 공동체에 널리 퍼진 편향된 지식

문제풀이

전문가들은 비전문 영역에서 특별한 강점이 없어서 그들에 대한 우리의 신뢰는 제한되고 초점이 맞춰져야 한다고 했지만 연구에 일생을 바친 전문가에 대한 어느 정도의 신뢰는 필요하다는 내용의 글로, 평생을 자연 세계에 관한 난제를 처리한 전문가에 대한 신뢰가 없으면 그들에 의해 제공되는 정보를 모를 것이라는 내용이 되어야 한다. 따라서 밑줄 친 'whether to make ready for the morning commute or not'가 의미하는 바로 가장 적절한 것은 ② 'readily applicable information offered by specialized experts(전문화된 전문가에 의해 제공되는 손쉽게 적용할 수 있는 정보)'이다.

구조 다시보기

도입	과학자들은 비전문 영역에서는 특별한 강점이 없음
전개	어떤 상황에서는 과학자들이 비전문가에게서 배울 수 있음

결과	전문가에 대한 우리의 신뢰는 제한되고 초점이 맞춰져야 함
반론	하지만 연구에 일생을 바친 전문가에 대한 어느 정도의 신뢰는 필요함

어휘·어구

purchase 강점, 유리한 지반
moral 도덕적인
ethical 윤리적인
qualified 자격이 있는
comment 논평, 언급
reform 개혁, 개선
physicist 물리학자
colony 집단
collapse 붕괴
feature 특징
expertise 전문 지식
relevant 관련 있는
domain 영역
ignorance 무지
Arctic 북극의
assessment 평가
degree 정도
designate 지정하다
devote 바치다
sort out ~을 처리하다
questionable 의심스러운
popularize 대중화하다
readily 손쉽게
applicable 적용되는
crucial 중대한
practical 실용적인
biased 편향된

정답률 63%

9. ② 환경 기자의 역할

직독/직해

There is an African proverb / that says, /
아프리카 속담이 있다 / 말하는 /
'Till the lions have their historians, /
사자들은 그들의 역사가를 갖게 될 때까지 /
tales of hunting will always glorify the hunter'.
사냥 이야기는 언제나 사냥꾼을 미화할 것이라고
The proverb is about power, control and law making.
그 속담은 권력, 통제, 법 제정에 관한 것이다
Environmental journalists have to play the role /
환경 기자는 역할을 해야 한다 /
of the 'lion's historians'. '사자의 역사가'의
They have to put across /
그들은 이해시켜야 한다 /
the point of view of the environment /
환경에 대한 관점을 /
to people who make the laws.
법을 제정하는 사람들에게
They have to be the voice of wild India.
그들은 인도의 야생 자연의 대변자여야 한다
The present rate of human consumption /
현재 인간의 소비율은 /
is completely unsustainable.
완전히 지속 불가능하다
Forest, wetlands, wastelands, coastal zones, eco-sensitive zones, /
숲, 습지, 황무지, 해안 지대, 환경 민감 지역 /
they are all seen as disposable /
그곳들은 모두 마음대로 이용할 수 있는 곳으로 여겨진다 /
for the accelerating demands of human population.
가속화되고 있는 인구 수요를 위해
But to ask for any change / in human behaviour /
하지만 어떤 변화든 요구하는 것은 / 인간의 행동에 /
— whether it be to cut down on consumption, /
소비를 줄이든 /
alter lifestyles / or decrease population growth — /
생활 방식을 바꾸든 / 또는 인구 증가를 줄이든 /
is seen as a violation of human rights.
인권 침해로 여겨진다
But at some point / human rights become 'wrongs'.
그러나 어느 시점에 / 인권은 '틀린 것'이 된다
It's time / we changed our thinking /
시간이다 / 우리가 우리의 생각을 바꿔야 할 /
so that there is no difference /
차이가 없도록 /
between the rights of humans and the rights of the rest of the environment.
인간의 권리와 나머지 환경의 권리 사이의

'사자들은 그들의 역사가를 갖게 될 때까지, 사냥 이야기는 언제나 사냥꾼을 미화할 것이다.'라고 말하는 아프리카 속담이 있다. 그 속담은 권력, 통제, 법 제정에 관한 것이다. 환경 기자는 '사자의 역사가' 역할을 해야 한다. 그들은 법을 제정하는 사람들에게 환경에 대한 관점을 이해시켜야 한다. 그들은 인도의 야생 자연의 대변자여야 한다. 현재 인간의 소비율은 완전히 지속 불가능하다. 숲, 습지, 황무지, 해안 지대, 환경 민감 지역, 그곳들은 모두 가속화되고 있는 인구 수요를 위해 마음대로 이용할 수 있는 곳으로 여겨진다. 하지만 소비를 줄이든, 생활 방식을 바꾸든, 또는 인구 증가를 줄이든, 인간의 행동에 어떤 변화든 요구하는 것은 인권 침해로 여겨진다. 그러나 어느 시점에 인권은 '틀린 것'이 된다. 인간의 권리와 나머지 환경의 권리 사이에 차이가 없도록 우리의 생각을 바꿔야 할 시간이다.

① 한 종의 생물학적 진화의 역사를 알아내는 것
② **자연을 위해 지속 가능한 인간의 행동으로 전환을 촉구하는 것**
③ 널리 퍼진 인권 침해에 맞서 싸우는 것
④ 더 드러나지 않은 사람들을 위해서 역사를 다시 쓰는 것
⑤ 환경법 제정자들의 권한을 제한하는 것

문제풀이

환경 기자는 환경법 제정자들에게 환경에 대한 관점을 이해시키고 야생 자연의 대변자 역할을 해야 한다고 하면서, 인간이 자연을 지속불가능한 마음대로 이용할 수 있는 곳으로 여겨서는 안 되고 인권과 나머지 환경의 권리 사이에 차이가 없도록 우리의 생각을 바꿔야 한다고 했다. 따라서 밑줄 친 'the role of the 'lion's historians'가 의미하는 바로 가장 적절한 것은 ② 'urging a shift to sustainable human behaviour for nature(자연을 위해 지속가능한 인간의 행동으로 전환을 촉구하는 것)'이다.

어휘·어구

glorify 미화하다, 기리다
put across ~을 이해시키다
consumption 소비
unsustainable 지속 불가능한
wasteland 황무지
eco-sensitive 환경에 민감한
disposable 마음대로 이용할 수 있는
accelerating 가속화되고 있는
cut down on ~을 줄이다
alter 바꾸다
violation 침해, 위반
uncover 알아내다, 적발하다
biological 생물학의
evolution 진화
urge 촉구하다
sustainable 지속 가능한
widespread 널리 퍼진
restrict 제한하다

정답률 82%

10. ④ 디저트를 먹는 Chloe와 할머니

직독/직해

When the tea tray was being carried /
찻쟁반이 옮겨지고 있을 때 /
across the room / to their table, /
방을 가로질러 / 그들의 테이블로 /
Chloe's eyes rounded / Chloe의 눈은 휘둥그레졌다 /
and she almost gasped out loud.
그리고 그녀는 크게 헉하는 숨 소리를 낼 뻔했다
There were lots of tiny desserts and mini
작은 디저트와 미니 샌드위치와 비스킷처럼 생긴 작은 것들이 많이 있었다
sandwiches and small biscuit-looking things.
Where to start? 뭐부터 먹을까?
Where to start? 뭐부터 먹을까?
Her grandmother smiled / 그녀의 할머니는 미소를 지었다 /
and winked at her / from across the table.
그리고 그녀에게 윙크했다 / 테이블 건너편에서
Chloe winked back. Chloe도 윙크했다
She took a sip of the sweet tea and waited /
그녀는 달콤한 차를 한 모금 마시며 기다렸다 /
for her grandmother / to make the first move.
할머니가 / 먼저 행동하기를
She carefully mirrored her grandmother's actions /
그녀는 조심스럽게 자신의 할머니의 행동을 따라 했다 /
and started with a small, delicate sandwich.
그리고 작고 아기자기한 샌드위치로 시작했다
It was good. 그것은 맛있었다
She ate it up and selected another.
그녀는 그것을 다 먹고 다른 것을 선택했다
After a time, / 얼마 후에 /
all the sandwiches were eaten up /
모든 샌드위치를 다 먹어 버렸다 /
and Chloe boldly chose the biscuit-looking thing /
그리고 Chloe는 비스킷처럼 생긴 것을 대담하게 선택했다 /
before her grandmother. 그녀의 할머니보다 먼저
"Aren't the scones lovely, dear?"
스콘이 맛있지 않니, 얘야?
asked her grandmother, / 그녀의 할머니가 물었다 /
as she spread cream and jam on hers.
그녀는 자신의 것에 크림과 잼을 바르면서
Scones, was that what they were called?
스콘, 그게 그것들의 이름인가?
Chloe had already started to eat hers /
Chloe는 이미 자신의 것을 먹기 시작했다 /
without the cream and jam; / 크림과 잼을 바르지 않고 /
in fact, it was mostly all / in her mouth already.
사실, 그것은 거의 대부분이 있었다 / 이미 그녀의 입안에

찻쟁반이 방을 가로질러 그들의 테이블로 옮겨지고 있을 때, Chloe의 눈은 휘둥그레졌고, 그녀는 크게 헉하는 숨 소리를 낼 뻔했다. 작은 디저트와 미니 샌드위치와 비스킷처럼 생긴 작은 것들이 많이 있었다. 뭐부터 먹을까? 뭐부터 먹을까? 그녀의 할머니는 테이블 건너편에서 미소를 지으며 ① 그녀에게 윙크했다. Chloe도 윙크했다. ② 그녀는 달콤한 차를 한 모금 마시며 할머니가 먼저 행동하기를 기다렸다. ③ 그녀는 조심스럽게 할머니의 행동을 따라 하면서 작고 아기자기한 샌드위치로 시작했다. 그것은 맛있었다. 그녀는 그것을 다 먹고 다른 것을 선택했다. 얼마 후에 모든 샌드위치를 다 먹어 버리고서 Chloe는 비스킷처럼 생긴 것을 할머니보다 먼저 대담하게 선택했다. ④ 그녀는 자신의 스콘에 크림과 잼을 바르면서 "스콘이 맛있지 않니, 얘야?"라고 그녀의 할머니가 물었다. 스콘, 그게 그것들의 이름인가? Chloe는 크림과 잼을 바르지 않고 이미 자신의 것을 먹기 시작했는데, 사실, 그것은 거의 대부분이 이미 ⑤ 그녀의 입안에 있었다.

문제풀이

①, ②, ③, ⑤는 Chloe를 가리키고, ④는 Chloe의 할머니를 가리킨다.

어휘·어구

gasp 헉하고 숨을 쉬다
take a sip 한 모금 마시다
delicate 정교한
boldly 대담하게

본문 023쪽

문법 플러스 4. 동사의 시제

A. 1. causes
2. shows
3. met
4. gone
5. had lost
6. will have been
7. broke out

1 [해석]▶ Newton은 중력 때문에 물체가 낙하한다고 믿었다.
[해설]▶ 과학적 사실과 진리는 시제일치를 받지 않고, 항상 현재시제를 사용한다.

2 [해석]▶ Sam은 Sally가 파티에 나타난다면 기쁠 것이다.
[해설]▶ 조건과 시간을 나타내는 부사절은 미래 의미를 현재시제로 나타낸다.

3 [해석]▶ 그는 그녀를 지난주에 만났는데, 첫눈에 사랑하게 되었다.
[해설]▶ 과거를 뚜렷하게 나타내는 부사(구)[ago, yesterday, last week ~]가 있는 문장은 현재완료가 아닌, 과거시제로 나타내야 한다.

4 [해석]▶ Sally는 런던에 가고 없다. 그녀는 지금 여기 없다.
[해설]▶ have gone to는 '~에 가고 여기 없다'는 의미이고, has been to는 '~에 다녀왔다'는 의미이다.

5 [해석]▶ Sally는 집에 왔을 때, 자신의 집 열쇠를 잃어버린 것을 알았다.
[해설]▶ 과거 이전의 일에 대해 말할 때는 과거완료형을 사용한다.

6 [해석]▶ 이번 주 일요일까지 베키와 나는 함께한 지 100일이 되었다.
[해설]▶ 미래의 특정 시점까지 계속을 나타내고 싶을 때는 미래완료형이 사용된다.

7 [해석]▶ 나는 프랑스 혁명이 1789년에 발생한 것으로 배웠다.
[해설]▶ 역사적 사실은 시제일치에 따르지 않고 항상 과거시제로 사용한다.

본문 023쪽

B. 1. freezes
2. gets
3. started
4. hasn't shown
5. hadn't
6. leaves
7. moves

1 [해석]▶ 물은 100도에 끓고, 0도에 언다.
[해설]▶ 과학적 사실은 현재시제를 사용한다.

2 [해석]▶ Sally가 집에 도착할 무렵에는 그녀의 아버지가 파리를 향해 떠났을 것이다.
[해설]▶ 시간과 조건 부사절은 미래 의미를 현재시제로 나타낸다.

3 [해석]▶ 영화는 5분 전부터 시작하였다.
[해설]▶ 과거를 뚜렷하게 나타내는 부사(ago)가 있는 문장은 현재완료가 아닌 과거시제로 나타내야 한다.

4 [해석]▶ 그는 30분 전에 도착하기로 되어 있는데, 아직도 도착하지 않았다.
[해설]▶ 과거의 행위나 상태가 현재에 미치는 경우 현재완료형을 사용한다.

5 [해석]▶ 그들은 예약을 하지 않아서 테이블을 구하지 못했다.
[해설]▶ 과거 이전에 일어난 일은 과거완료형으로 나타낸다.

6 [해석]▶ 그 비행기는 오늘밤 9시에 파리로 떠난다.
[해설]▶ 일정상 확실한 미래는 현재형이나 현재진행형으로 미래를 나타낼 수 있다.

7 [해석]▶ 갈릴레오는 지구가 태양 주위를 돈다고 믿었다.
[해설]▶ 불변의 진리나 과학적 사실은 시제 일치가 적용되지 않고 현재시제로 사용한다.

본문 024쪽

숙어 플러스 4. 수능 필수 숙어 4회

1. charge 2. likely
3. tired 4. bear

05. 글의 요지

본문 026쪽

Day 05

1. ① 2. ⑤ 3. ⑤ 4. ① 5. ②
6. ② 7. ① 8. ① 9. ① 10. ①

대표 기출 ① 도시에서 효율적인 운송 수단

직독/직해

Urban delivery vehicles / can be adapted /
도시의 배달 운송 수단은 / 조정될 수 있는데 /
to better suit the density of urban distribution, /
도시 배치의 밀집 상태에 더 잘 맞도록 /
which often involves smaller vehicles such as vans, / including bicycles.
거기에는 흔히 밴과 같은 더 작은 운송 수단을 포함하는데 / 자전거도 포함된다
The latter have the potential / to become a preferred 'last-mile' vehicle, /
후자(자전거)는 가능성이 있다 / 선호되는 '최종 단계' 운송 수단이 될 /
particularly in high-density and congested areas.
특히 밀도가 높고 혼잡한 지역에서
In locations where bicycle use is high, / such as the Netherlands, /
자전거 사용이 많은 지역에서는 / 네덜란드와 같이 /
delivery bicycles are also used / to carry personal cargo (e.g. groceries).
배달 자전거가 또한 사용된다 / 개인의 짐(예를 들어 식료품)을 운반하는 데도
Due to their low acquisition and maintenance costs, /
낮은 구매와 유지 비용 때문에 /
cargo bicycles convey much potential /
짐 자전거는 많은 잠재력을 전달한다 /
in developed and developing countries alike, /
선진국에서 개발도상국에서 똑같이 /
such as the becak (a three-wheeled bicycle) in Indonesia.
그리고 인도네시아의 베짝(바퀴가 세 개 달린 자전거)과 같이
Services using electrically assisted delivery tricycles /
전기 보조 배달용 세발자전거를 이용하는 서비스는 /
have been successfully implemented in France /
프랑스에서 성공적으로 시행되었다 /
and are gradually being adopted across Europe /
그리고 유럽 전역에서 서서히 도입되고 있다 /
for services as varied as parcel and catering deliveries.
그리고 소포나 음식 배달과 같은 다양한 서비스를 위해
Using bicycles as cargo vehicles / is particularly encouraged /
자전거를 화물 운송 수단으로 사용하는 것은 / 특히 권장된다 /
when combined with policies /
정책과 결합할 때 /
that restrict motor vehicle access to specific areas of a city, /
도시의 특정 지역에 차량 접근을 제한하는 /
such as downtown or commercial districts, /
도심이나 상업 지구처럼 /
or with the extension of dedicated bike lanes.
또는 자전거 전용 도로의 확장과 (결합할 때)

도시의 배달 운송 수단은 도시 배치의 밀집 상태에 더 잘 맞도록 조정될

수 있는데, 거기에는 흔히 밴과 같은 더 작은 운송 수단을 포함하는데, 자전거도 포함된다. 후자는 특히 밀도가 높고 혼잡한 지역에서 선호되는 '최종 단계' 운송 수단이 될 가능성이 있다. 네덜란드와 같이 자전거 사용이 많은 지역에서는 배달 자전거가 또한 개인의 짐(예를 들어 식료품)을 운반하는 데도 사용된다. 낮은 구매와 유지 비용 때문에 짐 자전거는 선진국에서 그리고 인도네시아의 베짝(바퀴가 세 개 달린 자전거)과 같이 개발도상국에서 똑같이 많은 잠재력을 전달한다. 전기 보조 배달용 세발자전거를 이용하는 서비스는 프랑스에서 성공적으로 시행되었고 소포나 음식 배달과 같은 다양한 서비스를 위해 유럽 전역에서 서서히 도입되고 있다. 자전거를 화물 운송 수단으로 사용하는 것은 도심이나 상업 지구처럼 도시의 특정 지역에 차량 접근을 제한하는 정책이나 자전거 전용 도로의 확장과 결합할 때 특히 권장된다.

문제풀이

밀도가 높고 혼잡한 도심에서 자전거가 최종 단계 운송 수단이 될 가능성이 있으며, 여러 나라에서 자전거를 운송 수단으로 사용하는 서비스가 서서히 도입되고 있다는 내용의 글이다. 따라서 글의 요지로 가장 적절한 것은 ① '도시에서 자전거는 효율적인 배송 수단으로 사용될 수 있다.'이다.

어휘·어구

urban 도시의
vehicle 운송 수단, 차량
adapt 맞추다 조정하다
density 밀집 상태
distribution 배치, 분포
congested 혼잡한
cargo 짐, 화물
acquisition 인수, 습득
maintenance 유지
convey 전달하다, 운반하다
assist 보조하다
implement 시행하다
gradually 서서히
adopt 도입하다, 채택하다
encourage 장려하다, 권장하다
restrict 제한하다
access 접근
commercial district 상업 지구
extension 확장
dedicated 전용의

1. ① 정보의 양보다는 유용한 사용이 중요함

직독/직해

Many people say /
많은 이들이 말한다 /
that we should take full advantage of the privileges of the Internet /
인터넷의 특혜를 충분히 활용해야 한다고 /
by forever learning more and more.
끊임없이 점점 더 많이 배움으로써
They see no limit to / how much information a person ought to consume /
그들은 ~에 대한 제한을 두지 않는다 / 한 사람이 얼마나 많은 정보를 소비해야 하는지
and never acknowledge the emotional and psychological cost /
그리고 감정적, 심리적 비용을 결코 인정하지 않는다 /
of cramming facts into our brains.
우리의 뇌에 사실을 잔뜩 밀어 넣는 데 드는
If we aren't using the wealth of available data /
만약 우리가 이용 가능한 그 풍부한 데이터를 이용하지 않는다면 /
to make ourselves more productive and useful to society, /
우리 자신을 사회에 더 생산적이고 유용하게 하는 데에 /
what's the point of having it?
그것을 가지고 있는 것이 무슨 소용이 있는가
While access to information is a privilege, / it's also a burden.
정보를 이용할 수 있다는 것은 특혜지만 / 그것은 또한 부담이다
This is especially true / when we treat being well-read as an obligation /
이것은 특히 그렇다 / 우리가 박식한 것을 의무로 취급할 때 /
that can't be escaped.
피할 수 없는
Constant exposure to upsetting news can be traumatic.
마음을 상하게 만드는 뉴스를 끊임없이 접하면 정신적 외상을 입을 수 있다
An unending flood of information makes it hard /
끝없이 쇄도하는 정보는 어렵게 만든다 /
to pause and reflect on anything you've learned.
잠시 멈춰, 배운 어떤 것이든 되돌아보는 것을
At some point, / even the most voracious of readers needs to pull the plug /
어느 시점에서는 / 가장 열심인 독자라도 플러그를 뽑을 필요가 있다 /
and stop the constant drip of facts, figures, and meaningless Internet fights.
그리고 사실, 수치, 그리고 무의미한 인터넷 싸움이 끊임없이 쏟아지는 것을 멈추게 해야 할
We're living in an era of information overload /
우리는 정보 과부하의 시대에 살고 있다 /
— and the solution is not to learn more /
해결책은 더 많은 것을 배우는 것이 아니라 /
but to step back and consume a smaller amount of data /
한 걸음 물러나 더 적은 양의 데이터를 소비하는 것이다 /
in a more meaningful way.
더 의미 있게

끊임없이 점점 더 많이 배움으로써 인터넷의 특혜를 충분히 활용해야 한다고 많은 이들이 말한다. 그들은 한 사람이 얼마나 많은 정보를 소비해야 하는지에 대한 제한을 두지 않으며, 우리의 뇌에 사실을 잔뜩 밀어 넣는 데 드는 감정적, 심리적 비용을 결코 인정하지 않는다. 만약 우리가 이용 가능한 그 풍부한 데이터를 우리 자신을 사회에 더 생산적이고 유용하게 하는 데에 이용하지 않는다면, 그것을 가지고 있는 것이 무슨 소용이 있는가? 정보를 이용할 수 있다는 것은 특혜지만, 그것은 또한 부담이다. 이것은 우리가 박식한 것을 피할 수 없는 의무로 취급할 때 특히 그렇다. 마음을 상하게 만드는 뉴스를 끊임없이 접하면 정신적 외상을 입을 수 있다. 끝없이 쇄도하는 정보로 인해 여러분은 잠시 멈춰, 배운 어떤 것이든 되돌아보는 것이 어려워진다. 어느 시점에서는 가장 열심인 독자라도 플러그를 뽑아서 사실, 수치, 그리고 무의미한 인터넷 싸움이 끊임없이 쏟아지는 것을 멈추게 해야 할 필요가 있다. 우리는 정보 과부하의 시대에 살고 있으며, 해결책은 더 많은 것을 배우는 것이 아니라 한 걸음 물러나 더 적은 양의 데이터를 더 의미 있게 소비하는 것이다.

문제풀이

인터넷의 도움으로 엄청난 정보를 습득할 수 있지만, 그 풍부한 데이터를 우리 자신을 사회에 더 생산적이고 유용하게 하는 데에 이용하지 않는다면 아무 소용이 없으므로 정보 과부하의 시대에서는 더 많은 것을 배우는 것보다 더 적은 양의 데이터를 더 의미 있게 소비할 필요가 있다는 내용의 글이다. 따라서 글의 요지로 가장 적절한 것은 ① '정보 습득의 양보다 정보의 유의미한 사용이 더 중요하다.'이다.

어휘·어구

take full advantage of ~을 충분히 활용하다
privilege 특혜
consume 소비하다
acknowledge 인정하다
psychological 심리적인
cram 밀어 넣다
productive 생산적인
treat 다루다
obligation 의무
constant 지속적인
exposure 노출
upsetting 속상하게 하는, 마음을 상하게 하는
traumatic 정신적 충격이 큰
pause 멈춤
reflect on ~을 되돌아보다
figure 수치
meaningless 무의미한
overload 과부하

2. ⑤ 조세 입법에 있어 중요한 것

직독/직해

Historically, / drafters of tax legislation /
역사적으로 / 조세 입법 입안자들은 /
are attentive to questions of economics and history, /
경제학과 역사 문제에는 주의를 기울인다 /
and less attentive to moral questions.
그리고 도덕적 질문에는 덜 주의를 기울인다
Questions of morality are often pushed to the side / in legislative debate, /
도덕성에 관한 질문은 종종 옆으로 미뤄지면서 / 입법 토론에서 /
labeled too controversial, too difficult to answer, /
너무 논란이 많거나, 대답하기 너무 어려운 것으로 분류된다 /
or, worst of all, / irrelevant to the project.
아니면 최악의 경우 / 계획과 무관한 것으로 (분류된다)
But, in fact, / the moral questions of taxation /
그러나 사실 / 조세의 도덕적 문제는 /
are at the very heart of the creation of tax laws.
세법을 만드는 바로 중심에 있다
Rather than irrelevant, / moral questions are fundamental / to the imposition of tax.
무관한 것이라기 보다는 / 도덕적 질문은 근본적이다 / 세금 부과에
Tax / is the application of a society's theories of distributive justice.
세금은 / 사회의 분배 정의 이론을 적용한 것이다
Economics can go a long way / towards helping a legislature determine /
경제학은 큰 도움이 될 수 있다 / 입법 기관이 결정하는 것을 돕는 것에 /
whether or not a particular tax law will help achieve a particular goal, /
특정 세법이 특정 목표를 달성하는 데 도움이 될지 말지를 /
but economics cannot, in a vacuum, identify the goal.
하지만 경제학이 고립되어 그 목표를 규명할 수는 없다.
Creating tax policy requires identifying a moral goal, /
조세 정책을 만드는 것은 도덕적 목표를 규명하는 것을 요구하는데 /
which is a task / that must involve ethics and moral analysis.
그것은 과업이다 / 윤리학과 도덕적 분석을 포함해야 하는

역사적으로, 조세 입법 입안자들은 경제학과 역사 문제에는 주의를 기울이고 도덕적 질문에는 덜 주의를 기울인다. 도덕성에 관한 질문은 종종 입법 토론에서 옆으로 미뤄지면서, 너무 논란이 많거나, 대답하기 너무 어렵거나, 아니면 최악의 경우, 계획과 무관한 것으로 분류된다. 그러나, 사실, 조세의 도덕적 문제는 세법을 만드는 바로 중심에 있다. 무관한 것이라기 보다는, 도덕적 질문은 세금 부과에 근본적이다. 세금은 사회의 분배 정의 이론을 적용한 것이다. 경제학은 입법 기관이 특정 세법이 특정 목표를 달성하는 데 도움이 될지 말지를 결정하는 것을 돕는 것에 큰 도움이 될 수 있지만, 경제학이 고립되어(=경제학만으로는) 그 목표를 규명할 수는 없다. 조세 정책을 만드는 것은 도덕적 목표를 규명하는 것을 요구하는데, 그것은 윤리학과 도덕적 분석을 포함해야 하는 과업이다.

문제풀이

도덕적 질문은 세금 부과에 근본적이라고 하면서, 조세 정책을 만들 때 윤리학과 도덕적 분석을 포함하는 도덕적 목표를 규명하는 것이 요구된다고 했다. 따라서 글의 요지로 가장 적절한 것은 ⑤ '세법을 만들 때 도덕적 목표를 설정하는 것이 중요하다.'이다.

어휘·어구

drafter 입안자
attentive to ~에 주의를 기울이는

moral 도덕적인
morality 도덕, 도덕성
legislative 입법의
debate 토론
label 분류하다
controversial 논란이 많은
irrelevant to ~과 무관한
taxation 조세
fundamental 근본적인
application 적용
distributive 분배적인
go a long way toward ~에 크게 도움이 되다
legislature 입법 기관, 입법부
in a vacuum 고립되어
identify 규명하다, 식별하다
ethics 윤리학
analysis 분석

정답률 91%

3. ⑤ 리더가 진실을 말해야 하는 이유

Giving honest information may be particularly relevant to integrity /
정직한 정보를 주는 것은 진실성과 특별히 관련되어 있을 수 있다 /
because honesty is so fundamental in discussions of trustworthiness.
정직이 신뢰성의 논의에서 매우 본질적이기 때문에
Unfortunately, / leaders are often reluctant to tell the truth.
유감스럽게도 / 리더들은 자주 진실을 말하는 것을 꺼린다
During times of crisis and change, / business leaders are often faced /
위기와 변화의 시간 동안 / 기업의 리더들은 자주 마주하게 된다 /
with the challenge of / either telling an uncomfortable truth, / remaining silent, /
(~하는) 도전에 / 불편한 진술을 말하거나 / 침묵을 유지하거나 /
or downplaying the severity of the situation.
또는 상황의 심각함을 가볍게 처리하는
There are plenty of other situations / in which, in the short term, /
많은 다른 상황이 있다 / 단기적으로는 /
it may be more comfortable / not to tell the truth to followers.
더 편할 수도 있는 / 추종자들에게 진실을 말하지 않는 것이
Ultimately, / however, / even dishonesty /
궁극적으로 / 하지만 / 심지어 부정직함도 /
that was meant to protect employee morale / will eventually be exposed, /
직원의 사기를 보호하고자 하는 / 결국 노출될 것이다 /
undermining trustworthiness / at a time /
신뢰성을 훼손시키면서 / 시간에 /
when commitment to the organization is most vital.
조직에 대한 헌신이 가장 중요한
Even concerted efforts at secrecy can backfire, /
비밀엄수에 합의한 노력조차 실패할 수 있다 /
as employees may simply "fill in the gaps" in their understanding /
직원들이 이해의 부족함을 채울 수 있기 때문에 /
with their own theories / about the leader's behavior.
자신만의 이론을 가지고 / 리더의 행동에 대한
Therefore, / leaders need to take steps /
그러므로 / 리더는 조치를 취할 필요가 있다 /
to explain the true reasons for their decisions /
자신의 결정에 대한 진실된 이유를 설명하려는 /
to those individuals affected by it,
그것에 의해 영향을 받는 그러한 개인들에게
leaving less room for negative interpretations of leader behavior.
리더의 행동에 대해 부정적 해석에 대한 여지를 덜 남기며

정직은 신뢰성의 논의에서 매우 본질적이기 때문에, 정직한 정보를 주는 것은 진실성과 특별히 관련되어 있을 수 있다. 유감스럽게도, 리더들은 자주 진실을 말하는 것을 꺼린다. 위기와 변화의 시간 동안 기업의 리더들은 불편한 진실을 말하거나 침묵을 유지하거나 상황의 심각함을 가볍게 처리하는 도전에 자주 마주하게 된다. 단기적으로는 추종자들에게 진실을 말하지 않는 것이 더 편할 수도 있는 많은 다른 상황이 있다. 하지만 궁극적으로 직원의 사기를 보호하고자 하는 부정직함도 결국 노출될 것이며 조직에 대한 헌신이 가장 중요한 시간에 신뢰성을 훼손시킨다. 직원들은 리더의 행동에 대한 자신만의 이론을 가지고 이해의 부족함을 채울 수 있기 때문에 비밀엄수에 합의한 노력조차 실패할 수 있다. 그러므로 리더는 그것에 의해 영향을 받는 그러한 개인들에게 자신의 결정에 대한 진실된 이유를 설명하려는 조치를 취할 필요가 있으며, 리더의 행동에 대해 부정적 해석에 대한 여지를 덜 남긴다.

문제풀이

단기적으로는 추종자들에게 진실을 말하지 않는 것이 더 편할 상황이 있긴 하지만, 결국 진실은 알려지게 되고 직원들의 사기를 떨어뜨리고 조직의 신뢰성을 훼손시키게 되기 때문에 리더는 구성원에게 진실을 알려야 한다는 내용의 글이다. 따라서 글의 요지로 가장 적절한 것은 ⑤ '리더는 조직 내 신뢰 유지를 위해 구성원에게 진실을 알려야 한다.'이다.

어휘·어구

relevant to ~에 관련된
integrity 진실성
fundamental 본질적인
trustworthiness 신뢰성
reluctant 꺼리는
downplay 경시하다, 얕보다
severity 가혹함
ultimately 궁극적으로
morale 사기, 의욕
undermine 해치다
commitment 헌신
vital 중요한
concerted 합의된
backfire 역효과를 낳다
interpretation 해석

정답률 61%

4. ① 주체적인 소비자가 되는 방법

Often overlooked, / but just as important a stakeholder, /
종종 간과된다 / 하지만 이해관계자만큼 중요한 것은 /
is the consumer / who plays a large role / in the notion of the privacy paradox.
소비자이다 / 큰 역할을 하는 / 개인 정보 역설이라는 개념에서
Consumer engagement levels in all manner of digital experiences and communities /
모든 방식의 디지털 경험과 공동체에서 소비자의 참여 수준은 /
have simply exploded / — and they show little or no signs of slowing.
그야말로 폭발적으로 증가했다 / 그리고 둔화될 기미를 거의 또는 전혀 보이지 않는다
There is an awareness among consumers, /
소비자들 사이에서는 인식이 있다 /
not only that their personal data helps / to drive the rich experiences /
자신들의 개인 정보가 도움이 된다는 것뿐만 아니라 / 풍부한 경험을 추진하는 데 /
that these companies provide, /
이런 회사들이 제공하는 /
but also that sharing this data is the price / you pay for these experiences, /
이 정보를 공유하는 것이 대가이기도 하다는 / 이런 경험에 대해 지불하는 /
in whole or in part.
전체로든 부분으로든
Without a better understanding /
더 잘 이해하지 못하면 /
of the what, when, and why of data collection and use, /
정보 수집 및 이용의 내용과 시기, 이유를 /
the consumer is often left feeling vulnerable and conflicted.
소비자는 종종 취약하고 갈등을 겪는다는 느낌을 받는다
"I love this restaurant-finder app on my phone, /
내 전화기에 있는 이 식당 검색 앱이 마음에 들어 /
but what happens to my data / if I press 'ok' /
하지만 내 정보에는 무슨 일이 일어나는가 / 'ok'를 누르면 /
when asked if that app can use my current location?"
그 앱이 내 현재 위치를 이용할 수 있느냐고 물을 때
Armed with tools / that can provide them options, /
도구로 무장된 / 그들에게 선택권을 제공할 수 있는 /
the consumer moves / from passive bystander to active participant.
소비자는 이동한다 / 수동적인 방관자에서 능동적인 참여자로

종종 간과되지만 이해관계자만큼 중요한 것은 개인 정보 역설이라는 개념에서 큰 역할을 하는 소비자이다. 모든 방식의 디지털 경험과 공동체에서 소비자의 참여 수준은 그야말로 폭발적으로 증가했으며, 둔화될 기미를 거의 또는 전혀 보이지 않는다. 소비자들 사이에서는 이런 회사들이 제공하는 풍부한 경험을 추진하는 데 자신들의 개인 정보가 도움이 된다는 것뿐만 아니라, 이 정보를 공유하는 것이 전체로든 부분으로든, 이런 경험에 대해 지불하는 대가이기도 하다는 인식이 있다. 정보 수집 및 이용의 내용과 시기, 이유를 더 잘 이해하지 못하면, 소비자는 종종 취약하고 갈등을 겪는다는 느낌을 받는다. '내 전화기에 있는 이 식당 검색 앱이 마음에 드는데, 그 앱이 내 현재 위치를 이용할 수 있느냐고 물을 때 'ok'를 누르면 내 정보에는 무슨 일이 일어나는가?' 그들에게 선택권을 제공할 수 있는 도구로 무장된 소비자는 수동적인 방관자에서 능동적인 참여자로 이동한다.

문제풀이

소비자는 개인 정보의 수집 및 이용의 내용과 시기, 그리고 이유에 대해 이해해야 능동적으로 참여하는 주체적인 소비자가 될 수 있다는 내용의 글이다. 따라서 글의 요지로 가장 적절한 것은 ① '개인 정보 제공의 속성을 심층적으로 이해하면 주체적 소비자가 된다.'이다.

어휘·어구

overlook 간과하다
consumer 소비자
notion 개념
paradox 역설
engagement 참여, 관여
explode 폭발하다, 폭발적으로 ~이 되다
awareness 인식
in whole or in part 전체로든 부분으로든
vulnerable 취약한
conflicted 갈등을 겪는
current 현재의
location 위치
armed with ~로 무장한
bystander 방관자
passive 수동적인
participant 참가자

정답률 90%

5. ② 인간의 지능 발달의 원인

To overcome death as the obstacle /
장애물로서의 죽음을 극복하기 위해 /
that was hindering the evolution of human intelligence, /
인간 지능의 진화를 방해하고 있었던 /
our ancestors developed the killer app /

우리 조상들은 킬러 앱을 개발했는데 /
that propelled our species forward, / ahead of all others: /
우리 종족을 앞으로 나아가게 했던 / 다른 모든 것들을 능가하여 /
namely, spoken and written language in words and maths.
즉, 말과 수학에서의 언문이다
I believe / communication was, and still is, our most valuable invention.
나는 믿는다 / 의사소통이 우리의 가장 가치 있는 발명품이었고 지금도 여전히 그렇다고
It has helped us preserve /
그것은 우리가 (~을) 보존하는 데 도움을 주어왔다 /
the knowledge, learning, discoveries and intelligence / we have gained /
지식, 학습, 발견과 지능을 / 우리가 얻어온 /
and pass them on / from person to person /
그리고 그것들을 물려주는 데 / 개인에서 개인으로 /
and from generation to generation.
그리고 대대로 (물려주는 데)
Imagine / if Einstein had had no way / of telling the rest of us /
상상해 보라 / 만약 아인슈타인이 방법이 없었다고 / 우리 모두에게 말할 /
about his remarkable understanding of the theory of relativity.
상대성 이론에 대한 자신의 놀라운 이해에 대해
In the absence of our incredible abilities to communicate, /
우리의 놀라운 의사소통 능력이 없다면 /
each and every one of us would need / to discover relativity on his or her own.
우리 각자 모두가 필요가 있을 것이다 / 스스로 상대성 (이론)을 발견할
Leaps of human intelligence have happened, / then, /
인간 지능의 도약은 발생해 왔다 / 그렇다면 /
as a response to the way / human society and culture developed.
방식에 대한 반응으로 / 인간 사회와 문화가 발전했던
A lot of our intelligence resulted from our interaction with each other, /
상당한 우리의 지능은 서로 간의 상호 작용에서 기인했다 /
and not just in response to our environments.
단지 우리의 환경에 대한 반응뿐만 아니라

인간 지능의 진화를 방해하고 있었던 장애물로서의 죽음을 극복하기 위해, 우리 조상들은 우리 종족을 다른 모든 것들을 능가하여 앞으로 나아가게 했던 킬러 앱을 개발했는데, 즉, 말과 수학에서의 언문이다. 나는 의사소통이 우리의 가장 가치 있는 발명품이었고 지금도 여전히 그렇다고 믿는다. 그것은 우리가 얻어온 지식, 학습, 발견과 지능을 우리가 보존하고 그것들을 개인에서 개인으로, 그리고 대대로 물려주는 데 도움을 주어왔다. 만약 아인슈타인이 상대성 이론에 대한 자신의 놀라운 이해에 대해 우리 모두에게 말할 방법이 없었다고 상상해 보라. 우리의 놀라운 의사소통 능력이 없다면 우리 각자 모두가 스스로 상대성 (이론)을 발견할 필요가 있을 것이다. 그렇다면 인간 지능의 도약은 인간 사회와 문화가 발전했던 방식에 대한 반응으로 발생해 왔다. 상당한 우리의 지능은 단지 우리의 환경에 대한 반응뿐만 아니라, 서로 간의 상호 작용에서 기인했다.

문제풀이

필자는 의사소통이 우리의 지식, 학습, 발견과 지능을 보존하고 물려주는 것을 도와주었다고 하면서 상당한 우리의 지능이 서로 간의 상호 작용에서 기인했다고 했으므로, 글의 요지로 가장 적절한 것은 ② '인간의 지능 발달은 상호 간 의사소통의 결과물이다.'이다

《 어휘·어구 》

overcome 극복하다
obstacle 장애물
hinder 방해하다
evolution 진화
ancestor 조상
propel 나아가게 하다, 몰고 가다
valuable 가치 있는
preserve 보존하다, 지키다
remarkable 놀랄 만한
relativity 상대성
incredible 믿을 수 없는, 믿기 힘든
leap 도약
interaction 상호 작용

정답률 86%

6. ② 인간이 지각하지 못하는 화학 신호로 가득 찬 세상

직독/직해

Just imagine / that we have invented special glasses /
그저 상상해 보라 / 우리가 특수 안경을 발명했다고 /
that give us the power to see the odorous world /
냄새로 가득한 세상을 보는 능력을 주는 /
the way that other organisms perceive it.
다른 유기체가 지각하는 방식으로
Put your pair on / and walk outside for just a moment.
여러분의 안경을 끼고 / 잠깐 밖을 거닐어 보라
As the bright sunlight hits our eyes, / we would encounter a world /
밝은 햇빛이 우리의 눈에 비칠 때 / 우리는 세상과 마주칠 것이다 /
far different from what we would normally expect.
우리가 평소 기대하는 바와 아주 다른
The air is full of molecules carried by breezes.
대기는 미풍에 의해 운반되는 분자로 가득하다
Chemical signals would flood our eyes /
화학 신호들이 우리의 눈에 물밀듯이 밀려들 것이다 /
just as surely / as sounds overwhelm our ears at a cocktail party.
아주 확실하게 / 칵테일파티에서 소리가 우리의 귀를 압도하는 것만큼이나
Stare at any plant / and you would see compounds /
어떤 식물을 응시하라 / 그러면 화합물을 볼 수 있을 것이다 /
being released into the air / from leaves, bark, and roots.
대기 중으로 방출되고 있는 / 나뭇잎, 나무껍질, 뿌리로부터
A squirrel in a tree exudes carbon dioxide and other compounds /
나무에 있는 다람쥐는 이산화 탄소와 다른 화합물을 발산한다 /
with each breath.
숨을 쉴 때마다
Glance along its brown body / and notice /
그것의 갈색 몸을 죽 훑어보라 / 그리고 주목하라 /
that specific points (scent glands) appear to be slowly releasing chemical signals.
특정 지점(냄새샘)이 서서히 화학 신호를 방출하는 것처럼 보이는 것에
If we could translate these signals into language, /
만약 우리가 이 신호들을 언어로 번역할 수 있다면 /
we would see phrases, sentences, statements, songs, and other messages /
우리는 구, 문장, 진술, 노래, 그리고 다른 메시지를 볼 것이다 /
waiting to be intercepted and interpreted.
가로채여(포착되어) 해석되기를 기다리고 있는

우리가 다른 유기체가 지각하는 방식으로 냄새로 가득한 세상을 보는 능력을 주는 특수 안경을 발명했다고 상상해 보라. 여러분의 안경을 끼고 잠깐 밖을 거닐어 보라. 밝은 햇빛이 우리의 눈에 비칠 때, 우리는 우리가 평소 기대하는 바와 아주 다른 세상과 마주칠 것이다. 대기는 미풍에 의해 운반되는 분자로 가득하다. 화학 신호들이 칵테일파티에서 소리가 우리의 귀를 압도하는 것만큼이나 아주 확실하게 우리의 눈에 물밀듯이 밀려들 것이다. 어떤 식물을 응시하더라도 나뭇잎, 나무껍질, 뿌리로부터 화합물이 대기 중으로 방출되고 있는 것을 볼 수 있을 것이다. 나무에 있는 다람쥐는 숨을 쉴 때마다 이산화 탄소와 다른 화합물을 발산한다. 그것의 갈색 몸을 죽 훑어보며 특정 지점(냄새샘)이 서서히 화학 신호를 방출하는 것처럼 보이는 것에 주목하라. 만약 우리가 이 신호들을 언어로 번역할 수 있다면, 우리는 구, 문장, 진술, 노래, 그리고 다른 메시지가 가로채여(포착되어) 해석되기를 기다리는 것을 볼 것이다.

문제풀이

냄새로 가득한 세상을 보는 능력을 주는 특수 안경을 끼고 보면, 대기가 분자로 가득 차 있는 것과 다양한 화학 신호를 볼 수 있고, 식물들이 화합물을 방출하는 것과 다람쥐가 다양한 화합물을 발산하는 것을 볼 수 있을 거라는 내용의 글이다. 따라서 글의 요지로 가장 적절한 것은 ② '세상은 인간이 지각하지 못하는 화학 신호로 가득 차 있다.'이다.

《 어휘·어구 》

odorous 냄새로 가득한
organism 유기체
perceive 지각하다, 인지하다
encounter 마주치다
molecule 분자
breeze 미풍, 산들바람
flood 물밀듯이 밀려들다, 쇄도하다
overwhelm 압도하다
stare at ~을 응시하다
compound 화합물
release 방출하다, 배출하다
bark 나무껍질
squirrel 다람쥐
carbon dioxide 이산화 탄소
glance 훑어보다
notice 주목하다
translate 번역하다
intercept 가로채다
interpret 해석하다

정답률 89%

7. ① 개인이 피하기 어려운 유해 환경 요인에 대한 대처

직독/직해

Environmental hazards include biological, physical, and chemical ones, /
환경 위험 요소는 생물학적, 물리적, 화학적인 위험 요소가 포함한다 /
along with the human behaviors /
인간의 행동과 함께 /
that promote or allow exposure.
노출을 촉진하거나 허용하는
Some environmental contaminants are difficult /
일부 환경적인 오염 물질은 어렵고 /
to avoid / 피하기가 /
(the breathing of polluted air, /
오염된 공기의 호흡 /
the drinking of chemically contaminated public drinking water, /
화학적으로 오염된 공공 식수의 음용 /
noise in open public spaces); /
개방된 공공장소에서의 소음 /
in these circumstances, / exposure is largely involuntary.
이런 상황에서 / 노출은 대개 자기도 모르게 이루어진다
Reduction or elimination of these factors /
이런 요소의 감소 또는 제거는 /
may require societal action, /
사회적 조치를 요구할지도 모른다 /
such as public awareness and public health measures.
대중의 인식 및 공중 보건 조치와 같은
In many countries, / 많은 국가에서 /
the fact that some environmental hazards are difficult /
일부 환경적 위험 요소가 어렵다는 사실은 /
to avoid at the individual level /
개인 차원에서 피하기 /
is felt to be more morally egregious /
도덕적으로 더 매우 나쁜 것으로 느껴진다 /
than those hazards /
그 위험 요소보다 /
that can be avoided.
피할 수 있는
Having no choice but to drink water /
물을 마시지 않을 수 없는 것은 /
contaminated with very high levels of arsenic, /
매우 높은 수준의 비소로 오염된 /
or being forced to passively breathe in tobacco smoke in restaurants, /

또는 식당에서 담배 연기를 수동적으로 들이마시도록 강요당하는 것은 /
outrages people / more than the personal choice /
사람들을 더 격노하게 한다 / 개인적인 선택보다 /
of whether an individual smokes tobacco.
개인이 담배를 피울지 말지에 대한
These factors are important / when one considers /
이런 요소들은 중요하다 / 고려할 때 /
how change (risk reduction) happens.
변화(위험 감소)가 어떻게 일어나는지를

환경 위험 요소는 생물학적, 물리적, 화학적인 위험 요소와 함께 노출을 촉진하거나 허용하는 인간의 행동을 포함한다. (오염된 공기의 호흡, 화학적으로 오염된 공공 식수의 음용, 개방된 공공장소에서의 소음처럼) 일부 환경적인 오염 물질은 피하기가 어렵고, 이런 상황에서 노출은 대개 자기도 모르게 이루어진다. 이런 요소의 감소 또는 제거는 대중의 인식 및 공중 보건 조치와 같은 사회적 조치를 요구할지도 모른다. 많은 국가에서, 일부 환경적 위험 요소가 개인 차원에서 피하기 어렵다는 사실은 피할 수 있는 그 위험 요소보다 도덕적으로 더 매우 나쁜 것으로 느껴진다. 매우 높은 수준의 비소로 오염된 물을 마시지 않을 수 없는 것이나, 식당에서 담배 연기를 수동적으로 들이마시도록 강요당하는 것은 개인이 담배를 피울지 말지에 대한 개인적인 선택보다 사람들을 더 격노하게 한다. 이런 요소들은 변화(위험 감소)가 어떻게 일어나는지를 고려할 때 중요하다.

문제풀이

개인 차원에서는 피하기 어려운 일부 환경적 위험 요소를 감소시키거나 제거하려면 대중의 인식 및 공중 보건 조치와 같은 사회적 조치를 필요로 한다는 내용의 글이다. 따라서 글의 요지로 가장 적절한 것은 ① '개인이 피하기 어려운 유해 환경 요인에 대해서는 사회적 대응이 필요하다.'이다.

《 어휘·어구 》

hazard 위험 (요소)
biological 생물학적인
promote 촉진하다
exposure 노출
contaminant 오염 물질
involuntary 자기도 모르게 하는
reduction 감소
elimination 제거
factor 요소
societal 사회의
awareness 의식, 관심
measure 조치
have no choice but to do ~하지 않을 수 없다
arsenic 비소
passively 수동적으로
outrage 격노하게 만들다

정답률 55%

8. ① 전문직과 사회의 관계

직독/직해

Historically, / the professions and society /
역사적으로 / 전문직과 사회는 /
have engaged in a negotiating process /
협상 과정에 관여해 왔다 /
intended to define the terms of their relationship.
그들의 관계의 조건들을 규정짓도록 의도된
At the heart of this process is the tension /
이러한 과정의 중심에는 긴장이 놓여있다 /
between the professions' pursuit of autonomy and the public's demand for accountability.
전문직의 자율성 추구와 대중의 책임에 대한 요구 사이의
Society's granting of power and privilege to the professions /
사회가 전문직에 권력과 특권을 부여한 것은 /
is premised on their willingness and ability /
그들의 의지와 능력을 전제로 한다 /
to contribute to social well-being /
사회 복지에 기여하는 /
and to conduct their affairs /
그리고 자신의 일을 수행하는 /
in a manner consistent with broader social values.
더 폭넓은 사회적 가치와 일치하는 방식으로
It has long been recognized /
오랫동안 인식되어 왔다 /
that the expertise and privileged position of professionals /
전문직의 전문지식과 특권적인 지위는 /
confer authority and power /
권위와 권력을 부여한다는 것이 /
that could readily be used /
쉽게 이용될 수 있는 /
to advance their own interests /
그들 자신의 이익을 도모하기 위해 /
at the expense of those they serve.
그들이 봉사하는 사람들을 희생하면서
As Edmund Burke observed two centuries ago, /
Edmund Burke가 두 세기 전에 말했듯이 /
"Men are qualified for civil liberty /
인간은 시민으로서의 자유를 누릴 자격이 부여된다 /
in exact proportion to their disposition /
그들의 성향에 정확히 비례해서 /
to put moral chains upon their own appetites."
자신의 욕구를 도덕적으로 통제하는
Autonomy has never been a one-way street /
자율성은 일방통행로였던 적이 없었다 /
and is never granted absolutely and irreversibly.
그리고 절대 절대적이고 뒤집을 수 없게 부여되는 것은 아니다

역사적으로 전문직과 사회는 그들의 관계의 조건들을 규정짓도록 의도된 협상 과정에 관여해 왔다. 이러한 과정의 중심에는 전문직의 자율성 추구와 대중의 책임에 대한 요구 사이의 긴장이 놓여있다. 사회가 전문직에 권력과 특권을 부여한 것은 사회 복지에 기여하고 더 폭넓은 사회적 가치와 일치하는 방식으로 자신의 일을 수행하는 그들의 의지와 능력을 전제로 한다. 전문직의 전문지식과 특권적인 지위는 그들이 봉사하는 사람들을 희생하면서 그들 자신의 이익을 도모하기 위해 쉽게 이용될 수 있는 권위와 권력을 부여한다는 것이 오랫동안 인식되어 왔다. Edmund Burke가 두 세기 전에 말했듯이, "인간은 자신의 욕구를 도덕적으로 통제하는 그들의 성향에 정확히 비례해서 시민으로서의 자유를 누릴 자격이 부여된다." 자율성은 일방통행로였던 적이 없었으며 절대 절대적이고 뒤집을 수 없게 부여되는 것은 아니다.

문제풀이

사회가 전문직에 부여한 권력과 특권은 그들이 사회 복지에 기여하고 사회적 가치와 부합하는 방식으로 그들의 일을 수행해야 한다는 책임을 전제로 한다는 내용의 글이다. 따라서 글의 요지로 가장 적절한 것은 ① '전문직에 부여되는 자율성은 그에 상응하는 사회적 책임을 수반한다.'이다.

《 어휘·어구 》

engage in ~에 관여하다
accountability 책임
grant 부여하다
contribute to ~에 기여하다
consistent with ~과 일치하는
expertise 전문지식
confer 주다, 부여하다
readily 쉽게
at the expense of ~을 희생하면서
be qualified for ~에 자격이 있다
in proportion to ~에 비례하여
disposition 성향
irreversibly 뒤집을 수 없게

정답률 89%

9. ① 음악 비평의 변화

직독/직해

Prior to file-sharing services, /
파일 공유 서비스 전에 /
music albums landed exclusively /
음악 앨범은 독점적으로 들어갔다 /
in the hands of music critics /
음악 비평가들의 손에 /
before their release. 발매 전에
These critics would listen to them well /
이 비평가들은 그것을 잘 듣곤 했다 /
before the general public could /
일반 대중들이 들을 수 있기 훨씬 전에 /
and preview them /
그리고 시사평을 쓰곤 했다 /
for the rest of the world / in their reviews.
나머지 사람들을 위해 / 자신의 비평에서
Once the internet made music easily accessible /
일단 인터넷을 통해 음악을 쉽게 접할 수 있게 되자 /
and allowed even advanced releases to spread /
그리고 미리 공개된 곡들이 퍼질 수 있게 되자 /
through online social networks, /
온라인 소셜 네트워크를 통해 /
availability of new music became democratized, /
신곡을 접할 수 있는 것이 민주화되었는데 /
which meant / critics no longer had unique access.
이것은 의미했다 / 비평가들이 더는 유일하게 접하지 않는다는 것을
That is, critics and laypeople alike /
말하자면, 비평가와 비전문가가 똑같이 /
could obtain new music simultaneously.
동시에 신곡을 얻을 수 있었다
Social media services also enabled people /
소셜 미디어 서비스는 또한 사람들이 ~하게 했다 /
to publicize their views on new songs, /
신곡에 대한 자신의 생각을 알리고 /
list their new favorite bands /
자신이 좋아하는 새로운 밴드의 목록을 작성하고 /
in their social media bios, /
자신의 소셜 미디어 약력에 /
and argue over new music endlessly /
그리고 신곡을 놓고 끝없이 논쟁할 수 있게 했다 /
on message boards. 메시지 게시판에서
The result was / 그 결과 ~였다 /
that critics now could access the opinions of the masses /
비평가들은 이제 대중의 의견을 접할 수 있었다 /
on a particular album / before writing their reviews.
특정 앨범에 관한 / 자신의 비평을 쓰기도 전에
Thus, instead of music reviews guiding popular opinion /
따라서 음악 비평이 여론을 인도하는 대신에 /
toward art / 예술에 관한 /
(as they did in preinternet times), /
그들이 인터넷 이전 시대에 했던 것처럼 /
music reviews began to reflect /
음악 비평은 반영하기 시작했다 /
— consciously or subconsciously — /
의식적으로든 또는 잠재 의식적으로든 /
public opinion. 여론을

파일 공유 서비스 전에, 음악 앨범은 발매 전에 음악 비평가들의 손에 독점적으로 들어갔다. 이 비평가들은 일반 대중들이 들을 수 있기 훨씬 전에 그것을 듣고 나머지 사람들을 위해 자신의 비평에서 시사평을 쓰곤 했다. 일단 인터넷을 통해 음악을 쉽게 접할 수 있게 되고, 미리 공개된 곡들이 온라인 소셜 네트워크를 통해 퍼질 수 있게 되자, 신곡을 접할 수 있는 것이 민주화되었는데, 이것은 비평가들이 더는 그들만이 유일하게 접하지 않는다는 것을 의미했다. 말하자면, 비평가와 비전문가가 똑같이 동시에 신곡을 얻을 수 있었다. 소셜 미디어 서비스는 또한 사람들이 신곡에 대한 자신의 생각을 알리고, 자신의 소셜 미디어 약력에 자신이 좋아하는 새로운 밴드의 목록을 작성하고, 메시지 게시판에서 신곡을 놓고 끝없이 논쟁할 수 있게 했다. 그 결과 비평가들은 이제 자신의 비평을 쓰기도 전에 특정 앨범에 관한 대중의 의견을 접할 수 있었다. 따라서 (그들이 인터넷 이전 시대에 했던 것처럼) 음악 비평이 예술에 관한 여론을 인도하는 대신에, 음악 비평은 의식적으로든 또는 잠재 의식적으로든 여론을 반영하기 시작했다.

문제풀이

파일 공유 서비스 전에는 음악 비평가가 일반 대중이 듣기 전에 먼저 신곡을 듣고 비평을 하여 그것에 관한 여론을 인도했지만, 온라인 소셜 네트워크를 통해 음악 비평가와 일반 대중이 동시에 신곡을

접할 수 있게 되면서 이전과는 달리 음악 비평이 대중의 의견을 반영하게 되었다는 내용의 글이다. 따라서 글의 요지로 가장 적절한 것은 ① '미디어 환경의 변화로 음악 비평이 대중의 영향을 받게 되었다.'이다.

《 어휘·어구 》

prior to ~이전에
file-sharing service 파일 공유 서비스
exclusively 독점적으로
critic 비평가
release 발매
preview 시사평을 쓰다
review 비평
accessible 접근 가능한
availability 입수 가능성
democratize 민주화하다
simultaneously 동시에
publicize 알리다
bio 약력, 경력
subconsciously 잠재 의식적으로

정답률 78%

10. ① 문자 기록을 이끈 고대 사회의 경제 활동

직독/직해

In retrospect, it might seem surprising /
돌이켜보면 그것은 놀라운 일로 보일지도 모른다 /
that something as mundane as the desire to count
양의 수를 세고자하는 욕구만큼 세속적인 것이
sheep / was the driving force for an advance as
/ 문자 언어처럼 근본적인 진보의 원동력이었다는 것은
fundamental as written language.
But the desire for written records has always
그러나 문자 기록에 대한 욕구는 언제나 경제 활동을 수반해 왔다 /
accompanied economic activity, /
since transactions are meaningless /
거래는 무의미하기 때문이다 /
unless you can clearly keep track of who owns what.
누가 무엇을 소유하고 있는지 명확하게 기억할 수 없다면
As such, early human writing is dominated by
이와 같이 초기 인간의 글쓰기는 수완을 발휘하는 것의 지배를 받는다 /
wheeling and dealing: /
a collection of bets, bills, and contracts.
내기, 계산서, 그리고 계약서의 모음과 같이
Long before we had the writings of the prophets, /
우리가 예언자들에 관한 기록을 갖기 훨씬 이전에 /
we had the writings of the profits.
우리는 이익에 대한 기록을 가졌다
In fact, many civilizations never got to the stage /
사실, 많은 문명이 그 단계에 결코 이르지 못했다 /
of recording and leaving behind the kinds of great
그런 위대한 문학 작품을 기록하고 그것을 뒤에 남기는 /
literary works /
that we often associate with the history of culture.
우리가 흔히 문화의 역사와 연관 짓는
What survives these ancient societies is, for the most part, a pile of receipts.
이런 고대 사회에서 살아남은 것은 대부분 영수증 더미이다
If it weren't for the commercial enterprises / that
상업적 기업이 없다면 / 그런 기록을 만들어내는 /
produced those records, /
we would know far, far less about the cultures that
우리는 그런 기록이 생겨난 문화에 대해 아주 훨씬 더 적게 알 것이다
they came from.

돌이켜보면, 양을 세고자 하는 욕망만큼 세속적인 것이 문자 언어처럼 근본적인 진보의 원동력이었다는 것은 놀라운 일로 보일지도 모른다. 그러나 문자 기록에 대한 욕구는 언제나 경제 활동을 수반해 왔는데, 왜냐하면 누가 무엇을 소유하는지 명확하게 추적할 수 없는 한 거래는 무의미하기 때문이다. 이와 같이 초기의 인간이 쓴 글의 우위를 수완을 발휘하는 것, 즉 내기, 어음, 계약서 더미가 차지하고 있다. 우리가 예언자들의 글을 갖기 훨씬 오래 전에, 우리는 수익에 대한 글을 가지고 있었다. 사실, 많은 문명들은 우리가 종종 문화의 역사와 연관 짓는 그러한 종류의 위대한 문학작품을 기록하고 남기는 단계에 이르지 못했다. 이러한 고대 사회에서 살아남은 것은 대부분 영수증 더미다. 만약 그 기록들을 만들어낸 상업적 사업이 아니었다면, 우리는 그것들이 속한 문화에 대해 훨씬 더 적게 알 것이다.

문제풀이

초기 인간의 글쓰기는 내기, 어음, 계약서와 같은 경제 활동과 관련된 것들이 주를 이뤘고 고대에서 살아남은 것들은 영수증 더미가 대부분으로 그런 기록들을 남기게 해준 상업적 활동이 없었다면 우리는 그 기록들이 속한 문화에 대해 훨씬 더 적게 알게 되었을 것이라는 내용이다. 이러한 글의 요지로 가장 적절한 것은 ① '고대 사회에서 경제 활동은 문자 기록의 원동력이었다.'이다.

《 어휘·어구 》

in retrospect 돌이켜보면
driving force 원동력
fundamental 근본적인
accompany 수반하다
transaction 거래
dominate 우위를 차지하다, 지배하다
wheeling and dealing 수완을 발휘하기
bill 어음, 지폐
associate with ~와 연관 짓다
commercial 상업의
enterprise 사업, 기업

본문 029쪽

문법 플러스 5. 동명사

A. 1. Setting
2. having done
3. learning
4. having been
5. her
6. being
7. dancing

1 [해석]▶ 목표를 세우고 포기하지 않는 것은 네가 인생에서 많은 일들을 성취하는 데 도움을 준다.
[해설]▶ 한 문장에서 동사가 두 개 나오면 안 된다. 그러므로 주어 역할을 하는 동명사구로 해야 한다.

2 [해석]▶ Sam은 그러한 어리석은 짓을 했다고 후회한다.
[해설]▶ regret는 동명사를 목적어로 취하며, 완료형 동명사(having done)는 문장의 술어동사의 시제(regrets)보다 한 시제 앞선 내용을 나타낼 때 사용한다. 「regret+동명사」는 '~한 것을 후회하다'는 의미이다.

3 [해석]▶ 이번 여름, 내 아들은 스쿠버 다이빙하는 법을 배우기를 매우 기대한다.
[해설]▶ look forward to(~을 기대하다)에서 to는 전치사이므로, 뒤에는 동명사가 나와야 한다.

4 [해석]▶ Sam은 그녀가 가수였다고 확신한다.
[해설]▶ 주절의 시제(is)는 현재이고, that 이하의 종속절의 시제(was)는 과거이므로 완료형 동명사로 나타내야 한다.

5 [해석]▶ 그는 그녀가 결백하다고 주장한다.
[해설]▶ 동명사의 의미상의 주어가 사람일 때는 소유격과 목적격을 모두 사용할 수 있다. her는 소유격이고 hers는 소유대명사이다. 소유대명사는 「소유격+명사」의 의미를 가지고 있다.

6 [해석]▶ 그 소년은 자신이 아이처럼 취급받는 것을 좋아하지 않는다.
[해설]▶ 소년이 아이처럼 취급받는 동작의 대상이므로 수동태로 나타내야 하는데, 주절의 시제가 현재(doesn't)이고, 종속절의 시제가 현재(is treated)이므로 단순 수동형 동명사를 사용해야 한다.

7 [해석]▶ 나는 지금 Sally와 춤을 추고 싶다.
[해설]▶ 동명사의 관용 표현 feel like -ing는 '~하고 싶다'는 의미이다.

본문 029쪽

B. 1. Understanding 2. fishing
3. succeeding 4. being
5. cars 6. being treated
7. crying

1 [해석]▶ 왜 역사적인 사건이 발생하는지 이해하는 것이 중요하다.
[해설]▶ 한 문장에서 동사가 두 개 나오면 안 된다. 또한 동명사는 문장에서 주어 역할을 할 수 있다.

2 [해석]▶ 나의 (직장) 상사는 주말 동안 낚시하는 것을 즐겼다.
[해설]▶ 동사 enjoy는 동명사를 목적어로 가질 수 있다.

3 [해석]▶ 인생의 성공의 열쇠 중 하나는 균형 감각을 가지고 사는 것이다.
[해설]▶ keys to ~는 '~에 대한 열쇠'라는 의미로 to는 전치사이므로 뒤에 동명사가 나온다.

4 [해석]▶ 그녀는 늦어서 미안함을 느낀다.
[해설]▶ 단순동명사는 주절의 시제와 that 이하의 종속절의 시제가 동일할 때 사용한다.

5 [해석]▶ 그 남자는 이곳에 차가 주차되는 것에 반대했다.
[해설]▶ 사물(car)을 동명사의 의미상의 주어로 사용할 때는 소유격으로 고치지 않고, 그대로 쓴다.

6 [해석]▶ Sally는 불공평하게 대접받는 것에 참지 못한다.
[해설]▶ Sally가 불공평하게 대접하는 주체가 아니라 대상이므로 동명사의 수동태로 나타내야 한다.

7 [해석]▶ 엎질러진 우유를 보고 울어봤자 소용없다.
[해설]▶ 동명사의 관용표현인 It's no use[good] -ing는 '~해도 소용없다'는 의미이다.

본문 030쪽

숙어 플러스 5. 수능 필수 숙어 5회

1. broken 2. into
3. about 4. for

06. 글의 주제

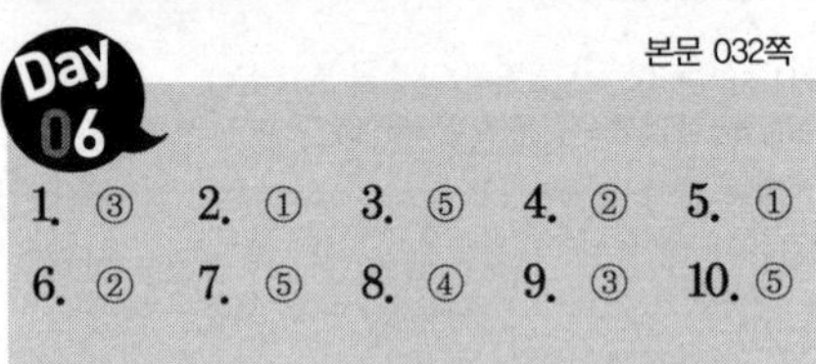

본문 032쪽

Day 06

1. ③ 2. ① 3. ⑤ 4. ② 5. ①
6. ② 7. ⑤ 8. ④ 9. ③ 10. ⑤

정답률 68%

대표 기출 ② 정보 공개의 이점

직독/직해

An important advantage of disclosure, /
공개의 중요한 이점은 /
as opposed to more aggressive forms of regulation, /
더 공격적인 형태의 규제와는 반대로 /
is its flexibility and respect / for the operation of free markets.
유연성과 존중이다 / 자유 시장의 작용에 대한
Regulatory mandates are blunt swords; / they tend to neglect diversity /
규제하는 명령은 뭉툭한 검인데 / 그것들은 다양성을 무시하는 경향이 있다 /
and may have serious unintended adverse effects.
그리고 의도하지 않은 심각한 역효과를 일으킬 수도 있다
For example, / energy efficiency requirements for appliances /
예를 들면 / 가전제품에 대한 에너지 효율 요건은 /
may produce goods / that work less well /
제품을 만들어 낼 수도 있다 / 덜 잘 작동하는 /
or that have characteristics / that consumers do not want.
또는 특징을 지닌 / 소비자가 원하지 않는
Information provision, / by contrast, / respects freedom of choice.
정보 제공은 / 그에 반해서 / 선택의 자유를 존중한다
If automobile manufacturers are required /
만약 자동차 제조업체가 ~해야 한다면 /
to measure and publicize the safety characteristics of cars, /
자동차의 안전 특징을 측정하고 공개해야 /
potential car purchasers can trade safety concerns /
잠재적인 자동차 구매자는 안전에 대한 걱정을 맞바꿀 수 있다 /
against other attributes, / such as price and styling.
다른 속성과 / 가격과 스타일 같은
If restaurant customers are informed of the calories in their meals, /
식당 손님들에게 식사에 들어 있는 열량을 알려주면 /
those who want to lose weight / can make use of the information, /
살을 빼고 싶은 사람들은 / 그 정보를 이용할 수 있다 /
leaving those who are unconcerned about calories unaffected.
열량에 신경 쓰지 않는 사람들은 영향을 받지 않은 채로 있게 된다
Disclosure does not interfere with, / and should even promote, /
공개는 방해하지 않고 / 그리고 심지어 촉진할 것이다 /
the autonomy (and quality) of individual decision-making.
개인 의사 결정의 자율성(과 품질)을

공개의 중요한 이점은 더 공격적인 형태의 규제와는 반대로 자유 시장의 작용에 대한 유연성과 존중이다. 규제하는 명령은 뭉툭한 검인데, 그것들은 다양성을 무시하는 경향이 있으며, 의도하지 않은 심각한 역효과를 일으킬 수도 있다. 예를 들면, 가전제품에 대한 에너지 효율 요건은 덜 잘 작동하거나 소비자가 원하지 않는 특징을 지닌 제품을 만들어 낼 수도 있다. 그에 반해서 정보 제공은 선택의 자유를 존중한다. 만약 자동차 제조업체가 자동차의 안전 특징을 측정하고 공개해야 한다면, 잠재적인 자동차 구매자는 가격과 스타일 같은 다른 속성과 안전에 대한 걱정을 맞바꿀 수 있다. 식당 손님들에게 식사에 들어 있는 열량을 알려주면, 살을 빼고 싶은 사람들은 그 정보를 이용할 수 있고, 열량에 신경 쓰지 않는 사람들은 영향을 받지 않은 채로 있게 된다. 공개는 개인 의사 결정의 자율성(과 품질)을 방해하지 않고 심지어 촉진할 것이다.

① 공공의 정보를 소비자가 접근 가능하게 만드는 과정
② 자유로운 선택을 보장하기 위해 정보를 공개하는 것의 이점
③ 기업들이 자유 시장에서 이윤을 늘리는 전략
④ 현재 산업 동향을 파악하고 분석할 필요성
⑤ 다양화된 시장이 합리적인 고객 선택에 미치는 영향

문제풀이

규제와는 반대로 정보 공개는 자유 시장에서 소비자가 자유롭게 의사 결정을 내릴 수 있는 자율성을 방해하지 않고 촉진한다는 내용의 글이다. 따라서 글의 주제로 가장 적절한 것은 ② 'benefits of publicizing information to ensure free choices(자유로운 선택을 보장하기 위해 정보를 공개하는 것의 이점)'이다.

구조 다시보기

도입(주제)	공개의 이점은 규제와 달리 자유 시장의 작용에 대한 유연성과 존중임
부연 1	규제하는 명령은 다양성을 무시하는 경향이 있고, 심각한 역효과를 일으킬 수 있음
예시 1	가전제품의 에너지 효율 규제는 품질에 문제가 있거나 원치 않는 특징의 제품을 만들어 낼 수도 있음
부연 2	정보 제공은 선택의 자유를 존중함
예시 1	자동차의 안정에 대한 특징 공개는 다른 속성과 안전에 대한 걱정을 맞바꿀 수 있음
예시 2	음식 열량 공개는 다이어트 중인 사람들만이 그 정보를 이용할 수 있음
결론	공개는 개인 의사 결정의 자율성을 촉진함

어휘·어구

disclosure 공개, 폭로
as opposed to ~와는 반대로
aggressive 공격적인
regulation 규제
flexibility 유연성
operation 작용
regulatory 규제하는
blunt 뭉툭한, 무딘
diversity 다양성
unintended 의도하지 않은
adverse effect 역효과, 부작용
efficiency 효율성
requirement 요건, 필요조건
appliance 가전제품
manufacturer 제조업체
publicize 알리다, 공표하다
attribute 특성
unaffected 영향을 받지 않는
interfere 방해하다
promote 촉진하다
accessible 접근 가능한
benefit 이점, 혜택
profit 이윤, 이익
diversify 다양화하다
reasonable 합리적인

정답률 82%

1. ③ 조기 직업 선택의 문제점

직독/직해

Most of us make our career choices / when we are about eighteen.
우리 대부분은 진로를 선택한다 / 열여덟 살쯤에
At eighteen, / you have limited experience, very limited skills /
열여덟 살에 / 여러분은 제한된 경험과 매우 제한적인 기술을 지니고 있다 /
and most of what you know /
그리고 여러분이 알고 있는 것의 대부분은 /
comes from your parents, your environment and the structured school system /
여러분의 부모, 여러분의 환경, 그리고 구조화된 학교 시스템으로부터 온다 /
you have gone through.
여러분이 경험한
You are usually slightly better at some skills /
여러분은 보통 몇 가지 기술에 약간 더 능숙하다 /
because you have spent a bit more time on them.
그것에 조금 더 많은 시간을 투자했기 때문에
Maybe someone in your environment was good at something /
아마도 여러분 주변에 있는 누군가가 어떤 것에 능숙할 수 있다 /
and passionate enough to get you interested /
그리고 여러분이 흥미를 느끼게 할 만큼 열정적이었을 수도 있다 /
in spending more time in that area.
그 분야에 더 많은 시간을 보내는 데
It is also possible / that you might have a specific physical feature /
또한 가능하다 / 여러분이 특정한 신체적 특징을 갖고 있을 수 있는 것이 /
— such as being tall — / that might make you better at certain activities, /
큰 키와 같은 / 여러분이 특정 활동을 더 잘하게 할 수도 있는 것이 /
such as playing basketball.
농구를 하는 것과 같은
In any case, / most people make a decision /
어쨌든 / 대부분 사람들이 결정을 내린다 /
regarding their career and direction in life /
그들의 삶의 진로와 방향에 대한 /
based on their limited experiences and biases /
그들의 제한된 경험과 편견을 바탕으로 /
in their childhood and teenage years.
유년기와 청소년기의
This decision will come to dominate their life / for many years to come.
이 결정은 그들의 삶을 지배하게 될 것이다 / 다가올 많은 세월 동안
No wonder so many get it wrong!
매우 많은 사람이 잘못된 결정을 내리는 것이 당연하다
It is easier to get it wrong / than to get it right, /
잘못된 결정을 내리기가 더 쉽다 / 올바른 결정을 내리기 보다 /
because statistically, there are more wrong ways than right ways.
통계적으로, 올바른 방법보다 잘못된 방법이 더 많기 때문에

우리 대부분은 열여덟 살쯤에 진로를 선택한다. 열여덟 살에 여러분은 제한된 경험과 매우 제한적인 기술을 지니고 있고, 여러분이 알고 있는 것의 대부분은 여러분의 부모, 여러분의 환경, 그리고 여러분이 경험한 구조화된 학교 시스템으로부터 온다. 여러분은 보통 몇 가지 기술에 약간 더 능숙한데, 그것에 조금 더 많은 시간을 투자했기 때문이다. 아마도 여러분 주변에 있는 누군가가 어떤 것에 능숙하고 여러분이 그 분야에 더 많은 시간을 보내는 데 더 흥미를 느끼게 할 만큼 열정적이었을 수도 있다. 또한 여러분은 농구를 하는 것과 같은 특정 활동을 더 잘하게 할 수도 있는 큰 키와 같은 특정한 신체적 특징을 갖고 있을 수도 있다. 어쨌든 대부분 사람들이 유년기와 청소년기의 제한된 경험과 편견을 바탕으로 삶의 진로와 방향에 대한 결정을 내린다. 이 결정은 다가올 많은 세월 동안 그들의 삶을 지배하게 될 것이다. 매우 많은 사람이 잘못된 결정을 내리는 것이 당연하다! 올바른 결정을 내리기보다 잘못된 결정을 내리기가 더 쉬운데, 이는 통계적으로, 올바른 방법보다 잘못된 방법이 더 많기 때문이다.

① 고용을 불안정하게 만드는 사회적 요인들
② 올바른 직업을 선택하는데 유용한 통계
③ 조기 직업 선택이 잘못될 수 있는 이유들
④ 가능한 한 빨리 자신의 적성을 찾아야 할 필요성
⑤ 직업 선택을 할 때 편견을 극복하는 방법

문제풀이

유년기와 청소년기의 제한된 경험과 편견을 바탕으로 지나치게 이른 나이에 진로를 결정하는 것은 올바른 결정을 내리기보다 잘못된 결정을 내리기가 더 쉽다는 내용의 글이다. 따라서 글의 주제로 가장 적절한 것은 ③ 'reasons that an early

career choice can go wrong(조기 직업 선택이 잘못될 수 있는 이유들)'이다.

《 어휘·어구 》

structure 구조
go through 경험하다
passionate 열정적인
physical 신체적인
feature 특징
regarding ~에 관한
base on ~에 근거하다
bias 편견

정답률 73%

2. ① 농업에서 경험적인 관찰 사용의 한계

직독/직해

Environmental learning occurs /
환경 학습은 일어난다 /

when farmers base decisions / on observations of "payoff" information.
농부들이 근거하여 결정할 때 / '이익' 정보에 대한 관찰에

They may observe their own or neighbors' farms, /
그들은 자신이나 이웃의 농장을 관찰할 수 있다 /

but it is the empirical results / they are using as a guide, /
하지만 경험의 결과이다 / 그들이 지침으로 삼는 것은 /

not the neighbors themselves.
이웃 자체가 아니라

They are looking at farming activities as experiments /
그들은 농업 활동을 실험으로 보고 있다 /

and assessing such factors /
그리고 요소를 평가하고 있다 /

as relative advantage, compatibility with existing resources, difficulty of use, and "trialability" /
상대적인 이점, 기존 자원과의 공존 가능성, 사용의 어려움, 그리고 '시험 가능성'과 같은 /

— how well can it be experimented with.
즉 얼마나 그것이 잘 실험될 수 있는가를 뜻하는

But / that criterion of "trialability" / turns out to be a real problem; /
그러나 / 그 '시험 가능성'의 기준은 / 진짜 문제인 것으로 밝혀지는데 /

it's true that farmers are always experimenting, /
농부들이 항상 실험하는 것은 사실이다 /

but working farms / are very flawed laboratories.
하지만 연구하는 농장은 / 매우 결함이 있는 연구실이다

Farmers cannot set up / the controlled conditions of professional test plots /
농부는 만들 수 없다 / 전문적인 시험장의 통제된 조건을 /

in research facilities.
연구 시설에서

Farmers also often confront / complex and difficult-to-observe phenomena /
농부는 종종 직면하기도 한다 / 복잡하고 관찰하기 어려운 현상에 /

that would be hard to manage / even if they could run controlled experiments.
관리하기 힘든 / 통제된 실험을 할 수 있다고 하더라도

Moreover / farmers can rarely acquire payoff information /
더욱이 / 농부는 이익 정보를 거의 얻을 수 없다 /

on more than a few of the production methods / they might use, /
몇 가지 생산 방법을 넘어서는 것에 관한 / 자신이 사용할 수 있는 /

which makes the criterion of "relative advantage" hard / to measure.
이는 '상대적 이점'의 기준을 어렵게 만든다 / 측정하기

환경 학습은 농부들이 '이익' 정보에 대한 관찰에 근거하여 결정할 때 일어난다. 그들은 자신이나 이웃의 농장을 관찰할 수 있지만, 그들이 지침으로 삼는 것은 이웃 자체가 아니라 경험의 결과이다. 그들은 농업 활동을 실험으로 보고 상대적인 이점, 기존 자원과의 공존 가능성, 사용의 어려움, 그리고 '시험 가능성', 즉 얼마나 그것이 잘 실험될 수 있는가와 같은 요소를 평가하고 있다. 그러나 그 '시험 가능성'의 기준은 진짜 문제인 것으로 밝혀지는데, 농부들이 항상 실험하는 것은 사실이지만, 연구하는 농장은 매우 결함이 있는 연구실이다. 농부는 연구 시설에서 전문적인 시험장의 통제된 조건을 만들 수 없다. 통제된 실험을 할 수 있다고 하더라도, 농부는 관리하기 힘든 복잡하고 관찰하기 어려운 현상에 종종 직면하기도 한다. 더욱이 농부는 자신이 사용할 수 있는 몇 가지 생산 방법을 넘어서는 것에 관한 이익 정보를 거의 얻을 수 없고, 이는 '상대적 이점'의 기준을 측정하기 어렵게 만든다.

① 농업에서 경험적인 관찰을 사용하는 것에 있어서의 한계
② 기존 농업 장비를 현대화하는 데 있어서의 문제
③ 농업 혁신에서 시험 가능성을 우선시해야 할 필요성
④ 농업에서 본능적 결정을 내려야 하는 것의 중요성
⑤ 예측할 수 없는 농업의 현상을 통제하는 방법

문제풀이

농부는 경험적 관찰의 결과를 지침으로 삼으며 어떤 농업 활동이 더 많은 이익을 가져다줄 지 평가하는데, 현실에서 농장은 결함이 있는 연구실로 여러 제약 때문에 경험적 관찰로 상대적 이점의 기준을 측정하는 데 어려움이 있다는 내용의 글이다. 따라서 글의 주제로 가장 적절한 것은 ① 'limitations of using empirical observations in farming(농업에서 경험적인 관찰을 사용하는 것에 있어서의 한계)'이다.

구조 다시보기

도입	환경 학습은 농부가 '이익' 정보에 대한 관찰에 근거하여 결정할 때 일어남
상술	농부는 경험의 결과를 지침으로 삼으며, 농업 활동을 실험으로 보며 여러 요소를 평가함
한계	'시험 가능성'의 기준이 문제인데, 연구하는 농장은 결함이 있는 연구실임
부연 1	연구 시설에서 전문적인 시험장의 통제된 조건을 만들 수 없음
부연 2	통제된 실험을 하더라도, 관리하기 힘든 현상에 직면하기도 함
부연 3	사용하는 몇 가지 생산 방법을 넘어서는 이익 정보를 얻을 수 없으며, 이것이 '상대적 이점'의 기준 측정을 어렵게 만듦

《 어휘·어구 》

observation 관찰
payoff 이익, 보상
assess 평가하다
relative 상대적인
advantage 장점
existing 기존의
trialability 시험 가능성
plot (특정 용도의) 터, 대지, 구성
flawed 결함이 있는
facility 시설
confront 직면하다
limitation 한계
prioritize 우선순위를 매기다
agricultural 농업의
unpredictable 예측할 수 없는

정답률 84%

3. ⑤ 신체 감각에 대한 뇌의 해석

직독/직해

From your brain's perspective, /
당신의 뇌의 관점에서 보면 /

your body is just another source of sensory input.
당신의 신체는 단지 감각 입력의 또 다른 원천일 뿐이다

Sensations from your heart and lungs, your metabolism, your changing temperature, and so on, /
당신의 심장과 폐, 신진대사, 변화하는 체온 등에서 생기는 감각은 /

are like ambiguous blobs.
여러 가지로 해석되는 형태가 뚜렷하지 않은 것들과 같다

These purely physical sensations inside your body /
당신의 신체 내의 그러한 순전히 신체적인 감각은 /

have no objective psychological meaning.
어떤 객관적 심리학적인 의미가 없다

Once your concepts enter the picture, / however, /
일단 당신의 개념이 맥락에 들어오면 / 그러나 /

those sensations may take on additional meaning.
그러한 감각은 추가적인 의미를 띨 수도 있다

If you feel an ache in your stomach / while sitting at the dinner table, /
만약 당신이 위의 통증을 느낀다면 / 저녁 식사 테이블에 앉아 있는 동안 /

you might experience it as hunger.
당신은 그것을 배고픔으로 경험할 수도 있다

If flu season is just around the corner, /
만약 독감 시기가 임박했다면 /

you might experience that same ache as nausea.
당신은 같은 통증을 메스꺼움으로 경험할 수도 있다

If you are a judge in a courtroom, / you might experience the ache /
만약 당신이 법정의 재판관이라면 / 당신은 그 통증을 경험할 수도 있다 /

as a gut feeling / that the defendant cannot be trusted.
직감으로 / 피고인이 의심스럽다는

In a given moment, / in a given context, / your brain uses concepts /
주어진 상황 / 주어진 맥락에서 / 당신의 뇌는 개념을 사용하고 /

to give meaning to internal sensations / as well as to external sensations /
내부의 감각에 의미를 부여하기 위해 / 외부의 감각뿐만 아니라 /

from the world, / all simultaneously.
세상으로부터 온 / 이 모든 것은 동시에 일어난다

From an aching stomach, /
위의 통증으로부터 /

your brain constructs an instance of hunger, nausea, or mistrust.
당신의 뇌는 배고픔, 메스꺼움, 불신의 사례를 구성한다

당신의 뇌의 관점에서 보면 당신의 신체는 단지 감각 입력의 또 다른 원천일 뿐이다. 당신의 심장과 폐, 신진대사, 변화하는 체온 등에서 생기는 감각은 여러 가지로 해석되는 형태가 뚜렷하지 않은 것들과 같다. 당신의 신체 내의 그러한 순전히 신체적인 감각은 어떤 객관적 심리학적인 의미가 없다. 그러나 일단 당신의 개념이 맥락에 들어오면, 그러한 감각은 추가적인 의미를 띨 수도 있다. 만약 당신이 저녁 식사 테이블에 앉아 있는 동안 위의 통증을 느낀다면, 당신은 그것을 배고픔으로 경험할 수도 있다. 만약 독감 시기가 임박했다면, 당신은 같은 통증을 메스꺼움으로 경험할 수도 있다. 만약 당신이 법정의 재판관이라면, 당신은 그 통증을 피고인이 의심스럽다는 직감으로 경험할 수도 있다. 주어진 상황, 주어진 맥락에서, 당신의 뇌는 세상으로부터 온 외부의 감각뿐만 아니라 내부의 감각에 의미를 부여하기 위해 개념을 사용하고, 이 모든 것은 동시에 일어난다. 위의 통증으로부터 당신의 뇌는 배고픔, 메스꺼움, 불신의 사례를 구성한다.

① 육체적 수행에 미치는 정신 건강의 영향
② 극단적인 감정 자극에 대한 생리적 반응
③ 어려운 상황에 대처하는 데 있어서 부정적인 감정의 역할
④ 다양한 전문적 맥락에서 객관성을 유지하는 것의 필요성
⑤ 문맥에 맞는 개념을 사용한 신체 감각에 대한 뇌의 해석

문제풀이

신체의 감각은 객관적 심리학적인 의미가 없지만, 일단 두뇌의 개념이 맥락에 들어오면 그러한 감각이 추가적인 의미를 지닐 수 있으므로 뇌는 주어진 상황, 주어진 맥락에서 신체 감각에 의미를 부여하기 위해 개념을 사용한다는 내용의 글이다. 따라서 글의 주제로 가장 적절한 것은 ⑤ 'brain's interpretation of bodily sensations using concepts in context(문맥에 맞는 개념을 사용한 신체 감각에 대한 뇌의 해석)'이다.

구조 다시보기

도입	신체적인 감각은 객관적 심리학적인 의미가 없음

전개	두뇌의 개념이 맥락에 들어오면 감각은 추가적 의미를 지닐 수 있음
예시	위의 통증은 상황에 따라 배고픔, 메스꺼움, 직감으로 여겨질 수 있음
결론	상황에 따라 뇌는 외부와 내부의 감각에 의미를 부여하기 위해 개념을 사용함

어휘·어구

perspective 관점
sensation 감각
metabolism 신진대사
and so on 기타 등등
ambiguous 모호한, 애매한
objective 객관적인
psychological 심리적인
additional 추가적인
just around the corner 임박하여
nausea 메스꺼움
courtroom 법정
gut feeling 직감
defendant 피고(인)
simultaneously 동시에
construct 구성하다
mistrust 불신

정답률 63%

4. ② 문화에 따라 달라지는 감정 표현

직독/직해

Considerable work by cultural psychologists and anthropologists / has shown /
문화 심리학자들과 인류학자들의 많은 연구는 / 보여준다 /
that there are indeed large and sometimes surprising differences /
정말로 크고, 때로는 놀랄만한 차이가 있다는 것을 /
in the words and concepts / that different cultures have for describing emotions, /
단어와 개념에 / 감정을 묘사하기 위해 서로 다른 문화가 가지고 있는 /
as well as in the social circumstances /
사회적 상황에서만이 아니라 /
that draw out the expression of particular emotions.
특정한 감정의 표현을 끌어내는
However, those data do not actually show /
그러나 그러한 데이터가 실제로 보여주는 것은 아닌데 /
that different cultures have different emotions, /
서로 다른 문화가 서로 다른 감정을 가지고 있다는 것을 /
if we think of emotions / as central, neurally implemented states.
만약 우리가 감정을 생각한다면 말이다 / 중추 신경의, 신경계에서 실행되는 상태라고
As for, say, color vision, / they just say that, /
예를 들면, 색 식별에 대해 데이터들은 / 단지 말해줄 뿐이다 /
despite the same internal processing architecture, /
체내에서 일어나는 동일한 처리 구성에도 불구하고 /
how we interpret, categorize, and name emotions / varies according to culture /
우리가 감정을 해석하고, 범주화하며 이름 붙이는 방식은 / 문화에 따라 다르다 /
and that we learn in a particular culture the social context /
그리고 사회적 상황을 특정 문화에서 배운다는 것을 /
in which it is appropriate to express emotions.
우리는 감정을 표현하는 것이 적절한
However, / the emotional states themselves / are likely to be quite invariant /
그러나 / 감정 상태 그 자체는 / 지극히 불변할 가능성이 있다 /
across cultures.
문화 전반에 걸쳐
In a sense, / we can think of a basic, culturally universal emotion set /
어떤 의미에서 / 우리는 기본적인, 문화적으로 보편적인 감정 모음을 생각할 수 있다 /
that is shaped by evolution / and implemented in the brain, /
진화에 의해 형성되어 / 그리고 두뇌에서 실행되는 /
but the links between such emotional states and stimuli, behavior, and other cognitive states /
하지만 그러한 감정 상태와 자극, 행동, 그리고 다른 인지 상태 간의 연관성은 /
are plastic and can be modified / by learning in a specific cultural context.
매우 바뀌기 쉬워 수정될 수 있다 / 특정 문화적 상황에서의 학습에 의해

문화 심리학자들과 인류학자들의 많은 연구는 특정한 감정의 표현을 끌어내는 사회적 상황에서만이 아니라 감정을 묘사하기 위해 서로 다른 문화가 가지고 있는 단어와 개념에 정말로 크고, 때로는 놀랄만한 차이가 있다는 것을 보여준다. 그러나 그러한 데이터가 서로 다른 문화가 서로 다른 감정을 가지고 있다는 것을 실제로 보여주는 것은 아닌데, 만약 우리가 감정을 중추 신경의, 즉 신경계에서 실행되는 상태라고 생각한다면 말이다. 예를 들면, 색 식별에 대해 데이터들은 단지, 체내에서 일어나는 동일한 처리 구성에도 불구하고, 우리가 감정을 해석하고, 범주화하며 이름 붙이는 방식은 문화에 따라 다르고, 우리는 감정을 표현하는 것이 적절한 사회적 상황을 특정 문화에서 배운다는 것을 말해줄 뿐이다. 그러나 감정 상태 그 자체는 문화 전반에 걸쳐 지극히 불변할 가능성이 있다. 어떤 의미에서 우리는 진화에 의해 형성되어 두뇌에서 실행되는 기본적인, 문화적으로 보편적인 감정 모음을 생각할 수 있지만, 그러한 감정 상태와 자극, 행동, 그리고 다른 인지 상태 간의 연관성은 매우 바뀌기 쉬워, 특정 문화적 상황에서의 학습에 의해 수정될 수 있다.

① 감정과 행동 사이의 근본적 연관성
② 감정에 대해 문화적으로 구성되는 표현
③ 세계적인 공용어를 통해 잘못 묘사되는 감정
④ 학문 영역 전반에 걸쳐 보편적으로 규정되는 감정
⑤ 문화적 상황을 학습하는 데 미치는 인식의 더 폭넓은 영향력

문제풀이

서로 다른 문화가 감정을 표현하기 위해 사용하는 단어와 개념에는 큰 차이가 있지만, 감정 상태 그 자체는 문화 전반에 걸쳐 보편적이고, 감정 상태와 자극, 행동, 다른 인지 상태 간의 연관성이 특정한 문화적 상황에서의 학습에 의해 수정될 수 있다는 내용의 글이다. 따라서 글의 주제로 가장 적절한 것은 ② 'culturally constructed representation of emotions(감정에 대해 문화적으로 구성되는 표현)'이다.

구조 다시보기

도입	많은 연구가 서로 다른 문화가 감정을 묘사하기 위해 사용하는 단어와 개념이 큰 차이가 있다는 것을 보여줌
전개	다른 문화가 다른 감정을 가진 것은 아님
예시	감정을 표현하는 것이 적절한 사회적 상황을 특정 문화에서 학습하게 됨
결론	감정 자체는 보편적이지만 특정한 문화적 상황에서 학습에 의해 수정될 수 있음

어휘·어구

considerable 상당한, 많은
psychologist 심리학자
describe 묘사하다
central 중추 신경의
neurally 신경으로
implement 시행하다
state 상태
as for ~에 관해 말하면
architecture 구조, 건축
interpret 해석하다
categorize 범주화하다
vary 다르다, 다양하다
context 상황, 맥락
appropriate 적절한
invariant 불변의, 변함없는
universal 보편적인
evolution 진화, 발전
plastic 바뀌기 쉬운, 가소성의
modify 수정하다
representation 표사
falsely 그릇되게, 옳지 않게
discipline 학문 (분야)

정답률 67%

5. ① 바로크 시대 회화의 특징

직독/직해

By the start of the 16th century, /
16세기 시작쯤에 /
the Renaissance movement had given birth to /
르네상스 운동은 일으켰다 /
the Protestant Reformation and an era of profound religious change.
종교 개혁과 심오한 종교적 변화의 시대를
The art of this period reflected the disruption / caused by this shift.
이 시기의 예술은 혼란을 반영했다 / 이런 변화에 의해 초래된
Appropriately named the Baroque, / meaning irregular or distorted, /
바로크라고 적절하게 이름 붙여진 / 불규칙적인 또는 왜곡된을 의미하는 /
European painting in the 16th century largely focused on /
16세기 유럽의 화법은 주로 초점을 두었다 /
capturing motion, drama, action, and powerful emotion.
움직임, 극적임, 행동, 그리고 강력한 감정을 포착하는 데
Painters employed the strong visual tools / of dramatic composition, /
화가들은 사용했다 강력한 시각적 도구들을 / 극적인 구도 /
intense contrast of light and dark, / and emotionally provocative subject matter /
강렬한 명암 대비 / 그리고 감정적으로 자극하는 소재의 /
to stir up feelings of disruption.
혼란의 감정을 불러일으키기 위해
Religious subjects were often portrayed / in this era /
종교적인 주제들은 흔히 묘사되었는데 / 이 시대에서 /
through new dramatic visual language, /
새로운 극적인 시각적 언어를 통해 /
a contrast to the reverential portrayal of religious figures / in earlier traditions.
종교적 인물들에 대한 경건한 묘사와 대조를 이루었다 / 이전의 전통에서의
In order to capture the social disruption /
사회적 혼란을 포착하기 위해서 /
surrounding Christianity and the Roman Catholic Church, /
기독교와 로마 가톨릭 교회를 둘러싼 /
many artists abandoned old standards of visual perfection /
많은 예술가들이 시각적인 완벽이라는 오래된 기준을 버렸다 /
from the Classical and Renaissance periods / in their portrayal of religious figures.
고전주의와 르네상스 시대로부터의 / 종교적 인물들에 대한 자신들의 묘사에 있어

16세기 시작쯤에 르네상스 운동은 종교 개혁과 심오한 종교적 변화의 시대를 일으켰다. 이 시기의 예술은 이런 변화에 의해 초래된 혼란을 반영했다. '불규칙적인 또는 왜곡된'을 의미하는, 바로크라고 적절하게 이름 붙여진, 16세기 유럽의 화법은 움직임, 극적임, 행동, 그리고 강력한 감정을 포착하는 데 주로 초점을 두었다. 화가들은 혼란의 감정을 불러일으키기 위해 극적인 구도, 강렬한 명암 대비, 그리고 감정적으로 자극하는 소재의 강력한 시각적 도구들을 사용했다. 종교적인 주제들은 새로운 극적인 시각적 언어를 통해 이 시대에서 흔히 묘사되었는데, 이는 이전의 전통에서의 종교적 인물들에 대한 경건한 묘사와 대조를 이루었다. 기독교와 로마 가톨릭 교회를 둘러싼 사회적 혼란을 포착하기 위해서 많은 예술가들이 종교적 인물들에 대한 자신들의 묘사에 있어 고전주의와 르네상스 시대로부터의 시각적인 완벽이라는 오래된 기준을 버렸다.

① 종교적 혼란에 의해 초래된 바로크 회화의 특징
② 시각적 완벽주의의 발달에 미친 바로크 양식의 영향
③ 르네상스 양식을 모방한 바로크 화가들의 노력

④ 분열된 사회를 안정시키는 데 있어 바로크 예술가들의 역할
⑤ 바로크 회화에 나오는 종교적 인물들을 이상화하는 이유

문제풀이

바로크 시대의 화법은 그 시기의 종교적 혼란을 반영하기 위해 극적인 구도, 강렬한 명암 대비, 그리고 강력한 시각적 도구들을 많이 사용했고 종교적 주제는 새로운 극적인 시각적 언어를 통해 묘사되었다고 하면서 바로크 회화의 특징을 이야기하고 있는 글이다. 따라서 주제로 가장 적절한 것은 ① 'characteristics of Baroque paintings caused by religious disruption(종교적 혼란에 의해 초래된 바로크 회화의 특징)'이다.

어휘·어구

give birth to ~을 일으키다, ~의 원인이 되다
era 시대
profound 심오한
religious 종교의
reflect 반영하다
disruption 혼란, 붕괴
shift 변화
appropriately 적당하게, 알맞게
irregular 불규칙적인
distorted 왜곡된
capture 포착하다
emotion 감정
employ 사용하다
dramatic composition 극적인 구도
intense 강력한
contrast 대비, 대조
provocative 도발적인, 자극적인
stir up 불러일으키다
portray 나타내다
reverential 경건한
portrayal 묘사
abandon 버리다
standard 기준
figure 인물
characteristic 특징
imitate 모방하다, 흉내 내다
stabilize 안정되다
idealize 이상화하다

정답률 66%

6. ② 사고 기술 교육의 한계

직독직해

Skills-based approaches to teaching critical thinking /
비판적 사고를 가르치는 데에 있어서 기술에 기반한 접근법은 /

now have a long history and literature, /
현재 오랜 역사와 문헌을 가지고 있다 /

but what has become clear through more than 25 years of work /
그러나 25년이 넘는 연구를 통해 명확해진 것은 /

on critical thinking theory and pedagogy /
비판적 사고 이론과 교수법에 대한 /

is that teaching students a set of thinking skills does not seem to be enough.
학생들에게 일련의 사고 기술을 가르치는 것으로는 충분하지 않아 보인다는 것이다

Students may learn to write an adequate article critique in one class, /
학생들은 어떤 수업에서 적절한 논문 비평을 쓰는 것을 배울 수도 있다 /

but fail to use those skills in another.
하지만 다른 수업에서 그 기술을 사용하지 못한다

They may learn how to evaluate research methodology /
그들은 연구 방법론을 평가하는 법을 배울 수도 있다 /

in other students' research designs, / but completely miss the flaws in their own.
다른 학생의 연구 설계에서 / 하지만 자기 자신의 것에서는 결함을 완전히 놓친다

They may learn to recognize thinking biases in the classroom, /
그들은 교실에서 사고 편향을 인식하는 것을 배울 수도 있다 /

but still use badly flawed reasoning in their own decision making.
하지만 자기 자신의 의사 결정에서는 여전히 심각한 결함이 있는 추론을 사용한다

Too often students think /
너무나 자주 학생들은 생각한다 /

our courses are either about memorizing a great deal of material, /
우리의 수업이 많은 양의 자료를 암기하는 것과 관련이 있다고 /

or about learning the rules for and playing one more idiosyncratic academic game.
또는 또 하나의 특유한 학문적 게임의 규칙을 배우고 그것(게임)을 하는 것과 관련이 있다고

Students regularly fail to understand / what we are trying to teach them /
학생들은 보통 이해하지 못한다 / 우리가 그들에게 가르치려 애쓰는 것을 /

or they fail to transfer and generalize thinking skills / across contexts and classes.
또는 그들은 사고 기술을 응용하고 일반화하지 못한다 / 상황과 수업 전반에 걸쳐

비판적 사고를 가르치는 데에 있어서 기술에 기반한 접근법은 현재 오랜 역사와 문헌을 가지고 있지만, 비판적 사고 이론과 교수법에 대한 25년이 넘는 연구를 통해 명확해진 것은 학생들에게 일련의 사고 기술을 가르치는 것으로는 충분하지 않아 보인다는 것이다. 학생들은 어떤 수업에서 적절한 논문 비평을 쓰는 것을 배울 수도 있지만, 다른 수업에서 그 기술을 사용하지 못한다. 그들은 다른 학생의 연구 설계에서 연구 방법론을 평가하는 법을 배울 수도 있지만, 자기 자신의 것에서는 결함을 완전히 놓친다. 그들은 교실에서 사고 편향을 인식하는 것을 배울 수도 있지만, 자기 자신의 의사 결정에서는 여전히 심각한 결함이 있는 추론을 사용한다. 너무나 자주 학생들은 우리의 수업이 많은 양의 자료를 암기하는 것과 관련이 있거나, 또 하나의 특유한 학문적 게임의 규칙을 배우고 그것(게임)을 하는 것과 관련이 있다고 생각한다. 학생들은 보통 우리가 그들에게 가르치려 애쓰는 것을 이해하지 못하거나 사고 기술을 상황과 수업 전반에 걸쳐 응용하고 일반화하지 못한다.

① 학교 학습에서 비판적 사고의 중요성
② 학생들에게 사고 기술을 가르치는 것의 한계
③ 학업성취도에 미치는 사고 편향의 영향
④ 교실에서의 다양한 교수법의 적용
⑤ 학생들의 비판적 사고 기술을 평가할 필요성

문제풀이

비판적 사고를 가르치는 데에 있어서 기술에 기반한 접근법은 비록 오랜 역사와 문헌을 지니고 있지만, 학생들에게 일련의 사고 기술을 가르치는 것만으로는 충분하지 않아 보인다는 내용의 글이다. 따라서 글의 주제로 가장 적절한 것은 ② 'limitations of teaching thinking skills to students(학생들에게 사고 기술을 가르치는 것의 한계)'이다.

구조 다시보기

주제	학생들에게 사고 기술을 가르치는 것으로는 충분하지 못함
예시	논문 비평, 연구 방법 평가, 사고 편향 등을 배울 수 있으나 적용을 잘 못함
주제 재진술	학생들은 사고 기술을 상황과 수업 전반에 걸쳐 응용하고 일반화하지 못함

어휘·어구

skills-based 기술에 기반한
approach 접근법
critical 비판적인
literature 문헌, 문학
adequate 적절한, 적당한
article critique 논문 비평
evaluate 평가하다
research methodology 연구 방법론
flaw 결함; 흠을 내다
recognize 인식하다
bias 편향
reasoning 추론
memorize 암기하다
transfer 응용하다, 옮기다
generalize 일반화하다
context 상황

정답률 77%

7. ⑤ 과학자들의 연구에서 패러다임의 역할

직독직해

Scientists *use* paradigms / rather than believing them.
과학자들은 패러다임을 사용한다 / 그것을 믿기보다는

The use of a paradigm in research /
연구에서 패러다임의 사용은 /

typically addresses related problems /
보통 관련된 문제들을 다룬다 /

by employing shared concepts, symbolic expressions, /
공유된 개념, 상징적인 표현을 사용함으로써 /

experimental and mathematical tools and procedures, /
실험적이고 수학적 도구와 절차를 (사용함으로써) /

and even some of the same theoretical statements.
그리고 심지어 동일한 이론적 진술의 일부를 (사용함으로써)

Scientists need only understand /
과학자들은 이해하기만 하면 된다 /

how to use these various elements /
이런 다양한 요소들을 사용하는 '방법'을 /

in ways that others would accept.
다른 사람들이 수용할만한 방식으로

These elements of shared practice / thus /
이런 공유된 실행의 요소들은 / 따라서 /

need not presuppose any comparable unity /
그 어떤 비슷한 통일성을 전제로 할 필요는 없다 /

in scientists' beliefs /
과학자들의 믿음에서 /

about what they are doing / when they use them.
그들이 하는 것에 관한 / 그들이 그것들을 사용할 때

Indeed, / one role of a paradigm /
실제로 / 패러다임의 한 가지 역할은 /

is to enable scientists to work successfully /
성공적으로 연구할 수 있게 하는 것이다 /

without having to provide a detailed account /
상세한 설명을 제공할 필요 없이 /

of what they are doing /
그들이 무엇을 하고 있는지(에 대한) /

or what they believe about it.
또는 그들이 그것에 대해 무엇을 믿고 있는지에 대한

Thomas Kuhn noted /
Thomas Kuhn이 언급했다 /

that scientists "can agree in their *identification* of a paradigm /
과학자들은 패러다임을 식별하는 데 있어서 일치할 수 있다 /

without agreeing on, or even attempting to produce, /
동의하거나, 심지어 그런 것을 만들어 내려고 시도조차 하지 않고도 /

a full *interpretation* or *rationalization* of it.
그것에 대한 완전한 '해석'이나 '이론적 설명'에

Lack of a standard interpretation or of an agreed reduction to rules /
표준적인 해석이나 규칙으로 축약되어 합의된 것이 없다 해도 /

will not prevent a paradigm from guiding research."
패러다임이 연구를 이끄는 것을 막지는 못할 것이다

과학자들은 패러다임을 믿기보다는 그것을 사용한다. 연구에서 패러다임의 사용은 보통 공유된 개념, 상징적인 표현, 실험적이고 수학적 도구와 절차, 그리고 심지어 동일한 이론적 진술의 일부를 사용함으로써 관련된 문제들을 다룬다. 과학자들은 다른 사람들이 수용할만한 방식으로 이런 다양한 요소들을 사용하는 '방법'을 이해하기만 하면 된다. 따라서 이런 공유된 실행의 요소들은 과학자들이 그것들을 사용할 때 그들이 하는 것

에 관한 그들의 믿음에서 그 어떤 비슷한 통일성을 전제로 할 필요는 없다. 실제로, 패러다임의 한 가지 역할은 과학자들이 그들이 무엇을 하고 있는지 또는 그들이 그것에 대해 무엇을 믿고 있는지에 대한 상세한 설명을 제공할 필요 없이 성공적으로 연구할 수 있게 하는 것이다. Thomas Kuhn이 언급하기를, 과학자들은 "패러다임에 대한 완전한 '해석'이나 '이론적 설명'에 동의하거나, 심지어 그런 것을 만들어 내려고 시도조차 하지 않고도, 그것을 '식별'하는 데 있어서 일치할 수 있다. 표준적인 해석이나 규칙으로 축약되어 합의된 것이 없다 해도 패러다임이 연구를 이끄는 것을 막지는 못할 것이다."

① 기존의 패러다임에서 새로운 이론을 이끌어 내는 데 있어서의 어려움
② 과학 분야에서 개인 믿음의 상당한 영향력
③ 혁신적인 패러다임의 등장을 촉진하는 핵심 요인
④ 비슷한 생각을 가진 연구원들을 분류하는 데 있어서 패러다임의 역할
⑤ 과학 연구에서 패러다임의 기능적인 측면

문제풀이

과학자들의 연구에서 패러다임은 믿음이 아니라 사용에 관련된 것이라고 하면서 과학자들이 패러다임을 어떻게 이용해야 하는지와 그 패러다임의 역할에 대해 설명하고 있는 글이다. 따라서 주제로 가장 적절한 것은 ⑤ 'functional aspects of a paradigm in scientific research(과학 연구에서 패러다임의 기능적인 측면)'이다.

어휘·어구

paradigm 패러다임, 이론적 테두리
typically 보통, 일반적으로
address 다루다
employ 사용하다
procedure 절차
theoretical 이론적인
statement 진술
element 요소
presuppose 전제로 하다
comparable 비슷한
unity 통일성
account 설명
identification 식별
interpretation 해석
rationalization 이론적 설명
draw 얻다, 도출해내다
novel 새로운
significant 상당한
field 분야
innovative 혁신적인
functional 기능적인
aspect 측면

정답률 66%

8. ④ 아동기와 청소년기의 놀이

직독직해

Children can move effortlessly /
아이들은 노력하지 않고도 이동할 수 있다 /
between play and absorption in a story, /
놀이와 이야기로의 몰입 사이를 /
as if both are forms of the same activity.
두 가지가 같은 활동의 형태인 것처럼
The taking of roles in a narratively structured game of pirates /
이야기식 구조의 해적 게임에서 역할을 맡는 것은 /
is not very different / than the taking of roles /
그다지 다르지 않다 / 역할을 맡는 것과 /
in identifying with characters / as one watches a movie.
등장인물과 동일시하며 / 영화를 감상하면서
It might be thought / 생각될 수도 있다 /
that, as they grow towards adolescence, /
그들이 청소년기로 자라나면서 /
people give up childhood play, / but this is not so.
사람들이 아동기의 놀이를 중단한다고 / 하지만 이는 그렇지 않다
Instead, / the bases and interests of this activity /
대신에 / 이러한 활동의 기반과 흥미가 /
change and develop / to playing and watching sports, /
바뀌어 발전한다 / 스포츠 활동과 관람으로 /
to the fiction of plays, novels, /
연극, 소설, 영화의 허구로 /
and movies, and nowadays to video games.
그리고 최근에는 비디오 게임으로
In fiction, / one can enter possible worlds.
허구 속에서 / 사람들은 있을법한 세계로 들어갈 수 있다
When we experience emotions / in such worlds, /
우리가 감정들을 경험할 때 / 그러한 세계에서 /
this is not a sign / 이는 징후는 아니다 /
that we are being incoherent or regressed.
우리가 일관되지 않다거나 퇴보하고 있다는
It derives / 그것은 비롯되는 것이다 /
from trying out metaphorical transformations of our selves /
우리 자신의 은유적 변신을 시도하는 것에서 /
in new ways, in new worlds, /
새로운 방식으로, 새로운 세계에서 /
in ways that can be moving and important to us.
우리에게 감동적이고 중요할 수 있는 방식으로

아이들은 놀이와 이야기로의 몰입이 같은 활동의 형태인 것처럼 노력하지 않고도 그 두 가지 사이를 이동할 수 있다. 이야기식 구조의 해적 게임에서 역할을 맡는 것은 영화를 감상하면서 등장인물과 동일시하며 역할을 맡는 것과 그다지 다르지 않다. 사람들이 청소년기로 자라나면서 아동기의 놀이를 중단한다고 생각될 수도 있겠지만, 이는 그렇지 않다. 대신에, 이러한 활동의 기반과 흥미가 바뀌어 스포츠 활동과 관람으로, 연극, 소설, 영화의 허구로, 그리고 최근에는 비디오 게임으로 발전한다. 허구 속에서 사람들은 있을법한 세계로 들어갈 수 있다. 그러한 세계에서 감정들을 경험할 때, 이는 우리가 일관되지 않다거나 퇴보하고 있다는 징후는 아니다. 그것은 새로운 방식으로, 새로운 세계에서, 우리에게 감동적이고 중요할 수 있는 방식으로 우리 자신의 은유적 변신을 시도하는 것에서 비롯되는 것이다.

① 놀이 유형과 정서적 안정성 사이의 관계
② 어린 시절에 가상의 등장인물과 동일시하는 이유
③ 청소년들이 좋은 독서 습관을 개발하도록 돕는 방법
④ 아동기 이후 바뀐 형태의 놀이에의 계속적인 참여
⑤ 이야기 구조가 독자의 상상력에 끼치는 영향

문제풀이

아이들이 청소년으로 성장하면서 아동기의 놀이를 중단하는 것이 아니라 놀이의 형태를 바꿔 계속해서 놀이에 참여하는 것이라는 이야기를 하고 있는 글이다. 따라서 글의 주제로 가장 적절한 것은 ④ 'continued engagement in altered forms of play after childhood(아동기 이후 바뀐 형태의 놀이에의 계속적인 참여)'이다.

구조 다시보기

도입	아이들은 놀이와 몰입 사이를 쉽게 이동함
주제	청소기가 되면서 아동기의 놀이를 중단하는 것은 아님
부연	아동기의 놀이가 스포츠 활동과 관람, 허구, 비디오 게임과 같은 다른 형태로 변화하는 것임
결론	우리가 일관성이 없거나 퇴보하는 것이 아니라 자아가 변신을 하는 것임

어휘·어구

effortlessly 노력하지 않고, 쉽게
absorption 몰입
narratively 이야기식으로
identify with ~와 동일시하다
adolescence 청소년기
base 기반, 기초
fiction 허구, 꾸며낸 이야기
regress 퇴행시키다, 퇴보시키다
derive from ~에서 비롯되다
try out ~을 시도하다, ~을 시험 삼아 해 보다
metaphorical 은유적인
transformation 변신
stability 안정, 안정성
engagement 참여, 관계함
altered 바뀐

정답률 62%

9. ③ 자동화된 시스템에서의 문제

직독직해

Difficulties arise / 어려움이 생겨난다 /
when we do not think of people and machines /
우리가 사람과 기계를 생각하지 않을 때 /
as collaborative systems, /
협업 시스템으로 /
but assign whatever tasks can be automated /
자동화될 수 있는 작업은 무엇이든 할당할 때 /
to the machines / 기계에 /
and leave the rest to people.
그리고 그 나머지를 사람들에게 맡길 때
This ends up requiring people /
이것은 결국 사람들에게 요구하게 된다 /
to behave in machine-like fashion, /
기계 같은 방식으로 행동할 것을 /
in ways that differ from human capabilities.
인간의 능력과 다른 방식으로
We expect people to monitor machines, /
우리는 사람들이 기계를 감시하기를 기대하는데 /
which means keeping alert for long periods, /
이것은 오랫동안 계속 경계를 하는 것을 의미하고 /
something we are bad at.
그것은 우리가 잘하지 못하는 것이다
We require people to do repeated operations /
우리는 사람들에게 반복적인 작업을 할 것을 요구하는데 /
with the extreme precision and accuracy /
극도의 정밀함과 정확성으로 /
required by machines, / 기계에 의해 요구되는 /
again something we are not good at.
그것은 또한 우리가 잘하지 못하는 것이다
When we divide up the machine and human components of a task /
우리가 어떤 과제의 기계적 구성 요소와 인간적 구성 요소를 나눌 때 /
in this way, / 이런 식으로 /
we fail to take advantage of human strengths and capabilities /
우리는 인간의 강점과 능력을 이용하지 못하고 /
but instead rely upon areas /
그 대신 영역에 의존하게 된다 /
where we are genetically, biologically unsuited.
유전적으로, 생물학적으로 부적합한
Yet, when people fail, / they are blamed.
그러나 사람들이 그러지 못할 때 / 그들은 비난을 받는다

우리가 사람과 기계를 협업 시스템으로 생각하지 않고 자동화될 수 있는 작업은 무엇이든 기계에 할당하고 그 나머지를 사람들에게 맡길 때 어려움이 생겨난다. 이것은 결국 사람들에게 기계 같은 방식으로, 다시 말하면 인간의 능력과 다른 방식으로 행동할 것을 요구하게 된다. 우리는 사람들이 기계를 감시하기를 기대하는데, 이것은 오랫동안 계속 경계를 하는 것을 의미하고, 그것은 우리가 잘하지 못하는 것이다. 우리는 사람들에게 기계에 의해 요구되는 극도의 정밀함과 정확성으로 반복적인 작업을 할 것을 요구하는데, 그것은 또한 우리가 잘하지 못하는 것이다. 우리가 이런 식으로 어떤 과제의 기계적 구성 요소와 인간적 구성 요소를 나눌 때, 우리는 인간의 강점과 능력을 이용하지 못하고, 그 대신 유전적으로, 생물학적으로 부적합한 영역에 의존하게 된다. 그러나 사람들이 그러지 못할 때, 그들은 비난을 받는다.

① 실패를 피하기 위해 인간의 약점을 극복하는 데 있어서 어려움
② 기계와 인간이 함께 일하게 하는 것의 혜택
③ 자동화된 시스템에서 인간에게 적합하지 않은 과제를 할당하는 것의 문제
④ 인간이 기계 자동화를 계속해서 추구하는 이유
⑤ 인간의 행동이 기계의 성능에 끼치는 영향

문제풀이

자동화될 수 있는 작업이 무엇이든 기계에 할당하고 그 나머지를 사람들에게 맡길 때, 인간에게 인간의 능력과 다른 방식으로 행동할 것을 요구하여 문제가 생긴다는 내용의 글이다. 따라서 글의 주제로 가장 적절한 것은 ③ 'issues of allocating unfit tasks to humans in automated systems(자동화된 시스템에서 인간에게 적합하지 않은 과제를 할당하는 것의 문제)'이다.

어휘·어구

collaborative 협업의, 협력적인
assign 할당하다
automate 자동화하다
end up -ing 결국 ~하게 되다
capability 능력
monitor 감시하다
alert 경계하는
precision 정밀함
accuracy 정확성
component 구성 요소
take advantage of ~을 이용하다
rely upon ~에 의존하다
genetically 유전적으로
biologically 생물학적으로
unsuited 부적합한
blame 비난하다
overcome 극복하다
benefit 이점, 혜택
allocate 할당하다
unfit 부적합한
pursue 추구하다
performance 성과

정답률 65%

10. ⑤ 도덕성에 미치는 유전자와 환경의 작용

직독/직해

Human beings do not enter the world as competent
인간은 유능한 도덕적 행위자로서 세상에 오지 않는다
moral agents.
Nor does everyone leave the world in that state.
또한 모든 이가 그 상태로 세상을 떠나지도 않는다
But somewhere in between, /
하지만 그 사이의 어딘가에서 /
most people acquire a bit of decency /
대부분의 사람들은 얼마간의 예의를 습득한다 /
that qualifies them for membership in the community
그들에게 도덕적 행위자 공동체의 구성원 자격을 주는
of moral agents.
Genes, development, and learning all /
유전자, 발달, 그리고 학습은 모두
contribute to the process of becoming a decent
예의 바른 인간이 되는 과정에 기여한다
human being.
The interaction between nature and nurture is,
하지만 천성과 양육 사이의 상호 작용은 매우 복잡하다 /
however, highly complex, /
and developmental biologists are only just beginning
그리고 발달 생물학자들은 간신히 이해하기 시작하고 있을 뿐이다
to grasp / just how complex it is.
/ 그것이 얼마나 복잡한지를
Without the context / provided by cells, organisms,
맥락이 없으면 / 세포, 유기체, 사회 집단, 그리고 문화에 의해 제공되는 /
social groups, and culture, /
DNA is inert. DNA는 비활성이다
Anyone who says that people are "genetically
사람들이 도덕적이도록 '유전적으로 프로그램이 짜여 있다'고 말하는 누구든 /
programmed" to be moral /
has an oversimplified view of how genes work.
유전자 작동 방식에 대해 너무 단순화된 견해를 가진 것이다
Genes and environment interact in ways that make
유전자와 환경은 생각하는 것을 무의미하게 만드는 방식으로 상호 작용한다 /
it nonsensical to think /
that the process of moral development in children,
아이들의 도덕적 발달 과정, 또는 다른 어떤 발달 과정이 /
or any other developmental process, /
can be discussed in terms of nature versus nurture.
천성 '대' 양육이라는 견지에서 논의될 수 있다고
Developmental biologists now know /
발달 생물학자들은 이제 안다 /
that it is really both, or nature through nurture.
그것이 진정 둘 다, 즉 양육을 '통한' 본성이라는 것을
A complete scientific explanation /
완전한 과학적 설명은 /
of moral evolution and development in the human
인간 종의 도덕적 진화와 발달에 대한
species / is a very long way off.
/ 까마득히 멀다

인간은 유능한 도덕적 행위자로 세상에 오지 않는다. 또한 모두가 그 상태로 세상을 떠나는 것도 아니다. 그러나 그 중간 어디에선가 대부분의 사람들은 도덕적 행위자들로 이루어진 공동체의 구성원으로서 그들에게 자격을 주는 약간의 예의를 습득한다. 유전, 발달, 학습은 모두 예의가 있는 인간이 되는 과정에 기여한다. 그러나 본성과 양육의 상호 작용은 매우 복잡하며, 발달 생물학자들은 그것이 얼마나 복잡한지 이제 막 파악하기 시작하고 있다. 세포, 유기체, 사회 집단, 문화에 의해 제공되는 문맥이 없다면, DNA는 비활성이다. 사람들이 도덕적으로 되도록 '유전적으로 프로그램이 되어 있다'고 말하는 누구나 유전자가 어떻게 작용하는지에 대해 지나치게 단순화된 견해를 가지고 있다. 유전자와 환경은 아이들의 도덕적 발달 과정, 또는 다른 발달 과정이 본성 대 양육의 관점에서 논의될 수 있다고 생각하는 것을 무의미하게 만드는 방식으로 상호 작용한다. 발달 생물학자들은 이제 그것이 정말로 둘 다라는 것을 알고 있고, 또는 양육을 통한 본성이라는 것을 알고 있다. 인간의 도덕적 진화와 발전에 대한 완전한 과학적 설명은 매우 멀리 떨어져 있다.

① 문화적 관점으로부터의 인간 도덕성의 진화
② 유전자의 진화 과정 연구에서의 어려움
③ 도덕적 행위자로서 아이들을 교육해야 할 필요성의 증가
④ 발달 생물학에서의 천성 대 양육 논쟁
⑤ 도덕 발달에서의 유전자와 환경의 복잡한 상호 작용

문제풀이

사람이 도덕성을 갖도록 프로그램되어 있다는 것은 지나치게 단순화된 견해로, 유전자와 환경은 아이들의 도덕적 발달 과정에서 상호 작용한다면서 인간의 도덕적 진화와 발전에 대한 완전한 과학적 설명은 아직 멀다고 이야기하고 있다. 따라서 글의 주제로 가장 적절한 것은 ⑤ 'complicated gene-environment interplay in moral development (도덕 발달에서의 유전자와 환경의 복잡한 상호 작용)'이다.

어휘·어구

competent 유능한
agent 행위자
acquire 얻다, 획득하다
qualify 자격을 주다
contribute 기여하다
decent 예의바른
nature 본성
nurture 양육
nonsensical 무의미한

본문 035쪽

문법 플러스 6. 부정사

A. 1. to emigrate
2. to pay
3. to get
4. to cooperate
5. to find
6. to carry
7. not to waste

1 [해석]▶ 그의 야망은 미국으로 이민 가는 것이다.
[해설]▶ to부정사가 문장 속에서 보어 역할을 하고 있다.

2 [해석]▶ 사람들은 새로운 세금을 지불하는 것을 거절할 것이다.
[해설]▶ refuse 동사는 to부정사를 목적어로 취한다.

3 [해석]▶ 이번 주 토요일에 있을 파티에 음식을 가져오는 것을 잊지 마.
[해설]▶ 미래에 대한 일을 말하고 있으므로 「forget+to부정사」를 사용해야 한다. 의미는 '~할 것을 잊다'는 의미이다.

4 [해석]▶ 협조하는 것을 그녀가 거부해 당황스러웠다.
[해설]▶ to부정사는 형용사처럼 문장 속에서 명사(refusal)를 수식할 수 있다.

5 [해석]▶ Peter는 집에 와서 자기의 집이 불이 난 것을 발견했다.
[해설]▶ '~에 와서 ~한 결과를 발견한 것이므로', to부정사의 부사적 용법 중에서 결과를 나타낸다.

6 [해석]▶ 그 상자는 내가 나를 수 있을 정도로 가볍다.
[해설]▶ A enough to B는 'B할 만큼 충분히 A하다'는 의미이다. carry의 목적어인 The case가 문장 앞에 간 것이므로 carry 뒤에 it을 또 쓰면 안 된다.

7 [해석]▶ 꿈을 실현하기 위해, 그들은 돈을 낭비하지 않기로 결심했다.
[해설]▶ to부정사의 부정은 not을 to부정사 앞에 쓴다.

본문 035쪽

B. 1. to report
2. to take
3. swimming
4. to modernize
5. To see
6. too fat
7. of

1 [해석]▶ 내 직업은 알리는 것이지 논평하거나 판단하는 것이 아니다.
[해설]▶ to부정사가 주어의 직업을 설명하는 주격보어 역할을 하고 있다.

2 [해석]▶ CEO의 연설 후에 15분간 휴식을 갖기로 했다.
[해설]▶ decide는 to부정사를 목적어로 취한다.

3 [해석]▶ 어렸을 때 이 강에서 수영한 것이 기억난다.
[해설]▶ 「remember+동명사」는 '(과거) ~했던 것을 기억하다'는 의미이다.

4 [해석]▶ 그 회사는 현대화를 하지 못한 것이 쇠퇴의 원인이 되었다.
[해설]▶ to부정사가 형용사처럼 문장 속에서 명사(The company's failure)를 수식하고 있다.

5 [해석]▶ 그녀가 걸어가는 것을 보면, 그녀가 맹인인 것을 알지 못할 것이다.

[해설]▶ to부정사는 문장 속에서 '~한다면(조건)'의 의미를 가질 수도 있다.

6 [해석]▶ 그 호랑이는 너무 살이 쪄서 나무를 올라갈 수 없다.
[해설]▶ too... to ~는 '너무 … 해서 ~할 수 없다'는 의미이다.

7 [해석]▶ 그렇게 불쌍한 아이들을 도와주다니 참 친절했구나.
[해설]▶ to부정사는 의미상의 주어를 쓸 수 있다. 의미상의 주어는 「for+목적격」으로 쓰며, kind, brave 등의 형용사 뒤에는 「of+목적격」을 의미상의 주어로 쓴다.

본문 036쪽

숙어 플러스 6. 수능 필수 숙어 6회

1. help	2. catch
3. check	4. across

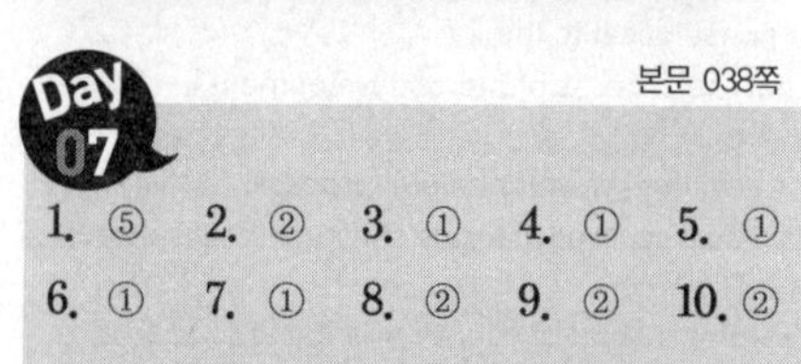

07. 글의 제목

Day 07

본문 038쪽

1. ⑤	2. ②	3. ①	4. ①	5. ①
6. ①	7. ①	8. ②	9. ②	10. ②

정답률 78%

대표 기출 ⑤ 뇌세포의 시각적 인식 방식

직독/직해

Different parts of the brain's visual system /
뇌의 시각 시스템의 다른 부분들은 /

get information on a need-to-know basis.
꼭 필요한 때 꼭 필요한 것만 알려주는 방식으로 정보를 얻는다

Cells that help your hand muscles reach out to an object /
여러분의 손 근육이 어떤 물체에 닿을 수 있도록 돕는 세포들은 /

need to know the size and location of the object, /
그 물체의 크기와 위치를 알아야 한다 /

but they don't need to know about color.
하지만 색에 대해서는 알 필요가 없다

They need to know a little about shape, / but not in great detail.
그것들은 모양에 대해 조금 알아야 한다 / 하지만 아주 자세히는 아니다

Cells that help you recognize people's faces / need to be extremely sensitive /
여러분이 사람의 얼굴을 인식하도록 돕는 세포는 / 극도로 예민해야 한다 /

to details of shape, / but they can pay less attention to location.
모양의 세부 사항에 / 하지만 위치에는 신경을 덜 쓸 수 있다

It is natural to assume /
추정하는 것은 당연하다 /

that anyone who sees an object / sees everything about it /
어떤 물체를 보는 사람은 누구든 / 그것에 관한 모든 것을 보고 있다고 /

— the shape, color, location, and movement.
모양, 색, 위치, 움직임 등

However, / one part of your brain sees its shape, / another sees color, /
그러나 / 여러분 뇌의 한 부분은 그것의 모양을 보고 / 다른 한 부분은 색깔을 보며 /

another detects location, / and another perceives movement.
또 다른 부분은 위치를 감지하고 / 또 다른 한 부분은 움직임을 인식한다

Consequently, / after localized brain damage, /
그 결과 / 국부적 뇌 손상 후 /

it is possible / to see certain aspects of an object / and not others.
가능하다 / 물체의 특정한 측면은 볼 수 있는 것이 / 다른 측면은 (볼 수 없는 것이)

Centuries ago, / people found it difficult /
수 세기 전에 / 사람들은 어려웠다 /

to imagine how someone could see an object / without seeing what color it is.
어떻게 누군가가 그 물체를 볼 수 있는지 상상하기가 / 색이 무엇인지 못 보면서

Even today, / you might find it surprising /
심지어 오늘날에도 / 여러분은 놀라워할 수 있다 /

to learn about people who see an object / without seeing where it is, /
물체를 보는 사람들에 대해 알게 되면 / 그것이 어디에 있는지 못 보면서 /

or see it / without seeing whether it is moving.
혹은 그것을 보거나 / 그것이 움직이고 있는지 못 보면서

뇌의 시각 시스템의 다른 부분들은 꼭 필요한 때 꼭 필요한 것만 알려주는 방식으로 정보를 얻는다. 여러분의 손 근육이 어떤 물체에 닿을 수 있도록 돕는 세포들은 그 물체의 크기와 위치를 알아야 하지만 색에 대해서는 알 필요가 없다. 그것들은 모양에 대해 조금 알아야 하지만, 아주 자세히는 아니다. 여러분이 사람의 얼굴을 인식하도록 돕는 세포는 모양의 세부 사항에 극도로 예민해야 하지만, 위치에는 신경을 덜 쓸 수 있다. 어떤 물체를 보는 사람은 누구든 모양, 색, 위치, 움직임 등 그것에 관한 모든 것을 보고 있다고 추정하는 것은 당연하다. 그러나 여러분 뇌의 한 부분은 그것의 모양을 보고, 다른 한 부분은 색깔을 보며, 또 다른 부분은 위치를 감지하고, 또 다른 한 부분은 움직임을 인식한다. 그 결과 국부적 뇌 손상 후 물체의 특정한 측면은 볼 수 있으면서 다른 측면은 볼 수 없는 것이 가능하다. 수 세기 전에 사람들은 어떻게 누군가가 색이 무엇인지 못 보면서 그 물체를 볼 수 있는지 상상하기가 어려웠다. 심지어 오늘날에도, 여러분은 물체가 어디에 있는지 못 보면서 그것을 보거나, 혹은 그것이 움직이고 있는지 못 보면서 그것을 보는 사람들에 대해 알게 되면 놀라워할 수 있다.

① 시각 시스템은 결코 우리의 신뢰를 배신하지 않는다!
② 색에 예민한 뇌세포의 비밀 임무
③ 맹점: 뇌에 관해 아직 알려지지 않은 것
④ 뇌세포가 자연의 회복 과정의 전형적 예가 되는 이유
⑤ 분리되고 독립적인: 뇌세포의 시각적 인식

문제풀이

뇌의 시각 시스템의 다른 부분들은 꼭 필요한 때 꼭 필요한 것만 알려 주는 방식으로 정보를 얻기 때문에 한 뇌세포가 인지하는 물체의 측면을 다른 뇌세포들은 인지하지 못한다고 하면서 시각과 관련된 각각의 뇌세포들의 독립적인 인식 능력에 대해 설명하고 있는 글이다. 이러한 글의 내용을 가장 잘 나타낸 제목으로는 ⑤ 'Separate and Independent: Brain Cells' Visual Perceptions (분리되고 독립적인: 뇌세포의 시각적 인식)'가 가장 적절하다.

어휘·어구

on a need-to-know basis 꼭 필요한 때 꼭 필요한 것만 알려주는 방식으로
cell 세포
extremely 극도로
sensitive 예민한
assume 추정하다
detect 감지하다
consequently 그 결과, 따라서
localized 국부적인
aspect 측면
betray 배신하다
exemplify 전형적인 예가 되다
recovery 회복

정답률 79%

1. ⑤ 동물 모방 의식을 보여주는 동굴 예술

직독/직해

In making sense of cave art, /
동굴 예술을 이해할 때 /

anthropologists have turned to surviving hunter-gatherer societies /
인류학자들은 현존하는 수렵·채집 사회에 관심을 두었다 /

that continue to paint inside caves, / particularly the San peoples, /
동굴 내부에 계속 그림을 그리는 / 특히 San족에 /

who live in communities across a wide region of southern Africa.
그들은 남부 아프리카의 넓은 지역에 걸쳐 공동체를 이루며 산다

What began to fascinate anthropologists / who studied the San /
인류학자들을 매료시키기 시작했던 것은 / San족을 연구하는 /

was their detailed imitations of the animals they hunt.
사냥하는 동물들에 대한 그들(San족)의 상세한 모방이었다

The hunters, / in some sense, / become animals /

사냥꾼들은 / 어떤 의미에서 / 동물이 된다 /

in order to make inferences about how their prey might behave.
자신의 사냥감이 어떻게 행동할 수 있을지에 관해 추론하기 위해

This spills over into ritual.
이것이 종교적 의식으로 번진다

The San use hyperventilation and rhythmic movement /
San족은 과호흡과 리듬 있는 동작을 사용한다 /

to create states of altered consciousness / as part of a shamanistic culture.
변환된 의식 상태를 만들기 위해서 / 주술적인 문화의 일환으로써

In the final stage of a trance, / Lewis-Williams writes, /
무아지경의 마지막 단계에서 / Lewis-Williams는 적고 있다 /

'people sometimes feel themselves to be turning into animals /
'사람들은 때때로 자신이 동물로 변하고 있다고 느낀다 /

and undergoing other frightening or exalting transformations'.
그리고 두렵게 하거나 의기양양하게 하는 다른 변신을 겪고 있다고 생각한다.'라고

For anthropologist Kim Hill, /
인류학자 Kim Hill에게 /

identifying and observing animals to eat and those to escape /
먹을 동물과 피해야 할 동물을 알아보고 관찰하는 것은 /

might merge into 'a single process' /
'단일 과정'으로 합쳐질 수도 있다 /

that sees animals as having humanlike intentions /
동물을 인간과 같은 의도를 가진 것으로 보는 /

that 'can influence and be influenced'.
'영향을 미칠 수 있고 영향을 받을 수 있는'

동굴 예술을 이해할 때, 인류학자들은 동굴 내부에 계속 그림을 그리는 현존하는 수렵·채집 사회, 특히 San족에 관심을 두었는데, 그들은 남부 아프리카의 넓은 지역에 걸쳐 공동체를 이루며 산다. San족을 연구하는 인류학자들을 매료시키기 시작했던 것은 사냥하는 동물들에 대한 그들(San족)의 상세한 모방이었다. 사냥꾼들은 자신의 사냥감이 어떻게 행동할 수 있을지에 관해 추론하기 위해 어떤 의미에서 동물이 된다. 이것이 종교적 의식으로 번진다. San 족은 주술적인 문화의 일환으로써 과호흡과 리듬 있는 동작을 사용하여 변환된 의식 상태를 만든다. Lewis-Williams는 무아지경의 마지막 단계에서 '사람들은 때때로 자신이 동물로 변하고 있으며, 두렵게 하거나 의기양양하게 하는 다른 변신을 겪고 있다고 생각한다.'라고 적고 있다. 인류학자 Kim Hill에게, 먹을 동물과 피해야 할 동물을 알아보고 관찰하는 것은 동물을 '영향을 미칠 수 있고 영향을 받을 수 있는', 인간과 같은 의도를 가진 것으로 보는 '단일 과정'으로 합쳐질 수도 있다.

① 동굴 벽화: 인간 창의성의 여명
② 동굴 예술을 통한 초기 인류의 의사소통
③ 동굴미술에서 묘사된 초기 인류의 고난
④ 조상에게 경의를 표하는 샤머니즘 문화
⑤ 동물 모방 의식과 동굴 미술의 이해

문제풀이

현존하는 수렵·채집 사회, 특히 San족이 동굴에 남긴 그림에서 San족은 자신들이 사냥한 동물들이 어떻게 행동하는지 추론하기 위해서 동물들을 상세히 모방하고 그 결과 동물로 변신하는 종교적 의식으로까지 발전하였다는 것을 인류학자들이 발견했다는 내용의 글이므로, 글의 제목으로 가장 적절한 것은 ⑤ 'Animal Imitation Rituals and Understanding Cave Art(동물 모방 의식과 동굴 미술의 이해)'이다.

어휘·어구

anthropologist 인류학자
particularly 특히
detailed 상세한
imitation 모방
inference 추론
prey 사냥감
spill 번지다
ritual 의식
rhythmic 율동적인
alter 바꾸다
consciousness 의식
turn into ~이 되다
undergo 겪다
frightening 두려움을 주는
transformation 변화
identify 알아보다
observe 관찰하다
merge into ~으로 합쳐지다
intention 의도

정답률 86%

2. ② 음악 연주에서 변주의 가치

직독/직해

Not only musicians and psychologists, /
음악가들과 심리학자들뿐만 아니라 /

but also committed music enthusiasts and experts /
열성적인 음악 애호가와 전문가도 /

often voice the opinion / that the beauty of music lies in an expressive deviation /
종종 의견을 낸다 / 음악의 아름다움은 표현상 벗어나는 데 있다고 /

from the exactly defined score.
정확히 정해진 악보로부터

Concert performances become interesting /
음악회 공연은 흥미롭다 /

and gain in attraction / from the fact /
그리고 매력을 얻는다 / 사실에서 /

that they go far beyond the information printed in the score.
악보에 인쇄된 정보를 훨씬 뛰어넘는다는

In his early studies on musical performance, / Carl Seashore discovered /
음악 연주에 관한 자신의 초기 연구에서 / Carl Seashore는 발견했다 /

that musicians only rarely play two equal notes / in exactly the same way.
음악가가 두 개의 동일한 음을 연주하는 경우가 거의 없다는 것을 / 정확히 같은 방식으로

Within the same metric structure, / there is a wide potential of variations /
동일한 미터 구조 내에서 / 광범위한 변화 가능성이 있다 /

in tempo, volume, tonal quality and intonation.
박자, 음량, 음질 및 인토네이션에 있어

Such variation is based on the composition /
이런 변화는 작품에 기초한다 /

but diverges from it individually.
하지만 개별적으로 그것으로부터 갈라진다

We generally call this 'expressivity'.
우리는 보통 이것을 '표현성'이라고 부른다

This explains / why we do not lose interest /
이것은 설명한다 / 우리가 흥미를 잃지 않는 이유를 /

when we hear / different artists perform the same piece of music.
우리가 들을 때 / 서로 다른 예술가가 동일한 곡을 연주하는 것을

It also explains / why it is worthwhile for following generations /
그것은 또한 설명한다 / 다음 세대가 가치 있는 이유를 /

to repeat the same repertoire.
같은 레퍼토리를 반복하는 것이

New, inspiring interpretations / help us to expand our understanding, /
새롭고 영감을 주는 해석은 / 우리가 이해를 넓히는 것을 돕는데 /

which serves to enrich and animate the music scene.
이는 음악계를 풍부하게 하고 생기를 불어넣는 역할을 한다

음악가들과 심리학자들뿐만 아니라, 열성적인 음악 애호가와 전문가도 음악의 아름다움은 정확히 정해진 악보로부터 표현상 벗어나는 데 있다고 종종 의견을 낸다. 음악회 공연은 악보에 인쇄된 정보를 훨씬 뛰어넘는다는 사실에서 흥미롭고 매력을 얻는다. Carl Seashore는 음악 연주에 관한 자신의 초기 연구에서 음악가가 정확히 같은 방식으로 두 개의 동일한 음을 연주하는 경우가 거의 없다는 것을 발견했다. 동일한 미터 구조 내에서, 박자, 음량, 음질 및 인토네이션에 있어 광범위한 변화 가능성이 있다. 이런 변화는 작품에 기초하지만, 개별적으로 그것으로부터 갈라진다. 우리는 보통 이것을 '표현성'이라고 부른다. 이것은 우리가 서로 다른 예술가가 동일한 곡을 연주하는 것을 들을 때 우리가 흥미를 잃지 않는 이유를 설명한다. 그것은 또한 다음 세대가 같은 레퍼토리를 반복하는 것이 가치 있는 이유를 설명한다. 새롭고 영감을 주는 해석은 우리가 이해를 넓히는 것을 돕는데, 이는 음악계를 풍부하게 하고 생기를 불어넣는 역할을 한다.

① 음악 비평에서 성공적인 경력을 이루는 방법
② 절대 같지 않음: 음악 연주에서 변주의 가치
③ 음악 치료에서 개인적 표현의 중요성
④ 냉정을 유지하라: 음악 연주할 때 무대공포증 극복하기
⑤ 클래식 음악 산업에서 무엇이 새로운가?

문제풀이

다른 예술가가 동일한 곡을 연주해도 다르게 표현되어 사람들이 흥미를 잃지 않게 해 주는데, 이런 표현성은 결국 사람들의 이해를 넓히는 것을 도와 음악계를 풍부하게 하고 생기 있게 한다고 하면서, 음악 연주에서 변주가 어떤 역할을 하는지에 관해 이야기하고 있는 글이다. 이러한 글의 내용을 가장 잘 나타낸 제목으로는 ② 'Never the Same: The Value of Variation in Music Performance(절대 같지 않음: 음악 연주에서 변주의 가치)'가 적절하다.

어휘·어구

committed 열성적인
enthusiast 열광적인 팬
expert 전문가
voice (말로) 나타내다, 표현하다
score 악보
expressive 나타내는, 표현력이 있는
attraction 매력
note 음, 음표
metric 미터(소절, 운율 등)
variation 변화, 변형
tonal 음조의
intonation 인토네이션(노래나 연주 시 의도한 음정에 정확히 도달했는지 여부)
composition (음악의) 작품
diverge 갈라지다
worthwhile 가치 있는
enrich 풍부하게 하다
animate 생기를 불어넣다
music scene 음악계

정답률 77%

3. ① 영양의 눈이 두개골의 측면에 위치하는 이유

직독/직해

On an antelope's skull, / the eye sockets are situated / on the side of the head.
영양의 두개골에서 / 눈구멍은 위치한다 / 머리의 측면에

This is because this animal spends a lot of its time / with its head bent down /
이것은 이 동물이 많은 시간을 보내기 때문이다 / 고개를 숙인 채 /

to eat a low-nutrient food: / grass.
영양가가 낮은 음식을 먹기 위해 / 즉 풀을

While the animal is busy grazing, / there will be predators out /
이 동물이 풀을 뜯느라 바쁜 동안 / 외부에는 포식자들이 있을 것이다 /

stalking for their food, /
먹이를 찾아 살그머니 접근하는 /

so the antelope needs the greatest possible range of vision /
그래서 영양은 가능한 최대 범위의 시야가 필요하다 /

so that it has the maximum chance of seeing its predator /
그것의 포식자를 알아차릴 수 있는 최대 가능성을 가지도록 /

and making an escape.
그리고 도망갈 수 있도록

With the eye sockets at the back of the head and on the side, /
눈구멍이 머리의 후면부와 측면부에 있어 /

it can see nearly 360° around itself.
그것은 자기 주변을 거의 360도 볼 수 있다

The eye of the antelope is also at the back of its head, /
또한 영양의 눈은 머리 후면부에 있다 /

giving it a long nose.
이는 그들에게 긴 코를 준다

If the eyes were at the front of the skull, / vision would be obscured /
만약 눈이 두개골의 앞쪽에 있다면 / 시야가 가려질 것이다 /

by long grass, / so its long nose also gives an evolutionary advantage.
긴 풀에 의해서 / 그래서 그것의 긴 코 또한 진화적 이점을 제공한다

영양의 두개골에서, 눈구멍은 머리의 측면에 위치한다. 이것은 이 동물이 영양가가 낮은 음식인 풀을 먹기 위해 고개를 숙인 채 많은 시간을 보내기 때문이다. 이 동물이 풀을 뜯느라 바쁜 동안, 외부에는 먹이를 찾아 살그머니 접근하는 포식자들이 있을 것이고, 그래서 영양은 그것의 포식자를 알아차리고 도망갈 수 있는 최대 가능성을 가지도록 가능한 최대 범위의 시야가 필요하다. 눈구멍이 머리의 후면부와 측면부에 있어, 그것은 자기 주변을 거의 360도 볼 수 있다. 또한 영양의 눈은 머리 후면부에 있어, 이는 그들에게 긴 코를 준다. 만약 눈이 두개골의 앞쪽에 있다면, 긴 풀에 시야가 가려질 것이고, 그래서 그것의 긴 코 또한 진화적 이점을 제공한다.

① 더 나은 포식자 탐지: 눈의 위치가 중요하다!
② 들판에서의 주요 방어 전술인 탈출
③ 눈이 가까울수록, 거리 인식은 덜 정확해 진다
④ 먹잇감과 포식자를 위한 윈윈 생존 전략
⑤ 왜 동물들은 인간보다 긴 코를 가질까요?

문제풀이

영양은 풀을 먹기 위해 고개를 숙인 채 많은 시간을 보내기 때문에, 외부에서 접근하는 포식자를 알아차리고 도망갈 수 있도록 최대 범위의 시야가 필요해서 눈의 위치가 머리의 후면부와 측면부에 있다는 내용의 글이다. 따라서 제목으로 가장 적절한 것은 ① Better Predator Detection: Eyes' Location Matters!(더 나은 포식자 탐지: 눈의 위치가 중요하다!)'이다.

《 어휘·어구 》

antelope 영양(동물)
skull 두개골
graze 풀을 뜯다
predator 포식자
stalk 몰래 접근하다
range 범위
eye socket 눈구멍
obscure 보기 어렵게 하다
evolutionary 진화의

4. ① 인간과 로봇의 혼합팀

직독/직해

The approach, *joint cognitive systems*, / treats a robot /
'결합 인지 시스템' 접근법은 / 로봇을 취급한다 /

as part of a human-machine team / where the intelligence is synergistic, /
인간-기계 팀의 일부로 / 지능이 상승하는 /

arising from the contributions of each agent.
각 행위자의 기여로 생겨나는

The team consists of at least one robot and one human /
그 팀은 적어도 로봇 한 개와 인간 한 명으로 구성된다 /

and is often called a *mixed team* /
흔히 '혼합팀'이라고 불린다 /

because it is a mixture of human and robot agents.
그 팀이 인간 행위자와 로봇 행위자가 혼합된 것이어서

Self-driving cars, / where a person turns on and off the driving, /
자율 주행차는 / 인간이 주행(엔진)을 켜고 끄는 /

is an example of a joint cognitive system.
결합 인지 시스템의 한 사례이다

Entertainment robots are examples of mixed teams /
오락용 로봇은 혼합팀의 사례이다 /

as are robots for telecommuting.
재택근무를 위한 로봇처럼

The design process concentrates /
설계 과정은 초점을 맞춘다 /

on how the agents will cooperate and coordinate with each other /
그 행위자들이 서로 협력하고 조정하는 방법에 /

to accomplish the team goals.
팀의 목표를 달성하기 위해

Rather than treating robots as peer agents /
로봇을 동료 행위자로 취급하기보다는 /

with their own completely independent agenda, /
그들 자체의 완전히 독립된 과제를 가진 /

joint cognitive systems approaches treat robots as helpers /
결합 인지 시스템 접근법은 로봇을 도움을 주는 존재로 취급한다 /

such as service animals or sheep dogs.
도우미 동물이나 양몰이 개처럼

In joint cognitive system designs, /
결합 인지 시스템 설계에서 /

artificial intelligence is used /
인공 지능이 사용된다 /

along with human-robot interaction principles / to create robots /
인간-로봇 상호 작용 원리와 함께 / 로봇을 만들기 위해 /

that can be intelligent enough to be good team members.
훌륭한 팀 구성원이 될 만큼 똑똑해질 수 있는

'결합 인지 시스템' 접근법은 로봇을 지능이 상승하고, 각 행위자의 기여로 생겨나는 인간-기계 팀의 일부로 취급한다. 그 팀은 적어도 로봇 한 개와 인간 한 명으로 구성되고 그 팀이 인간 행위자와 로봇 행위자가 혼합된 것이어서 흔히 '혼합팀'이라고 불린다. 인간이 주행(엔진)을 켜고 끄는 자율 주행차는 결합 인지 시스템의 한 사례이다. 오락용 로봇은 재택근무를 위한 로봇처럼 혼합팀의 사례이다. 설계 과정은 그 행위자들이 팀의 목표를 달성하기 위해 서로 협력하고 조정하는 방법에 초점을 맞춘다. 결합 인지 시스템 접근법은 로봇을 그들 자체의 완전히 독립된 과제를 가진 동료 행위자로 취급하기보다는 로봇을 도우미 동물이나 양몰이 개처럼 도움을 주는 존재로 취급한다. 결합 인지 시스템 설계에서 훌륭한 팀 구성원이 될 만큼 똑똑해질 수 있는 로봇을 만들기 위해 인공 지능이 인간-로봇 상호 작용 원리와 함께 사용된다.

① 함께하는 것이 더 낫다: 인간과 기계의 공동 작업
② 로봇은 인간 팀을 능가하기 위해 세력을 규합할 수 있을까?
③ 인간과 기계 간의 갈등에서 인간성의 상실
④ 전원 끄기: 로봇 파트너에게 아니라고 말할 시점과 방법
⑤ 도우미 동물에서 인간을 돕는 로봇 조력자로의 이동

문제풀이

인간과 로봇이 혼합팀이 되어 팀의 목표를 달성하기 위해 서로 협력하고 조정하는 데 초점을 맞추며, 로봇을 인간에게 도움을 주는 똑똑한 존재로 보는 결합 인지 시스템에 대한 글이다. 이러한 글의 내용을 가장 잘 나타낸 제목으로는 ① 'Better Together: Human and Machine Collaboration(함께하는 것이 더 낫다: 인간과 기계의 공동 작업)'이 가장 적절하다.

《 어휘·어구 》

approach 접근, 접근법
intelligence 지능, 이해력
synergistic (반응·효과 등이) 상승적인, 상조적인
arise 생기다, 발생하다
contribution 기여, 이바지
agent 행위자
consist of ~로 구성되다
telecommuting 재택근무
coordinate 조정하다
agenda 과제, 안건
service animal 도우미 동물(장애인을 돕도록 훈련받은 동물)
sheep dog 양몰이 개
artificial intelligence 인공 지능
interaction 상호 작용
principle 원칙, 원리
collaboration 협력
outperform 능가하다, 더 나은 결과를 내다

5. ① 챔팬지의 사냥 방식

직독/직해

Chimpanzees are known to / hunt and eat red colobus monkeys.
침팬지는 알려져 있다 / 붉은콜로부스 원숭이를 사냥해서 먹는 것으로

Although a solo male typically initiates a hunt, / others often join in, /
비록 수컷이 혼자 일반적으로 사냥을 시작하지만 / 다른 것들이 종종 합류한다 /

and hunting success is much higher /
그리고 사냥 성공률은 훨씬 더 높다 /

when chimps hunt as a group / rather than individually.
침팬지들이 집단으로서 사냥할 때 / 개별적으로 보다는

During the hunt, / chimpanzees adopt different roles: /
사냥 동안 / 침팬지들은 다른 역할들을 맡는데 /

one male might flush the monkeys / from their refuge, /
한 수컷은 원숭이들을 몰아낼 수도 있다 / 그것들의 은신처에서

while another blocks the escape route.
다른 침팬지가 탈출로를 막는 동안

Somewhere else, / an ambusher hides, / ready to make his deadly move.
어딘가 다른 곳에서는 / 복병이 숨어 / 자신의 치명적인 동작을 하려고 준비한다

Although this sounds a lot like teamwork, /
비록 이것이 매우 팀워크처럼 들리지만 /

recent work offers a simpler interpretation.
최근의 연구는 더 단순한 해석을 제공한다

Chimps are more likely to join others / for hunts /
침팬지들은 다른 침팬지들에 더 합류할 것이다 / 사냥을 위해서 /

because larger hunting groups increase /
더 큰 사냥 집단이 높이기 때문에 /

each *individual's* chance of catching a monkey — /
각 '개체(침팬지)'의 원숭이 한 마리를 잡을 가능성을 /

they aren't interested in collective goals.
그들은 집단적인 목표에는 관심이 없다

The appearance of specialised roles in the hunt / may also be an illusion: /
사냥에서의 전문화된 역할들의 출현 / 역시 착각일 수도 있는데 /

a simpler explanation / is that each chimp places himself /
더 단순한 설명은 / 각 침팬지가 자기 자신을 배치한다는 것이다 /

where his own chance of catching a monkey is highest, /
자신의 원숭이를 잡을 가능성이 가장 높은 곳에 /

relative to the positions the others have already taken.
다른 침팬지들이 이미 차지한 위치와 비교하여

Collaboration in chimps seems to emerge /
침팬지들의 협력은 나타나는 것처럼 보인다 /

from an 'every chimp for himself' mentality.
'자신을 위한 모든 침팬지'라는 사고방식에서

침팬지는 붉은콜로부스 원숭이를 사냥해서 먹는 것으로 알려져 있다. 비록 수컷이 혼자 일반적으로 사냥을 시작하지만, 다른 것들이 종종 합류하며, 사냥 성공률은 침팬지들이 개별적으로 보다는 집단으로서 사냥할 때 훨씬 더 높다. 사냥 동안 침팬지들은 다른 역할들을 맡는데, 다른 침팬지가 탈출로를 막는 동안 한 수컷(침팬지)은 원숭이들을 그것들의 은신처에서 몰아낼 수도 있다. 어딘가 다른 곳에서는 복병이 숨어 자신의 치명적인 동작을 하려고 준비한다. 비록 이것이 매우 팀워크처럼 들리지만, 최근의 연구는 더 단순한 해석을 제공한다. 침팬지들은 더 큰 사냥 집단이 각 '개체(침팬지)'의 원숭이 한 마리를 잡을 가능성을 높이기 때문에 사냥을 위해서 다른 침팬지들에 더 합류할 것이다. 그들은 집단적인 목표에는 관심이 없다. 사냥에서의 전문화된 역할들의 출현 역시 착각일 수도 있는데, 더 단순한 설명은 각 침팬지가 다른 침팬지들이 이미 차지한 위치와 비교하여 자신의 원숭이를 잡을 가능성이 가장 높은 곳에 자기 자신을 배치한다는 것이다. 침팬지들의 협력은 '자신을 위한 모든 침팬지'라는 사고방식에서 나타나는 것처럼 보인다.

① **침팬지 집단 사냥: 우리들을 위한 것이 아니라 나 자신을 위한 것**
② 침팬지가 집단 사냥을 위해 역할을 할당하는 데 있어서의 장애물
③ 한 마리의 이기적인 침팬지가 협동 집단 사냥을 망치는 방법
④ 다른 침팬지와 함께 사냥하는 것이 사회적 지위를 결정한다!
⑤ 협력적인 침팬지와 경쟁적인 침팬지 중 어느 것이 더 나은 사냥꾼인가?

문제풀이

침팬지가 붉은콜로부스 원숭이를 집단으로 사냥할 때 서로 역할을 배정해 팀워크가 있는 것처럼 행동하지만, 연구에 의하면 침팬지는 집단적인 목표에는 관심이 없고 각 개체가 원숭이를 잡을 확률을 높이기 위해 집단 사냥에 합류한다는 이야기를 하고 있는 글이다. 이러한 글의 내용을 가장 잘 나타낸 제목으로는 ① 'Chimps' Group Hunt: It's All about Myself, Not Ourselves(침팬지 집단 사냥: 우리들을 위한 것이 아니라 나 자신을 위한 것)'가 적절하다.

구조 다시보기

도입	침팬지는 붉은콜로부스 원숭이를 사냥해 먹음.
전개	서로 역할을 배정해 팀워크로 행동하는 것처럼 보임.
반전	집단적인 목표에는 관심이 없고 개체 이익을 고려함.
부연	사냥 시 보여주는 전문화된 역할 역시 착각일 수 있음.
결론	침팬지의 협력은 '자신을 위한 모든 침팬지'라는 사고방식에 기인함.

어휘·어구

hunt 사냥하다
typically 보통, 일반적으로
initiate 시작하다, 일으키다
adopt 쓰다, 취하다
flush 몰아내다
refuge 피난처
escape 탈출, 도피
route 길, 경로
deadly 치명적인
interpretation 해석
collective 집단적인
appearance 출현
specialised 전문적인, 전문화된
illusion 착각
relative to ~와 비교하여
collaboration 협력
emerge 드러나다
mentality 사고방식
assign 배치하다
selfish 이기적인
determine 결정하다
competitive 경쟁적인

정답률 87%

6. ① 생물 다양성 보존의 중요성

직독/직해

As much as we like to think of ourselves as being different and special, /
우리는 우리 자신을 다르고 특별한 존재인 것으로 생각하고 싶어 하지만 /
humans are a part of Earth's biosphere, / created within and by it.
인간은 지구의 생물권의 일부이다 / 그 안에서 그리고 그것에 의해 창조된
Ultimately, / it is the living, breathing elements of this world /
궁극적으로 / 이 세상의 살아 숨 쉬는 요소이다 /
that we need more / than inanimate supplies, / such as coal, gas, or bauxite ore.
우리에게 더 필요한 것은 / 무생물 공급품보다 / 석탄, 가스, 또는 보크사이트 광석과 같은
We can live without cars or beer cans, / but we cannot without food and oxygen.
우리는 자동차나 맥주 캔 없이는 살 수 있다 / 그러나 식량과 산소가 없으면 살 수 없다
As nations around the globe try to band together /
전 세계 국가가 협력하려 애쓰는 중에도 /
to attack the problems of greenhouse gas emissions /
온실가스의 배출 문제를 공략하기 위해 /
and the shrinking availability of fresh drinking water, /
그리고 줄어들고 있는, 신선한 식수의 가용성 (문제를 공략하기 위해) /
in all corners of the world / thousands of species quietly go extinct.
세계 곳곳에서 / 수천 종의 생물이 조용히 멸종되고 있다
E. O. Wilson, the renowned Harvard biologist, /
하버드 대학교의 저명한 생물학자인 E. O. Wilson은 /
recently presented the problem / our species faces / in a succinct law: /
최근에 문제를 제시했다 / 우리 인간이 직면하고 있는 / 간결한 법칙으로 /
"If you save the living environment, the biodiversity that we have left, /
'만약 여러분이 살아있는 환경, 즉 우리가 남겨 둔 생물 다양성을 구한다면 /
you will also automatically save the physical environment, too.
여러분은 자동으로 물리적 환경도 구할 것이다
But if you only save the physical environment, /
하지만 물리적 환경만 구한다면 /
you will ultimately lose both."
결국 두 가지 모두를 잃게 될 것이다

우리는 우리 자신을 다르고 특별한 존재인 것으로 생각하고 싶어 하지만, 인간은 지구 생물권 내에서 그것에 의해 창조된 생물권의 일부이다. 궁극적으로, 석탄, 가스, 또는 보크사이트 광석과 같은 무생물 공급품보다 우리에게 더 필요한 것은 이 세상의 살아 숨 쉬는 요소이다. 우리는 자동차나 맥주 캔 없이는 살 수 있지만, 식량과 산소가 없으면 살 수 없다. 전 세계 국가가 온실가스의 배출과 줄어들고 있는, 신선한 식수의 가용성 문제를 공략하기 위해 협력하려 애쓰는 중에도, 세계 곳곳에서 수천 종의 생물이 조용히 멸종되고 있다. 하버드 대학교의 저명한 생물학자인 E. O. Wilson은 우리 인간이 직면하고 있는 문제를 간결한 법칙으로 최근에 제시했다. '만약 여러분이 살아있는 환경, 즉 우리가 남겨 둔 생물 다양성을 구한다면, 여러분은 자동으로 물리적 환경도 구할 것이다. 하지만 물리적 환경만 구한다면, 결국 두 가지 모두를 잃게 될 것이다.'

① **지구를 구하기 위해 생물 다양성을 구하라**
② 생물 다양성을 위협하는 침입하는 외래종
③ 재생가능 에너지의 잠재력과 활용방안
④ 기후 변화에 대처하는 것은 갈 길이 멀다
⑤ 멸종 위기에 처한 종들을 보호하기 위한 전 세계적인 노력

문제풀이

인간은 지구 생물권 내에서 그것에 의해 창조된 생물권의 일부이므로, 인간에게 필요한 것은 무생물이 아니라 살아 숨 쉬는 요소이고, 살아있는 환경 즉 생물 다양성을 구한다면 자동으로 물리적 환경도 구할 것이라는 내용의 글이다. 따라서 글의 제목으로 가장 적절한 것은 ① 'Save Biodiversity to Save the Earth(지구를 구하기 위해 생물 다양성을 구하라)'이다.

어휘·어구

ultimately 궁극적으로, 결국
element (구성) 요소
inanimate 무생물의
bauxite 보크사이트
emission 배출(량)
shrink 줄다
availability 가용성, 사용 가능성
extinct 멸종한
renowned 저명한, 유명한
biodiversity 생물다양성
automatically 자동으로

정답률 52%

7. ① 기계가 대신할 수 없는 수리

직독/직해

Mending and restoring objects /
물건을 수리하고 복원하는 것은 /
often require even more creativity /
종종 훨씬 더 많은 창의력을 요구한다 /
than original production. 최초 제작보다
The preindustrial blacksmith made things /
산업화 이전의 대장장이는 물건을 만들었다 /
to order for people in his immediate community; /
주변에 사는 마을 사람들을 위해 주문에 맞춰 /
customizing the product, modifying or transforming it /
제품을 주문 제작하는 것, 그것을 수정하거나 변형하는 일이 /
according to the user, / was routine.
사용자에게 맞게 / 일상적이었다
Customers would bring things back /
고객들은 물건을 다시 가져다주곤 했고 /
if something went wrong; /
뭔가 잘못되면 /
repair was thus an extension of fabrication.
그래서 수리는 제조의 연장이었다
With industrialization and eventually with mass production, /
산업화와 결국 대량 생산이 이루어지면서 /
making things / 물건을 만드는 것은 /
became the province of machine tenders /
기계 관리자의 분야가 되었다 /
with limited knowledge.
제한된 지식을 가진
But repair continued to require /
하지만 수리에는 계속 요구되었다 /
a larger grasp of design and materials, /
설계와 재료에 대한 더 큰 이해가 /
an understanding of the whole and a comprehension of the designer's intentions.
전체에 대한 이해와 설계자의 의도에 대한 이해가
"Manufacturers all work /
제조업자들은 모두 일한다 /
by machinery or by vast subdivision of labour /
기계나 방대한 분업으로 /
and not, so to speak, by hand," /
말하자면 수작업으로 일하지는 않는다 /
an 1896 *Manual of Mending and Repairing* explained.
1896년의 'Manual of Mending and Repairing'는 설명한다
"But all repairing *must* be done by hand.
하지만 모든 수리는 손으로 '해야 한다'
We can make every detail of a watch or of a gun /
우리는 손목시계나 총의 모든 세부적인 것을 만들 수 있다 /
by machinery, / 기계로 /
but the machine cannot mend it when broken, /
하지만 기계는 그것을 수리할 수 없다 / 고장 났을 때 /
much less a clock or a pistol!"
시계나 권총은 말할 것도 없다

물건을 수리하고 복원하는 것은 종종 최초 제작보다 훨씬 더 많은 창의력을 요구한다. 산업화 이전의 대장장이는 주변에 사는 마을 사람들을 위해 주문에 맞춰 물건을 만들었고, 제품을 주문 제작하는 것, 즉 사용자에게 맞게 그것을 수정하거나 변형하는 일이 일상적이었다. 고객들은 뭔가 잘못되면 물건을 다시 가져다주곤 했고, 그래서 수리는 제조의 연장이었다. 산업화와 결국 대량 생산이 이루어지면서, 물건을 만드는 것은 제한된 지식을 가진 기계 관리자의 분야가 되었다. 하지만 수리에는 설계와 재료에 대한 더 큰 이해, 즉 전체에 대한 이해와 설계자의 의도에 대한 이해가 계속 요구되었다. 1896년의 'Manual of Mending and Repairing'는 "제조업자들은 모두 기계나 방대한 분업으로 일하고, 말하자면 수작업으로 일하지는 않는다."라고 설명한다. "하지만 모든 수리는 손으로 '해야' 한다. 우리는 기계로 손목시계나 총의 모든 세부적인 것을 만들 수 있지만, 고장 났을 때 기계는 그것을 수리할 수 없으며, 시계나 권총은 말할 것도 없다!"

① 현대의 대장장이에게 여전히 남겨진 것: 수리의 기술
② 수리의 기술이 어떻게 발전했는가에 관한 역사적 조사
③ 창의적인 수리공이 되는 방법: 조언과 아이디어
④ 수리의 과정: 만들고, 수정하고, 변형해라!
⑤ 산업화가 우리의 부서진 과거를 수리할 수 있을까?

문제풀이

과거에는 사용자에 맞게 물건을 제작했고 수리는 제작의 연장이었는데, 산업화와 대량 생산으로 물건 제작은 기계의 분야가 되었지만 수작업으로 해야 하는 수리는 인간의 분야로 남아있다는 내용의 글이다. 이러한 글의 내용을 가장 잘 나타낸 제목은 ① 'Still Left to the Modern Blacksmith: The Art of Repair(현대의 대장장이에게 여전히 남겨진 것: 수리의 기술)'이다.

《 어휘·어구 》

mend 수리하다, 고치다
restore 복원하다, 회복시키다
creativity 창의성
preindustrial 산업화 이전의
original 원래의
blacksmith 대장장이
immediate 아주 가까이에 있는
customize 주문 제작하다, 주인이 원하는 대로 만들다
modify 수정하다, 바꾸다
transform 변형시키다
extension 연장
fabrication 제작, 제조
grasp 이해
comprehension 이해(력)
intention 의도
manufacturer 제조자, 생산 회사
machinery 기계
subdivision of labour 분업
so to speak 말하자면
much less ~은 말할 것도 없이
pistol 권총
evolve 발달하다, 진화하다

정답률 59%

8. ② F. Yates의 대학 시절 일화

직독/직해

There is a story about F. Yates, /
F. Yates에 대한 이야기가 있다 /

a prominent UK statistician.
영국의 저명한 통계학자인

During his student years at St. John's College, Cambridge, /
Cambridge의 St. John's College에 다니던 학생 시절에 /

Yates had been keen on a form of sport.
Yates는 스포츠의 한 형태에 매우 관심이 많았다

It consisted of climbing /
그것은 올라 다니는 것으로 구성되었다 /

about the roofs and towers of the college buildings at night.
밤에 대학 건물들의 지붕과 탑들을

In particular, / 특히 /

the chapel of St. John's College has a massive neo-Gothic tower /
St. John's College 예배당에는 거대한 신고딕 양식의 탑이 있었다 /

adorned with statues of saints, /
성인들의 동상으로 장식된 /

and to Yates / it appeared obvious /
그리고 Yates에게는 / 분명해 보였다 /

that it would be more decorous /
그것이 더 품위 있어 보일 것이라는 것이 /

if these saints were properly attired in surplices.
이 성인들에게 적절하게 흰 가운을 입혀 주면

One night / he climbed up and did the job; /
어느 날 밤 / 그는 기어올라서 그 일을 했다 /

next morning / 다음날 아침 /

the result was generally much admired.
그 결과는 대체로 많은 칭찬을 받았다

But the College authorities were unappreciative /
하지만 대학 당국자들은 인정해 주지 않았다 /

and began to consider means /
그리고 방안에 대해 고려하기 시작했다 /

of divesting the saints of their newly acquired garments.
그 성인들에게서 새롭게 획득한 그들의 의복을 벗기는

This was not easy, / 이것은 쉽지 않았다 /

since they were well out of reach of any ordinary ladder.
그것들은 일반 사다리로는 도무지 닿을 수 없는 곳에 있었기 때문에

An attempt / to lift the surplices off from above, /
시도는 / 위에서부터 흰 가운을 들어 올리려는 /

using ropes with hooks attached, /
갈고리가 달린 밧줄을 사용하여 /

was unsuccessful. 성공하지 못했다

No progress was being made /
아무런 진전도 이루어지지 않았다 /

and eventually Yates came forward /
그리고 결국 Yates가 나섰다 /

and volunteered to climb up /
그리고 올라가겠다고 자원했다 /

in the daylight / and bring them down.
대낮에 / 그리고 그것들을 가져 내려오겠다고

This he did / to the admiration of the crowd /
그는 이일을 했다 / 군중들이 감탄하게도 /

that assembled. 모인

영국의 저명한 통계학자, F. Yates에 대한 이야기가 있다. Cambridge의 St. John's College에 다니던 학생 시절에, Yates는 스포츠의 한 형태에 매우 관심이 많았다. 그것은 밤에 대학 건물들의 지붕과 탑들을 올라 다니는 것으로 구성되었다. 특히, St. John's College 예배당에는 성인들의 동상으로 장식된 거대한 신고딕 양식의 탑이 있는데, Yates에게는 이 성인들에게 적절하게 흰 가운을 입혀 주면 더 품위 있어 보일 것이 분명해 보였다. 어느 날 밤 그는 기어올라서 그 일을 했으며, 다음날 아침 그 결과는 대체로 많은 칭찬을 받았다. 하지만 대학 당국자들은 인정해 주지 않았으며 그 성인들에게서, 새롭게 획득한 그들의 의복을 벗기는 방안에 대해 고려하기 시작했다. 그것들은 일반 사다리로는 도무지 닿을 수 없는 곳에 있었기 때문에, 이것은 쉽지 않았다. 갈고리가 달린 밧줄을 사용하여 위에서 흰 가운을 들어 올리려는 시도는 성공하지 못했다. 아무런 진전도 이루어지지 않았으며 결국 Yates가 나서서 대낮에 기어올라 그것들을 갖고 내려오겠다고 자원했다. 그는 이 일을 하여 모인 군중을 감탄하게 했다.

① St. John's 대학의 조각상에 대한 무서운 전설
② 자신이 만든 문제를 해결한 학생
③ 사람마다 다른 미의 기준
④ 범죄자를 찾아낸 영리한 교수
⑤ 신비로운 건축가의 성공 이야기

문제풀이

Yates가 학창 시절에 대학 예배당의 성인 동상 탑에 흰 가운을 입히는 일을 했고, 대학 당국자들이 흰 가운을 벗기려 했으나 모든 방법이 실패해서 Yates가 직접 다시 벗겼다는 내용의 글이므로, 글의 제목으로는 ② 'A Student Who Solved a Problem of His Own Making(자신이 만든 문제를 해결한 학생)'이 가장 적절하다.

《 어휘·어구 》

prominent 저명한
statistician 통계학자
keen 매우 관심이 많은, 열중하는
consist of ~로 구성되다
chapel 예배당
massive 거대한
neo-Gothic 신고딕 양식의
adorn 장식하다, 꾸미다
statue 동상, 조각상
saint 성인
attire (옷을) 차려 입히다
admire 칭찬하다, 감탄하다
authorities 당국자, 관계자
unappreciative 인정하지 않는
garment 의복
attempt 시도
hook 갈고리
progress 진전, 진척, 발전
eventually 결국
assemble 모이다, 조립하다

정답률 54%

9. ② 촉각의 본질

직독/직해

People don't usually think of touch /
사람들은 대개 촉각을 생각하지 않는다 /

as a temporal phenomenon, /
시간의 현상으로 /

but it is every bit as time-based / as it is spatial.
하지만 그것은 전적으로 시간 의존적이다 / 그것이 공간적인 만큼

You can carry out an experiment /
여러분은 실험을 할 수 있다 /

to see for yourself. 직접 보기 위해

Ask a friend / to cup his hand, /
친구에게 요청하라 / 손을 컵 모양으로 동그랗게 모아 쥐고 /

palm face up, / 손바닥이 위로 향하게 하고 /

and close his eyes. 그리고 눈을 감으라고

Place a small ordinary object / in his palm /
작은 평범한 물건을 올려놓아라 / 그의 손바닥에 /

— a ring, an eraser, anything will do — /
반지, 지우개, 무엇이든 괜찮은데 /

and ask him to identify it /
그리고 그것이 무엇인지 알아보라고 요청하라 /

without moving any part of his hand.
손의 어떤 부분도 움직이지 말고

He won't have a clue /
그는 어떤 단서도 잡지 못할 것이다 /

other than weight and maybe overall size.
무게와 아마 전체 크기 외에 다른

Then tell him to keep his eyes closed /
그러고 나서 그에게 눈을 감으라고 말하라 /

and move his fingers over the object.
그리고 그 물건 위로 손가락을 움직여보라고 (말하라)

He'll most likely identify it / at once.
그는 거의 틀림없이 그것을 알아낼 것이다 / 즉시

By allowing the fingers to move, /
손가락이 움직이게 함으로써 /

you've added time / to the sensory perception of touch.
여러분은 시간을 더했다 / 촉각이라는 감각적 지각에

There's a direct analogy /
직접적인 유사함이 있는데 /

between the fovea at the center of your retina and your fingertips, /
망막의 중심에 있는 중심와(窩)와 손가락 끝 사이에 /

both of which have high acuity.
둘 다 예민함이 높다는 것이다

Your ability to make complex use of touch, /
촉각을 복잡하게 사용하는 여러분의 능력은 /

such as buttoning your shirt /
어둠 속에서 셔츠 단추를 잠그는 것과 같이 /

or unlocking your front door in the dark, /
또는 현관문을 여는 것과 같이 /

depends on continuous time-varying patterns of touch sensation.
촉각이라는 감각의, 계속되는, 시간에 따라 달라지는 패턴에 의존한다

사람들은 대개 촉각을 시간의 현상으로 생각하지 않지만, 그것은 공간적인 만큼 전적으로 시간 의존적이다. 여러분은 직접 보기 위해 실험을 할 수 있다. 친구에게 손바닥이 위로 향하게 하고, 손을 컵 모양으로 동그랗게 모아 쥐고, 눈을 감으라고 요청하라. 그의 손바닥에 반지, 지우개, 무엇이든 작은 평범한 물건을 올려놓고 손의 어떤 부분도 움직이지 말고 그것이 무엇인지 알아보라고 요청하라. 그는 무게와 아마 전체 크기 외에 다른 어떤 단서도 잡지 못할 것이다. 그러고 나서 그에게 눈을 감고 그 물건 위로 손가락을 움직여보라고 말하라. 그는 거의 틀림없이 그것을 즉시 알아낼 것이다. 손가락이 움직이게 함으로써 여러분은 촉각이라는 감각적 지각에 시간을 더했다. 망막의 중심에 있는 중심와(窩)와 손가락 끝 사이에 직접적인 유사함이 있는데, 둘 다 예민함이 높다는 것이다. 어둠 속에서 셔츠 단추를 잠그거나 현관문을 여는 것과 같이 촉각을 복잡하게 사용하는 여러분의 능력은 촉각이라는 감각의, 계속되는, 시간에 따라 달라지는 패턴에 의존한다.

① 촉각과 움직임: 인간의 두 주요 요소
② 시간은 정말 중요하다: 촉각의 숨은 본질
③ 오감을 시기적절하게 사용하는 방법
④ 시간 개념 형성에 있어서 촉각의 역할
⑤ 지식의 촉진제로서 촉각의 놀라운 기능

문제풀이

손바닥에 올려둔 물건은 손의 어떤 부분도 움직이지 않으면 무엇인지 알 수 없지만 손가락을 움직여 만져보면 알아낼 수 있는데, 이것은 촉각이라는 감각적 지각에 시간을 더해서 지각이 가능해진 것이라는 이야기를 하고 있는 글이다. 이러한 글의 내용을 가장 잘 나타낸 제목으로는 ② 'Time Does Matter: A Hidden Essence of Touch(시간은 정말 중요하다: 촉각의 숨은 본질)'이 가장 적절하다.

《 어휘·어구 》

temporal 시간의
phenomenon 현상
every bit 전적으로, 어느 모로 보나
time-based 시간 의존적
spatial 공간적인
carry out ~을 수행하다
cup 손을 (컵 모양으로) 동그랗게 모아 쥐다
identify 알아내다
clue 단서
overall 전체의
sensory 감각적인
perception 지각, 인지
acuity 예민함
continuous 계속되는, 지속적인
time-varying 시간에 따라 달라지는
essence 본질
in a timely manner 시기적절하게
function 기능

정답률 69%

10. ② 생물다양성과 생태계 보존

직독/직해

Invasions of natural communities by
비토착종에 의한 자연 군집 침입은

non-indigenous species /

are currently rated as one of the most important
현재 가장 중요한 세계적 규모의 환경 문제 중 하나로 평가된다

global-scale environmental problems.

The loss of biodiversity has generated concern /
생물 다양성의 상실은 염려를 불러일으켰다 /

over the consequences for ecosystem functioning /
생태계 기능에 대한 결과에 대해 /

and thus understanding the relationship between
그에 따라 둘 사이의 관계 이해는 /

both / has become a major focus in ecological
지난 20년 동안의 생태계 연구에서 주요 초점이 되어왔다

research during the last two decades.

The "biodiversity-invasibility hypothesis" by Elton
Elton에 의한 '생물 다양성-침입성' 가설은 제안한다

suggests / that high diversity increases the
/ 높은 다양성이 군집의 경쟁력 있는 환경을 증가시킨다 /

competitive environment of communities /

and makes them more difficult to invade.
그리고 그들을 침략하기 어렵게 만든다

Numerous biodiversity experiments have been
수많은 생물 다양성 실험이 Elton의 시대 이후로 수행되어 왔다 /

conducted since Elton's time /

and several mechanisms have been proposed /
그리고 여러 방법이 제안되어 왔다 /

to explain the often observed negative relationship /
흔히 관찰되는 부정적 관계를 설명하기 위해 /

between diversity and invasibility.
다양성과 침입성 사이의

Beside the decreased chance of empty ecological
빈 생태적 지위의 가능성은 감소하지만

niches / but the increased probability of competitors
/ 침입 성공을 방지하는 경쟁자들의 가망성은 증가하는 것 이외에도 /

that prevent invasion success, /

diverse communities are assumed to use resources
다양한 군집은 자원을 더 완전하게 사용하는 것으로 여겨진다 /

more completely /

and, therefore, limit the ability of invaders to establish. 따라서 침입자가 확고히 자리 잡는 능력을 제한한다

Further, more diverse communities are believed
나아가, 더 다양한 군집은 더 안정적인 것으로 여겨진다 /

to be more stable /

because they use a broader range of niches than
그들이 종이 빈약한 군집보다 더 광범위한 생태적 지위를 사용하기 때문에

species-poor communities.

비토착종이 자연 공동체에 침입하는 것은 현재 가장 중요한 지구 규모의 환경 문제 중 하나로 평가되고 있다. 생물다양성의 상실은 생태계 기능의 결과에 대한 우려를 불러일으켰고, 따라서 두 가지 사이의 관계를 이해하는 것이 지난 20년 동안 생태학적 연구에 중요한 초점이 되었다. Elton에 의한 '생물 다양성-침입력 가설'은 높은 다양성이 공동체의 경쟁력 있는 환경을 증가시키고 침략을 더욱 어렵게 만든다는 것을 말한다. Elton 시대부터 수많은 생물다양성 실험이 실시되었으며, 다양성과 침입력 사이에 자주 관찰되는 부정적 관계를 설명하기 위한 몇 가지 메커니즘이 제안되었다. 빈 생태적 지위의 가능성은 감소하지만 침입 성공을 방지하는 경쟁자들의 가망성은 증가하는 것 이외에도, 다양한 군집은 자원을 더 완전하게 사용하여 침입자가 확고히 자리 잡는 능력을 제한하는 것으로 여겨진다. 게다가, 더 다양한 공동체는 종이 부족한 공동체보다 더 넓은 범위의 생태적 지위를 사용하기 때문에 더 안정적이라고 믿어진다.

문제풀이

다양성이 높은 군집이 침입종을 막는 경쟁자들의 가능성을 증가시키고 자원을 더 완전하게 사용해 침입자가 확고히 자리 잡는 능력을 제한할 것이라고 여겨진다고 했으며, 다양한 군집은 종이 빈약한 군집보다 더 광범위한 생태적 지위를 사용하기 때문에 더 안정적이라고 여겨진다고 했다. 이러한 글의 내용을 가장 잘 나타낸 제목으로는 ② 'Guardian of Ecology: Diversity Resists Invasion(생태의 수호자: 다양성이 침입을 저지하다)'가 적절하다.

《 어휘·어구 》

invasion 침입
biodiversity 생물다양성
generate 불러일으키다
consequence 결과
ecosystem 생태계
hypothesis 가설
competitive 경쟁의
diverse 다양한

본문 041쪽

문법 플러스 7. 분사, 분사구문

A. 1. inhabiting 2. interested 3. clawing
4. producing 5. Having found
6. closed 7. being

1 [해석]▶ 이런 측면에서 고려될 때, 초기 인류가 자신들의 세계에 살고 있는 인간 이외의 생명체들에 대하여 시각적으로 집착한 것은 깊은 의미를 띠게 된다.
[해설]▶ 주절의 술어동사인 becomes가 뒤에 있으므로 the nonhuman creatures를 수식하는 분사구가 이어져야 하는데, 뒤에 분사의 목적어인 their world가 있으므로, 능동의 의미를 나타내는 현재분사인 inhabiting이 어법상 적절하다.

2 [해석]▶ 그는 흥미로운 작가이고, 나는 그가 쓰는 주제에 대해 흥미가 많다.
[해설]▶ be interested in는 '~에 흥미를 느끼다'는 의미이다. 내가 흥미를 주는 것이 아니라, 흥미를 느끼는 것이므로 수동의 의미를 가지고 있는 과거분사로 표현해야 한다.

3 [해석]▶ Sam은 무언가가 그의 등위로 기어가는 것을 느꼈다.
[해설]▶ 목적어(something)와 목적격보어(clawing)가 능동관계이면 목적격보어를 현재분사를 쓴다.

4 [해석]▶ 세포는 모세포가 분열할 때 쌍둥이로 태어나고, 두 개의 딸세포를 생성한다.
[해설]▶ A cell is "born" as a twin when its mother cell divides, producing ~에서 producing은 주절의 주어를 의미상 주어로 하는 분사구문이다. 「접속사+주어+동사」인 and it produces~를 「접속사+주어」를 생략하고, 동사를 단순분사구문으로 바꾼 문장으로 producing이 어법상 적절하다.

5 [해석]▶ 호텔을 잡은 후, 그들은 저녁 먹을 곳을 찾았다.
[해설]▶ After they had found ~ 문장을 분사구문으로 고친 것이다. 주절의 시제보다 부사절의 시제가 앞설 때, 완료분사구문을 사용한다. 이 문장의 경우 주절의 시제는 과거, 부사절의 시제는 과거완료이다.

6 [해석]▶ 나는 눈을 감고서도 그것을 할 수 있다.
[해설]▶ 「with+목적어+분사」 구문은 '눈이 감긴 채'와 같이 목적어(my eyes)와 분사(closed)의 관계가 수동의 관계일 때는 분사를 과거분사를 쓴다.

7 [해석]▶ 가장 복잡한 세포조차도 그저 몇몇 부분만을 가지고 있는데, 각각은 세포 생명의 뚜렷하고, 명확한 측면을 맡고 있다.
[해설]▶ Even the most complex cell has only a small number of parts, each responsible for a distinct, well-defined aspect of cell life.에서 responsible은 and each is responsible~에서 each being responsible~로 고친 독립분사구문이다. 이 구문은 주절의 주어 the most complex cell과 and 이하의 다른 주절의 주어 each(=part)가 서로 다른 주어여서 주어(each)를 생략하지 않고 밝히고 있으며 동사 has와 is가 같은 현재시제이므로 is를 being으로 바꾼 구문이다. being을 생략할 수도 있다.

본문 041쪽

B. 1. associated 2. bored 3. waiting
4. Situated 5. Having seen
6. following 7. Not knowing

1 [해석]▶ 자신을 실험하는 과학자들은, 법률적으로는 아니지만, 직무상으로는 다른 사람들을 실험하는 것과 관련된 규제를 피할 수 있다.
[해설]▶ 분사구의 수식을 받는 명사구인 the restrictions가 associate가 나타내는 동작의 대상이므로 과거분사 associated가 어법상 적절하다.

2 [해석]▶ Sam의 일은 따분하다. 그래서 그는 지루해 한다.
[해설]▶ Sam이 지루함을 느끼게 되었으므로 수동의 의미를 가지고 있는 과거분사로 표현한다.

3 [해석]▶ 당신을 기다리게 해서 미안합니다.
[해설]▶ 목적어(you)와 목적격보어(waiting)가 능동 관계이므로 목적격보어를 현재분사로 표현한다. 목적어(you)가 기다리고 있는 중이므로 현재분사로 표현한다.

4 [해석]▶ 1300 미터 고도 지점에 위치해 있어, 그 도시는 일년내내 따뜻한 기후를 누린다.
[해설]▶ As the city is situated at ~의 부사절을 분사구문으로 바꾸면 (Being) Situated at ~이 된다.

5 [해석]▶ 사고를 보고난 후, 그녀는 차를 멈췄다.
[해설]▶ After she had seen an accident,~ 라는 부사절을 분사구문으로 바꾼 문장이다. 부사절은 과거완료, 주절은 과거이므로 완료분사구문으로 바꾸어야 한다.

6 [해석]▶ 그는 매일 개를 따르게 한 채 조깅을 한다.
[해설]▶ 「with+목적어+분사」 표현은 목적어와 분사의 관계가 능동이면 현재분사를 쓴다. 현재분사 following이 뒤에 목적어(him)를 가져오고 있다.

7 [해석]▶ 길을 몰랐기 때문에, 그들은 곧 길을 잃어 버렸다.
[해설]▶ 분사구문을 부정할 때는 부정어를 분사 바로 앞에 배치한다.

본문 042쪽

숙어 플러스 7. 수능 필수 숙어 7회

1. come 2. up
3. cope 4. count

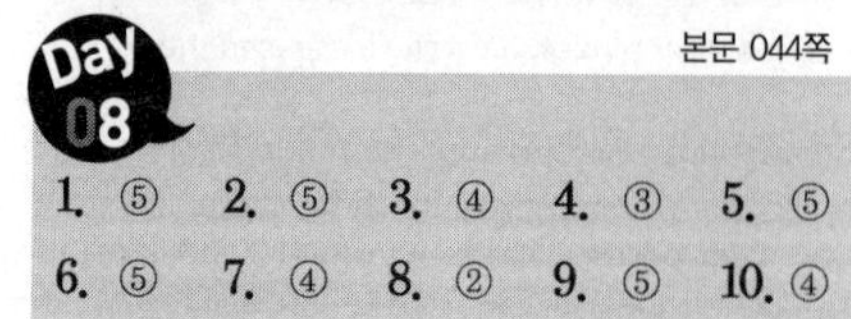

08. 도표 정보 파악

Day 08 본문 044쪽

1. ⑤	2. ⑤	3. ④	4. ③	5. ⑤
6. ⑤	7. ④	8. ②	9. ⑤	10. ④

정답률 94%

대표 기출 ④ 미국인이 선호하는 거주지 유형

직독/직해

The above graph shows /
위 그래프는 보여준다 /
the percentages of Americans' preferred type of place to live / by age group, /
미국인이 선호하는 거주지 유형의 비율을 / 연령대별로 /
based on a 2020 survey.
2020년 설문 조사를 기반으로
In each of the three age groups, /
각각 세 연령대에서 /
Town / Rural Area was the most preferred type of place to live.
읍내 / 시골 지역이 가장 선호되는 거주지 유형이었다
In the 18-34 year-olds group, /
18~34세 그룹에서는 /
the percentage of those who preferred Big / Small City / was higher /
대도시 / 소도시를 선호하는 사람들의 비율이 / 더 높았다 /
than that of those who preferred Suburb of Big / Small City.
대도시 / 소도시 교외를 선호하는 사람들의 비율보다
In the 35-54 year-olds group, /
35~54세 연령층에서는 /
the percentage of those who preferred Suburb of Big / Small City / exceeded /
대도시 / 소도시 교외를 선호하는 사람들의 비율이 / 앞질렀다 /
that of those who preferred Big/Small City.
대도시/소도시를 선호하는 사람들의 비율을
In the 55 year-olds and older group, /
55세 이상 연령층에서는 /
the percentage of those who chose Big / Small City /
대도시 / 소도시를 선택한 사람들의 비율이 /
among the three preferred types of place to live /
세 개의 선호하는 거주지 유형 중에서 /
was the lowest.
가장 낮았다
Each percentage of the three preferred types of place to live / was higher /
세 개의 선호하는 거주지 유형의 각각의 비율은 / 더 높았다 /
than 20% / across the three age groups.
20%보다 / 세 연령대에 걸쳐

위 그래프는 2020년 설문 조사를 기반으로 연령대별로 미국인이 선호하는 거주지 유형의 비율을 보여준다. ① 각각 세 연령대에서 읍내/시골 지역이 가장 선호되는 거주지 유형이었다. ② 18~34세 그룹에서는 대도시/소도시를 선호하는 사람들의 비율이 대도시/소도시 교외를 선호하는 사람들의 비율보다 더 높았다. ③ 35~54세 연령층에서는 대도시/소도시 교외를 선호하는 사람들의 비율이 대도시/소도시를 선호하는 사람들의 비율을 앞질렀다. ④ 55세 이상 연령층에서는 세 개의 선호하는 거주지 유형 중에서 대도시/소도시를 선택한 사람들의 비율이 가장 낮았다. ⑤ 세 개의 선호하는 거주지 유형의 각각의 비율은 세 연령대에 걸쳐 20%보다 더 높았다.

문제풀이

도표에 따르면, 55세 이상 연령층에서 대도시/소도시를 선택한 사람들의 비율은 26%로 두 번째로 낮았고 대도시/소도시 교외를 선택한 사람들의 비율이 22%로 가장 낮았다. 따라서 도표의 내용과 일치하지 않는 것은 ④이다.

어휘·어구

survey 조사하다; (설문) 조사
suburb 근교, 교외
town 읍내
rural 시골의
exceed 넘다, 초과하다

정답률 95%

1. ⑤ 미국 디지털 비디오 소비자 점유율

직독/직해

The graph above shows the share of U.S. digital video consumers /
위의 그래프는 미국 디지털 비디오 소비자의 점유율을 보여준다
who watched films/shows from three genres / between April 2021 and March 2022.
3개 장르의 영화/쇼를 시청한 / 2021년 4월부터 2022년 3월까지
"Thriller, Mystery, Crime" was the most watched genre /
'스릴러, 미스터리, 범죄'가 가장 많이 시청된 장르였다 /
by American adults with the percentage of 47, /
47%로 미국 성인들에 의해서 /
followed by "Horror" and "Science Fiction & Fantasy," /
'호러'와 '사이언스 픽션 & 판타지'가 뒤따랐다
which accounted for 39% and 35% respectively.
각각 39%, 35%를 차지하면서
In the 18–29 age group, / "Horror" was the most watched genre, /
18~29세 연령대에서는 / '호러'가 가장 많이 시청된 장르였다 /
while "Science Fiction & Fantasy" was the least watched genre.
반면에 '사이언스 픽션 & 판타지'가 가장 적게 시청된 장르였다
Each of the three genres was watched /
이 세 가지 장르 각각은 시청되었다 /
by more than 35 percent of the consumers / in the 30–49 age group.
30~49세 연령대의 소비자 중 35% 이상에 의해서
The percentage of people /
사람들의 비율은
who watched "Science Fiction & Fantasy" in the 30–49 age group /
30~49세 연령대에서 본 '사이언스 픽션 & 판타지'를 /
was the same as that in the 50-64 age group.
50~64세 연령대와 같았다
In the 50–64 age group, /
50~64세 연령대에서는 /
the percentage of those who watched "Thriller, Mystery, Crime"
'스릴러, 미스터리, 범죄'를 본 사람들의 비율이
was twice as large as the percentage of those who watched "Horror."
'공포'를 본 사람들의 비율의 2배이다.

위의 그래프는 2021년 4월부터 2022년 3월까지 3개 장르의 영화/쇼를 시청한 미국 디지털 비디오 소비자의 점유율을 나타낸 것이다. ① '스릴러, 미스터리, 범죄'는 47%로 미국 성인들이 가장 많이 본 장르였고, '호러'와 '사이언스 픽션 & 판타지'가 뒤따랐으며 각각 39%, 35%를 차지했다. ② 18~29세 연령대에서는 '호러'가 가장 많이 시청된 장르였고, '사이언스 픽션 & 판타지'가 가장 적게 시청된 장르였다. ③ 이 세 가지 장르 각각은 30~49세 연령대의 소비자 중 35% 이상이 시청했다. ④ '사이언스 픽션 & 판타지'를 30~49세 연령대에서 본 사람들의 비율은 50~64세 연령대와 같았다. ⑤ 50~64세 연령대에서는 '스릴러, 미스터리, 범죄'를 본 사람들의 비율이 '공포'를 본 사람들의 비율의 2배이다.

문제풀이

도표에 따르면 50~64세 연령대에서 '스릴러, 미스터리, 범죄'를 본 사람들의 비율은 52%이고, '공포'를 본 사람들의 비율이 37%이므로 '스릴러, 미스터리, 범죄'를 본 사람들의 비율은 '공포'를 본 사람들의 비율의 2배 이하이다. 따라서 도표의 내용과 일치하지 않는 것은 ⑤이다.

《 어휘·어구 》

share 점유율, 몫
genre (예술 작품의) 장르
account for (부분, 비율을) 차지하다

정답률 96%

2. ⑤ 가장 많은 재생에너지 발전 용량을 가진 유럽 상위 4개국

직독/직해

The graph above shows / the top four European countries /
위의 도표는 보여 준다 / 유럽의 상위 4개 국가를 /

with the most renewable energy generation capacity / in 2011 and in 2020.
가장 많은 재생에너지 발전 용량을 가진 / 2011년과 2020년에

Each of the four countries in the graph / had a higher /
그래프에 있는 4개 국가들은 각각 / 더 높았다 /

capacity to generate renewable energy in 2020 /
2020년 재생에너지 발전 용량이 /

than its respective capacity in 2011.
각각의 2011년 용량보다

Germany's capacity to generate renewable energy in 2011 /
독일의 2011년 재생에너지 발전 용량은 /

reached more than 50.0 gigawatts, / which was also the case in 2020.
50.0기가와트가 넘는 수준에 달했으며 / 이는 2020년에도 마찬가지였다

Among the countries above, / Spain ranked in second place /
위의 국가 중 / 스페인은 2위를 차지했다 /

in terms of renewable energy generation capacity in 2011 /
2011년 재생에너지 발전 용량 면에서 /

and remained in second place in 2020.
그리고 2020년에도 2위를 유지했다

The renewable energy generation capacity of Italy in 2020 /
2020년 이탈리아의 재생에너지 발전 용량은 /

was lower than that of Spain in the same year.
같은 해 스페인의 발전 용량보다 낮았다

The renewable energy generation capacity of France /
프랑스의 재생에너지 발전 용량은 /

was higher than that of Italy / in both 2011 and 2020.
이탈리아의 발전 용량보다 높았다 / 2011년과 2020년 모두

위의 도표는 2011년과 2020년에 가장 많은 재생에너지 발전 용량을 가진 유럽의 상위 4개 국가를 보여 준다. ① 그래프에 있는 4개 국가들은 각각 2020년 재생에너지 발전 용량이 각각의 2011년 용량보다 더 높았다. ② 독일의 2011년 재생에너지 발전 용량은 50.0기가와트가 넘는 수준에 달했으며, 이는 2020년에도 마찬가지였다. ③ 위의 국가 중, 스페인은 2011년 재생에너지 발전 용량 면에서 2위를 차지했고, 2020년에도 2위를 유지했다. ④ 2020년 이탈리아의 재생에너지 발전 용량은 같은 해 스페인의 발전 용량보다 낮았다. ⑤ 프랑스의 재생에너지 발전 용량은 2011년과 2020년 모두 이탈리아의 발전 용량보다 높았다.

문제풀이

도표에 따르면 프랑스의 재생에너지 발전 용량은 2011년에 이탈리아의 발전 용량보다 낮았으므로, 도표의 내용과 일치하지 않는 것은 ⑤이다.

《 어휘·어구 》

renewable energy 재생에너지
generation 발전
capacity 용량, 능력
rank 차지하다
in terms of ~ 면에서

정답률 91%

3. ④ 2016년 EU 국가들의 플라스틱 포장 쓰레기 처리법

직독/직해

The graph above shows the plastic packaging waste treatments /
위 그래프는 플라스틱 포장 쓰레기 처리법을 보여준다 /

in EU countries in 2016.
2016년 EU 국가들에서의

Among the six countries represented in the graph, /
그래프에 제시된 6개 국가 중에서 /

Germany had the highest amount of both recycling and energy recovery /
독일은 재활용과 에너지 재생 둘 다에서 가장 많은 양을 가졌다 /

while France had the highest amount of landfill.
반면 프랑스는 매립에서 가장 많은 양을 가졌다

In the United Kingdom, / the combined amount of energy recovery and landfill /
영국에서 / 에너지 재생과 매립을 합한 양은 /

was more than half the total amount of plastic packaging waste treated.
처리된 플라스틱 포장 쓰레기의 총량의 절반이 넘었다

In Italy, / plastic packaging waste recycled / and plastic packaging waste recovered for energy /
이탈리아에서 / 재활용된 플라스틱 포장 쓰레기와 / 에너지로 재생된 플라스틱 포장 쓰레기의 양은 /

each amounted to more than 800 thousand tons.
각각 80만톤이 넘었다

The amount of plastic packaging waste / used for energy recovery in France /
플라스틱 포장 쓰레기의 양은 / 프랑스에서 에너지 재생으로 사용된 /

was more than four times that of Spain.
스페인의 그것의 4배가 넘었다

The total amount of plastic packaging waste / treated in Poland /
플라스틱 포장 쓰레기의 총량은 / 폴란드에서 처리된 /

was less than the amount of plastic packaging waste /
플라스틱 포장 쓰레기의 양보다 적었다 /

recycled in the United Kingdom.
영국에서 재활용된

위 그래프는 2016년 EU 국가들에서의 플라스틱 포장 쓰레기 처리법을 보여준다. ① 그래프에 제시된 6개 국가 중에서, 독일은 재활용과 에너지 재생 둘 다에서 가장 많은 양을 가진 반면 프랑스는 매립에서 가장 많은 양을 가졌다. ② 영국에서, 에너지 재생과 매립을 합한 양은 처리된 플라스틱 포장 쓰레기의 총량의 절반이 넘었다. ③ 이탈리아에서 재활용된 플라스틱 포장 쓰레기와 에너지로 재생된 플라스틱 포장 쓰레기의 양은 각각 80만톤이 넘었다. ④ 프랑스에서 에너지 재생으로 사용된 플라스틱 포장 쓰레기의 양은 스페인의 그것의 4배가 넘었다. ⑤ 폴란드에서 처리된 플라스틱 포장 쓰레기의 총량은 영국에서 재활용된 플라스틱 포장 쓰레기의 양보다 적었다.

문제풀이

프랑스에서 에너지 재생으로 사용된 플라스틱 포장 쓰레기의 양은 97만 5천 톤이고, 스페인의 에너지 재생으로 사용된 플라스틱 포장 쓰레기의 양은 25만 톤으로 프랑스의 양은 스페인의 4배가 넘지 않는다. 따라서 ④ 'The amount of plastic packaging waste used for energy recovery in France was more than four times that of Spain.(프랑스에서 에너지 재생으로 사용된 플라스틱 포장 쓰레기의 양은 스페인의 그것의 4배가 넘었다.)'은 도표의 내용과 일치하지 않는다.

《 어휘·어구 》

treatment 취급
recovery 재생
landfill 쓰레기 매립

정답률 93%

4. ③ 거주자 특허 출원

직독/직해

The above tables show / the resident patent applications /
위의 표들은 보여준다 / 거주자 특허 출원을 /

per million population for the top 6 origins / in 2009 and in 2019.
상위 6개 출처에 대한 인구 100만 명당 / 2009년과 2019년에

The Republic of Korea, Japan, and Switzerland, / the top three origins in 2009, /
대한민국과 일본, 스위스는 / 2009년에 상위 3개 출처인 /

maintained their rankings in 2019.
2019년에도 그들의 순위를 유지했다

Germany, which sat fourth on the 2009 list /
2009년 명단에서 4위를 차지했던 독일은 /

with 891 resident patent applications per million population, /
인구 100만 명당 891건의 거주자 특허 출원으로 /

fell to fifth place on the 2019 list /
2019년 명단에서 5위로 떨어졌다 /

with 884 resident patent applications per million population.
인구 100만 명당 884건의 거주자 특허 출원으로

The U.S. fell from fifth place on the 2009 list to sixth place /
미국은 2009년 명단에서 5위에서 6위로 떨어졌는데 /

on the 2019 list, / showing a decrease /
2019년 명단에서는 / 감소를 보였다 /

in the number of resident patent applications per million population.
인구 100만 명당 거주자 특허 출원 건수에서

Among the top 6 origins which made the list in 2009, /
2009년에 명단에 들었던 상위 6개 출처 중에서는 /

Finland was the only origin / which did not make it again in 2019.
핀란드가 유일한 출처였다 / 2019년에 다시 순위에 들지 못한

On the other hand, /
반면 /

China, which did not make the list of the top 6 origins in 2009, /
2009년에 상위 6개 출처 명단에 오르지 못한 중국은 /

sat fourth on the 2019 list /
2019년 명단에서 4위를 차지했다 /

with 890 resident patent applications per million population.
인구 100만 명당 거주자 특허 출원 건수가 890건으로

위의 표들은 2009년과 2019년에 상위 6개 출처에 대한 인구 100만 명당 거주자 특허 출원을 보여준다. ① 2009년에 상위 3개 출처인 대한민국과 일본, 스위스는 2019년에도 그들의 순위를 유지했다. ② 인구 100만 명당 891건의 거주자 특허 출원으로 2009년 명단에서 4위를 차지했던 독일은 인구 100만 명당 884건의 거주자 특허 출원으로 2019년 명단에서 5위로 떨어졌다. ③ 미국은 2009년 명단에서 5위에서 2019년 명단에서는 6위로 떨어졌는데, 인구 100만 명당 거주자 특허 출원 건수에서 감소를 보였다. ④ 2009년에 명단에 들었던 상위 6개 출처 중에서는 핀란드가 2019년에 다시 순위에 들지 못한 유일한 출처였다. ⑤ 반면, 2009년에 상위 6개 출처 명단에 오르지 못한 중국은 인구 100만 명당 거주자 특허 출원 건수가 890건으로 2019년 명단에서 4위를 차지했다.

문제풀이

도표에 따르면, 미국은 2009년 명단에서 5위였다가 2019년 명단에서 6위로 떨어졌지만, 인구 100만 명당 거주민 특허 출원 건수는 733건에서 869건으로 증가했다. 따라서 ③은 표의 내용과 일치하지 않는다.

《 어휘·어구 》

resident 거주자, 주민
patent 특허
application 신청, 출원
population 인구
origin 출처, 기원
maintain 유지하다
ranking 순위, 등위
fall to ~로 떨어지다

5. ⑤ 연료 종류별 유럽 연합에서의 신차 점유율

직독/직해

The table above shows the share of new cars / in the EU /
위의 표는 신차 점유율을 보여준다 / 유럽 연합에서의 /
by fuel type / in 2018 and in 2020.
연료 종류에 따른 / 2018년과 2020년의
Compared to 2018, / the share of both gasoline and diesel cars /
2018년과 비교했을 때 / 가솔린차와 디젤차 모두 점유율이 /
decreased / in 2020.
감소했다 / 2020년에
However, / gasoline cars still held the largest share of new cars in 2020, /
하지만 / 가솔린차가 2020년에 여전히 가장 큰 신차 점유율을 차지했고 /
followed by diesel vehicles, /
그 뒤를 디젤차가 따랐는데 /
which made up more than a quarter of new cars / in the same year.
이는(디젤차는) 신차의 4분의 1보다 더 많이 차지했다 / 같은 해
Hybrid electric cars increased by 7.9 percentage points /
하이브리드 전기차는 7.9퍼센트포인트 증가했다 /
in the share of new cars / from 2018 to 2020.
신차 점유율이 / 2018년부터 2020년까지
In 2018, / the share of new cars powered by alternative fuels /
2018년에는 / 대체 연료에 의해 작동되는 신차 점유율이 /
was larger than that of battery electric cars, /
배터리 전기차의 그것보다 더 컸다 /
but in 2020, / the share of battery electric cars / was more than twice /
하지만 2020년에는 / 배터리 전기 차의 점유율이 / 두 배보다 더 많았다 /
that of cars using alternative fuels.
대체 연료를 사용하는 차량의 그것의
Plug-in hybrid vehicles were the only type of vehicle /
플러그인 하이브리드 차는 유일한 차종으로 /
which accounted for less than 1% of new cars in 2018, /
2018년에 신차의 1%보다 적게 차지했던 /
and their share remained the smallest / among all types of vehicle in 2020.
그리고 그것들의 점유율은 가장 적게 남아 있었다 / 2020년에 모든 차종 가운데

위의 표는 2018년과 2020년의 연료 종류별 유럽 연합에서의 신차 점유율을 보여준다. ① 2018년과 비교했을 때 가솔린차와 디젤차 모두 점유율이 2020년에 감소했다. ② 하지만 가솔린차가 2020년에 여전히 가장 큰 신차 점유율을 차지했고, 그 뒤를 디젤차가 따랐는데, 이는 같은 해 신차의 4분의 1보다 더 많이 차지했다. ③ 하이브리드 전기차는 2018년부터 2020년까지 신차 점유율이 7.9퍼센트포인트 증가했다. ④ 2018년에는 대체 연료에 의해 작동되는 신차 점유율이 배터리 전기차의 그것보다 더 컸지만, 2020년에는 배터리 전기 차의 점유율이 대체 연료를 사용하는 차량의 그것의 두 배보다 더 많았다. ⑤ 플러그인 하이브리드 차는 2018년에 신차의 1%보다 적게 차지했던 유일한 차종으로, 그것들의 점유율은 2020년에 모든 차종 가운데 가장 적게 남아 있었다.

문제풀이

도표에 따르면 플러그인 하이브리드 차는 2018년에 신차의 1%보다 적게 차지했던 유일한 차종인 건 맞지만 그것들의 점유율은 2020년에 모든 차종 가운데 두 번째로 적게 남아 있었다. 따라서 도표와 일치하지 않는 것은 ⑤이다.

어휘·어구

share 몫, 지분
fuel 연료
compared to ~와 비교하여
make up ~을 이루다[형성하다]
quarter 4분의 1
electric 전기의
alternative 대안적인, 대체의
vehicle 차량, 탈 것
remain 남아 있다

정답률 86%

6. ⑤ 차량 대 선박의 이산화 탄소 배출량

직독/직해

The graph above shows the CO_2 emissions from cars versus ships /
위 도표는 차량 대 선박의 이산화 탄소 배출량을 보여 준다 /
in Europe in 2019.
2019년 유럽에서
Among the eight countries, / the CO2 emissions from ships were larger /
8개국 중에서 / 선박의 이산화 탄소 배출량이 더 많았다 /
than those from cars / except for Belgium.
차량의 것보다 / 벨기에를 제외하고는
The Netherlands had the largest CO_2 emissions from both cars and ships, /
네덜란드가 차량과 선박 모두에서 이산화 탄소 배출량이 가장 많았다 /
whereas Sweden had the smallest CO_2 emissions from both.
반면에 스웨덴이 차량과 선박 모두에서 이산화 탄소 배출량이 가장 적었다
The CO_2 emissions from ships were larger in Spain /
선박에서 나온 이산화 탄소 배출량은 스페인에서 더 많았다 /
than in the United Kingdom, /
영국보다 /
but the CO_2 emissions from cars were larger in the United Kingdom than in Spain.
그러나 차량에서 나온 이산화 탄소 배출량은 스페인보다 영국에서 더 많았다
Germany's CO_2 emissions from ships were more than twice those of Sweden.
독일의 선박 이산화 탄소 배출량은 스웨덴의 선박 이산화 탄소 배출량의 두 배가 넘었다
The gap between the CO_2 emissions from cars and ships was the largest /
차량의 이산화 탄소 배출량과 선박의 이산화 탄소 배출량 사이의 격차는 가장 컸다 /
in the Netherlands / and the smallest in Italy and France.
네덜란드에서 / 그리고 이탈리아와 프랑스에서 가장 작았다

위 도표는 2019년 유럽에서 차량 대 선박의 이산화 탄소 배출량을 보여 준다. ① 8개국 중에서 벨기에를 제외하고는, 선박의 이산화 탄소 배출량이 차량의 것보다 더 많았다. ② 네덜란드가 차량과 선박 모두에서 이산화 탄소 배출량이 가장 많았고, 반면 스웨덴이 차량과 선박 모두에서 이산화 탄소 배출량이 가장 적었다. ③ 선박에서 나온 이산화 탄소 배출량은 영국보다 스페인에서 더 많았지만, 차량에서 나온 이산화 탄소 배출량은 스페인보다 영국에서 더 많았다. ④ 독일의 선박 이산화 탄소 배출량은 스웨덴의 선박 이산화 탄소 배출량의 두 배가 넘었다. ⑤ 차량의 이산화 탄소 배출량과 선박의 이산화 탄소 배출량 사이의 격차는 네덜란드에서 가장 컸고, 이탈리아와 프랑스에서 가장 작았다.

문제풀이

도표에 따르면 네덜란드에서의 차량의 이산화 탄소 배출량(16.7)과 선박의 이산화 탄소 배출량(19.9) 사이의 격차는 3.2이고, 스페인에서의 차량의 이산화 탄소 배출량(12.2)과 선박의 이산화 탄소 배출량(19.9) 사이의 격차는 4.9이므로 ⑤가 도표의 내용과 일치하지 않는다.

어휘·어구

emission 배출량
except for ~을 제외하고
gap 격차, 차이

7. ④ 세계 중산층의 점유율 비교

직독/직해

The above graphs show /
위 그래프들은 보여준다 /
the percentage share of the global middle class /
세계 중산층의 점유율을 /
by region / in 2015 and its projected share in 2025.
지역별로 / 2015년과 2025년에 예상된 점유율을
It is projected / that the share of the global middle class in Asia Pacific /
예상된다 / 아시아 태평양 지역의 세계 중산층 점유율은 /
will increase / from 46 percent in 2015 to 60 percent in 2025.
증가할 것으로 / 2015년에 46%로부터 2025년에는 60%로
The projected share of Asia Pacific in 2025, /
2025년의 아시아 태평양 지역의 예상 점유율은 /
the largest among the six regions, / is more / than three times that of Europe in the same year.
6개의 지역 중에서 가장 크며 / 더 많다 / 같은 해 유럽의 예상 점유율의 3배보다
The shares of Europe and North America / are both projected to decrease, /
유럽과 북미 지역의 점유율은 / 둘 다 감소할 것으로 예상된다 /
from 24 percent in 2015 to 16 percent in 2025 for Europe, /
유럽은 2015년에 24%로부터 2025년에 16%로 /
and from 11 percent in 2015 to 8 percent in 2025 for North America.
그리고 북미 지역은 2015년에 11%로부터 2025년에 8%로
Central and South America is not expected to change / from 2015 to 2025 / in its share of the global middle class.
중남미 지역은 변하지 않을 것으로 예상된다 / 2015년에서 2025년까지 / 세계 중산층 점유율에 있어서
In 2025, / the share of the Middle East and North Africa / will be larger / than that of sub-Saharan Africa, / as it was in 2015.
2025년에 / 중동 및 북아프리카의 점유율은 / 더 클 것이다 / 사하라 사막 이남의 아프리카의 점유율보다 / 2015년에 그랬듯이

위 그래프들은 지역별로 2015년 세계 중산층의 점유율과 2025년에 예상된 점유율을 보여준다. ① 아시아 태평양 지역의 세계 중산층 점유율은 2015년에 46%로부터 2025년에는 60%로 증가할 것으로 예상된다. ② 2025년의 아시아 태평양 지역의 예상 점유율은 6개의 지역 중에서 가장 크며, 같은 해 유럽의 예상 점유율의 3배보다 더 많다. ③ 유럽과 북미 지역의 점유율은, 유럽은 2015년에 24%로부터 2025년에 16%로, 북미 지역은 2015년에 11%로부터 2025년에 8%로, 둘 다 감소할 것으로 예상된다. ④ 중남미 지역은 세계 중산층 점유율에 있어서 2015년에서 2025년까지 변하지 않을 것으로 예상된다. ⑤ 2015년에 그랬듯이, 2025년에 중동 및 북아프리카의 점유율은 사하라 사막 이남의 아프리카의 점유율보다 더 클 것이다.

문제풀이

도표에 따르면, 중남미 지역은 세계 중산층의 점유율이 2015년에 9%였고 2025년의 예상된 점유율은 7%로, 2% 감소할 것으로 예상했다. 따라서 도표의 내용과 일치하지 않는 것은 ④이다.

어휘·어구

share 점유율
middle class 중산층
project 예상하다
sub-Saharan Africa 사하라 사막 이남의 아프리카

8. ② 미국 성인의 연령대별 책 소비

직독/직해

The above graph, / 위의 도표는 /
which was based on a survey conducted in 2019, /

2019년에 실시한 설문 조사에 기초한 /
shows the percentages of U.S. adults /
미국 성인의 비율을 보여 준다 /
by age group / 연령대별로 /
who said / they had read (or listened to) a book /
말한 / 그들이 책을 읽었(거나 들었)다고 /
in one or more of the formats /
한 개 이상의 형식으로 /
— print books, e-books, and audiobooks — /
종이책, 전자책, 오디오북 /
in the previous 12 months.
지난 12개월 동안
The percentage of people in the 18-29 group /
18~29세 그룹 사람들의 비율은 /
who said / they had read a print book / was 74%, /
말한 / 그들이 종이책을 읽었다고 / 74%였는데 /
which was the highest among the four groups.
이것은 4개의 연령대 중에서 가장 높았다
The percentage of people / who said /
사람들의 비율은 / 말한 /
they had read a print book / in the 50-64 group /
그들이 종이책을 읽었다고 / 50~64세 그룹에서 /
was higher / than that in the 65 and up group.
더 높았다 / 65세 이상 그룹의 비율보다
While 34% of people in the 18-29 group said /
18~29세 그룹의 34%의 사람들이 말한 반면에 /
they had read an e-book, /
그들이 전자책을 읽었다고 /
the percentage of people who said so /
그렇게 말한 사람들의 비율이 /
was below 20% / in the 65 and up group.
20% 미만이었다 / 65세 이상 그룹에서는
In all age groups, / the percentage of people /
모든 그룹에서 / 사람들의 비율은 /
who said / 말한 /
they had read an e-book / was higher /
그들이 전자책을 읽었다고 / 더 높았다 /
than that of people / who said /
사람들의 비율보다 / 말한 /
they had listened to an audiobook.
오디오북을 들었다고
Among the four age groups, /
4개의 그룹 중에서 /
the 30-49 group had the highest percentage of people /
30~49세 그룹이 사람들의 비율이 가장 높았다 /
who said / they had listened to an audiobook.
말한 / 그들이 오디오북을 들었다고

2019년에 실시한 설문 조사에 기초한 위의 도표는 지난 12개월 동안 종이책, 전자책, 오디오북 중 한 개 이상의 형식으로 책을 읽었(거나 들었)다고 말한 미국 성인의 비율을 연령대별로 보여 준다. ① 종이책을 읽었다고 말한 18~29세 그룹 사람들의 비율은 74%였는데, 이것은 4개의 연령대 중에서 가장 높았다. ② 50~64세 그룹에서 종이책을 읽었다고 말한 사람들의 비율은 65세 이상 그룹의 비율보다 더 높았다. ③ 18~29세 그룹의 34%의 사람들이 전자책을 읽었다고 말한 반면에, 65세 이상 그룹에서는 그렇게 말한 사람들의 비율이 20% 미만이었다. ④ 모든 그룹에서, 전자책을 읽었다고 말한 사람들의 비율은 오디오북을 들었다고 말한 사람들의 비율보다 더 높았다. ⑤ 4개의 그룹 중에서, 30~49세 그룹이 오디오북을 들었다고 말한 사람들의 비율이 가장 높았다.

문제풀이

도표에 따르면, 50~64세 그룹에서 종이책을 읽었다고 말한 사람들의 비율은 59%이고, 65세 이상 그룹에서 그렇게 말한 사람들의 비율은 63%이다. 따라서 도표의 내용과 일치하지 않는 것은 ②이다.

어휘·어구

be based on ~에 기초하다[근거하다]
survey 설문 조사
conduct 실시하다
format 형식
print book 종이책

정답률 93%

9. ⑤ 소매 판매의 온라인 점유율

직독/직해

The graph above shows the online shares of retail sales /
위의 도표는 소매 판매의 온라인 점유율을 보여준다 /
for each of six countries / in 2012 and in 2019.
여섯 국가 각각의 / 2012년과 2019년에
The online share of retail sales /
소매 판매의 온라인 점유율은 /
refers to the percentage of retail sales /
소매 판매의 비율을 나타내다 /
conducted online in a given country.
주어진 국가에서 온라인으로 이루어진
For each country, / 각 국가에서 /
its online share of retail sales in 2019 /
2019년의 소매 판매의 온라인 점유율은 /
was larger / than that in 2012.
더 컸다 / 2012년의 그것보다
Among the six countries, /
여섯 국가 중에서 /
the UK owned the largest online share of retail sales /
영국은 가장 큰 소매 판매의 온라인 점유율을 가졌다 /
with 19.7% / in 2019.
19.7%로 / 2019년에
In 2019, / 2019년에 /
the U.S. had the second largest online share of retail sales /
미국은 소매 판매의 온라인 점유율이 두 번째로 컸다 /
with 16.5%. 16.5%로
In 2012, / 2012년에 /
the online share of retail sales in the Netherlands /
네덜란드의 소매 판매의 온라인 점유율은 /
was larger than that in France, /
프랑스의 그것보다 더 컸다 /
whereas the reverse was true / in 2019.
반면 그 반대였다 / 2019년에는
In the case of Spain and Italy, /
스페인과 이탈리아의 경우에 /
the online share of retail sales in each country /
각 국가에서 소매 판매의 온라인 점유율이 /
was less than 5.0% / both in 2012 and in 2019.
5.0%보다 더 적었다 / 2012년과 2019년 둘 다에서

위의 도표는 2012년과 2019년에 여섯 국가 각각의 소매 판매의 온라인 점유율을 보여준다. 소매 판매의 온라인 점유율은 주어진 국가에서 온라인으로 이루어진 소매 판매의 비율을 나타낸다. ① 각 국가에서 2019년의 소매 판매의 온라인 점유율은 2012년의 그것보다 더 컸다. ② 여섯 국가 중에서 영국은 2019년에 19.7%로 가장 큰 소매 판매의 온라인 점유율을 가졌다. ③ 2019년에 미국은 16.5%로 소매 판매의 온라인 점유율이 두 번째로 컸다. ④ 2012년에 네덜란드의 소매 판매의 온라인 점유율은 프랑스의 그것보다 더 컸던 반면, 2019년에는 그 반대였다. ⑤ 스페인과 이탈리아의 경우에, 각 국가에서 소매 판매의 온라인 점유율이 2012년과 2019년 둘 다에서 5.0%에 미치지 못했다.

문제풀이

도표에 따르면, 2019년에 스페인의 소매 판매의 온라인 점유율은 5.4%로 5.0%보다 더 컸다. 따라서 도표의 내용과 일치하지 않는 것은 ⑤이다.

어휘·어구

share 점유율
retail sales 소매 판매
refer to ~을 나타내다
conduct 수행하다
reverse 반대

정답률 95%

10. ④ 세계 인구의 전기 이용

직독/직해

The above graph shows / the world population
위 도표는 보여준다 / 1997년과 2017년 세계 인구의 전기 이용 기회를
access to electricity in 1997 and in 2017.
The percentage of the total world population with
2017년의 전기를 이용할 수 있었던 총 세계 인구 비율은 /
electricity access in 2017 /
was 11 percentage points higher than that in 1997.
1997년의 비율보다 11퍼센트 포인트 높았다
Both in 1997 and in 2017, / 1997년과 2017년 두 해 모두 /
less than 80% of the rural population had access
시골 인구의 80 퍼센트 미만이 전기를 이용할 수 있었고 /
to electricity /
while over 90% of the urban population had access
반면에 90 퍼센트가 넘는 도시 인구가 전기를 이용할 수 있었다
to electricity.
In 1997, 36% of the rural population did not have
1997년에 시골인구의 36퍼센트가 전기를 이용할 수 없었고 /
electricity access /
while 5% of the urban population did not have
반면에 도시 인구의 5퍼센트가 전기를 이용할 수 없었다
access to electricity.
The percentage of the rural population without
2017년에 전기를 이용할 수 없었던 시골 인구의 비율은 /
electricity access in 2017 /
was 20 percentage points lower than that in 1997.
1997년의 비율보다 20퍼센트 포인트 더 낮았다
The percentage of the urban population without
전기를 이용할 수 없었던 도시 인구의 비율은
electricity access /
decreased from 5% in 1997 to 3% in 2017.
1997년 5퍼센트에서 2017년 3퍼센트로 감소했다

위 그래프는 1997년과 2017년의 세계 인구의 전기 이용을 보여준다. ① 2017년의 전기를 사용하는 세계 인구의 비율은 1997년보다 11 퍼센티지 포인트 높았다. ② 1997년과 2017년 모두, 시골 인구의 80% 미만이 전기를 이용했고 도시 인구의 90% 이상이 전기를 이용했다. ③ 1997년에 시골 인구의 36%가 전기 사용을 하지 않은 반면 도시 인구의 5%는 전기 사용을 하지 않았다. ④ 2017년에 전기 사용을 하지 않은 시골 인구의 비율은 1997년보다 20 퍼센티지 포인트 낮았다. ⑤ 전기 사용이 없었던 도시 인구의 비율은 1997년에 5%에서 2017년에 3%로 감소했다.

문제풀이

표에 따르면 전기를 사용할 수 없었던 시골 인구 비율은 2017년에 21퍼센트였고, 1997년에는 36퍼센트였으므로 그 비율은 2017년이 1997년보다 15퍼센트 포인트 낮았다. 따라서 표의 내용과 일치하지 않는 것은 ④이다.

어휘·어구

electricity 전기
rural 시골의
urban 도시의

본문 047쪽

문법 플러스 8. 준동사

A. 1. to have left
2. Having already seen
3. be
4. associated
5. opening
6. His
7. his not

1 [해석]▶ 그가 나라를 떠났다고 사람들은 믿는다.
[해설]▶ 주절의 시제(is)보다 종속절의 시제(left)가 앞서 있으므로, 완료형 부정사가 필요하다.

2 [해석]▶ 그녀는 그 영화를 두 번 봐서, 극장에 가기를 원치 않았다.
[해설]▶ 주절의 시제(didn't want: 과거) 보다 종속절의 시제(had seen: 과거완료)가 앞설 때는 완료분사구문을 쓴다.

3 [해석]▶ Sally는 방해를 받고 싶지 않아 전화를 차단했다.
[해설]▶ Sally가 전화 때문에 방해를 받는 것이므로 부정사의 수동태(to be p.p.)가 필요하다.

4 [해석]▶ 표현 형태로서 패션은 다수의 모호함을 담고 있어 개인이 특정한 옷과 연관된 의미를 다시 만들어낼 수 있게 한다.
[해설]▶ the meanings를 수식하는 과거분사구를 이끄는 associated가 어법상 적절하다. '연관된'이라는 의미로 앞의 명사 the meanings를 수식하는 과거분사가 나와야 하므로 associated가 적절하다.

5 [해석]▶ 패션은 또한 행동을 위한 공간을 열어주면서 다양한 방식으로 행동력을 강화할 수 있다.
[해설]▶ 앞 절 내용의 결과를 보여주는 분사구문을 이끄는 opening은 어법상 적절하다. '행동을 위한 공간을 열어주면서'라는 능동의 의미이므로, 현재분사 opening이 와야 한다.

6 [해석]▶ 내가 집에 갑자기 돌아온 것을 그가 알고 있는 것이 이상하다.
[해설]▶ 동명사가 문장의 주어로 문두에 나올 때는 소유격을 쓴다.

7 [해석]▶ 나는 그가 눈치 채지 못한 것이 놀랍다.
[해설]▶ 동명사의 부정은 의미상의 주어 바로 뒤에 not을 쓴다.

본문 047쪽

B. 1. having wasted
2. Having completed
3. being spoken to
4. taken
5. frustrated
6. of
7. Not wanting

1 [해석]▶ 당신의 시간을 낭비한 것에 대해 유감입니다.
[해설]▶ 주절의 주어는 현재시제이고, 종속절의 시제는 과거시제이다. 술어 동사의 시제보다 앞선 경우, 완료형 동명사를 사용한다.

2 [해석]▶ 그녀는 일을 마친 후, 휴가를 떠났다.
[해설]▶ 부사절의 시제가 주절의 시제보다 앞선 경우, 완료분사구문을 사용한다.

3 [해석]▶ Sam은 누군가 말을 걸지 않으면 말을 전혀 하지 않는다.
[해설]▶ 전치사 without 뒤에 동명사형이 나와야 하며, Sam이 말을 거는 주체가 아니라 대상이므로 동명사 수동태 「being+p.p.」형태로 나타내야 한다.

4 [해석]▶ 나는 Mark가 경찰에 끌려가는 것을 봤다.
[해설]▶ 지각동사 뒤에 목적어와 목적격보어가 수동 관계인 경우, 과거분사를 사용해야 한다.

5 [해석]▶ 그의 서툰 연기에 실망한 연극 연출가가 그를 향해 소리를 질렀다.
[해설]▶ 분사구문이 주절의 주어와 수동 관계이면 과거분사를 써야 한다. 연극 연출가가 그의 서툰 연기로 실망한 것이므로 수동의 의미를 드러내도록 과거분사를 써야 한다.

6 [해석]▶ 그가 휴대폰을 버스에 놓고 내린 것은 부주의한 일이었다.
[해설]▶ 부정사의 의미상의 주어는 「for+목적격」으로 나타내지만, 성품 형용사(careless)가 바로 앞에 나온 경우, 「of+목적격」으로 나타낸다.

7 [해석]▶ 대화를 중단시키고 싶지 않아서, 그는 조용히 서 있었다.
[해설]▶ to부정사 부정은 to부정사 바로 앞에 not을 쓴다.

본문 048쪽

숙어 플러스 8. 수능 필수 숙어 8회

1. to 2. harm
3. due 4. favor

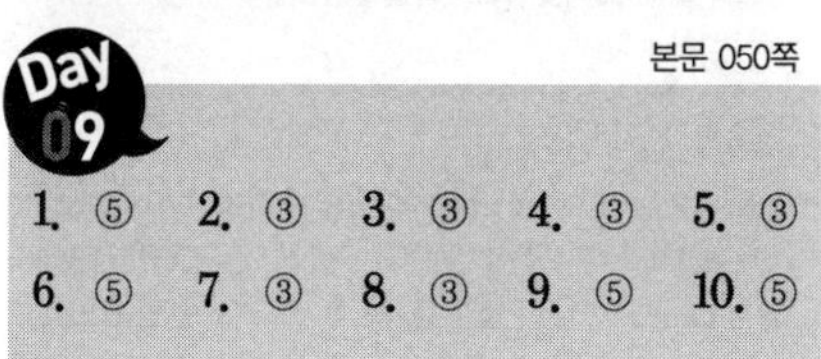

09. 내용 일치 · 불일치

Day 09 본문 050쪽

1. ⑤	2. ③	3. ③	4. ③	5. ③
6. ⑤	7. ③	8. ③	9. ⑤	10. ⑤

정답률 96%

대표 기출 ⑤ Niklas Luhmann

직독/직해

Niklas Luhmann, a renowned sociologist of the twentieth century, /
20세기의 유명한 사회학자인 Niklas Luhmann은 /
was born in Lüneburg, Germany in 1927.
독일 1927년에 Lüneburg에서 태어났다
After World War II, / he studied law / at the University of Freiburg until 1949.
제2차 세계 대전 이후 / 그는 법학을 공부했다 / 1949년까지 Freiburg 대학교에서
Early in his career, / he worked for the State of Lower Saxony, /
그의 경력 초기에 / 그는 State of Lower Saxony에서 일했는데 /
where he was in charge of educational reform.
그곳에서 그는 교육 개혁을 담당했다
In 1960–1961, / Luhmann had the chance /
1960년에서 1961년까지 / Luhmann은 기회가 있었는데 /
to study sociology at Harvard University, /
Harvard 대학교에서 사회학을 공부할 /
where he was influenced by Talcott Parsons, /
그곳에서 그는 Talcott Parsons의 영향을 받았다 /
one of the most famous social system theorists.
가장 유명한 사회 체계 이론가 중 한 명이었던
Later, / Luhmann developed his own social system theory.
나중에 / Luhmann은 그만의 사회 체계 이론을 개발했다
In 1968, / he became a professor of sociology / at the University of Bielefeld.
1968년에 / 그는 사회학 교수가 되었다 / Bielefeld 대학교에서
He researched a variety of subjects, / including mass media and law.
그는 다양한 주제를 연구했다 / 대중 매체와 법을 포함한
Although his books are known to be difficult to translate, /
비록 그의 책들이 번역하기 어렵다고 알려졌지만 /
they have in fact been widely translated into other languages.
사실 그것들은 다른 언어로 널리 번역되었다

20세기의 유명한 사회학자인 Niklas Luhmann은 1927년에 독일 Lüneburg에서 태어났다. ① 제2차 세계 대전 이후, 1949년까지 그는 Freiburg 대학교에서 법학을 공부했다. ② 그의 경력 초기에 그는 State of Lower Saxony에서 일했는데, 그곳에서 그는 교육 개혁을 담당했다. ③ 1960년에서 1961년까지 Luhmann은 Harvard 대학교에서 사회학을 공부할 기회가 있었는데, 그곳에서 그는 가장 유명한 사회 체계 이론가 중 한 명이었던 Talcott Parsons의 영향을 받았다. 나중에 Luhmann은 그만의 사회 체계 이론을 개발했다. 1968년에 그는 Bielefeld 대학교에서 사회학 교수가 되었다. ④ 그는 대중 매체와 법을 포함한 다양한 주제를 연구했다. ⑤ 비록 그의 책들이 번역하기 어렵다고 알려졌지만, 사실 그것들은 다른 언어로 널리 번역되었다.

문제풀이

'Although his books are known to be difficult to translate, they have in fact been widely translated into other languages.'에서 Luhmann의 책들이 번역하기 어렵다고 알려졌다고 했다. 따라서 글의 내용과 일치하지 않는 것은 ⑤이다.

어휘·어구

renowned 유명한, 명성 있는
sociologist 사회학자
be in charge of ~을 담당하다, 책임지다
reform 개혁
translate 번역하다

정답률 97%

1. ⑤ 미국 초상화의 아버지 Gilbert Stuart

직독/직해

Gilbert Stuart grew up in the American colony of Rhode Island /
Gilbert Stuart는 아메리카에 있는 Rhode Island 식민지에서 자랐다 /
before the United States was an independent nation.
미국이 독립 국가이기 전에
He traveled to Scotland, England, and Ireland to study art.
그는 미술을 공부하기 위해 스코틀랜드, 잉글랜드, 아일랜드로 갔다
He then returned to America /
그 후 그는 미국으로 돌아왔다 /
about the time the war for independence broke out, /
독립 전쟁이 발발했을 무렵 /
but he returned to Europe once again /
그러나 그는 유럽으로 다시 돌아갔다 /
because the war made his career as an artist difficult.
전쟁으로 인해 화가로서 일하는 것이 어려워져서
Even so, / he didn't find much success /
그랬음에도 / 그는 큰 성공을 거두지 못했다 /
until he came back to the United States in 1795, /
1795년 미국으로 돌아왔을 때까지 /
when he painted a portrait of George Washington.
그가 George Washington의 초상화를 그렸던
Stuart is called the "father of American portraiture" /
Stuart는 '미국 초상화의 아버지'로 불린다 /
because he painted pictures of all the famous people of early America.
그가 초기 미국의 모든 유명인의 초상화를 그렸기 때문에
One of his paintings of George Washington was hung in the White House.
그가 그린 George Washington의 그림 중 하나는 백악관에 걸렸다
The image of Washington on the U.S. one-ollar bill /
미국 1달러 지폐에 있는 Washington의 모습은 /
came from one of Stuart's most famous paintings of Washington.
Stuart의 가장 유명한 Washington 그림 중 하나에서 왔다
In 1824, / Stuart suffered a stroke / which left him partially paralyzed, /
1824년에 / Stuart는 뇌졸중을 겪었다 / 그를 부분적으로 마비되게 하였던 /
but he still continued to paint for two years / until his death on July 9, 1828.
그러나 2년 동안 여전히 그림을 계속 그렸다 / 1828년 7월 9일 사망할 때까지

Gilbert Stuart는 미국이 독립 국가이기 전에 아메리카에 있는 Rhode Island 식민지에서 자랐다. 그는 미술을 공부하기 위해 스코틀랜드, 잉글랜드, 아일랜드로 갔다. 그 후 그는 독립 전쟁이 발발했을 무렵 미국으로 돌아왔지만, 전쟁으로 인해 화가로서 일하는 것이 어려워져 유럽으로 다시 돌아갔다. 그랬음에도 1795년 미국으로 돌아와 George Washington의 초상화를 그릴 때까지 그는 큰 성공을 거두지 못했다. Stuart는 초기 미국의 모든 유명인의 초상화를 그렸기 때문에 '미국 초상화의 아버지'로 불린다. 그가 그린 George Washington의 그림 중 하나는 백악관에 걸렸다. 미국 1달러 지폐에 있는 Washington의 모습은 Stuart의 가장 유명한 Washington 그림 중 하나에서 왔다. Stuart는 1824년 뇌졸중을 겪어 부분적으로 마비되었지만, 1828년 7월 9일 사망할 때까지 2년 동안 여전히 그림을 계속 그렸다.

문제풀이

'In 1824, Stuart suffered a stroke which left him partially paralyzed, but he still continued to paint for two years until his death on July 9, 1828.'에서 Stuart가 뇌졸중에 걸려 부분적으로 마비되었지만, 사망할 때까지 2년 동안 여전히 그림을 계속 그렸다고 하였으므로 ⑤가 글의 내용과 일치하지 않는다.

어휘·어구

colony 식민지
break out (전쟁 등 안 좋은 일이) 발생하다
portrait 초상화
suffer 앓다
stroke 뇌졸중
partially 부분적으로
paralyze 마비시키다

정답률 98%

2. ③ Leon Festinger

직독/직해

Leon Festinger / was an American social psychologist.
Leon Festinger는 / 미국의 사회 심리학자였다
He was born in New York City in 1919 / to a Russian immigrant family.
그는 1919년에 뉴욕시의 (~에서) 태어났다 / 러시아인 이민자 가정에서
As a graduate student at the University of Iowa, /
아이오와 대학교의 대학원생으로서 /
Festinger was influenced by Kurt Lewin, / a leading social psychologist.
Festinger는 Kurt Lewin의 영향을 받았다 / 유명한 사회 심리학자인
After graduating from there, / he became a professor /
그곳에서 졸업한 이후, / 그는 교수가 되었다 /
at the Massachusetts Institute of Technology in 1945.
1945년에 매사추세츠 공과대학의 /
He later moved to Stanford University, /
나중에 그는 스탠퍼드 대학교로 옮겨 /
where he continued his work / in social psychology.
그곳에서 자신의 연구를 계속했다 / 사회 심리학에서
His theory of social comparison / earned him a good reputation.
자신의 사회 비교 이론으로 / 그는 좋은 평판을 얻었다
Festinger actively participated / in international scholarly cooperation.
Festinger는 적극적으로 참여했다 / 국제 학술 협력에
In the late 1970s, / he turned his interest / to the field of history.
1970년대 하반기에 / 그는 자신의 관심을 돌렸다 / 역사 분야로
He was one of the most cited psychologists / of the twentieth century.
그는 가장 많이 인용된 심리학자 중 한 명이었다 / 20세기에
Festinger's theories still play an important role / in psychology / today.
Festinger의 이론들은 여전히 중요한 역할을 한다 / 심리학에서 / 오늘날에도

Leon Festinger는 미국의 사회 심리학자였다. ① 그는 1919년에 뉴욕시의 러시아인 이민자 가정에서 태어났다. ② 아이오와 대학교의 대학원생으로서, Festinger는 유명한 사회 심리학자 Kurt Lewin의 영향을 받았다. 그곳에서 졸업한 이후, 그는 1945년에 매사추세츠 공과대학의 교수가 되었다. ③ 나중에 그는 스탠퍼드 대학교로 옮겨 그곳에서 자신의 사회 심리학 연구를 계속했다. 자신의 사회 비교 이론으로 그는 좋은 평판을 얻었다. ④ Festinger는 국제 학술 협력에 적극적으로 참여했다. ⑤ 1970년대 하반기에, 그는 역사 분야로 자신의 관심을 돌렸다. 그는 20세기에 가장 많이 인용된 심리학자 중 한 명이었다. Festinger의 이론들은 오늘날에도 여전히 심리학에서 중요한 역할을 한다.

문제풀이

'He later moved to Stanford University, where he continued his work in social psychology.'에서 Stanford 대학으로 옮겨 그곳에서 자신의 사회 심리학 연구를 계속했다고 했다. 따라서 글의 내용과 일치하지 않는 것은 ③이다.

어휘·어구

psychologist 심리학자
immigrant 이민자의
graduate 대학원의
comparison 비교
reputation 명성, 평판
scholarly 학술의
cite 인용하다

3. ③ Eric Carle의 삶

직독/직해

Eric Carle was an American writer and illustrator of children's literature.
Eric Carle은 미국 아동 문학 작가이자 삽화가였다

Born in Syracuse, New York, in 1929, / he moved with his parents to Germany /
1929년에 New York주의 Syracuse에서 태어난 / 그는 독일로 부모님과 함께 이사했다 /

when he was six years old.
6살 때

He was educated there, / and graduated from an art school in Stuttgart, Germany.
그는 그곳에서 교육을 받았다 / 그리고 독일 Stuttgart에 있는 예술 학교를 졸업했다

He moved back to the United States / and worked as a graphic designer /
그는 미국으로 돌아왔다 / 그리고 그래픽 디자이너로 일했다 /

at *The New York Times*.
The New York Times에서

In the mid-1960s, / children's author Bill Martin Jr. asked Carle /
1960년대 중반에 / 아동 작가 Bill Martin Jr.는 Carle에게 요청했다 /

to illustrate a book he was writing.
자신이 집필 중이던 책의 삽화를 그려달라고

In 1967, / they published their first collaboration: /
1967년에 / 그들은 그들의 첫 합작품을 출판했다 /

Brown Bear, Brown Bear, What Do You See?
'Brown Bear, Brown Bear, What Do You See?'를

His best-known work, *The Very Hungry Caterpillar*, /
그의 가장 잘 알려진 작품인 'The Very Hungry Caterpillar'는 /

has been translated / into more than 66 languages /
번역되었다 / 66개가 넘는 언어로 /

and sold over 50 million copies.
그리고 5천만 권이 넘게 팔렸다

In 2002, / Carle and his wife opened the Eric Carle Museum of Picture Book Art, /
2002년에 / Carle과 그의 아내는 Eric Carle Museum of Picture Book Art를 개관했다 /

which collects and features the work of children's book illustrators /
그것은 아동용 책 삽화가들의 작품을 수집하고 다룬다 /

from around the world.
전 세계로 부터

Eric Carle은 미국 아동 문학 작가이자 삽화가였다. 1929년에 New York주의 Syracuse에서 태어난 그는 6살 때 독일로 부모님과 함께 이사했다. 그는 그곳에서 교육을 받았고, 독일 Stuttgart에 있는 예술 학교를 졸업했다. 그는 미국으로 돌아와 The New York Times에서 그래픽 디자이너로 일했다. 1960년대 중반에 아동 작가 Bill Martin Jr.는 Carle에게 자신이 집필 중이던 책의 삽화를 그려달라고 요청했다. 1967년에 그들은 그들의 첫 합작품인 'Brown Bear, Brown Bear, What Do You See?'를 출판했다. 그의 가장 잘 알려진 작품인 'The Very Hungry Caterpillar'는 66개가 넘는 언어로 번역되었고 5천만 권이 넘게 팔렸다. 2002년에 Carle과 그의 아내는 Eric Carle Museum of Picture Book Art를 개관했고, 그것은 전 세계 아동용 책 삽화가들의 작품을 수집하고 다룬다.

문제풀이

'In 1967, they published their first collaboration: *Brown Bear, Brown Bear, What Do You See?*'에서 Bill Martin Jr.와의 첫 합작품을 출판한 것은 1960년대 중반이므로 ③은 글의 내용과 일치하지 않는다.

어휘·어구

illustrator 삽화가
literature 문학
graduate 졸업하다
illustrate 삽화를 넣다
collaboration 합작
translate 번역하다

4. ③ William Buckland

직독/직해

William Buckland (1784—1856) was well known /
William Buckland(1784-1856)는 잘 알려져 있다 /

as one of the greatest geologists / in his time.
가장 위대한 지질학자 중 한 명으로 / 그의 시대에

His birthplace, Axminster in Britain, / was rich with fossils, /
그의 출생지인 영국의 Axminster에는 / 화석이 풍부했다 /

and as a child, / he naturally became interested in fossils / while collecting them.
그리고 어린 시절 / 그는 자연스럽게 화석에 관심을 갖게 되었다 / 화석을 수집하면서

In 1801, / Buckland won a scholarship /
1801년에 / Buckland는 장학금을 받았다 /

and was admitted to Corpus Christi College, Oxford.
그리고 Oxford의 Corpus Christi 대학에 입학하였다

He developed his scientific knowledge there /
그는 그곳에서 과학 지식을 발전시켰다 /

while attending John Kidd's lectures / on mineralogy and chemistry.
John Kidd의 강의를 들으면서 / 광물학과 화학에 관한

After Kidd resigned his position, /
Kidd가 자신의 직위에서 사임한 후 /

Buckland was appointed his successor / at the college.
Buckland가 그의 후임자로 임명되었다 / 대학에서

Buckland used representative samples and large-scale geological maps /
Buckland는 대표 표본과 대축척 지질학 지도를 사용했는데 /

in his lectures, /
그의 강의에서 /

which made his lectures more lively.
그것이 그의 강의를 더 활기차게 만들어주었다

In 1824, / he announced the discovery of the bones of a giant creature, /
1824년 / 그는 거대한 생물의 뼈를 발견했다고 발표했다 /

and he named it *Megalosaurus*, or 'great lizard'.
그리고 그는 그것을 Megalosaurus 즉 '거대한 도마뱀'이라고 이름 붙였다

He won the prize / from the Geological Society /
그는 상을 받았다 / 지질학회로부터 /

due to his achievements in geology.
지질학에서의 그의 업적으로

William Buckland(1784-1856)는 그의 시대에 가장 위대한 지질학자 중 한 명으로 잘 알려져 있다. ① 그의 출생지인 영국의 Axminster에는 화석이 풍부했고, 어린 시절 그는 화석을 수집하면서 자연스럽게 화석에 관심을 갖게 되었다. 1801년에 Buckland는 장학금을 받고 Oxford의 Corpus Christi 대학에 입학하였다. ② 그는 그곳에서 광물학과 화학에 관한 John Kidd의 강의를 들으면서 과학 지식을 발전시켰다. ③ Kidd가 자신의 직위에서 사임한 후, Buckland가 대학에서 그의 후임자로 임명되었다. ④ Buckland는 그의 강의에서 대표 표본과 대축척 지질학 지도를 사용했는데, 그것이 그의 강의를 더 활기차게 만들어주었다. ⑤ 1824년, 그는 거대한 생물의 뼈를 발견했다고 발표했고, 그는 그것을 Megalosaurus 즉 '거대한 도마뱀'이라고 이름 붙였다. 그는 지질학에서의 그의 업적으로 지질학회로부터 상을 받았다.

문제풀이

'After Kidd resigned his position, Buckland was appointed his successor at the college.'에서 Kidd가 자신의 직위에서 사임한 후에 Buckland가 대학에서 그의 후임자로 임명되었다고 했으므로, ③은 글의 내용과 일치하지 않는다.

어휘·어구

geologist 지질학자
fossil 화석
scholarship 장학금
mineralogy 광물학
chemistry 화학
appoint 임명하다
successor 후임자, 계승자
representative sample 대표 표본
achievement 업적

5. ③ Antonia Brico

직독/직해

Antonia Brico was born in the Netherlands / in 1902 /
Antonia Brico는 네덜란드에서 태어났다 / 1902년에 /

and immigrated to the United States / at the age of six.
그리고 미국으로 이주했다 / 6살 때

After attending a park concert / when she was young, /
한 공원 콘서트에 참석한 후 / 그녀는 어렸을 때 /

she was so inspired / that she made up her mind /
그녀는 매우 영감을 받아서 / 그녀는 결심했다 /

to study music and become a conductor.
음악을 공부하고 지휘자가 되기로

In 1927, / she entered the Berlin State Academy of Music /
1927년에 / 그녀는 Berlin State Academy of Music에 입학했다 /

and became the first American to graduate from its master class / in conducting.
그리고 그곳의 마스터 클래스를 졸업한 최초의 미국인이 되었다 / 지휘 분야에서

In 1930, / Brico made her debut / as a professional conductor, /
1930년에 / Brico는 데뷔를 했고 / 전문 지휘자로서 /

for which she received positive reviews.
이로 인해 그녀는 긍정적인 평가를 받았다

She made an extensive European tour, /
그녀는 광범위한 유럽 순회공연을 떠났다 /

and during the tour / she was invited by Jean Sibelius /
그리고 그 공연 동안 / Jean Sibelius에 의해 초청받았다 /

to conduct the Helsinki Symphony Orchestra.
Helsinki Symphony Orchestra를 지휘하도록

Brico settled in Denver, / where she continued to work /
Brico는 Denver에 정착했다 / 그곳에서 그녀는 계속 일했다 /

as a conductor of the Denver Businessmen's Orchestra, /
Denver Businessmen's Orchestra의 지휘자로 /

later renamed the Brico Symphony Orchestra.
후에 Brico Symphony Orchestra로 다시 이름 지어진

In 1974, / her most famous student, folk singer

Judy Collins, /
1974년에 / 그녀의 가장 유명한 제자이자 포크 가수인 Judy Collins가 /
made a documentary film about her, / which was nominated for an Academy Award.
그녀에 대한 다큐멘터리 영화를 만들었고 / 그것은 아카데미상 후보에 올랐다

① Antonia Brico는 1902년에 네덜란드에서 태어나 6살 때 미국으로 이주했다. ② 그녀는 어렸을 때 한 공원 콘서트에 참석한 후, 매우 영감을 받아서 음악을 공부하고 지휘자가 되기로 결심했다. 1927년에 그녀는 Berlin State Academy of Music에 입학했고 지휘 분야에서 그곳의 마스터 클래스를 졸업한 최초의 미국인이 되었다. ③ 1930년에 Brico는 전문 지휘자로서 데뷔를 했고, 이로 인해 그녀는 긍정적인 평가를 받았다. 그녀는 광범위한 유럽 순회공연을 떠났고, 그 공연 동안 Jean Sibelius에 의해 Helsinki Symphony Orchestra를 지휘하도록 초청 받았다. ④ Brico는 Denver에 정착했고, 그곳에서 그녀는 후에 Brico Symphony Orchestra로 다시 이름 지어진 Denver Businessmen's Orchestra의 지휘자로 계속 일했다. ⑤ 1974년에 그녀의 가장 유명한 제자이자 포크 가수인 Judy Collins가 그녀에 대한 다큐멘터리 영화를 만들었고, 그것은 아카데미상 후보에 올랐다.

문제풀이

'In 1930, Brico made her debut as a professional conductor, for which she received positive reviews.'에서 1930년에 Brico는 전문 지휘자로서 데뷔를 했고 긍정적인 평가를 받았다고 했으므로, 글의 내용과 일치하지 않는 것은 ③이다.

어휘·어구

immigrate 이주해 오다
inspired 영감을 받은
make up one's mind 결심하다
conductor 지휘자
conduct 지휘하다
extensive 광범위한
settle 정착하다
nominate 지명하다, 추천하다

6. ⑤ 사진작가 Josef Sudek

직독/직해

Josef Sudek was born in the Czech Republic.
Josef Sudek은 체코 공화국에서 태어났다
Originally a bookbinder, / Sudek was badly injured during World War I, /
원래 제본 기술자였던 / Sudek은 제1차 세계 대전 중에 심하게 부상을 당했다 /
resulting in the loss of his right arm.
그 결과 그의 오른팔을 잃었다
After the injury, / he spent three years in various hospitals, /
그 부상 후 / 그는 여러 병원에서 3년을 보냈다 /
and began to take photographs out of boredom.
그리고 지루함을 느껴 사진을 찍기 시작했다
In 1922, / he enrolled at the State School of Graphic Arts in Prague, /
1922년 / 그는 Prague에 있는 State School of Graphic Arts에 등록했다 /
where he studied photography for two years.
그곳에서 그는 2년간 사진술을 공부했다
His army disability pension allowed him to make art /
그는 군인 장애 연금을 받아서 예술 창작을 할 수 있었다 /
without worrying about an income.
수입 걱정 없이
He photographed many night-scapes of Prague /
그는 Prague의 많은 야경을 사진에 담았다 /
and the wooded landscapes of Bohemia.
그리고 Bohemia의 나무가 우거진 풍경을
Sudek didn't let his disability get in the way / and, /
Sudek은 그의 장애가 그를 방해하도록 내버려 두지 않았다 / 그리고 /
despite having only one arm, / he used very heavy and bulky equipment.
팔이 하나밖에 없음에도 불구하고 / 그는 매우 무겁고 부피가 큰 장비를 사용했다
Often known as the 'Poet of Prague,' / Sudek never married, /
흔히 'Prague의 시인'으로 알려진 / Sudek은 결혼한 적이 없었다 /
and was a shy and retiring person.
그리고 수줍음이 많고 내성적인 사람이었다
He never appeared at his exhibition openings.
그는 자신의 전시회 개막식에 나타난 적이 없었다
He died on 15 September 1976, / when he was 80 years old.
그는 1976년 9월 15일에 사망했다 / 80세의 나이로

Josef Sudek은 체코 공화국에서 태어났다. 원래 제본 기술자였던 Sudek은 제1차 세계 대전 중에 심하게 부상을 당해 오른팔을 잃었다. 그 부상 후 그는 여러 병원에서 3년을 보냈고, 지루함을 느껴 사진을 찍기 시작했다. 1922년, Sudek은 Prague에 있는 State School of Graphic Arts에 등록하여 그곳에서 2년간 사진술을 공부했다. 그는 군인 장애 연금을 받아서 수입 걱정 없이 예술 창작을 할 수 있었다. 그는 Prague의 많은 야경과 Bohemia의 나무가 우거진 풍경을 사진에 담았다. Sudek은 그의 장애가 그를 방해하도록 내버려 두지 않았고 팔이 하나밖에 없음에도 불구하고 매우 무겁고 부피가 큰 장비를 사용했다. 흔히 'Prague의 시인'으로 알려진 Sudek은 결혼한 적이 없었으며 수줍음이 많고 내성적인 사람이었다. 그는 자신의 전시회 개막식에 나타난 적이 없었다. 그는 80세의 나이로 1976년 9월 15일에 사망했다.

문제풀이

'He never appeared at his exhibition openings.(그는 자신의 전시회 개막식에 나타난 적이 없었다.)'로 보아 ⑤는 글의 내용과 일치하지 않는다.

어휘·어구

bookbinder 책 제본 기술자
boredom 지루함
enroll 등록하다
disability pension 장애 연금
night-scape 야경
wooded 나무가 우거진
landscape 풍경
disability (신체적, 정신적) 장애
get in the way 방해되다
bulky 부피가 큰
equipment 장비
retiring 내성적인
exhibition 전시회
opening 개막식

7. ③ Donato Bramante

직독/직해

Donato Bramante, born in Fermignano, Italy, /
이탈리아 Fermignano에서 태어난 Donato Bramante는 /
began to paint early in his life.
인생에서 일찍부터 그림을 그리기 시작했다
His father encouraged him / to study painting.
그의 아버지는 그에게 권장했다 / 그림을 공부하도록
Later, / he worked /
후에 / 그는 일했다 /
as an assistant of Piero della Francesca in Urbino.
Urbino에서 Piero della Francesca의 조수로
Around 1480, / he built several churches /
1480년쯤 / 그는 몇 개의 교회들을 건축했다 /
in a new style / in Milan.
새로운 양식으로 / Milan에서
He had a close relationship with Leonardo da Vinci, /
그는 Leonardo da Vinci와 친밀한 관계를 맺었다 /
and they worked together in that city.
그리고 그들은 그 도시에서 함께 작업했다
Architecture became his main interest, /
건축이 그의 주된 관심사가 되었다 /
but he did not give up painting.
하지만, 그는 그림을 포기하지 않았다
Bramante moved to Rome in 1499 /
Bramante는 1499년에 Rome으로 이주했다 /
and participated in Pope Julius II's plan /
그리고 Pope Julius II의 계획에 참여했다 /
for the renewal of Rome.
Rome 재개발을 위한
He planned the new Basilica of St. Peter / in Rome /
그는 성 베드로 대성당의 새로운 바실리카를 구상했는데 / Rome에 있는 /
— one of the most ambitious building projects /
그것은 가장 야심적인 건축 프로젝트 중 하나였다 /
in the history of humankind. 인류 역사상
Bramante died on April 11, 1514 /
Bramante는 1514년 4월 11일에 죽었다 /
and was buried in Rome.
그리고 Rome에 묻혔다.
His buildings influenced other architects /
그의 건축물들은 다른 건축가들에게 영향을 끼쳤다 /
for centuries. 수 세기 동안

이탈리아 Fermignano에서 태어난 Donato Bramante는 인생에서 일찍부터 그림을 그리기 시작했다. 그의 아버지는 그에게 그림을 공부하도록 권장했다. 후에, ① 그는 Urbino에서 Piero della Francesca의 조수로 일했다. 1480년쯤, ② 그는 Milan에서 몇 개의 교회들을 새로운 양식으로 건축했다. 그는 Leonardo da Vinci와 친밀한 관계를 맺었으며, 그들은 그 도시에서 함께 작업했다. ③ 건축이 그의 주된 관심사가 되었지만, 그는 그림을 포기하지 않았다. Bramante는 1499년에 Rome으로 이주해서 ④ Pope Julius II의 Rome 재개발 계획에 참여했다. 그는 Rome에 있는 성 베드로 대성당의 새로운 바실리카를 구상했는데, 그것은 인류 역사상 가장 야심적인 건축 프로젝트 중 하나였다. Bramante는 1514년 4월 11일에 죽었으며 Rome에 묻혔다. ⑤ 그의 건축물들은 수 세기 동안 다른 건축가들에게 영향을 끼쳤다.

문제풀이

'Architecture became his main interest, but he did not give up painting.'에서 건축이 그의 주된 관심사가 되었지만 그는 그림을 포기하지 않았다고 했으므로, 글의 내용과 일치하지 않는 것은 ③이다.

어휘·어구

encourage 권장하다
assistant 조수
architecture 건축
pope 교황
renewal 재개발
basilica 바실리카 (끝 부분이 둥그렇고, 내부에 기둥이 두 줄로 서 있는 큰 교회나 회관)
ambitious 야심 있는
bury 묻다
architect 건축가

정답률 97%

8. ③ 육상 선수 Emil Zátopek

직독/직해

Emil Zátopek, a former Czech athlete, / is considered /
전직 체코 육상 선수였던 Emil Zátopek은 / 생각된다 /
one of the greatest long-distance runners ever.
역대 가장 위대한 장거리 선수 중 한 명이라고
He was also famous / for his distinctive running style.
그는 또한 유명했다 / 독특한 달리기 방식으로
While working in a shoe factory, /
신발 공장에서 일하던 동안 /
he participated in a 1,500-meter race /
그는 1,500m 경기에 참가했다 /

and won second place. 그리고 2등을 했다
After that event, / 그 경기 이후로 /
he took a more serious interest in running /
그는 달리기에 더 진지한 흥미를 느끼게 되었다 /
and devoted himself to it.
그리고 그것에 전념했다
At the 1952 Olympic Games in Helsinki, /
1952년 헬싱키에서 열린 올림픽 대회에서 /
he won three gold medals /
그는 3개의 금메달을 땄다 /
in the 5,000-meter and 10,000-meter races and in the marathon, /
5,000m, 10,000m 종목과 마라톤에서 /
breaking Olympic records / in each.
올림픽 기록을 깼다 / 각각의 종목에서
He was married to Dana Zátopková, /
그는 Dana Zátopková와 결혼했다 /
who was an Olympic gold medalist, too.
그녀도 올림픽 금메달리스트였다
Zátopek was also noted / for his friendly personality.
Zátopek은 또한 유명했다 / 그의 다정한 성격으로
In 1966, / Zátopek invited Ron Clarke, /
1966년에 Zátopek은 Ron Clarke를 초대했다 /
a great Australian runner /
위대한 호주 달리기 선수인 /
who had never won an Olympic gold medal, /
올림픽 금메달을 딴 적이 없던 /
to an athletic meeting in Prague.
프라하에서 열린 체전에
After the meeting, / 그 대회 이후에 /
he gave Clarke one of his gold medals / as a gift.
그는 Clarke에게 자신의 금메달 중 하나를 주었다 / 선물로

전직 체코 육상 선수였던 Emil Zátopek은 역대 가장 위대한 장거리 선수 중 한 명이라고 생각된다. ① 그는 또한 독특한 달리기 방식으로 유명했다. ② 신발 공장에서 일하던 동안 그는 1,500m 경기에 참가해서 2등을 했다. 그 경기 이후로 그는 달리기에 더 진지한 흥미를 느끼게 되어 그것에 전념했다. ③ 1952년 헬싱키에서 열린 올림픽 대회에서 그는 5,000m, 10,000m 종목과 마라톤에서 3개의 금메달을 땄는데, 각각의 종목에서 올림픽 기록을 깼다. ④ 그는 Dana Zátopková와 결혼했는데, 그녀도 올림픽 금메달리스트였다. Zátopek은 또한 그의 다정한 성격으로 유명했다. 1966년에 Zátopek은 올림픽 금메달을 딴 적이 없던 위대한 호주 달리기 선수인 Ron Clarke를 프라하에서 열린 체전에 초대했다. ⑤ 그 대회 이후에 그는 Clarke에게 자신의 금메달 중 하나를 선물로 주었다.

문제풀이

'At the 1952 Olympic Games in Helsinki, he won three gold medals in the 5,000-meter and 10,000-meter races and in the marathon, breaking Olympic records in each.'에서 1952년 헬싱키 올림픽 대회에서 Emil Zátopek이 5,000m, 10,000m 종목과 마라톤에서 3개의 금메달을 땄고, 각 종목에서 올림픽 기록을 깼다고 했다. 따라서 글의 내용과 일치하지 않는 것은 ③이다.

어휘·어구

athlete 육상 선수, 운동선수
distinctive 독특한
devote oneself to ~에 전념하다
noted for ~으로 유명한
personality 성격
athletic meeting 체전

9. ⑤ Frank Hyneman Knight

직독/직해

Frank Hyneman Knight was one of the most influential economists /
Frank Hyneman Knight는 가장 영향력 있는 경제학자들 중에 한 명이었다 /
of the twentieth century. 20세기의
After obtaining his Ph.D. /
박사 학위를 받은 후에 /
in 1916 at Cornell University, /
1916년에 Cornell 대학교에서 /
Knight taught / Knight는 가르쳤다 /
at Cornell, the University of Iowa, and the University of Chicago.
Cornell, Iowa, Chicago 대학교에서
Knight spent most of his career /
Knight는 경력의 대부분을 보냈다 /
at the University of Chicago.
Chicago 대학교에서
Some of his students at Chicago /
Chicago 대학교에서 그의 학생들 중 몇 명은 /
later received the Nobel Prize.
나중에 노벨상을 받았다
Knight is known as the author /
Knight는 저자로 알려져 있다 /
of the book *Risk, Uncertainty and Profit*, /
'Risk, Uncertainty and Profit'이라는 책의 /
a study of the role of the entrepreneur /
기업가의 역할에 대한 연구인 /
in economic life. 경제생활에서
He also wrote a brief introduction to economics /
그는 또한 간단한 경제학 개론서를 썼는데 /
entitled *The Economic Organization*, /
'The Economic Organization'이라는 제목의 /
which became a classic of microeconomic theory.
그것은 미시 경제학 이론의 고전이 되었다
But Knight was much more than an economist; /
그러나 Knight는 경제학자를 훨씬 넘었다 /
he was also a social philosopher.
그는 사회 철학자이기도 했다
Later in his career, / Knight developed his theories /
경력의 후반기에 / Knight는 자신의 이론을 개발했다 /
of freedom, democracy, and ethics.
자유, 민주주의와 윤리에 대한
After retiring in 1952, / Knight remained active /
1952년에 은퇴 후에도 / Knight는 여전히 적극적이었다 /
in teaching and writing.
가르치는 일과 글 쓰는 일에

① Frank Hyneman Knight는 20세기의 가장 영향력 있는 경제학자들 중에 한 명이었다. 1916년에 Cornell 대학교에서 박사 학위를 받은 후에, Knight는 Cornell, Iowa, Chicago 대학교에서 가르쳤다. ② Knight는 경력의 대부분을 University of Chicago에서 보냈다. ③ Chicago 대학교에서 그의 학생들 중 몇 명은 나중에 노벨상을 받았다. ④ Knight는 경제생활에서 기업가의 역할에 대한 연구인 'Risk, Uncertainty and Profit'이라는 책의 저자로 알려져 있다. 그는 또한 'The Economic Organization'이라는 제목의 간단한 경제학 개론서를 썼는데, 그것은 미시 경제학 이론의 고전이 되었다. 그러나 Knight는 경제학자를 훨씬 넘어 사회 철학자이기도 했다. Knight는 경력의 후반기에 자유, 민주주의와 윤리에 대한 자신의 이론을 개발했다. ⑤ 1952년에 은퇴 후에도 Knight는 가르치는 일과 글 쓰는 일에 여전히 적극적이었다.

문제풀이

'After retiring in 1952, Knight remained active in teaching and writing.'에서 Knight는 은퇴 후에 가르치는 일과 글 쓰는 일에 적극적이었다고 했다. 따라서 글의 내용과 일치하지 않는 것은 ⑤이다.

어휘·어구

influential 영향력 있는
economist 경제학자
be known as ~로 알려지다
author 저자
brief 간단한, 짧은
introduction 개론서
entitle 제목을 붙이다
microeconomic theory 미시 경제학 이론
philosopher 철학자
democracy 민주주의
retire 은퇴하다

10. ⑤ 나일강의 누에르족

직독/직해

The Nuer are one of the largest ethnic groups in South Sudan, /
Nuer 족은 South Sudan의 가장 큰 민족 집단 중 하나다 /
primarily residing in the Nile River Valley.
주로 Nile River Valley에 거주하는
The Nuer are a cattle-raising people, /
Nuer 족은 소를 기르는 민족으로 /
whose everyday lives revolve around their cattle.
그들의 일상생활은 자신들의 소를 중심으로 돌아간다
They have various terms related to cattle, /
그들에게는 소와 관련된 다양한 용어가 있다 /
so they can distinguish between hundreds of types of cows, /
그래서 그들은 수백 가지 유형의 소를 구별할 수 있다 /
based on color, markings, and shape of horns.
색상, 무늬, 그리고 뿔의 모양에 근거해서
They prefer to be called by the names of the cattle they raise.
그들은 자신이 기르는 소의 이름으로 불리는 것을 선호한다
The commonest daily foods for the Nuer are dairy products, /
Nuer 족에게 가장 일반적인 일상 음식은 유제품이다 /
especially milk for the young and soured milk, like yogurt, for adults.
특히 어린이들에게는 우유이고 어른에게는 요구르트와 같은 시큼한 우유이다
And wild fruits and nuts are favorite snacks for the Nuer.
그리고 야생 과일과 견과류는 Nuer 족이 특히 좋아하는 간식이다
The Nuer also have a culture of counting only older members of the family.
Nuer 족에게는 또한 집안의 나이가 든 구성원만 세는 문화가 있다
They believe that counting the number of children one has could result in misfortune /
그들은 어떤 사람이 가진 아이의 수를 세는 것은 불운을 가져온다고 믿는다 /
and prefer to report fewer children than they have.
그리고 자신이 가진 것보다 적은 수의 아이를 말하기를 선호한다

누에르족은 남수단에서 가장 큰 인종 집단 중 하나로, 주로 나일강에 거주한다. 누에르족은 소떼를 기르는 부족으로 그들의 일상생활은 소떼를 중심으로 돌아간다. 그들은 소떼와 관련된 다양한 용어들을 가지고 있어서, 색, 반점, 뿔의 모양에 근거해서 수백 가지 유형의 소를 구별할 수 있다. 그들은 자신들이 기르는 소떼의 이름으로 불리는 것을 선호한다. 누에르족의 가장 흔한 일상 음식은 유제품으로, 어린이들에게는 특히 우유이고 성인들에게는 요구르트와 같은 시큼한 우유이다. 그리고 야생 과일과 견과류들은 누에르족이 가장 좋아하는 간식이다. 누에르족은 또한 나이든 가족 구성원만 세는 문화를 가지고 있다. 그들은 아이의 수를 세는 것은 불운을 야기할 수 있다고 믿어서 그들이 가지고 있는 것보다 더 적은 수의 아이를 가지고 있다고 알리는 것을 선호한다.

문제풀이

'They believe that counting the number of children one has could result in misfortune and prefer to report fewer children than they have.'에서 아이의 수를 세는 것은 불운을 가져온다고 믿었다고 했으므로 글의 내용과 일치하지 않는 것은 ⑤이다.

어휘·어구

ethnic 인종의
reside 거주하다
term 용어
marking 반점, 무늬
dairy product 유제품
result in ~을 야기하다

본문 053쪽

문법 플러스 9. 조동사

A. 1. will be able to
2. tell
3. should have paid
4. take
5. point
6. not wake
7. might

1 [해석]▶ 너는 너의 숙제를 할 수 있을 것이다.
[해설]▶ 조동사는 두 개를 나란히 쓸 수 없다.

2 [해석]▶ 너는 그의 파티에 갈 수 없다고 그에게 말해두는 것이 좋겠다.
[해설]▶ 「had better+동사원형」은 '~하는 편이 낫다'는 의미이다.

3 [해석]▶ 나는 그에게 관심을 갖지 못한 것을 후회했다. 다르게 말하면, 나는 그를 더 잘 돌봤어야 했는데 그렇지 못했다.
[해설]▶ should have p.p.는 '~했어야 했는데'라는 의미로 과거의 하지 못한 일에 대한 유감이나 후회를 나타낸다.

4 [해석]▶ 그녀는 나에게 일을 떠나 휴식을 취할 것을 제안했다.
[해설]▶ 제안(suggest) 동사 다음의 that절에는 「should+동사원형」 또는 동사원형을 쓴다.

5 [해석]▶ 나는 우리가 현실에 계속해서 직면해야 한다는 것을 지적하지 않을 수 없다.
[해설]▶ 「cannot but+동사원형」은 '~하지 않을 수 없다(=~해야만 한다)'는 의미가 있다.

6 [해석]▶ 당신이 들어올 때 Billy를 깨우지 않는 것이 좋을 거예요.
[해설]▶ had better를 부정할 때는 바로 뒤에 not을 쓴다.

7 [해석]▶ 그는 내게 그날 저녁 나를 만나러 와도 되는지를 물었다.
[해설]▶ 조동사 may는 주절이 과거인 경우, 시제 일치의 규칙에 따라 종속절에 might를 써야 한다.

본문 053쪽

B. 1. do
2. smoke
3. needn't have cooked
4. should be
5. ride
6. not go
7. might

1 [해석]▶ 그 일은 잘 되어 갈 것이다.
[해설]▶ 조동사 뒤에는 동사원형이 나온다.

2 [해석]▶ 그는 파이프 담배를 피곤했다. 지금은 전자담배를 핀다.
[해설]▶ 「used to+동사원형」은 '(과거에는) ~했는데 (지금은) 그렇지 않다'는 의미가 있다.

3 [해석]▶ 그녀는 그렇게 많이 음식을 만들 필요가 없었다. 그러나 그녀는 음식을 많이 만들었다.
[해설]▶ needn't have p.p.는 '~할 필요가 없는데 ~했다'는 의미이다. don't need to부정사는 '~할 필요가 없다. (그래서 ~ 하지 않았다)'는 의미이다. 이 표현이 들어가면 문맥이 어색하다.

4 [해석]▶ 그는 회의가 연기되어야 한다고 제안했다.
[해설]▶ 제안(suggest) 명령, 요구, 주장을 나타내는 동사에 이어지는 that절에서는 「주어+(should)+동사원형」으로 쓴다.

5 [해석]▶ 나는 그 버스를 다시 타고 갈 바에, 차라리 5마일을 걸어서 학교에 가겠다.
[해설]▶ would rather A than B는 'B할 바에야 차라리 A할 것이다'는 의미로 A, B 자리에는 동사원형이 나와야 한다.

6 [해석]▶ 너는 건강이 매우 안 좋아 보여. 오늘은 일하러 가지 않는 것이 좋겠다.
[해설]▶ 「had better+동사원형」은 '~하는 편이 낫다'는 의미로 부정을 하려면 had better 바로 뒤에 not을 붙인다.

7 [해석]▶ Tom은 그녀가 내년이면 29살이 될 거라고 말했다.
[해설]▶ 조동사 may는 주절이 과거인 경우, 시제 일치의 규칙에 따라 종속절에 might를 써야 한다.

본문 054쪽

숙어 플러스 9. 수능 필수 숙어 9회

1. fall
2. fill
3. charge
4. over

10. 안내문

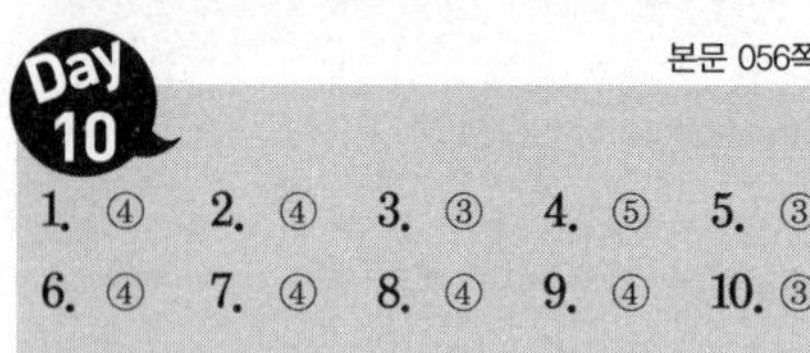

Day 10 본문 056쪽

1. ④ 2. ④ 3. ③ 4. ⑤ 5. ③
6. ④ 7. ④ 8. ④ 9. ④ 10. ③

정답률 97%

대표 기출 ② 보수 공사 공지

보수 공사 공지

Natural Jade 리조트는 투숙객들에게 더 나은 서비스를 제공하기 위해 계속적으로 시설을 향상시키고 있습니다. 그래서 저희는 아래 일정에 따라 리조트의 몇 개의 구역을 보수 공사하려고 합니다.

보수 공사 기간: 2022년 11월 21일부터 12월 18일까지
• 보수 공사는 오전 9시부터 오후 5시까지 매일 진행됩니다.

폐쇄될 구역: 체육관과 실내 수영장

추가 정보
• 모든 야외 여가 활동은 평소처럼 이용 가능할 것입니다.
• 투숙객들은 식당의 모든 식사에 대해 15%를 할인받을 것입니다.
• 투숙객들은 무료로 테니스장을 이용할 수 있습니다.

저희는 소음과 다른 불편함을 최소화하기 위해 모든 가능한 조치를 취할 것입니다. 이해해 주셔서 진심으로 감사드립니다.

문제풀이

'Renovations will take place every day from 9:00 a.m. to 5:00 p.m.'에서 보수 공사는 매일 진행된다고 했으므로, 안내문의 내용과 일치하지 않는 것은 ②이다.

어휘·어구

renovation 보수 공사
notice 공지
continually 계속적으로
improve 향상시키다
facility 시설
take place 진행되다, 일어나다
available 이용할 수 있는
for free 무료로, 공짜로
take measures 조치를 취하다
minimize 최소화하다, 축소하다
inconvenience 불편함
sincerely 진심으로

정답률 96%

1. ④ 2022 Valestown 재활용 포스터 대회

2022 Valestown 재활용 포스터 대회

올해의 Valestown 재활용 포스터 대회에 참여하여 여러분의 예술적 재능을 자랑하세요!

참가 기준
– Valestown의 고등학생만 참여할 수 있습니다.
– 참가자들은 '미래를 위한 재활용'이라는 주제를 사용해야 합니다.

출품작 양식
– 파일 양식: PDF만 가능
– 최대 파일 크기: 40MB

심사 기준
– 주제 활용 – 창의성 – 예술적 기술

세부 사항
– 출품작은 1인당 한 장의 포스터로 제한됩니다.
– 출품작은 12월 19일 오후 6시까지 웹사이트에 업로드되어야 합니다.
– 수상자는 12월 28일에 웹사이트에 발표될 것입니다.

더 많은 정보를 원하면 www.vtco.org를 방문하세요.

문제풀이

Valestown의 고등학생만 참여할 수 있고, 참가자는 '미래를 위한 재활용'이라는 주제를 사용해야 하며, 출품할 파일 양식은 PDF만 가능하고, 1인당 한 장의 포스터만 출품할 수 있다고 했다. 'Judging Criteria – Use of theme – Creativity – Artistic skill'에서 심사 기준은 주제 활용, 창의성, 예술적 기술이라고 했으므로, 심사 기준에 창의성이 포함된다. 따라서 안내문의 내용과 일치하는 것은 ④이다.

어휘·어구

contest 대회
show off ~을 자랑하다
artistic 예술의
talent 재능
guidline 가이드라인, 지침
participation 참가
theme 주제
submission 출품작
criterion 기준 (pl. criteria)

정답률 97%

2. ④ Glass Bottom Boat Adventure 안내문

Glass Bottom Boat Adventure

하루 종일 수족관 입장과 전용 유리 바닥 보트를 타고 우리 해양 수족관을 횡단하는 것을 즐기십시오. 당신은 우리 팀이 우리의 해양 종을 어떻게 돌보는지 볼 것이고 다른 시점에서 우리의 동물을 볼 것입니다.

비용:
• 성인(16세 이상): 80달러 / 어린이(4–15세): 65달러
• 활동 꾸러미: $8
• 활동 경로 지도, 돋보기, 그림 퍼즐 등을 포함합니다!

유의 사항:
• 0~3세 어린이는 보트 투어에 참여할 수 없습니다.
• 보트는 오전 10시부터 오후 4시까지 매시간 출발합니다.
• 적어도 보트 출발 20분 전에 도착하세요.

문제풀이

'Boat departs every hour from 10:00 a.m. – 4:00 p.m.'에서 보트는 오전 10시부터 오후 4시까지 매시간 출발한다고 하였으므로 안내문의 내용과 일치하지 않는 것은 ④이다.

어휘·어구

aquarium 수족관
exclusive 전용의, 독점적인
oceanarium 해양 수족관
marine 바다의, 해양의
point of view 시점, 관점
magnifying glass 돋보기, 확대경
depart 출발하다
prior to ~에 앞서, 먼저

정답률 94%

3. ③ Annual Car Wash Fundraiser 안내문

직독/직해

연례 세차 모금 행사

연례 세차 모금 행사에 참여하세요!
세차를 하고 집 없는 애완동물들을 돕기 위해 여러분의 역할을 하세요!

• **시간:** 11월 5일 토요일 오전 8시 30분 – 10시 30분
• **장소:** Cranberry College – Eastern Street 주차장
• **비용:** 차량 당 $10
(무료 음료는 대기실에서 제공됩니다.)
• 세차 시간 간격 – 30분 시간대 마다 10대의 세차 예약 가능:
• 오전 8:30 – 오전 9:00 • 오전 9:00 – 오전 9:30
• 오전 9:30 – 오전 10:00 • 오전 10:00 – 오전 10:30

세차하기 가장 편한 시간을 선택해주세요. 선택한 시간대가 지난 후 20분 후에 직접 차를 수거해야 합니다.

문제풀이

집 없는 애완동물을 돕기 위한 행사이고, 토요일 오전 2시간 동안 진행되며, 30분 시간대마다 10대의 세차 예약이 가능하고, 세차가 끝나면 직접 차를 가져가야 한다. 'A free beverage is offered in the waiting area.'에서 대기 장소에서 음료가 무료로 제공된다고 하였으므로 안내문의 내용과 일치하는 것은 ③이다.

어휘·어구

fundraiser 모금 행사
beverage 음료
time slot 시간대, 시간 간격
booking 예약
in person 몸소, 직접

정답률 97%

4. ⑤ 2022 K–차 문화 프로그램

2022 K–차 문화 프로그램

Evergreen 차 협회는 여러분을 제2회 연례 K–차 문화 프로그램으로 초대합니다! 오셔서 상쾌한 차 한 잔을 즐기시면서 전통 한국 차 문화에 대해 배우세요.

프로그램 포함 내용:
1) 한국의 차 문화 역사에 관한 짧은 동영상 시청하기
2) 한국 전통 차 의식('다도') 시연 관람하기
3) 그 의식에 직접 참가하기
4) 엄선된 여러 차를 쿠키와 함께 맛보기

일시: 9월 24일, 토요일, 오후 3시~오후 5시

장소: Evergreen 문화 센터

참가비: 1인당 20달러 (전통 찻잔 포함)

예약은 적어도 방문 하루 전에 온라인(www.egtsociety.or.kr)으로 되어야 합니다.

문제풀이

'Reservations should be made online (www.egtsociety.or.kr) at least one day before your visit.'에서 예약은 적어도 방문 하루 전에 되어야 한다고 했다. 따라서 안내문의 내용과 일치하지 않는 것은 ⑤이다.

어휘·어구

annual 연례의, 매년의
refreshing 상쾌한
demonstration 시연, 시범
ceremony 의식
participation fee 참가비

5. ③ 빅 데이터 전문가와 함께하는 직업의 날

직독/직해

빅 데이터 전문가와 함께하는 직업의 날

선도적인 IT 기업의 빅 데이터 전문가를 만나 보세요! 유명한 데이터 분석가이면서 베스트셀러 작가인 Jill Johnson은 Sovenhill 고등학교를 방문하여 빅 데이터 관련 직업에 대한 강의를 할 것입니다.

참가:
- Sovenhill 고등학교 학생만 참가 가능
- 학생 50명으로 제한됨

일시 및 장소:
- 10월 15일, 오전 10시부터 오전 11시 30분까지
- 도서관

등록: 신청서를 작성하기 위해서는 QR 코드를 스캔하세요.

주의사항:
- 강의 중에 음료수를 마시는 것은 허용되지 않습니다.
- 강의 후에 질의응답 시간이 이어질 것입니다.
- 모든 참석자는 강연자의 책 한 권을 무료로 받을 것입니다.

문제풀이

'Registration: Scan the QR code to fill in the application form.'에서 QR 코드를 스캔하여 신청서를 작성하라고 했다. 따라서 안내문의 내용과 일치하는 것은 ③이다.

어휘·어구

career 직업
analyst 분석가
author 작가
lecture 강의, 강연
fill in ~을 작성하다
application form 신청서
beverage 음료수
permit 허용하다

6. ④ Black Box Short Play Festival 안내문

직독/직해

Black Box 단편극 축제

연례 Black Box 단편극 축제가 여러분을 기다리고 있습니다. 이 축제는 신인 극작가의 작품이 무대에서 상연되게 해 줌으로써 그들을 소개하는 것이 목표입니다. 와서 즐겨 보세요!

날짜 및 장소
- 2022년 8월 12~14일
- The Black Box Theater, 5번가 530, New York

상연 일정

	금요일 8월 12일	토요일 8월 13일	일요일 8월 14일
The Midnight Salesmen	오후 8시	오후 2시	
Shrink to Fit		오후 8시	오후 2시
Casting the Villain Aside	오후 2시		오후 8시

티켓
- 조기 예매: 연극 당 10달러(2022년 7월 31일 이전 예매)
- 정가: 연극 당 15달러
- www.theblackboxtheater.com에서 온라인으로 티켓을 예매하십시오.

유의 사항
- 늦게 입장하는 것은 허용되지 않습니다.
- 10세 미만의 어린이는 입장할 수 없습니다.

문제풀이

'Early Bird: $10 per play (reserve before July 31, 2022)'에서 조기 예매시 관람료는 연극당 10달러라고 하였으므로 ④가 안내문의 내용과 일치하지 않는다.

어휘·어구

aim to ~하고자 하다
showcase 소개하다
performance 공연
reserve 예약하다
entry 참가
permit 허락하다

정답률 91%

7. ④ Newport Hackathon 2022에 관한 안내문

직독/직해

2022 Newport 해커톤

2022 Newport 해커톤은 창의성, 협력 그리고 혁신적 생각을 장려하기 위한 웹사이트 코딩 마라톤입니다.

행사 정보
- 누가: Newport University 학생
- 언제: 9월 23일 금요일 오후 1시~9월 24일 토요일 오전 9시
- 어디서: Newport University 학생 센터

참가 방법
- 여러분은 개인으로 또는 4명까지의 팀으로 참가할 수 있습니다.
- 여러분은 8월 23일부터 8월 31일 사이에 등록해야 합니다.

요구 사항과 규칙
- 참가자들은 행사 당일 공지되는 주제에 따라 웹사이트를 코딩하는 20시간을 갖게 됩니다.
- 제출물은 웹사이트를 설명하는 영상을 포함해야 합니다. (5분 미만의 길이)
- 참가자는 웹사이트를 개발하는 동안 공개된 소스 코드를 사용할 수 있습니다.

문제풀이

9월 23일 금요일 오후 1시와 토요일 오전 9시에 진행되고, 개인으로 또는 4명까지의 팀으로 참가할 수 있고, 8월 23일부터 8월 31일 사이에 등록해야 한다고 하였고, 제출하는 영상의 길이는 5분 미만이어야 한다고 하였다. 'Participants will have 20 hours to code a website according to the theme announced on the day of the event.'에서 주제가 행사 당일에 공지된다고 하였으므로 ④가 안내문의 내용과 일치한다.

어휘·어구

promote 장려하다
up to ~까지
register 등록하다
requirement 필요조건
participant 참가자
submission 제출물

정답률 96%

8. ④ 별똥별 보기 행사

직독/직해

별똥별 보기 행사

7월 24일 일요일에 오는, 희귀한 별똥별을 보고 싶으신가요? Downtown Central 과학 박물관은 그 생생한 경관을 볼 수 있는 최적의 장소입니다!

등록
- 온라인으로만 가능 — www.dcsm.org
- 7월 1일부터 7월 14일까지
- 참가자의 수는 50명으로 제한될 것입니다.

7월 24일 일정
- 오후 8시: 참가자들은 홀에서 모인 후에 옥상으로 이동할 것입니다.
- 오후 8시 30분: 안내원들이 별똥별을 관측하는 방법을 설명할 것입니다.
- 오후 9시~오후 11시: 우리는 별똥별을 본 경험을 공유할 것입니다.

공지 사항
- 행사가 기상 상황으로 인해 취소될 경우, 문자 메시지로 공지될 것입니다.
- 외부 음식과 음료는 허용되지 않습니다.

문제풀이

등록은 온라인으로만 가능하고, 참가자의 인원은 50명으로 제한되며, 참가자들은 오후 8시에 홀에서 모인 후 옥상으로 이동하고, 외부 음식과 음료는 허용되지 않는다고 했다. 'If the event is cancelled due to the weather conditions, notice will be given via text message.'에서 기상 상황으로 인한 행사 취소 시 문자 메시지로 공지될 것이라고 했으므로, 안내문의 내용과 일치하는 것은 ④이다.

어휘·어구

shooting star 별똥별, 유성
rare 희귀한
spot 장소
vivid 생생한
registration 등록
rooftop (건물의) 옥상
observe 관측하다
cancel 취소하다
via ~을 통해

9. ④ Sittka시 공영자전거 공유 서비스

Sittka시 공영자전거 공유 서비스

시를 탐방할 계획인가요?
이것이 그것을 하는 친환경적인 방법일 것입니다!

대여
- 저희 쉬운 앱을 통해 어디서든 등록하세요.
- 요금 지불은 오직 신용카드로만 할 수 있습니다.

요금
- 처음 30분은 무료
- 추가 30분마다 1달러

사용
- 자전거를 선택해서 그 자전거에 있는 QR 코드를 스캔하세요.
- 헬멧은 제공되지 않습니다.

반납
- 앱에 보이는 Green Zone에 자전거를 반납하세요.
- 자전거에 있는 OK 버튼을 눌러서 반납을 마치세요.

문제풀이

'Helmets are not provided.'에서 헬멧은 제공되지 않는다고 했으므로, 안내문의 내용과 일치하지 않는 것은 ④이다.

어휘·어구

explore 답사하다, 탐험하다
eco-friendly 친환경적인
register 등록하다
via ~을 통해
additional 추가의

10. ③ 디자인 대회

녹차 포장 디자인 대회

대회에서 TIIS Tea의 신제품 녹차 포장 상자를 디자인할 기회를 잡으세요!
마감일시: 2019년 12월 2일 오후 6시

참가자: Lokota County 주민들만
세부사항
• 저희 회사명 'TIIS Tea'가 디자인에 보여야 합니다.
• 대회 주제는 '녹차로 친환경하기'입니다.
• 출품작(JPG 포맷으로만)은 designmanager@tiistea.com으로 이메일로 제출해야 합니다.
평가 기준
• 기능성 • 창의성 • 친환경성
상
• 1등: 1,000달러 • 2등: 500달러 • 3등: 250달러
(1등 수상자의 서명이 포장 상자에 인쇄될 겁니다.)
대회에 관해 더 많이 알고 싶으시면 www.tiistea.com을 방문하세요.

문제풀이

출품작은 이메일로 제출해야 한다고 했으므로 안내문의 내용과 일치하지 않는 것은 ③이다.

어휘·어구

brand-new 신제품의
entry 출품작
submit 제출하다
functionality 기능성

본문 059쪽

문법 플러스 10. 수동태

A. 1. has been cleared
2. was put up with
3. was given
4. to be left
5. to sing
6. is said
7. suddenly disappeared

1 [해석]▶ 그 지역은 지뢰가 제거되었다.
[해설]▶ 현재완료수동태는 have been p.p 형태를 취한다.

2 [해석]▶ 그녀는 고통을 참았다.
[해설]▶ 동사구는 하나의 동사로 취급해 수동태를 만든다.

3 [해석]▶ 그는 말할 기회를 얻었다.
[해설]▶ 4형식 문장에서 간접목적어가 주어로 나온 수동태 문장인데 yesterday가 있으므로 was given으로 표현해야 한다.

4 [해석]▶ 소녀는 밤에 혼자 남기는 것을 무서워했다.
[해설]▶ to부정사의 수동태는 to be p.p.로 표현한다. 동명사 수동태로 나타내려면 be afraid of [being left]와 같이 of가 있어야 한다.

5 [해석]▶ 우리 아들이 한밤중에 혼자 노래했다.
[해설]▶ 지각동사는 수동태로 바꾸면 목적격보어가 to부정사 구조로 바뀐다.

6 [해석]▶ 사람들은 그녀가 신뢰할만한 사람이라고 말한다.
[해설]▶ say동사가 that절을 목적어로 갖는 경우, 수동태로 바꾸면 It is said that ~ 구조로 바뀐다.

7 [해석]▶ Sally가 갑자기 어둠속으로 사라졌다.
[해설]▶ 자동사(appear)는 수동태로 쓸 수 없다.

본문 059쪽

B. 1. has been collected
2. was called off
3. for
4. being dumped
5. to move
6. is thought
7. resemble

1 [해석]▶ 데이타는 수집되고 처리되어진 이후에만 유용할 수 있다.
[해설]▶ 현재완료 수동태는 has been p.p. 형태를 취한다.

2 [해석]▶ 그 야구 경기는 폭우로 인해 취소되었다.
[해설]▶ 동사구의 수동태 문장이다. be called off는 '~이 취소되다'는 의미이다.

3 [해석]▶ 그 야구 방망이는 아빠가 내게 사주셨다.
[해설]▶ buy동사가 들어간 4형식 문장을 3형식 문장으로 바꾸면 전치사 for가 간접목적어 앞에 붙는데, 수동태에서도 동일하게 적용된다.

4 [해석]▶ Sam은 차인 것을 어떻게 극복해야 할지 모른다.
[해설]▶ get over는 동명사를 목적어로 취하므로, get over 뒤에 동명사 수동태를 가져온다.

5 [해석]▶ 시냇물과 달리 빙하는 움직이는 것을 볼 수 없다.
[해설]▶ 지각동사의 목적격보어가 동사원형인 경우, 수동태로 바뀌면 「to+동사원형」이 된다.

6 [해석]▶ 유로화의 도입이 생활비의 상승을 초래했다고 생각한다.
[해설]▶ think동사가 that절을 목적어로 갖는 경우, 수동태로 바꾸면 It is thought that ~ 구조로 바뀐다.

7 [해석]▶ 너는 너의 엄마를 많이 닮았다.
[해설]▶ 타동사 resemble은 수동태로 바꿀 수 없다.

본문 060쪽

숙어 플러스 10. 수능 필수 숙어 10회

1 ahead	2. through
3. hand	4. influence

11. 어법 정확성 파악

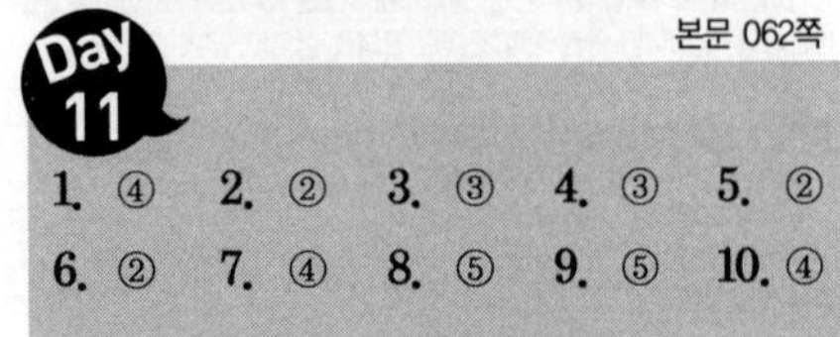

본문 062쪽

Day 11

1. ④	2. ②	3. ③	4. ③	5. ②
6. ②	7. ④	8. ⑤	9. ⑤	10. ④

정답률 40%

대표 기출 ② 패션의 역할

직독/직해

Trends constantly suggest new opportunities / for individuals / to restage themselves, /
유행은 새로운 기회를 계속해서 제시하고 / 사람들이 / 자신을 재조정할 /
representing occasions for change.
변화의 경우를 나타낸다
To understand / how trends can ultimately give individuals power and freedom, /
이해하기 위해서 / 유행이 궁극적으로 어떻게 개인에게 힘과 자유를 줄 수 있는지를 /
one must first discuss fashion's importance / as a basis for change.
먼저 패션의 중요성에 대해 논의해야 한다 / 변화를 위한 기본으로서의
The most common explanation offered by my informants /
나의 정보 제공자들이 제공한 가장 일반적인 설명은 /
as to why fashion is so appealing /
왜 패션이 그렇게도 매력적인가에 대해 /
is that it constitutes a kind of theatrical costumery.
그것이 일종의 연극적인 복장을 구성한다는 것이다
Clothes are part of how people present themselves to the world, /
옷은 사람들이 자신을 세상에 제시하는 방식의 일부이나 /
and fashion locates them in the present, /
그리고 패션은 그들을 현재에 위치시킨다 /
relative to what is happening in society / and to fashion's own history.
사회에서 일어나고 있는 일과 관련하여 / 그리고 패션 자체의 역사와 (관련하여)
As a form of expression, / fashion contains a host of ambiguities, /
표현 형태로서 / 패션은 다수의 모호함을 담고 있어 /
enabling individuals to recreate the meanings /
개인이 의미를 다시 만들어낼 수 있게 한다 /
associated with specific pieces of clothing.
특정한 옷과 연관된
Fashion is among the simplest and cheapest methods of self-expression: /
패션은 자기표현의 가장 단순하고 값싼 방법 중의 하나로 /
clothes can be inexpensively purchased /
옷은 값싸게 구매할 수 있으며 /
while making it easy to convey /
쉽게 전달할 수 있다 /
notions of wealth, intellectual stature, relaxation or environmental consciousness, /
부, 지적 능력, 휴식 혹은 환경 의식에 대한 개념을 /
even if none of these is true.
비록 이것 중 어느 것도 사실이 아니라 해도
Fashion can also strengthen agency / in various ways, /
패션은 또한 행동력을 강화할 수 있다 / 다양한 방식으로 /
opening up space for action.
행동을 위한 공간을 열어주면서

유행은 사람들이 자신을 재조정할 새로운 기회를 계속해서 제시하고, 변화의 경우를 나타낸다. 유행이 궁극적으로 어떻게 개인에게 힘과 자유를 줄 수 있는지를 이해하기 위해서 먼저 변화를 위한 기본으로서의 패션의 중요성에 대해 논의해야 한다. 왜 패션이 그렇게도 매력적인가에 대해 나의 정보 제공자들이 제공한 가장 일반적인 설명은 그것이 일종의 연극적인 복장을 구성한다는 것이다. 옷은 사람들이 자신을 세상에 제시하는 방식의 일부이고, 패션은 사회에서 일어나고 있는 일, 그리고 패션 자체의 역사와 관련하여 그들을 현재에 위치시킨다. 표현 형태로서 패션은 다수의 모호함을 담고 있어 개인이 특정한 옷과 연관된 의미를 다시 만들어낼 수 있게 한다. 패션은 자기표현의 가장 단순하고 값싼 방법 중의 하나로, 옷은 값싸게 구매할 수 있으며, 부, 지적 능력, 휴식 혹은 환경 의식에 대한 개념을, 비록 이것 중 어느 것도 사실이 아니라 해도, 쉽게 전달할 수 있다. 패션은 또한 행동을 위한 공간을 열어주면서 다양한 방식으로 행동력을 강화할 수 있다.

문제풀이

① **[접속사 that]**
뒤에 문장 성분을 모두 갖춘 완전한 문장이 왔으므로, 문장의 보어 역할을 하는 명사절을 이끄는 접속사 that이 온 것은 적절하다.

② **[재귀대명사]**
'사람들이 자신들을 세상에 제시하는'이라는 의미가 되어야 하는데 주어 people과 목적어가 가리키는 대상이 같으므로, them을 재귀대명사 themselves로 바꿔 써야 한다.

③ **[과거분사]**
'연관된'이라는 의미로 앞의 명사 the meanings를 수식하는 과거분사가 되어야 하므로, associated가 온 것은 적절하다.

④ **[부사]**
과거분사 purchased를 수식하므로 부사로 inexpensively가 온 것은 적절하다.

⑤ **[분사구문]**
분사구문이 와야 하는데, '행동을 위한 공간을 열어주면서'라는 능동의 의미이므로, 현재분사 opening이 온 것은 적절하다.

이렇게 풀자 어법상 틀린 부분을 찾는 문제는 밑줄이 있는 부분의 형태와 문맥을 보고 어법에 맞게 쓰였는지 확인해야 한다.
① that 뒤에 문장 성분을 모두 갖춘 완전한 절이 왔다면 that은 명사절을 이끄는 접속사로 쓰인 것이다.
② 주어와 목적어가 같은 사람을 가리킬 때 목적어로는 재귀대명사가 와야 한다.
③ 분사가 명사를 수식할 경우, 수동의 의미일 경우 과거분사가 오고 능동의 의미일 경우 현재분사가 온다.
④ 부사는 형용사(과거분사 / 현재분사)나 다른 부사를 수식할 수 있다. 또한 동사의 앞이나 뒤에서 동사를 수식하거나 문장의 앞뒤에서 문장 전체를 수식할 수 있다.
⑤ 분사구문에서 의미상 주어와의 관계가 능동일 때 현재분사가 와야 하고, 수동일 때 과거분사가 와야 한다.

어휘·어구

represent 나타내다, 표현하다
occasion 때, 경우
ultimately 궁극적으로, 결국
informant 정보 제공자
as to ~에 관해
appealing 매력적인
constitute 구성하다
costumery 복장
a host of 다수의
ambiguity 모호함
convey 전달하다
notion 개념
consciousness 의식
strengthen 강화하다

정답률 54%

1. ④ 지도자가 될 수 있게 해 주는 특성

직독직해

The idea / 생각은 /
that leaders *inherently* possess certain physical, intellectual, or personality traits /
지도자는 특정한 신체적, 지적, 혹은 성격적 특성을 '선천적으로' 가지고 있다는 /
that distinguish them from nonleaders / was the foundational belief /
그들을 지도자가 아닌 사람과 구별해 주는 / 기초적인 믿음이었다 /
of the trait-based approach to leadership.
리더십에 대한 특성 기반 접근법의
This approach dominated leadership research /
이 접근법은 리더십 연구를 지배했다 /
from the late 1800s until the mid-1940s /
1800년대 후반부터 1940년대 중반까지 /
and has experienced a resurgence of interest in the last couple of decades.
그리고 지난 몇십 년 동안 관심이 되살아나는 것을 경험했다
Early trait theorists believed / that some individuals are born with the traits /
초기 특성 이론가들은 믿었다 / 어떤 사람들은 특성을 가지고 태어난다고 /
that allow them to become great leaders.
위대한 지도자가 될 수 있게 해 주는
Thus, / early research in this area often presented the widely stated argument /
따라서 / 이 분야의 초기 연구는 널리 언급되는 주장을 자주 제시하였다 /
that "leaders are born, not made."
'지도자는 만들어지는 것이 아니라 태어나는 것'이라는
Also, / some of the earliest leadership studies were grounded in /
또한 / 초기 리더십 연구 중 일부는 ~에 기반을 두었다 /
what was referred to as the "great man" theory /
'위인' 이론이라 불리는 것(에) /
because researchers at the time focused on identifying traits of highly visible leaders in history /
이는 그 당시 연구자들이 역사에서 매우 눈에 띄는 지도자들의 특징을 확인하는 데 초점을 맞췄기 때문이다
who were typically male and associated with the aristocracy or political or military leadership.
일반적으로 남성이면서 귀족이거나 정치나 군대의 리더십과 관련이 있는
In more recent history, / numerous authors have acknowledged /
더 최근의 역사에서 / 수많은 저자들은 인정했다 /
that there are many enduring qualities, / whether innate or learned, /
많은 지속되는 자질이 있다는 것을 / 타고난 것이든 학습된 것이든 /
that contribute to leadership potential.
리더십 잠재력에 기여하는
These traits include such things as *drive, self-confidence, cognitive ability, conscientiousness, determination, intelligence, and integrity*.
이러한 특성에는 '추진력', '자신감', '인지 능력', '성실성', '결단력', '지능', 그리고 '청렴'과 같은 것이 포함된다

지도자는 그들을 지도자가 아닌 사람과 구별해 주는 특정한 신체적, 지적, 혹은 성격적 특성을 '선천적으로' 가지고 있다는 생각은 리더십에 대한 특성 기반 접근법의 기초적인 믿음이었다. 이 접근법은 1800년대 후반부터 1940년대 중반까지 리더십 연구를 지배했으며 지난 몇십 년 동안 관심이 되살아나는 것을 경험했다. 초기 특성 이론가들은, 어떤 사람들은 위대한 지도자가 될 수 있게 해 주는 특성을 가지고 태어난다고 믿었다. 따라서 이 분야의 초기 연구는 '지도자는 만들어지는 것이 아니라 태어나는 것'이라는 널리 언급되는 주장을 자주 제시하였다. 또한, 초기 리더십 연구 중 일부는 '위인' 이론이라 불리는 것에 기반을 두었는데, 이는 그 당시 연구자들이, 일반적으로 남성이면서 귀족이거나 정치나 군대의 리더십과 관련이 있는 역사에서 매우 눈에 띄는 지도자들의 특징을 확인하는 데 초점을 맞췄기 때문이다. 더 최근의 역사에서, 수많은 저자들은, 타고난 것이든 학습된 것이든, 리더십 잠재력에 기여하는 많은 지속되는 자질이 있다는 것을 인정했다. 이러한 특성에는 '추진력', '자신감', '인지 능력', '성실성', '결단력', '지능', 그리고 '청렴'과 같은 것이 포함된다.

문제풀이

① **[주어·동사의 수일치]**
동격절 'that leaders ~ nonleaders'의 수식을 받는 단수명사 the idea가 문장의 주어이므로 단수동사 was를 쓴 것은 올바른 용법이다.

② **[대명사]**
them의 앞의 복수명사 some individuals를 지칭하는 복수 대명사로 올바르게 사용되었다.

③ **[동격절 접속사 that]**
동격절 접속사 that은 '명사+that+완전한 문장'의 구조를 갖게 되는데, 이 문장에서는 명사 argument와 동격을 이루고, 그 뒤 문장 'leaders are born, not made'가 완전한 문장으로 올바르게 사용되었다.

④ **[능동태 vs. 수동태]**
'refer to A as B'는 'A를 B로 칭하다'의 뜻으로 'some of the earliest leadership studies were grounded in what referred to as the "great mean" theory'에서 referred to의 목적어가 보이지 않고 의미상으로도 '초기 리더십 연구 중 일부는 '위인' 이론이라 불리는 것에 기반을 두었다'가 되어 능동태의 의미인 '불렀다'가 아니라 '불리었다'인 수동의 의미가 되어야 하므로 'referred'를 수동형인 'was referred'로 고쳐야 한다.

⑤ **[부사절 접속사 whether]**
whether는 명사절과 부사절을 이끌 수 있는 접속사로 종종 'whether A or B'의 형태를 취할 수 있고, 특히 부사절에서는 앞의 주어와 일치하는 주어와 be동사를 생략할 수 있다. 이 문장에서는 'whether (they are) innate or learned'에서 they are가 생략된 형태로 올바르게 사용되었다.

어휘·어구

inherently 선천적으로
intellectual 지적인
personality 성격
trait 특성
distinguish A from B A와 B를 구별하다
approach 접근(법)
dominate 지배하다
argument 주장
be grounded in ~에 기반[기초]을 두다
be referred to as ~이라고 불리다
visible 명백한
be associated with ~와 관련 있다
numerous 수많은
endure 지속하다
contribute to ~의 원인이 되다
potential 잠재력
cognitive 인지 능력
determination 결단력
intelligence 지능
integrity 청렴, 고결

정답률 57%

2. ② 기업 윤리의 이해

직독직해

Recognizing ethical issues / is the most important step /
윤리적 문제를 인식하는 것은 / 가장 중요한 단계이다 /
in understanding business ethics.
기업 윤리를 이해하는 데
An ethical issue is an identifiable problem, situation, or opportunity /
윤리적 문제는 식별 가능한 문제, 상황 혹은 기회이다 /
that requires a person to choose from among several actions /
여러 행동 가운데에서 한 사람이 선택하기를 요구하는 /
that may be evaluated / as right or wrong, ethical or unethical.
평가받을 수 있는 / 옳거나 틀렸다고, 윤리적 혹은 비윤리적이라고
Learning how to choose from alternatives and

make a decision / requires /
대안 중에서 선택하고 결정하는 방법을 배우는 것은 / 요구한다 /

not only good personal values, /
훌륭한 개인적 가치관뿐만 아니라 /

but also knowledge competence in the business area of concern.
관계가 있는 비즈니스 분야에 대한 지식 역량도

Employees also need to know /
또한 직원들은 알아야 한다 /

when to rely on their organizations' policies and codes of ethics /
언제 자신이 속한 조직의 정책과 윤리 강령에 의존할지 /

or have discussions with co-workers or managers / on appropriate conduct.
또는 언제 동료나 관리자와 논의해야 할지를 / 적절한 행동에 대해

Ethical decision making is not always easy /
윤리적 의사결정이 언제나 쉬운 것은 아닌데 /

because there are always gray areas /
왜냐하면 회색 영역이 항상 있기 때문이다 /

that create dilemmas, / no matter how decisions are made.
딜레마를 만드는 / 결정이 어떻게 내려지든

For instance, / should an employee report / on a co-worker engaging in time theft?
예를 들면 / 직원은 보고해야 할까 / 시간 훔치기를 하는 동료에 관해

Should a salesperson leave out facts / about a product's poor safety record /
판매원은 사실을 생략해야 할까 / 어떤 제품의 안전 상태가 좋지 않다는 기록에 관한 /

in his presentation to a customer?
고객에게 프레젠테이션할 때

Such questions require the decision maker /
그런 질문은 의사결정자에게 요구한다 /

to evaluate the ethics of his or her choice /
자신이 선택한 윤리를 평가할 것을 /

and decide whether to ask for guidance.
그리고 지침을 요청할 것인지 아닐지의 여부를 결정할 것을

윤리적 문제를 인식하는 것은 기업 윤리를 이해하는 데 가장 중요한 단계이다. 윤리적 문제는 옳거나 틀렸다고, 윤리적 혹은 비윤리적이라고 평가받을 수 있는 여러 행동 가운데에서 한 사람이 선택하기를 요구하는 식별 가능한 문제, 상황 혹은 기회이다. 대안 중에서 선택하고 결정하는 방법을 배우는 것은 훌륭한 개인적 가치관뿐만 아니라 관계가 있는 비즈니스 분야에 대한 지식 역량도 요구한다. 또한 직원들은 언제 자신이 속한 조직의 정책과 윤리 강령에 의존할지 또는 언제 동료나 관리자와 적절한 행동에 대해 논의해야 할지를 알아야 한다. 윤리적 의사결정이 언제나 쉬운 것은 아닌데, 왜냐하면 결정이 어떻게 내려지든 딜레마를 만드는 회색 영역이 항상 있기 때문이다. 예를 들면, 직원은 시간 훔치기를 하는 동료에 관해 보고해야 할까? 판매원은 고객에게 프레젠테이션할 때 어떤 제품의 안전 상태가 좋지 않다는 기록에 관한 사실을 생략해야 할까? 그런 질문은 의사결정자가 자신이 선택한 윤리를 평가하여 지침을 요청할 것인지 아닐지의 여부를 결정할 것을 요구한다.

문제풀이

① **[수동태]**
several actions는 '평가받는' 수동적 대상이므로, 수동태가 되어야 한다. 따라서 be evaluated가 온 것은 적절하다.

② **[동명사]**
문장의 동사는 requires로 앞에는 주어가 와야 한다. 따라서 Learn을 주어가 될 수 있는 동명사구를 이끄는 동명사 Learning으로 고쳐야 한다.

③ **[병렬구조]**
when to에 이어지는 rely on과 등위접속사 or로 연결되어 마찬가지로 to에 이어지는 동사원형이 와야 하므로 have가 온 것은 적절하다.

④ **[관계대명사]**
뒤에 이어지는 절에서 주어 역할을 하며 선행사 gray areas를 수식하고 있으므로, 주격 관계대명사 that이 온 것은 적절하다.

⑤ **[whether+to부정사]**
decide의 목적어 역할을 하는 명사구가 와야 하는데, to부정사 앞의 의문사가 '~할 것인지 (아닌지)'라는 의미가 되어야 하므로, whether가 온 것은 적절하다.

이렇게 풀자 어법상 틀린 부분을 찾는 문제는 밑줄이 있는 부분의 형태와 문맥을 보고 어법에 맞게 쓰였는지 확인해야 한다.
① 「be동사+p.p.」에 밑줄이 있는 경우, 주어와의 관계를 파악하여 수동태로 쓰이는 것이 적절한지 살펴야 한다.
② 밑줄이 그어진 부분이 문장에서 어떤 역할을 하는지 파악해야 한다.
③ 컴마(,)나 등위접속사 다음에 밑줄이 있는 경우는 병렬구조가 아닌지 살펴본다.
④ 문장에서 관계대명사가 필요한 경우인지를 확인한 후, 선행사의 종류 및 격에 따라 적절하게 쓰였는지 살펴봐야 한다.
⑤ 의문사에 밑줄이 있는 경우 의미상 적절한 의문사가 쓰였는지 확인해야 한다.

어휘·어구

ethical 윤리적인
identifiable 식별 가능한
evaluate 평가하다
alternative 대안, 선택 가능한 것
competence 능력, 역량
rely on ~에 의존하다
appropriate 적절한
conduct 행동
dilemma 딜레마, 진퇴양난
engage in ~에 관여하다
leave out ~을 빼다

정답률 

3. ③ 스파이더 차트

직독/직해

The spider chart, / also called a radar chart, / is a form of line graph.
스파이더 차트는 / 방사형 차트라고도 불리는 / 선 그래프의 한 형태이다

It helps the researcher to represent their data / in a chart /
그것은 연구자가 그들의 데이터를 설명하도록 도와준다 / 차트로 /

that shows the relative size of a response / on one scale /
응답의 상대적 크기를 보여주는 / 하나의 척도에서 /

for interrelated variables.
상호 연관된 변수에 대해

Like the bar chart, / the data needs to have one scale /
막대그래프와 마찬가지로 / 데이터는 하나의 척도를 가져야 한다 /

which is common to all variables.
모든 변수에 공통인

The spider chart is drawn / with the variables spanning the chart, /
스파이더 차트는 그려지며 / 변수들이 차트에 걸치면서 /

creating a spider web.
거미줄을 만든다.

An example of this is seen / in a research study /
이것의 예는 보여진다 / 조사 연구에서 /

looking at self-reported confidence in year 7 students /
7학년 학생들의 스스로 보고된 자신감을 살펴본 /

across a range of subjects / taught in their first term in secondary school.
다양한 과목에 걸쳐 / 중등학교에서 첫 학기에 가르쳐진

The researcher takes the responses from a sample group /
연구자는 표본 집단으로부터 응답값들을 가져온다 /

and calculates the mean to plot on the spider chart.
그리고 스파이더 차트에 나타낼 평균치를 계산한다

The spider chart allows the researcher /
스파이더 차트는 연구자에게 허락한다 /

to easily compare and contrast the confidence level /
자신감 정도를 쉽게 비교하고 대조할 수 있도록

in different subjects for the sample group.
표본 집단의 여러 다른 과목에서의

The chart, / like the pie chart, / can then be broken down /
이 차트는 / 파이 차트와 마찬가지로 / 세분화될 수 있다 /

for different groups of students / within the study /
다른 학생 집단으로 / 연구 내의 /

to elicit further analysis of findings.
연구 결과의 추가 분석을 도출하기 위해

방사형 차트라고도 불리는 스파이더 차트는 선 그래프의 한 형태이다. 그것은 연구자가 상호 연관된 변수에 대해 하나의 척도에서 응답의 상대적 크기를 보여주는 차트로 그들의 데이터를 설명하도록 도와준다. 막대그래프와 마찬가지로 데이터는 모든 변수에 공통인 하나의 척도를 가져야 한다. 스파이더 차트는 변수들이 차트에 걸치면서 그려지며 거미줄을 만든다. 이것의 예는 중등학교에서 첫 학기에 가르쳐진 다양한 과목에 걸쳐 7학년 학생들의 스스로 보고된 자신감을 조사한 연구에서 보여진다. 연구자는 표본 집단으로부터 응답값들을 가져와 스파이더 차트에 나타낼 평균치를 계산한다. 스파이더 차트는 연구자가 표본 집단의 여러 다른 과목에서의 자신감 정도를 쉽게 비교하고 대조할 수 있도록 한다. 이후, 파이 차트와 마찬가지로, 이 차트는 연구 결과의 추가 분석을 도출하기 위해 연구 내의 다른 학생 집단으로 세분화될 수 있다.

문제풀이

① **[관계대명사 that]**
that은 a chart를 선행사로 하고, 동사 shows의 주어 역할을 하는 주격관계대명사로 올바르게 사용되었다.

② **[분사구문]**
전체 문장의 동사가 'is drawn'이고 접속사가 없으므로 creating은 결과를 나타내는 분사구문으로 올바르게 사용되었다.

③ **[정동사 VS 준동사]**
정동사 'is seen'과 'have taught'가 접속사나 관계사 없이 연결될 수 없다. 따라서 have taught는 앞의 명사 'a range of subjects'를 수식하는 분사가 되어야 한다. '가르쳐진'의 뜻을 지닌 수동의 의미가 되어야 하므로 'have taught'를 과거분사 taught로 고쳐야 한다.

④ **[병렬구문]**
'calculates'는 등위접속사 'and'에 의해서 앞의 동사 'takes'와 병렬을 이룬 동사로 올바르게 사용되었다.

⑤ **[to부정사]**
'to elicit'는 '도출하기 위해'의 뜻으로 목적의 의미인 to부정사구를 이끌고 있으므로 올바르게 사용되었다.

이렇게 풀자 어법 문제에서는 '정동사의 개수−1=접속사[관계사]'의 원칙을 적용하게 되면 쉽게 해결되는 문제가 많다. ①의 that은 관계대명사로 두 개의 정동사 helps와 shows를 연결하고 있고, ②의 creating은 준동사로 정동사 'is drawn'이 하나 있고 접속사나 관계사가 없으니 올바르게 사용되었다. ③의 have taught는 정동사의 형태로 이미 정동사 is seen이 있고, 접속사나 관계사가 없으므로 틀린 표현이다. ④의 calculates는 정동사 takes가 있고 접속사 and가 있으므로 올바른 표현이며, ⑤의 to elicit는 준동사로 정동사 can be broken이 있고 접속사나 관계사가 보이지 않으므로 올바르게 사용되었다.

어휘·어구

relative 상대적
response 응답
variable 변수
common 공통의
draw 그리다
span 걸치다
confidence 자신감
a range of 다양한

subject 과목
secondary 중등 교육의
calculate 계산하다
plot 나타내다, 표시하다
contrast 대조
elicit 알아내다
analysis 분석
finding 결과

4. ③ 생태계들의 구성과 범위

직독/직해

Ecosystems differ / in composition and extent.
생태계들은 다르다 / 구성과 범위가

They can be defined / as ranging /
그것들은 정의될 수 있다 / 범위에 이르는 것으로 /

from the communities and interactions of organisms / in your mouth /
유기체들의 군집과 상호 작용으로부터 / 여러분의 입속에 있는 /

or those in the canopy of a rain forest /
또는 열대 우림의 덮개 안에 있는 그것들에서부터 /

to all those in Earth's oceans.
지구의 바다에 있는 모든 그것들까지의

The processes governing them / differ in complexity and speed.
그것들을 지배하는 과정들은 / 복잡성과 속도의 면에서 다르다

There are systems that turn over in minutes, /
몇 분 안에 뒤바뀌는 시스템도 있다 /

and there are others / whose rhythmic time extends to hundreds of years.
그리고 다른 시스템도 있다 / 규칙적으로 순환하는 시간이 수백 년까지 이르는

Some ecosystems are extensive ('biomes', such as the African savanna); /
어떤 생태계는 광범위하고(아프리카 사바나 같은 '생물군계') /

some cover regions (river basins); /
어떤 생태계는 지역들에 걸쳐 있으며(강의 유역) /

many involve clusters of villages (micro-watersheds); /
많은 생태계가 마을 군집을 포함하고(작은 분수령들) /

others are confined to the level of a single village (the village pond).
다른 생태계들은 단 하나의 마을 차원으로 국한된다(마을 연못)

In each example / there is an element of indivisibility.
각각의 사례에는 / 불가분성이라는 요소가 있다

Divide an ecosystem into parts / by creating barriers, /
어떤 생태계를 부분들로 나누면 / 장벽을 만들어 /

and the sum of the productivity of the parts /
그리고 그 부분들의 생산성의 합은 /

will typically be found to be lower / than the productivity of the whole, /
일반적으로 더 낮다는 것이 밝혀질 것이다 / 전체의 생산성보다 /

other things being equal.
다른 것이 동일하다면

The mobility of biological populations / is a reason.
생물학적 개체군의 이동성이 / 하나의 이유이다

Safe passages, / for example, / enable migratory species to survive.
안전한 통행은 / 예를 들면 / 이동하는 생물 종들을 생존하게 한다

생태계들은 구성과 범위가 다르다. 그것들은 여러분의 입속에 있는 유기체들의 군집과 상호작용 또는 열대 우림의 덮개(최상부) 안에 있는 그것들에서부터 지구의 바다에 있는 모든 그것들까지의 범위에 이르는 것으로 정의될 수 있다. 그것들을 지배하는 과정들은 복잡성과 속도의 면에서 다르다. 몇 분 안에 뒤바뀌는 다른 시스템도 있고, 규칙적으로 순환하는 시간이 수백 년까지 이르는 시스템도 있다. 어떤 생태계는 광범위하고(아프리카 사바나 같은 '생물군계'), 어떤 생태계는 지역들에 걸쳐 있으며(강의 유역), 많은 생태계가 마을 군집을 포함하고(작은 분수령들), 다른 생태계들은 단 하나의 마을 차원으로 국한된다(마을 연못). 각각의 사례에는 불가분성이라는 요소가 있다. 어떤 생태계를 장벽을 만들어 부분들로 나누면, 그 부분들의 생산성의 합은 일반적으로, 다른 것이 동일하다면, 전체의 생산성보다 더 낮다는 것이 밝혀질 것이다. 생물학적 개체군의 이동성이 하나의 이유이다. 예를 들면, 안전한 통행은 이동하는 생물 종들을 생존하게 한다.

문제풀이

① **[지시대명사]**
앞에 있는 the communities and interactions of organisms를 지칭하는 지시대명사가 와야 하므로, those가 온 것은 적절하다.
② **[분사]**
The processes를 수식하는 분사가 와야 하는데 '지배하는'이라는 능동의 의미이므로, 현재분사 governing이 온 것은 적절하다.
③ **[관계대명사]**
선행사인 others를 수식하는 관계대명사절을 이끌면서 뒤에 있는 rhythmic time을 수식할 수 있는 소유격 관계대명사가 와야 하는 자리이다. 따라서 which를 whose로 고쳐야 한다.
④ **[분사구문]**
분사구문이 와야 하는데, 의미상의 주어가 other things로 '동일하다면'이라는 능동의 의미이므로, 현재분사 being이 온 것은 적절하다.
⑤ **[목적격보어]**
enable은 to부정사를 목적격보어로 취하는 동사이므로, to survive가 온 것은 적절하다.

● 이렇게 풀자 어법상 틀린 부분을 찾는 문제는 밑줄이 있는 부분의 형태와 문맥을 보고 어법에 맞게 쓰였는지 확인해야 한다.
① 지시대명사가 쓰인 경우, 앞 문장이나 절에서 가리키는 명사를 찾아서 수가 일치하는지 확인해야 한다.
② 분사가 명사를 수식할 경우, 수동의 의미일 경우 과거분사가 오고 능동의 의미일 경우 현재분사가 온다.
③ 문장에서 관계대명사가 필요한 경우인지를 확인한 후, 선행사의 종류 및 격에 따라 적절하게 쓰였는지 살펴봐야 한다.
④ 분사구문에서 의미상 주어와의 관계가 능동일 때 현재분사가 와야 하고, 수동일 때 과거분사가 와야 한다.
⑤ 동사의 종류에 따라 목적격보어로 to부정사가 오기도 하고 동사원형이 오기도 한다. 앞에 나온 동사를 잘 파악하여 어법에 맞는지 판단해야 한다.

《 어휘·어구 》

ecosystem 생태계
composition 구성
extent 범위
range from A to B A에서 B까지의 범위에 이르다
community 군집
organism 유기체
turn over 바뀌다
rhythmic 규칙적으로 순환하는
extend 연장되다
extensive 광범위한
biome (숲·사막 같은 특정 환경 내의) 생물 군계
river basin (강의) 유역
cluster 군집, 무리
watershed 분수령
confine 제한하다
indivisibility 불가분성
barrier 장벽
productivity 생산성
mobility 이동성
migratory 이동하는, 이주하는

5. ② 국가 통제주의와 자본주의에서의 독점 문제

직독/직해

The actual problems with monopolies / are caused by statism, / not capitalism.
독점의 실제 문제들은 / 국가 통제주의에 의해 발생된다 / 자본주의가 아니라

Under a statist social system, / taxes, subsidies, tariffs, and regulations /
국가 통제주의 사회 체제하에서 / 세금, 보조금, 관세와 규제가 /

often serve to protect existing large players / in the marketplace.
흔히 기존의 대기업들을 보호하는 역할을 한다 / 시장에서

Those players often use crony tactics / to retain or expand the protections: /
그런 기업들은 정실 전략을 흔히 사용한다 / (~와 같은) 보호책들을 유지하거나 확대하기 위해 /

a new tariff preventing foreign competition, /
외국과의 경쟁을 막는 새로운 관세 /

a subsidy making it harder / for new players to compete with them, /
더 어렵게 만드는 보조금 / 신규 기업들이 그들과 경쟁하는 것을 /

or a regulatory measure / that a large company has the resources / to comply with.
혹은 규제 조치와 같은 / 대기업이 자산을 가지고 있어 / 준수할 수 있는

Under a capitalist social system, / on the other hand, /
자본주의 사회 체제하에서는 / 반면에 /

the government has no say / in how dominant a company may become / in its industry /
정부는 발언권이 없다 / 기업이 얼마나 우위를 점하게 될지 / 그것의 산업에서 /

or how companies take over and merge / with one another.
혹은 어떻게 기업들이 인수하고 합병하는지에 관해 / 서로

Furthermore, / a capitalist society doesn't have /
뿐만 아니라 / 자본주의 사회는 가지고 있지 않다 /

rights-violating taxes, tariffs, subsidies, / or regulations favoring anybody /
권리를 침해하는 세금, 관세, 보조금 / 또는 누군가에게 유리한 규제를 /

nor does it have antitrust laws.
그것은 독점 금지법도 가지고 있지 않다

Under capitalism, / dominance can only be achieved /
자본주의하에서 / 우위는 오직 얻어질 수 있다 /

by becoming really good at / what you're doing.
정말 능숙해짐으로써 / 여러분이 하고 있는 것에

And to maintain dominance, /
그리고 우위를 유지하기 위해서 /

you have to continue to stay ahead of the competition, /
여러분은 계속해서 경쟁자를 앞서 있어야 하고 /

which sees your dominance and profits /
이는 여러분의 우위와 이익을 여긴다 /

as a sign that there is money / to be made by others as well.
또한 돈이 있다는 신호로 (여긴다) / 다른 사람들이 벌 수 있는

독점의 실제 문제들은 자본주의가 아니라 국가 통제주의에 의해 발생된다. 국가 통제주의 사회 체제하에서 세금, 보조금, 관세와 규제가 흔히 시장에서 기존의 대기업들을 보호하는 역할을 한다. 그런 기업들은 외국과의 경쟁을 막는 새로운 관세, 신규 기업들이 그들과 경쟁하는 것을 더 어렵게 만드는 보조금, 혹은 대기업이 자산을 가지고 있어 준수할 수 있는 규제 조치와 같은 보호책들을 유지하거나 확대하기 위해 정실 전략을 흔히 사용한다. 반면에 자본주의 사회 체제하에서는 정부가 기업이 그것의 산업에서 얼마나 우위를 점하게 될지, 혹은 어떻게 기업들이 서로 인수하고 합병하는지에 관해 발언권이 없다. 뿐만 아니라 자본주의 사회는 권리를 침해하는 세금, 관세, 보조금 또는 누군가에게 유리한 규제를 가지고 있지 않고 그것은 독점 금지법도 가지고 있지 않다. 자본주의하에서 우위는 여러분이 하고 있는 것에 정말 능숙해짐으로써 오직 얻어질 수 있다. 그리고 우위를 유지하기 위해서 여러분은 계속해서 경쟁자를 앞서 있어야 하고, 이는 여러분의 우위와 이익을 또한 다른 사람들이 벌 수 있는 돈이 있다는 신호로 여긴다.

문제풀이

① **[to부정사]**
앞에 가목적어 it이 나왔으므로, 진목적어로 쓰인 to부정사 to compete가 온 것은 적절하다.
② **[형용사 vs. 부사]**
의문사 how 다음에는 become의 보어 역할을 하는 형용사가 와야 하므로, dominantly를 dominant로 고쳐야 한다.

③ [현재분사 vs. 과거분사]
regulations를 수식하는 분사가 와야 하는데 '유리한'이라는 능동의 의미이므로, 현재분사 favoring이 온 것은 적절하다.
④ [관계대명사 what]
뒤에 목적어가 빠진 불완전한 절이 왔고 앞에 선행사가 없으므로, 선행사를 포함한 관계대명사 what이 온 것은 적절하다.
⑤ [접속사 that]
뒤에 모든 문장 성분을 갖춘 완전한 절이 왔고 앞의 명사 a sign과 동격인 명사절을 이끄는 접속사가 와야 하므로, that이 온 것은 적절하다.

이렇게 풀자 어법상 틀린 부분을 찾는 문제는 밑줄이 있는 부분의 형태와 문맥을 보고 어법에 맞게 쓰였는지 확인해야 한다.
① to부정사에 밑줄이 그어진 경우, 문장에서 어떤 역할을 하는지 파악해야 한다.
② 부사에 밑줄이 있는 경우, 형용사가 와야 하는 자리가 아닌지 확인해야 한다. 부사는 동사의 앞이나 뒤에서 동사를 수식하거나 문장의 앞뒤에서 문장 전체를 수식할 수 있으며, 또한 형용사나 다른 부사를 수식할 수 있다. 형용사는 명사를 수식하거나 문장의 보어로 쓰일 수 있다.
③ 분사가 명사를 수식할 경우, 수동의 의미일 경우 과거분사가 오고 능동의 의미일 경우 현재분사가 온다.
④ 관계대명사 what 뒤에는 주어나 목적어가 빠진 불완전한 문장이 와야 하고 앞에는 선행사가 없어야 하므로, what에 밑줄이 있는 경우 뒤에 온 문장이 성분을 모두 갖추고 있는지와 앞에 명사가 있는지 확인해야 한다.
⑤ that은 주어, 목적어, 보어 역할을 하는 명사절을 이끄는 접속사로 쓰일 수 있고, 동격의 명사절을 이끌기도 한다. that에 밑줄이 그어져 있을 경우, 명사절을 이끄는 접속사로 쓰인 것이 아닌지 판단하려면 뒤에 모든 문장 성분을 갖춘 완전한 절이 왔는지를 확인해야 한다.

《 어휘·어구 》

monopoly 독점
capitalism 자본주의
subsidy 보조금, 장려금
tariff 관세
regulation 규제
tactic 전략, 전술
retain 유지하다
expand 확대되다
regulatory 규제력을 지닌
comply 따르다
dominantly 지배적으로, 우세하게
take over 인수하다
merge 합병하다
violate 위반하다, 침해하다
dominance 우위
achieve 성취하다, 얻다
maintain 유지하다
profit 이익

6. ② 고대 그리스 음악의 소리

직독/직해

We don't know / what ancient Greek music sounded like, /
우리는 모른다 / 고대 그리스 음악이 어떤 소리를 냈는지 /
because there are no examples of it / in written or notated form, /
그것의 사례가 없기 때문에 / 기록되거나 악보에 적힌 형태로 되어 있는 /
nor has it survived in oral tradition.
그리고 그것은 구전으로도 살아남지 못했다
Much of it was probably improvised anyway, /
어쨌든 그것의 대부분은 아마도 즉흥적으로 연주되었을 것이다 /
within certain rules and conventions.
특정 규칙과 관례 내에서
So we are forced largely to guess at its basis /
그래서 우리는 주로 그것의 토대를 추측할 수밖에 없다 /
from the accounts of writers / such as Plato and Aristotle, /
작가들의 설명으로부터 / 플라톤과 아리스토텔레스와 같은 /
who were generally more concerned with writing about music /
그들은 음악에 대해 글을 쓰는 것에 대체로 더 관심이 있었다 /
as a philosophical and ethical exercise /
철학적이고 윤리적인 실천으로서의 /
than with providing a technical primer on its practice.
실제에 대한 기술적인 입문서를 제공하는 것보다
It seems Greek music was predominantly a vocal form, /
그리스 음악은 대개 성악 형식이었던 것으로 보인다 /
consisting of sung verse accompanied by instruments /
악기의 반주에 의해 노래되는 운문으로 구성된 /
such as the lyre or the plucked kithara (the root of 'guitar').
수금(竪琴)이나 튕기는 키타라('기타'의 뿌리)와 같은
In fact, / Plato considered music / in which the lyre and flute played alone /
사실 / 플라톤은 음악을 여겼다 / 수금(竪琴)과 피리만 연주되는 /
and not as the accompaniment of dance or song /
춤이나 노래의 반주로서가 아닌 /
to be 'exceedingly coarse and tasteless'.
'매우 조잡하고 무미건조하다'고
The melodies seem to have had a very limited pitch range, /
그 선율은 매우 제한된 음역을 가지고 있었던 것으로 보인다 /
since the instruments generally span only an octave, /
왜냐하면 그 악기들은 일반적으로 단지 한 옥타브에만 걸쳐 있기 때문이다 /
from one E (as we'd now define it) to the next.
한 E에서 (우리가 그것을 현재 정의하는 대로) 다음 E까지

우리는 고대 그리스 음악이 어떤 소리를 냈는지 알지 못하는데, 그 이유는 그것이 기록되거나 악보에 적힌 형태로 되어 있는 사례가 없고, 구전으로도 살아남지 못했기 때문이다. 어쨌든 그것의 대부분은 아마도 특정 규칙과 관례 내에서 즉흥적으로 연주되었을 것이다. 그래서 우리는 주로 플라톤과 아리스토텔레스와 같은 작가들의 설명으로부터 그것의 토대를 추측할 수밖에 없는데, 그들은 실제에 대한 기술적인 입문서를 제공하는 것보다 철학적이고 윤리적인 실천으로서의 음악에 대해 글을 쓰는 것에 대체로 더 관심이 있었다. 그리스 음악은 대개 성악 형식이었고, 수금(竪琴)이나 튕기는 키타라('기타'의 뿌리)와 같은 악기의 반주에 의해 노래되는 운문으로 구성되었던 것으로 보인다. 사실, 플라톤은 춤이나 노래의 반주로서가 아닌 수금(竪琴)과 피리만 연주되는 음악을 '매우 조잡하고 무미건조하다'고 여겼다. 그 선율은 매우 제한된 음역을 가지고 있었던 것으로 보이는데, 왜냐하면 그 악기들은 일반적으로 (우리가 그것을 현재 정의하는 대로)한 E에서 다음 E까지 단지 한 옥타브에만 걸쳐 있기 때문이다.

문제풀이

① [도치구문]
부정의 의미를 지닌 접속사 nor 다음에는 주어 동사가 도치되어야 하므로 올바르게 쓰였다.
② [비교구문]
as는 앞의 '~로서'의 의미를 지닌 자격을 나타내는 전치사 as와 연결된 것이 아니라 그 앞의 more와 연결된 비교 구문이므로 as를 than으로 바꿔야 한다.
③ [분사구문]
consisting of는 완전한 문장에 연결된 분사구문이고, consist는 자동사이므로 현재분사를 쓴 것은 올바른 용법이다.
④ [목적보어로 쓰인 to부정사]
consider는 '동사+목적어+to부정사'의 구조를 갖는 5형식 동사이므로 'to be'는 consider의 목적보어로 쓰인 to부정사로 올바르게 쓰였다.
⑤ [형용사 vs 부사]
generally는 동사 span을 수식한 부사로 올바르게 쓰였다.

《 어휘·어구 》

notate 악보에 적다
oral tradition 구전(口傳)
improvise 즉흥 연주를 하다
convention 관례, 관행, 약속
account 설명
be concerned with ~에 관심이 있다
philosophical 철학의
ethical 윤리적인
primer 입문서
predominantly 대개
consist of ~으로 구성되다
verse 운문
accompany 반주해 주다
instrument 악기
pluck (현악기를) 퉁기다, 뽑다
accompaniment 반주
exceedingly 매우
tasteless 무미건조한, 멋없는
melody 선율
limited 제한된
pitch range 음역
span 걸치다

7. ④ 세포 주기

직독/직해

Like whole individuals, / cells have a life span.
모든 개체처럼, / 세포도 수명을 가진다
During their life cycle (cell cycle), /
그것의 생애 주기(세포 주기) 동안에 /
cell size, shape, and metabolic activities /
세포의 크기, 모양, 물질대사 활동이 /
can change dramatically.
극적으로 바뀔 수 있다
A cell is "born" as a twin /
세포는 쌍둥이로 태어난다 /
when its mother cell divides, /
모세포가 나눠질 때 /
producing two daughter cells.
두 개의 딸세포를 생성하면서
Each daughter cell is smaller than the mother cell, /
각각의 딸세포는 모세포보다 더 작다 /
and except for unusual cases, / each grows /
그리고 특이한 경우를 제외하고는 / 각각 자란다 /
until it becomes as large as the mother cell was.
모세포의 크기만큼 커질 때까지
During this time, / 이 기간 동안에 /
the cell absorbs water, sugars, amino acids, and other nutrients /
세포는 물, 당, 아미노산, 그리고 다른 영양소들을 흡수한다 /
and assembles them / into new, living protoplasm.
그리고 그것들을 만든다 / 새로운 살아있는 원형질로
After the cell has grown to the proper size, /
세포가 적절한 크기로 자란 후 /
its metabolism shifts / 그것의 물질대사가 변화한다 /
as it either prepares to divide or matures and differentiates into a specialized cell.
그것은 분열할 준비를 하거나 성숙하여 특화된 세포로 분화하면서
Both growth and development require /
성장과 발달 둘 다 요구한다 /
a complex and dynamic set of interactions /
일련의 복잡하고 역동적인 상호 작용을 /
involving all cell parts.
모든 세포 부분을 포함하는

That cell metabolism and structure should be complex /
세포의 물질대사와 구조가 복잡해야 하는 것은 /

would not be surprising, / 놀라운 것이 아니다 /

but actually, they are rather simple and logical.
하지만 실제로 그것들은 아주 간단하고 논리적이다

Even the most complex cell has only a small number of parts, /
가장 복잡한 세포조차도 그저 소수의 부분만을 가지고 있는데 /

each responsible for a distinct, well-defined aspect of cell life.
각각은 세포 생명의 뚜렷하고, 명확한 측면을 맡고 있다

모든 개체처럼, 세포도 수명을 가진다. 그것의 생애 주기(세포 주기) 동안에, 세포의 크기, 모양, 물질대사 활동이 극적으로 바뀔 수 있다. 세포는 모세포가 두 개의 딸세포를 생성하면서 나눠질 때, 쌍둥이로 태어난다. 각각의 딸세포는 모세포보다 더 작고, 특이한 경우를 제외하고는 각각 모세포의 크기만큼 커질 때까지 자란다. 이 기간 동안에 세포는 물, 당, 아미노산, 그리고 다른 영양소들을 흡수하고 그것들을 새로운 살아있는 원형질로 만든다. 세포가 적절한 크기로 자란 후, 그것은 분열할 준비를 하거나 성숙하여 특화된 세포로 분화하면서 그것의 물질대사가 변화한다. 성장과 발달 둘 다 모든 세포 부분을 포함하는 일련의 복잡하고 역동적인 상호 작용을 요구한다. 세포의 물질대사와 구조가 복잡해야 하는 것은 놀라운 것이 아니겠지만, 실제로 그것들은 아주 간단하고 논리적이다. 가장 복잡한 세포조차도 그저 소수의 부분만을 가지고 있는데, 각각은 세포 생명의 뚜렷하고, 명확한 측면을 맡고 있다.

문제풀이

① [분사구문]
분사구문이 와야 하는데, '두 개의 딸세포를 생성하면서'라는 능동의 의미이므로, 현재분사 producing이 온 것은 적절하다.

② [대동사]
'컸다(was large)'는 의미의 모세포의 과거 사이즈를 지칭하는 대동사가 와야 하므로, was가 온 것은 적절하다. grows나 becomes를 받아 대동사 did를 사용하는 것은 의미상 적절하지 않다.

③ [병렬 구조]
부사절의 동사가 「either A or B(A나 B 둘 중 하나)」 구문으로 연결되어 있다. 이때 A와 B는 병렬 구조이고 B에서 두 동사가 and로 연결되어 있으므로 마찬가지로 3인칭 단수형인 differentiates가 온 것은 적절하다.

④ [접속사 that]
뒤에 모든 문장 성분을 갖춘 완전한 문장이 왔으므로, what은 적절하지 않다. 주어로 쓰인 명사절을 이끄는 접속사가 와야 하므로, what을 접속사 that으로 바꿔야 한다.

⑤ [분사구문]
분사구문 each being responsible ...에서 being이 생략되어 responsible이 온 것은 적절하다.

이렇게 풀자 어법상 틀린 부분을 찾는 문제는 밑줄이 있는 부분의 형태와 문맥을 보고 어법에 맞게 쓰였는지 확인해야 한다.
① 분사구문에서 의미상 주어와의 관계가 능동일 때 현재분사가 와야 하고, 수동일 때 과거분사가 와야 한다.
② be동사 뒤에 보어나 전치사구가 없다면 대동사일 가능성이 높다. 대동사는 be동사를 받으면 be동사를 시제와 인칭에 맞게 쓰고 일반동사를 받으면 do를 시제와 인칭에 맞게 써야 한다.
③ 「either A or B」 구문에서 A와 B의 문법적 형태가 같아야 한다.
④ what 뒤에는 주어나 목적어가 빠진 불완전한 문장이 와야 하므로, 뒤에 온 문장이 성분을 모두 갖추고 있는지 확인해야 한다.
⑤ 분사구문에서 being은 생략될 수 있다.

어휘·어구

individual 개인, 개체
life span 수명
dramatically 극적으로
absorb 흡수하다
amino acid 아미노산
assemble 조립하다
nutrient 영양소
proper 적절한
metabolism 물질대사
mature 성숙하다
differentiate 분화하다
logical 논리적인
distinct 뚜렷한
well-defined 명확한

정답률 59%

8. ⑤ 규칙성과 예측 가능성을 위한 도구

직독/직해

Most historians of science /
대부분의 과학 역사가들은 /

point to the need for a reliable calendar /
믿을 만한 달력의 필요성을 지적한다 /

to regulate agricultural activity /
농업 활동을 규제하기 위한 /

as the motivation for learning /
배우고자 하는 동기로 /

about what we now call astronomy, /
우리가 현재 천문학이라 부르는 것에 관해 /

the study of stars and planets.
별과 행성에 대한 연구인

Early astronomy provided information /
초기 천문학은 정보를 제공했다 /

about when to plant crops /
언제 작물을 심어야 하는지에 관한 /

and gave humans their first formal method /
그리고 인간에게 그들 최초의 공식적인 방법을 제공했다 /

of recording the passage of time.
시간의 흐름을 기록하는

Stonehenge, the 4,000-year-old ring of stones in southern Britain, /
영국 남부에 있는 4,000년 된 고리 모양을 한 돌들인 스톤헨지는 /

is perhaps the best-known monument /
아마도 가장 잘 알려진 기념비일 것이다 /

to the discovery of regularity and predictability /
규칙성과 예측 가능성의 발견에 대한 /

in the world / we inhabit.
세계에서 / 우리가 살고 있는

The great markers of Stonehenge point /
스톤헨지의 큰 표식은 나타낸다 /

to the spots on the horizon /
지평선의 장소를 /

where the sun rises at the solstices and equinoxes /
지점(至點)과 분점(分點)에서 태양이 뜨는 /

— the dates we still use /
우리가 여전히 사용하는 날짜인 /

to mark the beginnings of the seasons.
계절의 시작을 표시하기 위해

The stones may even have been used /
그 돌들은 심지어 사용되었을 수도 있다 /

to predict eclipses. (해 · 달의) 식(蝕)을 예측하는 데

The existence of Stonehenge, /
스톤헨지의 존재는 /

built by people without writing, /
글이 없던 시절 사람들이 지은 /

bears silent testimony /
말 없이 증언해 준다 /

both to the regularity of nature and to the ability of the human mind /
자연의 규칙성과 인간의 정신적 능력 둘 다를 /

to see behind immediate appearances /
눈앞에 보이는 모습의 이면을 보는 /

and discover deeper meanings in events.
그리고 사건에서 더 깊은 의미를 발견할 수 있는

대부분의 과학 역사가들은 별과 행성에 관한 연구, 즉 우리가 현재 천문학이라 부르는 것에 대해 배우고자 하는 동기로 농업 활동을 규제하기 위한 믿을 만한 달력의 필요성을 지적한다. 초기 천문학은 언제 작물을 심어야 하는지에 관한 정보를 제공하고 인간에게 시간의 흐름을 기록하는 그들 최초의 공식적인 방법을 제공했다. 영국 남부에 있는 4,000년 된 고리 모양을 한 돌들인 스톤헨지는 아마도 우리가 살고 있는 세계에서 규칙성과 예측 가능성의 발견에 대한 가장 잘 알려진 기념비일 것이다. 스톤헨지의 큰 표식은 우리가 계절의 시작을 표시하기 위해 여전히 사용하는 날짜인 지점(至點)과 분점(分點)에서 태양이 뜨는 지평선의 장소를 나타낸다. 그 돌들은 심지어 (해 · 달의) 식(蝕)을 예측하는 데 사용되었을 수도 있다. 글이 없던 시절 사람들이 지은 스톤헨지의 존재는 자연의 규칙성과 눈앞에 보이는 모습의 이면을 보고 사건에서 더 깊은 의미를 발견할 수 있는 인간의 정신적 능력 둘 다를 말 없이 증언해 준다.

문제풀이

① [대명사]
앞의 humans를 가리키면서 명사구 first formal method를 수식하는 소유격으로 사용되었으므로, 대명사 their가 온 것은 적절하다.

② [주어와 동사의 수일치]
주어가 Stonehenge이므로, 단수 동사가 와야 한다. 따라서 is가 온 것은 적절하다. the 4,000-year-old ring of stones in southern Britain은 Stonehenge를 부연 설명하는 동격어구이다.

③ [관계부사]
주어(the sun), 동사(rises), 부사구(at the solstices and equinoxes)를 모두 갖춘 완전한 절이 왔으므로, 선행사 the spots on the horizon을 수식하는 관계사절을 이끄는 관계부사 where가 온 것은 적절하다.

④ [수동태]
주어인 The stones가 사용되는 대상이므로, 수동태가 와야 한다. 따라서 may have been used가 온 것은 적절하다.

⑤ [병렬구조]
상관접속사 'both A and B' 구문에서 to see와 병렬구조인 to부정사가 B에 나와야 하므로, discovers를 discover로 고쳐야 한다.

이렇게 풀자 ① 대명사가 쓰인 경우, 앞 문장이나 절에서 가리키는 명사를 찾아서 수가 일치하는지, 문법에 맞는 격이 사용되었는지 확인한다.
② 동사에 밑줄이 있는 경우, 주어와 동사의 수일치를 묻는 문제인 경우가 많다. 따라서 주어를 분명히 파악하는 것이 중요하다.
③ 관계부사에 밑줄이 있는 경우, 뒤에 문장 성분을 모두 갖춘 완전한 문장이 왔는지 확인해야 한다.
④ 'be동사+p.p'에 밑줄이 있는 경우, 주어와의 관계를 파악하여 수동태로 쓰이는 것이 적절한지 살펴야 한다.
⑤ 'both A and B' 구문에서 A와 B는 문법적으로 대등한 관계여야 한다.

어휘·어구

point to ~을 지적하다, ~을 나타내다
reliable 믿을 만한
regulate 규제하다
agricultural 농업의
astronomy 천문학
passage 흐름
regularity 규칙성
predictability 예측 가능성
inhabit 살다
solstice 지점(至點)(태양이 적도로부터 북쪽 또는 남쪽으로 가장 치우쳤을 때)
equinox 분점(分點)(태양이 적도를 통과하는 점)
immediate 눈앞에 있는

9. ⑤ 자기를 실험하는 것의 장점과 단점

직독/직해

Regulations covering scientific experiments on human subjects /
인간 피험자들에 관한 과학 실험을 다루는 규제는 /
are strict. 엄격하다
Subjects must give their informed, written consent, /
피험자는 충분한 설명에 입각한 서면 동의를 해야 한다 /
and experimenters must submit their proposed experiments /
그리고 실험자는 자신들의 계획된 실험을 제출해야 한다 /
to thorough examination / by overseeing bodies.
철저한 정밀 조사를 / 감독 기관에 의한
Scientists who experiment on themselves /
자기 자신을 실험하는 과학자들은 /
can, functionally if not legally, / avoid the restrictions /
법률상으로는 아니지만 직무상으로는 / 규제를 피할 수 있다 /
associated with experimenting on other people.
다른 사람들을 실험하는 것과 관련된
They can also sidestep most of the ethical issues involved: /
그들은 또한 관련된 윤리적인 문제도 대부분 피할 수 있는데 /
nobody, presumably, is more aware of an experiment's potential hazards /
그것의 잠재적인 위험을 더 잘 알고 있는 사람은 짐작건대 없을 것이기 때문이다 /
than the scientist who devised it.
실험을 고안한 과학자보다
Nonetheless, / 그렇기는 하지만 /
experimenting on oneself remains deeply problematic.
자신을 실험하는 것은 여전히 문제가 많다
One obvious drawback is the danger involved; /
한 가지 분명한 문제점은 (실험에) 수반되는 위험인데 /
knowing that it exists /
그것이 존재한다는 것을 아는 것이 /
does nothing to reduce it.
그것을 줄이기 위해 어떤 일을 하는 것은 아니다
A less obvious drawback /
이보다 덜 분명한 문제점은 /
is the limited range of data /
제한된 범위의 데이터이다 /
that the experiment can generate.
실험이 만들어낼 수 있는
Human anatomy and physiology vary, /
인체의 해부학적 구조와 생리적 현상은 각기 다르다 /
in small but significant ways, /
사소하지만 의미 있는 방식으로 /
according to gender, age, lifestyle, and other factors.
성별, 나이, 생활 방식과 기타 요인에 따라
Experimental results derived from a single subject are, /
단 한 명의 피험자로부터 얻어진 실험 결과는 /
therefore, / 그러므로 /
of limited value; / there is no way to know /
가치가 제한적이며 / 알 방법이 없다 /
whether the subject's responses are typical or atypical /
그 피험자의 반응이 대표하는 것인지 아니면 이례적인 것인지 /
of the response of humans as a group.
집단으로서의 인간 반응을

인간 피험자들에 관한 과학 실험을 다루는 규제는 엄격하다. 피험자는 충분한 설명에 입각한 서면 동의를 해야 하고, 실험자는 자신들의 계획된 실험을 제출해 감독 기관에 의한 철저한 정밀 조사를 받아야 한다. 자기 자신을 실험하는 과학자들은, 법률상으로는 아니지만, 직무상으로는 다른 사람들을 실험하는 것과 관련된 규제를 피할 수 있다. 그들은 또한 관련된 윤리적인 문제도 대부분 피할 수 있는데, 실험을 고안한 과학자보다 그것의 잠재적인 위험을 더 잘 알고 있는 사람은 짐작건대 없을 것이기 때문이다. 그렇기는 하지만, 자신을 실험하는 것은 여전히 문제가 많다. 한 가지 분명한 문제점은 (실험에) 수반되는 위험인데, 위험이 존재한다는 것을 아는 것이 위험을 줄이기 위해 어떤 일을 하는 것은 아니다. 이보다 덜 분명한 문제점은 실험이 만들어낼 수 있는 제한된 범위의 데이터이다. 인체의 해부학적 구조와 생리적 현상은 성별, 나이, 생활 방식과 기타 요인에 따라 사소하지만, 의미 있는 방식으로 각기 다르다. 그러므로, 단 한 명의 피험자로부터 얻어진 실험 결과는 가치가 제한적이며, 그 피험자의 반응이 집단으로서의 인간 반응을 대표하는 것인지 아니면 이례적인 것인지 알 방법이 없다.

문제풀이

① [과거분사]
'관련된'이라는 수동의 의미로 명사 the restrictions를 수식하는 과거분사가 와야 하므로, associated가 온 것은 적절하다.
② [대명사]
앞의 an experiment를 가리키면서 동사 devised의 목적어로 사용되었으므로, 대명사 it이 온 것은 적절하다.
③ [부사]
형용사 problematic을 수식하는 부사로, deeply가 온 것은 적절하다.
④ [주어와 동사의 수일치]
주어가 Knowing that it exists로 동명사구이므로, 단수동사가 와야 한다. 따라서 does가 온 것은 적절하다.
⑤ [관계대명사 what]
밑줄 친 what이 이끄는 절이 모든 문장 성분을 갖춘 완전한 문장이므로, 관계대명사 what이 들어가는 것은 적절하지 않다. 문맥상 '~인지 아닌지'의 의미이므로, 접속사 whether로 고쳐 써야 한다.

이렇게 풀자 ① 분사가 명사를 수식할 경우, 수동의 의미일 경우 과거분사가 오고 능동의 의미일 경우 현재분사가 온다.
② 대명사가 쓰인 경우, 앞 문장이나 절에서 가리키는 명사를 찾아서 대명사의 수가 일치하는지, 문법에 맞는 대명사의 격이 사용되었는지 확인한다.
③ 부사는 동사의 앞이나 뒤에서 동사를 수식하거나 문장의 앞뒤에서 문장 전체를 수식할 수 있으며, 또한 형용사나 다른 부사를 수식할 수 있다.
④ 동사에 밑줄이 있는 경우, 주어와 동사의 수일치를 묻는 문제인 경우가 많다. 주어가 동명사구인 경우 단수동사가 와야 한다.
⑤ 관계대명사 what 뒤에는 주어나 목적어가 빠져 있는 불완전한 문장이 온다. 특히 관계대명사 what은 선행사를 포함하고 있으므로 문장에 선행사가 없어야 하며, 관계대명사절에서 주어나 목적어, 보어로 사용되어야 한다.

어휘·어구

regulation 규제
subject 대상, 피험자
strict 엄격한
submit 제출하다
proposed 제안된
rigorous 철저한, 엄격한
oversee 감독하다
functionally 기능적으로, 직무상으로
legally 법률적으로, 합법적으로
restriction 규제, 제한
associated with ~와 관련된
sidestep 피하다
ethical 윤리적인
presumably 짐작건대, 아마
potential 잠재적인
hazard 위험
devise 고안하다, 생각해 내다
drawback 문제점, 결점
derive from ~에서 얻다
typical 전형적인
atypical 이례적인

정답률 54%

10. ④ 초기 인류의 자연 세계와 인간 사회의 관계

직독/직해

Speculations about the meaning and purpose of
선사 시대 예술의 의미와 목적에 대한 고찰은 /
prehistoric art /
rely heavily on analogies / drawn with modern-day
유사점에 많이 의존한다 / 현대의 수렵 채집 사회와의 사이에서 끌어낸
hunter-gatherer societies.
Such primitive societies, / 그런 원시 사회는 /
as Steven Mithen emphasizes in *The Prehistory of the Modern Mind*, /
Steven Mithen이 'The Prehistory of the Modern Mind'에서 강조하듯이 /
tend to view man and beast, animal and plant, organic and inorganic spheres, /
인간과 짐승, 동물과 식물, 생물체의 영역과 무생물체의 영역을 여기는 경향이 있다 /
as participants in an integrated, animated totality.
통합적이고 살아 있는 총체에 대한 참여자로
The dual expressions of this tendency /
이런 경향이 표현된 두 가지가 /
are *anthropomorphism* (the practice of regarding animals as humans) /
'의인화'(동물을 인간으로 간주하는 관행) /
and *totemism* (the practice of regarding humans as animals), /
그리고 '토테미즘'(인간을 동물로 간주하는 관행)인데 /
both of which spread through the visual art and the mythology of primitive cultures.
이 두 가지는 원시 문화의 시각 예술과 신화에 널리 퍼져 있다
Thus the natural world is conceptualized / in terms of human social relations.
따라서 자연의 세계는 개념화된다 / 인간의 사회적 관계 측면에서
When considered in this light, /
이런 측면에서 고려될 때 /
the visual preoccupation of early humans with the nonhuman creatures /
초기 인류가 인간 이외의 생명체들에 대하여 시각적으로 집착한 것은 /
inhabiting their world / becomes profoundly meaningful.
자신들의 세계에 살고 있는 / 깊은 의미를 띠게 된다
Among hunter-gatherers, / 수렵 채집인들에게 /
animals are not only good to eat, they are also *good to think about*, /
동물은 먹기 좋은 대상일 뿐만 아니라, '생각해 보기에도 좋은' 대상이다 /
as Claude Lévi-Strauss has observed.
Claude Lévi-Strauss가 말했듯이
In the practice of totemism, / he has suggested, /
토템 신앙의 풍습에서 / 그는 말했다 /
an unlettered humanity "broods upon itself and its place in nature."
문맹의 인류는 "자연 속에서 자신과 자신의 위치에 대해 숙고한다."라고

선사 시대 예술의 의미와 목적에 대한 고찰은 현대의 수렵 채집 사회와의 사이에서 끌어낸 유사점에 많은 것을 의존한다. Steven Mithen이 'The Prehistory of the Modern Mind'에서 강조하듯이, 그런 원시 사회는 인간과 짐승, 동물과 식물, 생물체의 영역과 무생물체의 영역을 통합적이고 살아 있는 총체에 대한 참여자로 여기는 경향이 있다. 이런 경향이 표현된 두 가지가 '의인화'(동물을 인간으로 간주하는 관행)와 '토테미즘'(인간을 동물로 간주하는 관행)인데, 이 두 가지는 원시 문화의 시각 예술과 신화에 널리 퍼져 있다. 따라서 자연의 세계는 인간의 사회적 관계 측면에서 개념화된다. 이런 측면에서 고려될 때, 초기 인류가 자신들의 세계에 살고 있는 인간 이외의 생명체들에 대하여 시각적으로 집착한 것은 깊은 의미를 띠게 된다. 인류학자인 Claude Lévi-Strauss가 말했듯이 수렵 채집인들에게 동물은 먹기 좋은 대상일 뿐만 아니라, '생각해 보기에도 좋은' 대상이다. 토템 신앙의 풍습에서 문맹의 인류는 "자연 속에서의 자신과 자신의 위치에 대해 곰곰이 생각한다."라고 그는 말했다.

문제풀이

④가 속한 문장의 술어동사는 becomes이며, 밑줄 친 부분은 앞의 명사구 the nonhuman creatures를 수식하는 분사구가 되어야 하는데 뒤에 목적어인 their world가 있으므로 능동의 의미를 나타내는 현재분사 inhabiting이 되어야 한다. 따라서 inhabited를 inhabiting으로 고쳐야 한다.
① Speculations가 문장의 주어이므로 술어동사로서 복수형 동사 rely가 온 것은 적절하다.
② '~가 ...하듯이'라는 의미의 접속사로서 as의 쓰임이 적절하다.

③ 콤마(,) 다음에 이어지는 관계대명사 which는 앞의 절의 내용 전체를 선행사로 받는 계속용법으로서 쓰임이 적절하다.
⑤ 문장의 주어가 an unlettered humanity이므로 이에 대한 재귀대명사 itself의 쓰임이 적절하다.

이렇게 풀자_ 어법상 틀린 부분을 찾는 문제는 밑줄이 있는 부분의 형태와 문맥을 보고 어법에 맞게 쓰였는지 확인해야 한다. ① 주어와 동사의 수일치를, ② 접속사 as의 쓰임을, ③ 계속용법의 관계대명사 which의 쓰임을, ④ 현재분사구의 쓰임을, ⑤ 재귀대명사의 쓰임을 알아야 한다.

어휘·어구

draw an analogy with ~과의 유사점을 끌어내다
hunter-gatherer society 수렵 채집 사회
primitive 원시의, 원시 시대의
integrated 통합된
animated 살아 있는, 생기 있는
mythology 신화
conceptualize 개념화하다
preoccupation 집착, 열중
inhabit ~에 거주하다
observe (의견 · 소견 등을) 말하다, 관찰하다, 준수하다
unlettered 문맹의, 무지의

본문 065쪽

문법 플러스 11. 가정법

A. 1. had
2. had had
3. had taken
4. weren't
5. had had
6. Had she known
7. return

1 [해석]▶ 내가 약간의 돈을 가지고 있다면 그에게 그것을 빌려줄 텐데
[해설]▶ 가정법 과거는 현재 사실과 반대되는 것을 가정한다. 형태는 「If+주어+과거동사 ~, 주어+조동사 과거형+동사원형~」이다.

2 [해석]▶ 그가 농구공이 있었더라면 그는 게임을 시작했을 텐데.
[해설]▶ 가정법 과거완료는 과거의 사실과 반대되는 것을 가정한다. 형태는 「If+주어+had+과거분사 ~, 주어+조동사 과거형+have+과거분사~」이다.

3 [해석]▶ 그때 그녀가 나의 충고를 들었더라면 그녀는 아직 살아있을 텐데.
[해설]▶ 혼합가정법은 과거의 일이 현재에 영향을 미칠 때 사용한다. 형태는 「If+주어+had+과거분사 ~, 주어+조동사 과거형+동사원형~」이다.

4 [해석]▶ 그가 지금 여기에 없으면 좋으련만.
[해설]▶ 「I wish+가정법 과거」는 이루기 어려운 소망을 나타내며, 주절과 종속절이 나타내는 시제가 동일할 때 쓰인다.

5 [해석]▶ 그는 나쁜 소식을 들은 것처럼 보였다.
[해설]▶ 「as if+가정법과거완료」는 '마치 ~이었던 것처럼'이라는 의미이다. as if+가정법 과거완료는 주절보다 종속절의 시제가 앞선 경우에 사용한다.

6 [해석]▶ 만약 그것이 위험한 것을 알았더라면 그 산을 오르러 가지 않았을 텐데.
[해설]▶ 가정법 「If+주어+동사~」에서 If가 생략되면, 「동사+주어」로 문장이 도치된다.

7 [해석]▶ 그는 그녀에게 자기한테 빌려간 책을 돌려줄 것을 요구했다.
[해설]▶ 요구(demand)를 나타내는 동사에 이어지는 that절에서는 「주어+(should)+동사원형」을 쓴다.

본문 065쪽

B. 1. snowed
2. have prepared
3. be
4. hadn't quit
5. were
6. Had
7. settled

1 [해석]▶ 네 결혼식 날 눈이 오면 어떻게 할 거니?
[해설]▶ 가정법 과거 형태는 「If+주어+과거동사 ~, 주어+조동사 과거형+동사원형~」이다.

2 [해석]▶ 당신이 오는 것을 알았더라면, 저녁을 준비했을 텐데.
[해설]▶ 가정법 과거완료 형태는 「If+주어+had+과거분사 ~, 주어+조동사 과거형+have+과거분사~」이다.

3 [해석]▶ 당시에 네가 나의 충고를 따랐더라면, 지금은 행복했을 텐데.
[해설]▶ 혼합가정법은 과거의 일이 현재에 영향을 미칠 때 사용한다. 형태는 「If+주어+had+과거분사 ~, 주어+조동사 과거형+동사원형~」이다.

4 [해석]▶ 작년에 학교를 그만 두지 않았으면 좋았을 텐데.
[해설]▶ 「I wish+가정법 과거완료」는 이루기 어려운 소망을 나타내며 주절보다 종속절의 시제가 앞선 경우에 사용한다.

5 [해석]▶ Sally는 여왕처럼 행동한다. 사실 그녀는 여왕이 아니다.
[해설]▶ 「as if+가정법과거」는 '마치 ~인 것처럼'이라는 의미이다. 「as if+가정법 과거」는 주절과 종속절이 나타내는 시제가 동일할 때 쓰인다.

6 [해석]▶ Sam이 그녀에게 안전벨트를 차라고 말하지 않았더라면, 그녀는 더 심하게 다쳤을 텐데.
[해설]▶ 가정법 「If+주어+동사~」에서 If가 생략되면, 「동사+주어」로 문장이 도치된다.

7 [해석]▶ 당신은 부인과의 불화를 해소할 때입니다.
[해설]▶ It's time that ~ 뒤에는 가정법 과거 표현이 사용된다. 의미는 '~할 때이다'는 의미이다.

본문 066쪽

숙어 플러스 11. 수능 필수 숙어 11회

1 choice 2. nothing
3. detail 4. conclusion

12. 어휘 적절성 파악

Day 12 본문 068쪽

1. ⑤	2. ④	3. ⑤	4. ②	5. ④
6. ③	7. ④	8. ③	9. ⑤	10. ④

정답률 64%

대표 기출 ④ 스포츠의 정서적 격렬함

직독/직해

Sport can trigger an emotional response /
스포츠는 정서적 반응을 촉발할 수 있다 /
in its consumers / 그것의 소비자에게 /
of the kind rarely brought forth by other products.
다른 제품이 좀처럼 생산하지 않는 종류의
Imagine bank customers buying memorabilia /
은행 고객이 기념품을 산다고 상상해 보라 /
to show loyalty to their bank, /
그들 은행에 대한 충성심을 보여주기 위해서 /
or consumers identifying so strongly /
또는 고객이 매우 강한 동질감을 가져서 /
with their car insurance company /
그들 자동차 보험 회사에 대해 /
that they get a tattoo with its logo.
회사 로고로 문신을 한다고 (상상해 보라)
We know / that some sport followers are so passionate /
우리는 안다 / 일부 스포츠팬들이 매우 열정적이어서 /
about players, teams and the sport itself /
선수, 팀, 그리고 그 스포츠 자체에 /
that their interest borders on obsession.
그들의 관심이 집착에 아주 가깝다는 것을
This addiction provides the emotional glue /
이러한 중독은 정서적 접착제를 제공한다 /
that binds fans to teams, / 팬을 팀과 묶어주는 /
and maintains loyalty / 그리고 충성심을 유지하게 한다 /
even in the face of on-field failure.
심지어 구장에서 일어나는 실패에도
While most managers can only dream of having customers /
대부분의 운영자는 오직 고객을 가지기를 꿈꾸지만 /
that are as passionate about their products /
그들 제품에 열정적인 /
as sport fans, / 스포츠팬만큼 /
the emotion triggered by sport /
스포츠로 인해 촉발되는 감정은 /
can also have a negative impact.
또한 부정적인 영향을 끼칠 수 있다
Sport's emotional intensity can mean /
스포츠의 정서적 격렬함은 의미할 수 있다 /
that organisations have strong attachments to the past /
과거에 조직이 강한 애착을 가지고 있다는 것을 /
through nostalgia and club tradition.
향수와 클럽 전통을 통해
As a result, / they may ignore /
그 결과 / 그것은 무시할 수도 있다 /
efficiency, productivity / 효율성, 생산성 /
and the need to respond quickly /
그리고 신속하게 대응해야 할 필요성을 /
to changing market conditions.
변화하는 시장 상황에
For example, / 예를 들면 /

a proposal to change club colours /
클럽 색을 바꾸자는 제안은 /
in order to project a more attractive image /
더 매력적인 이미지를 투사하기 위해 /
may be defeated / 무산될지도 모른다 /
because it breaks a link with tradition.
그것이 전통과의 관계를 끊기 때문에

스포츠는 그것의 소비자에게 다른 제품이 좀처럼 생산하지 않는 종류의 정서적 반응을 촉발할 수 있다. 은행 고객이 그들 은행에 대한 충성심을 보여주기 위해서 기념품을 사거나, 고객이 그들 자동차 보험 회사에 대해 매우 강한 ① 동질감을 가져서 회사 로고로 문신을 한다고 상상해 보라. 우리는 일부 스포츠팬들이 선수, 팀, 그리고 그 스포츠 자체에 매우 ② 열정적이어서 그들의 관심이 집착에 아주 가깝다는 것을 안다. 이러한 중독은 팬을 팀과 묶어주는 정서적 접착제를 제공하고, 심지어 구장에서 일어나는 ③ 실패에도 충성심을 유지하게 한다. 대부분의 운영자는 스포츠팬만큼 그들 제품에 열정적인 고객을 가지기를 오직 꿈꾸지만, 스포츠로 인해 촉발되는 감정은 또한 부정적인 영향을 끼칠 수 있다. 스포츠의 정서적 격렬함은 조직이 향수와 클럽 전통을 통해 과거에 강한 애착을 가지고 있다는 것을 의미할 수 있다. 그 결과, 그것은 효율성, 생산성 그리고 변화하는 시장 상황에 신속하게 대응해야 할 필요성을 ④ 증가시킬(→ 무시할) 수도 있다. 예를 들면, 더 매력적인 이미지를 투사하기 위해 클럽 색을 바꾸자는 제안은 그것이 전통과의 관계를 끊기 때문에 ⑤ 무산될지도 모른다.

문제풀이

스포츠의 정서적 격렬함은 조직이 과거에 강한 애착을 가지는 것을 의미할 수 있다고 했고 더 매력적인 이미지를 위해 클럽 색을 바꾸자는 제안이 전통과의 관계를 끊기 때문에 무산될 수도 있다고 한 예를 보아, 조직이 효율성, 생산성 그리고 변화하는 시장 상황에 신속하게 대응할 필요성을 무시할 수 있다고 하는 것이 자연스럽다. 따라서 ④ 'increase(증가시키다)'를 'ignore(무시하다)'와 같은 낱말로 고쳐 써야 한다.

어휘·어구

trigger 촉발시키다
emotional 정서적인
consumer 고객
bring forth ~을 생산하다[낳다]
loyalty 충성(심)
identify with ~와 동질감을 갖다
insurance company 보험 회사
tattoo 문신
follower 팬, 열심히 따르는 사람
border on ~에 아주 가깝다
addiction 중독
glue 접착제
maintain 유지하다
passionate 열정적인, 열렬한
intensity 강렬함, 강도
attachment 애착(물)
nostalgia 향수
efficiency 효율
project 투사하다
attractive 매력적인
break a link with ~과의 관계를 끊다

정답률 58%

1. ⑤ 새로운 기술의 적응

직독/직해

Everywhere we turn / we hear about almighty "cyberspace"!
우리가 고개를 돌리는 모든 곳에서 / 우리는 전능하신 '사이버 공간'에 대해 듣는다
The hype promises /
과대광고는 약속한다 /
that we will leave our boring lives, put on goggles and body suits, /
우리가 지루한 삶을 떠나서 고글과 바디 수트를 착용할 것이라고 /
and enter some metallic, three-dimensional, multimedia otherworld.
그리고 어떤 금속성의, 3차원의, 멀티미디어로 만들어진 다른 세상으로 들어갈 (것이라고)
When the Industrial Revolution arrived / with its great innovation, the motor, /
산업 혁명이 도래했을 때 / 위대한 혁신인 모터와 함께 /
we didn't leave our world / to go to some remote motorspace!
우리는 우리의 세상을 떠나지 않았다 / 어떤 멀리 떨어진 모터 공간으로 가기 위해
On the contrary, / we brought the motors into our lives, /
그와는 반대로 / 우리는 모터를 우리 삶에 가져왔다 /
as automobiles, refrigerators, drill presses, and pencil sharpeners.
자동차, 냉장고, 드릴 프레스, 연필깎이와 같은 것들로
This absorption has been so complete /
이런 흡수는 너무 완전해서 /
that we refer to all these tools /
우리는 이 모든 도구를 지칭한다 /
with names that declare their usage, / not their "motorness."
그것들의 사용을 분명하게 밝히는 이름으로 / 그것들의 '모터성'이 아니라
These innovations led to a major socioeconomic movement /
이 혁신품들은 주요한 사회경제적 운동으로 이어졌다 /
precisely because they entered and affected profoundly our everyday lives.
그것들은 정확히 우리의 일상생활에 들어와 깊은 영향을 주었기 때문에
People have not changed fundamentally in thousands of years.
사람들은 수천 년간 근본적으로 변하지 않았다
Technology changes constantly.
기술은 계속해서 변화한다
It's the one / that must adapt to us.
바로 그것이다 / 우리에게 적응해야 하는 것은
That's exactly what will happen / with information technology and its devices /
그것이 바로 일어날 일이다 / 정보 기술과 그 장치들이 /
under human-centric computing.
인간 중심의 컴퓨터 사용 하에서
The longer we continue to believe /
우리가 계속해서 더 오래 믿게 될수록 /
that computers will take us to a magical new world, /
컴퓨터가 우리를 마법 같은 새로운 세상으로 데려다줄 것이라고 /
the longer we will delay / their natural fusion with our lives, /
우리는 더 오래 늦출 것인데 / 컴퓨터와 우리 삶의 자연스러운 융합을 /
the hallmark of every major movement /
이는 모든 주요 운동의 특징이다 /
that aspires to be called a socioeconomic revolution.
사회경제적 혁명이라고 불리기를 열망하는

우리가 고개를 돌리는 모든 곳에서 우리는 전능하신 '사이버공간'에 대해 듣는다! 과대광고는 우리가 지루한 삶을 떠나서 고글과 바디 수트를 착용하고, 어떤 금속성의, 3차원의, 멀티미디어로 만들어진 다른 세상으로 들어갈 것이라고 약속한다. 위대한 혁신인 모터와 함께 산업 혁명이 도래했을 때 우리는 어떤 ① 멀리 떨어진 모터 공간으로 가기 위해 우리의 세상을 떠나지 않았다! 그와는 반대로, 우리는 모터를 자동차, 냉장고, 드릴 프레스, 연필깎이와 같은 것들로 우리 삶에 가져왔다. 이런 ② 흡수는 너무 완전해서 우리는 그것들의 '모터성'이 아니라 그것들의 사용을 분명하게 밝히는 이름으로 이 모든 도구를 지칭한다. 이 혁신품들은 정확히 우리의 일상생활에 들어와 깊은 ③ 영향을 주었기 때문에 주요한 사회경제적 운동으로 이어졌다. 사람들은 수천 년간 근본적으로 변하지 않았다. 기술은 계속해서 변화한다. 우리에게 ④ 적응해야 하는 것은 바로 그것이다. 그것이 바로 정보 기술과 그 장치들이 인간 중심의 컴퓨터 사용 하에서 일어날 일이다. 컴퓨터가 우리를 마법 같은 새로운 세상으로 데려다줄 것이라고 계속해서 더 오래 믿게 될수록, 우리는 컴퓨터와 우리 삶의 자연스러운 융합을 더 오래 ⑤ 유지할(→ 늦출) 것인데, 이는 사회경제적 혁명이라고 불리기를 열망하는 모든 주요 운동의 특징이다.

문제풀이

새로운 기술이 나타날 때 우리가 그 기술로 가는 것이 아니라, 그 기술이 우리에게 적응해야 한다고 했으므로, 컴퓨터가 우리를 마법 같은 새로운 세상으로 데려다줄 것이라고 계속해서 더 오래 믿게 되면 우리는 컴퓨터와 우리 삶의 자연스러운 융합을 더 오래 늦출 것이라고 해야 한다. 따라서 ⑤ 'maintain(유지하다)'을 'delay(늦추다)'와 같은 낱말로 고쳐야 한다.

이렇게 풀자 'Technology changes constantly. It's the one that must adapt to us.(기술은 계속해서 변화한다. 우리에게 적응해야 하는 것은 바로 그것(기술)이다.)'에 '기술이 우리에게 적응해야 한다.'는 이 글의 중심 내용이 잘 드러나 있다. 'The longer we continue to believe that computers will take us to a magical new world(컴퓨터가 우리를 마법 같은 새로운 세상으로 데려다줄 것이라고 계속해서 더 오래 믿게 될수록)'은 주제와 반대되는 내용으로, 컴퓨터가 우리를 새로운 세상으로 데려다 줄 것이라고 오래 믿으면, 우리는 컴퓨터와 우리 삶의 융합을 더 오래 늦출 것이라고 추론할 수 있다.

어휘·어구

almighty 전능한
metallic 금속으로 된
three-dimensional 3차원의
remote 멀리 떨어진
absorption 흡수
refer to ~을 지칭하다
declare 선언하다, 분명하게 밝히다
precisely 정확히
profoundly 깊이
fundamentally 근본적으로
fusion 융합
aspire 열망하다

정답률 65%

2. ④ 음반에 대한 음악 공연자와 방송사들의 인식

직독/직해

Musical performers and their labor union did not perceive early recordings /
음악 공연자들과 그들의 노동조합은 초기 음반들을 인식하지 않았다 /
as a threat to their livelihoods /
자신들의 생계에 대한 위협으로 /
because the recordings were mostly of poor quality.
그 음반들이 대체로 음질이 좋지 않았기 때문에
It was not long before musicians began to wonder /
얼마 지나지 않아 음악가들은 궁금해하기 시작했다 /
whether recordings of popular artists or songs would undermine the demand for live music.
인기 있는 아티스트나 노래의 음반이 실황 음악에 대한 수요의 토대를 침식할까
For a time, / however, / recorded music was too scratchy /
한동안 / 그러나 / 녹음된 음악은 긁히는 소리가 매우 심했다 /
to pose a serious threat, /
심각한 위협을 제기하기에는 /
even though it played in commercial places and offered a few performers a way /
비록 그것이 상업적인 장소에서 재생되고 몇몇 연주자들에게 수단을 제공했음에도 불구하고 /
to supplement their income.
자신들의 수입을 보충할
Additionally, / during the early days of recording, /
게다가 / 녹음 초기에는 /
radio stations preferred using live musicians on

their programs.
라디오 방송국들이 실황 공연을 하는 음악가를 자신들의 프로그램에 활용하기를 선호했다

Sound from live performances was better quality, /
실황 공연의 소리가 음질이 더 좋았다 /

and stations at this time rarely used recordings.
그리고 이 시기 방송국들은 음반을 거의 사용하지 않았다

Broadcasters respected union demands for employment and decent wages, /
방송사들은 고용과 적절한 임금에 대한 노조의 요구를 존중했다 /

because the alterative use of recordings was even less attractive.
(실황 공연을) 대체하여 음반을 사용하는 것이 훨씬 덜 매력적이었기 때문에

They made efforts to employ orchestras, bands, and vocalists /
그들은 오케스트라, 악단, 그리고 가수를 고용하기 위해 애썼다 /

to perform on radio programs.
라디오 프로그램에서 공연할

There was relative balance between live music and technology /
실황 음악과 기술 사이에 상대적 균형이 있었다 /

in the early innovation stages.
초기의 혁신 단계에서는

With increased improvements in electrical recording, / however, /
전기 녹음이 점차 개선되면서 / 하지만 /

this balance soon changed.
이 균형은 곧 바뀌었다

음악 공연자들과 그들의 노동조합은 초기 음반들을 자신들의 생계에 대한 위협으로 인식하지 않았는데, 그 음반들이 대체로 음질이 좋지 않았기 때문이다. 얼마 지나지 않아 음악가들은 인기 있는 아티스트 노래의 음반이 실황 음악에 대한 수요의 토대를 ① 침식할까 궁금해하기 시작했다. 그러나 한동안, 녹음된 음악은 상업적인 장소에서 재생되고 몇몇 연주자들에게 자신들의 수입을 ② 보충할 수단을 제공했음에도 불구하고, 심각한 위협을 제기하기에는 긁히는 소리가 매우 심했다. 게다가 녹음 초기에는 라디오 방송국들이 실황 공연을 하는 음악가를 자신들의 프로그램에 활용하기를 ③ 선호했다. 실황 공연의 소리가 음질이 더 좋았고, 이 시기 방송국들은 음반을 거의 사용하지 않았다. 방송사들은 고용과 적절한 임금에 대한 노조의 요구를 ④ 거부했는데(→ 존중했는데), 이는 (실황 공연을) 대체하여 음반을 사용하는 것이 훨씬 덜 매력적이었기 때문이었다. 그들은 라디오 프로그램에서 공연할 오케스트라, 악단, 그리고 가수를 고용하기 위해 애썼다. 초기의 혁신 단계에서는 실황 음악과 기술 사이에 상대적 균형이 있었다. 하지만 전기 녹음이 점차 ⑤ 개선되면서 이 균형은 곧 바뀌었다.

문제풀이

초기 음반들은 실황 공연의 소리보다 음질이 좋지 않았기 때문에 음악 공연자들과 노동조합은 녹음된 음반에 대해서 위협을 느끼지 않았고, 라디오 방송국들도 녹음된 음반을 사용하기보다는 그들의 프로그램에서 실황 공연할 오케스트라, 악단, 그리고 가수를 고용하기 위해 애썼기 때문에 고용과 적절한 임금에 대한 음악 공연자 조합의 요구를 수용했다는 내용의 글이다. 따라서 ④ 'rejected(거부했다)'를 'respected(존중했다)'나 'accepted(수용했다)' 등의 어휘로 바꿔야 한다.

이렇게 풀자 문맥상 낱말의 쓰임을 묻는 문제에서는 밑줄 어휘의 주변 문맥을 보고 그 적절성을 점검할 필요가 있다. ① 'undermine (침식하다, 훼손하다)'는 그 뒤의 'however' 이하에서 녹음된 음악은 긁히는 소리가 매우 심했다는 내용으로 보아 '녹음 음악이 실황 음악에 대한 수요를 감소시키기에는 음질이 좋지 않았다는 의미이므로 적절하고, ② 'supplement(보충하다)'는 'even though'로 보아 녹음 음질이 좋지 않지만 어느 정도의 수입은 될 수 있었다는 내용이므로 적절하다.

어휘·어구

labor union 노동조합
perceive 인식하다
threat 위협
livelihood 생계
undermine 약화시키다
scratchy 긁히는
supplement 보충하다
additionally 게다가
performance 공연
rarely 거의
decent 적당한
wages 임금
attractive 매력적인
improvement 개선

정답률 61%

3. ⑤ 인터넷의 부정적인 면

직독/직해

Although the wonders of modern technology have provided people /
비록 현대 기술의 경이로운 것이 사람들에게 제공했지만 /

with opportunities beyond the wildest dreams of our ancestors, /
우리 선조들은 꿈에도 생각지 못한 기회를 /

the good, as usual, is weakened / by a downside.
항상 그렇듯이 좋은 점은 약해진다 / 부정적인 면에 의해

One of those downsides is /
그 부정적인 면 중 하나는 ~이다 /

that anyone who so chooses / can pick up the virtual megaphone /
그렇게 하기로 선택한 사람은 누구나 / 가상의 확성기를 집어 들 수 있다 /

that is the Internet / and put in their two cents /
인터넷이라는 / 그리고 의견을 말할 수 있다 /

on any of an infinite number of topics, /
무한히 많은 주제 중 어느 것에 대해서라도 /

regardless of their qualifications.
자신의 자격과 관계없이

After all, /on the Internet, / there are no regulations /
결국 / 인터넷에는 / 규제가 없다 /

preventing a kindergarten teacher from offering medical advice /
유치원 선생님이 의학적인 조언을 제공하는 것을 막는 /

or a physician from suggesting ways /
의사가 방법을 제안하는 것을 (막는) /

to safely make structural changes to your home.
여러분의 집에 안전하게 구조적인 변경을 할 수 있는

As a result, / misinformation gets disseminated as information, /
그 결과 / 잘못된 정보가 정보로 퍼져나가게 된다 /

and it is not always easy / to differentiate the two.
그리고 항상 쉽지만은 않다 / 그 둘을 구별하는 것이

This can be particularly frustrating for scientists, /
이것은 과학자에게 특히 좌절감을 줄 수 있는데 /

who spend their lives learning /
그들은 배우느라 인생을 보내지만 /

how to understand the intricacies of the world around them, /
자기 주변 세상의 복잡성을 이해하는 방법을 /

only to have their work summarily challenged by people /
결국 그들의 연구는 사람들에게 즉각 이의제기를 받게 된다 /

whose experience with the topic / can be measured in minutes.
그 주제에 대한 경험이 / 분 단위로 측정될 수 있는

This frustration is then amplified / by the fact /
그렇다면 이 좌절감은 증폭된다 / 사실에 의해 /

that, to the general public, / both the scientist and the challenger /
일반 대중들에게는 / 과학자와 도전자 둘 다 /

are awarded equal credibility.
똑같은 신뢰성을 부여받는다는

비록 현대 기술의 경이로운 것이 사람들에게 우리 선조들은 꿈에도 생각지 못한 기회를 제공했지만, 항상 그렇듯이 좋은 점은 부정적인 면에 의해 약해진다. 그 부정적인 면 중 하나는 그렇게 하기로 선택한 사람은 누구나 자신의 ① 자격과 관계없이 인터넷이라는 가상의 확성기를 집어 들고 무한히 많은 주제 중 어느 것에 대해서라도 의견을 말할 수 있다는 것이다. 결국, 인터넷에는 유치원 선생님이 의학적인 조언을 제공하거나 의사가 여러분의 집에 안전하게 구조적인 변경을 할 수 있는 방법을 제안하는 것을 ② 막는 규제가 없다. 그 결과, 잘못된 정보가 정보로 퍼져나가게 되고, 그 둘을 ③ 구별하는 것이 항상 쉽지만은 않다. 이것은 과학자에게 특히 좌절감을 줄 수 있는데, 그들은 자기 주변 세상의 복잡성을 이해하는 방법을 배우느라 인생을 보내지만 결국 그들의 연구는 그 주제에 대한 경험이 분 단위로 측정될 수 있는 사람들에게 즉석에서 ④ 이의제기를 받게 된다. 그렇다면 일반 대중들에게는 과학자와 도전자 둘 다 똑같은 신뢰성을 부여받는다는 사실에 의해 이 좌절감은 ⑤ 줄어든다(→ 증폭된다).

문제풀이

자격과 관계없이 누구나 어떤 주제에 관해서든 의견을 말할 수 있는 인터넷상에서, 주변 세상의 복잡성을 이해하는 법을 배우느라 인생을 보내는 과학자는 그 주제에 경험이 극히 적은 사람에게 즉석에서 이의제기를 받고 과학자와 도전자 둘 다에 대한 신뢰가 동등하게 부여받게 되었을 때 좌절감이 증폭될 것이다. 따라서 ⑤ 'diminished(줄어들다)'를 'amplified(증폭되다)'와 같은 낱말로 고쳐야 한다.

어휘·어구

wonder 경이로운 것
beyond the wildest dreams 꿈에도 생각지 못한
ancestor 조상, 선조
downside 부정적인 면
virtual 가상의
megaphone 확성기
infinite 무한한
regardless of ~에 관계없이
qualification 자격
regulation 규정, 규제
kindergarten 유치원
physician 의사, 내과 의사
differentiate 구별하다
frustrating 좌절감을 주는
summarily 즉석으로, 즉결로
diminish 줄어들다
credibility 신뢰성

정답률 40%

4. ② 전통적 양적 성장 개념의 변경 필요성

직독/직해

In poorer countries / many years of fast growth may be necessary /
가난한 나라에서는 / 수년 간의 빠른 성장이 필요할 수도 있다 /

to bring living standards up to acceptable levels.
생활 수준을 허용 가능한 수준으로 끌어올리기 위해

But growth is the means / to achieve desired goals, / not the end in itself.
그러나 성장은 수단이다 / 원하는 목표를 달성하기 위한 / 그 자체로 목적은 아니다

In the richer world / the whole idea of growth /
부유한 세계에서는 / 성장에 대한 개념 전체가

— at least as conventionally measured — / may need to be revised.
적어도 관습적으로 측정되는 것으로서의 / 개정될 필요가 있을지 모른다

In economies where services dominate, /
서비스가 지배하는 경제에서 /

goods and services / tailored to our individual needs /
재화와 서비스는 / 우리 개개인의 필요에 맞춘 /

will be what determine the advance of our societies.
우리 사회의 진보를 결정하는 것이 될 것이다

These could be anything / from genome-specific

medicines /
이것들은 어느 것이든 될 수 있다 / 게놈 맞춤형 약에서부터 /

to personalized care or tailored suits.
개별화된 관리 또는 맞춤 정장에 이르기까지

That is different / from more and more stuff, / an arms race of growth.
그것은 다르다 / 점점 더 많은 물건과는 / 즉 무기의 확대 경쟁과는

Instead, / it means improvements in quality, /
그 대신에 / 그것은 질적인 향상을 의미한다 /

something that GDP is ill equipped to measure.
즉 GDP가 잘 측정하지 못하는 것을 (의미한다)

Some fifty years ago /
약 50년 전 /

one US economist contrasted / what he called the "cowboy" economy, /
미국의 한 경제학자는 대조했다 / 그가 '카우보이' 경제라고 칭한 것을 /

bent on production, exploitation of resources, and pollution, /
생산, 자원의 착취, 오염에 집중하는 /

with the "spaceman" economy, /
'우주인' 경제와 /

in which quality and complexity replaced "throughput" /
그곳에서는 품질과 복합성이 '처리량'을 대체하였다 /

as the measure of success.
성공의 척도로

The move from manufacturing to services and from analog to digital /
제조업에서 서비스업으로 그리고 아날로그에서 디지털로의 이동은 /

is the shift from cowboy to spaceman.
카우보이에서 우주인으로의 전환이다

But we are still measuring the size of the lasso.
하지만 우리는 여전히 올가미 밧줄의 크기를 측정하고 있다

가난한 나라에서는 생활 수준을 허용 가능한 수준으로 끌어올리기 위해 수년간의 빠른 성장이 필요할 수도 있다. 그러나 성장은 원하는 목표를 달성하기 위한 수단이지, 그 자체로 ① 목적은 아니다. 부유한 세계에서는 적어도 관습적으로 측정되는 것으로서의 성장에 대한 개념 전체가 ② 유지될(→ 개정될) 필요가 있을지 모른다. 서비스가 지배하는 경제에서 우리 ③ 개개인의 필요에 맞춘 재화와 서비스는 우리 사회의 진보를 결정하는 것이 될 것이다. 이것들은 게놈 맞춤형 약에서부터 개별화된 관리 또는 맞춤 정장에 이르기까지 어느 것이든 될 수 있다. 그것은 점점 더 많은 물건, 즉 무기의 확대 경쟁과는 다르다. 그 대신에, 그것은 ④ 질적인 향상, 즉 GDP가 잘 측정하지 못하는 것을 의미한다. 약 50년 전 미국의 한 경제학자는 생산, 자원의 착취, 오염에 집중하는, 그가 '카우보이' 경제라고 칭한 것과 성공의 척도로 품질과 복합성이 '처리량'을 대체하는 '우주인' 경제를 대조했다. 제조업에서 서비스업으로 그리고 아날로그에서 디지털로의 ⑤ 이동은 카우보이에서 우주인으로의 전환이다. 하지만 우리는 여전히 올가미 밧줄의 크기를 측정하고 있다.

문제풀이

성장은 목적이 아니라 수단에 불과하고, 서비스가 지배적인 경제에서 개인의 필요에 맞춰진 재화와 서비스가 우리 사회의 발전을 결정하게 되므로, 양적인 성장이 아니라 질적인 성장에 초점을 맞춰야 한다는 내용의 글이다. 따라서 전통적인 양적 측정을 중시하는 성장의 개념을 '유지할 필요가 있을 것이다'가 아니라 '변경할 필요가 있다'라고 하는 것이 문맥상 자연스러우므로 ②의 'maintained(유지하다)'를 'revised(개정하다)'등의 어휘로 고쳐야 한다.

◎ 이렇게 풀자 난이도 1위의 문제로 각각의 낱말의 쓰임이 적절한지 한 문장, 한 문장 살펴볼 필요가 있다. ①의 'end'는 앞에 'means(수단)'라는 대조적인 단어가 언급되어 있고, 'in itself(그 자체로)'라는 표현과 결합되어 '성장은 수단이지 그 자체로 목적은 아니다'라는 의미로 올바르게 사용되었다. ②의 'maintained(유지하다)'는 뒷부분을 마저 읽어봐야 문맥상 적절성 여부를 판단할 수 있다. ③의 'individual(개개인의)'은 'tailored(맞춘)'로 보아 문맥상 적절하게 쓰였다. ④의 'quality(질)'는 'GDP is ill equipped to measure(GDP가 잘 측정하지 못한다)'로 보아 양과 대조적인 개념으로 올바르게 사용되었다. ⑤의 'move(이동)'는 'the shift(전환)'로 보아 올바르게 사용되었다. 글 전체의 내용으로 보아 양보다는 질을 추구하는 것이 옳다는 내용이므로 양적 측정을 중시하는 성장 개념을 바꿀 필요가 있다가 되어야 한다는 것을 알 수 있다.

어휘·어구

acceptable 받아들일 만한
achieve 달성하다
in oneself 그 자체로
revise 개정하다
dominate 지배하다
goods 상품, 재화
tailor 맞추다, 조정하다
determine 결정하다
personalized 개별화된
suit 정장
stuff 물건
exploitation 착취
replace 대체하다
manufacture 제조업
shift 전환

정답률 54%

5. ④ 자동차 수요 관리

직독/직해

In recent years / 최근 몇 년간 /

urban transport professionals globally have largely acquiesced to the view /
전 세계적으로 도시 교통 전문가들은 견해를 대체로 따랐다 /

that automobile demand in cities needs to be managed / rather than accommodated.
도시의 자동차 수요가 관리될 필요가 있다는 / 부응하기보다는

Rising incomes inevitably lead / to increases in motorization.
소득의 증가는 필연적으로 이어진다 / 자동차 보급의 증가로

Even without the imperative of climate change, /
기후 변화로 인한 불가피성이 없더라도 /

the physical constraints of densely inhabited cities /
인구 밀도가 높은 도시의 물리적 제약 /

and the corresponding demands of accessibility, mobility, safety, air pollution, and urban livability all /
그리고 그에 상응하는 접근성, 이동성, 안전, 대기 오염, 그리고 도시 거주 적합성에 대한 요구 모두가 /

limit the option of expanding road networks /
도로망을 확장하는 선택권을 제한한다 /

purely to accommodate this rising demand.
단지 이러한 증가하는 수요에 부응하기 위해

As a result, / as cities develop and their residents become more prosperous, /
그 결과 / 도시가 발전하고 도시의 거주자들이 더 부유해짐에 따라 /

persuading people to choose *not* to use cars /
사람들이 자동차를 사용하지 '않기로' 결정하도록 설득하는 것이 /

becomes an increasingly key focus of city managers and planners.
도시 관리자와 계획 설계자들의 핵심 중점 사항이 된다

Improving the quality of alternative options, /
대안적인 선택의 질을 향상하는 것이 /

such as walking, cycling, and public transport, /
걷기, 자전거 타기, 대중교통과 같은 /

is a central element of this strategy.
이 전략의 핵심 요소이다

However, / the most direct approach to managing automobile demand /
그러나 / 자동차 수요를 관리하는 가장 직접적인 접근 방법은 /

is making motorized travel more expensive /
자동차 여행을 더 비싸게 만드는 것이다 /

or restricting it with administrative rules.
또는 행정 규칙으로 그것을 제한하는 것이다

The contribution of motorized travel to climate change / reinforces this imperative.
자동차 여행이 기후 변화의 원인을 제공하는 것이 / 이런 불가피한 것을 강화한다

최근 몇 년간 전 세계적으로 도시 교통 전문가들은 도시의 자동차 수요에 부응하기보다는 관리될 필요가 있다는 견해를 대체로 따랐다. 소득의 증가는 필연적으로 자동차 보급의 증가로 이어진다. 기후 변화로 인한 불가피성이 없더라도, 인구 밀도가 높은 도시의 물리적 제약과 그에 상응하는 접근성, 이동성, 안전, 대기 오염, 그리고 도시 거주 적합성에 대한 요구 모두가 단지 이러한 증가하는 수요에 부응하기 위해 도로망을 확장하는 선택권을 ① 제한한다. 그 결과, 도시가 발전하고 도시의 거주자들이 더 부유해짐에 따라, 사람들이 자동차를 사용하지 '않기로' 결정하도록 ② 설득하는 것이 도시 관리자와 계획 설계자들의 핵심 중점 사항이 된다. 걷기, 자전거 타기, 대중교통과 같은 ③ 대안적인 선택의 질을 향상하는 것이 이 전략의 핵심 요소이다. 그러나 자동차 수요에 ④ 부응하는(→ (를) 관리하는) 가장 직접적인 접근 방법은 자동차 여행을 더 비싸게 만들거나 행정 규칙으로 그것을 제한하는 것이다. 자동차 여행이 기후 변화의 원인을 제공하는 것이 이런 불가피한 것을 ⑤ 강화한다.

문제풀이

최근 도시 교통 전문가들이 도시의 자동차 수요에 부응하기보다는 관리해야 한다는 견해를 따랐고, 사람들이 자동차를 사용하지 않도록 설득하는 것이 도시 관리자들과 도시 계획 설계자들의 핵심 중점 사항이 되었다고 했으므로, 자동차 여행을 더 비싸게 만들거나 행정 규칙으로 제한하는 것은 자동차 수요를 관리하는 방법이라고 하는 것이 자연스럽다. 따라서 ④ 'accommodating(부응하는)'은 'managing(관리하는)'과 같은 단어로 고쳐 써야 한다.

어휘·어구

urban 도시의
globally 전세계적으로
demand 수요, 요구
accommodate (요구 등에) 부응하다, 맞추다
income 수입
inevitably 불가피하게
motorization 자동차 보급, 전동화
densely inhabited 인구 밀도가 높은
corresponding 상응하는
accessibility 접근성, 접근
mobility 이동성
livability 거주 적합성, 살기 좋음
expand 확장하다
purely 단지, 다만
prosperous 번영하는
alternative 대안적인, 대체의
restrict 제한하다
administrative 행정의
reinforce 강화하다

정답률 42%

6. ③ 고객 점유율을 높이기

직독/직해

One of the most productive strategies / to build customer relationships /
가장 생산적인 전략들 중 하나는 / 고객과의 관계를 구축하기 위한 /

is to increase the firm's share of customer / rather than its market share.
회사의 고객 점유율을 높이는 것이다 / 그것의 시장 점유율보다

This strategy involves / abandoning the old notions of /
이러한 전략은 포함한다 / 오래된 인식을 버리는 것을 /

acquiring new customers and increasing transactions /
신규 고객들을 확보해서 거래를 늘린다는 /

to focus instead on / more fully serving the needs of existing customers.

대신에 ~것에 집중하기 위해서 / 기존 고객들의 요구를 더 완벽히 충족시키는

Financial services are a great example of this.
금융 서비스들이 이것의 좋은 예시이다

Most consumers purchase financial services / from different firms.
대부분의 소비자들은 금융 서비스를 구입한다 / 다른 회사들로부터

They bank at one institution, / purchase insurance from another, /
그들은 한 기관과 은행 거래를 하고 / 또 다른 기관으로부터 보험을 구매하며 /

and handle their investments elsewhere.
그리고 다른 곳에서 자산들의 투자금을 처리한다

To counter this purchasing pattern, /
이런 구매 패턴을 대항하기 위해서 /

many companies now offer all of these services / under one roof.
많은 회사들은 현재 이 모든 서비스를 제공한다 / 한곳에서

For example, / Regions Financial Corporation offers /
예를 들면 / Regions Financial Corporation은 제공한다 /

retail and commercial banking, trust, mortgage, and insurance products /
소매 및 상업 은행업, 신탁, 담보 대출, 그리고 보험 상품을 /

to customers / in a network of more than 1,500 offices.
고객들에게 / 1,500개가 넘는 지사의 네트워크에서

The company tries to more fully serve /
그 회사는 (~를) 더 완벽히 만족시키려고 노력하며 /

the financial needs of its current customers, /
그것의 현재 고객들의 금융적 요구를 /

thereby acquiring a larger share of each customer's financial business.
그것에 의해 각 고객의 금융 거래에서 더 큰 점유율을 획득한다

By creating these types of relationships, /
이런 유형의 관계를 형성함으로써 /

customers have little incentive / to seek out competitive firms /
고객들은 동기를 거의 갖지 않는다 / 경쟁 회사를 찾을 /

to fulfill their financial services needs.
자신들의 금융 서비스 요구를 충족시키기 위해

고객과의 관계를 구축하기 위한 가장 생산적인 전략들 중 하나는 회사의 시장 점유율보다 그것의 고객 점유율을 높이는 것이다. 이러한 전략은 대신에 기존 고객들의 요구를 더 완벽히 충족시키는 것에 집중하기 위해 신규 고객들을 ① 확보해서 거래를 늘린다는 오래된 인식을 버리는 것을 포함한다. 금융 서비스들이 이것의 좋은 예시이다. 대부분의 소비자들은 ② 다른 회사들로부터 금융 서비스를 구입한다. 그들은 한 기관과 은행 거래를 하고, 또 다른 기관으로부터 보험을 구매하며 다른 곳에서 자신들의 투자금을 처리한다. 이런 구매 패턴을 ③ 확고하게 하기(→ 대항하기) 위해서 많은 회사들은 현재 이 모든 서비스를 한곳에서 제공한다. 예를 들면, Regions Financial Corporation은 1,500개가 넘는 지사의 네트워크에서 고객들에게 소매 및 상업 은행업, 신탁, 담보 대출, 그리고 보험 상품을 제공한다. 그 회사는 그것의 ④ 현재 고객들의 금융적 요구를 더 완벽히 만족시키려고 노력하며, 그것에 의해 각 고객의 금융거래에서 더 큰 점유율을 획득한다. 이런 유형의 관계를 형성함으로써 고객들은 자신들의 금융 서비스 요구를 충족시키기 위해 경쟁 회사를 찾을 동기를 ⑤ 거의 갖지 않는다.

문제풀이

소비자들이 각기 다른 기관에서 은행 거래를 하고 보험을 구매하고 투자금을 처리하는 패턴에 대항하기 위해 많은 회사들이 이 모든 서비스를 한 곳에서 제공하고 있다는 것이 자연스러우므로, ③ 'solidify(확고하게 하다)'를 'counter(대항하다)'와 같은 단어로 바꿔 써야 한다.

구조 다시보기

도입	고객과의 관계 구축에 있어 가장 생산적인 전략은 고객 점유율을 높이는 것임.
부연	기존 고객들의 요구를 더 완벽히 충족시키는 것에 집중하기 위한 것임.
예시	각기 다른 곳에서 다른 금융 상품을 처리하는 것에 대항하여 모든 서비스를 한곳에서 제공함.
사례	Regions Financial Corporation은 1,500개가 넘는 지사의 네트워크에서 고객들에게 다양한 상품을 제공하여 각 고객의 금융 거래에서 더 큰 점유율 획득함.

어휘·어구

productive 생산적인
strategy 전략
involve 수반하다
acquire 얻다
transaction 거래
financial 금융의
institution 기관
insurance 보험
handle 처리하다, 다루다
investment 투자, 투자금
solidify 확고하게 하다
corporation 기업, 법인
retail 소매(小賣)
commercial 상업의, 상업적인
mortgage 대출, 융자
incentive 동기, 장려책
fulfill 다하다, 이행하다

7. ④ 기술의 발달과 그 결과 예측

직독/직해

Just as there's a tendency to glorify technological progress, /
기술의 발달을 미화하는 경향이 있는 것과 마찬가지로 /

there's a countertendency to expect the worst of every new tool or machine.
모든 새로운 도구나 기계에서 최악의 것을 예상하는 반대 경향도 있다

In Plato's *Phaedrus*, / Socrates bemoaned the development of writing.
플라톤의 *Phaedrus*에서 / 소크라테스는 글쓰기의 발전을 한탄했다

He feared / that, as people came to rely on the written word /
그는 우려했다 / 사람들이 글로 쓰인 말에 의존하게 됨에 따라 /

as a substitute for the knowledge / they used to carry inside their heads, /
지식에 대한 대체물로서 / 그들이 머릿속에 지니고 다니던 /

they would, / in the words of one of the dialogue's characters, /
그들은 / 대화의 등장인물 중 한 사람의 말처럼 /

"cease to exercise their memory and become forgetful."
기억력을 발휘하는 것을 멈추고 잘 잊어버리게 될 것이라고

And because they would be able to "receive a quantity of information /
그리고 그들은 많은 양의 정보를 받을 수 있을 것이기 때문에 /

without proper instruction," / they would "be thought very knowledgeable /
적절한 가르침 없이 / 그들은 매우 박식하다고 생각될 것이었다 /

when they are for the most part quite ignorant."
그들이 대체로 상당히 무지할 때도

They would be "filled with the conceit of wisdom / instead of real wisdom."
그들은 지혜의 자만심으로 가득 차 있게 될 것이었다 / 진정한 지혜 대신

Socrates wasn't wrong / — the new technology did often have the effects /
소크라테스가 틀리지는 않았다 / 새로운 기술은 자주 결과를 실제로 가져왔다 /

he feared / — but he was shortsighted.
그가 두려워했던 / 그러나 그는 근시안적이었다

He couldn't foresee the many ways /
그는 많은 방법을 예견할 수 없었다 /

that writing and reading would serve to spread information, /
쓰기와 읽기가 정보를 전파하는데 도움이 될 /

spark fresh ideas, and expand human knowledge / (if not wisdom).
신선한 생각을 촉발하며, 인간의 지식을 확장하는 데 / (지혜는 아닐지라도)

기술의 발달을 미화하는 경향이 있는 것과 마찬가지로, 모든 새로운 도구나 기계에서 최악의 것을 예상하는 반대 경향도 있다. 플라톤의 *Phaedrus*에서, 소크라테스는 글쓰기의 ① 발전을 한탄했다. 그는 사람들이 머릿속에 지니고 다니던 지식에 대한 ② 대체물로서, 글로 쓰인 말에 의존하게 됨에 따라, 대화의 등장인물 중 한 사람의 말처럼 그들은 '기억력을 발휘하는 것을 멈추고 잘 잊어버리게 될 것'이라고 우려했다. 그리고 그들은 '적절한 가르침 없이 많은 양의 정보를 ③ 받을' 수 있을 것이기 때문에, '대체로 상당히 무지할 때도 매우 박식하다고 생각될' 것이었다. 그들은 '진정한 지혜 대신 지혜의 자만심으로 가득 차 있게' 될 것이었다. 소크라테스가 ④ 맞지는(→ 틀리지는) 않아, 새로운 기술은 자주 그가 두려워했던 결과를 실제로 가져왔지만, 그는 근시안적이었다. 그는 쓰기와 읽기가 정보를 전파하고, 신선한 생각을 촉발하며, (지혜는 아닐지라도) 인간의 지식을 확장하는 데 도움이 될 많은 방법을 ⑤ 예견할 수 없었다.

문제풀이

사람들이 글로 쓰인 말에 의존하게 됨에 따라, 사람들은 잘 잊어버리게 될 것이고, 적절한 가르침 없이 많은 양의 정보를 획득할 수 있어서 상당히 무지할 때도 매우 박식하다고 여겨질 것이라고 하는 소크라테스의 의견이 언급된 후에 새로운 기술은 자주 그가 두려워했던 결과를 실제로 가져왔다고 했으므로 ④의 'right(맞는)'을 'wrong(틀린)'으로 바꾸어 '소크라테스가 틀리지는 않았다.'가 되어야 한다.

어휘·어구

tendency 경향
glorify 미화하다
progress 발달, 진보
countertendency 반대 경향
substitute 대체물
character 등장인물
cease 멈추다
a quantity of 많은
instruction 가르침, 훈련
knowledgeable 박식한
for the most part 대체로
ignorant 무지한
shortsighted 근시안적인
foresee 예견하다
serve 도움이 되다
spark 촉발하다
expand 확장하다

정답률 55%

8. ③ 유기농법의 단점

직독/직해

It has been suggested /
시사되어왔다 /

that "organic" methods, defined as those /
방식으로 정의되는 '유기농'법은 /

in which only natural products can be used as inputs, /
천연 제품들만 투입물로 사용되는 /

would be less damaging to the biosphere.
생물권에 해를 덜 끼친다고

Large-scale adoption of "organic" farming methods, /
'유기농' 경작 방식의 대규모 채택은 /

however, / 하지만 /

would reduce yields and increase production costs /
생산량을 줄이고 생산비를 증가시키게 된다 /

for many major crops.
많은 주요 작물의

Inorganic nitrogen supplies are essential /
무기질 질소 공급은 필수적인데 /

for maintaining moderate to high levels /
중상 수준으로 유지하는 데 /

of productivity for many of the non-leguminous crop species, /
많은 비(非)콩과 작물 종의 생산성을 /

because organic supplies of nitrogenous materials /
왜냐하면 그것은 질소성 물질의 유기적 공급이 /
often are either limited or more expensive /
자주 제한적이거나 더 비싸기 때문이다 /
than inorganic nitrogen fertilizers.
무기 질소 비료보다
In addition, / there are constraints /
게다가 / 제약이 있다 /
to the extensive use of either manure or legumes /
거름이나 콩과 식물의 광범위한 사용에는 /
as "green manure" crops.
'친환경적인 거름' 작물로
In many cases, / weed control can be very difficult /
많은 경우에 / 잡초 방제가 매우 어려울 수 있다 /
or require much hand labor /
또는 많은 손일이 필요할 수 있는데 /
if chemicals cannot be used, /
화학 물질이 사용될 수 없으면 /
and fewer people are willing to do this work /
그리고 이 작업을 기꺼이 하려는 사람이 더 적을 것이다 /
as societies become wealthier.
사회가 부유해짐에 따라
Some methods used in "organic" farming, /
'유기농' 경작에서 사용되는 몇 가지 방식들은 /
however, / 하지만 /
such as the sensible use of crop rotations /
돌려짓기의 합리적인 사용과 같은 /
and specific combinations of cropping and livestock enterprises, /
그리고 경작과 가축 경영의 특정한 조합(과 같은) /
can make important contributions /
중요한 기여를 할 수 있다 /
to the sustainability of rural ecosystems.
농촌 생태계의 지속 가능성에

천연 제품들만 투입물로 사용되는 방식으로 정의되는 '유기농'법은 생물권에 해를 덜 끼친다고 시사되어왔다. 하지만 '유기농' 경작 방식의 대규모 채택은 많은 주요 작물의 생산량을 ① 줄이고 생산비를 증가시키게 된다. 무기질 질소 공급은 많은 비(非)콩과 작물 종의 생산성을 중상 수준으로 유지하는 데 ② 필수적인데, 왜냐하면 그것은 질소성 물질의 유기적 공급이 무기 질소 비료보다 자주 제한적이거나 더 비싸기 때문이다. 게다가, '친환경적인 거름' 작물로 거름이나 콩과 식물의 광범위한 사용에는 ③ 이익(→ 제약)이 있다. 많은 경우에 화학 물질이 사용될 수 없으면 잡초 방제가 매우 어렵거나 많은 손일이 필요할 수 있는데, 사회가 부유해짐에 따라 이 작업을 기꺼이 하려는 사람이 ④ 더 적을 것이다. 하지만 돌려짓기의 합리적인 사용과 경작과 가축 경영의 특정한 조합과 같은 '유기농' 경작에서 사용되는 몇 가지 방식들은 농촌 생태계의 지속 가능성에 중요한 ⑤ 기여를 할 수 있다.

문제풀이

화학 물질을 사용하지 않으면 잡초 방제가 어렵고 손일이 많이 필요한데 그것을 하려는 사람이 더 적다고 했으므로, 거름이나 콩과 식물의 광범위한 사용의 제약이 있다고 하는 것이 자연스럽다. 따라서 ③ benefits(이점)를 constraints(제약)와 같은 낱말로 고쳐야 한다.

구조 다시보기

장점	유기농법은 생물권에 해를 덜 끼침
단점	유기농법의 채택은 주요 작물의 생산량을 줄이고 생산비를 증가시킴
근거 1	유기농법에 사용되는 질소성 물질의 유기적 공급이 제한적이거나 더 비쌈
근거 2	화학 물질을 사용하지 않으면 잡초 방제가 어렵고 손일이 많이 필요해서 광범위한 사용에 제약이 있음
반론	몇 가지 유기농법은 농촌 생태계의 지속 가능성에 중요한 기여를 함

어휘·어구

define 정의하다
input 투입(물)
biosphere 생물권
adoption 채택
yield 산출량, 생산량
inorganic 무기물의
maintain 유지하다
moderate 중간의
non-leguminous 비(非)콩과의
extensive 광범위한
be willing to do 기꺼이 ~하다
sensible 합리적인
crop rotation 돌려짓기
combination 조합
livestock 가축
enterprise 기업, 경영
contribution 기여, 이바지
sustainability 지속 가능성
ecosystem 생태계

정답률  73%

9. ⑤ 빛의 속도 측정에서 편승 효과의 발생

직독/직해

How the bandwagon effect occurs / is demonstrated /
편승 효과가 어떻게 발생하는지는 / 보여진다 /
by the history of measurements of the speed of light.
빛의 속도 측정의 역사로
Because this speed is the basis of the theory of relativity, /
이 빛의 속도는 상대성 이론의 기초여서 /
it's one of the most frequently and carefully measured quantities /
그것은 가장 자주 면밀하게 측정된 물리량 중 하나이다 /
in science. 과학에서
As far as we know, / 우리가 아는 한 /
the speed hasn't changed over time.
빛의 속도는 시간이 지나면서 이제껏 아무런 변함이 없었다
However, from 1870 to 1900, /
하지만 1870년부터 1900년까지 /
all the experiments found speeds /
모든 실험에서 속도가 발견되었다 /
that were too high. 너무 높은
Then, from 1900 to 1950, / the opposite happened /
그다음에, 1900년부터 1950년까지 / 그 반대 현상이 일어나 /
— all the experiments found speeds /
모든 실험에서 속도가 발견되었다 /
that were too low! 너무 낮은
This kind of error, / 이 형태의 오류를 /
where results are always on one side of the real value, /
결과가 항상 실제 값의 어느 한쪽에 있는 /
is called "bias." '편향'이라고 부른다
It probably happened / because over time, /
그것은 아마 일어났을 것이다 / 왜냐하면 시간이 흐르면서 /
experimenters subconsciously adjusted their results /
실험자들이 잠재의식적으로 결과를 조정했기 때문에 /
to match what they expected to find.
자신들이 발견할 것이라 예상한 것과 일치하도록
If a result fit what they expected, / they kept it.
만약 결과가 그들이 예상한 것과 일치하면 / 그들은 그것을 유지했다
If a result didn't fit, / they threw it out.
만약 결과가 일치하지 않으면 / 그들은 그것을 버렸다
They weren't being intentionally dishonest, /
그들은 의도적으로 부정직한 것은 아니었고 /
just influenced by the conventional wisdom.
단지 일반 통념에 의한 영향을 받았을 뿐이었다
The pattern only changed /
그 패턴은 바뀌었다 /
when someone had the courage /
누군가가 용기를 가졌을 때가 되어서야 /
to report what was actually measured /
실제로 측정된 것을 보고할 /
instead of what was expected.
예상된 것 대신에

편승 효과가 어떻게 발생하는지는 빛의 속도 측정의 역사로 보여진다. 이 빛의 속도는 상대성 이론의 기초여서, 과학에서 가장 자주 면밀하게 측정된 ① 물리량 중 하나이다. 우리가 아는 한, 빛의 속도는 시간이 지나면서 이제껏 아무런 변함이 없었다. 하지만 1870년부터 1900년까지 모든 실험에서 너무 높은 속도가 발견되었다. 그다음에, 1900년부터 1950년까지 그 ② 반대 현상이 일어나, 모든 실험에서 너무 낮은 속도가 발견되었다! 결과가 항상 실제 값의 어느 한쪽에 있는 이 형태의 오류를 '편향'이라고 부른다. 그것은 아마 시간이 흐르면서 실험자들이 자신들이 발견할 것이라 예상한 것과 일치하도록 잠재의식적으로 결과를 조정했기 때문에 일어났을 것이다. 만약 결과가 그들이 예상한 것과 ③ 일치하면, 그들은 그것을 유지했다. 만약 결과가 일치하지 않으면, 그들은 그것을 버렸다. 그들은 의도적으로 부정직한 것은 아니었고, 단지 일반 통념에 의한 ④ 영향을 받았을 뿐이었다. 그 패턴은 누군가가 예상된 것 대신에 실제로 측정된 것을 보고할 용기가 ⑤ 부족했을(→ 가졌을) 때가 되어서야 바뀌었다.

문제풀이

빛의 속도는 시간이 흘러도 일정하지만 실험자가 자신의 예상과 일치하도록 일반 통념에 의한 영향을 받아 조정해서 시대별로 빠르거나 느리게 측정되는 편향이 발생했다고 했으므로, 패턴이 바뀐 것은 누군가가 예상된 것이 아니라 실제로 측정된 것을 보고할 용기가 있을 때 일어났을 것이다. 따라서 ⑤ 'lacked(부족했다)'를 'had(가졌다)'와 같은 낱말로 바꿔 써야 한다.

구조 다시보기

도입	어떻게 편승 효과가 발생하는가?
예시	빛의 속도가 시대별로 빠르거나 느리게 측정되는 편향이 발생함
원인	실험자가 자신의 예상과 일치하도록 잠재 의식적으로 결과를 조정해서 일어난 것으로 예상됨
해결	예상이 아닌 실제 측정된 것을 보고할 수 있을 때에야 패턴이 바뀜

어휘·어구

demonstrate 증거를 들어가며 보여주다, 입증하다
measurement 측정
theory of relativity 상대성 이론
as far as ~하는 한
subconsciously 잠재의식적으로
adjust 조정하다
throw out ~을 거부하다
intentionally 고의로, 의도적으로
conventional wisdom 일반 통념, 속된 지혜
courage 용기

10. ④ 잘못된 선택의 오류

직독/직해

Suppose we know that Paula suffers from a severe phobia.
Paula가 극심한 공포증을 겪는다는 것을 우리가 안다고 가정하자
If we reason that Paula is afraid either of snakes or spiders, /
Paula가 뱀이나 거미 둘 중 하나를 두려워한다고 추론한다면, /
and then establish that she is not afraid of snakes, /
그러고 나서 그녀가 뱀을 두려워하지 않음을 규명한다면 /
we will conclude that Paula is afraid of spiders.
우리는 Paula가 거미를 두려워한다고 결론지을 것이다
However, our conclusion is reasonable /
그러나 우리의 결론은 타당하다 /
only if Paula's fear really does concern either snakes or spiders.
Paula의 두려움이 실제로 뱀이나 거미와 관계가 있는 경우에만
If we know only that Paula has a phobia, /
Paula가 공포증이 있다는 것만 안다면 /

then the fact that she's not afraid of snakes is
그녀가 뱀을 두려워하지 않는다는 사실은 전적으로 양립한다 /
entirely consistent /
with her being afraid of heights, water, dogs or the
그녀가 높은 곳, 물, 개, 또는 숫자 13을 두려워 한다는 것과
number thirteen.
More generally, / 더 일반적으로는 /
when we are presented with a list of alternative
우리에게 어떤 현상에 대한 일련의 대안적 설명이 제공될 때 /
explanations for some phenomenon, /
and are then persuaded that all but one of those
그런 다음 그 설명들 중 하나를 제외하고 모든 것이 부적절함을 확신한다면 /
explanations are unsatisfactory, /
we should pause to reflect.
우리는 멈춰서 심사숙고해야 한다
Before denying that the remaining explanation is
남아 있는 그 설명이 옳은 것이라는 것을 부정하기 전에 /
the correct one, /
consider whether other plausible options are
타당해 보이는 다른 선택 사항들이 무시되거나 간과되고 있는지를 고려해 보라
being ignored or overlooked.
The fallacy of false choice misleads /
잘못된 선택의 오류는 오도한다 /
when we're insufficiently attentive to an important
우리가 숨어 있는 중요한 가정에 불충분하게 주의를 기울이면
hidden assumption, /
that the choices which have been made explicit /
명백한 것으로 밝혀진 선택 사항들이 /
exhaust the sensible alternatives.
합리적인 대안을 고갈시키도록

Paula가 극심한 공포증을 겪는다는 것을 우리가 안다고 가정해 보자. Paula가 뱀이나 거미 둘 중 하나를 두려워한다고 추론한 다음, 그녀가 뱀을 두려워하지 않는다는 것을 ① 규명한다면, 우리는 Paula가 거미를 두려워한다고 결론지을 것이다. 그러나 우리의 결론은 실제로 Paula의 두려움이 뱀이나 거미 둘 중 하나와 관계가 있는 경우에만 타당하다. 만약 우리가 Paula가 공포증이 있다는 것만 알고 있다면, 그녀가 뱀을 두려워하지 않는다는 사실은 그녀가 높은 곳, 물, 개, 또는 숫자 13을 두려워한다는 것과 전적으로 ② 양립한다. 더 일반적으로는 우리에게 어떤 현상에 대한 일련의 대안적 설명이 제공되고, 그런 다음 그 설명들 중 하나를 제외하고는 모든 것이 ③ 적절하지 않다는 것을 확신한다면, 우리는 멈춰서 심사숙고해야 한다. 남아 있는 그 설명이 옳은 것이라는 것을 ④ 부정하기(→ 인정하기) 전에, 타당해 보이는 다른 선택 사항들이 무시되거나 간과되고 있는지를 고려해 보라. 잘못된 선택의 오류는, 우리가 숨어 있는 중요한 가정에 불충분하게 주의를 기울이면, 명백한 것으로 밝혀진 선택 사항들이 ⑤ 합리적인 대안을 고갈시키도록 오도한다.

문제풀이

어떤 현상에 대한 여러 가지 대안적 설명들 중에서 다른 모든 설명이 적절하지 않을 경우, 남은 하나의 설명이 옳다고 인정하기 전에 간과된 다른 타당한 설명이 있는지 고려해보라는 흐름이 되어야 자연스럽다. 따라서 ④ 'denying(부정하다)'은 'conceding(인정하다)'과 같은 말로 바꿔야 한다.

《 어휘·어구 》

phobia 공포증
establish 규명하다, 밝히다
concern 관계가 있다
consistent 양립하는
reflect 심사숙고하다
overlook 간과하다
mislead 오도하다, 잘못된 길로 이끌다
assumption 가정
explicit 명백한
exhaust 고갈시키다

본문 071쪽

문법 플러스 12. 대명사

A. 1. it
2. itself
3. hers
4. that
5. the other
6. what you like
7. it

1 [해석]▶ 그들은 또한 관련된 윤리적인 문제도 대부분 피할 수 있는데, 실험을 고안한 과학자보다 그것의 잠재적인 위험을 더 잘 알고 있는 사람은 아마 없을 것이기 때문이다.
[해설]▶ 앞서 언급된 an experiment를 대신하는 대명사가 와야 하므로 it이 어법상 적절하다.

2 [해석]▶ 토템 신앙의 풍습에서 문맹의 인류는 "자연 속에서의 자신과 자신의 위치에 대해 곰곰이 생각한다."라고 그는 말했다.
[해설]▶ 주어인 an unlettered humanity와 동일한 대상이므로 재귀대명사 itself가 어법상 적절하다.

3 [해석]▶ 그것은 그의 책이니? 아니오. 그것은 그녀의 책입니다.
[해설]▶ '그녀의 책'은 「소유격+명사」인 her book 또는 「소유대명사」 hers로 표현해야 한다.

4 [해석]▶ 사람들은 2030년이면 중국 경제는 미국 경제의 2.5배에 달할 거라고 말한다.
[해설]▶ '중국의 경제'와 '미국의 경제'를 비교하고 있다. the economy of US에서 단수명사 the economy의 반복을 피하기 위해서 지시대명사 that을 써도 된다.

5 [해석]▶ 우리는 강아지가 두 마리 있는데, 하나는 흰색이고, 다른 하나는 검정색이다.
[해설]▶ one…, the other ~는 '(둘 중에서) 하나는 …, 다른 하나는 ~'의 의미이다.

6 [해석]▶ 네 직업에 대해서 무엇을 가장 좋아하는지 말해 줄 수 있나요?
[해설]▶ What do you like most about your job?이라는 직접의문문을 앞 문장의 일부로 보내면 「의문사+주어+동사」의 어순으로 변한다.

7 [해석]▶ 어떤 의미에서 순수 미술 작품은 대중적인 소비를 위해 복제할 수 있기 때문에 가치 있게 여겨진다.
[해설]▶ 구체적인 명사구 the find art object를 가리키므로 it을 사용한다.

본문 071쪽

B. 1. write them down
2. themselves
3. yours
4. this
5. others
6. the others
7. some

1 [해석]▶ 아마도 목표에 집중하는 가장 효과적인 방법은 그것을 적는 것이다.
[해설]▶ 대명사가 목적어일 때, 「타동사+대명사+부사」의 어순으로 써야 한다.

2 [해석]▶ 옷은 사람들이 자신을 세상에 제시하는 방식의 일부이고, 패션은 사회에서 일어나고 있는 일, 그리고 패션 자체의 역사와 관련하여 그들을 현재에 위치시킨다.
[해설]▶ 주어인 people이 자신들을 세상에 보여주는 것이므로 재귀대명사인 themselves가 어법상 적절하다.

3 [해석]▶ 나는 내 연필을 가지고 있는데, 너는 네 것을 가지고 있니?
[해설]▶ 소유대명사(yours)는 「소유격(your)+명사(pencil)」를 대신하는 말이다.

4 [해석]▶ 내가 언급한 사진이 여기 이것이다.
[해설]▶ 지시대명사는 앞에 언급된 어구나 내용을 받는다. 가리키는 대상이 단수명사(the picture)이므로 지시대명사 this를 사용한다.

5 [해석]▶ 어떤 관광객들은 해변에 갔고, 다른 관광객들은 도시를 답사했다.
[해설]▶ some… others~는 '(막연한 다수 중) 일부는 …, 다른 일부는 ~'을 의미한다.

6 [해석]▶ 6권의 책이 있는데, 하나는 내 책이고, 나머지는 모두 남동생의 책이다.
[해설]▶ 한정된 6권 중에서 1권을 제외한 나머지 5권을 말하고 있으므로 the others로 표현해야 한다.

7 [해석]▶ 나에게 온 편지가 있나요? / 예, 몇 개 왔어요.
[해설]▶ any letters가 막연한 대상으로 복수명사이므로, 이것을 복수 대명사로 표현하려면 some을 사용한다.

본문 072쪽

숙어 플러스 12. 수능 필수 숙어 12회

1 effect	2. terms
3. time	4. mind

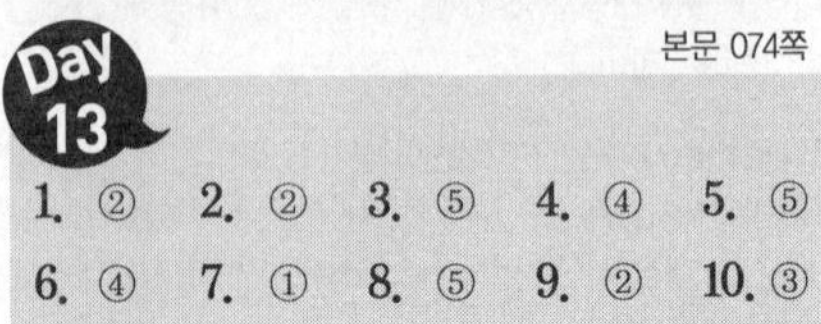

13. 빈칸 추론 (1) 어휘, 짧은 어구

본문 074쪽

1. ② 2. ② 3. ⑤ 4. ④ 5. ⑤
6. ④ 7. ① 8. ⑤ 9. ② 10. ③

정답률 47%

대표 기출 ② 스포츠 저널리스트 지위의 역설적인 측면

직독/직해

There is something deeply paradoxical /
아주 역설적인 것이 있다 /

about the professional status of sports journalism, /
스포츠 저널리즘의 전문적 지위에 대해서 /

especially in the medium of print.
특히 인쇄 매체에서

In discharging their usual responsibilities of description and commentary, /
기자들이 설명하고 논평하는 일상적인 자신의 책임을 이행할 때 /

reporters' accounts of sports events / are eagerly consulted by sports fans, /
스포츠 경기에 관한 기자들의 설명은 / 스포츠 팬들이 열심히 찾아보게 되며 /

while in their broader journalistic role of / covering sport in its many forms, /
반면에 그들의 더 폭넓은 저널리스트의 역할 안에서 / 여러 형식으로 스포츠를 취재하는

sports journalists / are among the most visible / of all contemporary writers.
스포츠 저널리스트는 / 가장 눈에 띄는 이들 가운데 있다 / 동시대의 모든 작가 중에서

The ruminations of the elite class of 'celebrity' sports journalists /
'유명인급' 스포츠 저널리스트 중 엘리트 계층의 숙고의 결과는 /

are much sought after by the major newspapers, /
주요 신문사들이 많이 찾게 되고 /

their lucrative contracts being the envy of colleagues /
그들의 수익성이 좋은 계약은 동료들의 부러움의 대상이 된다 /

in other 'disciplines' of journalism.
저널리즘의 다른 '부문'에 있는 (동료들의)

Yet sports journalists do not have a standing in their profession /
하지만 스포츠 저널리스트는 그들 전문성에서의 지위를 갖지 못한다 /

that corresponds to the size of their readerships or of their pay packets, /
그들의 독자 수나 급여 액수의 크기에 상응하는 (지위를) /

with the old saying /(now reaching the status of cliché) /
(이제는 상투적인 문구의 지위에 이르는) 옛말과 더불어 /

that sport is the 'toy department of the news media' / still readily to hand /
스포츠는 '뉴스 매체의 장난감 부서'라는 / 여전히 쉽게 건네지는

as a dismissal of the worth of what sports journalists do.
스포츠 저널리스트들이 하는 일의 가치를 묵살하는 말로

This reluctance to take sports journalism seriously /
이렇게 스포츠 저널리즘을 진지하게 여기기를 꺼리는 것은 /

produces the paradoxical outcome /
역설적인 결과를 얻는다 /

that sports newspaper writers are much read / but little admired.
스포츠 신문 작가들이 많이 읽힌다 / 하지만 거의 존경받지 못하는

스포츠 저널리즘의 전문적 지위에 대해서, 특히 인쇄 매체에서, 아주 역설적인 것이 있다. 기자들이 설명하고 논평하는 일상적인 자신의 책임을 이행할 때, 스포츠 팬들이 스포츠 경기에 관한 기자들의 설명을 열심히 찾아보는 반면, 여러 형식으로 스포츠를 취재하는 그들의 더 폭넓은 저널리스트의 역할 안에서 스포츠 저널리스트는 동시대의 모든 작가 중에서 가장 눈에 띄는 이들 가운데 있다. '유명인급' 스포츠 저널리스트 중 엘리트 계층의 숙고의 결과는 주요 신문사들이 많이 원하고, 그들의 수익성이 좋은 계약은 저널리즘의 다른 '부문'에 있는 동료들의 부러움의 대상이 된다. 하지만 스포츠 저널리스트는 스포츠는 스포츠 저널리스트들이 하는 일의 가치를 묵살하는 말로 여전히 쉽게 건네지는 '뉴스 매체의 장난감 부서'라는 (이제는 상투적인 문구의 지위에 이르는) 옛말과 더불어 그들의 독자 수나 급여 액수의 크기에 상응하는 그들 전문성에서의 지위를 갖지 못한다. 이렇게 스포츠 저널리즘을 진지하게 여기기를 꺼리는 것은 스포츠 신문 작가들이 많이 읽히지만 거의 존경받지 못하는 역설적인 결과를 얻는다.

① 돈을 받지 **② 존경받지** ③ 검열되지
④ 의문이 제기되지 ⑤ 논의되지

문제풀이

스포츠 저널리즘의 전문적 지위에 대해서는 역설적이라고 하면서, 스포츠 저널리스트들은 독자들이 그들의 글을 많이 찾아 읽고 신문사들도 많이 원하고 돈도 많이 벌지만, 뉴스 매체에서는 그들의 독자 수나 급여 규모의 액수에 상응하는 전문적인 지위를 갖지 못한다고 했다. 따라서 빈칸에는 ② 'admired'가 들어가서 빈칸을 포함한 문장이 '이렇게 스포츠 저널리즘을 진지하게 여기기를 꺼리는 것은 스포츠 신문 작가들이 많이 읽히지만 거의 존경받지 못하는 역설적인 결과를 얻는다.'가 되는 것이 적절하다.

어휘·어구

- **paradoxical** 역설적인
- **discharge responsibility** 책임을 다하다
- **medium** 매체
- **description** 설명, 서술, 묘사
- **commentary** 논평
- **accout** 설명
- **eagerly** 열심히
- **consult** 찾아보다
- **journalistic** 저널리스트[기자]의
- **cover** 취재하다
- **contemporary** 동시대의
- **rumination** 생각, 숙고의 결과
- **celebrity** 유명 인사
- **sought after** 많은 사람들이 원하는, 수요가 많은
- **contract** 계약
- **discipline** 부문, 분야
- **standing** 지위
- **correspond to** ~에 상응하다
- **readership** 독자 수[층]
- **pay packet** 급여 액수
- **cliché** 상투적인 문구
- **dismissal** 묵살
- **reluctance** 꺼림, 내키지 않음
- **paradoxical** 역설적인
- **outcome** 결과

1. ② 언어 혁신이 일어나는 장소

직독/직해

People have always wanted /
사람들은 언제나 원해 왔다 /

to be around other people / and to learn from them.
다른 사람들 주변에 있기를 / 그리고 그들로부터 배우기를

Cities have long been dynamos of social possibility, /
도시는 오래전부터 사회적 가능성의 발전기였다 /

foundries of art, music, and fashion.
예술, 음악, 패션의 주물 공장(이었다)

Slang, / or, if you prefer, / "lexical innovation," has always started in cities /
속어 / 혹은 여러분이 선호한다면 / '어휘의 혁신'은 언제나 도시에서 시작되었는데 /

an outgrowth of all those different people so frequently exposed to one another.
그 모든 별의별 사람이 그렇게도 빈번히 서로에게 접촉한 산물이다.

It spreads outward, / in a manner not unlike transmissible disease, /
그것은 밖으로 퍼져나가는데 / 전염성 질병과 다르지 않은 방식으로 /

which itself typically "takes off" in cities.
그 전염성 질병 자체도 보통 도시에서 '이륙한다'

If, / as the noted linguist Leonard Bloomfield argued, /
만약 / 유명한 언어학자 Leonard Bloomfield가 주장하듯 /

the way a person talks / is a "composite result of what he has heard before," /
어떤 사람이 말하는 방식이 / '그가 전에 들었던 것을 합성한 결과물'이라면 /

then language innovation would happen / where the most people heard /
언어 혁신은 일어날 것이다 / 가장 많은 사람이 가장 많은 타인의 말을 듣는 곳에서 /

and talked to the most other people.
그리고 가장 많은 다른 사람에게 말한 (곳에서)

Cities drive taste change /
도시는 취향 변화를 일으키는데 /

because they offer the greatest exposure to other people, /
그곳이 타인과 가장 많은 접촉을 제공하기 때문에 /

who not surprisingly are often the creative people / cities seem to attract.
그들은 놀랄 것도 없이 종종 창의적인 사람들이다 / 도시가 끌어들이는 듯 보이는

Media, ever more global, ever more far-reaching, /
그 어느 때보다 더 세계화된, 그 어느 때보다 더 멀리까지 미치는 미디어는 /

spread language faster to more people.
언어를 더 빨리 더 많은 사람에게 퍼뜨린다

사람들은 언제나 다른 사람들 주변에 있으며 그들로부터 배우기를 원해 왔다. 도시는 오래전부터 사회적 가능성의 발전기, 즉 예술, 음악, 패션의 주물 공장이었다. 속어, 혹은 여러분이 선호한다면 '어휘의 혁신'은 언제나 도시에서 시작되었는데, 그 모든 별의별 사람이 그렇게도 빈번히 서로에게 접촉한 산물이다. 그것은 전염성 질병과 다르지 않은 방식으로 밖으로 퍼져나가는데, 그 전염성 질병 자체도 보통 도시에서 '이륙한다.' 유명한 언어학자 Leonard Bloomfield가 주장하듯, 만약 어떤 사람이 말하는 방식이 '그가 전에 들었던 것을 합성한 결과물'이라면, 언어 혁신은 가장 많은 사람이 가장 많은 타인의 말을 듣고 가장 많은 다른 사람에게 말한 곳에서 일어날 것이다. 도시는 그곳이 타인과 가장 많은 접촉을 제공하기 때문에 취향 변화를 일으키는데, 그들은 놀랄 것도 없이 종종 도시가 끌어들이는 듯 보이는 창의적인 사람들이다. 그 어느 때보다 더 세계화된, 그 어느 때보다 더 멀리까지 미치는 미디어는 언어를 더 빨리 더 많은 사람에게 퍼뜨린다.

① 예술가들에게 풍부한 원재료를 공급하기
② 타인과 가장 많은 접촉을 제공하기
③ 속어 사용자들 사이에서 문화 충돌을 초래하기
④ 언어학자들에게 이상적인 연구 환경을 제공하기
⑤ 야심이 많은 외부인의 사회 이동을 줄이기

문제풀이

어휘의 혁신은 언제나 각양각색의 사람들이 서로 빈번히 접촉하게 되는 도시에서 생겨난다고 했고 taste change(취향 변화)는 어휘의 혁신이라고 할 수 있으므로, 빈칸에는 ② 'offer the greatest exposure to other people'이 들어가서 빈칸을 포함한 문장이 '도시는 그곳이 타인과 가장 많은 접촉을 제공하기 때문에 취향 변화를 일으키는데, 그들은 놀랄 것도 없이 종종 도시가 끌어들이는 듯 보이는 창의적인 사람들이다.'가 되는 것이 가장 적절하다.

이렇게 풀자 'if you prefer, "lexical innovation," has always started in cities — an outgrowth of all those different people so frequently exposed to one another(여러분이 선호한다면 '어휘의 혁신'은 언제

나 도시에서 시작되었는데, 그 모든 별의별 사람이 그렇게 도 빈번히 서로에게 접촉한 산물이다)'를 통해 taste change는 lexical innovation을 가리키는 말이라는 것을 알 수 있고, 빈칸에는 그것의 원인이 되는 'all those different people so frequently exposed to one another'와 의미가 통하는 내용이 와야 한다는 것을 알 수 있다.

《 어휘·어구 》

dynamo 발전기
slang 속어
outgrowth 자연스러운 결과, 산물
transmissible 전염성의
noted 유명한, 잘 알려져 있는
linguist 언어학자
composite 합성의
far-reaching 멀리 미치는
mobility 이동
source material 원재료
conflict 충돌, 갈등
ambitious 야심차게

2. ② 정치적 리스크의 불확실성

직독/직해

Much of what we call political risk / is in fact uncertainty.
우리가 정치적 리스크라고 부르는 것의 많은 부분은 / 사실 불확실성이다

This applies to all types of political risks, /
이것은 모든 유형의 정치적 리스크에 적용된다 /

from civil strife to expropriations to regulatory changes.
내란에서부터 몰수, 규제상의 변화에 이르기까지

Political risk, / unlike credit or market or operational risk, /
정치적 리스크는 / 신용, 시장 또는 운영 리스크와는 달리 /

can be unsystematic /
비체계적이다 /

and therefore more difficult to address in classic statistical terms.
그래서 전형적인 통계적 관점에서 처리하기가 더 어려울 수 있다

What is the probability / that terrorists will attack the United States again?
확률은 얼마나 되는가 / 테러리스트들이 미국을 다시 공격할

Unlike earthquakes or hurricanes, /
지진이나 허리케인과는 달리 /

political actors constantly adapt to overcome the barriers /
정치 행위자들은 장벽을 넘어서기 위해 끊임없이 적응한다 /

created by risk managers.
리스크 관리자들이 만든

When corporations structure foreign investments /
기업들이 해외 투자를 체계화할 때 /

to mitigate risks of expropriations, /
몰수의 리스크를 줄이기 위해 /

through international guarantees or legal contracts, /
국제적 보증이나 법적 계약을 통해 /

host governments seek out new forms of obstruction, /
(사업) 소재국 정부는 새로운 형태의 방해를 모색한다 /

such as creeping expropriation or regulatory discrimination, /
은밀히 진행되는 몰수나 규제상의 차별과 같은 /

that are very hard and legally costly to prove.
증명하기 매우 힘들고 법적으로 비용이 많이 드는

Observation of a risk changes the risk itself.
리스크를 관찰하면 리스크 자체가 변한다

There are ways to mitigate high-impact, low-probability events.
충격이 크지만 확률은 낮은 사건들을 줄이는 방법들이 있다

But analysis of these risks can be as much art as science.
그러나 이러한 리스크에 대한 분석은 과학일 수 있는 만큼이나 예술일 수 있다

우리가 정치적 리스크라고 부르는 것의 많은 부분은 사실 불확실성이다. 이것은 내란에서부터 몰수, 규제상의 변화에 이르기까지 모든 유형의 정치적 리스크에 적용된다. 신용, 시장 또는 운영 리스크와는 달리 정치적 리스크는 비체계적이고, 그래서 전형적인 통계적 관점에서 처리하기가 더 어려울 수 있다. 테러리스트들이 미국을 다시 공격할 확률은 얼마나 되는가? 지진이나 허리케인과는 달리, 정치 행위자들은 리스크 관리자들이 만든 장벽을 넘어서기 위해 끊임없이 적응한다. 기업들이 몰수의 리스크를 줄이기 위해 국제적 보증이나 법적 계약을 통해 해외 투자를 체계화할 때, (사업) 소재국 정부는 은밀히 진행되는 몰수나 규제상의 차별과 같은, 증명하기 매우 힘들고 법적으로 비용이 많이 드는 새로운 형태의 방해를 모색한다. 리스크를 관찰하면 리스크 자체가 변한다. 충격이 크지만 확률은 낮은 사건들을 줄이는 방법들이 있다. 그러나 이러한 리스크에 대한 분석은 과학일 수 있는 만큼이나 예술일 수 있다.

① 불공정 **② 불확실성**
③ 순환논리 ④ 모순
⑤ 의사소통의 오류

문제풀이

정치적 리스크는 체계가 없고 수치화하거나 예측하기 어려울 뿐만 아니라 계속해서 변한다는 내용의 글이다. 따라서 빈칸에는 ② 'uncertainty'가 들어가 빈칸을 포함한 문장이 '우리가 정치적 리스크라고 부르는 것의 많은 부분은 사실 불확실성이다.'가 되어야 한다.

이렇게 풀자 빈칸의 위치가 첫 문장인 경우에는 글의 주제문을 완성하는 문제이다. 반복적으로 등장하는 'political risk'가 글의 중심 소재인 것을 알 수 있고, 'Political risk, unlike credit or market or operational risk, can be unsystematic and therefore more difficult to address in classic statistical terms'에서 '정치적 위험이 비체계적이고 전형적인 통계적 관점에서 처리하기가 더 어렵다'고 언급하고 있으므로 이와 유사한 의미를 갖는 단어가 빈칸에 들어가야 한다는 것을 알 수 있다.

《 어휘·어구 》

uncertainty 불확실(성)
apply to ~에 적용되다
regulatory 규정하는
credit 신용
address 다루다
statistical 통계(학)상의
terms 관점
probability 확률
adapt to ~에 적응하다
barrier 장벽, 장애물
corporation (규모가 큰) 기업, 회사
guarantee 보증
contract 계약
seek out ~을 찾아내다
obstruction 방해
discrimination 차별
costly 많은 비용이 드는
impact 충격
analysis 분석

정답률 32%

3. ⑤ 생태 건강을 파괴하는 광물 또는 화합물의 채굴

직독/직해

Ecological health depends on keeping the surface of the earth /
생태 건강은 지표면을 유지하는 데 달려 있다 /

rich in humus and minerals /
부식토와 광물이 풍부한 상태로 /

so that it can provide a foundation for healthy plant and animal life.
그것이 동식물의 건강한 삶을 위한 토대를 제공할 수 있도록

The situation is disrupted / if the soil loses these raw materials /
그 상황은 붕괴한다 / 토양이 이러한 원료를 잃게 된다면 /

or if great quantities of contaminants are introduced into it.
또는 다량의 오염 물질이 그것(토양)에 유입되면

When man goes beneath the surface of the earth /
인간이 지표면 아래로 가서 /

and drags out minerals or other compounds /
그리고 광물이나 다른 화합물을 끄집어내면 /

that did not evolve as part of this system, / then problems follow.
이 시스템의 일부로 변하지 않은 / 문제가 뒤따른다

The mining of lead and cadmium are examples of this.
납과 카드뮴의 채굴이 이것의 예이다

Petroleum is also a substance /
석유 또한 물질이다 /

that has been dug out of the bowels of the earth /
지구의 내부에서 채굴되어 /

and introduced into the surface ecology by man.
그리고 인간에 의해 지표 생태계에 유입된 (물질이다)

Though it is formed from plant matter, /
비록 그것(석유)이 식물로부터 형성되지만 /

the highly reduced carbon compounds that result /
그로 인해 생기는 고도로 환원된 탄소 화합물은 /

are often toxic to living protoplasm.
살아 있는 원형질에 유독한 경우가 많다

In some cases / this is true of even very tiny amounts, /
몇몇 경우에는 / 심지어 매우 적은 양일 때도 이러하다 /

as in the case of "polychlorinated biphenyls," a petroleum product /
석유 생성 물질인 '폴리염화 바이페닐'의 경우에서처럼 /

which can cause cancer.
암을 유발할 수 있는

생태 건강은 지표면이 동식물의 건강한 삶을 위한 토대를 제공할 수 있도록 그것(지표면)을 부식토와 광물이 풍부한 상태로 유지하는 데 달려 있다. 토양이 이러한 원료를 잃거나 다량의 오염 물질이 그것(토양)에 유입되면 그 상황은 붕괴한다. 인간이 지표면 아래로 가서, 이 시스템의 일부로 변하지 않은 광물이나 다른 화합물을 끄집어내면, 문제가 뒤따른다. 납과 카드뮴의 채굴이 이것의 예이다. 석유 또한 인간에 의해 지구의 내부에서 채굴되어 지표 생태계에 유입된 물질이다. 비록 그것(석유)이 식물로부터 형성되지만, 그로 인해 생기는 고도로 환원된 탄소 화합물은 살아 있는 원형질에 유독한 경우가 많다. 암을 유발할 수 있는 석유 생성 물질인 '폴리염화 바이페닐'의 경우에서처럼, 몇몇 경우에는 심지어 매우 적은 양일 때도 이러하다.

① 그 위에 있는 식물의 수는 너무 빠르게 증가하면
② 그것이 인간에게 충분한 영양분을 제공하는 것을 멈춘다면
③ 기후 변화가 그것의 화학적 요소들을 변화시킨다면
④ 외래종들이 그 주변에 만연하고 자원을 고갈시킨다면
⑤ 다량의 오염 물질이 그것(토양)에 유입되면

문제풀이

생태 건강은 지표면에 부식토와 광물질이 풍부할 때 지켜지는데 인간이 지표면 아래로 가서 이 시스템의 일부로 변하지 않은 광물이나 다른 화합물을 지표 생태계로 끄집어내면 문제가 생기게 된다. 예를 들어 석유가 비록 식물로부터 형성되지만, 그로 인해 생기는 고도로 환원된 탄소 화합물은 아주 작은 양일 때도 살아 있는 원형질에 유독하다는 내용의 글이다. 따라서 빈칸에는 ⑤ 'great quantities of contaminants are introduced into it'이 들어가 빈칸을 포함한 문장이 '토양이 이러한 원료를 잃거나 다량의 오염 물질이 그것(토양)에 유입되면 그 상황은 붕괴한다.'가 되어야 한다.

이렇게 풀자 빈칸 완성 문제에서는 빈칸을 포함한 문장을 정확하게 분석하는 것이 중요하다. 빈칸을 포함한

문장은 'The situation is disrupted if the soil loses these raw materials or if ____'에서 'or'을 기준으로 'if 조건절'이 병렬되고 있으므로 어떤 조건에서 지표면의 상태가 악화되는지를 알아내야 한다. 빈칸 이하의 전개는 사람들이 지표면 생태계에 적합하지 않은 물질을 끌어내게 되면 생태 건강이 악화된다는 내용이므로 생태계에 적합하지 않은 물질 즉 오염 물질이 토양에 유입되면 생태 건강이 악화된다는 것을 파악할 수 있다.

어휘·어구

ecological health 생태 건강
foundation 토대
disrupt 붕괴되다
drag out 끄집어내다
compound 화합물
toxic 유독한, 치명적인

4. ④ 팬덤의 즐거움의 원천

직독/직해

Fans feel / for feeling's own sake.
팬은 느낀다 / 감정 그 자체를 위해서

They make meanings / beyond what seems to be on offer.
그들은 의미를 만들어낸다 / 제공되는 것으로 보이는 것을 넘어서

They build identities and experiences, /
그들은 정체성과 경험을 쌓는다 /

and make artistic creations of their own / to share with others.
그리고 그들 자신의 예술적 창작물을 만들어 내어 / 다른 사람들과 공유한다

A person can be an individual fan, /
한 사람은 개인적인 팬이 될 수 있다 /

feeling an "idealized connection with a star, /
'어떤 스타와 이상적인 연결을 느끼며 /

strong feelings of memory and nostalgia," /
기억과 향수의 강렬한 감정'(을 느끼며) /

and engaging in activities / like "collecting to develop a sense of self."
그리고 활동에 참여할 수 있다 / '자아감을 발달시키기 위한 모임'과 같은

But, more often, / individual experiences are embedded / in social contexts /
하지만 더 자주 / 개인적인 경험은 끼워 넣어져 있다 / 사회적인 맥락에 /

where other people with shared attachments /
애착을 공유하는 다른 사람들이 /

socialize around the object of their affections.
그들의 애정의 대상을 중심으로 교제하는

Much of the pleasure of fandom / comes from being connected to other fans.
팬덤의 즐거움 중 많은 부분은 / 다른 팬들과 관계를 맺는 것에서 온다

In their diaries, / Bostonians of the 1800s /
자신의 일기에서 / 1800년대의 보스턴 사람들은 /

described / being part of the crowds at concerts /
묘사했다 / 콘서트에 모인 군중의 일부가 되는 것을 /

as part of the pleasure of attendance.
참석의 기쁨의 일부로

A compelling argument can be made /
강력한 주장이 만들어질 수 있다 /

that what fans love / is less the object of their fandom /
팬이 사랑하는 것은 / 자신의 팬덤의 대상이라기보다 /

than the attachments to (and differentiations from) one another /
서로에 대한 애착(그리고 서로 간의 차이)이라는 /

that those affections afford.
그 애정이 제공할 수 있는

팬은 감정 그 자체를 위해서 느낀다. 그들은 제공되는 것으로 보이는 것을 넘어서 의미를 만들어낸다. 그들은 정체성과 경험을 쌓고, 그들 자신의 예술적 창작물을 만들어 내어 다른 사람들과 공유한다. 한 사람은 개인적인 팬이 되어, '어떤 스타와 이상적인 연결, 기억과 향수의 강렬한 감정'을 느끼며, '자아감을 발달시키기 위한 모임'과 같은 활동에 참여할 수 있다. 하지만 더 자주 개인적인 경험은 애착을 공유하는 다른 사람들이 그들의 애정의 대상을 중심으로 교제하는 사회적인 맥락에 끼워 넣어져 있다. 팬덤의 즐거움 중 많은 부분은 다른 팬들과 관계를 맺는 것에서 온다. 1800년대의 보스턴 사람들은 자신의 일기에서 콘서트에 모인 군중의 일부가 되는 것을 참석의 기쁨의 일부로 묘사했다. 팬이 사랑하는 것은 자신의 팬덤의 대상이라기보다 그 애정이 제공할 수 있는 서로에 대한 애착(그리고 서로 간의 차이)이라는 강력한 주장이 만들어질 수 있다.

① 세계적인 스타들 간의 협력으로 증진시킨다
② 스타와 잦은 개인적인 연락을 나누는 데서 기인한다
③ 팬이 자신의 아이돌과 함께 나이 들어갈수록 깊어진다
④ 다른 팬들과 관계를 맺는 것에서 온다
⑤ 스타가 미디어에 출연함으로써 고양된다

문제풀이

한 사람이 스타의 팬이 되면 흔히 개인적인 경험은 애정의 대상을 중심으로 교제하는 사회적인 맥락에 끼워 넣어져 있다고 했고, 팬이 사랑하는 것은 팬덤의 대상이라기보다는 팬들 서로에 대한 애착이라고 했다. 따라서 빈칸에는 다른 팬들과의 유대에 대한 내용인 ④ 'comes from being connected to other fans'가 들어가서, '팬덤의 즐거움 중 많은 부분은 다른 팬들과 관계를 맺는 것에서 온다.'가 되는 것이 가장 적절하다.

어휘·어구

for one's own sake ~자신을 위해
on offer 제공되는
identity 정체성
idealized 이상적인
nostalgia 향수
collecting 모임, 수집하기
context 상황, 맥락
attachment 애착
socialize 교제하다
affection 애정
attendance 참석
argument 주장
afford 제공하다
enhance 높이다
collaboration 공동 작업, 협력
frequent 잦은
heighten 고조되다
appearance 나타남, 출현

5. ⑤ 컴퓨터 미술가의 소멸

직독/직해

Young contemporary artists / who employ digital technologies in their practice /
젊은 현대 미술가들은 / 자신의 일에 디지털 기술을 사용하는 /

rarely make reference to computers.
컴퓨터를 거의 언급하지 않는다

For example, / 예를 들면 /

Wade Guyton, an abstractionist /
추상파 화가인 Wade Guyton은 /

who uses a word processing program and inkjet printers, /
워드 프로세싱 프로그램과 잉크젯식 프린터를 사용하는

does not call himself a computer artist.
자신을 컴퓨터 미술가라고 부르지 않는다

Moreover, / some critics, who admire his work, /
더욱이 / 그의 작품을 높이 평가하는 몇몇 비평가들은 /

are little concerned about his extensive use of computers /
그의 광범위한 컴퓨터 사용에 관해 거의 신경 쓰지 않는다 /

in the art-making process.
예술 창작 과정에서

This is a marked contrast / from three decades ago /
이것은 현저히 대조된다 / 30년 전과 /

when artists who utilized computers were labeled / by critics /
컴퓨터를 사용하는 미술가들이 낙인찍혔던 / 비평가들에 의해 /

— often disapprovingly — / as computer artists.
자주 탐탁지 않게 / 컴퓨터 아티스트라고

For the present generation of artists, /
현세대의 미술가들에게 /

the computer, or more appropriately, the laptop, /
컴퓨터, 또는 더욱 적절하는 휴대용 컴퓨터는 /

is one in a collection of integrated, portable digital technologies /
일련의 통합된, 휴대 가능한 디지털 기술 중 하나이다 /

that link their social and working life.
그들의 사회생활과 직업 생활을 연결하는

With tablets and cell phones surpassing personal computers in Internet usage, /
인터넷 사용에서 태블릿 컴퓨터와 휴대 전화가 개인용 컴퓨터를 능가하는 상황에서 /

and as slim digital devices resemble nothing like the room-sized mainframes and bulky desktop computers of previous decades, /
그리고 얇은 디지털 기기들이 수십 년 전의 방 크기의 중앙 컴퓨터와 부피가 큰 탁상용 컴퓨터와 전혀 닮지 않았기 때문에 /

it now appears / that the computer artist is finally extinct.
~으로 보인다 / 오늘날에는 컴퓨터 미술가가 결국 소멸한 것

자신의 일에 디지털 기술을 사용하는 젊은 현대 미술가들은 컴퓨터를 거의 언급하지 않는다. 예를 들면, 워드 프로세싱 프로그램과 잉크젯식 프린터를 사용하는 추상파 화가인 Wade Guyton은 자신을 컴퓨터 미술가라고 부르지 않는다. 더욱이, 그의 작품을 높이 평가하는 몇몇 비평가들은 예술 창작 과정에서 그의 광범위한 컴퓨터 사용에 관해 거의 신경 쓰지 않는다. 이것은 컴퓨터를 사용하는 미술가들이 비평가들에 의해, 자주 탐탁지 않게, 컴퓨터 아티스트라고 낙인찍혔던 30년 전과 현저히 대조된다. 현세대의 미술가들에게 컴퓨터, 또는 더욱 적절하는 휴대용 컴퓨터는, 그들의 사회생활과 직업 생활을 연결하는 일련의 통합된, 휴대 가능한 디지털 기술 중 하나이다. 인터넷 사용에서 태블릿 컴퓨터와 휴대 전화가 개인용 컴퓨터를 능가하는 상황에서, 그리고 얇은 디지털 기기들이 수십 년 전의 방 크기의 중앙 컴퓨터와 부피가 큰 탁상용 컴퓨터와 전혀 닮지 않았기 때문에, 오늘날에는 컴퓨터 미술가가 결국 소멸한 것으로 보인다.

① 깨어 있는 ② 영향력 있는 ③ 뚜렷이 다른
④ 골칫거리의 **⑤ 소멸한**

문제풀이

디지털 기술을 사용하는 젊은 현대 미술가들은 컴퓨터를 거의 언급하지 않고 과거와는 달리 비평가들도 창작 과정에서 컴퓨터 사용에 거의 신경을 쓰지 않고 있다고 하면서, 현세대의 미술가에게 컴퓨터는 그들의 사회생활과 직업 생활을 연결하는 통합된 휴대 가능한 디지털 기술 중 하나라고 했다. 따라서 휴대용 디지털 기기의 광범위한 사용으로 컴퓨터의 이용에 특별한 의미를 부과해서 컴퓨터 미술가라고 부르는 행태는 이제 없어졌다고 할 수 있으므로, 빈칸에는 ⑤ 'extinct'가 들어가서 빈칸을 포함한 문장이 '인터넷 사용에서 태블릿 컴퓨터와 휴대 전화가 개인용 컴퓨터를 능가하는 상황에서, 그리고 얇은 디지털 기기들이 수십 년 전의 방 크기의 중앙 컴퓨터와 부피가 큰 탁상용 컴퓨터와 전혀 닮지 않았기 때문에, 오늘날에는 컴퓨터 미술가가 결국 소멸한 것으로 보인다.'가 되는 것이 가장 적절하다.

어휘·어구

contemporary 현대의
employ 이용하다, 쓰다
make reference to ~을 언급하다
abstractionist 추상파 화가
inkjet 잉크젯식
critic 비평가

admire 존경하다, 칭찬하다
extensive 광범위한
marked 뚜렷한
decade 십년간
label 명명하다, 이름을 붙이다
disapprovingly 탐탁지 않게
appropriately 적절히
integrate 통합하다
portable 휴대 가능한, 들고 다닐 수 있는
surpass 능가하다
mainframe 중앙 컴퓨터
bulky 부피가 큰

정답률 47%

6. ④ 형식주의의 관점에서의 문학

직독/직해

The critic who wants to write about literature from a formalist perspective /
형식주의의 관점에서 문학에 관하여 글을 쓰고 싶어 하는 비평가는 /
must first be a close and careful reader /
먼저 면밀하고도 주의 깊은 독자가 되어야 한다 /
who examines all the elements of a text individually /
글의 모든 요소를 개별적으로 점검하고 /
and questions / how they come together to create a work of art.
그리고 질문하는 / 그것들이 어떻게 결합해서 예술 작품이 되는지에 대해
Such a reader, who respects the autonomy of a work, /
작품의 자율성을 존중하는 그런 독자는 /
achieves an understanding of it /
그것에 대한 이해를 성취한다 /
by looking inside it, / not outside it or beyond it.
그것의 내부를 들여다봄으로써 / 그것의 외부나 그것을 넘어서가 아니라
Instead of examining historical periods, author biographies, or literary styles, /
역사상의 시대, 작가의 전기, 혹은 문학적 양식을 검토하는 대신에 /
for example, / he or she will approach a text with the assumption /
예를 들면 / 그 사람은 (~라는) 추정으로 글에 접근할 것이다 /
that it is a self-contained entity /
글이 자족적인 실체이며 /
and that he or she is looking for the governing principles /
그리고 자신은 지배적인 원리를 찾고 있다는 /
that allow the text to reveal itself.
그 글이 스스로를 드러내도록 해 주는
For example, / 예를 들면 /
the correspondences / between the characters in James Joyce's short story "Araby" /
연관성은 / James Joyce의 단편 소설인 'Araby' 속의 등장인물들과 /
and the people he knew personally /
그리고 그가 개인적으로 알았던 사람들 사이의 /
may be interesting, /
흥미로울 수도 있다 /
but for the formalist / they are less relevant to understanding / how the story creates meaning /
하지만 그 형식주의자에게 / 그것들은 이해하는 데 덜 관련되어 있다 / 이야기가 의미를 만들어내는 방식을 /
than are other kinds of information /
다른 종류의 정보보다 /
that the story contains within itself.
그 이야기가 그 안에 포함하고 있는

형식주의의 관점에서 문학에 관하여 글을 쓰고 싶어 하는 비평가는 먼저 글의 모든 요소를 개별적으로 점검하고 그것들이 어떻게 결합해서 예술 작품이 되는지에 대해 질문하는 면밀하고도 주의 깊은 독자가 되어야 한다. 작품의 자율성을 존중하는 그런 독자는 그것의 외부나 그것을 넘어서가 아니라 그것의 내부를 들여다봄으로써 그것에 대한 이해를 성취한다. 예를 들면, 역사상의 시대, 작가의 전기, 혹은 문학적 양식을 검토하는 대신에, 그 사람은 글이 자족적인 실체이며, 자신은 그 글이 스스로를 드러내도록 해 주는 지배적인 원리를 찾고 있다는 추정으로 글에 접근할 것이다. 예를 들면, James Joyce의 단편 소설인 'Araby' 속의 등장인물들과 그가 개인적으로 알았던 사람들과의 연관성은 흥미로울 수도 있겠지만, 그 형식주의자에게 그것들은 그 이야기가 그 안에 포함하고 있는 다른 종류의 정보보다 이야기가 의미를 만들어내는 방식을 이해하는 데 덜 관련되어 있다.

① 자기 자신을 그것의 안과 밖 모두에 놓음
② 그것과 세상 사이에서 중간 지점을 찾음
③ 그 안에서 드러난 역사적인 현실을 찾아봄
④ 그것의 외부나 그것을 넘어서가 아니라 그것의 내부를 들여다 봄
⑤ 그것의 등장인물들의 문화적인 관련성을 탐구함

문제풀이

문학을 형식주의의 관점에서 보려면 글의 모든 요소들을 점검하고 그것들이 모여 예술 작품을 이루는 방식을 봐야 한다고 했고, 형식주의적 관점에서는 작품의 자율성이 중요하고 작품 외적인 것보다 작품 내 요소들이 더 의미 있다고 언급하고 있다. 따라서 빈칸에는 형식주의적인 독자의 특징인 ④ 'looking inside it, not outside it or beyond it'이 들어가서 빈칸을 포함한 문장이 '작품의 자율성을 존중하는 그런 독자는 그것의 외부나 그것을 넘어서가 아니라 그것의 내부를 들여다봄으로써 그것에 대한 이해를 성취한다.'가 되는 것이 적절하다.

어휘·어구

formalist 형식주의의; 형식주의자
element 요소
autonomy 자율성
biography 전기
literary 문학적인
assumption 추정
governing 지배하는
self-contained 자족적인
reveal 드러내다
correspondence 관련성
relevant 관련된
explore 탐구하다
relevance 관련성

정답률 67%

7. ① 유머의 특징

직독/직해

Humour involves not just practical disengagement /
유머는 실제적인 이탈을 수반할 뿐만 아니라 /
but cognitive disengagement.
인지적인 이탈도 (수반한다)
As long as something is funny, /
어떤 것이 재미있는 한 /
we are for the moment not concerned /
우리는 잠깐 관심을 두지 않는다 /
with whether it is real or fictional, true or false.
그것이 진짜인지 허구인지, 진실인지 거짓인지에 관해
This is why we give considerable leeway to people /
이것이 우리가 사람들에게 많은 여지를 주는 이유이다 /
telling funny stories.
재미있는 이야기를 하는
If they are getting extra laughs /
만일 그들이 추가 웃음을 얻고 있다면 /
by exaggerating the silliness of a situation /
상황의 어리석음을 과장해서 /
or even by making up a few details, /
혹은 심지어 몇 가지 세부 사항을 지어내서라도 /
we are happy to grant them comic licence, /
우리는 그들에게 기꺼이 희극적 파격 허락한다 /
a kind of poetic licence.
일종의 시적 파격을
Indeed, / someone listening to a funny story /
실제로 / 재미있는 이야기를 듣고 있는 누군가가 /
who tries to correct the teller /
말하는 사람을 바로잡으려고 하면 /
— 'No, he didn't spill the spaghetti on the keyboard and the monitor, /
아니야, 그는 스파게티를 키보드와 모니터에 쏟은 것이 아니라 /
just on the keyboard' — /
키보드에만 쏟았어 /
will probably be told by the other listeners /
아마 듣고 있는 다른 사람들로부터 말을 들을 것이다 /
to stop interrupting.
끼어들지 말라는
The creator of humour is putting ideas /
유머를 만드는 사람은 아이디어를 집어넣고 있는데 /
into people's heads / for the pleasure /
사람들의 머릿속에 / 재미를 위해서이지 /
those ideas will bring, /
그 아이디어가 가져다줄 /
not to provide accurate information.
정확한 정보를 제공하기 위해서가 아니다

유머는 실제적인 이탈뿐만 아니라 인지적인 이탈도 수반한다. 어떤 것이 재미있는 한, 우리는 잠깐 그것이 진짜인지 허구인지, 진실인지 거짓인지에 관해 관심을 두지 않는다. 이것이 우리가 재미있는 이야기를 하는 사람들에게 많은 여지를 주는 이유이다. 만일 그들이 상황의 어리석음을 과장하거나 심지어 몇 가지 세부 사항을 지어내서라도 추가 웃음을 얻고 있다면, 우리는 그들에게 기꺼이 희극적 파격, 일종의 시적 파격을 허락한다. 실제로, 재미있는 이야기를 듣고 있는 누군가가 '아니야, 그는 스파게티를 키보드와 모니터에 쏟은 것이 아니라 키보드에만 쏟았어.'라며 말하는 사람을 바로잡으려고 하면 그는 아마 듣고 있는 다른 사람들로부터 끼어들지 말라는 말을 들을 것이다. 유머를 만드는 사람은 사람들의 머릿속에 아이디어를 집어넣고 있는데, 그 아이디어가 가져다줄 재미를 위해서이지 정확한 정보를 제공하기 위해서가 아니다.

① 정확한 ② 상세한
③ 유용한 ④ 추가의
⑤ 대안적인

문제풀이

유머는 재미있는 한 과장이나 몇 가지 세부 사항을 지어내는 것도 허락하는 것으로, 재미있는 이야기를 할 때 틀린 내용을 바로잡으려고 하면 다른 사람에게서 끼어들지 말라는 말을 들을 것이라고 했다. 따라서 빈칸에는 'accurate'이 들어가서 빈칸을 포함한 문장이 '유머를 만드는 사람은 사람들의 머릿속에 아이디어를 집어넣고 있는데, 그 아이디어가 가져다줄 재미를 위해서이지 정확한 정보를 제공하기 위해서가 아니다.'가 되는 것이 적절하다.

어휘·어구

practical 실제적인, 실질적인
disengagement 이탈
as long as ~하는 한
concerned 관심이 있는, 걱정하는
fictional 허구적인
considerable 상당한, 많은
exaggerate 과장하다
silliness 어리석음, 바보짓
make up ~을 지어[만들어] 내다
grant 승인하다, 인정하다
licence (문학·예술상의) 파격
interrupt 끼어들다

정답률 47%

8. ⑤ 뉴스의 구성

직독/직해

News, especially in its televised form, / is constituted /
뉴스, 특히 텔레비전으로 방송되는 형태는 / 구성된다 /
not only by its choice of topics and stories /
그것이 선택하는 주제와 이야기뿐만 아니라 /
but by its verbal and visual idioms or modes of address.
그것의 언어적, 시각적 표현 양식이나 전달 방식에 의해서도
Presentational styles have been subject to a tension /
표현 방식은 긴장 상태에 영향을 받아 왔다 /
between an informational-educational purpose and the need to engage us entertainingly.
정보 제공 및 교육적 목적과 즐겁게 우리의 주의를 끌 필요성 사이의
While current affairs programmes are often 'serious' in tone /
시사 프로그램들이 종종 어조가 '진지'하지만 /
sticking to the 'rules' of balance, /
균형이라는 '규칙'을 고수하면서 /
more popular programmes adopt a friendly, lighter, idiom /
더 대중적인 프로그램들은 친근하고 더 가벼운 표현 방식을 채택하는데 /
in which we are invited to consider /
그 표현 양식에서 고려해 보게 된다 /
the impact of particular news items /
특정 뉴스 기사의 영향을 /
from the perspective of the 'average person in the street'.
우리는 '거리에 있는 보통 사람'의 관점에서
Indeed, / 사실 /
contemporary news construction has come to rely /
현대의 뉴스 구성은 의존하게 되었다 /
on an increased use of faster editing tempos /
더 빠른 편집 속도를 더 많이 이용하는 것에 /
and 'flashier' presentational styles /
와 '더 현란한' 표현 방식을 (더 많이 이용하는 것에) /
including the use of logos, sound-bites, rapid visual cuts /
로고, 짤막한 방송용 어구, 빠른 시각적 편집 화면을 이용하는 것을 포함한 /
and the 'star quality' of news readers.
그리고 뉴스 독자의 '스타성'을 (이용하는 것을 포함한)
Popular formats can be said to enhance understanding /
대중적인 구성은 이해를 향상시켰다고 할 수 있다 /
by engaging an audience /
시청자를 사로잡아 /
unwilling to endure the longer verbal orientation of older news formats.
장황한 언어를 지향하는 예전 뉴스 구성 방식을 견딜 의사가 없는
However, / they arguably work to reduce understanding /
그러나 / 그것은 아마 틀림없이 이해를 감소시키는 효과가 있다 /
by failing to provide the structural contexts for news events.
뉴스 사건에 관한 구조적 맥락을 제공하지 못함으로써 .

뉴스, 특히 텔레비전으로 방송되는 형태는 그것이 선택하는 주제와 이야기뿐만 아니라 그것의 언어적, 시각적 표현 양식이나 전달 방식에 의해서도 구성된다. 표현 방식은 정보 제공 및 교육적 목적과 즐겁게 우리의 주의를 끌 필요성 사이의 긴장 상태에 영향을 받아 왔다. 시사 프로그램들이 종종 균형이라는 '규칙'을 고수하면서 어조가 '진지'하지만, 더 대중적인 프로그램들은 친근하고 더 가벼운 표현 방식을 채택하는데 그 표현 양식에서 우리는 '거리에 있는 보통 사람'의 관점에서 특정 뉴스 기사의 영향을 고려해 보게 된다. 사실, 현대의 뉴스 구성은 로고, 짤막한 방송용 어구, 빠른 시각적 편집 화면, 그리고 뉴스 독자의 '스타성'을 이용하는 것을 포함한 더 빠른 편집 속도와 '더 현란한' 표현 방식을 더 많이 이용하는 것에 의존하게 되었다. 대중적인 구성은 장황한 언어를 지향하는 예전 뉴스 구성 방식을 견딜 의사가 없는 시청자를 사로잡아 이해를 향상시켰다고 할 수 있다. 그러나 그것은 뉴스 사건에 관한 구조적 맥락을 제공하지 못함으로써 아마 틀림없이 이해를 감소시키는 효과가 있다.

① 전통적인 표현 방식과 조화
② 최신 쟁점에 대한 신속하고도 온전한 보도
③ 제작자에 의해 선호되는 교육적 매체 내용
④ 오랫동안 지속되는 뉴스 기준에 대한 전념
⑤ 언어적, 시각적 표현 양식이나 전달 방식

문제풀이

뉴스, 특히 텔레비전의 뉴스가 내용뿐만 아니라 시각적인 편집 화면, 짤막한 방송용 어구 등을 이용하여 더 빠른 편집 템포와 현란한 표현 방식을 활용하여 시청자를 사로잡는다고 했다. 따라서 빈칸에는 ⑤ 'verbal and visual idioms or modes of address'가 들어가서 빈칸을 포함한 문장이 '뉴스, 특히 텔레비전으로 방송되는 형태는 그것이 선택하는 주제와 이야기뿐만 아니라 그것의 언어적, 시각적 표현 양식이나 전달 방식에 의해서도 구성된다.'가 되는 것이 적절하다.

이렇게 풀자 빈칸 뒤에 오는 내용에서 'While current affairs programmes are often 'serious' in tone sticking to the 'rules' of balance, more popular programmes adopt a friendly, lighter, idiom in which we are invited to consider the impact of particular news items from the perspective of the 'average person in the street'.(시사 프로그램들이 종종 균형이라는 '규칙'을 고수하면서 어조가 '진지'하지만, 더 대중적인 프로그램들은 친근하고 더 가벼운 표현 방식을 채택하는데 그 표현 방식에서 우리는 '거리에 있는 보통 사람'의 관점에서 특정 뉴스 기사의 영향을 고려해 보게 된다.)'와 'Indeed, contemporary news construction has come to rely on an increased use of faster editing tempos and 'flashier' presentational styles including the use of logos, sound-bites, rapid visual cuts and the 'star quality' of news readers.(사실, 현대의 뉴스 구성은 로고, 짤막한 방송용 어구, 빠른 시각적 편집 화면, 그리고 뉴스 독자의 '스타성'을 이용하는 것을 포함한 더 빠른 편집 속도와 '더 현란한 표현 방식을 더 많이 이용하는 것에 의존하게 되었다.)'에서 표현 양식이나 전달 방식에 대해 이야기하고 있다는 것을 알 수 있으므로, 표현 방식과 관련된 선택지가 답인 것을 유추해낼 수 있다.

어휘·어구

televise 텔레비전으로 방송하다
constitute 구성하다
presentational 표상적인
be subject to ~의 영향을 받다
engage (마음을) 사로잡다
entertainingly 즐겁게
current affairs programme 시사 프로그램
tone 어조
stick to ~을 고수하다
idiom 표현 양식, 관용구
perspective 관점
contemporary 현대의
construction 구성
flashy 현란한
sound-bite 짤막한 방송용 어구
format 구성, 포맷
enhance 높이다, 향상시키다
orientation 지향
arguably 아마 틀림없이
structural 구조적인
context 맥락, 상황
coordination 조화
display 표현, 표시
prompt 신속한
coverage 보도
commitment 전념

정답률 54%

9. ② 수메르 사회에서 사원의 역할과 문자의 발달

직독/직해

In the classic model of the Sumerian economy, /
수메르 경제의 전형적 모델에서 /
the temple functioned /
사원은 기능했다 /
as an administrative authority /
행정 당국으로서 /
governing commodity production, collection, and redistribution.
상품의 생산, 수집과 재분배를 관장하는
The discovery of administrative tablets /
행정용 판의 발견은 /
from the temple complexes at Uruk / suggests /
Uruk의 사원 단지에서 나온 행정용 판의 발견은 / 암시한다 /
that token use and consequently writing evolved /
상징의 사용, 그리고 결과적으로 글쓰기가 발달했다는 것을 /
as a tool of centralized economic governance.
중앙 집권화된 경제 지배의 도구로
Given the lack of archaeological evidence /
고고학적 증거가 없다는 것을 고려해 볼 때 /
from Uruk-period domestic sites, /
Uruk 시기 가정집의 터에서 나온 /
it is not clear / 분명하지 않다 /
whether individuals also used the system /
개인들이 또한 그 체계를 사용했는지는 /
for personal agreements.
개인적인 합의를 위해
For that matter, / it is not clear /
그 문제와 관련하여 / 분명하지 않다 /
how widespread literacy was / at its beginnings.
읽고 쓰는 능력이 얼마나 널리 퍼져 있었는지 / 그것의 초기에
The use of identifiable symbols and pictograms /
인식 가능한 기호와 그림 문자의 사용은 /
on the early tablets / 초기의 판에서의 /
is consistent with administrators needing a lexicon /
행정가들이 어휘 목록이 필요했던 것과 일치한다 /
that was mutually intelligible /
서로 이해할 수 있는 /
by literate and nonliterate parties.
읽고 쓸 줄 아는 쪽과 읽고 쓸 수 없는 쪽이
As cuneiform script became more abstract, /
쐐기 문자가 더 추상적으로 되면서 /
literacy must have become increasingly important /
읽고 쓰는 능력이 점점 더 중요해졌던 것이 틀림없다 /
to ensure one understood /
이해하고 있다는 것을 확실히 하기 위해 /
what he or she had agreed to.
자신이 합의했던 것을

수메르 경제의 전형적 모델에서 사원은 상품의 생산, 수집과 재분배를 관장하는 행정 당국으로서 기능했다. Uruk의 사원 단지에서 나온 행정용 판의 발견은 상징의 사용, 그리고 결과적으로 글쓰기가 중앙 집권화된 경제 지배의 도구로 발달했다는 것을 암시한다. Uruk 시기 가정집의 터에서 나온 고고학적 증거가 없다는 것을 고려해 볼 때, 개인들이 또한 개인적인 합의를 위해 그 체계를 사용했는지는 분명하지 않다. 그 문제와 관련하여, 읽고 쓰는 능력이 그것의 초기에 얼마나 널리 퍼져 있었는지 분명하지 않다. 초기의 판에서의 인식 가능한 기호와 그림 문자의 사용은 행정가들이 읽고 쓸 줄 아는 쪽과 읽고 쓸 수 없는 쪽이 서로 이해할 수 있는 어휘 목록이 필요했던 것과 일치한다. 쐐기 문자가 더 추상적으로 되면서, 읽고 쓰는 능력이 자신이 합의했던 것을 이해하고 있다는 것을 확실히 하기 위해 점점 더 중요해졌던 것이 틀림없다.

① 종교 행사 **② 개인적인 합의**
③ 공동의 책임 ④ 역사적 기록
⑤ 권력 이동

문제풀이

수메르 경제에서 글자가 중앙 집권화된 경제 지배의 도구로 발달했지만, 개인에게도 합의했던 것을 이해하고 있다는 것을 확실하게 하기 위해 점점 더 중요해졌다고 했다. 따라서 빈칸에는 ② 'personal agreements'가 들어가서 빈칸을 포함한 문장이 'Uruk 시기 가정집의 터에서 나온 고고

학적 증거가 없다는 것을 고려해 볼 때, 개인들이 또한 개인적인 합의를 위해 그 체계를 사용했는지는 분명하지 않다.'가 되는 것이 가장 적절하다.

《 어휘 · 어구 》

classic 전형적인, 고전적인
temple 사원
administrative 관리의, 행정의
authority 당국, 권위
govern 관장하다, 통치하다
commodity 상품, 물품
redistribution 재분배, 재배포
tablet 판, 평판(平板)
complex (건물) 단지, 복합 건물
token (구체적인 표식으로서의) 상징
evolve 발달하다, 진화하다
centralized 중앙 집권화된
given ~을 고려해 볼 때
domestic 가정의, 집안의, 국내의
for that matter 그 문제와 관련하여
widespread 널리 퍼진
literacy 읽고 쓰는 능력
identifiable 인식 가능한
pictogram 그림 문자
consistent with ~와 일치하는
administrator 관리자, 행정인
mutually 서로, 상호 간에, 공통으로
intelligible (쉽게) 이해할 수 있는
nonliterate 읽고 쓸 수 없는
abstract 추상적인
religious 종교의
communal 집단들이 관련된, 공동의

정답률 57%

10. ③ 환경의 영향을 받아 달라지는 생존 전략

직독/직해

Choosing similar friends / can have a rationale.
비슷한 친구를 고르는 것에는 / 논리적 근거가 있을 수 있다
Assessing the survivability of an environment /
어떤 환경의 존속 가능성을 평가하는 것은 /
can be risky / 위험할 수 있다 /
(if an environment turns out to be deadly, /
만약 어떤 환경이 치명적인 것으로 밝혀지면 /
for instance, / 예를 들면 /
it might be too late by the time you found out), /
그 사실을 알 무렵에는 너무 늦을 수도 있다 /
so humans have evolved the desire /
그래서 서로 비슷한 욕구를 발달시켜 왔다 /
to associate with similar individuals /
개인들과 함께하고자 하는 /
as a way to perform this function efficiently.
인간은 이 기능을 효율적으로 수행하기 위한 한 가지 방편으로
This is especially useful to a species /
이것은 종에게 특별히 유용하다 /
that lives in so many different sorts of environments.
매우 많은 유형의 환경에 사는
However, the carrying capacity of a given environment /
하지만 주어진 환경의 수용 능력은 /
places a limit on this strategy.
이 전략에 제한을 둔다
If resources are very limited, /
만약 자원이 매우 한정되어 있다면 /
the individuals who live in a particular place /
특정 장소에 사는 개인이 /
cannot all do the exact same thing /
모두 똑같은 것을 할 수는 없다 /
(for example, if there are few trees, /
예를 들어, 만약 나무가 거의 없다면 /
people cannot all live in tree houses, /
사람들이 모두 나무집에 살 수는 없으며 /
or if mangoes are in short supply, /
혹은 망고의 공급이 부족하면 /
people cannot all live /
사람들이 살 수는 없다 /
solely on a diet of mangoes).
모두 오직 망고를 먹는 식단으로만
A rational strategy would therefore sometimes /
따라서 합리적인 전략은 때로는 /
be to *avoid* similar members of one's species.
자신의 종의 비슷한 구성원들을 '피하는' 것이 될 것이다

비슷한 친구를 고르는 것에는 논리적 근거가 있을 수 있다. 어떤 환경의 존속 가능성을 평가하는 것은 위험할 수 있어서 (예를 들면, 만약 어떤 환경이 치명적인 것으로 밝혀지면, 그 사실을 알 무렵에는 너무 늦을 수도 있다), 인간은 이 기능을 효율적으로 수행하기 위한 한 가지 방편으로 서로 비슷한 개인들과 함께하고자 하는 욕구를 발달시켜 왔다. 이것은 매우 많은 유형의 환경에 사는 종에게 특별히 유용하다. 하지만 주어진 환경의 수용 능력은 이 전략에 제한을 둔다. 만약 자원이 매우 한정되어 있다면, 특정 장소에 사는 개인이 모두 똑같은 것을 할 수는 없다 (예를 들어, 만약 나무가 거의 없다면, 사람들이 모두 나무집에 살 수는 없으며, 혹은 망고의 공급이 부족하면, 사람들이 모두 오직 망고를 먹는 식단으로만 살 수는 없다). 따라서 합리적인 전략은 때로는 자신의 종의 비슷한 구성원들을 '피하는' 것이 될 것이다.

① 공동체의 예상 수요를 넘는다
② 다양한 생존의 수단에 의해 줄어든다
③ 이 전략에 제한을 둔다
④ 세상을 개인들에게 적합하게 만든다
⑤ 비슷하지 않은 구성원들과의 사회적 유대를 막는다

문제풀이

생존 가능성 평가가 위험할 수 있어서 생존 가능성을 높이려고 비슷한 구성원을 고르지만, 한정적 자원 때문에 인간은 이 생존 전략을 수정하여 비슷한 구성원을 피하는 전략을 갖기도 한다고 했다. 따라서 빈칸에는 ③ 'places a limit on this strategy'가 들어가서 빈칸을 포함한 문장이 '하지만 주어진 환경의 수용 능력은 이 전략에 제한을 둔다.'가 되는 것이 가장 적절하다.

구조 다시보기

주장	비슷한 친구를 고르는 것에는 논리적 근거가 있음
근거	생존 가능성 평가가 위험할 수 있어 생존 가능성을 높이기 위해서임
결론	다양한 유형의 환경에 사는 종에게 유용함
반론	자연이 한정된 환경에서 모든 개인이 같은 행동을 할 수 없음
반론의 결론	비슷한 구성원을 피하는 전략이 합리적임

《 어휘 · 어구 》

rationale 논리적 근거, 이유
assess 평가하다
survivability 생존 가능성
turn out ~으로 밝혀지다
deadly 치명적인
associate with ~와 함께하다, ~와 어울리다
efficiently 유효하게, 능률적으로
carrying capacity 수용 능력, 적재량
strategy 전략
limited 한정된
in short supply 공급이 부족한
solely 오로지, 단지
rational 합리적인, 이성적인
exceed 넘다, 초과하다
place a limit on ~에 제한을 두다
dissimilar 닮지 않은, 다른

본문 077쪽

문법 플러스 13. 관계대명사

A. 1. which 2. What 3. who
4. that 5. as 6. than
7. Whoever

1 [해석]▶ 이런 경향이 표현된 두 가지가 '의인화'(동물을 인간으로 간주하는 관행)와 '토테미즘'(인간을 동물로 간주하는 관행)인데, 이 두 가지는 원시 문화의 시각 예술과 신화에 널리 퍼져 있다.
[해설]▶ 앞에 있는 anthropomorphism (the practice of regarding animals as humans) and totemism (the practice of regarding humans as animals)를 가리키는 관계사이므로 which가 어법에 맞다.

2 [해석]▶ 인생에서 가장 중요한 것은 사랑이다.
[해설]▶ what은 선행사를 포함하고, what ~ in life가 주어부를 이루고, what절 안에서 what은 주어 역할을 하고 있다.

3 [해석]▶ 그녀는 그것을 친구와 상의했는데, 그녀의 친구는 변호사이다.
[해설]▶ 선행사는 her friend이고, 관계사 who가 선행사를 설명하는 계속적 용법으로 사용되었다.

4 [해석]▶ 나와 얘기했던 숙녀는 우리 이모야.
[해설]▶ 선행사가 사람(the lady)이고, 관계대명사는 전치사 with의 목적격 역할을 하고 있다. 이런 경우, 목적격 관계대명사 whom이나 that이 필요하다.

5 [해석]▶ 이것은 내가 잃어버린 시계와 같은 종류의 시계다.
[해설]▶ 선행사가 the same이 나온 경우, 유사 관계대명사 as를 쓴다.

6 [해석]▶ 그는 필요한 것보다 더 많은 돈을 가지고 있다.
[해설]▶ 선행사 앞에 비교급이 올 때, 유사관계대명사 than을 쓴다.

7 [해석]▶ 이 법을 어긴 사람은 누구든지 처벌을 받을 것이다. (Anyone who breaks this low~)
[해설]▶ 문맥상 이 법을 어긴 사람은 누구든지의 의미이므로 주어 역할을 하는 복합관계대명사 'whoever'가 필요하다.

본문 077쪽

B. 1. that 2. what 3. which
4. was 5. as 6. more
7. whichever

1 [해석]▶ 세포의 신진대사와 구조가 복잡해야 하는 것은 놀라운 것이 아니겠지만, 사실 그것들은 다소 간단하고 논리적이다.
[해설]▶ '~라는 것'이라는 뜻의 문장의 주어 역할을 하는 would 앞까지의 부분이 절의 모든 중요 구성 요소를 지니고 있으므로 관계사 what 대신 접속사 that을 써야 한다.

2 [해석]▶ 당신은 보지 않은 것을 믿을 수 있나요?
[해설]▶ 관계사절 앞에 선행사가 없고, 타동사 see의 목적어 역할을 하는 관계대명사가 필요하므로 선행사를 포함하고 있는 관계사 what이 필요하다.

3 [해석]▶ Sally는 빙판에서 넘어졌는데, 그것은 모두를 웃게 만들었다.
[해설]▶ 관계대명사 which가 선행사인 바로 앞 문장 전체를 설명하는 계속적 관계대명사 용법으로 사용되었다.

4 [해석]▶ 안내원으로 일하고 있던 그 남자는 새로운 직업을 찾는 중이었다.

4 [해석]▶ 안내원으로 일하고 있던 그 남자는 새로운 직업을 찾는 중이었다.
[해설]▶ 관계대명사절의 동사는 선행사(the man)와 수를 일치시킨다. 선행사가 단수명사이므로 단수동사를 써야 한다.

5 [해석]▶ 너를 도와줄 그런 친구를 선택해.
[해설]▶ 선행사가 such~인 경우, 유사관계대명사 as를 사용한다. as는 동사 will help의 주어 역할을 하고 있다.

6 [해석]▶ 그녀는 내가 가진 것보다 더 많은 책을 가지고 있다.
[해설]▶ 선행사 앞에 비교급이 올 때 유사관계대명사 than을 쓴다.

7 [해석]▶ 네 마음에 드는 것은 어느 것이든지 가져도 된다.
[해설]▶ 복합관계대명사 whichever는 선행사를 포함하고 있으며 '~하는 것은 어느 것이든지'의 의미로 타동사 like의 목적어 역할을 하고 있다.

본문 078쪽

숙어 플러스 13. 수능 필수 숙어 13회

1. touch	2. behind
3. after	4. for

14. 빈칸 추론 (2) 긴 어구, 문장

본문 080쪽

1. ⑤	2. ④	3. ①	4. ④	5. ②
6. ②	7. ①	8. ②	9. ①	10. ②

대표 기출 ① 벌들의 댄스 플로어에서 정보 교환의 결과

직독/직해

The entrance to a honeybee colony, / often referred to as the dancefloor, /
꿀벌 군집의 입구는 / 흔히 댄스 플로어(무도장)라고 일컫는데 /
is a market place for information /
정보를 교환하기 위한 시장이다 /
about the state of the colony and the environment outside the hive.
군집의 상태와 벌집 외부의 환경에 관한
Studying interactions on the dancefloor / provides us /
댄스 플로어에서의 상호 작용을 연구하는 것은 / 우리에게 제공한다 /
with a number of illustrative examples /
많은 예증이 되는 예시들을 /
of how individuals changing their own behavior /
어떻게 그들 자신의 행동을 바꾸는 개체들이 ~에 대한 /
in response to local information / allow the colony to regulate its workforce.
지역의 정보에 반응하여 / 군집이 그것의 노동력을 조절할 수 있도록 하는지에 (대한)
For example, / upon returning to their hive /
예를 들면 / 자신들의 벌집으로 돌아오자마자 /
honeybees that have collected water / search out a receiver bee /
물을 모아온 꿀벌들은 / 물을 받아줄 벌을 찾는다 /
to unload their water to within the hive.
자신들의 물을 벌집 안으로 넘겨주기 위해
If this search time is short /
만약 이 찾는 시간이 짧으면 /
then the returning bee is more likely to perform a waggle dance /
그 돌아오는 벌은 8자 춤을 출 가능성이 더 높다 /
to recruit others to the water source.
물이 있는 곳으로 데려갈 다른 벌들을 모집하기 위해 /
Conversely, / if this search time is long /
이와는 반대로 / 이 찾는 시간이 길면 /
then the bee is more likely to give up collecting water.
그러면 그 벌은 물을 모으러 가는 것을 포기할 가능성이 더 높다
Since receiver bees will only accept water / if they require it, /
물을 받는 벌들은 물을 받을 것이기 때문에 / 그들이 물이 필요할 때만 /
either for themselves / or to pass on to other bees and brood, /
자신들을 위해서든 / 또는 다른 벌들과 애벌레들에게 전해주기 위해서든 /
this unloading time is correlated with / the colony's overall need of water.
이런 물을 넘겨주는 시간은 상관관계가 있다 / 군집의 전반적인 물 수요와
Thus the individual water forager's response to unloading time /
그러므로 물을 넘겨주는 시간에 대한 개별적인 물 조달자의 반응은 /
(up or down) /
(시간이 늘어나든 혹은 줄어들든 간에) /
regulates water collection / in response to the colony's need.
물 수집을 조절한다 / 군집의 수요에 맞춰서

흔히 댄스 플로어라고 일컫는 꿀벌 군집의 입구는 군집의 상태와 벌집 외부의 환경에 관한 정보를 교환하기 위한 시장이다. 댄스 플로어에서의 상호 작용을 연구하는 것은 우리에게 지역의 정보에 반응하여 어떻게 그들 자신의 행동을 바꾸는 개체들이 군집이 그것의 노동력을 조절할 수 있도록 하는지에 대한 많은 예증이 되는 예시들을 제공한다. 예를 들면, 물을 모아온 꿀벌들은 자신들의 벌집으로 돌아오자마자 자신들의 물을 벌집 안으로 넘겨주기 위해 물을 받아줄 벌을 찾는다. 만약 이 (물을 받을 벌을) 찾는 시간이 짧으면, 그 돌아오는 벌은 물이 있는 곳으로 데려갈 다른 벌들을 모집하기 위해 8자 춤을 출 가능성이 더 높다. 이와는 반대로, 이 찾는 시간이 길면 그 벌은 물을 모으러 가는 것을 포기할 가능성이 더 높다. 물을 받는 벌들은 자신들을 위해서든 다른 벌들과 애벌레들에게 전해주기 위해서든, 물이 필요할 때만 물을 받을 것이기 때문에, 이런 물을 넘겨주는 시간은 군집의 전반적인 물 수요와 상관관계가 있다. 그러므로 (시간이 늘어나든 혹은 줄어들든 간에) 물을 넘겨주는 시간에 대한 개별적인 물 조달자의 반응은 군집의 수요에 맞춰서 물 수집을 조절한다.

① 군집이 군집의 노동력을 조절할 수 있게 하는지
② 거리를 측정하여 물이 있는 곳을 찾는지
③ 필요할 때 군집의 작업량을 줄이는지
④ 자신들 각자의 재능에 따라 일을 나누는지
⑤ 기본적인 의사소통 패턴을 습득하도록 일벌들을 훈련시키는지

문제풀이

빈칸 뒤에 이어지는 예에서 댄스 플로어에서 물을 넘겨주는 데 걸리는 시간에 따라 물을 조달하는 벌들의 행동이 달라지는데, 개별적인 벌들이 댄스 플로어(무도장)에서 정보를 교환하여 그것에 맞게 행동을 바꿈으로써 결국 군집 전체의 노동력을 조절하게 된다고 했다. 따라서 빈칸에는 ① 'allow the colony to regulate its workforce'가 들어가서 빈칸을 포함한 문장이 '댄스 플로어에서의 상호 작용을 연구하는 것은 우리에게 지역의 정보에 반응하여 어떻게 그들 자신의 행동을 바꾸는 개체들이 어떻게 군집이 그것의 노동력을 조절할 수 있도록 하는지에 대한 많은 예증이 되는 예시들을 제공한다.'가 되는 것이 가장 적절하다.

이렇게 풀자 빈칸 뒤에 이어지는 예와 그것에 대한 결론을 이야기하는 부분을 통해 빈칸에 들어갈 말을 추론할 수 있다. 'Thus the individual water forager's response to unloading time (up or down) regulates water collection in response to the colony's need.(그러므로 (시간이 늘어나든 혹은 줄어들든 간에) 물을 넘겨주는 시간에 대한 개별적인 물 조달자의 반응은 군집의 수요에 맞춰서 물 수집(량)을 조절한다.)'에서 'regulates water collection'에 해당하는 내용이 빈칸에 들어갈 내용과 같아야 한다. 물 수집을 조절하는 것이 노동력을 조절하는 것과 같은 의미라는 것을 알면 빈칸에 들어갈 말을 쉽게 추론할 수 있다.

어휘·어구

colony 군집, 집단
illustrative 예증이 되는
regulate 조절하다
unload 떠넘기다, (짐 등을) 내리다
waggle dance 8자의 춤(꿀벌이 꽃 등의 방향과 거리를 동료에게 알리는 동작)
workforce 노동력
workload 작업량, 업무량
respective 각각의

정답률 21%

1. ⑤ 시간에 대한 의식

직독/직해

We understand /
우리는 이해하는데 /
that the segregation of our consciousness into

present, past, and future /
우리의 의식을 현재, 과거, 미래로 분리하는 것이 /
is both a fiction and an oddly self-referential framework; /
허구이면서 이상하게도 자기 지시적인 틀이라는 것을 /
your present was part of your mother's future, /
당신의 현재는 당신의 어머니 미래의 일부였다 /
and your children's past will be in part your present.
그리고 당신 자녀의 과거는 당신 현재의 일부일 것이라는 것이다
Nothing is generally wrong / with structuring our consciousness of time /
일반적으로 잘못된 것이 전혀 없다 / 시간에 대한 우리의 의식을 구조화하는 것에는 /
in this conventional manner, / and it often works well enough.
이런 전통적인 방식으로 / 그리고 그것은 흔히 충분히 잘 작동한다
In the case of climate change, / however, /
기후 변화의 경우 / 하지만 /
the sharp division of time into past, present, and future /
시간을 과거, 현재, 미래로 분명하게 분리하는 것은 /
has been desperately misleading / and has, most importantly, hidden /
심하게 (사실을) 오도해왔다 / 그리고 가장 중요하게는 숨겨왔다 /
from view / the extent of the responsibility / of those of us alive now.
시야로부터 / 책임 정도[범위]를 / 지금 살아 있는 우리들의
The narrowing of our consciousness of time / smooths the way /
시간에 대한 우리의 의식을 좁히는 것은 / 길을 닦는다 /
to divorcing ourselves from responsibility / for developments /
책임으로부터 우리를 분리하는 / 발전에 대한
in the past and the future / with which our lives are in fact deeply intertwined.
과거와 미래의 / 그런데 사실 우리의 삶은 그것과 깊이 뒤얽혀 있다.
In the climate case, / 기후의 경우에는 /
it is not that we face the facts but then deny our responsibility.
우리가 사실을 직시하면서도 우리의 책임을 부인하는 것이 문제가 아니다
It is that the realities are obscured from view / by the partitioning of time, /
문제는 현실이 시야로부터 흐릿해지는 것이다 / 시간을 분리함으로써 /
and so questions of responsibility toward the past and future /
따라서 과거와 현재의 책임에 관한 질문이 /
do not arise naturally. 자연스럽게 생겨나지 않는 (것이다)

우리는 우리의 의식을 현재, 과거, 미래로 분리하는 것이 허구이면서 이상하게도 자기 지시적인 틀이라는 것을 이해하는데, 당신의 현재는 당신의 어머니 미래의 일부였고 당신 자녀의 과거는 당신 현재의 일부일 것이라는 것이다. 시간에 대한 우리의 의식을 이런 전통적인 방식으로 구조화하는 것에는 일반적으로 잘못된 것이 전혀 없으며 그것은 흔히 충분히 잘 작동한다. 하지만 기후 변화의 경우, 시간을 과거, 현재, 미래로 분명하게 분리하는 것은 심하게 (사실을) 오도해왔으며 가장 중요하게는 지금 살아 있는 우리들의 책임 정도[범위]를 시야로부터 숨겨왔다. 시간에 대한 우리의 의식을 좁히는 것은 사실 우리의 삶이 깊이 뒤얽혀 있는 과거와 미래의 발전에 대한 책임으로부터 우리를 분리하는 길을 닦는다. 기후의 경우에는 우리가 사실을 직시하면서도 우리의 책임을 부인하는 것이 문제가 아니다. 문제는 시간을 분리함으로써 현실이 시야로부터 흐릿해지고 따라서 과거와 현재의 책임에 관한 질문이 자연스럽게 생겨나지 않는 것이다.

① 우리의 모든 노력이 효과적인 것으로 증명되고 따라서 장려되는
② 충분한 과학적인 증거가 우리에게 제시되어온
③ 미래의 걱정이 현재의 필요보다 더욱 긴급한
④ 우리의 조상들이 다른 시간적 관점을 유지한
⑤ 우리가 사실을 직시하면서도 우리의 책임을 부인하는

문제풀이

우리가 의식을 현재, 과거, 미래로 분리하는 것은 허구이며 자기 지시적인 틀로 이해하는데, 일반적으로 이 방식으로 의식을 구조화하는 것은 충분히 잘 작동하지만 기후 변화의 경우에는 시간을 현재, 과거, 미래로 분명하게 구분하는 것이 사실을 오도하고 우리의 책임이 보이지 않게 가린다고 했다. it is not that 다음에는 이 내용의 반대 내용이 들어가야 하므로 빈칸에는 'we face the facts but then deny our responsibility'가 들어가서 빈칸을 포함한 문장이 ⑤ '기후의 경우에는 우리가 사실을 직시하면서도 우리의 책임을 부인하는 것이 문제가 아니다.'가 되는 것이 적절하다.

이렇게 풀자 'In the case of climate change, however, the sharp division of time into past, present, and future has been desperately misleading and has, most importantly, hidden from view the extent of the responsibility of those of us alive now.(하지만 기후 변화의 경우, 시간을 과거, 현재, 미래로 분명하게 분리하는 것은 심하게 (사실을) 오도해왔으며 가장 중요하게는 지금 살아 있는 우리들의 책임 정도를 시야로부터 숨겨왔다.)'를 통해 이 글이 시간을 현재, 과거, 미래로 구분하는 것이 사실을 제대로 못 보게 만들어 기후 변화의 책임을 부인하게 한다는 이야기를 하고 있다는 것을 알고 빈칸에는 이 글에서 이야기하는 바와 반대되는 내용이 들어가야 한다는 것을 알면 빈칸에 들어갈 말을 쉽게 유추할 수 있다.

어휘·어구

consciousness 의식
fiction 허구
oddly 이상하게
self-referential 자기 지시적인
framework 조직하다, 구조화하다
conventional 전통적인
division 구분, 분할
desperately 극심하게
misleading 호도하는, 오해의 소지가 있는
smooth the way to ~로 가는 길을 닦다
divorce 분리하다
partition 나누다, 분할하다
arise 생겨나다
sufficient 충분한
evidence 증거
urgent 긴급한
deny 부인하다

정답률 

2. ④ 과학적 발견의 장벽을 무너뜨리는 방법

직독/직해

Magical thinking, intellectual insecurity, and confirmation bias are all powerful barriers /
주술적 사고, 지적 불안, 그리고 확증 편향은 모두 강력한 장벽이다 /
to scientific discovery; /
과학적 발견에 대한
they blocked the eyes of generations of astronomers before Copernicus.
그것들은 코페르니쿠스 이전 여러 세대 천문학자들의 눈을 가렸다
But as twenty-first-century researchers have discovered, /
그러나 21세기 연구자들이 발견했듯이 /
these three barriers can all be destroyed / with a simple teaching trick: /
이 세 가지 장벽은 무너뜨릴 수 있다 / 모두 간단한 교수 기법으로 /
transporting our brain to an environment outside our own.
즉 우리의 뇌를 우리 자신 밖의 환경으로 이동시킴으로써
That environment can be a nature preserve many miles from our home, /
그 환경은 우리의 집으로부터 몇 마일 떨어진 자연 보호 구역이 될 수 있다 /
or a computer-simulated Mars, / or any other space /
또는 컴퓨터로 시뮬레이션한 화성 / 또는 다른 어떤 공간도 될 수 있다 /
that our ego doesn't associate directly with our health, social status, and material success.
우리의 자아가 우리의 건강, 사회적 지위, 그리고 물질적 성공과 직접 연관짓지 않는
In that environment, / 그런 환경에서 /
our ego will be less inclined to take the failure of its predictions personally.
우리의 자아는 자기의 예측이 틀린 것에 기분 상하는 경향이 덜할 것이다
Certainly, / our ego may feel a little upset /
분명히 / 우리의 자아는 약간 언짢은 느낌이 들 수도 있다 /
that its guesses about the nature preserve or Mars were wrong, /
그 자연 보호 구역이나 화성에 대한 자기의 추측이 틀렸다는 것에 /
but it was never really that invested in the guesses to begin with.
그러나 애초에 결코 그 추측에 실제로 그다지 관여를 하지 않았다
Why should it care too much about things /
왜 그것(자아)이 그런 것들에 대해 매우 많은 관심을 갖겠는가 /
that have no bearing on its own fame or well-being?
자신의 명성이나 행복과는 관계가 없는
So, / in that happy state of apathy, /
그래서 / 그러한 행복한 무관심 상태에서 /
our ego is less likely to get data manipulative, mentally threatened, or magically minded, /
우리의 자아는 데이터를 조작하거나, 정신적으로 위협받거나, 주술적으로 생각하게 될 가능성이 더 작아지게 되어 /
leaving the rest of our brain free to abandon failed hypotheses and venture new ones.
우리 뇌의 나머지 부분이 자유롭게 실패한 가설을 포기하고 새로운 가설을 과감하게 시도해 보게 한다

주술적 사고, 지적 불안, 그리고 확증 편향은 모두 과학적 발견에 대한 강력한 장벽이며, 그것들은 코페르니쿠스 이전 여러 세대 천문학자들의 눈을 가렸다. 그러나 21세기 연구자들이 발견했듯이, 이 세 가지 장벽은 모두 간단한 교수 기법으로 무너뜨릴 수 있는데, 그것은 우리의 뇌를 우리 자신 밖의 환경으로 이동시키는 것이다. 그 환경은 우리의 집으로부터 몇 마일 떨어진 자연 보호 구역이나, 컴퓨터로 시뮬레이션한 화성이나, 우리의 자아가 우리의 건강, 사회적 지위, 그리고 물질적 성공과 직접 연관짓지 않는 다른 어떤 공간도 될 수 있다. 그런 환경에서, 우리의 자아는 자기의 예측이 틀린 것에 기분 상하는 경향이 덜할 것이다. 분명히, 우리의 자아는 그 자연 보호 구역이나 화성에 대한 자기의 추측이 틀렸다는 것에 약간 언짢은 느낌이 들 수도 있지만, 애초에 결코 그 추측에 실제로 그다지 관여를 하지 않았다. 왜 그것(자아)이 자신의 명성이나 행복과는 관계가 없는 것들에 대해 매우 많은 관심을 갖겠는가? 그래서, 그러한 행복한 무관심 상태에서, 우리의 자아는 데이터를 조작하거나, 정신적으로 위협받거나, 주술적으로 생각하게 될 가능성이 더 작아지게 되어, 우리 뇌의 나머지 부분이 자유롭게 실패한 가설을 포기하고 새로운 가설을 과감하게 시도해 보게 한다.

① 불규칙적인 것을 제거하고 조화를 추구하게
② 나머지 데이터를 재구성하여 오류를 정당화하게
③ 지적 불안을 피하기 위해 장벽을 건설하게
④ 실패한 가설을 포기하고 새로운 가설을 과감하게 시도해 보게
⑤ 주변 환경을 조종하고 기존 아이디어를 지지하게

문제풀이

과학적 발견에 대한 장벽인 주술적 사고, 지적 불안, 확증 편향을 무너뜨리는 방법은 우리의 자아가 우리의 건강, 사회적 지위, 그리고 물질적 성공과 직접 연관짓지 않는 다른 공간으로 이동하는 것인데, 그런 환경에서는 자신의 추측이 틀렸다는 것에 크게 구애받지 않고 자유롭게 사고하게 된다는 내용의 글이다. 따라서 빈칸에는 ④ 'abandon failed hypotheses and venture new ones'가 들어가 빈칸을 포함한 문장이 '그래서, 그러한 행복한 무관심 상태에서, 우리의 자아는 데이터를 조작하거나, 정신적으로 위협받거나, 주술적으로 생각하게 될 가능성이 더 작아지게 되어, 우리 뇌의 나머지 부분이 자유롭게 실패한 가설을 포기하고 새로운 가설을 과감하게 시도해 보게 한다.'가 되어야 한다.

이렇게 풀자 빈칸 완성 문제에서는 'paraphrase(다른 말로 바꿔 표현 하기)'된 어구를 발견하게 되면 쉽게 답을 유추할 수 있다. 단서가 될 수 있는 문장 'transporting our brain to an environment outside our own.(우리의 뇌를 우리 자신 밖의 환경으로 이동시키는 것)'과 'In that environment, our ego will be less inclined to take the failure of its predictions

personally.(그런 환경에서, 우리의 자아는 자기의 예측이 틀린 것에 기분 상하는 경향이 덜할 것이다.)'에서 'predictions(예측)'를 'hypotheses(가설)'로 바꿔 쓴 것이라는 것을 파악하는 것이 중요하다.

《 어휘·어구 》

magical thinking 주술적 사고
insecurity 불안
confirmation bias 확증 편향 (자신의 신념과 일치하는 정보는 받아들이고 신념과 일치하지 않는 정보는 무시하는 경향)
barrier 장벽
blocked the eyes 눈을 가리다
preserve 보호하다
simulate 모의 실험하다
ego 자아
associate ~ with ... ~을 …와 연관시키다
inclined 하는 경향이 있는
prediction 예측
take ~ personally ~에 기분 상하다, ~을 기분 나쁘게 받아들이다
manipulative 조작하다
abandon 포기하다

정답률 44%

3. ① 우리의 믿음이 사실을 해석하는 방식에 영향을 미침

직독/직해

If you are unconvinced /
만약 여러분이 확신하지 못한다면 /
that our beliefs influence how we interpret facts, /
우리의 믿음이 우리가 사실을 해석하는 방식에 영향을 미친다는 것을
consider the example of the "flying horse."
'날고 있는 말'의 사례를 생각해보라
Depictions of galloping horses /
질주하는 말의 묘사는
from prehistoric times up until the mid-1800s /
선사 시대부터 1800년대 중반까지
typically showed horses' legs splayed while galloping, /
질주하는 동안 말의 다리가 벌어져 있는 것을 전형적으로 보여 준다 /
that is, / the front legs reaching far ahead /
즉 / 앞다리를 멀리 앞으로 내딛는 /
as the hind legs stretched far behind.
뒷다리를 뒤로 멀리 뻗은 채
People just "knew" / that's how horses galloped, /
사람들은 그저 '알고 있었다' / 그것이 말이 질주한 방식이라고 /
and that is how they "saw" them galloping.
그리고 그것이 그들이 말이 질주하는 것을 '보았던' 방식이다
Cavemen *saw* them this way, /
동굴 거주인들은 그것들을 이런 식으로 보았다 /
Aristotle *saw* them this way, /
아리스토텔레스도 그것들을 이런 식으로 보았다 /
and so did Victorian gentry.
빅토리아 시대의 상류층도 그랬다
But all of that ended /
그러나 그 모든 것은 끝이 났다 /
when, in 1878, Eadweard Muybridge published a set of twelve pictures /
1878년 Eadweard Muybridge가 열두 개 한 세트로 된 사진을 공개했을 때 /
he had taken of a galloping horse / in the space of less than half a second /
자신이 찍은 질주하는 한 마리 말의 / 0.5초도 안 되는 사이에
using twelve cameras hooked to wire triggers.
와이어 트리거에 연결된 열두 대의 카메라를 사용하여
Muybridge's photos showed clearly /
Muybridge의 사진은 분명히 보여 주었다 /
that a horse goes completely airborne in the third step of the gallop /
말이 보통 질주의 세 번째 스텝에서 완전히 공중에 뜬 채 가는 것을 /
with its legs *collected* beneath it, not splayed.
그것의 다리들이 벌어진 상태가 아니라, 밑에 '모아진' 상태로
It is called the moment of suspension.
그것은 부유의 순간이라고 불린다
Now even kids draw horses galloping this way.
지금은 아이들도 이런 식으로 질주하는 말을 그린다

만약 여러분이 우리의 믿음이 우리가 사실을 해석하는 방식에 영향을 미친다는 것을 확신하지 못한다면, '날고 있는 말'의 사례를 생각해보라. 선사 시대부터 1800년대 중반까지 질주하는 말의 묘사는 질주하는 동안 말의 다리가 벌어져 있는 것을, 즉 뒷다리를 뒤로 멀리 뻗은 채 앞다리를 멀리 앞으로 내딛는 모습을 전형적으로 보여 준다. 사람들은 그것이 말이 질주한 방식이라고 그저 '알고 있었고', 그것이 그들이 말이 질주하는 것을 '보았던' 방식이다. 동굴 거주인들은 그것들을 이런 식으로 '보았고', 아리스토텔레스도 그것들을 이런 식으로 '보았으며', 빅토리아 시대의 상류층도 그랬다. 그러나 그 모든 것은 1878년 Eadweard Muybridge가 와이어 트리거에 연결된 열두 대의 카메라를 사용하여 0.5초도 안 되는 사이에 자신이 찍은 열두 개 한 세트로 된, 질주하는 한 마리 말의 사진을 공개했을 때 끝이 났다. Muybridge의 사진은 말이 보통 질주의 세 번째 스텝에서 그것의 다리들이 벌어진 상태가 아니라, 밑에 '모아진' 상태로 완전히 공중에 뜬 채 가는 것을 분명히 보여 주었다. 그것은 부유의 순간이라고 불린다. 지금은 아이들도 이런 식으로 질주하는 말을 그린다.

① 우리의 믿음이 우리가 사실을 해석하는 방식에 영향을 미친다
② 우리가 보는 것은 우리의 과거 기억의 환상이다
③ 사진조차도 잘못된 시각적 인식을 초래할 수 있다
④ 좋고 나쁨을 판단하는 기준이 없다
⑤ 우리는 저항할 수 없는 증거에도 불구하고 직관을 고수한다

문제풀이

이 글은 말의 질주하는 모습을 선사 시대부터 1800년대 중반까지는 질주하는 동안 말의 다리가 벌어져 있다고 믿고 모든 사람들이 그렇게 보았으나, 1878년 Muybridge의 사진은 말이 보통 질주의 세 번째 스텝에서 그 다리를 모아진 상태로 완전히 공중에 뜬 채 가는 것을 보여 주었고, 지금은 아이들도 이런 식으로 질주하는 말을 그린다는 사례를 통해 사람들은 우리가 믿는대로 본다는 내용이다. 따라서 빈칸에는 '① our beliefs influence how we interpret facts'가 들어가 빈칸을 포함한 문장이 '만약 여러분이 우리의 믿음이 우리가 사실을 해석하는 방식에 영향을 미친다는 것을 확신하지 못한다면, '날고 있는 말'의 사례를 생각해보라.'가 되어야 한다.

구조 다시보기

주제	우리의 믿음이 우리가 사실을 해석하는 방식에 영향을 미침
예시 1	1800년대 중반까지는 말이 질주할 때 다리를 벌린다고 믿고 그렇게 봄
예시 2	1878년 사진 발표 후에는 말이 질주할 때 다리를 모은다는 것을 알게 되고 아이들도 그렇게 그림

《 어휘·어구 》

unconvinced 확신하지 않는
interpret 해석하다
depiction 서술
prehistoric 선사 시대의
hind legs 뒤쪽의 다리
suspension 공중에 떠 있기, 부유(浮遊), 일시적 정지

정답률 48%

4. ④ 의상 디자이너에 대한 인식 변화

직독/직해

There was nothing modern / about the idea of men making women's clothes /
현대적인 것이 전혀 없는데 / 남자가 여성복을 만든다는 생각에는 /
— we saw them doing it / for centuries in the past.
그들이 그 일을 하는 것을 보았다 / 우리는 과거 수 세기 동안
In the old days, / however, / the client was always primary /
옛날에는 / 그러나 / 항상 고객 위주였다 /
and her tailor was an obscure craftsman, / perhaps talented but perhaps not.
그리고 그녀의 재단사는 무명의 장인이었는데 / 아마 재능이 있었겠지만 없었을지도 모른다
She had her own ideas like any patron, / there were no fashion plates, /
그녀는 여느 후원자처럼 자신의 생각이 있었고 / 유행하는 옷의 본이 없었으며 /
and the tailor was simply at her service, /
그리고 재단사는 그저 그녀의 생각에 따랐다 /
perhaps with helpful suggestions / about what others were wearing.
아마 도움이 되는 제안을 가지고 / 다른 사람들이 입고 있는 것에 관한
Beginning in the late nineteenth century, /
19세기 후반에 시작하여 /
with the hugely successful rise of the artistic male couturier, /
예술적인 남성 고급 여성복 디자이너의 매우 성공적인 부흥과 함께 /
it was the designer / who became celebrated, /
바로 디자이너였다 / 유명해진 것은 /
and the client elevated / by his inspired attention.
그리고 고객은 치켜세워졌다 / 그의 영감 어린 관심에 의해
In a climate of admiration / for male artists and their female creations, /
경탄의 분위기에서 / 남성 예술가와 여성을 위한 그들의 창작물에 대한 /
the dress-designer first flourished / as the same sort of creator.
의상 디자이너는 처음으로 번영했다 / 같은 종류의 창작자로서
Instead of the old rule that dressmaking is a craft, /
의상 제작은 공예라는 옛 규칙 대신에 /
a modern connection between dress-design and art /
의상 디자인과 예술 간의 현대적 연결이 /
was invented / that had not been there before.
만들어졌다 / 예전에는 없던

남자가 여성복을 만든다는 생각에는 현대적인 것이 전혀 없는데, 우리는 과거 수 세기 동안 그들이 그 일을 하는 것을 보았다. 그러나 옛날에는 항상 고객 위주였고 그녀의 재단사는 무명의 장인이었는데, 아마 재능이 있었겠지만 없었을지도 모른다. 그녀는 여느 후원자처럼 자신의 생각이 있었고, 유행하는 옷의 본이 없었으며, 재단사는 아마 다른 사람들이 입고 있는 것에 관한 도움이 되는 제안을 가지고 그저 그녀의 생각에 따랐다. 예술적인 남성 고급 여성복 디자이너의 매우 성공적인 부흥과 함께 19세기 후반에 시작하여, 유명해진 것은 바로 디자이너였고, 고객은 그의 영감 어린 관심에 의해 치켜세워졌다. 남성 예술가와 여성을 위한 그들의 창작물에 대한 경탄의 분위기에서, 의상 디자이너는 처음으로 같은 종류의 창작자로서 번영했다. 의상 제작은 공예라는 옛 규칙 대신에, 예전에는 없던 의상 디자인과 예술 간의 현대적 연결이 만들어졌다.

① 패스트 패션을 주도하는 수익성이 있는 산업
② 마케팅 기술에 대한 광범위한 존중
③ 전통 디자인을 보존하는 공공 기관
④ 의상 디자인과 예술 간의 현대적 연결
⑤ 적정 가격의 의류를 만들어내기 위한 효율적인 체계

문제풀이

과거 수 세기 동안 재단사는 고객의 생각에 따라 옷을 만드는 무명의 장인이었지만, 19세기 후반부터 예술적인 남성 고급 여성복 디자이너가 매우 성공적으로 부흥하면서, 남성 예술가와 창작물에 대한 경탄의 분위기 속에서 그들이 창작자로서 번영했다고 했다. 따라서 빈칸에는 ④ 'a modern connection between dress-design and art'가 들어가서 빈칸을 포함한 문장이 '의상 제작은 공예라는 옛 규칙 대신에, 예전에는 없던 의상 디자인과 예술 간의 현대적 연결이 만들어졌다.'가 되는 것이 적절하다.

이렇게 풀자 'Beginning in the late nineteenth century, with the hugely successful rise of the artistic male couturier, it was the designer who became celebrated, and the client elevated by his inspired attention.(예술적인 남성 고급 여성복 디자이너의 매우 성공적인 부흥과 함께 19세기 후반에 시작하여, 유명해진 것은 바로 디자이너였고, 고객은 그의 영감 어린

관심에 의해 치켜세워졌다.)'과 'In a climate of admiration for male artists and their female creations, the dress-designer first flourished as the same sort of creator.(남성 예술가와 여성을 위한 그들의 창작물에 대한 경탄의 분위기에서, 의상 디자이너는 처음으로 같은 종류의 창작자로서 번영했다.)'를 통해 현대 의상 디자이너의 위상을 이해하면 쉽게 답을 찾을 수 있다.

어휘·어구

client 고객
primary 위주의, 우선의, 주요한
tailor 재단사
craftsman 장인
talented 재능 있는
fashion plate 유행하는 옷의 본
at one's service ~의 생각을 따르는
celebrated 유명한
elevated 치켜세워진
inspired 영감을 받은
flourish 번영하다, 번성하다
profitable 수익성이 있는
industry 산업
widespread 널리 퍼진
institution 기관
preserve 보존하다
efficient 효율적인
affordable (가격 등이) 알맞은

5. ② 제조업자들의 혁신 과정 설계 방식

직독/직해

Manufacturers design their innovation processes / around the way /
제조업자들은 자신들의 혁신 과정을 설계한다 / 방식에 맞춰 /

they think the process works.
그들이 생각하기에 그 과정이 작동되는

The vast majority of manufacturers still think /
대다수의 제조업자들은 여전히 생각한다 /

that product development and service development are always done /
제품 개발과 서비스 개발은 항상 이루어지며 /

by manufacturers, /
제조업자들에 의해 /

and that their job is always to find a need / and fill it /
그리고 자신들의 일은 항상 필요를 발견하고 / 그리고 그것을 채우는 것이라고 /

rather than to sometimes find and commercialize an innovation /
때때로 혁신을 발견하고 상업화하기보다는 /

that lead users have already developed.
리드유저가 이미 개발한

Accordingly, / manufacturers have set up market-research departments /
따라서 / 제조업자들은 시장 조사 부서를 설치해 왔다 /

to explore the needs of users in the target market, /
표적 시장에서 사용자들의 필요를 탐구하기 위한 /

product-development groups / to think up suitable products to address those needs, /
(그리고) 제품 개발 집단을 (설치해 왔다) / 그러한 필요에 대처하기에 적절한 제품을 고안하기 위한 /

and so forth. 및 기타 등등을 (설치해 왔다)

The needs and prototype solutions of lead users / — if encountered at all — /
리드유저의 필요와 시제품 해결책은 / 만약 정말 마주치기라도 한다면 /

are typically rejected / as outliers of no interest.
대체로 거부된다 / 전혀 흥미롭지 않은 아웃라이어로

Indeed, / when lead users' innovations do enter a firm's product line /
정말로 / 리드유저의 혁신이 그 회사의 제품 라인에 정말로 도입된다고 해도 /

— and they have been shown /
그리고 그것들이 입증된다고 해도 /

to be the actual source of many major innovations for many firms — /
많은 회사의 여러 주요 혁신의 실질적인 원천이 되는 것으로 /

they typically arrive with a lag / and by an unusual and unsystematic route.
그것은 대체로 지연된 채 도달한다 / 그리고 이례적이고 비체계적인 경로를 통해

제조업자들은 그들이 생각하기에 그 과정이 작동되는 방식에 맞춰 자신들의 혁신 과정을 설계한다. 대다수의 제조업자들은 제품 개발과 서비스 개발은 항상 제조업자들에 의해 이루어지며, 자신들의 일은 때때로 리드유저(시장 경향을 선도하는 사용자)가 이미 개발한 혁신을 발견하고 상업화하기보다는 항상 필요를 발견하고 그것을 채우는 것이라고 여전히 생각한다. 따라서 제조업자들은 표적 시장에서 사용자들의 필요를 탐구하기 위한 시장 조사 부서, 그러한 필요에 대처하기에 적절한 제품을 고안하기 위한 제품 개발 집단 및 기타 등등을 설치해 왔다. 리드유저의 필요와 시제품 해결책은, 만약 정말 맞닥뜨리기라도 한다면, 대체로 전혀 흥미롭지 않은 아웃라이어로 거부된다. 정말로, 리드유저의 혁신이 그 회사의 제품 라인에 정말로 도입된다고 해도 그리고 그것은 많은 회사의 여러 주요 혁신의 실질적인 원천으로서 입증된다고 해도 그것들은 대체로 지연된 채 그리고 이례적이고 비체계적인 경로를 통해 도착한다.

① 리드유저가 간과하는 경향이 있던
② 리드유저가 이미 개발한
③ 리드유저가 시장에서 맞닥뜨린
④ 다른 회사들이 자주 실행한
⑤ 사용자와 회사 둘 다 소중하게 여긴

문제풀이

제조업자들은 제품 개발과 서비스 개발은 제조업자들에 의해 이루어지며 그들이 (주도적으로) 시장을 분석하여 (소비자의) 필요를 발견하고 그것을 채우는 것으로 생각한다는 내용 다음에, 리드유저의 필요와 시제품 해결책은 중요하지 않은 것으로 거부되거나, 만일 제품 라인에 들어가게 된다고 하더라도 지연되고, 이례적이고 비체계적인 경로를 통해 이루어지게 마련이라는 내용이다. 이 문제에 나와 있는 rather than처럼 '부정'의 의미에 가까운 어구가 나올 경우에는 빈칸에 들어갈 내용이 글의 전반적인 요지와는 반대라는 점을 유의해야 한다. 따라서 빈칸에는 ② 'lead users have already developed'가 들어가서 빈칸을 포함한 문장이 '대다수의 제조업자들은 제품 개발과 서비스 개발은 항상 제조업자들에 의해 이루어지며, 자신들의 일은 때때로 리드유저가 이미 개발한 혁신을 발견하고 상업화하기보다는 항상 필요를 발견하고 그것을 채우는 것이라고 여전히 생각한다.'가 되는 것이 가장 적절하다.

이렇게 풀자 'The needs and prototype solutions of lead users — if encountered at all — are typically rejected as outliers of no interest.(리드유저의 필요와 시제품 해결책은, 만약 정말 마주치기라도 한다면, 대체로 전혀 흥미롭지 않은 아웃라이어로 거부된다.)'와 'Indeed, when lead users' innovations do enter a firm's product line — and they have been shown to be the actual source of many major innovations for many firms — they typically arrive with a lag and by an unusual and unsystematic route.(정말로, 리드유저의 혁신이 그 회사의 제품 라인에 정말로 도입된다고 해도 그리고 그것은 많은 회사의 여러 주요 혁신의 실질적인 원천으로서 입증된다고 해도 그것들은 대체로 지연된 채 그리고 이례적이고 비체계적인 경로를 통해 도착한다.)'를 통해 제조업자가 리드유저에 대해 어떻게 생각하는지를 알면 빈칸에 들어갈 말을 쉽게 유추해낼 수 있다.

어휘·어구

manufacturer 제조업자
innovation 혁신
the vast majority of 대다수의 ~
commercialize 상업화하다
accordingly 그래서, 따라서
address 대처하다
prototype 시제품, 시험 삼아 만들어 본 제품
encounter 맞닥뜨리다
lead user 리드유저, 시장 트렌드를 선도하는 사용자
outlier 아웃라이어, 해당 범위에서 많이 벗어나는 것
unsystematic 비체계적인
overlook 간과하다

정답률 36%

6. ② 음악 작품에서 전개부

직독/직해

Development can get very complicated and fanciful.
전개부는 매우 복잡하면서도 멋질 수가 있다

A fugue by Johann Sebastian Bach illustrates /
Johann Sebastian Bach의 푸가는 보여준다 /

how far this process could go, /
이 과정이 얼마나 효과를 보일 수 있을지를/

when a single melodic line, sometimes just a handful of notes, / was all /
하나의 멜로디 라인, 때로는 단지 몇 개 안 되는 음표가 / 전부였을 때 /

that the composer needed to create a brilliant work /
그 작곡가가 훌륭한 작품을 만들기 위해 필요한 /

containing lots of intricate development within a coherent structure.
통일성 있는 구조 내에서 많은 복잡한 전개부를 포함하는

Ludwig van Beethoven's famous Fifth Symphony provides /
Ludwig van Beethoven의 유명한 5번 교향곡은 제공한다 /

an exceptional example /
이례적일 정도로 뛰어난 사례를 /

of how much mileage a classical composer can get /
클래식 작곡가가 얼마나 많은 이익을 얻어낼 수 있는지에 대한 /

out of a few notes and a simple rhythmic tapping.
몇 개의 음표와 단순하며 리듬감 있는 두드림으로

The opening da-da-da-DUM that everyone has heard somewhere or another /
모든 사람이 어디에선가 들어본 시작 부분의 빠-바-바-밤은 /

appears in an incredible variety of ways /
엄청나게 다양한 방식으로 나타난다 /

throughout not only the opening movement, /
시작 악장뿐만 아니라 /

but the remaining three movements, /
남은 3악장 내내 /

like a kind of motto or a connective thread.
일종의 반복 악구나 연결 끈처럼

Just as we don't always see the intricate brushwork /
우리가 복잡한 붓놀림을 항상 볼 수 있는 것이 아니듯이 /

that goes into the creation of a painting, /
그림 작품 하나를 완성하는 데 들인 /

we may not always notice /
우리는 항상 알아보지는 못할 수도 있다 /

how Beethoven keeps finding fresh uses for his motto /
어떻게 Beethoven이 그의 반복 악구(모토)의 참신한 사용을 계속해서 발견하는지 /

or how he develops his material into a large, cohesive statement.
또는 어떻게 그가 그의 (음악) 재료를 거대하고 응집력 있는 진술로 전개하는지를

But a lot of the enjoyment / we get from that mighty symphony /
하지만 즐거움의 많은 부분은 / 그 강력한 교향곡에서 우리가 얻는 /

stems from the inventiveness behind it, /
그 이면의 독창성에서 생겨난다 /

the impressive development of musical ideas.
즉 음악적 아이디어의 인상적인 전개에서

전개부는 매우 복잡하면서도 멋질 수가 있다. Johann Sebastian Bach의 푸가는 하나의 멜로디 라인, 때로는 단지 몇 개 안 되는 음표가 그 작곡가가 통일성 있는 구조 내에서 많은 복잡한 전개부를 포함하는 훌

륭한 작품을 만들기 위해 필요한 전부였을 때, 이 과정이 얼마나 효과를 보일 수 있을지를 보여준다. Ludwig van Beethoven의 유명한 5번 교향곡은 클래식 작곡가가 몇 개의 음표와 단순하며 리듬감 있는 두드림으로 얼마나 많은 이익을 얻어낼 수 있는지에 대한 이례적일 정도로 뛰어난 사례를 제공한다. 모든 사람이 어디에선가 들어본 시작 부분의 빠-바-바-밤은 일종의 반복 악구나 연결 끈처럼, 시작 악장뿐만 아니라 남은 3악장 내내 놀라울 정도로 다양한 방식으로 나타난다. 우리가 그림 작품 하나를 완성하는 데 들인 복잡한 붓놀림을 항상 볼 수 있는 것이 아니듯이, 우리는 어떻게 Beethoven이 그의 반복 악구(모토)의 참신한 사용을 계속해서 발견하는지 또는 어떻게 그가 그의 (음악) 재료를 크고 거대하고 응집력 있는 진술로 전개하는지를 항상 알아보지는 못할 수도 있다. 하지만 그 강력한 교향곡에서 우리가 얻는 즐거움의 많은 부분은 그 이면의 독창성, 즉 음악적 아이디어의 인상적인 전개에서 생겨난다.

① 작곡가의 음악적 아이디어를 모순되게 만든다
② 놀라울 정도로 다양한 방식으로 나타난다
③ 광범위한 음악적 지식을 창의적으로 제공한다
④ 구조 내에서 상당히 차분한 상태를 유지한다
⑤ 자기 자신의 즐거움과 깊이 관련된다

문제풀이

Bach의 푸가가 하나의 멜로디 라인으로 복잡하게 전개되는 곡을 만들 수 있다는 것을 보여주었다는 예와 Beethoven의 5번 교향곡이 소수의 음표와 단순하며 리듬감 있는 두드림을 다양하게 전개하여 많은 이익을 얻어냈다는 예를 통해 시작 부분의 단순한 음이 나머지에서 반복되어 다양하게 나타날 수 있다는 것을 알 수 있다. 따라서 간단하고 단순한 음이라고 볼 수 있는 시작 부분의 빠-바-바-밤이 시작 악장뿐만 아니라 나머지 3악장 내내 엄청나게 다양한 방식으로 나타난다는 내용이 되어야 하므로, 빈칸에는 ② 'appears in an incredible variety of ways'가 들어가서 빈칸을 포함한 문장이 '모든 사람이 어디에선가 들어본 시작 부분의 빠-바-바-밤은 일종의 반복 악구나 연결 끈처럼, 시작 악장뿐만 아니라 남은 3악장 내내 놀라울 정도로 다양한 방식으로 나타난다.'가 되는 것이 적절하다.

구조 다시보기

주제	전개부는 복잡하면서 멋질 수 있음
사례 1	Bach의 푸가는 하나의 멜로디 라인이 있으면 복잡하게 전개되는 곡을 만들 수 있음을 보여줌
사례 2	Beethven의 5번 교향곡은 소수의 음표와 단순하며 리듬감 있는 두드림으로 많은 이익을 얻어냄
결론	강력한 교향곡에서 얻는 즐거움의 많은 부분은 음악적 아이디어의 인상적인 전개에서 생겨남

어휘·어구

development 전개부, 주제나 곡상(曲想)을 여러 각도에서 발전시킨 부분
complicated 복잡한
fanciful 멋진, 기발한
illustrate 보여주다
a handful of 소수의
note 음표
brilliant 훌륭한
exceptional 이례적일 정도로 우수한
mileage 이익
movement 악장
motto 반복 악구
material 제재
cohesive 응집력 있는, 결합시키는
stem from ~에서 생겨나다
inventiveness 독창적임
impressive 인상적인
contradictory 모순되는, 모순된
incredible 믿기 힘든
extensive 광범위한
fairly 상당히
associated 관련된

정답률 50%

7. ① 공유지 문제 해결책

직독/직해

Elinor Ostrom found / that there are several factors /
Elinor Ostrom은 알아냈다 / 몇 가지 요인이 있다는 것을 /
critical to bringing about stable institutional solutions /
안정적인 제도적 해결책을 가져오는 데 중요한 /
to the problem of the commons.
공유지의 문제에 대한
She pointed out, / for instance, /
그녀는 지적했다 / 예를 들면 /
that the actors affected by the rules /
영향을 받는 행위자들에게 /
for the use and care of resources /
자원의 사용 및 관리 규칙의 .
must have the right to participate in decisions /
결정에 참여할 권리가 있어야 한다고 /
to change the rules. 규칙을 바꾸는
For that reason, / 그러한 이유 때문에 /
the people who monitor and control the behavior of users /
이용자의 행동을 감시하고 통제하는 사람도 /
should also be users /
사용자여야 한다 /
and/or have been given a mandate by all users.
이고/이거나 모든 사용자에 의해서 위임을 받았어야 한다
This is a significant insight, / as it shows /
이것은 중요한 통찰인데 / 그것이 보여주기 때문이다 /
that prospects are poor for a centrally directed solution /
중앙 (정부) 통제적 해결책의 전망은 밝지가 않다는 것을 /
to the problem of the commons coming from a state power /
국가 권력에서 나오는 공유지 문제에 대한 /
in comparison with a local solution /
지역적인 해결책에 비해 /
for which users assume personal responsibility.
사용자가 개인적 책임을 지는
Ostrom also emphasizes /
Ostrom은 또한 강조한다 /
the importance of democratic decision processes /
민주적 의사결정 과정의 중요성을 /
and that all users must be given access to local forums /
그리고 모든 사용자에게 지역 포럼에 접근할 권한이 주어져야 한다고 /
for solving problems and conflicts among themselves.
그들 사이의 문제와 갈등을 해결하기 위한
Political institutions at central, regional, and local levels /
중앙, 지방 및 지역 차원의 정치적인 기관들은 /
must allow users / to devise their own regulations /
사용자가 ~할 수 있도록 해야 한다 / 자신들만의 규정을 고안하도록 /
and independently ensure observance.
독립적으로 준수할 수 있도록

Elinor Ostrom은 공유지의 문제에 대한 안정적인 제도적 해결책을 가져오는 데 중요한 몇 가지 요인이 있다는 것을 알아냈다. 예를 들면, 그녀는 자원의 사용 및 관리 규칙의 영향을 받는 행위자들에게 규칙을 변경하는 결정에 참여할 권리가 있어야 한다고 지적했다. 그러한 이유 때문에 이용자의 행동을 감시하고 통제하는 사람도 사용자이고, 사용자이거나 모든 사용자에 의해서 위임을 받았어야 한다. 이것은 중요한 통찰인데, 사용자가 개인적 책임을 지는 지역적인 해결책에 비해 국가 권력에서 나오는 공유지 문제에 대한 중앙 (정부) 통제적 해결책의 전망은 밝지가 않다는 것을 그것이 보여주기 때문이다. Ostrom은 또한 민주적 의사결정 과정의 중요성과 모든 사용자에게 그들 사이의 문제와 갈등을 해결하기 위한 지역 포럼에 접근할 권한이 주어져야 한다고 강조한다. 중앙, 지방 및 지역 차원의 정치적인 기관들은 사용자가 자신들만의 규정을 고안하고 독립적으로 준수할 수 있도록 해야 한다.

① 규칙을 바꾸는 결정에 참여할
② 자원에 대한 개인의 소유권을 주장할
③ 자신의 이익을 최대화하기 위해 그 자원을 이용할
④ 공동의 자원에 대한 자유로운 접근 권한을 요구할
⑤ 자신의 장점에 기반한 적당한 분배를 요청할

문제풀이

공유지 문제는 중앙 (정부) 통제적 해결책보다는 사용자 스스로 규정을 고안하고 준수할 수 있도록 해야 한다고 했으므로, 빈칸에는 ① 'participate in decisions to change the rules'가 들어가서 빈칸을 포함한 문장이 '예를 들면, 그녀는 자원의 사용 및 관리 규칙의 영향을 받는 행위자들에게 규칙을 바꾸는 결정에 참여할 권리가 있어야 한다고 지적했다.'가 되는 것이 적절하다.

이렇게 풀자 'Ostrom also emphasizes the importance of democratic decision processes and that all users must be given access to local forums for solving problems and conflicts among themselves.(Ostrom은 또한 민주적 의사결정 과정의 중요성과 모든 사용자에게 그들 사이의 문제와 갈등을 해결하기 위한 지역 포럼에 접근할 권한이 주어져야 한다고 강조한다.)'와 'Political institutions at central, regional, and local levels must allow users to devise their own regulations and independently ensure observance.(중앙, 지방 및 지역 차원의 정치적인 기관들은 사용자가 자신들만의 규정을 고안하고 독립적으로 준수할 수 있도록 해야 한다.)'를 통해 사용자 스스로 규정에 관한 결정에 접근할 권한을 주어야 한다는 이야기를 하고 있다는 것을 알면 빈칸에 들어갈 말을 추론해낼 수 있다.

어휘·어구

critical 중요한
bring about ~을 가져오다
stable 안정적인
institutional 제도적인
solution 해결책
point out ~을 지적하다
actor 행위자
monitor 감시하다
significant 중요한
insight 통찰(력)
prospect 전망
centrally directed 중앙 (정부) 통제적인
state power 국가 권력
in comparison with ~에 비해서
assume (권력·책임을) 맡다
emphasize 강조하다
access 접근권
political institution 정치 기관
devise 고안하다
regulation 규정
independently 독립적으로
observance 준수
ownership 소유(권)
profit 이익
communal 공동의
distribution 분배
merit 장점

8. ② 역사적 통찰의 특징

직독/직해

Precision and determinacy are a necessary requirement /
정확성과 확정성은 필수 요구조건이다 /
for all meaningful scientific debate, /
모든 의미 있는 과학 토론에 있어서 /
and progress in the sciences is, / to a large extent, /
그리고 과학에서의 발전은 ~이다 / 상당 부분 /
the ongoing process of achieving ever greater precision.
훨씬 더 높은 정확성을 달성하는 계속 진행 중인 과정이다
But historical representation puts a premium /

하지만 역사적 진술은 중요시하는데 /

on a proliferation of representations, /
진술의 증식을 /

hence / not on the refinement of one representation /
따라서 / 이는 한 가지 진술의 정제가 아닌 /

but on the production of an ever more varied set of representations.
훨씬 더 다양한 진술 집합의 생성을 (중시하는 것이다)

Historical insight is not a matter /
역사적 통찰은 문제가 아닌 /

of a continuous "narrowing down" of previous options, /
이전에 선택한 것들을 지속해서 '좁혀 가는 것'의 /

not of an approximation of the truth, /
진리에 근접함의 문제가 아닌 /

but, on the contrary, / 그와는 반대로 /

is an "explosion" of possible points of view.
가능한 관점들의 '폭발적 증가'이다

It therefore aims at the unmasking /
따라서 그것은 정체를 드러내는 것을 목표로 한다 /

of previous illusions of determinacy and precision /
확정성과 정확성에 대해 이전에 가진 환상의 /

by the production of new and alternative representations, /
새롭고 대안적인 진술의 생성에 의해 /

rather than at achieving truth / by a careful analysis /
진실에 도달하는 것이 아니라 / 신중한 분석에 의해 /

of what was right and wrong /
무엇이 옳고 틀렸는지에 대한 /

in those previous representations.
이전의 진술에서

And from this perspective, /
그리고 이런 관점에서 보자면 /

the development of historical insight /
역사적 통찰의 발전은 /

may indeed be regarded by the outsider /
외부인에게 진정 여겨질 수도 있다 /

as a process of creating ever more confusion, /
훨씬 더 많은 혼란을 만들어내는 과정으로 /

a continuous questioning of certainty and precision /
확실성과 정확성에 대한 지속적인 의문 제기로 /

seemingly achieved already, /
이미 성취한 것처럼 보이는 /

rather than, as in the sciences, /
과학에서처럼 /

an ever greater approximation to the truth.
진리에 훨씬 더 많이 근접함보다는

정확성과 확정성은 모든 의미 있는 과학 토론에 있어서 필수 요구조건이며, 과학에서의 발전은 상당 부분, 훨씬 더 높은 정확성을 달성하는 계속 진행 중인 과정이다. 하지만 역사적 진술은 진술의 증식을 중요시하는데, 따라서 이는 한 가지 진술의 정제가 아닌, 훨씬 더 다양한 진술 집합의 생성을 중시하는 것이다. 역사적 통찰은 이전에 선택한 것들을 지속해서 '좁혀 가는 것'의 문제, 즉 진리에 근접함의 문제가 아닌, 그와는 반대로 가능한 관점들의 '폭발적 증가'이다. 따라서 그것은 이전의 진술에서 무엇이 옳고 틀렸는지에 대한 신중한 분석에 의해 진실에 도달하는 것이 아니라, 새롭고 대안적인 진술의 생성에 의해 확정성과 정확성에 대해 이전에 가진 환상의 정체를 드러내는 것을 목표로 한다. 그리고 이런 관점에서 보자면, 역사적 통찰의 발전은 과학에서처럼 진리에 훨씬 더 많이 근접함보다는, 훨씬 더 많은 혼란을 만들어내는 과정, 즉 이미 성취한 것처럼 보이는 확실성과 정확성에 대한 지속적인 의문 제기로 외부인에게 진정 여겨질 수도 있다.

① 역사적인 진술을 평가하는 기준
② 이미 성취한 것처럼 보이는 확실성과 정확성
③ 어떤 사건에 대한 대안이 되는 해석의 가능성
④ 역사 저술에서 많은 관점 공존
⑤ 수집된 역사적 증거의 정확성과 신뢰성

문제풀이

과학에서는 정확성과 확정성이 중요한 반면 역사적 진술에서는 한 가지 진술의 정제가 아닌 훨씬 더 다양한 진술 집합의 생성을 중시한다고 하면서, 역사적 진술에서는 새롭고 대안적인 진술의 생성에 의해 확정성과 정확성에 대해 이전에 가진 환상의 정체를 드러내는 것이 목표라고 했다. 따라서 빈칸에는 ② 'certainty and precision seemingly achieved already'가 들어가서 빈칸을 포함한 문장이 '그리고 이런 관점에서 보자면, 역사적 통찰의 발전은 과학에서처럼 진리에 훨씬 더 많이 근접함보다는, 훨씬 더 많은 혼란을 만들어내는 과정, 즉 이미 성취한 것처럼 보이는 확실성과 정확성에 대한 지속적인 의문 제기로 외부인에게 진정 여겨질 수도 있다.'가 되는 것이 적절하다.

구조 다시보기

도입	과학에서는 정확성과 확정성이 필수 요구조건임
대조	역사적 진술은 한 가지 진술의 정제가 아닌 다양한 진술의 집합의 생성을 중시함
부연	역사적 통찰은 가능한 관점들의 폭발적 증가임
결론	역사적 통찰은 이미 성취한 것의 확실성과 정확성에 대해 이미 가진 환상의 정체를 드러내는 것이 목표임

어휘·어구

precision 정확성
determinacy 확정성
requirement 요구조건
meaningful 의미 있는, 중요한
debate 토론
progress 진보, 발전
to a large extent 상당 부분
ongoing 계속 진행 중인
representation 진술, 설명
put a premium on ~을 중시하다
refinement 정제, 개선
narrow down ~을 좁히다
approximation 근접
explosion 폭발적 증가
unmask 정체를 드러내다
illusion 환상, 착각
be regarded as ~으로 여겨지다
questioning 의문 제기
evaluate 평가하다
criterion 표준
alternative 대안이 되는
coexistence 공존
multiple 많은, 다수의
viewpoint 관점
reliability 신뢰성
evidence 증거

정답률 55%

9. ① 뇌 발달 과정

직독직해

Thanks to newly developed neuroimaging technology, /
새로 개발된 신경 촬영 기술 덕분에 /

we now have access to the specific brain changes /
우리는 이제 특정한 뇌 변화에 접근할 수 있게 되었다 /

that occur during learning.
학습하는 중에 발생하는

Even though all of our brains contain the same basic structures, /
비록 우리들의 뇌 모두는 같은 기본 구조로 되어 있더라도 /

our neural networks are as unique as our fingerprints.
우리의 신경망은 우리의 지문만큼이나 독특하다

The latest developmental neuroscience research has shown /
가장 최근의 발달 신경과학 연구는 보여준다 /

that the brain is much more malleable /
뇌가 훨씬 더 순응성이 있다는 것을 /

throughout life / 일생 동안 /

than previously assumed; /
이전에 가정했던 것보다 /

it develops / in response to its own processes, /
그것은 발달한다 / 자기 자신의 처리 과정에 반응하여 /

to its immediate and distant "environments," /
자신에게 인접한 '환경'과 멀리 떨어진 '환경'에 /

and to its past and current situations.
그리고 자신의 과거와 현재 상황에 (반응하여)

The brain seeks to create meaning /
뇌는 의미를 창조하려고 한다 /

through establishing or refining existing neural networks.
기존의 신경망을 확립하거나 개선하는 것을 통해

When we learn a new fact or skill, /
우리가 새로운 사실이나 기술을 학습할 때 /

our neurons communicate /
우리의 뉴런들은 소통한다 /

to form networks of connected information.
연결된 정보망을 형성하기 위해

Using this knowledge or skill /
이런 지식이나 기술을 사용하는 것은 /

results in structural changes /
구조적 변화를 초래한다 /

to allow similar future impulses /
앞으로 유사한 자극이 ~할 수 있게 하는 /

to travel more quickly and efficiently / than others.
더 빠르고 효율적으로 이동할 / 다른 것들보다

High-activity synaptic connections are stabilized and strengthened, /
고활동성 시냅스 연결이 안정화되고 강화되지만 /

while connections with relatively low use /
상대적으로 적게 사용되는 연결은 /

are weakened / 약해진다 /

and eventually pruned.
그리고 결국에는 잘린다

In this way, / our brains are sculpted /
이런 식으로 / 우리의 뇌는 형상이 만들어진다 /

by our own history of experiences.
우리의 경험의 이력에 의해

새로 개발된 신경 촬영 기술 덕분에, 우리는 이제 학습하는 중에 발생하는 특정한 뇌 변화에 접근할 수 있게 되었다. 비록 우리들의 뇌 모두는 같은 기본 구조로 되어 있더라도, 우리의 신경망은 우리의 지문만큼이나 독특하다. 가장 최근의 발달 신경과학 연구는 뇌가 이전에 가정했던 것보다 일생 훨씬 더 순응성이 있다는 것을 보여주며, 그것은 자기 자신의 처리 과정에, 자신에게 인접한 '환경'과 멀리 떨어진 '환경'에, 자신의 과거와 현재 상황에 반응하여 발달한다. 뇌는 기존의 신경망을 확립하거나 개선하는 것을 통해 의미를 창조하려고 한다. 우리가 새로운 사실이나 기술을 학습할 때, 우리의 뉴런들은 연결된 정보망을 형성하기 위해 소통한다. 이런 지식이나 기술을 사용하는 것은 앞으로 유사한 자극이 다른 것들보다 더 빠르고 효율적으로 이동할 수 있게 하는 구조적 변화를 초래한다. 고활동성 시냅스 연결이 안정화되고 강화되지만, 상대적으로 적게 사용되는 연결은 약해져서 결국에는 잘린다. 이런 식으로, 우리의 뇌는 우리의 경험의 이력에 의해 형상이 만들어진다.

① 우리의 경험의 이력에 의해 형상이 만들어진다
② 그것의 처음 구조를 유지하도록 설계된다
③ 최근의 기억을 강화하도록 맞춰진다
④ 다른 기관의 발달과 밀접히 결부된다
⑤ 논리적이고 창의적인 사고가 일어나는 장소로 묘사된다

문제풀이

뇌가 발달하는 과정에서 신경망의 확립이나 개선을 통해 고활동성의 시냅스 연결은 안정화되고 강화되지만, 상대적으로 그렇지 못한 연결은 약해져서 결국 잘린다고 했다. 이는 뇌의 신경망이 고활동성의 신경 연결로 구성된다는 것이므로, 빈칸에는 ① 'sculpted by our own history of experiences'가 들어가서 빈칸을 포함한 문장이 '이런 식으로, 우리의 뇌는 우리의 경험의 이력에 의해 형상이 만들어진다.'가 되는 것이 가장 적절하다.

이렇게 풀자 빈칸 추론 유형에서 빈칸이 지문의 맨 마지막에 놓인 경우 보통 글의 주제나 요지, 또는 글에서 이야기하고자 하는 결론이 들어가는 경우가 많다. 여기서는 빈칸 바로 앞 문장인 'High-activity synaptic connections are stabilized and strengthened, while connections with relatively low use are weakened and eventually pruned.(고활동성 시냅스 연결이 안정화

되고 강화되지만, 상대적으로 적게 사용되는 연결은 약해져서 결국에는 잘린다.)'을 통해 활동이 많은 신경 연결이 안정화되고 아닌 것은 연결이 없어진다는 것을 이해하면 빈칸에 들어갈 말을 유추해 낼 수 있다.

어휘·어구

neuroimaging 신경 촬영
have access to ~에 접근할 수 있다
neural 신경의
fingerprint 지문
previously 이전에
assume 추정하다
immediate 인접한, 당면한
establish 확립하다
refine 개선하다
existing 기존의
impulse 자극
high-activity 고활동성의
sculpt 형상을 만들다
maintain 유지하다
initial 처음의, 초기의
strengthen 강화하다
twin 결부시키다
organ 장기
portray 그리다, 묘사하다

정답률 43%

10. ② 교육 기술의 성공적인 통합

직독/직해

Successful integration of an educational technology /
교육 기술의 성공적인 통합은 /
is marked / 특징이다 /
by that technology being regarded / by users /
그 기술이 여겨지는 것이 / 사용자에 의해 /
as an unobtrusive facilitator of learning, instruction, or performance.
학습이나 교육, 혹은 수행의 눈에 띄지 않는 촉진자로
When the focus shifts / 초점이 옮겨갈 때 /
from the technology being used /
사용되고 있는 기술로부터 /
to the educational purpose that technology serves, /
기술이 이바지하는 교육적 목적으로 /
then that technology is becoming a comfortable and trusted element, /
그 기술은 편안하고 신뢰할 수 있는 요소가 되고 있다 /
and can be regarded /
그리고 여겨질 수 있다 /
as being successfully integrated.
성공적으로 통합되고 있다고
Few people give a second thought /
다시 생각하는 사람들은 거의 없다 /
to the use of a ball-point pen /
볼펜 사용법에 대해 /
although the mechanisms involved vary /
그 구조가 다양하지만 /
— some use a twist mechanism /
비록 (볼펜 중) 어떤 것들은 돌리는 방법을 사용하고 /
and some use a push button on top, /
그리고 어떤 것들은 위에 달린 누름단추를 사용하며 /
and there are other variations as well.
그리고 다른 변형된 방법들도 있지만
Personal computers have reached a similar level of familiarity /
개인용 컴퓨터는 비슷한 수준의 친숙함에 도달했다 /
for a great many users, / but certainly not for all.
꽤 많은 사용자에게 / 하지만 분명 모두에게 그렇지는 않다
New and emerging technologies /
새롭고 최근에 생겨난 기술은 /
often introduce both fascination and frustration with users.
흔히 사용자들에게 매력과 좌절감을 동시에 경험하게 한다
As long as the user's focus is on the technology itself /
사용자의 초점이 기술 그 자체에 맞춰져 있는 한 /
rather than its use / 기술의 사용이 아닌 /
in promoting learning, instruction, or performance, /
학습, 교육 혹은 수행을 촉진하는 데 있어서 /
then one ought not to conclude /
결론을 내리면 안 된다 /
that the technology has been successfully integrated /
그 기술이 성공적으로 통합되었다는 /
— at least for that user.
적어도 그 사용자에게는

교육 기술의 성공적인 통합은 그 기술이 사용자에 의해 학습이나 교육, 혹은 수행의 눈에 띄지 않는 촉진자로 여겨지는 것이 특징이다. 사용되고 있는 기술로부터 기술이 이바지하는 교육적 목적으로 초점이 옮겨갈 때, 그 기술은 편안하고 신뢰할 수 있는 요소가 되고 있으며, 성공적으로 통합되고 있다고 여겨질 수 있다. 비록 (볼펜 중) 어떤 것들은 돌리는 방법을 사용하고, 어떤 것들은 위에 달린 누름단추를 사용하며, 그리고 다른 변형된 방법들도 있지만, 볼펜 사용법에 대해 다시 생각하는 사람들은 거의 없다. 개인용 컴퓨터는 꽤 많은 사용자에게 (볼펜과) 비슷한 수준의 친숙함에 도달했지만, 분명 모두에게 그렇지는 않다. 새롭고 최근에 생겨난 기술은 흔히 사용자들에게 매력과 좌절감을 동시에 경험하게 한다. 학습, 교육 혹은 수행을 촉진하는 데 있어서 사용자의 초점이 기술의 사용이 아닌 기술 자체에 맞춰져 있는 한, 적어도 그 사용자에게는 그 기술이 성공적으로 통합되었다는 결론을 내리면 안 된다.

① 사용자가 성공적으로 그 기술에 대한 친숙함을 성취하는
② 사용자의 초점이 기술의 사용이 아닌 기술 자체에 맞춰져 있는
③ 사용자가 계속 구식의 교육 기술을 쓰는
④ 사용자가 모르는 사이에 그 기술의 오용에 익숙해지는
⑤ 다른 사용자와 상호 작용에 대한 사용자의 선호가 계속되는

문제풀이

사용되는 기술에서 기술이 이바지하는 교육적 목적으로 초점이 이동할 때 교육 기술이 성공적으로 통합되고 있다고 여겨질 수 있다고 했으므로, 사용자의 초점이 기술 자체에 맞춰져 있을 때 교육 기술이 성공적으로 통합되고 있지 않는다고 볼 수 있다. 따라서 빈칸에는 ② 'the user's focus is on the technology itself rather than its use'가 들어가서 빈칸을 포함한 문장이 '학습, 교육 혹은 수행을 촉진하는 데 있어서 사용자의 초점이 기술의 사용이 아닌 기술 자체에 맞춰져 있는 한, 적어도 그 사용자에게는 그 기술이 성공적으로 통합되었다는 결론을 내리면 안 된다.'가 되는 것이 가장 적절하다.

이렇게 풀자 이 글에서는 'When the focus shifts from the technology being used to the educational purpose that technology serves, then that technology is becoming a comfortable and trusted element, and can be regarded as being successfully integrated.(사용되고 있는 기술로부터 기술이 이바지하는 교육적 목적으로 초점이 옮겨갈 때, 그 기술은 편안하고 신뢰할 수 있는 요소가 되고 있으며, 성공적으로 통합되고 있다고 여겨질 수 있다.)'를 통해 언제 교육 기술이 성공적으로 통합되고 있다고 여겨지는지를 알면, 반대로 언제 교육 기술이 성공적으로 통합되지 않았다고 볼 수 있는지를 유추해 낼 수 있다.

어휘·어구

integration 통합
be regarded as ~로 여겨지다
facilitator 촉진자
serve 이바지하다
mechanism 구조, 방법
vary 다양하다
familiarity 친숙함
emerging 새롭게 생겨난
fascination 매력
frustration 좌절
promote 촉진하다
employ 쓰다, 이용하다
involuntarily 모르는 사이에
persist 계속되다

본문 083쪽

문법 플러스 14. 형용사, 부사

A. 1. do 2. alike 3. deeply
4. highly 5. Most 6. turn it up
7. old enough

1 [해석]▶ 왜 노인들이 혼자 사나요?
[해설]▶ 「the+형용사(elderly)」는 복수 보통명사(elderly people)를 나타낸다.

2 [해석]▶ 그들은 가족이 아니지만, 닮아 보인다.
[해설]▶ 형용사 alike는 서술적 용법으로 사용된다. look alike는 '~처럼 보이다'는 뜻이다.

3 [해석]▶ 그럼에도 불구하고, 자신을 실험하는 것은 여전히 매우 문제가 된다.
[해설]▶ 형용사 problematic을 수식하므로 부사 deeply가 어법상 적절하다.

4 [해석]▶ 나는 새로운 곳에 있다는 기대감이 가득했으며 매우 기분이 좋았다.
[해설]▶ 부사 highly는 very(매우)의 의미가 있다.

5 [해석]▶ 많은 사람들이 사과를 좋아한다.
[해설]▶ most(대부분의)가 형용사로서 바로 뒤의 복수명사 people을 수식하고 있다.

6 [해석]▶ 나는 그녀에게 볼륨을 높이라고 하지 않고, 낮추라고 말했다.
[해설]▶ 동사와 부사가 결합된 동사구에서 목적어가 대명사일 경우에는 「동사+대명사+부사」의 어순이 되어야 한다.

7 [해석]▶ 그는 그 프로그램을 보기에는 너무 어리다.
[해설]▶ enough가 형용사, 부사를 수식하는 경우, 「형용사[부사]+enough+to부정사」 순서로 나온다.

본문 083쪽

B. 1. talk 2. live 3. inexpensively
4. high 5. almost 6. put it off
7. ripe enough

1 [해석]▶ 영국 사람들은 날씨에 대해 많이 이야기한다.
[해설]▶ 「the+형용사(English)」가 복수 보통명사의 의미로 '영국 사람들'을 의미한다.

2 [해석]▶ 삼촌은 살아 있는 문어를 먹는 것을 좋아하십니다.
[해설]▶ live와 alive는 형용사로서 '살아 있는'의 의미이지만, 한정 용법으로 사용할 때는 live를 쓰고, be동사 뒤에 나와 서술 용법으로 사용할 때는 alive를 쓴다.

3 [해석]▶ 패션은 자기표현의 가장 단순하고 값싼 방법 중의 하나로, 옷은 값싸게 구매할 수 있으며, 부, 지적 능력, 휴식 혹은 환경 의식에 대한 개념을, 비록 이것 중 어느 것도 사실이 아니라 해도, 쉽게 전달할 수 있다.
[해설]▶ 과거분사 purchased를 수식하므로 부사 inexpensively가 어법상 적절하다.

4 [해석]▶ 내 형의 연은 하늘 높이 올랐다.
[해설]▶ high는 형용사와 부사의 형태가 같다. 이 문장에서

high(높이)는 부사로서 동사 rose를 수식하고 있다.

5 [해석]▶ 그녀는 좀처럼 약속 시간을 어기는 법이 없다.
[해설]▶ almost(거의)는 부사로서 다른 부사 always를 수식하고 있다. almost always는 '거의 항상'의 의미이다.

6 [해석]▶ 지금 과학 숙제를 해라. 내일까지 미루지 마.
[해설]▶ 동사(put)와 부사(off)가 결합된 동사구에서 목적어가 대명사일 경우에는 「동사+대명사+부사」의 어순이 되어야 한다.

7 [해석]▶ 저 토마토들은 먹을 수 있을 만큼 충분히 익지 않았다.
[해설]▶ enough가 형용사, 부사를 수식하는 경우, 「형용사[부사]+enough+to부정사」 순서로 나온다.

본문 084쪽

숙어 플러스 14. 수능 필수 숙어 14회

1. up 2. make
3. for 4. Needless

15. 흐름에 무관한 문장 찾기

Day 15

본문 086쪽

1. ③ 2. ④ 3. ④ 4. ③ 5. ③
6. ④ 7. ④ 8. ③ 9. ③ 10. ③

정답률 83%

대표 기출 ④ '수정 확대 가족'의 개념과 성격

Kinship ties continue / to be important today.
친족 간의 유대는 계속 ~하다 / 오늘날에 중요하다
In modern societies such as the United States /
미국과 같은 현대 사회에서 /
people frequently have family get-togethers, /
사람들이 자주 가족 모임을 갖는 /
they telephone their relatives regularly, /
그들은 자신의 친척에게 정기적으로 전화하고 /
and they provide their kin /
그리고 친족에게 제공한다 /
with a wide variety of services.
아주 다양한 도움을
Eugene Litwak has referred to this pattern of behaviour /
Eugene Litwak은 이런 행동 패턴을 언급했다 /
as the 'modified extended family'.
'수정 확대 가족'이라고
It is an extended family structure /
그것은 확대 가족 구조이다 /
because multigenerational ties are maintained, /
여러 세대의 유대 관계가 유지되기 때문에 /
but it is modified / 하지만 수정된 것이다 /
because it does not usually rest on co-residence /
그것은 보통 공동 거주에 기초를 두지 않기 때문에 /
between the generations / 세대 간 /
and most extended families do not act /
그리고 대부분의 확대 가족이 기능하지는 않기 때문에 /
as corporate groups. 공동 집단으로서
Although modified extended family members /
비록 수정 확대 가족의 구성원들이 /
often live close by, / 종종 가까이 살기는 하지만 /
the modified extended family does not require geographical proximity /
수정 확대 가족은 지리적인 근접이 필요치 않다 /
and ties are maintained /
그리고 유대 관계는 유지된다 /
even when kin are separated by considerable distances.
친척이 상당히 멀리 떨어져 있을 때조차도
The oldest member of the family /
그 가족의 최고 연장자가 /
makes the decisions / 결정을 내린다 /
on important issues, / 중요한 문제에 관해서는
no matter how far away family members live /
가족 구성원들이 아무리 멀리 떨어져 살더라도 /
from each other. 서로
In contrast to the traditional extended family /
전통적인 확대 가족과는 대조적으로 /
where kin always live in close proximity, /
친족이 언제나 아주 가까이서 사는 /
the members of modified extended families /
수정 확대 가족의 구성원들은 /
may freely move away from kin /
친족에게서 자유로이 멀리 이주해가서 /
to seek opportunities for occupational advancement.
직업상의 발전을 위한 기회를 추구할 수도 있다

친족 간의 유대는 오늘날에 계속 중요하다. 사람들이 자주 가족 모임을 갖는 미국과 같은 현대 사회에서, 그들은 자신의 친척에게 정기적으로 전화하고, 친족에게 아주 다양한 도움을 제공한다. ① Eugene Litwak은 이런 행동 패턴을 '수정 확대 가족'이라고 언급했다. ② 그것은 여러 세대의 유대 관계가 유지되기 때문에 확대 가족 구조이지만, 보통 세대 간 공동 거주에 기초를 두지 않고 대부분의 확대 가족이 공동 집단으로서 기능하지는 않기 때문에 수정된 것이다. ③ 비록 수정 확대 가족의 구성원들이 종종 가까이 살기는 하지만, 수정 확대 가족은 지리적인 근접이 필요치 않으며, 유대 관계는 친척이 상당히 멀리 떨어져 있어도 유지된다. ④ (가족 구성원들이 서로 아무리 멀리 떨어져 살더라도, 중요한 문제에 관해서는 그 가족의 최고 연장자가 결정을 내린다.) ⑤ 친족이 언제나 아주 가까이서 사는 전통적인 확대 가족과는 대조적으로, 수정 확대 가족의 구성원들은 친족에게서 자유로이 멀리 이주해가서 직업상의 발전을 위한 기회를 추구할 수도 있다.

문제풀이

지리적으로 가까이 살 필요는 없지만 유대 관계는 유지하는 '수정 확대 가족'의 특징에 대해 설명한 글이다. 따라서 가족의 최고 연장자의 결정권에 대한 내용인 ④는 전체 흐름과 관계가 없다.

이렇게 풀자 각 문장이 어색하지 않은지 갑자기 내용이 전환되거나 단절되지 않는지를 꼼꼼히 살피며 글을 읽도록 한다. 여기서는 수정 확대 가족의 지리적인 근접이 필요치 않다는 내용 다음에 가족의 최고 연장자가 중요한 문제에 대해 결정을 내린다는 내용이 오는 것은 어색하므로 ④가 정답임을 알 수 있다. 따라서 ④를 제외하고 ③과 ⑤를 연결해 보면 '비록 수정 확대 가족의 구성원들이 종종 가까이 살기는 하지만, 수정 확대 가족은 지리적인 근접이 필요치 않으며, 유대 관계는 친척이 상당히 멀리 떨어져 있어도 유지된다. 친척이 언제나 아주 가까이서 사는 전통적인 확대 가족과는 대조적으로, 수정 확대 가족의 구성원들은 친척에게서 자유로이 멀리 이주해 가서 직업상의 발전을 위한 기회를 추구할 수도 있다.'가 되어 글의 흐름이 자연스럽다는 것을 확인할 수 있다.

어휘·어구

kinship 친족
tie 유대 (관계)
get-together 모임
relative 친척, 친족
provide A with B A에게 B를 제공하다
refer to A as B A를 B라고 언급하다
modified 수정된
extended 확장된
rest on ~에 기초하다
co-residence 공동 거주
corporate 공동의
geographical 지리적인
considerable 상당한, 많은
occupational 직업상의
advancement 발전

정답률 82%

1. ③ 의사소통의 수단으로서의 목소리

직독/직해

Actors, singers, politicians and countless others /
배우들, 가수들, 정치가들, 그리고 무수한 다른 사람들은 /
recognise the power of the human voice / as a means of communication /
사람 목소리의 힘을 인정한다 / 의사소통의 수단으로서의 /
beyond the simple decoding of the words / that are used.
단어의 단순한 해독을 넘어서는 / 사용된
Learning to control your voice / and use it for different purposes / is, /
여러분의 목소리를 통제하고 / 그것을 다양한 목적을 위해 활용하는 것을 배우는 것은 / ~이다 /
therefore, / one of the most important skills to

develop /
그러므로 / 개발해야 할 가장 중요한 기술 중 하나 /
as an early career teacher. 경력 초기의 교사로서
The more confidently you give instructions, /
여러분이 더 자신 있게 지시 사항을 전달할수록 /
the higher the chance of a positive class response.
긍정적인 수업의 반응이 나올 가능성은 더 높다
There are times / when being able to project your voice loudly /
경우가 있다 / 목소리를 크게 내보낼 수 있는 것이 /
will be very useful / when working in school, /
아주 유용할 / 학교에서 일할 때 /
and knowing that you can cut through /
그리고 여러분이 (목소리로) 가를 수 있다는 것을 아는 것은 /
a noisy classroom, dinner hall or playground /
시끄러운 교실, 구내식당이나 운동장을 /
is a great skill to have. 갖춰야 할 훌륭한 기술이다
In order to address serious noise issues in school, /
교내의 심각한 소음 문제를 다루기 위해서는 /
students, parents and teachers should search for a solution together.
학생, 학부모, 교사가 함께 해결책을 찾아야 한다
However, / I would always advise /
하지만 / 나는 언제나 조언하고자 한다 /
that you use your loudest voice incredibly sparingly /
가장 큰 목소리는 놀랍도록 적게 써야 한다고 /
and avoid shouting as much as possible.
그리고 소리치는 것을 최대한 피해야 한다고
A quiet, authoritative and measured tone / has so much more impact /
조용하고 권위가 있으며 침착한 어조는 / 훨씬 더 큰 효과가 있다 /
than slightly panicked shouting.
약간 당황한 고함보다

배우들, 가수들, 정치가들, 그리고 무수한 다른 사람들은 사용된 단어의 단순한 해독을 넘어서는 의사소통의 수단으로서의 사람 목소리의 힘을 인정한다. 그러므로 여러분의 목소리를 통제하고 그것을 다양한 목적을 위해 활용하는 것을 배우는 것은 경력 초기의 교사로서 개발해야 할 가장 중요한 기술 중 하나이다. ① 여러분이 더 자신 있게 지시 사항을 전달할수록, 긍정적인 수업의 반응이 나올 가능성은 더 높다. ② 목소리를 크게 내보낼 수 있는 것이 학교에서 일할 때 아주 유용할 경우가 있으며, 여러분이 시끄러운 교실, 구내식당이나 운동장을 (목소리로) 가를 수 있다는 것을 아는 것은 갖춰야 할 훌륭한 기술이다. ③ (교내의 심각한 소음 문제를 다루기 위해서는 학생, 학부모, 교사가 함께 해결책을 찾아야 한다.) ④ 하지만 나는 가장 큰 목소리는 놀랍도록 적게 쓰고 소리치는 것을 최대한 피해야 한다고 언제나 조언하고자 한다. ⑤ 조용하고 권위가 있으며 침착한 어조는 약간 당황한 고함보다 훨씬 더 큰 효과가 있다

문제풀이

학교 현장에서 목소리를 크게 내보낼 수 있는 것은 매우 유용할 수 있지만, 조용하고 권위가 있으며 침착한 어조를 사용하는 것이 고함보다 훨씬 더 큰 효과가 있다는 내용의 글이다. 따라서 교내의 심각한 소음 문제를 다루기 위해서는 학생, 학부모, 교사가 함께 해결책을 찾아야 한다는 내용의 ③은 글의 흐름과 관계가 없다.

이렇게 풀자 각 문장이 어색하지 않은지 갑자기 내용이 전환되거나 단절되지 않는지를 꼼꼼히 살피며 글을 읽도록 한다. 여기서는 큰 목소리를 내는 것보다 조용하고 권위 있고 침착한 어조를 사용하는 것이 효과가 있다는 내용의 글인데 교내 소음 문제의 해결책에 관한 내용이 제시되는 것은 어색하므로 ③이 정답임을 알 수 있다. 따라서 ③을 제외하고 ②와 ④를 연결해 보면 '목소리를 크게 내보낼 수 있는 것이 학교에서 일할 때 아주 유용할 경우가 있으며, 여러분이 시끄러운 교실, 구내식당이나 운동장을 (목소리로) 가를 수 있다는 것을 아는 것은 갖춰야 할 훌륭한 기술이다. 하지만 나는 가장 큰 목소리는 놀랍도록 적게 쓰고 소리치는 것을 최대한 피해야 한다고 언제나 조언하고자 한다.'가 되어 글의 흐름이 자연스럽다는 것을 확인할 수 있다.

어휘·어구

politician 정치가
countless 무수한
decode (암호를) 해독하다
instruction 지시
address 다루다, 고심하다
incredibly 놀랍도록
sparingly 드물게, 인색하게
authoritative 권위가 있는
measured 신중한, 침착한
panicked 당황한

2. ④ 식품 보존 방식

직독/직해

Except for grains and sugars, / most foods humans eat are perishable.
곡물과 설탕을 제외하고 / 인간이 먹는 대부분의 식품은 부패하기 쉽다
They deteriorate in palatability, spoil, or become unhealthy /
그것들은 맛이 나빠지거나, 상하거나, 건강에 좋지 않게 된다 /
when stored for long periods.
장기간 보관될 때
Surplus animal and crop harvests, / however, / can be saved for future use /
수확한 잉여의 동물 및 농작물은 / 하지만 / 나중에 사용하기 위해 남겨 둘 수 있다 /
if appropriate methods of preservation are used.
적절한 보존 방법을 사용하면
The major ways of preserving foods are canning, freezing, drying, salting, and smoking.
식품을 보존하는 주요 방법은 통조림 가공, 냉동, 건조, 염장, 그리고 훈제이다
With all methods /
모든 방법에서 /
the aim is to kill or restrict the growth of harmful microbes or their toxins /
목표는 해로운 미생물의 성장이나 그것들의 독소를 없애거나 제한하는 것이다 /
and to slow or inactivate enzymes /
그리고 효소의 작용을 늦추거나 비활성화하는 것이다
that cause undesirable changes in food palatability.
음식의 맛에 바람직하지 않은 변화를 초래하는
Palatability is not static: / it is always changing, /
맛은 그대로 있지 않는다 / 그것은 늘 변한다 /
based on the state of the individual, /
개인의 상태에 따라 /
especially in regard to the time of food consumption.
특히 음식 섭취 시간과 관련하여
For further protection during long periods of storage, /
장기간 보관하는 동안 추가적인 보호를 위해 /
preserved food is placed either in sterile metal cans or glass jars /
보존되는 음식은 멸균한 금속 캔 또는 유리병에 담겨진다 /
or frozen in airtight paper or plastic containers.
또는 밀폐된 종이 또는 플라스틱 용기에 넣어 냉동한다

곡물과 설탕을 제외하고, 인간이 먹는 대부분의 식품은 부패하기 쉽다. 장기간 보관될 때, 그것들은 맛이 나빠지거나, 상하거나, 건강에 좋지 않게 된다. ① 하지만 적절한 보존 방법을 사용하면 수확한 잉여의 동물 및 농작물을 나중에 사용하기 위해 남겨 둘 수 있다. ② 식품을 보존하는 주요 방법은 통조림 가공, 냉동, 건조, 염장, 그리고 훈제이다. ③ 모든 방법에서 목표는 해로운 미생물의 성장이나 그것들의 독소를 없애거나 제한하고 음식의 맛에 바람직하지 않은 변화를 초래하는 효소의 작용을 늦추거나 비활성화하는 것이다. ④ (맛은 그대로 있지 않은데, 특히 음식 섭취 시간과 관련하여 개인의 상태에 따라 늘 변한다.) ⑤ 장기간 보관하는 동안 추가적인 보호를 위해, 보존되는 음식은 멸균한 금속 캔 또는 유리병에 담겨지거나 밀폐된 종이 또는 플라스틱 용기에 넣어 냉동한다.

문제풀이

인간이 먹는 대부분의 식품은 부패하기 쉽기 때문에 적절한 보존 방법을 사용하면 잉여의 동물 및 농작물을 나중에 사용하기 위해 남겨 둘 수 있는데 그 보존 방법으로는 통조림 가공, 냉동, 건조, 염장, 그리고 훈제 등이 있다. 이 모든 방법의 목표는 해로운 미생물의 성장이나 그것들의 독소를 없애거나 제한하는 것이고, 추가적인 보호를 위해서는 멸균한 금속 캔 또는 유리병에 담거나 밀폐된 종이 또는 플라스틱 용기에 넣어 냉동한다는 식품 보존 방법과 목표를 설명한 글이다. 그러나 맛은 음식 섭취 시간과 관련하여 개인의 상태에 따라 늘 변한다는 ④는 글의 흐름과 관련이 없는 문장이다.

어휘·어구

perishable 썩기 쉬운
spoil 상하다
surplus 나머지, 잉여
harvest 수확(물)
appropriate 적절한
preservation 보존
toxin 독소, 독성 물질
inactivate 비활성화
enzymes 효소
undesirable 바람직하지 못한
static 그대로의
preserved 보전되는
airtight paper 밀폐된 종이
container 용기

3. ④ 재해로부터 빨리 회복하는 식물의 능력

직독/직해

Because plants tend to recover from disasters more quickly / than animals, /
식물은 더 빠르게 재해로부터 회복하는 경향이 있어서 / 동물보다 /
they are essential / to the revitalization of damaged environments.
그것들은 필수적이다 / 손상된 환경의 소생에
Why do plants have this preferential ability / to recover from disaster?
왜 식물은 이 특별한 능력을 가지고 있을까 / 재해로부터 회복할 수 있는
It is largely because, / unlike animals, /
그것은 대체로 ~때문이다 / 동물과 달리 /
they can generate new organs and tissues / throughout their life cycle.
식물이 새로운 장기와 조직을 생성할 수 있기 / 생애 주기 동안 쭉
This ability is due to the activity of plant meristems /
이러한 능력은 식물의 분열 조직의 활동 때문이다 /
— regions of undifferentiated tissue in roots and shoots /
뿌리와 싹에 있는 분화되지 않은 세포 조직 부위의 (활동 때문이다) /
that can, / in response to specific cues, / differentiate into new tissues and organs.
즉 특정 신호에 반응하여 / 새 세포 조직과 기관으로 분화할 수 있는
If meristems are not damaged during disasters, / plants can recover /
만약 재해 시에 분열 조직이 손상되지 않는다면 / 식물은 회복할 수 있다 /
and ultimately transform the destroyed or barren environment.
그리고 파괴되거나 척박한 환경을 궁극적으로 바꿀 수 있다
You can see this phenomenon / on a smaller scale /
이러한 현상을 볼 수 있다 / 더 작은 규모로 /
when a tree struck by lightning forms new branches /
번개 맞은 나무가 새 가지를 형성할 때 /
that grow from the old scar.
오래된 상처에서 자라나는
In the form of forests and grasslands, / plants regulate the cycling of water /
숲과 초원의 형태로 / 식물은 물의 순환을 조절한다 /
and adjust the chemical composition of the atmosphere.
그리고 대기의 화학적 구성을 조절한다
In addition to regeneration or resprouting of

plants, /
식물의 재생이나 재발아에 더하여 /
disturbed areas can also recover through reseeding.
교란된 지역은 재파종을 통해서도 회복할 수 있다

식물은 동물보다 더 빠르게 재해로부터 회복하는 경향이 있어서 손상된 환경의 소생에 필수적이다. 왜 식물은 재해로부터 회복할 수 있는 이 특별한 능력을 가지고 있을까? 그것은 대체로 식물이 동물과 달리 생애 주기 동안 쭉 새로운 장기와 조직을 생성할 수 있기 때문이다. ① 이러한 능력은 식물의 분열 조직, 즉 특정 신호에 반응하여 새 세포 조직과 기관으로 분화할 수 있는, 뿌리와 싹에 있는 분화되지 않은 세포 조직 부위의 활동 때문이다. ② 만약 재해 시에 분열 조직이 손상되지 않는다면, 식물은 회복해서 파괴되거나 척박한 환경을 궁극적으로 바꿀 수 있다. ③ 번개 맞은 나무가 오래된 상처에서 자라나는 새 가지를 형성할 때 더 작은 규모로 이러한 현상을 볼 수 있다. ④ (숲과 초원의 형태로, 식물은 물의 순환을 조절하고 대기의 화학적 구성을 조절한다.) ⑤ 식물의 재생이나 재발아에 더하여, 교란된 지역은 재파종을 통해서도 회복할 수 있다.

문제풀이

동물과 달리 식물은 생애 주기 동안 쭉 새 세포 조직과 기관으로 분화할 수 있어서, 재해로부터 더 빠르게 회복하는 경향이 있다는 내용의 글이다. 따라서 식물은 물의 순환을 조절하고 대기의 화학적 구성을 조정한다고 하면서 식물의 역할에 대해 이야기하는 ④는 전체 흐름과 관계가 없다.

이렇게 풀자 각 문장이 어색하지 않은지 갑자기 내용이 전환되거나 단절되지 않는지를 꼼꼼히 살피며 글을 읽도록 한다. 여기서는 식물의 회복 능력에 관한 내용의 글인데 식물의 역할을 제시하는 것은 어색하므로 ④가 정답임을 알 수 있다. 따라서 ④를 제외하고 ③과 ⑤를 연결해 보면 '번개 맞은 나무가 오래된 상처에서 자라나는 새로운 가지를 형성할 때 더 작은 규모로 이러한 현상을 볼 수 있다. 식물의 재생이나 재발아 외에도, 교란된 지역은 재파종을 통해서도 회복할 수 있다.'가 되어 글의 흐름이 자연스럽다는 것을 확인할 수 있다.

어휘·어구

recover 회복하다
disaster 재해, 재난
preferential 특별한, 특혜의
generate 만들어 내다
organ 기관, 장기
tissue 세포 조직
life cycle 생애 주기
meristem 분열 조직
undifferentiated 분화되지 않은
shoot (새로 돋아난) 순, 싹
differentiate 분화하다
scar 흉터, 상처
regulate 조절하다
adjust 조절하다
composition 구성
regeneration 재생
resprouting 재발아
disturbed 교란된
reseeding 재파종

정답률 67%

4. ③ 서로 다른 가치를 지닌 다양한 형태의 에너지

직독/직해

Some forms of energy are more versatile / in their usefulness than others.
몇몇 형태의 에너지는 더 다용도이다 / 활용도에 있어 다른 에너지보다
For example, / we can use electricity for a myriad of applications, /
예를 들어 / 우리는 무수히 많은 용도로 전기를 사용할 수 있다 /
whereas the heat from burning coal is currently used /
반면에 석탄을 태워 얻은 열은 현재 주로 사용된다 /
mostly for stationary applications / like generating power.
주로 고정된 용도로 / 동력을 생산하는 것과 같은
When we turn the heat from burning coal into electricity, /
석탄을 태워 나오는 열을 전기로 바꿀 때 /
a substantial amount of energy is lost / due to the inefficiency of the process.
상당한 양의 에너지가 손실된다 / 공정의 비효율성으로 인해
But we are willing to accept that loss / because coal is relatively cheap, /
하지만 우리는 기꺼이 그 손실을 받아들인다 / 석탄이 상대적으로 저렴하기 때문에 /
and it would be difficult and inconvenient / to use burning coal *directly* /
그리고 어렵고 불편할 것이다 / 석탄을 태워 '즉시' 사용하는 것은 /
to power lights, computers, and refrigerators.
전등, 컴퓨터, 냉장고를 작동시키는 데
Finding an economical way to use coal / to produce carbon fibers /
석탄을 이용하는 경제적인 방법을 찾는 것은 / 탄소 섬유를 생산하기 위해
will help revitalize rural communities /
지역 사회를 소생시키는 데 도움을 줄 것이다 /
suffering from the decline in coal production.
석탄 생산의 감소로부터 고통 받고 있는
In effect, / we put a differing value / on different forms of energy, /
사실상 / 우리는 다른 가치를 부여하고 있다 / 다양한 형태의 에너지에 /
with electricity at the top of the value ladder, /
가치 사다리의 맨 위에 전기를 놓으며 /
liquid and gaseous fuels in the middle, / and coal or firewood at the bottom.
가운데에 액체와 기체 연료를 / 그리고 밑바닥에 석탄이나 장작을 (놓으며)
Solar and wind technologies have an advantage /
태양광과 풍력 기술은 장점이 있다 /
in that they produce high-value electricity directly.
높은 가치의 전기를 즉시 생산한다는 점에서

몇몇 형태의 에너지는 활용도에 있어 다른 에너지보다 더 다용도이다. 예를 들어, 우리는 전기를 무수히 많은 용도로 사용할 수 있는 반면, 석탄을 태워 얻은 열은 동력을 생산하는 것과 같은 고정된 용도로 현재 주로 사용된다. ① 석탄을 태워 나오는 열을 전기로 바꿀 때, 공정의 비효율성으로 인해 상당한 양의 에너지가 손실된다. ② 하지만 우리는 석탄이 상대적으로 저렴하기 때문에 기꺼이 그 손실을 받아들이고, 전등, 컴퓨터, 냉장고를 작동시키는 데 석탄을 태워 '즉시' 사용하는 것은 어렵고 불편할 것이다. ③ (탄소 섬유를 생산하기 위해 석탄을 이용하는 경제적인 방법을 찾는 것은 석탄 생산의 감소로부터 고통 받고 있는 지역 사회를 소생시키는 데 도움을 줄 것이다.) ④ 사실상, 우리는 가치 사다리의 맨 위에 전기를, 가운데에 액체와 기체 연료를, 밑바닥에 석탄이나 장작을 놓으며 다양한 형태의 에너지에 다른 가치를 부여하고 있다. ⑤ 태양광과 풍력 기술은 높은 가치의 전기를 즉시 생산한다는 점에서 장점이 있다.

문제풀이

석탄을 태워 나오는 열을 전기로 바꿀 때 공정의 비효율성으로 인해 상당한 에너지 손실이 있지만, 석탄이 상대적으로 저렴하기 때문에 그 손실을 받아들이는 것처럼, 다양한 형태의 에너지에 서로 다른 가치를 부여하고 있다는 내용의 글이다. 따라서 '탄소 섬유를 생산하기 위해 석탄을 사용하는 것이 지역 사회를 소생시키는 데 도움을 줄 것이다'라는 내용의 ③은 글의 전체 흐름과 관계가 없다.

어휘·어구

whereas 반면
currently 현재, 지금
stationary 고정된
a substantial amount of 상당히 많은 양
be willing to V (기꺼이) ~하려고 하다
inconvenient 불편한
firewood 장작
directly 즉시

정답률 82%

5. ③ 정보 수집과 동물의 의사 결정

직독/직해

The animal in a conflict between attacking a rival and fleeing /
상대를 공격하는 것과 도피하는 것 사이에서 갈등하는 동물은 /
may initially not have sufficient information /
처음에는 충분한 정보를 갖지 못할 수도 있다 /
to enable it to make a decision straight away.
즉시 결정을 내릴 수 있게 해줄 만큼
If the rival is likely to win the fight, /
만약 상대가 싸움에서 이길 것 같다면 /
then the optimal decision would be to give up immediately /
최적의 결정은 즉시 포기하는 것일 것이다 /
and not risk getting injured.
그리고 다칠 위험을 무릅쓰지 않는 (것일 것이다)
But if the rival is weak and easily defeatable, /
그러나 상대가 약해서 쉽게 이길만하다면 /
then there could be considerable benefit /
상당한 이익이 있을 수 있을 것이다 /
in going ahead and obtaining the territory, females, food or whatever is at stake.
싸워서 영역, 암컷, 먹이나 성패가 달린 것은 무엇이든 얻는 것에
Animals under normal circumstances / maintain a very constant body weight /
일반적인 상황에서 동물은 / 매우 일정한 체중을 유지한다 /
and they eat and drink enough for their needs / at regular intervals.
그리고 그들은 자신들에게 필요한 만큼 충분히 먹고 마신다 / 규칙적인 간격으로
By taking a little extra time / to collect information about the opponent, /
약간의 추가 시간을 들임으로써 / 상대에 대한 정보를 수집하는 데 /
the animal is more likely to reach a decision /
그 동물은 결정에 도달할 가능성이 더 크다
that maximizes its chances of winning /
이길 가능성을 최대화하는 /
than if it takes a decision without such information.
그런 정보 없이 결정을 내리는 경우보다 /
Many signals are now seen /
오늘날 많은 신호들이 간주되어 /
as having this information gathering or 'assessment' function, /
이런 정보 수집 또는 '평가' 기능을 갖는 것으로 /
directly contributing to the mechanism of the decision-making process /
의사 결정 과정의 메커니즘에 직접적으로 기여한다 /
by supplying vital information / about the likely outcomes of the various options.
매우 중요한 정보를 제공함으로써 / 다양한 선택의 가능한 결과에 관한

상대를 공격하는 것과 도피하는 것 사이에서 갈등하는 동물은 처음에는 즉시 결정을 내릴 수 있게 해줄 만큼 충분한 정보를 갖지 못할 수도 있다. ① 만약 상대가 싸움에서 이길 것 같다면, 최적의 결정은 즉시 포기하고 다칠 위험을 무릅쓰지 않는 것일 것이다. ② 그러나 상대가 약해서 쉽게 이길만하다면, 싸워서 영역, 암컷, 먹이나 성패가 달린 것은 무엇이든 얻는 것에 상당한 이익이 있을 수 있을 것이다. ③ (일반적인 상황에서 동물은 매우 일정한 체중을 유지하며, 그들은 규칙적인 간격으로 자신들에게 필요한 만큼 충분히 먹고 마신다.) ④ 상대에 대한 정보를 수집하는 데 약간의 추가 시간을 들임으로써, 그 동물은 그런 정보 없이 결정을 내리는 경우보다 이길 가능성을 최대화하는 결정에 도달할 가능성이 더 크다. ⑤ 오늘날 많은 신호들이 이런 정보 수집 또는 '평가' 기능을 갖는 것으로 간주되어, 다양한 선택의 가능한 결과에 관한 매우 중요한 정보를 제공함으로써 의사 결정 과정의 메커니즘에 직접적으로 기여한다.

문제풀이

공격할지 도망갈지 갈등 상황에 있는 동물이 의사 결정을 할 때 주변 신호를 통해 정보를 수집한다는 것과 추가 시간을 들여 상대에 대한 정보를 수집하는 것의 이점에 관한 글로, 일반적인 상황에서 동물은 매우 일정한 체중을 유지하고 규칙적인 간격으로 필요한 만큼 충분히 먹고 마신다는 내용의 ③은 전체 흐름과 관계가 없다.

● 이렇게 풀자 각 문장이 어색하지 않은지 갑자기 내용이 전환되거나 단절되지 않는지를 꼼꼼히 살피며 글을 읽도록 한다. 여기서는 상대가 약해서 이길만 하면 싸워서 큰 이익을 얻을 수 있다는 내용 다음에 일반적인 상황에서 동물의 체중 유지와 식습관에 관한 내용이 제시되는 것은 어색하므로 ③이 정답임을 알 수 있다. 따라서 ③을 제외하고 ②와 ④를 연결해 보면 '그러나 상대가 약해서 쉽게 이길만하다면, 싸워서 영역, 암컷, 먹이나 성패가 달린 것은 무엇이든 얻는 것에 상당한 이익이 있을 수 있을 것이다. 상대에 대한 정보를 수집하는 데 약간의 추가 시간을 들임으로써, 그 동물은 그런 정보 없이 결정을 내리는 경우보다 이길 가능성을 최대화하는 결정에 도달할 가능성이 더 크다.'가 되어 글의 흐름이 자연스럽다는 것을 확인할 수 있다.

어휘·어구

flee 도망가다
initially 처음에
sufficient 충분한
optimal 최적의
immediately 즉시
defeatable 이길 만한
considerable 상당한
territory 영역, 영토
be at stake 성패가 달려 있다
maintain 유지하다
constant 일정한
opponent 상대
maximize 최대화하다
assessment 평가
function 기능
vital 매우 중요한
outcome 결과

정답률 62%

6. ④ 초기 근대 유럽에서 철학과 과학의 특징

직독/직해

What characterizes philosophy and science / in early modern Europe /
철학과 과학을 특징짓는 것은 / 초기 근대 유럽에서 /

and marks a break from earlier traditions / is the concern /
그리고 이전의 전통으로부터 분리를 나타내는 (것은) / 관심이다 /

to tailor theories to evidence / rather than authority or tradition.
이론을 증거에 맞추려는 / 권위나 전통보다는

Galileo Galilei, Francis Bacon, René Descartes, and others /
Galileo Galilei, Francis Bacon, René Descartes와 다른 사람들은 /

formulated explanations /
설명을 정립했다 /

of the heavens, of the natural world around them, and of human nature and society /
하늘, 그들 주변의 자연 세계, 그리고 인간의 본성과 사회에 대한 (설명을) /

not by appealing to the proclamations of earlier thinkers.
이전 사상가들의 선언에 호소함으로써가 아니라

Nor were / religious principles and ecclesiastic dogma / their guiding lights.
아니었다 / 종교의 원칙과 교회의 교리도 또한 / 그들의 이끄는 빛이

Rather, / they took their lead from reason— /
오히려 / 그들은 이성을 따랐다 /

what some thinkers called "the light of nature"— / and experience.
일부 사상가들이 '자연의 빛'이라고 부르던 (이성을) / 그리고 경험을 (따랐다)

The fierce debates on the superiority of reason or experience / continued, /
이성이나 경험의 우월성에 대한 격렬한 논쟁이 / 계속되었다 /

but all serious thinkers / ultimately abandoned experience /
하지만 모든 진지한 사상가들은 / 궁극적으로 경험을 버렸다 /

in the development of modern science and philosophy.
근대 과학과 철학의 발전에 있어서

Whether they proceeded / according to the logic of deduction /
그들이 나아갔든 / 연역의 논리에 따라 /

or through the analysis of empirical data, /
혹은 경험적 자료 분석을 통해 (나아갔든) /

the modern scientific method / they developed /
근대의 과학적 방법은 / 그들이 발전시켰던 /

consists in testing theories / according to reason /
이론을 검증하는 것에 있다 / 이성에 따라 /

and in light of the available evidence.
그리고 이용 가능한 증거를 고려하여

초기 근대 유럽에서 철학과 과학을 특징짓고 이전의 전통으로부터 분리를 나타내는 것은 이론을 권위나 전통보다는 증거에 맞추려는 관심이다. ① Galileo Galilei, Francis Bacon, René Descartes와 다른 사람들은 이전 사상가들의 선언에 호소함으로써가 아니라 하늘, 그들 주변의 자연 세계, 그리고 인간의 본성과 사회에 대한 설명을 정립했다. ② 종교의 원칙과 교회의 교리도 또한 그들의 이끄는 빛이 아니었다. ③ 오히려, 그들은 일부 사상가들이 '자연의 빛'이라고 부르던 이성과 경험을 따랐다. ④ (이성이나 경험의 우월성에 대한 격렬한 논쟁이 계속되었지만 모든 진지한 사상가들은 근대 과학과 철학의 발전에 있어서 궁극적으로 경험을 버렸다.) ⑤ 그들이 연역의 논리에 따라 (나아갔든) 혹은 경험적 자료 분석을 통해 나아갔든, 그들이 발전시켰던 근대의 과학적 방법은 이성에 따라 그리고 이용 가능한 증거를 고려하여 이론을 검증하는 것에 있다.

문제풀이

초기 근대 유럽에서 철학과 과학을 특징짓고 이전의 전통으로부터 분리해 내는 것은 이론을 증거에 맞추려는 관심이라고 하면서 그 당시의 사상가들은 이성과 경험을 따랐다는 이야기를 하고 있는 글로, 모든 진지한 사상가들이 과학과 철학의 발전에 있어 결국 경험을 버렸다는 내용의 ④는 글의 흐름과 무관하다.

● 이렇게 풀자 각 문장이 어색하지 않은지 갑자기 내용이 전환되거나 단절되지 않는지를 꼼꼼히 살피며 글을 읽도록 한다. 여기서는 사상가들이 이성과 경험을 따랐다는 내용 다음에 모든 사상가들이 과학과 철학의 발전에 있어 궁극적으로 경험을 버렸다는 내용이 오는 것은 어색하므로 ④가 정답임을 알 수 있다. 따라서 ④를 제외하고 ③과 ⑤를 연결해 보면 '오히려, 그들은 일부 사상가들이 '자연의 빛'이라고 부르던 이성과 경험을 따랐다. 그들이 연역의 논리에 따라 (나아갔든) 혹은 경험적 자료 분석을 통해 나아갔든, 그들이 발전시켰던 근대의 과학적 방법은 이성에 따라 그리고 이용 가능한 증거를 고려하여 이론을 검증하는 것에 있다.'가 되어 글의 흐름이 자연스럽다는 것을 확인할 수 있다.

어휘·어구

characterize 특징짓다
philosophy 철학
tailor 맞추다
authority 권위
formulate 만들어 내다, 표현하다
appeal 호소하다
proclamation 선언
principle 원칙
fierce 격렬한
debate 토론
superiority 우월성
ultimately 궁극적으로
analysis 분석
empirical 경험에 의거한
consist in ~에 있다

정답률 74%

7. ④ 회사 간의 협력 형태의 변화

직독/직해

Since their introduction, /
도입된 이후로 /

information systems have substantially changed the way /
정보 시스템은 방식을 상당히 바꿔왔다 /

business is conducted. 사업이 시행되는

This is particularly true for business /
이는 사업에서 특히 그렇다 /

in the shape and form of cooperation /
협력 형태와 유형의 /

between firms that involves an integration of value chains /
가치 체인의 통합을 수반하는 회사 간의 /

across multiple units.
다수의 부문에 걸쳐

The resulting networks /
그 결과로 생겨나는 네트워크는 /

do not only cover the business units of a single firm /
단일 회사의 사업 부문을 포함할 뿐만 아니라 /

but typically also include multiple units from different firms.
보통 서로 다른 회사의 여러 부문을 포함하기도 한다

As a consequence, / 그 결과 /

firms do not only need to consider their internal organization /
회사는 그들 내부 조직에 주의를 기울일 필요가 있을 뿐만 아니라 /

in order to ensure sustainable business performance; /
지속 가능한 사업 성과를 보장하기 위해서는 /

they also need to take into account the entire ecosystem of units surrounding them.
자신들을 둘러싸고 있는 부문들의 전체 생태계를 고려하기도 해야 한다

Many major companies are fundamentally changing their business models /
많은 주요한 회사들은 자신들의 사업 모델을 근본적으로 변화시키고 있다 /

by focusing on profitable units /
수익성이 있는 부문에는 집중해서 /

and cutting off less profitable ones.
그리고 수익성이 낮은 부문은 잘라내서

In order to allow these different units to cooperate successfully, /
이 각기 다른 부문들이 성공적으로 협력할 수 있도록 하기 위해서는 /

the existence of a common platform is crucial.
공동 플랫폼의 존재가 매우 중요하다

정보 시스템은 도입된 이후로 사업 시행 방식을 상당히 바꿔왔다. ① 이는 특히 다수의 부문에 걸쳐 가치 체인의 통합을 수반하는 회사 간의 협력 형태와 유형의 사업에서 특히 그렇다. ② 그 결과로 생겨나는 네트워크는 단일 회사의 사업 부문을 포함할 뿐만 아니라, 보통 서로 다른 회사의 여러 부문을 포함하기도 한다. ③ 그 결과, 회사는 지속 가능한 사업 성과를 보장하기 위해서는 그들 내부 조직에 주의를 기울일 필요가 있을 뿐만 아니라, 자신들을 둘러싸고 있는 부문들의 전체 생태계를 고려하기도 해야 한다. ④ (많은 주요한 회사들은 수익성이 있는 부문에는 집중하고 수익성이 낮은 부문은 잘라내서 자신들의 사업 모델을 근본적으로 변화시키고 있다.) ⑤ 이 각기 다른 부문들이 성공적으로 협력할 수 있도록 하기 위해서는 공동 플랫폼의 존재가 매우 중요하다.

문제풀이

정보 시스템의 도입 이후, 회사 간의 협력 형태는 각기 다른 부문들을 통합하고 협력하는 방식으로 변화가 있어왔다는 내용의 글이다. 따라서 많은 주요한 회사가 수익성 있는 부문에 집중하고 수익성이 낮은 부문을 잘라내면서 사업 모델을 근본적으로 변화시키고 있다는 내용의 ④는 전체 글의 흐름과 관계가 없다.

● 이렇게 풀자 각 문장이 어색하지 않은지 갑자기 내용이 전환되거나 단절되지 않는지를 꼼꼼히 살피며 글을 읽도록 한다. 여기서는 부문들간의 통합 부문들간의 협력을 이야기하고 있는 문장 다음에, 회사가 수익성이 있는 부문에 집중하고 수익성이 낮은 부문은 잘라내며 사업 모

델을 바꾼다는 내용이 오는 것은 어색하므로 ④가 정답임을 알 수 있다. 따라서 ④를 제외하고 ③과 ⑤를 연결해 보면 '그 결과, 회사는 지속 가능한 사업 성과를 보장하기 위해서는 그들 내부 조직에 주의를 기울일 필요가 있을 뿐만 아니라, 자신들을 둘러싸고 있는 부문들의 전체 생태계를 고려하기도 해야 한다. 이 각기 다른 부문들이 성공적으로 협력할 수 있도록 하기 위해서는 공동 플랫폼의 존재가 매우 중요하다.'가 되어 글의 흐름이 자연스럽다는 것을 확인할 수 있다.

《 어휘·어구 》

substantially 상당히, 많이
cooperation 협력
integration 통합
value chain 가치 체인 (고객에 대한 제품이나 서비스의 창출 및 관리를 원활히 수행하는 기업 소속 직원의 그룹)
business unit 사업 부문
internal 내부의
sustainable 지속 가능한
take ~ into account ~을 고려하다
fundamentally 근본적으로, 기본적으로
profitable 수익성이 있는

정답률 56%

8. ③ 실효성이 없는 국제 인권 조약

직독/직해

A group of academics, / mainly political scientists, /
한 집단의 학자들은 / 주로 정치학자들인 /
assumed / 생각했다 /
that human rights treaties did *not* have any effect /
인권 조약이 아무런 영향을 미치지 '않는다'고 /
on the behavior of countries.
국가들의 행동에
Indeed, / these academics, /
사실 / 이러한 학자들은 /
who typically called themselves "realists," /
일반적으로 자신들을 '현실주의자'라고 부르는 /
assumed / 생각했다 /
that international law generally did not affect the behavior of states.
국제법이 국가들의 행동에 대개 영향을 미치지 않는다고
They saw the international arena /
그들은 국제적 활동 무대를 보았다 /
as a security competition among different states, /
여러 국가들 간의 안보 경쟁으로 /
a zerosum game /
제로섬 게임으로 /
in which one state's gain was another state's loss.
한 국가의 이득이 다른 국가의 손실인
International lawyers and human rights advocates assumed /
국제 변호사들과 인권 옹호자들은 생각했다 /
that human rights treaties caused /
인권 조약이 야기한다고
countries to improve their treatment of their citizens.
국가들로 하여금 자국민들에 대한 처우를 개선하도록
In such conditions, / states could gain little /
그런 상황에서 / 국가들이 얻을 수 있는 이득은 거의 없었다 /
by cooperating with each other /
서로 협력함으로써 /
— except in temporary military alliances or security agreements /
일시적인 군사 동맹이나 안보 협정 외에
that could fall apart at a moment's notice.
당장에라도 결렬될 수 있는
International law could play a minimal role or none at all, /
국제법은 최소한의 역할만 할 수 있거나 혹은 아무것도 할 수 없었다 /
and was perhaps just an illusion, a sophisticated kind of propaganda /
아마도 그것은 단지 환상, 어떤 정교한 선전이었다 /
— a set of rules that would be swept away /
즉 없어져 버릴 규칙들의 집합이었다
whenever the balance of power changed.
힘의 균형이 달라질 때마다

한 집단의 학자들, 주로 정치학자들은, 인권 조약이 국가들의 행동에 아무런 영향을 미치지 '않는다'고 생각했다. ① 사실, 일반적으로 자신들을 '현실주의자'라고 부르는 이러한 학자들은 국제법이 국가들의 행동에 대개 영향을 미치지 않는다고 생각했다. ② 그들은 국제적 활동 무대를 여러 국가들 간의 안보 경쟁, 즉 한 국가의 이득이 다른 국가의 손실인 제로섬 게임으로 보았다. ③ (국제 변호사들과 인권 옹호자들은 인권 조약이 국가들로 하여금 자국민들에 대한 처우를 개선하게 한다고 생각했다.) ④ 그런 상황에서, 국가들은 당장에라도 결렬될 수 있는 일시적인 군사 동맹이나 안보 협정 외에, 서로 협력함으로써 얻을 수 있는 이득은 거의 없었다. ⑤ 국제법은 최소한의 역할만 할 수 있거나 혹은 아무것도 할 수 없었으며, 아마도 그것은 단지 환상, 어떤 정교한 선전, 즉 힘의 균형이 달라질 때마다 없어져 버릴 규칙들의 집합이었다.

문제풀이

이 글은 정치학자들의 인권 조약과 국제법에 대한 인식에 대해 설명하고 있다. 그들은 인권 조약이 국가들의 행동에 아무런 영향을 미치지 않고, 국제법 역시 국가들의 행동에 영향을 미치지 않는다고 생각한다. 따라서 국제법은 단지 환상이나 선전에 불과하고 그 실효성이 전혀 없다는 내용의 글이다. 하지만 ③은 인권 조약이 국가들로 하여금 자국민들에 대한 처우를 개선하게 한다는 내용이므로 글의 전체 흐름에서 벗어난다.

《 어휘·어구 》

academic 학자, 교수
treaty 조약, 협정
competition 경쟁
zerosum game 제로섬 게임 (참가자 각각의 이득과 손실의 합이 제로가 되는 게임)
temporary 일시적인, 임시의
alliance 동맹, 연합
fall apart 무너지다
at a moment's notice 당장, 즉석에서
sophisticated 정교한
propaganda 선전, 선동
sweep away ~을 쓸어내다
advocate 옹호자

정답률 81%

9. ③ 조직 내에서 유머의 기능

직독/직해

Workers are united / by laughing /
직원들은 단합된다 / 웃음으로써 /
at shared events, /
공유된 사건에 대해서 /
even ones that may initially spark anger or conflict.
심지어 처음에 분노나 갈등을 유발할 수 있는 사건에 대해서도
Humor reframes potentially divisive events /
유머는 어쩌면 불화를 일으킬 수 있는 사건을 다시 구성한다 /
into merely "laughable" ones /
그저 '재미있는' 사건으로 /
which are put in perspective /
이해되는 /
as subservient to unifying values /
통합 가치에 도움이 된다고 /
held by organization members.
조직구성원들에 의해 간직되는
Repeatedly recounting humorous incidents /
유머러스한 사건들을 되풀이해서 이야기하는 것은 /

as subservient to unifying values /
통합 가치에 도움이 된다고 /
held by organization members.
조직 구성원들에 의해 간직되는
Repeatedly recounting humorous incidents /
유머러스한 사건들을 되풀이해서 이야기하는 것은 /
reinforces unity / based on key organizational values.
단합을 강화시킨다 / 조직의 핵심 가치에 기초한
One team told repeated stories /
한 팀이 이야기를 되풀이해서 했는데 /
about a dumpster fire, /
대형 쓰레기 수납기 화재에 관한 /
something that does not seem funny / on its face, /
재미있어 보이지 않는 것이다 / 표면적으로는 /
but the reactions of workers motivated to preserve safety /
하지만 안전을 지켜야겠다는 동기를 부여받게 된 직원들의 반응이 /
sparked laughter / 웃음을 유발했다 /
as the stories were shared multiple times /
그 이야기가 여러 번 공유되면서 /
by multiple parties in the workplace.
직장의 여러 당사자에 의해
Shared events that cause laughter /
웃음을 초래하는 공유된 사건은 /
can indicate a sense of belonging /
소속감을 나타낼 수 있다 /
since "you had to be there" /
왜냐하면 '여러분은 그곳에 있어야 했고' /
to see the humor in them, /
그 사건 속의 유머를 이해하려면 /
and non-members were not and do not.
그리고 조직 구성원이 아닌 사람들은 그러지 않았기에 그러지 못하기 때문이다
Since humor can easily capture people's attention, /
유머는 사람들의 관심을 쉽게 사로잡을 수 있어서 /
commercials tend to contain humorous elements, /
광고는 유머러스한 요소들을 포함하는 경향이 있다 /
such as funny faces and gestures.
웃긴 얼굴과 몸짓 같은
Instances of humor serve to enact bonds /
유머의 예는 유대감을 만드는 역할을 한다 /
among organization members.
조직 구성원들 간의
Understanding the humor / may even be required /
유머를 이해하는 것은 / 심지어 요구될지도 모른다 /
as an informal badge of membership in the organization.
조직의 구성원임을 나타내는 비공식적 신분증으로

직원들은 공유된 사건, 심지어 처음에 분노나 갈등을 유발할 수 있는 사건에 대해서도 웃음으로써 단합된다. 유머는 어쩌면 불화를 일으킬 수 있는 사건을, 조직 구성원들에 의해 간직되는 통합 가치에 도움이 된다고 이해되는 그저 '재미있는' 사건으로 다시 구성한다. 유머러스한 사건들을 되풀이해서 이야기하는 것은 조직의 핵심 가치에 기초한 단합을 강화시킨다. ① 한 팀이 대형 쓰레기 수납기 화재에 관한 이야기를 되풀이해서 했는데, 표면적으로는 재미있어 보이지 않는 것이지만, 그 이야기가 직장의 여러 당사자에 의해 여러 번 공유되면서 안전을 지켜야겠다는 동기를 부여받게 된 직원들의 반응이 웃음을 유발했다. ② 웃음을 초래하는 공유된 사건은 소속감을 나타낼 수 있는데, 이는 그 사건 속의 유머를 이해하려면 '여러분은 그곳에 있어야 했고' 조직 구성원이 아닌 사람들은 그러지 않았기에 그러지 못하기 때문이다. ③ (유머는 사람들의 관심을 쉽게 사로잡을 수 있어서, 광고는 웃긴 얼굴과 몸짓 같은, 유머러스한 요소들을 포함하는 경향이 있다.) ④ 유머의 예는 조직 구성원들 간의 유대감을 만드는 역할을 한다. ⑤ 심지어 유머를 이해하는 것은 조직의 구성원임을 나타내는 비공식적 신분증으로 요구될지도 모른다.

문제풀이

조직 내에서 유머러스한 사건들이 웃음을 유발할 수 있고 그것은 그 조직의 유대감을 형성하는 역할을 한다는 내용의 글인데, 광고에 유머러스한 요소를 포함하는 경향과 그 이유에 관한 내용인 ③은 글의 전체 흐름과 관계가 없다.

⊙ 이렇게 풀자 각 문장이 어색하지 않은지 갑자기 내용이 전환되거나 단절되지 않는지를 꼼꼼히 살피며 글을 읽도록 한다. 여기서는 웃음을 야기하는 공유된 사건은 소속감을 나타낼 수 있다는 내용 다음에, 광고에 유머러스한 요소를 포함하는 경향에 대한 내용이 오는 것은 어색하므로 ③이 정답임을 알 수 있다. 따라서 ③을 제외하

고 ②와 ④를 연결해 보면 '웃음을 초래하는 공유된 사건은 소속감을 나타낼 수 있는데, 이는 그 사건 속의 유머를 이해하려면 '여러분은 그곳에 있어야 했고' 조직 구성원이 아닌 사람들은 그러지 않았기에 그러지 못하기 때문이다. 유머의 예는 조직 구성원들 간의 유대감을 만드는 역할을 한다.'가 되어 글의 흐름이 자연스럽다는 것을 확인할 수 있다.

《 어휘 · 어구 》

initially 처음에
spark 유발하다
conflict 갈등
reframe 재구성하다
divisive 불화를 초래하는
merely 그저, 단지
put ~ in perspective ~을 전체적인 시각으로 보다
recount 이야기하다, 상술하다
incident 사건
reinforce 강화하다
based on ~에 기반하는
on one's face 표면적으로, 표면상
motivate 동기를 부여하다
preserve 지키다, 보존하다
multiple 다수의, 복합적인
party 무리, 당사자
indicate 나타내다
sense of belonging 소속감
commercial 광고
element 요소
enact 만들다, 제정하다
badge 신분증, 상징, 표지

정답률 68%

10. ③ 상반된 격언들의 모순

직독/직해

Although commonsense knowledge may have
상식적인 지식에는 장점이 있을 수 있지만, 그것에는 약점도 있다 /
merit, it also has weaknesses, /
not the least of which is that it often contradicts itself. 그중에서 중요한 것은 그것이 모순되는 경우가 많다는 것이다
For example, we hear / that people who are
예를 들어, 우리는 듣는다 / 비슷한 사람들이 서로 좋아하기 마련이라고 /
similar will like one another /
("Birds of a feather flock together") / 유유상종 /
but also that persons who are dissimilar will like
하지만 닮지 않은 사람들이 서로 좋아하기 마련이라는 말도 듣는다
each other / ("Opposites attract").
/ 정반대되는 사람들은 서로에게 끌린다
We are told that groups are wiser and smarter
우리는 집단이 개인보다 더 현명하고 더 똑똑하다는 말을 듣는다 /
than individuals /
("Two heads are better than one") /
두 사람의 지혜가 한 사람의 지혜보다 낫다 /
but also that group work inevitably produces poor
하지만 집단 작업이 불가피하게 좋지 않은 결과를 만든다는 말도 듣는다 /
results /
("Too many cooks spoil the broth").
요리사가 너무 많으면 수프를 망친다
Each of these contradictory statements may hold
이런 모순된 말들 각각은 사실일 수 있다
true / under particular conditions, /
/ 특정한 상황에서는 /
but without a clear statement of when they apply and when they do not, /
하지만 그것이 언제 적용되는지와 언제 적용되지 않는지에 관한 명확한 진술이 없으면 /
aphorisms provide little insight into relations
격언은 사람들 사이의 관계에 대한 통찰력을 거의 제공하지 못한다
among people.
That is why we heavily depend on aphorisms /
그것이 우리가 격언에 매우 의존하는 이유이다 /
whenever we face difficulties and challenges in the long journey of our lives.
삶의 긴 여정에서 어려움과 도전에 직면할 때마다
They provide even less guidance /
그것들은 거의 어떤 지침도 제공하지 못한다 /
in situations where we must make decisions.
우리가 결정을 내려야 하는 상황에서
For example, when facing a choice that entails
예를 들어, 위험을 수반하는 선택에 직면할 때
risk, / which guideline should we use — /
/ 우리는 어느 지침을 이용해야 하는가? /
"Nothing ventured, nothing gained" /
'모험하지 않으면 아무것도 얻을 수 없다' /
or "Better safe than sorry"?
또는 '나중에 후회하는 것보다 조심하는 것이 낫다'

상식적인 지식에는 장점이 있을 수 있지만, 그것 또한 약점이 있는데, 그 중 가장 중요한 것은 종종 그것이 스스로와 모순된다는 점이다. 예를 들어, 우리는 비슷한 사람들은 서로 좋아한다고("같은 깃털의 새들이 함께 모인다[유유상종]") 듣지만 또한 서로 비슷하지 않은 사람들도 서로를 좋아할 것이라고 듣는다("정반대되는 사람들이 서로에게 끌린다.")고도 듣는다. ① 우리는 집단이 개인보다 더 현명하고 영리하다고("두 머리가 하나의 머리보다 낫다[백지장도 맞들면 낫다]") 듣지만 또한 집단으로 하는 일은 필연적으로 나쁜 결과를 낳는다("요리사가 너무 많으면 국물을 망친다.[사공이 많으면 배가 산으로 올라간다.]")라고도 듣는다. ② 이러한 모순된 진술들은 각각 특정한 조건 하에서 진실일 수 있지만, 언제 적용하고 그렇지 않을지에 대한 명확한 진술이 없다면, 격언은 사람들 사이의 관계에 대한 통찰력을 거의 제공하지 못한다. ③ (그렇기 때문에 우리는 삶의 긴 여정에서 어려움과 도전에 직면할 때마다 격언에 크게 의존한다.) ④ 그것들은 우리가 결정을 내려야 하는 상황에서 훨씬 더 적은 지침을 제공한다. ⑤ 예를 들어, 위험을 수반하는 선택에 직면했을 때, "도전하지 않으면 얻는 것이 없다" 또는 "나중에 후회하는 것보다 조심하는 것이 낫다"중 우리는 어떤 지침을 사용해야 하는가?

문제풀이

서로 모순되는 상식적인 지식들은 각각 특정 조건 하에서는 진실일 수 있지만 그것을 언제 적용하고 언제 적용하지 않을지에 대한 명확한 진술이 없으면 결정을 내려야 하는 상황에서 아무런 통찰력을 제공하지 못한다는 내용이다. 하지만 ③은 그렇기 때문에 우리가 어려움에 직면할 때마다 격언에 의존한다는 의미로 글의 흐름과 어긋난다.

이렇게 풀자_ 갑작스런 내용의 등장으로 문장 간의 연결이 부자연스러운 곳을 찾아야 한다. 정답이 되는 무관한 문장은 그 전후의 문장에 쓰인 일부 어휘를 그대로 가져오는 경우가 많으므로 내용상의 흐름에 집중해서 글을 읽어야 한다. 여기서는 서로 모순되는 격언들이 언제 적용되고 언제 적용되지 않는지에 대한 명확한 진술이 없을 때 아무런 통찰을 제공하지 못한다는 문장 다음에, 그래서 우리가 어려움에 직면할 때 격언에 매우 의존한다는 내용이 오는 것은 부자연스러우므로 ③이 정답임을 알 수 있다. 무관한 문장에 쓰인 aphorisms가 글의 내용과 관련된 것처럼 해서 오답을 유도하는 점에 유의해야 한다.

《 어휘 · 어구 》

commonsense 상식의
contradict ~와 모순되다
dissimilar 닮지 않은, 다른
inevitably 필연적으로
spoil 망치다
contradictory 모순된
statement 진술
insight 통찰력

본문 089쪽

문법 플러스 15. 비교 구문

A. 1. diligent 2. much 3. the taller
4. novelists 5. best 6. than
7. less

1 [해석]▶ Sam은 그의 형만큼 부지런하다.
[해설]▶ 원급 비교는 「as+형용사/부사+as」의 형태이며, be동사의 보어 역할을 하므로 형용사를 써야 한다.

2 [해석]▶ Sally는 그녀의 친구들보다 더 현명하다.
[해설]▶ 비교급을 강조하는 경우 비교급 앞에 much, even, still, far, a lot 등을 쓴다.

3 [해석]▶ Peter는 2명 중에서 더 키가 크다.
[해설]▶ 비교급은 정관사 the를 붙이지 않지만, of the two가 나오면 비교급에 정관사 the를 붙인다.

4 [해석]▶ 그는 한국에서 가장 훌륭한 소설가 중의 한 명이다.
[해설]▶ 「one of the 최상급+ 복수명사」는 '가장 ~중의 하나'라는 의미이다.

5 [해석]▶ 네가 그녀를 제일 잘 아니까 네가 그녀에게 물어봐야 해.
[해설]▶ 최상급은 정관사 the를 붙이지만, 부사의 최상급은 정관사 the를 붙이지 않는다. best가 동사 know를 수식하고 있다.

6 [해석]▶ 어떤 것도 건강보다 더 소중하지는 않다.
[해설]▶ 부정주어 ~ 비교급 than은 '어떤 ~도 …보다 ~하지 않다'는 의미이다.

7 [해석]▶ 어린이는 적어도 하루에 8시간은 자야 한다.
[해설]▶ not less than은 '적어도'의 의미이다.

본문 089쪽

B. 1. as 2. prettier 3. the longer
4. boy 5. deepest 6. than
7. more

1 [해석]▶ Sally는 그녀의 언니만큼 아름답지는 않다.
[해설]▶ not as ~as…는 '…만큼 ~하지 않다'는 의미이다.

2 [해석]▶ Sarah는 Jane보다 더 예쁘다.
[해설]▶ 비교급 비교는 「비교급+than」의 형태를 취한다. than 앞에 비교급이 나와야 한다.

3 [해석]▶ 두 개의 펜 중에서 이것이 더 길다.
[해설]▶ of the two가 나오면 비교급에 정관사 the를 붙인다.

4 [해석]▶ Jack은 그의 반에서 가장 용감한 소년이다.
[해설]▶ 「as ~ as any+단수명사」(다른 어떤 …못지 않게 ~한)는 최상급의 의미를 가지고 있다.

5 [해석]▶ 이 호수는 이 지점이 가장 깊다.
[해설]▶ 동일 대상 내에서 최상급 비교는 정관사 the를 붙이지 않는다.

6 [해석]▶ 내게 있어서, 낚시만큼 재미있는 것은 없다.
[해설]▶ 부정주어 ~ 비교급 than은 '어떤 ~도 …보다 ~하지 않다'는 의미이다.

7 [해석]▶ Tom은 기껏해야 평범한 영업사원이다.
[해설]▶ not more than은 '단지, 기껏해야'의 의미이다.

본문 090쪽

숙어 플러스 15. 수능 필수 숙어 15회

1. no 2. of
3. contrary 4. hand

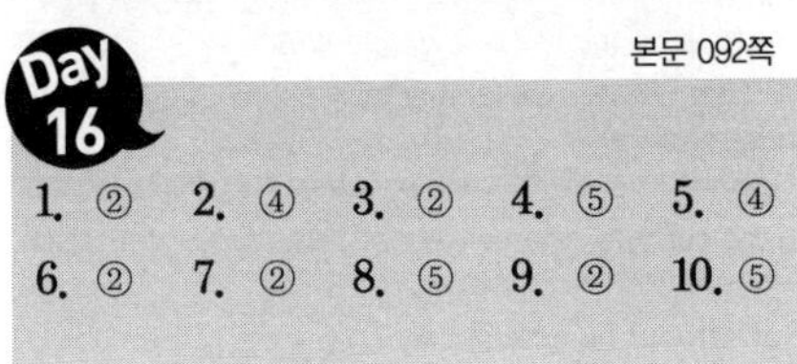

16. 문단 내 글의 순서 파악

본문 092쪽

1. ② 2. ④ 3. ② 4. ⑤ 5. ④
6. ② 7. ② 8. ⑤ 9. ② 10. ⑤

정답률 30%

대표 기출 ① 공간 기준의 상대적 크기

직독/직해

Spatial reference points / are larger than themselves.
공간 기준은 / 자신보다 더 크다

This isn't really a paradox: / landmarks are themselves, /
이것은 그다지 역설적이지 않은데 / 랜드마크는 그 자체이기도 하다 /

but they also define / 하지만 또한 규정하기도 한다 /

neighborhoods around themselves.
자기 주변 지역을

(A) In a paradigm / 한 전형적인 예에서 /

that has been repeated on many campuses, /
많은 캠퍼스에서 반복되어온 /

researchers first collect a list of campus landmarks /
연구원들은 캠퍼스 랜드마크의 목록을 수집한다 /

from students. 학생들에게서

Then / they ask another group of students /
그러고 나서 / 그들은 다른 학생 집단에게 요청한다 /

to estimate the distances / 거리를 추정하라고 /

between pairs of locations, / some to landmarks, /
짝을 이루는 장소 사이의 / 어떤 장소에서 랜드마크까지 /

some to ordinary buildings / on campus.
어떤 장소에서 일반 건물까지의 / 캠퍼스에 있는

(C) The remarkable finding is /
놀라운 결과는 ~이다 /

that distances from an ordinary location to a landmark /
일반 장소에서 랜드마크까지의 거리가 /

are judged shorter / 더 짧다고 추정된다는 것이다 /

than distances from a landmark to an ordinary location.
랜드마크에서 일반 장소까지의 거리보다

So, people would judge /
따라서 사람들은 추정할 것이다 /

the distance from Pierre's house to the Eiffel Tower /
Pierre의 집에서 에펠탑까지의 거리가 /

to be shorter / 더 짧다고 /

than the distance from the Eiffel Tower to Pierre's house.
에펠탑에서 Pierre의 집까지의 거리보다

Like black holes, / 블랙홀처럼 /

landmarks seem to pull ordinary locations /
랜드마크는 일반 장소를 끌어들이는 것처럼 보인다 /

toward themselves, / but ordinary places do not.
자신의 방향으로 / 하지만 일반 장소들은 그렇지 않다

(B) This asymmetry of distance estimates violates /
거리 추정에 관한 이러한 비대칭은 위반하는 것이다 /

the most elementary principles of Euclidean distance, /
가장 기본적인 유클리드 거리 법칙을 /

that the distance from A to B / must be the same /
A에서부터 B까지의 거리는 / 같아야 한다는 /

as the distance from B to A.
B에서부터 A까지의 거리와

Judgments of distance, then, /
그렇다면, 거리에 관한 판단은 /

are not necessarily coherent.
반드시 일관성이 있는 것은 아니다

공간 기준은 자신보다 더 크다. 이것은 그다지 역설적이지 않은데, 랜드마크는 그 자체이기도 하지만, 또한 자기 주변 지역을 규정하기도 한다.
(A) 많은 캠퍼스에서 반복되어온 한 전형적인 예에서, 연구원들은 학생들에게서 캠퍼스 랜드마크의 목록을 수집한다. 그러고 나서, 그들은 다른 학생 집단에게 짝을 이루는 장소 사이의 거리, 즉 캠퍼스에 있는 어떤 장소에서 랜드마크까지, 어떤 장소에서 일반 건물까지의 거리를 추정하라고 요청한다.
(C) 놀라운 결과는 일반 장소에서 랜드마크까지의 거리가 랜드마크에서 일반 장소까지의 거리보다 더 짧다고 추정된다는 것이다. 따라서 사람들은 Pierre의 집에서 에펠탑까지의 거리가 에펠탑에서 Pierre의 집까지의 거리보다 더 짧다고 추정할 것이다. 블랙홀처럼, 랜드마크는 일반 장소를 자신의 방향으로 끌어들이는 것처럼 보이지만, 일반 장소들은 그렇지 않다.
(B) 거리 추정에 관한 이러한 비대칭은, A에서부터 B까지의 거리는 B에서부터 A까지의 거리와 같아야 한다는 가장 기본적인 유클리드 거리 법칙을 위반하는 것이다. 그렇다면, 거리에 관한 판단은 반드시 일관성이 있는 것은 아니다.

문제풀이

공간 기준이 자신보다 더 크다고 하면서 랜드마크는 자신뿐만 아니라 그 주변도 규정한다고 한 주어진 글 다음에, 캠퍼스에서 이루어진 랜드마크에 관한 실험의 내용이 시작되는 (A)가 오고, 어떤 장소에서 랜드마크까지의 거리가 어떤 장소에서 일반 장소까지의 거리보다 더 짧게 추정된다고 하면서 (A)에서 언급된 실험의 결과를 설명하는 내용인 (C)가 온 후, 이어서 거리에 관한 판단이 반드시 일관성이 있는 것은 아니라고 하면서 그 실험의 의미를 정리하는 (B)가 오는 것이 가장 적절하다. 따라서 정답은 ①이다.

구조 다시보기

도입	공간 기준은 자신보다 더 큼
실험 내용	학생들에게 어떤 장소에서 랜드마크까지의 거리와 어떤 장소에서 일반 장소까지의 거리를 추정하라고 요청함
실험 결과	어떤 장소에서 랜드마크까지의 거리가 어떤 장소에서 일반 장소까지의 거리보다 더 짧게 추정되었음
결론	거리에 관한 판단이 반드시 일관성이 있는 것은 아님

어휘·어구

spatial 공간의
reference point (판단·비교용) 기준
paradox 역설
define 규정하다
paradigm 전형적인 예
estimate 추정하다, 추정
ordinary 평범한, 일반의
violate 위반하다
elementary 기본적인
coherent 일관성이 있는
remarkable 놀랄 만한

정답률 60%

1. ② 적응적 가소성

직독/직해

A fascinating species of water flea / exhibits a kind of flexibility /
물벼룩이라는 매혹적인 종은 / 일종의 유연성을 보인다 /

that evolutionary biologists call adaptive plasticity.
진화생물학자들이 '적응적 가소성'이라고 부르는

(A) That's a clever trick, / 그것은 영리한 요령인데 /

because producing spines and a helmet / is costly, in terms of energy, /
가시 돌기와 머리 투구를 만드는 것은 / 에너지 면에서는 비용이 많이 들기 때문이다 /

and conserving energy is essential / for an organism's ability /
그리고 에너지를 보존하는 것은 핵심적이기 때문이다 / 유기체의 능력을 위해 /

to survive and reproduce. 생존하고 번식하는

The water flea only expends the energy /
물벼룩은 오직 에너지를 사용한다 /

needed to produce spines and a helmet / when it needs to.
가시 돌기와 머리 투구를 만드는 데 필요한 / 필요할 때만

(B) If the baby water flea is developing into an adult /
만약 새끼 물벼룩이 성체로 발달하고 있으면 /

in water that includes the chemical signatures of creatures /
생물의 화학적인 (고유한) 특징을 포함하는 물에서 /

that prey on water fleas, /
물벼룩을 잡아먹는 /

it develops a helmet and spines / to defend itself against predators.
그것은 머리 투구와 가시 돌기를 발달시킨다 / 자신을 포식자로부터 지키기 위해서

If the water around it / doesn't include the chemical signatures of predators, /
만약 자신을 둘러싼 물이 / 포식자의 화학적인 특징을 포함하지 않으면 /

the water flea doesn't develop these protective devices.
그 물벼룩은 이 보호 장치를 발달시키지 않는다

(C) So it may well be that this plasticity is an adaptation: /
따라서 이 가소성은 아마 적응일 텐데 /

a trait that came to exist in a species /
생물 종에 존재하게 된 특징이다 /

because it contributed to reproductive fitness.
그것은 번식의 적합성에 기여하기 때문에

There are many cases, / across many species, / of adaptive plasticity.
많은 예가 있다 / 많은 종에 걸쳐 / 적응적 가소성의

Plasticity is conducive to fitness / if there is sufficient variation in the environment.
가소성은 적합성에 도움이 된다 / 환경에 충분한 차이가 있을 경우

물벼룩이라는 매혹적인 종은 진화생물학자들이 '적응적 가소성'이라고 부르는 일종의 유연성을 보인다.
(B) 만약 새끼 물벼룩이 물벼룩을 잡아먹는 생물의 화학적인 (고유한) 특징을 포함하는 물에서 성체로 발달하고 있으면, 그것은 자신을 포식자로부터 지키기 위해서 머리 투구와 가시 돌기를 발달시킨다. 만약 자신을 둘러싼 물이 포식자의 화학적인 특징을 포함하지 않으면, 그 물벼룩은 이 보호 장치를 발달시키지 않는다.
(A) 그것은 영리한 요령인데, 에너지 면에서는 가시 돌기와 머리 투구를 만드는 것은 비용이 많이 들고 에너지를 보존하는 것은 생존하고 번식하는 유기체의 능력을 위해 핵심적이기 때문이다. 물벼룩은 필요할 때만 가시 돌기와 머리 투구를 만드는 데 필요한 에너지를 사용한다.
(C) 따라서 이 가소성은 아마 적응일 텐데, 즉 그것은 번식의 적합성에 기여하기 때문에 생물 종에 존재하게 된 특징이다. 많은 종에 걸쳐 적응적 가소성의 많은 예가 있다. 가소성은 환경에 충분한 차이가 있을 경우 적합성에 도움이 된다.

문제풀이

물벼룩이 적응적 가소성이라 불리는 유연성을 보인다고 한 주어진 글 다음에, 그 구체적인 내용으로 포식자의 화학적인 특징을 포함하는 물에서 서식하는 물벼룩은 보호 장치를 발달시키지만 그렇지 않은 물에서는 보호 장치를 발달시키지 않는다고 한 (B)가 오고, (B)의 내용을 That으로 받아 그것이 에너지를 보존하기 위한 영리한 요령이라고 한 (A)가 온 후, 이어서 이런 가소성은 적응이라고 하면서 다른 종에서도 나타난다고 한 (C)가 오는 것이 적절하다. 따라서 정답은 ② '(B)-(A)-(C)'이다.

이렇게 풀자 우선 주어진 문장을 통해 무엇에 관한 글인지를 파악한 후, (A), (B), (C)의 핵심 내용을 정리하고 단서가 되는 연결사나 (대)명사에 유의하면서 연결 관계를 찾도록 한다. (A)의 'That(그것은)', (C)의 'So(따라서)'와 'this plasticity(이런 가소성)'가 글의 흐름의 단서가 되므로 이에 유의하면서 글을 읽도록 한다.

어휘·어구

fascinating 매혹적인
water flea 물벼룩
exhibit 보이다
evolutionary biologist 진화생물학자
flexibility 유연성
adaptive plasticity 적응적 가소성
in terms of ~면에서는
conserve 보존하다
organism 유기체
reproduce 번식하다
signature 특징
predator 포식자
may well 아마 ~일 것이다
contribute to ~에 기여하다
reproductive 번식의, 생식의
fitness 적합성
variation 차이, 변화

정답률 33%

2. ④ 승소 시 보수 약정

직독/직해

The most commonly known form of results-based pricing /
결과를 기반으로 한 가격 책정 중 가장 일반적으로 알려진 형태는 /

is a practice called *contingency pricing*, / used by lawyers.
'승소 시 보수 약정'이라고 불리는 관행이다 / 변호사가 사용하는

(C) Contingency pricing is the major way /
승소 시 보수 약정은 주요 방법이다 /

that personal injury and certain consumer cases are billed.
개인 상해 및 특정 소비자 소송에 대해 비용이 청구되는

In this approach, / lawyers do not receive fees or payment /
이런 방법에서 / 변호사는 수임료나 지불금을 받지 않는데 /

until the case is settled, / when they are paid a percentage of the money /
소송이 해결될 때까지 / 그때 그들은 금액의 일정 비율을 받는다 /

that the client receives.
의뢰인이 받는

(A) Therefore, / only an outcome in the client's favor is compensated.
그러므로 / 의뢰인에게 유리한 판결만 보수가 지불된다

From the client's point of view, / the pricing makes sense in part /
의뢰인의 관점에서 보자면 / 그 가격 책정은 부분적인 이유로 타당하다 /

because most clients in these cases /
왜냐하면 이런 소송의 의뢰인 대부분이 /

are unfamiliar with and possibly intimidated by law firms.
법률 사무소에 익숙하지 않고 아마도 겁을 먹을 수 있기 때문이다.

Their biggest fears are high fees / for a case /
그들의 가장 큰 두려움은 높은 수임료이다 / 소송에 대한 /

that may take years to settle.
해결하는 데 몇 년이 걸릴 수 있는

(B) By using contingency pricing, / clients are ensured /
승소 시 보수 약정을 사용함으로써 / 의뢰인은 보장받는다 /

that they pay no fees / until they receive a settlement.
수임료를 지불하지 않도록 / 합의금을 받을 때까지

In these and other instances of contingency pricing, /
승소 시 보수 약정의 이런 경우와 여타 경우에서 /

the economic value of the service is hard to determine / before the service, /
서비스의 경제적 가치는 측정하기 어렵다 / 서비스 전에 /

and providers develop a price /
그리고 공급자는 가격을 전달한다 /

that allows them to share / the risks and rewards of delivering value /
그들이 나눌 수 있게 하는 / 가치를 전달하는 위험과 보상을

to the buyer. 구매자에게

결과를 기반으로 한 가격 책정 중 가장 일반적으로 알려진 형태는 변호사가 사용하는 '승소 시 보수 약정'이라고 불리는 관행이다.
(C) 승소 시 보수 약정은 개인 상해 및 특정 소비자 소송에 대해 비용이 청구되는 주요 방법이다. 이런 방법에서 변호사는 소송이 해결될 때까지 수임료나 지불금을 받지 않는데, 그때 그들은 의뢰인이 받는 금액의 일정 비율을 받는다.
(A) 그러므로 의뢰인에게 유리한 판결만 보수가 지불된다. 의뢰인의 관점에서 보자면, 이런 소송의 의뢰인 대부분이 법률 사무소에 익숙하지 않고 아마도 겁을 먹을 수 있다는 부분적인 이유로 그 가격 책정은 타당하다. 그들의 가장 큰 두려움은 해결하는 데 몇 년이 걸릴 수 있는 소송에 대한 높은 수임료이다.
(B) 승소 시 보수 약정을 사용함으로써 의뢰인은 합의금을 받을 때까지 수임료를 지불하지 않도록 보장받는다. 승소 시 보수 약정의 이런 경우와 여타 경우에서 서비스의 경제적 가치는 서비스 전에 측정하기 어렵고, 공급자는 구매자에게 가치를 전달하는 위험과 보상을 그들이 나눌 수 있게 하는 가격을 전달한다.

문제풀이

변호사가 사용하는 '승소 시 보수 약정'의 개념을 소개한 주어진 글 다음에, 승소 시 보수 약정에서 변호사는 소송이 해결될 때까지 수임료를 받지 않는데, 그들은 의뢰인이 받는 금액의 일정 비율을 받는다는 내용의 (C)가 오고, Therefore로 시작하면서 그 결과 의뢰인에게 유리한 결과만 보수가 지불되는 데 의뢰인의 관점에서는 승소 시 보수 약정이 타당하다는 내용의 (A)가 온 후, 이어서 승소 시 보수 약정을 사용할 때 의뢰인과 변호사들에게 그리고 다른 경우에도 어떻게 적용되는지를 모두 정리하는 내용인 (B)가 오는 것이 적절하다. 따라서 정답은 ④ '(C)-(A)-(B)'이다.

어휘·어구

contingency pricing 승소 시 보수 약정
outcome 결과
compensate 보수를 지불하다
fee 수수료, 요금
make sense 타당하다
settle 해결하다
settlement 합의금
payment 지불금
reward 보상
approach 접근법

정답률 43%

3. ② 진화적 조정을 촉발한 직립 보행

직독/직해

Bipedalism, upright walking, started a chain of enormous evolutionary adjustments.
두 발 보행, 즉 직립 보행은 엄청난 진화적 조정을 연쇄적으로 촉발했다

It liberated hominin arms / for carrying weapons /
그것은 호미닌의 팔을 자유롭게 하였다 / 무기를 휴대할 수 있도록 /

and for taking food to group sites / instead of consuming it on the spot.
그리고 음식을 집단이 있는 장소로 가져갈 수 있도록 / 즉석에서 먹는 대신

But bipedalism was necessary to trigger hand dexterity and tool use.
그런데 두 발 보행은 손재주와 도구 사용을 촉발하기 위해 필요했다

(B) Hashimoto and co-workers concluded /
Hashimoto와 동료들은 결론지었다 /

that adaptations underlying tool use /
도구 사용의 기초가 되는 적응이 /

evolved independently of those required for human bipedalism /
인간의 두 발 보행에 필요한 적응과 독립적으로 진화했다고 (결론지었다) /

because in both humans and monkeys, each finger is represented separately /
인간과 원숭이 모두에서 각 손가락이 구분되어 나타나기 때문이다 /

in the primary sensorimotor cortex, /
1차 감각 운동 피질에서 /

just as the fingers are physically separated in the hand.
손에 있는 손가락이 물리적으로 나뉘어 있는 것처럼

(A) This creates the ability to use each digit independently /
이것은 각 손가락을 독립적으로 사용할 수 있는 능력을 만들어 낸다 /

in the complex manipulations required for tool use.
도구 사용에 필요한 복잡한 조작에서

But without bipedalism /
그러나 두 발 보행이 없다면 /

it would be impossible to use the trunk for leverage /
지렛대 역할을 하도록 몸통을 사용하는 것이 불가능할 것이다 /

in accelerating the hand during toolmaking and tool use.
도구 제작 및 도구 사용 중 손(놀림)을 가속화할 때

(C) Bipedalism also freed the mouth and teeth /
두 발 보행은 또한 입과 치아를 자유롭게 하였다 /

to develop a more complex call system / as the prerequisite of language.
더 복잡한 소리 신호 체계를 발전시키기 위해서 / 언어의 전제 조건으로서

These developments required larger brains /
이러한 발전으로 인해 더 큰 두뇌가 필요하게 되었다 /

whose energy cost eventually reached three times the level for chimpanzees, /
에너지 비용이 결국 침팬지의 3배 수준에 이르게 되는 /

accounting for up to one-sixth of the total basal metabolic rate.
총 기초 대사율의 최대 6분의 1을 차지하는

두 발 보행, 즉 직립 보행은 엄청난 진화적 조정을 연쇄적으로 촉발했다. 그것은 호미닌의 팔을 자유롭게 하여 무기를 휴대하고, 음식을 즉석에서 먹는 대신, 집단이 있는 장소로 가져갈 수 있게 해 주었다. 그런데 두 발 보행은 손재주와 도구 사용을 촉발하기 위해 필요했다.
(B) Hashimoto와 동료들은 도구 사용의 기초가 되는 적응이 인간의 두 발 보행에 필요한 적응과 독립적으로 진화했다고 결론지었는데, 인간과 원숭이 모두에서 손에 있는 손가락이 물리적으로 나뉘어 있는 것처럼 각 손가락도 1차 감각 운동 피질에서 구분되어 나타나기 때문이다.
(A) 이것은 도구 사용에 필요한 복잡한 조작에서 각 손가락을 독립적으로 사용할 수 있는 능력을 만들어 낸다. 그러나 두 발 보행이 없다면 도구 제작 및 도구 사용 중 손(놀림)을 가속화할 때 지렛대 역할을 하도록 몸통을 사용하는 것이 불가능할 것이다.
(C) 두 발 보행은 또한 입과 치아를 자유롭게 하여 언어의 전제 조건으로서 더 복잡한 소리 신호 체계를 발전시켰다. 이러한 발전으로 인해 에너지 비용이 결국 침팬지의 3배 수준에 이르러 총 기초 대사율의 최대 6분의 1을 차지하는 더 큰 두뇌가 필요하게 되었다.

문제풀이

직립보행이 팔을 자유롭게 하고 손재주와 도구 사용을 촉발하여 엄청난 진화적 조정을 야기했다는 주어진 글 다음에 인간의 도구 사용의 기초가 되는 적응이 두 발 보행에 필요한 적응과 상관없이 진화했다는 내용의 (B)가 이어지고, (B)의 마지막 부분에 인간과 원숭이 모두 손가락이 1차 감각 운동 피질에서 구분되어 나타난다는 내용을 'This'로 받아 도구 사용에 필요한 복잡한 조작에서 각 손가락을 독립적으로 사용할 수 있는 능력을 만들었다는 내용의 (A)가 이어지고, 직립 보행으로 인해 입과 치아를 자유롭게 하여 더 복잡한 소리 신호 체계가 발전하게 되었다는 내용의 (C)가 마지막으로 이어지는 것이 글의 순서로 적합하다. 따라서 정답은 ②이다.

이렇게 풀자 글의 순서 정하기 문제에서는 주어진 글의 소재와 전개 방향을 파악한 후, 지칭어나 연결사를 활용하여 주어진 글 바로 다음에 이어진 글과 그 다음에 이어질 글을 찾아 나가면 된다. 이 글은 'Bipedalism(두 발 보행)'이 팔의 자유와 손재주와 도구 사용을 촉발했다는 주어진 글 뒤에 손가락과 도구 사용에 관해 언급한 (A)와 (B)가 있고, 두 발 보행으로 인해 입과 치아를 자유롭게 했다는 (C)가 있으므로 (C)는 글의 마지막에 위치하고,

주어진 글 다음에는 (A)나 (B)가 와야 한다는 것을 알 수 있다. (A)의 지칭어 'This'가 각 손가락을 독립적으로 사용하게 해 주었다는 것으로 보아 주어진 문장 바로 다음에 올 수 없고 'This'는 (B)의 마지막 부분을 지칭한다는 것을 알 수 있다. 따라서 글의 순서는 '(B)-(A)-(C)'가 되어야 한다.

어휘·어구

upright walking 직립 보행
enormous 엄청난
evolutionary 진화의
adjustment 조정
liberate 해방시키다
on the spot 현장에서
complex 복잡한
manipulation 조작
accelerate 가속하다
adaptation 적응
underlying 기초를 이루는
separately 나뉘어 있는
primary 제1의
prerequisite 전제 조건
account for ~을 차지하다
basal metabolic rate 기초 대사율

정답률 69%

4. ⑤ 운하 건설에서 자연 수역의 수위 차이 보완 방법

직독/직해

When two natural bodies of water / stand at different levels, /
두 개의 자연 수역이 / 각기 다른 수위에 있을 때 /

building a canal between them / presents a complicated engineering problem.
그것들 사이에 운하를 건설하는 것은 / 복잡한 공학상의 문제를 야기한다

(C) To make up for the difference in level, /
그 수위의 차이를 보완하기 위해 /

engineers build one or more water "steps," / called locks, /
공학자들은 하나 이상의 물 '계단'을 만든다 / 로크라고 불리는 /

that carry ships or boats up or down / between the two levels.
배나 보트를 위아래로 운반하는 / 두 수위 사이에서

A lock is an artificial water basin.
로크는 인공의 물웅덩이이다.

It has a long rectangular shape /
그것은 긴 직사각형 모양이다 /

with concrete walls and a pair of gates at each end.
콘크리트 벽과 각 끝에 한 쌍의 문이 있는

(B) When a vessel is going upstream, / the upper gates stay closed /
선박이 상류로 갈 때 / 위쪽 문은 닫혀 있다 /

as the ship enters the lock at the lower water level.
더 낮은 수위에 있는 배가 잠금장치에 들어서는 동안

The downstream gates are then closed / and more water is pumped /
그러고 나서 하류의 문이 닫힌다 / 그리고 더 많은 물이 양수된다 /

into the basin.
웅덩이 안으로

The rising water lifts the vessel / to the level of the upper body of water.
올라간 물이 선박을 끌어 올린다 / 위쪽의 물 수위까지

(A) Then the upper gates open / and the ship passes through.
그러고 나서 위쪽 문이 열린다 / 그리고 배가 통과한다

For downstream passage, / the process works the opposite way.
하류 통행에서 / 그 과정은 반대 방식으로 작동한다

The ship enters the lock from the upper level, /
배가 위쪽 수위의 로크로 들어온다 /

and water is pumped from the lock / until the ship is in line with the lower level.
그리고 물이 로크로부터 양수된다 / 배가 더 낮은 수위와 같을 때까지

두 개의 자연 수역이 각기 다른 수위에 있을 때, 그것들 사이에 운하를 건설하는 것은 복잡한 공학상의 문제를 야기한다.
(C) 그 수위의 차이를 보완하기 위해 공학자들은 두 수위 사이에서 배나 보트를 위아래로 운반하는, 로크라고 불리는 하나 이상의 물 '계단'을 만든다. 로크는 인공의 물웅덩이이다. 그것은 콘크리트 벽과 각 끝에 한 쌍의 문이 있는 긴 직사각형 모양이다.
(B) 선박이 상류로 갈 때, 배가 더 낮은 수위에 있는 잠금장치에 들어서는 동안 위쪽 문은 닫혀 있다. 그러고 나서 하류의 문이 닫히고 더 많은 물이 웅덩이 안으로 양수된다. 올라간 물이 선박을 위쪽의 물 수위까지 끌어 올린다.
(A) 그러고 나서 위쪽 문이 열리고 배가 통과한다. 하류 통행에서, 그 과정은 반대 방식으로 작동한다. 배가 위쪽 수위의 로크로 들어오고, 배가 더 낮은 수위와 같을 때까지 물이 로크로부터 양수된다.

문제풀이

각기 다른 수위에 있는 두 개의 자연 수역 사이의 운하 건설은 복잡한 공학상의 문제를 야기한다는 내용의 주어진 글 다음에, 수위의 차이를 보완하기 위해 두 수위 사이에 인공적인 물웅덩이인 로크를 만든다는 내용의 (C)가 오고, 선박이 상류로 갈 때의 상황을 설명한 (B)가 오고 나서, 이어 그 후 배가 통과한다는 내용 다음에 상류에서 하류로 갈 때는 그와 반대로 작동한다는 내용의 (A)가 오는 것이 적절하다. 따라서 정답은 ⑤이다.

이렇게 풀자 우선 주어진 문장을 통해 무엇에 관한 글인지를 파악한 후, (A), (B), (C)의 핵심 내용을 정리하고 단서가 되는 연결사나 (대)명사에 유의하면서 연결 관계를 찾도록 한다. (A)의 'Then(그러고 나서)'와 'the opposite way(반대의 방식)', (B)의 'When a vessel is going upstream(선박이 상류로 갈 때)', (C)의 'the difference in level(그 수위의 차이)'가 글의 흐름의 단서가 되므로 이에 유의하면서 글을 읽도록 한다.

어휘·어구

canal 운하
downstream 하류의
passage 통행, 통과
opposite 정반대의
in line with ~과 같은
vessel (대형) 선박[배]
upstream 상류로
basin 웅덩이, 분지
make up for (손실 등을) 보상하다, 보전하다
artificial 인공적인

정답률 47%

5. ④ 디지털 세계의 잘못된 지시 전략

직독/직해

One common strategy and use of passive misdirection /
인식하지 못한 채 시선을 다른 곳으로 돌리게 하는 것에 대한 한 가지 흔한 전략과 사용은 /

in the digital world /
디지털 세계에서 /

comes through the use of repetition.
반복을 이용하여 이루어진다

(C) This digital misdirection strategy relies on the fact /
이러한 디지털 상에서 시선을 다른 곳으로 돌리게 하는 전략은 사실에 의존한다 /

that online users utilizing web browsers / to visit websites / have quickly learned /
웹 브라우저를 사용하는 온라인 사용자가 / 웹 사이트를 방문하기 위하여 / 바로 배웠다는 /

that the most basic ubiquitous navigational action /
가장 기본적이고 어디에서나 하는 탐색 동작이 /

is to click on a link or button / presented to them on a website.
링크나 버튼을 클릭하는 것이라는 것을 / 웹 사이트에서 그들에게 제시되는

(A) This action is repeated / over and over / to navigate their web browsers /
이 동작은 반복된다 / 여러 번 되풀이하여 / 그들의 웹 브라우저를 조종해 가기 위해 /

to the desired web page or action /
원하는 웹 페이지나 동작으로 /

until it becomes an almost immediate, reflexive action.
그것이 거의 즉각적이고 반사적인 동작으로 바뀔 때까지

Malicious online actors take advantage of this behavior /
악의적인 온라인 행위자들은 이러한 행동을 이용한다 /

to distract the user /
사용자의 관심을 다른 곳으로 돌리려고 /

from carefully examining the details of the web page /
웹 페이지의 세부 사항을 주의 깊게 검토하는 것으로부터 /

that might tip off the user / that there is something amiss about the website.
사용자에게 귀띔해 주는 / 웹 사이트에 어떤 잘못된 것이 있다고

(B) The website is designed / to focus the user's attention / on the action /
그 웹 사이트는 설계된다 / 사용자의 관심을 집중시키기 위해서 / 행동에 /

the malicious actor wants them to take / (e.g., click a link) /
악의적인 행위자가 사용자들이 수행하기를 원하는 / 예를 들어, 링크를 클릭하는 것 /

and to draw their attention / away from any details /
그리고 주의를 다른 곳으로 돌리도록 / 세부 사항으로부터 /

that might suggest to the user /
사용자에게 암시할 수 있는 /

that the website is not what it appears to be on the surface.
웹 사이트가 겉으로 보이는 것과 다르다는 것을

디지털 세계에서 인식하지 못한 채 시선을 다른 곳으로 돌리게 하는 것에 대한 한 가지 흔한 전략과 사용은 반복을 이용하여 이루어진다.
(C) 이러한 디지털 상에서 시선을 다른 곳으로 돌리게 하는 전략은 웹 사이트를 방문하기 위하여 웹 브라우저를 사용하는 온라인 사용자가 가장 기본적이고 어디에서나 하는 탐색 동작이 웹 사이트에서 그들에게 제시되는 링크나 버튼을 클릭하는 것이라는 것을 바로 배웠다는 사실에 의존한다.
(A) 이 동작은 원하는 웹 페이지나 동작으로 그들의 웹 브라우저를 조종해 가기 위해, 그것이 거의 즉각적이고 반사적인 동작으로 바뀔 때까지 여러 번 되풀이하여 반복된다. 악의적인 온라인 행위자들은 웹 사이트에 어떤 잘못된 것이 있다고 사용자에게 귀띔해 주는 웹 페이지의 세부 사항을 주의 깊게 검토하는 것으로부터 사용자의 관심을 다른 곳으로 돌리려고 이러한 행동을 이용한다.
(B) 그 웹 사이트는 악의적인 행위자가 사용자들이 수행하기를 원하는 행동에 사용자의 관심을 집중시키고 (예를 들어, 링크를 클릭하는 것) 사용자에게 웹 사이트가 겉으로 보이는 것과 다르다는 것을 암시할 수 있는 세부 사항으로부터 주의를 다른 곳으로 돌리도록 설계된다.

문제풀이

인식하지 못한 채 시선을 다른 곳으로 돌리게 하는 전략은 반복을 통해서 이루어진다는 내용의 주어진 글 다음에 이러한 전략은 온라인 사용자가 원하는 웹 사이트를 찾기 위해 그들에게 제시되는 링크나 버튼을 클릭하는 것을 배웠다는 사실에 의존한다는 내용의 (C)가 이어지고, 이 동작이 거의 즉각적이고 반사적인 동작이 될 때까지 반복되고, 악의적인 사용자는 웹 페이지의 잘못된 것을 알려주는 세부 사항을 온라인 사용자가 주의 깊게 살펴보지 못하도록 이러한 행동을 이용한다는 내용의 (A)가 이어진 다음, 그 악의적인 사용자가 링크 클릭과 같은 사용자들이 원하는 행동에 사용자의 관심을 집중시킴으로써 웹 사이트가 겉으로 보이는 것과 다르다는 것을 암시하는 세부 사항으로부터 주의를 다른 곳으로 돌리도록 설계된다는 내용의 (B)가 마지막으로 이어지는 것이 글의 순서로 가장 적절하다. 따라서 정답은 ④이다.

이렇게 풀자 (A)의 'this action'이나 (B)의 'The website'로 보아 (A)와 (B)는 주어진 문장 바로 다음에 이어질 수 없고, (C)의 'This digital misdirectin strategy'로 보아 주어진 문장 바로 다음에는 (C)가 와야 한다는 것을 알 수 있다. 또한 (A)의 'Malicious online actors'와 (B)의 'the malicious actor'로 보아 (A) 다음에 (B)가 이어져야 한다는 것을 알 수 있다. 따라서 주어진 글 다음에 이어질 글의 순서로 가장 적절한 것은 ④ '(C)-(A)-(B)'라는 것을 쉽게 알 수 있다.

어휘·어구

strategy 전략
passive 수동적인, 소극적인
misdirection 시선을 다른 곳으로 돌림, 그릇된 방향
come through ~을 이용하여 이루어지다
rely on ~에 의존[의지]하다
utilize 이용하다
ubiquitous 어디에나 있는
over and over 여러 번
navigate 조종하다
immediate 즉각적인
reflexive action 반사적인 동작
malicious 악의적인
take advantage of ~을 이용하다
distract 딴 데로 돌리다
detail 세부 사항

정답률 47%

6. ② 매몰 비용 오류의 장단점

직독/직해

In economics, / there is a principle known as the *sunk cost fallacy*.
경제학에서 / '매몰 비용 오류'라고 알려진 원리가 있다

The idea is / that when you are invested and have ownership in something, /
그 생각은 ~이다 / 여러분이 무언가에 투자하고 소유권을 가지면 /

you overvalue that thing.
여러분은 그것을 지나치게 중시한다는 것

(B) This leads people to continue on paths or pursuits /
이것은 사람들이 경로를 계속 따르거나 추구를 계속하게 한다 /

that should clearly be abandoned.
분명히 버려야 하는

For example, / people often remain in terrible relationships /
예를 들면 / 사람들은 종종 끔찍한 관계에 남아 있다 /

simply because they've invested a great deal of themselves into them.
그저 자신의 많은 것을 그 관계에 투여했기 때문에

Or someone may continue pouring money into a business /
아니면, 누군가는 사업에 계속 돈을 쏟아부을 수도 있다 /

that is clearly a bad idea in the market.
시장에서 분명히 나쁜 아이디어인

(A) Sometimes, the smartest thing a person can do / is quit.
때론 한 사람이 할 수 있는 가장 현명한 일은 / 그만두는 것일 수 있다

Although this is true, / it has also become a tired and played-out argument.
이것이 사실이더라도 / 그것은 또한 식상하고 효력이 떨어진 주장이 될 수 있다

Sunk cost doesn't always have to be a bad thing.
매몰 비용이 항상 나쁜 것은 아니다

(C) Actually, / you can leverage this human tendency / to your benefit.
사실 / 여러분은 이 인간적인 경향을 이용할 수 있다 / 여러분에게 득이 되도록

Like someone invests a great deal of money in a personal trainer /
확실히 많은 돈을 개인 트레이너에게 투자하는 사람처럼

to ensure they follow through on their commitment, /
자신이 자신의 약속을 끝까지 완수하기 위해 /

you, too, can invest a great deal up front /
여러분 또한 선지급으로 많은 돈을 투자할 수 있다 /

to ensure you stay on the path you want to be on.
여러분이 있고 싶은 경로에 확실히 있기 위해

경제학에서 '매몰 비용 오류'라고 알려진 원리가 있다. 그 생각은 여러분이 무언가에 투자하고 소유권을 가지면, 그것을 지나치게 중시한다는 것이다.
(B) 이것은 사람들이 분명히 버려야 하는 경로를 계속 따르거나 추구를 계속하게 한다. 예를 들면, 사람들은 그저 자신의 많은 것을 그 관계에 투여했기 때문에 종종 끔찍한 관계에 남아 있다. 아니면, 누군가는 시장에서 분명히 나쁜 아이디어인 사업에 계속 돈을 쏟아부을 수도 있다.
(A) 때론 한 사람이 할 수 있는 가장 현명한 일은 그만두는 것일 수 있다. 이것이 사실이더라도, 그것은 또한 식상하고 효력이 떨어진 주장이 될 수 있다. 매몰 비용이 항상 나쁜 것은 아니다.
(C) 사실, 여러분은 이 인간적인 경향을 여러분에게 득이 되도록 이용할 수 있다. 확실히 자신이 자신의 약속을 끝까지 완수하기 위해 많은 돈을 개인 트레이너에게 투자하는 사람처럼, 여러분 또한 여러분이 있고 싶은 경로에 확실히 있기 위해 선지급으로 많은 돈을 투자할 수 있다.

문제풀이

무언가에 투자하고 소유권을 가지면 그것에 지나친 가치를 부여하는 것을 매몰 비용 오류라고 한다는 내용의 주어진 글 다음에, 사람들이 버려야 하는 경로를 따르게 하는 매몰 비용의 문제점과 그 사례를 언급한 (B)가 오고, 매몰 비용 오류에 대처하는 방법은 중지하는 것이지만 매몰 비용도 긍정적 측면이 있다고 한 (A)가 온 후, 이어서 매몰 비용 오류가 득이 되는 사례를 제시한 (C)가 오는 것이 적절하다. 따라서 정답은 ②이다.

구조 다시보기

도입(정의)	어떤 것에 투자하여 소유권을 가지고 있으면 그것에 지나친 가치를 부여하는 것을 '매몰 비용 오류'라고 함
문제점	매몰 비용 오류는 사람들이 버려야 하는 경로를 따르게 함
해결책	매몰 비용 오류를 해결하는 가장 좋은 방법은 그만두는 것임
반전(장점)	계속 해야 하는 일에 선지급으로 많은 돈을 투자하는 것과 같은 상황에서는 매몰 비용 오류가 득이 될 수 있음

어휘·어구

sunk cost fallacy 매몰 비용 오류
ownership 소유권
overvalue 지나치게 중시하다, 과대평가하다
played-out 효력이 떨어진, 낡은
argument 주장
pursuit 일, 추구
abandon 그만두다, 폐기하다
a great deal of 많은 ~
follow through on ~을 완수하다
commitment 약속, 전념
up front 선지급으로

정답률 71%

7. ② 가격 인상의 결과

직독/직해

According to the market response model, /
시장 반응 모형에 따르면 /

it is increasing prices /
바로 가격의 인상이다 /

that drive providers to search for new sources, /
공급자가 새로운 공급원을 찾게 하는 것은 /

innovators to substitute, consumers to conserve, /
혁신가가 대체하게 하고, 소비자가 절약하게 하는 것은 /

and alternatives to emerge.
그리고 대안이 생기게 하는 것은

(B) Taxing certain goods or services, /
특정 재화나 용역에 세금을 부과하여 /

and so increasing prices, /
그리고 가격이 인상되면 /

should result in either decreased use of these resources /
이런 자원의 사용의 감소를 낳을 것이다 /

or creative innovation of new sources or options.
또는 새로운 공급원 또는 선택사항의 창조적 혁신을 (낳을 것이다)

The money raised through the tax /
세금을 매겨 조성된 돈은 /

can be used directly by the government /
정부에 의해 사용될 수 있다 /

either to supply services or to search for alternatives.
직접 서비스를 공급하거나 대안을 찾는 데

(A) Many examples of such "green taxes" exist.
그런 '환경세'의 많은 사례가 존재한다

Facing landfill costs, labor expenses, /
쓰레기 매립 비용, 인건비에 직면한 /

and related costs in the provision of garbage disposal, /
그리고 쓰레기 처리를 제공하는 데 관련된 비용(에 직면한) /

for example, / 예를 들면 /

some cities have required households /
일부 도시는 가정에 요구해왔다 /

to dispose of all waste in special trash bags, /
모든 쓰레기를 특별 쓰레기봉투에 담아 처리하도록 /

purchased by consumers themselves, /
소비자가 직접 구입한 /

and often costing a dollar or more each.
그리고 각각 흔히 1달러 혹은 그 이상씩 드는

(C) The results have been greatly increased recycling /
그 결과 재활용이 크게 증가했다 /

and more careful attention by consumers /
그리고 소비자가 더 세심한 주의를 기울이게 되었다 /

to packaging and waste.
포장과 쓰레기에

By internalizing the costs of trash to consumers, /
소비자에게 쓰레기 비용을 자기 것으로 되게 함으로써 /

there has been an observed decrease /
감소가 관찰되었다 /

in the flow of garbage from households.
가정에서 나오는 쓰레기 흐름의

시장 반응 모형에 따르면, 공급자가 새로운 공급원을 찾게 하고, 혁신가가 대체하게 하고, 소비자가 절약하게 하고, 대안이 생기게 하는 것은 바로 가격의 인상이다.
(B) 특정 재화나 용역에 세금을 부과하여 가격이 인상되면 이런 자원의 사용의 감소나 새로운 공급원 또는 선택사항의 창조적 혁신을 낳을 것이다. 세금을 매겨 조성된 돈은 정부에 의해 직접 서비스를 공급하거나 대안을 찾는 데 사용될 수 있다.
(A) 그런 '환경세'의 많은 사례가 존재한다. 예를 들면, 쓰레기 매립 비용, 인건비, 쓰레기 처리를 제공하는 데 관련된 비용에 직면한 일부 도시는 가정이 모든 쓰레기를 소비자가 직접 구입한, 각각 흔히 1달러 혹은 그 이상씩 드는 특별 쓰레기봉투에 담아 처리하도록 요구해왔다.
(C) 그 결과 재활용이 크게 증가했고 소비자가 포장과 쓰레기에 더 세심한 주의를 기울이게 되었다. 소비자에게 쓰레기 비용을 자기 것으로 되게 함으로써, 가정에서 나오는 쓰레기 흐름의 감소가 관찰되었다.

문제풀이

가격의 인상은 공급자, 혁신가 그리고 소비자가 대안을 모색하게 한다는 내용의 주어진 글 다음에, 특정 재화나 용역에 과세를 하면 자원의 사용을 줄이거나 새로운 공급이나 선택 사항의 창조적 혁신을 초래한다는 내용의 (B)가 오고, 그 사례로 '환경세'를 들면서 일부 도시들이 가정이 쓰레기를 처리할 때 비용을 부담해야 하는 쓰레기봉투를 사용하도록 했다는 내용의 (A)가 온 후, 이어서 그 결과 소비자가 직접 쓰레기 비용을 내게 해서 쓰레기 흐름이 감소했다는 내용의 (C)가 오는 것이 적절하다. 따라서 정답은 ②이다.

구조 다시보기

도입	가격 인상은 공급자, 혁신가, 그리고 소비자가 대안을 모색하게 함

전개	특정 재화나 용역에 과세하면 자원의 사용을 줄이거나 새로운 공급이나 선택 사항의 창조적 혁신을 초래함
예시	일부 도시들이 가정이 쓰레기를 처리할 때 직접 돈을 주고 구입해야 하는 쓰레기봉투를 사용하게 함
결과	재활용이 증가하고 소비자가 포장과 쓰레기에 주의를 기울여 쓰레기 흐름이 감소함

어휘·어구

innovator 혁신가
substitute 대체하다, 대용하다
conserve 아끼다, 아껴 쓰다
alternative 대안, 선택 가능한 것
emerge 생겨나다, 나오다
green tax 환경세
landfill 쓰레기 매립지
labor 노동, 근로
expense 비용, 돈
provision 공급, 제공
disposal 처리
dispose 처리하다
packaging 포장
internalize 내면화하다, 자기 것으로 하다

8. ⑤ 허구의 세계 vs. 현실의 세계

직독/직해

In spite of the likeness between the fictional and real world, /
허구의 세계와 현실의 세계 사이의 유사성에도 불구하고 /
the fictional world deviates from the real one /
허구의 세계는 현실의 세계에서 벗어난다 /
in one important respect.
한 가지 중요한 측면에서
(C) The existing world faced by the individual /
개인이 직면한 현존하는 세계는 /
is in principle / an infinite chaos of events and details /
원칙적으로 / 사건들과 세부 사항들의 무한한 혼돈 상태이다 /
before it is organized by a human mind.
인간의 정신에 의해 정리되기 전에는
This chaos only gets processed and modified /
이 혼돈 상태는 처리되고 수정된다 /
when perceived by a human mind.
인간의 정신에 의해 인식될 때에만
(B) Because of the inner qualities /
내적 특성 때문에 /
with which the individual is endowed /
개인이 부여받은 /
through heritage and environment, /
유산과 환경을 통해 /
the mind functions as a filter; /
그런 정신은 여과기 역할을 한다 /
every outside impression that passes through it /
그것을 통과하는 모든 외부의 인상이 /
is filtered and interpreted.
걸러지고 해석되는
However, / the world the reader encounters in literature /
하지만 / 문학에서 독자가 마주하는 세계는 /
is already processed and filtered /
이미 처리되고 여과되어 있다 /
by another consciousness.
또 다른 사람의 의식에 의해
(A) The author has selected the content /
작가는 내용을 선정했다 /
according to his own worldview and his own conception of relevance, /
자신의 세계관과 적절성에 대한 자신의 개념에 따라 /
in an attempt to be neutral and objective /
중립적이고 객관적이 되려는 시도로 /
or convey a subjective view on the world.
또는 세계에 대한 주관적인 시각을 전달하려는 (시도로)
Whatever the motives, /
동기가 무엇이든 상관없이 /
the author's subjective conception of the world stands /
세계에 대한 작가의 주관적인 개념은 존재한다 /
between the reader and the original, untouched world /
독자와 원래의 있는 그대로의 세계 사이에 /
on which the story is based.
이야기의 기반이 되는

허구의 세계와 현실의 세계 사이의 유사성에도 불구하고 허구의 세계는 한 가지 중요한 측면에서 현실의 세계에서 벗어난다.
(C) 개인이 직면한 현존하는 세계는 원칙적으로 인간의 정신에 의해 정리되기 전에는 사건들과 세부 사항들의 무한한 혼돈 상태이다. 이 혼돈 상태는 인간의 정신에 의해 인식될 때에만 처리되고 수정된다.
(B) 개인이 유산과 환경을 통해 부여받은 내적 특성 때문에 그런 정신은 그것을 통과하는 모든 외부의 인상이 걸러지고 해석되는 여과기 역할을 한다. 하지만 문학에서 독자가 마주하는 세계는 이미 또 다른 사람의 의식에 의해 처리되고 여과되어 있다.
(A) 작가는 중립적이고 객관적이 되려는, 또는 세계에 대한 주관적인 시각을 전달하려는 시도로 자신의 세계관과 적절성에 대한 자신의 개념에 따라 내용을 선정했다. 동기가 무엇이든 상관없이, 세계에 대한 작가의 주관적인 개념은 독자와 이야기의 기반이 되는 원래의 있는 그대로의 세계 사이에 존재한다.

문제풀이

허구의 세계가 한 가지 중요한 측면에서 현실의 세계에서 벗어난다고 한 주어진 글 다음에, 개인이 직면한 현실 세계는 혼돈 상태로 인간의 정신에 의해 인식될 때만 처리되고 수정된다는 내용의 (C)가 오고, 이어서 (C)에서 언급된 인간의 정신을 the mind로 받으며 그 정신은 모든 외부의 인상이 걸러지는 여과기 역할을 하지만 문학에서 세계는 이미 다른 사람에 의해 처리되고 여과되었다는 내용의 (B)가 온 후, 마지막으로 작가의 주관적인 개념에 의해 만들어진 세계에 대해 이야기하는 (A)가 오는 것이 가장 적절하다. 따라서 정답은 ⑤이다.

이렇게 풀자 우선 주어진 문장을 통해 무엇에 관한 글인지를 파악한 후, (A), (B), (C)의 핵심 내용을 정리하고 단서가 되는 연결사나 (대)명사에 유의하면서 연결 관계를 찾도록 한다. (A)의 'The author(그 작가는)', (B)의 'the mind(그런 정신)', (C)의 'The existing world(현존하는 세계는)'가 글의 흐름의 단서가 되므로 이에 유의하면서 글을 읽도록 한다.

어휘·어구

in spite of ~에도 불구하고
content 내용
relevance 적절, 타당성
in an attempt to ~하려는 시도로
neutral 중립적인
objective 객관적인
convey 전달하다
subjective 주관적인
untouched 손을 대지 않은
function 기능하다
encounter 맞닥뜨리다
consciousness 의식
in principle 원칙적으로
infinite 무한한
modify 수정하다
perceive 인지하다

9. ② 정치적 의도가 있는 전쟁의 속성

직독/직해

The objective of battle, / 전투의 목표 /
to "throw" the enemy and to make him defenseless, /
적군을 '격멸하고' 방어할 수 없는 상태로 만드는 것은 /
may temporarily blind commanders and even strategists /
일시적으로 지휘관과 심지어 전략가까지도 보지 못하게 할지도 모른다 /
to the larger purpose of war.
전쟁의 더 큰 목적을
War is never an isolated act, /
전쟁은 절대 고립된 행위가 아니며 /
nor is it ever only one decision.
또한 결코 단 하나의 결정도 아니다
(B) In the real world, / 실제 세계에서 /
war's larger purpose is always a political purpose.
전쟁의 더 큰 목적은 항상 정치적 목적이다
It transcends the use of force.
그것은 물리력의 사용을 초월한다
This insight was famously captured /
이런 통찰은 멋지게 포착되었다 /
by Clausewitz's most famous phrase, /
Clausewitz의 가장 유명한 구절에 의해 /
"War is a mere continuation of politics /
전쟁은 단지 정치를 계속하는 것이다 /
by other means." 다른 수단으로
(A) To be political, / 정치적이 되려면 /
a political entity or a representative of a political entity, /
정치적 실체나 정치적 실체의 대표자는 /
whatever its constitutional form, /
체제상의 형태가 무엇이든지, /
has to have an intention, a will.
의도, 즉 의지가 있어야 한다
That intention has to be clearly expressed.
그 의도는 분명히 표현되어야 한다
(C) And one side's will has to be transmitted /
그리고 한쪽의 의지는 전달되어야 한다 /
to the enemy / 적에게 /
at some point / during the confrontation /
어느 시점에 / 대치하는 동안 /
(it does not have to be publicly communicated).
그것이 공개적으로 전달될 필요는 없다
A violent act and its larger political intention /
폭력적인 행위와 그것의 더 큰 정치적 의도는 /
must also be attributed to one side /
또한 한쪽의 탓으로 돌려져야 한다 /
at some point / during the confrontation.
어느 시점에 / 대치하는 동안
History does not know of acts of war /
역사는 전쟁 행위에 대해 모른다 /
without eventual attribution.
궁극적인 귀인이 없는

전투의 목표, 즉 적군을 '격멸하고' 방어할 수 없는 상태로 만드는 것은 일시적으로 지휘관과 심지어 전략가까지도 전쟁의 더 큰 목적을 보지 못하게 할지도 모른다. 전쟁은 절대 고립된 행위가 아니며, 또한 결코 단 하나의 결정도 아니다.
(B) 실제 세계에서 전쟁의 더 큰 목적은 항상 정치적 목적이다. 그것은 물리력의 사용을 초월한다. 이런 통찰은 "전쟁은 다른 수단으로 단지 정치를 계속하는 것이다."라고 한 Clausewitz의 가장 유명한 구절에 의해 멋지게 포착되었다.
(A) 정치적이 되려면, 정치적 실체나 정치적 실체의 대표자는, 체제상의 형태가 무엇이든지, 의도, 즉 의지가 있어야 한다. 그 의도는 분명히 표현되어야 한다.
(C) 그리고 대치하는 동안 한쪽의 의지는 어느 시점에 적에게 전달되어야 한다(그것이 공개적으로 전달될 필요는 없다). 폭력적인 행위와 그것의 더 큰 정치적 의도 또한 대치하는 동안 어느 시점에 한쪽의 탓으로 돌려져야 한다. 역사는 궁극적인 귀인이 없는 전쟁 행위에 대해 모른다.

문제풀이

전쟁에는 적국을 격멸하고 무방비 상태로 만드는 것 이상의 목적이 있다는 내용의 주어진 글 다음에, 전쟁의 더 큰 목적은 정치적 목적이라고 밝히면서 그것은 물리력의 사용을 초월한다는 내용의 (B)가 오고, 이어서 정치적 목적을 가지기 위해서 대표자는 의지를 갖고 그것을 분명히 표현해야 한다는 내용의 (A)가 온 후, 마지막으로 (A)의 내용

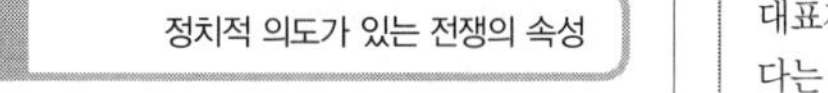

과 And로 연결하면서 분명한 의도의 표현에 대해 부연 설명하는 (C)가 오는 것이 가장 자연스럽다. 따라서 정답은 ②이다.

구조 다시보기

도입	전쟁에는 적국을 격멸하고 방어할 수 없는 상태로 만드는 것 이상의 목적이 있음
주제	전쟁의 더 큰 목적은 정치적 목적임
전개	• 정치적으로 되려면 정치적 실체나 그것의 대표자의 분명한 의도 표현이 필요함 • 대치하는 동안 의도를 상대에게 전달해야 함 • 폭력 행위, 정치적 의도가 한쪽 탓으로 돌려져야 함
결론	역사는 귀인이 없는 전쟁은 모름

어휘·어구

objective 목표
defenseless 방어할 수 없는
temporarily 일시적으로
commander 지휘관
strategist 전략가
isolated 고립된
representative 대표자
constitutional 체제[구성]상의, 헌법(상)의
intention 의도, 의사
capture 포착하다
phrase (간결한) 한마디, 어구
means 수단
transmit 전달하다, 전수하다
enemy 상대, 적
confrontation 대치, 대결
violent 폭력적인
be attributed to ~의 탓으로 돌려지다
eventual 궁극적인

정답률 49%

10. ⑤ 에너지 효율 투자에서 비용 효율

직독/직해

Experts have identified a large number of measures /
전문가들은 많은 수의 대책을 찾아냈다 /
that promote energy efficiency.
에너지 효율을 증진하는
Unfortunately / many of them are not cost effective.
안타깝게도 / 그중 많은 수는 비용 효율적이지 않다
This is a fundamental requirement /
이것은 기본적인 필요조건이다 /
for energy efficiency investment /
에너지 효율 투자의 /
from an economic perspective.
경제적 관점에서
(C) However, / the calculation of such cost effectiveness /
하지만 / 그런 비용 효과의 산정은 /
is not easy: / 쉽지 않은데 /
it is not simply a case / of looking at private costs /
그것은 단순히 ~경우가 아니기 때문이다 / 사적 비용을 살펴보는 /
and comparing them to the reductions achieved.
그리고 그것을 성취한 절감액과 비교하는
(B) There are significant externalities /
의미 있는 외부 효과가 있다 /
to take into account / 고려해야 할 /
and there are also macroeconomic effects.
그리고 거시 경제적 효과도 있다
For instance, / at the aggregate level, /
예를 들면 / 총체적 차원에서 /
improving the level of national energy efficiency /
국가의 에너지 효율 수준을 높이는 것은 /
has positive effects / on macroeconomic issues /
긍정적인 영향을 끼친다 / 거시 경제적 문제에 /
such as energy dependence, climate change, health, national competitiveness and reducing fuel poverty.
에너지 의존도, 기후 변화, 보건, 국가 경쟁력, 연료 빈곤을 감소시키는 것과 같은
(A) And this has direct repercussions /
그리고 이것은 직접적인 영향을 끼치는데 /
at the individual level: /
개인적 차원에서 /
households can reduce the cost of electricity and gas bills, /
가정은 전기 비용과 가스 요금을 줄일 수 있다 /
and improve their health and comfort, /
그리고 그들의 건강과 안락을 증진할 수 있다 /
while companies can increase their competitiveness and their productivity.
회사는 자체 경쟁력과 생산성을 증대시킬 수 있지만
Finally, / the market for energy efficiency /
결국 / 에너지 효율 시장은 /
could contribute to the economy /
경제에 기여할 수 있는 것이다 /
through job and firms creation.
일자리와 기업 창출을 통해

전문가들은 에너지 효율을 증진하는 많은 수의 대책을 찾아냈다. 안타깝게도 그중 많은 수는 비용 효율적이지 않다. 이것은 경제적 관점에서 에너지 효율 투자의 기본적인 필요조건이다.
(C) 하지만 그런 비용 효과의 산정은 쉽지 않은데, 그것은 단순히 사적 비용을 살펴보고 그것을 성취한 절감액과 비교하는 경우가 아니기 때문이다.
(B) 고려해야 할 의미 있는 외부 효과가 있고 거시 경제적 효과도 있다. 예를 들면 총체적 차원에서, 국가의 에너지 효율 수준을 높이는 것은 에너지 의존도, 기후 변화, 보건, 국가 경쟁력, 연료 빈곤을 감소시키는 것과 같은 거시 경제적 문제에 긍정적인 영향을 끼친다.
(A) 그리고 이것은 개인적 차원에서 직접적인 영향을 끼치는데, 즉 가정은 전기 비용과 가스 요금을 줄이고 그들의 건강과 안락을 증진할 수 있지만, 회사는 자체 경쟁력과 생산성을 증대시킬 수 있다. 결국, 에너지 효율 시장은 일자리와 기업 창출을 통해 경제에 기여할 수 있는 것이다.

문제풀이

비용 효율은 에너지 효율 투자의 기본적인 필요조건이라는 내용의 주어진 글 다음에, However로 시작하면서, 그런 비용 효율성의 산정은 어렵다는 내용의 (C)가 오고, 이어서 산정이 어려운 이유로 외부 효과와 거시 경제적 효과가 있다고 하면서 그 예를 든 (B)가 온 후, 마지막으로 이것이 개인적 차원에도 직접적인 영향을 미친다고 하면서 에너지 효율 시장이 일자리와 가업 창출을 통해 경제에 기여할 수 있다고 결론을 내리는 (A)가 오는 것이 가장 적절하다. 따라서 정답은 ⑤이다.

이렇게 풀자 우선 주어진 문장을 통해 무엇에 관한 글인지를 파악한 후, (A), (B), (C)의 핵심 내용을 정리하고 단서가 되는 연결사나 (대)명사에 유의하면서 연결 관계를 찾도록 한다. (A)의 'And this(그리고 이것은)', (B)의 'to take into account(고려해야 할)', (C)의 'However(하지만)'가 글의 흐름을 파악하는 단서가 되므로 이에 유의하면서 글을 읽도록 한다.

어휘·어구

expert 전문가
identify 찾다, 발견하다
measure 대책, 조치
promote 증진하다
efficiency 효율
fundamental 기본적인, 근본적인
perspective 관점
household 가정
bill 계산서, 청구서
competitiveness 경쟁력
contribute to ~에 기여하다
externality 외부 효과
take ~ into account ~을 고려하다
macroeconomic 거시 경제의

본문 095쪽

문법 플러스 16. 관계부사

A. 1. there 2. when 3. the way
4. where 5. from 6. that
7. whenever

1 [해석]▶ 결혼 후 아파트 한 채를 샀는데, 그곳에서 이후 10년간 살았다.
[해설]▶ 관계부사(where)는 「접속사(and)+부사(there)」의 역할을 한다.

2 [해석]▶ 네가 진정한 사랑을 찾을 시간이 올 것이다.
[해설]▶ 선행사가 시간(a time) 표현이 나오고 괄호 이하 부분이 완전한 문장이 나왔으므로 관계부사 when이 필요하다.

3 [해석]▶ 나는 그가 나를 보는 방식이 마음에 들지 않는다.
[해설]▶ 관계부사 how는 선행사(the way)와 함께 쓰지 않고 둘 중 하나만 써야 한다.

4 [해석]▶ 그들은 마침내 산 정상에 도달했는데, 그들은 그곳에서 주변에 구름을 제외하고 아무 것도 볼 수가 없었다.
[해설]▶ 선행사가 the mountaintop인 관계부사 where의 계속적 용법이다.

5 [해석]▶ 그것은 처방전에 있는 약을 받을 수 있는 자동판매기이다.
[해설]▶ 관계부사는 「전치사+관계대명사」로 바꾸어 쓸 수 있다. That's a vending machine where(= from which) you can get prescriptions drugs.

6 [해석]▶ 그들은 결정을 내려야 할 시간에 이르렀다.
[해설]▶ 관계부사 when 대신 that을 사용할 수 있다.

7 [해석]▶ 네가 필요할 때는 언제든지 전화해.
[해설]▶ 복합관계부사 whenever는 '~할 때는 언제나(= at any time when)'의 의미를 가지고 있다.

본문 095쪽

B. 1. there 2. why 3. the way
4. when 5. at 6. that
7. Wherever

1 [해석]▶ 우리는 마침내 지리산 정상에 도착했지만, 그곳에서 구름을 제외하고 아무 것도 볼 수 없었다.
[해설]▶ 관계부사는 접속사(but)+부사(there)로 바꿀 수 있다.

2 [해석]▶ 나는 Sally가 나의 초대를 왜 거절했는지 그 이유를 모른다.
[해설]▶ 이유를 나타내는 선행사(the reason)가 나오고 괄호 이하의 문장은 완전하므로 관계부사는 why가 필요하다.

3 [해석]▶ 나는 그녀가 나를 바라보는 방식이 맘에 든다.
[해설]▶ 선행사 the way나 관계부사 how는 '~하는 방식'의 의미를 가지고 있다. 주어진 문장은 I like the way.와 She looks at me in the way.라는 두 문장을 앞 문장의 the way를 선행사로 만들고, 뒷 문장의 in the way를 in which로 바꾼 문장이다.

4 [해석]▶ 내가 좋아하는 달은 2월인데, 그 달에 우리는 발렌타인데이를 기념한다.
[해설]▶ 선행사 the Fruary를 설명하는 관계부사 when의 계속적 용법이다.

5 [해석]▶ 이곳은 그녀가 스마트폰을 잃은 장소이다.
[해설]▶ 관계부사는 「전치사+관계대명사」로 바꾸어 쓸 수 있다. 주어진 문장은 This is the place where(= at which)

she lost her smartphone.에서 관계부사 where를 「전치사+관계대명사」로 바꾼 문장이다.

6 [해석]▶ 이것이 철새들이 길을 찾아가는 방법이다.
[해설]▶ 선행사가 the way(방식)는 관계부사 how와 함께 쓸 수 없다. 관계부사 how 대신 that을 쓸 수 있다.

7 [해석]▶ 네가 어디에 있든지 내가 너와 함께 있을게.
[해설]▶ 복합관계부사 wherever는 '~하는 곳은 어디나(= at any place where)의 의미가 있다.

본문 096쪽

숙어 플러스 16. 수능 필수 숙어 16회

1. order 2. placed
3. play 4. prevent

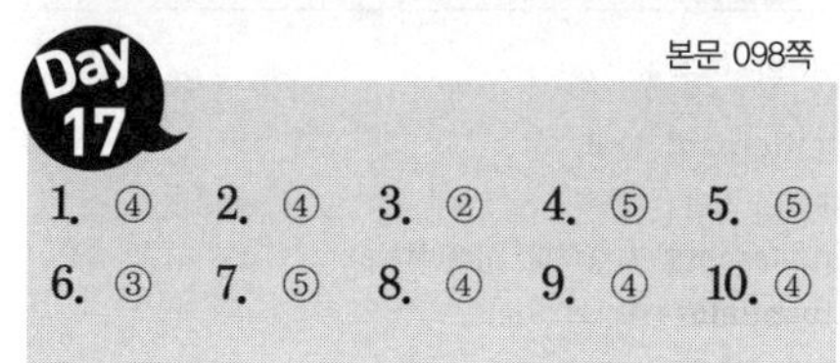

17. 주어진 문장의 위치 파악

Day 17 본문 098쪽

1. ④ 2. ④ 3. ② 4. ⑤ 5. ⑤
6. ③ 7. ⑤ 8. ④ 9. ④ 10. ④

정답률 54%

대표 기출 ⑤ 공원의 형태

직독/직해

Parks take the shape / demanded by the cultural concerns of their time.
공원은 형태를 갖는다 / 그것이 속한 시대의 문화적 관심사가 요구하는

Once parks are in place, / they are no inert stage /
일단 공원이 설치되면 / 그것은 비활성화된 단계가 아닌데 /

— their purposes and meanings are made and remade /
그것의 목적과 의미는 만들어지고 다시 만들어진다 /

by planners and by park users.
계획자와 공원 사용자에 의해서

Moments of park creation are particularly telling, / however, /
공원을 만드는 순간들은 특히 중요한데 / 하지만 /

for they reveal and actualize ideas /
왜냐하면 그것이 아이디어를 드러내고 실현하기 때문이다 /

about nature and its relationship to urban society.
자연과 도시 사회와 갖는 관계에 대한

Indeed, / what distinguishes a park / from the broader category of public space /
실제로 / 공원을 구별하는 것은 / 더 넓은 범주의 공공장소와

is the representation of nature / that parks are meant to embody.
자연의 표현이다 / 공원이 구현하고자 하는

Public spaces / include parks, concrete plazas, sidewalks, even indoor atriums.
공공장소는 / 공원, 콘크리트 광장, 보도, 심지어 실내 아트리움도 포함한다

Parks typically have trees, grass, and other plants / as their central features.
보통 공원에는 나무, 풀, 그리고 다른 식물들이 있다 / 그들의 중심적인 특색으로

When entering a city park, /
도시공원에 들어갈 때 /

people often imagine a sharp separation / from streets, cars, and buildings.
사람들은 종종 뚜렷한 분리를 상상한다 / 거리, 자동차, 그리고 건물과의

There's a reason for that: / traditionally, /
그것에는 이유가 있는데 / 전통적으로 /

park designers attempted to create such a feeling /
공원 설계자들은 그런 느낌을 만들어 내려고 시도했다 /

by planting tall trees at park boundaries, / building stone walls, /
공원 경계에 키가 큰 나무를 심고 / 돌담을 쌓고 /

and constructing other means of partition.
그리고 다른 칸막이 수단을 건설하여

What's behind this idea /
이 아이디어의 배후에는 /

is not only landscape architects' desire /
조경사의 욕구뿐만 아니라 /

to design aesthetically suggestive park spaces, /
미적인 암시가 있는 공원 공간을 설계하려는 /

but a much longer history of Western thought /
훨씬 더 오래된 서구 사상의 역사가 (있다) /

that envisions cities and nature / as antithetical spaces and oppositional forces.
도시와 자연을 상상하는 / 대조적인 공간과 반대 세력으로

공원은 그것이 속한 시대의 문화적 관심사가 요구하는 형태를 갖는다. 일단 공원이 설치되면, 그것은 비활성화된 단계가 아닌데 그것의 목적과 의미는 계획자와 공원 사용자에 의해서 만들어지고 다시 만들어진다. 하지만 공원을 만드는 순간들은 특히 중요한데, 왜냐하면 자연과 그것이 도시 사회와 갖는 관계에 대한 생각을 드러내고 실현하기 때문이다. (①) 실제로 공원을 더 넓은 범주의 공공장소와 구별하는 것은 공원이 구현하고자 하는 자연의 표현이다. (②) 공공장소는 공원, 콘크리트 광장, 보도, 심지어 실내 아트리움도 포함한다. (③) 보통 공원에는 그들의 중심적인 특색으로 나무, 풀, 그리고 다른 식물들이 있다. (④) 도시공원에 들어갈 때, 사람들은 종종 거리, 자동차, 그리고 건물과의 뚜렷한 분리를 상상한다. (⑤) 그것에는 이유가 있는데, 전통적으로 공원 설계자들은 공원 경계에 키가 큰 나무를 심고, 돌담을 쌓고, 다른 칸막이 수단을 건설하여 그런 느낌을 만들어 내려고 시도했다. 이 아이디어의 배후에는 미적인 암시가 있는 공원 공간을 설계하려는 조경사의 욕구뿐만 아니라 도시와 자연을 대조적인 공간과 반대 세력으로 상상하는 훨씬 더 오래된 서구 사상의 역사가 있다.

문제풀이

주어진 문장은 'that'에 이유가 있다고 하면서 그 이유로 공원 설계자들이 전통적으로 공원 경계에 나무를 심고 돌담 및 다른 칸막이 수단을 건설하여 그런 느낌을 만들려고 시도했다는 내용으로, 도시 공원에 들어갈 때 사람들이 도시의 사물들과는 뚜렷한 분리를 상상한다는 내용과 이 아이디어에는 미적인 공원 공간을 설계하려는 조경사의 욕구와 도시와 자연을 대조적인 공간으로 상상하는 서구 사상의 역사가 있다는 내용 사이인 ⑤에 들어가는 것이 적절하다. that은 ⑤ 앞 문장에서 언급된 '도시 공원에 들어갈 때 사람들이 종종 거리, 자동차, 그리고 건물과는 뚜렷한 분리를 상상하는 것'을 가리키고, such a feeling은 ⑤ 앞 문장에서 언급된 '공원과 도시의 사물이 분리되는 느낌'을 의미한다. ⑤ 뒤 문장의 the idea는 주어진 문장에서 언급된 '공원 경계에 큰 나무를 심고, 돌담을 쌓고, 다른 칸막이를 건설하는 것'을 가리킨다.

이렇게 풀자 내용의 논리적인 비약이나 단절이 일어나는 곳에 주어진 문장을 넣어 보고 글의 흐름이 자연스럽게 연결되는지 확인해 보면 답을 쉽게 찾을 수 있다. 여기서는 ⑤ 다음의 this idea가 앞에 나오지 않아서 단절이 일어났다. 따라서 주어진 문장을 ⑤에 넣어서 자연스럽게 연결되는지 확인해 본다.

어휘·어구

attempt to ~하려고 시도하다
boundary 영역
partition 칸막이
inert 비활성의
representation 표현, 묘사
embody 실현하다, 상징하다
landscape architect 조경사
envision 마음속에 그리다, 상상하다
oppositional 대조적인

정답률 56%

1. ④ 협상가들의 문제 해결 전략

직독/직해

Negotiators should try to find ways / to slice a large issue into smaller pieces, /
협상가들은 방법을 찾으려고 애써야 한다 / 큰 문제를 더 작은 조각으로 자르는 (방법을) /

known as using *salami tactics*.
'살라미 전략'을 사용하는 것으로 알려진

Issues that can be expressed in quantitative, measurable units / are easy to slice.
정량적이며 측정 가능한 단위로 표현될 수 있는 문제는 / 자르기 쉽다

For example, / compensation demands can be divided into /
예를 들면 / 보상 요구는 나누어질 수 있다 /
cents-per-hour increments / 시간당 센트 증가로 /
or lease rates can be quoted / as dollars per square foot.
또는 임대료는 견적을 낼 수 있다 / 평방 피트당 달러로
When working to fractionate issues of principle or precedent, /
원칙이나 판례의 쟁점을 세분화하는 작업을 할 때 /
parties may use the time horizon /
당사자들은 시간 지평을 사용할 수 있다 /
(when the principle goes into effect or how long it will last) /
(원칙이 효력을 발생하거나 지속되는 기간) /
as a way to fractionate the issue.
그 쟁점을 세분화하는 방법으로
It may be easier to reach an agreement /
합의에 도달하는 것이 더 쉬울 수 있다 /
when settlement terms don't have to be implemented / until months in the future.
합의 조건이 시행될 필요가 없을 때 / 앞으로 몇 개월까지
Another approach is to vary the number of ways /
또 다른 접근법은 방법의 수를 다양화하는 것이다 /
that the principle may be applied.
원칙이 적용될지도 모르는
For example, / a company may devise a family emergency leave plan /
예를 들면 / 회사는 가족 비상 휴가 계획을 고안할 수 있다 /
that allows employees the opportunity to be away from the company /
직원에게 회사를 비울 기회를 제공하는 /
for a period of no longer than three hours, / and no more than once a month, /
3시간 이내 기간 동안 / 그리고 한 달에 한 번 이하의 (기간 동안) /
for illness in the employee's immediate family.
직원의 직계 가족의 질병에 대해

협상가들은 '살라미 전략'을 사용하는 것으로 알려진, 큰 문제를 더 작은 조각으로 자르는 방법을 찾으려고 애써야 한다. (①) 정량적이며 측정할 수 있는 단위로 표현될 수 있는 문제는 자르기 쉽다. (②) 예를 들면, 보상 요구는 시간당 센트 증가로 나누거나 임대료는 평방 피트당 달러로 견적을 낼 수 있다. (③) 원칙이나 판례의 쟁점을 세분화하는 작업을 할 때, 당사자들은 그 쟁점을 세분화하는 방법으로 시간 지평(원칙이 효력을 발생하거나 지속되는 기간)을 사용할 수 있다. (④) 합의 조건이 앞으로 몇 개월까지 시행될 필요가 없을 때 합의에 도달하는 것이 더 쉬울 수 있다. 또 다른 접근법은 원칙이 적용될지도 모르는 방법의 수를 다양화하는 것이다. (⑤) 예를 들면, 회사는 직원의 직계 가족의 질병에 대해 직원에게 3시간 이내, 한 달에 한 번 이하의 기간 동안 회사를 비울 기회를 제공하는 가족 비상 휴가 계획을 고안할 수 있다.

문제풀이

주어진 문장은 합의 조건이 앞으로 몇 개월까지 시행될 필요가 없다면 합의에 도달하는 것이 더 쉬울 수 있다는 내용으로, 쟁점을 세분화하기 위해 원칙이 효력을 발휘하는 기간인 시간 지평을 사용하는 것에 대한 내용과 또 다른 접근법으로 원칙 적용이 가능한 방법의 수를 다양화하는 것에 대한 내용 사이인 ④에 들어가는 것이 적절하다.

이렇게 풀자 이 문제는 다른 문장 삽입 문제와는 달리 논리적인 비약이나 단절이 일어난 곳을 찾아야 하는 것이 아니라, 주어진 문장과 관련된 내용을 찾아 그 뒤에 주어진 문장을 사례로 넣어야 한다. 이 글에서 시간과 관련된 내용은 ④ 앞의 문장 밖에 없으므로 주어진 문장을 ④에 넣어서 자연스럽게 연결되는지 확인해 본다.

구조 다시보기

도입(주제)	협상가들은 큰 문제를 작게 자르는 방법을 찾으려 애씀
부연 1	정량적이고 측정할 수 있는 단위로 표현될 수 있는 문제는 자르기 쉬움
예시 1	보상 요구는 시간당 센트로, 임대료는 평방 피트당 달러로 견적을 냄
부연 2	원칙이나 판례의 쟁점을 세분화하는 작업에는 시간 지평을 사용할 수 있음
예시 2	합의 조건이 시행되기까지 시간이 몇 개월 남아 있을 때 합의에 도달이 더 쉬울 수 있음
부연 3	원칙이 적용될지도 모르는 방법의 수를 다양화함
예시 3	회사가 비상 휴가 계획을 구체적 기간이나 횟수를 제한할 수 있음

어휘·어구

settlement 합의
term 조건
implement 시행하다, 이행하다
negotiator 협상가
slice 자르다
tactic 전략
quantitative 양적인
compensation 보상
lease rates 임대료
quote 시세를 매기다
principle 원칙
precedent 관례, 전례
party 당사자
time horizon 시간 지평
devise 고안하다
emergency leave plan 비상 휴가 계획

정답률 64%

2. ④ 물 분자의 대기 순환 과정

직독/직해

Water molecules circulate through the atmosphere / as a result of evaporation.
물 분자는 대기를 순환한다 / 증발의 결과로
As water molecules rise high up in the atmosphere, /
물 분자가 대기 중으로 높이 상승하면 /
they may split up into their constituent chemical elements, hydrogen and oxygen, /
그것은 그것을 구성하는 화학 원소인 수소와 산소로 분해될 수도 있다 /
under the influence of sunlight.
햇빛의 영향을 받아
Whereas the much heavier oxygen either remains in the atmosphere /
훨씬 더 무거운 산소가 대기 중에 남아 있는 반면에 /
or is captured on the Earth's surface, /
혹은 지구 표면에 붙들리는 (반면에) /
the hydrogen tends to escape into space, /
수소는 우주로 빠져나가는 경향이 있다 /
because it is so light that Earth's gravity cannot retain it.
왜냐하면 수소가 너무 가벼워서 지구 중력이 그것을 붙잡아 둘 수 없기 때문에
As long as there was little or no free oxygen in the atmosphere /
유리 산소가 대기 중에 거의 없거나 전혀 없는 한 /
that could capture hydrogen / before it escaped into the cosmos, /
수소를 붙잡아 둘 수 있는 / 수소가 우주로 빠져나가기 전에 /
this process would have continued unhindered.
이 과정은 방해받지 않고 계속되었을 것이다
However, / after all the available materials on the Earth's surface, mostly iron, /
그러나 / 대부분이 철인, 지구 표면의 이용 가능한 모든 물질이 /
had combined with the free oxygen, / it began to appear in the atmosphere /
유리 산소와 결합한 후 / 그것은 대기 중에 모습을 드러내기 시작했다 /
in sizable quantities. 꽤 많은 양으로
As soon as this happened, / 이런 일이 일어나자마자 /
the free oxygen would have captured most of the free hydrogen /
유리 산소는 대부분의 유리 수소를 붙들어 두게 될 것이다 /
by forming water molecules again, / thus slowing down the loss of hydrogen.
다시 물 분자를 형성함으로써 / 그 결과 수소 손실을 늦추면서
Over the course of time, / 시간이 지남에 따라 /
this process would have helped to retain water on Earth, /
이 과정은 지구에 물을 보유하는 데 도움을 주었을 것이다 /
while it also contributed to the emergence of oxygen in the atmosphere.
게다가 그것은 동시에 대기 중의 산소 발생에도 기여했다

물 분자는 증발의 결과로 대기를 순환한다. (①) 물 분자가 대기 중으로 높이 상승하면, 그것은 햇빛의 영향을 받아 그것을 구성하는 화학 원소인 수소와 산소로 분해될 수도 있다. (②) 훨씬 더 무거운 산소가 대기 중에 남아 있거나 지구 표면에 붙들리는 반면에, 수소는 우주로 빠져나가는 경향이 있는데, 수소가 너무 가벼워서 지구 중력이 그것을 붙잡아 둘 수 없기 때문이다. (③) 수소가 우주로 빠져나가기 전에 수소를 붙잡아 둘 수 있는 유리 산소가 대기 중에 거의 없거나 전혀 없는 한, 이 과정은 방해받지 않고 계속되었을 것이다. (④) 그러나 대부분이 철인, 지구 표면의 이용 가능한 모든 물질이 유리 산소와 결합한 후, 그것은 대기 중에 꽤 많은 양으로 모습을 드러내기 시작했다. 이런 일이 일어나자마자 유리 산소는 다시 물 분자를 형성함으로써 대부분의 유리 수소를 붙들어 두어 그 결과 수소 손실을 늦추었을 것이다. (⑤) 시간이 지남에 따라, 이 과정은 지구에 물을 보유하는 데 도움을 주었을 것이고, 동시에 대기 중의 산소 발생에도 기여했다.

문제풀이

이 글은 증발의 결과로 물 분자가 대기를 순환하는 과정을 설명한 글이다. 물 분자가 대기 중으로 상승하면 물 분자는 수소와 산소로 분해되는 데, 무거운 산소는 대기 중에 남아 있지만, 수소는 너무 가벼워서 우주로 빠져 나가게 되는데 대기 상에 유리 산소가 있으면 우주로 빠져나가는 유리 수소를 붙들어 두어 다시 물 분자를 형성하게 된다고 설명하고 있다. 주어진 문장은 지구 표면의 모든 물질이 유리 산소와 결합한 후에, 그것(유리 산소)이 대기 중에 꽤 많이 나타난다는 내용으로, 주어진 문장의 'However'를 통해 이 문장의 앞에는 유리 산소가 대기 중에 거의 없다는 내용이 나와야 하고, 그 뒤에는 대기 중에 있는 유리 산소가 유리 수소를 붙들게 된다는 내용이 와야 하므로 주어진 문장은 ④에 들어가는 것이 가장 적절하다.

구조 다시보기

도입	물 분자는 증발의 결과로 대기를 순환함
전개	물 분자가 상승하면 산소 원자와 수소 원자로 분리됨
발전	무거운 산소 원자는 대기 중이나 지표면에 남아 있지만, 가벼운 수소 원자는 우주로 날아가 버림
전환	철과 같은 지표면의 물질과 결합한 후 상당히 많은 양의 유리 산소가 대기 중에 남아 있음
결론	대기 상에 남아 있는 유리 산소가 수소 원자를 붙잡아 물 분자를 형성함

어휘·어구

molecule 분자
circulate 순환하다
evaporation 증발
split up into ~으로 분해되다
constituent 구성하는
retain 붙잡아두다
free oxygen 유리 산소
free hydrogen 유리 수소
unhindered 방해받지 않는
sizable 꽤 많은
slow down 느리게 하다
emergence 발생

정답률 39%

3. ② 집단의 정의

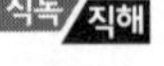

직독/직해

In everyday life, / we tend to see any collection of people as a group.
일상생활에서 / 우리는 어떤 사람들의 무리라도 하나의 집단으로 여기는 경향이 있다

However, / social psychologists use this term / more precisely.
하지만 / 사회 심리학자들은 이 용어를 사용한다 / 더 정확하게

In particular, / they define a group / as two or more people /
특히, / 그들은 집단을 정의한다 / 둘 이상의 사람들로 /

who interact with, and exert mutual influences on, each other.
서로 상호 작용을 하고, 상호 간의 영향력을 발휘하는

It is this sense of mutual interaction or inter-dependence for a common purpose /
바로 이런 공동의 목적을 위한 서로의 상호 작용 또는 상호 의존감이다 /

which distinguishes the members of a group /
집단의 구성원들을 구별해내는 것은 /

from a mere aggregation of individuals.
단순한 개인들의 집합으로부터

For example, / as Kenneth Hodge observed, /
예를 들면 / Kenneth Hodge가 말한 것과 같이 /

a collection of people / who happen to go for a swim after work / on the same day each week /
사람들의 무리는 / 일을 마치고 우연히 수영을 하러 가는 / 매주 똑같은 날에 /

does not, strictly speaking, constitute a group /
엄밀히 말하면 집단을 구성하지 않는데 /

because these swimmers do not interact with each other / in a structured manner.
이런 수영하는 사람들은 서로 상호 작용하지 않기 때문이다 / 구조적인 방식으로

By contrast, / a squad of young competitive swimmers /
그에 반해서 / 경쟁하는 어린 수영 선수들의 팀은 /

who train every morning / before going to school / *is* a group /
매일 아침 훈련하는 / 학교에 가기 전에 / 집단'이다' /

because they not only share a common objective / (training for competition) /
공동의 목표를 공유할 뿐만 아니라 / (경기를 위한 훈련) /

but also interact with each other / in formal ways /
서로 상호 작용하기 때문에 / 공식적인 방식으로 /

(e.g., by warming up together beforehand).
(예를 들면, 미리 함께 워밍업을 함)

It is this sense of people coming together / to achieve a common objective /
바로 사람들이 함께 모이는 이런 생각이다 / 공동의 목표를 달성하기 위해 /

that defines a "team".
'팀'을 정의하는 것은

일상생활에서 우리는 어떤 사람들의 무리라도 하나의 집단으로 여기는 경향이 있다. (①) 하지만 사회 심리학자들은 이 용어를 더 정확하게 사용한다. (②) 특히, 그들은 서로 상호 작용을 하고, 상호 간의 영향력을 발휘하는 둘 이상의 사람들로 집단을 정의한다. 집단의 구성원들을 단순한 개인들의 집합으로부터 구별해내는 것은 바로 이런 공동의 목적을 위한 서로의 상호 작용 또는 상호 의존감이다. (③) 예를 들면, Kenneth Hodge가 말한 것과 같이, 매주 똑같은 날에 일을 마치고 우연히 수영을 하러 가는 사람들의 무리는 엄밀히 말하면 집단을 구성하지 않는데, 이런 수영하는 사람들은 구조적인 방식으로 서로 상호 작용하지 않기 때문이다. (④) 그에 반해서, 매일 아침 학교에 가기 전에 훈련하는, 경쟁하는 어린 수영 선수들의 팀은 공동의 목표(경기를 위한 훈련)를 공유할 뿐만 아니라 공식적인 방식(예를 들면, 미리 함께 워밍업을 함)으로 상호 작용하기 때문에 집단'이다'. (⑤) '팀'을 정의하는 것은 바로 공동의 목표를 달성하기 위해 사람들이 함께 모이는 이런 생각이다.

문제풀이

주어진 문장은 그들이 집단을 서로 상호 작용하고 서로 영향력을 발휘하는 둘 이상의 사람들로 정의 내렸다는 내용으로, 사회 심리학자들은 집단을 더 정확하게 사용한다는 내용과 집단 구성원의 특징이 이런 공동의 목적을 위한 서로의 상호 작용 또는 상호 의존감이라고 한 문장 사이인 ②에 오는 것이 적절하다. 주어진 문장의 they는 ② 앞의 문장의 social psychologist를 가리킨다.

○ 이렇게 풀자 내용의 논리적인 비약이나 단절이 일어나는 곳에 주어진 문장을 넣어 보고 글의 흐름이 자연스럽게 연결되는지 확인해 보면 답을 쉽게 찾을 수 있다. ② 다음 문장의 this sense에 해당하는 내용이 앞 문장에는 나오지 않아 흐름에 단절이 일어났다. 따라서 주어진 문장을 ②에 넣어서 자연스럽게 연결되는지 확인해 본다. this sense는 주어진 문장에서 언급한 '서로 상호 작용을 하고, 상호 간의 영향력을 발휘하는 감각'을 가리킨다.

어휘·어구

define A as B A를 B로 정의하다
interact 상호 작용하다
mutual 서로의
social psychologist 사회 심리학자
term 용어
precisely 정확하게
distinguish 구별하다
aggregation 집합
constitute 구성하다
structured 구조화된
squad 팀
observe 말하다
competitive 경쟁을 하는
objective 목표
competition 경기
beforehand 사전에, 미리

정답률 40%

4. ⑤ 편리성과 보안의 관계

직독/직해

Each new wave of technology / is intended to enhance user convenience, /
각각의 새로운 기술의 물결은 / 사용자 편의성을 향상하려는 의도이다 /

as well as improve security, /
보안을 향상할 뿐만 아니라 /

but sometimes these do not necessarily go hand-in-hand.
하지만 가끔 이것들이 반드시 같이 진행되지는 않는다

For example, / the transition from magnetic stripe to embedded chip /
예를 들면 / 마그네틱 띠에서 내장형 칩으로의 전환은 /

slightly slowed down transactions, /
거래(의 속도)를 약간 늦췄는데 /

sometimes frustrating customers in a hurry.
때때로 바쁜 고객을 좌절시켰다

Make a service too burdensome, / and the potential customer will go elsewhere.
서비스를 너무 부담스럽게 만들면 / 잠재 고객은 다른 곳으로 갈 것이다

This obstacle applies / at several levels.
이러한 장벽은 적용된다 / 몇몇 수준에서

Passwords, double-key identification, /
비밀번호, 이중 키 확인, /

and biometrics such as fingerprint-, iris-, and voice recognition /
그리고 지문, 홍채 및 음성 인식과 같은 생체 인식은 /

are all ways / of keeping the account details hidden / from potential fraudsters, /
모두 (~하는) 방법이다 / 계정 세부 정보를 숨겨 주는 / 잠재적인 사기꾼으로부터 /

of keeping your data dark.
즉 여러분의 데이터를 비밀로 유지해주는

But / they all inevitably add a burden / to the use of the account.
그러나 / 그것들은 모두 불가피하게 부담을 가중한다 / 계좌 사용에

On top of the hurdles introduced / in accessing his or her money, /
도입되어진 난관에 더해 / 자신의 돈에 접근하는 데 있어서 /

if a suspected fraud is detected, /
만약 의심스러운 사기가 탐지되면 /

the account holder has to deal with the phone call asking /
계좌 주인은 전화 통화에 응해야만 한다 /

if he or she made the suspicious transactions.
본인이 그 의심스러운 거래를 했는지를 묻는 내용의

This is all useful at some level — /
이것은 모두 어느 정도 유용하며 /

indeed, it can be reassuring /
실제로, 안심될 수는 있다 /

knowing that your bank is keeping alert / to protect you — /
여러분의 은행이 경계를 늦추지 않고 있다는 것을 알게 되어 / 여러분을 보호하기 위해 /

but it becomes tiresome / if too many such calls are received.
하지만 그것은 성가신 일이 된다 / 그런 전화를 너무 많이 받으면

각각의 새로운 기술의 물결은 보안을 향상할 뿐만 아니라, 사용자 편의성을 향상하려는 의도이지만, 가끔 이것들이 반드시 같이 진행되지는 않는다. 예를 들면, 마그네틱 띠에서 내장형 칩으로의 전환은 거래(의 속도)를 약간 늦췄는데, 때때로 바쁜 고객을 좌절시켰다. (①) 서비스를 너무 부담스럽게 만들면, 잠재 고객은 다른 곳으로 갈 것이다. (②) 이러한 장벽은 몇몇 수준에서 적용된다. (③) 비밀번호, 이중 키 확인, 지문, 홍채 및 음성 인식과 같은 생체 인식은 모두 잠재적인 사기꾼으로부터 계정 세부 정보를 숨겨 주는, 즉 여러분의 데이터를 비밀로 유지해주는 방법이다. (④) 그러나 그것들은 모두 불가피하게 계좌 사용에 부담을 가중한다. (⑤) 자신의 돈에 접근하는 데 있어서 도입되어진 난관에 더해, 만약 의심스러운 사기가 탐지되면, 계좌 주인은 본인이 그 의심스러운 거래를 했는지를 묻는 내용의 전화 통화에 응해야만 한다. 이것은 모두 어느 정도 유용하며, 실제로, 여러분의 은행이 여러분을 보호하기 위해 경계를 늦추지 않고 있다는 것을 알게 되어 안심될 수는 있지만, 그런 전화를 너무 많이 받으면 성가신 일이 된다.

문제풀이

주어진 문장은 자신의 돈에 접근할 때 도입된 난관에 더해 사기가 의심되면 계좌 주인은 그 의심스러운 거래를 했는지를 묻는 전화 통화를 해야 한다는 내용으로, 사기꾼으로부터 데이터를 비밀로 유지해주는 방법이 계좌 사용에 부담을 가중한다는 내용과 이것이 어느 정도 도움을 주고 안심시켜줄 수는 있지만, 그런 전화가 성가실 수도 있다는 내용 사이인 ⑤에 들어가는 것이 적절하다. ⑤ 뒤의 문장에서 such calls가 가리키는 것은 주어진 문장에서 언급한 의심스러운 거래를 했는지 계좌 주인에게 묻는 전화를 가리킨다.

어휘·어구

hurdle 장애, 난관
access 접근하다
suspected 미심쩍은
detect 감지하다, 탐지하다
account 계좌
deal with ~을 다루다[처리하다]
transaction 거래
enhance 높이다, 향상시키다
embedded 내장형의
slightly 약간, 조금
frustrate 좌절감을 주다
burdensome 부담스러운
obstacle 장애, 장애물
identification 식별
biometrics 생체 인식
fraudster 사기꾼[범]
inevitably 필연적으로
reassuring 안심시키는
tiresome 귀찮은, 성가신

정답률 44%

5. ⑤ 영국에서의 패션 디자인의 맞춤복에서 기성복으로 전환

직독/직해

Earliest indications of the need for inspiration for fashion direction /
패션 경향의 영감에 대한 요구의 초기 징후들은 /
are possibly evidenced / by a number of British manufacturers /
아마도 보인다 / 많은 영국 제조업자들에 의한 것으로 /
visiting the United States / in around 1825 / where they were much inspired /
미국을 방문한 / 1825년경에 / 그곳에서 그들은 많은 영감을 받았다 /
by lightweight wool blend fabrics / produced for outerwear.
경량 울 혼방 옷감에 / 겉옷용으로 제작되는
The ready-to-wear sector was established / much earlier in America /
기성복 부문은 확립되었다 / 미국에서 훨씬 이전에 /
than in Britain / and with it came new challenges.
영국보다 / 그리고 그로 인해 새로운 도전이 생겨났다
Previously garments were custom-made / by skilled individuals /
이전에 의복은 맞춤 제작되었다 / 숙련된 사람들에 의해 /
who later became known as or recognized as being fashion designers.
나중에 패션 디자이너로 알려지거나 인정받은
These handmade garments / that are now accepted /
이 수제 의류는 / 지금은 인정되고 있는 /
as being the fashion garments of that time / were only made for those /
그 당시 상류 사회 의상으로 / 오직 사람들을 위해서만 만들어졌다 /
with the means to pay for them.
그것을 지불할 수 있는 수단을 가진
The lesser-privileged mass market wore /
특권을 덜 가진 일반 대중들은 입었다 /
homemade and handed down garments.
집에서 만들고 물려받은 옷을
Later, / by the end of the industrial revolution, /
나중에 / 산업 혁명이 끝나갈 무렵 /
fashion was more readily available and affordable to all classes.
패션은 모든 계층에게 더욱 쉽게 이용할 수 있고 구매 가능하게 되었다
By now / designers worked predominately within factories /
그즈음에 / 디자이너들은 주로 공장에서 일했다 /
and no longer designed for individuals but for mass markets.
그리고 더 이상 개인을 위해서가 아닌 대량 판매 시장을 위해서 디자인했다
Thus / the direct communication link between the designer and client /
그러므로 / 디자이너와 고객 사이의 직접적인 소통 연결이 /
no longer existed /
더 이상 존재하지 않았다 /
and designers had to rely on anticipating the needs and desires /
그리고 디자이너들은 필요와 욕구를 예상하는 것에 의존해야만 했다.
of the new fashion consumer.
새로운 패션 소비자의

패션 경향의 영감에 대한 요구의 초기 징후들은 아마도 1825년경에 미국을 방문하여 겉옷용으로 제작되는 경량 울 혼방 옷감에 많은 영감을 받은 많은 영국 제조업자들에 의한 것으로 보인다. 기성복 부문은 영국보다 미국에서 훨씬 이전에 확립되었고 그로 인해 새로운 도전이 생겨났다. (①) 이전에 의복은 나중에 패션 디자이너로 알려지거나 인정받은 숙련된 사람들에 의해 맞춤 제작되었다. (②) 그 당시 상류 사회 의상으로 지금은 인정되고 있는 이 수제 의류는 오직 그것을 지불할 수 있는 수단을 가진 사람들을 위해서만 만들어졌다. (③) 특권을 덜 가진 일반 대중들은 집에서 만들고 물려받은 옷을 입었다. (④) 나중에 산업 혁명이 끝나갈 무렵, 패션은 모든 계층에게 더욱 쉽게 이용할 수 있고 구매 가능하게 되었다. (⑤) 그즈음에 디자이너들은 주로 공장에서 일했고 더 이상 개인을 위해서가 아닌 대량 판매 시장을 위해서 디자인했다. 그러므로 디자이너와 고객 사이의 직접적인 소통 연결이 더 이상 존재하지 않았고 디자이너들은 새로운 패션 소비자의 필요와 욕구를 예상하는 것에 의존해야만 했다.

문제풀이

주어진 문장은 'By now'로 시작하여 '그즈음에 디자이너들은 공장에서 일했고 대량 판매 시장을 위해서 디자인했다'는 내용으로 산업 혁명이 끝날 무렵에 패션이 개인을 위한 맞춤 제작에서 모든 계층에서 더욱 쉽게 이용할 수 있고 구매 가능하게 되었다는 내용과 그러므로 디자이너와 고객 사이의 직접적인 소통 연결이 더 이상 존재하지 않았다는 내용 사이에 오는 것이 적절하므로 ⑤에 들어가는 것이 가장 적절하다.

이렇게 풀자 내용의 논리적인 비약이나 단절이 일어나는 곳에 주어진 문장을 넣어 보고 글의 흐름이 자연스럽게 연결되는지 확인해 보면 답을 쉽게 찾을 수 있다. ⑤의 인과 관계를 나타내는 연결사 'Thus' 뒤의 내용과 그 앞의 내용은 원인 결과가 되어야 하는데 산업 혁명이 끝나갈 무렵, 모든 계층이 패션을 이용할 수 있었다는 내용과 디자이너와 고객 사이의 직접적인 소통 연결이 더 이상 존재하지 않았다는 내용은 인과 관계로 볼 수 없다. 따라서 주어진 문장이 들어가야 글의 흐름이 자연스럽게 연결되어야 한다는 것을 알 수 있다.

어휘·어구

indication 징후
inspiration 영감
lightweight 가벼운, 경량의
blend 혼합, 혼방
fabric 옷감
sector 부문
previously 이전의
garment 의복
recognize 인정하다
hand down 물려주다
industrial revolution 산업 혁명
readily 쉽게
affordable 구매 가능한, (가격이) 알맞은
anticipate 예상하다

6. ③ 집단 탐지의 역학

직독/직해

The dynamics of collective detection / have an interesting feature.
집단 탐지의 역학에는 / 재미있는 특징이 있다
Which cue(s) do individuals use / as evidence of predator attack?
개체들은 어느 단서를 사용하는가 / 포식자 공격의 증거로써
In some cases, / when an individual detects a predator, /
어떤 경우에는 / 한 마리의 개체가 포식자를 감지할 때 /
its best response is to seek shelter.
그것의 최선의 반응은 피난처를 찾는 것이다
Departure from the group / may signal danger to nonvigilant animals /
무리로부터의 이탈은 / 경계하지 않는 동물들에게 위험 신호를 보낼 수도 있다 /
and cause / what appears to be a coordinated flushing of prey from the area.
그리고 야기할 수도 있다 / 먹잇감 동물이 그 구역에서 조직화되어 날아오르는 것으로 보이는 것을
Studies on dark-eyed juncos (a type of bird) / support the view /
(새의 한 종류인) 검은 눈 검은방울새에 대한 연구는 / 견해를 지지해 준다 /
that nonvigilant animals attend to departures of individual group mates /
경계하지 않는 동물들이 무리 친구들의 개별적 이탈에 주목한다는 /
but that the departure of multiple individuals / causes a greater escape response /
하지만 여러 개체의 이탈은 / 더 큰 탈출 반응을 야기할 수 있다는 /
in the nonvigilant individuals.
경계하지 않는 동물에게
This makes sense / from the perspective of information reliability.
이것은 타당하다 / 정보 신뢰성의 관점에서 보면
If one group member departs, /
만약 무리의 구성원 하나가 이탈한다면 /
it might have done so for a number of reasons /
그것은 여러 이유로 그렇게 했을 수 있다 /
that have little to do with predation threat.
포식 위협과 관계가 거의 없는
If nonvigilant animals escaped / each time a single member left the group, /
만약 경계하지 않는 동물들이 도망한다면 / 단 하나의 구성원이 무리를 떠날 때마다 /
they would frequently respond / when there was no predator (a false alarm).
그것들은 종종 반응할 것이다 / 포식자가 전혀 없는 (가짜 경보인) 때에도
On the other hand, / when several individuals depart the group at the same time, /
반면에 / 여러 개체가 동시에 무리를 이탈할 때 /
a true threat is much more likely to be present.
진짜 위협이 있을 가능성이 훨씬 더 크다

집단 탐지의 역학에는 재미있는 특징이 있다. 개체들은 어느 단서를 포식자 공격의 증거로써 사용하는가? 어떤 경우에는 한 마리의 개체가 포식자를 감지할 때 그것의 최선의 반응은 피난처를 찾는 것이다. (①) 무리로부터의 이탈은 경계하지 않는 동물들에게 위험 신호를 보내서 먹잇감 동물이 그 구역에서 조직화되어 날아오르는 것으로 보이는 것을 야기할 수도 있다. (②) (새의 한 종류인) 검은 눈 검은방울새에 대한 연구는 경계하지 않는 동물들이 무리 친구들의 개별적 이탈에 주목하지만 여러 개체의 이탈은 경계하지 않는 동물에게 더 큰 탈출 반응을 야기할 수 있다는 견해를 지지해 준다. (③) 이것은 정보 신뢰성의 관점에서 보면 타당하다. (④) 만약 무리의 구성원 하나가 이탈한다면, 포식 위협과 관계가 거의 없는 여러 이유로 그렇게 했을 수 있다. (⑤) 만약 경계하지 않는 동물들이 단 하나의 구성원이 무리를 떠날 때마다 도망한다면, 그것들은 포식자가 전혀 없는 (가짜 경보인) 때에도 종종 반응할 것이다. 반면에 여러 개체가 동시에 무리를 이탈할 때, 진짜 위협이 있을 가능성이 훨씬 더 크다.

문제풀이

주어진 문장은 이것이(This) 정보 신뢰성의 관점에서 타당하다는 내용으로, 주어진 문장의 This가 무엇을 가리키는지 찾아본다. ③ 앞부분에 개별적 이탈과 여러 개체의 이탈에 대해 다른 동물들의 반응이 다르다는 내용을 기술하고 있으므로 이 부분이 주어진 문장의 This를 가리킨다. ③ 뒤의 내용은 정보 신뢰성에 관한 부연 설명이 나오므로 주어진 문장은 ③에 오는 것이 가장 적절하다.

어휘·어구

cue 단서
make sense 이치에 맞다, 타당하다
reliability 신뢰성
dynamics 역학
collective 집단적인
detection 감지
feature 특징
shelter 은신처
departure 이탈
coordinate 조직화하다, 조정하다
flush ~을 쫓아내다 (*n.* flushing 날아오름)
junco 검은방울새(의 일종)
have little to do with ~과 관계가 거의 없다
predation 포식
threat 위협, 위험
predator 포식자

7. ⑤ 공장에 로봇 도입을 두려워하는 직원을 위해 할 일

직독/직해

Introduction of robots into factories, /
로봇을 공장에 도입하는 것은 /
while employment of human workers is being reduced, /
인간 노동자의 고용이 줄어들면서 /
creates worry and fear.

걱정과 두려움을 불러일으킨다
It is the responsibility of management /
경영진의 책임이다 /
to prevent or, at least, to ease these fears.
이런 두려움을 예방하거나 적어도 완화하는 것은
For example, / 예를 들면 /
robots could be introduced only in new plants /
로봇은 새로운 공장에만 도입될 수 있다 /
rather than replacing humans in existing assembly lines.
기존의 조립 라인에서 인간을 대체하는 대신
Workers should be included in the planning for new factories /
노동자는 새로운 공장을 계획하는 데 포함되어야 하는데 /
or the introduction of robots into existing plants, /
또는 기존의 공장에 로봇을 도입하는 데 (포함되어야 하는데) /
so they can participate in the process.
그렇게 해서 그들은 그 과정에 참여할 수 있다
It may be that robots are needed /
로봇이 필요할 수도 있다 /
to reduce manufacturing costs /
제조비용을 낮추기 위해 /
so that the company remains competitive, /
회사가 경쟁력을 유지하도록 /
but planning for such cost reductions /
그런 원가절감을 위한 계획은 /
should be done jointly by labor and management.
노사가 공동으로 해야 한다
Retraining current employees for new positions within the company /
회사 내 새로운 직책을 위해 현재 직원을 재교육하는 것은 /
will also greatly reduce their fear of being laid off.
해고를 당하는 것에 대한 두려움도 또한 크게 줄여줄 것이다.
Since robots are particularly good at highly repetitive simple motions, /
로봇은 특히 고도로 반복적인 단순 동작을 잘하기 때문에 /
the replaced human workers should be moved to positions /
대체된 인간 노동자는 위치로 옮겨져야 한다 /
where judgment and decisions beyond the abilities of robots /
로봇의 능력을 넘어선 판단과 결정이/
are required. 필요한

로봇을 공장에 도입하는 것은, 인간 노동자의 고용이 줄어들면서 걱정과 두려움을 불러일으킨다. (①) 이런 두려움을 예방하거나 적어도 완화하는 것은 경영진의 책임이다. (②) 예를 들면 로봇은 기존의 조립 라인에서 인간을 대체하는 대신 새로운 공장에만 도입될 수 있다. (③) 노동자는 새로운 공장을 계획하거나 기존의 공장에 로봇을 도입하는 데 포함되어야 하는데, 그렇게 해서 그들은 그 과정에 참여할 수 있다. (④) 회사가 경쟁력을 유지하도록 제조비용을 낮추기 위해 로봇이 필요할 수도 있지만, 그런 원가절감을 위한 계획은 노사가 공동으로 해야 한다. (⑤) 회사 내 새로운 직책을 위해 현재 직원을 재교육하는 것은 해고를 당하는 것에 대한 두려움도 또한 크게 줄여줄 것이다. 로봇은 특히 고도로 반복적인 단순 동작을 잘하기 때문에 대체된 인간 노동자는 로봇의 능력을 넘어선 판단과 결정이 필요한 위치로 옮겨져야 한다.

문제풀이

주어진 문장은 사내 새 직책을 위해 현재 직원을 재교육하는 것이 해고에 대한 두려움을 줄여준다는 내용으로, 직원을 참여시켜 노사가 공동으로 계획해야 한다는 내용과 단순 동작의 반복을 잘하는 로봇의 능력을 넘어선 판단과 결정이 필요한 위치로 인간 노동자가 가야 한다는 내용 사이인 ⑤에 들어가는 것이 가장 적절하다.

이렇게 풀자 내용의 논리적인 비약이나 단절이 일어나는 곳에 주어진 문장을 넣어 보고 글의 흐름이 자연스럽게 연결되는지 확인해 보면 답을 쉽게 찾을 수 있다. 로봇 도입에 대한 계획을 노사가 공동으로 해야 한다는 내용 바로 다음에 인간 노동자가 로봇의 능력을 넘어선 판단과 결정이 필요한 위치로 옮겨져야 한다는 내용이 오는 것은 어색하다. 따라서 주어진 문장을 ⑤에 넣어서 자연스럽게 연결되는지 확인해 본다.

어휘·어구

current 현재의
employee 직원, 피고용자
lay ~ off ~를 해고하다
introduction 도입
employment 고용
management 경영, 경영진
plant 공장
replace 대체하다
existing 기존의
assembly 조립
manufacture 제조하다
competitive 경쟁력이 있는
jointly 공동으로
repetitive 반복적인

정답률 47%

8. ④ 영화의 가치

직독/직해

Cinema is valuable / not for its ability /
영화는 가치가 있다 / 능력 때문이 아니라 /
to make visible the hidden outlines of our reality, /
우리 현실의 보이지 않는 윤곽을 보이도록 만드는 /
but for its ability to reveal what reality itself veils /
현실 자체가 가리고 있는 것을 드러내는 능력 때문에 /
— the dimension of fantasy.
즉 환상의 차원
This is why, / to a person, /
이것이 이유이다 / 사람에게
the first great theorists of film decried /
처음의 위대한 영화 이론가들이 공공연히 비난한 /
the introduction of sound and other technical innovations (such as color) /
소리와 (색채와 같은) 다른 기술 혁신의 도입을 /
that pushed film in the direction of realism.
영화를 사실주의쪽으로 밀어붙였던
Since cinema was an entirely fantasmatic art, /
영화는 전적으로 환상의 예술이었기 때문에 /
these innovations were completely unnecessary.
이런 혁신은 완전히 불필요했다
And what's worse, / they could do /
그리고 설상가상으로 / 그것들은 할 수 있을 뿐이었다 /
nothing but turn filmmakers and audiences away from the fantasmatic dimension of cinema, /
영화 제작자와 관객을 영화의 환상의 차원에서 멀어지게 할 뿐 /
potentially transforming film into a mere delivery device /
잠재적으로 영화를 단순한 전달 수단으로 변형시키면서 /
for representations of reality.
현실의 표현을 위한
As long as the irrealism of the silent black and white film predominated, /
무성 흑백 영화의 비현실주의가 지배하는 한 /
one could not take filmic fantasies for representations of reality.
영화적 환상을 현실에 대한 표현으로 착각할 수 없었다.
But sound and color threatened to create just such an illusion, /
하지만 소리와 색채는 바로 그런 착각을 만들겠다고 위협하여 /
thereby destroying the very essence of film art.
그렇게 함으로써 영화 예술의 바로 그 본질을 파괴했다
As Rudolf Arnheim puts it, /
Rudolf Arnheim이 표현한 것처럼 /
"The creative power of the artist can only come into play /
예술가의 창의적 힘은 ~만 발휘될 수 있다 /
where reality and the medium of representation do not coincide."
현실과 묘사의 수단이 일치하지 않는 곳에서

영화는 우리 현실의 보이지 않는 윤곽을 보이도록 만드는 능력 때문이 아니라 현실 자체가 가리고 있는 것, 즉 환상의 차원을 드러내는 능력 때문에 가치가 있다. (①) 이것이 처음의 위대한 영화 이론가들이 영화를 사실주의쪽으로 밀어붙였던 소리와 (색채와 같은) 다른 기술 혁신의 도입을 공공연히 비난한 이유이다. (②) 영화는 전적으로 환상의 예술이었기 때문에 이런 혁신은 완전히 불필요했다. (③) 그리고 설상가상으로 그것들은 잠재적으로 영화를 현실의 표현을 위한 단순한 전달 수단으로 변형시키면서, 영화 제작자와 관객을 영화의 환상의 차원에서 멀어지게 할 수 있을 뿐이었다. (④) 무성 흑백 영화의 비현실주의가 지배하는 한 영화적 환상을 현실에 대한 표현으로 착각할 수 없었다. 하지만 소리와 색채는 바로 그런 착각을 만들겠다고 위협하여 영화 예술의 바로 그 본질을 파괴했다. (⑤) Rudolf Arnheim이 표현한 것처럼 "예술가의 창의적 힘은 현실과 묘사의 수단이 일치하지 않는 곳에서만 발휘될 수 있다."

문제풀이

주어진 문장은 무성 흑백 영화의 비현실주의가 지배하는 동안 영화적 환상을 현실에 대한 표현으로 착각할 수 없었다는 내용으로, But으로 시작하면서 소리와 색채가 그런 착각을 만들겠다고 위협해서 영화 예술의 그 본질을 파괴했다는 내용 앞인 ④에 들어가는 것이 적절하다. ④ 뒤의 such an illusion은 주어진 문장의 '영화적 환상을 현실에 대한 표현으로 착각'을 가리킨다.

이렇게 풀자 마찬가지로 내용의 논리적인 비약이나 단절이 일어나는 곳에 주어진 문장을 넣어 보고 글의 흐름이 자연스럽게 연결되는지 확인해 보면 되는데, ④ 다음에 나온 'such an illusion'에 해당하는 내용이 ④ 앞에 나오지 않아 단절이 일어났다. 따라서 주어진 문장을 ④에 넣어서 자연스럽게 연결되는지 확인해 본다.

어휘·어구

irrealism 비현실주의
take A for B A를 B라고 생각하다
predominate 지배하다
representation 표현
valuable 가치가 있는
veil 가리다
dimension 차원
reveal 드러내다
innovation 혁신
realism 사실주의
entirely 전적으로
potentially 잠재적으로
transform 변형시키다
illusion 착각
come into play 작동하다
coincide 일치하다

정답률 54%

9. ④ 나쁜(bad)과 사악한(wicked)의 차이

직독/직해

Imagine / I tell you that Maddy is bad.
상상해 보라 / 내가 여러분에게 Maddy는 나쁘다고 말한다고
Perhaps you infer from my intonation, or the context /
아마 여러분은 내 억양이나 상황에서 추론한다 /
in which we are talking, / that I mean morally bad.
우리가 말하고 있는 / 내 뜻이 도덕상 나쁘다는 것이라고
Additionally, / you will probably infer /
게다가 / 아마 여러분은 추론할 것이다 /
that I am disapproving of Maddy, / or saying /
내가 Maddy를 못마땅해하고 있다고 / 혹은 말하고 있다고 /
that I think / you should disapprove of her, or similar, /
내 생각에 / 여러분이 그녀를 못마땅해하거나 그와 비슷해야 한다고 /
given typical linguistic conventions /
일반적인 언어 관행을 고려해 볼 때 /
and assuming I am sincere.
그리고 내가 진심이라고 가정해 볼 때
However, / you might not get a more detailed sense /

그러나 / 여러분은 더 자세하게 인식하지 못할지도 모르는데 /
of the particular sorts of way / in which Maddy is bad, /
특정 유형의 방식에 대해서는 / Maddy가 나쁜 /
her typical character traits, and the like, /
그녀의 일반적인 성격 특성 등 /
since people can be bad in many ways.
사람들은 여러 방면에서 나쁠 수도 있기 때문이다
In contrast, / if I say that Maddy is wicked, /
그에 반해 / 만약 내가 Maddy는 사악하다고 말한다면 /
then you get more of a sense /
그렇다면 여러분은 더 인식하게 된다 /
of her typical actions and attitudes to others.
다른 사람들에 대한 그녀의 일반적인 행동과 태도를
The word 'wicked' is more specific / than 'bad'.
'사악한'이라는 말은 더 구체적이다 / '나쁜'보다
I have still not exactly pinpointed Maddy's character /
나는 여전히 Maddy의 성격을 정확하게 지적하지 않았다 /
since wickedness takes many forms.
사악함은 많은 형태들을 띠기 때문에
But there is more detail nevertheless, /
하지만 그럼에도 불구하고 더 많은 세부 사항이 있다 /
perhaps a stronger connotation of the sort of person /
아마도 사람 유형에 대한 더 두드러진 함축인 /
Maddy is. Maddy의
In addition, / 게다가 /
and again assuming typical linguistic conventions, /
그리고 다시 일반적인 언어 관행을 가정하면 /
you should also get a sense /
여러분은 또한 인식할 것이다 /
that I am disapproving of Maddy, /
내가 Maddy를 못마땅해하고 있다고 /
or saying / 또는 말하고 있다고 /
that you should disapprove of her, or similar, /
여러분이 그녀를 못마땅해하거나 그와 비슷해야 한다고 /
assuming that we are still discussing her moral character.
우리가 여전히 그녀의 도덕적 성격을 논하고 있다고 가정하면서

내가 여러분에게 Maddy는 나쁘다고 말한다고 상상해 보라. 아마 여러분은 내 억양이나 우리가 말하고 있는 상황에서 내 뜻이 도덕상 나쁘다는 것이라고 추론한다. 게다가 여러분은 아마, 일반적인 언어 관행을 고려해 볼 때 그리고 내가 진심이라고 가정해 볼 때, 내가 Maddy를 못마땅해하고 있다고, 혹은 내 생각에 여러분이 그녀를 못마땅해하거나 그와 비슷해야 한다고 내가 말하고 있다고, 추론할 것이다. (①) 그러나 여러분은 Maddy가 나쁜 특정 유형의 방식, 그녀의 일반적인 성격 특성 등에 대해서는 더 자세하게 인식하지 못할지도 모르는데, 사람들은 여러 방면에서 나쁠 수도 있기 때문이다. (②) 그에 반해, 만약 내가 Maddy는 사악하다고 말한다면, 그렇다면 여러분은 다른 사람들에 대한 그녀의 일반적인 행동과 태도를 더 인식하게 된다. (③) '사악한'이라는 말은 '나쁜'보다 더 구체적이다. (④) 사악함은 많은 형태들을 띠기 때문에 나는 여전히 Maddy의 성격을 정확하게 지적하지 않았다. 하지만 그럼에도 불구하고 더 많은 세부 사항, 아마도 Maddy의 사람 유형에 대한 더 두드러진 함축이 있다. (⑤) 게다가, 그리고 다시 일반적인 언어 관행을 가정하면, 여러분은 또한, 우리가 여전히 그녀의 도덕적 성격을 논하고 있다고 가정하면서, 내가 Maddy를 못마땅해하고 있다고, 또는 여러분이 그녀를 못마땅해하거나 그와 비슷해야 한다고 내가 말하고 있다고 인식할 것이다.

문제풀이

주어진 문장은 사악함은 많은 형태가 있어서 나는 여전히 Maddy의 성격을 정확하게 지적하지 않았다는 내용으로, '사악한'이 '나쁜'보다 더 구체적이라는 내용과 그럼에도 불구하고 더 많은 세부사항 아마 Maddy의 사람 유형에 대한 더 두드러진 함축이 있다는 내용의 사이인 ④에 오는 것이 적절하다.

이렇게 풀자 내용의 논리적인 비약이나 단절이 일어나는 곳에 주어진 문장을 넣어 보고 글의 흐름이 자연스럽게 연결되는지 확인해 보면 답을 쉽게 찾을 수 있다. 여기서는 ④ 바로 앞 문장과 뒤 문장은 비슷한 내용으로 뒤 문장이 But으로 시작해서 nevertheless와 연결되는 것이 어색하다. 따라서 주어진 문장은 ④에 들어가는 것이 가장 적절하다.

《 어휘·어구 》

pinpoint 정확하게 지적[묘사]하다
wickedness 사악
infer 추론하다
intonation 억양
morally 도덕적으로
disapprove of ~을 못마땅해 하다
linguistic 언어의
convention 관행
sincere 진실된, 진정한
trait 특성
attitude 태도

정답률 69%

10. ④ 저작권의 특징

직독 직해

Designers draw on their experience of design /
디자이너들은 자신의 디자인 경험에 의지한다 /
when approaching a new project.
새로운 프로젝트에 접근할 때
This includes the use of previous designs /
이것에는 기존의 디자인의 활용이 포함된다 /
that they know work /
그들이 생각하기에 효과가 있는 /
— both / designs that they have created themselves /
둘 다 / 그들이 직접 만들었던 디자인 /
and those that others have created.
그리고 다른 사람들이 만들었던 디자인
Others' creations often spark inspiration /
다른 사람들의 창작물은 종종 영감을 불러일으킨다 /
that also leads to new ideas and innovation.
새로운 아이디어와 혁신으로도 이어지는
This is well known and understood.
이는 잘 알려져 있고 이해된다
However, / 하지만 /
the expression of an idea is protected by copyright, /
어떤 아이디어의 표현은 저작권에 의해 보호된다 /
and people who infringe on that copyright /
그리고 그 저작권을 침해하는 사람들은 /
can be taken to court and prosecuted.
고소되어 기소될 수 있다
Note / that copyright covers the expression of an idea /
주목하라 / 저작권은 아이디어의 표현을 다룬다는 점에 /
and not the idea itself.
그리고 아이디어 그 자체를 다루지는 않는다는 점에
This means, / for example, /
이것은 의미한다 / 예를 들면 /
that while there are numerous smartphones /
모두 많은 스마트폰이 있지만 /
all with similar functionality, /
비슷한 기능을 가진 /
this does not represent an infringement of copyright /
이것이 저작권 침해를 나타내지 않는다는 것을 /
as the idea has been expressed / in different ways /
그 아이디어가 표현되었기 때문에 / 다른 방식으로 /
and it is the expression / that has been copyrighted.
그리고 그 표현이기 때문에 / 저작권 보호를 받은 것은
Copyright is free / 저작권은 무료이다 /
and is automatically invested in the author, /
그리고 그 저작자에게 자동으로 부여된다 /
for instance, / the writer of a book or a programmer /
예를 들면 / 어떤 책의 저자나 프로그래머(에게) /
who develops a program, /
프로그램을 개발하는 /
unless they sign the copyright over to someone else.
저작권을 다른 누군가에게 양도하지 않는 한

디자이너들은 새로운 프로젝트에 접근할 때 자신의 디자인 경험에 의지한다. 이것에는 그들이 생각하기에 효과가 있는 기존의 디자인, 즉 그들이 직접 만들었던 디자인과 다른 사람들이 만들었던 디자인을 둘 다 활용하는 것이 포함된다. (①) 다른 사람들의 창작물은 종종 새로운 아이디어와 혁신으로도 이어지는 영감을 불러일으킨다. (②) 이는 잘 알려져 있고 이해된다. (③) 하지만 어떤 아이디어의 표현은 저작권에 의해 보호되며, 그 저작권을 침해하는 사람들은 고소되어 기소될 수 있다. (④) 저작권은 아이디어의 표현을 다루지, 아이디어 그 자체를 다루지는 않는다는 점에 주목하라. 이것은 예를 들면, 모두 비슷한 기능을 가진 많은 스마트폰이 있지만, 그 아이디어가 다른 방식으로 표현되었고 저작권 보호를 받은 것은 그 표현이기 때문에 이것이 저작권 침해를 나타내지 않는다는 것을 의미한다. (⑤) 저작권은 무료이며 저작자, 예를 들면 어떤 책의 저자나 프로그램을 개발하는 프로그래머가 저작권을 다른 누군가에게 양도하지 않는 한 그 저작자에게 자동으로 부여된다.

문제풀이

주어진 문장은 저작권은 아이디어 그 자체가 아닌 아이디어의 표현을 다룬다는 내용으로, 많은 기능이 유사한 스마트폰은 그 아이디어가 서로 다른 방식으로 표현되었고 저작권 보호를 받은 것은 그 표현이기 때문에 이것이 저작권 침해를 나타내지 않는다는 사실을 예로 든 문장 앞인 ④에 오는 것이 적절하다.

이렇게 풀자 마찬가지로 내용의 논리적인 비약이나 단절이 일어나는 곳을 찾으면 되는데, ④ 다음의 This가 가리키는 것이 ④ 앞에서 나오지 않았다. 따라서 주어진 문장을 ④에 넣어서 자연스럽게 연결되는지 확인해 보면 된다. ④ 다음의 This는 주어진 문장의 'copyright covers the expression of an idea and not the idea itself'를 가리킨다.

《 어휘·어구 》

copyright 저작권, 저작권을 보호하다
draw on ~에 의지하다
inspiration 영감
numerous 많은
functionality 기능
represent 나타내다
infringement 침해
automatically 자동으로
invest 부여하다, 투자하다
sign over ~을 양도하다

본문 101쪽

문법 플러스 17. 병렬 구조

A. 1. swallows 2. eating 3. act
4. but 5. differentiates
6. mine 7. that

1 [해석]▶ 그것은 번개 같이 재빠르게 턱을 벌려 경계를 하고 있지 않던 먹이를 붙잡아 머리부터 먼저 삼킨다.
[해설]▶ 등위접속사 and가 동사(seizes, swallows)를 병렬 구조로 연결하고 있다.

2 [해석]▶ 그녀는 이탈리아에 가서 매일 훌륭한 파스타를 요리를 먹고 싶어 한다.
[해설]▶ look forward to는 '~을 기대하다'의 의미로, 목적어로 동명사를 가져온다. 본문의 문장은 look forward to +[동명사] and [동명사]인 병렬 구조를 이루고 있다.

3 [해석]▶ 하지만 이제 디지털 시대의 도구들은 우리에게 정보를 쉽게 얻고, 공유하고, 새로운 방식으로 행동할 수 있는 방법을 제공한다.
[해설]▶ 등위접속사 and가 to부정사 to easily get, (to) share, and (to) act를 를 병렬 구조로 연결하고 있다.

4 [해석]▶ 몽골 제국은 통일된 국가가 아니라, 군사력에 의해 하나로 묶인 광대한 영토의 집합이었다.
[해설]▶ not A but B는 'A가 아니라 B'라는 의미이며, A와 B가 명사구가 나와 병렬 구조로 연결되어 있다.

5 [해석]▶ 세포가 적절한 크기로 성장한 후, 세포는 분열 또는 성숙을 준비하고 특화된 세포로 분화하면서 신진대사

가 변화한다.
[해설]▶ either A or B 구조에서 A와 B에 오는 말은 병렬 구조를 이루어야 하므로 prepares와 마찬가지로 matures and differentiates~를 쓰는 것이 어법상 적절하다.

6 [해석]▶ 그의 아이디어는 내 아이디어보다 더 낫다.
[해설]▶ 비교 구문에서도 병렬 구조를 지켜야 한다. His idea와 mine(= my idea)를 비교하고 있으므로 mine이 나와야 한다.

7 [해석]▶ 도쿄의 인구는 서울의 인구보다 더 많다.
[해설]▶ 비교 구문이 병렬 구조를 이루는 경우, 명사의 반복(the population)을 피하기 위해 that을 쓴다.

본문 101쪽

B. 1. humorous 2. playing 3. study
4. nor 5. has 6. hers
7. that

1 [해석]▶ Sally는 똑똑하고 아름다우며 재미있다.
[해설]▶ A(형용사), B(형용사), and C(형용사)가 병렬 구조를 이루고 있다.

2 [해석]▶ 어른들은 음식을 준비하고 아이들을 지키며, 배구 경기하느라 바빴다.
[해설]▶ busy+목적어+(in) A, B, and C의 병렬 구조이다. A, B처럼 C에도 동명사가 들어가야 한다.

3 [해석]▶ 그는 런던 대학에 들어가 이 박사님 밑에서 공부하기를 희망한다.
[해설]▶ hopes to go ~ and (to) study의 병렬 구조이다.

4 [해석]▶ Peter나 그의 아내도 이사 가는 것에 대해 아무 말도 하지 않았다.
[해설]▶ Neither A nor B는 'A도 B도 둘 다 아닌'의 의미이다.

5 [해석]▶ 너와 네 누나 중 한 명은 여기에 남아야 한다.
[해설]▶ either A or B는 'B'에 동사의 수를 일치시킨다.

6 [해석]▶ 나의 스마트폰은 색상과 모양에서 그녀의 것과 비슷해.
[해설]▶ 비교 구문에서도 병렬 구조를 지켜야 한다. my smartphone과 hers(= her smartphone)를 비교하고 있다.

7 [해석]▶ 일본은 전자 제품의 생산이 증가했지만, 일본의 증가는 한국의 그것보다 더 작았다.
[해설]▶ 비교 구문이 병렬 구조를 이루는 경우, 명사의 반복(the increase)을 피하기 위해 that을 쓴다.

본문 102쪽

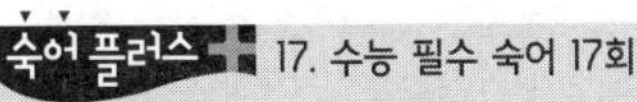

17. 수능 필수 숙어 17회

1. rich 2. risk
3. see 4. show

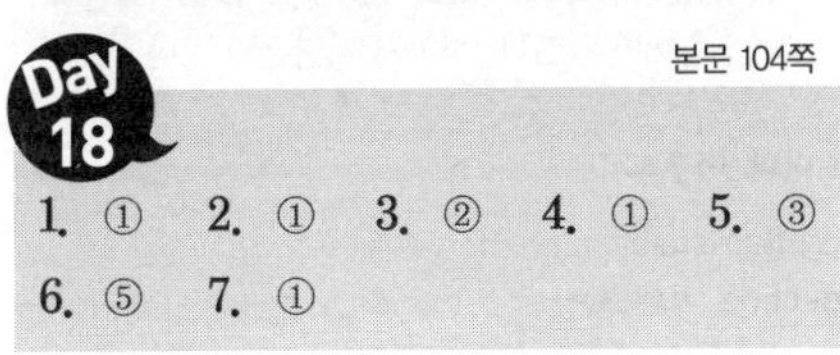

Day 18 본문 104쪽

1. ① 2. ① 3. ② 4. ① 5. ③
6. ⑤ 7. ①

정답률 58%

대표 기출 ③ 영국 귀족에게 나무 심기의 의의

직독/직해

The idea that *planting* trees could have a social or political significance /
나무를 '심기'가 사회적이거나 정치적인 의의가 있을 수도 있다는 생각은 /
appears to have been invented by the English, /
영국인들에 의해 고안된 것처럼 보인다 /
though it has since spread widely.
비록 이후에 그것이 널리 퍼지기는 했지만
According to Keith Thomas's history *Man and the Natural World*, /
Keith Thomas의 역사서인 'Man and the Natural World'에 따르면 /
seventeenth- and eighteenth-century aristocrats /
17, 18세기의 귀족들은 /
began planting hardwood trees, / usually in lines, /
활엽수를 심기 시작했다 / 대개 줄을 지어 /
to declare / 선언하기 위해 /
the extent of their property /
자신의 재산 범위를 /
and the permanence of their claim to it.
그리고 그것에 대한 자신의 권리의 영속성을
"What can be more pleasant," /
무엇이 더 즐거울 수 있는가 /
the editor of a magazine for gentlemen /
신사들을 위한 잡지의 그 편집자는 /
asked his readers, / 자신의 독자들에게 물었다 /
"than to have the bounds and limits of your own property /
여러분 자신의 재산 경계와 한계가 ~하게 하는 것보다 /
preserved and continued from age to age /
대대로 보존되고 지속되게 /
by the testimony of such living and growing witnesses?"
그렇게 살아 있고 성장하는 증인들의 증언에 의해
Planting trees had the additional advantage /
나무를 심기는 추가적인 이점을 가졌는데 /
of being regarded as a patriotic act, /
애국적인 행동으로 여겨지는 /
for the Crown had declared /
왜냐하면 군주가 선언했기 때문이었다 /
a severe shortage of the hardwood /
단단한 목재의 극심한 부족을 /
on which the Royal Navy depended.
영국 해군이 의존하는

➡ For English aristocrats, / 영국 귀족들에게 /
planting trees served as statements /
나무를 심기는 표현의 역할을 했다 /
to mark the lasting ownership of their land, /
자신의 땅에 대한 지속적인 소유권을 표시하는 /
and it was also considered /
그리고 그것은 또한 여겨졌다 /
to be an exhibition of their loyalty to the nation.
국가에 대한 그들의 충성심을 표현하는 것으로

나무를 '심기'가 사회적이거나 정치적인 의의가 있을 수도 있다는 생각은, 비록 이후에 널리 퍼지기는 했지만, 영국인들에 의해 고안된 것처럼 보인다. Keith Thomas의 역사서인 'Man and the Natural World'에 따르면, 17, 18세기의 귀족들은 자신의 재산 범위와 그것에 대한 자신의 권리의 영속성을 선언하기 위해 대개 줄을 지어 활엽수를 심기 시작했다. 신사들을 위한 잡지의 그 편집자는 자신의 독자들에게 "그렇게 살아 있고 성장하는 증인들의 증언에 의해 여러분 자신의 재산 경계와 한계가 대대로 보존되고 지속되게 하는 것보다 무엇이 더 즐거울 수 있는가?"라고 물었다. 나무를 심기는 애국적인 행동으로 여겨지는 추가적인 이점을 가졌는데, 왜냐하면 군주가 영국 해군이 의존하는 단단한 목재의 극심한 부족을 선언했기 때문이었다.

➡ 영국 귀족들에게, 나무를 심기는 자신의 땅에 대한 (A) 지속적인 소유권을 표시하는 표현의 역할을 했고, 그것은 또한 국가에 대한 그들의 충성심을 (B) 표현하는 것으로 여겨졌다.

① 불안정한 – 확인 ② 불안정한 – 과장
③ **지속적인 – 표현** ④ 지속적인 – 조작
⑤ 공식적인 – 정당화

문제풀이

17세기와 18세기 영국 귀족들은 자신의 재산 범위를 표시하고 그 재산에 대한 자신의 권리의 영속성을 선언하기 위해 줄 지어 활엽수를 심기 시작했고, 또한 단단한 목재가 부족하다는 군주의 선포에 대한 애국적인 행동으로 나무를 심었다고 했다. 따라서 요약문의 빈칸 (A)에는 'lasting(지속적인)'이 (B)에는 'exhibition(표현)'이 오는 것이 적절하다.

이렇게 풀자 요약문의 내용을 먼저 파악하고 난 뒤 글을 읽으면서 빈칸에 들어갈 알맞은 말을 찾아야 한다. 영국 귀족들에게 나무심기가 어떤 역할을 한 것인지를 파악하는 데 중점을 두고 글을 읽는다. 'seventeenth- and eighteenth-century aristocrats began planting hardwood trees, usually in lines, to declare the extent of their property and the permanence of their claim to it(17, 18세기의 귀족들은 자신의 재산 범위와 그것에 대한 자신의 권리의 영속성을 선언하기 위해 대개 줄을 지어 활엽수를 심기 시작했다)'을 통해 요약문의 빈칸 (A)에 들어갈 말을, 'Planting trees had the additional advantage of being regarded as a patriotic act, for the Crown had declared a severe shortage of the hardwood on which the Royal Navy depended.(나무를 심기는 애국적인 행동으로 여겨지는 추가적인 이점을 가졌는데, 왜냐하면 군주가 영국 해군이 의존하는 단단한 목재의 극심한 부족을 선언했기 때문이었다.)'를 통해 요약문의 빈칸 (B)에 들어갈 말을 유추해낼 수 있다.

어휘·어구

political 정치적
significance 의의, 중요성
hardwood tree 활엽수
property 재산
extent 정도, 범위
permanence 영속성
claim 권리
editor 편집자
bound 경계(선)
testimony 증언
witness 증인, 목격자
severe 극심한, 심각한
shortage 부족
statement 표현
loyalty 충성심

1. ① 장인 정신

직독/직해

"Craftsmanship" may suggest a way of life /
'장인 정신'은 삶의 방식을 제시할지도 모른다 /
that declined with the arrival of industrial society /
— but this is misleading.

산업 사회의 도래와 함께 쇠퇴한 / 하지만 이것은 오해의 소지가 있다

Craftsmanship names an enduring, basic human impulse, /
장인 정신은 지속적이고 기본적인 인간의 충동을 (말한다) /

the desire to do a job well / for its own sake.
일을 잘하고자 하는 욕구를 (말한다) / 그것 자체를 위해

Craftsmanship cuts a far wider swath / than skilled manual labor; /
장인 정신은 훨씬 더 넓은 구획을 자르는데 / 숙련된 육체노동보다 /

it serves the computer programmer, the doctor, and the artist; /
그것은 컴퓨터 프로그래머, 의사, 예술가에게 도움이 되고 /

parenting improves / when it is practiced as a skilled craft, / as does citizenship.
양육은 향상된다 / 그것이 숙련된 기술로서 실천될 때 / 시민 의식과 마찬가지로

In all these domains, / craftsmanship focuses on objective standards, /
이 모든 영역에서 / 장인 정신은 객관적인 기준에 초점을 맞춘다 /

on the thing in itself. 그 자체의 것에

Social and economic conditions, / however, /
사회적, 경제적 조건은 / 하지만 /

often stand in the way of the craftsman's discipline and commitment: /
종종 장인의 수련과 전념을 방해하는데 /

schools may fail to provide the tools / to do good work, /
학교는 도구를 제공하지 못할 수 있다 / 일을 잘하기 위한 /

and workplaces may not truly value the aspiration for quality.
그리고 직장은 품질에 대한 열망을 진정으로 가치 있게 여기지 않을 수 있다

And though craftsmanship can reward an individual /
그리고 비록 장인 정신이 개인에게 보상을 줄 수 있지만 /

with a sense of pride in work, / this reward is not simple.
일에 대한 자부심으로 / 이 보상은 단순하지 않다

The craftsman often faces conflicting objective standards of excellence; /
장인은 흔히 뛰어남에 대한 상충되는 객관적 기준에 마주하며 /

the desire to do something well for its own sake /
어떤 일 그 자체를 위해 그것을 잘하려는 욕구는 /

can be weakened / by competitive pressure, by frustration, or by obsession.
약화될 수 있다 / 경쟁적 압력에 의해, 좌절에 의해 또는 집착에 의해

➡ Craftsmanship, / 장인 정신은 /

a human desire / that has persisted over time in diverse contexts, /
즉 인간의 욕구인데 / 다양한 상황에서 시간이 지남에 따라 지속되어 온 /

often encounters factors / that limit its full development.
흔히 요소들과 맞닥뜨린다 / 그 완전한 발전을 제한하는

'장인 정신'은 산업 사회의 도래와 함께 쇠퇴한 삶의 방식을 제시할지도 모르지만, 이것은 오해의 소지가 있다. 장인 정신은 지속적이고 기본적인 인간의 충동, 즉 일 자체를 위해 그것을 잘하고자 하는 욕구를 말한다. 장인 정신은 숙련된 육체노동보다 훨씬 더 넓은 구획을 자르는데, 그것은 컴퓨터 프로그래머, 의사, 예술가에게 도움이 되고, 시민 의식과 마찬가지로 그것이 숙련된 기술로서 실천될 때 양육은 향상된다. 이 모든 영역에서 장인 정신은 객관적인 기준, 즉 그 자체의 것에 초점을 맞춘다. 하지만 사회적, 경제적 조건은 종종 장인의 수련과 전념을 방해하는데, 즉 학교는 일을 잘하기 위한 도구를 제공하지 못할 수 있고, 직장은 품질에 대한 열망을 진정으로 가치 있게 여기지 않을 수 있다. 그리고 비록 장인 정신이 일에 대한 자부심으로 개인에게 보상을 줄 수 있지만, 이 보상은 단순하지 않다. 장인은 흔히 뛰어남에 대한 상충되는 객관적 기준에 마주하며, 어떤 일 그 자체를 위해 그것을 잘하려는 욕구는 경쟁적 압력에 의해, 좌절에 의해 또는 집착에 의해 약화될 수 있다.

➡ 다양한 상황에서 시간이 지남에 따라 (A) 지속되어 온 인간의 욕구인 장인 정신은 흔히 그 완전한 발전을 (B) 제한하는 요소들과 맞닥뜨린다.

	(A)	(B)
①	**지속되었다**	**제한하다**
②	지속되었다	양성하다
③	발달했다	가속화하다
④	줄어들었다	형성하다
⑤	줄어들었다	제한하다

문제풀이

장인 정신은 일 자체를 위해 그것을 잘하고자 하는 욕구를 말하는 것으로 여러 분야에서 도움을 주는 것으로서 존재해 왔지만, 사회적, 경제적 조건은 종종 장인의 수련과 전념을 방해하고 장인은 뛰어남에 대한 상충되는 객관적 기준에 마주하며 장인 정신은 경쟁적 압력, 좌절, 집착에 의해 약화될 수 있다고 했다. 따라서 요약문의 빈칸 (A)에는 'persisted(지속되었다)'와 (B)에는 'limit(제한하다)'가 들어가야 한다. 따라서 정답은 ①이다.

어휘·어구

craftsmanship 장인 정신, 손재주
decline 쇠퇴하다
misleading 오해의 소지가 있는
name 말하다, 지정하다
enduring 지속적인
impulse 충동
for one's own sake ~ 자체를 위한
parenting 양육
craft 기술
citizenship 시민 의식
domain 영역
objective 객관적인
stand in the way of ~을 방해하다
discipline 수련, 훈육
commitment 전념
aspiration 열망
conflicting 상충되는
obsession 집착
encounter 맞닥뜨리다, 직면하다
factor 요소

정답률 69%

2. ① 두 가지 설명에 대한 철학적 이론

직독/직해

Philip Kitcher and Wesley Salmon have suggested /
Philip Kitcher와 Wesley Salmon은 제안했다 /

that there are two possible alternatives /
두 개의 가능한 대안이 있다고 /

among philosophical theories of explanation.
설명에 대한 철학적 이론 중

One is the view / 한 가지는 견해이다 /

that scientific explanation consists in the *unification* of broad bodies of phenomena /
과학적 설명이 광범위하게 많은 현상을 '통합'하는 데 있다는 /

under a minimal number of generalizations.
최소한으로 적은 수의 일반화 하에

According to this view, /
이 견해에 따르면 /

the (or perhaps, a) goal of science /
과학의 목표(혹은 어쩌면 한 가지 목표)는 /

is to construct an economical framework of laws or generalizations /
법칙이나 일반화의 경제적인 틀을 만드는 것이다 /

that are capable of subsuming all observable phenomena.
모든 관찰할 수 있는 현상을 포섭할 수 있는

Scientific explanations organize and systematize /
과학적 설명은 조직하고 체계화하는데 /

our knowledge of the empirical world; /
경험적 세상에 대한 우리의 지식을 /

the more economical the systematization, /
체계화가 더 경제적일수록 /

the deeper our understanding of what is explained.
설명되는 것에 대한 우리의 이해는 더 깊어진다

The other view is the *causal/mechanical* approach.
다른 관점은 '인과 관계적/기계론적' 접근이다

According to it, / 그것에 따르면 /

a scientific explanation of a phenomenon /
어떤 현상에 대한 과학적인 설명은 /

consists of uncovering the mechanisms /
메커니즘을 밝혀내는 것으로 이루어져 있다 /

that produced the phenomenon of interest.
관심 있는 그 현상을 생산해낸

This view sees the explanation of individual events /
이런 관점은 개별 사건들에 대한 설명을 본다 /

as primary, / 일차적으로 /

with the explanation of generalizations flowing from them.
일반화에 대한 설명이 그것들에서 흘러나온다고

That is, / the explanation of scientific generalizations /
즉 / 과학적 일반화에 대한 설명은 /

comes from the causal mechanisms /
인과적 메커니즘에서 나온다 /

that produce the regularities.
규칙성을 만들어 내는

➡ Scientific explanations can be made /
과학적 설명은 만들어질 수 있다 /

either by seeking the least number of principles /
최소한의 원리를 찾음으로써 /

covering all observations /
모든 관찰에 적용되는 /

or by finding general patterns /
또는 일반적인 양식을 발견함으로써 /

drawn from individual phenomena.
개별 현상으로부터 도출된

Philip Kitcher와 Wesley Salmon은 설명에 대한 철학적 이론 중 두 개의 가능한 대안이 있다고 제안했다. 한 가지는 과학적 설명이 최소한으로 적은 수의 일반화 하에 광범위하게 많은 현상을 '통합'하는 데 있다는 견해이다. 이 견해에 따르면 과학의 목표(혹은 어쩌면 한 가지 목표)는 모든 관찰할 수 있는 현상을 포섭할 수 있는 법칙이나 일반화의 경제적인 틀을 만드는 것이다. 과학적 설명은 경험적 세상에 대한 우리의 지식을 조직하고 체계화하는데, 체계화가 더 경제적일수록, 설명되는 것에 대한 우리의 이해는 더 깊어진다. 다른 관점은 '인과 관계적/기계론적' 접근이다. 그것에 따르면, 어떤 현상에 대한 과학적인 설명은 관심 있는 그 현상을 생산해 낸 메커니즘을 밝혀내는 것으로 이루어져 있다. 이런 관점은 개별 사건들에 대한 설명을 일차적으로 보고, 일반화에 대한 설명이 그것들에서 흘러나온다고 본다. 즉, 과학적 일반화에 대한 설명은 규칙성을 만들어 내는 인과적 메커니즘에서 나온다.

➡ 과학적 설명은 모든 관찰에 적용되는 (A) 최소한의 원리를 찾거나 개별 현상으로부터 도출된 일반적인 (B) 양식을 발견함으로써 만들어질 수 있다.

① **최소한의 ...... 양식**		② 고정된 ...... 특성
③ 제한된 ...... 기능		④ 고정된 ...... 규칙
⑤ 최소한의 ...... 추정		

문제풀이

설명에 대한 철학적 이론 중 두 가지 대안에 관한 글로, 한 가지는 과학적 설명은 최소한으로 적은 수의 일반화 하에 광범위하게 많은 현상들을 통합하는 데 있다는 것이고 다른 하나는 인과 관계적/기계론적 접근으로 과학적 일반화에 대한 설명은 개별 현상에서 대한 설명에서 규칙성을 만들어 내는 인과적 메커니즘에서 나온다고 했다. 따라서 요약문의 빈칸 (A)에는 'least(최소한의)'가, (B)에는 'patterns(양식)'이 들어가야 한다.

이렇게 풀자 요약문의 내용을 먼저 파악하고 난 뒤 글을 읽으면서 빈칸에 들어갈 알맞은 말을 찾아야 한다. 과학적 설명에 대한 철학적 이론 두 가지의 특징을 파악하는 데 중점을 두고 글을 읽는다. 'One is the view that scientific explanation consists in the *unification* of broad bodies of phenomena under a minimal number of generalizations.(한 가지는 과학적 설명이 최소한으로 적은 수의 일반화 하에 광범위하게 많은 현상을 '통합'하는 데 있다는 견해이다.)'를 통해 (A)에 들어갈 말을, 'According to it, a scientific explanation of a phenomenon consists of uncovering the mechanisms that produced the phenomenon of interest.(그것에 따르면, 어떤 현상에 대한 과학적인 설명은 관심 있는 그 현상을 생산해낸 메커니즘을 밝혀내는 것으로 이루어져 있다)'와 'That is, the explanation of scientific generalizations comes from the causal mechanisms that produce the regularities.(즉, 과학적 일반화에 대한 설명은 규칙성을 만들어 내는 인과적

> 메커니즘에서 나온다.)'를 통해 요약문의 빈칸 (B)에 들어갈 말을 유추해낼 수 있다.

《 어휘 · 어구 》

philosophical 철학의
consist in ~에 있다
unification 통합
body 많은 양
phenomenon 현상
minimal 최소의
generalization 일반화
construct 구성하다
framework 틀
be capable of ~할 수 있다
observable 관찰할 수 있는
organize 정리하다
systematize 체계화하다
causal 인과관계의
mechanical 기계론적인
approach 접근법
consist of ~을 구성되다
uncover 밝혀내다
mechanism 메커니즘, 구조
primary 일차적인
regularity 규칙성

정답률 79%

3. ② 마술 기법의 모방과 비밀 누설

Perhaps not surprisingly, /
아마도 당연히 /

given how long magicians have been developing their craft, /
마술사들이 자신들의 기술을 얼마나 오랫동안 발전시켜 왔는지를 생각해 보면 /

a lot of creativity in magic is of the tweaking variety /
마술에 존재하는 많은 창의성은 살짝 변화를 준 다양성에 관한 것이다 /

— some of the most skilled and inventive magicians gained fame /
가장 숙련되고 창의적인 마술사 중의 일부는 명성을 얻었다

by refining the execution of tricks /
마술 기법의 실행을 정교하게 함으로써 /

that have been known for decades, or sometimes centuries.
수십 년 혹은 때로는 수 세기 동안 알려져 온

Nevil Maskelyne, one of magic's old masters, claimed /
마술의 옛 거장 중 한 명인 Nevil Maskelyne은 주장했다 /

that "the difficulty of producing a new magical effect /
새로운 마술적 효과를 내는 어려움은

is about equivalent /
거의 같은 것이다 /

to that of inventing a new proposition in Euclid."
유클리드 기하학에서 새로운 명제를 만들어 내는 어려움과

Whether it's because there's little that's completely new, /
완전히 새로운 것이 거의 없기 때문이든 /

or for some other reason, /
아니면 어떤 다른 이유 때문이든 /

magicians seem to worry less about imitation.
마술사는 모방에 대해 덜 걱정하는 것으로 보인다

They do, however, worry a lot about *traitors* /
하지만 그들은 '배신자'들에 대해 정말로 걱정한다 /

— those magicians /
마술사들에 대해 /

who expose the secrets behind a trick to the public.
마술 기법 뒤에 숨겨진 비밀을 대중에게 누설하는

Once a trick is exposed in this way, /
이런 식으로 하나의 마술 기법이 누설되면 /

its value as "magic" is destroyed, /
'마술'로서 그것의 가치가 없어진다 /

and this harms everyone in the industry.
그리고 이것은 그 업계에 종사하는 모든 사람에게 피해를 준다

For this reason, / 이런 이유로 /

magicians' norms are focused mostly on punishing magicians /
마술사들의 규범은 마술사를 처벌하는 데 주로 초점이 맞춰져 있다 /

who expose tricks to the public /
마술 기법을 대중에게 누설하는 /

— even if the trick is the exposer's own invention.
비록 그 마술 기법이 그 누설자 자신이 발명한 것이라고 하더라도

➡ Magicians, / having long refined existing tricks, /
마술사들은 / 오랫동안 기존의 마술 기법을 정교하게 다듬어 온 /

are not much worried /
그다지 걱정하지 않는다 /

about copying tricks, / but they are very strict /
마술 기법을 모방하는 것에 대해 / 하지만 그들은 매우 엄격하다 /

about disclosing the methods of tricks /
마술 기법의 방법을 누설하는 것에 대해 /

as it damages their industry.
그것(누설)이 자신들의 업계에 피해를 주기 때문에

아마도 당연히, 마술사들이 자신들의 기술을 얼마나 오랫동안 발전시켜 왔는지를 생각해 보면, 마술에 존재하는 많은 창의성은 살짝 변화를 준 다양성에 관한 것인데, 가장 숙련되고 창의적인 마술사 중의 일부는 수십 년 혹은 때로는 수 세기 동안 알려져 온 마술 기법의 실행을 정교하게 함으로써 명성을 얻었다. 마술의 옛 거장 중 한 명인 Nevil Maskelyne은 '새로운 마술적 효과를 내는 어려움은 유클리드 기하학에서 새로운 명제를 만들어 내는 어려움과 거의 같은 것이다.'라고 주장했다. 완전히 새로운 것이 거의 없기 때문이든, 아니면 어떤 다른 이유 때문이든, 마술사는 모방에 대해 덜 걱정하는 것으로 보인다. 하지만 그들은 '배신자', 즉 마술 기법 뒤에 숨겨진 비밀을 대중에게 누설하는 마술사들에 대해 정말로 걱정한다. 이런 식으로 하나의 마술 기법이 누설되면 '마술'로서 그것의 가치가 없어지고, 이것은 그 업계에 종사하는 모든 사람에게 피해를 준다. 이런 이유로, 마술사들의 규범은, 비록 그 마술 기법이 그 누설자 자신이 발명한 것이라고 하더라도, 마술 기법을 대중에게 누설하는 마술사를 처벌하는 데 주로 초점이 맞춰져 있다.

➡ 오랫동안 기존의 마술 기법을 정교하게 다듬어 온 마술사들은 마술 기법을 (A) 모방하는 것에 대해 그다지 걱정하지 않지만, 그들은 그것(누설)이 자신들의 업계에 피해를 주기 때문에 마술 기법의 방법을 (B) 누설하는 것에 대해 매우 엄격하다.

(A)		(B)	(A)		(B)
① 모방하는	……	혼합하는	**② 모방하는**	**……**	**누설하는**
③ 비판하는	……	왜곡하는	④ 수정하는	……	평가하는
⑤ 수정하는	……	과소평가하는			

문제풀이

마술사들은 새로운 기술을 만들기 보다는 기존 마술 기법의 실행을 정교하게 다듬어 왔기 때문에 모방에 대해 덜 걱정하지만, 마술 기법 뒤에 숨겨진 비밀이 누설되면 마술로서의 가치가 없어지고 그 업계에 종사하는 사람들에게 피해를 주기 때문에 마술 기법을 대중에게 누설하는 마술사를 처벌하려고 한다는 내용의 글이므로, 요약문의 빈칸 (A)에는 'copying(모방하는)'이, (B)에는 'disclosing(누설하는)'이 들어가는 것이 가장 적절하다.

이렇게 풀자 요약문의 완성 문제는 본문에 요약문의 빈칸에 들어갈 어휘와 유사한 어휘가 있는 경우가 많다. 이 문제에서는 'imitation(모방)'과 'expose(누설하다)'가 빈칸에 들어갈 어휘의 결정적인 단서가 된다.

《 어휘 · 어구 》

craft 기술
variety 다양(성)
inventive 창의적인
refine 다듬다
execution 실행
equivalent to ~에 동등한, ~와 같은
proposition 명제
norm 규범
disclose 폭로하다

정답률 51%

4. ① 컴퓨터 정보 처리의 장단점

직독/직해

The computer has, / to a considerable extent, /
컴퓨터는 / 상당한 정도로 /

solved the problem /
문제를 해결했다 /

of acquiring, preserving, and retrieving information.
정보를 얻고, 보존하고, 추출하는

Data can be stored /
데이터는 저장될 수 있다 /

in effectively unlimited quantities and in manageable form.
사실상 무한량으로, 그리고 관리가 쉬운 형태로

The computer makes available a range of data /
컴퓨터는 다양한 데이터를 이용 가능하게 한다 /

unattainable in the age of books.
책의 시대에서는 얻을 수 없는

It packages it effectively; /
그것은 그것을 효과적으로 짜임새 있게 담는다 /

style is no longer needed /
방식은 더는 필요하지 않다 /

to make it accessible, /
그것을 이용할 수 있게 만들기 위한 /

nor is memorization.
암기도 또한 필요하지 않다

In dealing with a single decision /
단 한 가지 결정을 다룰 때 /

separated from its context, /
맥락과 분리된 /

the computer supplies tools /
컴퓨터는 도구들을 제공한다 /

unimaginable even a decade ago.
10년 전만 해도 상상이 불가능했던

But it also diminishes perspective.
그러나 그것은 또한 관점을 감소시킨다

Because information is so accessible and communication instantaneous, /
정보에 매우 접근하기 쉽고 의사소통이 순간적이기 때문에

there is a diminution of focus /
관심 집중이 감소한다

on its significance, or even on the definition /
그것의 중요성이나 정의에 대해서 /

of what is significant. 심지어 중요한 것의

This dynamic may encourage policymakers /
이러한 역학은 정책 입안자들이 ~하게 할 수 있다 /

to wait for an issue to arise /
쟁점이 생겨나기를 기다리게 하고 /

rather than anticipate it, /
쟁점을 예상하기보다는 /

and to regard moments of decision /
그리고 결정의 순간을 간주하게 할 수 있다 /

as a series of isolated events /
일련의 고립되어 일어나는 일로 /

rather than part of a historical continuum.
역사적인 연속의 일부라기보다는

When this happens, /
이러한 일이 일어나면 /

manipulation of information replaces reflection /
정보의 조작이 숙고를 대체한다 /

as the principal policy tool.
주요한 정책 도구로서의

➡ Although the computer is clearly competent /
컴퓨터는 명백히 유능하지만 /

at handling information in a decontextualized way, /
탈맥락화된 방식으로 정보를 처리하는 데 있어서 /

it interferes with our making comprehensive judgments /
그것은 우리의 종합적인 판단을 방해한다

related to the broader context, /
더 광범위한 맥락과 관련된 /

as can be seen in policymaking processes.
정책 결정 과정에서 볼 수 있는 것처럼

컴퓨터는 정보를 얻고, 보존하고, 추출하는 문제를 상당한 정도로 해결했다. 데이터는 사실상 무한량으로, 그리고 관리가 쉬운 형태로 저장될 수 있다. 컴퓨터는 책의 시대에서는 얻을 수 없는 다양한 데이터를 이용 가능하게 한다. 그것은 그것을 효과적으로 짜임새 있게 담고, 그것을 이용할 수 있게 만들기 위한 방식은 더는 필요하지 않으며 암기도 또한 필요하지 않다. 맥락과 분리된 단 한 가지 결정을 다룰 때 컴퓨터는 10년 전만 해도 상상이 불가능했던 도구들을 제공한다. 그러나 그것은 또한 관점을 감소시킨다. 정보에 매우 접근하기 쉽고 의사소통이 순간적이기 때문에, 그것의 중요성이나 심지어 중요한 것의 정의에 대해서 관심 집중이 감소한다. 이러한 역학은 정책 입안자들이 쟁점을 예상하기보다는 생겨나기를 기다리게 하고, 결정의 순간을 역사적인 연속의 일부라기보다는 일련의 고립되어 일어나는 일로 간주하게 할 수 있다. 이러한 일이 일어나면, 정보의 조작이 주요한 정책 도구로서의 숙고를 대체한다.

➡ 컴퓨터는 탈맥락화된 방식으로 정보를 처리하는 데 있어서 명백히 (A) 유능하지만, 정책 결정 과정에서 볼 수 있는 것처럼 더 광범위한 맥락과 관련된 우리의 (B) 종합적인 판단은 방해한다.

	(A)	(B)		(A)	(B)
①	**유능한**	**– 종합적인**	②	지배적인	– 편향된
③	불완전한	– 잘 아는	④	인상적인	– 합법적인
⑤	비효율적인	– 시기적절한			

문제풀이

컴퓨터가 맥락과 분리된 단 한 가지 결정을 다룰 때 다양한 정보를 더 쉽게 처리할 수 있게 해 주지만, 맥락을 고려해서 정책을 결정해야 할 때는 결정의 순간을 역사적인 연속의 일부라기보다는 일련의 고립되어 일어나는 일로 간주하게 하여 정보 조작 같은 문제를 가져온다고 했다. 따라서 요약문의 빈칸 (A)에는 'competent(유능한)'와 (B)에는 'comprehensive(종합적인)'이 들어가는 것이 적절하므로, 정답은 ①이다.

⊙ 이렇게 풀자 요약문의 내용을 먼저 파악하고 난 뒤 글을 읽으면서 빈칸에 들어갈 알맞은 말을 찾아야 한다. 컴퓨터가 탈맥락화된 방식으로 정보를 처리할 때의 장단점을 파악하는 데 중점을 두고 글을 읽는다. 'The computer makes available a range of data unattainable in the age of books.(컴퓨터는 책의 시대에서는 얻을 수 없는 다양한 데이터를 이용 가능하게 한다.)', 'In dealing with a single decision separated from its context, the computer supplies tools unimaginable even a decade ago.(맥락과 분리된 단 한 가지 결정을 다룰 때 컴퓨터는 10년 전만 해도 상상이 불가능했던 도구들을 제공한다.)'를 통해 빈칸 (A)에 들어갈 말을, 'This dynamic may encourage policymakers to wait for an issue to arise rather than anticipate it, and to regard moments of decision as a series of isolated events rather than part of a historical continuum.(이러한 역학은 정책 입안자들이 쟁점을 예상하기보다는 생겨나기를 기다리게 하고, 결정의 순간을 역사적인 연속의 일부라기보다는 일련의 고립되어 일어나는 일로 간주하게 할 수 있다.)'를 통해 빈칸 (B)에 들어갈 말을 유추해낼 수 있다.

《 어휘·어구 》

considerable 상당한
acquire 얻다
effectively 사실상, 효과적으로
a range of 다양한
unattainable 얻을 수 없는
package 짜임새 있게 담다
deal with ~을 처리하다[다루다]
diminish 감소시키다
perspective 관점
instantaneous 순간적인
significance 중요성
anticipate 예상하다
regard A as B A를 B라고 간주하다
continuum 연속체
manipulation 조작
reflection 숙고
principal 주요한
decontextualize 탈맥락화하다
interfere with ~을 방해하다

정답률 

5. ③ 다른 문화의 정치 권력 이해

직독/직해

From a cross-cultural perspective /
비교 문화적 관점에서 /
the equation between public leadership and dominance /
대중적인 지도력과 지배력 사이의 방정식은 /
is questionable. 의문이 있다
What does one mean by 'dominance'?
'지배력'이 무엇을 의미하는가
Does it indicate coercion?
그것이 강제를 나타내는 것인가
Or control over 'the most valued'?
또는 '가장 가치 있는 것'에 대한 통제인가
'Political' systems may be /
'정치적' 시스템은 ~일지도 모른다 /
about both, either, or conceivably neither.
둘 다에 관한 것일지도, 둘 중 하나에 관한 것일지도, 또는 아마도 둘 다에 관한 것이 아닐지도
The idea of 'control' would be a bothersome one /
'통제'라는 생각은 성가신 것일 텐데, /
for many peoples, / 많은 부족에게는 /
as for instance among many native peoples of Amazonia /
예를 들면 아마존의 많은 원주민 부족 사이에서처럼 /
where all members of a community are fond of their personal autonomy /
공동체의 모든 구성원이 개인의 자율성을 좋아하는 /
and notably allergic to any obvious expression of control or coercion.
그리고 통제나 강제가 명확하게 표현되는 어떤 것이든 현저히 싫어하는
The conception of political power as a coercive force, /
'강제적인' 힘으로서 정치 권력이라는 개념은 /
while it may be a Western fixation, / is not a universal.
서양의 고정 관념일 수도 있지만 / 보편적인 것이 아니다
It is very unusual / for an Amazonian leader /
매우 흔치 않은 일이다 / 아마존의 지도자가 /
to give an order. 명령을 내리는 것은
If many peoples do not view political power /
만약 많은 부족이 정치 권력을 여기지 않는다면 /
as a coercive force, / *nor as the most valued domain*, /
강제적인 힘으로, / '또한 가장 가치 있는 영역으로' /
then the leap from 'the political' to 'domination' (as coercion), /
그러면 '정치적인 것'에서 (강제로서의) '지배'로의 도약은 /
and from there to 'domination of women', /
'그리고 거기에서' '여성에 대한 지배'로 (도약은) /
is a shaky one. 불안정한 것이다
As Marilyn Strathern has remarked, /
Marilyn Strathern이 말한 것처럼 /
the notions of 'the political' and 'political personhood' /
'정치적인 것'과 '정치적 개성'이라는 개념은 /
are cultural obsessions of our own, /
우리 자신의 문화적 강박 관념이다 /
a bias long reflected in anthropological constructs.
인류학적 구성 개념에 오랜 시간 반영된 편견인
➡ It is misguided / 잘못 이해된 것이다 /
to understand political power in other cultures /
다른 문화에서의 정치 권력을 이해하는 것은 /
through our own notion of it /
그것에 대한 우리 자신의 개념을 통해 /
because ideas of political power are not uniform /
정치 권력에 관한 생각은 획일적이지 않기 때문에 /
across cultures. 문화에 따라

비교 문화적 관점에서 대중적인 지도력과 지배력 사이의 방정식은 의문이 있다. '지배력'이 무엇을 의미하는가? 그것이 강제를 나타내는 것인가? 또는 '가장 가치 있는 것'에 대한 통제인가? '정치적' 시스템은 둘 다에 관한 것일지도, 둘 중 하나에 관한 것일지도, 또는 아마도 둘 다에 관한 것이 아닐지도 모른다. '통제'라는 생각은 많은 부족에게는 성가신 것일 텐데, 예를 들면 공동체의 모든 구성원이 개인의 자율성을 좋아하고 통제나 강제가 명확하게 표현되는 어떤 것이든 현저히 싫어하는 아마존의 많은 원주민 부족 사이에서처럼 말이다. 서양의 고정 관념일 수도 있지만, '강제적인' 힘으로서 정치 권력이라는 개념은 보편적인 것이 아니다. 아마존의 지도자가 명령을 내리는 것은 매우 흔치 않은 일이다. 만약 많은 부족이 정치 권력을 강제적인 힘으로, '또한 가장 가치 있는 영역으로' 여기지 않는다면, 그러면 '정치적인 것'에서 (강제로서의) '지배'로, '그리고 거기에서' '여성에 대한 지배'로의 도약은 불안정한 것이다. Marilyn Strathern이 말한 것처럼, '정치적인 것'과 '정치적 개성'이라는 개념은 우리 자신의 문화적 강박 관념으로, 인류학적 구성 개념에 오랜 시간 반영된 편견이다.

➡ 정치 권력에 관한 생각은 문화에 따라 (B) 획일적이지 않기 때문에 정치 권력에 대한 우리 자신의 개념을 통해 다른 문화에서의 정치 권력을 이해하는 것은 (A) 잘못 이해된 것이다.

① 합리적인	– 융통성 있는	② 적절한	– 아주 흔한
③ **잘못 이해한**	**– 획일적인**	④ 불합리한	– 다양한
⑤ 효과적인	– 객관적인		

문제풀이

서양은 정치 권력을 '강제적인 힘'으로 여기지만 아마존의 많은 원주민 부족은 정치 권력을 그렇게 여기지 않는다고 하면서, 정치 권력에 관한 생각은 보편적인 것이 아니기 때문에 다른 문화의 정치 권력을 서양의 개념에 따라 이해하는 것은 잘못된 것이라는 이야기를 하고 있다. 따라서 요약문의 빈칸 (A)에는 'misguided(잘못 이해된)'가 (B)에는 'uniform(획인적인)'이 들어가야 한다. 정답은 ③이다.

《 어휘·어구 》

equation 방정식
dominance 지배력
questionable 의심스러운
conceivably 아마도, 생각건대
bothersome 성가신
allergic to ~을 몹시 싫어하는
conception 개념
fixation 고정 관념
universal 보편적인 것
domain 영역, 범위
domination 지배, 우세
shaky 불안정한
personhood 개성
obsession 강박 관념
bias 편견
construct 구성 개념
rational 합리적인
flexible 유연한
commonplace 아주 흔한
uniform 획일적인
unreasonable 불합리한
objective 객관적인

정답률 

6. ⑤ 코끼리의 인사 행동

직독/직해

Because elephant groups break up and reunite
코끼리 집단은 예컨대 매우 자주 헤어지고 재결합하기 때문에 /
very frequently — for instance, /
in response to variation in food availability — /
먹이의 이용 가능성의 변화에 대응하여 /
reunions are more important in elephant society
코끼리 사회에서는 영장류들 사이에서 보다 재결합이 더 중요하다
than among primates.
And the species has evolved elaborate greeting

그래서 이 좋은 정교한 인사 행동을 진화시켜 왔다 /
behaviors, /
the form of which reflects the strength of the
그 형태는 개체들 사이의 사회적 유대감의 강도를 반영한다 /
social bond between the individuals /
(much like how you might merely shake hands
with a long-standing acquaintance /
마치 여러분이 오래 전부터 알고 지내온 지인들과는 단지 악수만 하는 방식과 같이 /
but hug a close friend you have not seen in a while,
and maybe even tear up).
하지만 한동안 못 본 친한 친구는 껴안고, 어쩌면 눈물까지 흘릴 수도 있는 것처럼
Elephants may greet each other /
코끼리는 서로 인사를 할 수 있다 /
simply by reaching their trunks into each other's
단순히 코를 서로의 입안으로 갖다 대면서 /
mouths, /
possibly equivalent to a human peck on the cheek.
아마도 사람들이 뺨에 가볍게 입 맞추는 것과 같이
However, after long absences, /
그러나 오랜 공백 후에 /
members of family and bond groups greet one
가족이나 친밀 집단의 구성원들은 서로에게 인사한다 /
another /
with incredibly theatrical displays.
믿을 수 없을 정도로 극적인 모습으로
The fact that the intensity reflects the duration of
강렬함이 떨어져 있었던 시간의 길이를 반영한다는 사실은 /
the separation /
as well as the level of intimacy / 친밀도뿐만 아니라 /
suggests that elephants have a sense of time as
well. 코끼리들에게 시간적 감각도 있다는 것을 암시한다
To human eyes, these greetings strike a familiar
사람들의 눈에 이런 인사 행위는 공감을 불러일으킨다
chord.
I'm reminded of the joyous reunions /
나는 즐거운 상봉 장면이 생각난다 /
so visible in the arrivals area of an international
국제공항 터미널 도착 구역에서 쉽게 볼 수 있는
airport terminal.

예를 들어 코끼리 집단은 식량 가용성의 변화에 대응하면서 아주 자주 헤어졌다가 재결합하기 때문에, 재결합은 영장류 사이에서보다 코끼리 사회에서 더 중요하다. 그리고 그 좋은 정교한 인사 행위를 진화시켜 왔는데, 그 형태는 개체들 사이의 사회적 유대감의 강도를 반영한다(여러분이 오래된 지인과 악수만 하지만 한동안 못 본 친한 친구를 껴안고, 어쩌면 눈물까지 흘릴 수도 있는 것과 아주 비슷하다). 코끼리는 단순히 코를 서로의 입에 닿게 함으로써 서로에게 인사를 할 수도 있는데, 이는 아마도 사람이 뺨에 가벼운 입맞춤을 하는 것과 동일한 것일 수 있다. 하지만 오랜 부재 후에, 가족과 유대를 맺은 집단의 구성원들은 믿을 수 없을 정도의 극적인 표현으로 서로에게 인사를 한다. 강도는 친밀감의 수준뿐만 아니라 이별의 지속시간을 반영한다는 사실은 코끼리들이 시간의식도 가지고 있음을 시사한다. 사람의 눈에는 이런 인사 행위가 친숙한 공감을 일으킨다. 나는 국제공항 터미널 도착 구역에서 쉽게 볼 수 있는 즐거운 재회가 생각난다.

➡ 코끼리들의 진화된 인사 행동은 그들이 사회적으로 얼마나 많이 (A) 유대감을 갖고 있으며 얼마나 오래 (B) 떨어져 있었는지를 나타내주는 지표로서 역할을 할 수 있다.

① 경쟁력 있는 — 따로 떨어진
② 유대감을 가진 — 멸종 위기에 처한
③ 책임감 있는 — 고립된
④ 경쟁력 있는 — 연합한
⑤ 유대감을 가진 — 떨어져 있는

문제풀이

코끼리는 정교한 인사 행위를 진화시켜왔는데 그것들은 서로 헤어졌다가 다시 만날 때 친밀감의 수준과 이별의 지속 시간에 따라 인사의 강도가 다르다고 했다. 따라서 (A)에는 'tied(유대감을 가진)'가, (B)에는 'parted(떨어져 있는)'가 들어가는 것이 가장 적절하다. 정답은 ⑤이다.

《 어휘·어구 》

reunite 재결합하다
variation 변화
primate 영장류
elaborate 정교한
social bond 사회적 유대
long-standing 오래된
equivalent 동등한 것
theatrical 연극 같은, 과장된
intimacy 친밀함
strike a chord 뭔가 생각나게 하다

정답률 74%

7. ① 즉각적인 생산물을 선호하는 경향

직독/직해

Biological organisms, / 생물학적 유기체들은 /
including human societies both with and without
시장 시스템이 있는 인간 사회와 시장 시스템이 없는 인간 사회를 포함하여
market systems, / discount distant outputs /
/ 멀리 떨어진 생산물의 가치를 더 낮게 본다 /
over those available at the present time /
현재 이용할 수 있는 생산물보다 /
based on risks associated with an uncertain future.
불확실한 미래와 연관된 위험에 근거해서
As the timing of inputs and outputs varies greatly /
투입물과 생산물의 시점이 상당히 다양하기 때문에 /
depending on the type of energy, / 에너지 유형에 따라 /
there is a strong case to incorporate time / when
시간을 통합하려는 강력한 사례가 있다 / 대체 에너지를 평가할 때
assessing energy alternatives.
For example, / the energy output from solar panels
예를 들어 / 태양 전지나 풍력 엔진으로부터 나오는 에너지 생산량은 /
or wind power engines, /
where most investment happens / before they begin
대부분의 투자가 이뤄지는 / 에너지를 생산하기 전에
producing, / may need to be assessed differently /
/ 다르게 평가되어야 할 수도 있는데 /
when compared to most fossil fuel extraction
대부분의 화석 연료 추출 기술과 비교했을 때
technologies, / where a large proportion of the
/ 에너지 생산의 많은 비율이 훨씬 빨리 나오며 /
energy output comes much sooner, /
and a larger (relative) proportion of inputs is applied /
(상대적으로) 더 큰 비율의 투입이 적용되고 /
during the extraction process, / and not upfront.
추출 과정 동안 / 선행 투자되지 않는다
Thus fossil fuels, / particularly oil and natural gas, /
따라서 화석 연료 / 특히 석유와 천연가스는 /
in addition to having energy quality advantages /
에너지 품질 장점을 가지고 있는 것 외에도 /
(cost, storability, transportability, etc.) /
(비용, 저장성, 운반성 등등) /
over many renewable technologies, / also have a
많은 재생 가능한 기술들보다 / 또한 '시간적인 장점'을 갖는다
"temporal advantage" / after accounting for human
/ 그것은 인간의 행동적 선호의 설명에 비추어 볼 때
behavioral preference / for current consumption/return.
/ 현재의 소비/수익에 대한
Due to the fact / that people tend to favor more
사실 때문에 / 사람들이 더 즉각적인 생산물을 선호하는 경향이 있는 /
immediate outputs, /
fossil fuels are more competitive / than renewable
화석 연료는 더 경쟁력이 있다 / 재생 가능한 대체 에너지보다
energy alternatives / in regards to the distance
/ 투입과 생산 간의 거리 면에서
between inputs and outputs.

시장 시스템이 있는 인간 사회와 시장 시스템이 없는 인간 사회를 포함하여 생물학적 유기체들은 불확실한 미래와 연관된 위험에 근거해서 현재 이용할 수 있는 생산물보다 멀리 떨어진 생산물의 가치를 더 낮게 본다. 에너지 유형에 따라 투입물과 생산물의 시점이 상당히 다양하기 때문에, 대체 에너지를 평가할 때 시간을 통합하려는 강력한 사례가 있다. 예를 들어, 에너지를 생산하기 전에 대부분의 투자가 이뤄지는 태양 전지나 풍력 엔진으로부터 나오는 에너지 생산량은, 대부분의 화석 연료 추출 기술과 비교했을 때 다르게 평가되어야 할 수도 있는데, (화석 연료 추출 기술에서는) 에너지 생산의 많은 비율이 훨씬 빨리 나오며, (상대적으로) 더 큰 비율의 투입이 추출 과정 동안 적용되고, 선행 투자되지 않는다. 따라서 화석 연료, 특히 석유와 천연가스는, 많은 재생 가능한 기술들보다 에너지 품질 장점(비용, 저장성, 운반성 등등)을 가지고 있는 것 외에도, 그것은 현재의 소비/수익에 대한 인간의 행동적 선호의 설명에 비추어 볼 때 '시간적인 장점' 또한 갖는다.

➡ 사람들이 더 (A) 즉각적인 생산물을 선호하는 경향이 있는 사실 때문에, 화석 연료가 투입과 생산 간의 거리 면에서 재생 가능한 대체 에너지보다 더 (B) 경쟁력이 있다.

① 즉각적인 – 경쟁력 있는
② 이용 가능한 – 비싼
③ 지체된 – 경쟁력 있는
④ 편리한 – 비싼
⑤ 풍부한 – 경쟁력 있는

문제풀이

사람들은 시간상으로 멀리 떨어진 생산물의 가치를 더 낮게 보는 경향이 있고, 시간상으로 훨씬 빨리 나오는 생산물을 선호하기 때문에 재생 가능한 대체 에너지보다 바로 얻을 수 있는 화석 연료를 선호한다는 내용이다. 이는 사람들이 더 즉각적인 것을 선호하므로, 화석연료가 대체에너지보다 더 경쟁력이 있다는 문장으로 요약할수 있다. 따라서 (A)에는 'immediate(즉각적인)'가, (B)에는 'competitive(경쟁력 있는)'가 들어가야 한다.

이렇게 풀자_ 글의 주제문인 'Biological organisms, including human societies both with and without market systems, discount distant outputs over those available at the present time based on risks associated with an uncertain future.(시장 시스템이 있는 인간 사회와 시장 시스템이 없는 인간 사회를 포함하여 생물학적 유기체들은 불확실한 미래와 연관된 위험에 근거해서 현재 이용할 수 있는 생산물보다 멀리 떨어진 생산물의 가치를 더 낮게 본다.)'가 글의 요약문의 빈칸에 들어갈 말을 찾는 단서이다.

《 어휘·어구 》

associated with ~와 관련된
incorporate 통합하다
alternative 대체(의)
extraction 추출
proportion 비율
storability 저장성
transportability 운반성
renewable 재생 가능한
temporal 시간의
account for 설명하다

본문 107쪽

문법 플러스 18. 수의 일치

A. 1. are
2. are
3. contain
4. have
5. was
6. think
7. that

1 [해석]▶ 한 유명한 교수와 한 음악가가 그 문제를 토론하고 있다.
[해설]▶ 수 일치의 기본 원칙은 복수주어는 복수동사를 사용한다.

2 [해석]▶ 불쾌한 주제와 상황들을 무시함으로써 갈등을 피하는 가정들은 그것으로 인해 더 강해지는 것이 아니라 더 약해진다.

[해설]▶ 관계사절(that~)로 주어, 동사가 멀리 떨어져 있는 경우 주어를 잘 찾아 동사의 수를 일치시켜야 한다. 주어는 families로 복수주어이므로 복수동사가 나와야 한다.

3 [해석]▶ 아이들은 폭력이 담겨 있는 TV 프로그램을 봐서는 안 된다.
[해설]▶ 관계대명사절 안의 동사는 선행사의 수에 일치시킨다. 선행사가 복수주어(TV programs)이면 복수동사(contain)를 사용해야 한다.

4 [해석]▶ 아름다운 잔디, 초목, 아름다운 연못이 있는 곳이 바로 골프장이다.
[해설]▶ It... that ~ 강조 구문에서 주어가 강조되면, that 바로 뒤의 동사는 강조된 주어에 맞게 수를 일치시킨다. 강조된 주어가 복수주어 golf courses이므로 복수동사 have가 나와야 한다.

5 [해석]▶ 그녀가 죽고 난 후에야, 나는 그녀의 고마움을 알 수 있었다.
[해설]▶ 도치 구문(only after her death)은 뒤에 나오는 주어(I)에 맞게 수를 일치시킨다.

6 [해석]▶ 그녀의 친구 중 일부는 그녀가 스마트워치 때문에 일하고 저축하는 것은 어리석은 일이라고 생각한다. 하지만 나는 그들의 생각에 동의하지 않는다.
[해설]▶ some of ~이 주어로 쓰인 경우, 동사는 of 뒤에 나오는 명사(구)의 수에 일치시킨다.

7 [해석]▶ 토끼의 꼬리는 고양이의 꼬리보다 더 짧다.
[해설]▶ 토끼의 꼬리(the tail)과 고양이의 꼬리를 비교하고 있으므로, 고양이의 꼬리를 나타내는 대명사는 단수로 표현해야 한다.

본문 107쪽

B. 1. is
2. is
3. have
4. is
5. does
6. are
7. it

1 [해석]▶한 유명한 교수 겸 음악가가 전화로 통화를 하고 있다.
[해설]▶ 관사를 한 번만 사용했으므로 동일 인물을 나타낸다. 단수주어는 단수동사를 사용해야 한다.

2 [해석]▶ 신체에 보석을 치장하는 관습은 고대부터 그랬다.
[해설]▶ 분사구(decorating~)가 주어 the custom을 수식하고 있다. 주어가 단어주어(the custom)이므로, 단수동사를 사용해야 한다.

3 [해석]▶ 의사들이 지난 3개월 동안 그 약을 복용한 암 환자들을 접촉하고 있다.
[해설]▶ 관계대명사절 안의 동사는 선행사의 수에 일치시킨다. 선행사가 복수명사 patients이므로 복수동사가 나와야 한다.

4 [해석]▶ 우리집 근처에는 지하철역이 없다.
[해설]▶ There be ~ 구문에서 주어는 be동사 뒤에 나온 어구이다. 주어가 단수명사 subway station이므로 단수동사를 써야 한다.

5 [해석]▶ Sam은 좀처럼 사람들에 대해 험담하지 않는다.
[해설]▶ 부정어(seldom)가 문장 가장 앞에 나와 주어와 동사가 도치된 문장이다. 주어가 Sam이므로 단수동사 does가 나와야 한다.

6 [해석]▶ 선반의 대부분이 비워있다.
[해설]▶ most of ~이 주어로 쓰인 경우, 동사는 of 뒤에 나오는 명사(구)의 수에 일치시킨다.

7 [해석]▶ 명사를 대신하는 대명사는 그 명사의 수와 일치해야 한다.
[해설]▶ 갈등을 공개적으로 표출하는 것은 가정의 문제를 처리하고 그것을 접근 가능한 범위 안에 두는 훌륭한 방법이다.
[해설]▶ 괄호의 대명사가 지칭한 것은 family conflict이므로 단수 대명사가 필요하다.

본문 108쪽

숙어 플러스 18. 수능 필수 숙어 18회

1. stand	2. stayed
3. out	4. off

19. 장문의 이해 (1)

본문 110쪽

Day 19

1. ① 2. ④ 3. ② 4. ③ 5. ③
6. ④ 7. ⑤ 8. ④

대표 기출 사생활에 대한 권리의 개념 변화

직독/직해

The right to privacy / 사생활에 대한 권리는 /
may extend only to the point /
정도까지만 연장될 수 있다 /
where it does not restrict /
한정하지 않는 /
someone else's right to freedom of expression or right to information.
다른 사람의 표현의 자유에 대한 권리나 정보에 대한 권리를
The scope of the right to privacy / is similarly restricted /
사생활에 대한 권리의 범위는 / 유사하게 한정된다 /
by the general interest / 공공 이익에 의해 /
in preventing crime or in promoting public health.
범죄 예방이나 공중 보건 증진에 있어서
However, / 그러나 /
when we move away from the property-based notion of a right /
우리가 속성에 기반을 둔 권리 개념에서 옮겨갈 때 /
[where the right to privacy would protect, for example, images and personality], /
예를 들면, 사생활에 대한 권리가 이미지와 인격을 보호할 개념 /
to modern notions of private and family life, /
사생활과 가족의 생활이라는 현대적 개념으로 /
we find it easier / to establish the limits of the right.
우리는 더 쉽다는 것을 알게 된다 / 그 권리의 한계를 확립하기가
This is, of course, / 이것은 물론 ~이다
the strength of the notion of privacy, /
사생활 개념의 강점이다 /
in that it can adapt to meet changing expectations /
변화하는 기대에 대처하기 위해 조정될 수 있다는 점에서 /
and technological advances.
그리고 기술 진보에 대처하기 위해
In sum, *what* is privacy today?
요약해 보면, 오늘날 사생활이란 '무엇'인가
The concept includes a claim /
그 개념은 주장을 포함한다 /
that we should be unobserved, /
우리가 감시당하지 않아야 한다는 /
and that certain information and images about us /
우리에 관한 특정 정보와 이미지가 /
should not be circulated without our permission.
우리의 허락 없이 유포되어서는 안 된다는
Why did these privacy claims arise?
'왜' 이러한 사생활 주장들이 생겨나게 되었는가
They arose because powerful people took offence /
그것은 영향력 있는 사람들이 불쾌감을 느꼈기 때문에 생겼다 /
at such observation. 그렇게 감시당하는 것에
Furthermore, / 더욱이 /
privacy incorporated the need /
사생활은 필요성을 포함했고 /
to protect the family, home, and correspondence /
가족, 가정, 그리고 서신을 보호할 /
from arbitrary interference /
임의적인 간섭으로부터 /

and, in addition, / 또한 /
there has been a determination /
확고한 의지가 있었다 /
to protect honour and reputation.
명예와 명성을 보호하려는
How is privacy protected?
사생활은 '어떻게' 보호되는가
Historically, / privacy was protected /
역사적으로 / 사생활은 보호되었다 /
by restricting circulation of the damaging material.
피해를 주는 자료의 유포를 한정해서
But / 하지만 /
if the concept of privacy first became interesting legally /
만약 사생활 개념이 처음 법적으로 관심을 끌게 되었다면 /
as a response to reproductions of images /
이미지 재생산에 대한 대응으로 /
through photography and newspapers, /
사진과 신문을 통한 /
more recent technological advances, /
더 근래의 기술 발전은 /
such as data storage, digital images, and the Internet, /
자료 저장, 디지털 이미지, 그리고 인터넷과 같은 /
pose new threats to privacy.
사생활에 대해 새로운 위협을 제기한다
The right to privacy is now being reinterpreted /
사생활에 대한 권리는 이제 재해석되고 있다 /
to meet those challenges.
그런 어려운 점들에 대처하기 위해

사생활에 대한 권리는 다른 사람의 표현의 자유에 대한 권리나 정보에 대한 권리를 한정하지 않는 정도까지만 연장될 수 있다. 사생활에 대한 권리의 범위는 범죄 예방이나 공중 보건 증진에 있어서 공공 이익에 의해 (a) 유사하게 한정된다. 그러나 우리가 속성에 기반을 둔 권리 개념(예를 들면, 사생활에 대한 권리가 이미지와 인격을 보호할 개념)에서 사생활과 가족의 생활이라는 현대적 개념으로 옮겨갈 때, 우리는 그 권리의 한계를 확립하기가 (b) 더 쉽다는(→ 더 어렵다는) 것을 알게 된다. 이것은 물론 변화하는 기대와 기술 진보에 대처하기 위해 조정될 수 있다는 점에서, 사생활 개념의 강점이다.
요약해 보면, 오늘날 사생활이란 '무엇'인가? 그 개념은 우리가 감시당하지 않아야 한다는 주장과, 우리에 관한 특정 정보와 이미지가 우리의 허락 없이 (c) 유포되어서는 안 된다는 주장을 포함한다. '왜' 이러한 사생활 주장들이 생겨나게 되었는가? 그것은 영향력 있는 사람들이 그렇게 감시당하는 것에 불쾌감을 느꼈기 때문에 생겼다. 더욱이 사생활은 가족, 가정, 그리고 서신을 임의적인 (d) 간섭으로부터 보호할 필요성을 포함했고, 또한 명예와 명성을 보호하려는 확고한 의지가 있었다. 사생활은 '어떻게' 보호되는가? 역사적으로 사생활은 피해를 주는 자료의 유포를 한정해서 보호되었다. 하지만 만약 사생활 개념이 사진과 신문을 통한 이미지 재생산에 대한 대응으로 처음 법적으로 관심을 끌게 되었다면, 자료 저장, 디지털 이미지, 그리고 인터넷과 같은 더 근래의 기술 발전은 사생활에 대해 새로운 위협을 (e) 제기한다. 사생활에 대한 권리는 이제 그런 어려운 점들에 대처하기 위해 재해석되고 있다.

어휘·어구

extend 연장하다, 확대하다
restrict 한정하다, 제한하다
scope 범위
general interest 공공 이익
promote 촉진하다, 증진하다
property-based 속성에 기반을 둔
notion 개념
in that ~라는 점에서
unobserved 눈에 띄지 않는
circulate 유포하다
arise 생기다
take offence 불쾌감을 느끼다
incorporate 포함하다
correspondence 서신 (교환)
interference 간섭, 방해
determination 확고한 의지, 결심
reputation 평판
damaging 피해를 주는
legally 법적으로
reproduction 재생산
pose (문제 등을) 제기하다
threat 위협
reinterpret 재해석하다
challenge (어려운) 문제, 도전
side effect 부작용
legal 법률의
conflict 갈등
loose 느슨한
regulation 구제, 규정
intervention 개입, 간섭

정답률 
41. ③

① 사생활 보호 기술의 부작용
② 사생활 보호 주장과 갈등의 법률적 영역
③ **사생활에 대한 권리: 발전하는 개념과 관행**
④ 더 느슨한 사생활 규제로부터 누가 정말 이득을 보는가?
⑤ 적을수록 더 좋다: 사생활에 있어서 국가의 개입을 줄여라!

문제풀이

사생활에 대한 권리의 적용에 있어서 범위는 한정되는데, 그것의 개념이 변화하는 기대와 기술 발전에 따라 생겨나는 여러 문제에 대처하기 위해 바뀌고 있다는 이야기를 하고 있는 글이다. 이러한 글의 내용을 가장 잘 나타낸 제목으로는 ③ 'The Right to Privacy: Evolving Concepts and Practices(사생활에 대한 권리: 발전하는 개념과 관행)'가 적절하다.

정답률 
42. ②

문제풀이

사생활에 대한 권리의 개념이 변화하는 기대와 기술 발전에 따라 생겨나는 새로운 여러 위협에 대처하기 위해 재해석되고 있다고 했으므로, 그것이 속성에 기반을 둔 개념에서 사생활과 가족의 생활이라는 현대적 개념으로 바뀌면서 그 권리의 한계를 설정하기가 더 어려워졌다고 하는 것이 자연스럽다. 따라서 (b) 'easier(더 쉬운)'를 'harder(더 어려운)'와 같은 낱말로 바꿔 써야 한다.

1~2 판단할 때, 단순한 공식의 중요성

직독/직해

There is evidence / 증거가 있다 /
that even very simple algorithms can outperform expert judgement /
심지어 매우 간단한 알고리즘도 전문가의 판단을 능가할 수 있다는 /
on simple prediction problems. 단순한 예측 문제에 대한
For example, / algorithms have proved more accurate than humans /
예를 들면 / 알고리즘이 인간보다 더 정확하다는 것이 증명했다 /
in predicting / whether a prisoner released on parole /
예측하는데 / 가석방으로 풀려난 죄수가 /
will go on to commit another crime, /
계속 다른 범죄를 저지를 것인지 /
or in predicting / whether a potential candidate will perform well /
또는 예측하는 데 / 잠재적인 지원자가 일을 잘할 것인지를 /
in a job in future. 장차 직장에서
In over 100 studies across many different domains, / half of all cases show /
많은 다른 영역에 걸친 100개가 넘는 연구에서 / 모든 경우의 절반은 보여준다 /
simple formulas make better significant predictions / than human experts, /
단순한 공식이 중요한 예측을 더 잘한다는 것을 / 인간 전문가보다 /
and the remainder (except a very small handful), / show a tie between the two.
그리고 그 나머지(아주 적은 소수를 제외하고)는 / 둘 사이의 무승부를 보여준다
When there are a lot of different factors involved /
관련된 많은 다른 요인이 있을 때 /
and a situation is very uncertain, / simple formulas can win out /
그리고 상황이 매우 불확실할 때 / 단순한 공식이 승리할 수 있다 /
by focusing on the most important factors / and being consistent, /
가장 중요한 요소에 초점을 맞추으로써 / 그리고 일관성을 유지함으로써 /
while human judgement is too easily influenced /
반면에 인간의 판단은 너무 쉽게 영향을 받는다 /
by particularly salient and perhaps irrelevant considerations.
특히 두드러지고 아마도 무관한 고려 사항에 의해
A similar idea is supported by further evidence /
유사한 아이디어가 추가적인 증거에 의해 뒷받침 받는다 /
that 'checklists' can improve the quality of expert decisions / in a range of domains
'체크리스트'가 전문가의 판단의 질을 향상할 수 있다는 (증거에 의해) / 다양한 영역에서 /
by ensuring that important steps or considerations aren't missed /
중요한 조치나 고려 사항을 놓치지 않도록 함으로써 /
when people are feeling overloaded.
사람들이 일이 너무 많다고 느낄 때
For example, / treating patients in intensive care /
예를 들면 / 집중 치료 중인 환자를 치료하는 것은 /
can require hundreds of small actions per day, /
하루에 수백 가지의 작은 조치를 필요로 할 수 있다 /
and one small error could cost a life.
그런데 작은 실수 하나는 목숨을 잃게 할 수 있다
Using checklists / to ensure that no crucial steps are missed /
체크리스트를 사용하는 것은 / 어떤 중요한 단계도 놓치지 않기 위해 /
has proved to be remarkably effective / in a range of medical contexts, /
현저하게 효과적이라는 것이 입증되었다 / 다양한 의학적 상황에서 /
from preventing live infections to reducing pneumonia.
당면한 감염을 예방하는 것에서부터 폐렴을 줄이는 것에 이르기까지

심지어 매우 간단한 알고리즘도 단순한 예측 문제에 대한 전문가의 판단을 능가할 수 있다는 증거가 있다. 예를 들면, 가석방으로 풀려난 죄수가 계속 다른 범죄를 저지를 것인지 예측하거나, 잠재적인 지원자가 장차 직장에서 일을 잘할 것인지를 예측하는 데 알고리즘이 인간보다 더 (a) 정확하다는 것이 증명했다. 많은 다른 영역에 걸친 100개가 넘는 연구에서, 모든 경우의 절반은 단순한 공식이 인간 전문가보다 중요한 예측을 (b) 더 잘하고, 그 나머지(아주 적은 소수를 제외하고)는 둘 사이의 무승부를 보여준다. 관련된 많은 다른 요인이 있고 상황이 매우 불확실할 때, 가장 중요한 요소에 초점을 맞추고 일관성을 유지함으로써 단순한 공식이 승리할 수 있는 반면, 인간의 판단은 특히 두드러지고 아마도 (c) 무관한 고려 사항에 의해 너무 쉽게 영향을 받는다. 사람들이 (d) 편안하다고(→ 일이 너무 많다고) 느낄 때 중요한 조치나 고려 사항을 놓치지 않도록 함으로써 '체크리스트'가 다양한 영역에서 전문가의 판단의 질을 향상할 수 있다는 추가적인 증거가 유사한 아이디어를 뒷받침한다. 예를 들면, 집중 치료 중인 환자를 치료하는 것은 하루에 수백 가지의 작은 조치를 필요로 할 수 있으며, 작은 실수 하나는 목숨을 잃게 할 수 있다. 어떤 중요한 단계도 놓치지 않기 위해 체크리스트를 사용하는 것은 당면한 감염을 예방하는 것에서부터 폐렴을 줄이는 것에 이르기까지 다양한 의학적 상황에서 현저하게 (e) 효과적이라는 것이 입증되었다.

어휘·어구

outperform 능가하다, 더 나은 결과를 내다
accurate 정확한
commit (범죄를) 저지르다, 범하다
potential 잠재적인
candidate 후보, 지원자
domain 영역
remainder 나머지
handful 몇 안 되는 수

consistent 일관성이 있는
irrelevant 무관한
intensive care 집중 치료
cost 희생시키다, 잃게 하다
crucial 중요한
remarkably 현저하게, 뚜렷하게
live 당면한, 생생한
infection 감염
formula 공식
prioritise 우선순위를 매기다

구조 다시보기

증거 1	의사 결정할 때 간단한 공식의 힘 1: 매우 간단한 알고리즘조차도 간단한 예측 문제에 대한 전문가의 판단을 능가할 수 있음
예시	가석방된 죄수가 다른 범죄를 저지를 것인지 예측하는 문제와 잠재적인 후보자가 장차 직장에서 일을 잘할 것인지 예측하는 문제에서 알고리즘이 인간보다 더 정확하다는 것이 입증됨
증거 2	의사 결정할 때 간단한 공식의 힘 2: 다양한 영역의 100개가 넘는 사례 연구에서, 모든 사례의 절반은 단순한 공식이 인간 전문가보다 예측을 더 잘했고, 나머지는 무승부를 보여줌
주제	관련된 여러 요인이 있을 때 중요한 요소에 초점을 맞추고 일관성을 유지하는 간단한 공식은 무관한 고려 사항에 쉽게 영향을 받는 인간의 판단을 이길 수 있음
증거 3	의사 결정할 때 간단한 공식의 힘 3: 체크리스트를 마련해서 이용하면 다양한 영역에서 전문가의 결정의 질을 향상할 수 있음
예시	많은 조치가 필요한 집중 치료 중인 환자를 치료할 때 중요한 단계를 놓치지 않게 체크리스트를 사용하는 것이 효과적임

정답률 57%

1. ①

① **의사 결정을 할 때의 간단한 공식의 힘**
② 항상 우선순위를 매겨라: 빅 데이터 관리 방법
③ 알고리즘의 실수: 단순함의 신화
④ 준비하라! 만약의 경우를 대비해 체크리스트를 만들라
⑤ 인간의 판단이 알고리즘을 이기는 방법

문제풀이

모든 사례의 절반은 간단한 공식이 인간 전문가보다 중요한 예측을 더 잘했고, 사람들은 업무가 과중하다고 느낄 때 중요한 조치나 고려 사항을 놓치지 않도록 체크리스트를 마련하는 것이 전문가의 결정의 질을 향상시킬 수 있다는 내용의 글이다. 이러한 글의 내용을 가장 잘 나타낸 제목으로는 ① 'The Power of Simple Formulas in Decision Making(의사 결정을 할 때의 단순한 공식의 힘)'이 적절하다.

정답률 62%

2. ④

문제풀이

집중 치료를 받는 환자에게 하루에 수백 가지의 작은 조치가 필요한 상황에서 어떤 중요한 것도 놓치지 않기 위해 체크리스트가 필요하다고 했는데, 이는 사람들이 처리할 일이 많을 때 중요한 조치를 놓치지 않도록 체크리스트를 만든다는 의미이다. 따라서 (d) 'relaxed(편안한)'를 'overloaded(일이 너무 많은)'와 같은 낱말로 바꾸어야 한다.

3~4 언어의 분류적 특성

직독/직해

Classifying things together into groups / is something /
사물들을 묶어서 그룹으로 분류하는 것은 / 일이다 /
we do all the time, / and it isn't hard / to see why.
우리가 늘 하는 / 그리고 어렵지 않다 / 그 이유를 이해하는 것은
Imagine trying to shop in a supermarket /
쇼핑하려고 한다고 상상해 보라 /
where the food was arranged / in random order /
배열된 슈퍼마켓에서 / 무작위로 /
on the shelves: / 음식이 진열대에 /
tomato soup next to the white bread / in one aisle, /
흰 빵 옆에 토마토 수프가 있고 / 한 통로에서는 /
chicken soup in the back next to the 60-watt light bulbs, /
치킨 수프는 뒤쪽에 있는 60와트 백열전구 옆에 있고 /
one brand of cream cheese in front and another /
한 크림치즈 브랜드는 앞쪽에, 또 다른 하나는 /
in aisle 8 near the cookies.
쿠키 근처의 8번 통로에 있다
The task of finding what you want /
여러분이 원하는 것을 찾는 일은 /
would be time-consuming and extremely difficult, /
시간이 많이 걸리고 매우 어려울 것이다 /
if not impossible.
불가능하지는 않아도
In the case of a supermarket, /
슈퍼마켓의 경우 /
someone had to design the system of classification.
누군가는 분류 체계를 설계해야 했다
But there is also a ready-made system of classification /
그러나 또한 기성의 분류 체계도 있다 /
embodied in our language.
우리 언어에 포함되어 있는
The word "dog," / for example, /
'개'라는 단어는 / 예를 들면 /
groups together a certain class of animals /
특정 부류의 동물들을 함께 분류한다 /
and distinguishes them from other animals.
그리고 다른 동물들과 구별한다
Such a grouping may seem too obvious /
그런 분류가 너무 명백하게 보일 수 있다 /
to be called a classification, /
분류라고 불리기에는 /
but this is only /
하지만 이것은 단지 ~이다 /
because you have already mastered the word.
여러분이 이미 그 단어를 숙달했기 때문
As a child learning to speak, /
말하기를 배우는 아이로서 /
you had to work hard /
여러분은 열심히 노력해야 했다 /
to learn the system of classification /
분류 체계를 배우려고 /
your parents were trying to teach you.
여러분은 부모님이 가르쳐주려 애썼던
Before you got the hang of it, /
여러분이 그것을 이해하기 전에 /
you probably made mistakes, /
여러분은 아마 실수를 했을 것이다 /
like calling the cat a dog.
고양이를 개라고 부르는 것과 같은
If you hadn't learned to speak, /
만일 여러분이 말하기를 배우지 않았다면 /
the whole world would seem like the unorganized supermarket; /
온 세상이 정돈되지 않은 슈퍼마켓처럼 보일 것이다 /
you would be in the position of an infant, /
여러분은 유아의 입장에 있을 것이다 /
for whom every object is new and unfamiliar.
모든 물건이 새롭고 낯선
In learning the principles of classification, / therefore, /
분류의 원칙을 배울 때 / 따라서 /
we'll be learning about the structure /
우리는 구조에 대해 배우고 있는 것이다 /
that lies at the core of our language.
언어의 핵심에 놓여 있는

사물들을 묶어서 그룹으로 분류하는 것은 우리가 늘 하는 일이며, 그 이유를 이해하는 것은 어렵지 않다. 음식이 진열대에 무작위로 배열된 슈퍼마켓에서 쇼핑하려고 한다고 상상해 보라. 한 통로에서는 흰 빵 옆에 토마토 수프가 있고, 치킨 수프는 뒤쪽에 있는 60와트 백열전구 옆에 있고, 한 크림치즈 브랜드는 앞쪽에, 또 다른 하나는 쿠키 근처의 8번 통로에 있다. 여러분이 원하는 것을 찾는 일은, 불가능하지는 않아도, (a) 시간이 많이 걸리고 매우 어려울 것이다. 슈퍼마켓의 경우, 누군가는 분류 체계를 (b) 설계해야 했다. 그러나 또한 우리 언어에 포함되어 있는 기성의 분류 체계도 있다. 예를 들면, '개'라는 단어는 특정 부류의 동물들을 함께 분류하여 다른 동물들과 구별한다. 분류라고 불리기에는 그런 분류가 너무 (c) 추상적이게(→ 명백하게) 보일 수 있지만, 이것은 단지 여러분이 이미 그 단어를 숙달했기 때문이다. 말하기를 배우는 아이로서, 여러분은 부모님이 가르쳐주려 애썼던 분류 체계를 (d) 배우려고 열심히 노력해야 했다. 여러분이 그것을 이해하기 전에, 아마 고양이를 개라고 부르는 것과 같은 실수를 했을 것이다. 만일 여러분이 말하기를 배우지 않았다면, 온 세상이 (e) 정돈되지 않은 슈퍼마켓처럼 보일 것이다. 여러분은 모든 물건이 새롭고 낯선 유아의 입장에 있을 것이다. 따라서 분류의 원칙을 배울 때, 우리는 언어의 핵심에 놓여 있는 구조에 대해 배우고 있는 것이다.

어휘·어구

classify A into B A를 B로 분류하다
arrange 배열하다, 정리하다
random 무작위의, 임의로
aisle 통로
light bulb 백열 전구
time-consuming 시간이 많이 걸리는
classification 분류
ready-made 이미 만들어진
embody 포함하다, 담다
distinguish A from B A를 B로부터 구별하다
abstract 추상적인
get the hang of ~을 이해하다
unorganized 잘 정돈되지 않은
infant 유아
unfamiliar 낯선
principle 원칙, 원리
core 핵심
strategy 전략
inherent 내재된
categorization 범주화

정답률 64%

3. ②

① 판매와 어학학습에서 전략의 유사성
② **분류: 언어의 내재된 특징**
③ 범주화를 통한 언어학적 문제 탐구
④ 이미 만들어진 분류 체계가 정말 더 나은가?
⑤ 언어교육에서 분류 사용의 딜레마

문제풀이

언어에는 이미 분류에 연관된 개념이 포함되어 있기 때문에 분류에 대한 개념 이해는 언어를 배우는 과정에서 습득할 수 있다는 내용의 글이다. 이러한 글의 내용을 가장 잘 나타낸 제목으로는 ② 'Classification: An Inherent Characteristic of Language(분류: 언어의 내재된 특징)'가 적절하다.

정답률 61%

4. ③

문제풀이

뒤에서 분류를 이해하기 전에는 고양이를 개라고 부르는 것과 같은 실수를 했다고 했으므로, 단어

를 숙달했다면 '개'라는 단어가 특정 부류의 동물들을 함께 분류하여 다른 동물과 구분하는 것이 명백하다고 하는 것이 적절하다. 따라서 (c) 'abstract(추상적인)'는 'obvious(명백한)'와 같은 낱말로 고쳐 써야 한다.

5~6 동물 행동의 복잡성

직독/직해

Our irresistible tendency to see things /
사물을 보는 우리의 억누를 수 없는 경향 /
in human terms / 인간의 관점에서 /
— that we are often mistaken /
우리가 종종 잘못 생각하는 것은 /
in attributing complex human motives and processing abilities to other species — /
다른 종들에게 복잡한 인간의 동기와 처리 능력이 있다고 /
does not mean / 의미하지는 않는다 /
that an animal's behavior is not, in fact, complex.
동물의 행동이 실제로 복잡하지 않다는 것을
Rather, it means / 오히려 그것은 의미한다 /
that the complexity of the animal's behavior /
동물 행동의 복잡성이 /
is not purely a product of its internal complexity.
순전히 그것의 내적 복잡성의 산물이 아니라는 것을
Herbert Simon's "parable of the ant" /
Herbert Simon의 '개미 우화'는 /
makes this point very clearly.
이러한 점을 매우 명확하게 해 준다
Imagine an ant walking along a beach, /
한 마리의 개미가 해변을 따라 걷고 있는 것을 상상하라 /
and visualize tracking the trajectory of the ant /
그리고 그 이동 경로를 추적하는 것을 머릿속에 그려보라 /
as it moves. 그것이 이동함에 따라
The trajectory would show a lot of twists and turns, /
그 이동 경로는 많이 구부러지고 방향이 바뀔 것이다 /
and would be very irregular and complicated.
그리고 매우 불규칙하고 복잡할 것이다
One could then suppose /
그렇다면 가정할 수 있을 것이다 /
that the ant had equally complicated internal navigational abilities, /
그 개미에게 똑같이 복잡한 내적인 항행 능력이 있다고 /
and work out / what these were likely to be /
그리고 알아낼 수 있을 것이다 / 이것이 무엇일 수 있는지를 /
by analyzing the trajectory /
그 이동 경로를 분석함으로써 /
to infer the rules and mechanisms /
규칙과 구조를 추론하기 위해 /
that could produce such a complex navigational path.
그런 복잡한 항행 경로를 만들어 낼 수 있는
The complexity of the trajectory, however, /
그러나 그 이동 경로의 복잡성은 /
"is really a complexity in the surface of the beach, /
실제로 해변 지면에서의 복잡성이지 /
not a complexity in the ant."
그 개미의 내적 복잡성이 아니다
In reality, / 사실 /
the ant may be using a set of very simple rules: /
그 개미는 일련의 매우 단순한 규칙들을 사용하고 있을 수도 있는데 /
it is the interaction of these rules with the environment /
바로 이 규칙들과 환경의 상호 작용이다 /
that actually produces the complex trajectory, /
그 복잡한 이동 경로를 실제로 만들어 내는 것은 /
not the ant alone. 그 개미 혼자서는 아니다
Put more generally, /
좀 더 일반적으로 말하자면 /
the parable of the ant illustrates /
개미 우화는 보여준다 /
that there is no necessary correlation /
필연적인 상관관계가 없음을 /
between the complexity of an observed behavior and the complexity of the mechanism /
관찰된 행동의 복잡성과 구조의 복잡성 사이의 /
that produces it. 그것을 만들어 내는

인간의 관점에서 사물을 보는 우리의 억누를 수 없는 경향, 즉 다른 종들에게 복잡한 인간의 동기와 처리 능력이 있다고 우리가 종종 잘못 생각하는 것은 동물의 행동이 실제로 복잡하지 않다는 것을 의미하지는 않는다. 오히려 그것은 동물 행동의 복잡성이 순전히 그것의 내적 복잡성의 (a) 산물이 아니라는 것을 의미한다. Herbert Simon의 '개미 우화'는 이러한 점을 매우 명확하게 해 준다. 한 마리의 개미가 해변을 따라 걷고 있는 것을 상상하고, 그 개미가 이동함에 따라 그 이동 경로를 추적하는 것을 (b) 머릿속에 그려보라. 그 이동 경로는 많이 구부러지고 방향이 바뀌고, 매우 불규칙하고 복잡할 것이다. 그렇다면 그 개미에게 똑같이 복잡한 (c) 내적인 항행 능력이 있다고 가정하고, 그런 복잡한 항행 경로를 만들어 낼 수 있는 규칙과 구조를 추론하기 위해 그 이동 경로를 분석함으로써 이것이 무엇일 수 있는지를 알아낼 수 있을 것이다. 그러나 그 이동 경로의 복잡성은 '실제로 해변 지면에서의 복잡성이지 그 개미의 내적 복잡성이 아니다.' 사실 그 개미는 일련의 매우 (d) 복잡한(→ 단순한) 규칙들을 사용하고 있을 수도 있는데, 그 복잡한 이동 경로를 실제로 만들어 내는 것은 바로 이 규칙들과 환경의 상호 작용이지, 그 개미 혼자서는 아니다. 좀 더 일반적으로 말하자면, 개미 우화는 (e) 관찰된 행동의 복잡성과 그것을 만들어 내는 구조의 복잡성 사이의 필연적인 상관관계가 없음을 보여준다.

《어휘·어구》

irresistible 억누를 수 없는
tendency 경향
term 관점
attribute (성질 등이) 있다고 생각하다
purely 순전히, 전적으로
visualize 머릿속에 그리다
irregular 불규칙적인
complicated 복잡한
navigational 항행의, 항해의
analyze 분석하다
infer 추론하다
mechanism 구조
interaction 상호 작용
correlation 상관관계

정답률  66%

5. ③

① 환경 복잡성의 신비한 문을 열라!
② 인간과 동물의 평화로운 공존
③ **동물 행동의 복잡성을 만드는 것은 무엇인가?**
④ 동물의 딜레마: 인간 세계에서 자신의 길 찾기
⑤ 인간 행동 복잡성에 끼치는 환경의 영향

문제풀이

인간의 관점에서 보면 동물의 행동이 복잡한 것으로 보일지도 모르지만, 실제로 동물의 단순한 행동 규칙이 환경과 상호 작용하면서 동물의 행동이 복잡한 것처럼 보이는 것이라는 내용의 글이다. 이러한 글의 내용을 가장 잘 나타낸 제목으로는 ③ 'What Makes the Complexity of Animal Behavior?(동물 행동의 복잡성을 만드는 것은 무엇인가?)'이다.

정답률  73%

6. ④

문제풀이

개미의 이동 경로의 복잡성은 개미의 내적 복잡성이 아니며 동물의 단순한 행동 규칙이 환경과 상호 작용할 때 그것이 복잡한 이동 경로를 만들어 낼 수 있다고 했으므로, 그 규칙은 복잡한 내적 항행 능력을 반영하는 복잡한 규칙이 아니다. 따라서 (d) 'complex(복잡한)'를 'simple(단순한)'과 같은 낱말로 바꿔 써야 한다.

○ 이렇게 풀자 먼저 글의 주제와 흐름을 파악한 뒤 밑줄 친 어휘가 포함된 문장 전후 문맥을 파악해서 적절하게 쓰였는지를 판단하면 된다. 'The complexity of the trajectory, however, "is really a complexity in the surface of the beach, not a complexity in the ant."(그러나 그 이동 경로의 복잡성은 '실제로 해변 지면에서의 복잡성이지 그 개미의 내적 복잡성이 아니다.')'와 'it is the interaction of these rules with the environment that actually produces the complex trajectory, not the ant alone(그 복잡한 이동 경로를 실제로 만들어 내는 것은 바로 이 규칙들과 환경의 상호 작용이지, 그 개미 혼자서는 아니다)'를 통해 개미가 복잡하지 않은 규칙을 사용하고 있다는 것을 알면 (d) complex가 적절하지 않다는 것을 알 수 있다.

7~8 과학 학습에서 체험보다 중요한 사고

직독/직해

For quite some time, science educators believed /
상당 기간 동안, 과학 교육자들은 믿었다 /
that "hands-on" activities were the answer to children's understanding /
'직접 해보는' 활동이 아이들이 이해하는 것에 대한 대답이라고 /
through their participation in science-related activities. 과학 관련 활동에 참여하는 것을 통해
Many teachers believed / 많은 교사들은 믿었다 /
that students merely engaging in activities and manipulating objects /
학생들이 단지 활동에 참여하고 사물을 조작하는 것만으로 /
would organize the information to be gained and the knowledge to be understood /
얻게 되는 정보와 이해하게 되는 지식을 체계화할 것이라고 /
into concept comprehension. 개념 이해로
Educators began to notice /
교육자들은 깨닫기 시작했다 /
that the pendulum had swung too far to the "hands-on" component of inquiry /
'직접 해보는' 탐구의 요소 쪽으로 추가 너무 많이 기울었다는 것을 /
as they realized / 깨달으면서 /
that the knowledge was not inherent in the materials themselves, /
지식이 자료 자체에 내재되어 있는 것이 아니라 /
but in the thought and metacognition about what students had done in the activity.
학생들이 그 활동에서 한 것에 대한 생각과 초(超)인지에 있다는 것을 깨달으면서
We now know that "hands-on" is a dangerous phrase / when speaking about learning science.
이제 우리는 '직접 해보는 것'이 위험한 문구라는 것을 안다 / 과학을 배우는 것에 대해 말할 때
The missing ingredient is the "minds-on" part of the instructional experience.
누락된 요소는 교육 경험의 '사고를 요구하는' 부분이다
Uncertainty about the knowledge intended in any activity / comes from each student's re-creation of concepts — /
어떤 활동에서든 의도된 지식에 대한 불확실성은 / 각 학생의 개념 재창조에서 비롯된다 /
and discussing, thinking, arguing, listening, and evaluating one's own preconceptions /
그리고 자신의 선입견에 대해 토론하고, 사고하고, 논쟁하고, 듣고, 평가하는 것을 통해서 /
after the activities, / 그 활동들 이후에 /
under the leadership of a thoughtful teacher, /
사려 깊은 선생님의 지도하에 /
can bring this about. 이것을 가져올 수 있다
After all, a food fight is a hands-on activity, /
결국, 음식물 던지기 장난은 직접 해보는 활동이다 /
but about all you would learn /
하지만 여러분이 배우게 되는 것은 /

was something about the aerodynamics of flying
으깬 감자를 날리는 공기 역학에 관한 것이었다
mashed potatoes!
Our view of what students need to build their knowledge and theories /
지식과 이론을 구축하기 위해 학생들이 필요로 하는 것에 대한 우리의 견해는 /
about the natural world / 자연 세계에 대한 /
extends far beyond a "hands-on activity."
'직접 해보는 활동'을 훨씬 넘어서는 것이다
While it is important for students to use and interact with materials in science class, /
과학 수업에서 학생들이 재료를 사용하고 상호 작용하는 것이 중요하기는 하지만 /
the learning comes from the sense-making of students' "hands-on" experiences.
학습은 '직접 해보는' 학생들의 경험에 대해 의미를 부여하는 것으로부터 나온다

한동안, 과학 교육자들은 "직접 해 보는" 활동들이 아이들의 과학 관련 활동 참여를 통한 자신들의 이해에 대한 답변이었다고 믿었다. 많은 교사들은 단순히 활동과 물체를 (a) 다루는 일에 참여한 학생들이 얻게 될 정보와 이해될 지식을 체계화해서 개념 이해를 하게 된다고 믿었다. 교육자들은 지식이 재료 자체에 (b) 내재된 것이 아니라 학생들이 활동에서 했던 것들에 대한 생각과 초인지에 내재해 있다는 것을 깨달으면서, "직접 해 보는" 요소 쪽으로 연구의 추가 너무 멀리 흔들렸다는 것을 간파하기 시작했다. 우리는 이제 과학을 배우는 것에 관해 말할 때 "직접 해 보는 것"이 위험한 말이라는 것을 알고 있다. (c) 빠져 있는 요소는 교육 경험의 "생각해 보는" 부분이다. 어떤 활동에서든 의도된 지식에 대한 (d) 불확실성은 각 학생의 개념에 대한 재창조에서 나오며, 활동 후에 사려 깊은 교사의 지도력 하에서, 토론하고, 생각해보고, 논쟁하고, 귀담아듣고, 자기 자신의 예상을 평가하는 것이 이를 불러일으킬 수 있다. 결국 음식 싸움은 직접 해 보는 활동이지만, 여러분이 배우게 되는 것이라곤 으깬 감자의 공기역학에 관한 것이었다! 학생들이 자연 세계에 대한 자신들의 지식과 이론을 수립하기 위해 필요한 것에 대한 우리의 견해는 "직접 해 보는 활동"을 훨씬 넘어서까지 (e) 확대된다. 학생들이 과학 수업에서 재료를 사용하고 재료와 상호작용하는 것이 중요하지만 학습은 학생들의 "직접 해 보는" 경험에 대한 감각으로부터 나온다.

어휘·어구

hands-on 직접 해보는
engage in ~에 참여하다
comprehension 이해
component 요소
inquiry 탐구, 연구
ingredient 요소, 성분
instructional 교육의
evaluate 평가하다
preconception 선입견
bring about ~을 유발하다
mash 으깨다

7. ⑤

① 창의력의 원천으로서 '직접 해보는' 활동
② 활동 중심의 학습이 과학 교육에 들어오다!
③ 과학 수업에서 학생들이 가장 좋아하는 것을 알아내라
④ 즐거움과 학습: 분리될 때 더 효과적이다
⑤ 과학 수업에서 '사고를 요하는' 학습을 켜라

문제풀이

한동안 과학 교육자들은 학생들이 정보와 지식을 '직접 해보는' 활동을 통해 체계화해 개념 이해를 하게 된다고 믿었지만 거기에는 교육 경험의 '생각해보는' 부분이 빠져 있었으며, 과학 수업에서 재료를 사용하고 재료와 상호 작용 하는 것이 중요하지만 학습은 그런 활동 경험을 넘어서 사고를 바탕으로 개념의 재창조를 통해 이뤄진다는 내용의 글이다. 이러한 글의 내용을 가장 잘 나타낸 제목으로는 ⑤ 'Turn "Minds-on" Learning On in Science Class(과학 수업에서 '사고를 요하는' 학습을 켜라)'가 적절하다.

이렇게 풀자_ 글의 주제를 정확히 파악하여 주제를 간결하게 잘 드러내는 포괄적이고 상징적인 것이 제목이 되어야 한다. 'While it is important for students to use and interact with materials in science class, the learning comes from the sense-making of students' "hands-on" experiences.(과학 수업에서 학생들이 재료를 사용하고 상호 작용하는 것이 중요하기는 하지만, 학습은 '직접 해보는' 학생들의 경험에 대한 감각으로부터 나온다.)'에 글의 주제가 잘 드러나 있다.

정답률 53%

8. ④

문제풀이

활동 후 토론, 사고, 논쟁 등을 통한 개념에 대한 재창조를 통해 얻을 수 있는 것은 (d) 'Uncertainty (불확실성)'이 아니라 'Clarity(명료성)' 등의 단어가 되어야 한다.

본문 113쪽

문법 플러스 19. 접속사, 전치사

A. 1. as 2. study 3. nor
4. that 5. as 6. when
7. whatever

1 [해석]▶ 수요가 늘어남에 따라, 가격도 오른다.
[해설]▶ 「according to」는 뒤에 구가 나오고, 「according as」는 뒤에 절이 나온다.

2 [해석]▶ 나는 그 대학에 입학해 Kim 박사님 지도하에 공부하기를 원한다.
[해설]▶ 「주어+동사+ to go~ and (to) study~」 문장 구조이다. 등위접속사(and)가 to부정사와 to부정사를 병렬 구조로 연결하고 있다.

3 [해석]▶ 어떻게 너도 Sam도 나의 파티에 오지 않을 수 있니?
[해설]▶ 상관접속사 neither A not B는 'A도 B도 아닌'의 의미이다.

4 [해석]▶ 왜 패션이 그렇게도 매력적인가에 대해 나의 정보 제공자들이 제공한 가장 일반적인 설명은 그것이 일종의 연극적인 복장을 구성한다는 것이다.
[해설]▶ that 이하의 절은 동사 is의 보어 역할을 하는 명사절을 이끌고 있으며, that 이하의 it~costumery가 완전한 문장을 이루고 있으므로 접속사 that이 어법상 적절하다.

5 [해석]▶ Steven Mithen이 'The Prehistory of the Modern Mind'에서 강조하듯이, 그런 원시 사회는 인간과 짐승, 동물과 식물, 생물체의 영역과 무생물체의 영역을 통합적이고 살아 있는 총체에 대한 참여자로 여기는 경향이 있다.
[해설]▶ 문맥상 '~하듯이'라는 의미로 부사절을 이끄는 접속사가 필요하므로 as가 어법상 적절하다.

6 [해석]▶ 그는 집에 오자마자, 불평하기 시작했다.
[해설]▶ 「hardly(scarcely) 과거완료 when(before) 과거시제」 구문은 '~하자마자 …하다'는 의미이다.

7 [해석]▶ 무슨 일이 나더라도, 나는 너를 지지하겠다.
[해설]▶ 「의문사+ever」는 양보의 부사절을 이끌 수 있으며, whatever happens는 '무슨 일이 일어나더라도'의 의미이다.

본문 113쪽

B. 1. due to 2. making 3. but
4. whether 5. Because 6. than
7. Wherever

1 [해석]▶ 폭설 때문에 모든 야외 활동은 취소되었다.
[해설]▶ due to는 '~ 때문에'의 의미를 가지고 있으며 뒤에 구(heavy snow)를 가져온다. because는 뒤에 절이 나온다.

2 [해석]▶ 그는 학교에서 어학 실력을 향상하고 친구를 사귀는 데 집중했다.
[해설]▶ concentrate on+[동명사+접속사(and)+동명사]가 병렬 구조를 이룬 문장이다.

3 [해석]▶ 그들의 영광은 성취에 있지 않고, 희생에 있다.
[해설]▶ not A but B는 'A가 아니라 B'다는 의미이다.

4 [해석]▶ 따라서, 단 한 명의 피험자로부터 얻어진 실험 결과는 가치가 제한적이며, 그 피험자의 반응이 집단으로서의 인간 반응을 대표하는 것인지 아니면 이례적인 것인지 알 방법이 없다.
[해설]▶ know의 목적어 역할을 하는 명사절을 유도해야 하는데, 완전한 형태의 절이 이어지고 문맥상 의문을 나타내고 있으므로 어법상 whether가 적절하다.

5 [해석]▶ 모든 것들은 서로 연관되어 있기 때문에, 한 지역의 변화는 다른 지역에 영향을 줄지도 모른다.
[해설]▶ Because 뒤에는 주어, 동사로 이루어진 절이 나오고, Because of 뒤에는 구가 나온다.

6 [해석]▶ 세차를 끝마치자마자 비가 내리기 시작했다.
[해설]▶ no sooner... than ~ 구문은 '…하자마자 ~하다'는 의미이다.

7 [해석]▶ 그녀가 어디를 가더라도, 나는 바로 여기서 그녀를 기다리겠다.
[해설]▶ 「wherever+주어+동사」는 '(주어가) 어디로 ~하더라도'라는 양보의 의미이다.

본문 114쪽

숙어 플러스 19. 수능 필수 숙어 19회

1. take 2. turns
3. extent 4. down

20. 장문의 이해 (2)

Day 20 본문 116쪽

1. ⑤ 2. ② 3. ③ 4. ③ 5. ③
6. ② 7. ③ 8. ⑤ 9. ④ 10. ③
11. ② 12. ③

대표 기출 아빠에게 준 생일 선물

직독/직해

(A) "Hailey, be careful!" / Camila yelled uneasily, /
Hailey, 조심해! / Camila는 걱정되어 소리쳤다 /

watching her sister carrying a huge cake to the table.
여동생이 테이블로 큰 케이크를 들고 오는 것을 보며

"Don't worry, Camila," / Hailey responded, smiling.
걱정하지 마, Camila / Hailey는 웃으며 대답했다

Camila relaxed / only when Hailey had safely placed the cake on the party table.
Camila는 안심했다 / Hailey가 케이크를 파티 테이블에 안전하게 올려 두었을 때 비로소 /

"Dad will be here shortly.
곧 아빠가 오실 거야

What gift did you buy for his birthday?" / Camila asked out of interest.
너는 아빠 생일을 위해 무슨 선물을 샀니? / Camila는 호기심에서 물었다

"Dad will be surprised to find out what it is!" / Hailey answered with a wink.
그게 뭔지 알면 아빠가 깜짝 놀라실걸! / Hailey는 윙크하면서 대답했다

(D) "I bet you bought a wallet or a watch for him," / Camila said.
분명 너는 아빠에게 줄 지갑이나 시계를 샀을 거야 / Camila가 말했다

In reply, / Hailey answered, / "No. I bought something much more personal. /
대답하면서 / Hailey는 대답했다 / 아니 / 난 훨씬 더 개인적인 걸 샀어 /

By the way, / there's something you should know about Dad..."
그건 그렇고 / 네가 아빠에 대해 알아야 할 게 있어…

They were suddenly interrupted / by the doorbell ringing.
그들의 대화는 갑자기 중단되었다 / 초인종이 울려서

It was their dad / and they were overjoyed to see him.
그들의 아빠였다 / 그리고 그들은 그를 보고 매우 기뻐했다

"My lovely ladies, / thank you for inviting me to your place / for my birthday."
사랑하는 내 딸들 / 너희들 집에 초대해줘서 고맙구나 / 내 생일에

He walked in joyfully, / hugging his daughters.
그는 기뻐하면서 걸어 들어왔다 / 딸들을 안았다

They all walked into the dining room, /
그들은 모두 식당(방)으로 들어갔고 /

where he was greeted / with a rainbow-colored birthday cake and fifty red roses.
그곳에서 그는 환영받았다 무지개색 생일 케이크와 50송이의 빨간 장미로

(C) "Happy birthday! / You're fifty today, / Dad. / We love you!"
생신 축하드려요! / 오늘은 쉰 살이네요 / 아빠 / 우린 아빠를 사랑해요!

Camila said / before her sister handed him a small parcel.
Camila가 말했다 / 그녀의 동생이 그에게 작은 꾸러미를 건네기 전에

When he opened it, / he discovered a pair of glasses inside.
그가 그것을 열었을 때 / 그는 안에서 안경을 발견했다

"Hailey, / Dad doesn't have eyesight problems," / Camila said, puzzled.
Hailey / 아빠는 시력에 문제가 없어 / Camila가 어리둥절해하며 말했다

"Actually Camila, / I recently found out /
사실은 Camila / 난 최근에 알게 되었어 /

he has long been suffering from color blindness.
아빠가 오래전부터 색맹을 앓고 있다는 것을

He's kept it a secret / so as not to worry us," / Hailey explained.
아빠는 그것을 비밀로 해왔어 / 우리를 걱정시키지 않기 위해 / Hailey가 설명했다

(B) "Dad, / these glasses can help correct your red-green color blindness," /
아빠 / 이 안경은 적록색맹을 교정하는 데 도움이 될 수도 있어요 /

said Hailey.
Hailey가 말했다

He slowly put them on, / and stared at the birthday presents on the table.
그는 천천히 그것을 쓰고 / 테이블 위에 있는 생일 선물을 바라보았다

Seeing vivid red and green colors for the first time ever, /
지금껏 처음으로 선명한 빨강색과 초록색을 보고서 /

he started to cry.
그는 울기 시작했다

"Incredible! / Look at those wonderful colors!" / He shouted in amazement.
믿을 수가 없구나! / 저 경이로운 색들을 봐! / 그는 깜짝 놀라 소리쳤다

Hailey told him in tears, / "Dad, I'm glad /
Hailey는 눈물을 흘리면서 그에게 말했다 / 아빠 / 전 기뻐요 /

you can now finally enjoy the true beauty of rainbows and roses.
전 아빠가 이제 마침내 무지개와 장미의 진정한 아름다움을 즐기실 수 있어서

Red represents love / and green represents health.
빨간색은 사랑을 나타내요 / 그리고 초록색은 건강을 나타내요

You deserve both."
아빠는 둘 다 누릴 자격이 있어요

Camila nodded, / seeing /
Camila는 고개를 끄덕이며 / 알게 되었다 /

how happy her gift of the glasses had made their dad.
그녀의 안경 선물이 그들의 아빠를 얼마나 행복하게 했는지

(A) "Hailey, 조심해!" Camila는 여동생이 테이블로 큰 케이크를 들고 오는 것을 보며 걱정되어 소리쳤다. "걱정하지 마, Camila." Hailey는 웃으며 대답했다. Camila는 Hailey가 파티 테이블에 케이크를 안전하게 올려 두었을 때 비로소 안심했다. "곧 아빠가 오실 거야. (a) 너는 아빠 생일을 위해 무슨 선물을 샀니?" Camila는 호기심에서 물었다. "그게 뭔지 알면 아빠가 깜짝 놀라실걸!" Hailey는 윙크하면서 대답했다.
(D) "분명 (d) 너는 아빠에게 줄 지갑이나 시계를 샀을 거야."라고 Camila가 말했다. 대답하면서 Hailey는 "아니. 난 훨씬 더 개인적인 걸 샀어. 그건 그렇고 (e) 네가 아빠에 대해 알아야 할 게 있어…"라고 대답했다. 초인종이 울려서 그들의 대화는 갑자기 중단되었다. 그들의 아빠였고 그들은 그를 보고 매우 기뻐했다. "사랑하는 내 딸들, 내 생일에 너희들 집에 초대해줘서 고맙구나." 그는 기뻐하면서 걸어 들어와 딸들을 안았다. 그들은 모두 다이닝 룸으로 들어갔고, 그곳에서 그는 무지개색 생일 케이크와 50송이의 빨간 장미로 환영받았다.
(C) "생신 축하드려요! 오늘은 쉰 살이네요, 아빠. 우린 아빠를 사랑해요!"라고 (c) 그녀의 동생이 그에게 작은 꾸러미를 건네기 전에 Camila가 말했다. 그가 그것을 열었을 때 그는 안에서 안경을 발견했다. "Hailey, 아빠는 시력에 문제가 없어."라고 Camila가 어리둥절해하며 말했다. "사실은 Camila, 난 아빠가 오래전부터 색맹을 앓고 있다는 것을 최근에 알게 되었어. 아빠는 우리를 걱정시키지 않기 위해 그것을 비밀로 해왔어."라고 Hailey가 설명했다.
(B) "아빠, 이 안경은 적록색맹을 교정하는 데 도움이 될 수도 있어요."라고 Hailey가 말했다. 그는 천천히 그것을 쓰고, 테이블 위에 있는 생일 선물을 바라보았다. 지금껏 처음으로 선명한 빨강색과 초록색을 보고서 그는 울기 시작했다. "믿을 수가 없구나! 저 경이로운 색들을 봐!" 그는 깜짝 놀라 소리쳤다. Hailey는 눈물을 흘리면서 그에게 말했다. "아빠, 전 아빠가 이제 마침내 무지개와 장미의 진정한 아름다움을 즐기실 수 있어서 기뻐요. 빨간색은 사랑을 나타내고 초록색은 건강을 나타내요. 아빠는 둘 다 누릴 자격이 있어요." Camila는 고개를 끄덕이며, (b) 그녀의 안경 선물이 그들의 아빠를 얼마나 행복하게 했는지 알게 되었다.

《 어휘·어구 》

yell 소리치다
out of interest 호기심에서
be surprised to ~하기로 되어 있다
correct 교정하다
color blindness 색맹
vivid 선명한
represent 나타내다
incredible 믿을 수 없는
parcel 꾸러미, 소포
puzzled 어리둥절하여
suffer from ~을 앓다
wallet 지갑
watch 시계
personal 개인적인
interrupt 방해하다, 중단시키다
overjoyed 매우 기쁜

43. ⑤

문제풀이

Camila와 Hailey가 아빠의 생일을 파티를 준비하면서 생일 선물에 관해 이야기하는 주어진 글 (A) 다음에, 생일 선물에 대한 대화를 이어가던 중 그들의 아버지가 그들의 집에 와서 환영받았다는 내용인 (D)가 오고, 이어서 아빠가 오래 전부터 색맹을 앓고 있다는 사실을 비밀로 해온 것을 Hailey가 알게 되어 아빠를 위해 색맹 교정 안경을 생일 선물로 드렸다는 내용인 (C)가 온 후, 안경을 쓴 아빠가 선명한 색들을 보고 매우 행복해했다는 내용인 (B)가 오는 것이 적절하다. 정답은 ⑤ '(D)−(C)−(B)'이다.

44. ⑤

문제풀이

(a), (b), (c), (d)는 모두 Hailey를 가리키지만, (e)는 Camila를 가리킨다. 따라서 정답은 ⑤이다.

45. ④

문제풀이

"My lovely ladies, thank you for inviting me to your place for my birthday."에서 아빠가 자기 생일에 Camila와 Hailey의 집에 자신을 초대해줘서 고맙다고 했으므로, 글에 관한 내용으로 적절하지 않은 것은 ④이다.

1~3 Van Gogh의 '해바라기'를 보기 위한 여정

직독/직해

(A) Walking out of Charing Cross Station in London, /
런던의 채링크로스 역에서 나와 걸으면서 /

Emilia and her traveling companion, Layla, / already felt their hearts pounding.
Emilia와 그녀의 여행 동반자인 Layla는 / 벌써 심장이 뛰는 것을 느꼈다

It was the second day / of their European summer trip.
둘째 날이었다 / 그들의 여름 유럽 여행의

They were about to visit / one of the world's most

famous art galleries.
그들은 막 방문하려고 했다 / 세계에서 가장 유명한 미술관 중 하나를

The two of them started hurrying / with excitement.
그들 두 사람은 서두르기 시작했다 / 신이 나서

Suddenly, Emilia shouted, / "Look! / There it is!
갑자기 Emilia가 소리쳤다 / 봐 / 저기야

We're finally at the National Gallery!"
우리는 드디어 내셔널 갤러리에 도착했어

Layla laughed and responded, / "Your dream's finally come true!"
Layla는 웃으며 대답했다 / 네 꿈이 드디어 이루어졌구나

(D) Upon entering the National Gallery, / Emilia knew exactly where to go first.
내셔널 갤러리에 들어가자마자 / Emilia는 정확하게 알았다 / 우선 어디로 가야 할지를

She grabbed Layla's hand / and dragged her hurriedly /
그녀는 Layla의 손을 꼭 잡았다 / 그리고 바삐 그녀를 끌고 갔다 /

to find van Gogh's *Sunflowers*.
van Gogh의 '해바라기'를 찾으러

It was Emilia's favorite painting /
그것은 Emilia가 제일 좋아하는 그림이었다 /

and had inspired her to become a painter.
그리고 그녀가 화가가 되도록 영감을 준 것이었다

Emilia loved his use of bright colors and light.
Emilia는 그의 밝은색과 빛의 사용을 매우 좋아했다

She couldn't wait to finally see his masterpiece / in person.
그녀는 그의 걸작을 드디어 빨리 보고 싶어 했다 / 직접

"It'll be amazing to see /
보는 것은 엄청날 거야 /

how he communicated the feelings of isolation and loneliness / in his work," /
그가 고립과 고독의 느낌을 전달한 방식을 / 자기 작품에서 /

she said eagerly.
그녀는 기대하며 말했다

(C) However, / after searching all the exhibition rooms, /
하지만 / 모든 전시실을 찾아본 후 /

Emilia and Layla couldn't find van Gogh's masterpiece anywhere.
Emilia와 Layla는 van Gogh의 걸작을 어디에서도 찾을 수가 없었다

"That's weird.
이상하네

Van Gogh's *Sunflowers* should be here.
van Gogh의 '해바라기'는 여기 있어야 하는데

Where is it?"
그것이 어디에 있지

Emilia looked upset, / but Layla kept calm and said, /
Emilia는 속상해 보였다 / 하지만 Layla는 침착함을 유지하며 말했다 /

"Maybe you've missed a notice / about it.
아마도 네가 공지를 놓쳤을 거야 / 그것에 대한

Check the National Gallery app."
내셔널 갤러리의 앱을 확인해

Emilia checked it quickly.
Emilia는 빠르게 그것을 확인했다

Then, she sighed, / "*Sunflowers* isn't here!
그런 다음, 그녀는 한숨을 쉬며 / '해바라기'는 이곳에 없어

It's been lent to a different gallery / for a special exhibition.
그것은 다른 미술관에 대여되었어 / 특별 전시회를 위해

I can't believe / I didn't check!"
나는 믿을 수가 없어 / 내가 확인을 안 했다는 걸

(B) "Don't lose hope yet!
아직 희망을 잃지 말아

Which gallery is the special exhibition at?" / Layla asked.
특별 전시회는 어느 미술관에서 하는 거야 / Layla는 물었다

Emilia responded, / "Well, his *Sunflowers* is still in England, /
Emilia는 대답했다 / 음, 그의 '해바라기'는 여전히 영국에 있어 /

but it's at a gallery in Liverpool.
하지만 그것은 리버풀의 미술관에 있어

That's a long way, / isn't it?"
거기는 거리가 멀지 / 그렇지 않아

After a quick search on her phone, / Layla stated,
전화로 빠르게 검색해 본 다음에 / Layla는 대답했다

"No! / It's only two hours to Liverpool / by train.
아니야 / 리버풀까지 겨우 두 시간 걸려 / 기차로

The next train leaves / in an hour.
다음 기차는 떠나 / 한 시간 후에

Why don't we take it?"
그걸 타는 게 어때

After considering the idea, / Emilia, now relieved, responded, /
그 생각을 고려해 본 다음 / 이제 마음이 놓인 Emilia는 대답했다 /

"Yeah, / but you always wanted / to see Rembrandt's paintings.
응 / 그런데 너는 항상 원했잖아 / Rembrandt의 그림을 보길

Let's do that first, Layla!
그것을 먼저 하자, Layla!

Then, after lunch, / we can catch the next train."
그런 다음에, 점심 먹고 나서 / 그다음 기차를 탈 수 있어

Layla smiled brightly.
Layla가 밝게 웃었다

(A) 런던의 채링크로스 역에서 나와 걸으면서, Emilia와 그녀의 여행 동반자인 Layla는 벌써 심장이 뛰는 것을 느꼈다. 그들의 여름 유럽의 여행 둘째 날이었다. 그들은 세계에서 가장 유명한 미술관 중 하나를 막 방문하려고 했다. 그들 두 사람은 신이 나서 서두르기 시작했다. 갑자기 Emilia가 "봐! 저기야! 우리는 드디어 내셔널 갤러리에 도착했어!"라고 소리쳤다. Layla는 웃으며, "(a) 네 꿈이 드디어 이루어졌구나!"라고 대답했다.
(D) 내셔널 갤러리에 들어가자마자, Emilia는 우선 어디로 가야 할지를 정확하게 알았다. (e) 그녀는 van Gogh의 '해바라기'를 찾으러 Layla의 손을 꼭 잡고 바삐 그녀를 끌고 갔다. 그것은 Emilia가 제일 좋아하는 그림이자 그녀가 화가가 되도록 영감을 준 것이었다. Emilia는 그의 밝은색과 빛의 사용을 매우 좋아했다. 그녀는 그의 걸작을 드디어 직접 빨리 보고 싶어 했다. 그녀는 "그가 자기 작품에서 고립과 고독의 느낌을 전달한 방식을 보는 것은 엄청날 거야."라고 기대하며 말했다.
(C) 하지만 모든 전시실을 찾아본 후, Emilia와 Layla는 van Gogh의 걸작을 어디에서도 찾을 수가 없었다. "이상하네. van Gogh의 '해바라기'는 여기 있어야 하는데. 그것이 어디에 있지?" Emilia는 속상해 보였지만, Layla는 침착함을 유지하며 "아마도 (c) 네가 그것에 대한 공지를 놓쳤을 거야. 내셔널 갤러리의 앱을 확인해."라고 말했다. Emilia는 빠르게 그것을 확인했다. 그런 다음, 그녀는 한숨을 쉬며, "'해바라기'는 이곳에 없어! 그것은 특별 전시회를 위해 다른 미술관에 대여되었어. (d) 나는 내가 확인을 안 했다는 걸 믿을 수가 없어!"라고 말했다.
(B) Layla는 "아직 희망을 잃지 말아! 특별 전시회는 어느 미술관에서 하는 거야?"라고 물었다. Emilia는 "응, 그의 '해바라기'는 여전히 영국에 있지만, 그것은 리버풀의 미술관에 있어. 거기는 거리가 멀지, 그렇지 않아?"라고 대답했다. 전화로 빠르게 검색해 본 다음에, Layla는 "아니야! 리버풀까지 기차로 겨우 두 시간 걸려. 다음 기차는 한 시간 후에 떠나. 그걸 타는 게 어때?"라고 말했다. 그 생각을 고려해 본 다음, 이제 마음이 놓인 Emilia는 "응, 그런데 (b) 너는 항상 Rembrandt의 그림을 보길 원했잖아. 그것을 먼저 하자, Layla! 그런 다음에, 점심 먹고 나서, 그다음 기차를 탈 수 있어."라고 대답했다. Layla가 밝게 웃었다.

《 어휘·어구 》

companion 동행
pound (가슴이) 쿵쿵 뛰다
be about to 막 ~하려고 하다
exhibition 전시회, 전시
relieved 마음이 놓인, 안심한
masterpiece 걸작
weird 이상한
calm 차분한
notice 공고문, 안내문
upon v-ing ~하자마자
grab 붙잡다
inspire 영감을 주다
in person 직접
isolation 고립
loneliness 고독
eagerly 갈망하여

1. ⑤

문제풀이

영국 여행 중인 Emilia와 Layla가 내셔널 갤러리에 도착했다는 내용의 (A) 다음에, Emilia는 직접 보기를 열망했던 van Gogh의 '해바라기'를 보러 갔다는 내용의 (D)가 오고, 이어서 미술관 전체를 찾아보았지만 '해바라기'를 찾을 수 없었고, Emilia가 그 그림이 다른 미술관에 대여되었다는 사실을 알게 되는 내용의 (C)가 온 후, 그 그림이 기차로 두 시간 거리에 있는 리버풀의 미술관에 전시된 것을 알게 되고, 다음 기차를 타고 리버풀로 가자고 Layla가 제안하는 내용인 (B)가 오는 것이 가장 적절하다. 따라서 정답은 ⑤이다.

2. ②

문제풀이

(a), (c), (d), (e)는 모두 Emilia를 가리키지만, (b)는 Layla를 가리킨다. 따라서 정답은 ②이다.

3. ③

문제풀이

'Then, after lunch, we can catch the next train.'에서 Emilia는 점심 식사 후에 기차를 타자고 Layla에게 제안했으므로, 글에 관한 내용으로 적절하지 않은 것은 ③이다.

4~6 태권도 연습에 나오지 못한 Cora

직독/직해

(A) In the gym, / 체육관에서 /

members of the taekwondo club were busy practicing.
태권도 동아리 회원들이 연습하느라 바빴다

Some were trying to kick / as high as they could, /
일부는 발차기하기 위해 애쓰고 있었다 / 가능한 한 높이 /

and some were striking the sparring pad.
그리고 일부는 겨루기 패드 치기를 하고 있었다

Anna, the head of the club, /
동아리 회장인 Anna는 /

was teaching the new members basic moves.
신입 회원들에게 기본 동작을 가르치고 있었다

Close by, / her friend Jane was assisting Anna.
바로 옆에서 / 그녀의 친구인 Jane이 Anna를 도와주고 있었다

Jane noticed / that Anna was glancing /
Jane은 알아차렸다 / Anna가 힐끗 보고 있는 것을 /

at the entrance door of the gym.
체육관의 출입문을

She seemed to be expecting someone.
그녀는 누군가를 기대하고 있는 것처럼 보였다

At last, / when Anna took a break, /
마침내 / Anna가 휴식을 취할 때 /

Jane came over to her and asked, /
Jane이 그녀에게 다가와서 /

"Hey, / are you waiting for Cora?"
"얘, / 너 Cora를 기다리니?"라고 물었다

(C) Anna answered the question / by nodding uneasily.
Anna는 그 질문에 답했다 / 걱정스럽게 고개를 끄덕임으로써

In fact, / Jane knew / what her friend was thinking.
사실 / Jane은 알고 있었다 / 자신의 친구가 무엇을 생각하고 있는지

Cora was a new member, /
Cora는 신입 회원인데 /

whom Anna had personally invited to join the club.
그녀에게 Anna가 동아리에 가입하라고 직접 요청했었다

Anna really liked her.
Anna는 그녀를 정말로 좋아했다

Although her budget was tight, /
자신의 예산이 빠듯했지만 /

Anna bought Cora a taekwondo uniform.
Anna는 Cora에게 태권도 도복을 사 주었다

When she received it, / Cora thanked her and promised, /
그녀가 그것을 받을 때 / Cora는 그녀에게 고마움을 표하면서 약속했다 /

"I'll come to practice / and work hard every day."
연습하러 올 거야 / 그리고 매일 열심히 할 거야

However, / unexpectedly, /
그러나 / 예상과 달리 /

she came to practice only once /
그녀는 연습하러 단 한 번만 왔다 /

and then never showed up again.
그리고 그러고 나서 다시는 나타나지 않았다

(D) Since Cora had missed several practices, /
Cora가 여러 번 연습에 빠져서 /

Anna wondered / what could have happened.
Anna는 궁금해했다 / 무슨 일이 있는지

Jane, / on the other hand, /
Jane은 / 반면 /

was disappointed and said judgingly, /
실망하여 판단하듯이 말했다 /

"Still waiting for her, huh?
아직 그 애를 기다리는 거야, 응?

I can't believe / you don't feel disappointed or angry.
나는 믿을 수가 없어 / 네가 실망하거나 화를 느끼지 않는 것을

Why don't you forget about her?" / Anna replied, /
그 애에 대해 잊어버리는 것이 어때 / Anna는 대답했다 /

"Well, / I know /
음 / 난 알아 /

most newcomers don't keep their commitment to the club, /
대다수의 신입생이 동아리에 대한 약속을 지키지 않는 것은 /

but I thought / that Cora would be different.
하지만 나는 생각했어 / Cora는 다를 거라고

She said / she would come every day and practice."
그 애는 말했어 / 매일 와서 연습할 거라고

Just as Jane was about to respond to her, /
Jane이 바로 막 그녀에게 응답하려 했을 때 /

the door swung open.
문이 활짝 열렸다

There she was!
거기에 그녀가 있었다

(B) Cora walked in / like a wounded soldier /
Cora는 걸어 들어왔다 / 부상당한 군인처럼 /

with bandages on her face and arms.
얼굴과 양팔에 붕대를 하고서

Surprised, / Anna and Jane simply looked at her /
놀라서 / Anna와 Jane은 그녀를 바라볼 뿐이었다 /

with their eyes wide open.
두 눈을 크게 뜨고

Cora explained, / "I'm sorry I've been absent.
Cora는 설명했다 / "계속 못 와서 미안해.

I got into a bicycle accident, / and I was in the hospital /
난 자전거 사고가 났어 / 그리고 입원해 있었어 /

for two days. 이틀간

Finally, / the doctor gave me the okay to practice."
드디어 / 의사 선생님이 나에게 연습해도 좋다는 동의를 해 주셨어

Anna said excitedly, / "No problem! / We're thrilled /
Anna가 흥분하여 말했다 / "괜찮아 / 우리는 신이 나 /

to have you back!"
네가 돌아오게 되어서

Then, Jane gave Anna an apologetic look, /
그때, Jane이 Anna에게 사과하는 표정을 해 보였다 /

and she responded /
그리고 그녀는 답했다 /

with a friendly pat on Jane's shoulder.
Jane의 어깨를 다정하게 쳐서

체육관에서, 태권도 동아리 회원들이 연습하느라 바빴다. 일부는 가능한 한 높이 발차기하기 위해 애쓰고 있었고, 일부는 겨루기 패드 치기를 하고 있었다. 동아리 회장인 Anna는 신입 회원들에게 기본 동작을 가르치고 있었다. 바로 옆에서 그녀의 친구인 Jane이 Anna를 도와주고 있었다. Jane은 Anna가 체육관의 출입문을 힐끗 보고 있는 것을 알아차렸다. 그녀는 누군가를 기대하고 있는 것처럼 보였다. 마침내, Anna가 휴식을 취할 때 Jane이 (a) 그녀에게 다가와서 "얘, 너 Cora를 기다리니?"라고 물었다.

(C) Anna는 걱정스럽게 고개를 끄덕임으로써 그 질문에 답했다. 사실, Jane은 자신의 친구가 무엇을 생각하고 있는지 알고 있었다. Cora는 신입 회원인데, 그녀에게 Anna가 동아리에 가입하라고 직접 요청했었다. Anna는 (c) 그녀를 정말로 좋아했다. 자신의 예산이 빠듯했지만, Anna는 Cora에게 태권도 도복을 사 주었다. 그것을 받을 때, Cora는 그녀에게 고마움을 표하면서 "매일 연습하러 와서 열심히 할 거야."라고 약속했다. 그러나 예상과 달리, 그녀는 연습하러 단 한 번만 왔고 그러고 나서 다시는 나타나지 않았다.

(D) Cora가 여러 번 연습에 빠져서 Anna는 무슨 일이 있는지 궁금해했다. 반면 Jane은 실망하여 "아직 그 애를 기다리는 거야, 응? 나는 (d) 네가 실망하거나 화를 느끼지 않는 것을 믿을 수가 없어. 그 애에 대해 잊어버리는 것이 어때?"라고 판단하듯이 말했다. Anna는 "음, 난 대다수의 신입생이 동아리에 대한 약속을 지키지 않는 것은 알지만, Cora는 다를 거라고 생각했어. 그 애는 매일 와서 연습할 거라고 말했어."라고 대답했다. Jane이 바로 막 (e) 그녀에게 응답하려 했을 때, 문이 활짝 열렸다. 거기에 그녀가 있었다!

(B) Cora는 얼굴과 양팔에 붕대를 하고서 부상당한 군인처럼 걸어 들어왔다. 놀라서 Anna와 Jane은 두 눈을 크게 뜨고 그녀를 바라볼 뿐이었다. Cora는 "계속 못 와서 미안해. 난 자전거 사고가 나서 이틀간 입원해 있었어. 드디어 의사 선생님이 나에게 연습해도 좋다는 동의를 해 주셨어."라고 설명했다. Anna가 "괜찮아! 우리는 네가 돌아오게 되어 신이 나."라고 흥분하여 말했다. 그때, Jane이 Anna에게 사과하는 표정을 해 보였고 (b) 그녀는 Jane의 어깨를 다정하게 쳐서 답했다.

《 어휘·어구 》

sparring (권투·태권도 등) 스파링, 겨루기
assist 돕다
glance 흘낏[휙] 보다
bandage 붕대
thrilled 아주 신이 난
apologetic 사과하는
uneasily 걱정하여
budget 예산, 비용
show up 나타나다
judgingly 판단으로
commitment 전념, 헌신
swing open 활짝 열리다

정답률 95%

4. ③

문제풀이

태권도 동아리 연습 모임이 있는 체육관에서 Jane이 Anna에게 Cora를 기다리고 있는지 물었다는 내용의 주어진 글 다음에, Anna가 그렇다고 응답했고 매일 연습하겠다는 약속과는 달리 Cora는 한 번밖에 나오지 않았다는 내용의 (C)가 오고, 이어서 Anna는 Cora에게 무슨 일이 일어난 것인지 궁금해 했지만 Jane은 실망하며 Anna에게 Cora에 대해 잊어버리라고 말했고 둘이 대화하던 중 문이 열렸다는 내용의 (D)가 오고, 얼굴과 양팔에 붕대를 감고 Cora가 걸어 들어왔다는 내용의 (B)가 오는 것이 가장 적절하다. 따라서 정답은 ③이다.

5. ③

문제풀이

(a), (b), (d), (e)는 모두 Anna를 가리키지만, (c)는 Cora를 가리킨다. 따라서 정답은 ③이다.

6. ②

문제풀이

'Cora walked in like a wounded soldier with bandages on her face and arms. Surprised, Anna and Jane simply looked at her with their eyes wide open.'에서 Cora가 들어왔을 때 Anna와 Jane은 그녀를 보고 놀라서 눈을 크게 뜨고 바라봤다고 했다. 따라서 글의 내용과 일치하지 않는 것은 ②이다.

7~9 Felix의 가정 경찰관 놀이

직독/직해

(A) In this area, / heavy snow in winter /
이 지역에서는 / 겨울에 폭설이 /

was not uncommon. 흔하지 않은 일이 아니었다

Sometimes it poured down for hours and hours /
때때로 몇 시간 동안 쏟아졌다 /

and piled up very high. 그리고 매우 높이 쌓였다

Then, no one could go out.
그러고 나서는 아무도 외출할 수 없었다

Today too, because of the heavy snow, /
오늘 또한 폭설 때문에 /

Mom was doing her office work / at the kitchen table.
엄마는 사무실 업무를 보고 있었다 / 주방 식탁에서

Felix, the high schooler, /
고등학생인 Felix는 /

had to take online classes / in his room.
온라인 수업을 들어야 했다 / 자신의 방에서

Five-year-old Sean, / 다섯 살인 Sean은 /

who normally went to kindergarten, /
보통 때는 유치원에 가던 /

was sneaking around in the house /
집안 여기저기를 몰래 돌아다니고 있었다 /

playing home policeman.
가정 경찰관 놀이를 하며

The kindergartener wanted to know /
그 유치원생은 알고 싶었다 /

what his family members were up to, /
가족들이 무엇을 하는지 /

and was checking up on everyone.
그래서 모두를 확인하고 있었다

(C) While checking on his family, /
가족을 확인하는 동안 /

Sean interfered in their business / as if it was his own.
Sean은 그들의 일에 간섭했다 / 마치 그것이 자기 자신의 일인 것처럼

This time, the playful and curious boy was interested /
이번에는 그 장난기 많고 호기심 많은 남자아이가 관심을 보였는데 /

in his brother Felix, / 형 Felix에게 /

who committed himself to studying /
그는 공부에 전념했다 /

no matter where he was. 그가 어디에 있든지

Sean secretly looked inside his brother's room from the door, /
Sean은 문에서 형의 방을 몰래 보고서는 /

and shouted toward the kitchen where Mom was working, /
엄마가 일하고 있는 주방을 향해 소리쳤다 /

"Mom, Felix isn't studying.
엄마, Felix가 공부를 하지 않고 있어요

He's just watching a funny video."
그는 그저 재미있는 영상을 보고 있을 뿐이에요.

Sean was naughtily smiling at his brother.
Sean은 형을 향해 짓궂게 웃고 있었다

(D) Felix was mad / Felix는 매우 화가 났다 /

because his little brother was bothering him.
자신의 어린 동생이 자신을 성가시게 하고 있어서

Felix was studying science /
Felix는 과학을 공부하고 있었다 /
using a video posted on the school web site.
학교 웹사이트에 올라온 영상을 이용해서
He made an angry face / at the naughty boy.
그는 화난 표정을 지었다 / 그 개구쟁이 남자아이를 향해
Right then, Mom asked loudly from the kitchen, /
바로 그때 엄마가 주방에서 큰소리로 물었다 /
"What are you doing, / Felix?"
무얼 하고 있어 / Felix
Felix's room was located next to the kitchen, /
Felix의 방은 주방 옆에 있었다 /
and he could hear Mom clearly.
그리고 그는 엄마의 말을 분명히 들을 수 있었다
"I'm watching a lecture video / for my science class."
전 동영상을 보고 있어요 / 과학 수업의
Felix argued against Sean's accusation /
Felix는 Sean의 비난을 반박했다 /
and mischievously stuck his tongue out /
그리고 장난기 있게 자신의 혀를 내밀었다 /
at his little brother. 어린 동생에게
[B] "All right. 그러게
I'm sure / you're doing your work." /
난 확신해 / 넌 네 공부를 하고 있을 거라고 /
Mom replied, / and then sharply added a question.
엄마가 대답했다 / 그리고 나서 빠르게 질문을 추가했다
"Sean, / what are *you* doing?"
Sean / '넌' 무엇을 하고 있니
Sean's face immediately became blank, /
Sean은 즉시 멍한 표정이 되었다 /
and he said, / "Nothing."
그리고, 그는 말했다 / 아무것도 안 해요
"Come here, Honey, / and you can help me."
이리로 와, 얘야 / 그러면 날 도와줄 수 있어
Sean ran to the kitchen / right away.
Sean은 주방으로 달려갔다 / 곧장
"What can I do for you, / Mom?"
내가 무엇을 도와줄까요 / 엄마
His voice was high, / and Felix could sense /
그의 목청은 높았다 / 그리고 Felix는 감지할 수 있었다 /
that his brother was excited.
동생이 신이 났다는 것을
Felix was pleased / to get rid of the policeman, /
Felix는 기뻤다 / 경찰관을 제거해서 /
and now he could concentrate on the lesson, /
그리고 이제 그는 수업에 집중할 수 있었다 /
at least till Sean came back.
적어도 Sean이 돌아올 때까지

(A) 이 지역에서는 겨울에 폭설이 흔하지 않은 일이 아니었다. 때때로 몇 시간 동안 쏟아져 매우 높이 쌓였다. 그러고 나서는 아무도 외출할 수 없었다. 오늘 또한 폭설 때문에 엄마는 주방 식탁에서 사무실 업무를 보고 있었다. 고등학생인 Felix는 자신의 방에서 온라인 수업을 들어야 했다. 보통 때는 유치원에 가던 다섯 살인 Sean은 가정 경찰관 놀이를 하며 집안 여기저기를 몰래 돌아다니고 있었다. (a) 그 유치원생은 가족들이 무엇을 하는지 알고 싶어서, 모두를 확인하고 있었다.
(C) Sean은 가족을 확인하는 동안 그는 마치 그들의 일이 자기 자신의 일인 것처럼 간섭했다. 이번에는 (c) 그 장난기 많고 호기심 많은 남자아이가 형 Felix에게 관심을 보였는데, 그는 어디에 있든지 공부에 전념했다. Sean은 문에서 형의 방을 몰래 보고서는, 엄마가 일하고 있는 주방을 향해 "엄마, Felix가 공부를 하지 않고 있어요. 그는 그저 재미있는 영상을 보고 있을 뿐이에요."라고 소리쳤다. Sean은 형을 향해 짓궂게 웃고 있었다.
(D) Felix는 (d) 자신의 어린 동생이 자신을 성가시게 하고 있어서 매우 화가 났다. Felix는 학교 웹사이트에 올라온 영상을 이용해서 과학을 공부하고 있었다. 그는 그 개구쟁이 남자아이를 향해 화난 표정을 지었다. 바로 그때 엄마가 주방에서 큰소리로 "무얼 하고 있어, Felix?"라고 물었다. Felix의 방은 주방 옆에 있었고, 그는 엄마의 말을 분명히 들을 수 있었다. "과학 수업의 동영상을 보고 있어요." Felix는 Sean의 비난을 반박하고는 장난기 있게 어린 동생에게 (e) 자신의 혀를 내밀었다.
(B) "그러게, 난 네가 네 공부를 하고 있을 거라고 확신해."라고 엄마가 대답하고 나서 빠르게 질문을 추가했다. "Sean, '넌' 무엇을 하고 있니?" Sean은 즉시 멍한 표정이 되었고, 그는 "아무것도 안 해요."라고 말했다. "이리로 와, 얘야. 그러면 날 도와줄 수 있어." Sean은 곧장 주방으로 달려갔다. "내가 무엇을 도와줄까요, 엄마?" 그의 목청은 높았고, Felix는 동생이 신이 났다는 것을 감지할 수 있었다. Felix는 (b) 경찰관을 제거해서 기뻤고, 적어도 Sean이 돌아올 때까지 이제 그는 수업에 집중할 수 있었다.

《 어휘 · 어구 》
uncommon 흔하지 않은, 드문
pile up 쌓이다
kindergarten 유치원
sneak 몰래 다니다
up to ~을 하고 있는
check up on ~가 제대로 하고 있는지 확인하다
immediately 즉시
blank 멍한
get rid of ~을 제거하다
concentrate on ~에 집중하다
interfere 간섭하다
commit oneself to ~에 전념하다
bother 성가시게 하다
naughty 개구쟁이인, 장난꾸러기인
accusation 비난, 고발
stick out ~을 내밀다

정답률 92%

7. ③

문제풀이

폭설 때문에 가족 모두가 집에 있자 5살인 Sean이 경찰관 놀이를 하며 가족들이 무엇을 하는지 확인하러 집안 여기저기를 몰래 돌아다녔다는 내용의 (A) 다음에, Sean이 형 Felix의 방을 들여다보면서 엄마에게 형이 공부를 하지 않고 재미있는 영상을 보고 있다고 거짓으로 말하는 내용의 (C)가 오고, 이어서 Felix가 엄마에게 과학 수업의 강의 영상을 보며 과학 공부를 하고 있다고 말하는 내용의 (D)가 온 후, 엄마가 도움을 요청하려고 Sean을 불러서 Felix가 동생에게서 벗어나게 되어 기뻐했다는 내용의 (B)가 오는 것이 적절하다. 따라서 정답은 ③이다.

정답률 87%

8. ⑤

문제풀이

(a), (b), (c), (d)는 모두 동생 Sean을 가리키고, (e)는 Felix를 가리킨다. 따라서 정답은 ⑤이다.

정답률 92%

9. ④

문제풀이

'Felix was studying science using a video posted on the school web site.'에서 Felix는 학교 웹사이트에 올라온 동영상을 이용해서 과학 공부를 하고 있었다고 했다. 따라서 글의 내용으로 적절하지 않은 것은 ④이다.

10~12 연어를 보고 용기를 낸 전 챔피언

직독/직해

[A] The colors of the trees looked like they were on
나무들의 색깔이 마치 불이 붙은 것처럼 보였다 /
fire, /
the reds and oranges competing with the yellows
빨간색과 오렌지색이 노란색 및 황금색과 다투고 있었다
and golds.
This was Nina's favorite season, /
이때가 Nina가 가장 좋아하는 계절이었다 /
but she remained silent for hours while Marie was
하지만 그녀는 Marie가 운전하는 동안 몇 시간 동안 침묵하고 있었다
driving.
Nina had been heartbroken after losing her
Nina는 챔피언 벨트를 잃은 뒤 상심해 있었다
championship belt.
Now a former champion, / 이제 전 챔피언으로 /
she was thinking of retiring from boxing.
그녀는 권투에서 은퇴를 생각하고 있었다
Marie, her long-time friend and trainer, shared
오랜 친구이자 트레이너인 Marie는 그녀의 고통을 함께 나눴다
her pain.
After another silent hour, Marie and Nina saw a
sign: Sauble Falls.
침묵의 한 시간이 또 지난 후 Marie와 Nina는 'Sauble 폭포'라는 표지판을 보았다
Marie thought this would be a good place for them
Marie는 이곳이 그들이 멈추기에 좋은 장소라고 생각했다
to stop.
[C] Marie pulled over into the parking lot.
Marie는 주차장으로 들어가 차를 댔다
Marie and Nina went down a path to watch the
Marie와 Nina는 폭포를 구경하기 위해 길을 내려갔다
falls.
Another sign: / 또 다른 표지판이 있었다 /
Watch Your Step. Rocks Are Slippery.
발걸음 조심하세요. 바위가 미끄럽습니다.
They found the falls spilling out in various layers of
그들은 겹겹의 다양한 바위에서 폭포가 쏟아져 나오는 것을 발견했다
rock.
No one was there except them.
거기에는 그들 말고는 아무도 없었다
"Look at them!" 저것들 좀 봐!
Marie pointed to movement in the water /
Marie는 물속의 움직임을 가리켰다 /
moving toward the falls. 폭포를 향해 이동하는
Hundreds of fish tails were flashing and catching
수 백 개의 물고기 꼬리가 번쩍거리고 태양으로부터 빛을 받고 있었다 /
light from the sun, /
moving upstream. 상류로 이동하며
Beneath them in the water, / 자신들 발밑 물속에서 /
they saw salmon slowly moving their bodies.
그들은 연어들이 천천히 몸을 움직이는 것을 봤다
[D] While Marie and Nina kept watching the
salmon, / a big one suddenly leapt.
Marie와 Nina가 연어를 지켜보고 있는 동안 / 큰 놈 하나가 갑자기 뛰어 올랐다
It threw itself up and over the rushing water above,
그것은 급류 위로 몸을 솟구쳐 넘어가려고 했지만, 소용없었다
but in vain.
They were standing without a word and watching
그들은 말 한 마디 없이 선채 물고기들이 애쓰는 것을 지켜봤다
the fish struggling.
Another jumped, / its body spinning until it made it
또 한 마리가 뛰었다 / 폭포를 넘을 때까지 녀석의 몸이 빙글빙글 돌았다
over the falls.
Another one leapt / and was washed back by the
또 한 마리가 뛰었다 / 그리고 물의 힘에 의해 다시 쓸려갔다
power of the water.
Watching the salmon, / Marie noticed Nina fixing
her eyes on their continuing challenge.
연어를 보면서 / Marie는 Nina가 그들의 계속된 도전에 눈을 고정하는 것을 알아챘다
Nina's heart was beating fast at each leap and twist.
각각의 도약과 회전에 Nina의 심장은 빠르게 고동쳤다
[B] Then, with a great push, / a small one turned a
그 때 크게 박차고 올라 / 작은 연어 하나가 완전히 한 바퀴 돌았다 /
complete circle /
and made it over the falls. 그리고 폭포를 넘어 갔다
"He made it!" / Nina shouted at the success with
녀석이 해냈어 / Nina는 그 성공에 감탄하며 외쳤다

admiration.

More salmon then followed and succeeded.
그런 다음 더 많은 연어가 뒤따랐고 성공했다

She felt ashamed to be looking at them.
그녀는 그것들을 바라보며 부끄러웠다

After a moment, she turned to Marie and said,
잠시 후 그녀는 Marie를 돌아보며 말했다

"Giving up is not in my vocabulary.
포기하는 것은 내 어휘에는 없어

Marie, I'll get my championship belt back."
Marie, 나는 내 챔피언 벨트를 되찾을 거야

Marie nodded with a bright smile.
Marie는 밝게 미소 지으며 끄덕였다

"Our training begins tomorrow.
내일 우리의 트레이닝 시작이다

It's going to be tough. 쉽지 않을 거야.

Are you ready?" 준비는 됐니?

Walking up the path and back to the car, /
길을 걸어 올라가 차로 돌아가며 /

they could still hear the fish splashing in the water.
그들은 여전히 물고기들이 물에서 첨벙거리는 것을 들을 수 있었다

(A) 나무들의 색깔은 마치 불이 붙은 것처럼 보였고, 붉은 색과 주황색은 노란색 및 금색과 경쟁하고 있었다. 이 시기는 Nina가 가장 좋아하는 계절이었지만 Marie가 운전하는 동안 그녀는 몇 시간 동안 침묵을 지켰다. Nina는 챔피언 벨트를 잃은 뒤에 가슴이 아팠다. 이제 전 챔피언으로서 그녀는 권투에서 은퇴할 생각을 하고 있었다. 오랜 친구이자 트레이너인 Marie는 고통을 함께 했다. 또 한 시간이 지난 후에, Marie와 Nina는 'Sauble 폭포'라는 표지판을 보았다. Marie는 이곳이 (a) 그들이 멈추기에 좋은 장소라고 생각했다.

(C) Marie는 주차장에다 차를 세웠다. Marie와 Nina는 폭포를 구경하기 위해 길을 내려갔다. '발걸음을 조심하십시오. 바위가 미끄럽습니다.'라는 다른 표지판이 있었다. (d) 그들은 여러 층의 바위에서 넘쳐흐르는 폭포를 발견했다. 그들 외에는 아무도 없었다. "저것들 좀 봐!" Marie는 물속에서 폭포 쪽으로 움직이는 움직임을 가리켰다. 수백 마리의 물고기 꼬리가 번쩍이며 태양으로부터 빛을 받으면서 상류로 이동하고 있었다. 그들 밑에 있는 물속에서 그들은 연어가 천천히 몸을 움직이는 것을 보았다.

(D) Marie와 Nina가 연어를 계속 보고 있는 동안, 갑자기 큰 것이 뛰어올랐다. 그것은 위쪽에서 밀려오는 물 위로 몸을 던졌지만 허사였다. (e) 그들은 말없이 서서 물고기가 애쓰는 것을 보고 있었다. 또 다른 한 마리가 뛰어 올랐는데 그것의 몸이 폭포위로 올라가는 것을 성공할 때까지 빙글빙글 돌았다. 또 다른 한 마리가 뛰어올랐다가 물의 힘에 의해 뒤로 휩쓸려갔다. 연어를 지켜보던 Marie는 Nina가 그들의 계속되는 도전에 시선을 고정시키고 있는 것을 알아차렸다. (연어들이) 뛰어올라 뒤틀릴 때마다 Nina의 심장이 빠르게 뛰고 있었다.

(B) 그런 다음 크게 밀면서 작은 한 마리가 온전히 한 바퀴를 돈 다음 폭포 위로 가는 데 성공했다. "이 연어가 해냈어!" Nina는 탄복하며 그 성공을 향해 외쳤다. 그런 다음 더 많은 연어가 뒤따라 성공했다. 그녀는 (b) 그들을 보는 것이 부끄러웠다. 잠시 후, 그녀는 Marie에게 돌아서서 "포기란 말은 내 어휘에는 없어. Marie, 나는 내 챔피언 벨트를 다시 가져올 거야."라고 말했다. Marie는 밝게 미소 지으며 고개를 끄덕였다. "우리의 훈련은 내일 시작이야. 그것은 힘들 거야. 준비됐어?" 길을 올라와서 다시 차로 걸어가면서 (c) 그들은 여전히 물속에서 물고기들이 물을 튀기는 소리를 들을 수 있었다.

《 어휘·어구 》

heartbroken 가슴이 아픈
make it 성공하다
admiration 탄성
pull over 길 한쪽으로 차를 대다
slippery 미끄러운
spill out 넘쳐흐르다
layer 층, 겹
upstream 상류로
salmon 연어
leap 뛰어오르다
struggle 애쓰다
spin 빙글빙글 돌다
wash 휩쓸다
beat (심장이) 뛰다

정답률 93%

10. ③

문제풀이

챔피언 벨트를 잃고 상심한 Nina가 친구이자 트레이너인 Marie가 운전하는 차를 타고 가다가 폭포 표지판을 보고 잠시 머무르기로 했다는 내용의 주어진 글 다음에, 두 사람이 폭포를 보고 물속에서 상류로 이동하는 연어를 봤다는 내용의 (C)가 오고, 계속해서 폭포를 뛰어넘으려고 도전하는 연어를 지켜보며 Nina의 가슴이 뛰었다는 내용의 (D)가 온 후, Nina가 연어의 모습을 보고 자신을 부끄러워하며 다시 챔피언벨트를 찾기로 결심했다는 내용의 (B)가 오는 것이 가장 적절하다. 따라서 정답은 ③이다.

정답률 93%

11. ②

문제풀이

(a), (c), (d), (e)는 Marie와 Nina를 가리키지만, (b)는 연어들을 가리킨다. 따라서 정답은 ②이다.

정답률 92%

12. ③

문제풀이

(B)에서 Nina는 계속 도전하는 연어를 보고 자신을 부끄러워하며 챔피언 벨트를 되찾아 오겠다고 결심한다. "Giving up is not in my vocabulary. Marie, I'll get my championship belt back." ("포기하는 것은 내 어휘에는 없어. Marie, 나는 내 챔피언 벨트를 되찾을 거야.")라고 했으므로, 윗글에 관한 내용으로 적절하지 않은 것은 ③이다.

본문 119쪽

문법 플러스 20. 특수 구문

A. 1. could they
2. does Sam
3. comes the writer
4. who
5. do
6. Not every
7. do

1 [해석]▶ 그들은 앞을 전혀 볼 수 없었을 뿐만 아니라 지치고 병이 들어서 더 이상 걸을 수가 없었다.
[해설]▶ 부정어구(not only)가 문장 앞에 오면 「주어+(조)동사」가 도치된다.

2 [해석]▶ 단지 그의 가족에 대한 사랑 때문에 Sam은 그렇게 힘든 일을 했다.
[해설]▶ Only가 포함된 어구가 문장 앞에 오면 「주어+(조)동사」가 도치된다.

3 [해석]▶ 이곳에 그 작가가 와!
[해설]▶ 장소와 방향을 나타내는 부사(here)가 문장 앞에 오면 주어와 동사가 도치된다.

4 [해석]▶ 우리가 가야할 길을 닦은 사람들은 끊임없는 시행착오를 거쳤던 바로 그러한 탐험가들이다.
[해설]▶ It ~ that 강조 구문으로서 those explores가 강조되고 있다. 강조되는 어구가 사람을 가리키므로 that 대신 who를 사용할 수 있다.

5 [해석]▶ 롤링의 책이 초자연적 생명체를 담고 있는 것은 사실이다.
[해설]▶ 조동사 do를 사용하여 동사를 강조할 수 있다. 주어가 복수이므로 do를 써야 한다.

6 [해석]▶ 인터넷에 있는 모든 뉴스가 다 진실인 것은 아니다.
[해설]▶ 전체를 나타내는 어구가 not과 함께 쓰이면 부분 부정의 의미를 나타낸다. not every는 '전부 ~인 것 은 아니다'의 의미이다.

7 [해석]▶ 나의 단짝, Sally는 나보다 더 피아노를 잘 친다.
[해설]▶ 일반동사로 시작하는 어구가 반복되면 대동사 do를 사용하여 생략한다. play를 반복 사용하지 않기 위해 대동사를 사용할 수 있는데, 주어가 I이므로, do를 써야 한다.

본문 119쪽

B. 1. had she
2. can rest
3. are the poor
4. which
5. the very
6. Not everyone
7. was

1 [해석]▶ 그녀가 가자마자 그는 그녀를 욕하기 시작했다.
[해설]▶ 부정어구(hardly)가 문두에 나오면 「주어+(조)동사」가 도치된다.

2 [해석]▶ 열심히 일한 후에만 진정으로 휴식을 즐길 수 있다.
[해설]▶ Only가 포함된 어구가 문장 앞에 오면 「주어+(조)동사」가 도치된다. 이 문장에서 rest는 '휴식'이라는 말로 주어 역할을 하고 있다.

3 [해석]▶ 마음이 가난한 사람은 복이 있다.
[해설]▶ 보어가 문장의 앞에 오면, 주어와 be동사가 도치된다.

4 [해석]▶ 우리가 매우 불쾌하다고 생각한 것은 바로 그녀가 한 말이 아니었다.
[해설]▶ It ~ that 강조 구문으로서, 강조 대상이 사물(not her remarks)이면 that 대신 which를 사용할 수 있다.

5 [해석]▶ 그녀는 며칠 전 나를 도와주었던 바로 그 여인이다.
[해설]▶ 명사를 강조하고 싶은 때는 the very를 사용하여 명사를 강조할 수 있다.

6 [해석]▶ 당신이 나를 싫어해도 괜찮아요, 모든 사람이 좋은 취향을 가진 건 아니니깐요.
[해설]▶ not everyone은 '모두 다 ~인 것은 아니다'라는 부분 부정의 의미이다.

7 [해석]▶ 각각의 딸세포는 모세포보다 작으며, 특이한 경우를 제외하고는 모세포만큼 커질 때까지 자란다.
[해설]▶ as the mother cell was large에서 was는 large가 생략된 대동사로 볼 수 있다.

본문 120쪽

숙어 플러스 20. 수능 필수 숙어 20회

1. turn	2. pressure
3. down	4. up

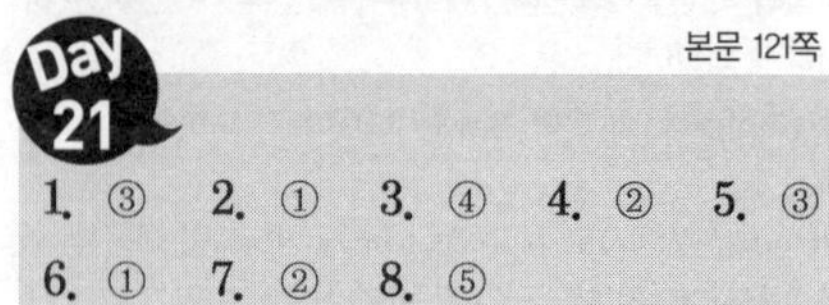

미니 고난도 Test 1회

Day 21

본문 121쪽

1. ③ 2. ① 3. ④ 4. ② 5. ③
6. ① 7. ② 8. ⑤

정답률 26%

1. ③ 학습 가능한 타인에 대한 감정

직독/직해

In the Indian language of pali, /
인도 팔리어에서 /

mettā means benevolence, kindness or tenderness.
*mettā*는 자비심, 친절 혹은 다정함을 의미한다

It is one of the most important ideas in Buddhism.
그것은 불교에서 가장 중요한 관념 중 하나다

Buddhism recommends a daily ritual meditation / (known as mettā bhāvanā) /
불교에서는 매일 의례적으로 하는 명상을 권한다 / (*mettā bhāvanā*로 알려진) /

to foster this attitude.
이러한 태도를 기르기 위해

The meditation begins with a call /
명상은 요구로 시작한다 /

to think carefully every morning of /
매일 아침 ~을 사려 깊게 생각하라는 /

an individual with whom one tends to get irritated /
짜증이 나게 되는 어떤 한 사람을 /

or to whom one feels aggressive or cold /
또는 공격적인 혹은 냉담한 기분이 들게 하는 /

and / — in place of one's normal hostile impulses — /
그리고 / 평소의 적대적인 충동 대신 /

to rehearse kindly messages / like 'I hope you will find peace' /
친절한 메시지를 기꺼이 연습하라는 / 나는 당신이 평안을 찾길 바랍니다와 같은 /

or 'I wish you to be free from suffering'.
또는 나는 당신이 고통에서 벗어나기를 기원합니다와 같은

This practice can be extended outwards /
이 수행은 밖으로 확장될 수 있다 /

ultimately to include pretty much everyone on Earth.
결국 지상의 거의 모든 사람을 포함하도록

The background assumption is that, / with the right stimulus, /
그 배경이 되는 가정은 ~ 것이다 / 적절한 자극으로 /

our feelings towards people are not fixed and unalterable, /
사람들을 향한 우리의 감정이 고정되어 바뀔 수 없는게 아니라 /

but open to deliberate change and improvement.
의도적인 변화와 개선의 여지가 있다는 (것이다)

Compassion is a learnable skill, / and we need to direct it /
연민은 학습 가능한 기술이다 / 그리고 우리는 그것을 향하게 할 필요가 있다 /

as much towards those we are tempted to dismiss and detest /
우리가 무시하고 혐오하고 싶은 마음이 생기는 사람에게도 /

as to those we love.
우리가 사랑하는 사람에게 만큼이나

인도 팔리어에서 *mettā*는 자비심, 친절 혹은 다정함을 의미한다. 그것은 불교에서 가장 중요한 관념 중 하나다. 불교에서는 이러한 태도를 기르기 위해 매일 의례적으로 하는 (*mettā bhāvanā*로 알려진) 명상을 권한다. 명상은 짜증이 나게 하거나, 공격적인 혹은 냉담한 기분이 들게 하는 경향이 있는 어떤 한 사람을 매일 아침 사려 깊게 생각하고, 평소의 적대적인 충동 대신 '나는 당신이 평안을 찾길 바랍니다.' 또는 '나는 당신이 고통에서 벗어나기를 기원합니다.'와 같은 메시지를 기꺼이 연습하라는 요구로 시작한다. 이 수행은 밖으로 확장되어 결국 지상의 거의 모든 사람을 포함할 수 있다. 그 배경이 되는 가정은 적절한 자극으로 사람들을 향한 우리의 감정이 고정되어 바뀔 수 없는게 아니라 의도적인 변화와 개선의 여지가 있다는 것이다. 연민은 학습 가능한 기술이며, 우리가 사랑하는 사람에게 만큼이나 우리가 무시하고 혐오하고 싶은 마음이 생기는 사람에게도 그것을 향하게 할 필요가 있다.

① 창의성 ② 긴장 완화 **③ 연민**
④ 정당화 ⑤ 권한 부여한

문제풀이

미워하거나 싫어하는 사람들이 평안을 갖기를 바라고, 고통에서 벗어나기를 기원하는 명상을 하게 되면 타인에 대한 감정이 의도적으로 변화하고 개선의 여지가 있다는 내용의 글이다. 따라서 빈칸에는 ③ 'Compassion'이 들어가 빈칸을 포함한 문장이 '연민은 학습 가능한 기술이며, 우리가 사랑하는 사람에게 만큼이나 우리가 무시하고 혐오하고 싶은 마음이 생기는 사람에게도 그것을 향하게 할 필요가 있다.'가 되는 것이 적절하다.

이렇게 풀자 빈칸 완성 문제는 글 전체의 주제를 파악하고, 빈칸 전후의 문장에서 단서를 찾으면 된다. 빈칸 바로 앞의 'The background assumption is that, with the right stimulus, our feelings towards people are not fixed and unalterable, but open to deliberate change and improvement.'에서 다른 사람들을 향한 우리의 감정이 의도적인 변화와 개선의 여지가 있다는 것이라고 하였고, 빈칸이 학습 가능한 기술이라고 하였으므로, 빈칸에는 '다른 사람들을 향한 우리의 감정'에 해당하는 말인 'compassion'이 들어가야 한다는 것을 알 수 있다.

구조 다시보기

도입	인도 팔리어에서 *mettā*는 불교의 중요한 관념 중 하나인데 자비심, 친절, 다정함을 의미함
전개	불교에서는 명상을 통해 다른 사람들에 대한 부정적인 감정을 자비심과 사랑의 메시지로 바꾸도록 연습하라고 요구함
부연	사람들을 향한 우리의 감정은 바뀔 수 있고 개선될 수 있음
결론	연민은 학습 가능한 기술임

《어휘·어구》

benevolence 자비심
kindness 친절
tenderness 다정함
Buddhism 불교
recommend 권하다, 추천하다
ritual 의례적인
meditation 명상
foster 기르다
irritated 짜증이 난
aggressive 공격적인
in place of ~대신에
hostile 적대적인
impulse 충동
extend 확장하다
ultimately 결국, 궁극적으로
assumption 가정
unalterable 바꿀 수 없는
deliberate 의도적인, 계획적인
improvement 개선
be tempted to ~하고 싶은 마음이 생기다
dismiss 무시하다
detest 혐오하다

정답률 57%

2. ① 평등의 개념

직독/직해

Since human beings are at once both similar and different, /
인간은 동시에 비슷하고 다르기도 해서 /

they should be treated equally / because of both.
그들은 동등하게 대우받아야 한다 / 두 가지 모두 때문에

Such a view, / 그런 견해는 /

which grounds equality not in human uniformity /
평등의 기초를 인간의 획일성이 아닌 /

but in the interplay of uniformity and difference, /
획일성과 차이의 상호 작용에 두는 /

builds difference into the very concept of equality, /
평등이라는 바로 그 개념에 차이를 만들어 내고 /

breaks the traditional equation of equality with similarity, /
전통적으로 평등을 유사성과 동일시하는 것을 깨뜨리며 /

and is immune to monist distortion.
그리고 일원론적 왜곡을 면한다

Once the basis of equality changes / so does its content.
일단 평등의 기초가 바뀌면 / 그것의 내용도 그렇다

Equality involves equal freedom or opportunity /
평등은 동등한 자유나 기회를 포함한다 /

to be different, / 서로 다를 /

and treating human beings equally /
그리고 인간을 동등하게 취급하는 것은 /

requires us to take into account /
우리가 고려하도록 요구한다 /

both their similarities and differences.
그들의 유사성과 차이점을 둘 다

When the latter are not relevant, /
후자가 관련이 없을 때 /

equality entails uniform or identical treatment; /
평등은 균일하거나 똑같은 대우를 수반하고 /

when they are, / it requires differential treatment.
차이점이 관련이 있을 때 / 그것은 차이를 나타내는 대우를 필요로 한다

Equal rights do not mean identical rights, /
평등한 권리는 똑같은 권리를 의미하지 않는데 /

for individuals with different cultural backgrounds and needs /
왜냐하면 서로 다른 문화적 배경과 요구를 가진 개인들이 /

might require different rights / to enjoy equality /
다른 권리를 요구할지도 모르기 때문이다 / 평등을 누릴 /

in respect of whatever happens to be the content of their rights.
우연히 그들의 권리의 내용이 되는 어떤 것이든 그것에 관해서

Equality involves not just rejection of irrelevant differences /
평등은 무관한 차이들에 대한 거부뿐만 아니라 /

as is commonly argued, / 보통 주장되듯이 /

but also full recognition of legitimate and relevant ones.
합법적이고 관련 있는 차이들에 대한 완전한 인정도 포함한다

인간은 동시에 비슷하고 다르기도 해서 두 가지 모두 때문에 동등하게 대우받아야 한다. 평등의 기반을 인간의 획일성이 아닌 획일성과 차이의 상호 작용에 두는 그런 견해는 평등이라는 바로 그 개념에 차이를 만들어 내고, 전통적으로 평등을 유사성과 동일시하는 것을 깨뜨리며, 일원론적 왜곡을 면하게 된다. 일단 평등의 기초가 바뀌면 그것의 내용도 그렇다. 평등은 서로 다를 동등한 자유나 기회를 포함하고, 인간을 동등하게 취급하는 것은 우리가 그들의 유사성과 차이점을 둘 다 고려하도록 요구한다. 후자가 관련이 없을 때 평등은 균일하거나 똑같은 대우를 수반하고, 차이점이 관련이 있을 때 그것은 차이를 나타내는 대우를 필요로 한다. 평등한 권리는 똑같은 권리를 의미하지 않는데, 왜냐하면 서로 다른 문화적 배경과 요구를 가진 개인들이 우연히 그들의 권리의 내용이 되는 어떤 것이든 그것에 관해서 평등을 누릴 다른 권리를 요구할지도 모르기 때문이다. 평등은 보통 주장되듯이 무관한 차이들에 대한 거부뿐만 아니라 합법적이고 관련 있는 차이들에 대한 완전한 인정도 포함한다.

① 평등을 누릴 다른 권리를 요구할
② 평등을 위해서 자신의 자유를 포기할
③ 불평등에 관한 동일한 인식을 기꺼이 받아들일
④ 사회 구조에서 자신의 위치를 더 쉽게 받아들일
⑤ 완전한 이해를 얻기 위해서 관련이 있는 차이점을 거부할

문제풀이

평등의 기반을 유사성과 획일성이 아닌 유사성과

차이점의 상호 작용에 두면 서로 간의 차이를 고려한 서로 다른 대우를 포함할 수 있게 된다고 했으므로, 평등한 권리란 똑같은 권리를 의미하는 게 아니기 때문에 서로 다른 권리를 요구할 수 있는 것이라고 해야 한다. 따라서 빈칸에는 ① 'require different rights to enjoy equality'가 들어가서, 빈칸을 포함한 문장이 '평등한 권리는 똑같은 권리를 의미하지 않는데, 왜냐하면 서로 다른 문화적 배경과 요구를 가진 개인들이 우연히 그들의 권리의 내용이 되는 어떤 것이든 그것에 관해서 평등을 누릴 다른 권리를 요구할지도 모르기 때문이다.'가 되는 것이 가장 적절하다.

어휘·어구

at once 동시에
equally 평등하게
ground A in B A의 기반을 B에 두다
uniformity 획일성
interplay 상호 작용
concept 개념
equation 동일시, 방정식
immune (질병이나 공격 등을) 면한
distortion 왜곡
content 내용
take into account ~을 고려하다
the latter 후자
relevant 관련이 있는
identical 동일한
differential 차이를 나타내는
in respect of ~에 관해서
rejection 거부
legitimate 합법적인, 타당한
abandon 버리다
perception 인지

정답률 69%

3. ④ 특정 체제에서 성공한 사람들은 그 체제를 정당화함

직독/직해

Research has shown / that individuals /
연구는 보여 주어 왔다 / 개인들은 /
— especially those who have benefited from a particular system /
특히 특정 체제로부터 이득을 얻어 왔던 사람들 /
— are prone to support and rationalize the status quo, /
현재 상태를 지지하고 합리화하는 경향이 있다는 것을 /
even if there are clear problems.
비록 분명한 문제들이 존재하더라도
These people justify systemic inequity with familiar phrases /
이러한 사람들은 익숙한 문구로 체제상의 불공평을 정당화한다 /
like "If you just work hard enough you can pull yourself up by your bootstraps."
'만약 네가 충분히 일하기만 하면, 너는 스스로의 힘으로 해낼 수 있다'라는
A branch of psychology /
심리학의 한 분야는 /
called *system justification theory* / describes /
체제 정당화 이론이라 불리는 / 묘사한다 /
how people tend to see social, economic, and political systems /
어떻게 사람들이 사회적, 경제적, 정치적 체제들을 여기는 경향이 있는지를 /
as good, fair, and legitimate /
좋고, 공정하며, 옳은 것으로 /
if they have succeeded as a result of those systems.
만약 사람들이 그러한 체제의 결과로 성공했다면
According to Erin Godfrey, /
Erin Godfrey에 의하면 /
a professor of applied psychology at New York University, /
뉴욕 대학교의 응용 심리학 교수인 /
"The people who are at the top /
정상에 있는 사람들은 /
want to believe in meritocracy /
능력주의를 믿고 싶어 한다 /
because it means that they deserve their successes."
이는 그것이 그들이 스스로의 성공을 누릴 자격이 있다는 것을 의미하기 때문이다
Indeed, / it is not surprising /
실제로 / 놀랍지 않다 /
that there exists a general consensus /
보편적인 합의가 존재한다는 것은 /
across social class /
사회 계층에 걸쳐 /
about the definition and the results of meritocracy.
능력주의의 정의와 결과에 대해
Those who are in an advantaged position in society /
사회에서 유리한 지위에 있는 사람들은 /
are more likely to believe /
더 믿을 가능성이 있다 /
the system is fair / and see no reason to change it.
그 체제가 공정하다고 / 그리고 그것을 바꿀 이유가 없다고 여길

연구는 개인들, 특히 특정 체제로부터 이득을 얻어 왔던 사람들은 비록 분명한 문제들이 존재하더라도 현재 상태를 지지하고 합리화하는 경향이 있다는 것을 보여 주어 왔다. ① 이러한 사람들은 '만약 네가 충분히 일하기만 하면, 너는 스스로의 힘으로 해낼 수 있다'라는 익숙한 문구로 체제상의 불공평을 정당화한다. ② '체제 정당화 이론'이라 불리는 심리학의 한 분야는 만약 사람들이 그러한 체제의 결과로 성공했다면 어떻게 그들이 사회적, 경제적, 정치적 체제들을 좋고, 공정하며, 옳은 것으로 여기는 경향이 있는지를 설명한다. ③ 뉴욕 대학교의 응용 심리학 교수인 Erin Godfrey에 의하면, "정상에 있는 사람들은 능력주의를 믿고 싶어 하는데, 이는 그것이 그들이 스스로의 성공을 누릴 자격이 있다는 것을 의미하기 때문이다." ④ (실제로, 능력주의의 정의와 결과에 대해 사회 계층에 걸쳐 보편적인 합의가 존재한다는 것은 놀랍지 않다.) ⑤ 사회에서 유리한 지위에 있는 사람들은 그 체제가 공정하다고 믿으며 그것을 바꿀 이유가 없다고 여길 가능성이 더 높다.

문제풀이

특정 체제에서 성공한 사람들은 비록 그 체제에 분명한 문제점이 있다 할지라도, 그 현재 체제를 지지하고 정당화하며, 능력이 있으면 성공할 수 있다는 능력주의를 믿고 싶어하는 경향이 있다는 내용의 글인데, 능력주의의 정의와 결과에 대한 보편적 합의가 존재한다는 내용의 ④는 글의 전체 흐름과 관계가 없다.

이렇게 풀자 전체 글의 흐름과 관계 없는 문장을 고르는 문제는 대개 첫 문장이 주제문이고 나머지 문장들이 뒷받침 문장이다. 각각의 뒷받침 문장들이 주제문과 관련 있는지 여부를 확인하면 흐름과 관계없는 문장을 쉽게 찾을 수 있다. 특히 주제문에 등장한 표현과 같거나 유사한 표현들을 찾아보면 쉽게 답을 유추할 수 있다. 이 문제에서는 첫 문장의 'nationalize the status quo(현재 상태를 합리화하다)', ①의 'justify systemic inequity(체제상의 불공평을 정당화하다)', ②의 'system justification theory(체제 정당화 이론)', ③의 'they deserve their sucesses(그들은 성공을 누릴 자격이 있다)', ⑤의 'the system is fair(그 체제가 공정하다)'등이 모두 성공한 사람들은 현재 체제를 정당화한다는 표현이다. 따라서 이런 내용이 없는 ④가 글의 흐름과 관계없다는 것을 쉽게 유추할 수 있다.

어휘·어구

individual 각각의, 개개의
be prone to do ~하기 쉽다
rationalize 합리화하다
by one's bootstrap 혼자 힘으로
justify 정당화하다
inequity 불공평
legitimate 정당한, 옳은
deserve 받을 만하다
consensus 합의
definition 정의

정답률 55%

4. ② 인간과 동물이 공유하는 특성

직독/직해

In the fifth century *B.C.E.*, / 기원전 5세기에 /
the Greek philosopher Protagoras pronounced, /
그리스의 철학자 프로타고라스는 선언했다 /
"Man is the measure of all things."
사람은 만물의 척도이다
In other words, / we feel entitled to ask the world, /
다시 말해 / 우리는 세상을 향해 물어볼 자격이 있다고 느낀다 /
"What good are you?"
당신은 무슨 쓸모인가
(B) We assume / that we are the world's standard, /
우리는 생각한다 / 우리가 세상의 기준이라고 /
that all things should be compared to us.
즉 모든 것이 우리와 비교되어야 한다고
Such an assumption makes us / overlook a lot.
그러한 추정은 우리가 ~하게 한다 / 많은 것을 간과하게
(A) Abilities said to "make us human" /
'우리를 인간답게 만들어준다고' 말해지는 능력들 /
— empathy, communication, grief, toolmaking, and so on — /
공감, 의사소통, 슬픔, 도구 만들기 등은 /
all exist to varying degrees /
모두 존재들에게도 다양한 정도로 존재한다 /
among other minds sharing the world with us.
우리와 세상을 공유하는 다른 지력을 지닌
Animals with backbones (fishes, amphibians, reptiles, birds, and mammals) all /
척추동물(어류, 양서류, 파충류, 조류, 포유류)은 모두 /
share the same basic skeleton, organs, nervous systems, hormones, and behaviors.
똑같은 기본 골격, 장기, 신경계, 호르몬, 행동을 공유한다
(C) Just as / different models of automobiles each /
~인 것과 마찬가지로 / 서로 다른 자동차의 모델들이 각각 /
have an engine, drive train, four wheels, doors, and seats, /
엔진, 동력 전달 체계, 네 바퀴, 문, 좌석을 가지고 있는 /
we differ / 우리는 다르다 /
mainly in terms of our outside contours and a few internal tweaks.
주로 우리의 외부 윤곽과 몇 가지 내부적인 조정 면에서
But like naive car buyers, /
그러나 순진한 자동차 구매자들처럼 /
most people see only animals' varied exteriors.
대부분의 사람은 단지 동물들의 다양한 겉모습만을 본다.

기원전 5세기에, 그리스의 철학자 프로타고라스는 "사람은 만물의 척도이다."라고 선언했다. 다시 말해, 우리는 세상을 향해 "당신은 무슨 쓸모인가?"라고 물어볼 자격이 있다고 느낀다.
(B) 우리는 우리가 세상의 기준이라고, 즉 모든 것이 우리와 비교되어야 한다고 생각한다. 그러한 추정은 우리가 많은 것을 간과하게 한다.
(A) '우리를 인간답게 만들어준다고' 말해지는 능력들, 즉 공감, 의사소통, 슬픔, 도구 만들기 등은 모두 우리와 세상을 공유하는 다른 지력을 지닌 존재들에게도 다양한 정도로 존재한다. 척추동물(어류, 양서류, 파충류, 조류, 포유류)은 모두 똑같은 기본 골격, 장기, 신경계, 호르몬, 행동을 공유한다.
(C) 서로 다른 자동차의 모델들이 각각 엔진, 동력 전달 체계, 네 바퀴, 문, 좌석을 가지고 있는 것과 마찬가지로, 우리는 주로 우리의 외부 윤곽과 몇 가지 내부적인 조정 면에서 다르다. 그러나 순진한 자동차 구매자들처럼, 대부분의 사람은 단지 동물들의 다양한 겉모습만을 본다.

문제풀이

프로타고라스의 '사람은 만물의 척도이다'라는 말을 제시한 주어진 글 다음에, 사람이 세상의 기준이라고 여기는 것이 많은 것을 간과하게 만든다는 내용의 (B)가 오고, (B)에서 언급한 사람들이 간과하는 것에 관한 내용을 소개하면서 인간에게만 있다고 여겨지는 공감, 의사소통 등의 능력은 인간 아닌 다른 존재들에게도 있고 척추동물은 신체

적으로도 동일한 특징을 공유한다는 내용의 (A)가 온 후, 마지막으로 서로 다른 자동차들도 기본 사양이 같은 것처럼 인간과 동물도 겉만 다른데 사람들은 겉모습만 본다는 내용의 (C)가 오는 것이 가장 적절하다. 따라서 정답은 ②이다.

《 어휘·어구 》

philosopher 철학자
pronounce 선언하다
measure 척도
entitled to ~할 자격이 있는
empathy 공감
grief 슬픔
backbone 척추, 등뼈
amphibian 양서류
reptile 파충류
mammal 포유류
skeleton 골격
organ 장기
nervous system 신경계
assume 생각하다, 추정하다
standard 기준, 표준
assumption 가정
overlook 간과하다
in terms of ~ 면에서, ~에 관해서는
drive train 동력 전달 체계
naive 순진한
exterior 겉모습

정답률 62%

5. ③ 거짓말과 진실을 말하는 방식의 차이

직독/직해

There are several broad differences in the way /
방식에는 몇 가지 큰 차이가 있다
that liars and truth tellers discuss events.
거짓말하는 사람들과 진실을 말하는 사람들이 사건들에 관해 이야기하는
One difference / is that liars say less overall /
한 가지 차이점은 / 거짓말하는 사람들이 전반적으로 말을 덜 한다는 것이다 /
than truth tellers. 진실을 말하는 사람들보다
If you are telling the truth, /
당신이 진실을 말하고 있다면 /
the details of what happened / are obvious.
일어난 일의 세부 내용은 / 분명하다
If you are lying, / it is not easy /
당신이 거짓말을 하고 있다면 / 쉽지 않다 /
to conjure up lots of details.
많은 세부 내용을 떠올리기가
Interestingly, / truth tellers talk *less* /
흥미롭게도 / 진실을 말하는 사람들은 '덜' 이야기한다 /
about their emotions / than liars do.
그들의 감정에 관해 / 거짓말하는 사람들보다
That is because / when you recall a real memory, /
그것은 ~ 때문이다 / 당신이 실제 기억을 떠올리면 /
you begin to reexperience /
당신은 다시 경험하기 시작하기 (때문이다) /
some of the emotion from that event.
그 사건에서 느꼈던 일부 감정을
As a result, / that emotion feels obvious to you /
그 결과 / 그 감정은 당신에게 분명하게 느껴진다 /
(and would be obvious to anyone watching you).
그리고 당신을 보는 누구에게라도 분명할 것이다
If you are lying, though, /
하지만 만약 당신이 거짓말을 하고 있다면 /
you don't really experience that emotion, /
당신은 그 감정을 실제로 경험하지 못한다 /
so you describe it instead.
그래서 당신은 대신에 그 감정을 묘사하게 된다

Truth tellers also talk about themselves /
진실을 말하는 사람들은 또한 자신에 관해 더 많이 이야기한다 /
more than liars, / 거짓말하는 사람보다 /
because people telling the truth are more focused /
진실을 말하는 사람들은 더 집중하기 때문이다 /
on their own memories / than liars are /
자신의 기억에 / 거짓말하는 사람들보다 /
(who are also thinking / 그들은 또한 생각한다 /
about how their story is being perceived /
그들의 이야기가 어떻게 인식되는지에 관해 /
by others). 다른 사람들에 의해

거짓말하는 사람들과 진실을 말하는 사람들이 사건들에 관해 이야기하는 방식에는 몇 가지 큰 차이가 있다. 한 가지 차이점은 거짓말하는 사람들이 전반적으로 진실을 말하는 사람들보다 말을 덜 한다는 것이다. 당신이 진실을 말하고 있다면, 일어난 일의 세부 내용은 분명하다. (①) 당신이 거짓말을 하고 있다면, 많은 세부 내용을 떠올리기가 쉽지 않다. (②) 흥미롭게도, 진실을 말하는 사람들은 거짓말하는 사람들보다 그들의 감정에 관해 '덜' 이야기한다. (③) 그것은 당신이 실제 기억을 떠올리면, 당신은 그 사건에서 느꼈던 일부 감정을 다시 경험하기 시작하기 때문이다. 그 결과, 그 감정은 당신에게 분명하게 느껴진다(그리고 당신을 보는 누구에게라도 분명할 것이다). (④) 하지만 만약 당신이 거짓말을 하고 있다면, 그 감정을 실제로 경험하지 못하므로 당신은 대신에 그 감정을 묘사하게 된다. (⑤) 진실을 말하는 사람들은 또한 거짓말하는 사람보다 자신에 관해 더 많이 이야기하는데, 그 이유는 진실을 말하는 사람들은 거짓말하는 사람들보다 자신의 기억에 더 집중하기 때문이다(그들은 또한 그들의 이야기가 다른 사람들에 의해 어떻게 인식되는지에 관해 생각한다).

문제풀이

③ 뒤의 문장은 'As a result'로 보아 앞 문장에 대한 결과를 서술하는 문장임을 알 수 있다. 따라서 'As a result'로 시작하는 문장 앞에는 원인에 대한 내용이 나와야 한다. 또한 주어진 문장의 'That'은 ③ 앞의 문장에서 언급된 '진실을 말하는 사람들이 그들의 감정에 관해 덜 이야기하는 것'을 가리키므로, 주어진 문장은 ③에 들어가는 것이 가장 적절하다.

이렇게 풀자 주어진 문장의 위치를 찾는 문제의 경우, 문장 간의 흐름이 단절된 곳이나 주어진 문장에 쓰인 대명사와 연결어가 주요 단서가 된다. 이 지문에서는 주어진 문장에서 쓰인 대명사 'That'과 ③ 뒤의 문장에 쓰인 'As a result'의 의미를 파악하면, 주어진 문장의 위치를 쉽게 찾을 수 있다.

《 어휘·어구 》

recall 생각해 내다, 기억하다
broad 넓은
discuss 이야기하다, 논의하다
detail 세부 내용
obvious 분명한, 명백한

정답률 64%

6. ① 동료를 구하는 쥐

직독/직해

In 2010 / scientists conducted a rat experiment.
2010년에 / 과학자들은 쥐 실험을 했다
They locked a rat in a tiny cage, /
그들은 쥐 한 마리를 작은 우리에 가두고 /
placed the cage within a much larger cell /
그 우리를 훨씬 더 큰 방 안에 두었다 /
and allowed another rat to roam freely through that cell.
그리고 또 다른 쥐가 그 방을 자유롭게 돌아다닐 수 있게 했다
The caged rat gave out distress signals, /
우리에 갇힌 쥐는 조난 신호를 보냈다 /
which caused the free rat also to exhibit /
이것은 자유로운 쥐 또한 보이게 했다 /
signs of anxiety and stress.
불안과 스트레스의 징후를

In most cases, / 대부분의 경우에 /
the free rat proceeded to help her trapped companion, /
자유로운 쥐는 결국 갇힌 동료를 돕게 되었다 /
and after several attempts /
그리고 몇 번의 시도 후 /
usually succeeded in opening the cage /
대개는 우리를 여는 데 성공했다 /
and liberating the prisoner.
그리고 갇힌 쥐를 풀어주는 데 (성공했다)
The researchers then repeated the experiment, /
그러고 나서 연구원들이 실험을 반복했다 /
this time placing chocolate / in the cell.
이번에는 초콜릿을 놓고 / 방 안에
The free rat now had to choose /
이제 자유로운 쥐는 선택해야 했다 /
between either liberating the prisoner, /
갇힌 쥐를 풀어주거나 /
or enjoying the chocolate all by herself.
아니면 혼자서 초콜릿을 먹는 것 사이에서
Many rats preferred to first free their companion /
많은 쥐가 먼저 동료를 풀어주는 것을 선호했다 /
and share the chocolate /
그리고 초콜릿을 나눠 먹는 것을 (선호했다) /
(though a few behaved more selfishly, /
하지만 몇 마리는 더 이기적으로 행동했다 /
proving perhaps / 이것은 어쩌면 증명하면서 /
that some rats are meaner than others).
어떤 쥐들이 다른 쥐들보다 더 인색하다는 것을
➡ In a series of experiments, /
일련의 실험에서 /
when the free rats witnessed /
자유로운 쥐들이 목격했을 때 /
their fellow in a state of anguish in a cage, /
우리에 갇힌 자신의 동료가 고통의 상태에 있는 것을 /
they tended to rescue their companion, /
그들은 자신의 동료를 구하려는 경향이 있었다 /
even delaying eating chocolate.
심지어 초콜릿을 먹는 것을 미루면서까지

2010년에 과학자들은 쥐 실험을 했다. 그들은 쥐 한 마리를 작은 우리에 가두고, 그 우리를 훨씬 더 큰 방 안에 두고는 또 다른 쥐가 그 방을 자유롭게 돌아다닐 수 있게 했다. 우리에 갇힌 쥐는 조난 신호를 보냈는데, 이것은 자유로운 쥐 또한 불안과 스트레스의 징후를 보이게 했다. 대부분의 경우에, 자유로운 쥐는 결국 갇힌 동료를 돕게 되었고, 몇 번의 시도 후 대개는 우리를 열고 갇힌 쥐를 풀어주는 데 성공했다. 그러고 나서 이번에는 연구원들이 방 안에 초콜릿을 놓고 실험을 반복했다. 이제 자유로운 쥐는 갇힌 쥐를 풀어주거나 혼자서 초콜릿을 먹는 것 사이에서 선택해야 했다. 많은 쥐가 먼저 동료를 풀어주고 나서, 초콜릿을 나눠 먹는 것을 선호했다 (하지만 몇 마리는 더 이기적으로 행동했고, 이것은 어쩌면 어떤 쥐들이 다른 쥐들보다 더 인색하다는 것을 증명했다).

➡ 일련의 실험에서, 자유로운 쥐들이 우리에 갇힌 자신의 동료가 (A) 고통의 상태에 있는 것을 목격했을 때, 그들은 심지어 초콜릿을 먹는 것을 (B) 미루면서까지 자신의 동료를 구하려는 경향이 있었다.

① 고통 — 미루면서　② 고통 — 우선시하면서
③ 흥분 — 우선시하면서　④ 지루함 — 거부하면서
⑤ 지루함 — 미루면서

문제풀이

방 안을 자유롭게 돌아다닐 수 있는 쥐가 우리에 갇힌 동료를 볼 경우, 대부분의 쥐는 동료가 보내는 조난 신호를 인지하고 난 후 동료를 구하는 경향이 있고, 심지어 초콜릿이 있는 방 안에서 같은 실험을 했을 때조차도 동료를 풀어주고 초콜릿을 나눠 먹는 것을 선호했다는 실험 결과를 통해, 요약문의 빈칸 (A)에는 'anguish(고통)'가, (B)에는 'delaying(미루면서)'이 들어가는 것이 가장 적절함을 알 수 있다.

《 어휘·어구 》

conduct 수행하다
cell 방
roam 돌아다니다
distress signal 조난 신호
exhibit 보이다

anxiety 불안, 염려
proceed to ~이 되다, ~에 이르다
companion 동료
attempt 시도
succeed in ~에 성공하다
liberate 해방시키다, 자유롭게 해주다
behave 행동하다
selfishly 이기적으로
mean 인색한
anguish 고통
prioritize 우선시하다
boredom 지루함

구조 다시보기

실험 내용	우리에 갇힌 쥐와 자유롭게 돌아다니는 쥐에 대한 실험
실험 1	우리에 갇힌 쥐가 자유롭게 돌아다니는 쥐에게 조난 신호를 보냄 → 우리에 갇힌 쥐를 풀어줌
실험 2	방 안에 초콜릿이 있는 상황에서 같은 실험을 진행함 → 우리에 갇힌 쥐를 풀어주고 같이 초콜릿을 먹는 것을 선호함

7~8 연구에서 주의해야 할 점

직독/직해

In studies examining the effectiveness of vitamin C, /
비타민 C의 효과를 조사하는 연구에서 /
researchers typically divide the subjects /
연구원들은 일반적으로 피험자들을 나눈다 /
into two groups. 두 집단으로
One group (the experimental group) receives a vitamin C supplement, /
한 집단(실험군)은 비타민 C 보충제를 받는다 /
and the other (the control group) does not.
그리고 다른 집단(통제군)은 안 받는다
Researchers observe both groups / to determine /
연구원들은 두 집단 모두를 관찰한다 / 판단을 내리기 위해 /
whether one group has fewer or shorter colds /
한 집단이 감기에 더 적게 또는 더 짧게 걸리는지를 /
than the other. 다른 집단보다
The following discussion describes some of the pitfalls /
이어지는 논의는 함정 중 일부를 기술한다 /
inherent in an experiment of this kind /
이런 종류의 실험에 내재되어 있는 /
and ways to avoid them. 그리고 이를 피하는 방법을
In sorting subjects into two groups, /
피험자를 두 집단으로 분류할 때 /
researchers must ensure /
연구원들은 반드시 ~해야 한다
that each person has an equal chance of being assigned /
각 개인이 배정될 확률이 똑같도록 /
to either the experimental group or the control group.
실험군 또는 통제군 둘 중 한 곳에
This is accomplished by randomization; /
이는 무작위 추출에 의해 달성되는데 /
that is, the subjects are chosen randomly /
즉 피험자는 무작위로 선정된다 /
from the same population /
동일 모집단에서 /
by flipping a coin or some other method involving chance.
동전 던지기나 우연이 포함된 어떤 다른 방법에 의해
Randomization helps to ensure /
무작위 추출은 반드시 도움이 된다 /
that results reflect the treatment /
결과에 처리가 반영되도록 하는 데 /
and not factors /
그리고 요인은 반영되지 않도록 하는 데 /
that might influence the grouping of subjects.
피험자의 분류에 영향을 줄지도 모르는
Importantly, /
중요한 것은 /
the two groups of people must be similar /
두 집단의 사람들이 비슷해야 한다는 것이다 /
and must have the same track record /
그리고 똑같은 기록을 가지고 있어야 한다는 것이다 /
with respect to colds /
감기와 관련하여 /
to rule out the possibility /
가능성을 배제하기 위해 /
that observed differences in the rate, severity, or duration of colds /
감기의 비율, 심각성, 또는 지속 기간에서 관찰된 차이가 /
might have occurred anyway.
어떤 식으로든 일어났을지도 모른다는
If, for example, the control group would normally catch twice as many colds as the experimental group, /
예를 들면, 통제군이 보통 실험군보다 감기에 무려 두 배나 많이 걸리면,
then the findings prove nothing.
연구 결과는 아무것도 입증하지 못한다
In experiments involving a nutrient, /
영양분을 포함하는 실험에서 /
the diets of both groups must also be different, /
두 집단의 식단 또한 달라야 한다 /
especially with respect to the nutrient being studied.
연구 중인 영양분에 관련하여 특히 (그래야 한다)
If those in the experimental group were receiving less vitamin C /
실험군에 속한 사람들이 비타민 C를 적게 섭취하고 있었다면 /
from their usual diet, /
평소 식단에서
then any effects of the supplement /
보충제의 어떤 효과도 /
may not be apparent.
분명하지 않을 수 있다

비타민 C의 효과를 조사하는 연구에서, 연구원들은 일반적으로 피험자들을 두 집단으로 나눈다. 한 집단(실험군)은 비타민 C 보충제를 받고 다른 집단(통제군)은 안 받는다. 연구원들은 한 집단이 다른 집단보다 감기에 더 적게 또는 더 짧게 걸리는지를 판단을 내리기 위해 두 집단 모두를 관찰한다. 이어지는 논의는 이런 종류의 실험에 내재되어 있는 함정 중 일부와 이를 (a) 피하는 방법을 기술한다. 피험자를 두 집단으로 분류할 때, 연구원들은 반드시 각 개인이 실험군 또는 통제군 둘 중 한 곳에 배정될 확률이 (b) 똑같도록 해야 한다. 이는 무작위 추출에 의해 달성되는데 즉 피험자는 동전 던지기나 우연이 포함된 어떤 다른 방법에 의해 동일 모집단에서 무작위로 선정된다. 무작위 추출은 반드시 결과에 처리가 반영되도록, 피험자의 분류에 영향을 줄지도 모르는 요인은 반영되지 않도록 하는 데 도움이 된다. 중요한 것은, 감기의 비율, 심각성, 또는 지속 기간에서 관찰된 차이가 어떤 식으로든 일어났을지도 모른다는 가능성을 (c) 배제하기 위해 감기와 관련하여 두 집단의 사람들이 비슷하고 똑같은 기록을 가지고 있어야 한다는 것이다. 예를 들면, 통제군이 보통 실험군보다 감기에 무려 두 배나 많이 걸리면, 연구 결과는 (d) 아무것도 입증하지 못한다. 영양분을 포함하는 실험에서, 두 집단의 식단 또한 (e) 달라야 (→ 비슷해야) 하며, 연구 중인 영양분에 관련하여 특히 그래야 한다. 실험군에 속한 사람들이 평소 식단에서 비타민 C를 적게 섭취하고 있었다면, 보충제의 어떤 효과도 분명하지 않을 수 있다.

어휘·어구

subject 피험자, 실험 대상
experimental group 실험군, 실험 집단
supplement 보충제
control group 통제 집단, 통제군
inherent 내재한
assign 배정하다
randomization 무작위 추출
population 모집단
flip (동전 등을) 던지다
track record 기록, 행적, 실적
with respect to ~과 관련하여
rule out ~을 배제하다
severity 심각성
finding 연구 결과
nutrient 영양분
apparent 명백한
faulty 불완전한, 잘못된
irrelevant 무관한, 관련 없는
in-depth 철저하고 상세한, 면밀한
analysis 분석

정답률 

7. ②

① 완벽한 계획과 불완전한 결과: 연구에 있어 슬픈 현실
② 관련 없는 요인이 결과에 영향을 미치지 않도록 하라!
③ 실험 연구에 참여하는 인간 피험자들을 보호하라!
④ 어떤 영양분이 감기를 더 잘 예방할 수 있을까?
⑤ 영양에 대한 면밀한 분석: 인간의 건강을 위한 핵심 요소

문제풀이

비타민 C의 효과를 조사하는 연구에서 연구원들이 피험자들을 실험군과 통제군으로 나눌 때, 피험자의 분류가 결과에 영향을 미치지 않도록 각 개인이 둘 중 한 곳에 배정될 확률이 같도록 무작위로 배정해야 하고, 두 집단의 사람들이 감기와 관련하여 비슷하고 같은 기록을 가지고 있도록 해야 한다는 내용의 글이다. 이러한 글의 내용을 가장 잘 나타낸 제목으로는 ② 'Don't Let Irrelevant Factors Influence the Results!(관련 없는 요인이 결과에 영향을 미치지 않도록 하라!)'가 가장 적절하다.

정답률 

8. ⑤

문제풀이

연구를 할 때, 연구 결과에 외부 요인이 영향을 미치지 않도록 실험군과 통제군을 임의로 분류하는 것과 감기와 관련된 비슷한 기록을 가지고 있는 것이 중요하다고 했다. 따라서 영양분을 포함하는 실험에서도 두 집단의 식단이 다르면 비타민 C 보충제의 효과를 분명하게 알 수 없기 때문에 두 집단의 식단은 비슷하거나 같아야 하므로, (e) 'different(다른)'를 'similar(비슷한)'와 같은 낱말로 바꾸어야 한다.

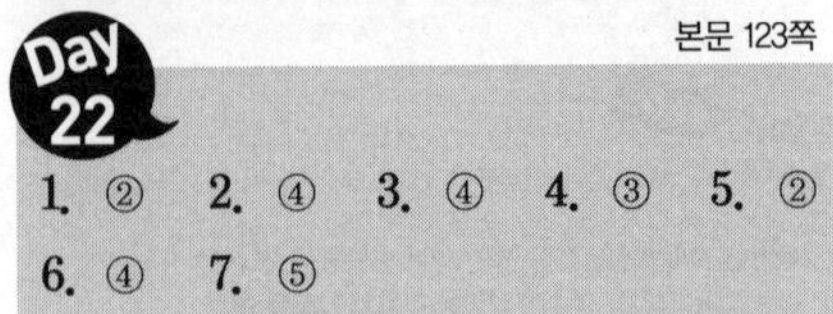

본문 123쪽

1. ② 2. ④ 3. ④ 4. ③ 5. ②
6. ④ 7. ⑤

정답률 39%

1. ② 유전 공학이 자연의 다양성에 끼치는 긍정적인 영향

직독/직해

Genetic engineering followed by cloning /
복제로 이어지는 유전 공학은 /
to distribute many identical animals or plants /
많은 똑같은 동물들이나 식물들을 퍼뜨리기 위한 /
is sometimes seen as a threat / to the diversity of nature.
때때로 위협으로 간주된다 / 자연의 다양성에 대한
However, humans have been replacing diverse natural habitats /
하지만 인간은 다양한 자연 서식지를 대체해 오고 있다 /
with artificial monoculture / for millennia.
인위적인 단일 경작으로 / 수천 년 동안
Most natural habitats in the advanced nations /
선진국에 있는 자연 서식지의 대부분은 /
have already been replaced / 이미 대체되었다 /
with some form of artificial environment /
어떤 형태의 인위적인 환경으로 /
based on mass production or repetition.
대량 생산 혹은 반복에 기반을 둔
The real threat to biodiversity / is surely the need /
생물 다양성에 대한 진정한 위협은 / 필요성임이 확실하다 /
to convert ever more of our planet /
지구의 더 많은 부분을 전환해야 할 /
into production zones / 생산 지대로 /
to feed the ever-increasing human population.
계속 늘어나는 인구에 식량을 공급하기 위해
The cloning and transgenic alteration of domestic animals /
가축의 복제와 이식 유전자에 의한 변형은 /
makes little difference / to the overall situation.
거의 변화를 만들어내지 않는다 / 전반적인 상황에
Conversely, / the renewed interest in genetics /
반대로 / 유전학에 관한 새로워진 관심은 /
has led to a growing awareness /
인식을 점점 키웠다 /
that there are many wild plants and animals /
많은 야생 동식물이 있다는 /
with interesting or useful genetic properties /
흥미롭거나 유용한 유전 특성을 가진 /
that could be used / 이용될 수 있는 /
for a variety of as-yet-unknown purposes.
아직 알려지지 않은 다양한 목적을 위해
This has led in turn to a realization /
이것은 결국 깨닫게 해 주었다 /
that we should avoid destroying natural ecosystems /
우리가 자연 생태계를 파괴하는 것을 피해야 한다는 것을 /
because they may harbor tomorrow's drugs /
그것들이 미래의 약을 품고 있을 수도 있으므로 /
against cancer, malaria, or obesity.
자연 생태계가 암이나 말라리아 또는 비만에 맞서는

많은 똑같은 동물들이나 식물들을 퍼뜨리기 위한 복제로 이어지는 유전 공학은 때때로 자연의 다양성에 대한 위협으로 간주된다. 하지만 인간은 수천 년 동안 인위적인 단일 경작으로 다양한 자연 서식지를 대체해 오고 있다. 선진국에 있는 자연 서식지의 대부분은 대량 생산 혹은 반복에 기반을 둔 어떤 형태의 인위적인 환경으로 이미 대체되었다. 생물 다양성에 대한 진정한 위협은 계속 늘어나는 인구에 식량을 공급하기 위해 지구의 더 많은 부분을 생산 지대로 전환해야 할 필요성임이 확실하다. 가축의 복제와 이식 유전자에 의한 변형은 전반적인 상황에 거의 변화를 만들어내지 않는다. 반대로, 유전학에 관한 새로워진 관심은 아직 알려지지 않은 다양한 목적을 위해 이용될 수 있는 흥미롭거나 유용한 유전 특성을 가진 많은 야생 동식물이 있다는 인식을 점점 키웠다. 이것은 결국 자연 생태계가 암이나 말라리아 또는 비만에 맞서는 미래의 약을 품고 있을 수도 있으므로 자연 생태계를 파괴하는 것을 피해야 한다는 것을 깨닫게 해 주었다.

① 생태계는 유전적으로 프로그램되어 있다
② 자연 생태계를 파괴하는 것을 피해야 한다
③ 유전자 변형 생물을 만드는 것을 중단할 필요가 있다
④ 인위적인 생물은 자연환경에서 생존할 수 있다
⑤ 살아있는 것들은 자신의 물리적 환경에 적응한다

문제풀이

유전 공학이 때때로 자연의 다양성에 대한 위협으로 간주되지만, 수천 년 동안 이어진 인위적인 단일 경작이 생물 다양성의 진정한 위협이며 가축 복제와 이식 유전자에 의한 변형은 전반적인 상황에 거의 변화를 주지 않고 오히려 유전학 덕분에 치료 약과 같이 앞으로 다양하게 이용될 수 있는 유전 특성을 가진 야생 생물에 관심과 인식이 커지게 되었고 자연 생태계 보존에 대한 인식을 주었다고 했다. 따라서 빈칸에는 ② 'we should avoid destroying natural ecosystems'가 들어가서, 빈칸을 포함한 문장이 '이것은 결국 자연 생태계가 암이나 말라리아 또는 비만을 치료하는 미래의 약을 품고 있을 수도 있으므로 자연 생태계를 파괴하는 것을 피해야 한다는 것을 깨닫게 해 주었다.'가 되는 것이 가장 적절하다.

어휘·어구

genetic engineering 유전 공학
cloning 복제
distribute 퍼뜨리다
identical 똑같은
threat 위협
diversity 다양성
habitat 서식지
artificial 인위적인
convert 전환하다
transgenic 이식 유전자에 의한
alteration 변형
domestic 사육되는
overall 전반적인
conversely 반대로
property 특성
in turn 결국
harbor (계획, 생각 등을) 품다
cancer 암
obesity 비만
genetically modified 유전자가 조작된
organism 생물

정답률 39%

2. ④ 점진적 개선을 나타내는 프로토피아

직독/직해

Protopia is a state of becoming, / rather than a destination.
프로토피아는 되어가는 상태이다 / 목적지이기보다는
It is a process. 그것은 과정이다
In the protopian mode, / things are better today /
프로토피아적인 방식에서는 / 오늘 상황이 더 낫다 /
than they were yesterday, / although only a little better.
어제보다 / 비록 단지 약간 더 나아졌을 뿐이더라도
It is incremental improvement or mild progress.
그것은 점진적인 개선이나 가벼운 진보이다
The "pro" in protopian stems /
프로토피아적이라는 말에서 '프로'는 유래한다 /
from the notions of process and progress.
과정과 진보라는 개념에서
This subtle progress is not dramatic, not exciting.
이 미묘한 진보는 극적이지도 않으며 자극적이지도 않다
It is easy to miss / because a protopia generates /
그것을 놓치기 쉽다 / 프로토피아는 발생시키기 때문에 /
almost as many new problems as new benefits.
거의 새로운 이점만큼 많은 새로운 문제를
The problems of today were caused /
오늘의 문제는 야기한 것이다 /
by yesterday's technological successes, /
어제의 기술적 성공이 /
and the technological solutions to today's problems /
그리고 오늘의 문제에 대한 기술적 해결책은 /
will cause the problems of tomorrow.
내일의 문제를 야기할 것이다
This circular expansion of both problems and solutions hides /
문제와 해결책 모두의 이러한 순환적 팽창은 보이지 않게 한다 /
a steady accumulation of small net benefits /
작은 순이익의 꾸준한 축적을 /
over time. 시간이 지나면서
Ever since the Enlightenment and the invention of science, /
계몽주의와 과학의 발명 이래로 계속 /
we've managed to create a tiny bit more /
우리는 조금 더 많은 것을 만들어냈다 /
than we've destroyed each year.
매년 파괴해 온 것보다
But that few percent positive difference is compounded /
하지만 그 작은 몇 퍼센트의 긍정적인 차이는 조합된다 /
over decades / into what we might call civilization.
수십 년에 걸쳐 / 우리가 문명이라고 부를 수 있는 것으로
Its benefits never star in movies.
그것의 이익은 영화에서 주연을 맡아 돋보이는 법이 없다

프로토피아는 목적지이기보다는 되어가는 상태이다. 그것은 과정이다. 프로토피아적인 방식에서는 어제보다 오늘, 비록 단지 약간 더 나아졌을 뿐이더라도, 상황이 더 낫다. 그것은 점진적인 개선이나 가벼운 진보이다. 프로토피아적이라는 말에서 '프로'는 과정과 진보라는 개념에서 유래한다. 이 미묘한 진보는 극적이지도 않으며 자극적이지도 않다. 프로토피아는 거의 새로운 이점만큼 많은 새로운 문제를 발생시키기 때문에 그것을 놓치기 쉽다. 오늘의 문제는 어제의 기술적 성공이 야기한 것이고, 오늘의 문제에 대한 기술적 해결책은 내일의 문제를 야기할 것이다. 문제와 해결책 모두의 이러한 순환적 팽창은 시간이 지나면서 작은 순이익이 꾸준히 축적되는 것을 감추었다. 계몽주의와 과학의 발명 이래로 계속, 우리는 매년 파괴해 온 것보다 조금 더 많은 것을 만들어냈다. 하지만 그 작은 몇 퍼센트의 긍정적인 차이는 수십 년에 걸쳐 우리가 문명이라고 부를 수 있는 것으로 조합된다. 그것의 이익은 영화에서 주연을 맡아 돋보이는 법이 없다.

① 현재의 혁신 한계를 감춘다
② 자신 있게 미래를 예측하는 것을 어렵게 한다
③ 프로토피아적인 문명을 빨리 이루도록 우리에게 동기부여를 한다
④ 시간이 지나면서 작은 순이익이 꾸준히 축적되는 것을 감추었다
⑤ 기술적 성공에서 상당한 변화를 만든다

문제풀이

프로토피아는 약간일 뿐이라도 상황이 과거보다 더 향상되는 과정을 의미하는 말로, 미묘한 진보는 잘 드러나지 않고 어제의 성공이 오늘의 문제를 만들고 오늘의 문제를 해결한 성공이 내일의 문제를 유발하는 문제와 해결책의 순환적 팽창으로 인해 잘 보이지는 않지만 조금이나마 이전보다 나은 것이 쌓여서 문명이란 것을 이룩해왔다고 했다. 따라서 빈칸에는 ④ 'hides a steady accumulation of small net benefits over time'이 들어가서 빈칸을 포함한 문장이 '문제와 해결책 모두의 이러한 순환적 팽창은 시간이 지나면서 작은 순이익이 꾸준히 축적되는 것을 감추었다.'가 되는 것이 가장 적절하다.

이렇게 풀자 'It is easy to miss because a protopia generates almost as many new problems as new benefits.(프로토피아는 거의 새로운 이점만큼 많은 새로운 문제를 발생시키기 때문에 그것을 놓치기 쉽다.)'와 'The problems of today were caused by yesterday's technological successes, and the technological solutions to today's problems will cause the problems of tomorrow.(오늘의 문제는 어제의 기술적 성공이 야기한 것이고, 오늘의 문제에 대한 기술적 해결책은 내일의 문제를 야기할 것이다.)'를 통해 이 글에서 시간이 흐르면서 약간씩 개선이 쌓이는 것은 놓치기 쉽다는 이야기를 하고 있다는 것을 알면 빈칸에 들어갈 말을 유추해낼 수 있다.

《 어휘·어구 》

state 상태
mode 방식
stem from ~에서 유래하다
notion 개념
subtle 미묘한
generate 발생시키다
circular 순환적인
expansion 팽창, 확장
ever since ~이래로 계속
enlightenment 계몽주의
civilization 문명
star 주연을 맡아 돋보이다
conceal 감추다
predict 예상하다
accumulation 축적
considerable 상당한, 많은

정답률 78%

3. ④ 항공 교통 관제 시스템 보안 강화의 중요성

직독/직해

Cyber attacks on air traffic control systems /
항공 교통 관제 시스템에 대한 사이버 공격은 /
have become a leading security concern.
안보의 주요 우려 사항이 되었다
The federal government released a report in 2009 /
2009년에 연방 정부는 보고서를 내놓았다 /
stating / 기술한 /
that the nation's air traffic control system /
국가의 항공 교통 관제 시스템이 /
is vulnerable to a cyber attack /
사이버 공격에 취약하다고 /
that could interrupt communication with pilots /
조종사들과의 통신을 방해할 수 있는 /
and alter the flight information /
그리고 비행 정보를 변경할 수 있는 /
used to separate aircraft /
항공기를 서로 떼어 놓는 데 사용되는 /
as they approach an airport.
그들이 공항에 접근할 때
The report found numerous security problems /
이 보고서는 수많은 보안 문제를 발견했다 /
in airline computer systems, /
항공사 컴퓨터 시스템에서의 /
including easy-to-crack passwords and unencrypted file folders, /
쉽게 풀 수 있는 암호와 암호화되지 않은 파일 폴더를 포함한 /
issues that could give invaders easy access.
즉 침입자에게 쉬운 접근을 줄 수 있는 문제점들을
A cyber attack on air traffic / has the potential /
항공 교통에 대한 사이버 공격은 / 가능성을 가지고 있다 /
to kill many people / 많은 사람을 죽일 수 있는 /
and could cripple the country's entire airline industry.
그리고 국가 전체 항공 산업을 무력하게 만들 수 있다
Unprecedented declines in consumer demand /
소비자 수요의 전례 없는 감소는 /
impacted the profitability of the airline industry, /
항공 산업의 수익성에 영향을 미쳤다 /
changing the face of aircraft travel /
항공기 여행의 면모를 바꿔 놓으면서 /
for the foreseeable future. 예측할 수 있는 미래의
Tightening airline computer security /
항공사 컴퓨터 보안을 강화하는 것이 /
could be even more important /
훨씬 더 중요할 수도 있다 /
than conducting security screenings of passengers, /
승객에 대한 보안 검사를 하는 것보다 /
because in an increasingly cyber-oriented world, /
왜냐하면 점점 더 사이버 지향적인 세계에서 /
plane hijackers of the future /
미래의 비행기 납치범들은 /
may not even be on board.
비행기에 탑승해 있지 않을 수도 있기 때문에

항공 교통 관제 시스템에 대한 사이버 공격은 안보의 주요 우려 사항이 되었다. ① 2009년에 연방 정부는 국가의 항공 교통 관제 시스템이 조종사들과의 통신을 방해하고 항공기가 공항에 접근할 때 그것들을 서로 떼어 놓는 데 사용되는 비행 정보를 변경할 수 있는 사이버 공격에 취약하다고 기술한 보고서를 내놓았다. ② 이 보고서는 쉽게 풀 수 있는 암호와 암호화되지 않은 파일 폴더, 즉 침입자에게 쉬운 접근을 줄 수 있는 문제점을 포함한 항공사 컴퓨터 시스템에서의 수많은 보안 문제를 발견했다. ③ 항공 교통에 대한 사이버 공격은 많은 사람을 죽일 수 있는 가능성을 가지고 있으며, 국가 전체 항공 산업을 무력하게 만들 수 있다. ④ (소비자 수요의 전례 없는 감소는 항공 산업의 수익성에 영향을 미쳤고, 예측할 수 있는 미래 항공기 여행의 면모를 바꿔 놓았다.) ⑤ 점점 더 사이버 지향적인 세계에서 미래의 비행기 납치범들은 비행기에 탑승해 있지 않을 수도 있기 때문에 항공사 컴퓨터 보안을 강화하는 것이 승객에 대한 보안 검사를 하는 것보다 훨씬 더 중요할 수도 있다.

문제풀이

이 글은 항공 교통 관제 시스템에 대한 사이버 공격이 안보의 주요 우려 사항이 되었다는 내용의 글이다. 하지만 ④는 소비자 수요의 전례 없는 감소가 항공 산업의 수익성에 영향을 미쳤다는 내용이므로 글의 전체 흐름에서 벗어난다.

이렇게 풀자 전체 글의 흐름과 관계없는 문장을 고르는 문제는 대개 첫 문장이 주제문이고 나머지 문장들이 뒷받침 문장이다. 각각의 뒷받침 문장들이 주제문과 관련 있는지 여부를 확인하면 흐름과 관계없는 문장을 쉽게 찾을 수 있다. '항공 교통 관제 시스템에 대한 사이버 공격이 안보의 주요 우려 사항이 되었다.'는 첫 문장이 주제문이다. ①, ②는 그에 대한 보고서에 관한 내용이고, ③은 그 보고서에 따른 우려 사항이 언급되었으며, ⑤는 컴퓨터 보안을 강화하는 것이 중요하다는 결론 문장이지만, ④는 항공 산업의 수익에 관한 내용으로 사이버 공격에 대한 보안 강화와는 관련이 없다.

《 어휘·어구 》

air traffic 항공 교통
leading 주요한, 주된
security 안보, 보안
concern 우려 사항, 관심사
release 내놓다, 발표[공개]하다, 출시하다
vulnerable 취약한
aircraft 항공기
airline 항공사
crack 풀다
access 접근
unprecedented 전례 없는
profitability 수익성
foreseeable 예측할 수 있는
hijacker 납치범
on board 탑승한, 승차한

정답률 58%

4. ③ 협상에 있어 시간적 제약

직독/직해

Any negotiation is bounded / in terms of time /
어떤 협상이든 제한되어 있는데 / 시간이라는 측면에서 /
allocated to it, / 거기에 할당된 /
and time constraints are especially important /
그리고 시간 제약이 특히 중요하다 /
when it comes to constitutional negotiations.
헌법 협상에 관해서는
Constitutions are typically, / though not always, /
헌법은 일반적으로 / 비록 항상 그렇건 아니지만 /
adopted in moments of high political drama, /
고도의 정치적 드라마의 순간에 채택된다 /
perhaps even violent crisis.
어쩌면 심지어 격렬한 위기의 (순간에)
Often there are upstream constraints /
종종 외적인 제약이 있다 /
that limit the amount of time / available to drafters /
시간의 양을 제한하는 / 입안자에게 이용 가능한
—deadlines / 즉 마감 기한 /
that are exogenously fixed and cannot be evaded.
외적인 요인으로 정해져 있는 그리고 피할 수 없는
These constraints may be helpful /
이러한 제약은 도움이 될지도 모른다 /
to facilitate agreement, /
합의를 촉진하는 데 /
as they put pressure on parties / to come to agreement.
그것들은 당사자들에게 압력을 가하기 때문에 / 합의에 이르도록
But they also bound the negotiation /
그러나 그 제약은 또한 협상을 제한한다 /
and prevent the parties /
그리고 당사자들이 ~하는 것을 막는다 /
from spelling out a complete set of arrangements, /
일련의 완전한 합의를 상세히 기술하는 것을 /
and so the constitutional bargain will of necessity be incomplete.
그래서 헌법 협상은 필연적으로 불완전하게 될 것이다
Negotiators may focus only on the largest, most salient issues, /
협상자들은 가장 크고 가장 두드러진 문제에만 집중할지도 모른다
leaving more minor ones unresolved.
더 사소한 것들은 풀리지 않은 채로 내버려 두면서
Time pressures contribute to the introduction of structural mistakes /
시간 압박은 구조적 오류가 들어오는 원인이 되며 /
in the constitutional text, / 헌법 전문에 /
seeding pitfalls for the immediate post-constitution-making period.
헌법 제정 직후 시기 위험의 씨앗이 된다

어떤 협상이든 거기에 할당된 시간이라는 측면에서 제한되어 있는데, 헌법 협상에 관해서는 시간 제약이 특히 중요하다. (①) 헌법은 비록 항상 그렇건 아니지만, 일반적으로 고도의 정치적 드라마, 어쩌면 심지어 격렬한 위기의 순간에 채택된다. (②) 종종 입안자에게 이용 가능한 시간의 양을 제한하는 외적인 제약, 즉 외적인 요인으로 정해져 있으며 피할 수 없는 마감 기한이 있다. (③) 이러한 제약은 당사자들에게 합의에 이르도록 압력을 가하기 때문에 합의를 촉진하는 데 도움이 될지도 모른다. 그러나 그 제약은 또한 협상을 제한하고 당사자들이 일련의 완전한 합의를 상세히 기술하는 것을 막아, 헌법 협상은 필연적으로 불완전하게 될 것이다. (④) 협상자들은 가장 크고 가장 두드러진 문제에만 집중하고 더 사소한 것들은 풀리지 않은 채로 내버려 둔다. (⑤) 시간 압박은 헌법 전문에 구조적 오류가 들어오는 원인이 되며 헌법 제정 직후 시기 위험의 씨앗이 된다.

문제풀이

주어진 문장은 제약이 합의에 이르도록 압력을 가해 합의를 촉진하는 데 도움이 될 수 있다는 내용으로 이용 가능한 시간의 양을 제한하는 외적인 제약을 언급한 문장과 But으로 시작하면서 헌법 협상의 단점을 이야기하고 있는 문장 사이인 ③에 오는 것이 가장 적절하다.

구조 다시보기

도입	헌법 협상에 있어 시간 제약이 중요함
주제	헌법은 보통 피할 수 없는 마감 기한이 있음

장점	마감 기한은 합의를 촉진하는 데 도움이 됨
단점	시간 제약으로 헌법 협상은 불완전하게 됨

어휘·어구

constraint 제약
facilitate 촉진하다
put pressure on ~에 압력을 가하다
party 당사자
negotiation 협상
bind 얽매다, 의무를 지우다
allocate 할당하다
when it comes to ~에 관한 한
constitutional 헌법의
adopt 채택하다
violent 격렬한
upstream constraint 외적인 제약
drafter 입안자
evade 피하다, 모면하다
prevent A from -ing A가 ~하는 것을 막다
spell out ~을 상세히 설명하다
unresolved 미해결의
pitfall 위험, 곤란

5~7 할머니 댁의 옥수수 수확을 도운 아이들

직독/직해

(A) The children arrived / at sunrise /
아이들은 도착했다 / 해가 뜰 때 /
at their grandmother's house.
할머니 댁에
They always gathered / at this time of year /
그들은 항상 모였다 / 이맘때에 /
to assist with her corn harvest.
그녀의 옥수수 수확을 도우려고
In return, / their grandmother would reward them /
보답으로 / 그들의 할머니는 그들에게 보답하곤 했다 /
with a present / and by cooking a delicious feast.
선물로 / 그리고 맛있는 진수성찬을 차림으로써
The children were all in great spirits.
아이들은 모두 아주 활기가 있었다
But not Sally. 그러나 Sally는 그렇지 않았다
She disliked working in the corn field /
그녀는 옥수수밭에서 일하는 것을 싫어했다 /
as she hated the heat and the dust.
그녀는 더위와 먼지를 싫어해서
She sat silently / as the others took a sack each /
그녀는 조용히 앉아 있었다 / 다른 아이들이 각자 자루를 가지고 /
and then sang their way to the field.
그러고 나서 노래를 부르며 밭으로 향할 갈 때
(C) They reached the field /
그들은 들판에 도착했다 /
and started to work happily.
그리고 행복하게 일하기 시작했다
Soon after, / Sally joined them / with her sack.
곧 / Sally는 그들과 함께했다 / 자신의 자루를 가지고
Around mid-morning, / their grandmother came /
오전의 중반쯤 / 할머니는 왔다 /
with ice-cold lemonade and peach pie.
얼음처럼 차가운 레모네이드와 복숭아 파이를 가지고
After finishing, / the children continued working /
다 먹고 난 뒤에 / 아이들은 계속 일했다 /
until the sun was high and their sacks were bursting.
해가 높게 뜨고 자루가 터질 때까지
Each child had to make three trips / to the granary.
아이들은 각자 세 번 이동해야 했다 / 곡물창고로
Grandmother was impressed by their efforts /
할머니는 그들의 노력에 감동하였다 /
and she wanted to give them presents accordingly.
그래서 그녀는 그들에게 선물을 주고 싶어 했다
(B) Sally just wanted / Sally는 그냥 원했다 /
to get her present and leave the field /
그녀의 선물을 받고 밭을 떠나길 /
because she was starting to get hot and feel irritated.
그녀는 덥고 짜증이 나기 시작해서
She had only filled her sack twice, /
그녀는 자루를 두 번만 채웠다 /
but the others were now taking their third sacks /
하지만 다른 아이들은 이제 세 번째 자루를 나르고 있었다 /
to the granary. 곡물창고로
Sally sighed heavily. Sally는 한숨을 푹 내쉬었다
Then an idea struck her.
그때 그녀에게 한 가지 생각이 떠올랐다
To make the sack lighter and speed things up, /
자루를 더 가볍게 만들고 일의 속도를 높이기 위해 /
she quickly filled her last sack / with corn stalks.
그녀는 마지막 자루를 빠르게 채웠다 / 옥수수 줄기로
Sally reached the granary first, /
Sally는 곡물창고에 가장 먼저 도착했다 /
and her grandmother asked her /
그리고 할머니는 그녀에게 요청했다 /
to put aside the final load /
마지막에 가져온 짐을 한쪽에 놓으라고 /
and write her name on it.
그리고 그 위에 그녀의 이름을 쓰라고
(D) Grandmother asked the other children /
할머니는 다른 아이들에게도 ~하게 했다 /
to do the same thing. 똑같이 하게
Then, all of the children enjoyed /
그런 다음 아이들은 즐겼다 /
their grandmother's delicious lunch.
모두 할머니의 맛있는 점심을
"I am so pleased with your work," / she told them /
난 너희들이 한 일 때문에 매우 기뻐 / 할머니가 그들에게 말했다 /
after lunch. 점심 식사 후에
"This year, / you can all take home your final load /
올해에는 / 너희들 모두 마지막에 가져온 짐을 집에 가져가도록 해 /
as a present!" 선물로
The children cheered for joy, / gladly thanked her, /
아이들은 기뻐서 환호했다 / 기꺼이 감사하다고 했다 /
and lifted their sacks to take home.
그리고 자신들의 자루를 들어 올려 집으로 가져갔다
Sally was terribly disappointed.
Sally는 굉장히 실망했다
There was nothing but useless corn stalks / in her sack.
쓸모없는 옥수수 줄기 외에는 아무것도 없었다 / 그녀의 자루에는
She then made the long walk home, /
그러고 나서 그녀는 먼 길을 걸어 집으로 갔다 /
pretending that she was carrying a heavy load.
자신이 무거운 짐이라도 가지고 가는 척하면서

(A) 해가 뜰 때 아이들은 할머니 댁에 도착했다. 이맘때에 그들은 항상 그녀의 옥수수 수확을 도우려고 모였다. 보답으로, 그들의 할머니는 선물로 그리고 맛있는 진수성찬을 차림으로써 그들에게 보답하곤 했다. 아이들은 모두 아주 활기가 있었다. 그러나 Sally는 그렇지 않았다. 그녀는 더위와 먼지를 싫어해서 옥수수밭에서 일하는 것을 싫어했다. 다른 아이들이 각자 자루를 가지고 노래를 부르며 밭으로 향해 갈 때 (a) 그녀는 조용히 앉아 있었다.
(C) 그들은 들판에 도착해서 행복하게 일하기 시작했다. 곧, Sally는 자신의 자루를 가지고 그들과 함께했다. 오전의 중반쯤 할머니는 얼음처럼 차가운 레모네이드와 복숭아 파이를 가지고 왔다. 다 먹고 난 뒤에, 아이들은 해가 높게 뜨고 자루가 터질 때까지 계속 일했다. 아이들은 각자 곡물창고로 세 번 이동해야 했다. 할머니는 그들의 노력에 감동하였고, 그래서 (d) 그녀는 그들에게 선물을 주고 싶어 했다.
(B) Sally는 덥고 짜증이 나기 시작해서 그냥 그녀의 선물을 받고 밭을 떠나길 원했다. (b) 그녀는 자루를 두 번만 채웠지만, 다른 아이들은 이제 세 번째 자루를 곡물창고로 나르고 있었다. Sally는 한숨을 푹 내쉬었다. 그때 그녀에게 한 가지 생각이 떠올랐다. 자루를 더 가볍게 만들고 일의 속도를 높이기 위해, 그녀는 마지막 자루를 옥수수 줄기로 빠르게 채웠다. Sally는 곡물창고에 가장 먼저 도착했고, 할머니는 (c) 그녀에게 마지막에 가져온 짐을 한쪽에 놓고 그 위에 그녀의 이름을 쓰라고 요청했다.
(D) 할머니는 다른 아이들에게도 똑같이 하게 했다. 그런 다음 아이들은 모두 할머니의 맛있는 점심을 즐겼다. "난 너희들이 한 일 때문에 매우 기뻐. 올해에는 너희들 모두 마지막에 가져온 짐을 선물로 집에 가져가도록 해."라고 점심 식사 후에 할머니가 그들에게 말했다. 아이들은 기뻐서 환호했고, 기꺼이 감사하다고 했으며, 자신들의 자루를 들어 올려 집으로 가져갔다. Sally는 굉장히 실망했다. (e) 그녀의 자루에는 쓸모없는 옥수수 줄기 외에는 아무것도 없었다. 그러고 나서 그녀는 자신이 무거운 짐이라도 가지고 가는 척하면서 먼 길을 걸어 집으로 갔다.

어휘·어구

assist with ~을 돕다
harvest 수확
in return 보답으로
reward 보답하다, 사례하다
feast 진수성찬
in spirits 활기 있게
sack 자루
irritated 짜증이 난
sigh 한숨 쉬다
put aside ~을 한쪽에 두다
load 짐
burst 터지다
accordingly 그래서, 그에 맞춰
terribly 몹시
nothing but 오직, 단지 ~일 뿐인
pretend ~인 체하다

5. ②

문제풀이

할머니의 옥수수 수확을 돕기 위해 할머니 댁에 도착한 아이들이 활기차게 자루를 들고 밭으로 갔지만 Sally는 조용히 앉아 있었다는 내용의 주어진 글 다음에, 곧 Sally도 자신의 자루를 가지고 함께 일했고 열심히 일하는 아이들의 노력에 감동한 할머니가 아이들에게 선물을 주길 원했다는 내용의 (C)가 오고, 덥고 짜증이 나기 시작한 Sally가 마지막 자루를 가벼운 옥수수 줄기로 채워 가장 먼저 일을 끝낸 뒤에 할머니가 시키는 대로 마지막 자루에 자신의 이름을 썼다는 (B)가 온 후, 각자 마지막에 가져온 자루를 선물로 가지고 가라는 할머니의 말에 실망한 Sally가 옥수수 줄기만 들어 있는 자루를 가지고 집으로 갔다는 내용의 (D)가 오는 것이 적절하다. 따라서 정답은 ②이다.

6. ④

문제풀이

(a), (b), (c), (e) 모두 Sally를 가리키지만 (d)는 할머니를 가리킨다. 따라서 정답은 ④이다.

7. ⑤

문제풀이

'She then made the long walk home, pretending that she was carrying a heavy load.'에서 Sally는 옥수수 줄기가 담긴 가벼운 자루를 무거운 척하며 집으로 가지고 갔다고 했다. 따라서 글에 관한 내용으로 적절하지 않은 것은 ⑤이다.

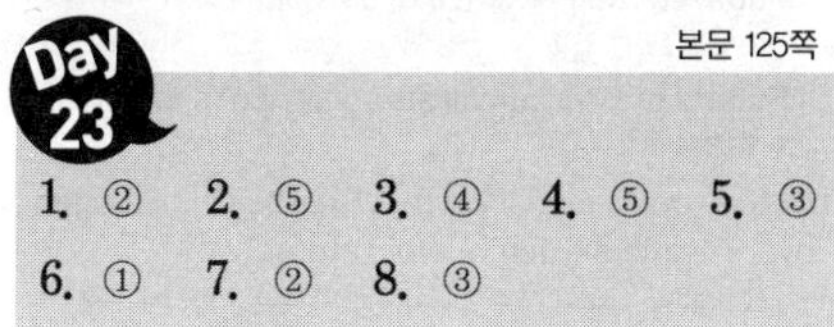

미니 고난도 Test 3회

Day 23 본문 125쪽

1. ② 2. ⑤ 3. ④ 4. ⑤ 5. ③
6. ① 7. ② 8. ③

정답률 33%

1. ② 유라시아 내에의 높은 작물 확산 가능성

직독/직해

Not only was Eurasia by chance blessed / with biological abundance, /
유라시아는 우연히 축복받았을 뿐만 아니라 / 생물학적인 풍부함으로 /

but the very orientation of the continent / greatly promoted the spread of crops /
그 대륙의 바로 그 방향은 / 농작물들의 확산을 크게 촉진했다

between distant regions.
멀리 떨어진 지역 간의

When the supercontinent Pangea fragmented, / it was torn apart along rifts /
초대륙 판게아가 조각났을 때 / 갈라진 틈을 따라 분열되었다 /

that just so happened to leave /
그것은 그저 우연히 남겨두게 되었던 /

Eurasia as a broad landmass running in an east-west direction — /
유라시아를 동서 방향으로 가로지르는 넓은 땅덩어리로 /

the entire continent stretches more / than a third of the way around the world, /
그 전체 대륙은 더 많이 뻗어있다 / 세계를 둘러싼 거리의 3분의 1보다 /

but mostly within a relatively narrow range of latitudes.
그러나 대부분 상대적으로 좁은 위도의 범위 내에서

As it is the latitude on the Earth /
바로 그 지구의 위도이기 때문에 /

that largely determines the climate and length of the growing season, /
기후와 성장 계절의 길이를 주로 결정하는 것이 /

crops domesticated in one part of Eurasia / can be transplanted /
유라시아의 한 지역에서 재배되는 농작물들은 / 옮겨 심겨질 수 있다

across the continent / with only minimal need for adaptation to the new locale.
대륙을 가로질러 / 새로운 장소에의 적응에 대한 단지 최소한의 필요만 지닌 채

Thus wheat cultivation spread readily /
따라서 밀 재배는 손쉽게 퍼져나갔다 /

from the uplands of Turkey / throughout Mesopotamia, /
터키의 고지대로부터 / 메소포타미아 전역을 통과해 /

to Europe, and all the way round to India, / for example.
유럽으로, 그리고 인도에 이르기까지 / 예를 들면

The twin continents of the Americas, / by contrast, /
아메리카의 한 쌍의 대륙은 / 대조적으로 /

lie in a north-south direction.
북남 방향으로 놓여 있다

Here, / the spreading of crops originally domesticated / in one region to another /
이곳에서는 / 본래 재배된 농작물들이 퍼지는 것은 / 한 지역에서 또 다른 지역으로 /

led to a much harder process of re-adapting the plant species /
식물종을 재적응시키는 훨씬 더 어려운 과정을 초래했다 /

to different growing conditions.
다른 성장 환경에

유라시아는 우연히 생물학적인 풍부함으로 축복받았을 뿐만 아니라 그 대륙의 바로 그 방향은 멀리 떨어진 지역 간의 농작물들의 확산을 크게 촉진했다. 초대륙 판게아가 조각났을 때, 그것은 유라시아를 동서 방향으로 가로지르는 넓은 땅덩어리로 그저 우연히 남겨두게 되었던 갈라진 틈을 따라 잘라졌다. 그 전체 대륙은 세계를 둘러싼 거리의 3분의 1보다 더 많이, 그러나 대부분 상대적으로 좁은 위도의 범위 내에서 뻗어있다. 바로 그 지구의 위도가 기후와 성장 계절의 길이를 주로 결정하기 때문에, 유라시아의 한 지역에서 재배되는 농작물들은 새로운 장소에의 적응에 대한 단지 최소한의 필요만 지닌 채 대륙을 가로질러 옮겨 심겨질 수 있다. 따라서 예를 들면 밀 재배는 터키의 고지대로부터 메소포타미아 전역, 유럽으로, 그리고 인도에 이르기까지 손쉽게 퍼져나갔다. 대조적으로 아메리카의 한 쌍의 대륙은 북남 방향으로 놓여 있다. 이곳에서는 한 지역에서 본래 재배된 농작물들이 또 다른 지역으로 퍼지는 것은 식물종을 다른 성장 환경에 재적응시키는 훨씬 더 어려운 과정을 초래했다.

① 고립 **② 방향** ③ 다양성
④ 보호 ⑤ 불안정

문제풀이

유라시아는 동서 방향으로 가로지르는 넓은 땅덩어리, 즉 좁은 위도 범위 내에서 뻗어 있기 때문에 한 지역에서 재배되는 작물들은 대륙을 가로질러 새로운 장소에 옮겨 심겨질 수 있었다고 했다. 따라서 유라시아의 동서 방향으로 긴 것이 작물의 확산을 촉진했다고 볼 수 있으므로, 빈칸에는 ② 'orientation'이 들어가서 빈칸을 포함한 문장이 '유라시아는 우연히 생물학적인 풍부함으로 축복받았을 뿐만 아니라 그 대륙의 바로 그 방향은 멀리 떨어진 지역 간의 작물들의 확산을 크게 촉진했다.'가 되는 것이 가장 적절하다.

어휘·어구

- **by chance** 우연히, 뜻밖에
- **biological** 생물학의
- **abundance** 풍부
- **continent** 대륙
- **promote** 촉진하다
- **tear apart** ~을 분열시키다[떼어 놓다]
- **landmass** 광활한 토지, 대륙
- **relatively** 상대적으로
- **latitude** 위도
- **domesticate** 재배하다
- **transplant** 옮겨 심다, 이식하다
- **adaptation** 적응
- **cultivation** 경작, 재배
- **upland** 고지대

정답률 27%

2. ⑤ 돌연변이의 축적

직독/직해

Imagine / some mutation appears /
상상해 보라 / 어떤 돌연변이가 나타난다고 /

which makes animals spontaneously die / at the age of 50.
동물들을 저절로 죽게 만드는 / 50세에

This is unambiguously disadvantageous— / but only very slightly so.
이것은 분명히 불리하지만 / 아주 약간만 그렇다

More than 99 per cent of animals / carrying this mutation /
99퍼센트가 넘는 동물들은 / 이 돌연변이를 지닌 /

will never experience its ill effects /
절대 그것의 부작용을 경험하지 못할 것이다 /

because they will die / before it has a chance to act.
그것들이 죽을 것이기 때문에 / 그것이 작용할 기회를 갖기 전에

This means / that it's pretty likely to remain in the population — /
이는 의미하는데 / 그것이 개체군에 남아 있을 가능성이 꽤 있다는 것을 /

not because it's good, /
그것이 좋아서가 아니라 /

but because the 'force of natural selection' at such advanced ages /
그러한 고령에 '자연 선택의 힘'이 /

is not strong enough to get rid of it.
그것을 없애 버릴 수 있을 만큼 충분히 강하지 않기 때문이다

Conversely, / if a mutation killed the animals at two years, /
반대로 / 만일 한 돌연변이가 2세에 동물들을 죽여서 /

striking them down /
그것들의 목숨을 앗아 간다면 /

when many could reasonably expect / to still be alive and producing children, /
다수가 마땅히 예상할 수 있을 때 / 여전히 살아서 새끼를 낳을 것이라 /

evolution would get rid of it very promptly: /
진화는 그것을 매우 빠르게 제거할 것이다 /

animals with the mutation / would soon be outcompeted /
그 돌연변이를 지닌 동물들은 / 곧 경쟁에서 뒤처지게 될 것인데 /

by those fortunate / enough not to have it, /
운이 좋은 것들에 의해 / 그것을 가지지 않을 만큼 충분히 /

because the force of natural selection is powerful /
왜냐하면 자연 선택의 힘이 강력하기 때문이다 /

in the years up to and including reproductive age.
번식 연령을 포함해서 (그 연령에) 이르기까지 여러 해 동안

Thus, / problematic mutations can accumulate, /
따라서 / 문제가 되는 돌연변이들은 축적될 수 있다 /

just so long as they only affect animals /
그것들이 동물들에게 겨우 영향을 주는 한 /

after they're old enough to have reproduced.
동물들이 번식했었을 만큼 충분히 나이가 든 후에야

동물들을 50세에 저절로 죽게 만드는 어떤 돌연변이가 나타난다고 상상해 보라. 이것은 분명히 불리하지만 아주 약간만 그렇다. 이 돌연변이를 지닌 99퍼센트가 넘는 동물들은 그것이 작용할 기회를 갖기 전에 그것들이 죽을 것이기 때문에 절대 그것의 부작용을 경험하지 못할 것이다. 이는 그것이 개체군에 남아 있을 가능성이 꽤 있다는 것을 의미하는데, 그것이 좋아서가 아니라, 그러한 고령에 '자연 선택의 힘'이 그것을 없애 버릴 수 있을 만큼 충분히 강하지 않기 때문이다. 반대로, 만일 한 돌연변이가 2세에 동물들을 죽여서, 다수가 여전히 살아서 새끼를 낳을 것이라 마땅히 예상할 수 있을 때 그것들의 목숨을 앗아 간다면, 진화는 그것을 매우 빠르게 제거할 것이다. 그 돌연변이를 지닌 동물들은 그것을 가지지 않을 만큼 충분히 운이 좋은 것들에 의해 곧 경쟁에서 뒤처지게 될 것인데, 왜냐하면 번식 연령을 포함해서 (그 연령에) 이르기까지 여러 해 동안 자연 선택의 힘이 강력하기 때문이다. 따라서 문제가 되는 돌연변이들은 동물들이 번식했었을 만큼 충분히 나이가 든 후에야 그것들이 동물들에게 겨우 영향을 주는 한, 축적될 수 있다.

① 자연 선택의 힘은 동물이 나이가 들수록 증가한다
② 그들의 축적은 주로 그들의 진화적 이점 때문이다
③ 진화는 동물의 번식 성공을 억제함으로써 작동한다
④ 동물들은 그들의 능력의 감소를 신속하게 보충할 수 있다
⑤ 동물들이 번식했었을 만큼 충분히 나이가 든 후에야 그것들이 동물들에게 겨우 영향을 준다

문제풀이

번식 연령 이후인 고령에 돌연변이가 나타나면 자연 선택의 힘이 그것을 없앨 수 있을 만큼 충분히 강하지 않아서 그것이 개체군에 남아 있을 가능성이 높다고 했고, 반대로 번식 연령 이전에 돌연 변이가 나타나면 돌연변이를 지닌 동물은 그렇지 않은 것들에 의해 경쟁에서 뒤쳐질 것이라고 했다. 이는 번식 연령 이후에 이 돌연변이 특성이 발현되어야 돌연변이가 남아 있을 수 있다는 의미이므로, 빈칸에는 ⑤ 'they only affect animals after they're old enough to have reproduced'가 들어가서 빈칸을 포함한 문장이 '따라서 문제가 되는 돌연변이들은 동물들이 번식했었을 만큼 충분히 나이가 든 후에야 그것들이 동물들에게 겨우 영향을 주는 한, 축적될 수 있다.'가 되는 것이 적절하다.

구조 다시보기

도입	50세에 저절로 죽는 돌연변이를 지닌 동물은 돌연변이가 개체군에 남아 있을 가능성이 큼.
부연	2세에 죽는 돌연변이를 지닌 동물은 그렇지 않은 동물과의 경쟁에서 뒤처지게 됨.

결론	돌연변이는 동물이 번식한 후 동물에 영향을 주면 축적될 수 있음.

어휘·어구

spontaneously 자발적으로, 자연스럽게
unambiguously 분명하게
disadvantageous 불리한
slightly 약간, 조금
get rid of ~을 없애다[제거하다]
conversely 정반대로
reasonably 상당히, 꽤
promptly 즉시, 지체 없이
outcompete ~보다 경쟁에서 우월하다
up to ~까지
reproductive 번식의, 생식의
problematic 문제가 있는
accumulate 모으다, 축적하다
so long as ~하는 한
evolutionary 진화의
benefit 혜택, 이득
suppress 억누르다, 억제하다
compensate for 보상하다, 보충하다
decline 감소

정답률 64%

3. ④ 탐지견 훈련 방식

When a dog is trained / 개가 훈련받을 때 /
to detect drugs, explosives, contraband, or other items, / 마약, 폭발물, 밀수품, 또는 다른 물건들을 탐지하도록 /
the trainer doesn't actually teach the dog / 조련사는 실제로 개에게 가르치지 않는데 /
how to smell; / the dog already knows / 냄새를 맡는 법을 / 개는 이미 알고 있다 /
how to discriminate one scent from another. 한 가지 냄새를 다른 냄새와 구별하는 법을
Rather, the dog is trained / 오히려 개는 훈련받는다 /
to become emotionally aroused / 정서적으로 자극을 받도록 /
by one smell versus another. 다른 냄새에 비해 한 가지 냄새에 의해
In the step-by-step training process, / 단계별 훈련 과정에서 /
the trainer attaches an "emotional charge" to a 조련사는 특정한 냄새에 '정서적 흥분'을 부착한다 /
particular scent /
so that the dog is drawn to it above all others. 개가 모든 다른 냄새보다 그것에 끌리도록
And then the dog is trained / 그리고 그런 다음에 개는 훈련된다 /
to search out the desired item on cue, / 마침 때에 맞추어 원하는 물건을 찾도록 /
so that the trainer can control or release the behavior. 그래서 조련사는 그 행동을 통제하거나 풀어줄 수 있다
This emotional arousal is also / 이러한 정서적 자극은 또한 ~이다 /
why playing tug with a dog / 개와 잡아당기는 놀이를 하는 것이 /
is a more powerful emotional reward / 더 강력한 감정적 보상이 되는 이유이다 /
in a training regime / 훈련 관리 체계에서 /
than just giving a dog a food treat, / 단순히 개에게 특별한 음식을 주는 것보다는 /
since the trainer invests more emotion into a game 왜냐하면 조련사가 당기기 게임에 더 많은 감정을 투자하기 때문이다
of tug.
As long as the trainer gives the dog a food reward 조련사가 정기적으로 개에게 먹이 보상을 주는 한
regularly, / the dog can understand / 개는 이해할 수 있다 /
its "good" behavior results in rewards. 자신의 '좋은' 행동이 보상을 초래한다는 것을
From a dog's point of view, / 개의 관점에서 볼 때 /
the tug toy is compelling / 그 잡아당기기 장난감은 흥미를 돋운다 /
because the trainer is "upset" by the toy. 조련사가 장난감에 의해 '화가 나기' 때문에

개가 마약, 폭발물, 밀수품, 또는 다른 물건들을 탐지하도록 훈련받을 때, 조련사는 실제로 개에게 냄새를 맡는 법을 가르치지 않는데, 개는 이미 한 가지 냄새를 다른 냄새와 구별하는 법을 알고 있기 때문이다. 오히려 개는 다른 냄새에 비해 한 가지 냄새에 의해 정서적으로 자극을 받도록 훈련받는다. ① 단계별 훈련 과정에서 조련사는 개가 모든 다른 냄새보다 특정한 냄새에 끌리도록 그 냄새에 '정서적 흥분'을 부착한다. ② 그리고 그런 다음에 개는 마침 때에 맞추어 원하는 물건을 찾도록 훈련되어서 조련사는 그 행동을 통제하거나 풀어줄 수 있다. ③ 이러한 정서적 자극은 또한 조련사가 개와 잡아당기는 놀이를 하는 것이 단순히 개에게 특별한 음식을 주는 것보다는 훈련 관리 체계에서 더 강력한 감정적 보상이 되는 이유인데, 왜냐하면 조련사가 당기기 게임에 더 많은 감정을 투자하기 때문이다. ④ (조련사가 정기적으로 개에게 먹이 보상을 주는 한, 개는 자신의 '좋은' 행동이 보상을 초래한다는 것을 이해할 수 있다.) ⑤ 개의 관점에서 볼 때, 그 잡아당기기 장난감은 조련사가 장난감에 의해 '화가 나기' 때문에 흥미를 돋운다.

문제풀이

탐지견을 훈련시킬 때 냄새를 맡는 법을 가르치기보다는 특정한 냄새에 정서적 자극을 받게 만든다는 내용의 글인데, 조련사가 정기적으로 개에게 먹이 보상을 주면 개가 자신의 좋은 행동 때문에 보상을 받았다고 이해한다는 내용의 ④는 전체 글의 흐름과 관계가 없다.

이렇게 풀자_ 각 문장의 연결이 어색하지 않은지 갑자기 내용이 전환되거나 단절되지 않는지를 꼼꼼히 살피며 글을 읽도록 한다. 여기서는 정서적 자극이 개에게 음식을 주는 것보다 훈련 관리체계에서 더 강력한 감정적 보상이 되는 이유는 조련사가 당기기 게임에 더 많은 감정을 투자하기 때문이라고 한 내용 뒤에 개들이 먹이 보상을 이해하는 방식에 대한 내용이 오는 것은 어색하므로 ④가 정답임을 알 수 있다. 따라서 ④를 제외하고 ③과 ⑤를 연결해 보면 '이러한 정서적 자극은 또한 조련사가 개와 잡아당기는 놀이를 하는 것이 단순히 개에게 특별한 음식을 주는 것보다는 훈련 관리체계에서 더 강력한 감정적 보상이 되는 이유인데, 왜냐하면 조련사가 당기기 게임에 더 많은 감정을 투자하기 때문이다. 개의 관점에서 볼 때, 그 잡아당기기 장난감은 조련사가 장난감에 의해 '화가 나기' 때문에 흥미를 돋운다.'가 되어 글의 흐름이 자연스럽다는 것을 확인할 수 있다.

어휘·어구

detect 탐지하다
explosive 폭발물
discriminate 구별하다
scent 냄새
arouse 자극하다
step-by-step 단계적인
attach 부착하다
emotional charge 정서적 흥분
on cue 마침 때에 맞추어
release 풀어주다
arousal 자극
reward 보상
regime 관리 체계
compelling 흥미를 돋우는

정답률 58%

4. ⑤ 당 분자가 갈색으로 변하는 이유

The reason why any sugar molecule / 당 분자가 ~하는 이유는 /
— whether in cocoa bean or pan or anywhere else / 카카오 열매 안이나 냄비 안, 혹은 다른 어디에 있든 /
— turns brown when heated / 가열되었을 때 갈색으로 변하는 /
is to do with the presence of carbon. 탄소의 존재와 관련이 있다
(C) Sugars are carbohydrates, / which is to say / 당은 탄수화물인데 / 이것은 말한다 /
that they are made of carbon ("carbo-"), hydrogen ("hydr-"), and oxygen ("-ate") atoms. 당이 탄소("carbo-"), 수소("hydr-") 그리고 산소("-ate") 원자들로 이루어졌다는 것을
When heated, / 가열되었을 때 /
these long molecules disintegrate into smaller units, / 이 긴 분자들은 더 작은 단위들로 분해되고 /
some of which are so small / that they evaporate / 이 중 일부는 너무 작아서 / 증발한다 /
(which accounts for the lovely smell). (이것은 좋은 냄새가 나는 이유를 설명해 준다)
(B) On the whole, / it is the carbon-rich molecules / 대체로 / 탄소가 풍부한 분자이다 /
that are larger, / 더 큰 것이 /
so these get left behind, / 그래서 이것이 남게 되고 /
and within these there is a structure / 이 안에는 구조가 있다 /
called a carbon-carbon double bond. 탄소-탄소 이중 결합이라 불리는
This chemical structure absorbs light. 이 화학 구조는 빛을 흡수한다
In small amounts / 적은 양에서 /
it gives the caramelizing sugar a yellow-brown color. 그것은 캐러멜화된 당에 황갈색을 띠게 한다
(A) Further roasting will turn some of the sugar into pure carbon / 더 로스팅하면 일부 당이 순수 탄소로 변하는데 /
(double bonds all round), / (사방에 이중 결합이 있는) /
which creates a burnt flavor and a dark-brown color. 그것은 탄 맛과 진갈색을 만들어 낸다
Complete roasting results in charcoal: / 완전히 로스팅하면 숯이 된다 /
all of the sugar has become carbon, / which is black. 모든 당이 탄소가 되고 / 검은색이 된다

카카오 열매 안이나 냄비 안, 혹은 다른 어디에 있든, 가열되었을 때 당 분자가 갈색으로 변하는 이유는 탄소의 존재와 관련이 있다.
(C) 당은 탄수화물인데, 이것은 당이 탄소("carbo-"), 수소("hydr-") 그리고 산소("-ate") 원자들로 이루어졌다는 것을 말한다. 가열되었을 때, 이 긴 분자들은 더 작은 단위들로 분해되고, 이 중 일부는 너무 작아서 증발한다(이것은 좋은 냄새가 나는 이유를 설명해 준다).
(B) 대체로, 더 큰 것이 탄소가 풍부한 분자라서, 이것이 남게 되고, 이 안에는 탄소-탄소 이중 결합이라 불리는 구조가 있다. 이 화학 구조는 빛을 흡수한다. 양이 적을 때 그것은 캐러멜화된 당에 황갈색을 띠게 한다.
(A) 더 로스팅하면 일부 당이 (사방에 이중 결합이 있는) 순수 탄소로 변하는데, 그것은 탄 맛과 진갈색을 만들어 낸다. 완전히 로스팅하면 숯이 된다. 모든 당이 탄소가 되고, 검은색이 된다.

문제풀이

가열되었을 때 당 분자가 갈색으로 변하는 이유는 탄소의 존재와 관련이 있다는 주어진 글 다음에, 당은 탄소, 수소, 산소 원자들로 이루어진 탄수화물이고, 가열되었을 때 어떤 화학적 변화들이 있는지를 설명하는 (C)가 오고, (C)의 뒤에서 언급된 '작은 분자들은 증발한다'라는 내용을 받아 큰 분자들에 대한 설명을 이끄는 (B)가 온 뒤, 마지막으로 더 로스팅을 하면 일부 당이 순수 탄소로 변한다는 내용인 (A)가 오는 것이 가장 적절하다.

어휘·어구

molecule 분자
be to do with ~와 관련이 있다
presence 존재

carbon 탄소
pure 순수한
burnt (불에) 탄
flavor 맛
charcoal 숯
on the whole 대체로, 전반적으로
structure 구조
chemical 화학적인
absorb 흡수하다
caramelize 캐러멜이 되다
carbohydrate 탄수화물
hydrogen 수소
oxygen 산소
atom 원자
disintegrate 해체되다, 산산조각나다
evaporate 증발하다
account for ~을 설명하다

5. ③ 수를 이용한 크기 비교

직독/직해

We sometimes solve number problems /
때때로 우리는 수 문제를 풀기도 한다 /
almost without realizing it. 거의 깨닫지도 못한 채
For example, / suppose /
예를 들면 / 가정해 보라 /
you are conducting a meeting / and you want to ensure /
여러분이 회의를 주관하고 있다고 / 그리고 확실히 원한다고 /
that everyone there has a copy of the agenda.
그곳에 있는 모든 사람이 의제가 담긴 사본을 갖길
You can deal with this /
여러분은 이것을 해결할 수 있다 /
by labelling each copy of the handout in turn /
그 유인물의 각 사본에 차례대로 적음으로써 /
with the initials of each of those present.
참석한 사람들 각자의 이름 첫 글자들을
As long as you do not run out of copies /
사본이 떨어지지 않는 한 /
before completing this process, / you will know /
이 과정을 끝내기 전에 / 여러분은 알 것이다 /
that you have a sufficient number to go around.
사람들에게 돌아갈 충분한 수의 사본을 갖고 있다는 것을
You have then solved this problem /
그렇다면 여러분은 이 문제를 해결한 것이다 /
without resorting to arithmetic /
산수에 의존하지 않고 /
and without explicit counting.
그리고 명시적인 수 세기 없이
There are numbers at work for us / here all the same /
우리에게 영향을 주고 있는 수가 있다 / 여전히 여기에는 /
and they allow precise comparison of one collection with another, /
그리고 그것이 하나의 집합과 다른 집합을 정확히 비교할 수 있게 하는데 /
even though the members that make up the collections /
그 집합을 구성하는 수들이 /
could have entirely different characters, /
완전히 다른 특징을 가질 수 있어도 /
as is the case here, / 여기의 경우처럼 그러하다 /
where one set is a collection of people, /
한 세트는 사람들의 집합이고 /
while the other consists of pieces of paper.
반면에 다른 세트는 종이로 구성된
What numbers allow us to do /
수가 우리가 할 수 있게 하는 것은 /
is to compare the relative size of one set / with another.
한 세트의 상대적인 크기를 비교하는 것이다 / 다른 세트와

때때로 우리는 거의 깨닫지도 못한 채 수 문제를 풀기도 한다. (①) 예를 들면, 여러분이 회의를 주관하고 있고 그곳에 있는 모든 사람이 의제가 담긴 사본을 확실히 갖길 원한다고 가정해 보라. (②) 여러분은 그 유인물의 각 사본에 참석한 사람들 각자의 이름 첫 글자들을 차례대로 적음으로써 이것을 해결할 수 있다. (③) 이 과정을 끝내기 전에 사본이 떨어지지 않는 한, 여러분은 사람들에게 돌아갈 충분한 수의 사본을 갖고 있다는 것을 알 것이다. 그렇다면 여러분은 산수에 의존하지 않고, 명시적인 수 세기 없이 이 문제를 해결한 것이다. (④) 그래도 여기에는 우리에게 영향을 주고 있는 수가 있고 그것이 하나의 집합과 다른 집합을 정확히 비교할 수 있게 하는데, 그 집합을 구성하는 것들이 한 세트는 사람들의 집합이고 다른 세트는 종이로 구성된 여기의 경우처럼 완전히 다른 특징을 가질 수 있어도 그러하다. (⑤) 수가 우리가 할 수 있게 하는 것은 한 세트의 상대적인 크기를 다른 세트와 비교하는 것이다.

문제풀이

주어진 문장은 이 과정을 끝내기 전에 사본이 떨어지지 않는 한 충분한 수의 사본이 있다는 것을 알 것이라는 내용으로, 유인물 사본이 충분하게 있는지 알기 위해 그것들에 참석자의 이름 첫 글자를 적어서 해결할 수 있다는 내용과 산수와 수 세기 없이 문제를 해결한 것이라는 내용 사이인 ③에 오는 것이 적절하다. 주어진 문장에서 'this process'는 '사람들에게 유인물 사본을 확실히 갖게 하기 위해 참석자 각자의 이름 첫 글자들을 적는 과정'을 의미하므로, 그 과정을 자세히 언급한 문장 뒤에 와야 한다.

구조 다시보기

도입	인식하지 못한 채 푸는 수 문제가 있음
예시	회의 시 모든 참석자에게 유인물을 배부할 때, 사본에 이름 첫 글자 적어 해결하기
주제	수를 통해 다른 특징을 가진 집합의 상대적 크기 비교 가능

어휘·어구

as long as ~하는 한
run out of ~이 떨어지다
sufficient 충분한
go around (사람들에게 몫이) 돌아가다
conduct a meeting 회의를 주관하다
agenda 의제, 안건
handout 유인물
initial 이름의 첫 글자
resort to ~에 의지하다
explicit 명시적인
all the same 그래도, 여전히
comparison 비교
make up ~을 구성하다
character 특징, 특성, 인격, 성격
consist of ~으로 구성되다
relative 상대적인

정답률 71%

6. ① 거짓말 할 때 뇌 변화에 관한 실험

직독/직해

A few scientists from Duke University and University College London / 듀크 대학과 런던 대학의 몇몇 과학자들은 /
decided to find out / what happens inside our brains /
알아내기로 결정했다 / 우리의 뇌 안에서 무슨 일이 일어나는지 /
when we lie. 우리가 거짓말을 할 때
They put people into an fMRI machine /
그들은 사람들을 기능적 자기 공명 영상(fMRI) 기계에 넣었다 /
and had them play a game / 그리고 게임을 하게 했다 /
where they lied to their partner.
그 사람들이 자신의 파트너에게 거짓말을 하는
The first time people told a lie, /
사람들이 처음 거짓말을 했을 때 /
the amygdala weighed in. 편도체가 관여했다
It released chemicals / that give us that familiar fear, /
그것은 화학 물질을 분비했다 / 우리에게 그 익숙한 공포감을 주는 /
that sinking sense of guilt we get / when we lie.
우리가 갖게 되는 그 무거운 죄책감을 주는 / 우리가 거짓말을 할 때
But then the researchers went one step further.
하지만 그러고 나서 연구자들은 한 단계 더 나아갔다
They rewarded people for lying.
그들은 사람들에게 거짓말에 대한 보상을 주었다
They gave them a small monetary reward /
그들은 그들에게 작은 금전적 보상을 주었다 /
for deceiving their partner / 파트너를 속인 것에 대해 /
without them knowing they'd been lied to.
자신이 속았다는 점을 그들이 모르게
Once people started getting rewarded /
일단 사람들이 보상을 받기 시작하자 /
for lying and not getting caught, /
거짓말을 하고 들통이 나지 않은 것에 대해 /
that amygdala-driven sense of guilt /
그 편도체에 의해 유발된 죄책감이 /
started to fade. 사라지기 시작했다
Interestingly, / it faded most markedly /
흥미롭게도 / 그것은 가장 현저하게 사라졌다 /
when the lie would hurt someone else /
거짓말이 다른 누군가에게는 해가 될 때 /
but help the person telling it.
하지만 그것을 말하는 사람에게 도움이 될 때
So people started telling bigger and bigger lies.
따라서 사람들은 점점 더 큰 거짓말을 하기 시작했다
Despite being small at the beginning, /
초기에는 작음에도 불구하고 /
engagement in dishonest acts /
부정직한 행위를 하는 것은 /
may trigger a process / 과정을 유발할 수도 있다 /
that leads to larger acts of dishonesty later on.
이후에 더 큰 부정직한 행위로 계속 이어지는
➡ The experiment above suggests /
위 실험은 보여 준다 /
that when people receive a prize for lying, /
사람들이 거짓말을 하는 것에 대해 상을 받으면 /
their brain chemistry changes, /
그들의 뇌 화학 작용이 변하고 /
affecting their sense of guilt / 그들의 죄책감에 영향을 주어 /
and facilitating engagement in bigger lies.
더 큰 거짓말을 하도록 촉진한다는 것을

듀크 대학과 런던 대학의 몇몇 과학자들은 우리가 거짓말을 할 때 우리의 뇌 안에서 무슨 일이 일어나는지 알아내기로 결정했다. 그들은 사람들을 기능적 자기 공명 영상(fMRI) 기계에 넣고 그 사람들이 자신의 파트너에게 거짓말을 하는 게임을 하게 했다. 사람들이 처음 거짓말을 했을 때 편도체가 관여했다. 그것은 우리에게 그 익숙한 공포감, 우리가 거짓말을 할 때 갖게 되는 그 무거운 죄책감을 주는 화학 물질을 분비했다. 하지만 그러고 나서 연구자들은 한 단계 더 나아갔다. 그들은 사람들에게 거짓말에 대한 보상을 주었다. 그들은 파트너를 자신이 속았다는 점을 모르게 속인 것에 대해 그들에게 작은 금전적 보상을 주었다. 일단 사람들이 거짓말을 하고 들통이 나지 않은 것에 대해 보상을 받기 시작하자, 그 편도체에 의해 유발된 죄책감이 사라지기 시작했다. 흥미롭게도, 그것은 거짓말이 다른 누군가에게는 해가 되지만 그것을 말하는 사람에게 도움이 될 때 가장 현저하게 사라졌다. 따라서 사람들은 점점 더 큰 거짓말을 하기 시작했다. 초기에는 작음에도 불구하고, 부정직한 행위를 하는 것은 이후에 더 큰 부정직한 행위로 계속 이어지는 과정을 유발할 수도 있다.

➡ 위 실험은 사람들이 거짓말을 하는 것에 대해 (A) 상을 받으면, 그들의 뇌 화학 작용이 변하고, 그들의 죄책감에 영향을 주어 더 큰 거짓말을 하도록 (B) 촉진한다는 것을 보여 준다.

① 상 — 촉진한다 ② 상 — 막다
③ 이익 — 저해하다 ④ 불이익 — 장려한다
⑤ 불이익 — 억제한다

문제풀이

처음에 거짓말을 했을 때에는 편도체에서 죄책감을 유발하는 화학 물질을 분비하지만, 거짓말에 대한 금전적 보상이 주어졌을 때에는 편도체에 의해 유발된 죄책감이 사라진다는 것으로 보아, 요약문의 빈칸 (A)에는 'prize(상)'가, (B)에는 'facilitating(촉진한다)'이 들어가는 것이 가장 적절하다.

어휘·어구

weigh in ~에 관여하다
release 방출하다
monetary 금전의
deceive 속이다, 기만하다
fade 바래지다, 사라지다
markedly 현저하게, 두드러지게
engagement 참여, 개입
dishonesty 부정행위, 불성실
affect ~에 영향을 미치다
facilitate 촉진하다

7~8 속이는 소리 내는 자와 듣는 자의 공진화

직독/직해

Evolutionary biologist Richard Dawkins and zoologist John Krebs, /
진화 생물학자인 Richard Dawkins와 동물학자인 John Krebs는 /

in a now classic 1978 paper, / point out /
지금은 고전이 된 1978년 논문에서 / 지적한다 /

that deceptive signaling is, itself, an evolutionary adaptation, /
기만적인 신호 보내기가 그 자체로 진화적 적응이라고 /

a trait that developed in our earliest animal ancestors, /
즉 우리의 가장 초기의 동물 조상에서 발달했던 특성이라고 /

to gain survival and reproductive benefits.
생존과 번식의 이득을 얻기 위해

(Think about / how hostile mammalian and avian vocalizations are built /
~에 대해 생각해 봐라 / 어떻게 적대적인 포유동물과 조류의 발성이 형성되는지 /

upon size bluffing / through lowered pitch and noisy growling — /
크기 허세 부리기에 기반을 두고 / 낮아진 음조와 시끄러운 으르렁거림을 통해 /

a "dishonest signal.")
즉 '속임수의 신호' (를 통해)

According to Dawkins and Krebs, / such false signaling is found /
Dawkins와 Krebs에 따르면 /그러한 거짓 신호 보내기는 발견된다 /

in *all* animal communication: /
'모든' 동물의 의사소통에서 /

the colors flashed by butterflies, / the calls of crickets, /
나비에 의해 휙 내보여지는 색깔 / 귀뚜라미의 울음소리 /

the pheromones released by moths and ants, /
나방과 개미에 의해 방출되는 페로몬 /

the body postures of lizards, and our acoustic signals.
도마뱀의 몸자세, 그리고 우리의 음향 신호

Nature is deceitful.
자연은 기만적이다

Creatures will do / what they can to *not die* — /
생물체들은 할 것이다 / '죽지 않기' 위해 그들이 할 수 있는 것을 /

at least until they've succeeded /
적어도 그들이 성공해 낼 때까지 /

in winning a mate and passing along their genes.
짝을 얻고 자신들의 유전자를 물려주는 것에

But / at the same time, / Dawkins and Krebs tell us, /
하지만 / 동시에 / Dawkins와 Krebs가 우리에게 말하기를 /

the *receivers* of deceptive signals undergo /
기만적인 신호의 '수신자들'은 겪는다 /

their own coevolutionary "selection pressure" / for *detecting* false communications.
그들 자신의 공진화적 '선택압'을 (겪는다) / 거짓의 의사소통을 '감지하기' 위해

The coevolution of voice and ear / initiated a biological "arms race."
목소리와 귀의 공진화가 / 생물학적인 '군비 경쟁'을 시작했다

The "manipulating" vocalizer evolves, / over vast spans of evolutionary time, /
'조작하는' 소리를 내는 자는 진화시킨다 / 진화적 시간의 방대한 기간에 걸쳐 /

finer and finer means for faking, /
속이기 위한 점점 더 정교한 수단을 /

by acquiring greater neurological control / over the vocal apparatus.
더 큰 신경학적 통제를 얻음으로써 / 발성 기관에 관한

Meanwhile, / the listener, / who has his own survival concerns, / gets better /
한편 / 듣는 자는 / 자신만의 생존 염려가 있는 / 더 잘하게 된다 /

at picking out the particular blend of pitch, rhythm, timbre and volume /
음, 리듬, 음색, 그리고 음량의 특정한 조합을 가려내는 것을 /

that marks the vocalizer as a deceiver.
소리 내는 자를 기만자로 특징짓는

This compels / the sender to further refine his "manipulations," /
이것은 강요한다 / 발신자가 자신의 '조작'을 더 정교화하도록 /

which creates further pressure on the receiver /
이는 수신자에게 더한 압박을 만들어 낸다 /

to improve his acoustic "mindreading."
자신의 음향적 '독심술'을 향상하도록

진화 생물학자인 Richard Dawkins와 동물학자인 John Krebs는 지금은 고전이 된 1978년 논문에서 기만적인 신호 보내기가 그 자체로 진화적 적응, 즉 생존과 번식의 이득을 얻기 위해 우리의 가장 초기의 동물 조상에서 발달했던 특성이라고 지적한다. (어떻게 적대적인 포유동물과 조류의 발성이 낮아진 음조와 시끄러운 으르렁거림, 즉 '속임수의 신호'를 통해 크기 허세 부리기에 기반을 두고 형성되는지에 대해 생각해 봐라.) Dawkins와 Krebs에 따르면, 그러한 거짓 신호 보내기는 '모든' 동물의 의사소통, 즉 나비에 의해 휙 내보여지는 색깔, 귀뚜라미의 울음소리, 나방과 개미에 의해 방출되는 페로몬, 도마뱀의 몸자세, 그리고 우리의 음향 신호에서(a) 발견된다. 자연은 기만적이다. 생물체들은 적어도 그들이 짝을 얻고 자신들의 유전자를 물려주는 것에 (b) 성공해 낼 때까지, '죽지 않기' 위해 그들이 할 수 있는 것을 할 것이다. 하지만 동시에 Dawkins와 Krebs가 우리에게 말하기를, 기만적인 신호의 '수신자들'은 거짓의 의사소통을 '감지하기' 위해 그들 자신의 공진화적 '선택압'을 겪는다. 목소리와 귀의 공진화가 생물학적인 '군비 경쟁'을 시작했다. '조작하는' 소리를 내는 자는 발성 기관에 관한 더 큰 신경학적 통제를 (c) 버림(→ 얻음)으로써, 속이기 위한 점점 더 정교한 수단을 진화적 시간의 방대한 기간에 걸쳐 진화시킨다. 한편 자신만의 생존 염려가 있는 듣는 자는 소리 내는 자를 기만자로 특징짓는 음, 리듬, 음색, 그리고 음량의 특정한 조합을 가려내는 것을 (d) 더 잘하게 된다. 이것은 발신자가 자신의 '조작'을 더 정교화하도록 (e) 강요하며, 이는 수신자에게 자신의 음향적 '독심술'을 향상하도록 더한 압박을 만들어 낸다.

어휘·어구

evolutionary biologist 진화 생물학자
zoologist 동물학자
paper 논문
point out 지적하다
deceptive 기만하는, 속이는
adaptation 적응
ancestor 조상
reproductive 번식의
benefit 혜택, 이득
hostile 적대적인
mammalian 포유류의
avian 새의
growling 으르렁거리는
false 가짜의
cricket 귀뚜라미
pheromone 페로몬, 동종 유인 호르몬
moth 나방
lizard 도마뱀
acoustic 음향의
deceitful 기만적인, 부정직한
gene 유전자
undergo 겪다
coevolutionary 공진화의
detect 감지하다
initiate 시작하다, 개시하다
manipulate 조종하다
vast 방대한, 막대한
span 기간, 시간
neurological 신경의, 신경학의
compel 강요하다
trustworthiness 신뢰성, 신용
competition 경쟁
on-going 계속 진행 중인
migration 이주

정답률 

7. ②

① 경고 신호의 신뢰도 저하: 기만 비용
② **속이는 소리 내는 자와 듣는 자의 진화적 경쟁**
③ 속임수의 정글에서 소리 내는 자가 항상 승리자이다!
④ 동물의 세계에서 가장 강한 자만이 거짓 신호를 보낸다.
⑤ 자연에서 진행 중인 군비 경쟁: 이주의 주요 원인

문제풀이

생물체는 생존과 번식의 이득을 얻기 위해 기만적 신호를 보내지만 동시에 그 기만적 신호의 수신자들은 거짓 의사소통을 감지하기 위해 진화하는데, 이때 조작하는 소리를 내는 자는 속이기 위해 점점 더 정교한 수단을 오랜 시간에 걸쳐 진화시키며 듣는 자도 따라서 가려내는 것을 더 잘하게 된다고 했다. 이렇게 기만적 신호의 소리 내는 자와 듣는 자가 같이 진화하는 상황을 가장 잘 나타낸 제목으로는 ② 'Evolutionary Competition Between Deceiving Vocalizers and Detectors(속이는 소리 내는 자와 듣는 자의 진화적 경쟁)'가 적절하다.

정답률 

8. ③

문제풀이

속이는 소리 내는 자의 거짓 의사소통을 감지하기 위해 듣는 자도 공진화함에 따라, 소리 내는 자는 더 잘 속이기 위해서 발성 기관에 관한 더 큰 신경학적 통제를 얻을 것이다. 따라서 (c) 'abandoning(버림)'을 'acquiring(얻음)'과 같은 낱말로 바꿔 써야 한다.

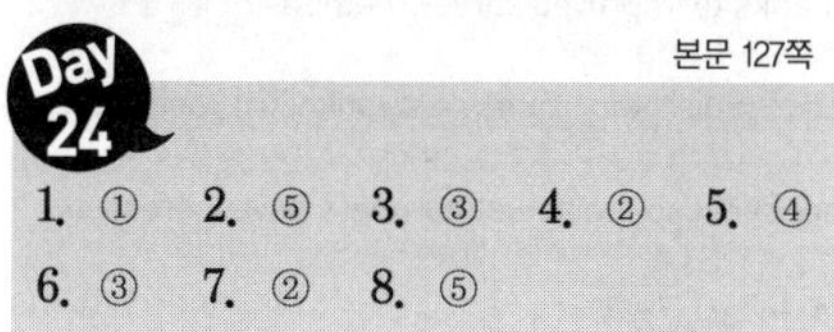

미니 고난도 Test 4회

본문 127쪽

1. ① 2. ⑤ 3. ③ 4. ② 5. ④
6. ③ 7. ② 8. ⑤

정답률 44%

1. ① 신피질의 특징

직독/직해

When you are born, / your neocortex knows almost nothing.
여러분이 태어날 때 / 여러분의 신피질은 거의 아무것도 모른다

It doesn't know any words, / what buildings are like, / how to use a computer, /
그것은 어떠한 단어도 모른다 / 건물이 어떤지 (모른다) / 컴퓨터를 어떻게 사용하는지 (모른다) /

or what a door is / and how it moves on hinges.
또는 문이 무엇인지 (모른다) / 그리고 그것이 경첩에서 어떻게 움직이는지를 (모른다)

It has to learn countless things.
그것은 셀 수 없이 많은 것을 배워야 한다

The overall structure of the neocortex / is not random.
신피질의 전체적인 구조는 / 무작위적이지 않다

Its size, the number of regions it has, /
그것의 크기, 그것이 가지고 있는 영역들의 수 /

and how they are connected together / is largely determined by our genes.
그리고 어떻게 그것들이 함께 연결되어 있는지는 / 우리의 유전자에 의해 주로 결정된다

For example, / genes determine /
예를 들면 / 유전자는 결정한다 /

what parts of the neocortex are connected to the eyes, /
신피질의 어떤 부분들이 눈과 연결되어 있는지 /

what other parts are connected to the ears, /
어떤 다른 부분들이 귀와 연결되어 있는지 /

and how those parts connect to each other.
그리고 어떻게 그 부분들이 서로 연결되는지를 /

Therefore, / we can say / that the neocortex is structured /
따라서 / 우리는 말할 수 있다 / 신피질은 구조화되어 있다고 /

at birth / to see, hear, and even learn language.
태어날 때 / 보고 듣고 심지어 언어를 배울 수 있도록

But it is also true / that the neocortex doesn't know / what it will see, /
그러나 또한 사실이다 / 신피질은 모르는 것 / 그것이 무엇을 볼지 /

what it will hear, / and what specific languages it might learn.
그것이 무엇을 들을지 / 그리고 그것이 무슨 특정한 언어를 배울지

We can think of the neocortex / as starting life /
우리는 신피질을 생각할 수 있다 / 삶을 시작하는 것으로 /

having some built-in assumptions about the world /
세상에 대한 어떤 내재된 가정을 (가졌지만) /

but knowing nothing in particular.
하지만 특별히 아는 것은 없이

Through experience, / it learns a rich and complicated model of the world.
경험을 통해 / 그것은 풍부하고 복잡한 세상 모형을 배운다

여러분이 태어날 때, 여러분의 신피질은 거의 아무것도 모른다. 그것은 어떤 단어도, 건물이 어떤지, 컴퓨터를 어떻게 사용하는지, 또는 문이 무엇이며 그것이 경첩에서 어떻게 움직이는지를 모른다. 그것은 셀 수 없이 많은 것을 배워야 한다. 신피질의 전체적인 구조는 무작위적이지 않다. 그것의 크기, 그것이 가지고 있는 영역들의 수와 어떻게 그것들이 함께 연결되어 있는지는 우리의 유전자에 의해 주로 결정된다. 예를 들면, 유전자는 신피질의 어떤 부분들이 눈과 연결되어 있는지, 어떤 다른 부분들이 귀와 연결되어 있는지, 그리고 어떻게 그 부분들이 서로 연결되는지를 결정한다. 따라서 우리는 신피질은 태어날 때 보고 듣고 심지어 언어를 배울 수 있도록 구조화되어 있다고 말할 수 있다. 그러나 신피질은 그것이 무엇을 볼지, 그것이 무엇을 들을지와 그것이 무슨 특정한 언어를 배울지 모르는 것 또한 사실이다. 우리는 신피질이 세상에 대한 어떤 내재된 가정을 가졌지만 특별히 아는 것이 없이 삶을 시작하는 것으로 생각할 수 있다. 경험을 통해 그것은 풍부하고 복잡한 세상 모형을 배운다.

① 세상에 대한 어떤 내재된 가정을 가진
② 유전자와 환경 사이에 충돌을 일으킨
③ 효율적으로 사전 지식을 재처리할 수 있는
④ 뇌의 구조와 처리 능력을 조절하는
⑤ 유전자의 결정된 세계에 맞서 끈질기게 싸워서

문제풀이

신피질은 태어날 때 보고, 듣고, 언어를 배울 수 있게 유전적으로 구조화되어 있지만 무엇을 보고 듣고, 어떤 언어를 배울지는 모른다고 했으므로, 빈칸에는 ① 'having some built-in assumptions about the world'이 들어가서 빈칸을 포함한 문장이 '우리는 신피질이 세상에 대한 어떤 내재된 가정을 가졌지만 특별히 아는 것이 없이 삶을 시작하는 것으로 생각할 수 있다.'가 되는 것이 가장 적절하다.

어휘·어구

hinge 경첩
overall 종합적인, 전체의
random 무작위의
specific 구체적인
complicated 복잡한
assumption 가정
conflict 갈등, 충돌
efficiently 효율적으로
persistently 끈질기게, 고집스레

정답률 46%

2. ⑤ 데이터 축적의 가치

직독/직해

In the longer term, / 더 장기적으로 /

by bringing together enough data and enough computing power, / 충분한 데이터와 충분한 컴퓨팅 능력을 결합시킴으로써 /

the data-giants could hack /
거대 데이터 기업들은 해킹할 수 있다 /

the deepest secrets of life, /
삶의 가장 깊숙한 비밀들을 /

and then use this knowledge /
그리고 이 지식을 사용할 수 있다 /

not just to make choices for us or manipulate us, /
우리를 위해 선택하거나 우리를 조종할 뿐만 아니라 /

but also to re-engineer organic life /
유기적 생명체를 재설계하기 위해 /

and to create inorganic life forms.
그리고 비유기적 생명체를 만들어내기 위해

Selling advertisements may be necessary /
광고를 판매하는 것은 필요할 수 있다 /

to sustain the giants / 거대 기업들을 지탱하기 위해 /

in the short term, / 단기적으로 /

but they often evaluate apps, products and companies /
하지만 그들은 종종 앱, 제품, 그리고 회사들을 평가한다 /

according to the data they harvest /
그것들이 수집하는 데이터에 따라 /

rather than according to the money they generate.
그것들이 창출하는 돈에 따라서 라기보다는 오히려

A popular app may lack a business model /
인기 있는 앱은 비즈니스 모델이 없을 수 있다 /

and may even lose money /
그리고 심지어 돈을 잃을 수도 있다 /

in the short term, / but as long as it sucks data, /
단기적으로는 / 하지만 그것이 데이터를 빨아들이는 한 /

it could be worth billions.
그것은 수십억의 가치가 있을 수도 있다

Even if you don't know /
심지어 여러분이 모른다 할지라도 /

how to cash in on the data today, /
오늘날 데이터로 어떻게 돈을 벌지 /

it is worth having it / because it might hold the key /
그것을 보유할 가치가 있다 / 그것이 열쇠를 가지고 있을지도 모르기 때문에 /

to controlling and shaping life / in the future.
삶을 통제하고 형성할 수 있는 / 미래에

I don't know for certain / 나는 확실히 알지는 못한다 /

that the data-giants explicitly think about it /
거대 데이터 기업들이 그것에 관해 명시적으로 생각하는지 /

in such terms, / but their actions indicate /
그런 관점에서 / 하지만 그들의 행동은 보여준다 /

that they value the accumulation of data /
그들이 데이터의 축적을 가치 있게 여긴다는 것을 /

more than mere dollars and cents.
단지 돈보다 더

더 장기적으로, 충분한 데이터와 충분한 컴퓨팅 능력을 결합시킴으로써 거대 데이터 기업들은 삶의 가장 깊숙한 비밀들을 해킹할 수 있고, 이 지식을 우리를 위해 선택하거나 우리를 조종할 뿐만 아니라 유기적 생명체를 재설계하고 비유기적 생명체를 만들어내기 위해 사용할 수 있다. 광고를 판매하는 것은 단기적으로 거대 기업들을 지탱하기 위해 필요할 수 있지만, 거대 기업들은 종종 앱, 제품, 그리고 회사들을 그것들이 창출하는 돈에 따라서 라기보다는 오히려 그것들이 수집하는 데이터에 따라 평가한다. 인기 있는 앱은 비즈니스 모델이 없고 단기적으로는 심지어 돈을 잃을 수도 있지만, 그것이 데이터를 빨아들이는 한 수십억의 가치가 있을 수도 있다. 심지어 여러분이 오늘날 데이터로 어떻게 돈을 벌지 모른다 할지라도, 데이터가 미래에는 삶을 통제하고 형성할 수 있는 열쇠를 가지고 있을지도 모르기 때문에 그것을 보유할 가치가 있다. 나는 거대 데이터 기업들이 데이터에 관해 그런 관점에서 명시적으로 생각하는지 확실히 알지는 못하지만, 그들의 행동은 그들이 데이터의 축적을 단지 돈보다 더 가치 있게 여긴다는 것을 보여준다.

① 데이터의 민주화에 대한 필요성을 인정한다
② 단기간의 손실의 장기적인 영향을 과소평가한다
③ 데이터를 귀중한 자산이 아닌, 기업의 부산물로 취급한다
④ 광고를 팔아 이윤을 낼 수 있는 수익에만 집중한다
⑤ 데이터의 축적을 단지 돈보다 더 가치 있게 여긴다

문제풀이

거대 데이터 기업들은 앱이나 제품 등이 창출하는 돈보다는 그것들이 수집하는 데이터에 따라 평가를 하고, 인기 있는 앱이 돈을 잃을지라도 데이터를 갖게 되는 한 수십억의 가치가 있을 수 있기 때문에 데이터를 보유하는 것이 중요하다는 내용이다. 따라서 빈칸에 ⑤ 'value the accumulation of data more than mere dollars and cents'가 들어가서 빈칸이 포함되는 문장이 '나는 거대 데이터 기업들이 데이터에 관해 그런 관점에서 명시적으로 생각하는지 확실히 알지는 못하지만, 그들의 행동은 그들이 데이터의 축적을 단지 돈보다 더 가치 있게 여긴다는 것을 보여준다.'가 되는 것이 가장 적절하다.

이렇게 풀자 빈칸 바로 앞 문장인 'Even if you don't know how to cash in on the data today, it is worth having it because it might hold the key to controlling and shaping life in the future.(심지어 여러분이 오늘날 데이터로 어떻게 돈을 벌지 모른다 할지라도, 데이터가 미래에는 삶을 통제하고 형성할 수 있는 열쇠를 가지고 있을지도 모르기 때문에 그것을 보유할 가치가 있다.)'로 보아 거대 데이터 기업들은 데이터의 축적을 돈보다 가치 있게 여긴다는 것을 추론할 수 있다.

어휘·어구

in the long term 장기적으로
bring together ~을 묶다, 합치다
hack 해킹하다
manipulate 조종하다
re-engineer 재설계하다

organic 유기적인, 유기물의
inorganic 비유기적인, 무기물의
advertisement 광고
sustain 지속하다
in the short term 단기적으로
evaluate 평가하다
harvest 거둬들이다, 획득하다
generate 발생시키다, 생성하다
suck 빨아들이다
shape 형성하다
explicitly 명시적으로
acknowledge 인정하다
democratization 민주화
underestimate 과소평가하다
by-product 부산물
operation 기업, 사업체
valuable 귀중한
asset 자산
return 이익
accumulation 축적

정답률 69%

3. ③ 신체적 우수함을 추구하는 예술과 스포츠

직독/직해

In the case of classical music performance, /
클래식 곡 연주의 경우에 /
notwithstanding the perhaps increased psychological pressure /
아마 가중된 심리적 압박에도 불구하고 /
to achieve "perfection," / to a large extent /
'완벽'에 이르려는 / 상당한 정도까지 /
it is the participation in a physical pursuit of excellence /
바로 탁월함을 신체적으로 추구하는 것에서의 관여이다 /
that links art to sports.
예술을 스포츠와 연결해 주는 것은
Musicians and athletes both /
음악가들과 운동선수들은 모두 /
must attempt to create mistake-free performances /
실수 없는 수행을 만들어 내려고 시도해야 한다 /
that require finely tuned neural and muscle control /
세밀하게 조절된 신경과 근육의 통제를 필요로 하는 /
enabled by countless hours of practice.
셀 수 없이 많은 시간 동안의 연습을 통해 가능해지는.
For both activities, / disciplining the body and mind is central /
두 활동 모두에서 / 신체와 정신을 훈련시키는 것이 핵심적이다 /
to achieving / 달성하는 데에 있어서 /
what is typically considered a successful performance.
일반적으로 성공적인 수행이라고 여겨지는 것을
Standard descriptions of the actions of the muscles /
근육의 움직임에 대한 일반적 기술은 /
controlling the hand / 손을 통제하는 /
can give a misleading impression /
잘못된 인상을 줄 수 있다 /
of the degree / 정도에 대해 /
to which the fingers can be controlled independently.
손가락이 독립적으로 통제될 수 있는
Indeed one might assume /
사실 사람들은 생각할 수 있다 /
that one of the prime objectives of art, / as in sports, /
예술의 주된 목표 중 하나가 / 스포츠에서처럼 /
is to win recognition / 인정받는 것이라고 /
for the artist/performer's technical physical ability.
예술가/연주자가 가진 신체의 기술적 능력에 대해
Thus, in essence, / 따라서 본질적으로 /
even music becomes a competition for performers, /
연주자에게는 음악조차도 경쟁이 되어서 /
who compete against their own bodies, /
그들은 자기 자신의 신체와 겨룬다 /
if not those of others, / 다른 사람의 신체는 아닐지라도
in attaining recognition for their performances.
자기 자신의 연주에 대한 인정을 얻는 과정에서

클래식 곡 연주의 경우에 아마 '완벽'에 이르려는 가중된 심리적 압박에도 불구하고, 상당한 정도까지, 예술을 스포츠와 연결해 주는 것은 바로 탁월함을 신체적으로 추구하는 것에 관여한다는 것이다. ① 음악가들과 운동선수들은 모두, 셀 수 없이 많은 시간 동안의 연습을 통해 가능해지는, 세밀하게 조절된 신경과 근육의 통제를 필요로 하는 실수 없는 수행을 만들어내려고 시도해야 한다. ② 두 활동 모두에서, 신체와 정신을 훈련시키는 것이 일반적으로 성공적인 수행이라고 여겨지는 것을 달성하는 데에 있어서 핵심적이다. ③ (손을 통제하는 근육의 움직임에 대한 일반적 기술은 손가락이 독립적으로 통제될 수 있는 정도에 대해 잘못된 인상을 줄 수 있다.) ④ 사실 사람들은 예술의 주된 목표 중 하나가 스포츠에서처럼 예술가/연주자가 가진 신체의 기술적 능력에 대해 인정받는 것이라고 생각할 수 있다. ⑤ 따라서 본질적으로 연주자에게는 음악조차도 경쟁이 되어서, 그들은 자기 자신의 연주에 대한 인정을 얻는 과정에서 다른 사람의 신체는 아닐지라도 자기 자신의 신체와 겨룬다.

문제풀이

예술과 스포츠는 모두 신체적으로 탁월함을 추구한다는 내용의 글이다. 따라서 손을 통제하는 근육의 움직임에 대한 기술이 손가락이 개별적으로 통제될 수 있는 정도에 오해를 불러일으킬 수 있다는 내용의 ③은 글의 내용과 관계가 없다.

이렇게 풀자 각 문장이 어색하지 않은지 갑자기 내용이 전환되거나 단절되지 않는지를 꼼꼼히 살피며 글을 읽도록 한다. 여기서는 예술과 스포츠 활동에서 신체와 정신의 훈련이 중요하다는 내용 다음에 손 근육의 움직임이 손가락이 개별적으로 통제될 정도에 오해를 줄 수 있다는 내용이 오는 것은 어색하므로 ③이 정답임을 알 수 있다. 따라서 ③을 제외하고 ②와 ④를 연결해 보면 '두 활동 모두에서, 신체와 정신을 훈련하는 것이 일반적으로 성공적인 수행이라고 여겨지는 것을 달성하는 데에 있어서 핵심적이다. 사실 사람들은 예술의 주된 목표 중 하나가 스포츠에서처럼 예술가/연주자가 가진 신체의 기술적 능력에 대해 인정받는 것이라고 생각할 수 있다.'가 되어 글의 흐름이 자연스럽다는 것을 확인할 수 있다.

어휘·어구

notwithstanding ~에도 불구하고
pursuit 추구
finely 섬세하게, 정교하게
neural 신경의
countless 셀 수 없이 많은
discipline 단련하다
misleading 오해의 소지가 있는
impression 인상
objective 목표
competition 경쟁
attain 이루다, 획득하다

4. ② 오랑우탄 개체 수의 감소

직독/직해

In the 1980s and '90s, / some conservationists predicted /
1980년대와 90년대에 / 몇몇 환경 보호 활동가들은 예측했다 /
that orangutans would go extinct /
오랑우탄이 멸종될 것으로 /
in the wild within 20 or 30 years.
20년이나 30년 이내에 야생에서
Fortunately that didn't happen.
다행히 그런 일은 발생하지 않았다
Many thousands more orangutans /
수천 마리나 더 많은 오랑우탄이 /
are now known to exist /
현재 현존하는 것으로 알려져 있다 /
than were recognized / at the turn of the millennium.
인지되었던 것보다 / 밀레니엄의 전환기에
(B) This doesn't mean /
이것이 의미하는 것은 아니다 /
that all is well in the orangutans' world.
오랑우탄의 세계에 아무 문제가 없다는 것을
The higher figures come /
더 높은 수치는 나온 것이다 /
thanks to improved survey methods /
향상된 조사 기법들 덕분에 /
and the discovery of previously unknown populations, /
그리고 이전에는 알려지지 않았던 개체들의 발견 (덕분에) /
not because the actual numbers have increased.
실제 개체 수가 증가했기 때문이 아니라.
(A) In fact, / 실제로 /
the overall population of orangutans has fallen /
오랑우탄의 전체 개체 수는 감소했다 /
by at least 80 percent / in the past 75 years.
적어도 80% / 지난 75년 동안
It's indicative of the difficulty of orangutan research /
오랑우탄 연구의 어려움을 보여준다 /
that scientist Erik Meijaard is willing to say /
과학자인 Erik Meijaard가 말하는 것을 개의치 않는 것은 /
only that between 40,000 and 100,000 live on Borneo.
40,000마리에서 100,000마리 사이의 오랑우탄이 보르네오섬에 살고 있다고만
Conservationists on Sumatra estimate /
수마트라섬의 환경 보호 활동가들은 추측한다 /
that only 14,000 survive there.
단지 14,000마리만 거기에서 생존하고 있다고
(C) Much of this loss has been driven /
이런 감소의 많은 부분은 초래되었다 /
by habitat destruction from logging /
벌목으로 인한 서식지 파괴에 의해 /
and the rapid spread of vast plantations of oil palm, /
그리고 기름 야자나무의 광대한 재배 농장의 급속한 확산(으로 인해) /
the fruit of which is sold to make oil /
기름을 만들기 위해 판매되는 열매인 /
used in cooking and in many food products.
요리와 많은 식품에 사용되는

1980년대와 90년대에, 몇몇 환경 보호 활동가들은 오랑우탄이 20년이나 30년 이내에 야생에서 멸종될 것으로 예측했다. 다행히 그런 일은 발생하지 않았다. 밀레니엄의 전환기에 인지되었던 것보다 수천 마리나 더 많은 오랑우탄이 현재 현존하는 것으로 알려져 있다.
(B) 이것이 오랑우탄의 세계에 아무 문제가 없다는 것을 의미하는 것은 아니다. 더 높은 수치는 실제 개체 수가 증가했기 때문이 아니라, 향상된 조사 기법들과 이전에는 알려지지 않았던 개체들의 발견 덕분에 나온 것이다.
(A) 실제로, 오랑우탄의 전체 개체 수는 지난 75년 동안 적어도 80% 감소했다. 과학자인 Erik Meijaard가 40,000마리에서 100,000마리 사이의 오랑우탄이 보르네오섬에 살고 있다고만 말하는 것을 개의치 않는 것은 오랑우탄 연구의 어려움을 보여준다. 수마트라섬의 환경 보호 활동가들은 단지 14,000마리만 거기에서 생존하고 있다고 추측한다.
(C) 이런 감소의 많은 부분은 벌목으로 인한 서식지 파괴와, 요리와 많은 식품에 사용되는 기름을 만들기 위해 판매되는 열매를 맺는 기름 야자나무의 광대한 재배 농장의 급속한 확산 때문에 초래되었다.

문제풀이

환경 보호 활동가들의 예측과는 달리 더 많은 오랑우탄이 현존한다는 주어진 글 다음에, 예상보다 더 많은 수가 존재한다는 것은 향상된 조사 기법과 새로운 개체들의 발견 덕분이라는 내용의 (B)가 오고, 오랑우탄의 감소한 개체 수에 관해 구체적으로 진술하는 (A)가 온 뒤, 감소의 원인에 관해 설명하는 (C)가 마지막에 오는 것이 가장 적절하다.

이렇게 풀자 (B)의 'This'는 주어진 문장의 뒷부분에 서술된 '수천 마리나 더 많은 오랑우탄이 현존하는 것으로 알려져 있다'를 받기 때문에 주어진 문장 뒤에 (B)가 와야 하고, (C)의 'loss'는 (A)에서 언급된 오랑우탄의 전체 개체 수가 감소했다는 것을 의미하므로 (A) 뒤에 (C)가 와야 한다.

어휘·어구

conservationist 환경 보호 활동가
predict 예측하다

go extinct 멸종되다
indicative ~을 나타내는
be willing to do 기꺼이 ~하다
estimate 추정하다
figure 수치
thanks to ~ 덕분에
survey method 조사 방법
habitat 서식지
destruction 파괴
logging 벌목
vast 방대한
plantation 농장
oil palm 기름 야자나무

5. ④ 진화하는 영화 문법

직독/직해

Film has no grammar. 영화는 문법을 가지고 있지 않다
There are, however, some vaguely defined rules of usage / 하지만 어렴풋이 정의된 몇 가지 규칙이 있다 /
in cinematic language, / and the syntax of film — / 영화 언어 사용에 관한 / 그리고 영화의 문법 /
its systematic arrangement — / orders these rules / 그것의 체계적인 방식은 / 이 규칙들을 정리한다 /
and indicates relationships among them. 그리고 그것들 사이의 관계를 나타낸다
As with written and spoken languages, / 문어와 구어에서처럼 /
it is important to remember / 기억하는 것이 중요하다 /
that the syntax of film is a result of its usage, / 영화의 문법은 그것에서의 사용의 결과물이라는 것을 /
not a determinant of it. 그것의 결정 요인은 아니라는 것을
There is nothing preordained / about film syntax. 미리 정해진 것은 아무것도 없다 / 영화 문법에 관해
Rather, / it evolved naturally / 오히려 / 그것은 자연스럽게 진화했다 /
as certain devices were found / 어떤 방법이 밝혀지면서 /
in practice to be both workable and useful. 실제로 운용할 수 있고 유용하다는 것이
Like the syntax of written and spoken language, / 문어와 구어의 문법처럼 /
the syntax of film is an organic development, / 영화의 문법은 자연스럽게 성장한 것으로 /
descriptive rather than prescriptive, / 규범적이지 않고 기술적이다 /
and it has changed considerably over the years. 그리고 그것은 수년 간 많이 바뀌었다
"Hollywood Grammar" may sound laughable now, / '할리우드 문법'은 지금은 웃기게 들릴 수도 있다 /
but during the thirties, forties, and early fifties / 하지만 30년대, 40년대, 50년대 초반에는 /
it was an accurate model of the way / 그것은 방식의 정확한 모델이었다 /
Hollywood films were constructed. 할리우드 영화가 제작되는

영화는 문법을 가지고 있지 않다. (①) 하지만 영화 언어 사용에 관한 어렴풋이 정의된 몇 가지 규칙이 있고, 영화의 문법, 즉 그것의 체계적인 방식은 이 규칙들을 정리하고 그것들 사이의 관계를 나타낸다. (②) 문어와 구어에서처럼, 영화의 문법은 그것에서의 사용의 결과물이지 그것의 결정 요인은 아니라는 것을 기억하는 것이 중요하다. (③) 영화 문법에 관해 미리 정해진 것은 아무것도 없다. (④) 오히려, 그것은 어떤 방법이 실제로 운용할 수 있고 유용하다는 것이 밝혀지면서 자연스럽게 진화했다. 문어와 구어의 문법처럼, 영화의 문법은 자연스럽게 성장한 것으로 규범적이지 않고 기술적이고, 수년 간 많이 바뀌었다. (⑤) '할리우드 문법'은 지금은 웃기게 들릴 수도 있지만, 30년대, 40년대, 50년대 초반에는 할리우드 영화가 제작되는 방식의 정확한 모델이었다.

문제풀이

주어진 문장은 Rather로 시작하며 영화 문법이 실제 운용할 수 있고 유용하다는 것이 밝혀지면서 자연스럽게 진화했다는 내용으로, 영화 문법이 미리 정해진 것이 아니라는 내용과 영화 문법의 자연스러운 진화에 대한 설명 사이인 ④에 오는 것이 적절하다.

이렇게 풀자 내용의 논리적인 비약이나 단절이 일어나는 곳에 주어진 문장을 넣어 보고 글의 흐름이 자연스럽게 연결되는지 확인해 보면 답을 쉽게 찾을 수 있다. 영화 문법에 관해 미리 정해진 것이 없다는 내용 다음에 영화 문법이 규범적이지 않고 수년 간 많이 바뀌었다는 내용이 오는 것은 어색하다. 따라서 주어진 문장을 ④에 넣어서 자연스럽게 연결되는지 확인해 본다.

어휘·어구

in practice 실제로
device 방법, 장치
workable 운용할 수 있는
vaguely 어렴풋이
cinematic 영화의
syntax 문법, 통사론
indicate 나타내다
determinant 결정 요인
organic 자연스러운, 서서히 생기는
descriptive 기술적인
prescriptive 규범적인
accurate 정확한
construct 건설하다

6~8 급류 타기를 하는 Sophia와 친구들

직독/직해

(A) Fighting against the force of the water / 물의 힘에 맞서 싸우는 것은 /
was a thrilling challenge. 긴장감 있는 도전이었다
Sophia tried to keep herself planted firmly in the boat, / Sophia는 배에 굳건히 자리 잡고 있으려고 애썼다 /
paying attention to the waves / 물결에 주목하면서 /
crashing against the rocks. 바위에 부딪히는
As the water got rougher, / 물이 더 거칠어지자 /
she was forced to paddle harder / 그녀는 더 열심히 노를 저을 수밖에 없었다 /
to keep the waves from tossing her into the water. 물결이 자기를 물속으로 던지지 못하게
Her friends Mia and Rebecca were paddling eagerly / 그녀의 친구들인 Mia와 Rebecca는 열심히 노를 젓고 있었다 /
behind her / 그녀의 뒤에서 /
to balance the boat. 보트의 균형을 맞추려고
They were soaked / from all of the spray. 그들은 흠뻑 젖었다 / 모든 물보라로
Mia shouted to Sophia, / "Are you OK? / Mia는 Sophia에게 외쳤다 / 너는 괜찮니 /
Aren't you scared?" 너는 무섭지 않니
(C) "I'm great!" / Sophia shouted back excitedly. 나는 좋아 / Sophia는 신나서 되받아 외쳤다
Even though the boat was getting thrown around, / 보트가 이리저리 내던져지고 있었지만 /
the girls managed to avoid / hitting any rocks. 그 여자들은 간신히 피했다 / 어떤 바위에도 부딪치는 것을
Suddenly, / 갑자기 /
almost as quickly as the water had got rougher, / 거의 물이 더 거칠어졌던 것처럼 그만큼 /
the river seemed to calm down, / 강이 진정해지는 것처럼 보였다 /
and they all felt relaxed. 그리고 그들은 모두 긴장을 풀었다
With a sigh of relief, / Sophia looked around. 안도의 한숨을 쉬면서 / Sophia는 주위를 둘러보았다
"Wow! What a wonderful view!" / she shouted. 우와! 정말 경치가 멋지다 / 그녀는 소리쳤다
The scenery around them / was breathtaking. 그들 주변의 경치는 / 숨이 멎을 정도였다
Everyone was speechless. 모두가 말이 없었다
As they enjoyed the emerald green Rocky Mountains, / 그들이 에메랄드빛 녹색인 Rocky 산맥을 즐길 때 /
Mia said, / Mia가 말했다 /
"No wonder rafting is the best thing / 급류 타기는 최고의 일인 것은 당연해 /
to do in Colorado!" Colorado에서 하는
(D) Agreeing with her friend, / 친구에게 동의하면서 /
Rebecca gave a thumbs-up. Rebecca는 엄지를 들어 올렸다
"Sophia, your choice was excellent!" / she said / Sophia, 네 선택은 훌륭했어 / 그녀는 말했다 /
with a delighted smile. 기쁨의 미소를 띠면서
"I thought you were afraid of water, / though, / 나는 네가 물을 무서워한다고 생각했어 / 그런데 /
Sophia," / Mia said. Sophia / Mia가 말했다
Sophia explained, / "Well, I was / Sophia는 설명했다 / 음, 나는 무서워했었지 /
before I started rafting. 급류 타기를 시작하기 전에는
But I graduate from college / in a few months. 그렇지만 나는 대학을 졸업해 / 몇 달 뒤에
And, before I do, / 그리고, 그렇게 하기 전에 /
I wanted to do something really adventurous / 나는 진짜 모험적인 것을 해 보고 싶었어 /
to test my bravery. 내 용기를 시험해 볼
I thought / that if I did something completely crazy, / 나는 생각했어 / 만약 내가 완전히 미친 짓을 하면
it might give me more confidence / 그것이 나에게 더 많은 자신감을 줄 거라고 /
when I'm interviewing for jobs." 내가 취업 면접을 볼 때
Now they could see / why she had suggested going rafting. 이제 그들은 알 수 있었다 / 왜 그녀가 급류 타기를 하러 가자고 제안했는지
(B) "You've got a good point. 네 말에 일리가 있어
It's a real advantage / to graduate from college / 정말 이득이야 / 대학을 졸업하는 것은 /
with the mindset of a daring adventurer," / 대담한 모험가의 마음가짐으로 /
Mia said. Mia가 말했다
Rebecca quickly added, / Rebecca는 재빨리 덧붙였다 /
"That's why I went to Mongolia / 그것이 내가 몽골에 간 이유야 /
before I started my first job / out of college. 첫 직장 생활을 시작하기 전에 / 내가 대학을 나와서
Teaching English there for two months / 그곳에서 두 달 동안 영어를 가르친 것은 /
was a big challenge / for me. 큰 도전이었어 / 나에게
But I learned a lot / from the experience. 하지만 나는 많이 배웠어 / 그 경험에서
It really gave me the courage / to try anything in life." 것은 정말 용기를 내게 주었어 / 인생에서 무슨 일이든 시도해 볼
Listening to her friends, / 친구들의 말을 들으면서 /
Sophia looked at her own reflection in the water / Sophia는 물에 비친 자기 자신의 모습을 보았다 /
and saw a confident young woman / 그리고 자신감 있는 젊은 여자를 보았다 /
smiling back at her.

자신에게 미소를 되돌려주는

(A) 물의 힘에 맞서 싸우는 것은 긴장감 있는 도전이었다. Sophia는 바위에 부딪히는 물결에 주목하면서 배에 굳건히 자리 잡고 있으려고 애썼다. 물이 더 거칠어지자, 그녀는 물결이 자기를 물속으로 던지지 못하게 더 열심히 노를 저을 수밖에 없었다. 그녀의 친구들인 Mia와 Rebecca는 보트의 균형을 맞추려고 그녀의 뒤에서 열심히 노를 젓고 있었다. 그들은 모든 물보라로 흠뻑 젖었다. Mia는 Sophia에게 "너는 괜찮니? (a) 너는 무섭지 않니?"라고 외쳤다.
(C) "나는 좋아!"라고 Sophia는 신나서 되받아 외쳤다. 보트가 이리저리 내던져지고 있었지만 그 여자들은 어떤 바위에도 부딪치는 것을 간신히 피했다. 갑자기, 물이 더 거칠어졌던 것처럼 거의 그만큼 빨리 강이 잔잔해지는 것처럼 보였고, 그들은 모두 긴장을 풀었다. 안도의 한숨을 쉬면서, Sophia는 주위를 둘러보았다. "우와! 정말 경치가 멋지다!"라고 (d) 그녀는 소리쳤다. 그들 주변의 경치는 숨이 멎을 정도였다. 모두가 말이 없었다. 그들이 에메랄드빛 녹색인 Rocky 산맥을 즐길 때, Mia가 말했다. "급류 타기는 Colorado에서 하는 최고의 일인 것은 당연해!"
(D) 친구에게 동의하면서 Rebecca는 엄지를 들어 올렸다. "Sophia, 네 선택은 훌륭했어!"라고 그녀는 기쁨의 미소를 띠면서 말했다. "그런데, 나는 네가 물을 무서워한다고 생각했어, Sophia."라고 Mia가 말했다. Sophia는 "음, 급류 타기를 시작하기 전에는 무서워했었지. 그렇지만 나는 몇 달 뒤에 대학을 졸업해. 그리고, 그렇게 하기 전에, 나는 내 용기를 시험해 볼 진짜 모험적인 것을 해 보고 싶었어. 나는 만약 내가 완전히 미친 짓을 하면 취업 면접을 볼 때 그것이 (e) 나에게 더 많은 자신감을 줄 거라고 생각했어."라고 설명했다. 이제 그들은 왜 그녀가 급류 타기를 하러 가자고 제안했는지 알 수 있었다.
(B) "네 말에 일리가 있어. 대담한 모험가의 마음가짐으로 대학을 졸업하는 것은 정말 이득이야."라고 Mia가 말했다. Rebecca는 "그것이 내가 대학을 나와서 첫 직장 생활을 시작하기 전에 몽골에 간 이유야. 그곳에서 두 달 동안 영어를 가르친 것은 나에게 큰 도전이었어. 하지만 (b) 나는 그 경험에서 많이 배웠어. 그것은 정말 인생에서 무슨 일이든 시도해 볼 용기를 내게 주었어."라고 재빨리 덧붙였다. 친구들의 말을 들으면서, Sophia는 물에 비친 (c) 자기 자신의 모습을 보았고 자신에게 미소를 되돌려주는 자신감 있는 젊은 여자를 보았다.

《 어휘·어구 》

thrilling 긴장감 있는
plant 자리를 잡다
crash 세게 부딪치다
rough 거친
toss 내던지다
eagerly 열심히
soaked 흠뻑 젖은
spray 물보라
graduate from ~를 졸업하다
mindset 마음가짐
daring 대담한
courage 용기
reflection (물이나 거울 등에 비친) 모습[상]
manage to do 간신히 ~하다
calm down 진정하다
a sigh of relief 안도의 한숨
scenery 경치
breathtaking 숨이 멎을 정도로 멋진
speechless 말을 못하는, 말로 표현할 수 없는
delighted 기뻐하는
bravery 용감(성)

6. ③

문제풀이

Sophia와 친구 Mia와 Rebecca는 배에서 거친 물결에 맞서 노를 저었고, Mia가 Sophia에게 괜찮은지를 물었다는 내용의 주어진 글 다음에, 이에 Sophia가 괜찮다고 대답했고 잔잔한 강에 도착해서 모두 긴장을 풀고 주변의 멋진 경치를 보며 감탄했다는 내용인 (C)가 오고, 이어서 Sophia가 급류 타기를 하기로 한 이유를 설명하면서 이런 모험적인 것을 해 보면 취업 면접할 때 더 자신감이 생길 거라고 생각했다고 말했다는 내용의 (D)가 온 후, 마지막으로 Rebecca가 자기도 그런 생각으로 몽골에 가서 두 달 간 영어를 가르치는 큰 도전을 해 본 후 인생에서 무슨 일이든 시도해 볼 용기를 얻게 된다고 말했다는 내용의 (B)가 오는 것이 가장 적절하다. 따라서 정답은 ③이다.

정답률 87%

7. ②

문제풀이

(a), (c), (d), (e)는 모두 Sophia를 가리키지만, (b)는 Rebecca를 가리킨다. 따라서 정답은 ②이다.

정답률 81%

8. ⑤

문제풀이

'And, before I do, I wanted to do something really adventurous to test my bravery.'에서 Sophia는 대학 졸업 전에 용기를 시험할 모험을 하길 원했다고 했으므로, 글의 내용으로 적절하지 않은 것은 ⑤이다.

시험 직전까지 꼭 챙겨 봐야 할 영어 오답 Note

틀린 문제를 붙이고 틀린 이유, 몰랐던 단어, 숙어와 문장을 정리하여 나만의 오답노트를 작성해보세요.
꾸준히 작성한 오답노트를 유형별로 분류해보면 자신이 자주 틀리는 유형이 무엇인지, 어떤 실수가 반복되는지 알 수 있어, 자신의 약점을 파악하고 고쳐나가는 데 큰 도움이 됩니다.

시험명 2021년 4월 경기 교육청 **번호** 29 **유형** 어법 문제

2021년 4월 고3 경기교육청

29. 다음 글의 밑줄 친 부분 중, 어법상 틀린 것은? [3점]

The world's first complex writing form, Sumerian cuneiform, followed an evolutionary path, moving around 3500 BCE from pictographic to ideographic representations, from the depiction of objects to ① that of abstract notions. Sumerian cuneiform was a linear writing system, its symbols usually ② set in columns, read from top to bottom and from left to right. This regimentation was a form of abstraction: the world is not a linear place, and objects do not organize ③ themselves horizontally or vertically in real life. Early rock paintings, thought to have been created for ritual purposes, were possibly shaped and organized ④ to follow the walls of the cave, or the desires of the painters, who may have organized them symbolically, or artistically, or even randomly. Yet after cuneiform, virtually every form of script that has emerged has been set out in rows with a clear beginning and endpoint. So ⑤ uniformly is this expectation, indeed, that the odd exception is noteworthy, and generally established for a specific purpose.

* cuneiform: 쐐기 문자 ** regimentation: 조직화

✓ 왜 틀렸나

- □ 단어 / 숙어가 어려움
- □ 문장을 해석하지 못함
- □ 글 내용을 이해하지 못함
- ☑ 문법 사항이 어려움
- □ 기타 (   )

정답 & 오답

***정답**

⑤ 'so 형용사/부사 that' 구문에서 'so 형용사/부사' 부분이 강조되어 도치된 문장이다. 여기서 uniformly는 be동사의 보어이다. 따라서 ★ 부사 uniformly를 형용사 uniform으로 바꿔야 한다.

***내가 고른 오답**

③ 타동사의 목적어가 주어와 같을 경우에는 재귀대명사를 써야 한다.
★ 주어 objects와 목적어가 같으므로, 재귀대명사는 themselves를 사용함.

해석이 안 되거나 어려웠던 문장

1) Sumerian cuneiform was a linear writing system, its symbols usually set in columns, read from top to bottom and from left to right. : 주절의 주어와 분사구문의 주어가 다른 독립분사 구문이다.

2) So uniformly is this expectation, indeed, that the odd exception is noteworthy, ~: 도치 문장으로서 정치된 문장으로 써 보면 'this expection is so uniformly that ~'이 된다.

몰랐던 단어 / 숙어 / 표현 정리

- □ pictographic 상형 문자의
- □ ideographic 표의 문자의
- □ abstract 추상적인
- □ linear 선형의
- □ from top to bottom 위에서 아래로
- □

1. 틀린 문제를 복사해서 붙입니다.
2. 왜 틀렸는지 체크합니다. 단어가 모자라서였는지, 해석이 안 되어서였는지, 아니면 내용을 이해하지 못해서였는지 생각해보고 틀린 이유를 중심으로 오답노트를 기록하세요.
3. 정답을 확인한 뒤 내가 고른 오답은 무엇이고, 틀린 이유가 무엇이었는지 써보세요. 틀린 이유를 확실히 파악해야 같은 실수를 반복하지 않습니다.
4. 해석이 안 돼서 건너뛰었거나 구조를 제대로 파악하지 못한 문장을 쓰고 해설편의 직독직해를 참고하여 분석해 보세요. 복습한 문장들이 차곡차곡 쌓여서 독해력의 바탕이 되어줄 것입니다.
5. 몰랐던 단어, 숙어를 정리하고 복습하세요. 오답노트에 따로 정리해 둔 단어는 시험 직전에 다시 한 번 꼭 확인하세요.

뒷면에 있는 오답노트 양식을 가위로 잘라내 복사하거나, PDF 파일을 프린트하여 사용하세요.
골드교육 홈페이지(www.goldedu.co.kr)에서 오답노트의 PDF 파일을 무료로 다운받을 수 있습니다.

시험명	번호	유형

틀린 문제 붙이기

✓ 왜 틀렸나

- ☐ 단어 / 숙어가 어려움
- ☐ 문장을 해석하지 못함
- ☐ 글 내용을 이해하지 못함
- ☐ 문법 사항이 어려움
- ☐ 기타 (   )

정답 & 오답

*정답

*내가 고른 오답

해석이 안 되거나 어려웠던 문장

몰랐던 단어 / 숙어 / 표현 정리

- ☐
- ☐
- ☐
- ☐
- ☐
- ☐
- ☐
- ☐
- ☐
- ☐